THE LIBYAN ANARCHY

Society of Biblical Literature

Writings from the Ancient World

Theodore J. Lewis, General Editor

Editorial Board

Number 21

The Libyan Anarchy:
Inscriptions from Egypt's Third Intermediate Period
by Robert K. Ritner
Edited by Edward Wente

THE LIBYAN ANARCHY: INSCRIPTIONS FROM EGYPT'S THIRD INTERMEDIATE PERIOD

Translated with an Introduction and Notes
by
Robert K. Ritner

Edited by
Edward Wente

Society of Biblical Literature
Atlanta

THE LIBYAN ANARCHY:
INSCRIPTIONS FROM EGYPT'S
THIRD INTERMEDIATE PERIOD

Library of Congress Cataloging-in-Publication Data

Ritner, Robert Kriech, 1953–
  The Libyan anarchy: inscriptions from Egypt's Third Intermediate Period / by Robert K. Ritner.
      p. cm. — (Writings from the ancient world ; no. 21)
  English with Egyptian texts in transliteration and translation.
  Includes bibliographical references and index.
  ISBN-13: 978-1-58983-174-2 (paper binding : alk. paper)
  ISBN-10: 1-58983-174-8 (paper binding : alk. paper)
1. Egypt—History—To 332 B.C.—Sources. 2. Inscriptions, Egyptian—Translations into English. I. Title. II. Series.
  DT89.R58 2009
  932'.015—dc22   2005016971

17 16 15 14 13 12 11 10 09   5 4 3 2 1
Printed in the United States of America on acid-free, recycled paper
conforming to ANSI/NISO Z39.48-1992 (R1997) and ISO 9706:1994
standards for paper permanence.

For Neil Jordan Krakauer

𓉼𓏃 𓃾𓏇𓎼𓏤

(Pyramid Texts 1455a)

CONTENTS

Following General Records, entries are grouped by dynasties under individual reigns. Entries listed in parentheses refer the reader to relevant sections of the General Records.

II. DYNASTY XXI

SERIES EDITOR'S FOREWORD

Writings from the Ancient World is designed to provide up-to-date, readable English translations of writings recovered from the ancient Near East. The series is intended to serve the interests of general readers, students, and educators who wish to explore the ancient Near Eastern roots of Western civilization or to compare these earliest written expressions of human thought and activity with writings from other parts of the world. It should also be useful to scholars in the humanities or social sciences who need clear, reliable translations of ancient Near Eastern materials for comparative purposes. Specialists in particular areas of the ancient Near East who need access to texts in the scripts and languages of other areas will also find these translations helpful. Given the wide range of materials translated in the series, different volumes will appeal to different interests. But these translations make available to all readers of English the world's earliest traditions as well as valuable sources of information on daily life, history, religion, and so forth in the preclassical world.

The translators of the various volumes in this series are specialists in the particular languages and have based their work on the original sources and the most recent research. In their translations they attempt to convey as much as possible of the original texts in a fluent, current English. In the introductions, notes, glossaries, maps, and chronological tables, they aim to provide the essential information for an appreciation of these ancient documents.

The ancient Near East reached from Egypt to Iran and, for the purposes of our volumes, ranged in time from the invention of writing (by 3000 B.C.E.) to the conquests of Alexander the Great (ca. 330 B.C.E.). The cultures represented within these limits include especially Egyptian, Sumerian, Babylonian, Assyrian, Hittite, Ugaritic, Aramean, Phoenician, and Israelite.

It is hoped that Writings from the Ancient World will eventually produce translations from most of the many different genres attested in these cultures: letters (official and private), myths, diplomatic documents, hymns, law collections, monumental inscriptions, tales, and administrative records, to mention but a few.

Significant funding was made available by the Society of Biblical Literature for the preparation of this volume. In addition, those involved in preparing this volume have received financial and clerical assistance from their respective institutions. Were it not for these expressions of confidence in our work, the arduous tasks of preparation, translation, editing, and publication could not have been accomplished or even undertaken.

It is the hope of all who have worked with the Writings from the Ancient World series that our translations will open up new horizons and deepen the humanity of all who read these volumes.

Theodore J. Lewis
The Johns Hopkins University

ABBREVIATIONS

ÄAT	Ägypten und Altes Testament
ABM	*Annual of the Brooklyn Museum*
AcOr	*Acta Orientalia*
AegLeo	Aegyptiaca Leodiensia
ÄF	Ägyptologische Forschungen
AH	Aegyptica Helvetica
AJSL	*American Journal of Semitic Languages and Literature*
AnOr	Analecta Orientalia
BdÉ	Bibliothèque d'Étude
Bib	*Biblica*
BiAeg	Bibliotheca Aegyptia
BIE	*Bulletin de l'Institute d'Égypt*
BIFAO	*Bulletin de l'Institut Français d'Archéologie Orientale*
BiOr	*Bibliotheca Orientalis*
BSÉG	*Bulletin de la Société d'Égyptologie Genève*
BSFE	*Bulletin de la Société française d'Égyptologie*
BSFFT	*Bulletin de la Société française des Fouilles de Tanis*
BzÄe	Beiträge zur Ägyptologie
CdÉ	*Chronique d'Égypte*
CdK	*Cahiers de Karnak*
CGC	Catalogue General du Musee du Caire
CRAIBL	*Comptes rendus de l'Académie des Inscriptions et Belles-lettres*
CRIPEL	*Cahier de Recherches de l'Institut de Papyrologie et d'Égyptologie de Lille*
DMOA	Documenta et monumenta orientis antiqui
EEF	Egypt Exploration Fund
Enchoria	*Enchoria: Zeitschrift für Demotistik und Koptologie*
FIFAO	Fouilles de l'Institut français d'archéologie orientale
GM	*Göttinger Miszellen*
HÄB	Hildesheimer Ägyptologische Beiträge

IFAO	L'Institut Français d'Archéologie Orientale
JAOS	*Journal of the American Oriental Society*
JARCE	*Journal of the American Research Center in Egypt*
JEA	*Journal of Egyptian Archaeology*
JEOL	*Jaarbericht van het Vooraziatisch-egyptisch Genootschap Ex Oriente Lux*
JNES	*Journal of Near Eastern Studies*
JSOT	*Journal for the Study of the Old Testament*
JSSEA	*Journal of the Society for the Study of Egyptian Antiquities*
Kêmi	*Kêmi: Revue de philologie et d'archéologie égyptienne et coptes*
Kush	*Kush: Journal of the Sudan Antiquities Service*
LÄe	Helck, Wolfgang, Eberhard Otto, and Wolfhart Westendorf, eds. 1975–92. *Lexikon der Ägyptologie.* 7 vols. Wiesbaden: Harrassowitz.
LingAeg	*Lingua Aegyptia: Journal of Egyptian Language Studies*
MÄS	Münchner ägyptologische Studien
MDAIK	*Mitteilungen des Deutschen Archäologischen Instituts, Abteilung Kairo*
MIFAO	Mémoires publiés par les membres de l'Institut Français d'Archéologie Orientale
MIO	*Mitteilungen des Instituts für Orientforschung*
NARCE	*Newsletter of the American Research Center in Egypt*
OBO	Orbis Biblicus et Orientalis
OIC	Oriental Institute Communications
OIP	Oriental Institute Publications
OLA	Orientalia Lovaniensia Analecta
OLZ	*Orientalistische Literaturzeitung*
OrSuec	*Orientalia Suecana*
PÄe	Probleme der Ägyptologie
PIFAO	Publications de l'Institut Français d'Archéologie Orientale du Caire
PSBA	*Proceedings of the Society of Biblical Archaeology*
RdÉ	*Revue d'Égyptologie*
RHJE	*Revue de l'histoire juive en Egypt*
RIDA	*Revue Internationale des Droits de l'Antiquité*
RT	*Recueil de travaux relatifs à la philologie et à l'archéologie égyptiennes et assyriennes*
SAK	*Studien zur Altägyptischen Kultur*
SAOC	Studies in Ancient Oriental Civilizations
SASAE	Supplément aux Annales du service des antiquités de l'Égypte
SBLWAW	Society of Biblical Literature Writings from the Ancient World

SPAW	*Sitzungsberichte der Preussischen Akademie der Wissenschaften*
StudAeg	Studia Aegyptiaca
UGAÄ	Untersuchungen zur Geschichte und Altertumskunde Ägyptens
VA	*Varia Aegyptiaca*
VT	*Vetus Testamentum*
YES	Yale Egyptological Studies
ZÄS	*Zeitschrift für ägyptische Sprache und Altertumskunde*

INTRODUCTION

THE HISTORY AND HISTORIOGRAPHY OF THE "LIBYAN ANARCHY"

Contemporary with the Israelite kingdom of Solomon and David, the Nubian conqueror Piye (Piankhy), and the Assyrian Assurbanipal, Egypt's Third Intermediate Period is of critical interest not only to Egyptologists but also to biblical historians, Africanists, and Assyriologists. Spanning six centuries and as many dynasties, the turbulent era extended from approximately 1100 to 650 B.C.E., from the inception of the divided Dynasty XXI until the reunification of the kingdom in the first reign of Dynasty XXVI. As its traditional designation indicates, this "intermediate period" represents an age of decentralization between the stable New Kingdom and the later Saite "Renaissance." Characterized by ever-increasing political fragmentation under rulers styled variously as priest-kings, great generals, and lineage chiefs, the Third Intermediate Period is commonly disparaged as "the Libyan Anarchy," with reference to the ethnicity of its foreign rulers, who were descended from Libyan mercenaries.

The standard history of this complex period remains K. A. Kitchen's *The Third Intermediate Period in Egypt,* first published in 1973, revised in a second edition of 1986, and given an additional preface in 1995. As an aid to the reader, each selection in this volume is keyed to the relevant historical discussion in Kitchen's text. Since the initial appearance of Kitchen's study, certain scholars (most notably the "Birmingham School" of A. Leahy, D. Aston, and J. Taylor) have offered differing reconstructions of Dynasty XXIII both in terms of its composition (adding Takelot II) and location (Thebes rather than Leontopolis). It is beyond the scope of this volume of translations to critique these many suggestions, but references to them will be found in the individual textual bibliographies and in Kitchen's 1995 preface.

The Libyan character of the era has been recognized only gradually. In the outlandish names of its contemporary rulers, the first generations of Egyptologists thought to have found evidence of an intrusive Mesopotamian or Elamite dynasty, with Osorkon a variant of Sargon, Takelot for Tiglath, Namlot for Nimrod, Sheshonq meaning "man of Shushan" (Susa), and Iuwelot (Aourot) for Babylonian Ardu. Although the Libyan identity of this dynasty was established by L. Stern in 1883 on the basis of the Pasenhor genealogy (text 2 in this collection), consensus was not reached until 1908, when W. Max Müller identified the supposedly Babylonian royal names as Berber. The inexpensive reissue of outdated, public-domain histories such as H. Brugsch's *Egypt under the Pharaohs* (1996 [orig. 1902]) has, ironically, reintroduced such obsolete theory to the general reading public.

If the Libyan origin of Dynasties XXII–XXIV was then explicitly recognized in such pivotal studies as J. Yoyotte's "Les Principautés du Delta au temps de l'anarchie libyenne" (1961), the potential Libyan component of Dynasties XXI–XXVI was all but ignored. The ethnic connections of Dynasty XXI have now become apparent with improved publications of the temple of Khonsu, revealing both the Libyan names of its Theban founder's children and the direct familial link between Dynasties XXI and XXII. Long recognized as the continuation of Dynasty XXIV, Dynasty XXVI has been acknowledged to have Libyan ancestry, but swayed by the dynasty's official, nationalistic propaganda in imagery and text, scholars have paid little attention to this fact. In modern times at least, depictions of Third Intermediate Period rulers in traditional guise has had the effect the authors intended, and in general histories such as the *Cambridge Ancient History*, rulers of Libyan descent are assumed to be thoroughly Egyptianized, "Egyptian by birth and upbringing." Despite such confidence, anomalies unique to the era characterize both the ruling families and the prevailing culture. The search for an ethnic Libyan dimension underlying these peculiarities was first undertaken by A. Leahy in 1985 ("The Libyan Period in Egypt: An Essay in Interpretation") and by the present author in a series of lectures and articles from 1988 onward. While studies of tribalism have long been central to Near Eastern and Mesopotamian scholarship, Egyptology has shown scant interest in the issue. This volume gathers much of the documentary evidence for a projected future analysis of "Libya in Egypt," tracing the history of Egyptian and Libyan interactions.

Obvious ethnic influence has been noted in the retention of Libyan names, lineage titles, and dress, whereby the most prominent offices are held by "Chiefs of the Meshwesh tribe" represented with alien names and feathers in their hair. The retention of tribal structure, with its basis in kinship confederations, is indicated not only by the multiplicity of tribal titles but by a concomitant—and tolerated—political fragmentation (or decentralization) that perverts traditional notions of a united Egyptian kingship. Following the anthropological pattern of "segmentary lineages," collateral royal families descended from a common ruling ancestor were initially unified, then allied, and ultimately in competition. Within the bureaucracy, royal families enforced a monopoly on regional military and administrative offices, so that normal institutional promotion now became subordinated to claims of kinship status. Emphasis on kinship also motivated exogamous marriage alliances (1 Kgs 3:1; 9:16), previously anathema to Egyptian royalty, and the new development of extended genealogies. Such genealogies typically constitute "history" for tribal societies, and within Egypt the practice often served to link an individual to the dynastic family, thereby assuring status and rights of office. In response, native elites employed the same technique to record long-standing familial control of temple offices, giving rise to the priestly "caste system" encountered by Herodotus (2.143, 164, and 37, end) in the fifth century B.C.E.

Probable Libyan influence is to be found in the numerous "donation stelae" recording gifts of landed endowments (comparable to the modern Islamic *waqf*) for the support of religious institutions. Although this custom originated in the early New Kingdom, it is only in the Third Intermediate Period that examples proliferate, with an abrupt disappearance after Dynasty XXVI. The most characteristic texts of the era, these stelae provide critical information regarding chronology, political geography, dominant personalities, local cults, and contemporary economics. They are limited almost exclusively to Delta areas of major Libyan settlement, and their frequent depiction of Libyan chiefs serving as intermediaries in the donation may reflect the custom of tribal, rather than pharaonic, ownership of community lands.

Other innovations suggested to be Libyan in origin are modifications in burial practices, favoring family interments within temple precincts over individual burials in isolated cemeteries, and a supposed "disintegration" of linguistic and orthographic conventions. Such linguistic changes are in large measure a normal development from standards current in the preceding Ramesside age, the primary stylistic model for the Third Intermediate Period before the archaizing renaissance initiated by the Nubian and Saite courts. As in Ramesside Egypt, formal temple inscriptions on relief and statuary employ classic Middle Egyptian hieroglyphs mixed in varying degrees with Late Egyptian, the current vernacular that was employed in personal and legal texts typically inscribed on papyrus in the cursive hieratic script. The use of both Late Egyptian and hieratic expands throughout the period, particularly in the newly prominent oracular and donation decrees that are at once monumental and legal records. Innovation here is only in format; these inscriptions are simply copies on stone of vernacular legal decrees drafted in standard fashion on papyrus.

The political division of the country under Libyan rule did allow the chancellery styles of north and south to develop in divergent ways, leading to the Demotic language and script in the former and "abnormal hieratic" in the latter. Many antecedents to Demotic terms and formulary can be found throughout the current corpus and are signaled in the notes. These antecedents are relevant not only to Egyptologists, since they have been shown to underlie the derivative formularies adopted in imperial Aramaic contracts within Persian Egypt. Following the Saite victory over their southern Nubian opponents, the gradual imposition of Demotic throughout the country served as a major unifying force and marks the linguistic termination of the Third Intermediate Period. The Berber language once spoken by members of the Libyan elite was never written, and only names and a few titles are preserved in transcription within Egyptian texts. Those found in this volume are gathered in a concluding index.

In social history as in language the Ramesside age provided the necessary preconditions for the Third Intermediate Period. Beginning in the reign of Seti I (ca. 1321–1304 B.C.E.), a series of military campaigns against the Meshwesh, Libu, and smaller tribes marked the first serious hostilities on Egypt's western border since the Middle Kingdom, some six centuries earlier. Detailed campaign records from the reigns of Merneptah and Rameses III describe organized Libyan invasions abetted by contingents of "Sea Peoples," roving marauders of various ethnicities who were to destroy most Late Bronze Age Mediterranean cultures. Egypt alone withstood these broad population movements, and defeated warriors were impressed into the Egyptian military. The pastoral Libyans, who had traveled with families and flocks, were settled by tribe under their own leaders in isolated regional camps in an ancient "reservation" system. Mercenaries were recruited from the camps, and over time individual Libyan families rose within the ranks and adopted aspects of Egyptian culture, although in varying degrees. In the late Ramesside age, Libyan bands might still terrorize the west bank of Thebes while their cousins maintained the Egyptian defense.

Having withdrawn to their Delta capital of Piramesses, the later Ramesside rulers increasingly abandoned the administration of Upper Egypt to the high priests of Thebes. A mismanaged attempt to suppress the overweening pontiff Amonhotep about year 9 of Rameses XI began with an invasion of Thebes by the viceroy of Nubia, who in turn had to be dislodged by the military commander Herihor, sent from the Libyan camp at el-Hibeh near the city of Heracleopolis. By year 19, an official renaissance ("repeating of births") proclaimed a condominium between a theocratic state in the south, from Elephantine to el-Hibeh, and a royal dynasty in the north. Although in the person of Rameses XI Dynasty XX lingered for a few years in Piramesses, the divided Dynasty XXI had begun, with military high priests adopting royal titularies at Thebes and their close relatives ruling as kings in Tanis (biblical Zoan), a port suburb of the Ramesside capital remade as a "northern Thebes." This ascendancy of the priesthood at the expense of a unified monarchy has exerted undue influence in Egyptian historiography. Disregarding the unique historical circumstances that produced the Theban "priest-kings," scholars have generalized the political situation of Dynasty XXI to explain the motives of Akhenaton's "anticlerical" revolution in Dynasty XVIII. On the contrary, increased manifestations of religious fervor in the Libyan era seem the direct result of Akhenaton's challenge and the counterrevolution of "popular piety" in Ramesside times. It is in late Dynasty XVIII through Dynasty XX also that origins may be found for the most common "magico-religious" practices of the Third Intermediate Period: the use of judicial oracles and healing stelae. Often disparaged as reflecting an increase in magic and superstition, such practices indicate only a quantitative, not a qualitative, change in religious norms and were firmly based in the belief that divinity held ultimate earthly authority to resolve policies, disputes, and illness. In this respect, the theologians of the Libyan era were not dissimilar to those at Amarna. The theocracy of Amon is most closely paralleled by that of Aton.

The Ramesside age also bequeathed to its successor the problem of tomb robbery, and it is ostensibly for this reason that the whole of the Theban Dynasty XXI was preoccupied with the rewrapping and reburial of earlier royal mummies. That the mummies were interred minus their gold accouterments suggests that the motivation may have had more to do with the defection of the Nubian viceroy and the loss of the Nubian gold mines. The suspicion seems confirmed by the quantity of gold (and Merneptah's reused sarcophagus) discovered by P. Montet in 1939 in the unplundered royal tombs at Tanis. Generally overlooked in favor of Tutankhamon's riches, these finds are among the great treasures of the Cairo Museum. Toward the end of this dynasty, intermarriage with new Libyan families is apparent in the accession of "Osorkon the Elder" and the political prominence of Sheshonq, the Great Chief of the Ma (an abbreviation for Meshwesh), who obtained the throne as Sheshonq I, founder of Dynasty XXII. Although formerly resident in Bubastis, the new king maintained his capital in the metropolis of Tanis.

While the preceding dynasty betrayed few signs of Libyan ethnicity, Sheshonq and his descendants were not reticent in their preference for ethnic names, titles, and feathers, and it was not until his fifth year that Thebes acknowledged the Great Chief of the Ma as its legitimate pharaoh. In an attempt to restore unity to the country, Sheshonq appointed his own son as high priest and royal representative at Thebes, a practice emulated by the following four rulers and applied to lesser offices as well. Known to the Bible as Shishak without an "n," a common variant of the name also found in Egyptian records, Sheshonq led the one major foreign campaign of the period, recorded on the Bubastite Portal at Karnak and in 1 Kgs 14:25–26. Conducted as a razzia for plunder rather than imperial conquest, Sheshonq's military foray recalls tribal custom rather than New Kingdom colonialism. So successful was the raid that his successor Osorkon I was still able to dedicate over 1,500,000 lb troy weight of gold and silver to the gods of Heliopolis and Thebes, not including sums donated to the family seat at Bubastis and other shrines at Hermopolis, Silê, and elsewhere.

Disunity within the kingdom first appears in the reign of Osorkon II, the fourth independent ruler of the dynasty. Despite an oracular request that his sons might retain control of the offices of kingship, hereditary princedoms, the high priesthoods of Thebes and Heracleopolis, and the chieftainship of the Ma "without a brother being resentful of his brother," his own cousin Harsiese established a collateral, if ephemeral, "sub-dynasty" at Thebes. Harsiese's heirs would contest the office of Theban pontiff with Tanite princes for several generations, most notably during the prolonged travails of the high priest Osorkon, the ill-fated but persistent son of Takelot II, successor to Osorkon II. Probably in reaction to the politicization of that office, the ancient female role of God's Wife of Amon is granted new status, rapidly supplanting the traditional authority of the Theban high priest. From Osorkon II onward, the post is held by a royal but unmarried princess, allied to the ruling house and unable to produce a competing line. With the death of Takelot II, dynastic competition was formalized with the appearance of Dynasty XXIII, traditionally derived from the Tanite line and associated with Leontopolis and minor kingdoms at Heracleopolis and Hermopolis. As with the lineage of Harsiese, Dynasty XXIII probably represents a collateral branch of Dynasty XXII.

From the accession of its founder, Pedubast I, Dynasty XXIII is linked closely, but not exclusively, with Thebes. Whatever may have been its territorial ambitions, the new dynasty, like the old, was soon bounded by proliferating petty states subject to "Kings of Upper and Lower Egypt," hereditary princes, and Great Chiefs of the Ma or Libu tribes. The final five Tanite pharaohs (Sheshonq III and IV, Pamiu, Sheshonq V, and Osorkon IV) controlled diminishing territory about the ancestral capital, and dona-tion stelae from the reign of Sheshonq V document the expansion of a nascent Libu "Kingdom of the West" based in Sais. In the absence of inter-nal political cohesion, it is hardly surprising that Egypt could provide no united support for Israelite resistance against the powerful threat of Assyria (2 Kgs 17:4). As an influx of somewhat assimilated Libu tribesmen con-tested the northern authority of Dynasty XXII, so the southern dominance of Dynasty XXIII faced almost simultaneous challenge from an aggressive, and partly Egyptianized, Cushite dynasty centered at Napata in modern Sudanese Nubia. After a mere four reigns, Dynasty XXIII's Osorkon III, contemporary of Sheshonq V, will have found an expanding Nubian presence at Aswan or beyond, seemingly encouraged by anti-Libyan sentiment at Thebes. By the following reign of Takelot III, the Nubian Kashta was acknowledged from Elephantine to Thebes and may then have installed his daughter Amonardis as the adopted successor of the God's Wife Shepenwepet, daughter of Osorkon III.

In response to the evolving face of foreign domination, a broad cultural revision gained momentum in the chancellery and thereafter in linguistic and artistic media. First attested in the formal titularies of Osorkon III and Sheshonq V, the movement represents a conscious rejection of the florid Ramesside cultural model that had inspired the Libyan era for over three centuries in favor of a spare, archaizing style that evoked ancient glory with obvious nationalistic implications. Thus while his predecessor had been crowned as "Usimaʿre-setepenre, Pamiu, beloved of Amon, Son of Bastet, the god, ruler of Thebes," Sheshonq V was most often simply "Aakheperre, Sheshonq," employing a Dynasty XVIII prenomen. In keeping with Old and Middle Kingdom practice, a single epithet ("Great of Strength") served for all his other throne names. At about the same time, designations of tribal affinity fall into disfavor, so that Great Chiefs of the Ma become "Great Chiefs," and in Memphite sacerdotal circles Egyptian names displace Libyan ones. With the continual atrophy of Dynasties XXII and XXIII, the Egyptian revival passes ironically into the hands of the Nubian Dynasty XXV and the Libyan Dynasties XXIV and XXVI at Sais. Each would exploit native cultural conventions as propaganda to show themselves as true Egyptians and their opponents as alien impostors.

The clearest examples of such propaganda are found in the records of the Cushite invader Piye, whose name was formerly read Piankhy. Piye's dynasty was probably born of a fortunate concatenation of events: the defection of the Nubian viceroy and the lapse of pharaonic control; the continued presence of a privileged Egyptian priesthood; and the presence or arrival of a local Nubian elite. Enlarging upon his father Kashta's success in Upper Egypt, Piye claimed in his third regnal year to be the divinely sanctioned overlord selecting lesser chiefs and kings in Egypt. Like earlier texts from this dynasty such as that of queen regnant Katimala, the document displays a claim to Egyptian kingship, a single-minded devotion to Amon, and a preference for Ramesside vernacular and style. In the wake of his victorious campaign of year 21, however, his pious claims of authority are now composed in classical Middle Egyptian, and his opposing kings and chiefs are stigmatized as ritually unclean. The contest between Nubian and Libyan would continue for a century. Although Piye's adversary Tefnakht was temporarily defeated, his Saite kingdom absorbed the Delta as Dynasty XXIV under his heir Bakenrenef, who was in turn slain by Piye's heir Shabako. Egypt would be subject to Nubian stewardship for three further reigns, but unity was illusory. Regional Libyan polities were never

eliminated, and power was retained by local rulers such as the native Theban priest Montuemhat, virtual king of Upper Egypt.

Throughout the period of Cushite hegemony, the threat of Assyrian expansion prompted a series of desultory campaigns and diplomatic
missions recorded in Assyrian annals and biblical chronicles (2 Kgs 17:4;
19:9; Isa 37:9). In 671 B.C.E., Esarhaddon successfully invaded Egypt, driving Taharqa southward and confirming local dynasts, a pattern repeated
by Assurbanipal in 667/666. A subsequent, quelled revolt left only Necho
and his son Psametik of Sais as Assyrian vassal kings in the Delta, while
Tanwetamani assumed the throne in Napata. If, in his campaign of 664
and its formal record ("Dream Stela"), Tanwetamani sought to imitate his
ancestor Piye, he was far less successful. Although Necho was slain, the
destructive Assyrian counterattack in 663 forever ended Nubian rule and
established Psametik as the preeminent king within Egypt. Before the
end of Assurbanipal's reign, Psametik had expelled the Assyrians, and in
his ninth year Psametik installed his daughter Nitocris as God's Wife in
Thebes, effectively unifying the country. Rarely accorded the appreciation
it deserves, Psametik's Dynasty XXVI represents more than the ultimate
triumph of Tefnakht's Saite lineage. By a deliberately paced imposition
of national officials, conventions, and the Demotic language and script,
Psametik eliminated tribal and regional factionalism and nurtured a coherent cultural renaissance that would redefine and maintain the essential
elements of Egyptian society—even in the face of repeated foreign occupation—until the triumph of Christianity. This was no small feat for a ruler
of Libyan extraction.

THE TRANSLATIONS

While the complex history of the period has been reconstructed from
an array of scattered primary sources, the sources themselves are often difficult to consult, available only in obscure or obsolete editions. Many are
incompletely published, most are in need of careful revision, and few are
in English. Several of the texts have a significance extending far beyond
their own period. The single most important copy of royal jubilee rituals
forms part of this corpus, but these reliefs have never been fully assembled
or translated. Aside from a technical study of biographies from Dynasties
XXII and XXIII (Jansen-Winkeln 1985), no thorough collection of Third
Intermediate Period inscriptions now exists in any language, and the non-
specialist is left with only the highly selective excerpts included in J. H.
Breasted's *Ancient Records of Egypt* (1906–7). The discovery of significant
new texts, as well as recent improvements in grammar and lexicography,
readily justifies a new and expanded collection. As the period covers six
centuries, the volume is necessarily representative, not exhaustive, but it

does contain the primary documents of the Libyan era, comprising every significant genre and material as well as all relevant texts formerly translated by Breasted.

Temple scenes carved in stone (e.g., nos. 39, 53, 56, 58–60, 155, 159, 166) demonstrate continuity and innovation with regard to earlier religious tradition, the contemporary prominence of sites and cults, and the geographic range of individual regimes. Such monumental works necessarily overlap with the category of formal royal inscriptions appearing on reliefs, stelae, stone or bronze statuary, and even clay bricks and seals (e.g., nos. 15, 31, 48, 98, 151). Royal sponsorship is explicit or implied in the carved oracular petitions (e.g., nos. 28, 30, 33, 35, 40–41, 69) and donation stelae (e.g., nos. 13–14, 62, 80, 86–88, 102–6) on behalf of community temples and personnel. The sacerdotal class served by these documents is also represented in the genealogies (nos. 1–5), priestly annals and inundation records (nos. 6–9), reburial dockets (nos. 19, 29, 36), papyrus and stone magical texts (nos. 10–11), and Serapeum votive stelae for the deceased Apis bull (nos. 89, 94–97, 131–37, 165, 175). For all ranks within the literate elite, purely personal documentation was expressed publicly in genealogies, magical, votive, and donation stelae, and graffiti (e.g., nos. 22, 25, 63, 70, 83) and more privately in tomb inscriptions on walls, coffins, bandages, and equipment (e.g., nos. 37, 44, 54–55, 68, 73, 81, 91, 101, 117, 124). Completing the categories are personal letters and literary accounts on papyrus (nos. 18, 21, 26–27) and miscellaneous small objects (e.g., nos. 67, 107, 114, 118–20, 122–23, 129–30, 148, 167). Inscriptions vary greatly in length, and while some are more important for their findspot than their content, all have been selected for their historical or cultural significance. After a selection of general records representative of the broader era, documents are presented in roughly chronological order, by reign within individual dynasties. Strict chronological ordering is not suitable, as dynasties frequently overlap.

The present volume marks a break in format with earlier Egyptological contributions to Writings from the Ancient World by including transliteration, a convention already employed within the series for Mesopotamian, Aramaic, Hebrew, and Ugaritic documents. Given the complexities of the Third Intermediate Period writing system, with group writing, phonetic spellings, and a mixture of Middle and Late Egyptian, a full transliteration is necessary to justify revised translations and interpretations. As many of the texts have never been edited with transliteration, it is hoped that this will provide a primary service for scholars and students. In any case, it will allow the reader to see rather than intuit the assumptions made by the translator.

Begun with the support of the Morse Fellowship for Scholarly Research in 1995–96 while I was at Yale University, this project has been the beneficiary of continued encouragement and sound advice. In particular, Edward F. Wente's meticulous editorial acumen has eliminated errors both typographic and philological. Richard Jasnow volunteered hours scouring the volume for inconsistencies and mistakes in the text and the revised transliteration font. Those that remain are my fault alone. To the former series editor, the late Simon B. Parker, I am indebted for sustained endorsement and indulgence with format modifications, and I am grateful to the current editor, Theodore J. Lewis, for examining the manuscript multiple times with insight and improvement. For assistance with the Phoenician texts, I thank Dennis Pardee of the Oriental Institute and Richard Steiner of Yeshiva University. I have received much-appreciated assistance from Bob Buller of SBL Press, who has, with meticulous attention to detail, transformed almost two hundred files into a coherent manuscript. John Larson, Museum Archivist of the Oriental Institute, provided access to critical photographs and early handcopies, and I am grateful for his personal and professional support. My deepest gratitude is due my family, including my parents, Robert and Margaret, and most especially Dr. Neil J. Krakauer, whose untimely passing has prevented him from seeing the completion of a project whose progress he had enlivened for a half dozen years. I can only hope that the result is worthy of the dedicatee, "great Star who has brought his attributes unto the nether world and traverses what is therein" (Book of the Dead 180).

CONVENTIONS USED IN THE TRANSLITERATIONS AND TRANSLATIONS

[ ]	encloses damaged sections restored by the editor
( )	encloses sections supplied by the editor for clarity and omissions
{ }	encloses sections to be deleted
< >	encloses sections found in variant copies
...	indicates lost or unintelligible sections
l.p.h.	"life, prosperity, and health!" a pious exclamation following mention of the king or palace
NN	insertion of a variable personal or divine name
no./nos.	number/numbers
var.	variant

For clarity in genealogies, female names are prefaced by "the woman," corresponding to the feminine determinative in the Egyptian scripts.

Translations of the stereotyped phrase dỉ.n≠ỉ n≠k are rendered either "To you I have given" or "Thus I have given to you," depending upon English diction or poetic parallelism with other nominal ("emphatic") forms. For the latter translation, see Hoch 1995, §149.

I

GENERAL RECORDS

A. GENEALOGIES

1. KHONSU ROOF GENEALOGIES OF A PRIESTLY INDUCTION:
THE INTERRELATIONSHIP OF DYNASTIES XXI–XXII

The roof of the large Khonsu temple, or "Bennet," at the southern edge of the Karnak enclosure was a favorite site for pious graffiti during the Libyan Period. On one roofing slab, two adjacent hieroglyphic graffiti recorded the induction of a God's Father of Khonsu named Ankhefenkhonsu in the reign of Takelot III. Originally copied by Lepsius as a single inscription, the graffiti, which joined almost end to end, were subsequently recognized by Daressy as distinct but related texts with identical date. On the basis of comparable terminology in the Karnak Priestly Annals (no. 9), which record the inductions of the same rank of priests of the neighboring cult of Amon, it can be inferred that the righthand graffito relates the speech and genealogy of the inductee, while the lefthand text presents the name and pedigree of his sponsor. The typical format of the Karnak texts, however, combines these elements in a single inscription. A falcon-headed vase, representing a cultic utensil of the priestly office of Khonsu, was sketched beside the lefthand graffiti above a short text offering a blessing or curse upon the potential reader. The roofing slab is now lost, and no measurements or photograph are available.

The historical significance of the graffiti was not recognized until 1977, when Yoyotte demonstrated that the inductee's ancestors included the Meshwesh Chief Namlot, father of the founder of Dynasty XXII, and the lady Mehetemweskhet, who was mother of both this Namlot and King Osorkon ("The Elder"), the fifth ruler of Dynasty XXI. Thus a Libyan dignitary had assumed the throne several decades before his nephew

Sheshonq I, providing a direct familial link to the subsequent Meshwesh Dynasty XXII. Sections of this genealogy left untranslated by Yoyotte show that Osorkon's legitimacy derived from his mother Mehetemweskhet, descended from the Theban high priest and sometime king, Menkheperre of Dynasty XXI. From Takelot III to Menkheperre, the lineage of Ankhefenkhonsu extends back over 250 years.

This is the first integral translation. For the texts and partial translations, see Daressy 1896, 51–52, §III; Yoyotte 1976–77, 39–54; Graefe 1981, 1:112–14 (no. 130). See Kitchen 1986, 323 §282; 357 §319; 534–35 §437; 573–74 §505; and 581 §521.

RIGHTHAND GENEALOGY

(1) ḥsb.t 7.(t) tp(y) šmw n.(t) ny-sw.t bỉ.ty [Wsr-Mꜣꜥ.t-Rꜥ Stp-n-ʾImn sꜣ Rꜥ T̲krỉwt hrw pn b]s [ỉt]-nt̲r mrỉ-nt̲r [...] (2) [...] n H̱nsw m Wꜣs.t Nfr-ḥtp ḥm-nt̲r Mnw ꜥnḫ≠f-n-H̱nsw d̲d≠f ỉ ʾImn-Rꜥ ny-sw.t nt̲r.w [...] n.w ḫfn. w H̱r sꜣ ꜣs.t [...] (3) [...] (4) [...] (5) ḥm-nt̲r 2-nw [...] n H̱nsw m Wꜣs. t Nfr-ḥtp sš ḥw.t-nt̲r [...] ʾIp.t-s.wt D̲d-H̱nsw-ỉw≠f-ꜥnḫ mꜣꜥ-ḫrw ḥm.t≠f [tꜣ šr.t n(?)] (6) ḫꜣw.ty ḫtmw bỉ.ty H̱nsw-s[...]-mr≠f(?)[1] [mꜣꜥ-ḫrw(?)] Nsy-pr-nbw mꜣꜥ.(t)-ḫrw rnn Nb≠s-[...]-n-ꜣs.t mꜣꜥ.t-ḫrw [ỉt]≠s wr ꜥꜣ nꜣ Mꜥ.w ꜥꜣ qꜥḥ² (7) Pꜣ-šr-n-ꜣs.t mꜣꜥ-ḫrw sꜣ Rywrhꜣnꜣ mꜣꜥ-ḫrw sꜣ R[y]tysꜣ mꜣꜥ-ḫrw mw.t≠f Tꜣ-šr.t-n-ꜣs.t mꜣꜥ.t-ḫrw sꜣ.t n Rywrhꜣ(8)nꜣ mꜣꜥ-ḫrw pꜣ nḫtỉw mw.t≠f Tꜣ-šꜣꜥ-n-ḫpr mꜣꜥ.t-ḫrw tꜣ ḥm.t nt̲r n Pr-ꜥꜣ Wsỉrkn pꜣ šr n Mḫ.t-(m)-wsḫ.t mꜣꜥ.t-ḫrw ỉt≠f [...] (9) mw.t n Pꜣ-šr-n-ꜣs.t mꜣꜥ-ḫrw [...] T̲n.t-[tꜣ]-nt̲r.t mꜣꜥ.t-ḫrw tꜣ šr.t n Pꜣ-dỉw-Nbw.t mꜣꜥ-ḫrw sꜣ Nꜣsꜣ[r]tỉ [mꜣꜥ-ḫrw pꜣ šr n] (10) [Nꜣmꜣ]rtỉ mꜣꜥ-ḫrw pꜣ [wr ꜥꜣ nꜣ M]ꜥ.w ỉt mw.t[≠f] Nsy-[...³ pꜣ šr(?)] n Tꜣ-šr.t-n-Dỉdỉ (11) [tꜣ šr.t n(?)] ỉmy-rꜣ pr-ḥd n Pr-ꜥꜣ ʾIbrš[..]-ꜣs.t mꜣꜥ.(t)-ḫrw tꜣ šr.t n D̲d-D̲ḥwty-ỉw≠s-ꜥnḫ mꜣꜥ.t-ḫrw sꜣ.t ḥm-nt̲r ʾImn [...] (12) [...] ḥm-nt̲r ʾImn-Rꜥ ny-sw.t nt̲r. w ỉmy-rꜣ pr-ḥd n nb tꜣ.wy Šd-s(w)-D̲ḥwty mꜣꜥ-ḫrw sꜣ n ḥm-nt̲r nt̲r.t nb.t [...]ỉwḫ(?) ỉmy-rꜣ pr-ḥd n nb tꜣ.wy [...] (13) [... sꜣ ...] D̲d-Mw.t-[ỉw≠s-ꜥnḫ mꜣꜥ.t-ḫrw] mw.t≠s [...]-ḥtp.tỉ mꜣꜥ.t-ḫrw tꜣ šr.t mw.t⁴ (n.t) ḥm-nt̲r tp(y) (n) ʾImn-Rꜥ ny-sw.t nt̲r.w Mn-ḫpr-Rꜥ

(1) Regnal year 7, first month of summer, of the King of Upper and Lower Egypt, [Usimaꜥre-setepenamon, Son of Re, Takelot (III). On this day there was in]ducted the God's [Father], the beloved of the god, [...] (2) [...] of Khonsu in Thebes Neferhotep, the prophet of Min, Ankhefenkhonsu, who says: "O Amon-Re, King of the Gods, [...] of hundreds of thousands, Horus son of Isis [...] (3) [...] (4) [... born of] (5) the Second Prophet [and ...] of Khonsu in Thebes Neferhotep and temple scribe [and ...] of Karnak, Djedkhonsiuefankh, the justified, whose wife was [the daughter of (?)] (6) the leader and seal-bearer of the King of Lower Egypt, Khonsus[...]meref (?),[1] [the justified (?)], the woman Nespernebu, the justified, who was raised by the woman Nebes[...]enese, the justified,

whose [father was the Great Chief of] the Ma (Meshwesh), the district chief,[2] (7) Pasherenese, the justified,

son of Riwerhan (II), the justified,

son of Ritchisa, the justified, while his mother was the woman Tasheritenese, the justified,

daughter of Riwerha(8)n (I), the justified, the Victorious,

whose mother was the woman Tashaenkheper, the justified, the god's wife of Pharaoh Osorkon,

the son of the woman Mehet(em)weskhet, the justified, whose father was [...]

(9) while the mother of Pasherenese, the justified, was the woman Ten[ta]neteret, the justified,

the daughter of Patinebu, the justified,

son of Nasa[lo]t, [the justified],

(10) [the son of Nam]lot, the justified, the [Great Chief of the] Ma,

the father of whose mother was Nes[...],[3]

[the son (?)] of the woman Tasheritendidi,

(11) [the daughter of (?)] the overseer of the treasury of Pharaoh, Ibresh[... and whose mother was (?) the woman ...]ese,

the daughter of the woman Djeddjehutyiuesankh, the justified,

the daughter of the prophet of Amon [...] (12) [...] prophet of Amon-Re, King of the Gods, overseer of the treasury of the Lord of the Two Lands, Shedsudjheuty, the justified,

son of the prophet of the goddess, Lady of [...]..., overseer of the treasury of the Lord of the Two Lands, [...] (13) [...],

[son of the woman] Djedmut[iuesankh, the justified],

whose mother was the woman [...]hetepti, the justified,

the half-sister by the same mother[4] of the First Prophet of Amon-Re, King of the Gods, Menkheperre."

LEFTHAND GENEALOGY

(1) ḥsb.t 7.(t) tp(y) šmw (n.t) ny-sw.t bỉ.ty nb t3.wy Wsr-M3ꜥ.t-Rꜥ Stp-n-ꜣImn s3 Rꜥ Tk[rỉw]t hrw pn nfr [n bs ỉt-nṯr][5] n Ḫnsw m W3s.t Nfr-ḥtp ỉn ỉt-nṯr [...] (2) [...] Ḫnsw wn{n}ḫ[6] ḥr s3 3-nw n Ḫnsw m W3s.t Nfr-ḥtp n ḥw.t-nṯr Ḫnsw-Dḥwty wnḫ (3) [...] nṯr.w nb.w [...] (4) [...] (5) [...]wḫ[...] n Ḫnsw m W3s.t Nfr-ḥtp t3(ỉ)-ḫw[7] ḥr [wnmy ...] (6) ḥm-nṯr [...] ꜣIp.t-s.wt qbḥw (n) Ḫnsw m Bnn.(t) ḥm-nṯr ỉmy-3bd≠f n pr Ḫnsw ḥr s3 [3?]-nw [...] n Ḫnsw-Dḥwty wnḫ ḥr s3 3-nw [...] (7) n Ḫnsw m W3s.t Nfr-ḥtp n [Ḫnsw?]-Dḥwty wnḫ (n) Ḫnsw-Dḥwty wr p3 ỉr sḫr≠f šsp mnḫ.t n ny-sw.t [...] (8) [...] ỉmy-3bd≠f [n] ꜣIp.t ḥr s3 3-nw šd[8] n dw3.t-nṯr n ꜣImn Nb.t-ḫpr m3ꜥ-ḥrw s3 t3(ỉ)-ḫw ḥr wnmy n (9) Ḫnsw m W3s.t Nfr-ḥtp t3(ỉ)-ḫw ḥr wnmy n ny-sw.t Ns-pr-Nbw m3ꜥ-ḥrw s3 mỉ-nn ꜥnḫ≠f-(n)-Ḫnsw m3ꜥ-ḥrw s3 mỉ-nn ꜣIw≠f-[n]-Ḫnsw m3ꜥ-ḥrw s3 (10) mỉ-nn Ns-Ḫnsw m3ꜥ-ḥrw s3 mỉ-nn P3-dỉ-

Ḥnsw mȝꜥ-ḫrw sȝ (mỉ-nn) ꜣIw⸗f-n-Ḥnsw mȝꜥ-ḫrw sȝ mỉ-nn Šd-s(w)-Ḥnsw
mȝꜥ-ḫrw sȝ mỉ-nn (11) Dỉ-Ḥnsw mȝꜥ-ḫrw sȝ mỉ-nn Pȝ-s-ꜥȝ-ḫꜥ mȝꜥ-ḫrw sȝ
mỉ-nn Ḥnsw-ms mȝꜥ-ḫrw sȝ mỉ-nn sš ḥw.t-nṯr n pr Ḥnsw Wnn-[nfr?] mȝꜥ-
ḫrw mw.t⸗f (12) nb.t pr šps.(t) Ns-Ḥnsw-pȝ-ẖrd [sȝ.t] wp ꜥȝ.wy Nw.t m
ꜣIp.t-s.wt⁹ qbḥw n Ḥnsw m Bnn.(t) sš ḥw.t-nṯr Ḥnsw-pȝ-ẖrd

(1) Regnal year 7, first month of summer, of the King of Upper and
Lower Egypt, Usimaꜥre-setepenamon, Son of Re, Take[lo]t (III). On this
good day [of inducting the God's Father]⁵ of Khonsu in Thebes Neferhotep
by the God's Father [...] (2) [... of] Khonsu, and stolist⁶ for the third phyle
of Khonsu in Thebes Neferhotep of the temple of Khonsu-Thoth, and stolist
(3) [...] all the gods [...] (4) [...] (5) [...] of Khonsu in Thebes Neferhotep,
the fanbearer⁷ on [the right of ...,] (6) prophet of [... in] Karnak, libation
priest of Khonsu in Bennet (the Khonsu temple at Karnak), prophet and
priest on monthly service in the estate of Khonsu for the [third (?)] phyle,
[...] of Khonsu-Thoth, and stolist for the third phyle [...] (7) of Khonsu
in Thebes Neferhotep and of [Khonsu(?)]-Thoth, stolist of Khonsu-Thoth
the great, the maker of his plans, clothing bearer of the King, [...] (8) [...]
priest on monthly service of the goddess Ipet for the third phyle, the reciter
(?)⁸ for the Divine Votaress of Amon, Nebetkheper, the justified,
    son of the fanbearer on the right of (9) Khonsu in Thebes Neferhotep
and fanbearer on the right of the King, Nespernebu, the justified,
    son of the similarly titled Ankhef(en)khonsu, the justified,
    son of the similarly titled Iuef[en]khonsu (II), the justified,
    son of (10) the similarly titled Neskhonsu, the justified,
    son of the similarly titled Padikhonsu, the justified,
    son of (the similarly titled) Iuefenkhonsu (I), the justified,
    son of the similarly titled Shedsukhonsu, the justified,
    son of the similarly titled (11) Dikhonsu, the justified,
    son of the similarly titled Pasaakha, the justified,
    son of the similarly titled Khonsumes, the justified,
    son of the similarly titled, temple scribe of the estate of Khonsu, Wen-
[nefer(?)], the justified,
    while his mother (12) was the housewife and noblewoman, Neskhon-
supakhered, [daughter of] the one who opens the doors of Nut in Karnak,⁹
libation priest of Khonsu in Bennet, and temple scribe, Khonsupa-khered.

COMPANION TEXT WITH DRAWING OF FALCON-HEADED VASE

    ḏd Ḥnsw m [Wȝs.t Nfr-ḥtp ...] (2) ỉr pȝ nty-ỉw⸗f [...] (3) ỉw⸗f ḥr ḥs.t
n.[(t) Ḥnsw m Wȝs.t Nfr-ḥtp ...] (4) r wdn sȝ pn ỉw [pȝ nty-ỉw⸗f ... p](5)n
ỉw⸗f ḥr t(ȝ) š[ꜥ.t n Ḥnsw m Wȝs.t] (6) Nfr-ḥtp n(n) sȝ⸗f r s[.t⸗f ...]

    There has said Khonsu in [Thebes Neferhotep ...] (2) "As for the one

There has said Khonsu in [Thebes Neferhotep ...] (2) "As for the one who will [...], (3) he shall be in the favor of [Khonsu in Thebes Neferhotep ...] (3) regarding the installation of this son, while [the one who will ...] this [...], (5) he is subject to the sl[aughter of Khonsu in Thebes] (6) Neferhotep; his son shall not be in [his] po[sition...]."

NOTES

1. The titles in line 6 preceding the name of Nespernebu belong to a male relative whose name probably survives in the signs Ḫnsw-s[...]-mr≠f.

2. For the title, first noted in Dynasty XXI and attested in Dynasty XXII from Sheshonq I until (approximately) Takelot II, see Yoyotte 1976–77, 42–43 and 52, nn. 8–9. Examples occur in the Larger Dakhleh Stela (no. 43) and the Apanage Stela (no. 69) and on the coffin lid of Djedptahiuefankh (no. 44).

3. The maternal genealogy of Pasherenese here skips a generation, since the mother of Chief Namlot has already been cited at the conclusion of the paternal genealogy in line 8 with respect to his (half?) brother King Osorkon. The lost name at the end of line 8 could well be Sheshonq (A), making Namlot and Osorkon full brothers.

4. Literally, "child of the (same) mother"; cf. Crum 1939, 197a and 585a (ϢⲚⲘⲀⲀⲨ); Zauzich 1968, 2:303 n. 834.

5. For the basic format, see the Karnak Priestly Annals in Kruchten 1989, 12–23.

6. Cf. Wb. I, 323–34 "to clothe," and note the priest's additional title "clothing bearer" (literally, "taker of clothing").

7. Graefe (1981, 1:112) read ṯ₃(ỉ)-sr.t in lines 5, 8, and 9.

8. Determined by a man with upraised arms (reciting praises?).

9. Title designating the shrine attendant as "opener of the heavenly doors" in Karnak.

RIGHTHAND GENEALOGY OF ANKHEFENKHONSU

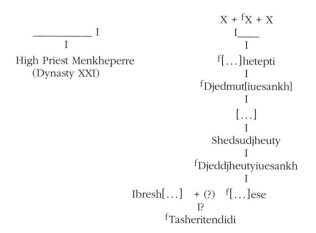

X + ᶠX + X

———————— I

I

High Priest Menkheperre
(Dynasty XXI)

I

ᶠ[...]hetepti
I
ᶠDjedmut[iuesankh]
I
[...]
I
Shedsudjheuty
I
ᶠDjeddjheutyiuesankh
I
Ibresh[...]   + (?)   ᶠ[...]ese
I?
ᶠTasheritendidi

RIGHTHAND GENEALOGY OF ANKHEFENKHONSU

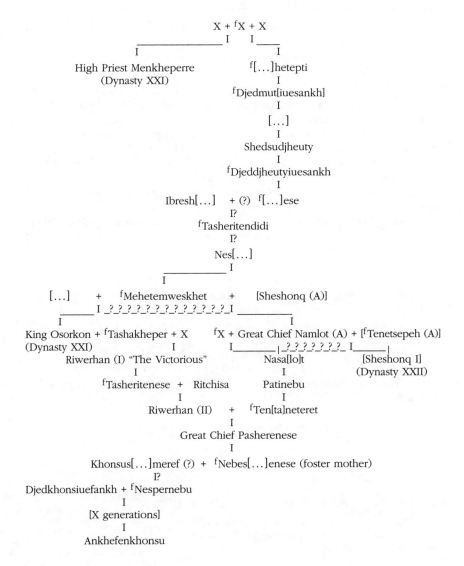

2. SERAPEUM STELA OF PASENHOR: THE ROYAL GENEALOGY OF DYNASTY XXII (S. LOUVRE IM 2846, CAT. NO. 31)

No document has proved more significant for the history of Dynasty XXII than the small limestone stela of Pasenhor (0.29 m high, 0.185 m wide, 0.052 m thick) erected in the catacombs of the Memphite Serapeum at the death of the sacred Apis bull in year 37 of Sheshonq V (ca. 731 B.C.E.) and discovered by Mariette on 26 February 1852. In conformity with contemporary practice, the votive stela provides a lengthy genealogy of its dedicant (formerly read Horpasen), who traces his lineage through fifteen preceding generations. In the sixth generation before the God's Father, the genealogy joins the royal line of Dynasty XXII and thus provides both filiation and marriages for the first four kings of the Bubastite dynasty as well as the patriarchal ancestors for an additional six generations, ending with "the Libyan Buyuwawa."

As recognized by Stern in 1883,[1] the stela settles the formerly "much-vexed question of the nationality of the Bubastites,"[2] whom early Egyptologists had identified variously as Assyrians, Chaldeans, Elamites, Syrians, or other eastern Mesopotamian Semites. Despite Stern's compelling arguments, consensus would not be reached until 1921, when W. Max Müller identified Berber elements in the names and vocabulary of the period.[3]

This is the first integral translation. Text and bibliography in Malinine, Posener, and Vercoutter 1968, 30–31 (no. 31) and pl. 10; translation of horizontal section only in Breasted 1906–7, 4:393–99 §§785–92. Commentary, and revised dating under Sheshonq V, in Kitchen 1986, 105–10 §§85–88; 285 §239; and 488 (table 19).

In the lunette are two vertical texts surrounding the representation of a standing Pȝ-sn-Ḥr[4] facing the embalmed bull labelled Wsỉr Ḥp "Osiris Apis."

RIGHTHAND TEXT FACING PASENHOR

(1) d̠(d).t.n[5] sȝ-mr≠f[6] ỉnk Ḥr mk ỉt≠f Wsỉr r nw≠f mk wỉ mỉ mk(2)≠ỉ ỉt≠ỉ Wsỉr r nw≠f hȝ rmt̠ nb pꜥ.t nb.t (3) rḫy.t ḥnmm.t nb(.t) ỉnk ny.t-sw.t n d̠.t ỉw≠ỉ ḥr ns.t n.t ỉt(4)≠ỉ Wsỉr ny.t-sw.t≠f m Ḥw.t-šsr[7] (5) ỉtt[8] wr m Ḥw.t-ḫtm-sꜥḥ≠f[9] sꜥḥ(6)≠f m Ḥw.t-wt̠s.t mȝ ỉr≠f (7) tn rḫy.t ḥnmm.t nb(.t) m wsḫ.t ỉnk (8) ny.t-sw.t n d̠.t ỉw≠ỉ ḥr ns.t n(.t) (9) ỉt≠ỉ Wsỉr ỉnk sȝ-mr≠f (10) mdt≠ỉ ḥr ỉt≠ỉ Wsỉr

(1) That which[5] the "son-who-loves"[6] said: "I am Horus who protects his father Osiris at his critical time. Protect me as (2) I protect my father Osiris at his critical time. Hail, all people, all patricians, (3) all commoners, all humanity! Mine is the kingship of eternity. I am seated on the throne of (4) my father Osiris, his kingship being in the Mansion of the Arrow.[7]

(5) The Great One has taken possession[8] of the Mansion of Sealing His Mummy,[9] even while his mummy (6) is in the Mansion of Elevation. See, then, (7) all you commoners and sunfolk in the broad hall! Mine is (8) the kingship of eternity. I am seated on the throne of (9) my father Osiris. I am a 'son-who-loves.' (10) It is on behalf of my father Osiris that I speak."

LEFTHAND TEXT FACING APIS

(1) dd-mdw ìnk s3≠f Ḥr sswn n≠f ḫfty.w≠f (2) sm3ꜥ r≠f ḫrw≠f (3) s3-mr≠f ḥm-N.t ìt-nṯr[10] P3-sn-Ḥr (4) s3 mr-mšꜥ Ḥm-Ptḥ m3ꜥ-(5)ḫrw ꜥnḫ ḏ.t

(1) Recitation: "I am his son Horus, who incinerates for him his enemies, (2) who justifies his voice." (3) The "son-who-loves," prophet of Neith, God's Father[10] Pasenhor, (4) son of the general Hemptah, the (5) justified, living forever.

MAIN TEXT, HORIZONTAL

(1) sḫn nṯr pn n ìt≠f Ptḥ n ḥsb.t 12.t 3bd 4 pr.t sw 4 n ny-sw.t ꜥ3-Ḫpr-Rꜥ (2) s3 Rꜥ Ššq dì ꜥnḫ ms.tw≠f n ḥsb.t 11.t n ḥm≠f ḥtp≠f ḥr s.t≠f (3) m t3-dsr n ḥsb.t 37.t 3bd 3 3ḫ.t sw 27 n ḥm≠f

dì≠f ꜥnḫ wd3 snb 3w(.t)-ìb n (4) s3-mr≠f ḥm-N.t ìt-nṯr[10] P3-sn-Ḥr s3 ḥ3.ty-ꜥ mr-Šmꜥy mr-ḥm.w-nṯr m Ḥnn-ny-sw.t mr-(5)mšꜥ Ḥm-Ptḥ ms.n ḥm(.t)-nṯr Ḥw.t-Ḥr Nb(.t) Ḥnn-ny-sw.t sn.t≠f nb.t pr ꜣìrt.w-r-r≠w (6) s3 mì-nn P3-sn-Ḥr ms.n ḫrp ìḥy.w n Ḥr(y)-š≠f ny-sw.t t3.wy ḥq(3) ìdb.wy (7) Ptpt-dd-s s3 mì-nn Ḥm-Ptḥ ìr.n mì-nn[11] T3-n-km.t s3 mì-nn (8) Wḏ-Ptḥ-ꜥnḫ≠f ìr.n ḥm(.t)-nṯr Ḥw.t-Ḥr Nb(.t) Ḥnn-ny-sw.t s3.t ny-sw.t nb.t pr Tì-n.t-spḥ (s3) s3 ny-sw.t mì-nn N3mr3tì (9) ìr.n ḫrp ìḥy.w n Ḥr(y)-š≠f ny-sw.t t3.wy ḥq(3) ìdb.wy Ṯ-n.t-spḥ s3 nb t3.wy Wsrkn ìr.n Wḏ-Mw.t-ꜥnḫ≠s s3 ny-sw.t Tkrìwṯ (10) mw.t-nṯr K3ps s3 ny-sw.t Wsrkn mw.t-nṯr T3-šd-Ḫnsw s3 ny-sw.t Ššnq mw.t-nṯr Kr-(11)ꜥmꜥ.t (s3) ìt-nṯr wr ꜥ3 N3mr3tì mw.t-nṯr Ṯ-n.t-spḥ s3 mì-nn Ššnq ìr.n mw.t ny-sw.t (12) Mḫ(w).t-n-wšḫ.t s3 mì-nn P3-ꜥḥwt(y) s3 mì-nn Nb-nšì s3 mì-nn (13) M3w3s3n s3 Tḥn Bwyww3w3 mn sp-2 (14) w3ḫ sp-2 dd sp-2 w3ḏ sp-2 m Pr-Ḥr(y)-š≠f ny-sw.t t3.wy ḥq(3) ìdb.wy m s wꜥ s3 s (15) wꜥ[12] nn sk r nḥḥ sp-2 ḏ.t sp-2 m Ḥnn-ny-sw.t

(1) This god (Apis) joined with his father Ptah in regnal year 12, fourth month of winter, day 4, of King Aakheperre, (2) Son of Re, Shesho(n)q (V), given life, being born in regnal year 11 of His Majesty, and resting upon his seat (3) in the necropolis in regnal year 37, third month of inundation, day 27 of His Majesty.

May he give life, prosperity, health, and joy to (4) the son-whom-he-loves, prophet of Neith, and God's Father[10] Pasenhor,

son of the mayor, overseer of Upper Egypt, overseer of prophets in Heracleopolis, (5) the general Hemptah, and born of the prophetess of Hathor, Lady of Heracleopolis, his sister, the housewife Ithores,

(6) son of the like-titled Pasenhor, and born of the chief of sistrum players of Herishef, King of the Two Lands, ruler of the Two Banks, (7) the woman Petpetdedes,

son of the like-titled Hemptah, and born by the like-titled[11] woman Tchankeme,

son of the like-titled (8) Wedjptahankhef, and born by the prophetess of Hathor, Lady of Heracleopolis, the royal daughter, the housewife Tenetsepeh,

(son) of the royal son, the like-titled Namlot, (9) and born by the chief of sistrum players of Herishef, King of the Two Lands, Ruler of the Two Banks, the woman Tenetsepeh,

son of the Lord of the Two Lands Osorkon, and born by the woman Wedjmutankhes,

son of King Takelot (10) and the God's Mother Kapes,

son of King Osorkon and the God's Mother Tashedkhonsu,

son of King Sheshonq and the God's Mother (11) Karoama,

(son) of the God's Father, great chief Namlot and the God's Mother Tenetsepeh,

son of the like-titled Sheshonq, and born by the king's mother (12) Mehetemweskhet,

son of the like-titled Pahuty,

son of the like-titled Nebneshi,

son of the like-titled (13) Mawasen,

son of the Libyan Buyuwawa,

firm! (14) stable! enduring! flourishing! in the temple of Herishef, King of the Two Lands, Ruler of the Two Banks, being one man the son of one (15) man[12] without interruption forever! and ever! in Heracleopolis.

NOTES

1. See Stern 1883, 15–26.

2. Brugsch 1996, vii and 365 n. 1.

3. Müller 1921, 193–97 (note the defense of Stern in col. 195); 1908, 361–63. For the supposed Asian identifications, see Oppert 1873, 2:183; Haigh 1877, 38–40, 64–71; Renouf 1891, 599–603; Revillout 1899, 367–75; Petrie 1905b, 231–32; and Caminos 1958, 12–13.

4. For the reading of the name as Pasenhor, and not the formerly accepted Horpasen, see Leahy 1983, 37–48.

5. Phonetically written ḏt-n for the past relative form, "that which NN said."

6. Title of the ritual impersonator of the deity Horus.

7. For Ḥw.t-šsr, see Gauthier 1925–31, 4:134: a locality or sanctuary in the fifteenth Upper Egyptian nome (Wn.t) or a name for the major local temple of Thoth (Ashmunein).

8. For ỉt m "to take possession of," see Gunn 1941, 147–48. The geminated verb probably represents a nominal form, with emphasis on following adverbial

expressions. The wording indicates that Horus (the great one) has performed the proper burial ritual of his father Osiris (Apis), and he may thus ascend the throne.

9. Cf. (?) Gauthier 1925–31, 4:120: Ḥw.t-ḫtm (?), a region of Memphis attested in the Fourth Dynasty.

10. Contra Breasted, who interpreted all the signs after s3-mr⸗f as a writing of "prophet of Neith." The reading "God's Father" is also recognized by Kitchen 1986, 105.

11. The implication is that Tchankeme held the same feminine titles as her son's wife, Petpetdedes, while the elder Pasenhor and Hemptah (like Wedjptah-ankhef and Nimlot) held the same masculine titles as their descendant, the junior Hemptah. On the basis of this text, Legrain challenged the traditional interpretation of mỉ-nn ("like-titled" lit., "like this") in favor of a supposed title "manoun" ("of similar lineage?"), but his argument is vitiated by a conflation of personalities, genealogies, dates, and the tendency of different monuments to highlight differing titles. See Legrain 1909a, 1–10; and cf. Bierbrier 1975, xiv–xv, with the remarks of Leahy 1992, 148. The increasingly common expression is first attested in Dynasty XXII; see Erman and Grapow 1926–63, 2:37/11.

12. The phrase wꜥ s3 wꜥ "one man the son of one man" is a recognized idiom for paternal succession (Erman and Grapow 1926–63, 1:274/10). The patrilineal aspect is strengthened in the Pasenhor stela by the unique addition of the word s "man." Examples are gathered by Jansen-Winkeln 1991a, 53–56, although the author's proposed exceptions to the standard translation are not problematic and his reinterpretation unacceptable. The detailing of a long genealogy concludes with a double description of the stemma from descendants to ascendants (sons of sons) and from ascendants to descendants (fathers of fathers): "with one man the son of one man in this house, being the fathers of fathers since the time of the ancestors." Contra Jansen-Winkeln (1991a, 55), the text makes excellent sense; each man is both son and father in an unbroken succession. The same explanation holds for his second instance: "I am the son of great prophets, one man the son of one man since antiquity." The author's odd refusal to allow a predicative relationship between wꜥ and s3 (one = the son of one) ignores the basic usage of s3 "son" in Egyptian filiations (NN s3 NN meaning "NN = the son of NN"), serving as the pattern for the present construction. The unexceptional presence of the initial preposition m "being (one man the son of one man)" hardly renders this interpretation "völlig ausgeschlossen."

STEMMA OF PASENHOR

The Libyan Buyuwawa
I
great chief Mawasen
I
great chief Nebneshi
I
great chief Pahuty
I

great chief Sheshonq	+	king's mother Mehetemweskhet
	I	
great chief Namlot	+	fTenetsepeh
	I	
King Sheshonq (I)	+	fKaroama
	I	
King Osorkon (I)	+	fTashedkhonsu
	I	
King Takelot (I)	+	fKapes
	I	
King Osorkon (II)	+	fWedjmutankhes
	I	
Prince Namlot	+	fTenetsepeh
	I	
Mayor Wedjptahankhef	+	Princess Tenetsepeh
	I	
Mayor Hemptah	+	fTchankeme
	I	
Mayor Pasenhor	+	fPetpetdedes
	I	
Mayor Hemptah	+	his sister Ithores
	I	

The son-who-loves, prophet of Neith, God's Father Pasenhor

3. THE GENEALOGY OF THE MEMPHITE PRIESTLY ELITE
(BERLIN 23673)

Carved in four registers on white limestone (0.90 m long x 0.45 m high), the Berlin genealogy lists sixty generations of a single family of Memphite priests who held office from the contemporary reign of Sheshonq V backwards to the time of Montuhotep I and possibly earlier, a span of at least thirteen hundred years.[1] On the right, a now-lost figure of the king faced four smaller registers, each containing fifteen advancing priests wearing panther skins, carrying flails, and labeled by title, name, and often by reign. For ease of modern transport, the surface relief has been removed from a block once part of the corner of a larger room wall. Traces of mortar on the upper left edge indicate the perpendicular join of the adjacent corner block. The emphasis upon paternal genealogy in the professional priesthood recalls the statement of Herodotus (2.142–143), who was shown temple votive statues representing 345 generations of the priestly caste. The images of priests on the Memphite block may represent similar statues in a temple setting.

As preserved, the Berlin table provides the primary evidence for the succession of Memphite high priests for Dynasty XXI and much of the New and Middle Kingdoms, though earlier generations seem to exhibit the "telescoping" otherwise typical of oral genealogies. Thus, only a single pontiff is noted for a period of roughly 150 years between Amonemnisut (reg. 1, no. 15) and Rameses II (reg. 2, no. 2). Some of these discrepancies may be explained if the relief was continued onto the adjoining block around the left corner, a practice well-attested though relatively infrequent. The Dynasty XXI sequence is paralleled on a stela from the Serapeum (S. Louvre 96), whose genealogy diverges in the reign of Sheshonq I by following the senior son and heir of the high priest Shedsunefertum (reg. 1, no. 9). The Berlin genealogy does not always cite an individual's highest title, and neither Shedsunefertum nor his father Ankhefensakhmet ("A") is designated as high priest. The family's loss of the office of Memphite pontiff was a result of the formal political program of Osorkon II (see Kitchen 1986, 193 §155; and the king's Philadelphia-Cairo Statue, no. 74). Names distinguished by capital letters follow the system of Kitchen; lowercase letters are given to individuals not in Kitchen.

For the text, see Borchardt 1935, 96–112 and pls. 2–2a; 1932, 618–22. For discussion, see Redford 1986, 63–64; Wente 1967b, 155–56; Kees 1962, 146–49; Gardiner 1961, 50, 160, and 443; Wilson 1977, 125–29; Kemp 1983, 155; and Kitchen 1986, 69–71 §56; 187–92 §§151–53; 487 (table 18); and 560 §474.

LABEL FOR KING
    ḏd≠f(?) dmḏ.n.tw wr.w-ḫrp.w-ḥm.w² n ny-sw.t Šš(n)q mꜣꜥ-ḫrw

He said (?): "The 'Chiefs of Master-craftsmen'² are united for King Shesho(n)q, the justified."

LABELS FOR FILES OF PRIESTS
    (1/1) ỉt-nṯr Ptḥ ḥm-nṯr Sḥm.t ꜥnḫ≠f-n-Sḥm.t sꜣ (1/2) n ḥm-nṯr Sḥm.t Pꜣ-ḥm-nṯr sꜣ (1/3) n ḥm-nṯr Sḥm.t Pꜣ-šr-Sḥm.t sꜣ (1/4) n ḥm-nṯr³ ḥry-sštꜣ s.t wr.t Pꜣ-ḥm-nṯr sꜣ (1/5) n ḥm-nṯr [ꜥḥm(?)⁴] m Ḥm Sꜣ-Sḥm.t sꜣ (1/6) n ḥm-nṯr Sḥm.t Pꜣ-ḥm-nṯr sꜣ (1/7) n ḥm-nṯr ḥry-sštꜣ s.t wr.t ỉw≠f-ꜥꜣ-n-P(t)ḥ sꜣ (1/8) n ḥm-nṯr ḥry-sštꜣ s.t wr.t Pꜣ-ḥm-nṯr sꜣ (1/9) n ḥm-nṯr ḥry-sštꜣ s.t wr.t Šd-(sw)-Nfr-tm sꜣ (1/10) n ḥm-nṯr ꜥnḫ≠f-n-Sḥm.t sꜣ (1/11) n ḥry-sštꜣ s.t wr.t ḥm-nṯr […] ꜥšꜣ-ḫt sꜣ (1/12) n ḥm-nṯr Pp m rk ny-sw.t Pꜣ-sbꜣ-ḫꜥ-(n)-Nỉw.t sꜣ (1/13) n wr-ḫrp.w-ḥm.w (Ḥr)-sꜣ-ꜣs.t m rk ny-sw.t Pꜣ-sbꜣ-ḫꜥ-(n)-Nỉw.t sꜣ (1/14) n wr-ḫrp.w-ḥm.w Pp m rk ny-sw.t ꜥꜣ-ḫpr-Rꜥ Stp-n-ỉ[mn] sꜣ (1/15) n wr-

ḥrp.w-ḥm.w ꜥš3-ḫt m rk ny-sw.t ꜣImn-m-ny-sw.t[5] s3 (...?) (2/1) n wr-ḫrp.
w-ḥm.w Ptḥ-m-3ḫ.t [... s3] (2/2) n wr-ḫrp.w-ḥm.w Nfr-rnp.t m rk ny-sw.t
Wsr-m3ꜥ.t-Rꜥ-stp-n-Rꜥ s3 (2/3) n wr-ḫrp.w-ḥm.w Ptḥ-m-3ḫ.t m rk ny-sw.t
Wsr-m3ꜥ.t-Rꜥ-stp-n-Rꜥ (s3) (2/4) n wr-ḫrp.w-ḥm.w [...]nšn.t m rk ny-sw.t
Wsr-m3ꜥ.t-Rꜥ-stp-n-Rꜥ (s3) (2/5) n ꜣt-nṯr ꜣImn m ꜣIp.t-s.wt ꜣmy-r3 k3.wt n
Wsr-m3ꜥ.t-Rꜥ-stp-n-Rꜥ Ptḥ-ḥtp s3 (2/6) n wr-ḫrp.w-ḥm.w Nṯr.wy-ḥtp m rk
ny-sw.t Mn-m3ꜥ.t-Rꜥ s3 (2/7) n wr-ḫrp.w-ḥm.w Skr-m-s3꞊f m rk ny-sw.t
Mn-m3ꜥ.t-Rꜥ s3 (2/8) n wr-ḫrp.w-ḥm.w Ty m rk ny-sw.t Ḏsr-ḫpr(.w)-Rꜥ Stp-
n-Rꜥ s3 (2/9) n ꜣt-nṯr ꜣImn-Rꜥ nb [n ꜣI]p.t-s.wt Skr-m-s3꞊f s3 (2/10) n ꜣt-nṯr
Sḫm.t wꜥb n ny-sw.t ꜣt-nṯr ꜣIy ꜣIpw s3 (2/11) n wr-ḫrp.w-ḥm.w Wr-mr m
rk ny-sw.t Nb-m3ꜥ.t-Rꜥ s3 (2/12) n wr-ḫrp.w-ḥm.w Pn-p3-nbs m rk ny-sw.t
Nb-m3ꜥ.t-Rꜥ s3 (2/13) n ꜣt-nṯr ḥry-sšt3 Ptḥ Nḥmm-Ptḥ s3 (2/14) n s(t)m n Ptḥ
wr-m3ꜥ.w[6] m rk ny-sw.t Mn-ḫpr-Rꜥ s3 (2/15) [n ... s3] (...?) (3/1) n ꜣt-nṯr
Ty s3 (3/2) n wr-ḫrp.w-ḥm.w P3-ꜣmy-rd m rk ny-sw.t Ḏsr-k3-Rꜥ s3 (3/3) n
ꜣt-nṯr ḥry-sšt(3) n Ptḥ Ty s3 (3/4) n wr-ḫrp.w-ḥm.w Mnṯ(w) m rk ny-sw.t
Nb-pḥ.ty-Rꜥ s3 (3/5) n ꜣt-nṯr wr-m3ꜥ.w ꜣIwnw Ḥr-m3ꜥ-ḫrw m rk ny-sw.t ꜣIpp
s3 (3/6) n s(t)m n Ptḥ Wr-ḥtp m rk ny-sw.t Š3rk s3 (3/7) n ꜣt-nṯr Ḥr-s3-3s.t
s3 (3/8) n ꜣt-nṯr ꜣIrmr s3 (3/9) n ꜣt-nṯr K3-Ḥp s3 (3/10) n wꜥb ḫr(y)-ḥb(.
t) Ḥr-m-ḥtp [s3] (3/11) n ꜣt-nṯr ḥry-sšt3 n Ptḥ Ptḥ-m-ḥ3.t s3 (3/12) n s(t)m
n Ptḥ P3-sr m rk ny-sw.t ꜥ3-qn[7] s3 (3/13) n wr-ḫrp.w-ḥm.w Sr-mt(?)[8] m rk
ny-sw.t ꜣIby s3 (3/14) [n ... s3] (3/15) [n ... s3] (...?) (4/1) n wr-ḫrp.w-ḥm.w
[W]ḫt(?)[9] m rk ny-sw.t Ḥꜥ-k3-Rꜥ (s3) (4/2) n ꜣt-nṯr ḥm-nṯr Sbk Sḥtp-ꜣb-snb
s3 (4/3) n wr-ḫrp.w-ḥm.w ꜥnḫ-Nbw-k3.w-Rꜥ m rk ny-sw.t Ḥꜥ-k3-Rꜥ s3 (4/4)
n wr-ḫrp.w-ḥm.w ꜥnḫ-Ḥꜥ-k3-Rꜥ m rk ny-sw.t Nbw-k3.w-Rꜥ s3 (4/5) n wr-
ḫrp.w-ḥm.w ꜥnḫ-Sḥtp-ꜣb-Rꜥ m rk ny-sw.t Ḥpr-k3-Rꜥ s3 (4/6) n ꜣt-nṯr ꜣmy-r3
nꜣ.wt t3ty Nṯr.wy-ḥtp m rk ny-sw.t Sḥtp-ꜣb-Rꜥ s3 (4/7) n ꜣt-nṯr ḥry ḥm.w ḫrp
ꜣ3.t nb.(t) n ny-sw.t Skr-m-ḥb s3 (4/8) n [...] ḥm-nṯr S3t.t nb.(t) ꜥnḫ-t3.wy
Nb-nfr.w s3 (4/9) n wꜥb ḫr(y)-ḥb(.t) Mnw-m-ḥb s3 (4/10) n ꜣt-nṯr Ptḥ-ḥtp
s3 (4/11) n ꜣt-nṯr ḥry-sšt(3) n Ptḥ Nḥmm s3 (4/12) n ꜣt-nṯr ḥry-sšt(3) n Ptḥ
Mn-m-ḥ3.t s3 (4/13) n wr-ḫrp.w-ḥm.w Ptḥ-m-ḥb m rk ny-sw.t Nb-ḥp.t-Rꜥ[10]
s3 (4/14) [n ... s3] (4/15) [n ... s3] (...?)

(1/1) The God's Father of Ptah and prophet of Sakhmet, Ankhefensakhmet ("b"), son (1/2) of the prophet of Sakhmet, Pahemnetcher ("d"),
son (1/3) of the prophet of Sakhmet, Pasher(en)sakhmet, son (1/4) of the
prophet[3] and chief of secrets of the sanctuary, Pahemnetcher ("c"), son
(1/5) of the prophet [of the image (?)[4]] in Letopolis, Sisakhmet, son (1/6) of
the prophet of Sakhmet, Pahemnetcher ("b"), son (1/7) of the prophet and
chief of secrets of the sanctuary, Iwefaaenp(t)ah, son (1/8) of the prophet
and chief of secrets of the sanctuary, Pahemnetcher ("a"), son (1/9) of
the prophet and chief of secrets of the sanctuary, Shed(su)nefertum, son
(1/10) of the prophet, Ankhefensakhmet ("A"), son (1/11) of the chief of
secrets of the sanctuary and prophet [...], Ashachet ("B"), son (1/12) of the

prophet, Pepi ("B"), in the reign of King Pseusennes (I), son (1/13) of the Chief of Master-craftsmen, (Hor)siese ("J"), in the reign of King Pseusennes (I), son (1/14) of the Chief of Master-craftsmen, Pepi ("A"), in the reign of Aakheperre Setepena[mon] (= Pseusennes I), son (1/15) of the Chief of Master-craftsmen, Ashachet ("A"), in the reign of King Amonemnisut,[5] son (continuation on missing block?) (2/1) of the Chief of Master-craftsmen, Ptahemachet ("b"), [..., son] (2/2) of the Chief of Master-craftsmen, Nefer-renpet, in the reign of King Usimaᶜresetepenre (= Rameses II), son (2/3) of the Chief of Master-craftsmen, Ptahemachet ("a"), in the reign of King Usimaᶜresetepenre (= Rameses II), (son) (2/4) of the Chief of Master-crafts-men, [...]neshnet (?), in the reign of King Usimaᶜresetepenre (= Rameses II), (son) (2/5) of the God's Father of Amon in Karnak, overseer of works of Usimaᶜresetepenre (= Rameses II), Ptahhotep, son (2/6) of the Chief of Master-craftsmen, Netcherwyhotep ("b"), in the reign of King Menmaatre (= Seti I), son (2/7) of the Chief of Master-craftsmen, Sokaremsaf ("b"), in the reign of King Menmaatre (= Seti I), son (2/8) of the Chief of Mas-ter-craftsmen, Tiye ("c"), in the reign of King Djeserkheperre Setepenre (=Horemheb), son (2/9) of the God's Father of Amon-Re, Lord [of Kar]nak, Sokaremsaf ("a"), son (2/10) of the God's Father of Sakhmet, *wab*-priest of the king and God's Father Ay, Ipu, son (2/11) of the Chief of Master-craftsmen, Wermer, in the reign of King Nebmaatre (= Amonhotep III), son (2/12) of the Chief of Master-craftsmen, Penpanebes, in the reign of King Nebmaatre (= Amonhotep III), (son) (2/13) of the God's Father and chief of secrets of Ptah, Nehememptah, son (2/14) of the *setem*-priest of Ptah, the chief of seers,[6] in the reign of King Menkheperre (= Tuth-mosis III), son (2/15) [of ....] (continuation on missing block?) (3/1) of the God's Father Tiye ("b"), son (3/2) of the Chief of Master-craftsmen, Paimired, in the reign of King Djeserkare (= Amonhotep I), son (3/3) of the God's Father and chief of secrets of Ptah, Tiye ("a"), son (3/4) of the Chief of Master-craftsmen, Montu, in the reign of King Nebpehtyre (= Ahmose), son (3/5) of the God's Father and chief of seers of Heliopolis, Hormaakheru, in the reign of King Apophis, son (3/6) of the *setem*-priest of Ptah, Werhotep, in the reign of King Sharek (=? Salatis), son (3/7) of the God's Father, Horsiese, son (3/8) of the God's Father, Irmer, son (3/9) of the God's Father, Kahap, son (3/10) of the *wab*-priest and lector priest, Horemhotep, [son] (3/11) of the God's Father and chief of secrets of Ptah, Ptahemhat, son (3/12) of the *setem*-priest of Ptah, Paser, in the reign of King Aaqen,[7] son (3/13) of the Chief of Master-craftsmen, Sermut (?),[8] in the reign of King Iby, son (3/14) [of ..., son] (3/15) [of ..., son] (continuation on missing block?) (4/1) of the Chief of Master-craftsmen, Wehket (?),[9] in the reign of King Khakare (= Senwosret III), son (4/2) of the God's Father and prophet of Sobek, Sehetepibseneb, son (4/3) of the Chief of Master-craftsmen, Ankhnubkhaure, in the reign of King Khakare

(= Senwosret III), son (4/4) of the Chief of Master-craftsmen, Ankhkhakare, in the reign of King Nubkhaure (= Amonemhat II), son (4/5) of the Chief of Master-craftsmen, Ankhsehetepibre, in the reign of King Kheperkare (= Senwosret I), son (4/6) of the God's Father, overseer of the city and vizier, Netcherwyhotep ("a"), in the reign of King Sehetepibre (= Amonemhat I), son (4/7) of the God's Father, overseer of craftsmen, and controller of every office of the king, Sokaremheb, son (4/8) of [the … and] prophet of Satis, Lady of Ankh-Tawy, Nebneferu, son (4/9) of the *wab*-priest and lector priest, Minemheb, son (4/10) of the God's Father, Ptahhotep, son (4/11) of the God's Father and chief of secrets of Ptah, Nehemem, son (4/12) of the God's Father and chief of secrets of Ptah, Minemhat, son (4/13) of the Chief of Master-craftsmen, Ptahemheb, in the reign of of King Nebhepetre[10] (= Montuhotep I), son (4/14) [of …, son] (4/15) [of …] (continuation on missing block?).

NOTES

1. Redford (1986, 63) suggests Sheshonq IV (ca. 793–787), but following the succession of known high priests after Shedsunefertum, the eighth subsequent generation (the time of Ankhefensakhmet "b" of col. 1/1) falls in the time of Pamiu and Sheshonq V (ca. 760); see Kitchen 1986, 487, table 18.
2. Title of the high priest of Memphis.
3. Borchardt translated "God's Father."
4. Borchardt restored ꜥḥm, "image/falcon."
5. Following Grdseloff 1947b, 207–11; versus Borchardt 1935, 99, who read ꜣImn-m-îp.t-rsy.t "Amenophthis."
6. Title of the high priest of Heliopolis.
7. The inclusion of the discredited Hyksos kings Apophis, Sharek, and Aaqen demonstrates the unbroken line of the priestly ancestors, not the perceived legitimacy of the Hyksos themselves. The name Aaqen has been transformed from "Great of Valor" to "Valiant Ass."
8. So copied by Borchardt, who transliterated Šr-gm (?).
9. So Borchardt; traces unclear.
10. Borchardt read Nb-ḫrw-Rꜥ.

4. THE STATUE GENEALOGY OF BASA
CHICAGO OIM 10729

Purchased by J. H. Breasted in Cairo in 1919, the limestone block statue of Basa (IV) of Dendera depicts the prelate seated on a stepped base with his legs drawn up before his chest and his arms crossed over his knees. He is fully enveloped within a cloak, from which only the head and hands protrude and which provides a surface for an extensive biographical text of thirty-two lines, listing the owner's numerous titles as well as the names and titles of twenty-six generations of paternal ascendants and four maternal ascendants. On the basis of style and genealogical reckoning, the statue can be assigned to the late Twenty-Second or Twenty-Third Dynasty, allowing for nineteen generations from Basa IV to his famous ancestor, Nebwenenef, the Theban high priest of Amon appointed by Rameses II in his first regnal year. This extended genealogy, which offers unique testimony for the Denderite temple hierarchy from the New Kingdom through the Third Intermediate Period, should be compared with the preceding Genealogy of the Memphite Priestly Elite (Berlin 23673). Like the Memphite list, the text of Basa serves to justify the hereditary source and legitimacy of the incumbent's many income-generating offices. Presumably placed within the local temple precinct, Basa's statue served as a public record of individual and family status.

Featured prominently on the front of the statue is a tableau of Basa, in ceremonial leopard skin, worshiping the enthroned Osiris and standing Isis; at either shoulder appears a smaller vignette of Basa kneeling before a mummiform Osiris. A skyline of stars frames scenes and texts on the front and lateral surfaces. The statue's maximum dimensions measure 41.0 cm in height by 21.4 cm in width by 24.4 cm in depth.

For the text, translation and discussion, see Ritner 1994, 205–26.

CENTRAL TABLEAU: BASA ADORES OSIRIS AND ISIS

Above Basa
(1) ḥm-nṯr 3-nw n (2) Ḥw.t-Ḥr Nb.(t) ʾIwn.t (3) ḥry-[sš]t3 mnḫ.(t) (4) s[š ḥw.]t-[nṯ]r B3s3
Third Prophet of (2) Hathor, Lady of Dendera, (3) overseer of secrets of clothing (stolist priest), (4) temple scribe, Basa.

Before Osiris
(1) ḏd-mdw ỉn Wsỉr Wn-(2)nfr ḥr(y)-ỉb ʾIwn.t nṯr ʿ3 (3) ḥq3 ḏ.t
Recitation by Osiris On-(2)nophris, resident in Dendera, great god, (3) ruler of eternity.

Before Isis
ḏd-mdw ỉn 3s.t wr.(t) mw.t-nṯr ḥr(y.t)-ỉb ʾIwn.t Nb.(t) p.t ḥnw.t nṯr.w
Recitation by Isis the great, the God's Mother, resident in Dendera, Lady of heaven, Mistress of the Gods.

VIGNETTE ON RIGHT SHOULDER

Above Kneeling Basa
(1) ḥm-nṯr 3-nw n Ḥw.t-Ḥr Nb.(t) ʾIwn.t ḥry-sšt3 (2) mnḫ.(t) sš ḥw.t-nṯr B3s3

Third Prophet of Hathor, Lady of Dendera, overseer of secrets (2) of clothing, temple scribe, Basa.

Before Osiris
    Wsîr ḥr(y)-îb ᵓIwn.t
    Osiris resident in Dendera.

VIGNETTE ON LEFT SHOULDER

Above Kneeling Basa
    (1) [ḥm-nṯr 3-nw n] Ḥw.t-Ḥr Nb.(t) ᵓIwn.t ḥry-sštȝ (2) [mnḫ.(t) sš] ḥw.t-nṯr Bȝsȝ
    Third Prophet of Hathor, Lady of Dendera, overseer of secrets (2) of clothing, temple scribe, Basa.

Before Osiris
    [Wsîr ḥr(y)-îb ᵓIwn.t]
    Osiris resident in Dendera.

GENEALOGICAL TEXT
    (Front: eight vertical columns below tableau) (1) ḥm-nṯr 3-nw n Ḥw.t-Ḥr Nb.(t) ᵓIwn.t ḥry-sštȝ n nṯr.w nṯr.wt nb.w ᵓIwn.t wᶜb-ᶜ.wy wȝḫ (2) mnḫ.(t) n pr pn sš ḥw.t-nṯr sš wbȝ sš šn sš {ḫt}-(3) tȝ¹ ḥw.t-nṯr n pr Ḥw.t-Ḥr Nb.(t) ᵓIwn.t wn ᶜȝ.wy p.tᶻ n nṯr.w nṯr.wt nb.w m ᵓIwn.t îmy-rȝ dî (4) ḥtp.w-nṯr.w nb.w ḥr s.tᶻs sḥtp nṯr m dbḥ.[w] îmy-(5)rȝ snṯ wrᶻ n Nb.(t) p.t ḥm-nṯr îmy-wnw.tᶻf n sȝ 3-nw îmy-rȝ šnᶻ îmy-(6) s.t-ᶜ{ȝ}² ḥr sȝ tp(y) sȝ 3-nw îmy-rȝ wᶜb Šḫm.t îmy-rȝ îḫ ḥry ḥm.t (7) îmy-ȝbd ḥr sȝ tp(y) sȝ 2-nw sȝ 3-nw sȝ 4-nw n pr Ḥw.t-Ḥr Nb.(t) ᵓIwn.t ḥm-nṯr (8) Ḥw.t-Ḥr ḥry s.t-wr.t ḥm-nṯr Rᶜ ḥr(y)-îb ᵓIwn.t ḥm-nṯr n ᵓImn ḥr(y)-îb (right side: nine vertical columns, final three below vignette) (9) [ᵓIw]n.t ḥm-[nṯr] Wsîr ny-sw.t nṯr. w ḥm-nṯr Wsîr-Skr ḥm-nṯr Ptḥ Šḫm.t (10) ḥr(y)-îb ᵓIwn.t ḥm-nṯr n Wsîr-Ḥmȝq ḥm-nṯr Mnw-kȝ-mw.tᶻf ḥr(y)-îb ᵓIwn.t ḥm-nṯr (11) n mdw-ᶜnḫ n Ḥw.t-Ḥr Smȝ-Tȝ.wy ḥm-nṯr n ᵓImn-m-ᵓIp.t ḥr(y)-îb ᵓIwn.t sḥtp ḥm.tᶻsȝ îhy smȝ-îr(w)⁴ (12) wᶜb îqr îmȝḫ ḥr Nb.(t) ᵓIwn.t Bȝsȝ sȝ ḥm-nṯr sḥtp ḥm.tᶻsȝ (13) ḥm-nṯr n mdw-ᶜnḫ n Ḥw.t-Ḥr îmy-rȝ îḫ n pr Ḥw.t-Ḥr Nb.(t) ᵓIwn.t Ḏd-Ḥr-îwᶻf-ᶜnḫ (14) mȝᶜ-ḫrw
    sȝ mî-nw Bȝsȝ mȝᶜ-ḫrw
    sȝ mî-nw ḥm Nbw.t ḥnk îmy-rȝ šnᶻ îmy-(15) s.t-ᶜ² ḥr sȝ 3-nw Ns-pȝ-ḥrd (16) mȝᶜ-ḫrw
    sȝ ḥm Nbw.t wᶜb (ḥb?)-îtr⁵ wr 15-(17)n.t⁶ îmy-rȝ ḥm.w-nṯr Nb.(t) ᵓIwn. t îmy-rȝ snṯ (back: six vertical columns) (18) wrᶻ Nb.t p.t ḥm-nṯr 3-nw n Ḥw.t-Ḥr Nb.(t) [ᵓIw]n.t ḥry-sštȝ mnḫ.(t) ḥm-nṯr Ḥw.t-Ḥr ḥry s.t-wr.t ḥm-nṯr n Wsîr ny-sw.t (19) nṯr.w wn ᶜȝ.wy p.tᶻ n nṯr.w îmy.(w) ᵓIwn.t sḥtp nṯr m

dbḥ{n}.w ḥm-nṯr P(ꜣ)-Rꜥ ḥr(y)-ỉb ʾIwn.t (20) ḥm-nṯr Mnw-kꜣ-mw.t≠f ỉmy-rꜣ
šn.d² ỉmy-s.t-n.t-ꜥ² ḥr sꜣ 3-nw sḥtp ḥm.t≠sꜣ ỉḥy smꜣ ỉr(w)⁴ ỉmꜣḫ ḫr Nb.(t)
ʾIwn.t (21) Bꜣsꜣ

    sꜣ mỉ-nw Ḏd-Ḥr-ỉw≠f-ꜥnḫ mꜣꜥ-ḫrw
    sꜣ mỉ-nw Bꜣsꜣ mꜣꜥ-ḫrw
    sꜣ mỉ-nw Ns-(22)p(ꜣ)-ḫrd mꜣꜥ-ḫrw
    sꜣ mỉ-nw Pnpn mꜣꜥ-ḫrw
    sꜣ mỉ-nw Ns-kꜣ-f(ꜣy)-ꜥ
    sꜣ mỉ-nn ʾImn-m-ʾIp.t mꜣꜥ-ḫrw
    sꜣ (23) mỉ-nw P(ꜣ)-ꜥn-ḫr-Mꜣꜥ.t mꜣꜥ-ḫrw
    sꜣ mỉ-nw Wḏꜣ≠f-r-wy mꜣꜥ-ḫrw
    sꜣ mỉ-nw P(ꜣ)-Nḥs mꜣꜥ-ḫrw
    sꜣ mỉ-nw (left side: nine vertical columns, initial three below vignette)
(24) ʾImn-šd≠f mꜣꜥ-ḫrw
    sꜣ mỉ-nw Pꜣ-n-nw-(25)Nbw.(t)-r≠f mꜣꜥ-ḫrw
    sꜣ mỉ-nw Sꜣ-Ḥ.wt-Ḥr mꜣꜥ-ḫrw
    sꜣ (26) ḥm-nṯr tp(y) n Ḥw.t-Ḥr Nb.(t) ʾIwn.t Ḥꜥy (27) mꜣꜥ-ḫrw
    sꜣ mỉ-nw Smꜣ-tꜣ.wy mꜣꜥ-ḫrw
    sꜣ ḥm-nṯr tp(y) n ʾImn-Rꜥ ny-sw.t nṯr.w Nb-wnn(≠f) (28) mꜣꜥ-ḫrw
    sꜣ ḥm-nṯr tp(y) n Ḥw.t-Ḥr Nb.(t) ʾIwn.t ỉmy-rꜣ ỉḫ ỉmy-rꜣ sḫ.t ỉmy-rꜣ
šnw.t Smꜣ-tꜣ.wy mꜣꜥ-ḫrw
    sꜣ (29) mỉ-nw Sꜣ-n-Ḥw.t-Ḥr mꜣꜥ-ḫrw
    sꜣ mỉ-nn ʾImn-ḥtp
    sꜣ mỉ-nw Sꜣ-Ḥw.t-Ḥr
    (30) sꜣ mỉ-nw Nfr mꜣꜥ-ḫrw
    sꜣ mỉ-nw ỉmy-rꜣ gs-pr Dd mꜣꜥ-ḫrw
    ỉr.n nb.(t)-pr ỉḥy.t n (31) ʾImn-Rꜥ ḥm.(t) n Nb.(t) ʾIwn.t Tꜣy≠s-mr-dn
sꜣ.t ḥm-nṯr Ḥw.t-Ḥr Nb.(t) ʾIwn.t ḫꜣ.ty-ꜥ (32) n ʾIwn.t P(ꜣ)-dỉ-Nb.ty
    sꜣ mỉ-nw Ḏd-Ḥnsw-ỉw≠f-ꜥnḫ
    sꜣ mỉ-nw Ns-pꜣ-ỉḥy mꜣꜥ-ḫrw

(1) Third Prophet of Hathor, Lady of Dendera, overseer of secrets of all
the gods and goddesses of Dendera, pure one of hands, stolist (2) priest of
this temple, temple scribe, scribe of the forecourt, scribe of investigation,
scribe of the temple (3) cadaster[1] of the estate of Hathor, Lady of Dendera,
he who opens the doors of heaven[2] of all the gods and goddesses in Dendera, overseer of providing (4) all divine offerings in her (Hathor's) place,
he who pacifies the deity with necessities, over(5)seer of the great plan[2] of
the Lady of heaven, prophet and astrologer priest of the third phyle, lesonis
(inspector) priest,[2] (6) acolyte[2] for the first phyle and third phyle, overseer
of *wab*-priests of Sakhmet, overseer of cattle, overseer of craftsmen, (7)
monthly priest for the first phyle, second phyle, third phyle, and fourth
phyle of the estate of Hathor, Lady of Dendera, prophet (8) of Hathor,

overseer of the sanctuary, prophet of Re, resident in Dendera, prophet of Amon, resident in (*right side,* 9) Dendera, prophet of Osiris, King of the Gods, prophet of Osiris-Sokar, prophet of Ptah and Sakhmet, (10) resident in Dendera, prophet of Osiris, the Bandaged One, prophet of Min, Bull of His Mother, resident in Dendera, prophet (11) of the living staff of Hathor and Sematawy, prophet of Amonemope, resident in Dendera, pacifier of Her Majesty,[3] sistrum player, he who unites the forms,[4] (12) excellent *wab*-priest, revered one before the Lady of Dendera, Basa (IV),

son of the prophet, pacifier of Her Majesty,[3] (13) prophet of the living staff of Hathor, overseer of cattle of the estate of Hathor, Lady of Dendera, Djedhoriuefankh (II) (14), the justified,

son of the similarly titled Basa (III), the justified,

son of the similarly titled prophet of the Golden One (Hathor), offering priest, lesonis priest,[2] (15) acolyte[2] for the third phyle, Nespakhered (II), (16) the justified,

son of the prophet of the Golden One, *wab*-priest of the river festival,[5] great one of the half-month,[6] (17) overseer of the prophets of the Lady of Dendera, overseer of the great plan[2] (*back,* 18) of the Lady of heaven, Third Prophet of Hathor, Lady of Dendera, overseer of secrets of clothing, prophet of Hathor, overseer of the sanctuary, prophet of Osiris, King (19) of the Gods, he who opens the doors of heaven[2] of the Gods who are in Dendera, he who pacifies the deity with necessities, prophet of Pre, resident in Dendera, (20) prophet of Min, Bull of His Mother, lesonis priest,[2] acolyte[2] for the third phyle, pacifier of Her Majesty,[3] sistrum player, he who unites the forms,[4] revered one before the Lady of Dendera, (21) Basa (II),

son of the similarly titled Djedhoriuefankh (I), the justified,

son of the similarly titled Basa (I), the justified,

son of the similarly titled Nes-(22)pakhered (I), the justified,

son of the similarly titled Penpen, the justified,

son of the similarly titled Neskafaya,

son of the similarly titled Amonemope, the justified,

son of (23) the similarly titled Paankhermaat, the justified,

son of the similarly titled Wedjaefarou, the justified,

son of the similarly titled Panehsy, the justified,

son of the similarly titled (*left side,* 24) Amonshedef, the justified,

son of the similarly titled Pennu-(25)nebuterof, the justified,

son of the similarly titled Sihathor (II), the justified,

son of (26) the First Prophet of Hathor, Lady of Dendera, Khay, (27) the justified,

son of the similarly titled Sematawy (II), the justified,

son of the First Prophet of Amon-Re, King of the Gods, Nebwenn(ef), (28) the justified, son of the First Prophet of Hathor, Lady of Dendera, overseer of cattle, overseer of fields, overseer of the granary, Sematawy (I), the justified,

son of (29) the similarly titled Sinhathor, the justified,

son of the similarly titled Amonhotep,

son of the similarly titled Sihathor (I),

(30) son of the similarly titled Nefer, the justified,

son of the similarly titled overseer of the work center, Ded, the justified;

born by the housewife, the sistrum player of (31) Amon-Re, the servant of the Lady of Dendera, Tayesmerden,

daughter of the prophet of Hathor, Lady of Dendera, the mayor (32) of Dendera, Padinebty,

son of the similarly titled Djedkhonsuiuefankh,

son of the similarly titled Nespaihy, the justified.

NOTES

1. A local variant of the late priestly title well-attested on contemporary block statues from the Theban area, sš t3 (n Pr-ʾImn).

2. Otherwise noted as a distinctively Theban title.

3. The title occurs in lines 11, 12, and 20. Registered in Erman and Grapow 1926–63, 4:222/15, this is one of the few distinctive titles of the Denderite temple hierarchy attested on later private monuments from the site.

4. For this title in lines 11 and 20, see the fuller writings in Erman and Grapow 1926–63, 3:447/14–15, where it is identified simply as a Greco-Roman priestly title in Dendera.

5. Cf. Erman and Grapow 1926–63, 1:146/16, the festival of šsp îtr ("Receiving the Nile").

6. For the reading, see Erman and Grapow 1926–63, 4:147/1 smd.t(?).

GENEALOGY OF BASA

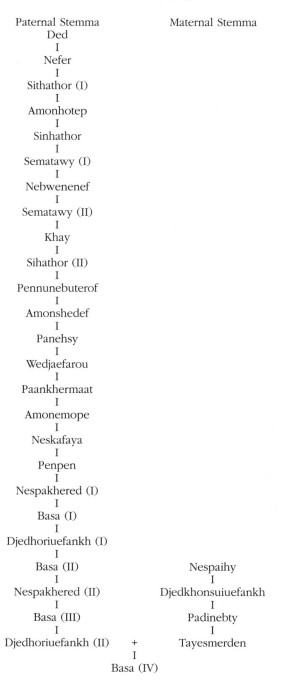

Paternal Stemma
Ded
I
Nefer
I
Sithathor (I)
I
Amonhotep
I
Sinhathor
I
Sematawy (I)
I
Nebwenenef
I
Sematawy (II)
I
Khay
I
Sihathor (II)
I
Pennunebuterof
I
Amonshedef
I
Panehsy
I
Wedjaefarou
I
Paankhermaat
I
Amonemope
I
Neskafaya
I
Penpen
I
Nespakhered (I)
I
Basa (I)
I
Djedhoriuefankh (I)
I

Maternal Stemma

Basa (II)   Nespaihy
I   I
Nespakhered (II)   Djedkhonsuiuefankh
I   I
Basa (III)   Padinebty
I   I
Djedhoriuefankh (II) + Tayesmerden
I
Basa (IV)

5. FUNERARY STELA OF TAFABART
CAIRO JdE 21797

Excavated by Mariette at the northern necropolis of Abydos, the lime-stone memorial stela of the chantress Tafabart measures only 0.45 m high by 0.23 m wide. Despite its relatively small size, the stela has attained disproportionate significance as purported evidence for the obligatory vir-ginity of a class of minor chantresses, assumed to perpetuate their office exclusively by adoption. The suggestion that these attendant "chantresses of the Residence of Amon" imitated the cultic virginity of their superior, the Divine Votaress in Thebes, derives from an inaccurate translation of the genealogy of Tafabart. By suppressing the father's name and invert-ing the names and titles of the women Tamin and Titchauawyese, the standard discussion of the passage implies two mothers for Tafabart, one natural and the other adoptive. More likely, the housewife Titchauawyese is Tafabart's paternal grandmother, and only Tamin is noted as mother for the chantress. Both mother and daughter hold the same professional title, and the former was obviously married and not a virgin.[1] The round-topped stela contains a lunette scene of adoration above six horizontal lines of hieroglyphic text, still incompletely published. On purely stylistic grounds, the stela is dated ca. 600 B.C.E.

For the text, see A. Mariette 1982a [orig. 1880], 483 no. 1281. For trans-lation and discussion, see Ritner 1998, 85–90; superseding Yoyotte 1962, 43–52 (esp. 45); and Munro 1973, 284.

LUNETTE SCENE

Below a winged disk, two women adore a hawk-headed Re (R⁽) followed by the goddess "Isis the great, the God's Mother" (3s.t wr.t mw.t ntr).

LABEL FOR THE TAFABART
    ḥs.(t) (n.t) ḫn (n) 'Imn T3f3brt
    The chantress of the Residence of Amon, Tafabart.

LABEL FOR TAFABART'S MOTHER
    ḥs.(t) (n.t) ḫn (n) 'Imn T(n).t-Mnw[2]
    The chantress of the Residence of Amon, Tamin.[2]

GENEALOGY OF TAFABART
    ḥtp dỉ ny-sw.t (n) Wsỉr …[3] dỉ≠f …[3] n ḥs.(t) (n.t) ḫn (n) 'Imn T3f3brt
    m3⁽.(t)-ḫrw s3.t Ptḥ-ỉ-ỉr-dỉ-sw[4] m3⁽-ḫrw ms nb.(t)-pr
    Tỉ-t3w-⁽.wy-3s.t m3⁽.(t)-ḫrw mw.t≠s ḥs.(t) (n.t) ḫn (n) 'Imn T(n).t-Mnw
    m3⁽.(t)-ḫrw

An offering that the king gives to Osiris …[3] that he might give …[3] to the chantress of the Residence of Amon, Tafabart, the justified, daughter of Ptahirdies,[4] the justified, who was himself born of the housewife Titchauawyese, the justified, while her (Tafabart's) mother is the chantress of the Residence of Amon, Tamin, the justified.

GENEALOGICAL CHART

```
          Titchauawyese
               I
         Ptahirdies      +       Tamin
               I
           Tafabart
```

NOTES

1. Some evidence does exist for the practice of professional adoption among the highest female servants of the Votaress; see Assmann 1977, 15–17.

2. Munro read T3-(dỉ.t)-Mnw.

3. Partial text cited only in Munro.

4. Munro read ʾIˁḥ-ỉ-ỉr-dỉ-sw.

6. FUNERARY STELA OF KAROAMA
CHICAGO OIM 1352

This gessoed and painted stela (29.0 x 20.5 x 2.5 cm) is one of a dozen round-topped wooden funerary monuments recovered by Quibell's excavations of an intrusive Dynasty XXII cemetery at the Ramesseum. With arms upraised in adoration, the deceased worships an enthroned Re-Horachty. While the small stela is traditional in form, Libyan features are notable in the woman's name and perhaps in the paternal genealogy, which, though relatively brief, is more extensive than in comparable stelae. It is striking that the parentage of her father and husband is noted but not the name of her own mother. Karoama's spousal title is one that has received much discussion in Egyptology, with translations varying from "concubine" to "secondary wife."

Publication with transcription and photo in Quibell 1898, 11, 17, and pl. XXI, no. 9.

ḏd-mdw (ỉ)n Rˁ Ḥr-3ḫ.ty ḥry nṯr.w (2) dỉ≠f ḥtp.w ḏf3w n Wsỉr nb.t pr (3) K3r3mˁ m3ˁ.t-ḥrw s3.t n ỉt-nṯr ḥm ʾImn Ḥr-s3-3s.t (4) m3ˁ-ḥrw s3 n mỉ-nn Mr-Ḫnsw m3ˁ-ḥrw ḥbs.(t) n.(t) (5) mry-nṯr ỉdnw n pr ʾImn Sr-(6)Ḏḥwty s3 n Ḥr-Ḥby.t

Recitation by Re-Horachty, chief of the gods. (2) May he give provisions and foodstuffs to the Osiris and housewife (3) Karoama, the justified,

daughter of the God's Father and prophet of Amon, Harsiese, (4) the justified, son of the similarly titled Merkhonsu, the justified, and spouse of the
(5) God's Beloved and deputy of the estate of Amon, Ser(6)djeheuty, son
of Horkheby.

B. PRIESTLY ANNALS AND GRAFFITI

7. THEBAN NILE LEVEL RECORDS

Engraved at varying heights on the West face of the Karnak Temple
quay (now beneath the wooden entrance ramp), these forty-five inscriptions record by their position the maximum flood level attained during
each dated inundation. Early theories suggesting a strict chronological
basis for their carved arrangement must be disregarded, as the determin-
ing factor was inundation height, not dynastic succession. The texts span
the entire period of the "Libyan Anarchy," from the reign of Sheshonq I to
that of Psametik I. Numbers assigned to each inscription follow the initial
ordering by Legrain and are not in strict historical sequence. The height of
each inscription is indicated above or below a zero point corresponding
to the pavement of the Karnak hypostyle hall.

For the position of the quay inscriptions, see Nelson 1941, pl. XIV, fig.
10 (Karnak O. 102). For the texts, see von Beckerath 1966, 43–55; updating
Legrain 1896b, 111–18; 1896a, 119–21. Documentary photographs cited in
von Beckerath 1966, 43 n. 8, are Chicago Oriental Institute photos 8744–45.
See also Lauffray, Sauneron, and Traunecker 1975, 58–65; Breasted 1906–7,
4:339–43 §§693–98; 303–4 §§793–94; 451–53 §§885–88; and the citations in
Kitchen 1986, 513, index.

SHESHONQ I

Text No. 3 (see Kitchen 1986, 288 n. 257; height -0.21 m)
    p3 ḥ'py (n) ḥsb.t 5(.t) ny-sw.t bỉ.ty Ḥd-ḫpr-R'-stp-n-R' s3 R' Šš(n)q
mrỉ-ʾImn s3 3s.t
    The inundation of regnal year 5 of the King of Upper and Lower
Egypt, Hedjkheperre-setepenre, Son of Re, Sheshonq, beloved of Amon,
Son of Isis.

Text No. 1 (height +0.07 m)
    p3 ḥ'py (n) ḥsb.t 6(.t) ny-sw.t bỉ.ty nb t3.wy Ḥd-ḫpr-R'-stp-n-R' s3 R'
nb ḫ'.w Šš(n)q mrỉ-ʾImn [...]

The inundation of regnal year 6 of the King of Upper and Lower Egypt, Lord of the Two Lands, Hedjkheperre-setepenre, Son of Re, Lord of Diadems, Sheshonq, beloved of Amon, [...]

OSORKON I

Text No. 2 (see Kitchen 1986, 307 §265; height +0.09 m)
p3 ḥ‘py (n) ḥsb.t 12(.t) ny-sw.t bỉ.ty Sḫm-ḫpr-R‘-stp-n-R‘ s3 R‘ nb ḫ‘.w Wsrkn mrỉ-’Imn
The inundation of regnal year 12 of the King of Upper and Lower Egypt, Sekhemkheperre-setepenre, Son of Re, Lord of Diadems, Osorkon, beloved of Amon.

TAKELOT I

Text No. 16 (see von Beckerath 1966, 46; Kitchen 1986, 121 §96; height +0.16 m)
p3 ḥ‘py (n) ḥsb.t 5(.t) ḥm-nṯr tp(y) n ’Imn ’Iwwrỉtỉ m3‘-ḫrw s3 ny-sw.t nb t3.wy Wsỉrkn mrỉ-’Imn
The inundation of regnal year 5; First Prophet of Amon, Iuwelot, the justified, royal son of the Lord of the Two Lands, Osorkon, beloved of Amon.

Text No. 20 (see von Beckerath 1966, 46; Kitchen 1986, 121 §96; height +0.67 m)
[p3 ḥ‘py (n) ḥsb.t ...(.t) ḥm-nṯr tp(y) n ’Imn ’Iwwrỉt̲ly m3‘-ḫrw s3 ny-sw.t nb t3.wy Wsỉrkn mrỉ-’Imn dỉ ‘nḫ mỉ R‘ d̲.t
[The inundation of regnal year...; First Prophet of Amon, Iuwelo]t, the justified, royal son of the Lord of the Two Lands, Osorkon, beloved of Amon, given life like Re, forever.

Text No. 21 (see von Beckerath 1966, 46; Kitchen 1986, 121 §96; height +0.10 m)
[p3 ḥ‘py (n) ḥsb.t ...(.t) ḥm-nṯr tp(y) n ’Imn ’Iwwrỉt̲ly m3‘-ḫrw s3 ny-sw.t nb t3.wy Wsỉrkn mrỉ-’Imn
[The inundation of regnal year...; First Prophet of Amon, Iuwelo]t, the justified, royal son of the Lord of the Two Lands, Osorkon, beloved of Amon.

Text No. 17 (see Kitchen 1986, 121 §96; height -0.38 m)
p3 ḥ‘py (n) ḥsb.t 8(.t) ḥm-nṯr tp(y) n ’Imn-R‘ ny-sw.t nṯr.w Ns-b3-{nb}-D̲d m3‘-ḫrw s3 ny-sw.t nb t3.wy Wsỉrkn mrỉ-’Imn

The inundation of regnal year 8; First Prophet of Amon-Re, King of the Gods, Smendes, the justified, royal son of the Lord of the Two Lands, Osorkon, beloved of Amon.

Text No. 18 (see Kitchen 1986, 121 §96; height -0.52 m)

p3 ḥᶜpy (n) ḥsb.t 14(.t) ḥm-nṯr tp(y) n ᵓImn-Rᶜ ny-sw.t nṯr.w Ns-b3-{nb}-Ḏd m3ᶜ-ḥrw s3 ny-sw.t nb t3.wy Wsrkn mrỉ-ᵓImn

The inundation of regnal year 14; First Prophet of Amon-Re, King of the Gods, Smendes, the justified, royal son of the Lord of the Two Lands, Osorkon, beloved of Amon.

Text No. 19 (see Kitchen 1986, 121 §96; height -0.92 m)

p3 ḥᶜpy (n) ḥsb.t [...(.t)] ḥm-nṯr tp(y) n ᵓImn-Rᶜ ny-sw.t nṯr.w Ns-b3-{nb}-Ḏd m3ᶜ-ḥrw s3 ny-sw.t nb t3.wy Wsrkn mrỉ-ᵓImn

The inundation of regnal year [...]; First Prophet of Amon-Re, King of the Gods, Smendes, the justified, royal son of the Lord of the Two Lands, Osorkon, beloved of Amon.

OSORKON II (?) (OR III?)

Text No. 8 (corrected by slightly higher text no. 9; see von Beckerath 1966, 45; Kitchen 1986, 94 §75; height +0.15 m)

p3 ḥᶜpy (n) ḥsb.t 12(.t)[1] ny-sw.t bỉ.ty nb t3.wy Wsr-m3ᶜ.t-Rᶜ-stp-n-ᵓImn s3 Rᶜ nb ḥᶜ.w Wsỉ[rkn] mrỉ-ᵓImn

The inundation of regnal year 12[1] of the King of Upper and Lower Egypt, Lord of the Two Lands, Usimaᶜre-setepenamon, Son of Re, Lord of Diadems, Oso[rkon], beloved of Amon.

Text No. 9 (see Kitchen 1986, 94 §75; height +0.25 m)

p3 ḥᶜpy (n) ḥsb.t 12(.t) ny-sw.t bỉ.ty nb t3.wy Wsr-m3ᶜ.t-Rᶜ-stp-n-ᵓImn s3 Rᶜ nb ḥᶜ.w Wsỉrkn mrỉ-ᵓImn

The inundation of regnal year 12 of the King of Upper and Lower Egypt, Lord of the Two Lands, Usimaᶜre-setepenamon, Son of Re, Lord of Diadems, Osorkon, beloved of Amon.

Text No. 10 (see Kitchen 1986, 353 §314; height -0.19 m)

p3 ḥᶜpy (n) ḥsb.t [10(?) +] 3(.t) ny-sw.t bỉ.ty nb t3.wy Wsr-mᶜ3.t-Rᶜ[-stp-n-ᵓImn] [...]

The inundation of regnal year [1]3 (?) of the King of Upper and Lower Egypt, Lord of the Two Lands, Usimaᶜre-[setepenamon], [...]

Text No. 11 (see Kitchen 1986, 94 §75; and 353 §314; height -0.27 m)
p3 ḥꜥpy (n) ḥsb.t 21(.t) ny-sw.t bỉ.ty nb t3.wy Wsr-mꜥ3.t-Rꜥ-stp-n-ꞋImn
s3 Rꜥ nb ḫꜥ.w Wsỉ[r]k[n] mrỉ-ꞋImn
The inundation of regnal year 21 of the King of Upper and Lower
Egypt, Lord of the Two Lands, Usimaꜥre-setepenamon, Son of Re, Lord of
Diadems, Oso[r]ko[n], beloved of Amon.

Text No. 12 (see Kitchen 1986, 94 §75; and 353 §314; height -0.29 m)
p3 ḥꜥpy (n) ḥsb.t 22(.t) ny-sw.t bỉ.ty[2] nb t3.wy Wsr-m3ꜥ.t-Rꜥ-stp-n-ꞋImn
s3 Rꜥ nb ḫꜥ.w Wsỉ[r]k[n] mrỉ-ꞋImn
The inundation of regnal year 22 of the King of Upper and Lower
Egypt,[2] Lord of the Two Lands, Usimaꜥre-setepenamon, Son of Re, Lord of
Diadems, Oso[r]ko[n], beloved of Amon.

Text No. 15 (see von Beckerath 1966, 46; height -0.345 m)
[p3 ḥꜥpy (n) ḥsb.t ... ny-sw.t bỉ.ty] [Wsr-m3ꜥ.t]-Rꜥ[-stp-n]-ꞋI[mn] s3 Rꜥ
[Wsỉrkn mrỉ-ꞋImn(?)]
[The inundation of regnal year ... of the King of Upper and Lower
Egypt,] [Usimaꜥ]re-[setepen]a[mon], Son of Re, [Osorkon, beloved of Amon
(?)].

SHESHONQ III

Text No. 23 (see Kitchen 1986, 87–88 §68; 335 §296; height +0.09 m)
p3 ḥꜥpy (n) ḥsb.t 6(.t) ny-sw.t bỉ.ty Wsr-m3ꜥ.t-Rꜥ-stp-n-ꞋImn s3 Rꜥ
Šš(n)q mrỉ-ꞋImn dỉ ꜥnḫ ḥm-ntr tp(y) (n) ꞋImn-Rꜥ ny-sw.t ntr.w Ḥr-s3-3s.t
m3ꜥ-ḫrw
The inundation of regnal year 6 of the King of Upper and Lower Egypt,
Usimaꜥre-setepenamon, Son of Re, Sheshonq, beloved of Amon, given life;
First Prophet of Amon-Re, King of the Gods, Harsiese, the justified.

Text No. 24 (see Kitchen 1986, 102 n. 88, 134–36 §§106–7; height -0.15 m)
p3 ḥꜥpy (n) ḥsb.t 12(.t) nty (m) ḥsb.t 5(.t) ny-sw.t bỉ.ty Wsr-m3ꜥ.t-Rꜥ-
stp-n-ꞋImn s3 Rꜥ P3-dỉ-[B3st.t] mrỉ-ꞋImn s3 3s.t dỉ ꜥnḫ d.t ḥm-ntr tp(y) (n)
ꞋImn-Rꜥ ny-sw.t ntr.w Ḥr-s3-3s.t [m3ꜥ-ḫrw]
The inundation of regnal year 12, which is regnal year 5 of the King
of Upper and Lower Egypt, Usimaꜥre-setepenamon, Son of Re, Pedu[bast],
beloved of Amon, Son of Isis, given life forever; First Prophet of Amon-Re,
King of the Gods, Harsiese, [the justified].

Text No. 22 (see Kitchen 1986, 107 §86; 339 n. 531 [wrongly said to be year 29]; height +0.30 m)

p3 ḥꜥpy (n) ḥsb.t 39(.t) ny-sw.t bỉ.ty Wsr-m3ꜥ.t-Rꜥ-stp-n-Rꜥ s3 Rꜥ Šš(n)q mrỉ-ꜣImn s3 B3st.t dỉ ꜥnḫ (m) h(3w) ḥm-nṯr tp(y) (n) ꜣImn-Rꜥ ny-sw.t nṯr. w Wsrkn

The inundation of regnal year 39 of the King of Upper and Lower Egypt, Usimaꜥre-setepenre, Son of Re, Sheshonq, beloved of Amon, Son of Bastet, given life, in the time of the First Prophet of Amon-Re, King of the Gods, Osorkon.

PEDUBAST I AND IUPUT I

Text No. 26 (see Kitchen 1986, 124 §98; height -0.33 m)

p3 ḥꜥpy (n) ḥsb.t 16(.t) ny-sw.t bỉ.ty P3-dỉ-B3st.t mrỉ-ꜣImn nty (m) ḥsb.t 2(.t) ny-sw.t bỉ.ty ꜣIwpwtỉ mrỉ-ꜣImn

The inundation of regnal year 16 of the King of Upper and Lower Egypt, Pedubast, beloved of Amon, which is regnal year 2 of the King of Upper and Lower Egypt, Iuput, beloved of Amon.

Text No. 28 (see Kitchen 1986, 124 §98; height -0.435 m)

p3 ḥꜥpy (n) ḥsb.t 18(.t) ny-sw.t (bỉ.ty) nb t3.wy P3-dỉ-B3st.t mrỉ-ꜣImn nty (m h3w) ḥm-nṯr tp(y) (n) ꜣImn [Ḥr-s3-]3s.t

The inundation of regnal year 18 of the King of Upper (and Lower) Egypt, Lord of the Two Lands, Pedubast, beloved of Amon, which is (in the time of) the First Prophet of Amon, [Harsi]ese.

Text No. 27 (see Kitchen 1986, 124 §98; height -0.18 m)

p3 ḥꜥpy (n) ḥsb.t 19(.t) ny-sw.t bỉ.ty nb t3.wy P3-dỉ-B3st.t mrỉ-ꜣImn (m) h(3w) ḥm-nṯr tp(y) (n) ꜣImn Ḥr-s3-[3s.t] m3ꜥ-ḫrw

The inundation of regnal year 19 of the King of Upper and Lower Egypt, Lord of the Two Lands, Pedubast, beloved of Amon, in the time of the First Prophet of Amon, Harsi[ese], the justified.

Text No. 29 (see Kitchen 1986, 124 §98; height -0.42 m)

p3 ḥꜥpy (n) ḥsb.t 23(.t) ny-sw.t bỉ.ty P3-dỉ-B3st.t mrỉ-ꜣImn (m) h(3w) ḥm-nṯr tp(y) (n) ꜣImn Ṯkrtỉ

The inundation of regnal year 23 of the King of Upper and Lower Egypt, Pedubast, beloved of Amon, in the time of the First Prophet of Amon, Takelot.

SHESHONQ VI

Text No. 25 (see Kitchen 1986, 125 §99; for renumbering of Sheshonq IV as VI, see Kitchen 1995, xxvi, xxxiii–iv; height +0.23 m)

p3 ḥˤpy (n) ḥsb.t 6(.t) ny-sw.t bỉ.ty Wsr-m3ˤ.t-Rˤ-mrỉ-ʾImn s3 Rˤ Šš(n)q mrỉ-ʾImn (m) h(3w) ḥm-nṯr tp(y) (n) ʾImn Ṯkrỉwtỉ

The inundation of regnal year 6 of the King of Upper and Lower Egypt, Usimaˤre-meriamon, Son of Re, Sheshonq, beloved of Amon, in the time of the First Prophet of Amon, Takelot.

OSORKON III

Text No. 5 (the second highest level recorded, corresponding to the king's flood text in Luxor temple; see Kitchen 1986, 92 §73; height +0.785 m)

p3 ḥˤpy (n) ḥsb.t 3(.t) ḫr ḥm (n) ny-sw.t bỉ.ty Wsr-m3ˤ.t-Rˤ-stp-n-ʾImn s3 Rˤ Wsỉrkn mrỉ-ʾImn s3 3s.t dỉ ˤnḫ mỉ Rˤ ḏ.t mw.t≠f ḥm.t ny-sw.t wr.t [Kmˤmˤ mrỉ-mw.t]

The inundation of regnal year 3 under the Majesty of the King of Upper and Lower Egypt, Usimaˤre-setepenamon, Son of Re, Osorkon, beloved of Amon, Son of Isis, given life like Re, forever, whose mother is the great queen [Kamama, beloved of Mut].

Text No. 6 (height + 0.185 m)

p3 ḥˤpy (n) ḥsb.t 5(.t) ny-sw.t bỉ.ty Wsr-m3ˤ.t-Rˤ-stp-n-ʾImn s3 Rˤ Wsỉrkn mrỉ-ʾImn mw.t≠f ḥm.t ny-sw.t wr.t Kmˤmˤ mrỉ-mw.t

The inundation of regnal year 5 of the King of Upper and Lower Egypt, Usimaˤre-setepenamon, Son of Re, Osorkon, beloved of Amon, whose mother is the great queen Kamama, beloved of Mut.

Text No. 7 (height + 0.15 m)

p3 ḥˤpy (n) ḥsb.t 6(.t) ny-sw.t bỉ.ty Wsr-m3ˤ.t-Rˤ-stp-n-ʾImn s3 Rˤ Wsỉrkn mrỉ-ʾImn mw.t≠f ḥm.t ny-sw.t wr.t Kmˤmˤ mrỉ-mw.t

The inundation of regnal year 6 of the King of Upper and Lower Egypt, Usimaˤre-setepenamon, Son of Re, Osorkon, beloved of Amon, whose mother is the great queen Kamama, beloved of Mut.

Text No. 13 (see Kitchen 1986, 92–93 §73; 353 §314; height +0.715 m)

p3 ḥˤpy (n) ḥsb.t 28(.t) ḥm n ny-sw.t bỉ.ty Wsr-m3ˤ.t-Rˤ-stp-n-ʾImn s3 Rˤ Wsỉrkn mrỉ-ʾImn s3 3s.t ntr ḥq3 W3s.t nty m ḥsb.t 5(.t) n(.t) s3≠f (2) [Wsr-m3ˤ.t-]Rˤ-stp-[n-]Imn] s3 Rˤ Ṯkrtỉ mrỉ-ʾImn s3 3s.t nṯr ḥq3 W3s.t ˤnḫ ḏ.t

The inundation of regnal year 28 of the Majesty of the King of Upper and Lower Egypt, Usimaˤre-setepenamon, Son of Re, Osorkon, beloved of Amon, Son of Isis, the god, ruler of Thebes, which is regnal year 5 of his son (2) [Usima⁽re-setep[enamon], Son of Re, Takelot (III), beloved of Amon, Son of Isis, the god, ruler of Thebes, living forever.

Text No. 14 (see Kitchen 1986, 353 n. 627; height: -0.26 m)
    p3 ḥ⁽py (n) ḥsb.t 29(.t) ny-sw.t bỉ.ty nb t3.wy Wsr-m3⁽.t-R⁽-stp-n-ʾImn
    The inundation of regnal year 29 of the King of Upper and Lower Egypt, Lord of the Two Lands, Usima⁽re-setepenamon.

TAKELOT III

Text No. 4 (see Kitchen 1986, 95 §76; height -0.355 m)
    [p3 ḥ⁽py] (n) ḥsb.t 6(.t) ny-sw.t bỉ.ty nb t3.wy Ṯkrtỉ mrỉ-ʾImn s3 3s.t mw.t≠f T-n.t-S3ỉ m3⁽-ḥrw
    [The inundation] of regnal year 6 of the King of Upper and Lower Egypt, Lord of the Two Lands, Takelot, beloved of Amon, Son of Isis, whose mother is Tentsai, the justified.

SHABAKO

Text No. 30 (see Kitchen 1986, 379 §340; height +0.29 m)
    ḥsb.t 2(.t) ḥr ḥm n Ḥr Sbq t3.wy Nb.ty Sbq t3.wy Ḥr-nbw Sbq t3.wy ny-sw.t bỉ.ty Nfr-k3-R⁽ s3 R⁽ [Š3]b3k3 [dỉ] ⁽nḫ ḏ.t (2) mry ʾImn-R⁽ nb ns.wt t3.wy mry Mnṯ-R⁽ nb W3s.t ḥ⁽py wr ỉt nṯr.w mḥ 20 šsp 1 db⁽
    Regnal year 2 under the Majesty of Horus: "He who blesses the Two Lands"; The Two Ladies: "He who blesses the Two Lands"; The Golden Horus: "He who blesses the Two Lands"; the King of Upper and Lower Egypt, Neferkare, Son of Re, [Sha]bako, [given] life forever, (2) beloved of Amon-Re, Lord of the Thrones of the Two Lands, beloved of Montu-Re, Lord of Thebes, and Hapi (the Inundation) the great, father of the gods: 20 cubits, 1 palm and a digit.

Text No. 31 (see Kitchen 1986, 381 §343; height +0.23 m)
    [p3 ḥ⁽py(?)] (n) ḥsb.t 4(.t) [ḥr] ḥm n ny-sw.t bỉ.ty Nfr-k3-R⁽ s3 R⁽ Š3b3k3 mrỉ-ʾImn wr Nwn wr
    [The inundation (?)] of regnal year 4 [under] the Majesty of the King of Upper and Lower Egypt, Neferkare, Son of Re, Shabako, beloved of Amon the great and Nun the great.

Text No. 32 (see Kitchen 1986, 381 §343; height +0.04 m)
    [p3 ḥ⁽py(?) (n) ḥsb.t ... ḥr] ḥm n Ḥr S[bq t3.wy Nb.ty] Sbq t3.wy Ḥr-nbw Sbq t3.wy ny-sw.t bỉ.ty Nfr-k3-R⁽ s3 R⁽ Š3b3k3 mrỉ-ʾImn wr Nwn wr
    [The inundation (?) of regnal year ... under] the Majesty of Horus: "He who [blesses the Two Lands"; The Two Ladies:] "He who blesses the Two

Lands"; The Golden Horus: "He who blesses the Two Lands"; the King of Upper and Lower Egypt, Neferkare, Son of Re, Shabako, beloved of Amon the great and Nun the great.

SHEBITKU

Text No. 33 (see Kitchen 1986, 383 §345; height +0.04 m)

ḥsb.t 3.t 3bd 1 šmw sw 5 ḫr ḥm n Ḥr K3 nḫt ḫꜥ m W3s.t ny-sw.t bἰ.ty Nb.ty Ḏd ḫꜥ[.w] Ḥr-nbw Ḏd-k3.w-Rꜥ s3 Rꜥ mr≠f Š3b3t3k3 (2) mry ꜣImn-Rꜥ nb ns.wt t3.wy sk rf ḫꜥ ḥm≠f m ny-sw.t3 m ḥw.t n.t ꜣImn rdἰ.n≠f n≠f ḫꜥ≠f n t3.wy mἰ Ḥr ḥr (3) ns.t Rꜥ [... rdἰ] n≠f ἰt≠f ꜣImn wr ḥꜥpy ꜥ3 wr wr ḥꜥpy m h(3w)≠f (mḥ) 20 ššp 2

Regnal year 3, first month of summer, day 5, under the Majesty of Horus: "Strong Bull Appearing in Thebes"; the King of Upper and Lower Egypt, The Two Ladies: "Enduring of Appearances"; The Golden Horus; Djedkaure, Son of Re, whom he ("Re") loves, Shebitku, (2) beloved of Amon-Re, Lord of the Thrones of the Two Lands. Now then, His Majesty appeared as king[3] in the temple of Amon, who had given to him his accession in the Two Lands like Horus on (3) the throne of Re [...] since his father Amon the great [had given] to him a very great inundation. The extent of the inundation in his time: 20 (cubits) and 2 palms.

TAHARQA

Text No. 35 (the first of two records for the extraordinary flood of year 6, made before an unexpected further ascent of the Nile; see Kitchen 1986, 388–89 §349; height +0.77 m)

p3 ḥꜥpy (n) ḥsb.t 6(.t) ḫr ḥm n ny-sw.t bἰ.ty Ḫw-Nfr-tm-Rꜥ s3 Rꜥ T3hrq ꜥnḫ ḏ.t mry Nwn wr ꜣImn wr Ḥꜥpy ἰt nṯr.w ḏ3ḏ3.t (2) tp.t nwy rdἰ n≠f ἰt≠f ꜣImn n mr(w.t) snfr h3w≠f

The inundation of regnal year 6 under the Majesty of the King of Upper and Lower Egypt, Khunefertumre, Son of Re, Taharqa, living forever, beloved of Nun the great, Amon the great, Hapi the father of the gods, and the council (2) in charge of the flood, which his father Amon gave to him in a desire to benefit his reign.

Text No. 34 (the highest level recorded on the quay, corresponding to the flood inscription of Kawa Stela V; see Kitchen 1986, 388–89 §349; height +0.84 m)

ḥsb.t 6(.t) ny-sw.t T3hrq mry ꜣImn wr

Regnal year 6 of king Taharqa, beloved of Amon the great.

Text No. 36 (see Kitchen 1986, 389 §349; height +0.28 m)

pꜣ ḥꜥpy (n) ḥsb.t 7(.t) ḫr ḥm n ny-sw.t bỉ.ty Ḥw-Nfr-tm-Rꜥ sꜣ Rꜥ Tꜣhrq ꜥnḫ ḏ.t mry Nwn wr ʾImn wr Ḥꜥpy ỉt nṯr.w ḏꜣḏꜣ.t (2) tp.t nwy rdỉ n≠f ỉt≠f ʾImn n mr(w.t) snfr hꜣw≠f

The inundation of regnal year 7 under the Majesty of the King of Upper and Lower Egypt, Khunefertumre, Son of Re, Taharqa, living forever, beloved of Nun the great, Amon the great, Hapi the father of the gods, and the council (2) in charge of the flood, which his father Amon gave to him in a desire to benefit his reign.

Text No. 37 (see Kitchen 1986, 389 §349; height +0.28 m)

pꜣ ḥꜥpy (n) ḥsb.t 8(.t) ḫr ḥm n ny-sw.t bỉ.ty Ḥw-Nfr-tm-Rꜥ sꜣ Rꜥ Tꜣhrq ꜥnḫ ḏ.t mry Nwn [wr] ʾImn wr Ḥꜥpy ỉt nṯr.w ḏꜣḏꜣ.t (2) tp(.t) nwy rdỉ n≠f ỉt≠f ʾImn [n mr(w.t)] snfr hꜣ(w)≠f

The inundation of regnal year 8 under the Majesty of the King of Upper and Lower Egypt, Khunefertumre, Son of Re, Taharqa, living forever, beloved of Nun [the great], Amon the great, Hapi the father of the gods, and the council (2) in charge of the flood, which his father Amon gave to him [in a desire] to benefit his reign.

Text No. 38 (see Kitchen 1986, 389 §349; height +0.28 m)

pꜣ ḥꜥpy (n) ḥsb.t 9.t (n) sꜣ Rꜥ Tꜣhrq ꜥnḫ ḏ.t mry Nwn wr ʾImn wr

The inundation of regnal year 9 of the Son of Re, Taharqa, living forever, beloved of Nun the great and Amon the great.

PSAMETIK I

Text No. 39 (height +0.46 m)

pꜣ ḥꜥpy (n) ḥsb.t 10(.t) ḫr ḥm n ny-sw.t bỉ.ty Wꜣ-ỉb-Rꜥ sꜣ Rꜥ Psmtk ꜥnḫ ḏ.t mry Nwn wr ʾImn wr Ḥꜥpy ỉt nṯr.w ḏꜣḏꜣ.t (2) tp(.t) nwy rdỉ n≠f ỉt≠f ʾImn snfr [h]ꜣw≠f

The inundation of regnal year 10 under the Majesty of the King of Upper and Lower Egypt, Wahibre, Son of Re, Psametik, living forever, beloved of Nun the great, Amon the great, Hapi the father of the gods, and the council (2) in charge of the flood, which his father Amon gave to him to benefit his reign.

Text No. 40 (height +0.285 m)

pꜣ ḥꜥpy (n) ḥsb.t 11(.t) ḫr ḥm n ny-sw.t bỉ.ty [Wꜣ-ỉb]-Rꜥ sꜣ Rꜥ Psmtk ꜥnḫ ḏ.t mry Nwn wr ʾImn wr Ḥꜥpy ỉt nṯr.w ḏꜣḏꜣ.t (2) tp(.t) nwy rdỉ n≠f ỉt≠f ʾImn snfr [h]ꜣw≠f

The inundation of regnal year 11 under the Majesty of the King of Upper and Lower Egypt, [Wahib]re, Son of Re, Psametik, living forever, beloved of Nun the great, Amon the great, Hapi the father of the gods, and the council (2) in charge of the flood, which his father Amon gave to him to benefit his reign.

Text No. 41 (height +0.155 m)
p3 ḥꜥpy (n) ḥsb.t 17(.t) ḫr ḥm n ny-sw.t bỉ.ty W3ḥ-ỉb-Rꜥ s3 Rꜥ Psmṯk ꜥnḫ ḏ.t mry Nwn wr ꜣImn (wr) Ḥꜥpy ỉt nṯr.w ḏ3ḏ3.t (2) tp.t nwy rdỉ n≠f ỉt≠f ꜣImn n mr(w.t) snfr h3w≠f mḥ 20 ḏbꜥ 5
The inundation of regnal year 17 under the Majesty of the King of Upper and Lower Egypt, Wahibre, Son of Re, Psametik, living forever, beloved of Nun the great, Amon (the great), Hapi the father of the gods, and the council (2) in charge of the flood, which his father Amon gave to him in a desire to benefit his reign: 20 cubits and 5 digits.

Text No. 42 (height +0.25 m)
p3 ḥꜥpy (n) ḥsb.t 19(.t) ḫr ḥm n ny-sw.t bỉ.ty nb t3.wy W3ḥ-ỉb-Rꜥ s3 Rꜥ Psmṯk ꜥnḫ ḏ.t mry Nwn wr ꜣImn wr Ḥꜥpy ỉt nṯr.w (2) ḏ3ḏ3.t tp(.t) nwy rdỉ n≠f ỉt≠f ꜣImn n mr(w.t) snfr h3w≠f
The inundation of regnal year 19 under the Majesty of the King of Upper and Lower Egypt, Lord of the Two Lands, Wahibre, Son of Re, Psametik, living forever, beloved of Nun the great, Amon the great, Hapi the father of the gods, and (2) the council in charge of the flood, which his father Amon gave to him in a desire to benefit his reign.

UNASSIGNED; DYNASTIES XXII–XXIII

UNASSIGNED; DYNASTIES XXII–XXIII

Text No. 43 (height -0.185 m)
p3 ḥꜥpy (n) ḥsb.t 3(.t) ny-sw.t bỉ.ty nb t3.wy [...] mrỉ-ꜣImn [...]
The inundation of regnal year 3 of the King of Upper and Lower Egypt, Lord of the Two Lands, [...] beloved of Amon, [...].

Text No. 44 (height -0.24 m)
[p3 ḥꜥpy (n) ḥsb.t] 6(.t) ny-sw.t bỉ.ty [...]-Rꜥ mrỉ-ꜣImn s3 Rꜥ [...] h(3w) ḥm nṯr tp(y) n ꜣImn [...]
[The inundation of regnal year] 6 of the King of Upper and Lower Egypt, [...]-re, beloved of Amon, Son of Re, [...], in the time of the First Prophet of Amon, [...]

Text No. 45 (height -0.32 m)
p3 ḥꜥpy (n) ḥsb.t 15 [+x](.t) ny-sw.t bỉ.ty [...] s3 Rꜥ [...] mrỉ-ꜣImn
The inundation of regnal year 15 [+x] (of) the King of Upper and Lower Egypt, [...], Son of Re, [...], beloved of Amon.

NOTES
1. Date added above line, superseded by adjacent text 9.
2. Written with a seated king lacking the distinguishing crown. Or read simply ny-sw.t nb tȝ.wy "King and Lord of the Two Lands."
3. Copied by Legrain but ignored by von Beckerath without comment.

8. THE HELIOPOLITAN ANNALS OF DYNASTY XXII

Found reused in a staircase platform of the Fatimid gateway Bab el-Nasr in Cairo, an eroded white limestone block (104 cm x 64 cm x 36.5 cm) preserves a portion of once-lengthy annals recording royal benefactions at Heliopolis, the biblical On. The preserved section notes donations by Pamiu and a predecessor, probably the newly identified Sheshonq IV, whose titles include the distinctive epithet "Ruler of Heliopolis." The textual orientation suggests that a lost facing section detailed grants by Pamiu's successor, Sheshonq V, so that the original inscription would have documented over half a century of rule by Dynasty XXII. Engraved annals are characteristic of the period, providing legitimacy for claims both sacerdotal (Karnak Priestly Annals and the Chronicle of Prince Osorkon) and royal (Taharqa's Kawa Stelae). Consciously anachronistic in format, the annals evoke Old Kingdom precedents.

For the texts, translation, and discussion, see Bickel, Gabolde, and Tallet 1998, 31–56.

Text I in Vertical Columns
(1–9) [...] (10) [...] pr.w [...] (11–14) [...] (15) [...] m [...] (16) [... Šȝšnq [mrỉ-ʾImn] sȝ [Bȝst.t(?)]¹ (17) [...] (18) [...] m [ḫr]-ỉb (19–40) [...]

(1–9) [...] (10) [...] houses [...] (11–14) [...] (15) [...] in [...] (16) [...] Sheshonq, [beloved of Amon,] Son of [Bastet (?)],¹ (17) [...] (18) [...] in the midst of (19–40) [...].

Text II in Horizontal Bands
(1) [...] sȝ Rᶜ Pȝ-mỉ(w) dỉ ᶜnḫ ḏ.t ỉr.n⸗f m mnw⸗f n bȝ.w ʾIwnw nb.w Ḥw.t-ᶜȝ.t m-ḫnt ʾIwnw smn.t n⸗sn ḥtp-nṯr n rᶜ nb ḥb nb n Ḥw.t-ᶜȝ.t m ȝw.t ḏ.t [...] hȝ⸗sn mỉ Rᶜ ḏ.t
(2) [... Pȝ-mỉ(w)] ᶜnḫ ḏ.t wn wḏ⸗f [...] ḥw.t-[nṯr] n.t ỉt⸗f r mrr⸗f ỉr.t ḥtp-nṯr n bȝ.w ʾIwnw m [wḥ]m wḥm sp-2 rnp.t rnp.t ḫft mȝ ḥm⸗f ḥ.t⸗f sḥtp.n² ḥm⸗f t(ȝ)-n.t hȝw ḥr wdn.w m-ḫȝw wn.t ỉm m-bȝḥ ỉm n rᶜ nb [...]

(1) [...], Son of Re, Pamiu, given life forever. As his monument for the Souls of Heliopolis, lords of the Great Temple that dominates Heliopolis, he has established for them an endowment offering for every day and

every festival of the Great Temple for the duration of eternity, [...] around them like Re forever.

(2) [Pamiu], living forever. His command was to [enrich (?)] the temple of his father according to his desire to make an endowment offering for the Souls of Heliopolis, repeatedly from year to year, as His Majesty examines his property. His Majesty has funded[2] the expenses for the offerings even in excess of what had been there, in the divine presence there daily [...].

TEXT III IN VERTICAL COLUMNS

(1–10) [...]

(11) [ḥsb.t 3.(t) s3] Rꜥ [P3-mî(w) îr.n≠f m mnw≠f n ... smn.t n≠... ḥtp-ntr ...] (12) [...] (13) [... db]n 20 [...] m ᾽Iwnw n [...] (14) 3ḥ.t dbn [...] 1/4 [...] ḫ.t n.t nb [...] nb Ḏw-[...] prr [m ...] (15) m [᾽Iwnw(?)] r [ḥt]p-[ntr ...] ḥr(y)-îb [...] Ḥtp.t [...] (16) s3 Rꜥ P3-mî(w) îr.n≠f m mnw≠f n [ît≠f Ptḥ(?)] smn.t n≠f ḥtp-ntr n rꜥ nb m [3w.t ḏ.t (?) ...] (17) n sw.t ḥq3.t 15.(t) [...] prr m t3 ꜥ.t n.(t) înn.t [...] (18) ḫd dbn 36 ḥr ḥtr≠f nw[y] n p3 ḥḏ3 ps(î) mrw r3 [...]

(19) ḥsb.t 4.(t) s3 Rꜥ P3-[mî(w)] îr.n≠f m mnw≠f n b3.w ᾽Iwnw smn. t n≠sn ḥtp-ntr n rꜥ nb [...] ît(?) prr (20) m t3 m3w.t mḥ.t ḫd dbn 17 n [...] n.t pr n [...] îr n ḫd dbn 20 prr m [...] (21) t3 Ḥw.t-ꜥ3.t ḫnt(y).t ᾽Iwnw [s]r 9 n tp-3bd prr m t3 îs.t r ḫ3w.t ntr ꜥ3b.t [ꜥ3.t ...]

(22) ḥsb.t 5.(t) s3 Rꜥ [P3-mî(w)] îr.n≠f m mnw≠f n b3.w ᾽Iwnw smn. t n≠sn ḥtp-ntr n rꜥ nb [...] (23) [...] prr m n3 š<3.w n Rꜥ m ḏ[d.t ḥm]≠f dî ꜥnḫ ḏd w3s mî Rꜥ [ḏ.t] (24) s3 Rꜥ [P3-mî(w)] îr.n≠f m mnw≠f n Tm ḥr(y)-îb nîw.t≠f n psḏ.t ꜥ3.t m ᾽Ip.t smn[.t] (25) n≠sn ḥtp-ntr n rꜥ nb m [ḫ]3w wn.t îm m-b3ḥ n.t-[ꜥ(?) ...] (26) ḥmt ḥnq.t [...] îm rꜥ nb prr m p3 [...] (27) [... smn.t n]≠sn ḥtp-ntr îm rꜥ nb îr n≠sn s3 Rꜥ P3-mî(w) [dî] ꜥnḫ [ḏd w3s mî Rꜥ] ḏ.t

(28) [ḥsb].t [6.(t) s3 Rꜥ] P3-[mî(w)] îr.n≠f m mnw≠f n b3.w ᾽Iwnw smn. t n≠sn ḥtp-ntr n rꜥ nb [...] (29) [...] (30) [...] rꜥ nb [...] (31) [...] s3 Rꜥ P3-mî(w) [îr.n≠f m mnw≠f] (32) [n ... s]mn.t n≠f ḥtp-[ntr ...] prr m [...] (33) [...] ḥtp-[ntr](?) [...] ḫ[mt ḥn]q.t [...] (34) [...]

(35) ḥsb.t [7].(t) s3 Rꜥ P3-[m]î(w) îr.n≠f m mn[w≠f n ...] (36) w[... s3 Rꜥ] P[3-mî(w) ...]

(36–40) [...]

(1–10) [...]

(11) [Regnal year 3 of the Son] of Re, [Pamiu. As his monument for ... he established for ... an endowment offering ...] (12) [consisting of ...] (13) [...] 20 *deben* [...] in Heliopolis for [...] (14) field of [...] *deben* and 1/4 [...] property of the lord [...] the Lord of the Mountain of [...], issued [from ...] (15) in [Heliopolis (?)] for the endowment offering [of ...] who is resident in [...] Hetepet [...]. (16) The Son of Re, Pamiu: as his monument for [his father Ptah, (?)] he has established for him a daily endowment

offering for [the duration of eternity (?), … consisting] (17) of 15 sacks of wheat […] issued from the department of income, […], (18) 36 *deben* of silver regarding its annual levy collected for payment,[3] cooked food desirable to the mouth […]

(19) Regnal year 4 of the Son of Re, Pa[miu]. As his monument for the Souls of Heliopolis, he has established for them a daily endowment offering [… consisting of] grain issued (20) from the northern island-land; 17 *deben* of silver of […] of the house of […], which amounts to 20 *deben* of silver issued from [… for] (21) the Great Temple that dominates Heliopolis; 9 geese monthly issued from the supply house for the divine altar and the [great] offering […].

(22) Regnal year 5 of the Son of Re, [Pamiu]. As his monument for the Souls of Heliopolis, he has established for them a daily endowment offering [… consisting of] (23) […] issued from the granaries of Re, in accordance with what [was said by] His [Majesty], given life, stability, and dominion like Re [forever.] (24) The Son of Re, [Pamiu]: as his monument for Atum, resident in his city, and for the great Ennead in Opet, he has established (25) for them a daily endowment offering in excess of what had been there, in the divine presence for the rituals (?) […] (26) drink and beer […] there every day, issued from the […] (27) [… establishing for] them an endowment offering there daily, which was done for them by the Son of Re, Pamiu, [given] life, [stability, and dominion like Re] forever.

(28) [Regnal] year [6 of the Son of Re,] Pa[miu]. As his monument for the Souls of Heliopolis, he has established for them a daily endowment offering [consisting of …] (29) […] (30) […] daily […] (31) […]. The Son of Re, Pamiu: [as his monument] (32) [for …,] he established for him an endowment offering [… consisting of …] issued from […] (33) […] [endowment] offering (?) […] drink and beer […] (34) […].

(35) Regnal year 7] of the Son of Re, Pamiu. As his monument for […] (36) [.... The Son of Re], P[amiu …]

(36–40) […]

NOTES

1. The traces may be compared with the cartouche of Sheshonq IV on his canopic vase, where the small sign for s3 appears above the "n" of Sheshonq. Here there is no room for the epithet "the god, ruler of Heliopolis." The editors associate the damaged cartouche with Sheshonq III.

2. Literally, "satisfied."

3. Literally, "the silver/money."

9. KARNAK PRIESTLY ANNALS

Like the Theban flood records from the Karnak quay, the Karnak Priestly Annals provide basic chronological documentation spanning most of the Libyan Period, from Pseusennes I of Dynasty XXI (text 3A) to the Nubian Kashta of incipient Dynasty XXV (text 31). Inscribed on rectangular pilaster (?) blocks from the central "Akh-menu" shrine of Thutmose III, the annals follow a standard format that combines the categories of formal inscription and private graffiti. Following a specific date in the reign of the locally acknowledged monarch, the texts record the "day of induction" of priestly candidates into the shrine or "great and noble places" of Amon-Re at Karnak. Successive entries may note the "repetition of favor" within the priestly hierarchy. More elaborate examples mention the sacerdotal agent who introduced the candidate and conclude with the latter's "inaugural speech" proclaiming the omnipotence of the Theban deity.

In addition to furnishing evidence for the length of individual reigns and pontificates, the annals document the first use of "Pharaoh" as a formal title (text 3B, reign of Siamon), show initial Theban reluctance to acknowledge the Libyan Sheshonq I as anything more than a "Great Chief of the Ma" (text 4), contain one of the final attestations for the embattled Prince Osorkon "B" (text 7), and attest to the local disregard of Dynasty XXII after the reign of Sheshonq III and to the rising influence of Nubia in later Dynasty XXIII (text 31). By the nature of the texts, religious concerns are prominent. Located at the heart of Karnak, the older Akh-menu chapel seems to have served as the contemporary sanctuary and repository of the cult image of Amon. It is thus natural that initiates recorded here their "elevation" allowing access to this earthly "heaven" and the radiant statue within it (see texts 2 and 7). If correctly understood, text 7 also provides the first documentation of asceticism among the Egyptian priesthood, with abstinence from food, drink, and sleep as a consequence of induction.

The texts are in all cases mere "fragments" found on scattered blocks by Legrain during 1898–99 and are often carved in enigmatic and damaged script. With the exception of the stones containing texts 1–2 (Cairo JdE 36494) and text 7 (Cairo JdE 36493), all blocks have been lost, and it was only the rediscovery of the excavator's paper squeezes that allowed a republication of the difficult inscriptions by Kruchten in 1989. The few induction speeches are particularly obscure, and the published translations diverge sharply. The following translations of these passages are necessarily provisional and are offered with due reservation. Texts from the same series in the Fitzwilliam Museum at Cambridge were signaled by Daressy in 1913 and are included here as texts 45 and 46. As some twenty texts are of uncertain date, the traditional (nonchronological) order has been retained.

For the texts, translations, and discussion, see Kruchten 1989; Kitchen 1993, 308–9; Jansen-Winkeln 1991b, 765–71; 1985, 223–28, 566–70, text A 21; 1990, 173–77; Breasted 1906–7, 4:388–89 §§775–77 (no. 7); and Legrain 1900a, 51–63. For the Fitzwilliam texts, see also Daressy 1913, 131–32. See Kitchen 1986, 11 n. 39; 131 §103.

TEXT 1 (CAIRO JdE 36494): PEDUBAST I
See Kitchen 1986, 337–38 §298. On the same block with text 2.

(1a) [... hrw n] bs [...]

(1b) ḥsb.t 7.(t) tp(y) šmw n ny-sw.t Pꜣ-dỉ-Bꜣs.t mrỉ-ʾImn hrw n bs sꜣ⸗f ỉt-nṯr n ʾImn Pꜣ-dỉw-ʾImn.t¹ mꜣꜥ-ḫrw r nꜣ s.wt n Mw.t Ḫnsw [Mnṯw Mꜣꜥ.t(?)

wḥm²] (2) ḥs.t n ḥsb.t 8.(t) n ny-sw.t pn hrw n bs ỉt-nṯr n ʾImn Pꜣ-dỉw-ʾImn.t¹ mꜣꜥ-ḫrw sꜣ Mḥ-ʾImn-ḥꜣ.t¹ sꜣ Pꜣ-mꜥrw [mꜣꜥ-ḫrw sꜣ]

(3) Pꜣ-nbꜣ mꜣꜥ-ḫrw sꜣ ʾImn-m-sꜣ⸗f sꜣ Ḫnsw-ḫw mꜣꜥ-ḫrw r nꜣ s.wt ꜥꜣ.w(t) šps.w(t) n.(t) ʾImn

dd⸗f ỉ ỉwy[.w ḫpr.w²] (4) m-ḫt ꜥq.w n.{t} ʾIp.t-s.wt psd.t pw n.t ꜥnḫ.(w) stꜣ.w wỉꜣ n bꜣ wr šms ʾImn nn ḥb(ỉ.t) n ỉwr.t (5) mꜥr.wy šm ḥr mw⸗f mḥ-ỉb pw n hn sw n kꜣ⸗f m(w)nf n ḥr(y) ỉw ỉsf[.t]

(6) ỉw.n⸗f n nty m sꜣw-ꜥ dwn.n⸗f³ nty m g(ꜣ)ḥ ndr⸗f ꜥ⸗ỉ

dd(?)⸗f⁴ ḥr mꜣꜣ dsr⸗f ḥnm.w m ỉs.t Rꜥ (7) ꜥr nḥm.k(wỉ) rmt.w ḥnbb n psd.t⁵ nn sr sꜥr⸗f spr⸗ỉ nn mw.t⸗ỉ sn.w⸗(ỉ) ḫꜣ⸗ỉ ỉs nn (8) km ḫfn.w dmd pr.w⁶ n šms ʾImn¹

(1a) [... day of] induction [...]

(1b) Regnal year 7, first month of summer, of King Pedubast (I), beloved of Amon: the day of induction of his son, the God's Father of Amon, Padiamonet,¹ the justified, into the places of Mut, Khon[su, Montu, and Maat (?).

Repetition² of] (2) favor in regnal year 8 of this king: the day of induction of the God's Father of Amon, Padiamonet,¹ the justified, son of Mehamonhat, son of Pamaru, [the justified, son of] (3) Paneba, the justified, son of Amonemsaef, son of Khonsukhu, the justified, into the great and noble places of Amon.

He said: "O you who come, [who come into being²] (4) hereafter and who enter into Karnak, that is to say, (into) the Ennead of the living, and who haul the bark of the great ram (Amon), serve Amon without diminishing the offering bread! (5) How fortunate is the one who is loyal to him! He (Amon) is the confidant of the one who bends himself to his (Amon's) ka-spirit, the protector of the victim of injustice or evil. (6) As he has come to the one who is helpless ("broken of hand"), so he has raised up³ the one who is weary. May he take my hand."

He (Padiamonet) said[4] at the sight of his (Amon's) holiness, when the members of the crew of Re are (7) elevated: "I am saved, O people who enter into the Ennead.[5] There is no official who forwards my petition. My mother and (my) brothers are not behind me (as protectors). Indeed, there is no (8) profit of hundreds of thousands that can total the surplus[6] of the service of Amon."[1]

Text 2 (Cairo JdE 36494): Pedubast I
See Kitchen 1986, 124 §98; 337–38 §298.

(1) ḥsb.t 8.(t) tp(y) šmw sw 19 (n) s3 Rꜥ P3-dỉ-B3s.t mrỉ-ʾImn hrw n bs ḥm-nṯr n ʾImn-Rꜥ ny-sw.t nṯr.w ỉmy-r3 nỉ.wwt t3ty t3y.ty s3b ỉry Nḫn ḥm-nṯr n [M3ꜥ.t ...] (2) sšm n b(w)-nfr t3 r-ḏr≠f[7] wḥꜥ q(3)s n ḥnmm.t ỉmy-r3 sr.w tp(y) sꜥḥ.w P3-nty-ỉw≠f-ꜥnḫ nb ỉm3ḫ s3 (ḥm)-nṯr n ʾImn-Rꜥ ny-sw.t nṯr.w ỉmy-r3 nỉ.wwt t3ty r3 t3 nḏ ỉm(y)≠f ꜥ3 wr ḥr [...] (3) ꜥḥ Hrỉ m3ꜥ-ḫrw ms.n nb.t pr šps.t T3-rš.wy ꜥnḫ.tỉ r t3 g3y.t ꜥ3.t šps.(t) n.(t) ʾImn ỉn ḥm-nṯr tp(y) n ʾImn ỉmy-r3 mḏ Šmꜥw Ḥr-s3-3s.t [... ỉ](4)m≠f m33≠f ʾImn m sšm≠f pw ḏsr ỉmn r nṯr.w

ỉb≠ỉ sp 2 nḫ≠k ḫpr.(w) ḫf(t) m33≠ỉ sšt3 n ỉmy W3s.t dg3[≠ỉ] 3ḫ [...][8] (5) s.wt m sn.t r ỉtn≠f m Nw.t ỉ3.t wr.t ḫnm.t m ỉwf≠ỉ nn dr≠s r nḥḥ s3(?) M3ꜥ.t swꜥb [...] pr.w [...]

(1) Regnal year 8, first month of summer, day 19, of the Son of Re, Pedubast (I), beloved of Amon: the day of induction of the prophet of Amon-Re, King of the Gods, overseer of cities, vizier, the one of the portal, judge, supervisor of Nekhen (Hierakonpolis), prophet of [Maat, ...]

(2) he who leads the entire land toward goodness,[7] who resolves difficulties ("loosens what is bound") for humanity, the overseer of officials, first of nobles, Panetiuefankh, the possessor of reverence, son of the prophet of Amon-Re, King of the Gods, overseer of cities, vizier, the "door of the land", who protects those in it, the great door-leaf at [...] (3) the palace, Hori, the justified, and who was born of the housewife and noble lady, Tareshwy, who yet lives, into the great and noble shrine of Amon by the First Prophet of Amon, magnate of the "Ten of Upper Egypt," Harsiese, [...] (4) in it, so that he might see Amon in this holy cult image of his, which is more hidden than those of the other gods.

"My heart, my heart! What you have wished has occurred, as I saw the secret image of the one who is in Thebes, and I viewed the brilliance [...][8] (5) places, conforming to his disk in heaven. The great office has become a part of myself; it cannot be taken away forever. The protection (?) of Maat purifies [...] surplus [...]."

Text 3A: Menkheperre (and Pseusennes I)
See Kitchen 1986, 14 §12 (iii); 270 §226.

(1) ḥsb.t 40.(t) 3bd 3 šmw hrw n sỉp pr ʾImn-Rˁ ny-sw.t nṯr.w (2) pr ʾImn-(m)-ʾIp.t pr Mw.t pr Ḫnsw pr Ptḥ rsy ỉnb≠f m W3s.t (3) pr Mntw nb W3s.t pr M3ˁ.t ỉn⁹ ḥm-nṯr tp(y) n ʾImn-Rˁ ny-sw.t nṯr.(w) Mn-ḫpr-Rˁ (4) s3 ny-sw.t P3-nḏm mrỉ-ʾImn m-ḫt dd m ḥr n ḥm-nṯr 4-nw n ʾImn-Rˁ ny-sw.t nṯr.w (5) ḥm-nṯr n Mnṯ(w)-Rˁ nb W3s.t ḥry t3y.w šḥtpy ḫ3.t ʾImn T3y-nfr m3ˁ-ḫrw (6) s3 ḥm-nṯr 4-nw n ʾImn-[Rˁ] ḥm-nṯr n Mnṯ(w) nb W3s.t Nsy-p3-ḥr-n-Mw.t m3ˁ-ḫrw

(1) Regnal year 40, month 3 of summer: the day of inspecting the temple of Amon-Re, King of the Gods, (2) the temple of Amon(em)ope, the temple of Mut, the temple of Khonsu, the temple of Ptah, who is south of his wall, in Thebes, (3) the temple of Montu, Lord of Thebes, and the temple of Maat by⁹ the First Prophet of Amon-Re, King of the Gods, Menkheperre, (4) son of King Pinedjem (I), beloved of Amon, after assignment was given to the Fourth Prophet of Amon-Re, King of the Gods, (5) prophet of Montu-Re, Lord of Thebes, and chief thurifer before Amon, Tchainefer, the justified, (6) son of the Fourth Prophet of Amon-[Re], and prophet of Montu, Lord of Thebes, Nesipaherenmut, the justified.

Text 3B: Osorkon ("The Elder"), Siamon, and Pseusennes II (?)
See Kitchen 1986, 7 §4; 11 §7 n. 39; 12 §9; 13 §10; 203 §167 (iii, v); 278 §233; 284 §238; 422 §388 (56); 423 §390 (83); and §391 (86).

(1) ḥsb.t 2.(t) tp(y) šmw sw 20 ḫr ḥm n ny-sw.t bỉ.ty nb t3.wy ˁ3-ḫpr-Rˁ-stp-n-Rˁ s3 Rˁ [Wsrkn …] (2) hrw n bs ỉt-nṯr n ʾImn-Rˁ ny-sw.t nṯr.w sš ḥw.t-nṯr n Mw.t wr.t nb.(t) ʾIšrw ḥry sš wḏḥ(w) n pr ʾImn [… Ns]-p3-nfr-ḥr (m3ˁ)-ḫrw s3 ʾIw≠f-n-ʾImn m3ˁ-ḫrw r t3 [g3y.t ˁ3.t] (3) šps.t n ʾImn-Rˁ ny-sw.t nṯr.w r rd nb n ḥm.w-nṯr

(3b) ḥsb.t 17.(t) tp(y) šmw ḫr ḥm n ny-sw.t bỉ.ty nb t3.wy pr-ˁ3¹⁰ S3-ʾImn hrw n bs ỉt-nṯr [n] (4) ʾImn-Rˁ ny-sw.t nṯr.w sš ḥw.t-nṯr n Mw.t wr.t nb.(t) ʾIšr(w) ḥry sš wḏḥ(w) n pr ʾImn Ḥrỉ (m3ˁ)-ḫrw s3 ḥm-nṯr n ʾImn-Rˁ ny-sw.t nṯr.w ḥry sš ḥw.t-nṯr n pr ʾImn ỉmy-r3 sš.(w) ḥw.wt-nṯr n3 nṯr.w (5) nb.w n.w Šmˁw Mḥw Ns-p3-nfr-ḥr m3ˁ-ḫrw r t3 g3y[.t ˁ3.t] šps.t n [ʾImn-Rˁ ny-sw.t nṯr.w] r [rd nb n ḥm.w-nṯr(?) …]

(6) ḥsb.t 13.(t) 3bd 3 pr.t sw 10 […]¹¹

(1) Regnal year 2, first month of summer, day 20, under the Majesty of the King of Upper and Lower Egypt, Lord of the Two Lands, Aakheperre-setepenre, Son of Re, [Osorkon ("The Elder") …]: (2) the day of induction of the God's Father of Amon-Re, King of the Gods, the temple scribe of Mut the great, Lady of Asheru, and chief of scribes of the offering table of the estate of Amon [.... Nes]paneferher, the justified, son of Iuefenamon,

the justified, into the [great and] (3) noble [shrine] of Amon-Re, King of the Gods, and into any designated place of the prophets.

(3b) Regnal year 17, first month of summer, under the Majesty of the King of Upper and Lower Egypt, Lord of the Two Lands, Pharaoh[10] Siamon: the day of induction of the God's Father [of] (4) Amon-Re, King of the Gods, the temple scribe of Mut the great, Lady of Asheru, and chief of scribes of the offering table of the estate of Amon, Hori, the justified, son of the prophet of Amon-Re, King of the Gods, chief temple scribe of the estate of Amon, and overseer of temple scribes of (5) all the gods of Upper and Lower Egypt, Nespaneferher, the justified, into the [great] and noble shrine of [Amon-Re, King of the Gods,] and into [any designated place of the prophets (?).]

(6) Regnal year 13, month 3 of summer, day 10 [of Pseusennes II (?) ...][11]

TEXT 4: SHESHONQ I (AS CHIEF OF MA AND KING)
See Kitchen 1986, 288 §242.

(1) [ḥsb.t ... ḥrw n bs ...] pr [...] pr [...] pr [...ʾImn]-ḥtp mꜣꜥ-ḫrw sꜣ ỉt-nṯr n ʾI[m]n-[Rꜥ ny-sw.t nṯr.w ... r tꜣ gꜣy.t ꜥꜣ.t] (2) šps.t n ʾImn-Rꜥ ny-sw.t nṯr.w n ḥnw pr≠f

(3) ḥsb.t 2.(t) ꜣbd 3 ꜣḫ.t sw 7 n wr ꜥꜣ n Mꜥ Šꜣšꜣ(n)q mꜣꜥ-ḥrw ḥrw n bs [...]

(4) ḥsb.t 13.(t) ꜣbd 3 pr.t sw 9 n ny-sw.t Ššnq mrỉ-ʾImn mꜣꜥ-[ḥrw] wḥm [ḥs.t m ḥsb.t ...]

(1) [Regnal year ... the day of induction of ...] of the temple [of ...] of the temple [of ...] of the temple [of ... Amon]hotep, the justified, son of the God's Father of Amon-Re, King of the Gods, ... into the great] (2) and noble [shrine] of Amon-Re, King of the Gods, within his temple.

(3) Regnal year 2, month 3 of Inundation, day 7, of the Great Chief of the Ma, Sheshonq (I), the justified: the day of induction of [...]

(4) Regnal year 13, month 3 of winter, day 9, of King Sheshonq (I), beloved of Amon, the justified. Repetition of [favor in regnal year ...]

TEXT 5: OSORKON II, TAKELOT II, AND SHESHONQ III
See Kitchen 1986, 131 §103; 338 §298 n. 526 (attributing lines 2–3 to Pedubast I).

(1) [ḥsb.t ...] ny-sw.[t W]sỉ(r)kn [mrỉ-ʾImn] ḥrw n [bs ...]

(2) ḥsb.t 14.(t) tp(y) šmw n ny-sw.t Wsr-mꜣꜥ.t-Rꜥ-stp-n-ʾImn sꜣ Rꜥ [...]

(3) ḥsb.t 23.(t) tp(y) šmw n ny-sw.t Wsr-mꜣꜥ.t-Rꜥ-[stp-n]-ʾI[mn ...]

(4) wḥm ḥs.t≠f ḥsb.t 11.(t) tp(y) š[mw ...]

(5) ḥsb.t [...] (6) [... Wsr]-mꜣꜥ.t-Rꜥ-stp-n-Rꜥ sꜣ Rꜥ Ššnq mrỉ-ʾImn sꜣ Bꜣst.t nṯr ḥqꜣ ʾIwnw ꜥnḫ ḏ.t (7) [...] mꜣꜥ-ḥrw r tꜣ.ty n nỉw.t rsy.t r swꜣḏ [...]

(1) Regnal year ...] of King [O]sorkon (II?), [beloved of Amon,]: the day of [induction of ...]

(2) Regnal year 14, first month of summer, of King Usimaʿre-setepena-mon, Son of Re, [(Osorkon II) ...]

(3) Regnal year 23, first month of summer, of King Usimaʿre-[setepen]a[mon, (Osorkon II) ...]

(4) Repetition of his favor in regnal year 11 (of Takelot II), first month of s[ummer ...]

(5) Regnal year [...] (6) [... Usi]maʿre-setepenamon, Son of Re, Sheshonq (III), beloved of Amon, son of Bastet, the god, ruler of Heliopo-lis, living forever. (7) [...] the justified, to be Vizier of the Southern City, in order to make prosper [...]

TEXT 6: OSORKON II (?)
Related to text 5 (?); see Legrain 1900a, 55; Payraudeau 2003, 250–55. See Kitchen 1986, 131 §103.

(1) [ḥsb.t ...] ḥm n ny-sw.t bỉ.ty nb t3.wy Wsr-m3ʿ.t-Rʿ-stp-n-ʾImn s3 Rʿ nb ḫʿ.w [... ḥrw n bs ...] (2) [... ʾImn-Rʿ ny-sw.t nt̲r.w ỉdnw n pr Mw.t wr.t nb.(t) ʾIšr[w] Ḥr m3ʿ-ḫrw s3 ỉt-ntr (n) ʾImn-Rʿ ny-sw.t [ntr.w ...]¹² (3) [... ʾImn(?)]-Rʿ ʿnḫ≠f-n-Mw.t m3ʿ-ḫrw ỉr.n{n} ỉḥy.(t) n.(t) ʾImn-Rʿ T3-b3k.(t)-n-Mw.t m3ʿ.t-ḫrw [s3.t ...] (4) [...] n pr [ʾI]mn ḥry sš ḥw.t-ntr pr ʾImn Ḥr m3ʿ-ḫrw [s3 ...] n [ʾImn-Rʿ] ny-sw.t ntr.[w] ḥry [...]

(1) [Regnal year ... of] the Majesty of the King of Upper and Lower Egypt, Lord of the Two Lands, Usimaʿre-setepenamon, Son of Re, Lord of Diadems, [(Osorkon II?) ...: the day of induction of ...]

(2) [... of A]mon-Re, King of the Gods, deputy of the estate of Mut the great, Lady of Asher[u], Hor, the justified, son of the God's Father of Amon-Re, King of [the Gods ...]¹² (3) [... Amon]-Re, Ankhefenmut, the justified, born by the sistrum-player of Amon-Re, Tabaketenmut, the justi-fied, [daughter of ...] (4) [...] of the estate of [A]mon, chief temple scribe of the estate of Amon, Hor, the justified, [son of ...] of [Amon-Re,] King of the God[s], and chief of [...]

TEXT 7 (CAIRO JdE 36493): SHESHONQ III
See Kitchen 1986, 340 §300 and n. 540.

(1) ḥsb.t 39.(t) tpy šmw sw 26 ḥr ḥm n ny-sw.t bỉ.ty nb t3.wy s3 Rʿ Šš(n)q mrỉ-ʾImn s3 B3st.t ʿnḫ d̲.t

ỉst ḥm-ntr tp(y) n ʾImn-Rʿ ny-sw.t ntr.w ỉmy-r3 Šmʿw h3w.ty Wsỉrkn [s3 ny-sw.t] (2) Tkrt mrỉ-ʾImn ʿnḫ d̲.t m ḥnw W3s.t ḥr ỉr.t ḥb ʾImn n ỉb wʿ ḫft sn≠f ỉmy-r3 mšʿ n (Ḥw.t)-nn-ny-sw.t h3w.ty B3k-n-Ptḥ ntr.w nb.w ḥtp.(w) m-[dỉ](3)≠sn¹³ ḥr sḫr ʿh3 nb r≠sn hrw pn n bs t3y.ty s3b ỉmy-r3 nỉw.t t3ty [wr] n [M]ꜥ Ḥr-s3-3s.t s3 ḥsk(w) ḥm B3st.t ḥm Ḥry-š≠f(?) m T3-š ny-sw.t t3.[wy … P3(?)-]

(4)ḥn-3s.t¹⁴ r t3 g3y.t¹⁵ ꜥ3.t šps.(t) n.(t) ʾImn p.t pw nn snỉ-ḥwd m ỉw.ty pḥ≠s m ḥm≠f m ỉw.w ỉwy(w)¹⁶

ḏd≠f m (5) ỉb≠ỉ […]≠k [..]k ḏr b3ḥ n ꜥr≠(ỉ) šd≠k(wỉ)¹⁷ wnn p3 sr ḥw m pr-ꜥnḫ dỉ≠k ḫ3.w m ḥtp-nṯr ḥr tm.t≠(ỉ?)¹⁸ ỉ(w)≠k šn.tw n m3ꜥ.t wr.t sp-2 ḥr(y.t)-tp≠k ḫpr.t m […] (6) ḏr.t […]ỉb ḥr tbs ꜥ.t nb.(t) ỉm≠ỉ r nw nb tm≠(ỉ) 3ꜥꜥ n≠ỉ n tr n 3ꜥꜥ sdḥr.t(w) t mw m r3≠ỉ ꜥnḫ.tw ỉm ḥr≠k t3ỉ r ỉqḥ Nw.t(?)¹⁹ [r] (7) m33 Šw ỉm≠s ỉst m3ꜥ-ḫrw≠k(wỉ)²⁰ mỉ m3.n≠ỉ ḫnty. w≠f wr.w m nỉw.t nb.(t) n ny-sw.t n{w} T3-Mḥw sp3.wt≠f n s3b-sš.w m-ḫnw ʾIdḥw²¹ ḥr s3 tỉ.t≠f m Tm ḫnt(y) Nꜥr.t (8) ỉst n(t)sn²² ḫ3bs.w 3ḫ.ty m W3s.t

mỉ r≠k snsn ḥnꜥs ḫnm n≠s ỉr.t wnm.t m ꜥḥm(?)²³ ỉ-nḫ≠w n≠n ꜥnḫ r šs≠n mḥw≠n ḫpr m ršw […] (9) [w]ỉ ḥr≠s m smr ḥft≠k n(n) th≠(ỉ) m wḏ.t.n≠k m[ỉ] sšm≠k (w)ỉ r ḥry(?)≠f tp t3 ḥr spḥr k3≠ỉ m psḏ.t ḥr-nty ỉr wnn sw3ḫ.tw≠ỉ n rs-tp ḥr ḥ.wt […]

(1) Regnal year 39, first month of summer, day 26, under the Majesty of the King of Upper and Lower Egypt, Lord of the Two Lands, Son of Re, Sesho(n)q (III), beloved of Amon, Son of Bastet, living forever.

Now, the First Prophet of Amon-Re, King of the Gods, the overseer of Upper Egypt and leader, Osorkon (B), [son of King] (2) Takelot (II), beloved of Amon, living forever, was in Thebes performing the festival of Amon in concord with his brother, the general of Heracleopolis and leader, Bakenptah, while all the gods were satisfied with (3) them¹³ in overthrowing everyone who fought against them.

This day of inducting the one of the portal, judge, overseer of the city, vizier and [Chief] of the [M]a, Harsiese (E), son of the *ḥesek*-priest (of Osiris in Abydos), prophet of Bastet, prophet of Harsaphes (?) in the Faiyum, King of the Two [Lands, … Pa(?)-](4)henese,¹⁴ into the great and noble shrine¹⁵ of Amon. It is heaven without defect, being unreachable by the ignorant one among the visitors who come.¹⁶

He said: "It is (5) my heart […] you […] previously, when I had not ascended. I am saved!¹⁷ It is in the House of Life (scriptorium) that the predestined one is protected. May you grant an abundance of offerings because of my negation (?),¹⁸ while you are embraced by Maat, the doubly great, with your uraeus become as […] (6) hand, […] pricking every limb of mine at every moment, so that I do not fall asleep at the time of sleeping, and bread and water are made bitter in my mouth. One lives by means of them because of you, when taken to penetrate heaven (?)¹⁹ to (7) see Shu within it. Now I am justified,²⁰ inasmuch as I have seen his great cult images in every city of the King of Lower Egypt, his nomes of recreation within the Delta swamp,²¹ after his image as Atum, Foremost of the Heracleopolite nome. (8) Now, it is they[22] who are the starry firmament of the Horizon dweller in Thebes.

Come then and fraternize with it (Thebes)! Unite with it, the Right Eye that is the cult image (?)[23] that has been beseeched for us regarding life, for our well-being, with the result that our care has become joy. [...] (9) [...] me bearing it, as a courtier before you. I shall not transgress what you have commanded inasmuch as you guide me to be his superior (?) on earth, causing my *ka*-spirit to circulate among the Ennead, because if it is the case that I am made to endure because of vigilance regarding offerings [...]"

TEXT 8: UNCERTAIN DATE

(1) [ḥsb.t ... hrw n] bs ỉt-nṯr n ᵓImn-Rˁ ny-sw.t nṯr.w ˁnḫ-pȝ-ẖrd sȝ mỉ-nn Pȝ-mỉw sȝ mỉ-nn ˁnḫ-pȝ-ẖrd mȝˁ-ḫrw sȝ ḥm-nṯr n ᵓImn ḥry sš ḥw.t-nṯr n pr ᵓImn Ḏd-Mw.t-ỉw≠f-ˁnḫ mȝˁ-ḫrw sȝ mỉ-nn Ḥr mȝˁ-[ḫrw ...]

(2) [ḥsb.t ...] hrw pn n bs ỉt-nṯr mr-nṯr Pȝ-dỉ-ᵓImn.t sȝ mỉ-nn Pȝ-mỉw sȝ mỉ-nn ˁnḫ-pȝ-ẖrd mȝˁ-ḫrw sȝ ḥm-nṯr n ᵓImn ḥry sš ḥw.t-nṯr n pr ᵓImn Ḏd-Mw.t-ỉw≠f-ˁnḫ mȝˁ-ḫrw sȝ mỉ-nn Ḥr mȝˁ-ḫrw r nȝ s.wt [...]

(3) [ḥsb.t ...] hrw p[n n] bs ỉt-nṯr mr-nṯr Ḏ[d]-Bȝst.t-ỉw≠[f]-ˁnḫ sȝ mỉ-nn Pȝ-mỉw sȝ mỉ-nn ˁnḫ-pȝ-ẖrd mȝˁ-ḫrw sȝ ḥm-nṯr n ᵓImn ḥry sš ḥw.t-nṯr n pr ᵓImn Ḏd-Mw.t-ỉw≠[f]-ˁnḫ [mȝˁ-ḫrw] sȝ [mỉ-nn] Ḥr [mȝˁ-ḫrw ...]

(1) [Regnal year ...: the day of] induction of the God's Father of Amon-Re, King of the Gods, Ankhpakhered, son of the similarly titled Pamiu, son of the similarly titled Ankhpakhered, the justified, son of the prophet of Amon, chief temple scribe of the estate of Amon, Djedmutiuefankh, the justified, son of the similarly titled Hor, the justified, [...]

(2) [Regnal year ...]: this day of induction of the God's Father, whom the god loves, Padiamonet, son of the similarly titled Pamiu, son of the similarly titled Ankhpakhered, the justified, son of the prophet of Amon, chief temple scribe of the estate of Amon, Djedmutiuefankh, the justified, son of the similarly titled Hor, the justified, into the places [...]

(3) [Regnal year ...]: this day [of] induction of the God's Father, whom the god loves, Dj[ed]bastetiuefankh, son of the similarly titled Pamiu, son of the similarly titled Ankhpakhered, the justified, son of the prophet of Amon, chief temple scribe of the estate of Amon, Djedmutiu[ef]ankh, [the justified], son of [the similarly titled] Hor, [the justified, ...]

TEXT 9: UNCERTAIN DATE

(1) [ḥsb.t ...] hrw (n) bs [...]

(2) [... ᵓImn-]-n-ỉn.t mȝˁ-ḫrw sȝ [ỉt]-nṯr [...]

(3) [ḥsb.t ...] tp(y) šmw sw 15 n ny-sw.t [...]

(1) [Regnal year ...]: the day of induction of [...]

(2) [... Amon]emonet, the justified, son of the God's Father [...]

(3) [Regnal year ...], first month of summer, day 15, of King [...]

TEXT 10: UNCERTAIN DATE

(x+1) [...]...[...]

(x+2) [...] rmṯ.w wꜥ.w nb.w [...]n [...][24]

(x+3) [...]≠f r wpš ꜣḫ.t ỉw≠ỉ m nḫn qn(ỉ) m [...]š [...]

(x+4) [...] ḥr ỉb≠ỉ dỉ≠ỉ dbḥ mn≠ỉ n.t-ꜥ sn.n≠ỉ [...]

(x+5) [...] nfr≠ỉ r [...]

(x+1) [...]...[...]

(x+2) ["...] all people alone [...][24]

(x+3) [...] him to illuminate the horizon, while I was a valiant youth in [...]

(x+4) [...] in my heart. I gave requisitions, persevering (in) the regulations, having surpassed [...]

(x+5) [...] while I was better than [...]"

TEXT 11: SHESHONQ III
See Kitchen 1986, 335 §296.

(1) [ḥsb.t ...] Wsr-mꜣꜥ.t-Rꜥ-stp-n-ʾImn sꜣ Rꜥ Šš(n)q mrỉ-ʾImn sꜣ Bꜣst.t [... hrw n bs ...]

(2) [...] sꜣ 3-nw Pꜣ-dỉ-ʾImn mꜣꜥ-ḫrw r s.wt ꜥꜣ.(wt) šps.(wt) n.(t) [ʾImn ...]

(1) [Regnal year ... of King] Usimaꜥre-setepenamon, Son of Re, Sheshonq (III), beloved of Amon, Son of Bastet, [... : the day of induction of ...]

(2) [...] of the third phyle, Padiamon, the justified, into the great and noble places of [Amon ...]

TEXT 12: OSORKON I, II, OR III
Correct Kitchen 1986, 483, table 15 (Rudpamut to Padimut).

(1) [ḥsb.t ...] sꜣ Rꜥ Wsỉrkn mrỉ-ʾImn ꜥnḫ [ḏ.t hrw n bs ...]

(2) [...] sꜣ ḥm-nṯr (n) ʾImn-Rꜥ ny-sw.t nṯr.[w] ỉmy-rꜣ nỉw.[w]t tꜣty rwḏw [ꜥꜣ] Pꜣ-[dỉ]-Mw.t [...]

(1) [Regnal year ... of King ...], Son of Re, Osorkon, beloved of Amon, living [forever: the day of induction of ...]

(2) [...] son of the prophet of Amon-Re, King of the God[s], overseer of cities, vizier and great agent, Pa[di]mut [...]

Text 13: Unknown Date
(1) [...] pr ꜣImn Ḏd-Ḏḥwty-ỉw≠f-ꜥnḫ sꜣ n ỉt-nṯr mr-nṯr rmn pꜣ [...]
(1) [...] of the estate of Amon, Djeddjehutyiuefankh, son of the God's
Father, whom the god loves, who shoulders the [...]

Text 14: Osorkon I, II, or III
See Kitchen 1986, 305 §264 n. 347.
(1) [ḥsb.t ... hrw] n bs ỉt-nṯr n ꜣImn Ns-Pꜣw.ty-tꜣ.wy mꜣꜥ-ḫrw (r) n(ꜣ)
[s].wt ꜥꜣ.(wt) šps.(wt) n.(t) [ꜣImn ...]
(2) [... Ns]-Pꜣw.ty-tꜣ.wy mꜣꜥ-ḫrw sꜣ wꜥb n pr ꜣImn ꜣImn-Mw.t mꜣꜥ-ḫrw
sꜣ wꜥb Ns-ꜣImn [...]
(3) [ḥsb.t ... hrw n] bs sꜣ≠f 2-(nw) ỉt-nṯr n ꜣImn Pꜣ-dỉ-[...]
(4) [ḥsb.t ...] Wsrkn mrỉ-ꜣImn [...]

(1) [Regnal year ...: the day] of induction of the God's Father of Amon,
Nespautytawy, the justified, (into) the great and noble places of [Amon
...]
(2) [... Nes]pautytawy, the justified, son of the *wab*-priest of the estate
of Amon, Amonmut, the justified, son of the *wab*-priest, Nesamon [...]
(3) [Regnal year ...: the day of] induction of his second son, the God's
Father of Amon, Padi[...]
(4) [Regnal year ... of King ...] Osorkon, beloved of Amon, [...]

Text 15: Uncertain Date
(1) [ḥsb.t ... hrw n bs ỉt-nṯr n] ꜣImn-Rꜥ ny-sw.t [nṯr.w ...] (2) [...r≠]w
mꜣꜥ-ḫrw sꜣ mỉ-[nn ...] (3) [...].w m mnḫ m [...] (4) [...] ꜣIp.t-s.wt ḥr ḥw
qmꜣ≠f [...] (5) [...] mꜣꜥ.t r smnḫ≠f nḏ [...] (6) [...].w≠f ḥr [...]m[...] (7) [...]
mꜣ.w≠f [...] (8) [...]k sꜣ [...]

(1) [Regnal year ...: the day of induction of the God's Father of] Amon-
Re, King of [the Gods, ...] (2) [... ...er]ou, the justified, son of the similarly
titled [...] (3) [...] being excellent in [...] (4) [...] Karnak, in protecting
what he has created [...] (5) [...] Maat, in order to embellish it and protect
[...] (6) [...] his [...] upon [...] (7) [...] his rays [...] (8) [...]k, son of [...]

Text 16: Osorkon III (?)
(1) [ḥsb.t ... Wsr]kn [mrỉ-ꜣImn] ms [Kmꜥmꜥ mrỉ-mw.t(?) ...] (2) [...] n
mꜣꜥ Ns-pꜣ-[...] (3) [...] r [t]ꜣ gꜣy.t ꜥꜣ.(t) šps.(t) (4) [n ꜣImn ...]ỉ ꜣḫ [...]
(5) ỉn ḥm-nṯr [...]
(1) [Regnal year ... of King ... Osor]kon (III?), [beloved of Amon,]
born of [Kamama, beloved of Mut (?) ...] (2) [...] of Maat, Nespa[...] (3)
[...] to the great and noble shrine(4) [of Amon ...] effective [...] (5) by the
prophet of [...]

TEXT 17: OSORKON I WITH RETROSPECTIVE MENTION OF PSEUSENNES II (?)
See Kitchen 1986, 305 §264. Cf. texts 34 and 37.
(1) [...] r p3 r-ỉr.t ... ʾỈ[m]n [...]
(1a) ḥsb.t 1.(t) [...] n[y-sw.t] [W]sỉ[r]kn mrỉ-ʾImn hrw [n bs]
(2) [...] ỉt-nṯr n ʾImn Ns-P3w.ty-t3.wy m3ꜥ-ḫrw s3 Ḥr-ḫby.t m3ꜥ-ḫrw s3
[ʾIw⸗f-n-Ḥnsw ...] (3) [...] n ny-sw.t P3-sb3-ḫꜥ-n-[Nỉw.t mrỉ]-ʾImn [...]

(1) [...] to the one who made ... A[mo]n [...]
(1a) Regnal year 1, [...] of K[ing O]so[r]kon (I), beloved of Amon: the
day [of induction ...] (2) [...] the God's Father of Amon, Nespautytawy, the
justified, son of Horkhebi, the justified, son of [Iwefenkhonsu ...] (3) [...]
of King Pseusen[nes], [beloved of] Amon, [...]

TEXT 18: OSORKON III (?)
(1) [... NN ...] n[y-sw.t] bỉ.ty Wsr-m3ꜥ.t-Rꜥ mrỉ-ʾImn m3ꜥ-ḫrw s3 ḥm-
nṯr [3]-nw (n) ʾỈ[mn Nb-nṯr.w(?)...] (2) [...] h[rw n] bs⸗f r n3 s.wt ꜥ3.w(t)
m-ḫnw [...] (3) [...] s3 ʾIw⸗[f-n]-Ḥnsw [...]
(1) [... of] the King of Upper and Lower Egypt, Usimaꜥre, beloved of
Amon, the justified, son of the Third Prophet of A[mon, Nebnetcheru (?),
...] (2) [...] the day of inducting him into the great places within [...] (3)
[...] son of Iw[efen]khonsu, [...]

TEXT 19: SHESHONQ III
See Kitchen 1986, 131 §103 and 335 §296.
(1) [ḥsb.t ...] Šš(n)q [mrỉ-ʾỈmn (m) h3w ḥm-nṯr tp(y) n ʾImn-Rꜥ ny-sw.t
nṯr.w [...] (2) [...] P3-ṯnf m3ꜥ-ḫrw ỉy.n⸗ỉ [...] (3) [... ʾỈ]mn-[Rꜥ] ny-sw.t nṯr.
w P3-ṯn[f ...]
(1) [Regnal year ... of King] Sheshonq (III), [beloved of A]mon, (in)
the time of the First Prophet of Amon-Re, King of the Gods, [...] (2) [...]
Patchenef, the justified. "I have come [...] (3) [... of A]mon-[Re], King of
the Gods, Patchenef, [...]"

TEXT 20: UNCERTAIN DATE
(1) [...] m h3w ḥm-nṯr tp(y) n ʾImn-Rꜥ ny-sw.t nṯr.w [...] (2) [...] s3 ḥry
sš.(w) ḥw.t-nṯr n pr ʾImn Ḥr m3ꜥ-ḫrw s3 ḥm-nṯr (n) ʾỈ[mn ...]
(1) [...] in the time of the First Prophet of Amon-Re, King of the Gods,
[...]
(2) [...] son of the chief temple scribe of the estate of Amon, Hor, the
justified, son of the prophet of A[mon...]

TEXT 21: UNCERTAIN DATE

(x+1) [...]... mꜣꜥ-ḫrw sꜣ [ḥry(?)] ꜥꜣ.w n [...] (x+2) [...] ḥm-nṯr n Mw.t sš pr-ḥḏ (n) pr ʾImn sš ḥw.t-nṯr n Mw.t wr.(t) nb.(t) ʾIšrw sš [...] (x+3) [...] Ns-[pꜣ]-q(ꜣ)-šw.ty r tꜣ s.t ꜥꜣ.(t) šps.(t) n.(t) ʾImn-Rꜥ ny-sw.t nṯr.w

wḥm [ḥs.t ḥsb.t ...]

(x+1) [...]..., the justified, son of the [chief] porter of [...] (x+2) [...] prophet of Mut, scribe of the treasury of the estate of Amon, temple scribe of Mut the great, Lady of Asheru, scribe of [...] (x+3) [...] Nespekashuty to the great and noble place of Amon-Re, King of the Gods.

Repetition of [favor in regnal year ...]

TEXT 22: UNCERTAIN DATE

(x+1) [...]ỉ-m-ḥb m dỉ Ḫnsw ḏs≠f[25] (x+2) [...] ỉt-nṯr (n) ʾImn-Rꜥ ny-sw.t nṯr.[w] Ḏ(d)-Ḫnsw-ỉw≠f-ꜥnḫ mꜣꜥ-ḫrw

(x+1) [... ...]emheb, as one whom Khonsu himself installed.[25] (x+2) [...] God's Father of Amon-Re, King of the God[s], Djedkhonsuiuefankh, the justified.

TEXT 23: HARSIESE (OSORKON II) OR LATER
Cf. Kitchen 1986, 315 §§273–74

(1) [...] ꜣs.t-wr.t mꜣꜥ.t-ḫrw sꜣ.t nb tꜣ.wy [Ḥr-sꜣ]-ꜣs.t mrỉ-ʾImn ꜥnḫ ḏ.t [...] (2) [... hrw n] bs≠f r tꜣ gꜣy.t ꜥꜣ.t šps.(t) n.(t) ʾImn

ḏd≠f wsr.t≠k ỉm [...] (3) [...] s.t-rꜣ≠tn r≠ỉ ḥr wꜣ.wt≠f štꜣ.w(t) m p.[t] mk sḏm≠f spr.t≠tn n ḥm[≠f ...]

(1) [...] Isetweret (A), the justified, daughter of the Lord of the Two Lands, [Harsi]ese (A), beloved of Amon, living forever. [...] (2) [... the day of] inducting him into the great and noble shrine of Amon.

He said: "Your (Amon's) power which is in [...] (3) [...] your (plural) utterance regarding me concerning his secret paths in heaven. Behold, he has heard your petitions; [he] is not ignorant [...]"

TEXT 24: UNCERTAIN DATE

(x+1) [...]ḏtk mꜣꜥ-ḫrw sꜣ ḥm-nṯr n ʾImn-Rꜥ ny-sw.t nṯr.w [...] (x+2) [...] ʾImn-Rꜥ ny-sw.t nṯr.w n ḥs.(t) ny-sw.t m-ḫt [...] (x+3) [...] ḥm-nṯr 2-nw (n) ʾImn-Rꜥ ny-sw.t nṯr.w Pꜣ-šr-n-ꜣs.t [...]

(x+1) [...]djetchek, the justified, son of the prophet of Amon-Re, King of the Gods, [...] (x+2) [...] Amon-Re, King of the Gods, by royal favor after [...] (x+3) [...] Second Prophet (of) Amon-Re, King of the Gods, Pasherenese [...]

TEXT 25: UNCERTAIN DATE

[ḥsb.t ...] hrw pn n bs ḥm-nṯr n ʾImn m ʾIp.t-s.wt sš [...]

[Regnal year …]: the day of inducting the prophet of Amon in Karnak, scribe of [...]

TEXTS 26 + 27: TAKELOT II
See Kitchen 1986, 331 §292 n. 486.

ḥsb.t 11.(t) tp(y) šmw sw 25 ḥr ḥm n nb t3.wy [Tkr]t hrw pn n bs ît-nṯr mrî-nṯr wn ʿ3.wy n.w p.t m ʾIp.t-s.wt [...]

Regnal year 11, first month of summer, day 25, under the Majesty of the Lord of the Two Lands, [Takelo]t: this day of inducting the God's Father, whom the god loves, the opener of the doors of heaven (shrine opener) in Karnak, [...]

TEXT 28: UNCERTAIN DATE
See Kitchen 1986, 131 §103.

(1) [ḥsb.t …] sw 4 (n) ny-sw.t bî.ty nb t3.wy Wsr-m3ʿ.t-Rʿ-stp-n-ʾImn s3 Rʿ [...] mrî-ʾImn [...] (2) [...] Ns-p3-ḥr-n-t(3)-ḥ3.t m3ʿ-ḫrw s3 n (ît)-nṯr mrî-nṯr îmy-r3 pr.wy-ḥḏ [...]

(1) [Regnal year …] day 4 (of) the King of Upper and Lower Egypt, Lord of the Two Lands, Usimaʿre-setepenamon, Son of Re, [...], beloved of Amon. [...] (2) [...] Nespaherentahat, the justified, son of the God's (Father), whom the god loves, the overseer of the double treasury of [...]

TEXT 29: UNCERTAIN DATE

(x+1) [...] nîw.t(?) n [...] (x+2) [...] m 15-n.t(?) ḥm-[nṯr ...] (x+3) [...] rsy.w ḥm-nṯr n Ḫnm-Rʿ nb [...] (x+4) [...]ḥ≠tn qm3 nîw.t

ḏd-mdw ḥm-nṯr [...] (x+5) [... r] t3 g3y.t ʿ3.t šps.(t) n.(t) ʾImn [...] (x+6) [...] r sḫt≠k ḫpr [...] (x+7) [...] ʿq≠î [...]

(x+1) [...] city (?) of [...] (x+2) [...] in the half-month festival (?), the prophet [...] (x+3) [...] southern, prophet of Khnum-Re, Lord of [...]

(x+4) [...] your [...], who created the City (Thebes).

Recitation of the prophet [...] (x+5) [... into] the great and noble shrine of Amon: "[...] (x+6) [...] in order to snare you. [...] happen [...]

(x+7) [...] may I enter [...]"

TEXT 30: UNCERTAIN DATE

(1) [ḥsb.t …] n [ḥ]m (n) ny-sw.t bî.ty nb t3.wy [...] (2) [...] B3k-n-Ḫnsw m3ʿ-ḫrw s3 ît-nṯr n ʾImn-Rʿ ny-sw.t [nṯr.w ...] (3) [... n ʾImn-Rʿ ny-sw.t] nṯr. w Ḥr-s3-3s.t m3ʿ-[ḫrw] s3 ît-nṯr n ʾImn-Rʿ ny-sw.t nṯr.w [...]

(1) [Regnal year …] of the [Maj]esty of the King of Upper and Lower Egypt, Lord of the Two Lands, [...](2) [...] Bakenkhonsu, the justified, son of the God's Father of Amon-Re, King of the [Gods, ...] (3) [... of Amon-

Re, King] of the Gods, Harsiese, the justified, son of the God's Father of
Amon-Re, King of the Gods, [...]

TEXT 31: KASHTA
For discussion, see Priese 1970, 16–18.
    ḥsb.t 1.(t) n.(t) N(y)-mꜣꜥ.t-Rꜥ [...]
    Regnal year 1 of Nimaꜥre [...].

TEXT 32: SHESHONQ III
See Kitchen 1986, 335 §296.
    (1) [ḥsb.t ...] n ny-sw.t bἰ.ty Wsr-mꜣꜥ.t-Rꜥ-stp-n-ʾImn sꜣ Rꜥ Ššnq mrἰ-
ʾImn hrw pn [n bs ...] (2) [... ʾIp.t]-s.wt ʾImn-m-ἰn.t sꜣ (ἰt)-nṯr mrἰ-nṯr wn
ꜥꜣ.wy n.w p.t [...] (3) [...] ḥm-nṯr ʾImn-Rꜥ ny-sw.t nṯr.w ḥm-nṯr ἰm[y]-ꜣb[dꜣf
...]

    (1) [Regnal year ...] of the King of Upper and Lower Egypt, Usimaꜥre-
setepenamon, Son of Re, Sheshonq (III), beloved of Amon: this day
[of induction of ...] (2) [... of Kar]nak, Amonemonet, son of the God's
(Father), whom the god loves, the opener of the doors of heaven (shrine
opener) [...]
    (3) [...] prophet of Amon-Re, King of the Gods, prophet on monthly
service [...]

TEXT 33: PINEDJEM II AND SIAMON
See Kitchen 1986, 11 §7; 12 §9; 278 §233 n. 206; 423 §390 (81).
    (1) [...]m.w tꜣ [...] m mnw(?) s.t [...] (2) [... ἰn ḥm-nṯr tp(y) n ʾImn]
Pꜣy-ndm mꜣꜥ-ḥrw sꜣ n Mn-ḫpr-Rꜥ mꜣꜥ-ḥrw
    ḥsb.t 14.(t) ꜣbd 4 šmw sw 5 n ny-sw.t [Sꜣ]-ʾI[mn ...]

    (1) [...] the [...] as a monument (?), the place [...] (2) [... by the First
Prophet of Amon,] Pinedjem (II), the justified, son of Menkheperre, the
justified.
    Regnal year 14, month 4 of summer, day 5, of King [Si]a[mon ...]

TEXT 34: OSORKON I
See Kitchen 1986, 305 §264. Cf. texts 17 and 37.
    (1) [...] Ns-Pꜣw.ty-tꜣ.wy mꜣꜥ-ḥrw sꜣ Ḥr-ḫby.t mꜣꜥ-ḥrw sꜣ ʾIw⸗f-n-Ḫnsw
mꜣꜥ-ḥrw ḥr ʾImn r ts pꜣ [...] (2) [...] Ḥr-ḫby.t mꜣꜥ-ḥrw r nꜣ s.wt ꜥꜣ.w(t) n.(t)
ʾImn ἰn ḥm-nṯr tp(y) n ʾImn Ššnq [...]
    (1) [...] Nespautytawy, the justified, son of Horkhebi, the justified, son
of Iwefenkhonsu, the justified, bearing Amon in order to support the [...]
(2) [...] Horkhebi, the justified, into the great places of Amon by the First
Prophet of Amon, Sheshonq (II).

TEXT 35: OSORKON I
See Kitchen 1986, 305 §264.
(1) [ḥsb.t ... sw x+] 3 (n) ny-sw.t Sḫm-ḫpr-Rꜥ-stp-n-[Rꜥ ...] (2) [... Mwt] wr.(t) nb.(t) ꜣIšrw ḥm-nṯr 3-nw n Ḫnsw m Wꜣs.t Nfr-ḥtp ḥm-nṯr n Mnṯ(w) nb ꜣIwny [...] (3) [...] ꜣImn-[Rꜥ] ḥm-nṯr 3-[nw n] Ḫ[n]sw [...]

(1) [Regnal year ... day x+] 3 (of) King Sekhemkheperre-setepen[re ...] (2) [... of Mut] the great, Lady of Asheru, Third Prophet of Khonsu in Thebes, Neferhotep, and prophet of Montu, Lord of Armant [...] (3) [... of] Amon-[Re], Third Prophet of Kh[on]su [...]

TEXT 36: UNCERTAIN DATE
(1) [...] ît-nṯr n ꜣImn ḥm-nṯr [...]
(2) [ḥsb.t] 15.(t) tp(y) ꜣḫ.t [...]

(1) [...] the God's Father of Amon and prophet [...]
(2) [Regnal year] 15, first month of Inundation [...]

TEXT 37: OSORKON I
See Kitchen 1986, 305 §264. Cf. texts 17 and 34.
(1) [ḥsb.t ...] hrw (n) bs [...] (2) [...] Ns-Pꜣw.ty-tꜣ.wy mꜣꜥ-ḫrw sꜣ ḥm-nṯr n ꜣImn-Rꜥ ny-sw.t nṯr.w Ḥr-[ḫby.t ...] (3) [... ꜣI]mn-[Rꜥ] ny-sw.t nṯr.w Pꜣ-dî-Mw.t mꜣꜥ-ḫrw sꜣ ḥm-nṯr (n) ꜣImn-Rꜥ [...]

(1) [Regnal year ...]: the day of induction [of ...] (2) [...] Nespau-tytawy, the justified, son of the prophet of Amon-Re, King of the Gods, Hor[khebi...]
(3) [... of A]mon-Re, King of the Gods, Padimut, the justified, son of the prophet of Amon-Re [...]

TEXT 38: UNCERTAIN DATE
(1) [...] mꜣꜥ-ḫrw [h]rw (n) bs [...] (2) [... ꜣImn-Rꜥ ny-sw.t] nṯr.w n ḥsb.t 10.(t) tp(y) šmw sw 22 [+x ...]

(1) [...], the justified: the day of induction [of ...] (2) [... of Amon-Re, King of] the Gods, in regnal year 10, first month of summer, day 22 [+ x ...]

TEXT 39: UNCERTAIN DATE
(1) [...] Ḏd-[ꜣs].t-îw≠f-ꜥnḫ mꜣꜥ-ḫrw sꜣ ḥm-nṯr n ꜣImn-Rꜥ ny-sw.t nṯr.w îmy-rꜣ pr-ḥḏ n nb tꜣ.wy ny-sw.t [bî.ty ...] (2) [... ꜣI]mn m-ḫnw n pr≠f šps r tꜣ s.t n ît.w≠f

(1) [...] Djedeseiuefankh, the justified, son of the prophet of Amon-Re, King of the Gods, and overseer of the treasury of the Lord of the Two Lands and King of Upper [and Lower Egypt ...] (2) [... of A]mon in the interior of his noble estate into the place of his ancestors.

Text 40: Retrospective Mention of Osorkon I (?)

(1) [...] ḥm-nṯr n ʾImn-Rꜥ ny-sw.t nṯr.w ỉmy-rꜣ nỉw.t ṯꜣty [...] (2) [... sꜣ ny-sw.t nb tꜣ.wy] Wsỉrkn mrỉ-ʾImn mw.t≠s ḥr(y.t) šps.w(t) ꜥnḫ≠s-n-Ptḥ mꜣꜥ.t-ḫrw [...]

(1) [...] prophet of Amon-Re, King of the Gods, overseer of the city and vizier [...] (2) [... royal son of the Lord of the Two Lands,] Osorkon, beloved of Amon, whose mother is the chief of noble ladies, Ankhe-senptah, the justified, [...]

Text 41: Uncertain Date

(1) [...] Ḏd-Ḥnsw-ỉw≠f-ꜥnḫ [...] (2) [... r nꜣ s.wt] ꜥꜣ.[w(t)] špš.w(t) n [ʾImn ...]

(1) [...] Djedkhonsuiuefankh [...] (2) [... to the] great and nobles [places] of [Amon ...]

Text 42: Uncertain Date

[... ʾImn]-n-ỉp.t mꜣꜥ-ḫrw [...]

[... Amon]emope, the justifed [...]

Text 43: Uncertain Date

[...] ỉr.n{n} ḥm-nṯr tp(y) n ʾImn-Rꜥ ny-sw.t nṯr.w [...]

[...] made by the First Prophet of Amon-Re, King of the Gods, [...]

Text 44: Sheshonq III
See Kitchen 1986, 335 §296.

(1) [...] Mnṯ(w)-ḥtp mꜣꜥ-ḫrw r tꜣ gꜣy.t ꜥꜣ.(t) šps.(t) n ʾI[mn]-Rꜥ [...]

(2) [ḥsb.t ...] sw 9 (n) ḥm n Ššnq mrỉ-ʾImn sꜣ Bꜣst.t nṯr ḥqꜣ ʾIwnw ꜥnḫ ḏ.t (m) h(ꜣw) n ḥm-nṯr tp(y) (n) ʾImn-Rꜥ ny-sw.t nṯr.w [...]

(3) [...] ʾImn-Rꜥ sš ḥw.t-nṯr n pr ʾImn Ḥr-ḫby.t sꜣ n ḥm-nṯr n ʾImn-Rꜥ [...](4) [... sš] šꜥ.[t] ny-sw.t Nb-nṯr.w r nꜣ s.wt ꜥꜣ.(wt) šps.(wt) n ʾImn m [...]

(5) [ḥsb.t ... ny-sw].t [...] mrỉ-ʾImn ꜥnḫ ḏ.t (hrw) n bs [...]

(1) [...] Montuhotep, the justified, into the great and noble shrine of A[mon]-Re [...]

(2) [Regnal year ...] day 9 of the Majesty of Sheshonq (III), beloved of Amon, Son of Bastet, the god, ruler of Heliopolis, living forever, in the time of the First Prophet of Amon-Re, King of the Gods, [...] (3) [...] of Amon-Re, and temple scribe of the estate of Amon, Horkhebi, son of the prophet of Amon-Re [...] (4) [...] letter [scribe] of the king, Nebnetcheru, into the great and noble places of Amon in [...]

(5) [Regnal year ... of King] [...], beloved of Amon, living forever: (the day) of induction [of ...]

Text 45 (Fitzwilliam 391 = M. E SS 67): Osorkon II, Sheshonq III, and Osorkon III
See Kitchen 1986, 131 §103.

(1) [ḥsb.t ...] hrw (n) bs [...]

(2) [ḥsb.t ...] s3 Rʿ Wsîrkn mrî-ʾImn hrw (n) bs [...]

(3) [ḥsb.t ... ny-sw].t Wsr-m3ʿ.t-Rʿ-stp-n-ʾImn s3 Rʿ Ššnq mrî-ʾImn hrw [n bs ...]

(4) [ḥsb.t ... ny-sw].t Wsr-m3ʿ.t-Rʿ-(stp-n)-ʾImn s3 Rʿ W[sîrkn] mrî-ʾImn [hrw n bs ....]

(5) [ḥsb.t ... ny-sw.t] Wsr-m3ʿ.t-[Rʿ]-(stp-n)-ʾImn [s3] Rʿ [Wsîrkn mrî-ʾImn hrw n bs ....]

(1) [Regnal year ...]: the day of induction [of ...]

(2) [Regnal year ... of King ...] Son of Re, Osorkon (II), beloved of Amon: the day of induction [of ...]

(3) [Regnal year ... of Kin]g Usimaʿre-setepenamon, Son of Re, Sheshonq (III), beloved of Amon: the day [of induction of ...]

(4) [Regnal year ... of Kin]g Usimaʿre-(setepen)amon, Son of Re, O[sorkon (III)], beloved of Amon: [the day of induction of ...]

(5) [Regnal year ... of King] Usimaʿre-(setepen)amon, Son of Re, [Osorkon (III), beloved of Amon: the day of induction of ...]

Text 46 (Fitzwilliam 392 = M. E SS 68): Uncertain Date
See Kitchen 1986, 131 §103.

(1) [... Nb]-ntr.w s3 Nsy-r-ʾImn m3ʿ-ḫrw r n3 s.wt [ʿ3.wt šps.wt n ʾImn ...] (2) [... hrw n b]s sš wt[26] Nb-ntr.w r t3 g3y.t ʿ3.(t) šps.(t) n.(t) ʾImn în ḥm-ntr tp(y) n ʾI[mn ...] (3) [...] Nḫt-t3(y)≠f-mw.t s3 ḥm-ntr (n) ʾImn-Rʿ ny-sw.t ntr.w pr [...] sš wt[26] T3[...]

(4) [wḥm] ḥs.t≠f (m) ḥsb.t 18.(t) tp(y) šmw sw 6 n ny-sw.t Wsr-m3ʿ.t-Rʿ-stp-n-ʾImn s3 Rʿ [... mrî-]ʾI[mn ...] (5) [...] în ḥm-ntr tp(y) n ʾImn-[Rʿ ...

ḏd≠f ...] (6) [...] nîw.t ḫnm≠k(wî) (m) rš [...]

(1) [... Neb]netcheru, son of Nesieramon, the justified, into the [great and noble] places [of Amon ...] (2) [...: the day of induc]tion of the scribe of embalming,[26] Nebnetcheru, into the great and noble shrine of Amon by the First Prophet of A[mon ...] (3) [...] Nakhtefmut, son of the prophet of Amon-Re, King of the Gods, of the estate [...], the scribe of embalming,[26] Ta[...]

(4) [Repetition] of his favor in year 18, first month of summer, day 6, of King Usimaʿre-setepenamon, Son of Re, [..., beloved of] A[mon ...] (5) [...] by the First Prophet of Amon-[Re ...

He said: "...] (6) [...] the City (Thebes), while I am embued with joy [...]."

NOTES

1. Amon is written with an irrelevant final "t" throughout this text. Kitchen accepted the spelling in the personal name as "Pediamonet." For another example, see text 8, line 2.

2. Restoration following Jansen-Winkeln.

3. Both Kruchten and Jansen-Winkeln understood ỉw n≠f and dwn n≠f with following datives.

4. Following Jansen-Winkeln, who insisted upon the reading ḏd≠f rather than ḏs≠f, as read by Kruchten and Legrain.

5. The translation is highly uncertain, chosen in preference to an abrupt change to second person. Jansen-Winkeln interpreted the sentence as the direct speech of Amon to the candidate: "May you save the people who enter into the Ennead." Inversely, Kruchten considered the speech a statement of the candidate to Amon: "You save the man...." Jansen-Winkeln's reading of ḥnbb is certain, as opposed to Kruchten's suggested emendations.

6. Generally following the interpretation of Jansen-Winkeln 1990, 175–77.

7. Following Jansen-Winkeln; cf. 1985, 227–28; 1991b, col. 768.

8. Kruchten's reading of lines 4–5 as ȝḫ s.wt is not possible; see Jansen-Winkeln 1991b, col. 768.

9. The investigation is instigated in the name of Menkheperre but conducted by the subordinate Fourth Prophet.

10. This is the earliest use of Pr-ꜥȝ "Pharaoh" as a royal title. Contra Hodjash and Berlev 1994, 135, there is no reason to assume that the text is posthumous for the king and dynasty.

11. For the suggested dating, see Kitchen 1986, 13 §10.

12. Against Kruchten's analysis of this text as two distinct entries, see Jansen-Winkeln 1991b, col. 768.

13. So Kruchten; Kitchen (1995, 340 n. 540) restored [... wn-ỉn] (3)≠sn ḥr sḫr "Then they overthrew...."

14. Kruchten suggests the unattested [Pȝ-s](4)ḥn-ȝs.t; Kitchen, following Legrain, restored a mother's name [Tȝ-](4)ḥn-ȝs.t.

15. So all copyists except Kruchten, who read ns.t.

16. Kruchten interpreted the line as a vocative ("Come, O you who come") before the candidate's speech.

17. Provisional translation. For the association of (likely technical expressions) for "ascent" (ꜥr) into the shrine and subsequent "salvation" (nḥm/šd), cf. text 1, line 7.

18. Kruchten read tm(ȝ).t≠ỉ "my mat." The candidate notes his abstinence from sleep and food in the following line.

19. Following the text copy of James. For the candidate's view of the shrine as Nut ("heaven") in these texts, see text 2, line 5, and the related Karnak Graffito of Hori (no. 83).

20. All passages taken as first-person Old Perfectives were understood by Kruchten as statements in the second person.

21. A reference to the restricted Delta authority of Sheshonq III?

22. A space was left empty for the uncarved "t."

23. For Thebes as the image of the Eye of Re, see The Chronicle of Prince Osorkon (no. 82), §I, lines 33 and 38, and the Karnak Graffito of Hori (no. 83). Kruchten translated: "when it has welcomed the western form which is Sokar."

24. For this text, see Jansen-Winkeln 1991b, col. 768.

25. For the idiom, see Jansen-Winkeln 1991b, cols. 768–69.

26. Kruchten read sš šꜥ.t (?) "secretary (?)." Perhaps sš ḥsb "reckoning scribe" should be read.

10. FOUR CLERICAL GRAFFITI FROM THE KHONSU TEMPLE ROOF
(NOS. 10, 11, 121, AND 19)

Throughout the Third Intermediate Period, the Khonsu temple at Karnak was the most imposing contemporary construction in Thebes, and its roof served as a favored locale for commemorative graffiti. Some three hundred graffiti have been collected, with approximately ninety being purely representational, while others record official events, family genealogies, and personal devotions. Most of the graffiti remain unpublished, awaiting a formal edition announced by Helen Jacquet-Gordon. The four texts treated here derive from a preliminary study by Jacquet-Gordon and are listed by her enumeration. Contrary to practice elsewhere, the texts were carved not by pilgrims but by local members of the clergy of Khonsu. Each inscription is accompanied by the carved representation of feet, either bare or shod, to indicate the enduring presence of the individual. As a style of devotional graffiti, such footprints would continue until the closing of the native temples, and the last recorded Demotic inscription followed just such a pattern (Philae 377).[1] The four Khonsu graffiti record several generations of priests belonging to one family, starting in the reign of a Sheshonq (III or IV?) and including the unique mention of a later local Pharaoh Iny, whose date and identification remain unknown. For other graffiti from this site, see the Khonsu Temple Graffito of Osorkon I (no. 61) and the Khonsu Roof Genealogies of a Priestly Induction (no. 1).

For the texts, photos, translation (of nos. 10 and 11 only), and commentary, see Jacquet-Gordon 1979, 167–83 and plates XXVII–XXIX; 2004, 49, 55–56 and plates 46 and 54–56; see Kitchen 1986, 97–98 §§78–79 (no. XVI) and 342 n. 551.

NUMBER 10

The hieratic inscription occupies a quadrant measuring 35 cm in length by 14 cm high. The pair of feet, provided with sandals, measures 27 cm in length and is 10 cm below the text. The graffito is adjacent to no. 11 on the same roofing slab (E 2).

(1) ḥsb.t 4.(t) ꜣbd 2 šmw sw 26 (n) Pr-ꜥꜣ Šꜣšꜣq mrỉ-ʾImn² (2) ỉr.n ỉt-nṯr
n Ḫnsw Ḏd-ỉꜥḥꜣ sꜣ n Ḫnsw-m-ḥb sꜣ n Pn-tꜣ-wp.t

(3) ḏd Ḫnsw m Wꜣs.t Nfr-ḥtp pꜣ nṯr ꜥꜣ wr (n) šꜣꜥ (n) ḫpr⁴ pꜣ (4) nty-
ỉw≠f ft pꜣ dgꜣs n Ḏd-ỉꜥḥ pꜣ(y≠ỉ) (5) bꜣkỉ ỉw(≠ỉ) ftt rn≠f n bnbn pꜣ(y≠ỉ)
pr ꜥꜣ šps[y] (6) ỉw[≠ỉ] tm dỉ.t sꜣ≠f ỉ (= r) tꜣ s.t n ỉt≠f

(1) Regnal year 4, month 2 of summer, day 26 (of) Pharaoh Sheshonq
(III?) beloved of Amon.² (2) Made by the God's Father of Khonsu, Djediah,³ son of Khonsuemheb, son of Pentawepet.

(3) Khonsu in Thebes Neferhotep, the very great god since the beginning of creation,⁴ has said: "The one (4) who will efface the footprint of
Djediah, my (5) servant, I shall efface his name from the Benben, my great
and noble house, (6) and I shall not place his son in the position of his
father."

NUMBER 11

The hieratic inscription occupies a quadrant measuring 22 cm in length
by 8 cm in height. The pair of feet are bare with toes indicated, measure 24
cm in length, and are carved 19 cm below the text. The graffito is adjacent
to no. 10 on the same roofing slab (E 2).

(1) ḥsb.t 5.(t) ꜣbd 3 šmw sw 10 n Pr-ꜥꜣ ʾIny⁵ (2) sꜣ ꜣs.t mrỉ-ʾImn ꜥnḫ
wḏꜣ snb rꜥ nb⁶ (3) ỉr.n wꜥb n Ḫnsw Ḏd-ỉꜥḥ sꜣ Ḫnsw-(4)[m-ḥb(?)⁷ sꜣ] Ḏd-ỉꜥḥ
sꜣ Ḫnsw-[m]-ḥb sꜣ (5) [Pn-tꜣ-wp.t ...]

(1) Regnal year 5, month 3 of summer, day 10 of Pharaoh Iny,⁵ (2) Son
of Isis, beloved of Amon, l.p.h. every day!⁶ (3) Made by the *wab*-priest
of Khonsu, Djediah, son of Khonsu(4)[emheb(?),⁷ son of] Djediah, son of
Khonsu[em]heb, son of (5) [Pentawepet ...]

NUMBER 121

Dimensions not given. The undated hieratic inscription and bare feet
are enclosed within a sketched rectangle. The graffito is carved on slab C
5, on the opposite side of the roof from nos. 10, 11, and 19. See Jacquet-
Gordon 1979, 177, 179 fig. 4, and plate XXIXA.

(1) wꜥb (n) Ḫnsw Ḏd-Ḫnsw-ỉw≠f-ꜥnḫ sꜣ Ḫnsw-(2)m-ḥb sꜣ Pn-[tꜣ]-wp.t
sꜣ Ns-[Ḫn]sw-pꜣ-ḫrd

(3) [ḏd Ḫnsw] m Wꜣs.t Nfr-[ḥtp] ỉw≠(ỉ) ftt pꜣ (4) [rn n pꜣ nty-ỉ]w≠f ftt
[pꜣ dgꜣ]s (n) Ḏd-Ḫnsw-(5)ỉw≠f-ꜥnḫ [sꜣ Ḫnsw-m-ḥb pꜣ] wꜥb n [Ḫnsw]

(1) The *wab*-priest of Khonsu, Djedkhonsuiuefankh, son of Khonsu
(2)emheb, son of Pen[ta]wepet, son of Nes[khon]supakhered.

(3) [Khonsu] in Thebes Nefer[hotep has said]: "I shall efface the (4)
[name of the one who] will efface [the foot]print of Djedkhonsu(5)iuefankh,
[son of Khonsuemheb, the] *wab*-priest of [Khonsu."]

NUMBER 19

Dimensions not given. The undated hieroglyphic inscription corresponds to the style of graffiti from Dynasties XXV–XXVI. The text forms two perpendicular columns beside a pair of bare feet and is carved on the same roofing slab as nos. 10 and 11 (E 2). See Jacquet-Gordon 1979, 177, 179 fig. 5, and plate XXIXB.

(1) ỉr.n ỉt-nṯr n Ḫnsw ʾIr.t-Ḥr-r⸗w (2) sꜣ ỉt-nṯr (n) Ḫnsw Ḏd-ỉꜥḥ

(1) Made by the God's Father of Khonsu, Irethorerou, (2) son of the God's Father of Khonsu, Djediah.

GENEALOGY OF THE FAMILY OF DJEDIAH

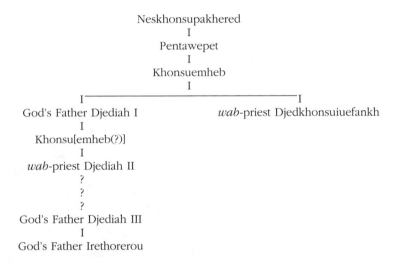

```
                    Neskhonsupakhered
                           I
                      Pentawepet
                           I
                    Khonsuemheb
                           I
  I────────────────────────────────────I
God's Father Djediah I        wab-priest Djedkhonsuiuefankh
        I
Khonsu[emheb(?)]
        I
wab-priest Djediah II
        ?
        ?
        ?
God's Father Djediah III
        I
God's Father Irethorerou
```

NOTES

1. Griffith 1937, 106.

2. See the discussion in Jacquet-Gordon 1979, 178–83. Kitchen preferred Sheshonq IV.

3. The name could also be a sportive writing of Ḏd-Ḫnsw; see Jacquet-Gordon 1979, 176–77 n. 1.

4. An epithet commonly applied to Amon; see the Oracular Decree Preserving the Property of Maatkare (B) (no. 40), line x +2, for the full writing, and the Karnak Sanctuary Blocks of Taharqa, First Amon Hymn, line 2 (no. 149), for the abbreviated writing. The epithet survives in Greek as "the very great deity who was the first to appear"; see Bernand 1981, 2:30–31 and 38.

5. Iny is suggested to be the successor of Rudamon in von Beckerath 1997, 94, 96, and 98. For further possible attestations of Iny, see Yoyotte 1989, 125–30.

6. The common expression need not be taken as Old Perfectives, contra Gardiner 1999, 230 §313 and 295 §378; see the list of obvious nouns in Gebel es-Silsilah Quarry Stela No. 100 (text no. 47), line 30: ꜥnḫ wḏꜣ snb qn(ỉ) nḫt.w "(to whom be) life, prosperity, health, valor, and victories!"

7. Name restored on the basis of papponymy, with sons named after grand-fathers.

C. MAGICAL TEXTS

11. MAGICAL HEALING STELAE:
CIPPI OF "HORUS ON THE CROCODILES"

Magical stelae offering protection and cure against the bite of noxious animals—particularly snakes and scorpions—are first attested in Dynasty XVIII, but it is in the late Ramesside and Third Intermediate Period that they attain a standardized form that would survive into Greco-Roman times and even influence developing Christian iconography. In the earliest examples, a profile figure of the archer deity Shed ("The Savior") tramples crocodiles while grasping animals of the desert, traditional symbols of threatening chaos. During the Libyan Period, the central deity becomes Horus-Shed (often reinterpreted as "Horus the Reciter"), who is now represented frontally. Chicago Oriental Institute 10738 presents a transitional figure, with body in profile and head in frontal relief. A subordinate scene characteristic of examples from this period retains the profile figure of Shed, who shoots fleeing desert animals from a chariot drawn by griffins. Each "cippus" of Horus depicts additional files of healing deities and contains one or more standardized

Chicago OIM 10738

texts. The texts were not read, but water poured over the inscriptions was collected and drunk to allay pain.

Several surviving cippi were made for prominent individuals of the Libyan Period. Chicago Oriental Institute 10738 is inscribed for a king born of a lady Isetemkheb ([…].t m3ꜥ-ḫrw ỉr{t}.n 3s.t-n-Ḥb), perhaps Isetemkheb "C," mother of the Theban rulers Smendes II and Pinedjem II of Dynasty XXI. The final -t within the royal cartouche could correspond to a spelling of the nomen of Smendes (Ns-B3-nb-Dd.t), though this ephemeral pontiff is not otherwise attested with royal honors. Brooklyn 57.21.2 was intended to protect "those in the house of the Son of Re, Osorkon, beloved of Amon," one of the four kings of that name in Dynasty XXII, and the funerary residence of crown prince Sheshonq (D), son of Osorkon II, was guarded by a cippus interred in his grave at Mit Rahina. An example from the Karnak storage magazines (KTA CS VIII 67) served a local prophet of Amon and overseer of priests of Sakhmet. The name of the owner of Chicago Field Museum 31737 was intentionally erased, although surviving titles include "phylarch" (ḥry-tp s3) and "stolist" ([šsp(?)]-mnḫ.t). Unedited cippi belonged to Nakhtefmut (A), great-grandson of Sheshonq I and Fourth Prophet of Amon in the reign of Osorkon II (Paris private collection), to the "follower of She-who-is-united of the estate of Amon" (šms ḫnm.t n pr ꜣImn), Ankhefenkhonsu (former Černý collection), and to a certain Amonemope (IFAO collection).

With figures of Bastet and Horus sculpted in the round (14 cm high) on either side of a smaller image perhaps of Bes, the magical statue group Cairo 9430 differs from standard cippi, but the reverse of its back support displays typical cippus scenes and texts, which proclaim that "all lands, all deserts, mountains and waters and what is in them are under the feet of Horus, the son of Isis."[1] The inscriptions of this healing sculpture close with the wish: "May his name remain before his father Harsaphes, King of the Two Lands, the Chief of the Ma, Pamiu, son of the Lord of the Two Lands, Sheshonq, beloved of Amon." Found at Sais (Sa el-Hagar), the monument may have belonged to the future king Pamiu while still only a prince under Sheshonq III. The summarily carved stela is in need of re-edition, and the identity of Pamiu has been questioned by Yoyotte, but the rough traces here seem to justify the original editor's reading.

Unlike other translations in this volume, the following renditions of standard texts A–C represent a compilation from various sources. Texts A–C are represented on Field Museum 31737; Text B alone on Brooklyn 57.21.2, Chicago Oriental Institute 10738, and Cairo 9430; and Text C alone on KTA CS VIII 67. Text A invokes Horus and his magical skill against the minions of Seth on land and water, text B addresses the solar creator for protection against the confederates of the serpent Apep, and the rarer text C threatens Maga, the crocodile offspring of Seth.

For the various stelae dating to the Third Intermediate Period, see Berlandini 1980, 235–45 and pls. LIV–LV (KTA CS VIII 67), with an overview of documentation on 236 n. 2 and 244 n. 1; Ritner 1989, 103–16 (Field Museum Chicago 31737 and general history); Jacquet-Gordon 1965–66, 53–64 (Brooklyn 57.21.2); Seele 1947, 43–52 (Chicago OI 10738); Badawi 1956, 153–77 and pls. I–XVI (esp. 177 and pl. XV.C); Yoyotte 1988a, 171–74; Bruyère 1952,145–46 (Černý stela); Daressy 1903, 37–39 and pl. XI (Cairo 9430); and Fazzini 1988, 10–11. See Kitchen 1986, 102–3 §82 n. 89; 141 §113; 326 §286; and 563–64 §482.

TEXT A

ỉnd̲-ḥr⸗k nt̲r s3 nt̲r ỉnd̲-ḥr⸗k ỉwꜥw s3 ỉwꜥw ỉnd̲-ḥr⸗k k3 s3 k3 ms.n ḫ.t nt̲r.t ỉnd̲-ḥr⸗k Ḥr pr m Wsỉr ms.n 3s.t d̲d.n⸗ỉ m rn⸗k šd.n⸗ỉ[2] m ḥk3.w⸗k d̲d.n⸗ỉ m 3ḫw⸗k[3] šn.n⸗ỉ m mdw⸗k[4] qm3.n⸗k ḥm.t⸗k[5] pw(y) ỉmy r3⸗k wd̲ n⸗k ỉt⸗k Gb rdỉ n⸗k mw.t⸗k Nw.t rdỉ n⸗k mw.t⸗k 3s.t sb3 n⸗k ḥm n Ḫn.ty-Ḫm r ỉr s3⸗k r wḥm mk.t⸗k r ḥtm r3 n d̲df.wt nb.(t) ỉmy.w p.t ỉmy.w t3 ỉmy.w mw r sꜥnḫ rmt̲.w r sḥtp nt̲r.w r s3ḫ Rꜥ m sns.w⸗k

mỉ n⸗ỉ 3s[6] sp-2 m hrw pn mỉ ỉr⸗k ḥm m dp.t nt̲r ḫsf⸗k n⸗ỉ m3ỉ nb ḥr mrw msḫ.w nb ḥr ỉtrw[7] r3 nb psḥ m tpḥ.t⸗sn ỉr⸗k sn n⸗ỉ mỉ ꜥr.w ḥr mrw mỉ sd qrḥ.t m-ḫt mr.t[8] šd⸗k n⸗ỉ t3 mtw.t nty m ꜥ.t nb.(t) n.(t) NN[9] s3w ỉft mdw⸗k ḥr⸗s mk nỉs.tw rn⸗k m hrw pn[10] sḫpr n⸗ỉ qf3.w⸗k m ḥk3.w⸗k sq3 n⸗ỉ 3ḫ.w⸗k[11] sꜥnḫ⸗k nty m g3w ḥty.t dỉ(w)[12] n⸗k ỉ3w ỉn rḫy.t dw3.tw M3ꜥ. t m ỉrw⸗k nỉs.tw nt̲r m mỉt.t⸗k m ꜥš rn⸗k m hrw pn ỉnk Ḥr-Šd

"Hail to you, God, son of a God! Hail to you, heir, son of an heir! Hail to you, bull, son of a bull, born of the divine womb! Hail to you, Horus, come forth from Osiris, born of Isis! As I have spoken by means of your name, so I have I recited by means of your magic.[2] As I have spoken by means of your spells,[3] so I have enchanted by means of your words[4] that you created. It is your magical skill[5] which is in your mouth, which your father Geb has ordained for you, which your mother Nut gave to you, which your mother Isis gave to you, which the Majesty of the One Foremost of Letopolis taught to you in order to make your protection, in order to renew your safeguard, in order to seal the mouth of every reptile that is in heaven, in earth, or in the water, to cause mankind to live, to pacify the gods, and to beatify Re by means of your praises.

Come to me! Hurry[6] today, inasmuch as you ply the rudder in the divine boat! May you repel for me every lion on the desert, every crocodile on the river,[7] every mouth that bites in their holes. May you make them for me like the pebbles on the desert, like the potsherds along the street.[8] May you extract for me the poison that is in any limb of NN.[9] Beware lest your words concerning it be disparaged. Behold, your name is summoned today.[10] Create for me your prestige by means of your magic. Exalt for me your spells.[11] May you revive the one whose throat is constricted since praises have been given[12] to you by the populace, Maat is adored in your form, and god is summoned in your likeness by calling your name today: I am Horus the Savior/Reciter."

TEXT B

ỉ ỉȝw rnpỉ sw r nw≠f nḥḥ ỉr ḥwn dỉ≠k ỉw n≠ỉ Ḏḥwty ḥr ḫrw≠ỉ[13] sḫm≠f n≠ỉ Nḥȝ-ḥr mk Wsỉr ḥr mw ỉr.t Ḥr m-ᶜ≠f ᶜpy wr m ḫfᶜ≠f[14] m fȝ(ỉ) ḥr≠tn ỉmy.w mw r snỉ Wsỉr ḥr≠tn mtn sw r Ḏdw šrỉ rȝ≠tn ḏbȝ ḥngg≠tn[15] ḥȝ≠k sbỉ m fȝ(ỉ) ḥr≠k r Wsỉr[16] ỉw Rᶜ ḥr tṣ≠f r wỉȝ≠f r mȝȝ psḏ.t n.t Ḥr-ᶜḥȝ nȝ nb.w dwȝ.t ᶜḥᶜ ḥr bḥn≠k ỉy ỉn Nḥȝ-ḥr[17] pnᶜ ḥr≠tn dd ḥr ȝt≠tn ḫtm rȝ≠tn ỉn Rᶜ ḏbȝ ḥngg≠tn ỉn Sḫm.t šᶜd≠tn[18] ỉn Ḏḥwty šp ỉr.wy≠tn ỉn Ḥkȝ pȝ 4 nṯr. w ᶜȝ.w nty ỉr sȝ ḥr Wsỉr ntsn ỉr sȝ n nty ḥr mw n pȝ hrw[19] ḫrw bgȝ m ḥw.t N.t ỉm ᶜȝ m rȝ n mỉw nṯr.w ḥr ptr sp-2 ḥr ȝbdw ms.tw≠f[20] ḥm n≠ỉ nmt.t≠k sbỉ ỉnk Ḫnm nb Ḥw.t-wr.t sȝw m wḥm nkn≠k m 2-nw sp ḥr nn ỉr n≠k m-bȝḥ psḏ.t ᶜȝ.t ḫsf r≠k ḥm n≠ỉ ỉnk nṯr

hy sp-2 ỉ Rᶜ ỉs n sḏm.n≠k ḫrw bgȝ m-ḏr wḫȝ ḥr wḏb pwy n Nḏy.t[21] sgb ᶜȝ (m) rȝ nṯr nb nṯr.t nb.(t) nṯr.w ᶜȝ.w n nḥw ḥr pȝ qn ỉr.n≠k pȝ sbỉ ỉr ḏw mk Rᶜ nšn ḫᶜr ḥr≠s wḏ≠f ỉr.t šᶜd≠k ḥȝ≠k sbỉ

"O aged one, who rejuvenates himself in his season, old man who becomes a youth! May you send to me Thoth at my call,[13] so that he might repel for me the Rough-faced one (Apep). Behold, Osiris is on the water, and the Eye of Horus is with him, with the great scarab in his grasp.[14] Do not lift up your heads, O you who are in the water, so that Osiris may pass by you! Behold, he is bound for Busiris. Your mouths are gagged; your gullets[15] are stopped up. Back, O enemy! Do not lift up your head against Osiris![16] Re is raising himself into his barge to see the Ennead of Egyptian Babylon (the old quarter of modern Cairo), the lords of the underworld, who wait to slaughter you. The Rough-faced one has come;[17] turn yourselves upside down, being placed on your backs! Your mouths are sealed by Re; your gullets are stopped up by Sakhmet; you are slaughtered[18] by Thoth; your eyes are blinded by Heka, the four great gods who make protection for Osiris. It is they who make protection for the one who is on the water today.[19] A wailing cry is in the temple of Neith! A great shriek is in the mouth of the cat! The gods scrutinize the *abdju*-fish at its birth.[20] Turn your steps away from me, O enemy! I am Khnum, lord of Hawara. Beware! Do not repeat your injury a second time because of that which was done to you before the great Ennead. Retreat, turn back from me! I am the god!

Hail, hail, O Re! Have you not heard the wailing cry since evening upon this shore of Nedyet?[21] A great cry is in the mouth of every god and every goddess, since the great gods are in mourning because of the injury that you have inflicted, O enemy and evildoer. Behold, Re is raging and furious because of it, and he has given order to carry out your slaughter. Back, O enemy!"

TEXT C

hy sp-2 ỉ pr m dwȝ.t wbn m Nnw sḥd tȝ.wy m ỉr.wy⸗f mk mnỉ⸗k wn tw r wỉȝ⸗k m ȝw.t-ỉb nḏ ḥm rn⸗k[22]

nḥm.n⸗ỉ nmt.t⸗k Mᶜgȝ[23] sḥtḥt.n⸗ỉ nmt.t⸗k sbỉ ḏd.tw n⸗k ỉr.wy⸗k m ḥḏ nṯr ỉm⸗f Rᶜ[24] hȝ⸗k qȝb pwy n mḥt(w) n(n) ḥᶜ.w⸗k ḥpr⸗k ỉm⸗f npy pwy ḥm r⸗k ỉn Rᶜ ỉw⸗ỉ rḫ.kwỉ ỉr.n⸗k ḏw hy sp-2 ỉ sp-2 pȝ nty m ỉw.t sȝw tw r tkn r ḥᶜ.w nṯr ỉr ỉw⸗k r NN ỉw⸗k r Wsỉr ỉw⸗f ḥr mw ỉr.t Ḥr m-ḫt⸗f šp ḥr⸗k sḥtḥt nmt.t⸗k ḥm tw Mᶜgȝ Wsỉr ṯs r⸗k m ʾIwnw ỉw⸗k sḫr.t n⸗k sbỉ r hȝ nn sḫm⸗k m rmṯ.w nb smsm.w nb ỉᶜw.t mnmn.t nb.(t) nty ḥr mw n NN[25] ḥrw bgȝ m ḥw.t N.t ỉm ᶜȝ m rȝ n mỉw ḥr nn ỉr Mᶜgȝ nn wḏ pw n ỉr.s Sbk[26] ᶜȝ pr r⸗k rdỉ.n⸗f nkn ḏ.t⸗k sȝw sbq.wy(?)⸗k[27] sḥw bȝw ỉr.w r⸗k m-ḫnw sp ḥpr r⸗k nw n⸗k r⸗k ḥm r⸗k n⸗ỉ swȝw⸗k n⸗ỉ ỉnk Ḫnm ỉy.n⸗ỉ m ʾIwnw m wp.t Spȝ[28] ỉnk ỉnq ᶜ⸗f[29]

"Hail, hail, O he who has come forth from the underworld, who has risen in the Abyss, who has illuminated the Two Lands with his eyes! Behold, you have moored. Hasten to your barge in joy to protect against the one who is ignorant of your name.[22]

As I have taken away your stride, O Maga,[23] so I have turned back your stride, O enemy! Let it be said to you that your eyes are white, the god in them being Re.[24] Back, O that coil of intestines! You do not have a body in which you might exist! O that mass of guts, retreat—so says Re. I know that you have done evil. Hail, hail! O he who is coming! Beware of attacking the god's flesh! If you come against NN, you shall come against Osiris, since he is on the water, with the Eye of Horus following him. May you be blinded! Turn back your stride! Retreat, Maga, for Osiris has risen against you in Heliopolis. You are fallen over, O enemy, backwards. You shall not have power over any people, any horses, any flocks or herds that are on the water, belonging to NN.[25] A wailing cry is in the temple of Neith; a great shriek is in the mouth of the cat because of this which Maga has done. It was not commanded to do it. Sobek[26] the great has come forth against you, and he has caused that your body be injured by cutting off your legs,[27] and the punishment to be inflicted upon you has been assembled from among the remainder of what might happen to you. Watch out for yourself! Retreat from me! May you pass away from me! I am Khnum. I have come from Heliopolis on the business of Sepa.[28] I am the one whose hand clenches."[29]

NOTES

1. Miscopied in the edition of Daressy. For the magical symbolism, see Ritner 1993b, 119–36.

2. Variant in Field 31737: šn.n≠ỉ "I have enchanted." For the following list of terms for enchantment, see Ritner 1993b, 40–41.

3. Variant in Cairo 9401: ḏd.n≠ỉ m ḏd≠k ȝḫ.n≠ỉ m ȝḫw≠k "As I have spoken by means of your speech, so I have cast spells by means of your spells."

4. Variant in Cairo 9401 and 9402: šn.n≠ỉ m šd≠k "I have enchanted by means of your recitation."

5. Variant in Cairo 9401 and 9402: ḥkȝ "magic."

6. Variant in Field 31737 and Cairo 9402: stȝ.wy "Hurry."

7. Cairo 9401 and 9402 add: ḥfȝ.w nb ḏȝr.t nb ḏdf.t nb psḥ m rȝ≠sn ḏdb m sd/psḏ≠sn "every snake, every scorpion, every reptile which bite with their mouth, which sting with their tail/back."

8. Symbolic allusion to execration rites entailing the breaking of pots and figures; see Ritner 1993b, 151.

9. The owner's name is inserted here. Field 31737 has the erased [...] ỉr.n{n} ȝs.t [...], "born by Ese."

10. Variants substitute mk rn≠k ỉm m hrw pn "Behold, your name is there today."

11. For this passage, see Ritner 1993b, 32. n. 144.

12. Variant: ḏd.tw.

13. Variant in Field 31737 and Cairo 9402: mdw≠ỉ "my word(s)."

14. Later variants have a long addition: "May he who is on the water go forth safely. If one attacks him who is on the water, then one attacks the Eye of Horus which would weep likewise. Back, dead ones who are in the water, that enemy whether male or female dead, male or female adversary, etc."

15. Brooklyn 57.21.2 reads: "Your gullets, O those among you, are stopped up, so that [Osiris] may pass. Osiris is risen to see the Ennead, the lords of Egyptian Babylon, the lords of the underworld."

16. OI 10738 reads "Don't raise your heads against Osiris who is on the water." There are numerous variants.

17. Variants: "The Rough-faced one will not come"; "If the Rough-faced one comes."

18. Later variants: šꜥd ns.t≠tn "your tongue is cut out."

19. Brooklyn 57.21.2 concludes: pȝ 4 nṯr.w ꜥȝ.w ỉr sȝ≠ỉ ḥr mw tȝ pr nty ḥr mw [... ỉ]my pr sȝ Rꜥ Wsỉrkn mrỉ-ʾỉmn w[ḏȝ] "the four great gods who make my protection on water and land so that the one who is on the water [from among (?)] those in the house of the Son of Re, Osorkon, beloved of Amon, might go forth safely."

20. The prophetic *abdju*-fish guided the barge of Re and warned of the approach of Apep.

21. The place where Osiris was slain by Seth.

22. Following Field 31737, but copies differ. Brooklyn 60.73 has ḫfty≠k ḫr n(n) nḏ ḫm rn≠k wr "Your enemy is fallen; there is no one to greet who is ignorant of your great name." Cairo 9402 has r nḏnd n rḫ rn≠k "in order to consult with the one who knows your name."

23. The crocodile Maga is termed sȝ Stš "son of Seth" in later variants.

24. The animal is blinded by the sun's glare? Following Cairo 9402 and Field 31737. Brooklyn 60.73 and KTA CS VIII 67 have m w3dw3d "Do not flourish!"

25. Cut out on Field 31737, leaving only [...] ỉr.n{n} 3s.t "[...] born by Ese."

26. The crocodile Sobek is sent against his evil counterpart, Maga.

27. KTA CS VIII 67 reads: sp.(ty)≠k "your lips."

28. For this passage regarding Sepa, the sacred centipede, see Ritner 1990b, 167–68.

29. Perhaps a reference to the depicted act of throttling hostile animals.

12. ORACULAR AMULETIC DECREE
(P. BM 10730)

Probably intended for the protection of young children of prominent families, "oracular amuletic decrees" are a terrestrial counterpart to funerary oracles, promising the recipient a lifetime of security from a fairly standardized list of ills, both natural and demonic. The texts are inscribed in highly cursive script on long, narrow strips of papyrus subsequently rolled and worn as a phylactery within tubular amulets suspended from the neck. Reflecting the contemporary vogue for judicial oracles, the twenty-two published examples share format, vocabulary, and temple patronage with other divine pronouncements of the era and are unique to the Third Intermediate Period. One decree is said to have been found at Saqqara, although most are likely to derive from the Thebaid. A single royal example provides the only internal evidence of date and demonstrates the nonexclusive, "popular" nature of post-Ramesside royal religious practice. Of uncertain provenance, this British Museum example measures 1.47 m in length by .08 m in width and is designed for a prince and future general of a Pharaoh Osorkon, probably Osorkon I.

For the text, translation, and discussion, see Edwards 1960, xiii–xiv, 47–50 and plates XVI–XVII. For the genre, see also Bohleke 1997, 155–67; Ryholt 1993, 189–98; and Fischer-Elfert 1996, 129–44.

[dd NN ... ỉw≠ỉ šd NN mw.t≠f NN p3y≠ỉ b3k ... ỉw≠ỉ] šd≠f r [...] (2) [...]f [...] Ḥnsw nb [...] (3) n3 nṯr.w ᶜ3y.w n.w p.t t3 dw3.[t] (4) ỉw≠ỉ dỉ.t ndm n≠f p3 ᶜq nty ỉw≠f wn(5)[m≠f ỉw]≠ỉ dỉ.t ndm n≠f [p3 mw] nty (6) [ỉw≠f swr≠f ...] (7) ᶜ3 p3 nty ỉw≠f nfr n≠f ḥr≠f ỉw≠[ỉ] (8) [shr] n≠f ʾImn Mw.t Ḥnsw (9) [n3] nṯr.w wr.w ỉw≠ỉ dỉ.t ḥtp≠w (10) n≠f ỉw≠ỉ [šd]≠f ỉ (=r) [...] (11) [ỉ(=r)] ḥk3 nb t3 ḫ3s.t nb ỉw≠ỉ šd(12)≠f r t3 ᶜršn Ḫ3rw (13) t3 ᶜršn Kšy (14) bn ỉw≠ỉ dỉ.t ḫpr≠w [m-dỉ≠f m h(3)w] (15) nb ᶜnḫ ỉw≠ỉ šd≠f r sbḫ (16) r k{n}mn ỉ-ỉr wd3.t (17) m h(3)w nb ᶜnḫ ỉw≠ỉ šd≠f (18) m dr.t n3 nṯr.w nty t3ỉ wᶜ (19) m šb.t wᶜ ỉw≠ỉ dỉ.t šb(20).t(w)≠f (m) ỉ3d.t (< 3.t) nb.t ỉw≠ỉ shr (21) n≠f Mnw Ḥr 3s.t Gbty (22) ỉw≠ỉ šd.t≠f¹ ỉ(=r) n3y≠w b3.w (23) ỉw≠ỉ dỉ.t ššp≠w m-dr.t≠f² m šsp (24) nfr ỉw≠ỉ dỉ.t dỉ≠w sw ḥr (25) n3 mỉ.wt nfr.(wt) ᶜnḫ snb (26) ỉw≠ỉ dỉ.t n≠f {m}³ ᶜnḫ wd3 snb ᶜḥᶜ q3(ỉ) ỉ3w.t

ꜥꜣ.(t) (27) nfr.(t) ỉw⸗ỉ dỉ.t nꜣy⸗f ḥsw.(t) (28) mr(w.t) m-ẖnw ḥꜣ.ty (29) Pr-
ꜥꜣ Wsỉrkn (30) mrỉ-ʾImn pꜣy⸗ỉ šr nfr (31) ỉw⸗ỉ hrḥr r⸗f ỉw bn ỉw⸗ỉ (32)
ṯṯ mt(r) gr(33)ḥ nw nb ỉw⸗ỉ dỉ.t (34) ḥ(ꜣ)b sw Pr-ꜥꜣ Wsỉr(35)kn mrỉ-ʾImn
pꜣy⸗ỉ šr (36) nfr (r)-ḥꜣ.t mšꜥ.w ꜥꜣy.w mtw⸗f (37) ꜥn n⸗f smỉ nb nfr ꜥḏ(?)
(38) md.t nb.t nfr.(t) ỉw⸗ỉ wn (39) ḫ.t nꜣy⸗f ḥbs.(w)⁴ ỉ(=r) ms (40) ḥrd.w
ꜥḥꜣwty.(w) ḥrd.w (41) ḥm.(w)t m mw pr m ḥꜥ.w{t}⸗f⁵ (42) ỉw⸗ỉ dỉ.t ꜥnḫ⸗w
ỉw⸗ỉ dỉ.t snb⸗(w) (43) ỉw⸗ỉ dỉ.t ꜥꜣy⸗w ỉw⸗ỉ dỉ.t ỉry(44)⸗w sbq ỉw⸗ỉ dỉ.t
mnḫ⸗w (45) ỉw⸗ỉ dỉ.t mtr ḥꜣ.ty (46) Pr-ꜥꜣ Wsỉrkn (47) mrỉ-ʾImn pꜣy⸗ỉ šr
nfr (48) m-ỉm⸗w (m) kꜣ.t nb.t ỉw Pr-ꜥꜣ (49) Wsỉrkn mrỉ-ʾImn (50) pꜣy⸗ỉ
šr nfr ꜥnḫ snb (51) nḫt wsr.tw⁶ pḥty (52) ỉw wr ḥkꜣy⁷ nb.t Pr-Wꜣḏ.(t) (53)
smn ḥr tp⸗f ỉw wr nb (54) tꜣ nb ḫꜣs.t nb.(t) ḏd n⸗f ỉry (55) ỉw mdw⸗f ḥr
tp tꜣ⸗sn(?)⁸

(56) ỉw⸗ỉ snb tp⸗(f) nb ḏꜣ(ḏꜣ⸗f) (57) ỉw⸗ỉ snb nḥb.t⸗f (58) ỉw⸗ỉ snb
pꜣy⸗f hny (59) r ḏr⸗f ỉw⸗ỉ snb ḥꜥ.w{t}(60)⸗f nb.{t} ꜥ.t⸗f nb.t šꜣꜥ (61) tp⸗f r
tb.t⸗f (62) ỉw⸗ỉ dỉ mḥ pꜣy⸗ỉ ḥr.tw (63) ꜥꜣ wr špsy ꜥnḫ snb ỉm⸗f (64) ỉw⸗ỉ
m sꜣ⸗f rꜥ nb sp-2 ỉw⸗ỉ ỉr n⸗f (65) ỉry-mšꜥ nfr (m) s.t nb.(t) nty (66) ỉw⸗f
šmỉ ỉr-r⸗w sḫ (67) nb nty ỉw⸗f ꜥq ḥr-r⸗w (68) ỉw⸗ỉ šd⸗f (ḥr) pꜣ ỉmw nꜣ
(69) ḫt(r).w pꜣ ꜥḏ (70) ỉw⸗ỉ dỉ.t mḥ pꜣy⸗ỉ ḥr.tw (71) ꜥꜣ wr šps m-ỉm⸗f
ỉw⸗ỉ m sꜣ⸗f (72) rꜥ nb sp-2

(73) ỉ-ỉr m ḏd.w n pꜣ (74) nṯr ꜥꜣ wr n šꜣꜥ ḫpr⁹

[There has said the deity NN: "... I shall save NN, whose mother is
NN, my servant ... I shall] save him from [...] (2) [...] him [...] Khonsu,
Lord of [...] (3) the great gods of heaven, earth, and the underworld. (4)
I shall sweeten for him the bread that he will eat. (5) I [shall] sweeten for
him [the water] that (6) [he will drink ...] (7) great, what will be good for
him because of it. [I] shall (8) [propitiate] for him Amon, Mut, and Khonsu,
(9) [the] great gods. I shall cause that they be gracious (10) to him. I shall
[save] him from [...] (11) [and from] all magic of every land and foreign
country. I shall save (12) him from the Syrian lentigo (13) and the Cushite
lentigo. (14) I shall not allow them to occur [to him at any period] (15) of
life. I shall save him from leprosy (16) and from blindness that the Sound
Eye suffered (17) at any period of life. I shall save him (18) from the gods
who seize one in (19) substitution for another. I shall allow (2) that one be
substituted for him at all times. I shall propitiate (21) for him Min, Horus,
and Isis of Coptos. (22) I shall save¹ him from their wrathful manifestations.
(23) I shall cause that they receive things from him² in a good reception.
(24) I shall cause that they place him on (25) the good paths of life and
health. (26) I shall give³ to him life, prosperity, and health, a long lifetime,
and a great and goodly old age. (27)

I shall place favor and (28) love for him within the heart (29) of Pharaoh Osorkon, (30) beloved of Amon, my good son. (31) I shall guard
him; nor shall I (32) relax at midday, (33) night, or at any time. I shall

cause (34) Pharaoh Osorkon (35), beloved of Amon, my good son, (36) to send him at the head of great armies, and he (37) will send back to him every report that is good to hear (?) (38) and all good tidings. I shall open (39) the wombs of his concubines[4] to give birth to (40) male children and female children (41) as seed come forth from his body.[5] (42) I shall cause that they live. I shall cause that they be healthy. (43) I shall cause that they mature. (44) I shall cause that they be clever. I shall cause that they be trustworthy. (45) I shall cause that the heart (46) of Pharaoh Osorkon, (47) beloved of Amon, my good son, (48) be satisfied with them in every work, while Pharaoh (49) Osorkon, beloved of Amon, (50) my good son, is alive, healthy, (51) victorious, and powerful[6] of strength, (52) with "Great of Magic,"[7] Lady of Buto, (53) affixed upon his head, and while every chief (54) of every land and every foreign country says to him: 'I shall act!' (55) and while his mace is atop their (?)[8] lands.

(56) I shall make healthy his whole head and skull. (57) I shall make healthy his neck. (58) I shall make healthy his entire frame. (59) I shall make healthy his whole body (60) and all his limbs from (61) his head to his soles. (62) I shall cause that my (63) very great and noble oracle of life and health take control of him, (64) with me being his protection every day! I shall be for him (65) a good traveling companion in all places (66) to which he will go and all shrines (67) into which he will enter. (68) I shall save him whether on boat, (69) chariots, or the desert edge. (70) I shall cause that my (71) very great and noble oracle take control of him, with me being his protection (72) every day!"

(73) Made in accordance with the statements of the (74) very great god since the beginning of creation.[9]

NOTES

1. Phonetic spelling with change of d to t; cf. Demotic šty.

2. Edwards translates "accept (offerings) from his hand"; cf. Chassinat 1935, 54 line 8: "you shall receive them from him (m-dr.t≠f) in a good reception."

3. Perhaps using a precursor of the Demotic direct-object marker.

4. For the opening of the womb, see Ritner 1984b, 209–21.

5. Treated as a feminine word by conflation with ḥ.t, Coptic ϨΗΤ≠.

6. Generic stative ending as in Demotic.

7. Designation of the uraeus and crown as Edjo, tutelary goddess of Lower Egypt.

8. The standard phrase is "while his mace is above their heads"; cf. Chassinat 1935, 54 line 9.

9. This common epithet of oracular gods recurs throughout this book. For discussion, see Edwards 1955, 96–98. Unknown to Edwards, the expression is translated into Ptolemaic Greek as "the very great deity who was the first to appear"; see Bernand 1981, 2:30–40, nos. 112–13.

D. DONATION STELAE

13. DONATION STELA OF NIUMATEPED

This lost and fragmentary donation stela, formerly in the Nahman antiquities dealership in Cairo, is included for its clear depiction of Libyan tribal
authorities usurping the traditional pharaonic role as land donor to the gods.
The monument is dated to Sheshonq V and probably derives from Kom
Firin within the nascent "Chiefdom of the Libu" in the western Delta. In the
lunette, the goddess Sakhmet and her son Heka, god of magic, receive an
offering of field from a chief of the Libu while another tribal figure raises
his hands in adoration behind him and a smaller figure of the beneficiary
precedes him. Both Libyans wear erect feathers in their hair as emblems of
tribal rank and bear exotic names. A further, broken Libyan word preserves
part of a place or personal name. While the lunette is inscribed in hieroglyphs, the body of the text is in hieratic. The lost text will have detailed a
donation of revenue-producing territory to the local deities for the support
of the temple functionary depicted before the chief.

Drawing after Spiegelberg 1920, plate V.

For the text, translation, and discussion, see Spiegelberg 1920, 57–58 and pl. V; Yoyotte 1961, 143 §30. See also Meeks 1979a, 670 (no. 22.10.8). See Kitchen 1986, 351 §311; 1995, xxvi.

LABEL FOR SAKHMET

dd-mdw în Sḫm.t
Recitation by Sakhmet.

LABEL FOR HEKA

Ḥkꜣ (2) [...]wydyn[1] Ḥkꜣ pꜣ ẖrd
Heka (2) [...]wydyn,[1] Heka the child.

LABEL FOR THE LIBU CHIEF

wr ꜥꜣ n Rb(w) [Nꜣy]wmꜣtpd
Great Chief of the Libu, Niumateped.

LABEL FOR ADORING LIBYAN

Wtîr(2)y   Wetery.

MAIN TEXT

(1) ḥsb.t 8.t (n.t) [ny-sw.t] bî.ty Šš(n)q sꜣ Bꜣst.t mrî-ꜣImn nṯr ḥqꜣ Wꜣs.t îw wr ꜥꜣ n Yrbꜣ(2)yw ... (3) .... ꜣḥ.t ... (4) ...[...]

Regnal year 8 of [the King of Upper] and Lower Egypt, Sheshonq (V), Son of Bastet, beloved of Amon, the god, ruler of Thebes, while the Great Chief of the Libu (2) ... (3) .... field .... (4) ...[...]

NOTE

1. Libyan personal or place name.

14. DONATION STELA STRASSBURG 1588

Donation stelae comprise the most characteristic genre of Third Intermediate Period texts, and dated examples are grouped by reign throughout this volume. This small round-topped limestone stela (0.195 x 0.255 m), summarily carved with three lines of hieratic text, provides a simple example of the type, with obvious Libyan features. The lunette scene depicts Thoth adored by a Libyan chief and a smaller male figure. From the Delta, perhaps the cult site of Thoth at Damanhur (Hermopolis Parva), the stela is dated to year 6 of an unnamed ruler. The monument is notable for its simple style and the prominence of the Meshwesh functionary Natimru, who combines Egyptian religious authority with Libyan civil service. Where understood, Meshwesh titles are invariably military (cf. the untranslated "matwaher" below, no. 43), but this text preserves a unique example of a bureaucratic scribe affiliated with the tribe. As the Libyan dialects were not written and only sporadic terms appear in Egyptian transcription,[1] Natimru's dictations (or translations) will have been in Egyptian.

Publication with transcription and photo in Spiegelberg 1920, 57 and pl. IV (right). See also Meeks 1979a, 665, no. 22.0.6.

LABEL FOR LIBYAN DYNAST

Pk-w3-ỉw-š3(?)[2]

Pkoish (?)[2]

MAIN TEXT

(1) ḥsb.t 6.(t) ḥmk3 3ḥ.wt st3.t 5 n Ḏḥwty (m-dỉ) ḥm-nṯr n

ʾImn-(2)Rˁ ny-sw.t nṯr.w sš šˁ.t n3 Mˁ.w N3-tỉ-m-rw[2]

(1) Regnal year 6. Donation[3] of 5 arouras of field to Thoth by the prophet of Amon-(2)Re, King of the Gods, and letter scribe of the Ma, Natimru.[2]

NOTES

1. A supposed papyrus of "Qeheq war chants" in Turin has never been authenticated; see Botti 1900, 161–69; Müller 1910, 127; and Bates 1970 [orig. 1914], 76 n. 2: "E. Schiaparelli is there said to have found a papyrus containing 'Qeheq war-songs in the Libyan language, transcribed in hieratic.' Since 1900 no more has been heard of this remarkable discovery nor has Dr. Schiaparelli condescended to answer my enquiries concerning it."

2. A non-Egyptian name, presumably Meshwesh. Spiegelberg combined the name of line 2 with the label written between the donor and Thoth to create the outlandish N3-tỉ-m-rw-pk-w3-ỉw-š3(?), but see Yoyotte 1961, 140 n. 2.

3. For the variant spelling of ḥnq as ḥm-k3, see Gardiner 1948, 111–13; Meeks 1979a, 626.

II

DYNASTY XXI

A. SMENDES

15. GENERAL AND HIGH PRIEST HERIHOR AT KARNAK
(CAIRO JDE 42190)

Prior to his appropriation of royal titulary and regalia, but after his conquest of Thebes for the distant Rameses XI, the great general Herihor had
a statue of himself erected in the dromos of the Karnak temple. Depicted
in the traditional guise of a learned scribe, as adapted for Ramesside taste,
Herihor wears a huge pectoral over a rippled belly revealed by a sheer
garment with pleated sleeves. He sits cross-legged with a papyrus unrolled
upon his lap. The now-headless statue carved from gray granite measures
90 cm and was recovered in 1904 from the Karnak "cachette" that held
disused statuary buried in Ptolemaic times. Herihor's inscriptions reflect
this volatile era not only by his exceptional titles but by the curse directed
against any who might remove his memorial. It is striking that Herihor's
"lord" is exclusively Amon, with no reference to Rameses XI.

For the text and translation, see Lefebvre 1926, 63–68; and Georges
Legrain 1909b, 59 and pl. LII; noted in Meeks 1979a, 682. See Kitchen 1986,
248 §209 n. 31.

On the Unrolled Papyrus

di.w m ḥs n nb nṯr.w pꜣ.wty tꜣ.wy (2) dî≠f ꜥḥꜥ qꜣî m-ẖnw ḥw.t-nṯr≠f
mî ꜣẖ≠(3)î n kꜣ≠f îw tw(t)≠(î) mn r (4) ẖft-ẖr≠f[1] wšd.n≠f s(w) m ẖꜥꜥ≠f
(5) [n] kꜣ n îry-pꜥ.t ḥꜣ.ty-ꜥ ḥm-nṯr tp(y) (6) [n] ꜣImn-Rꜥ ny-sw.t nṯr.w îmy-rꜣ
nî.wt tꜣty (7) [sꜣ ny-sw.t] n Kš îmy-rꜣ mšꜥ (8) [w]r n.{w} Šmꜥw Mḥw sḥtp
tꜣ.wy (9) n nb≠f ꜣImn Ḥr(y)-Ḥr mꜣꜥ-[ẖrw]

Placed as a favor of the Lord of the Gods, the primeval one of the
Two Lands, (2) so that he might grant a long lifetime within his temple

81

inasmuch as I was effective (3) for his *ka*-spirit, with my statue enduring in (4) his presence,[1] having saluted him in his processional appearance, (5) [for] the *ka*-spirit of the Hereditary Prince and Count, the First Prophet (6) [of] Amon-Re, King of the Gods, the overseer of the city and vizier, (7) [the king's son] of Cush, the [great] general (8) of Upper and Lower Egypt, who pacifies the Two Lands (9) for his lord Amon, Herihor, the justified.

ABOUT THE BASE

îry-pꜥ.t ḥr(y)-tp t3.wy smr ꜥ3 m t3 ḏr≠f t3ty wp-M3ꜥ.t sḏm md.w rḫy. t Šmꜥw îmy-r3 ḫ3s.wt rsy.w îr 3ḫ.w m pr ᵓImn ḫrp n≠f t3 nb dmḏ ḥm-nṯr tp(y) n ᵓImn-Rꜥ ny-sw.t nṯrw Ḥr(y)-Ḥr m3ꜥ-ḫrw ḏd≠f îr rmṯ nb nty-îw≠f rwî p3y twt ḥr s.t≠f m-ḫt rnp.wt qnw.w îw≠f m b3.w n ᵓImn Mw.t Ḥnsw bn ḫpr rn≠f m p3 t3 n Km.t mt≠f n ḥq(r) n îb(y)

The Hereditary Prince and superior of the Two Lands, the great courtier in the entire land, the vizier who determines Maat, who hears the words of the plebeians of Upper Egypt, the overseer of southern foreign lands, who makes benefactions in the estate of Amon, who administers for him the whole entire land, the First Prophet of Amon-Re, King of the Gods, Herihor, the justified, who says: "As for any man who will remove this statue from its place after many years, he is subject to the wrath of Amon, Mut, and Khonsu. His name shall not exist in the land of Egypt. May he die of hunger and of thirst."

NOTE

1. Or, "in his dromos."

16. THE KINGSHIP OF HERIHOR IN THE GREAT HYPOSTYLE HALL AT KARNAK

The royal titulary of Herihor is confined to the precincts of Karnak, appearing in both the great Hypostyle Hall and in the forecourt of the associated Khonsu temple. Fragmentary restoration inscriptions added to the southern end of the east wall of the Hypostyle Hall and on ten worn column bases record Herihor's prenomen (First Prophet of Amon) and nomen (Herihor, son of Amon). The random placement of the surviving column-base inscriptions (columns 22, 32, 40, 42, 49, 57, 60, 62, and 63) suggests that similar texts once adorned all columns in the hall. Despite the restricted attestations of Herihor's kingship, his elevation of the priestly title within a royal cartouche is extraordinary and anticipates the pharaonic claims of subsequent pontiffs of Dynasty XXI.

For the texts and translation, see Roth 1983, 43–53; Kitchen 1975–90, 1:730; and Barguet 1962, 60. See Kitchen 1986, 20 §17 and 569 §496.

EAST WALL MARGIN INSCRIPTION

[…] nb [t3.wy] nb [ỉr.(t) ḫ.t] ḥm-nṯr tp(y) n ꜣImn s3 Rꜥ nb ḫꜥ.w Ḥry-Ḥr s3 ꜣImn m pr ỉt₌f ꜣImn-Rꜥ ny-sw.t nṯr.[w] dỉ ₌[f] ꜥnḫ ḏd w3s snb n ny-sw.t bỉ.ty ḥm-nṯr [t]p(y) [n ꜣImn s3 Rꜥ nb ḫꜥ.w Ḥry-Ḥr s3 ꜣImn]

[…] Lord of [the Two Lands], Lord of [ritual performance], the First Prophet of Amon, the Son of Re, Lord of Diadems, Herihor, son of Amon, in the house of his father, Amon-Re, King of the Gods, so that [he] might grant life, stability, dominion, and health to the King of Upper and Lower Egypt, the First Prophet [of Amon, the Son of Re, Lord of Diadems, Herihor, son of Amon.]

COMPOSITE TEXT OF COLUMN BASES

ḥm-nṯr tp(y) n ꜣImn s3 Rꜥ nb ḫꜥ.w [Ḥry-Ḥr] s3 ꜣImn sm3w mnw ỉr.n{n} ny-sw.t bỉ.ty nb t3.wy nb ỉr.(t) ḫ.t ḥm-nṯr tp(y) n ꜣImn s3 Rꜥ nb ḫꜥ.w [Ḥry-Ḥr] s3 ꜣImn m pr ỉt₌[f] ꜣImn-Rꜥ ḥq3 nṯr.w [dỉ₌f ꜥnḫ ḏd w3s]

The First Prophet of Amon, the Son of Re, Lord of Diadems, [Herihor], son of Amon: A renewal of monuments that the King of Upper and Lower Egypt, Lord of the Two Lands, Lord of ritual performance, the First Prophet of Amon, the Son of Re, Lord of Diadems, [Herihor], son of Amon, made in the house of [his] father, Amon-Re, ruler of the gods, [so that he might grant life, stability, and dominion.]

17. THE LIBYAN ANCESTRY OF HERIHOR

Among the scenes in the forecourt of the Khonsu temple at Karnak that depict the general Herihor as "priest-king," two provide indirect but compelling evidence of his Libyan background. A relief on the south wall shows the general offering to Horus of "The Camp," a designation of the fortress of el-Hibeh employed in contemporary correspondence. Beneath a protective vulture, Herihor offers wine and a bouquet to the enthroned Horus, followed by a "mother goddess" equated with Isis by her crown and a graffito. The unique scene probably records Herihor's devotion to the deities of his home military base, one of the many colonies of Libyan mercenaries established by the Ramesside rulers.

Along the west wall of the forecourt, Herihor commissioned an elaborate processional scene of his family members, following the royal precedent established by Rameses II and III at Luxor, the Ramesseum, and Medinet Habu. In two lengthy registers, Herihor's wife and nineteen named sons appear above nineteen daughters, only four of whom are named. Although most of his sons bear Egyptian names, the names of six are unmistakably Libyan: Masaharta (7), Masaqaharta (8), […]mena (15), Nawasun (16), Osorkon (17), and Madenen (19). The name Masaharta will reappear three generations later among the Theban high priests, while Osorkon recurs throughout Dynasties XXI–XXIII as a favored royal appellation. In contrast to these later Libyan dynasts, Herihor and his contemporaries *seem* quite "Egyptianized," although their formal records may mask other distinctive ethnic features. Perhaps it is significant that it is Herihor's junior sons, born after his initial career advancement, who are given Libyan names. The inscription for the eighteenth prince has been recut for a son of the later high priest and king Pinedjem I.

For the texts and translations, see Epigraphic Survey 1979, xiii–iv, 4, 11–13, and pls. 14 and 26; Porter and Moss 1927–51, 2:230 §§16.III.2 and 18.III. See Kitchen 1986, 252–53 §211, 540–41 §444; 1995, xvii §L.

I. KING HERIHOR OFFERS TO HORUS OF THE CAMP

Label for Horus
Ḥr [ḥry-ỉb] pȝ ỉh (2) nṯr ꜥȝ [nb] Mȝꜥ.t (3) dỉ.n≠(ỉ) n≠k [ꜥnḫ] wȝs
Horus [who is resident in] "The Camp," (2) the great god, [lord] of Maat: (3) "Thus I have given to you [life] and dominion."

Label for the Mother Goddess, Isis
Ḥnw.t ms.ṯ (2) dỉ≠s snb nb (3) ȝw.t-ỉb nb mỉ Rꜥ (4) [dỉ]≠s snb nb
The Mistress of Birth. (2) May she give all health (3) and all joy like Re. (4) [May] she [give] all health.

Graffito
ȝs.t   Isis.

Label for Protective Vulture
Wȝḏy.t   Edjo.

Label for Herihor
Nb tȝ.wy [ḥ]m-[nṯ]r tp(y) n ʾImn (2) [nb ḫꜥ].w Ḥr(y)-Ḥr sȝ ʾImn (3) dỉ ꜥnḫ ḏd wȝs mỉ Rꜥ ḏ.t nḥḥ (4) sȝ [ꜥnḫ] ḏd wȝs (5) ḥnq m ỉrp
The Lord of the Two Lands, the First Prophet of Amon, (2) [the Lord of Diadem]s, Herihor, son of Amon, (3) given life, stability, and dominion like Re forever and ever. (4) The protection of [life,] stability, and dominion (is behind him). (5) Offering wine.

II. THE FAMILY PROCESSION

Label for Queen Nodjmet
[ỉry.t-pꜥ].t wr.t ḥs.w(t) ḥnw.t tȝ.wy nb.t ỉȝm.(t) bnr mr(w).t wr.[t] ḫnr. t n.(t) ʾImn-Rꜥ (2) ny-sw.t nṯr.[w] ḥm.t ny-sw.t wr.t mr.(t)≠f Ndm.t mȝꜥ. t-ḫrw

The [Hereditary Princess,] whose favor is great, the Mistress of the Two Lands, possessor of charm, sweetly beloved, chief of the musical troupe of Amon-Re, (2) King of the Gods, the great royal wife whom he loves, Nodjmet, the justified.

The First Prince

(3) s3 ny-sw.t n ḥ.(t)≠f [mr≠f] ỉmy-r3 pr wr n ʾImn ḥm-nṯr n Mw.t ḥm-nṯr [...] n ʾImn ỉmy-r3 ssy(m.wt) (4) n nb t3.wy ḥ3w.ty ʿnḫ[≠f-n-Mw.t m3ʿ-ḫrw]

(3) The king's bodily son, [whom he loves,] the chief steward of Amon, prophet of Mut, the [...] Prophet of Amon, overseer of horses (4) of the Lord of the Two Lands, and leader, Ankh[efenmut, the justified.]

The Second Prince

(5) s3 ny-sw.t n ḥ.(t)≠f ḥm-[nṯr] 3-nw [n] ʾI[m]n ḥm-nṯr n ʾIn-ḥr ḥm-nṯr n Ḥr Bḥd.t[y] ỉmy-r3 (ỉ)ḥ.[w n] (6) P3-Rʿ ʿnḫ≠f-n-ʾImn m3ʿ-ḫrw

(5) The king's bodily son, the Third Prophet [of] Amon, prophet of Onuris, prophet of Horus the Behdedite, and overseer of cattle [of] (6) Pre, Ankhefenamon, the justified.

The Third Prince

(7) s3 ny-sw.t n ḥ.(t)≠f ỉmy-r3 [...] (8) [n] ʾImn-Rʿ ny-sw.t nṯr.w [...] smr [...].t (9) P3-nfr (10) m3ʿ-ḫrw

(7) The king's bodily son, the overseer of [...] (8) [of] Amon-Re, King of the Gods, [...] courtier [...], (9) Panefer, (10) the justified.

The Fourth Prince

(11) s3 ny-sw.t n ḥ.t≠f mr≠f ʾIt≠(ỉ)-ʾImn m3ʿ-ḫrw

(11) The king's bodily son, Iotiamon, the justified.

The Fifth Prince

(12) s3 ny-sw.t n ḥ.t≠f (13) ʾImn-ḥr-wnmy≠f m3ʿ-ḫrw

(12) The king's bodily son, (13) Amonherwenemef, the justified.

The Sixth Prince

(14) s3 ny-sw.t n ḥ.t≠f (15) Tḫwy m3ʿ-ḫrw

(14) The king's bodily son, (15) Tekhwi, the justified.

The Seventh Prince

(16) s3 ny-sw.t n ḥ.t≠f (17) M3s3h3rtỉ m3ʿ-ḫrw

(16) The king's bodily son, (17) Masaharta, the justified.

The Eighth Prince
   (18) s3 ny-sw.t n ḥ.t≠f (19) M3s3q3h3rtỉ (m3ꜥ-ḫrw)
   (18) The king's bodily son, (19) Masaqaharta, (the justified).

The Ninth Prince
   (20) s3 ny-sw.t n ḥ.t≠f (21) P3-šd-Ḫnsw m3ꜥ-ḫrw
   (20) The king's bodily son, (21) Pashedkhonsu, the justified.

The Tenth Prince
   (22) [s3] ny-[sw.t n ḥ].t≠f (23) [...]-nfr m3ꜥ-ḫrw
   (22) The king's [bodily son], (23) [...]nefer, the justified.

The Eleventh Prince
   (24) s3 ny-sw.t n ḥ.t≠f (25) ᾽Imn-ḥr-ḫpš≠f m3ꜥ-[ḫrw]
   (24) The king's bodily son, (25) Amonherkhepeshef, the justified.

The Twelfth Prince
   (26) s3 ny-sw.t [n] ḥ.t≠f (27) Ḥr-Ḫby.t m3[ꜥ-ḫrw]
   (26) The king's bodily son, (27) Horkhebi, the justified.

The Thirteenth Prince
   (28) s3 ny-sw.t [n] ḥ.t≠f (29) [...]ỉtḫ [m3ꜥ]-ḫrw
   (28) The king's bodily son, (29) [....]itekh, the justified.

The Fourteenth Prince
   (30) s3 ny-sw.t [n] ḥ.t≠f (31) [Bỉ]k-ntry m3ꜥ-ḫrw
   (30) The king's bodily son, (31) Biknetery, the justified.

The Fifteenth Prince
   (32) s3 ny-sw.t n ḥ.t≠f (33) [...]mn3 m3ꜥ-ḫrw
   (32) The king's bodily son, (33) [...]mena, the justified.

The Sixteenth Prince
   (34) s3 ny-sw.t [n] ḥ.t≠f (35) N3w3swn3y [m3ꜥ-ḫrw]
   (34) The king's bodily son, (35) Nawasun, [the justified.]

The Seventeenth Prince
   (36) s3 ny-sw.t n ḥ.t≠f (37) W3s3ỉrk3n3 [m3ꜥ-ḫrw]
   (36) The king's bodily son, (37) Osorkon, [the justified.]

The Eighteenth Prince
   (38) s3 [ny-sw.t] n ḥ.t≠f (39) ỉt-nṯr n ᾽Imn Nsy-p3-nfr-ḥr m3ꜥ-ḫrw s3
P3y-nḏm m3ꜥ-ḫrw

(38) The [king's] bodily son, (39) the God's Father of Amon, Nespaneferher, the justified, son of Pinedjem, the justified.

The Ninteenth Prince

(40) [s3 ny-sw.t n ẖ.t≠f] (41) M3dnn3 m3ꜥ-ḫrw
(40) [The king's bodily son,] (41) Madenen, the justified.

The First Princess

(42) s3.t ny-sw.t [n.t ẖ.t]≠f šmꜥy.[t n.t ꜣImn wr.t ḫnr.t [n.(t) Ḫnsw šps.
t Šm-sbq].t
(42) The king's [bodily] daughter, chantress [of] Amon, chief of the
musical troupe [of Khonsu, and noble lady, Shemsebek].

The Second Princess

(43) [s3.t] ny-[sw.t n.t ẖ.t]≠f Nsy.t m3ꜥ.t-ḫrw
(43) The king's [bodily daughter], Nesit, the justified.

The Third Princess

(44) [s3.t ny-sw.t n.t ẖ.t≠f …]n-wr.w m3ꜥ.t-ḫrw
(44) [The king's bodily daughter, …]enweru, the justified.

The Fourth Princess

(45) [s3.t ny-sw.t n.t] ẖ.t≠f Ḥ[nw].t-n.(t)-t3-nb m3ꜥ.t-ḫrw
(45) [The king's] bodily [daughter], Henutentaneb, the justified.

18. THE VOYAGE OF WENAMON
(P. MOSCOW 120)

Composed in the nonliterary Late Egyptian vernacular typical of
administrative accounts, the report of Wenamon nonetheless features an
engaging plot, scenic descriptions, complex speeches, and passages of
irony. As a result, scholars have differed over whether it is a genuine docu-
ment with extraordinary style or a literary fiction of extraordinary realism.
The format of the papyrus itself conforms to that of official documents.
Whatever its category, the report well illustrates the beginning of Dynasty
XXI, with a divided Egypt ruled in the south by the high priest Herihor at
Thebes and in the north by Smendes and his queen Tanetamon at Tanis.
Probably still acknowledged tacitly in the initial dating formula is the last
Ramesside king of Dynasty XX: the largely irrelevant Rameses XI residing
at Per-Rameses and dismissed in columns 2/51–53 as a mere mortal. The
regnal date designates the "renaissance era" of the joint rule of Rameses
and Herihor, or perhaps the new condominium of Herihor and Smendes.
Egyptian authority in the Levant is in clear decline, as indicated both by

Wenamon's abject dependence upon foreign whim (rather than Egyptian garrisons) and by the Byblite ruler's haughty attitude toward Wenamon and the earlier emissaries of Rameses XI. The narrative ends abruptly at the end of column 2, and the amount of missing text is unknown. A fragmentary account is recorded on the verso of the papyrus, at a right angle to the text of the recto. The papyrus derives from el-Hibeh, the northern administrative center of the Theban high priest.

For the text, translations, and discussions, see Gardiner 1932, 61–76; Lichtheim 1973–80, 224–30; E. F. Wente in Simpson 1973, 142–55; Helck 1986, cols. 1215–17; Winand 1987; and Schipper 2005. The transliteration adopted here treats Gardiner's transcribed "dots" as the signs for which they are intended. See Kitchen 1986, 5 §2, 8 §5, 17 §14, 49 §42, 248–52 §§209–10, 417 §379, 428 §395, 570 §497; 1995, xvi §J.

(1/1) ḥsb.t 5.(t) 3bd 4 šmw sw 16 hrw n wd̠y i̯-i̯r sms{m}(w) h3y.(t) Wn-ʾImn n Pr ʾImn (1/2) [nb ns.wt] t3.wy r in t[3] t̠.t n p3 wi3 ꜥ3 špsy n ʾImn-Rꜥ ny-sw.t ntr.w nty ḥr-tp (1/3) [i̯(t)r.w nty rn≠f (m) ʾI]mn-wsr-ḫ3.t hrw n spr i̯-i̯r≠i̯ r D̠ꜥn.t r p3 (1/4) [nty Nsy-sw-B3-nb]-D̠d.(t) Ti̯-n.t-ʾImn im iw≠i̯ di̯.t n≠w n3 w3ḫ.w (< wḫ3.w) n.(w) ʾImn-Rꜥ ny-sw.t ntr.w iw≠w (1/5) di̯.t ꜥš.tw≠w m-b3ḫ≠w iw≠w d̠d iry sp-2 m p3 (i̯)-d̠d ʾImn-Rꜥ ny-sw.t ntr.w p3(1/6)[y]≠n [nb]

iw≠i̯ ir š3ꜥ-(m) 3bd 4 šmw iw≠i̯ m-ḫnw D̠ꜥn.t iw Nsy-sw-B3-nb-D̠d.(t) (1/7) Ti̯-n.t-ʾImn wd̠y≠i̯ irm ḥry mnšw Mngbt iw≠i̯ h3y r (1/8) p3 ym ꜥ3 n Ḫ3r n tpy šmw sw 1¹ iw≠i̯ spr r Dyr wꜥ dmi̯ n (1/9) T̠kr iw Bdr p3y≠f wr di̯.t in.tw n≠i̯ ꜥq.w 50 irp msḫ (1/10) 1 m3s.t n.(t) iḥ 1 iw wꜥ rmt n t3y≠i̯ byr wꜥr iw t3y≠f nbw (1/11) [tbw] 1 [ir] n dbn 5 ḥd̠ tbw 4 ir n dbn 20 ḥd̠ ꜥrfy dbn 11 (1/12) [dmd n p3 it3y]≠f nbw dbn 5 ḥd̠ dbn 31

iw≠i̯ dwn m t3y dw3w iw≠i̯ šmi̯ r (1/13) p3 nty p3 wr n-im iw≠i̯ d̠d n≠f tw≠i̯ t3y.tw n t3y≠k mr.(t) ḥr mntk p3 wr n p3y t3 ḥr (1/14) mntk p3y≠f smt(r)y w3ḫ (< wḫ3) p3y≠i̯ ḥd̠ y3 ir p3 ḥd̠ nsy-sw ʾImn-Rꜥ (1/15) ny-sw.t ntr.w p3 nb n n3 t3.w nsy-sw Nsy-sw-B3-nb-D̠d.(t) nsy-sw Ḥry-Ḥr p3y≠i̯ nb n3 k.t-ḫ.w (1/16) ꜥ3y.w n Km.t mntk sw nsy-s.t Wrt nsy-s.t Mkmr nsy-s.t T̠kr(1/17)-Bꜥr p3 wr n Kpn

iw≠f d̠d n≠i̯ (i̯)n dns≠k (i̯)n mnḫ≠k² ḥr ptri̯ bw-i̯r≠i̯ (1/18) ꜥ3m n t3y wšb.t i̯-d̠d≠k n≠i̯ h3n3 it3y iw nsy-sw p3y≠i̯ t3 p3 h3y (1/19) r t3y≠k byr mtw≠f t3y p3y≠k ḥd̠ wnw-iw≠i̯ d̠b3≠f n≠k m p3y≠i̯ wd3 š3ꜥ.tw≠w (1/20) gm p3y≠k it3y n rn≠f y3 ir p3 it3y it3y tw mntk sw nsy-sw (1/21) t3y≠k byr i̯-i̯r(y) nh3y h3rw.w d(y) q3i̯ n≠i̯ w3ḫ≠i̯ sw

iw≠i̯ ir hrw 9 iw≠i̯ mni̯(1/22).tw (m) t3y≠f mr.(t) iw≠i̯ šmi̯ q3i̯ n≠f iw≠i̯ d̠d n≠f mk bw-pw≠k gm p3y≠i̯ ḥd̠ (1/23) [i̯]ḫ [wd̠y]≠k (w)i̯ irm n3 ḥry.w mnšw irm n3 šm (r) ym iw≠f d̠d n≠i̯ gr tw (1/24) [iw≠k w3ḫ g]m p3[y≠k ḥd̠ …] sd̠m t3y[≠i̯] md.t mtw≠k ir i̯-d̠d]≠i̯ n≠k iw m-i̯r (1/25) […] sd̠m […] p3 nty-iw≠k i̯[m] iw≠k mḥ [m] n3y≠w k3ry.w mtw≠k mḥ mi̯ […]

(1/26) [… šꜣꜥ].tw≠w šmꞽ (r) wꜣḫ pꜣy≠w ꞽtꜣy ꞽ[tꜣy s.t …] (1/27) [… sḏ]r (ḥr) tꜣ mr.(t)ꜣ [m]k ꞽ[w≠k(?) … ꞽw≠ꞽ spr r] (1/28) [D]r

ꞽw≠ꞽ pr m Ḏr m šsp ḥḏ […] (1/29) […]≠k Ṯkr-Bꜥ(r) pꜣ wr n Kpn[…] (1/30) [… b]yr ꞽw≠ꞽ gm ḥḏ dbn 30 ꞽm≠s ꞽw≠ꞽ mḥ ꞽm≠w [ꞽw≠ꞽ ḏd n nꜣ nb.w n tꜣ byr mḥ≠ꞽ m] (1/31) pꜣy≠tn ḥḏ ꞽw≠f wꜣḫ m-dꞽ≠ꞽ [šꜣ]ꜥ ꞽ-ꞽr≠tn gm pꜣ[y≠ꞽ ḥḏ m rꜣ-pw pꜣ ꞽtꜣy] (1/32) ꞽtꜣy sw bw-pw≠ꞽ ꞽtꜣy≠tn ꞽw≠ꞽ r ꞽtꜣy.t≠f wpw mnt(t)n ꞽw[≠tn …]w≠ꞽ r […]

(1/33) ꞽw≠w šm n≠w ꞽw≠ꞽ ḥb n≠ꞽ [m] ꞽm(ꜣ)w (r) sp{r}.(t) (n.t) pꜣ y[m] (ḥr) tꜣ mr.(t) (n.t) Kp[n] ꞽw[≠ꞽ …] (1/34) […] ʾImn-(n)-tꜣ-mꞽ.t ꞽw≠ꞽ dꞽ.t ꜣḫ.t≠f m-ẖnw≠f ꞽw pꜣ [wr] n Kpn ḥꜣb n≠ꞽ r ḏd [ꞽ]-r[wꞽꜣ tw]k [m] (1/35) [tꜣ]y[≠ꞽ] mr.(t) ꞽw≠ꞽ ḥꜣb n≠f r ḏd ꞽ-ꞽr[≠ꞽ šmꞽ n≠ꞽ r] tn(w) […]n≠ꞽ šm[ꞽ] (1/36) […] ꞽr [wn m-dꞽ≠k byr(?)] r ẖn.t≠(ꞽ) ꞽmy tꜣ[y.](1/37)tw≠(ꞽ) r Km.t [ꜥ]n [ꞽ]w≠ꞽ ꞽr hrw 29 n tꜣy≠f mr[.(t) ꞽw ꞽ-ꞽr]≠f nw ḥꜣb n≠ꞽ m mn.t r ḏd ꞽ-rw(1/38)ꞽꜣ twk (m) tꜣy≠ꞽ mr.(t)

ḥr ꞽr sw wdn (n) nꜣy≠f nṯr.w [ꞽ]w pꜣ nṯr tꜣy wꜥ ꜥddꞽ ꜥꜣ (n) nꜣy≠f (1/39) ꜥddꞽ.w ꜥꜣy.wꜣ ꞽw≠f dꞽ.t≠f ḫ̱ꜣw.t ꞽw≠f⁵ ḏd n≠f ꞽny [pꜣ] nṯr r ḥry ꞽny pꜣ ꞽpw.ty nty ḥr-r≠f (1/40) (ꞽ)n ʾImn ꞽ-wḏy sw mntf ꞽ-dꞽ ꞽw≠f ꞽw ꞽ-ꞽr pꜣ ḫꜣw.t ḫꜣw.t m pꜣy grḥ ꞽw g(1/41)my≠ꞽ wꜥ byr ꞽw ḥr≠s r Km.t ꞽw ꜣtp≠ꞽ pꜣy≠ꞽ ꞽnk nb r≠s ꞽw ꞽ-ꞽr≠ꞽ nw (1/42) r pꜣ kky r ḏd ḥꜣy≠f ꜣtp≠ꞽ pꜣ nṯr r tm dꞽ.t ptrꞽ sw k.t ꞽr.t

ꞽw pꜣ (1/43) ꞽmy-rꜣ mr.(t) ꞽy n≠ꞽ r ḏd smn tw šꜣꜥ dwꜣw ḥr≠f n pꜣ wr ꞽw≠ꞽ ḏd n≠f nn (= ꞽn)⁶ mntk pꜣ nty ꞽ-(1/44)ꞽr≠f nw ꞽy n≠ꞽ m mn.t r ḏd ꞽ-rwꞽꜣ twk (m) tꜣy≠ꞽ mr.(t) nn (= ꞽn) ꞽ-ꞽr≠k ḏd smn tw m pꜣ grḥ (1/45) r dꞽ.t wḏ tꜣ byr ꞽ-gm≠ꞽ mtw≠k ꞽy ḏd ḥn≠k n≠k ꜥn ꞽw≠f šmꞽ ꞽw≠f ḏd.t≠f n (1/46) pꜣ wr ꞽw pꜣ wr ḥꜣb n pꜣ ḥry mnšw n tꜣ byr r ḏd smn tw šꜣꜥ dwꜣw ḥr≠f n (1/47) pꜣ wr

ꞽw dwꜣw ḫpr ꞽw≠f ḥꜣb ꞽw≠f ꞽtꜣy≠ꞽ r ḥry ꞽw pꜣ nṯr ḥtp.w m pꜣ ꞽm(ꜣ)w (1/48) nty sw ꞽm≠f (ḥr) sp.t (n.t) pꜣ ym ꞽw≠ꞽ gm.t≠f ḥms (m) tꜣy≠f ꜥrt.(t) ꞽw ḫꜥ ꜣt.(1/49)t≠f r wꜥ sšd ꞽw ꞽ-ꞽr n(ꜣ) hꜣn.w n pꜣ ym ꜥꜣ n Ḥꜣr ẖ(wꞽ) r mkẖꜣ(1/50){ḥꜣ}≠f ꞽw≠ꞽ ḏd n≠f sfty ʾImn ꞽw≠f ḏd n≠ꞽ wr r pꜣ hrw m-ḏr ꞽw≠k n pꜣ nty (1/51) ʾImn ꞽm ꞽw≠ꞽ ḏd n≠f 5 ꜣbd (n) ḥꜣ(r)w r pꜣy ꞽw≠f ḏd n≠ꞽ mk mntk mꜣꜥ.tw sw tn(w) pꜣ (1/52) wꜣḫ n ʾImn nty m ḏr.t≠k sw tnw tꜣ šꜥ.(t) n.(t) pꜣ ḥm-nṯr tp(y) n ʾImn nty m ḏr.t≠k ꞽw≠ꞽ ḏd (1/53) n≠f dꞽ≠ꞽ s.t n Nsy-sw-Bꜣ-nb-Ḏd.(t) Tꞽ-n.t-ʾImn ꞽw≠f ḥdn r ꞽqr sp-2 ꞽw≠f ḏd n≠ꞽ ḥr mk wḥꜣ.w (1/54) šꜥ.w(t) mn n ḏr.t≠k sw tnw pꜣ ꞽmw⁷ n ꜥš ꞽ-dꞽ n≠k Nsy-sw-Bꜣ-nb-Ḏd.(t) sw tnw (1/55) tꜣy≠f ꞽs.t Ḥꜣr.w nn ꞽ-ꞽr≠f ḥn≠k n pꜣy ḥry mnšw drꞽdrꞽ r rdꞽ.t ḥdb≠f (1/56) tw mtw≠w ḫꜣꜥ≠k r pꜣ ym wnw-ꞽ-ꞽr≠w wꜣḫ pꜣ nṯr m-ḏr nym mntk m-rꜣ-ꜥ ꞽ-ꞽr≠w (1/57) wꜣḫ≠k m-ḏr nym ꞽn≠f n≠ꞽ

ꞽw≠ꞽ ḏd n≠f nn (= ꞽn) bn ꞽmw n Km.t ẖr ꞽs.t n.(t) Km.t nꜣ nty ḥn(ꞽ) (1/58) ḥr Nsy-sw-Bꜣ-nb-Ḏd.(t) nn wn (m)-dꞽ≠f ꞽs.wt Ḥꜣr ꞽw≠f ḏd n≠ꞽ nn (= ꞽn) mn 20 n mnšw (1/59) d(y) n tꜣy≠ꞽ mr.(t) ꞽw≠w n ḫbr ꞽrm Nsy-sw-Bꜣ-nb-Ḏd.(t) ꞽr pꜣy Dddnꜣ (2/1) pꜣ ky ꞽ-sš≠k r≠f nn (= ꞽn) mn k.t 50 n byr n-ꞽm ꞽw≠w n ḫbr (2/2) ꞽrm Wrktr ꞽw ꞽ-ꞽr≠w ꞽtḥ r pꜣy≠f pr

ỉw≠ỉ gr n t3y wnw.t (2/3) ꜥ3.t ỉw≠f wšb dd n≠ỉ ỉ-ỉr≠k ỉy ḥr ỉḫ n sḥn
ỉw≠ỉ dd n≠f ỉ-ỉr≠ỉ ỉy (2/4) m-s3 t3 t̠.t n p3 wỉ3 ꜥ3 špsy n ᵓImn-Rꜥ ny-sw.t
nt̠r.w ỉ-ỉr p3y≠k ỉt ỉ(2/5)-ỉr p3 ỉt n p3y≠k ỉt ỉw≠k ỉr≠f m-r3-ꜥ8 ỉn≠ỉ n≠f
ỉw≠f dd n≠ỉ mntw ỉ-ỉr sw m m3ꜥ.t (2/6) ỉw≠k dỉ.t n≠ỉ n ỉr≠s{w} mtw≠ỉ
ỉr≠s{w} y3 ỉ-ỉr n3y≠ỉ ỉr p3y sḥn ỉw dỉ (2/7) Pr-ꜥ3 ꜥnḫ wd̠3 snb ỉn.tw 6 byr.
w ỉw≠w 3tp n 3ḫ.t n Km.t ỉw≠w šw r n3y≠w (2/8) wd̠3.w mntk ỉḫ p3 (ỉ)-
ỉn≠k n≠ỉ gr ỉnk

ỉw≠f dỉ.t ỉn.tw ꜥr.(t) h3(r)w (n.t) n3y≠f ỉty.w (2/9) ỉw≠f dỉ.t ꜥš.tw≠s
m-b3ḥ≠ỉ ỉw≠w gm 1000 n dbn n ḫd nty nb r t3y≠f ꜥr.(t) (2/10) ỉw≠f dd n≠ỉ
ỉr p3 ḥq3 n Km.t p3 nb p3y≠ỉ ḥr ỉnk p3y≠f b3kỉ m-r3-ꜥ (2/11) nn (= ỉn) wn
ỉ-ỉr≠f dỉ.t ỉn.tw ḫd nbw r dd ỉ-ỉr p3 sḥn n ᵓImn nn (= ỉn) f3y (2/12) mrk.
w p3 wn≠w ỉr≠f n p3y≠ỉ ỉt ỉr ỉnk gr ỉnk nn ỉnk p3y≠k (2/13) b3kỉ nn ỉnk
b3kỉ n p3 (ỉ)-ỉr wd̠≠k m r3-ꜥ ỉw≠ỉ ꜥš sgp r p3 (2/14) Rbrn ỉ-ỉr t3 p.t wn ỉw
n3 ḫt.w d(y) ḫ3ꜥ (ḥr) sp.t (n.t) p3 ym ỉmy.(2/15)tw n≠ỉ n3 ḫt3.w ỉ-ỉn≠k r
t3y n3y≠k byr.w nty ḥr n3y≠k ḫt.w r (Km.t) (2/16) ỉmy.tw n≠ỉ n3 nwḥ.[w
ỉ]-ỉn≠k [r mr n3 ꜥš].w nty ỉw≠ỉ šꜥd≠w r ỉr≠w n≠k (2/17) [...] nty ỉw≠ỉ (r)
ỉr≠w n≠k (n) n3 ḫt3.w (n.w) n3y≠k (2/18) byr.w mtw n3 tpy.w dns mtw≠w
s3w mtw≠k mt n≠k ḥr-ỉb p3 ym (2/19) mk ỉ-ỉr ᵓImn ḫrw m t3 p.t ỉw dỉ≠f
Swtḫ m rk≠f ḥr ỉ-ỉr ᵓImn (2/20) grg n n3 t3.w dr.w ỉ-ỉr≠f grg≠w ỉw grg≠f
p3 t3 n Km.t p3 ỉw≠k n-ỉm ḥr-(2/21)h3.t ḥr ỉ-ỉr mnḫ pr ỉm≠f r pḥ r p3 nty
tw≠ỉ ỉm ḥr ỉ-ỉr sb3 pr (2/22) n-ỉm≠f r pḥ r p3 nty tw≠ỉ ỉm ỉḫ n3 mšꜥ.(w)
swg3.(w) ỉ-dỉ≠w ỉr≠k

ỉw≠ỉ dd n≠f (2/23) ꜥd3ỉ bn mšꜥ.(w) swg3.(w) ỉwn3 n(3) nty tw≠ỉ
ỉm≠w mn ỉmw nb ḥr-tp ỉ(t)rw ỉw (2/24) bn nsy-s.t ᵓImn mntf p3 ym ḥr
mntf p3 Rbrn nty tw≠k dd ỉnk sw ỉ-ỉr≠f (2/25) rwd n ᵓImn-wsr-ḫ3.t p3 nb
n ỉmw nb y3 ỉn≠f n ᵓImn-Rꜥ ny-sw.t nt̠r.w dd n Ḥry(2/26)-Ḥr p3y≠ỉ nb ỉ-
wd̠ (w)ỉ ỉw≠f dỉ.t ỉw≠ỉ ḥr p3y ntr ꜥ3 ḥr ptrỉ dỉ≠k ỉr (2/27) p3y ntr ꜥ3 p3y
hrw 29 ỉw≠f mnỉ (m) t3y≠k mr.(t) ỉw bw rḫ≠k nn (= ỉn) sw d(y) nn (=
ỉn) bn sw p3 nty (2/28) wnw≠f9 tw≠k ꜥḥꜥ.tw r ỉr šw(y) n p3 Rbrn m-dr
ᵓImn p3y≠f nb ỉr p3y≠k dd wnw n3 (2/29) ny.w-sw.t h3w.tyw dỉ.t ỉn.tw ḫd
nbw h3n3 wn (m)-dỉ≠w ꜥnḫ snb wnw bn ỉw≠w dỉ.t ỉn.tw n3 (3)ḫ.t (2/30)
ỉ-ỉr≠w dỉ.t ỉn.tw n3 3ḫ.t (r)-db3 ꜥnḫ snb (n) n3y≠k ỉt.w ḥr ỉr ᵓImn-Rꜥ ny-
sw.t nt̠r.w mntf p3 (2/31) nb n p3 ꜥnḫ snb ḥr mntf p3 nb (n) n3y≠k ỉty.w
ỉr≠w p3y≠w ꜥḥꜥ(w) n ꜥnḫ ỉw≠w wdn (2/32) n ᵓImn mntk m-r3-ꜥ mntk b3kỉ
n ᵓImn ỉr ỉw≠k dd ỉry sp-2 n ᵓImn mtw≠k ꜥrꜥr p3y≠f (2/33) sḥn ỉw≠k ꜥnḫ
mtw≠k wd̠3 mtw≠k snb mtw≠k nfr n p3y≠k t3 (r) dr.w≠f n3y≠k rmt̠.w m-ỉr
mr n≠k (2/34) nkt n ᵓImn-Rꜥ (ny-sw.t) nt̠r.w y3 m3ỉ mr 3ḫ.t≠f ỉmy ỉn.tw
n≠ỉ p3y≠k sš h3(2/35)b≠ỉ sw n Nsy-sw-B3-nb-D̠d.(t) Tỉ-n.t-ᵓImn n3 sn{n}ty.
w t3 ỉ-dỉ ᵓImn n p3 mḥ.t(y) n p3y≠f t3 (2/36) mtw≠w dỉ.t ỉn.tw p3 nty nb
ỉw≠ỉ h3b≠f n≠w r dd ỉmy ỉn.tw≠f šꜥ ỉ-ỉr.t≠ỉ šmỉ r rsy mtw≠ỉ dỉ.t (2/37)
ỉn.tw n≠k p3y≠k g3b nb sp-2 m-r3-ꜥ ỉn≠ỉ n≠f

ỉw≠f dỉ.t t3y≠ỉ šꜥ.t m dr.t p3y≠f ỉpw.ty ỉw≠f 3tp t3 pỉ(2/38)pỉ.t p3 tp
n t3 ḫ3.t p3 tp n p3 pḥw ỉrm ky 4 ḫt md̠ḥ dmd̠ 7 ỉw≠f dỉ.t ỉn.tw≠w r Km.t

(2/39) ỉw p3y≠f ỉpw.ty šm r Km.t ỉy n≠ỉ r Ḫ3r n tpy pr.t ỉw dỉ Nsy-sw-B3-nb-Ḏd.(t) Tỉ-n.t-ʾImn ỉn.tw (2/40) nbw ṯbw 4 k3kmn 1 ḥḏ ṯbw 5 ḥbsw n šs-ny-sw.t ʿ 10 šmʿ.(t) nfr.(t) ḫrd 10 nʿʿ qn (2/41) 500 dḥrỉ n ỉḥ 500 nwḥ. w 500 ʿršn ḫ3r 20 rm.w mst3 30 ỉw≠s dỉ.t ỉn.tw n≠ỉ ḥbsw (2/42) šmʿ.(t) nfr.(t) ʿ 5 šmʿ.(t) nfr.(t) ḫrd 5 ʿršn ḫ3r 1 rm.w mst(ỉ) 5[10] ỉw p3 wr ršỉ.t ỉw≠f ʿrʿr (2/43) s 300 ỉḥ ḥwty 300 ỉw≠f dỉ.t wḥm.w r ḫ3.t≠w r rdỉ.t šʿd≠w n3 ḫt.w ỉw≠w šʿd≠w ỉw≠w ỉr pr.t ỉm (2/44) ḫ3ʿ

ỉr 3bd 3 šmw ỉw≠w ỉtḥ≠w (r) sp.t (n.t) p3 ym ỉw p3 wr pr ỉw≠f ʿḥʿ ḥr-r≠w ỉw≠f h3b n≠ỉ (2/45) r ḏd mỉ ḫr ỉr tw≠ỉ ms{b} q3ỉ n≠f ỉw t3 ḥ3b.(t) n.(t) t3y≠f srpt h(3)y r≠ỉ ỉw Pn-ʾImn (2/46) wʿ wḏ3 ỉw mntf sw ỉr ỉwd≠ỉ r ḏd t3 ḥ3b.(t) n.(t) Pr-ʿ3 ʿnḫ wḏ3 snb p3y≠k nb h3y.tw r≠k ỉw≠f[11] ḫdn (2/47) r≠f r ḏd ḫ3ʿ sw n≠k ỉw≠ỉ ms{b} q3ỉ n≠f ỉw≠f wšb ḏd n≠ỉ ptrỉ p3 sḫn ỉ-ỉr n3(2/48)y≠ỉ ỉt.w ḥr-ḫ3.t ỉ-ỉr≠ỉ sw ỉw bw-pw≠k ỉr n≠ỉ p3 wnw n3y≠k ỉt.w ỉr≠f n≠ỉ gr mntk ptrỉ pḥ (2/49) p3 pḥw n t3y≠k t.t ỉw≠f w3ḥ ỉ-ỉr n h3ty≠ỉ mtw≠k ỉy r 3tp≠s ḫr nn (= ỉn) bn ỉw≠w dỉ.t≠s{w} n≠k (2/50) m-ỉr ỉy r ptrỉ t3 ḥry.(t) n.(t) p3 ym wnn ỉw≠k ptrỉ t3 ḥry.(t) n.(t) p3 ym ỉw≠k ptr(2/51)ỉ t3y≠ỉ ḥʿ≠ỉ y3 bw-pw≠ỉ ỉr n≠k p3 (ỉ)-ỉr≠w (n) n3 ỉpw.tyw n Ḫʿ.w-m-W3s. t[12] m-ḏr ỉr≠w 17 n rnp.t (2/52) n p3y t3 ỉ-ỉr≠w mt (m) s.wt≠w ỉw≠f ḏd n p3y≠f wb3 t3y sw ỉmy ptrỉ≠f t3y≠w mʿḥʿ.t nty s.t (2/53) sḏrỉ n-ỉm≠s

ỉw≠ỉ ḏd n≠f m-ỉr dỉ.t ptrỉ≠ỉ sw ỉr Ḫʿ.(w)-m-W3s.t rmt.w n(3) (ỉ)-h3b≠f n≠k n ỉpw.tyw ḫr rmt (2/54) ḥʿ≠f bn mntk wʿ (n) n3y≠f ỉpw.tyw ỉw ỉw≠k ḏd ḥn≠k ptrỉ≠k n3y≠k ỉry.w ỉst bw-ỉr≠k ršỉ (2/55) mtw≠k dỉ.t [ỉr]≠tw n≠k wʿ wḏy mtw≠k ḏd ḥr-r≠f h3b n≠ỉ ʾImn-Rʿ ny-sw.t nṯr.w ʾImn-(n)-t3-mỉ.t p3y≠f ỉpw(2/56).ty [ʿnḫ] wḏ3 snb ḥnʿ Wn-ʾImn p3y≠f ỉpw.ty (n) rmt m-s3 t3 t.t n p3 wỉ3 ʿ3 špsy n ʾImn-Rʿ ny-sw.t nṯr.w šʿd(2/57)≠ỉ sw 3tp≠ỉ sw ʿpr≠ỉ sw (m) n3y≠ỉ byr.w n3y≠ỉ ỉs.wt dỉ≠ỉ pḥ≠w r Km.t r dbḥ n≠ỉ (2/58) 50 n rnp.t n.(t) ʿnḫ m-ḏr ʾImn m-ḫ[3]w p3y≠ỉ š3y mtw ḫpr≠f ỉr m-s3 ky h3(r)w mtw wʿ ỉpw.ty ỉy (2/59) m p3 t3 n Km.t ỉw≠f rḫ sš.w mtw≠f ʿš rn≠k ḥr p3 wḏy ỉw≠k šsp mw ỉmn.t mỉ-qd n(3) nṯr.w nty (2/60) d(y)

ỉw≠f ḏd n≠ỉ mtr.(t) ʿ3.t n.(t) md.t t3y (ỉ)-ḏḏ≠k n≠ỉ ỉw≠ỉ ḏd n≠f ỉr n3 qnw ỉ-ḏḏ≠k n≠ỉ ỉr ỉw≠ỉ pḥ r (2/61) p3 nty p3 ḥm-nṯr tp(y) n ʾImn ỉm mtw≠f ptrỉ p3y≠k sḫn m (=ỉn) p3y≠k sḫn ỉ-ỉr ỉtḥ (2/62) n≠k nkt

ỉw≠ỉ šmỉ n≠ỉ (r) sp{r}.(t) (n.t) p3 ym r p3 nty n3 ḫt.w ỉm w3ḥ ỉw≠ỉ nw r 11 n b(2/63)yr ỉw≠w n-ỉw n p3 ym ỉw nsy-s.t n3 Ṯkr.w r ḏd ḏdḥ sw m d3y byr.w (2/64) m-dỉ≠f r p3 t3 n Km.t ỉw≠ỉ ḫpr ḥms.tw rmw ỉw p3 sš šʿ.(t) n p3 wr ỉy n≠ỉ r-bnr (2/65) ỉw≠f ḏd n≠ỉ ỉḥ r≠k ỉw≠ỉ ḏd n≠f nn (= ỉn) bw-ỉr≠k ptrỉ n3 g3š.w ỉ-ỉr ỉr sp 2 n h3y r Km.t (2/66) ptrỉ s.t ỉw≠w nʿy r qbḥ(w) š3ʿ.tw ỉḥ ỉy ỉw≠ỉ d(y) ḫ3ʿ.tw ḫr nn (=ỉn) bw-ỉr≠k ptrỉ n3 ỉw (2/67) r ḏdḥ≠ỉ ʿn

ỉw≠f šmỉ ỉw≠f ḏd.t≠f n p3 wr ỉw p3 wr ḫpr rmw m-ḏr n3 md.(w)t ỉ-ḏḏ≠w n≠f ỉw≠w (2/68) mr ỉw≠f dỉ.t ỉw n≠ỉ p3y≠f sš šʿ.(t) r-bnr ỉw ỉn≠f n≠ỉ ỉrp msḥ 2 ỉyr 1 ỉw≠f dỉ.t ỉn.tw (2/69) n≠ỉ Tỉ-n.t-nỉw.t wʿ.(t) ḥsy.(t) n.(t) Km.t ỉw≠s m-dỉ≠f r ḏd ḥsy n≠f m d3y t3y h3ty≠f sḫr.w ỉw≠f h3b n≠ỉ

(2/70) r ḏd wnm swrî m dꜣy tꜣy ḥꜣty≠k sḥr.w îw≠k sḏm pꜣ nty nb îw≠î ḏd.t≠f n dwꜣw

îw dwꜣw (2/71) ḫpr îw≠f dî.t ꜥš.tw n pꜣy≠f mwꜥd îw≠f ꜥḥꜥ m-ḥnw≠w îw≠f ḏd (n) nꜣ Ṯkr.(w) îḫ nꜣy≠tn mšꜥ.w (2/72) îw≠w ḏd n≠f î-îr≠n îy m-sꜣ nꜣ byr.w qnqn nty tw≠k wḏ≠w r Km.t m nꜣy≠n îry.w n ṯtt (2/73) îw≠f ḏd n≠w bn îw≠î rḫ ḏdḥ pꜣ îpw.ty n ꜣImn m-ḫnw pꜣy≠î tꜣ îmî.tw wḏ≠î sw mtw≠tn šmî m-sꜣ≠f (2/74) r ḏdḥ≠f

îw≠f ꜣtp≠î îw≠f wḏ≠î îm r tꜣ mr.(t) n.(t) pꜣ ym îw pꜣ tꜣw ḥwꜣ.t≠(î) r pꜣ tꜣ n (2/75) ꜣIrsꜣ[13] îw nꜣy tꜣ dmî.t pr r≠î r ḥdb≠î îw≠î wꜣšꜣ.t≠(î) îwd≠w r pꜣ nty Ḫꜣtîbꜣ (2/76) tꜣ wr.(t) n.(t) pꜣ dmî îm îw≠î gm.t≠s m-dr pr≠s n pꜣy≠s wꜥ pr îw≠s n ꜥq m pꜣy≠s ky îw≠î (2/77) wšd≠s îw≠î ḏd (n) nꜣ rmṯ. w nty ꜥḥꜥ.(w) qꜣî n≠s nn (=în) mn wꜥ n-îm≠tn îw≠f sḏm md.wt Km.t îw wꜥ (2/78) n-îm≠w ḏd tw≠î sḏm îw≠î ḏd n≠f î-ḏd n tꜣy≠î ḥnw.t wn≠î sḏm šꜣꜥ nîw.t r pꜣ nty ꜣImn îm r ḏd î-îr.tw (2/79) grg n dmî nb î-îr.tw mꜣꜥ.t n pꜣ tꜣ n ꜣIrsꜣ îst î-îr.tw îr grg rꜥ nb d(y)

îw≠s ḏd yꜣ îḫ m (2/80) pꜣy≠k ḏd.t≠f îw≠î ḏd n≠s îr îw pꜣ ym qnd mtw pꜣ tꜣw ḥwꜣ.t≠(î) r pꜣ tꜣ nty tw≠t îm≠f (2/81) nn (= în) îw≠t dî.t šsp≠w n ḥꜣ.t≠î r ḥdb≠î îw înk îpw.ty n ꜣImn mk ptrî înk îꜣ≠tw (= îw≠tw) wꜣḫ≠î (2/82) šꜣꜥ hꜣ(r)w nb îr tꜣy≠î îs.t n pꜣ wr n Kpn nty s.t wꜣḫ ḥdb sw nn (= în) bn îw pꜣy≠s nb gm (2/83) 10 n îs.t m-dî≠t mtw≠f ḥdb≠w gr mntf îw≠s dî.t ꜥš.tw n nꜣ rmṯ.w îꜣ≠tw (= îw≠tw) sꜥḥꜥ≠w îw≠s ḏd n≠î sḏr n≠k [...]

(vo. 1) r rdî.t rḫ.tw pꜣ nty nb î-dî Nꜣ-ḥr-[...] în.tw≠f (n) Nsy-sw-pꜣ-krm (vo. 2) šꜣw 8 dn šb.t [...]

(1/1) Regnal year 5, month 4 of summer, day 16, the day of departure made by Wenamon, the elder of the portal of the estate of Amon, (1/2) [Lord of the Thrones] of the Two Lands, in order to bring back the timber for the great and noble bark of Amon-Re, King of the Gods, which is upon (1/3) [the river and whose name is] Amon-user-hat. On the day when I had arrived at Tanis at the (1/4) [place where Smendes] and Tanetamon were, I gave to them the dispatches of Amon-Re, King of the Gods, and they (1/5) had them read aloud in their presence, and they said: "I shall act, I shall act in accordance with that which Amon-Re, King of the Gods, (1/6) our [lord], has said."

And I spent from month 4 of summer within Tanis. Then Smendes (1/7) and Tanetamon sent me off with the ship's captain Mengebet, and I went down to (1/8) the great Syrian sea in the first month of summer, day 1.[1] I arrived at Dor, a town of (1/9) the Tcheker, and Badir, its prince, had 50 loaves, 1 jug of wine, (1/10), and 1 haunch of beef brought to me. Then a man of my ship fled, having stolen 1 golden (1/11) [jar] amounting to 5 *deben,* 4 silver jars amounting to 20 *deben,* and a bag of 11 *deben* of silver, (1/12) [with the total of what] he [stole being] 5 *deben* of gold and 31 *deben* of silver.

And I arose on that morning, and I went to (1/13) the place where the prince was, and I said to him: "I have been robbed in your harbor. Now you are the prince of this land. Now (1/14) *you* are its investigator. Search for my money! But really, as regards the money, it belongs to Amon-Re, (1/15) King of the Gods, the Lord of the Lands. It belongs to Smendes; it belongs to Herihor, my lord, and the other (1/16) magnates of Egypt. It is yours. It belongs to Warti; it belongs to Mekamer; it belongs to Tcheker-baal, the prince of Byblos."

And he said to me: "Whether you are distraught or trustworthy,[2] now look, I cannot (1/18) understand this response that you have said to me. If it had been a thief who belonged to my land who had gone down (1/19) to your ship and stolen your money, I would replace it for you from my storehouse until (1/20) your thief, whatever his name, had been found. But really, as regards the thief who robbed you, he is yours. He belongs to (1/21) your ship. Spend a few days here near me so that I may search for him."

And I spent 9 days moored (1/22) in his harbor. Then I went before him and I said to him: "Look, you have not found my money. (1/23) Please [send] me [off] with the ship's captains and those who go to sea." And he said to me: "Be silent! (1/24) [If you wish to] find your [money …] listen to my [words and do what] I [say] to you, but do not (1/25) […] listen to […] the place where you are. You will take possession of their boats (?), and you will be paid in full like […] (1/26) [… until] they go to search for their thief who [robbed them …] (1/27) [… Spend the] night at the harbor.[3] Look, [you will (?) …]" … And I arrived at] (1/28) Tyre.

And I left from Tyre at first light […] (1/29) […] Tchekerbaal, the prince of Byblos […] (1/30) […] a ship, and I found 30 *deben* of silver in it, and I took possession of it. [I said to the ship's owners: "I have taken possession of] (1/31) your money. It will remain with me [until] you have found my [money or the thief] (1/32) who stole it. I have not robbed you, although I shall rob him. But as for you, [you] shall […] me to […]."

(1/33) Then they went away and I celebrated by myself [in] a tent on the seashore at the harbor of Byblos. And [I found a] (1/34) [hiding place for] Amon-of-the-Road and I placed his possessions within it. Then the [prince] of Byblos sent word to me, saying: "Get [yourself out of] (1/35) [my] harbor!" And I sent word to him, saying: "Where [should I go]? […] I […] go […] (1/36) […] If [you if have a ship] to transport me, let me be taken (1/37) back to Egypt." And I spent 29 days in his harbor, [although] daily he spent time sending word to me, saying: "Get (1/38) yourself out of my harbor!"

Now when he offered to his gods, the god (Amon) seized a great seer from among his (1/39) great seers,[4] and he caused him to be in an ecstatic state. He[5] said to him:

"Bring up the god!

Bring the messenger who bears him! (1/40)

It is Amon who has sent him.

It is he who has caused that he come."

But the ecstatic became ecstatic on that night only after I had found (1/41) a ship heading for Egypt, and I had loaded all my belongings onto it, and I had watched (1/42) for darkness to fall so that I might put the god on board in order to prevent another eye from seeing him.

And the (1/43) harbor-master came to me, saying: "Stay until morning—so says the prince!" And I said to him: "Are you[6] not the one who (1/44) daily spent time coming to me, saying: 'Get yourself out of my harbor'? Are you saying 'Stay tonight,' (1/45) just to allow the ship that I have found to depart, and then you will come back, saying: 'Be off with you,' again?" Then he went and told it to (1/46) the prince, and the prince sent word to the captain of the ship, saying: "Stay until morning—so says (1/47) the prince!"

Morning came and he sent word and took me up while the god rested in the tent (1/48) where he was on the seashore. I found him seated in his high chamber with his back set (1/49) against a window, while behind his head crashed the waves of the great Syrian sea. (1/50) I said to him: "Amon be merciful!" He said to me: "How long has it been until today since you came from the place where (1/51) Amon is?" I said to him: "Five full months until today." He said to me: "Indeed, you are correct. Where is the (1/52) dispatch of Amon that is in your possession? Where is the letter of the First Prophet of Amon that is in your possession?" I said (1/53) to him: "I gave them to Smendes and Tanetamon." And he became very irritated, and he said to me: "Now look, neither dispatches nor (1/54) letters, nothing is in your possession. Where is the pinewood ship[7] that Smendes gave to you? Where is (1/55) its Syrian crew? Has he entrusted you to this foreign ship's captain just to have him kill (1/56) you and have them throw you into the sea? With whom would the god be sought? And you also, (1/57) with whom would you also be sought?" So he said to me.

And I said to him: "Is it not an Egyptian ship? Now, they are Egyptian crews that sail (1/58) under Smendes. He has no Syrian crews." He said to me: "Are there not 20 cargo ships (1/59) here in my harbor that are in partnership with Smendes? As for that Sidon, (2/1) the other place that you have passed, are there not another 50 ships there that are in partnership (2/2) with Warkatel, although it is to his house that they haul?"

And I was silent at that important moment. (2/3) And he responded, saying to me: "On what commission have you come?" I said to him: (2/4) "It is in pursuit of the timber for the great and noble bark of Amon-Re, King of the Gods, that I have come. What your father did, and what (2/5) the father of your father did, you shall do also."[8] So I said to him. He said to me: "It is they who did it, truly. (2/6) If you pay me for doing it then I shall do it. But really, mine did this commission only after (2/7) Pharaoh, l.p.h., had caused 5 ships to be brought, which had been loaded with the products of Egypt and then were unloaded into their (2/8) storehouses. As for you, what is it that you have brought to me for my part?"

He had the daily ledger of his ancestors brought, (2/9) and he had it read aloud in my presence. They found 1,000 *deben* of silver and all manner of things on his ledger. (2/10) He said to me: "Were the ruler of Egypt the lord of what is mine, and I his servant as well, (2/11) would he have caused silver and gold to be brought to say: 'Perform the commission of Amon!'? Wasn't it the delivery (2/12) of royal gifts that he used to perform for my father? Now as for me myself, I am not your (2/13) servant, nor am I the servant of the one who sent you either. If I but cry out to the (2/14) Lebanon, heaven opens with the logs lying right here on the seashore! Give (2/15) me the sails that you brought to take your ships laden with your logs to Egypt. (2/16) Give me the ropes [that] you brought [to bind the pines] that I am to cut down in order to make them for you. (2/17) [...] that I am to make for you for the sails for your (2/18) ships, and the yards may be too heavy and may break, and you may die in the midst of the sea. (2/19) Look, Amon thunders in the sky only since he placed Seth at his side. Now (2/20) all lands has Amon founded. He founded them only after he had first founded the land of Egypt, the one from which you have come. (2/21) Thus virtues came forth from it just to reach the place where I am. Thus learning came forth (2/22) from it just to reach the place where I am. What is the sense of these foolish wanderings that they have made you do?"

I said to him: (2/23) "Wrong! They are not foolish wanderings that I am on! There is not any ship upon the river that (2/24) does not belong to Amon. His is the sea and his is the Lebanon, about which you say: 'It is mine.' It is (2/25) a nursery just for Amon-user-hat, the lord of every ship. But really, he—that is Amon-Re, King of the Gods—said in speaking to Herihor, (2/26) my lord: 'Send me off!' And he caused that I come bearing this great god. Now look, you have caused (2/27) this god to spend these 29 days moored in your harbor, without your knowing whether he was here or whether he was not the one whom (2/28) he is.⁹ You are waiting to haggle over the Lebanon with Amon, its lord. As for your saying that the (2/29) former kings used to send silver and gold, if they had possessed life and health they would not have sent those things. (2/30) It was instead of life and health that they sent those things to your fathers. Now, as for Amon-Re, King of the Gods, *he* is the (2/31) lord of life and health. Now *he* is the lord of your fathers. They spent their lifetimes offering (2/32) to Amon. You also, *you* are a servant of Amon. If you say 'I shall act, I shall act' to Amon, and you accomplish his commission, you will live; you will prosper; you will be healthy; and you will be fortunate in your entire land and your people. Do not covet for yourself (2/34) the property of Amon-Re, King of the Gods! For really, a lion loves his property! Let your scribe be brought to me so that (2/35) I might send him to Smendes and Tanetamon, the foundations whom Amon has placed in the north of his land, (2/36) and they will have everything brought. I shall send him to them, saying: 'Let it be brought until I return to the south, and then I shall have (2/37) absolutely all your expenses brought back to you in turn.'" So I said to him.

He placed my letter in the hand of his messenger, and he loaded the (2/38) keel, the bow-post, and the stern-post together with another 4 hewn logs, for a total of 7, and he had them brought to Egypt. (2/39) His messenger went to Egypt and returned to me in Syria in the first month of winter, Smendes and Tanetamon having sent: (2/40) 4 jars and 1 vessel of gold, 5 silver jars, 10 articles of clothing of royal linen, 10 veils of sheer cloth of good quality, 500 mats of smooth linen, (2/41) 500 ox-hides, 500 ropes, 20 sacks of lentils, and 30 baskets of fish. And she had brought to me: (2/42) 5 articles of clothing of sheer cloth of good quality, 5 veils of sheer cloth of good quality, 1 sack of lentils, and 5 baskets of fish.[10] Then the prince rejoiced, and he supplied (2/43) 300 men and 300 oxen, and he assigned heralds over them to have them cut down the logs. And they cut them down, and they spent the winter (2/44) lying there.

In month 3 of summer, they dragged them to the seashore. The prince went out and stood by them, and he sent word to me, (2/45) saying: "Come!" Now when I was conducted near to him, the shadow of his lotus fan fell upon me, and Penamon, (2/46) a cupbearer who belonged to him, intervened, saying: "The shadow of Pharaoh, l.p.h., your lord, has fallen upon you." And he[11] became angry (2/47) at him, saying: "Leave him alone!" I was conducted near to him, and he responded, saying to me: "Look, the commission that (2/48) my fathers did previously, I have done it—even though you, for your part, have not done for me what your fathers used to do for me. Look, (2/49) the last of your lumber has arrived and is in place. Do as I wish and come to load it, for will it not be given to you? (2/50) Do not come to look upon the terror of the sea! Were you to look upon the terror of the sea, you would look upon (2/51) my own. For really, I have not done to you what was done to the messengers of Khaemwase,[12] when they had spent 17 years (2/52) in this land. In their jobs they died." And he said to his cupbearer: "Take him! Let him see their tomb in which they (2/53) lie."

And I said to him: "Don't make me see it! As for Khaemwese, they were but men whom he sent to you as messengers, and he himself a man. (2/54) You do not have here one of his messengers, that you should say: 'You should go and see your fellows.' Why do you not rejoice (2/55) and have [made] for yourself a stela and say upon it: 'Amon-Re, King of the Gods, sent to me Amon-of-the-Road, his messenger, (2/56) l.p.h., together with Wenamon, his human messenger, in pursuit of the timber for the great and noble bark of Amon-Re, King of the Gods. I cut (2/57) it down. I loaded it. I equipped him with my ships and crews. I caused that they reach Egypt in order to beseech for myself (2/58) 50 years of life from Amon over and above my allotted fate.' And should it happen after another day that a messenger comes (2/59) from the land of Egypt who knows writings and he reads your name on the stela, you will receive water in the west like the gods who (2/60) are there."

He said to me: "This is a great testimony of words that you have said to me." I said to him: "Regarding the many things that you have said to me, if I reach (2/61) the place where the First Prophet of Amon is, and he sees your commission, it is your commission that will draw (2/62) profit to you."

Then I went off to the seashore to the spot where the logs were placed. I caught sight of 11 (2/63) ships coming in from the sea that were under the control of the Tcheker, who were saying: "Imprison him! Do not let a ship (2/64) of his head for the land of Egypt!" Then I sat down weeping. The secretary of the prince came out to me, (2/65) and he said to me: "What's with you?" I said to him: "Do you not see the migratory birds who have already made two descents into Egypt? (2/66) Look at them going to the cool water region. Until what comes about shall I be abandoned here? Now do you not see the ones coming (2/67) to imprison me again?

Then he went and he told it to the prince. The prince began to weep because of the words that were told to him, for they were (2/68) painful. He sent his secretary out to me, bringing me 2 jugs of wine and 1 sheep. And he sent (2/69) to me Tanetniut, an Egyptian songstress whom he had, saying: "Sing for him! Do not allow his heart to obsess upon affairs." And he sent word to me, (2/70) saying: "Eat! Drink! Do not allow your heart to obsess upon affairs. You will hear whatever I shall say in the morning."

The morning (2/71) came, and he had his assembly summoned. He stood in their midst and he said to the Tcheker: "What is the meaning of your journeys?" (2/72) They said to him: "It is in pursuit of the blasted ships that you are sending to Egypt together with our adversaries that we have come." (2/73) He said to them: "I will not be able to imprison the messenger of Amon within my land. Let me send him off, and you go after him (2/74) to imprison him."

He had me board, and he sent me off from there at the harbor of the sea. The wind blew me to the land of (2/75) Alasiya.[13] The people of the harbor came out against me in order to kill me, and I forced my way through them to the place where Hatiba, (2/76) the princess of the town, was. I found her when she had gone out of one of her houses and was in the act of entering into her other one. I (2/77) hailed her, and I said to the people who were standing near to her: "Is there not one among you who understands the Egyptian language?" And one among them said: "I understand." I said to him: "Say to my lady: 'I have heard as far as Thebes, in the place where Amon is, that even as (2/79) injustice is done in every town, so justice is done in the land of Alasiya.' Is injustice done daily even here?"

Then she said: "Really, what is the meaning of (2/80) your saying that?" I said to her: "If the sea rages and the wind blows me to the land where you are, (2/81) will you let them greet me so to kill me, although I am a messenger of Amon? Look here, as for me, I shall be sought (2/82) for all time. As for this crew of the prince of Byblos, whom they are seeking to kill, will not its lord find 10 (2/83) crews belonging to you and kill them then for his part?" Then she caused that the men be summoned and they were arraigned. She said to me: "Spend the night." [...]

Verso

(1) To let it be known: Everything that Naher[...] had brought to Nespakarm: (2) coriander 8 baskets (?), cucumbers [...]

NOTES

1. The dates in the text have been considered irreconcilable as written, but a solution without emendation is posed by Egberts 1991, 57–67. Wenamon will have reached Tanis, probably from el-Hibeh, in month 4 of summer and then waited in the northern capital for a further eight months, departing for Syria in the first month of the following summer. Egberts's revisions of this scheme in 1998, 93–108, concern only the setting of the initial date within the "renaissance era" of Rameses XI and assume an inversion of the traditional order of Herihor and Piankh. For response to this theory, see Kitchen 1995, xiv–xvii §§A-K.

2. Literally, "Are you heavy (or) are you excellent?" For the translation "whether ... whether," see Gardiner 1999, 164 §217. The term dns typically has negative nuances ("burdened, irksome"), while mnḫ is uniformly positive. Previous translations have reversed the nuances.

3. The prince warns Wenamon not to appropriate Tcheker property as compensation lest he be repaid only to be pursued in turn as a thief. Wenamon does exactly what he has been warned against, with predictable results.

4. The term for "medium" is written as the common Egyptian word for "youth," but on the basis of context it has been suggested to represent a Semitic word for "seer," perhaps related to Aramaic ʿddn; for discussion and bibliography, see Hoch 1994, 86–87.

5. The seer speaks to the prince of Byblos.

6. Variously interpreted by modern editors, the particle nn is here taken in most contexts to represent the older interrogative particle în. Within this text the particle is commonly used in rhetorical questions expecting the answer "yes," often

a negative construction in English (Egyptian "are you" corresponding to English "are you not"). For discussion, see Gardiner 1999, 65a.

7. The abbreviated writing with wood determinative, not found in dictionaries, appears also in the Funerary Decree of Amon for Princess Neskhons (no. 35 below), lines 95, 97, and 100.

8. Or, "Just as your father acted, so the father of your father acted. You will do it also." For the parallel nominal clauses, cf. col. 2/78–79.

9. Literally, "Is he here (or) is he not the one who he is?"

10. In addition to the monarchs' loan for paying Tchekerbaal, Tanetamon has provided supplies for Wenamon personally.

11. Tchekerbaal reproaches his Egyptian cupbearer, who had implied that Wenamon's true protector and "Pharaoh" is the Byblite ruler. In Egyptian imagery, "to shade" signifies "to protect" (cf. Coptic ⲢϪⲀⲈⲒⲂⲈⲤ).

12. The throne name of Rameses XI, here noted disrespectfully as a simple individual without royal cartouche or epithets. Egberts (1998, 102, states that Rameses XI is described as deceased in the following passage ("he was a man himself"), but *no grammatical past-tense marker* is employed in the phrase "and he himself a man" (ḫr rmṯ ḥꜥ ꜥf).

13. Cyprus.

19. THE REBURIAL OF ROYAL MUMMIES UNDER HERIHOR

Dynasty XXI is noted for its preoccupation with the rewrapping and reburial of the royal mummies of the New Kingdom, an enterprise that began with Herihor and continued beyond the first decade of the reign of Sheshonq I of the subsequent dynasty. While a few burial renewals are known from Dynasty XVIII (the tomb of Tutankhamon restored shortly after its robbery and Horemheb's renewal of Thutmose IV after the Amarna turmoil), a formal campaign of reburial occurs only after the systematic plundering of private tombs in the late Ramesside age. The degree to which royal tombs had been pillaged is unclear, and the Dynasty XXI reburials may in fact constitute official plundering rather than a devotional response to prior robbery. Deprived of grave goods and ornamentation, the rewrapped mummies of Seti I and Rameses II would each be "renewed" three times, ultimately becoming members of the group cache installed in the family tomb of Pinedjem II (DB 320). Hieratic dockets on the kings' wooden coffins record the various moves. The inscription of Herihor on the mummy of Rameses II was washed off and surcharged by a later text of Siamon. Beyond the initial lines, the traces of the original inscription are obscure.

For the texts and translations, see Maspero 1889, 553, 557 (fig. 15) and plates Xb and XII (retouched); Daressy 1909, 30 and 32 and pls. XVIII and XXII; Reeves 1990, 234; Thomas 1966, 249 §2a–b and 262, nn. 4–9; Černý

1946, 26–27; and Peet 1928, 65 n. 4. See Kitchen 1986, 17 §14, 251–52 §210 and 417 §379, 2–3.

THE MUMMY OF KING SETI I OF DYNASTY XIX (CAIRO JDE 61019).

ḥsb.t 6.(t) ꜣbd 2 ꜣḫ.t sw 7 hrw n wḏ ỉr.n t̠ꜣ.ty ỉmy-rꜣ mš[ꜥ wr][1] (2) ḥm-nt̠r tpy n ꜣImn-Rꜥ ny-sw.t nt̠r.w Ḥr(y)-Ḥr r wḥm (3) q(r)ỉs n ny-sw.t Mn-Mꜣꜥ.t-Rꜥ ꜥnḫ wḏꜣ snb sꜣ Rꜥ Sty-mry-Ptḥ[2] (4) ỉn rwḏw Ḥr-n-ꜣImn-pnꜥ⸗f mnḫ[3] Pꜣ-Rꜥ-pꜣy⸗w-ỉt

Regnal year 6, month 2 of Inundation, day 7: the day when the vizier, the [great] general,[1] (2) and the First Prophet of Amon-Re, King of the Gods, Herihor issued a dispatch to restore (3) the burial of King Men-maatre, l.p.h., the Son of Re, Seti (I) beloved of Ptah,[2] (4) by the agent Herenamonpenaf and the cadet[3] Prepayuit.

THE MUMMY OF RAMESES II OF DYNASTY XIX (CAIRO JDE 61020).

ḥsb.t 6.(t) ꜣbd 3 pr.t[4] sw 15 hrw n wḏ ỉ-ỉr t̠ꜣ.ty(?)[5] ỉmy-rꜣ [mšꜥ] (2) wr n tꜣ [r] dr⸗[f] ḥm-nt̠r tpy n ꜣImn-Rꜥ ny-sw.t nt̠r.w (3) Ḥry-Ḥr wr mnw [...]... ꜣImn-ḥtp(?)[...] m pꜣ ḫr (4) [r wḥm] qrꜣs n ny-sw.t Wsr-Mꜣꜥ.t-Rꜥ-stp-n-Rꜥ ...[...] (5) [...] wḥm [...] pꜣ [...] nt̠ry mrỉ.t wr mnw ws(6)t.t [...] dr [...]ḫ. w⸗s ỉmn.t(?) Wꜣs.t(?) mm [...] šꜣbyty.w (7) ꜥšꜣy mnḫ.w [...] ỉwn[ꜣ ..] m-dỉ⸗ỉ r m[...]y bꜣk [...] bw [...] t̠ꜣ.ty šꜣꜥ (8) [...] tꜣ drỉ⸗[f] ỉw [...] qm⸗f [...]k[...]k [..]m[..] m ḫr(y)

Regnal year 6, month 3 of winter,[4] day 15, the day when the vizier (?),[5] the (2) great general of the entire land, the First Prophet of Amon-Re, King of the Gods, (3) Herihor, whose monuments are great [...] issued a dispatch [...] Amonhotep (?) [...] the royal tomb (4) [to renew] the burial of King Usermaatre-setepenre ...[...] (5) [...] renew [...] the divine [...] harbor, great of monuments, document (6) [...] remove its [...] west (?) of Thebes (?) among [...] (7) many effective *shawabti*-figures [...] not [...] with me to [...] work [...] not [...] vizier. (8) The entire land began [...] he completed [...] above.

NOTES
1. The conclusion of this line, disputed by Peet, is confirmed by E. F. Wente, personal communication.
2. Daressy added ꜥnḫ wḏꜣ snb "l.p.h.," invisible on photographs and not read by Maspero.
3. A junior member of the military or priesthood.
4. So Maspero's hand copy, but read ꜣḫ.t "Inundation" by Daressy.
5. Daressy read ny-sw.t. The appearance of that title, if accurate, would contradict the statement that Herihor did not use royal titles in these dockets (Kitchen 1986, 251 n. 42).

20. THE DIBABIEH QUARRY STELA OF SMENDES

A hieroglyphic stela carved on a pillar in the western gallery of the limestone quarries at Dibabieh, near the town of Gebelein, preserved a rare mention of Smendes in Upper Egypt. Below a winged disk, the stela was framed by vertical bands of text recording the titles of the king, although only the right band remained for modern copyists. In addorsed scenes above the primary inscription, Smendes was depicted worshiping Amon and Khonsu on the right and Amon and Mut on the left. The main text of seventeen lines adopts the standard *Königsnovelle* format, in which the king is informed of disturbance and promptly orders corrective action. Particularly noteworthy is the royal presence at Memphis (rather than at Tanis) and the destructive flooding of Luxor temple, encountered again during the tenure of Osorkon III. A broken passage in line 15 suggests a census of project workers, noting deaths and new births. The primary textual edition is in places unreliable, but the stela is now destroyed below the cornice and winged disk (personal communication, James A. Harrell, 19 October 1999).

For the text and translations, see Daressy 1888, 133–38; Maspero 1889, 675–76; Breasted 1906–7, 4:308–9 §§627–30; and von Beckerath 1984, 97. See Kitchen 1986, 255–56 §§213–14, 287 §241, and 428 §395.

FRAMING BAND

ntr nfr nb t3.wy nb ỉr.(t) ḫ.t Ḥd-ḫpr-Rˤ-stp-n-Rˤ s3 Rˤ nb ḫˤ.w Ns-b3-(nb)-Ḏd.t mrỉ-ʾImn dỉ ˤnḫ ḏd w3s mỉ Rˤ

The Good God, Lord of the Two Lands, Lord of ritual performance, Hedjkheperre-setepenre, the Son of Re, Lord of Diadems, Smendes, beloved of Amon, given life, stability, and dominion like Re.

RIGHTHAND SCENE

Label for Amon

ḏd-mdw ỉn ʾImn-Rˤ nb ns.wt t3.wy ḫnt(y) ʾIp.t-s.wt ntr ˤ3 nb p.t (2) ḏd-mdw ỉn ʾImn-Rˤ p3w.ty t3.wy ntr pw ḫpr m sp tp(y) dỉ≠f ˤnḫ

Recitation by Amon-Re, Lord of the Thrones of the Two Lands, Foremost of Karnak, the great god, lord of heaven. (2) Recitation by Amon-Re, the primeval one of the Two Lands. He is the god who came into existence on the first occasion. May he give life.

Label for Khonsu

ḏd-mdw ỉn Ḫnsw nb M3ˤ.t sm3 M3ˤ.t

Recitation by Khonsu, lord of Maat, united with Maat.

Label for the King

ntr nfr nb t3.wy Ḥd-ḫpr-Rꜥ-stp-n-Rꜥ s3 Rꜥ nb ḫꜥ.w Ns-b3-(nb)-Ḏd.t mrỉ-
ʾImn m3[...] Ḥr-3ḫ.ty(?) [...]n r ny-sw.t nb [...] dỉ ꜥnḫ ḏd w3s nb snb nb
mỉ Rꜥ

The Good God, Lord of the Two Lands, Hedjkheperre-setepenre, the
Son of Re, Lord of Diadems, Smendes, beloved of Amon, [...] Horachty (?)
[...] more than any king [...], given all life, stability, and dominion and all
health like Re.

LEFTHAND SCENE

Label for Amon

[ḏd-mdw ỉn ʾImn-Rꜥ ...] ḫnt(y) ʾIp.t-s.wt [...] (2) ḏd-mdw ỉn ʾImn-Rꜥ
nb ns.wt t3.wy ḫnt(y) ʾIp.t-s.wt wr n nṯr.w dỉ≠f qn(ỉ)

[Recitation by Amon-Re, ...] Foremost of Karnak, [...] (2) Recitation by
Amon-Re, Lord of the Thrones of the Two Lands, Foremost of Karnak, the
greatest of the gods. May he give valor.

MAIN TEXT

(1) ꜥnḫ Ḥr k3 nḫt mry Rꜥ swsr ʾImn ḫpš≠f r sq(3) M3ꜥ.t Nb.ty sḫm pḥ.ty
ḫ(wỉ) rqy.w≠f bh3t.w≠f¹ ḥpt m [... Ḥr-nbw] (2) ḫsf dndn ny-sw.t bỉ.ty nb
t3.wy nb ỉr.(t) ḫ.t ḥq3 t3.wy Ḥd-ḫpr-Rꜥ-stp-n-Rꜥ s3 Rꜥ nb ḫꜥ.w mỉ ʾImn-Rꜥ
ny-sw.t nṯr.w wr [ny.t]-sw.t [Ns-b3-(nb)-Ḏd.t mrỉ-ʾImn dỉ ꜥnḫ] (3) ḏd w3s
mỉ Rꜥ ḏ.t

ỉstw ḥm≠f n dmỉ Ḥw.t-k3-Ptḥ ḫnw≠f šps n qn(ỉ) nḫt mỉ Rꜥ [... r pr Ptḥ]
(4) nb ꜥnḫ-t3.wy Sḫm.t ꜥ3.(t) mry.(t) Ptḥ [...] Mntw psḏ.t ỉmy≠w ʾInb-ỉty²

ỉstw ḥm≠f sndm m w3[rḫ ỉw.tw r ḏd n] (5) ḥm≠f ỉw ꜥ ỉn.t³ wn m dr.w
n.(w) ʾIp.t-rsy.t ỉr.n{n} ny-sw.t Mn-ḫpr-Rꜥ w3[y r w3s ...] (6) wn mḥy.(t) ꜥ3.t
ỉqḥw wr m-[ḫnw]≠f r s3tw ꜥ3 n ḥw.t-nṯr wdb≠f ḫnt[y ...]

[ỉstw ḏd ḥm≠f] (7) n≠sn ỉr mdt pw ḏd.t m ḥr≠ỉ n(n) ḫ.t pw m rkw⁴
ḥm≠ỉ (r)-ḏr≠s mỉt.t ỉry m ḥm [...] (8) ḫw (m) (ỉ)3d3.(t)⁵ ỉm wnn ꜥ pw ḥtr
ḥr tr n rnp.t ḥr smd.ty n[...] (9) m ḥm ḫ.(t)≠ỉ(?) nn r-3w m rwty n ỉty

wn-ỉn ḥm≠f r[dỉ ỉw(?) ỉmy-r3 ỉqd](10).w s 3000 ḥnꜥ≠sn m stp n rḫw.w
n.(w) ḥm≠f wḏ.n ḥm≠f m ḥr≠sn š3ỉs r r[sy(?) ...] (11) sm.t [...] ḫnty.w n.w
ḥm≠f m ỉry-rd.wy (r) sḫpr ꜥḫꜥ.w m [...]

(12) mt(r).t [...] m qdw.t ḫ3.t pn⁶ m rkw sn.w r h3(r)w ʾIn.ty ỉ[...] (13)
ḥw.t-nṯr n.(t) Mnt(w) nb Ḏr.ty ndrỉ≠sn wḏ pn dd mn ḥm≠f [...] (14) ḫt⁷ m
ḫꜥ.w n≠s(n) tp-3bd spr wḏ≠f r sdsr k3.wt n.t wḏ [...] (15) m ḥsbw wnw nḫn
ḥr mnd n mw.t≠f r š3[ꜥ ...] (16) ỉry m mỉt.t≠f m rkw tp(y).w-ꜥ

ỉstw ḥm≠f sn m sp-2 mỉ Ḏḥwty [...](17)m.w r b(w)-ỉqr ỉsw ỉry m
qn(ỉ) nḫt ḫꜥ ḥr s.t Ḥr⁸ [ḏ.t]

(1) Long live the Horus: "Strong Bull, beloved of Re, whose strong arm Amon has strengthened to elevate Maat"; The Two Ladies: "He whose strength is powerful, who smites those who would rebel against him, with those who would flee from him[1] grasped by [...]"; The Golden Horus:] (2) "He who repels wrath"; the King of Upper and Lower Egypt, Lord of the Two Lands, Lord of ritual performance, ruler of the Two Lands, Hedj-kheperre-setepenre, the Son of Re, Lord of diadems like Amon-Re, King of the Gods, great of king[ship], [Smendes, beloved of Amon, given life,] (3) stability, and dominion like Re forever.

Now His Majesty was in the city of Memphis, his noble residence of valor and victory like Re [... He went (?) to the estate of Ptah,] (4) lord of Ankh-Tawy, and Sakhmet the great, the beloved of Ptah [...], Montu and the Ennead who are in the "Wall of the Sovereign."[2]

Now His Majesty was seated in the columned [hall, and one came to say to] (5) His Majesty: "The canal bed[3] that formed the borders of Luxor temple and that was made by King Menkheperre (Thutmosis III) is fallen [into ruin. ...] (6) There is a great flood and a strong current with[in] it on the great pavement of the temple. It has encircled the front [...]."

[Now His Majesty said] (7) to them: "If it is a matter said before me, yet it is not something at all in the experience[4] of My Majesty, anything similar being unknown [...] (8) protect from the calamity[5] there. It was a canal harnessed seasonally for the borders of [...] (9) in ignorance of my property (?), all these being remote from the sovereign."

Then His Majesty [sent architects] (10) and 3,000 men with them, comprising the best of the comrades of His Majesty. To them His Majesty commanded: "Go to [the south (?) ...] (11) desert [...] the commanders of His Majesty as subordinates at his heels to create heaps (of stones) in [the quarry (?) ...] (12) witness [...] in the vicinity of this[6] quarry from the time of those who have passed away until today, Gebelein [...] (13) the temple of Montu, lord of Tod. They engraved this decree that causes that His Majesty remain [...] (14) excavated[7] by themselves monthly. His command arrived to sanctify the works of the decree [...] (15) in reckoning those who had passed away and the child at the breast of his mother up to [... Never was anything] (16) done similarly in the time of the ancestors.

Now His Majesty passed by a second time like Thoth [... the ...](17) people in a state of excellence, the reward for this being valor and victory and appearance in glory upon the throne of Horus[8] [forever].

NOTES

1. The term is attested in Hellenistic times (Erman and Grapow 1926–63, 1:467/11) and derives from an older verb "to flee" (1:467/8).

2. The royal precinct at Memphis; see Zibelius 1978, 42–43.

3. Taken as înb "wall" by Breasted. For the meaning "bed" of a river or canal, see Meeks 1980–82, 2:34, no. 78.0354.

4. Literally, "time."

5. The term's literal meaning of "pestilent water" (associated with dew or pouring rain) is clearly relevant here.

6. Daressy copies a masculine for an expected feminine form.

7. For ḥt "carve" (Erman and Grapow 1926–63, 3:347–48) or ḥtt/ḫtt "pluck/extract" (3:403). Perhaps one might restore [ḥt]ḥt < ḥdḥd "to examine"; see Lesko 1982–90, 2:214.

8. Copied by Daressy as ꜣ. For the phrase, cf. the conclusions of Kawa Stelae IV and VII (nos. 161, 164 below).

21. AN INCRIMINATING LETTER TO THE GENERAL AND HIGH PRIEST PIANKH (P. BM 10375)

Political instability during the concluding years of Dynasty XX had entailed the military suppression of an ambitious Theban pontiff, Amonhotep, and invasions of Thebes by maurading Libyan and Nubian troops. Yet more significant was the subsequent revolt of the Nubian viceroy, Pinehsy, that effectively deprived Egypt of access to its southern gold mines. Following the deposed Amonhotep, Theban high priests are invariably generals, descendants of Libyan mercenaries. Piankh, the probable successor of Herihor, certainly was more actively engaged in a failed Nubian reconquest than in theological matters. Characteristically, it is only his title of general that appears on the address of a letter sent from the administrators of the Theban necropolis that bears witness to the instigation of a new official policy for replacing lost finances: the systematic plundering of older tombs. Part of a now-dispersed archive of correspondence known collectively as the "Late Ramesside Letters," letter 28 derives from the fortified mortuary temple of Rameses III at Medinet Habu that housed the necropolis administration under the senior scribes Thutmose, known also as Tcharoy, and his son, Butehamon.

After customary greetings to the general on campaign in Nubia and discussion of the delivery of clothing for the war effort, the workmen note their compliance with Piankh's unprecedented request to uncover an ancient tomb and preserve it intact for his arrival. The ominous implications of the letter are strengthened by Piankh's personal correspondence (letters 21, 34, and 35) with Thutmose, his own agent, and Herihor's widow Nodjmet, termed "our mistress" by the workmen, ordering that two snooping policemen "be placed in two baskets and thrown into the river at night—but do not let anyone in the land find out!"

For the text and translations, see Wente 1990, 194–95 (and cf. 183–84); 1967b, 59–65; Černý 1939, 44–48a; 1973, 364; and Reeves and Wilkinson

1996, 204–5. See Kitchen 1986, 19 §16 and 253 §211. For the relative positions of Herihor and Piankh, see Kitchen 1995, xiv–xvii §§A-K.

t3y ḫwy ny-sw.t ḥr wnmy sš ny-sw.t ỉmy-r3 mšꜥ ḥm-nṯr tp(y) n ʾImn-Rꜥ
(2) [ny-sw.t nṯr.w] s3 [ny-sw.t] n Kš ỉmy-[r3] ḫ3s.w[t] rsy.w(t) ỉmy-r3 šnw.
wt n šnw.wt Pr-ꜥ3 ꜥnḫ wd3 snb (3) [ḥ3.wty P3y-]ꜥnḫ n pd.wt Pr-ꜥ3 ꜥnḫ wd3
snb (m) p3 ꜥ3 2 n ỉs.t sš Bw-th3(4)-ʾI[m]n n pr (= p3) [ḫ]r s3w [K3r3 n3 rmṯ.
w ỉs.t]

m ꜥnḫ wd3 snb m ḥs.t ʾImn-Rꜥ ny-sw.t nṯr.w tw.n dd n ʾImn-Rꜥ (5) ny-
sw.t nṯr.w Mw.t Ḫ[n]sw nṯr.w nb.w W3s.t P3-Rꜥ-Ḥr-3ḫ.ty m wbn꞊f m ḥtp꞊f
n ʾImn (6) ḫnm nḥḥ¹ ḥnꜥ psd.t꞊f n3 Ḥmny.w ꜥ3y.w špsy {r-}nty ḥtp (m) Ḫft-
ḥr-nb꞊s² Mr꞊s-gr.t (7) ḥnw.t ʾImnt.t n3 nṯr.w n p3 t3 {r-}nty tw꞊k m-ḫnw꞊f
ỉmy n꞊k ꜥnḫ wd3 snb ꜥḥꜥ(w) q3 ỉ3w.t ꜥ3.t (8) nfr.t ỉmy n꞊k ḥs[.wt qnw.(t)
ꜥš3.(t) m-b3ḥ] ʾIm[n]-Rꜥ [n]y-sw.t nṯr.w p[3]y꞊[k] nb ꜥnḫ wd3 snb mtw ỉmn
ỉn꞊k (9) ỉw꞊k wd3.tỉ mtw꞊k mḫ qn꞊k m Nỉw.t mtw꞊n mḫ ỉr.t꞊n m ptr꞊k
ỉw꞊k ỉy.tỉ ꜥnḫ wd3 snb rꜥ nb sp-2

(10) ḥnꜥ dd sdm꞊n md.w nb ỉ-h3b n꞊n p3y꞊n nb ḥr-r꞊w p3 h3b ỉ-ỉr.tw
n꞊n (11) t3y šꜥ.t m dr.t Ḥrỉ p3 Šrdn p3y šms n p3y꞊n nb ỉw sš Bw-th3-ʾImn
(12) d3ỉ ỉw꞊f šsp꞊s n꞊f m tpy šmw (sw) 18 ỉw꞊ỉ twt p3 ꜥ3 2 n ỉs.t sš Bw-
th3-ʾImn s3w K3r3 (13) n3 rmṯ.w ỉs.t pr (= p3) ḫr ỉw꞊ỉ ꜥḥꜥ m-ḫnw꞊w ỉw꞊ỉ
ꜥš꞊s n꞊w ỉw꞊w {r-}dd ỉry꞊n sp-2 (14) m p3 ỉ-dd p3y꞊n nb m p3y꞊w ꜥ3 m
p3y꞊w šrỉ ḥr wnn tw꞊ỉ (m) nꜥy m Nỉw.t (r) ỉn n3 (15) rmṯ.w {r-}nty ḥms.
w m-ỉm ỉw꞊ỉ gm rmṯ ỉs.t ʾImn-p3-nfr Ḥr-ʾImn-pnꜥ꞊f p3y rmṯ 2 (16) ỉ-wnw
dy r-q3r p3y꞊w nb m p3 t3 rsy ỉw꞊w {r-}dd n꞊ỉ tw꞊n ỉy.tỉ m p3y꞊n nb r-rdỉ
(17) ỉw꞊n r p3 nty tw꞊tn ỉm ỉw dỉ꞊f ỉn꞊n wꜥ.(t) šꜥ.t

ỉw sš Bw-th3-ʾImn šsp t3 šꜥ.t (18) ỉw꞊ỉ ꜥš n p3 ꜥ3 2 n ỉs.t p3y s3w n3 rmṯ.
w pr (= p3) ḫr {r-}nty (r)-ḫ3.t꞊w m p3y꞊w ꜥ3 m p3y꞊w šrỉ (19) ỉw꞊ỉ ꜥš꞊s
n꞊w ỉw꞊w dd ỉry꞊n sp-2 m p3 ỉ-dd p3y꞊n nb ỉw ỉ-ỉr t3y šꜥ.t spr r-r꞊n m
(20) {m} tpy šmw sw 20

ḥr sdm꞊n p3 h3b ỉ-ỉr n꞊n p3y꞊n nb r-dd m-ỉr nny m p3y šḫn ỉ(21)n꞊f
m p3y꞊n nb mtw꞊f tm³ dd ỉḫ m p3 sḫr n h3b ỉ-ỉr꞊(ỉ) n꞊tn ḥr{y}-ḫ3.t ỉw꞊ỉ
m ḫnty (22) r-dd ỉmy ỉn.tw nhy (n) n3 ḥbs.w gm ỉ-ỉr꞊tn dỉ ỉw꞊w m-s3꞊ỉ
ỉw꞊ỉ wd.k(wỉ) ỉn꞊f m p3y꞊n nb

(23) ỉst bw-ỉr sš Dḥwty-ms n pr (= p3) ḫr {r-}dd n꞊k smỉ m p3 w3ḥ
(<wḥ3) ỉ-ỉr꞊n ꜥq3ỉ ỉw꞊n tm (24) gm 3s ỉw꞊f ḫpr mt n꞊f m-d3ỉ (<m-dr)
pḥ꞊n Nỉw.t m-d3ỉ (<m-dr) dd꞊w n꞊f tw꞊k wd.(tw) ỉw bw-ỉr.t꞊n (25) pḥ
t3y꞊n ḥnw.t ỉw꞊s dd n sš T3r3y⁴ n p3 ḫr r-dd dd꞊f⁵ n꞊k mỉ m-s3꞊ỉ ỉw꞊n
sw3d (= swd) n3 ḥbs.w (26) n t3y꞊n ḥnw.t ỉw꞊s dd n sš T3r3y (ỉ)n bn tw꞊k
m nꜥy ỉrm{꞊w} n3 ḥbs.w ḥr mntk ỉ-ỉr꞊k sw3d꞊[w] (= swd꞊w) (27) n p3y꞊k
nb ỉn꞊s n꞊f m t3y꞊n ḥnw.t

ḥr m-s3 wꜥ 10,000 n b3kỉ.w n p3y꞊n nb ỉw꞊w sdm n꞊f mỉ-qd꞊n (28)
y[3] tw꞊n [ꜥr]ꜥr šn.w nb n p3y꞊n nb tw꞊n s3w n꞊f bw-ỉr꞊n bꜥ⁶ m šn nb
(29) s3wy {r-}nty [tw]꞊n ỉr.t꞊w ḥr ỉr ʾImn-Rꜥ ny-sw.t nṯr.w p3y꞊k nb dỉ n꞊n

ḥs.t r-ḥr≠k m mît.t (vo. 1) înn bn î-îr≠n bȝk n≠k m îb ḫȝ.ty≠n îw≠n hȝb r rdî ʿȝm (<ʿm) pȝy≠n nb

(vo. 2) ky dd n rmṯ.w îs.t pr (= pȝ) ḥr ʿȝ špsy n nb≠n sdm≠n md.w nb î-hȝb n≠n (vo. 3) pȝy≠n nb ḫr-r≠w pȝ hȝb î-îr n≠n pȝy≠n nb r-dd ḥnw (t)n îr (vo. 4) n≠î wʿ šḥn îw bw-pwy≠tn šmⁿ⁷ n≠f ʿn mtw≠tn wȝḥ≠f (<wḫȝ≠f) î-îr.t≠(î) spr r-r≠tn (vo. 5) în≠f m pȝy≠n nb îry.[tw]≠f îḫ pȝ nty tw≠(t)n rḫ sw îw wn≠tn îm≠f ʿnⁿ⁸ î-wȝḥ sw n≠tn (vo. 6) m-îr ḥnw n≠f î[n]≠f m pȝy≠n nb

îr pȝy sšⁿ⁹ î-wn dy (r)-ḫȝ.t≠n îw mntf (vo. 7) pȝ nty dî îw≠f rḫ wʿ ḥyⁿ¹⁰ îw≠f m rmṯ ʿȝ îw mtr s(w) pȝy≠f ît sw îrm≠k (vo. 8) ḥr wnn≠f wȝḥ tȝ mtr.(t) m-bȝḥ≠n m-rȝ-ʿ îw≠n îr šȝʿ 10 n hȝrw r 20 îw≠f (vo. 9) ptr wʿ ḥy m mn.t î-îr.t≠f gm

ḥr ptr hȝ(vo. 10)b≠k r-dd wn wʿ s.t m nȝ s.wt ḫȝ.tyw mtw≠tn sȝw tȝy≠s ḫtm.(t) î-îr.t≠(î) (vo. 11) îy în≠f (m) pȝy≠n nb tw≠n îr šḥn.w î-îr≠n dî gm≠k sw wȝḥ (vo. 12) grg.tw pȝ nty tw≠n rḫ sw mtw≠k wd sš Tȝrȝy n pr (= pȝ) ḥr r rdî îw≠f ptr(vo. 13)≠f n≠n wʿ ḥy yȝ tw≠n dî šm îw≠n ḫtḫt îw bw rḫ≠n s.t rd.wy(vo. 14)≠n

ḥr îry n≠k ʾImn-Rʿ ny-sw.t nṯr.w nfr nb bn îw≠k ȝty m (n)kt îw≠î hȝb r rdî (vo. 15) ʿ[ȝm] (<ʿm) pȝy≠n nb m-dr.t Mdȝî Hȝd-nḫt n pȝ ḥr m tpy šmw sw 29

(vo. 16) pȝ îmy-rȝ mšʿ n Pr-ʿȝ ʿnḫ wdȝ snb (m) n(ȝ) ḥnty.w n pr (= pȝ) ḥr

To the royal fanbearer on the righthand side, the royal scribe, general, and First Prophet of Amon-Re, (2) [King of the Gods,] the [King's] Son of Cush, Overseer of southern foreign lands, granary overseer of the granaries of Pharaoh, l.p.h., (3) [the leader] of the archery troops of Pharaoh, l.p.h., [Pi]ankh, from the two foremen of the construction crew, the necropolis scribe Bute(4)hamon, the guard [Kar, and the men of the construction crew]:

"In life, prosperity, and health! In the favor of Amon-Re, King of the Gods! We say each and every day to Amon-Re, (5) King of the Gods, to Mut, Khonsu, and all the gods of Thebes, to Pre-Horachty at his rising and at his setting, to Amon, (6) United with Eternity,[1] together with his Ennead, to the great and noble Ogdoad who rest in Khefet-her-nebes,[2] to Merseger, (7) Mistress of the West, and to the gods of the land in which you are: 'Give to you life, prosperity, and health, a long lifetime and an advanced and goodly old age! (8) Give to you many numerous favors in the presence of Amon-Re, King of the Gods, your lord, l.p.h.! And may Amon bring you back (9) safe, and you fill your embrace with Thebes, and we fill our eyes with the sight of you, when you have returned, alive, prosperous, and healthy!'

(10) And further: We have heeded all matters concerning which our lord has sent word to us. Regarding our having been sent (11) this letter by the hand of Hori the Sherden, this attendant of our lord, the scribe Butehamon (12) crossed over and he received it from him in the first month of summer, day 18. And I assembled the two foremen of the construction crew, the scribe Butehamon, the guard Kar, (13) and the men of the construction crew of the royal tomb, and I stood among them, and I read it aloud to them. Then they said, "We shall act, we shall act (14) in accordance with that which our lord has said!" including both their eldest and their youngest. Now I was going from Thebes bringing back the (15) men who were staying there, and I found the crewmen Amonpanefer and Heramonpenaf, these two men (16) who had been there beside their lord in the southland. Then they said to me: "We have returned. It is our lord who has caused (17) us to come to the place where you are, having had us bring a letter."

Then the scribe Butehamon received the letter. I called out to the two foremen of the construction crew, this guard and the men of the royal tomb who were under their authority, including both their eldest and their youngest. (19) I read it aloud to them, and they said, "We shall act, we shall act in accordance with that which our lord has said!" while it was in the (20) first month of summer, day 20, that this letter reached us.

Now we have heeded the task that our lord has assigned to us, saying: "Do not be lax in this commission!" So said (21) our lord. And he should not[3] say: "What is the status of the task that I assigned to you previously when I was going southward, (22) saying: 'Have some of the readily found cloth brought. When I have departed, you should send them after me'?" So said our lord.

(23) Cannot the necropolis scribe Thutmose report to you about our having searched for a transport ship? We did not (24) find one quickly, and he was about to die when we reached Thebes and when he was told that you had departed before we had (25) reached our mistress. And she spoke to the necropolis scribe Tcharoy,[4] saying "He[5] said to you: 'Come after me!'" And we delivered the clothing (26) to our mistress, and she said to the scribe Tcharoy: "Are you not going with the clothing? Now you are the one who should deliver [them] (27) to your lord." So our mistress said to him.

Now even beyond a myriad of servants of our lord who heed him like us, (28) we really carry out all the commissions of our lord. We are attentive to him. Do we not respect[6] every commission (29) of his that we perform? Now Amon-Re, King of the Gods, your lord, will grant favor to us in your sight accordingly. (vo. 1) If it is not in accordance with the desire of our hearts that we work for you, we shall send word to inform our lord.

(vo. 2) Another statement of the men of the construction crew of the great and noble royal tomb to our lord: We have heeded every matter concerning which (vo. 3) our lord has sent word to us. Regarding our lord's having sent word to us, saying: "May you go and perform (vo. 4) for me a construction task that you have never yet attempted,[7] and you should seek it out until I reach you," (vo. 5) so said our lord, just what does it mean, "the one that you know, since you have been in it already"?[8] "Leave it alone! (vo. 6) Do not tamper with it." So said our lord.

As for this scribe[9] who used to be here in charge of us, whereas he is (vo. 7) the one who can provide it, knowing a marker[10] and being a prominent man whose father has vouched for him, he is with you. (vo. 8) Now when he has placed the evidence before us also, we shall spend from 10 to 20 days while he looks for a marker daily until he finds one.

Now look, you have sent word to us, saying: "Uncover a tomb among the ancestral tombs and preserve its seal until I return." So said our lord. We are performing commissions. We shall cause that you find it left alone (vo. 12) and ready—the one that we know. And you should dispatch the necropolis scribe Tcharoy to have him come that he might look (vo. 13) for a marker for us. Really, we are setting out and going astray, since we do not know where to put our feet. (vo. 14)

Now may Amon-Re, King of the Gods, do everything good for you. You will not lack for anything. And I have sent word to (vo. 15) inform our lord by the hand of the necropolis policeman Hadnakht in the first month of summer, day 29.

Address: (vo. 16) The general of Pharaoh, l.p.h., from the captains of the necropolis.

NOTES

1. Amon of Medinet Habu.

2. "She who is before her lord," an area of western Thebes including the Dynasty XVIII temple of the Ogdoad at Medinet Habu. For discussion, see Nims 1955, 113 and 118.

3. In this and the following paragraph, the workmen protest that Piankh should not berate them about the clothing shipment since that duty was reassigned to Thutmose, who is now with the general in Nubia.

4. A nickname of the necropolis scribe Thutmose mentioned at the beginning of the paragraph.

5. Piankh.

6. Or "We do not reject any commission of his that we perform." For the rare term bˤ, see Wente 1967a, 63 n. y.

7. Literally, "to go on/for" a task; cf. the Demotic Instructions of 'Onchsheshonqy, col. 12/21.

8. In indignant protest, the workers ask why Piankh has suggested that they have already entered a tomb that they know and need to be reminded not to dis-

turb it. The tomb that they know is again mentioned in vo. 12, where it is stressed that it remains unviolated.

9. The workers are referring to the necropolis scribe Thutmose/Tcharoy.

10. Formerly translated as "inspector," the term ḥy has been reinterpreted as a testimonial document or physical marker; see Groll 1974, 171.

B. PINEDJEM I, HIGH PRIEST OF AMON AND KING

22. THEBAN GRAFFITI OF HIGH PRIEST PINEDJEM I

Expanding upon the pretensions of his predecessors Herihor and Piankh, the Theban pontiff and generalissimo Pinedjem I steadily acquired the epithets, trappings, and ultimately the full titulary of pharaonic status. In perhaps his earliest record, he invokes his deceased father in company with his four brothers on a scene in Luxor temple. A later graffito on the same wall depicts him officiating before the Theban triad. Although he is still entitled "First Prophet of Amon," his accompanying three daughters are styled "bodily daughter of the king," with the eldest daughter's name enclosed within a royal cartouche and both elder siblings called "Lady of the Two Lands." Pinedjem's mother is cited in a further, unfortunately damaged, inscription on a column from the same temple. At neighboring Karnak, Pinedjem reinscribed the sphinxes along the processional entrance to the temple, adopting the exclusively royal epithet "lord of ritual performance" and boasting that his works exceeded those of any king.

I. COMMEMORATION OF THE DECEASED PIANKH

Luxor forecourt of Rameses II, eastern end of the south wall (Nelson Key Plans A 81a). For the texts and translations, see Daressy 1892, 32–33; Gauthier 1914, 3:245; Taylor 1998, 1145, and Porter and Moss 1927–51, 2:307, §27.III.1; Chicago Oriental Institute photo 9216. See Kitchen 1986, 41–42 §37, 257–58 §215.

Four Men Adore Amon, behind Whom Stands Nodjmet, Wife of the Deceased High Priest and King Herihor

dwȝ.t n ʾImn-Rᶜ ḫnty [ʾIp.t-sw.t] n kȝ n [ḥm-ntr tp(y)] n ʾImn-Rᶜ ny-sw.t ntr.w wp tȝ.wy hȝw.ty Pȝ(y)-ᶜnḫ ir.n sȝ≠f sᶜnḫ rn≠f imy-rȝ ní.wt tȝty ḥm-ntr tp(y) n ʾImn-Rᶜ ny-sw.t ntr.w imy-rȝ mšᶜ wr n tȝ dr≠f hȝw.ty[1] Pȝ(y)-ndm sȝ≠f ḥm-ntr 2-nw ʾImn Ḥqȝ-nfr mȝᶜ-ḫrw sȝ≠f stm m ḥw.t-ny-sw.t Ḥqȝ-mȝᶜ. t[2] mȝᶜ-ḫrw sȝ≠f imy-rȝ iḥ imy-rȝ pr wr ʾImn ḥm-ntr n Mw.t ᶜnḫ≠f-(n)-Mw.t mȝᶜ-ḫrw

Adoration to Amon-Re, Foremost of [Karnak,] for the *ka*-spirit of [the First Prophet] of Amon-Re, King of the Gods, who judges the Two Lands,

the leader, Piankh, made by his son who causes his name to live, the overseer of the city and vizier, the First Prophet of Amon-Re, King of the Gods,
the great general of the entire land, the leader,[1] Pinedjem, together with
his son, the Second Prophet of Amon, Hekanefer, the justified, together
with his son, the *setem*-priest in Medinet Habu, Hekamaat,[2] the justified,
together with his son, the overseer of cattle, the great steward of Amon
and the prophet of Mut, Ankhefenmut, the justified.

Label for Amon

ʾImn-Rˁ ny-sw.t nṯr.w ʾImn m ỉn.t dỉ≠f ˁḥˁ [qȝỉ m-ẖnw] Wȝs.t (n) nb.t
pr wr ẖnr.t [n.t] ʾImn Ndm.t

Amon-Re, King of the Gods, Amon in the Valley. May he grant [a long]
lifetime [within] Thebes to the lady of the house, the chief of the musical
troupe [of] Amon, Nodjmet.

II. Pinedjem and His Three Daughters Adore the Theban Triad

Luxor forecourt of Rameses II, eastern end of the south wall (Nelson
Key Plans A 70a). For the texts and translations, see Epigraphic Survey
1998, 52–54 and pls. 199–200; Daressy 1892, 3:32–33; Gauthier 1914, 245;
Wente 1967b, 167–68; Gardiner 1962, 68–69; and Porter and Moss 1927–51,
2:307, §27.III.2; Chicago Oriental Institute photo 9168. See Kitchen 1986, 45
§40, 55 §46, and 257–58 §215.

Label for Enthroned Amon

ʾImn-Rˁ ms sw ḏs≠f nṯr [ˁȝ] (2) dỉ.n≠(ỉ) n≠k qny nb nḫt nb (3) dỉ.n≠(ỉ)
n≠k ˁnḫ ḏd wȝs snb nb

Amon, who bore himself, the [great] god. (2) "Thus I have given to
you all valor and all victory. (3) Thus I have given to you all life, stability,
dominion, and all health."

Label for Ithyphallic Amon

ʾImn-[Rˁ] kȝ-[mw.t≠f ḫnt(y)] (2) ỉp.t≠f (3) ʾImn-Rˁ [ḫnt(y)] ʾIp.t-sw.t

Amon-[Re], Ka[mutef, Foremost of] (2) his Opet. (3) Amon-Re, [Fore-
most of] Karnak.

Label for Mut

Mw.t wr.t nb.(t) (2) ʾIšrw ỉr.t Rˁ (3) ḥnw.t nṯr.w nb.w

Mut the great, the Lady of (2) Asheru, the eye of Re, (3) the Mistress
of all the gods.

Label for Khonsu

Ḫnsw m (2) Wȝs.t Nfr-ḥtp nṯr ˁȝ (3) [ḥry-ỉb] ʾI[p.t-sw].t

Khonsu (2) in Thebes, Neferhotep, the great god, (3) resident in Karnak.

Label for Pinedjem I
îry-pꜥ.t ḥr(y)-tp tꜣ.wy ḥm-ntr tp(y) n ʾImn-Rꜥ (2) ny-sw.t ntr.w Pꜣy-ndm mꜣꜥ-ḫrw sꜣ Pꜣy-ꜥnḫ mꜣꜥ-ḫrw (3) îr.t sntr qbḥw n ʾImn-Rꜥ nb ns.wt tꜣ.wy
The Hereditary Prince and superior of the Two Lands, the First Prophet of Amon-Re, (2) King of the Gods, Pinedjem, the justified, son of Piankh, the justified. (3) Censing and making a libation for Amon-Re, Lord of the Thrones of the Two Lands.

Label for Maatkare (A)
sꜣ.t ny-sw.t n.(t) ẖ.t≠f mrî.(t)≠f ḥm.t-ntr (2) n.(t) ʾImn nb.(t) tꜣ.wy Mꜣꜥ.t-kꜣ-Rꜥ
The bodily daughter of the king, his beloved, the God's Wife (2) of Amon and Lady of the Two Lands, Maatkare.

Label for Henuttawy (B)
sꜣ.t ny-sw.t n.(t) ẖ.t≠f mrî.(t)≠f (2) šmꜥ(y).t n.(t) ʾImn-Rꜥ ny-sw.t ntr.w nb.(t) tꜣ.wy (3) Ḥnw.t-tꜣ.wy mꜣꜥ.t-ḫrw
The bodily daughter of the king, his beloved, (2) the chantress of Amon-Re, King of the Gods, the Lady of the Two Lands, (3) Henuttawy, the justified.

Label for Nedjemmut
sꜣ.t ny-sw.t n.(t) ẖ.t≠f mrî.(t)≠f (2) ḥry.(t) ḫnr.t{îw} n.(t) ʾImn Nḏm-mw.t mꜣꜥ.t-ḫrw
The bodily daughter of the king, his beloved, (2) the chief of the musical troupe of Amon, Nedjemmut, the justified.

III. Luxor Second Court
Hieratic text about the shaft (not base) of the first northern column of western grouping (Nelson, Key Plans C 94). For the texts and translations, see Daressy 1910, 185; Gauthier 1914, 3:246; Taylor 1998, 1149–55; and Wente 1967b, 160. See Kitchen 1986, 45 §39, 53 §45, 257–58 §215, and 536 §438.

(1) ḥm-ntr tpy n ʾImn-Rꜥ ny-sw.t [ntr.w] Pꜣ(y)-ndm sꜣ (2) [ḥm-ntr] tpy n ʾImn-Rꜥ ny-sw.t ntr.[w] Pꜣ(y)-ꜥnḫ mw.t≠f (3) wr.(t) ḫnî[.t] n.(t) ʾImn [...] ꜥnḫ wdꜣ snb Ḥ[rr.t(?)]ꜣ (4) ḏd≠f [...]f [...]m tꜣy≠k [...]ny [...] smꜣꜥ (5) [...]
The First Prophet of Amon-Re, King of the [Gods], Pinedjem, son of (2) the First [Prophet] of Amon-Re, King of the Gods, Piankh, whose mother

is (3) the chief of the musical troupe of Amon [...] l.p.h., H[rere (B)],³ (4) who says: "[...] your [...] justify (5) [..]."

IV. KARNAK INSCRIPTIONS ADDED TO THE CRIOSPHINXES OF RAMESES II CONNECTING THE FIRST PYLON TO THE QUAY

For the texts and translations, see Barguet 1962, 42; Daressy 1892, 30; Gauthier 1914, 3:247; and Breasted 1906–7, 4:312 §635. See Kitchen 1986, 258 §215.

ꜥnḫ ḥm-nṯr tp(y) n ʾImn-Rꜥ ny-sw.t nṯr.w nb ỉr.(t) ḫ.t Pꜣy-nḏm sꜣ Pꜣy-ꜥnḫ ḏḏ≠f ỉnk wr mnw.w ꜥꜣ bỉꜣw.t m-ḫnw ʾIp.t-s.wt nb nḫt sꜥꜣ≠ỉ ʾImn wr r nṯr.w nb.w ỉr≠ỉ n≠f mnw.w ꜥꜣ.w wr.w m ḥḏ nbw ḫt ḥr rn≠ỉ n ḏ.t tꜣ pn q(ꜣỉ) r ꜣw≠f wsḫ≠f ỉmy ỉr n≠f s nb mỉ ỉr.n≠ỉ smn≠ỉ rn≠ỉ ḥr-tp tꜣ m-bꜣḥ ʾImn ỉnk ꜣḫ n kꜣ≠f r ḥḥ.w m sp n(n) ny-sw.t ỉrr ỉr.(t)≠ỉ

Long live the First Prophet of Amon-Re, King of the Gods, the lord of ritual performance, Pinedjem, son of Piankh, who says: "I am one who has grandiose monuments and great wonders within Karnak, a lord of victory. I have magnified Amon more greatly than all other gods. I have made great and magnificent monuments for him in silver and gold, engraved in my name forever. This land is exalted in its length and breadth. Let everyone act for him as I have done. I have established my name upon earth in the presence of Amon. I have been one who is beneficial to his *ka*-spirit more than millions of times. There is no king who has done what I have done."

NOTES

1. So Gauthier, copied ꜥꜣ.wy by Daressy. Confirmed by photo.
2. So Kitchen, copied Ḥqꜣ-ꜥꜣ by Daressy. Confirmed by photo.
3. For the proposed reading, see Kitchen 1986, 53 and 536; Bierbrier 1973, 311; and Taylor 1998, 1149–50; but cf. Jansen-Winkeln 1997, 59–60, who opted for an alternate reading Nḏm[.t].

23. PINEDJEM I—THE TRANSITION TO ROYAL STATUS (KARNAK STATUARY)

I. CAIRO JdE 42191

The notion of "priest-king" is well-illustrated by this kneeling figure of Pinedjem I, who is designated simply as high priest yet wears the royal *nemes*-headdress while offering two jugs in traditional royal posture. In year 16, Pinedjem would adopt not only the regalia but also the formal titles of royalty. The broken basalt statue, now lacking its base, measures 27 cm and was recovered in 1904 from the Karnak "cachette" of disused statuary. For the text, see Legrain 1909b, 60 and pl. LIII. See Kitchen 1986, 4 §2 n. 8, and 258 §215.

Inscription on Each Upper Arm of the King
ḥm-nṯr tp(y) n ʾImn Pȝy-nḏm sȝ Pȝy-ʿnḫ
The First Prophet of Amon, Pinedjem, son of Piankh.

II. Colossus Standing in the First Court of Karnak
    Often attributed to Rameses II, this colossus is inscribed for Pinedjem
I, in whose reign the abandoned Ramesside statue was completed. The
red granite colossus, which now measures about 11 m high, was discovered beneath collapsed stones of the Second Pylon. It depicts the king in
the form of a crowned Osiris holding the crook and flail, while a smaller
figure of a queen stands before him between his legs. Under the pedestal,
an original cartouche of Rameses II was usurped by Rameses VI, above
which Pinedjem added his own inscription. For the texts and translations,
see Habachi 1972, 16–20 and pl. 2; and Barguet 1962, 55. See Kitchen 1986,
257–58 §215 and 570 §498.

Below Base
    ḥm-nṯr tp(y) n ʾImn-Rʿ (2) ny-sw.t nṯr.w Pȝ(y)-nḏm sȝ Pȝ(y)-ʿnḫ
    The First Prophet of Amon-Re, (2) King of the Gods, Pinedjem, son
of Piankh.

West Side of Base
    [...] n ît≠(î) ʾImn n mrw.t sʿnḫ rn≠î m pr≠f [...]
    [...] for my father Amon through the desire to make my name live in
his estate [...]

East Side of Base
    [ʾImn]-Rʿ [ḫnty] ʾIp.t-sw.t îr.ty ny-sw.t n tȝ pn [...]≠f [î]w≠f [...]î nb
[...]
    [Amon]-Re, [Foremost] of Karnak, the two eyes of the king in this land
[...]

Fecundity Figures on Base (composite text)
    ḏd-mdw în≠(î) [n≠k ... ḥm-nṯr tp(y) n] (2) ʾImn-Rʿ [...] (3) Pȝ(y)-nḏm
sȝ Pȝy-[ʿnḫ ...]
    Recitation: "[To you] I have brought [... the First Prophet of] (2) Amon-
Re, [...] (3) Pinedjem, son of Pi[ankh ...]."

Dorsal Pillar Flanking Inscriptions beneath a Scene of Pinedjem Offering
to the Enthroned Amon (composite text)
    ʿnḫ ḥm-nṯr tp(y) n ʾImn-Rʿ ny-sw.t nṯr.w Pȝy-nḏm sȝ ḥm-nṯr tp(y) n
ʾImn-Rʿ ny-sw.t nṯr.w Pȝy-ʿnḫ mȝʿ-ḫrw m dî.t ʾImn ḏs≠f îr.n≠f m mnw n
ît≠f ʾImn-Rʿ nb ns.wt tȝ.wy [...]

Long live the First Prophet of Amon-Re, King of the Gods, Pinedjem, son of the First Prophet of Amon-Re, King of the Gods, Piankh, the justi-fied, as granted by Amon himself. As a monument for his father Amon-Re, Lord of the Thrones of the Two Lands, he made [...]

24. THE REBURIAL OF ROYAL MUMMIES UNDER PINEDJEM I

From year 6 of Smendes through year 8 of Pseusennes I, the high priest—and later king—Pinedjem I was actively engaged in the "renewal" of New Kingdom royal burials. Rewrapped mummies, deprived of expen-sive tomb furnishings and all gilt decoration, were deposited in collective caches in the tombs of Seti I (KV 17), Amonhotep II (KV 35), and the crag-tomb of Queen Inhapi, wife of Seqenenre-Tao II of Dynasty XVII (perhaps WN A "Bab el-Muallaq"). Approximately sixty years after Pinedjem, the Seti burials were transferred to the Inhapi cache (year 10 of Siamon), and some forty years even later (after year 11 of Sheshonq I) this consolidated grouping was moved for a final time to the family tomb of the high priest Pinedjem II (DB 320). Here they rested until their discovery by grave rob-bers in 1881.

The "re-Osirification" of the nobility of the empire may have been motivated by more than the purely pious concerns traditionally invoked. With the loss of Nubian gold mines, the older royal tombs became verita-ble "bank deposits" for contemporary authorities. Pinedjem's constructions were perhaps financed by "recycled" treasure, and his own burial cer-tainly benefited from the appropriation of ancient equipment. The use of treasurers as inspection agents is probably not without significance. A rep-resentative selection of docket notations from DB 320 is presented here. All are hieratic inscriptions written on the wooden coffins or linen bandages of the royal mummies.

For the history and interpretations of the royal burials, see Jansen-Winkeln 1995b, 62–78; Kitchen 1995, xvii–xix; and Reeves and Wilkinson 1996, 194–207.

I. Pinedjem I as Theban High Priest until Year 15 of Smendes

For the texts and translations, see Maspero 1889, 545–46 (fig. 14), 536–37 (fig. 8), 563–64 (fig. 19), and 560 (fig. 18); Reeves 1990, 229–30 and 234–35; Thomas 1966, 249 §4a–b, 250 §§7–8, and 262 nn. 11–13 and 17–26; Kees 1964, 24; and Breasted 1906–7, 4:312–14 §§637–38, 640 and 642 (wrongly dated year 17). See Kitchen 1986, 257 §215; 418 §381, 9–10; 419 §382, 25–26 (wrongly R. III); and 587 §535.

The Mummy of King Thutmose II of Dynasty XVIII (linen docket)

ḥsb.t 6.(t) ꜣbd 3 pr.t sw 7 hrw pn wḏ.n ḥm-nṯr tpy n ʾImn-Rꜥ ny-sw.t
nṯr.w Pꜣy-nḏm sꜣ n ḥm-nṯr tp(y) n ʾImn Pꜣy-ꜥnḫ ỉmy-rꜣ pr-ḫd wr Pꜣy-nfr-ḥr
(2) r wḥm smꜣw-(tꜣ)[1] n ny-sw.t ꜥꜣ-(ḫpr)-n-Rꜥ ꜥnḫ wḏꜣ snb

Regnal year 6, month 3 of winter, day 7. On this day, the First Prophet
of Amon-Re, King of the Gods, Pinedjem, son of the First Prophet of Amon,
Piankh, dispatched the chief treasurer Pineferher (2) to renew the interment[1] of King Aa(kheper)enre, l.p.h.

The Mummy of King Amonhotep I of Dynasty XVIII (coffin docket)

ḥsb.t 6.(t) ꜣbd 4 pr.t sw 7 hrw pn ỉw wḏ.n ḥm-nṯr tpy n ʾImn-Rꜥ ny-
sw.t nṯr.w Pꜣy-nḏm sꜣ n ḥm-nṯr tp(y) (n) ʾImn {Pꜣy-nḏm sꜣ}[2] Pꜣy-ꜥnḫ (2) r
wḥm qrs n ny-sw.t Ḏsr-kꜣ-Rꜥ sꜣ Rꜥ ʾImn-ḥtp ꜥnḫ wḏꜣ snb ỉn ỉmy-rꜣ pr-ḫd
Pꜣ[y-nfr-ḥr(?)]

Regnal year 6, month 4 of winter, day 7. On this day, the First Prophet
of Amon-Re, King of the Gods, Pinedjem, son of the First Prophet of
Amon, {Pinedjem, son of}[2] Piankh, issued a dispatch (2) to renew the burial
of King Djeserkare, the Son of Re, Amonhotep, l.p.h., by the treasurer
Pi[neferher (?)].

The Mummy of King Rameses III of Dynasty XX (linen docket)

ḥsb.t 13.(t)[3] ꜣbd 2 šmw sw 27 hrw pn ỉw wḏ.n ḥm-nṯr tpy n (2) ʾImn-Rꜥ
ny-sw.t nṯr.w Pꜣy-nḏm sꜣ n ḥm-nṯr tpy n ʾImn Pꜣy-ꜥnḫ (3) sš ḥw.t-nṯr Ḏsr-
sw-Ḥnsw sš m s.t Mꜣꜥ.t[4] Bw-thꜣ-ʾImn (4) r rdỉ.t Wsỉr[5] (n) ny-sw.t Wsr-Mꜣꜥ.
t-Rꜥ-mrỉ-ʾImn ꜥnḫ wḏꜣ snb mn wꜣḥ ḏ.t

Regnal year 13,[3] month 2 of summer, day 27. On this day, the First
Prophet of (2) Amon-Re, King of the Gods, Pinedjem, son of the First
Prophet of Amon, Piankh, dispatched (3) the temple scribe Djesersuk-
honsu and the necropolis[4] scribe Butehamon (4) to give Osiris-status[5] to
King Usermaatre-meriamon, l.p.h., with the result that he remains and
endures forever.

The Second Reburial of King Rameses II of Dynasty XIX (linen docket)

ḥsb.t 15.(t)[6] ꜣbd 3 ꜣḫ.t[7] sw 6 hrw n ỉn.(t) Wsỉr (2) ny-sw.t Wsr-Mꜣꜥ.t-
Rꜥ-stp-n-Rꜥ ꜥnḫ wḏꜣ snb (r) wḥm≠f r (3) qꜣ(r)ỉs≠f (m) pꜣ ḥr n Wsỉr ny-sw.t
(4) Mn-Mꜣꜥ.t-Rꜥ Sty ꜥnḫ wḏꜣ snb ỉn ḥm-nṯr tp(y) n ʾImn (5) Pꜣy-nḏm

Regnal year 15,[6] month 3 of Inundation,[7] day 6. The day of bringing
the Osiris, (2) King Usermaatre-setepenre, l.p.h., to renew him and to (3)
bury him in the royal tomb of the Osiris, King (4) Menmaatre Seti (I), l.p.h.,
by the First Prophet of Amon, (5) Pinedjem.

II. Pinedjem as King in Year 16 of Smendes

This docket, added directly beneath that of year 6 of Smendes, indicates an abrupt change in the titulary of Pinedjem I, who is now "king" while his son Masaharta (A) has inherited his father's former office of Theban pontiff. For the text and translation, see Maspero 1889, 536–37 (fig. 8); Reeves 1990, 236; Thomas 1966, 251 §14 and 263 nn. 34–35; Breasted 1906–7, 4:315 §647. See Kitchen 1986, 258 §216 and 419 §383, 27.

The Second Reburial of King Amonhotep I (coffin docket).

ḥsb.t 16.(t) 3bd 4 pr.t sw 11 ỉw wḏ.n ḥm-nṯr tpy n ᵓImn-Rᶜ ny-sw.t nṯr. w M3s3h3r3tỉ s3 n (2) ny-sw.t P3y-nḏm r wḥm qrs n nṯr pn ỉn sš pr-ḥḏ sš ḥw.t-nṯr Pn-ᵓImn s3 Swty-ms

Regnal year 16, month 4 of winter, day 11. The First Prophet of Amon-Re, King of the Gods, Masaharta, son of (2) King Pinedjem, issued a dispatch to renew the burial of this god by the treasury scribe and temple scribe, Penamon, son of Sutymes.

III. Pinedjem I as King under Pseusennes I

Adopting the regnal years of the Tanite ruler Pseusennes I, this linen docket records the latest attestation of Pinedjem I, buried soon thereafter in a former coffin of Tuthmosis I "recycled" for contemporary nobility. For the texts and translations, see Maspero 1889, 534 (fig. 7) and 538 (fig. 9); Reeves 1990, 236; Thomas 1966, 250 §12a–b and 263 nn. 29–30; Kees 1964, 24; and Breasted 1906–7, 4:314–15 §§645–46. See Kitchen 1986, 77–78 §62 (for the attribution of the regnal date to Pseusennes I), 262 §219, and 420 §386.

The Mummy of King Ahmose I, Founder of Dynasty XVIII (linen docket)

ḥsb.t 8.(t) 3bd 3 pr.t sw 29 ỉw wḏ.n ny-sw.t bỉ.ty nb t3.wy Ḫpr-ḫᶜ-Rᶜ-stp-n-ᵓImn ᶜnḫ wḏ3 snb (2) P3y-nḏm mry-ᵓImn ᶜnḫ wḏ3 snb r rdỉ.t Wsỉr n Wsỉr ny-sw.t Nb-pḥ.(ty)-Rᶜ ᶜnḫ wḏ3 snb

Regnal year 8, month 3 of winter, day 29. The King of Upper and Lower Egypt, Lord of the Two Lands, Kheperkhare-setepenamon, l.p.h., (2) Pinedjem, beloved of Amon, l.p.h., issued a dispatch to give Osiris-status to the Osiris, King Nebpehtyre, l.p.h.

The Mummy of Prince Siamon, Son of King Ahmose I (linen docket)

ḥsb.t 8.(t) 3bd 3 pr.t sw 29 ỉw wḏ.n ḥm≠f ᶜnḫ wḏ3 snb (2) r rdỉ.t Wsỉr n s3 ny-sw.t S3-ᵓImn

Regnal year 8, month 3 of winter, day 29. His Majesty, l.p.h., issued a dispatch (2) to give Osiris-status to the Prince Siamon.

NOTES

1. Read sm3 qrs by Thomas. See Reeves 1990, 230.
2. Dittography.
3. Misread as year 14 by Maspero.
4. "The Place of Maat," Deir el-Medina and the Theban necropolis.
5. For the expression, see Reeves 1990, 230.
6. Misread as year 17 by Maspero, followed by Breasted.
7. Misread as pr.t by Maspero.

25. THE ATTAINMENT OF ROYALTY: THE VOTIVE STELA OF WENNEFER, PRIEST OF COPTOS (CAIRO JdE 71902)

Unambiguous evidence of Pinedjem's adoption of royal status is afforded by a private stela that derives from Coptos, proof also of the acceptance of his kingship beyond the narrow confines of Thebes. On the obverse, Pinedjem I is depicted with full pharaonic regalia and titulary followed by his wife, Queen Henuttawy (A). Pinedjem offers incense and a libation to a standing figure of Osiris, while Henuttawy raises a sistrum in adoration. Pinedjem is given a proper prenomen and nomen within cartouches, and no mention is made of his office of Theban high priest. On the reverse, the lunette is divided into two registers, with the kneeling Wennefer depicted in flanking scenes adoring the solar bark above addorsed scenes of the priest before Osiris, Anubis, and Thoth (left) and his father before the Coptite triad (right). A unique biographical text details Wennefer's training, career, and ritual responsibilities. The exceptional prominence of Osiris reflects the "Osirification" of the local cult. Acquired by the Cairo Museum in 1939, the limestone stela of Wennefer measures 121.5 by 95 by 13 cm, with the loss of its lower portion. The stela was recut from an earlier New Kingdom private monument belonging to a military commander, and traces of the original text remain on the thickness.

For the texts and translation, see Abdallah 1984, 65–72 and pls. XVI–XVII; and Iversen 1996, 213–14. See Kitchen 1986, 259 §216 n. 88; 570 §498; 1995, xv.

I. Front

A. Labels

Label for Osiris, King, and Queen
Wsîr nb nḥḥ ḥr(y)-îb (2) Gbtyw (3) dî≠f pr.t-ḥrw (m) t ḥnq.t k3.[w] 3pd.w [ḥ].t nb.(t) nfr.t w‘b.t (4) (n) ntr nfr Ḫpr-ḫ‘-R‘-stp-[n]-'Imn (5) s3 R‘ P3y-nḏm mrî-'Imn (6) dî≠f t ḥnq.t k3.(w) 3pd.(w) sntr qbḥw (7) ḥ.t nb.t nfr.t w‘b.t r‘ nb (8) (n) s3.t ny-sw.t m3‘.t wr.t ḫnr.t (9) n 'Imn-R‘ ny-sw.t ntr.

w ḥry.(t) šps.wt ny-sw.t mw.t ny-sw.t (10) nb.t tȝ.wy dwȝ.t Ḥw.t-Ḥr Ḥnw. t-tȝ.wy (11) mȝꜥ.t-ḫrw

Osiris, Lord of eternity, resident in (2) Coptos. (3) May he give invocation offerings consisting of bread, beer, oxen, fowl, and everything good and pure (4) to the Good God Kheperkhare-setepenamon, (5) Son of Re, Pinedjem, beloved of Amon. (6) May he give bread, beer, oxen, fowl, incense, cool water, (7) and everything good and pure every day (8) to the genuine royal daughter, the chief of the musical troupe (9) of Amon-Re, King of the Gods, superior of the royal ladies, royal mother, (10) the Lady of the Two Lands, the votaress of Hathor, Henuttawy, (11) the justified.

Label for Scene
    îr.t snṯr qbḥw
    Censing and making a libation.

B. Main Text

(1) ḥtp dî ny-sw.t (n) Wsîr ḫnt(y) ʾImnt.t nb ȝbḏw Wn-nfr ḥqȝ ꜥnḫ.w nṯr ꜥȝ ḥr(y)-îb Gbtyw Ḥr-sȝ-ȝs.t (2) [ȝs.t wr.t] mw.[t] nṯr nb.t p.t ḥnw.t nṯr.w dî⸗sn pr.t-ḫrw (m) ḫȝ m t ḫȝ m ḥnq.t ḫȝ m kȝ.w ḫȝ m ȝpd.w ḫȝ m (3) [snṯr ḫȝ m qbḥw ...] ḫȝ m îrt.t ḫȝ m mrḥ.t nb.(t) ḫȝ m šs mnḫ.t ḫȝ m ḥtp.t (4) [...] ꜥȝ ny-sw.t nb [tȝ.wy] nb îr.t ḫ.t (5) [... Pȝy-nḏm ...] ȝbḏw(?)

An offering that the king gives to Osiris, Foremost of the West, Lord of Abydos, Onnophris, ruler of the living, the great god, resident in Coptos, and to Horus, son of Isis, and to (2) [Isis the great,] the God's Mother, the lady of heaven, the mistress of all the gods, so that they might give invocation offerings consisting of a thousand loaves of bread, a thousand jugs of beer, a thousand cuts of oxen, a thousand cuts of fowl, a thousand units of (3) [incense, a thousand jars of cool water, ...] a thousand jars of milk, a thousand jars of all kinds of oil, a thousand pieces of alabaster and clothing, a thousand bundles (4) [..] great [...] the king, Lord [of the Two Lands,] Lord of ritual performance, (5) [... Pinedjem ....] Abydos (?).

II. REVERSE

A. Upper Lunette

Label for Enthroned Amon-Re in Solar Bark
    ḥtp dî ny-sw.t n (2) ʾImn-Rꜥ Ḥr-ȝḫ.ty nṯr ꜥȝ nb p.t (3) ḥn ḥr Rꜥ (4) n nḥḥ nb ḥnky.t(?) (5) ḥnk [...] ḥpt⸗k (6) rꜥ nb îr (7) ȝbdw (8) mkt(?) nb [...] sd⸗k (9) n dd.t ḥr.(t) n kȝ n (10) ḥm-nṯr Wn-nfr sȝ ît-nṯr wꜥb-ꜥ.(wy) n Mnw (11) Mrl-ît⸗f(?)¹] mȝꜥ-ḫrw îr.(t).n Tȝ-rnn.(t) [...] n Mnw
    An offering that the king gives to (2) Amon-Re Horachty, the great god, lord of heaven. (3) Steering for Re (4) forever, the lord of the bier (?); (5)

offering [...] your oar (6) daily. May the (7) sacred *Abdju*-fish make (8) all protection (?) [...] conveying you, (9) that the sky gives to the *ka*-spirit of (10) the prophet Wennefer, son of the God's Father and pure-handed one of Min, (11) Mer[-itef(?)¹], the justified, borne by Tarenenet, the [...] of Min.

On the Prow of the Ship
ꜣs.t wr.(t) mw.t nṯr (2) Nb.t-ḥw.t
Isis the great, the God's Mother. (2) Nephthys.

Label for Thoth as Baboon on Prow
ḏd-mdw în Ḏḥwty nb nyny (2) nṯr ꜥꜣ îmy Ḥmnw (3) dî.(t) îꜣw.w n ḥr⸗k nfr
Recitation by Thoth, lord of greeting, (2) the great god who is in Hermopolis: (3) "Giving praises to your beautiful face."

Label for Wennefer
dwꜣ n ʾImn-Rꜥ Tm (2) Ḥr-[ꜣḫ.ty] ḏꜣ(î) p.t n kꜣ n (3) ḥm-nṯr 2-nw n Mnw Wn(4)-nfr mꜣꜥ-ḫrw
Adoration of Amon-Re Atum (2) Hor[achty], who crosses the heaven, for the *ka*-spirit of (3) the Second Prophet of Min, Wen(4)nefer, the justified.

B. Lower Register

Lefthand Scene

Label for Osiris
ḥtp dî ny-sw.t n Wsîr (2) ḫnty (3) ʾImnt.t nb nḥḥ (4) ḥqꜣ ḏ.t
An offering that the king gives to Osiris, (2) Foremost (3) of the West, lord of eternity, (5) ruler of infinity.

Label for Anubis
ʾInp(w) nb tꜣ ḏsr
Anubis, lord of the sacred land.

Label for Thoth
ḥtp dî ny-sw.t n Ḏḥwty nb Ḥmnw
An offering that the King gives to Thoth, lord of Hermopolis.

Label for Wennefer
rdî.(t) î(ꜣ)w n kꜣ⸗k (2) nb ʾImnt.t dî⸗f tꜣw (3) qbḥw snṯr n (4) Wsîr ḥm-nṯr n (5) Mnw Wnn-(6)nfr (7) sꜣ⸗f wꜥb Wsîr (8) Ḥr-ms

Giving praises to your *ka*-spirit, (2) O lord of the West, so that he might give breezes, (3) cool water, and incense to (4) the Osiris, the prophet of Min, Wen(6)nefer (7) and his son, the *wab*-priest, the Osiris (8) Harmose.

Righthand Scene

Label for Min
　　Mnw Gbtyw (2) nṯr ꜥꜣ nb p.t
　　Min of Coptos, (2) the great god, lord of heaven.

Label for Isis
　　Ꜣs.t wr.(t) mw.t nṯr
　　Isis the great, the God's Mother.

Label for Horus
　　[Ḥr nḏ ỉ]t=f
　　[Horus, the protector of] his father.

Label for Wennefer's Father
　　ḥtp dỉ ny-sw.t n Mnw (2) dỉ=f qbḥw snṯr (3) n Wsỉr ḥm-nṯr (4) Mr-ỉt=f(?)[1] (5) sꜣ=f Wn-nfr
　　An offering that the king gives to Min, (2) so that he might give cool water and incense (3) to the Osiris, the prophet (4) Meritef (?),[1] (5) and his son Wennefer.

III. Main Text
　　(1) ḥm-nṯr 2-nw (n) Mnw Wnn-nfr ḏd=f ỉ ḥm.w-nṯr wꜥb.w ḥry.w-ḥb.(t) ỉt.w-nṯr ỉmy.[w]-rꜣ [pr][1] n.w ḥw.t-nṯr ḏd=ỉ n=[tn][1] dỉ=ỉ rḫ=tn qỉ=ỉ (2) wn=(ỉ) tp tꜣ n(y)-wỉ Gbtyw ḥr ỉt=(ỉ) mw.t=(ỉ) (m) ms n wndw.t n.(t) pr=sꜣ (s)ḫprw=ỉ m ỉ[d]w ḥr sꜣtw nỉw.t=s ỉ[...] ỉqr sbꜣ m ỉr (3) sš m pr=s drp.w=ỉ m ḥw.t-nṯr=s bw-rḫ=(ỉ) qn ỉwf[1] n ꜣt[1] ỉr=ỉ (m) pꜣy=s wbꜣ sḫpr [...] sqr.k(w)ỉꜣ ỉ(4)rt.t n.(t) mw.t=ỉ nꜣy=sn mhn.w tꜣy=ỉ mnꜥ.(t) ỉr=ỉ wꜥb ḥr ḏr.t ỉt=ỉ [... mꜣꜣ].k(wỉ?) (ỉn?) ḥm.w-nṯr (5) ỉr=ỉ ḥny n ḫꜣ.t nṯr pn ỉmy.w-rꜣ sbꜣ.w[4] m pr=s ỉr=ỉ sš mdꜣ.t nṯr wp rꜣ m-bꜣḥ=sn[5] ỉr=ỉ [...] smꜣy n(6)[b]d sḫr ḫꜣ(k)-ỉb bwt nšm.t rdỉ n sḏ.t ds mn ḥr tp=f tw.ỉ bs.kwỉ r ỉt-nṯr (m) s.t n ỉt.w=(ỉ) ỉr=ỉ ḥm-nṯr rmn (7) [s]šm.w wdn m-ꜥ(?) sš m sty ḥb.w ỉn=ỉ nṯr r šb s(w)ꜣ=ỉ nṯr.w nb.w ỉw=(ỉ) dwꜣ n nṯr nb ḥr rn=f nn sḫm.t[4] wꜥ ỉm=sn ỉnk (8) [ꜣḫ n(?)] kꜣ=sn ỉnk wꜥb rḫ bs štꜣ.w nn ḫpr=s{w} ỉwd ḏd tp-rd n wnw.(t) sšm ỉy ḥr-sꜣ=ỉ (9) [..]=ỉ mtr.(t) nb.t nn ḥm=ỉ ỉn.w nb ḏd=ỉ [...] nb [...] dỉ.n=ỉ wrr.(t) ḥr tp n nb=s smn šw.ty[1] m ꜥ[..]ꜣ ỉr=(ỉ) (10) [...] mnḫ.t (m) nḏ.(t)-ḥr[1] m wdn(?) m tꜣ s.t ỉr=ỉ ḥw.t-nṯr m [... r]mn=s ts=ỉ sšdw mnꜥ. t wḏꜣ.w n šnb.t=f [...]m stꜣ qb(11)[ḥw(?) ...] n psḏ.t ỉkꜣbw (< ỉꜣkbw) m nb.w ỉn.t pꜣ wḥm ny-sw.t n Skr nb r ḏr ỉmỉ nỉs.tw=(ỉ) m-bꜣḥ nṯr ꜥꜣ (12)

[...] r wsḫ.t Rs-w[d]ȝ[1] šbn.k(wỉ) (m) nṯr.w qr.(t)yw ḥm-nṯr Wnn-nfr m ḫȝ.t ȝḫ.w rwd rn≠ỉ (13) [...] n-dr pȝw.ty

ḏd≠f n≠tn ḏȝmw ỉw≠sn ỉst wỉ (14) [...] dm≠tn rn≠ỉ ỉm≠tn nn ỉr [...] m ḏd≠f (15) [...] Ḥby.t smỉ n tỉ[...]

Vertical labels for missing figures: (16) [...] (17) šmꜥy.t n [... Tȝ-r](18)nn.(t) nb.(t) [pr(?)] (19) šmꜥy.t n ʾImn [...] (20) Mw.t-ḥtp(?)[1] [...]

The Second Prophet of Min, Wennefer, who says: "O prophets, *wab*-priests, lector priests, God's Fathers, and stewards[1] of the temple! Let me speak to you,[1] so that I might let you know my character (2) when I was on earth. I belonged to Coptos through my father and my mother as a child of the inhabitants of her[2] house. I grew up as a boy on the soil of her city, [...] excellently instructed in the act of (3) writing in her house, with my meals in her temple. I did not know the embrace of flesh[1] in the time[1] that I spent in her forecourt, when [I was?] brought up. I was consecrated (?)[3] (4) with the milk of my mother, its milk jars being my nurse. I acted as *wab*-priest under the direction of my father [...] observed by (?) the prophets. (5) I acted as a prominent officer of this god, the headmaster of teachers[4] in her temple. I acted as a scribe of the divine book who performed the "opening of the mouth" ritual in their presence.[5] I [enchanted] the confederacy of (6) the Evil One, overthrowing the disaffected one, the abomination of the sacred bark of Osiris, who was given to the fire with a knife fixed atop his head. I was initiated into the rank of God's Father in the position of my fathers. I acted as a prophet who shouldered the (7) cult statues, offering through writings and by means of festival perfumes. I brought the god to the food offerings. I paid honor to all the gods, and I adored every god by name, without forgetting[4] anyone among them. I am one (8) [who was beneficial for (?)] their *ka*-spirits. I am a *wab*-priest, who knows secret matters of initiation, without it becoming dispersed, who gives instructions to the temple priesthood, who guides the one who comes after me. (9) I [...] every instruction, without forgetting any dues that I should give [...]. I placed the crown on the head of its lord, affixing the two plumes[1] at [...]. I made (10) [...] clothing as a gift[1] in offering in the place. I made the temple as a [...] its domain. I tied on the fillet, the counterpoise and the amulets on his breast [...] pouring cool (11) water (?) [...] for the Ennead, mourning as the lords of the Valley. O, first royal herald of Sokar, the Lord of All, let me be summoned into the presence of the great god (12) [...] at the hall of the One who Awakens Soundly[1] while I consort with the cavern-dwelling gods, the prophet Wennefer being at the head of the blessed dead. May my name endure (13) [...] since the primeval time,"

and who says to you (further): "O generations to come, truly, I am [...]
(14) [...] May you pronounce my name among you, without doing [evil (?)]
in saying it (15) [...] Khemmis report to [...]."

(16) [...], (17) The chantress of [... Ta](18)renenet, the lady [of the
house (?)] (19) The chantress of Amon, [...] (20) Muthotep (?)¹ [...]

NOTES
    1. Not so read by the editor.
    2. Throughout the text, the city of Coptos is personified as "she."
    3. Or read s(i)qr.k(w)i "I was enriched (by)". Iversen read [...] ... dp≠i i(4)rt.
t n.(t) mw.t m n3y≠sn mhn.w n.w t3y≠i mn.(t) "[...] ... I tasted mother's-milk from
the jugs of my nurse."
    4. Following Iversen's corrected reading.
    5. Contra Iversen, who read m wm.t≠sn "in its thickness, entirely." For m-b3ḥ
written similarly, see line 11.

26. A LETTER FROM EL-HIBEH REGARDING HIGH PRIEST MASAHARTA
(P. STRASBOURG 21)

In 1895, sixteen private letters of Dynasty XXI were purchased from a
dealer in Luxor. Internal evidence indicates that all derived from el-Hibeh,
the northernmost fortified dependency and likely ancestral home of the
contemporary Theban pontiffs. The correspondence constitutes an archive
of prominent clergy of the local deity "He of the Camp," who is depicted
as a form of Horus in a relief of Herihor at the Theban Khonsu temple
(no. 16). One letter is of particular historical interest, as it represents a
petition to the ancestral deity on behalf of the ailing high priest Masaharta.
Despite his status within the Theban Amon cult, Masaharta is styled simply
a servant and ward of this local god. Written by one of Masaharta's brothers to the "noble prophet" in el-Hibeh, the fragmentary letter probably
requested a formal oracular pronouncement, comparable to the "oracular
amuletic decrees" of the period. The request for a prolonged life was
unsuccessful, and Masaharta predeceased his father. The high priest was
succeeded by his brother Menkheperre, who may be the author of the
Strasbourg letter.
    For the text, translations and discussion, see Spiegelberg 1917a, 1–30,
esp. 13–14 and pls. 5–6; Wente 1990, 208; Černý 1962, 46; Ryholt 1993,
189–98; and Fischer-Elfert 1996, 129–44. See Kitchen 1986, 259 §217.

[... M3s3h3rti p3] b[3]k [n P(3)-ln-p3-(2)ih3y [nty] mr dd šd (3)
sw snb sw i-rwy mr nb nty im≠f (4) nfr.(w) m-b3ḥ P(3)-[n]-p3-ih3y p3(5)y≠i nb m
p3y≠f šd M[3]s3h3yrti (6) mtw≠f snb≠f mtw≠f di.t n≠f ʿnḫ wd3 snb ʿḥʿ(w)

q3(ỉ) (7) ỉ3w.t ꜥ3.t mtw≠f sḏm n ḥrw n (8) M3s3h3yrtỉ p3y≠f ḫrd p3y≠f (vo. 1) sḫpr mtw≠f šd sn≠(ỉ) (vo. 2) p3y b3k s3wy mtw≠f (vo. 3) snb≠f mtw≠f dỉ.t≠f n≠ỉ m spr (vo. 4) mỉ-qd [md.t] nb.(t) nfr.(t) (vo. 5) ỉ-ỉr [n≠ỉ p3]y≠ỉ nb

(vo. 6) ḥm-nṯr pn šps P(3)-n-p3-ỉh3y nṯr ꜥ3 ḥr(y)-ỉb p[3?] ỉ[h3y ...]

[... regarding Masaharta, the] servant [of] "He of the (2) Camp," [who is] ill, saying: "Save (3) him! Cure him! Remove all illness that is in him, (4) with the result that he is well before 'He of the Camp,' (5) my lord, through his saving Masaharta! (6) And he should cure him, and give him life, prosperity, health, a long lifetime, (7) and a prolonged old age! And he should heed the plea of (8) Masaharta, his son and his (vo. 1) ward! And he should save my brother, (vo. 2) this servant of his, and (vo. 3) cure him and give him back to me by petition (vo. 4) just like every good [thing] (vo. 5) that my lord has done [for me]!"

Address: (vo. 6) This noble Prophet of "He of the Camp," the great god resident in [the Camp ...].

27. A LETTER TO EL-HIBEH FROM HIGH PRIEST MENKHEPERRE
(P. MOSCOW 5660)

Deriving from the same archive as the Strasbourg correspondence (no. 26), the Moscow letter of Menkheperre documents the priest's new status following the death of his ailing brother Masaharta. The high priest writes to the temple of el-Hibeh regarding favorable pronouncements on his behalf made by the family's ancestral deity, "He of the Camp." Menkheperre's authority over all the armies of Egypt recalls that of Herihor, while his claim to be a divine son is a distinctly royal affectation.

For the text, translations and discussion, see Posener 1982, 134–38 and pl. XIV, 1; Wente 1990, 208–9; Ryholt 1993, 189–98; and Fischer-Elfert 1996, 129–44. See Kitchen 1986, 573 §503.

[... P(3)-n-p3]-ỉh3y nṯr ꜥ3 ḥr(y)-ỉb (2) [p3 ỉh3y n] s3≠[f mrỉy≠f ḥm-nṯr tpy n (3) [ʾImn-Rꜥ] ny-sw.t nṯr.w ỉmy-r3 mšꜥ wr Šmꜥw Mḥy (4) h3w.ty Mn-ḫpr-Rꜥ nty (m)-h3.t n3 mšꜥ.w ꜥ3y.w n.(w) (5) Km.t (r)-ḏr≠w sḏm≠ỉ p3 ḫr n n3 sḫr.w nfr.w (6) [bỉ3y.t(?)] ꜥ3[y.t(?)] ỉ-sr≠[f] m-ꜥq[3]y≠ỉ ỉw≠ỉ [...]

[(To) ... "He of the] Camp," the great god resident in (2) [the Camp, from his beloved] son, the First Prophet of (3) [Amon-Re,] King of the Gods, the great general of Upper and Lower Egypt (4) and leader, Menkheperre, who is at the head of the great armies of (5) Egypt in their entirety. I have heeded the account of the good decisions (6) and great [oracles (?)] that [he] has foretold with respect to me, and I [...].

C. AMONEMNISUT

28. THE BANISHMENT STELA
(LOUVRE C. 256)

One of the few documents dated to the brief reign of Neferkare Amonemnisut, this black granite monument (1.275 m x .82 m) is known also as the Maunier Stela, after the French consul who discovered it within the Karnak precinct in 1860. The text records, in year 25 of Smendes, the installation of the Theban high priest Menkheperre, a junior son of Pinedjem I and successor of Masaharta. The new high priest is represented as being summoned by Amon himself to displace an unnamed rival and to restore harmony to the god's domain. Such evidence of factional conflict within Thebes prefigures the later hostilities under the high priest Osorkon (B) in Dynasty XXII. The motivation for the stela is not Menkhepere's accession but his consolidation of power, as is evident from the transcript of a subsequent oracular consultation that forms the bulk of the text.

Now banished to the Kharga Oasis, the defeated faction of "quarrelsome servants" is formally forgiven and recalled by Amon with the full agreement of Menkheperre, whose secure authority and Theban connections are emphasized at the conclusion of the text. To introduce the issue of divine forgiveness, Menkheperre recites a hymn extolling the deity's unrivalled power and consequent propensity for mercy. By implication, Amon's clerical representative displays similar qualities. In the broken lunette, a figure of Menkheperre in sacerdotal panther skin offers incense to Amon.

For the text and translations, see von Beckerath 1968, 7–36 and pl. 1; and Breasted 1906–7, 4:316–20 §§650–58. See Kitchen 1986, 14–15 §12, 25–26 §§22–23, 29–30 §25, 69 §55, 255 §213, 260–62 §§217–18, and 573 §503.

LABEL FOR AMON

['Imn-Rˤ ...] (2) dỉ≠f ˤnḫ wḏꜣ snb nḏm-ỉb rˤ nb

[Amon-Re ...] (2) May he give life, prosperity, health, and happiness every day.

MAIN TEXT

(1) ḥsb.t 25.(t) ꜣbd 3 šmw sw 29 ḫft ḥb 'Imn-Rˤ ny-sw.t nṯr.w m ḫb≠f [nfr n 'Ip.t-ḥm.t≠s ...] (2) Ns-ḫr m-qꜣb≠sn ỉry wn-ỉn ḥm n nṯr pn šps 'I[mn-Rˤ ny-sw.t nṯr.w ḥr ḫˤ ...] (3) Wꜣs.t ˤḥˤ ỉr.n≠f wꜣ.t r nꜣ sš.w rwd.w rmṯ.w [...]

(4) ḥsb.t 25.(t) tpy ꜣḫ.t [sw] 2 [+x hrw pn ḫr.tly ḥm n nṯr pn šps 'Imn-Rˤ nb ns.wt tꜣ.wy [...] (5) ỉb≠[s]n mn [...] ˤšꜣ≠sn [...] ḥm-nṯr tp(y) n 'Imn-Rˤ

ny-sw.t nṯr.w ỉmy-rȝ mšꜥ wr Mn-ḫpr-[Rꜥ] mȝꜥ-ḫrw sȝ ny-sw.t Pȝ(y)-nḏm
mrỉ-ʾImn [mȝ]ꜥ-[ḫrw …] (6) m ḥn≠f […] ỉry rd.wy≠f ỉb≠sn ḥꜥ.w n mr(w.
t)≠f ỉy.n≠f r rsy m qny nḫt r shr tȝ dr rqy≠f rdỉ≠f wnn […] r [… mỉ] (7)
wnn≠sn m rk Rꜥ

spr.n≠f r Nỉw.t m ỉb ḥr šsp.n sw ḏȝmw.w n.w Wȝs.t ḥr nhm wp.t ḥr-
ḥȝ.t≠f sḫꜥⁱ (n) ḥm n nṯr pn šps nb nṯr.w ʾImn-Rꜥ nb ns.wt tȝ.wy m […] (8)
ḥn≠f sw r wr sp-2 smn≠f sw r s.t ỉt≠f m ḥm-nṯr tp(y) n ʾImn-Rꜥ ny-sw.t nṯr.
w ỉmy-rȝ mšꜥ wr n.{w} Šmꜥw Mḥw sr.n≠f n≠f bỉȝ.wt² qn.w(t) nfr.w(t) n
pȝ.tw mȝȝ≠w ḏr-bȝḥ

ḫr ỉ[r m-ḫt ḥsb.t …] (9) ȝbd 4 šmw hrw 5 ḥry.(w rnp.t) ms.(t) ȝs.t ḫft
ḥb ʾImn m wp-rnp.tȝ sḫꜥⁱ n ḥm n nṯr pn šps nb nṯr.w ʾImn-Rꜥ ny-sw.t nṯr.
w nꜥy r nȝ wsḫ.w(t) ꜥȝ.w(t) n.(t) pr ʾImn ḥtp m-bȝḥ pȝ ḏȝḏȝwy n ʾImn
stȝ.n≠f [r ḥm]-n[ṯr tp(y)] (10) n ʾImn-Rꜥ ny-sw.t nṯr.w ỉmy-rȝ mšꜥ wr Mn-
ḫpr-Rꜥ mȝꜥ-ḫrw wšd≠f sw r wr sp-2 m sp.w ꜥšȝ wȝḫ n≠f m [ḥ]r≠f⁴ m [ḫ].
wt nfr.(w)t

ꜥḥꜥ.n wḥm n≠f ḥm-nṯr tp(y) n ʾImn-Rꜥ Mn-ḫpr-Rꜥ mȝꜥ-ḫrw m ḏd pȝy≠ỉ
nb nfr wnn md.(t) ỉw ỉw.tw (r) wḥm≠s m-bȝḥ

(11) ꜥḥꜥ.n pȝ nṯr ꜥȝ hnn r wr sp-2

ꜥḥꜥ.n wḥm.n≠f spr r pȝ nṯr ꜥȝ m ḏd pȝy≠ỉ nb nfr tȝ md.(t) nȝ bȝk.w tt.w
ỉ-qnd≠k r-r≠sn nty m Wḥȝ.t tȝ(y) nt.(t) smn.t≠w r≠s⁵

ꜥḥꜥ.n pȝ nṯr ꜥȝ (12) hnn r wr sp-2

ỉsk ỉmy-rȝ mšꜥ pn ꜥ.wy≠f m ỉ(ȝw) ḥr dwȝ nb≠f mỉ ỉt ḥr wḥm n sȝ≠(f)
ḏs≠f

ỉnd-ḥr≠k ỉr nty nb qmȝ wnn.t nb.(t)
ỉt nṯr.w ms nȝ nṯr.wt
grg s.t m nỉw.wt spȝ.wt
wtt (13) tȝy.w ms ḥm.wt
ỉr ꜥnḫ n ḥr nb
H̱nmw pw qd r mnḫ
tȝw n ꜥnḫ s[t n] mḥy.t
Ḥ[ꜥ]p[y] wr ꜥnḫ.tw m kȝ≠f
ỉr ḥr.(t) nṯr.w rmṯ.w
šw n hrw ỉ(ꜥ)ḥ mšr(w)
ḏȝỉ p.t (14) ỉwty wrd.n≠f
wr bȝw sḫm sw r Sḫm.t
mỉ ḫ.t m ḏꜥw
q(ȝỉ) ḥtpy ḥn⁶ [sw] n sn sw
ꜥn sw r snfr mn
n ptr≠[f m] rmṯ.w nn mḫ≠f (< ḫm≠f) ḥr nb
ḥr sḏm≠f (15) n s ḥḥ.w m-ỉm≠sn
ỉn-nym tȝy≠f šp.t≠k
ỉs dr[≠f nšny(?)] bȝw≠k

ỉw≠k sḏm n ḫrw≠ỉ m pȝ hrw mt(w)k ḥtp r nȝ bȝk.w ṯṯ.w ỉ-ḫȝꜥ≠k r (16) Wḫȝ.t mtw≠tw ỉn.t≠w r Km.t

ꜥḥꜥ.n pȝ nṯr ꜥȝ hnn r wr sp-2

ꜥḥꜥ.n wḥm.n≠f m ḏd pȝy≠ỉ nb nfr ỉr pȝ nty nb r-wḏ≠k r ỉn≠f tw≠tw ḏd ḥtp≠[k r≠sn] r [ḏ.t]

ꜥḥꜥ.n pȝ nṯr ꜥȝ hnn r wr sp-2

ꜥḥꜥ.n wḥm.n≠f (17) spr r pȝ nṯr ꜥȝ m ḏd pȝy≠ỉ nb nfr ỉw≠k ỉr wḏ.t ꜥȝ.t ḥr rn≠k r tm dỉ.t [ỉ]n.t[w] r[mṯ].w nb n pȝ tȝ r tȝ wȝ.t n.(t) Wḫȝ.t r tm […] šȝꜥ-m pȝ hrw r ḥry

(18) ꜥḥꜥ.n pȝ nṯr ꜥȝ hnn r wr sp-2

ꜥḥꜥ.n wḥm.n≠f m ḏd tw≠k ḏd ỉr s(y) m wḏ.t ḥr ꜥḥꜥy [n ỉnr(?) …] smn m nỉw.t≠k mn wȝḥ [r ḏ].t

[ꜥḥꜥ.n] pȝ [nṯr ꜥȝ hn]n r [wr sp]-2

ꜥḥꜥ.n wḥm n≠f ḥm-nṯr tp(y) n ʾImn (19) Mn-ḫpr-Rꜥ mȝꜥ-ḫrw m ḏd pȝy≠ỉ nb nfr pȝy≠k wḏ r ḫḫ.w n.(w) sp ḥr pȝ wḏ n ỉt mw.t mhȝw.t nb.(t) ỉw mdw≠ỉ n ḥr m-bȝḥ ỉnk ḥm≠k n mȝꜥ.t ȝḫ n kȝ≠k (20) ỉḥwn n nỉw.t≠k sḫpr≠ỉ m ḏfȝw≠k swr≠k ỉw≠ỉ m ḥ.t qd≠k m swḥ.t wḏ≠k(w)ỉ (r) ỉr ḥꜥꜥ.(t) n.(t) rmt.w≠k ỉmy.tw ỉr≠ỉ ꜥḥꜥ(w) nfr (21) m šmsy kȝ≠k wꜥb.tw wḏȝ.tw r ḫnw≠k nb ỉmy rd.wy≠ỉ ḥr mꜥtn≠k sꜥqȝ wỉ ḥr wȝ.t≠k ỉ-wȝḥ ỉb≠ỉ ḥr mk.(t)≠f r ỉr [ḫ.t]≠k (22) ỉmy ỉr≠ỉ ỉmȝḫw-ḥry nfr m ḥtp ỉw≠ỉ wȝḥ.tw ꜥnḫ. tw m pr≠k šps mỉ ḥsy nb ỉr m qd≠ỉ (19) ꜥḥꜥ.n pȝ ḥm-nṯr tp(y) n ʾImn Mn-ḫpr-Rꜥ mȝꜥ-ḫrw spr r pȝ nṯr ꜥȝ m ḏd ỉry rmt.w nb nty ỉw≠w wḥm m-bȝḥ≠k r-ḏd smȝ≠k rmt.w ꜥnḫ.w ỉw≠k (r) ḫf≠f (< fḫ≠f) ỉw≠k (r) ḥdb≠f

ꜥḥꜥ.n pȝ nṯr ꜥȝ hnn r wr sp-2

(1) Regnal year 25, month 3 of summer, day 29, at the time of the festival of Amon-Re, King of the Gods, in his [beautiful] festival [of Epiphi … while the official] (2) Neshor was among them. The Majesty of this noble god [Amon-Re, King of the Gods, made a processional appearance …. in (?)] (3) Thebes. Then he made a path to the scribes, the agents, and the people […]

(4) Regnal year 25, first month of Inundation, [day] 2 [+x. On this day occurred the] oracle of the Majesty of this noble god Amon-Re, Lord of the Thrones of the Two Lands, […] people […] (5) their hearts firm, […] they were numerous […] the First Prophet of Amon-Re, King of the Gods, the great general, Menkheperre, the justified, son of King Pinedjem (I), beloved of Amon, the justified […] (6) when he went […] attendant at his heels, with their hearts joyful through love of him. In valor and victory he came southward to make the land content, to drive out his opponent, and to cause that […] be […, and that things be] (7) as they were in the reign of Re.

When he arrived at the city with contented heart, then the young men of Thebes received him in acclamation, with a crowd of men and women before him. There occurred the processional appearance[1] of the Majesty of this noble god, the Lord of the Gods, Amon-Re, Lord of the Thrones of the Two Lands, in […], (8) while he (Amon) charged him firmly as he established him in the position of his father as the First Prophet of Amon-Re, King of the Gods, and great general of Upper and Lower Egypt, having foretold for him many good wonders[2] that had not been seen previously.

Now after regnal year […], (9) month 4 of summer, the five epagomenal days: the birthday of Isis, at the time of the festival of Amon at the opening of the year,[3] there occurred the processional appearance[1] of the Majesty of this noble god, the Lord of the Gods, Amon-Re, King of the Gods. Going[1] to the great columned halls of the estate of Amon. Resting[1] before the processional chapel of Amon. He drew near to the [First Prophet of] (10) Amon-Re, King of the Gods, the great general, Menkheperre, the justified. He worshiped him greatly, many times, offering to him in his [presence][4] with good things.

Then the First Prophet of Amon-Re, Menkheperre, the justified, reported to him saying: "My good lord, is there a matter that one should report in the divine presence?"

(11) Then the great god nodded in agreement very fervently.

Then he again approached the great god, saying: "My good lord, is it the matter of the quarrelsome servants at whom you were angered and who are in the oasis in which people are confined?"[5]

Then the great god (12) nodded in agreement very fervently.

Now this general had his arms upraised in praise, adoring his lord like a father reporting to his own son:

"Hail to you, who made everything, who created all that exists,
Father of the gods, who bore the goddesses,
Who settled them in the towns and districts,
Who begot (13) males, who bore females,
Who made the life of everyone.
He is Khnum, who fashions to effect,
The breath of life, the [fragrance] of the North Wind,
The great Inundation, by whose food one lives,
Who has made the necessities of the gods and mankind,
The sunlight of day, the moon at evening,
Who crosses the sky without (14) wearying.
Great of wrath, he is more powerful than Sakhmet,
Like the fiery blast in a stormwind.
Highly forgiving, [he] returns quickly[6] to the one who entreats him;
He turns back to heal the sick,
For he watches over mankind, without forgetting anyone;
Thus he listens (15) to millions of men among them.

Who will withstand your displeasure,
Or will dispel [the fury of] your wrath?

Will you listen to my voice today and be forgiving toward the quarrelsome servants whom you banished (16) to the oasis, and let them be
brought back to Egypt?"

Then the great god nodded in agreement very fervently.

Then he spoke again, saying: "My good lord, as for everyone whom
you have commanded to be brought, is it said that [you] are forgiving
[toward them forever]?"

Then the great god nodded in agreement very fervently.

Then he again (17) approached the great god, saying: "My good lord,
will you issue a great decree in your name to prevent any people of the
land being brought away to the oasis and to prevent [...] from today forward?"

(18) Then the great god nodded in agreement very fervently.

Then he spoke again, saying: "Do you say: 'Issue it as a decree upon a
stela [of stone (?) ...],' erected in your city, fixed and enduring forever?"

[Then] the [great god nodded] in agreement very [fervently].

Then the First Prophet of Amon, (19) Menkheperre, the justified, again
spoke to him, saying: "My good lord, is then your command for all time,
and is then the command for father, mother, and the entire family? My
statement is in full contentment in the divine presence. I am your true servant, who is effective for your *ka*-spirit, (20) a youth of your city, having
been raised on your food and drink while I was in the womb, whom you
fashioned in the egg, ordained to make your people rejoice. Let me spend
a goodly lifetime (21) in serving your *ka*-spirit, being pure and safe from
all that you despise. Place my feet upon your path, direct me upon your
path, set my heart in its proper position to perform your [ritual]. (22) Let
me attain the good state of being revered in peace, remaining and living in
your noble estate like every saint who has acted in my manner."

(23) Then the First Prophet of Amon, Menkheperre, the justified,
approached the great god, saying: "As for everyone who will report before
you so as to say: 'Slay living people!' will you destroy him, will you kill
him?"

Then the great god nodded in agreement very fervently.

NOTES
1. Narrative infinitive.
2. The term can also signify "oracles."
3. The lost regnal date corresponds to one of the few years of Amonemnisut,
successor of Smendes, and falls at the transition to the New Year ("Opening of the
Year") on the fourth of the five epagomenal days, the birthday of Isis. For discussion, see von Beckerath 1968, 17 and 33.

4. Contra von Beckerath 1968, 18, the traditional restoration "before him" is not "senseless" here.

5. Literally, "to which one is affixed/firmly placed." Unrecognized by von Beckerath, the preceding t3(y) is the required copula, separating the relative clause from its antecedent, as is typical in Late Egyptian, Demotic, and Coptic.

6. The word should be restored following Erman and Grapow 1926–63, 3:103, in parallel with the synonym ˤn "return" paired in this couplet.

D. PSEUSENNES I

29. TITLES OF THE TANITE PRIEST-KING PSEUSENNES I

Owing to the poor conditions for preservation in the Delta, the primary monuments of Tanite rule are typically the work of Theban contemporaries, who acknowledge northern regnal years but rarely names or titles. Even the most prolific monarch of Dynasty XXI, Pseusennes I, is best attested only by brief inscriptions at the capital, deriving from temple ruins and his unplundered tomb, discovered in 1939. Although no works of Pseusennes have been recovered from Thebes, both his name ("The star that has arisen in Thebes") and his titulary stress Theban associations. Yet more striking is the king's adoption of the title of high priest of Amon, either within or accompanying the royal cartouche. Royal authority is explicitly "of Amon's giving," reflecting the official theocracy of the period.

For the texts and translations, see Montet 1966, 41 and pl. IV.14; 1951, 136, 177, and pl. CXI. See Kitchen 1986, 262–63 §220.

A. LIMESTONE TEMPLE DEDICATION BLOCK, RECOVERED FROM THE SACRED LAKE AT TANIS

(1) [... ỉr]≠f ḥw.t-nṯr m ỉ[nr] ḥ[ḍ[nf[r n ˤ]nw [...] (2) [...] ny-sw.t bỉ.ty ḥm-nṯr tp(y) n ʾImn-Rˤ ny-sw.t nṯr.w P3-sb3-ḫˤ-n-nỉw.t dỉ [ˤnḫ mỉ Rˤ ḏ.t]

(1) [...] He [made] a temple of good white Tura limestone [...] (2) [...] The King of Upper and Lower Egypt, the First Prophet of Amon-Re, King of the Gods, Pseusennes, given [life like Re forever.]

B. COLLAR CLASP (NO. 482) FROM THE TOMB OF PSEUSENNES

(1) ˤnḫ Ḥr k3 nḫt m dd[1] ʾImn (2) wsr f3w sḫˤ m W3s.t Nb.ty wr mnw (3) m ʾIp.t-s.wt nb pḥ.ty wˤf t3.wy (4) w3ḫ ny.t-sw.t mỉ Rˤ m p.t Ḥr-nbw sm3 ḫpr.w2 dr (5) psḏ.t psḏ.t (ỉ)t m sḫm≠f m t3.w nb.w (6) ny-sw.t bỉ.ty nb t3.wy ˤ3-ḫpr-Rˤ-stp-n-ʾImn s3 Rˤ (7) ḥm-nṯr tp(y) n ʾImn-Rˤ ny-sw.t nṯr. w P3-sb3-ḫˤ-n-nỉw.t

(1) Long live the Horus: "Strong Bull of Amon's giving,[1] (2) rich in splendor, who was made manifest in Thebes"; the Two Ladies: "Great of

monuments (3) in Karnak, Lord of strength, who subdues the Two Lands, (4) enduring of kingship like Re in heaven"; the Horus of Gold: "He who unites the manifestations,[2] who repels (5) the Nine Bows, who seizes by his power from all the lands"; (6) the King of Upper and Lower Egypt, Lord of the Two Lands, Aakheperre-setepenamon, the Son of Re, (7) the First Prophet of Amon-Re, King of the Gods, Pseusennes.

NOTES

1. Contra von Beckerath 1984, 98 and 100 n. 3, who read m ʿ.wy ʾImn "in the arms of Amon."

2. Montet read t3.w "lands," employing the late cryptographic value of the sign.

30. ORACULAR PROPERTY SETTLEMENT OF MENKHEPERRE (KHONSU TEMPLE COLUMN 1)

Added to the west face of column 1 of the Khonsu temple's court is an inscription of more than fifty lines recording the oracular confirmation of a joint purchase of property by Amon and his high priest Menkheperre from over two dozen Theban residents. The god's estate pays 60 percent, with the remaining 40 percent paid by the high priest himself. As Kitchen has noted, the transaction suggests an act of expropriation with overly generous terms to avoid friction, perhaps in deference to the earlier conflicts of Menkheperre's tenure noted in The Banishment Stela (no. 28).

For the text, translation, and discussion, see Epigraphic Survey 1981, 17–20 and pl. 133; and Kitchen 1984, 85. See Kitchen 1986, 270 n. 162 §226 and 573 §503.

(1) [...]t [...] (2) [...] p3y≠f nfr m t3y [w]sḫ[.t ...] (3) [... Mn]-ḫpr-[Rꜥ] m3ꜥ-ḫrw s3 ny-sw.t P3y-nḏm mrỉ-ʾImn p3 [...] (4) [... n] ʾImn-Rꜥ ny-sw.t nṯr. w ḥm.t-nṯr n p3 ḥr n ʾImn T̲-n.t-Nbw.t ḥm.t-nṯr [...] (5) [... n]3 ḥrd.w n ỉt-nṯr sš mšꜥ ʾI[ry]-ꜥ3 [m3ꜥ-ḫrw] s3 sm[sw(?) ... ỉ-](6)ỉr≠[ỉ] n≠s r wn m n3 [ỉwꜥ. w(?) ...] (7) m-b3ḥ p3 nṯr ꜥ3 [... ʾImn]-Rꜥ ny-sw.t nṯr.w sš sḫn n n pr [ʾI]mn sš šꜥ.(t) Ḥrỉ m3ꜥ-ḫrw

[... ḥm-nṯr tp(y)] (8) n ʾImn-Rꜥ ny-sw.t nṯr.w ỉmy-r3 mšꜥ.w [wr n.w Šmꜥw Mḥw] Mn-ḫpr-Rꜥ m3ꜥ-ḫrw m-b3ḥ p3 nṯr ꜥ3 m ḏd p3y≠ỉ nb nfr ḏd ʾI[mn]-Rꜥ [ny-sw.t] nṯr.w p3 [nṯr ꜥ3] (9) wr n šꜥ3 ḫpr [...]p r p3 dbn n ḥḏ ptrỉ≠ỉ 100 n dbn n ḥmt ḫ3.ty n [...] ḥrp.t dbn [...] t3ỉ[... r] (10) p3 dr m p3 hrw [...] ỉp.t 3.(t) n bd.ty ḫ3.ty n ỉt≠ỉ

ḏd [ḥm]-n[ṯr tp(y) n ʾImn-Rꜥ ny-sw.t nṯr.w ... Mn-ḫpr-Rꜥ m3ꜥ-ḫrw] (11) m-b3ḥ nṯr pn ỉr ʾImn-Rꜥ ny-sw.t nṯr.w pnꜥ≠f r rmt nb m n3 ỉwꜥ.w nty ꜥḥꜥ m-b3ḥ Ḫnsw-m-W3s.t Nfr-ḥtp p3y≠ỉ nb [ỉw]≠w ḏ[d] (12) šsp≠ỉ nk.t n ꜥd3 m-dỉ n3 rwḏw.w n Mn-ḫpr-Rꜥ m3ꜥ-ḫrw ỉw bw-pw≠w šsp≠f

ḏd [...]t t3 [...] (13) m bw wꜥ šsp.n≠n p3 5 [ḥ3r] (n) bd.(t)y r p3 [dr ỉrw
m 100 dbn] ḥm.t (r) p3 dbn n ḥḏ [...] (14) ỉn≠w

ḏd ḥm nt̠r tp(y) [n ꜣImn-Rꜥ ny-sw.t nt̠r.w Mn-ḫpr-Rꜥ m3ꜥ-ḫrw m-b3ḥ
nt̠r pn] ỉ[r] n3 [ỉwꜥ.w (?) ...] (15) [...] dỉ.n≠w 1/10 n p3y n[...] n3 [...] (16)
[...] ỉw≠f n ḫ3.ty n [... Mn]-ḫpr[-Rꜥ m3ꜥ-ḫrw(?) ...] rd (< dr) [...] (17) [...]
n t3y ꜥ3.t n3 r[d.w(?) ...]f [...] (18) [m-b3ḥ] p3 nt̠r ꜥ3 wn [...] t3 m [...] (19)
[...] r p3 ỉw¹

ꜥḥꜥ.[n ḥm nt̠r t]p(y) n [ꜣI]mn-Rꜥ ny-sw.t nt̠r.w Mn-ḫpr-Rꜥ m3ꜥ-ḫrw ḏd
m-b3ḥ p3 nt̠r ꜥ3 m ḏd p3y≠ỉ nb nfr [...] (20) [...] dỉ≠f dny.t [...]

[ꜥḥꜥ.n p3] (21) nt̠r [ꜥ3] nꜥ n ḫ[3]≠f²

[ḏd ḥm nt̠r tp(y) n ꜣImn-Rꜥ ny-sw.t nt̠r.w Mn-ḫpr-Rꜥ m3ꜥ-ḫrw m-b3ḥ nt̠r
pn ...] t3(?) nb [...] (22) ỉw r-ḏb3 ḥḏ r-ḏb3 [...]

[ꜥḥꜥ.n wḥm.n ḥm nt̠r tp(y) n ꜣImn-Rꜥ ny-sw.t nt̠r.w Mn-ḫpr-Rꜥ m3ꜥ-ḫrw
m-b3ḥ p3] (23) nt̠r ꜥ3 m ḏd p3y≠ỉ nb nfr [...] t3y [...] (24) nmḥy³ n[b ...]

[ꜥḥꜥ.n p3] nt̠r ꜥ3 (25) hn r wr sp-2 m sp.w ꜥš3

ꜥḥꜥ.[n wḥ]m.n ḥm nt̠r tp(y) [n ꜣI]mn-[Rꜥ] ny-sw.t nt̠r.w Mn-ḫpr-Rꜥ m3ꜥ-
ḫrw s3 ny-sw.t [nb t3.wy P3y-nḏm m ḏḏ] (26) ptr n t3y rmt̠.t nmḥy.w n Nỉw.
t rdỉ.tw n≠w ḥḏ [r-ḏ]b[3] p3 ỉw ỉw [...] (27) ỉ[r]my ꜥ3 p3 ḥḏ m[-dr.t] ꜣImn-Rꜥ
ny-sw.t nt̠r.w p3 nt̠r ꜥ3 ỉmy s.t r p3 dbn n ḥḏ 60 n dbn n ḥm.t dỉ≠ỉ 40 n
ḫ3.ty(28)w r[dỉ]≠ỉ 5 ḥ3r n bd.(t) [r] p3 rd ỉw 3 ḥ3r p3 dỉ p3 t3 r p3 rd ḫ3.ty
n ḥ3r 2 ỉ[r ḥr].w nb nty ỉw≠w ḏd mdw (29) m p3 sḫr ỉ-ỉryw [ꜣImn]-Rꜥ ḏs≠f
m dw3.t r-s3 dw3.t ỉ-ỉr Ḥnsw-m-W3s.t Nfr-ḥtp dỉ ꜥq(?)≠f [... ỉr ...] nb sr.[w
nb] (30) m mỉt.t nty ỉw≠w [m]d[w m] p3 ỉw ỉw bn n3 ḫrd.w n Mr.t̠-ꜣImn
m3ꜥ.t-ḫrw ỉm≠w [... ḥr] gs.wy r-[ḫ]nꜥ (31) n3 ỉwꜥ.(w) n ꜣIry-ꜥ3 [m3ꜥ-ḫrw ...]
m-b3ḥ nt̠r pn rdỉ.tw n≠w⁴ ḥḏ r-ḏb3 p3 ỉw r-ḏd m-b3ḥ p3 nt̠r ꜥ3 šsp.(32)n≠n
p3 [ḥḏ m-dỉ s3] ny-sw.t tw≠n mḥ.tw m-ỉm≠f

n3 ỉwꜥ.w n T̠n.t-srr m3ꜥ.t-ḫrw ḥm.t dbn 305 (33) ỉrw n dr 30 [1/2 ...
T3-ỉwnrr m3ꜥ.t-ḫrw] n p3y≠s ḥrd 3 wꜥ nb 101 1/2 dbn

T3y≠ỉ-nḏm.t m3ꜥ.t-ḫrw mw.t≠s T3-ỉwnr[r] m3ꜥ.t-ḫrw m 101 dbn 1/2

(34) Ḥnw.t-nḏm.t m3ꜥ.t-ḫrw mw.t≠s [T3-ỉwnrr m3ꜥ.t-ḫrw m] 101 dbn
1/2 m-dỉ swnw Nsy-P3w.ty-t3.wy

r-ḥnꜥ sn ỉt≠f Ḥry m3ꜥ-ḫrw mw.t≠f T3-ỉwnrr m3ꜥ.t-ḫrw

ỉwꜥ.[w] (35) n q(r)s⁵ n T̠n.(t)-[...] p3 3 ỉwꜥ.w m-dỉ [ꜥ]3 P3y≠ỉ-nb-n-ꜥdd
n p3 qwr n pr ꜣImn 300 [+ 600 +] (36) 5 dbn [...]

[NN m3ꜥ.t-ḫrw] mw.t≠s Mw.t-n-ꜣIp.t m3ꜥ.t-ḫrw n 305 dbn ỉrw n dr m 30
1/2 m-dỉ sš ꜥnḫ≠f-n-Mw.t Ḫꜥ-[...] (37) r-ḥnꜥ [...]

[NN] m3ꜥ.t-ḫrw mw.t≠s Mw.t-n-ꜣIp.t m3ꜥ.t-ḫrw n 305 dbn ỉr[w] n rd (<
dr) m 30 1/2 wp.t≠sn

Ḥry m3ꜥ-ḫrw mw.t≠f [T3-](38)[ỉwnrr m3ꜥ.t-ḫrw]

[NN m3ꜥ.t-ḫrw] mw.t≠s T3-mỉmỉ.t m3ꜥ.t-ḫrw n 152 1/2 (dbn)

[P3-]w3ḫ m3ꜥ-ḫrw mw.t≠f T3-[šr].t-n-3s.t m[w.t]≠s Ṯn.t-ʾImn [m3ꜥ.t-ḫrw
...] (39) [...]

ʾI[rly-ꜥ3 m3ꜥ-ḫrw mw.t≠f ʾIry.t-ꜥ3 m3ꜥ.t-ḫrw 305 dbn ỉrw n rd (sic. < dr)
m 30 1/2 wp.t≠sn
    W3.t-n-ꜥ3 [...] (40) [...]
    ỉt-nṯr n ʾImn Nsy-P3w.ty-t3.wy m3ꜥ-ḫrw s3 P3-sr m3ꜥ-ḫrw n 43 1/2 (dbn)
    T3-pš.t s3.t P3-sr m3ꜥ-[ḫrw n 40](41)[+ 3 1/2 (dbn)]
    [NN s3/s3.t] P3-sr m3ꜥ-ḫrw m-dr.t≠f n 43 1/2 (dbn)
    r dmd Nsy-P3w.ty-t3.wy m3ꜥ-ḫrw n 130 1/2 (dbn)⁶
    Ḥr-ms m3ꜥ-ḫrw s3 P3-sr [m3ꜥ-ḫrw] (42) [...]
    [NN m3ꜥ.t-ḫrw] mw.t≠s [...]ḫ[...] m3ꜥ.(t)-ḫrw s3.[t] [...] m3ꜥ-ḫrw n 43
1/2 (dbn)
    Ḥry-ỉmw(?) m3ꜥ.(t)-ḫrw s3.(t) ʾIry-ꜥ3 m3ꜥ-ḫrw mw.t≠s ʾI[ry.t-ꜥ3 m3ꜥ.
t-ḫrw ...] (43) [...]
    [...] n Nsy-P3w.ty-t3.wy m3ꜥ-ḫrw n ỉwꜥ n q(r)s n 305 dbn
    ỉt-nṯr sš mšꜥ [...] (44) [...]
    [... n3y]≠s(?) ḫrd.w n 305 m-dỉ sš ḥtp-nṯr Pn-š-[n-ꜥb(?)] m3ꜥ-ḫrw s3
ʾIm[n-ḫ]tp [m3ꜥ-ḫrw ...] (45) [...] (46) [...] (47) [...]
    (48) [...] P3[y-ndm] m3ꜥ-ḫrw r-[ḫ]nꜥ n3 n[mḥy.w(?) n Nỉw.t ...] (49)
[...]
    [NN m3ꜥ.t-ḫrw] mw.t≠s Ṯn.t-3s.t m3ꜥ.t-ḫrw s3.t P3-gs m3ꜥ-ḫrw r-ḫnꜥ
sn.t≠s N[...]
    (50) [...] Šd-n-dw3.t m3ꜥ.t-ḫrw m-dr.[t] sš Nsy-ʾImn m3ꜥ-ḫrw r-ḫnꜥ [...]
    (51) [... NN] m3ꜥ.t-ḫrw s3≠s 3 n Ḥr-(m)-nỉw.t≠f dbn 305
n3 [...]
    (52) [...] P3-šd [m3ꜥ-ḫrw] s3 [...]

(1) [...] (2) his beauty in this court [...] (3) [...] Menkheperre, the
justified, son of King Pinedjem (I), beloved of Amon, the [...] (4) [... of]
Amon-Re, King of the Gods; the Priestess of the countenance of Amon,
Tanetnubt; the Priestess of [...] (5) [...] the children of the God's Father and
army scribe Iryaa, [the justified], eldest (?) son of [...] (6) [which I] made
for her to be as the [heirs (?) ...] (7) in the presence of the great god [and
the (?) ... of Amon]-Re, King of the Gods, the administrative scribe of the
estate of Amon and letter writer, Hori, the justified.
    [There came the First Prophet] (8) of Amon-Re, King of the Gods, the
[great] general [of Upper and Lower Egypt,] Menkheperre, the justified, into
the presence of the great god, saying: "My good lord, Amon-Re, [King] of
the Gods, the very [great god] (9) since the beginning of creation, has said
[...] regarding the *deben* of silver. I have recognized 100 *deben* of silver
over and above [the] assessment of *deben* [...] this (?) [... per] (10) shawl
today [...] 3 *oipe* of emmer over and above my grain."

There said [the First] Prophet [of Amon-Re, King of the Gods, … Men-kheperre, the justified,] (11) in the presence of this god: "Will Amon-Re, King of the Gods, turn himself away from any man among the heirs who will stand in litigation in the presence of Khonsu-in-Thebes Neferhotep, my lord, saying (12) falsely: 'I received property from the agents of Men-kheperre, the justified,' when they have not received it?" There said […] the […] (13) with one accord: "We have received the 5 [sacks] of emmer per [shawl evaluated at 100] copper [deben] per deben of silver […]," (14) so they said.

There said the First Prophet [of Amon-Re, King of the Gods, Men-kheperre, the justified, in the presence of this god]: "As for the [heirs (?) …] (15) […] they have given 1/10 of this […] the […] (16) […] although it is over and above […] Menkheperre, [the justified, (?) …] shawl […] (17) […] of this size. The shawls (?) […] (18) [in the presence of] the great god, there is […] land in […] (19) […] per plot of land."[1]

Then the First [Prophet] of Amon-Re, King of the Gods, Menkheperre, the justified, said in the presence of the great god, saying: "My good lord, […] (20) […] he gave a share […]."

Then the] (21) [great] god disagreed.[2]

[There said the First Prophet of Amon-Re, King of the Gods, Men-kheperre, the justified, in the presence of this god …] any land (?) […] (22) the plot of land in exchange for silver, in exchange for […]

[Then the First Prophet of Amon-Re, King of the Gods, Menkheperre, the justified, repeated in the presence of the] (23) great god, saying: "My good lord, […] this […] (24) every free[3] man […]

[Then the] great god (25) nodded in agreement very fervently, many times.

Then the First Prophet of Amon-[Re], King of the Gods, Menkheperre, the justified, royal son of the [Lord of the Two Lands, Pinedjem (I)] repeated, saying: (26) "Look after these people, free men of Thebes. Let silver payment be given to them in exchange for the plot of land, while […] (27) Let the silver payment be great from Amon-Re, King of the Gods, the great god. Give it, per deben of silver, at 60 deben of copper, and I shall give the 40 (deben) over and above (28) them. I shall give 5 sacks of emmer [per] shawl, though it is 3 sacks that the country gives per shawl—an excess of 2 sacks. As for any[one] who will dispute (29) the arrangement that [Amon]-Re himself has made, whether tomorrow or after tomorrow, Khonsu-in-Thebes Neferhotep will cause that he enter (?) [… As for] any [… or any] official (30) likewise who will [contest] the plot of land, with the children of Meretamon not being among them, [… on] both sides together with (31) the heirs of Iryaa, [the justified …] in the presence of this god. Let silver payment be given to them[4] in exchange for the plot of land, saying in the presence of the great god: 'We have received (32) the [silver payment from the] royal son; we are thereby paid in full.' "

The heirs of Tanetserer, the justified: 305 *deben*, (33) amounting to 30 [1/2] shawls [...Taiunrer, the justified] for her 3 children. Each one: 101 1/2 *deben.*

Tainodjmet, the justified, whose mother is Taiunrer, the justified: 101 1/2 *deben.*

Henutnodjmet, the justified, whose mother is [Taiunrer, the justified]: 101 1/2 *deben* in the possession of Nespautytawy,

together with his maternal uncle Hory, the justified, whose mother is Taiunrer, the justified.

Heirs-(35)of-burial[5] of Tanet[...] the three inheritances in the possession of Painebenadjed, chief of the miners of the estate of Amon: 905 (36) *deben* [...]

[NN, the justified], whose mother is Mutenipet, the justified: 305 *deben* amounting to 30 1/2 shawls in the possession of the scribe Ankhefenmut, Kha[...], (37) together with [...]

[NN], the justified, whose mother is Mutenipet, the justified: 305 *deben* amounting to 30 1/2 shawls. Their specification:

Hory, the justified, whose mother is [Ta(38)iunrer, the justified.]

[NN, the justified], whose mother is Tamimi, the justified: 152 1/2.

Pawah, the justified, whose mother is Tasherenese, whose mother is Tanetamon, [the justified ...] (39) [...]

Iryaa, the justified, whose mother is Irytaa, the justified: 305 *deben* amounting to 30 1/2 shawls. Their specification:

Watenaa [...] (40) [...]

The God's Father of Amon, Nespautytawy, the justified, son of Paser, the justified: 43 1/2

Tapeshet, daughter of Paser, the justified: [43] (41) [1/2]

[NN, son/daughter of] Paser, the justified, in his possession: 43 1/2

In sum for Nespautytawy, the justified: 130 1/2.[6]

Harmose, the justified, son of Paser, [the justified] (42) [...]

[NN, the justified], whose mother is [...], the justified, daughter of [NN], the justified: 43 1/2

Heriimu (?), the justified, daughter of Iryaa, the justified, whose mother is Irytaa, [the justified ...] (43) [...]

[...] for Nespautytawy, the justified, as an heir-of-burial: 305 *deben.*

The God's Father and army scribe [...] (44) [...]

[...] her (?) children: 305 *deben* in the possession of the scribe of the divine offerings, Pensh[enab (?)], the justified, son of Amon[hotep, [the justified ...] (45) [...] (46) [...] (47) [...]

(48) [...] King Pinedjem, the justified, together with the free [men of Thebes ...] (49) [...]

[NN, the justified], whose mother is Tanetese, the justified, the daughter of Pages, the justified, together with her brother N[...]

(50) [...] Shedenduat, the justified, in the possession of the scribe Nesamon, the justified, together with [...]

(51) [... NN], the justified, her 3 sons by Haremniutef: 305 *deben*. The [...]

(52) [...] Pashed, [the justified], son of [...]

NOTES

1. The term is probably to be associated with the coalesced terms for "island, mound, field" (Erman and Grapow 1926–63, 1:26/9–11 and 47).

2. Literally, "moved backward." For the techniques of Egyptian oracles, see Černý 1962, 35–48.

3. This is the first attestation of later Demotic terminology; see Thompson 1940, 74–75.

4. The published translation has "They were given payment...," but the form rdỉ.tw n≠w is identical to that in line 26.

5. For the institution, see Kitchen 1986, 333 n. 498.

6. Nespautytawy receives his own 43 1/2 *deben* share and controls those of two siblings for a total of 130 1/2 *deben*.

31. THE ROYAL TITULARY OF MENKHEPERRE (A) AT EAST KARNAK

To the east of Karnak temple, below the ruins of a quadrant of houses probably associated with the construction work of Taharqa, recent Canadian excavations have recovered stamped bricks of an earlier Dynasty XXI structure. These bricks, like others at el-Hibeh, Shurafa, and Gebelein, attest to an extensive building campaign of the high priest Menkheperre (A), second son and heir of the high priest and king Pinedjem I. At el-Hibeh, bricks of Menkheperre include the title "King of Upper and Lower Egypt," an assumption of royalty now attested at East Karnak. Here Menkheperre commonly enclosed his name in cartouches, with his prenomen being simply "First Prophet of Amon," following the pattern of Herihor. Isolated, and perhaps earlier, bricks name him as the son of King Pinedjem I or pair his cartouche with that of his queen, Istemkheb (C).

For the texts and translations, see Redford 1981, 17 and pl. 3; 1983, 221 and pl. 30. The unpublished text (8.5 x 19.5 cm) of the single "Type 3" brick (35 x 17.5 x 10.5 cm) was confirmed by D. B. Redford, personal communication. See Kitchen 1986, 262 §219, 269–70 §226, and 572 §501.

TYPES 1 (FACING RIGHT) AND 2 (FACING LEFT)
    ḥm-nṯr tp(y) n ʾImn (2) Mn-ḫpr-Rᶜ

The First Prophet of Amon, (2) Menkheperre.

TYPE 3 (ONE EXAMPLE, FACING RIGHT)

ḥm-nṯr tp(y) n ʾImn Mn-ḫpr-Rᶜ (2) sꜣ ny-sw.t Pꜣy-nḏm mrỉ-ʾImn

The First Prophet of Amon, Menkheperre, (2) son of King Pinedjem (I), beloved of Amon.

TYPE 4 (TWO EXAMPLES, FACING LEFT)

Mn-ḫpr-Rᶜ (2) ꜣs.t-m-Ḫby.t

Menkheperre. (2) Istemkheb (C).

32. KARNAK RESTORATION STELA OF MENKHEPERRE (CAIRO STELA 3/12/24/2)

Near the end of his pontificate in year 48 of Pseusennes I, the high priest Menkheperre erected a new enclosure wall about the northeast precinct of Karnak to prevent the encroachment of the adjacent town upon the sacred territory of Amon. The pontiff's benefaction is recorded on a sandstone stela (130 x 105 cm), discovered reused within the east colonnade built by Taharqa in Dynasty XXV. In the lunette, the high priest offers to the Theban triad while standing between the deities and a female personification of the city, shown reversed or "excluded" from the ritual scene. A similar posture is shown on a Dynasty XX stela of Siptah discovered at Karnak (Lauffray, Sauneron, and Traunecker 1975, pl. IX).

For the texts and translation, see Barguet 1962, 36–38 and pl. 32; Gauthier 1914, 3:265 §V; and Porter and Moss 1927–51, 2:210. See Kitchen 1986, 14 §12, 270 §226.

LABEL FOR DISK WITH PENDANT URAEI

Bḥd.ty

The Behdedite.

LABEL FOR AMON

ʾImn-Rᶜ nb ns.wt tꜣ.wy ḫnty (2) ʾIp.t-s.wt (3) dỉ.n≠(ỉ) n≠k [...][1]

Amon-Re, Lord of the Thrones of the Two Lands, Foremost of (2) Karnak. (3) To you I have given [...].[1]

LABEL FOR MUT

Mw.t ḥnw.t nṯr.w (2) nb.w

Mut, Mistress of all the gods.

LABEL FOR KHONSU

Ḫnsw m Wꜣs.t Nfr-ḥtp (2) sꜣ ḫꜣ[≠f ...][1] mỉ Rᶜ

Khonsu in Thebes, Neferhotep. (2) Protection is around [him ...]¹ like Re.

LABEL FOR MENKHEPERRE

[rdỉ.t ỉrp?] n ỉt≠f(?)¹ ḥm-nṯr tp(y) n ᵓImn-Rᶜ (2) ny-sw.t nṯr.w ỉmy-rȝ mš̌ᶜ wr tp n ḥḥ.w Mn-ḫpr-Rᶜ sȝ ny-[sw.t nb] tȝ.wy (3) Pȝy-nḏm mrỉ-ᵓImn [...]¹

[Offering wine (?)] to his father (?).¹ The First Prophet of Amon-Re, (2) King of the Gods, the great general and chief of millions, Menkheperre, son of the King and [Lord] of the Two Lands, (3) Pinedjem (I), beloved of Amon [...].¹

MAIN TEXT

ḥsb.t 48.(t) š̌ȝᶜ kȝ.t m ỉr.t n (= m) mȝwy.(t) ỉn ḥm-nṯr tp(y) n ᵓImn-Rᶜ ny-sw.t nṯr.w Mn-ḫpr-Rᶜ mȝᶜ-ḫrw sȝ ny-sw.t Pȝy-nḏm mrỉ-ᵓImn m pr ỉt≠f ᵓImn-Rᶜ n[b] ns[.wt] tȝ.[wy ḫnty] (2) ᵓIp.t-s.wt ỉr.n≠f sbty ᶜȝ wr mḥt ᵓIp.t-s.wt r-š̌ȝᶜ pȝ ḏȝḏȝ rsy n ᵓImn r pr-ḥḏ mḥt n pr ᵓImn n mr(w.t) sḥȝ[p] (3) ḥ.wt-nṯr n ỉt≠f ᵓImn-[Rᶜ twr]ỉ r hȝw-mr m-ḫt gm≠f sw qd m pr.w nȝ rmṯ[.w] (4) n pȝ tȝ [m]n m ws[ḫ].w pr ᵓImn tȝ ḫȝt.t ỉr.n≠f (sw) m mȝwy.(t) m sbty qd m bḫn [...]² (5) Wȝs.t n nb≠s sᶜȝ r rw.ty r pr ỉt≠f ᵓImn n mr(w.t) smnḫ pr n smnḫ m pr≠f [mỉ Ḥr] (6) nḏ≠f ỉt≠f ỉswy ỉry m ỉr.(t) nn ns.[w]t≠f ḥr(y)-tp tȝ ỉmy ḏd≠f m ᵓIp.t-s.wt mn [r nḥḥ]

Regnal year 48, the beginning of the work of renovation by the First Prophet of Amon-Re, King of the Gods, Menkheperre, the justified, son of King Pinedjem (I), beloved of Amon, in the house of his father Amon-Re, Lord of the Thrones of the Two Lands, [Foremost of] (2) Karnak. He made a very great wall on the north of Karnak from the southern processional chapel of Amon to the northern treasury of the estate of Amon, specifically through the desire to mask (3) the temple of his father Amon-[Re so as to exclude] the profane masses, when he found it built over previously by houses of the people (4) of the land installed in the open courts of the estate of Amon. He renewed it with a wall built of greywacke, [separating (?)]² (5) Thebes for her lord, offering defensive protection outside of the estate of his father Amon through the desire to ennoble the estate of him who is ennobled in his estate, [as did Horus] (6) when he protected his father, with the associated reward for doing this being his thrones upon earth. May he be enduring in Karnak, remaining [forever!]

NOTES

1. Unclear traces on the small published photograph.

2. Barguet restored [ḫft-ḥr-]Wȝs.t-n-nb≠s sᶜš̌ȝ and translated "the people of Thebes being driven out...."

E. AMONEMOPE OR SIAMON

33. SETTLEMENT TEXT OF HENUTTAWY (C)
(PYLON X AT KARNAK)

Dated to either Amonemope or Siamon, this inscription on the north face of the Tenth Pylon at Karnak once consisted of some fifty long horizontal lines, of which twenty-seven now survive in ruinous condition. The lost first ten lines were partially copied and paraphrased by Champollion, whose remarks were republished and supplemented by Maspero. The fragmentary text preserves the record of several judicial oracles conducted during the pontificate of Pinedjem II to secure the property rights of Theban patricians Henuttawy (C) and her daughter Isetemkheb (E). Through questions prompted by the junior prophet Tchaynefer, the oracle reviews and confirms property settlements made by the former high priest Smendes II and his sister/wife Henuttawy C, both children of Isetemkheb C, with regard to their daughter Isetemkheb E. The document reflects a fear of internal family litigation and was seemingly designed to separate Isetemkheb's interests from those of her prominent half-sister Neskhons (A), wife of the current high priest Pinedjem II and Smendes's daughter by a secondary marriage to a niece. For Neskhons A, with implications of her combative nature, see the Funerary Decree of Amon for Princess Neskhons (no. 35). In the transition from regnal year 5 to 6, the questioner Tchaynefer is promoted from Third to Second Prophet of Amon. As in similar oracular procedures, the "questions" are expressed as declarative statements to which the deity assents.

For the text, translation, and discussion, see Maspero 1889, 704–6; Gardiner 1962, 57–64; and Porter and Moss 1972, 187 (580). These editions were supplemented by Chicago Oriental Institute photo 5739 and Oriental Institute Museum photos 745–46, and copies inked by Charles Nims. See Kitchen 1986, 40 §36, 56–57 §§46–47, 63 §51, 65 §52, and 277 §233.

(1) [... šḫꜥ ꞽn pꜣ nṯr ꜥꜣ(?)] m tr n dwꜣ.t m stꜣ[1] nṯr ꞽn ḥm-nṯr tp(y) n ꞽImn-Rꜥ ny-sw.t nṯr.w Pꜣy-nḏm mꜣꜥ-ḫrw sꜣ Mn-ḫpr-Rꜥ mꜣꜥ-ḫrw stꜣ[2] r ḥm-nṯr tp(y) n ꞽImn-Rꜥ ny-sw.t nṯr.w Pꜣy-nḏm mꜣꜥ-ḫrw ... [...] (2) ꜣs.t-m-Ḥb ... [...][3] (3) Ḥnw.t-tꜣ.wy ... [...] (4) sr.w ḥm.w-nṯr ꞽt.w-nṯr wꜥb.w ḥry.w-ḥb sš.w ... [...]

(5) ḥsb.t 5.(t) tpy ꜣḫ.t sw 1 hrw pn m pr ꞽImn-Rꜥ ny-sw.t nṯr.w ... [...] (6) ꞽy ꞽn ḥm-nṯr 3-nw n ꞽImn Ṯꜣy-nf[r mꜣꜥ-ḫrw sꜣ] Nsy-pꜣ-ḫr-n-Mw.t mꜣꜥ-ḫrw ... [...] (7) ... n Ḥnw.t-tꜣ.wy mw.t≠s ꜣs.t-m-Ḥb mꜣꜥ.t-ḫrw ... [...][4]

(8) ḥsb.t 6.(t) ꜣbd 3 šmw sw 19 ... [...] (9) nfr.w ḥr≠f Pꜣy-nḏm mꜣꜥ-ḫrw pꜣy≠tn[5] bꜣk ꞽn[6] Ḥnw.t-tꜣ.wy mꜣꜥ.t-ḫrw mw.t≠s ꜣs.t-m-Ḥb mꜣꜥ.t-ḫrw tꜣy ḥry.

t wr.(t) ḫnr.t tp.t n.(t) ᵓImn ... [...] (10) Ḥnw.t-t3.wy m3ᶜ.t-ḫrw mw.t≠s 3s.t-
m-Ḥb m3ᶜ.t-ḫrw t3y≠tn b3k.t n s3≠s n s3 n s3≠s n s3.t≠s n s3.t n.(t) s3.t≠s r
tm [...] (11) [...] (12) nty îw≠sn kt[kt nk.t îm≠w ... mt](13)w≠tn ḫtm ᵓImn.t
r-ḫ3.t≠w [...] t3 wd [î-îr ᵓImn-Rᶜ Mw.t] Ḥnsw (14) n3 nṯr.w ᶜ3.w n n3 3[ḫ.wt
...].w ḫnᶜ n3 3ḫ.wt (15) îmî [...] sîp [... mtw≠tn] smn ...⁷ (16) ...⁷ [...] 3ḫ.w
nmḫ.w n [...] Ḥr-m-3ḫ.t m3ᶜ-ḫrw [...] nḫt (17) p3 [...] îr n3(?) [...] (18) [...
mtw≠tn] fd[k]≠w m p3 t3 (19) bn îw≠t[n dî n≠sn] s.wt≠[sn]

ᶜḥᶜ.n t3 [psd.t dd(?) ... dî] (20) îr.t(w)≠f m ḥtp.w-[nṯr(?)] î(=r) dî.t≠f n
Ḥnw.t-t3.wy m3ᶜ.t-ḫrw [...] n pr ᵓImn [...]

[ᶜḥᶜ.n wḫ](21)m ḥm-nṯr 2-nw n ᵓImn T3y-nfr m3ᶜ-ḫrw s3 Nsy-[p3-ḫr-n-
Mw.t m3ᶜ-ḫrw spr m-b3ḥ p3 nṯr ᶜ3 m dd p3y≠î nb nfr ... n3y]≠s ḥrd.w
wšd r wr sp-2 în p3y nṯr

ᶜḥᶜ.n wḥm.n≠f spr m-b3ḥ p3 nṯr ᶜ3 m dd p3y(22)≠î nb nfr îr rmṯ.w nb
nty îw≠w dd îrm Ḥnw.t-t3.wy m3ᶜ.t-ḫrw [îrm 3s.t-m-Ḥb m3ᶜ.t-ḫrw ...]
[wšd r wr sp-2 în p3y nṯr]

[ᶜḥᶜ.n wḥm.n≠f spr m-b3ḥ] p3 nṯr ᶜ3 m dd p3y≠î nb nfr îr t3 wd î-îr
ᵓImn-Rᶜ ny-sw.t nṯr.w n n3 3ḫ.w nmḫ.w î-în (23) Ḥnw.t-t3.wy m3ᶜ.t-ḫrw r
swn m sw3.w n t3 q3y.t p3 ww n ᵓIwn[8 ...] ᶜd3 [... î-dî] Nsy-B3-nb-Dd.(t)
m3ᶜ-ḫrw îr.t(w)≠f n Nsy-Ḥnsw m3ᶜ.t-ḫrw t3(y)≠f šr.t [...] dî≠f pš.t≠f n b3k
b3k.t ḥm.t dḥr (24) ḫbs.w pr k3m.w 3ḫ.t n sḫ.t nty nb [nk.t nb ... Nsy-B]3-
nb-Dd.(t) m3ᶜ-ḫrw î-[h(3)y] r≠f n ḫ.wt n.(t) 3s.t-n-Ḥb t3(y)≠f mw.t n Ḥnw.
t-t3.wy⁹ m3ᶜ-ḫrw îw≠k dî.t≠f n 3s.t-(m)-Ḥb t3y šr.t n (25) Nsy-B3-nb-Dd.(t)
m3ᶜ-ḫrw îw≠k tm dî.t ḫpr [...] pr.w nb nty î[w≠w ...]
[wšd r wr sp-2 în p3y nṯr]

[ᶜḥᶜ.n wḥm.n≠f spr m-b3ḥ p3 nṯr ᶜ3 m dd p3y≠î nb nfr î]r rmṯ.w nb
nty îw≠w dd îrm Ḥnw.t-t3.wy m3ᶜ.t-ḫrw îrm 3s.t-m-Ḥb t3y≠s šr.t ḥr-n t3y
pš.t n.(t) Nsy-B3-nb-Dd.(t) m3ᶜ-ḫrw (26) î-h(3)y r≠f n ḫ.wt n.(t) 3s.t-m-Ḥb
t3(y)≠f mw.t r [...] ...⁷ [... m]tw≠tw gm.t≠[f] îw≠[f] m3ᶜ îmy≠tw dî.t n≠f [...]
b3k mtw≠f (27) ᶜnḫ(?) n 3s.t-m-Ḥb wn n Ḥnw.t-t3.wy m3ᶜ.t-ḫrw mtw≠w
dî.t n≠s [... Mw.t w]r nb.(t) ᵓIšrw [Ḥnsw] Nfr-ḥtp n3 nṯr.w [ᶜ3.w ... Ḥn]sw
n3 nṯr.w ᶜ3.[w ...] (28) [ᵓImn-Rᶜ ny-sw.t nṯr.w p3y nṯr ᶜ3 wr n] š3ᶜ ḫpr Mw.t
Ḥnsw n3 nṯr.w [ᶜ3.w ...] m(?) m3ᶜ-ḫrw Ḥnw.t-t3.wy m3ᶜ.t-ḫrw t3[y≠n b3k.
t(?) ...] (29) [...] ᵓImn-Rᶜ ny-sw.t nṯr.w p3[y nṯr] ᶜ3 [wr n š3ᶜ] ḫpr [...] îw≠tn
fdk rn≠w n p3 t3 [îw≠tn tm dî.t rwd]≠w îm≠s îr t3 md.t bîn.t nt.(t) îr ᶜ3
nb n mšᶜ [n3y≠w ît.w] n3y≠w mw.wt n3y(30)≠w ḫrd.w p3(y)≠w sn t3(y)≠w
sn.t rmṯ nb (n) wndw nb îw≠w n pt[... t3y wd.t ... dî.t ḥr(?)] w3.t n¹⁰ md.t
nb nt.(t) ḥr≠s îw≠tn îr n≠w [btw î]w≠tn ḥdb≠w îw≠tn fdk rn≠w n p3 t3
îw≠tn tm dî.t rwd≠w îm≠s

dd [ᵓImn-Rᶜ] (31) ny-sw.t nṯr.w p3y nṯr ᶜ3 wr n [š3ᶜ ḫpr Mw.t] Ḥnsw n3
nṯr.w ᶜ3.w îw≠n phr [ḫ3.t≠w¹¹ ...]

[ᶜḥᶜ.n wḥm.n≠f spr m-b3ḥ p3 nṯr ᶜ3 m dd p3y≠î nb nfr ... Ḥnw.t-t3.wy
m3ᶜ.t-ḫrw t3y šr.t n.(t)] 3s.t-m-Ḥb r tm 3ᶜᶜ≠s r tm [îr.t n≠s md.t nb.(t)] bîn.
t nt.(t) îw≠w 3ḫw îm≠s îw îr p3 nty îw≠f wn dd.t mtw≠f dnn ḥd(32)b

Ḥnw.t-t3.wy m3ꜥ.t-ḫrw t3(y)⸗tn b3k.t r ỉr.(t) n⸗s md.(t) nb.(t) bỉn.t ỉw[⸗tn ... ʾImn-Rꜥ ny-sw.t nṯr.w] p3y nṯr ꜥ3 wr n š3ꜥ ḫpr Mw.t Ḫnsw n3 nṯr.w ꜥ3.w [n]3.w(?) Ḥnw.t-t3.wy m3ꜥ.t-ḫrw t3y šr.t n.(t) 3s.t-m-Ḥb t3(y)⸗tn b3k.t ỉw⸗tn dỉ.t wd3⸗w

ḏd ʾImn-Rꜥ ny-sw.t nṯr.w p3y (33) nṯr ꜥ3 wr n š3ꜥ ḫpr Mw.t Ḫnsw n3 nṯr. w ꜥ3.w ỉr ꜥ3 nb n mšꜥ t3(y)⸗f mw.t t3(y)⸗f [sn.t ...] n [wn]ḏw nb [...]

[ꜥḥꜥ.n wḥm.n⸗f spr m-b3ḥ p3 nṯr ꜥ3 m ḏd p3y⸗ỉ nb nfr ỉr ...] r⸗s ỉw⸗tn ḏd n[..]3ỉ ỉw⸗tn ỉr n[3y⸗tn] b3w ꜥ3.w dns.[w ỉr]-r⸗w mỉt.t⸗s m wḏ n ʾImn-Rꜥ ny-sw.t nṯr.w p3y (34) nṯr ꜥ3 wr n š3ꜥ ḫpr Mw.t Ḫnsw n3 nṯr.w ꜥ3.w ḥtp ḥr p3 t3 n ḥḏ n pr ʾImn [...] nty wnmy ỉ3by n p3 nṯr ꜥ3 n ḥsb.t 8.(t) 3bd 2[+2(?)] 3ḫ.t [...] ỉw sn.t ky ỉwꜥ ỉw nsy n3 rmṯ.w ỉ-dỉ n3 pr.w n 3s.t-m-Ḥb pr ỉm⸗w m dw3.(t) ḥr-s3 dw3.(t) r ḏd mn n⸗tn p3 pr ỉwn(3) (35) ḥr dỉ⸗n sw n ky ỉw⸗tn dỉ.t n ḥr n rwḏw [...] rwḏw nb n Nỉw.t [...] ḏd.t nt.(t) ỉr n3 ỉwꜥ.w ỉr⸗f r dỉ.t dỉ⸗w ...[...]

[ḏd ʾImn-Rꜥ ny-sw.t nṯr.w p3y nṯr ꜥ3 wr] n š3ꜥ ḫpr ỉw⸗ỉ smn n3 pr.w ỉ-swn 3s.t-m-Ḥb m-ꜥ nb⸗sn n Ḥnw.t-t3.wy m3ꜥ.t-ḫrw t3(y)⸗s šr.t m-dỉ.t (= m-ḏr.t) Ḥnw.t-t3.wy m3ꜥ.t-ḫrw t3(y)⸗ỉ b3k.t (36) m-ḏr.t s3 n s3⸗s ỉwꜥ n ỉwꜥ⸗s ms n ms.w⸗s r nḥḥ ḏ.t

ḏd ʾImn-Rꜥ ny-sw.t nṯr.w p3y [nṯr ꜥ3 wr n š3ꜥ ḫpr ... w]ḏ n pr dw3.t-nṯr n ʾImn mtw⸗tw ḫ...[...] ỉr⸗f(?) ỉmy dỉ⸗s n⸗w

ḏd ʾImn-Rꜥ ny-sw.t nṯr.w p3y nṯr ꜥ3 wr n š3ꜥ ḫpr ỉr p3 sš n pr dw3.t-nṯr n ʾImn nty ỉw⸗f ḥ3p (37) t3y wḏ r n3 ḥrd.w n ḥrd.w n Ḥnw.t-t3.wy m3ꜥ.t-ḫrw mtw⸗f ft sš.w ỉm⸗s n mr⸗f ỉr n⸗w [... ỉw⸗n ỉr n3y⸗n] b3w ꜥ3.w dns.w ỉr-r⸗w mỉ[t.t⸗s m wḏ n ʾImn-Rꜥ ny-sw.t nṯr.w p3y nṯr ꜥ3 wr n š3ꜥ ḫpr Mw.t Ḫnsw n3 nṯr.w ꜥ3.w ...]

(1) [... Processional appearance by the great god (?)] at the time of morning in a procession[1] of the god by the First Prophet of Amon-Re, King of the Gods, Pinedjem (II), the justified, son of Menkhepere, the justified. Approaching[2] the First Prophet of Amon-Re, King of the Gods, Pinedjem, the justified, ... [...] (2) Isetemkheb ...[...][3] (3) Hennuttawy (C) ... [...] (4) officials, prophets, God's Fathers, *wab*-priests, lector priests, scribes, ... [...] (5) Regnal year 5, first month of Inundation, day 1: On this day in the estate of Amon-Re, King of the Gods, ... [...] (6) Then came the Third Prophet of Amon, Tchaynefer, [the justified, son of] Nespaherenmut, the justified, ... [...] (7) ... for Henuttawy, whose mother is Isetemkheb (C), the justified, ... [...][4]

(8) Regnal year 6, third month of summer, day 19 ... ["...] (9) good," so says Pinedjem, the justified, your[5] servant. "Henuttawy, the justified, whose mother is Isetemkheb, the justified, this first great chief of the musical troupe of Amon, has purchased[6] ... [...] (10) Henuttawy, the justified, whose mother is Isetemkheb, the justified, your servant, to her son, to the son of her son, to her daughter, to the daughter of her daughter, in order

to prevent [...] (11) [...] (12) [...] who will tamper [with anything among them ...] (13) and will you close the west in front of them [...] this decree [made by Amon-Re, Mut and] Khonsu, (14) the great gods, for the [fields ...] them together with the fields? (15) Make [...] inspection [... and will you] establish their sons in their places, with the result that they are rich[7] (16) and honored [...] favor (?)[7] [...] private fields for [...] Horemakhet, the justified [...] strong (17) the [...] make the [...] (18) [... and will you] cut them out from the land? You will not [give them their] places?"

Then the [Ennead said (?): ... cause] (20) it to be made into endowment offerings (?) to give it to Henuttawy, the justified [...] of the estate of Amon [...]

[Then] (21) the Second Prophet of Amon Tchaynefer, the justified, son of Nes[paherenmut, the justified,] again [approached into the presence of the great god, saying: "My good lord, ...] her children."

Very favorable response by this god.

Then he again approached into the presence of the great god, saying: "My (22) good lord, as for every man who will dispute with Henuttawy, the justified, [and with Isetemkheb, the justified, ...]

[Very favorable response by this god.]

[Then he again approached into the presence of] the great god, saying: "My good lord, as for the decree that Amon-Re, King of the Gods, has made for the private fields that (23) Henuttawy, the justified, has purchased in the region of the highland of the district of Iunu[8] [...] falsehood [... that] Smendes (II), the justified, [caused] to be made for Neskhons (A), the justified, his daughter, [...] he gave his 1/2 share of male servants, female servants, copper, leather, (24) clothing, house, gardens, country field, everything [and all property ...] Smendes, the justifed, which he inherited from the property of Isetemkheb (C), his mother, to Henuttawy (C),[9] the justified, will you give it to Isetemkheb (E), this daughter of (25) Smendes, the justified; will you not allow it to happen that [...] any houses that [they will ...]?"

[Very favorable response by this god.]

[Then he again approached into the presence of the great god, saying: "My good lord,] as for every man who will dispute with Henuttawy, the justified, and with Isetemkheb, her daughter, concerning this 1/2 share of Smendes, the justifed, (26) which he inherited from the property of Isetemkheb, his mother, so as to [...] in their possession[7] [...] and they find [him] justified, let one give to him [...] servant and he will (27) swear (?) to Isetemkheb: 'Make an inventory for Henuttawy, the justified,' and they will give to her [... Mut], the great, the Lady of Asheru, [and Khonsu]-Neferhotep, the [great] gods [...] Khonsu the great gods [...] (28) [Amon-Re, King of the Gods, this very great god since] the beginning of creation, Mut and Khonsu, the [great] gods [...] in (?) justification Henuttawy, the justified, [our servant (?) ...] (29) [...] Amon-Re, King of the Gods, this [very] great [god since the beginning of] creation, [...] will you cut out their names from the land; [will you not allow] them [to flourish] in them? As for the evil thing that any military commander, [their fathers,] their mothers, their (30) children, their brother, their sister, or any man of any sort who are in [...] will do [... this decree ... to set] aside10 anything that is in it, will you [punish] them; will you kill them; will you cut out their names from the land; will you not allow them to flourish in them?"

Then said [Amon-Re,] (31) King of the Gods, this very great god since [the beginning of creation, Mut] and Khonsu, the great gods: "We will turn [their hearts11 ...]

[Then he again approached into the presence of the great god, saying: "My good lord, ... Henuttawy, the justified, this daughter of] Isetemkheb, not to injure her nor to [do to her anything] evil by which they may make mischief, whereas for the one who will neglect what is said, and who will strive to kill (32) Henuttawy, the justified, your servant, or to do anything evil to her; will [you] ... Amon-Re, King of the Gods,] this very great god since the beginning of creation, Mut and Khonsu, the great gods? But those belonging to (?) Henuttawy, the justified, this daughter of Isetemkheb, your servant, will you cause that they be safe?"

Then said Amon-Re, King of the Gods, this (33) very great god since the beginning of creation, Mut and Khonsu, the great gods: "As for any military commander, his mother, his sister, [...] of any sort, [...]"

[Then he again approached into the presence of the great god, saying: "My good lord, as for ...] against her, will you say [...]; will you inflict your great and heavy wrath upon them, with a written copy of it in a decree of Amon-Re, King of the Gods, this (34) very great god since the beginning of creation, and of Mut and Khonsu, the great gods, who rest upon the silver pavement of the temple of Amon? [...] who are on the right and left of the great god in regnal year 8, month 4 (?) of Inundation, [...] when the sister of another heir who belongs to the people who sold the houses to Isetemkheb comes forth from them tomorrow or after tomorrow to say: 'The house is not yours, (35) so we shall sell it to another,' will you charge an agent [...] any agent of Thebes [...] statement that the heirs will make to cause that they give ...[...]?"

[Then said Amon-Re, King of the Gods, this very great god] since the beginning of creation: "I shall confirm the houses that Isetemkheb purchased from their owners for Henuttawy, the justified, her daughter, in the possession of Henuttawy, the justified, my servant, (36) and in the possession of the son of her son, the heir of her heir, the offspring of her offspring forever and ever."

Then said Amon-Re, King of the Gods, this [very great god since the beginning of creation: " ...] decree of the estate of the Divine Votaress of

Amon, and one should …[…] do it (?). Let her give to them."

Then said Amon-Re, King of the Gods, this very great god since the beginning of creation: "As for the scribe of the estate of the Divine Votaress of Amon who will conceal (37) this decree from the children of the children of Henuttawy, the justified, and who will erase writings from it through his desire to do to them [injury (?) …, we shall inflict our] great and heavy wrath upon them, with written copy [of it in a decree of Amon-Re, King of the Gods, this very great god since the beginning of creation, and of Mut and Khonsu, the great gods, …]"

NOTES

1. So Champollion, but perhaps pḥ-ntr as suggested by Nims. For this oracular procedure, see Ritner 1993b, 214–20.

2. A signal of approval by the divine statue.

3. Here Champollion's paraphrase notes that Isetemkheb is frequently mentioned with regard to buildings and exchanges of money.

4. Here Champollion's paraphrase notes references to much property (misunderstood as gifts) belonging to Henuttawy, daughter of Isetemkheb.

5. The plural address throughout the text is directed to the Theban triad: Amon, Mut, and Khonsu.

6. Taken as a past tense în NN (r swn) "purchased" (cf. lines 22–23); Gardiner translated as the imperative "Bring!"

7. The translation follows Gardiner; the text is illegible on both the photos and published handcopy.

8. The incomplete geographical name could be Armant, Esna, Dendera, or Heliopolis.

9. Gardiner mistakenly read "Neskhons." Property given by Smendes II to his sister and wife Henuttawy C as inheritance from their common mother, Isetemkheb C, is to be transferred to their daughter Isetemkheb E.

10. Perhaps using a direct object marker as in Demotic.

11. Literally, "enchant their hearts"; for the idiom, see Ritner 1993b, 66–67.

F. SIAMON

34. THE TITLES OF NESKHONS (A), WIFE OF PINEDJEM II

The wealth and influence of the Theban family of "priest-kings" was consolidated by marriage alliances and the concomitant accumulation of priestly endowments. High priest Pinedjem II married both his sister Isetemkheb (D) and his niece Neskhons (A), whose inherited benefices were retained by the family and further supplemented by an array of income-generating sinecures within and beyond Thebes. Isetemkheb held honorary positions in almost one-third of the provinces of Upper

Egypt, including offices in Thebes, Cusae, Akhmim, Abydos, Thinis, and el-Kab.

The titles of Neskhons are somewhat less extensive but of more historical interest. In addition to customary titles indicating her prominence within the feminine clergy and musical troupe (formerly translated "harim") of Amon in Thebes, Neskhons is provided with income from positions in Aswan and Nubia. In conjunction with the latter, Neskhons is given the extraordinary titles of Viceroy of Cush and overseer of southern foreign lands, former administrative positions rendered moot by the loss of Nubia after the revolt of Panehsy but retained optimistically by Herihor and Piankh. While Neskhons cannot have administered Nubia, her positions may have entailed revenue from imposed duties on southern trade.

I. HIERATIC LINEN DOCKET FOUND ON THE SHROUD COVERING THE COFFIN OF RAMESES IX

For the text and translations, see Maspero 1889, 567; Thomas 1966, 251 and 263 n. 44; and Gauthier 1914, 3:276 §X. See Kitchen 1986, 66 §53, 275–76 §232, and 422 §389.

în.(t) îr.n wr.(t) ḫnr.wt tp(y).(wt) n.(t) ᵓImn ḥm.(t)-nṯr n.(t) ᵓImn-ḫnm-Wȝs.t Nsy-Ḫnsw mȝꜥ.t-ḫrw (m) ḥsb.t 5.(t)

Gift that the chief of the principal musical troupes of Amon, prophetess of Amon, United with Thebes,[1] Neskhons, the justified, made in regnal year 5.

II. HIERATIC WALL DOCKET RECORDING THE BURIAL OF NESKHONS, INSCRIBED ON THE RIGHT DOOR-JAMB AT THE BOTTOM OF THE TOMB SHAFT (DB 320).

For the text and translations, see Maspero 1889, 520–22; Černý 1946, 25–26; Thomas 1966, 251 and 263 nn. 45–46; and Gauthier 1914, 3:281 §IX C. See Kitchen 1986, 66 §53, 275–76 §232, and 422 §389.

ḥsb.t 5.(t) ȝbd 4 šmw sw 21 (2) hrw n qrs ḥry.(t) šps.wt Nsy-Ḫnsw (3) în ît-nṯr n ᵓImn îmy-rȝ pr ḥd Dd-Ḫnsw-îw⸗f-ꜥnḫ [sȝ] Pȝy-nḏm (4) ḥm-nṯr n ᵓImn-Rꜥ ny-sw.t nṯr.w ꜥnḫ⸗f-n-ᵓImn (5) [smsw] h(ȝ)y.t Nsy-pȝy-[...] (6) ît-nṯr n ᵓImn îmy-rȝ mšꜥ[2] Nsy-pȝ-qȝ(î)-šw.ty (7) nȝ ḥtm.wt nty ḥr tȝy s.t [...] (8) tȝ ḥtm.t îmy-rȝ pr ḥd Dd-Ḫnsw-îw⸗f-ꜥnḫ (9) tȝ ḥtm.t sš pr-ḥd Nsy-swl[...]

Regnal year 5, month 4 of summer, day 21, (2) the day of burial of the chief of the noble ladies, Neskhons, (3) by the God's Father of Amon and overseer of the treasury, Djedkhonsuiuefankh, [son of] Pinedjem, (4) and the prophet of Amon-Re, King of the Gods, Ankhefenamon, (5) [and the elder] of the portal, Nespay[...], (6) and the God's Father of Amon and general,[2] Nespakashuty. (7) The seals that are on this place [...]: (8) The seal of the overseer of the treasury, Djedkhonsuiuefankh, (9) and the seal of the treasury scribe, Nes[...].

III. AMELIA B. EDWARDS TABLET (UNIVERSITY COLLEGE LONDON 14226)

Before an offering table, Neskhons raises a pot of incense to a standing, mummiform Osiris. The painted, wooden stela measures 39.5 cm x 22 cm and derives from Deir el-Bahari tomb 320. For the text and translations, see Stewart 1983, 3 and pl. 47; Petrie 1905b, 218; Gunn 1955, 83–84 n. 4; and Gauthier 1914, 3:281 §XXIX E. See Kitchen 1986, 66 §53, 275–76 §232, and 422 §389.

Label for Osiris

ḏd-mdw î(n) Wsîr ḫnty ʾImnty.w (2) îmy ȝbḏw (3) ḥqȝ ḏ.t

Recitation by Osiris, (2) Foremost of the Westerners, (3) he who is in Abydos, (3) Ruler of Eternity.

Label for Neskhons

Wsîr wr.t ḫnr.wt tp(y).(w)t n.(t) ʾImn-Rᶜ ny-sw.t nṯr.w (2) ḥm.t-nṯr n.(t) Ḫnmw nb Qbḥw sȝ.(t) ny-sw.t n Kšy (3) îmy.(t)-rȝ ḫȝs.wt rsy.w(t)³ ḥm.t-nṯr n.(t) Nb.(t)-ḥtp.(t)⁴ n.(t) Srwd.t (4) ḥry.(t) tî.wt-šps Nsy-Ḫnsw mȝᶜ.t-ḫrw

The Osiris, chief of the principal musical troupes of Amon-Re, King of the Gods, (2) prophetess of Khnum, Lord of the Cataract District, King's Daughter of Cush, (3) overseer of southern³ foreign lands, prophetess of the goddess Nebethetepet⁴ of Serwedet, (4) and chief of the noble ladies, Neskhons, the justified.

NOTES

1. Amon of the Ramesseum, contra Kitchen, p. 276, who identified the site with Medinet Habu. See Erman and Grapow 1926–63, 3:379/5.

2. For the reading mšᶜ, see Černý 1946, 26 n. 3 and 28.

3. Read šmᶜw by Gunn 1955, 84. The titles are feminine adaptations of traditional designations of the viceroy of Cush.

4. For the goddess in this passage, see Vandier 1966, 134.

35. FUNERARY DECREE OF AMON FOR PRINCESS NESKHONS (A)
(P. CAIRO 58032)

Opening with an extended hymn that has been termed by Vernus the official "credo" of the contemporary theocratic state, this hieratic decree guarantees divine status and protection in the afterlife for Princess Neskhons, daughter of Smendes, the founder of Dynasty XXI, and wife and niece of the Theban pontiff Pinedjem II. The papyrus text is closely paralleled on a hieratic writing board inscribed for Neskhons (Cairo 46891); both were discovered in 1881 in the Deir el-Bahari family tomb (DB 320) in which they had been interred during the reign of King Siamon and which thereafter served as a burial cache for the collected royal mummies.

Though not formally punctuated, the poetic hymn comprises roughly equal stanzas of parallel "thought-units," each concluding with a reference to the creator's formation of, or authority over, the earth. The decree records the official pronouncement of the oracle of Amon of Karnak, unique creator, divine patron of the dynasty, and ultimate ruler as "the King of Upper and Lower Egypt, Amon-Re, King of the Gods" (line 39). A similar decree accompanied Pinedjem II (Cairo 58033), whose protection—from a deceased Neskhons—is also guaranteed in his wife's own oracle. Whatever might be the implications for the personality of Neskhons, such concern for surviving family members need not reflect misogyny but general fear of empowered ghosts, who might inflict illness and death if slighted.

For the text, translation, and discussion, see Assmann 1975, 308–12 (no. 131, hymn only); Gunn 1955, 83–105 (decree only); Maspero 1889, 594–614; Vernus in Association française d'action artistique 1987, 103–4 (discussion of official credo); and Golénischeff 1927, 169–96. See Kitchen 1986, 65–66 §53 and 277 §233.

(1) nṯr pn šps(y) nb nṯr.w nb.w
ʾImn-Rˁ nb ns.(w)t tȝ.wy ḫnty ʾIp.t-s.wt
(2) bȝ šps(y) ḫpr m ḥȝ.t
nṯr ˤȝ ˤnḫ m mȝˤ.t
pȝw.ty tpy ms pȝw(3).tyw
ḫpr nṯr nb ỉm≠f
wˤ wˤ.w ỉr wnn.w
šȝˤ tȝ m sp tpy

(4) štȝw msy.w ˤšȝy ḫpry.w
nn rḫ.tw bs≠f
sḫm šps(y) mrw.(5)ty šfy.ty
wsr m ḫˤˤ.w≠f
nb fȝw sḫm ḫprỉ
ḫpr ḫprỉ (6) nb n ḫprỉ≠f
šȝˤ ḫpr nn wpw-ḥr≠f
sḫḏ tȝ m sp tpy

ỉtn wr (7) ḥȝy sty.wt
dỉ≠f sw ˤnḫ ḥr nb
ḏȝy ḥr.t nn n≠f wrd
(8) dwȝw sp-2 nt.w-ˤ≠f mn
nḥḥ nhȝp≠f m ỉḥwn
ỉny (9) ḏr.w n nḥḥ
pḫr ḥr.t ḫns dwȝ.t
r sḫḏ tȝ.wy qȝm.n≠f (< qmȝ.n≠f)

nṯr (10) nṯrỉ nbỉ sw ḏs≠f
ỉry p.t t3 m ỉb≠f
wr wry.w ꜥ3 n (11) n3 ꜥ3y.w
wr wr≠f r nṯr.w
k3 rnpỉ dm ḫn.ty
(12) s3dd t3.wy m rn≠f wr
ỉw nḥḥ ḥr wsr≠f
ỉny pḥ n ḏ.t
(13) nṯr wr m š3ꜥ ḫpr
ỉty t3.wy m nḫt≠f

šfy h3w.ty dnỉny (= tnỉ) ḫprỉ
(14) ỉ3m.ty r nṯr.w nb.w
m3ỉ ḥsy ḥr ds.t (= ṯs.t) wḏ3.ty
(15) nb nbỉ r ḫfty.w≠f
nwn wr bs sw r nw≠f
r (16) sꜥnḫ pr ḥr nḥp≠f
nmt ḥr.t pḫr dw3.t
ḫḏ t3 r ꜥ≠f n (17) sf

nb pḥ.ty ḏsr šfy.(t)
sšt3.n m3w.w(t)≠f ḏ.t≠f
wnm.ty(18)≠f ỉ3b.ty≠f ỉtn ỉꜥḥ
p.t t3 3bḫ m nfr.wt≠f
(19) ny-sw.t mnḫ ỉwty nny
wrd ỉb n wbn ḥtp
pr rmṯ.w m (20) nṯr.ty≠f
nṯr.w m tp.w-r3≠f
ỉr k3.w š3ꜥ df3w
q(21)3m (< qm3) wnn.w nb

nḥḥy sbby rnp.wt
nn ḏr.w ꜥḥꜥ(w)≠f
ỉ3w (22) rnpỉ sbby nḥḥ
nḥḥ ỉr ỉḥwn≠f
ꜥš3y ỉr.w(t) (23) wr ꜥnḫ.w
sšm ḥḥ (m) psḏ≠f
nb ꜥnḫ dd (n) mr≠f
šnw n (24) t3 ḥr s.t-ḥr≠f

wḏy ỉry ỉwty ḥnn.w
nn sk.ty ỉr.(t).n≠f nb
ḥn-ỉn(25)ỉw rn bnrỉ mr(w)y.(t)

dw3w ḥr nb r nḫt≠f
(26) wr nrỉ ꜥ3 pḥ.ty
nt̲r nb ḥr snd.t≠f
k3 rnpỉ dr (27) nḫnwy.w (< n3 ḫnn.w)
nḫt ꜥ ḥ(w)ỉ ḫfty.w≠f
nt̲r pn š3ꜥ t3 m sḫr.w≠f

b3 (28) psd m wd̲3.ty≠f
b3y.ty ḫpr (m) ḫprỉ.w
d̲sry ỉwty rḫ (29) sw
ny-sw.t pw ỉr ny.w-sw.t
tsỉ t3.w m wd̲y ỉr.n≠f
nt̲r.w nt̲r.wt m (30) ks(w) n b3w≠f
n ꜥ3 n šfy.t≠f
ỉy m h3.t km.n≠f pḥ(w)
š3ꜥ.(31)n≠f t3.w m sḫr.w≠f

št3 ḫprỉ nn rḫ.tw≠f
ỉmn sw r nt̲r.w nb.w
ỉtn (32) sw m ỉtn nn rḫ.tw≠f
sh3p sw r pr ỉm≠f
tk3 sty.(33)w wr ḥdd.w
dg3ỉ.tw m-ḫnw dg3ỉ≠f
wrš.tw ḥr (34) m33≠f nn s3(ỉ).tw n-ỉm≠f
ḥd̲ t3 ḥr nb.w r nḫt≠f

tḫ(35)n ḫꜥꜥ.w m-ḫnw psd̲.t
3bw.(t)≠f n (= m) nt̲r nb
ỉw nwn (36) ḫnty mḥy(t.t) m-ḫnw nt̲r pn št3
ỉr wd̲y.w≠f n ḥḥ n ḥḥ.w
nn (37) mnmn d̲r.t≠f
drỉ ḥr.tw mnḫ wd̲y.w≠f ỉwty wh3ỉ (38) sp≠f
dd ꜥḥꜥ(w) qb rnp.wt m (= n) p3 nty (m) ḥs.wt≠f
nḫỉ nfr n dỉ (39) sw m ỉb≠f nbỉ n nḥḥ d̲.t
ny-sw.t bỉ.ty ꜣImn-Rꜥ ny-sw.t nt̲r.w nb p.t t3 mw dw.(40)w
š3ꜥ t3 m ḫprỉ≠f
wr sw stn sw r nt̲r.w nb.w n p3w.t tpy

(41) (r)-nty wd̲y ꜣImn-Rꜥ ny-sw.t nt̲r.w p3 nt̲r ꜥ3 wr n š3ꜥ ḫpr p3y≠f
ḥr.tw ꜥ3 wr šp(42)s(y) r ntrỉ Ns-Ḫnsw t3 šr.(t) T3-ḫnw.t-D̲ḥwty n (= m)
ỉmnt.t r ntrỉ≠s m ḥr.t-ntr
(43) d̲d ꜣImn-Rꜥ ny-sw.t nt̲r.w p3 ntr ꜥ3 wr n š3ꜥ ḫpr ỉw≠ỉ ntrỉ Ns-Ḫnsw
t3y šr.(t) T3-ḫnw(44).t-D̲ḥwty n (= m) ỉmnt.t ỉw≠ỉ ntrỉ≠s m ḥr.t-ntr ỉw≠ỉ

dỉ.t šsp≠s mw ỉmnt.t ỉw≠ỉ dỉ.t (45) šsp≠s ḥtp.w m ḥr.t-nṯr ỉw≠ỉ nṯrỉ bȝ≠s
ḥȝ.t≠s m ḥr.t-nṯr ỉw bn ỉw≠ỉ dỉ.t (46) ỉr.tw sḥtm bȝ≠s m ḥr.t-nṯr ꜥn sp-2
ỉw≠ỉ nṯrỉ≠s m ḥr.t-nṯr mỉ-qd nṯr nb nṯr(47).t nb.(t) nty nṯrỉ mỉ-qd nty nb¹
nkt nb nty nṯrỉ m ḥr.t-nṯr ỉw≠ỉ dỉ.t šsp s(y) nṯr nb (48) nṯr.t nb.(t) nkt nb
nty nb nṯrỉ m ḥr.t-nṯr ỉw≠ỉ dỉ.t šsp s(y) nȝ nty (m) wnḏw nb m ḥr.t-nṯr (49)
m šsp nfr ỉw≠ỉ dỉ.t ỉr≠(w) n≠s md.(t) nb.(t) nfr.t nt.(t) ḫpr m-dỉ rmṯ.w m
pȝy≠f ḫpr (50) m pȝy qȝ(ỉ) ỉ-ḫpr m-dỉ≠s mtw≠w tȝy.t≠f r ḥr.t-nṯr mtw≠w
nṯrỉ{n}≠f² mtw≠w ỉr (51) n≠f nkt nb nfr m-ỉm mtw≠w dỉ.t šsp≠f mw ḥtp.w
mtw≠w dỉ.t šsp≠f tȝy≠f pwỉȝ.(t) (= pȝw.t) (52) m pȝ ḫpr pwỉȝ.(t) (= pȝw.
t) tȝ šsp nȝ nty nṯrỉ mtw≠w dỉ.t šsp≠f ḥtp-nṯr m pȝ ḫpr ḥtp-nṯr pȝ (53) šsp
nȝ nty nṯrỉ

ḏd ʾImn-Rꜥ ny-sw.t nṯr.w pȝ nṯr ꜥȝ wr n šȝꜥ ḫpr ỉw≠ỉ dỉ.t ỉr (54) Ns-
Ḥnsw tȝy šr.(t) n Tȝ-ḥn(w.t)-Ḏḥwty pȝ qȝ(ỉ) wnm pȝ qȝỉ swrỉ³ (55) ỉ-ỉr
nṯr nb nṯr.t nb.(t) nty nṯrỉ m ḥr.t-nṯr ỉw≠ỉ dỉ.t ỉr Ns-Ḥnsw qȝ(ỉ) nb nfr ỉ-
(56)ḫpr m-dỉ nṯr nb nṯr.t nb.(t) ỉ-ỉr nṯrỉ m ḥr.t-nṯr mtw≠ỉ šd Pȝ-nḏm pȝy≠ỉ
bȝk(57)ỉ r ḫnw nb n btȝ r ḏbȝ.t≠f ỉw bn-ỉw≠w ỉr btȝ n⁴ Ns-Ḥnsw r btȝ nb
n ḥr.t-nṯr (58) r ḏbȝ.t≠f ỉw≠ỉ dỉ.t pr pȝy≠s bȝ ỉw≠ỉ dỉ.t ꜥq≠f m ḏd ỉb≠f ỉw
bn-ỉȝ.tw šnꜥ≠f

ḏd (59) ʾImn-Rꜥ ny-sw.t nṯr.w pȝ nṯr ꜥȝ wr n šȝꜥ ḫpr ỉw≠ỉ pḥr ḥȝ.ty⁵
n Ns-Ḥnsw tȝy šr.(t) n Tȝ-ḥn(w.t)-Ḏḥwty (60) ỉw bn-ỉw≠s ỉr md.(t) nb.t
bỉn.(t) r⁶ Pȝ-nḏm pȝ šr n ȝs.t-m-Ḥby.t ỉw≠ỉ pḥr ḥȝ.ty≠s (61) ỉw bn-ỉw≠ỉ
dỉ.t ḥbȝỉ≠s m pȝy≠f ꜥḥꜥ(w) ỉw bn-ỉw≠ỉ dỉ.t dỉ≠s ḥbȝỉ≠w m pȝy≠f ꜥḥꜥ(w)
ỉw≠ỉ (62) pḥr ḥȝ.ty≠s ỉw bn-ỉw≠ỉ dỉ.t ỉr≠s n≠f md.(t) nb.(t) bỉn.(t) r ḥȝ.ty
rmṯ ỉw≠f ꜥnḫ ỉw≠ỉ pḥr (63) ḥȝ.ty≠s ỉw bn-ỉw≠ỉ dỉ.t dỉ≠s ỉr≠w n≠f md.(t)
nb.(t) nt.(t) dḥrỉ (r) ḥȝ.ty rmṯ ỉw≠f ꜥnḫ

(64) ḏd ʾImn-Rꜥ ny-sw.t nṯr.w pȝ nṯr ꜥȝ wr n šȝꜥ ḫpr ỉw≠ỉ dỉ.t ḫpr ỉw
bn-ỉw≠s wȝḫ (< wḫȝ) md.(t) nb.t bỉn.(t) n (65) Pȝ-nḏm pȝ šr n ȝs.t-m-Ḥby.
t n (= m) md.(t) nb.(t) n mt ỉw≠ỉ pḥr ḥȝ.ty≠s ỉw bn-ỉw≠s ỉr n≠f md.(t)
(66) nb.(t) nkt nb nty nb nty ỉr btȝ r rmṯ.w ỉw bn-ỉw≠s dỉ.t ỉr s.t n≠f nṯr
nb nṯr.t nb.(t) nty nṯrỉ (67) ȝḫ nb ȝḫ.(t) nb.(t) nty nṯrỉ ỉw bn-ỉw≠s dỉ.t ỉr
s.t n≠f nȝ nty (n) wnḏw nb nty nb nty ỉr sḫr.w (68) nty nb nty ỉ-ỉr≠w sḏm
ḫrw≠w ḫr-m-dỉ nȝ nty (n) wnḏw nb ỉw≠ỉ pḥr ḥȝ.ty≠s r wȝḫ n≠f (69) nfr
ỉw≠f ḥr-tp tȝ ỉw≠ỉ dỉ.t ḫpr ỉw wȝḫ (< wḫȝ) n≠f ꜥḥꜥ(w) qȝỉ sp-2 ỉw≠f ḥr-
tp tȝ ỉw≠f ꜥnḫ snb ỉw≠f nḫt (70) wsr pḥ.ty pȝ nty-ỉw≠s ỉr≠f ỉw≠ỉ dỉ.t ḫpr
ỉw wȝḫ n≠f md.(t) nb.(t) nfr.t pȝ nty-ỉw≠s (71) ỉr≠f n (= m) s.t nb.(t) nty-
ỉw≠w sḏm ḫrw≠s m-ỉm≠w ỉw≠ỉ dỉ.t ḫpr ỉw bn-ỉw≠s wȝḫ n≠f md.(t) nb.t
bỉn.t (n) wnḏw nb (72) nty ỉr btȝ r rmṯ.w nty ỉr dḥrỉ ḥȝ.ty r Pȝ-nḏm pȝ šr
n ȝs.t-m-Ḥby.t ỉw≠ỉ dỉ.t ḫpr (73) ỉw bn-ỉw≠s wȝḫ (< wḫȝ) md.(t) nb.(t) n
bỉn.t md.(t) nb.(t) n mt md.(t) nb.(t) n bỉn.t (n) wnḏw nb nty ỉr dḥrỉ (74)
ḥȝ.ty n rmṯ mtw≠w ỉr btȝ r rmṯ (n) rmṯ nb nty ỉb n≠w Pȝ-nḏm ỉw ỉ (= ỉr)⁷
ḥȝ.ty≠f dḥrỉ (75) n≠w m pȝ⁸ md.(t) bỉn.(t) ḫpr m-dỉ≠w ỉw≠ỉ dỉ.t ḫpr ỉw
pȝ nty m sšr m-dỉ ḥȝ.ty n Ns-Ḥnsw m-dỉ pȝy≠s (76) bȝ ỉw bn-ỉr ḥȝ.ty≠s
gȝwȝšȝ ỉm≠f ỉw bn-ỉr pȝy≠s bȝ gȝwȝšȝ ỉm≠f ỉw bn-ỉw≠f gȝwȝ(77)šȝ m-dỉ

Ns-Ḥnsw n (= m) q3ỉ nb n g3w3š3 nty ḫpr m-dỉ p3 rmṯ ỉw≠f m p3y sḫr (78)
ỉ-ḫpr m-dỉ≠s ỉw≠f nṯrỉ m ḥr.t-nṯr ỉw≠f (n) wnḏw nb ỉw bn-ỉw≠f ỉr md.(t)
bỉn.t m-dỉ Ns(y)-sw-Ḥnsw (79) (m) q3ỉ nb nty ḫpr m-dỉ rmṯ ỉw≠f (m) p3y
sḫr ỉ-ḫpr m-dỉ≠s mtw≠f ḫpr m ỉb h3r m-dỉ≠s (80) m p3 ḫpr md.(t) nb.t nfr.
t ꜥḥꜥ(w) q3ỉ sp-2 ỉw≠f ḥr-tp t3 ỉw≠f nḫt wsr pḥ.ty m p3 nty-ỉw≠f ḫpr (81)
m-dỉ P3-nḏm ỉw bn-ỉ3.tw ḫb3ỉ m p3y≠f ꜥḥꜥ(w) ỉw bn-ỉr md.(t) nb.(t) bỉn.
t (n) wnḏw nb nty ỉr (82) bt3 r rmṯ nty dḥrỉ (r) h3.ty rmṯ ḫpr m-dỉ P3-nḏm
ỉw bn-ỉw≠w ḫpr m-dỉ n3y≠f ḥm.wt m-dỉ n3y(83)≠f ḥrd.w m-dỉ n3y≠f sn.w
m-dỉ ꜣI-t3.wy m-dỉ Ns-t3-nb.(t)-ꜣIšrw m-dỉ M3s3h3rtỉ[9] (84) m-dỉ T3y-nfr n3
ḥrd.w n Ns(y)-sw-Ḥnsw ỉw bn-ỉw≠w ḫpr m-dỉ n3y≠s sn.w ỉw≠ỉ dỉ.t ḫpr
ỉw p3 nty (85) 3ḫ n≠s (m) q3(ỉ) nb mtw≠f mdn n≠s (m) q3(ỉ) nb n mdn
nty ḫpr m-dỉ rmṯ (86) ỉw≠f m p3y sḫr ỉ-ḫpr m-dỉ≠s m p3[8] md.(t) nb.(t)
nfr.t ꜥḥꜥ(w) q3ỉ sp-2 ḫpr m-dỉ P3-nḏm m sšr sp-2 (87) m-dỉ n3y≠f ḥm.wt
m-dỉ n3y≠f ḥrd.w m-dỉ n3y≠f sn.w m-dỉ n3 ḥrd.w n Ns(y)-sw-Ḥnsw m-dỉ
n3y≠s sn.w

(88) ḏd ꜣImn-Rꜥ ny-sw.t nṯr.w p3 nṯr ꜥ3 wr n š3ꜥ ḫpr ỉr nty nb nkt nb[10]
q3ỉ nb nty ḫpr m-dỉ rmṯ ỉw≠f n (= m) (89) p3y sḫr ỉ-ḫpr m-dỉ≠s mtw≠f
nṯrỉ ỉm≠w ỉw≠ỉ dỉ.t ḫpr≠w m-dỉ≠s ỉw≠ỉ dỉ.t ḏd.tw wr[11] ḥs Rꜥ n (= m)
(90) rn≠ỉ ỉw bn-ỉ3.tw šḥtm b3≠s m ḥr.t-nṯr ꜥn sp-2

ḏd ꜣImn-Rꜥ ny-sw.t nṯr.w p3 nṯr ꜥ3 wr n š3(91)ꜥ ḫpr ỉr md.(t) nb.(t)
nt.(t) ỉw≠w nfr n Ns(y)-sw-Ḥnsw mtw≠w nṯrỉ≠s mtw≠w dỉ.t šsp≠s mw
ḥtp.w ỉ-(92)šḥm≠w ỉ (=r) ḏd≠w m-b3ḥ≠ỉ ḥr-m-dỉ n3 ḏd≠w ỉw≠ỉ ỉr≠w
n≠s ḏr≠w ỉw mn (m)-dỉ≠w spp(y) (93) ỉr md.(t) nfr.t ỉ-ḏd≠w m-b3ḥ≠ỉ r
Ns(y)-sw-Ḥnsw ỉw≠ỉ ỉr≠w n≠s (m) trỉ nb[12] t3 p.t smn.tw (94) ỉw šw pr ỉw
bn-ỉr md.(t) bỉn.t pḥ≠s n md.(t) nb.t bỉn.t nt.(t) pḥ r rmṯ nty (95) m p3y
q3ỉ nty Ns(y)-sw-Ḥnsw ỉm≠f (m) trỉ nb t3 p.t smn.tw ỉw šw pr ỉw mw ḥr
ỉmw.w (96) ỉr md.(t) nb.(t) ỉ-ḏd≠w m-b3ḥ≠ỉ r-ḏd ỉ-ỉry s.t n≠s ḫr-m-dỉ n3
šḥm≠w ỉ (= r) ḏd≠w m-b3ḥ≠ỉ ỉw≠w (97) nfr.w ỉw≠ỉ ỉr≠w n≠s (m) trỉ nb
t3 p.t smn.tw ỉw šw pr ỉw mw ḥr ỉmw.w š3ꜥ p3 hrw (98) r ḥry[10] ỉr md.(t)
nb.(t) nt.(t) bỉn.(t) n rmṯ ỉw≠f m p3y q3ỉ ḫpr m-dỉ≠s ỉ-šḥm≠w ỉ (= r) (99)
ḏd≠w m-b3ḥ≠ỉ ḥr-m-dỉ n3 ḏd≠w ỉw≠ỉ r wỉ3.t≠w[13] ỉ-ỉr≠s ḏr≠w ỉw mn
(m)-dỉ≠w spp(y) (100) (m) trỉ nb t3 p.t smn.tw ỉw šw pr ỉw mw ḥr ỉmw.
w š3ꜥ-n p3 hrw r ḥry

(101) ḏd ꜣImn-Rꜥ ny-sw.t nṯr.w p3 nṯr ꜥ3 wr n š3ꜥ ḫpr ỉw≠ỉ dỉ.t ḏd.tw
wr[11] ḥs Rꜥ n (= m) rn≠ỉ (102) ỉw bn-ỉw≠ỉ dỉ.t ḫpr n≠s spp(y) n md.(t)
nb.(t) nfr.t nt.(t) ḫpr m-dỉ rmṯ ỉ-ḫpr (m) p3y q3ỉ nty Ns-Ḥnsw (103) ỉm≠f
ỉw≠ỉ dỉ.t šsp≠s ḥtp.w t ꜥq.w ḥnq.t mw ḥw3w ỉrp šdḥ ỉrt.(t) dg3ỉ.w (104)
ỉw≠ỉ dỉ.t šsp≠s 3ḫ.t nb.(t) nkt nb nty nb nfr n rmṯ ỉw≠f m p3y q3ỉ nty
Ns(y)-sw-Ḥnsw (105) m-ỉm≠f mtw≠f ỉr ḥs.w mtw≠w nṯrỉ≠f ỉw≠ỉ dỉ.t šsp≠s
mỉ-qd nṯr nb nṯr.t nb.(t) nkt nb nty šsp ỉw≠w nṯrỉ≠w m ḥr.t-nṯr (106) ỉw≠ỉ
dỉ.t šsp≠s ḥtp.(w)-nṯr≠s (r)-ḥ.t.w[10] n nṯr.w

ḏd ꜣImn-Rꜥ ny-sw.t nṯr.w p3 nṯr ꜥ3 wr n š3ꜥ ḫpr (107) ỉr p3y ḏd ỉ-ỉr≠w
ḥtp n sḫ.wt n ꜣIwr 3ḫ.wt n sḫ.wt n ꜣIwr nn (= ỉn) md.(t) (108) nfr.t n rmṯ

ỉw≠f (m) p3y q3ỉ nty nty Ns(y)-sw-Ḫnsw n-ỉm≠f m p3y.tw ỉr≠f[14] ỉw≠ỉ dỉ.t
ḥtp n (109) sḫ.wt n ꞽIwr 3ḥ.wt n sḫ.(w)t (n) ꞽIwr n Ns(y)-sw-Ḫnsw t3 šr.(t)
n.(t) T3-ḫnw.(t)-Ḏḥwty m p3 (110) ḫpr {m} p3 nty-ỉw≠f nfr n≠s {m} p3y ỉw
bn sw šrỉ.{t} ỉwn3 m p3 ḫpr p3 nty-ỉw≠f nfr (111) n≠s p3y

ḏd ꞽImn-Rꜥ ny-sw.t nt̠r.w p3 nt̠r ꜥ3 wr (n) š3ꜥ ḫpr ỉr md.(t) nb.(t) nfr.
t ỉ-ḏd≠w (112) m-b3ḥ≠ỉ r-ḏd ỉ-ỉr s.t (n) Ns(y)-sw-Ḫnsw t3 šr.(t) n.(t) T3-
ḫnw.(t)-Ḏḥwty ỉw≠ỉ ỉr≠w n≠s ỉw bn s.t šrỉ (113) ỉwn3 ỉw bn-ỉw≠w t̠3y.
t≠w dr≠w ỉw bn-ỉw≠w ḥb3 n-ỉm≠w {n} ꜥn sp-2 (m) trỉ nb t3 (114) p.t smn.
tw ỉw šw pr wpw ỉw≠s šsp≠w ỉw≠w ꜥš3y m ꜥ3.w p3 nty nb ỉw≠f nfr n≠s
(115) mỉ qd rmt̠ nb nt̠r nb nty nt̠rỉ.w mtw≠w pr mtw≠w ꜥq mtw≠w šmỉ r
s.t nb.(t) n mr≠w

(116) ḏd ꞽImn-Rꜥ ny-sw.t nt̠r.w p3 nt̠r ꜥ3 wr (n) š3ꜥ ḫpr ỉr md.(t) nb.(t)
nfr.t ỉ-ḏd≠tw m-b3ḥ≠ỉ r-ḏd ỉw≠k ỉr≠w (117) n P3-nḏm p3y šr n 3s.t-m-Ḫby.
t p3y≠ỉ b3kỉ n3y≠f ḥm.wt n3y≠f ḥrd.w n3y≠f sn.w (118) rmt̠ nb nty ỉb≠f
n≠w ỉw ỉ (= ỉr)[7] h3.ty≠f dḥrỉ n≠w m p3[8] md.(t) bỉn.t ḫpr m-dỉ≠w ỉw≠ỉ
(119) wḏ p3y≠ỉ ḥr-tw ꜥ3 wr šps r s.t nb.(t) nt.(t) ỉ-ỉr n3 md.(wt) nfr.w(t)
ḫpr m-dỉ {n} (120) P3-nḏm m-dỉ (n3y≠f)[2] ḥm.wt m-dỉ n3y≠f ḥrd.w m-dỉ
n3y≠f sn.w m-dỉ rmt̠ nb nty ỉb≠f n≠w m {r} p3(121)y.tw šmỉ ỉm r-ḏd ỉ-ỉr
s.t ḫr-tw n ꞽImn-Rꜥ ny-sw.t nt̠r.w p3 nt̠r ꜥ3 wr n š3ꜥ ḫpr (122) mtw≠ỉ dỉ.t
dỉ≠w ḫpr≠w

ỉn p3y nt̠r ꜥ3

This noble god, lord of all the gods,
Amon-Re, Lord of the Thrones of the Two Lands, Foremost of Karnak,
(2) The noble *ba*-spirit who came into being in the beginning,
The great god who lives on Maat,
The first primeval one, who bore the primeval ones,
(3) From whom every god came into being,
The singly unique one who made what exists,
Who began the earth in the first instant.

(4) Secret of birth and numerous of forms,
Whose hidden image is unknown,
August power, beloved (5) and revered,
Mighty in his glorious appearances,
Lord of magnificence, powerful of form,
From whose form (6) all forms were formed,
Who began formation, when there was nothing but him,
Who enlightened the earth in the first instant.

Great solar disk, (7) with streaming rays,
Presenting himself so that everyone might live,
He who crosses the firmament without wearying,

(8) Morning by morning, his custom is fixed.
Elderly one, rising as a youth in the early morning,
Who attains (9) the limits of eternity,
Encircles the firmament and traverses the underworld,
To enlighten the Two Lands, which he has created.

Divine (10) god, who fashioned himself,
Who made heaven and earth in his heart,
Greatest of the great, grandest of (11) the grand,
Great one, greater than the gods,
Youthful bull, with sharp-pointed horns,
At whose great name the Two Lands (12) tremble,
Under whose might eternity comes about,
Who brings an end to infinity,
(13) Great god, who began creation,
Who seized the Two Lands with his strength.

Ram-faced, exalted of form,
(14) More gracious than all the gods,
Wild-eyed lion elevating the two Healthy Eyes,
(15) Lord of flame against his enemies,
Great Abyss, who surges forth at his time,
To (16) enliven what has come from his potter's wheel,
Who bestrides the firmament, who encircles the underworld,
When earth lightens, again at his station of (17) yesterday.

Lord of strength, sacred of dignity,
Whose body his radiance has hidden,
Whose right eye (18) and left eye are the solar disk and the moon,
Heaven and earth being compounded with his radiant beauty,
(19) Excellent King, who does not slack,
Concerned for rising and setting,
From whose (20) two divine eyes mankind came forth,
And the gods from the utterances of his mouth,
Who made foodstuffs, who initiated nourishment,
Who created (21) all that exists.

Eternal one, who traverses the years,
Without limits to his lifespan,
Aged (22) and rejuvenated, who traverses eternity,
Elderly one, who begets his youth,
With multiple eyes (23) and many ears,
Who guides the millions by his shining,

Lord of life, who gives to whom he wishes,
(24) Under whose authority is the circuit of the earth.

Who commands to act, who is without opposition,
With no destruction of anything that he has done,
Pleasant (25) in name and sweet in love,
To entreat whom everyone arises early,
(26) Great in terror and grand in strength,
With every god having fear of him,
Youthful bull, who repels the (27) brawlers,
Strong armed, who smites his enemies,
This god, who began the earth by his resolutions.

Ba-spirit, (28) who shines by his two Healthy Eyes,
He of *ba*-spirit, who became manifest forms,
Holy one, who cannot be known,
(29) He is the King who made the Kings,
Who knit together the lands by the command that he has made,
While the gods and goddesses (30) bow to his might,
Through the greatness of his respect,
He who came forth in the beginning, he has completed the end,
Having begun (31) the lands by his resolutions.

Secret of form, who is unknown,
Who has hidden himself from all the gods,
Who has set (32) himself apart as the solar disk, yet who is unknown,
Who has concealed himself from what has come forth from him,
Glowing torch, (33) great in brilliance,
Within whose sight one sees,
The day is spent (34) beholding him, without being sated by him,
When earth lightens, everyone will entreat him.

Brilliant in (35) appearances in the midst of the Ennead,
His distinctive essence in every god,
The Abyss waters come, (36) the north wind goes south, within this
    secret god,
Who makes his commands for millions of millions,
(37) Whose hand does not tremble,
With inflexible oracles, effective in his commands, whose deeds do
    not fail,
(38) Who grants the lifetime and doubles the years for the one in his
    favor,
A good helper for the one who places (39) him in his heart,

A protector forever and ever,
The King of Upper and Lower Egypt, Amon-Re, King of the Gods,
Lord of heaven, earth, water, and the mountains,
(40) Who began the earth by his transformation,
Greater is he, more distinguished is he, than all the gods of the first
    primeval time.

(41) To wit: Amon-Re, King of the Gods, the very great god since the
beginning of creation, has dispatched his very great and noble oracle (42)
to deify Neskhons, the daughter of Tahenuttheuty, in the West, and to deify
her in the necropolis.

(43) Amon-Re, King of the Gods, the very great god since the beginning of creation, has said: "I shall deify Neskhons, this daughter of
Tahenu(44)ttheuty, in the west. I shall deify her in the necropolis. I shall
cause that she receive water of the west. I shall cause (45) that she receive
offerings in the necropolis. I shall deify her *ba*-spirit and her corpse in the
necropolis, whereas I shall not allow (46) her *ba*-spirit to be destroyed in
the necropolis, ever! I shall deify her in the necropolis like every god or
(47) every goddess who is divine, and like everyone[1] and everything that
is divine in the necropolis. I shall cause that every god (48) and every goddess, everyone and everything that is divine in the necropolis, receive her.
I shall cause that all those who are of any sort in the necropolis receive
her (49) in a good reception. I shall cause that there be done for her every
good thing that happens to a person when he comes to be (50) in this
condition that has happened to her, and he is taken to the necropolis, and
he is deified,[2] and there is done (51) for him every good thing there, and
he is caused to receive water and offerings, and he is caused to receive his
pat-cake (52) in the event that it is a *pat*-cake that those who are divine
receive, and he is caused to receive an endowment offering in the event
that it is an endowment offering (53) that those who are divine receive."

Amon-Re, King of the Gods, the very great god since the beginning of creation, has said: "I shall cause (54) Neskhons, this daughter of
Tahenuttheuty, to eat and drink in the same manner[3] (55) as every god
or every goddess who is divine in the necropolis. I shall cause Neskhons
to experience every good condition that (56) happens to every god and
every goddess who has become divine in the necropolis, and I shall save
Pinedjem, my servant, (57) from any accusation of wrongdoing concerning him, while Neskhons will not be punished[4] regarding any wrongdoing
of the necropolis (58) concerning him. I shall cause her *ba*-spirit to go
forth; I shall cause it to enter, as its desire prompts, whereas it will not be
hindered."

(59) Amon-Re, King of the Gods, the very great god since the beginning of creation, has said: "I shall enchant the heart[5] of Neskhons, this

daughter of Tahenuttheuty, (60) and she will not do anything evil against[6] Pinedjem, the son of Isetemkheb. I shall enchant her heart, (61) and I shall not permit her to diminish his lifetime, nor shall I permit her to cause that his lifetime be diminished. I shall (62) enchant her heart, and I shall not permit her to do to him anything harmful to the heart of a living man. I shall enchant (63) her heart, and I shall not permit her to have done to him anything that is grievous to a living man."

(64) Amon-Re, King of the Gods, the very great god since the begin-ning of creation, has said: "I shall cause it to happen that she will not seek anything evil for (65) Pinedjem, the son of Isetemkheb, in any deadly mat-ter. I shall enchant her heart, and she will not do to him anything spoken, (66) anything physical or anything whatever that does injury to people; nor will she cause any god or any goddess who is divine to do it to him, (67) nor any male or female blessed spirit who is divine; nor will she cause those who are of any sort to do it to him, neither anyone who exercises authority, (68) anyone whose voice is heard, nor indeed those who are of any sort. I shall enchant her heart to seek for him (69) good things while he is on earth. I shall cause it to happen that it is only seeking for him a very long lifetime—while he is on earth, being alive and healthy, being strong (70) and mighty—that she will do. I shall cause it to happen that it is only seeking for him everything good that she (71) will do, in every place in which her voice will be heard. I shall cause it to happen that she will not seek for him anything evil of any sort (72) that does injury to people, that is grievous to Pinedjem, the son of Isetemkheb. I shall cause it to happen (73) that she will not seek anything evil, anything deadly or anything evil of any sort that is grievous (74) to a man and does injury to a man, against any man for whom Pinedjem has affection and for whom he would[7] be grieved (75) if[8] an evil matter happened to them. I shall cause it to happen that what is in good order shall be with the heart of Neskhons and with her (76) *ba*-spirit, and that her heart will not turn away from him, and that her *ba*-spirit will not turn away from him, and that he will not turn away (77) from Neskhons in any manner of turning away that happens to a man when he is in this state (78) that has happened to her, while he is divine in the necropolis or existing in any fashion; and that he will not do anything evil to Neskhons (79) in any manner that happens to a man when he is in this state that has happened to her; and he shall be of satis-fied heart with regard to her, (80) in the event that everything good, a very long lifetime while he is on earth, and being strong and mighty, is what will happen (81) to Pinedjem, and that his lifetime will not be diminished, and that nothing evil of any kind that (82) injures a man or that is grievous to a man will happen to Pinedjem, and that they will not happen to his wives, to his (83) children, to his brethren, to Itawi, to Nestanebetasheru, to Masaharta[9] (84) or to Tchainefer, the children of Neskhons, and that

they will not happen to her brethren. I shall cause it to happen that what is (85) beneficial be hers in every manner, and that it give comfort to her in every manner of giving comfort that happens with a man (86) who is in this state that has happened to her, provided that[8] everything good and a very long lifetime happen to Pinedjem in every respect, (87) as well as to his wives, to his children, to his brethren, to the children of Neskhons, and to her brethren."

(88) Amon-Re, King of the Gods, the very great god since the beginning of creation, has said: "As for any and everything[10] of any manner that happens to a man who is in (89) this state that has happened to her, and by which he is deified, I shall cause them to happen to her. I shall cause that 'Great[11] is the favor of Re' be said in (90) my name, while her *ba*-spirit will not be destroyed in the necropolis, ever!"

Amon-Re, King of the Gods, the very great god since the beginning of (91) creation, has said: "As for anything that will be good for Neskhons, and that will deify her, and that will cause her to receive water and offerings, and that (92) they have forgotten to mention before me, as well as those things they have mentioned, I shall do them for her entirely, without exception. (93) As for everything good that they have mentioned before me regarding Neskhons, I shall do them for her so long as[12] the sky is fixed (94) and the sun goes forth, and nothing evil will assail her from among anything evil that assails a man who is (95) in this condition in which Neskhons is, so long as the sky is fixed, the sun goes forth and water supports boats. (96) As for everything that they have mentioned before me, saying: 'Do them for her,' as well as those things that they have forgotten to mention before me and that will be (97) good, I shall do them for her so long as the sky is fixed, the sun goes forth and water supports boats, from today (98) forward.[10] As for everything that is bad for a man who is in this condition that has happened to her, and that they have forgotten to (99) mention before me as well as those things they have mentioned, I shall distance them[13] from her entirely, without exception, (100) so long as the sky is fixed, the sun goes forth and water supports boats, from today forward."

(101) Amon-Re, King of the Gods, the very great god since the beginning of creation, has said: "I shall cause that 'Great[11] is the favor of Re' be said in my name, (102) and I shall not create for her a shortcoming of anything good that happens to a man who has come to be in this condition in which Neskhons (103) is. I shall cause her to receive offerings of bread loaves, beer, water, sweet drink, wine, pomegranate-wine, milk, and fruit. (104) I shall cause her to receive everything and anything that is good for a man who is in this condition in which Neskhons (105) is, and who becomes a saint and who is deified. I shall cause her to receive (such), like any god, any goddess or anything that receives, being divine

in the necropolis. (106) I shall cause that she receive endowment offerings in conformity with[10] the gods."

Amon-Re, King of the Gods, the very great god since the beginning of creation, has said: (107) "As for this mention that they made of an offering of the Field of Reeds and plots of the Fields of Reeds, is it a good thing (108) for a man who is in this condition in which Neskhons is, when one does it?[14] I shall give offerings of (109) the Field of Reeds and plots of the Fields of Reeds to Neskhons, the daughter of Tahenuttheuty, in the (110) event that it is what will be good for her, and in no small quantity in the event that it is what will be good (111) for her."

Amon-Re, King of the Gods, the very great god since the beginning of creation, has said: "As for everything good that they have mentioned (112) before me, saying: 'Do them for Neskhons, the daughter of Tahenuttheuty,' I shall do them for her, and in no small quantity, (113) while absolutely none of them shall be taken away, nor will they be diminished ever, so long as the (114) sky is fixed and the sun goes forth, but rather she shall receive them, they being numerous to the extent of whatever will be good for her, (115) like every man and every god who is divine, and who go forth and who enter and who go to any place of their preference."

(116) Amon-Re, King of the Gods, the very great god since the beginning of creation, has said: "As for everything good that has been mentioned before me, saying: 'Will you do them (117) for Pinedjem, this son of Isetemkheb, my servant, his wives, his children, his brethren, (118) and any man for whom Pinedjem has affection and for whom he would[7] be grieved if[8] an evil matter happened to them,' I shall (119) dispatch my very great and noble oracle to every place where the good things will accrue to (120) Pinedjem, to his[2] wives, to his children, to his brethren, and to any man for whom he has affection, when (121) one goes there, saying: 'Do them, O oracle of Amon-Re, King of the Gods, the very great god since the beginning of creation,' (122) and I shall cause that they be made to happen."

Thus says this great god.

NOTES

1. Written nb nty throughout the text, as often in hieratic documents of this period; cf. Wenamon, col. 2/9.

2. The Cairo hieratic board preserves the correct reading.

3. Literally, "to make the manner of eating and the manner of drinking" done by any god or goddess. The expression continues in Demotic (Setna I, col. 5/17) and in Coptic ⲡϬⲓⲛⲟⲩⲱⲙ, ⲡϬⲓⲛⲥⲱ.

4. Literally, "to do what is abominated to" Neskhons. Considered a mistake by Gunn (1955, 89), the idiom signifies "to punish."

5. For the idiom, see Ritner 1993b, 66–67, contra Gunn 1955, 89 §II n. 1. Gunn's translation, "turn her heart," implies a predisposition on the part of Neskhons for vengeance and would require *ỉw≠ỉ dỉ.t pḥr ḥꜣ.ty≠s.

6. Gunn 1955, 89–90 §IV n. 2, read "t" as a final feminine marker for the expected preposition "r" copied by Golenischeff. The hieratic board, however, writes a clear "r" at this point. Other questionable examples of "r" do correspond to final feminine endings after the determinative, thus anticipating Demotic practice.

7. For the meaning, see Edwards 1955, 98–99.

8. Literally, "in the (event that) evil happen"; see Gunn 1946, 93.

9. A Libyan name born by three prominent males of Dynasty XXI.

10. The phraseology anticipates Demotic usage.

11. The writing, which resembles the number 70, anticipates the "abnormal hieratic" of Dynasty XXV. The expression is perhaps the incipit of a traditional prayer.

12. Literally, "at every time (that)."

13. Read rwỉ.t≠w by Gunn 1955, 93 n. 6, who noted the unexpected presence of a feminine ending. But cf. the standard Late Egyptian term wỉꜣ.tw in Erman and Grapow 1926–63, 1:272/4, with similar determinative and meaning.

14. Amon restates the oracular question, asking whether it is proper to mention prospective allotments of underworld fields ("Fields of Reeds").

36. THE REBURIAL OF ROYAL MUMMIES UNDER SIAMON

In the tenth year of Siamon, after sixty years of lying within the tomb of Seti I (KV 17), the royal mummies of Rameses I and II were moved together with Seti himself to the ancient crag-tomb of Queen Inhapi. This represented the third reburial for Rameses II and the second for Rameses I. All three kings would be moved again some forty years later to the collective cache in the family tomb of Pinedjem II (DB 320). Coffin dockets record two associated events, three days apart. On the 17th, an oracle of the goddess Mut authorized the move, which was duly enacted on the 20th, the same day as the burial of Pinedjem II in DB 320. Presumably, similar dockets were recorded for both dates on the coffins of all three kings, but only the first docket now survives on the fragmentary coffin of Rameses I.

For the texts and translations, see Maspero 1889, 551–54, 557–60; Daressy 1909, 27, 30–31, 33, and pls. XVI, XIX, XXII–XXIII; Thomas 1966, 252–53, 263 nn. 50–61; Breasted 1906–7, 4:335–36 §§690–92; Černý 1946, 26–30; and Reeves 1990, 237–39. See Kitchen 1986, 10–11 §7, 277–78 §233.

I. Composite Text from the Coffins of Rameses I, Seti I, and Rameses II

ḥsb.t 10.t[1] ꜣbd 4 pr.t sw 17[2] n ny-sw.t Sꜣ-ꜣImn[3] hrw n ỉn.(t) ny-sw.t Mn-pḥ.t(y)-Rꜥ (var. Mn-Mꜣꜥ.t-Rꜥ Sty-mry-Ptḥ ꜥnḫ wḏꜣ snb var. Wsr-Mꜣꜥ.t-Rꜥ pꜣ nṯr ꜥꜣ) r-bnr m-ẖnw pꜣy ẖr n ny-sw.t Mn-Mꜣꜥ.t-Rꜥ Sty-mry-Ptḥ[4] ỉ (= r)

ḏd sꜥq⸗f r pꜣy qꜣy n ꞋIn-Ḥꜥpy nty (m) s.t ꜥꜣ.t[5] ỉn ḥm-nṯr n ꞋImn-Rꜥ ny-sw.t
nṯr.w ꜥnḫ⸗f-n-ꞋImn sꜣ Bꜣky ỉt-nṯr n ꞋImn-Rꜥ ny-sw.t nṯr.w ḥm-nṯr 3-nw n
Ḫnsw-m-Wꜣs.t Nfr-ḥtp sš sḫn n pr ꞋImn-Rꜥ ny-sw.t nṯr.w stm n Tꜣ-ḥw.t-Wsr-
Mꜣꜥ.t-Rꜥ-stp-n-Rꜥ m pr ꞋImn ỉmy-rꜣ mšꜥ[6] n Tꜣ-s.t-mry.(t)-Ḏḥwty[7] sš rwḏw ꜥꜣ
Nsy-pꜣ-qꜣ(ỉ)-šw.ty sꜣ Bꜣk-n-Ḫnsw m-ḫt ḏd Mw.t tꜣ ḥr(y.t) s.t wr.t pꜣ nty m
sšrw m-bꜣḥ⸗ỉ ỉw mn sḫr nb n-ỉm⸗f[8] m pꜣy⸗w ỉn.t⸗w r-bnr m-ḫnw pꜣy ḫr
nty s.t ỉm⸗f mtwtw sꜥq.t⸗w r pꜣy qꜣy n ꞋIn-Ḥꜥpy nty (m) s.t ꜥꜣ.t nty ꞋImn-
ḥtp ỉm ḥtp

Regnal year 10,[1] month 4 of winter, day 17[2] of King Siamon,[3] the day
of bringing King Menpehtyre (Rameses I; var. Menmaatre, Seti beloved of
Ptah, l.p.h.; var. Usermaatre-setepenre, the great god) out from within this
royal tomb of King Menmaatre, Seti (I) beloved of Ptah,[4] in order to cause
him to enter into this crag-tomb of (Queen) Inhapi, which is an important
place,[5] by the prophet of Amon-Re, King of the Gods, Ankhefenamon,
son of Baki, and by the God's Father of Amon-Re, King of the Gods, the
Third Prophet of Khonsu in Thebes, Neferhotep, the scribe of commissions of the estate of Amon-Re, King of the Gods, the *setem*-priest of the
Mansion of Usermaatre-setepenre in the estate of Amon, the general[6] of
The-place-beloved-of-Thoth,[7] the scribe and senior agent, Nespakashuty,
son of Bakenkhonsu, after the goddess Mut, the superior of the Great Place
said: "What is fine in my presence, without any harm in it,[8] is their bringing
them out from within this royal tomb in which they are, and their causing
them to enter into this crag-tomb of (Queen) Inhapi, which is an important
place, and in which Amonhotep (I) rests."

II. Composite Text from the Coffins of Seti I and Rameses II

ḥsb.t 10.t[9] ꜣbd 4 pr.t sw 20 hrw (n) sꜥq nṯr r s.t⸗f r rdỉ.t[10] ḥtp n tꜣy
ḥw.t nḥḥ nt.(t)[11] ꞋImn-ḥtp pꜣ ỉb-ỉb (n) ꞋImn m ꜥnḫ wḏꜣ snb ỉn ỉt-nṯr n
ꞋImn ỉmy-rꜣ pr ḥḏ Ḏd-ꞋImn-ỉw⸗f-ꜥnḫ ỉt-nṯr n ꞋImn[12] ḥm-nṯr 3-nw n Mw.t[13]
Ꞌ Iw⸗f-n-ꞋImn sꜣ Nsy-sw-pꜣ-qꜣ(ỉ)-šw.ty ỉt-nṯr n ꞋImn Wn-nfr sꜣ Mntw-m-Wꜣs.
t ỉt-nṯr n ꞋImn [...]

Regnal year 10,[9] month 4 of winter, day 20, the day of causing the
god to enter into his place to be put[10] to rest in this "Mansion of Eternity"
in which[11] Amonhotep (I), the favorite of Amon, is in life, prosperity, and
health, by the God's Father of Amon and overseer of the treasury, Djedamoniuefankh, and by the God's Father of Amon[12] and Third Prophet of Mut,[13]
Iuefenamon, son of Nespakashuty, and by the God's Father of Amon, Wennefer, son of Montuemwaset, and by the God's Father of Amon [...]

NOTES
    1. Misread 16 by Maspero 1889 and Daressy 1909; see Černý 1946, 26, 28.
    2. Misread as 13 on the coffins of Rameses I and Seti I by Maspero 1889 and
Daressy 1909; see Černý 1946, 28.

3. The phrase "of King Siamon" is omitted on the coffin of Rameses II.

4. Thus on the coffins of Rameses I and II. The Seti text has m-ḫnw pꜣy⸗f ḥr "from within his royal tomb."

5. An addition nty ꜣImn-ḥtp ỉm ḥtp "and in which Amonhotep (I) rests" is found only on the Rameses I coffin.

6. For the reading mšꜥ, not ḫtmw (as Maspero 1889 and Daressy 1909), see Černý 1946, 26 n. 3, 28.

7. For the locality, see the references gathered in Černý 1946, 28 n.5.

8. Thomas and Reeves translated, "That which was in good condition in my care, there has been no injury to it…," converting a marked circumstantial to a main clause. See the discussion in Thomas 1966, 252.

9. Misread 16 by Maspero 1889 and Daressy 1909; see Černý 1946, 28.

10. Thus on the Seti I coffin. The Rameses II text has the variant ỉ (=r) dỉ.t.

11. Translations by Breasted and Černý 1946 have interpreted the form nty as a genitive, "the tomb of Amonhotep," but the tomb is rather that of Inhapi "in which" Amonhotep either "rests" (docket of day 17) or "is in life," etc. (docket of day 20).

12. The conclusion follows the fuller text of Rameses II. After the mention of Djedamoniuefankh, the Seti I coffin inverts the order of Wennefer and Iuefenamon: "by the God's Father of Amon, Wennefer, and by the God's Father of Amon and Third Prophet of Mut, Iuefenamon [son of Nespakashuty …]."

13. So Černý 1946, 28. Maspero 1889, followed by Daressy 1909 and Breasted 1906–7, read Ḫnsw "Khonsu" in the Seti text and an erroneous "f" in that of Rameses II.

37. THE BURIAL OF PINEDJEM II:
WALL DOCKETS OF DEIR EL-BAHARI TOMB 320

On the same day that the royal mummies of Rameses I and II and Seti I were reinterred in the crag-tomb of Queen Inhapi in year 10 of Siamon, the newly deceased high priest of Amon, Pinedjem II, was laid to rest in the usurped New Kingdom tomb that would serve as his family's crypt and, ultimately, as the collective cache for the oft-moved royal mummies. Two wall dockets on the left jamb of the doorway just off the tomb shaft record the burial. The first text was discontinued for lack of space and repeated lower on the same wall. Agents involved in the burial (Nespakashuty, Wennefer, and Ankhefenamon) appear also in the Inhapi dockets.

For the texts and translations, see Maspero 1889, 520–22; Černý 1946, 26–27 (recollation and improved translation); Thomas 1966, 253, 263 nn. 63–65; and Reeves 1990, 188, 239. See Kitchen 1986, 10–11 §7, 277–78 §233.

I. DOCKET 1

ḥsb.t 10.t[1] ꜣbd 4 pr.t sw 20 hrw n qrs [Wsỉ]r

Regnal year 10,[1] month 4 of winter, day 20, the day of burial of the [Osiris].

I. DOCKET 2

ḥsb.t 10.t[1] ꜣbd 4 pr.t sw 20 hrw n qrs (2) Wsỉr ḥm-nṯr tpy n ꜣImn-Rꜥ ny-sw.t nṯr.w ỉmy-rꜣ mšꜥ[2] wr ḥꜣw.ty Pꜣy-nḏm (3) ỉn ỉt-nṯr n ꜣImn ỉmy-rꜣ pr ḥḏ Ḏd-Ḫnsw-ỉw≠f-ꜥnḫ ỉt-nṯr n ꜣImn sš mšꜥ rwḏw ꜥꜣ Nsy-pꜣ-qꜣ(ỉ)-šw.ty ḥm-nṯr[3] n ꜣImn [ꜥnḫ≠f]-n-ꜣImn[4] (4) ỉt-nṯr n ꜣImn Wnn-nfr ỉn sš ny-sw.t (m) s.t Mꜣꜥ.t Bꜣk-n-Mw.t[5] ꜥꜣ n ỉs.t Pꜣ-dỉ-ꜣImn[6] ꜥꜣ n ỉs.t ꜣImn-ms (5) ỉt-nṯr n ꜣImn ḥr(y) sštꜣ.w Pꜣ-dỉ-ꜣImn sꜣ ꜥnḫ≠f-n-Ḫnsw

Regnal year 10,[1] month 4 of winter, day 20, the day of burial (2) of the Osiris, the First Prophet of Amon-Re, King of the Gods, the great general[2] and leader, Pinedjem (II), (3) by the God's Father of Amon and overseer of the treasury, Djedkhonsuiuefankh, the God's Father of Amon, scribe of the army and senior agent, Nespakashuty, the prophet[3] of Amon, [Ankhef]enamon,[4] (4) and the God's Father of Amon, Wennefer, and by the royal necropolis scribe, Bakenmut,[5] the foreman of the construction crew, Padiamon,[6] the foreman of the construction crew, Amonmose, (5) and the God's Father of Amon and chief of secrets, Padiamon, son of Ankhefenkhonsu.

NOTES

1. Misread 16 by Maspero 1889 and Daressy 1909; see Černý 1946, 26, 28.
2. For the reading mšꜥ in lines 2–3, see Černý 1946, 26 n. 3 and 28.
3. So Černý 1946, 27, contra Maspero's ꜣbd wḥm (?).
4. So Thomas 1966, 263 n. 64. This prophet of Amon is mentioned before Nespakashuty on the contemporary coffin dockets of day 17.
5. So Černý 1946, 27, contra Maspero's Bꜣk "Bak." Bakenmut is scribe of the "Place of Truth," the name of the Theban necropolis.
6. So Černý 1946, 27, contra Maspero's Pꜣ-dỉ-Ḥr "Padihor."

38. A MEMPHITE LAND SALE UNDER SIAMON
(COLLÈGE ST. JOSEPH DES FRÈRES DES ÉCOLES CHRÉTIENNES AU CAIRE)

Recovered from the ruins of Fustat, this round-topped limestone stela measures 30 cm high by 20 cm wide. On the right of the lunette, King Siamon offers wine to the Memphite deities Ptah and Sakhmet. The decorative format recalls that of donation stelae, but the text records a private sale of land between members of the temple estate of Ptah.

For the text, see Munier 1922, 361–66; Pirenne and van de Walle 1937, 41–43; noted in Meeks 1979a, 687. See Kitchen 1986, 279 §234.

LABEL FOR PTAH
Ptḥ nb mꜣꜥ.t
Ptah, Lord of Maat.

LABEL FOR SAKHMET

Shm.t ꜥ3.(t) mrỉ.(t) Ptḥ

Sakhmet the great, beloved of Ptah.

LABEL FOR SIAMON

[nṯr] nfr (2) Nṯr-ḫpr-Rꜥ mrỉ-ʾImn (3) rdỉ.t ỉrp

The Good [God], (2) Netcherkheperre, beloved of Amon. (3) Giving wine.

MAIN TEXT

(1) ḥsb.t 16.(t) ȝbd 3 ȝḫ.t sw 4 ḫr ḥm (n) ny-sw.t bỉ.ty Nṯr-ḫpr-Rꜥ mrỉ-ʾImn sȝ Rꜥ Sȝ-ʾImn mrỉ-ʾImn (2) hrw pn hnk ḥḏ ỉ-ỉr mḥ ḥḏ n ḥw.t nbw[1] n Ptḥ ʾIty (3) n wꜥb ḫry-ḥb.(t) (n) Ptḥ ꜥnḫ≠f-n-Ḫnsw[2] sȝ ḥry ỉry-sš.w Pȝ-sbȝt[y]³ (4) n(3) n[t]ly m šnw.wt n.(t) pr Ptḥ r-ḏbȝ ȝḫ.t stȝ.t 2 m ww n (5) Pȝ-bꜥḥ.t(y) n Mn-nfr n pȝ ỉmn.t n (6) pȝ kȝm n Tȝ-ỉȝ.t ỉw≠ỉ ḫȝꜥ n≠f (7) ḥḏ dbn 2 qd.t 2.(t) wḥm r-ḏbȝ ȝḫ.t nty m Pȝ-(8)bꜥ(ꜥ)ḥ.t(y) n Mn-nfr m-dỉ wꜥb ḫry-ḥb.(t) n Ptḥ Sḫ.t-ꜥȝ.(t)-Ḥry⁴ ȝḫ.t stȝ.t 2 ỉw≠ỉ dỉ ḥḏ dbn 1

Regnal year 16, month 3 of Inundation, day 4, under the Majesty of the King of Upper and Lower Egypt, Netcherkheperre, Son of Re, Siamon, beloved of Amon. (2) On this day there was a transaction of silver made by the silversmith in the goldsmiths' workshop[1] of Ptah, Ity, (3) to the *wab*-priest and lector priest of Ptah, Ankhefenkhonsu,[2] son of Pasebaty,[3] the chief archivist (4) of those (documents) that are in the granaries of the estate of Ptah, in exchange for 2 *arouras* of field in the district of (5) "The Flooded Land" of Memphis on the west of (6) the garden of the woman Taiat, while I (Ity) measured out for him (7) 2 *deben* and 2 *kite* of silver, and furthermore, in exchange for the field that is in "The Flooded Land" of Memphis in the possession of the *wab*-priest and lector priest of Ptah, Sekhaathor,[4] being 2 *arouras* of field, while I gave 1 *deben* of silver.

NOTES

1. Literally "filler of silver in the House of Gold."

2. Misread Ptah-ankh-ef-en-khensou by earlier editors. The title "*wab*-priest and lector priest of Ptah" appears again in line 8.

3. Or Pȝ-dwȝt[y] "Paduaty."

4. Or Ḥry stm ꜥȝ "Hori, the great *setem*-priest."

39. TANITE VICTORY RELIEF

A variation on the conventional motif of "Pharaoh smiting his enemies" is preserved on a fragmentary calcite bas-relief recovered from a ruined construction of Pseusennes I and Siamon east of the main temple axis at Tanis. King Siamon is depicted in the traditional act of raising his (lost) mace to strike an enemy whom he grasps by the hair. In contrast to typical scenes displaying defeated Nubians and Libyans, the enemy's ethnic marker is here a double axe, indicative of an Aegean or Philistine warrior. The unusual scene may substantiate the biblical account in 1 Kgs 9:16, which records an unnamed pharaoh's conquest of Gezer, subsequently given to Solomon as dowry with a royal princess.

For the relief and discussion, see Montet 1947, 36 and pl. 9a; 1941, 195–96. See Kitchen 1986, 278 §234, 280–81 §235 (esp. 280 n. 222 for additional bibliography), and 574 §506.

CARTOUCHE OF SIAMON
   S3-ʾImn mrî-[ʾImn]
   Siamon, beloved of [Amon].

G. PSEUSENNES II

40. ORACULAR DECREE PRESERVING THE PROPERTY OF MAATKARE (B)

Engraved on the west wing of the northern face of the Seventh Pylon at Karnak is the transcript of an oracular decree guaranteeing Theban property rights for the princess and queen Maatkare (B), daughter of Pseusennes II and primary wife of Osorkon I. Approximately two-thirds of the initial text has been lost, leaving eight fragmentary horizontal lines. Owing to the loss of the upper sections, the date of the oracle is uncertain; the range of possibilities encompasses the reigns of Pseusennes II, Sheshonq I, and Osorkon I. The decree should be compared with the Apanage Stela of Iuwelot (no. 69), who succeeded her own son Sheshonq (II) as high priest of Amon. The oracle was certainly conducted by the contemporary high priest, and the document may well date to the pontificate of the second Sheshonq, serving as a confirmation of his maternal inheritance.

The inscription was discovered by Mariette in 1874, with subsequent publications by himself (1875 [1982a]), Brugsch (1877), Lauth (1879), and Maspero (1877; 1889). Text and early bibliography are found in Maspero 1889, 694–95; with text corrections, translation, and discussion in Gardiner 1962, 64–69; and Černý 1942, 126–33. An English translation of the obsolete analysis of Brugsch has been reissued in Brugsch 1996, 373–75. See Kitchen 1986, 60–61 §49 and 306 §265.

   16+ lines lost [...]
   (1+x) [wḥm dd-în≠f m-bȝḥ¹ ʾImn-Rˤ ny-sw.t nṯr.w pȝy nṯr ˤȝ wr n šȝˤ n

ḫpr Mw.t Ḫnsw] n3 ntr.w ꜥ3.w [... nkt] nb [n wnḏw] nb [î-]dî n≠s n3 rmṯ.w n
p3 t3 î-[... n3 rmṯ.w n] (2+x) p3 t3 î-t3(î)≠s n šrî.t n ḥ.t≠w îw≠tn smn(t)≠w
n≠s nkt nb nmḥw îw≠[t]n [smn.t≠w m-ḏr.t s3≠s s3 n s3≠s s3.t≠s s3.t n s3.t≠s
ms n m]s.w≠s š3ꜥ r-ḫt nḥḥ

ḏd ꞌImn-Rꜥ ny-sw.t ntr.w p3y ntr ꜥ3 wr n š3ꜥ n ḫpr Mw.t Ḫnsw n3 ntr.w
[ꜥ3.w îw≠n smn.t≠w] (3+x) ny-sw.t nb ḥm-ntr tp(y) n ꞌImn nb ꜥ3 n mšꜥ nb
n mšꜥ rmṯ n wnḏw nb îw≠w n ꜥḥ3wty.w îw≠w n ḥm.wt nt-îw≠w îr sḫr.
w îr [š3]ꜥ n3 nty-îw≠w îr sḫr.w ḥr-s3 î-smn nkt nb n wnḏw nb î-în M3ꜥ.
t-k3-Rꜥ m3ꜥ.t-ḫrw s3.t n ny-sw.t P3-sb3-ḫꜥ-n-Nîw.t mrî-ꞌImn [m snnw≠s3 (m)
ꜥ Šmꜥ ... m-dî n3 rmṯ.w(?)]

(4+x) n p3 t3 ḥnꜥ nkt nb n wnḏw nb î-dî n≠s n3 rmṯ.w n p3 t3 î-t3(î)≠s
n šrî.t n ḥ.t≠w î-smn.(t)≠w m-ḏr.t≠s îw≠{t}n3 smn.t≠w m-ḏr.t s3≠s s3 n s3≠s
s3.t≠s s3.t n s3.t≠s ms n ms.(w)≠s š3ꜥ r-ḫt nḥḥ

wḥm [dd-în≠f m-b3ḥ[1] ꞌImn-Rꜥ ny-sw.t ntr.]w p3y ntr ꜥ3 wr [n š3]ꜥ (5+x)
n ḫpr Mw.t Ḫnsw n3 ntr.w ꜥ3.w ḥdb[5] rmt nb n wnḏw nb n p3 t3 ḏr≠f îw≠w
n ꜥḥ3wty.w îw≠w n ḥm.wt nt-îw≠w mdty (n) nkt nb n wnḏw nb î-în{n}
M3ꜥ.t-k3-Rꜥ s3.t ny-sw.t P3-sb3-ḫꜥ-n-Nîw.t mrî-ꞌImn m snnw≠s (m) ꜥ Šmꜥ
ḥnꜥ p3 nkt [nb n wnḏw nb î-dî n≠s n3] rmṯ.w (6+x) (n) p3 t3 î-t3(î)≠s n
šrî.t n ḥ.t≠w n3 nty-îw≠w ktkt nkt n-îm≠w n dw3 ḥr-s3 dw3 îw≠(t)n3 îr
n3y≠(t)n3 b3.w ꜥ3.w dns.w[5] î-r≠w îw bn-îw≠(t)n3 ḥtp n≠w [gr]

[wšd[6]] r wr sp-2 în p3y ntr ꜥ3 Mw.t Ḫnsw n3 ntr.w ꜥ3.w

ḏd ꞌImn-Rꜥ ny-sw.t ntr.w p3y ntr ꜥ3 [wr n š3ꜥ n ḫpr Mw.t Ḫnsw n3] ntr.
w ꜥ3.w (7+x) îw≠n ḥdb rmṯ nb n wnḏw nb n p3 t3 ḏr≠f îw≠w n ꜥḥ3wty.w
îw≠w n ḥm.wt nt-îw≠w mdty n nkt nb n wnḏw nb [î-în{n} M3ꜥ.t-k3-Rꜥ s3.t
ny-sw.t P3-sb3-ḫꜥ-n-Nîw.t mrî-ꞌImn[7] m snnw]≠s (m) ꜥ Šmꜥ ḥnꜥ p3 nkt nb n
wnḏw nb î-dî n≠s n(3) rmṯ.w n p3 t3 î-t3(î)≠s n [šrî.t n ḥ.t≠w n3 nty-îw≠w
ktkt nkt n-îm≠w]

(8+x) n dw3 ḥr-s3 dw3 îw≠n îr n3y≠n b3.w ꜥ3.w dns.w î-r≠w îw bn-
îw≠n ḥtp n≠w gr îw≠n [dî] šr.t≠w n p3 îtn[8] îw≠w [m b3.w(?) n p3y ntr ꜥ3]
Mw.t [Ḫ]n[sw] n3 ntr.w ꜥ3.w

16+ lines lost [...]

(1+x) [Again he said before[1] Amon-Re, King of the Gods, this very
great god since the beginning of creation, Mut and Khonsu], the great
gods: ["...] Any[thing of] any [sort that] the people of the land sold to her
and that [she purchased from (?) the people of](2+x) the land or that she
acquired as a child from their property, will you confirm them for her? Any
private property, will you [confirm them in the possession of her son, the
son of her son, her daughter, the daughter of her daughter, the child of]
her children throughout eternity?"

Then said Amon-Re, King of the Gods, this very great god since the
beginning of creation, Mut and Khonsu, the [great] gods: ["We shall confirm
them.] (3+x) Any king, any First Prophet of Amon, any army commander

of the military, people of any sort whether male or female who shall exercise authority, even up to those who will exercise authority hereafter to confirm anything of any sort that Maatkare, the justified, royal daughter of Pseusennes (II), beloved of Amon, purchased [at her price[2] (in) the territory of Upper Egypt ... from the people (?)] (4+x) of the land, together with anything of any sort that the people of the land sold to her or that she acquired as a child from their property, so as to confirm them in her possession, we[3] shall confirm them in the possession of her son, the son of her son, her daughter, the daughter of her daughter, the child of her children throughout eternity."

Again [he said before[1] Amon-Re, King of the God]s, this very great god [since the beginning] (5+x) of creation, Mut and Khonsu, the great gods: "Kill[4] any person of any sort in the entire land whether male or female who will contest anything of any sort that Maatkare, the royal daughter of the Lord of the Two Lands, Pseusennes (II), beloved of Amon, purchased by her price in the territory of Upper Egypt, together with [any]thing [of any sort that the] people (6+x) of the land [sold to her] or that she acquired as a child from their property. Those who will tamper with a thing among them tomorrow or after tomorrow, will you[3] inflict your[3] great and burdensome[5] wrath upon them, without forgiving them [either]?"

Very favorable [response[6]] by this great god, Mut and Khonsu, the great gods.

Then said Amon-Re, King of the Gods, this [very] great god [since the beginning of creation, Mut and Khonsu, the] great gods: (7+x) "We shall kill any person of any sort in the entire land whether male or female who will contest anything of any sort [that Maatkare, the royal daughter of Pseusennes (II), beloved of Amon,[7] purchased by] her [price] (in) the territory of Upper Egypt, together with anything of any sort that the people of the land sold to her or that she acquired as [a child from their property. Those who will tamper with a thing among them] (8+x) tomorrow or after tomorrow, we shall inflict our great and burdensome wrath upon them, without forgiving them either. We shall put their noses into the ground,[8] as they are [subject to the wrath (?) of this great god,] Mut and Khonsu, the great gods."

NOTES

1. For the restoration, see the Abydos Stela of Sheshonq I (no. 41), line 2.

2. For the expression "to purchase at her price" in lines 3, 5, and 7, see Černý 1942, 126–33.

3. For the engraver's confusion of the suffix pronouns tn "you" and n "we," see Gardiner 1962, 65.

4. Cf. the phraseology (posed as a question) in the Abydos Stela of Sheshonq I (no. 41), lines 2–3.

5. For the spelling in lines 6 and 8 (found also in The Voyage of Wenamon [no. 18]), see Junge 1996, 41.

6. Restored following the Abydos Stela of Sheshonq I (no. 41), line 2. Or restore hnn "Nodding in agreement"; cf. The Banishment Stela (no. 28), lines 11, 12, and *passim*.

7. Following Gardiner 1962, 67. Maspero restores [ỉ-ỉn{n}≠s m snnw]≠s.

8. Violators are to be "overthrown"; for the magical significance of the terminology, see Ritner 1993b, 168–71.

41. ABYDOS STELA OF GREAT CHIEF SHESHONQ
FOR HIS FATHER NAMLOT
(S. CAIRO JdE 66285)

The stela preserves the judicial transcript of an oracle of Theban Amon conducted by Pseusennes II on behalf of the Meshwesh Chief Sheshonq (B), the future Sheshonq I, followed by a formal contractual account of Namlot's funerary endowment. Made of red granite, the slab now measures 1.5 m x 1.52 m, with its upper portion missing. No document displays so clearly the impending ascension of the family of Dynasty XXII, long intermarried with the declining Tanite line (see the Khonsu Roof Genealogies, no. 1). Sheshonq's presumption to demand inclusion in royal festivals as "co-partner" is unprecedented. Dynastic transition would be further eased by the marriage of Sheshonq's heir Osorkon (I) to Maatkare (B), daughter of the pliant Pseusennes, who sponsored the following oracle (see no. 40 for the marriage).

The primary text edition and translation is Blackman 1941, 83–95 and pls. 10–12a, replacing Breasted 1906–7, 4:328–33 §§674–87. A thoroughly obsolete interpretation appears in Revillout 1899, 168–79 (styling Sheshonq a Chaldean satrap!). Partial translation is found in Vernus 1987, 106–7. An English translation of the obsolete analysis of Brugsch has been reissued in Brugsch 1996, 370–73. For economic studies, see Baer 1962, 25–45; and Janssen 1975, 530–31. See Kitchen 1986, 285–86 §239.

[....] (1) wr ꜥ3 n wr.w Šš3nq m3ꜥ-ḫrw p3(y)≠f šr ḥr s.t 3ḫ.w ḫr ỉt≠f ỉw≠k dỉ [sꜥ3]≠f nfr.w≠f m nỉw.t n T3-wr ḫft-ḥr-n Rs-wd3 ỉw≠k dỉ ỉm3ḫ≠f r ššp[1] kḥkḥ ỉw s3≠f (2) mn ḥr-s3 ỉr(y)≠w ỉw≠k dỉ.t ỉ3m≠f ḥb.w n ḥm≠f ḥr ššp nḫt dmd m sp wꜥ [2]

wšd wr sp-2 ỉn p3y nṯr ꜥ3

ꜥḥꜥ.n wḥmy dd-ỉn≠f m-b3ḥ p3y nṯr ꜥ3 p3(y)≠ỉ nb nfr ỉw≠k ḫdb p3 (3) ꜥ3 n mšꜥ p3 ḥtyw p3 sš p3 rwdw p3 ỉpwty nb h(3)b.w nb n wp.t r sḫ.t nty ỉw≠w r t3(ỉ) nk.t n p3y ḫnty[3] n Wsỉr wr ꜥ3 n Mꜥ Nm3rt m3ꜥ-ḫrw s3 Mḥ.t-n-wsḫ.t m3ꜥ.t-ḫrw nty m 3bdw (4) rmṯ.t nb nty ỉw≠w ḫb n p3(y)≠f ḥtp.w-nṯr n 3ḫ.wt≠f rmṯ.t≠f n mnmn(.t)≠f k3m≠f ꜥ3b.t≠f nb ḥm.w-k3≠f nb ỉw≠k ỉr.t[4] n3y≠k b3.w ꜥ3.w dr.w r-r≠w r n3y≠w ḥm.wt (5) n3y≠w ẖrd.w wšd în p3y ntr ꜥ3

wn-în ḥm≠f ḥr snn t3 m-b3ḥ≠f dd-în ḥm≠f m3ꜥ≠k ḥrw Šš3nq m3ꜥ-ḥrw
p3 wr ꜥ3 n Mꜥ wr n wr.w p3(y)≠î ꜥ3 ḥnꜥ nty nb ḥr mw≠k (6) mš≠k mî
îr(y)≠w dr-nty ḥs tw ꜥImn-Rꜥ ny-sw.t nṯr.w ḥr îr.n≠k nb n ît≠k îw≠k r šsp
kḥkḥ mn.tw ḥr tp t3 îw îwꜥ.w≠k ḥr s.t≠k r nḥḥ

wn-în ḥm≠f wd p3 ḥnty n Wsîr wr ꜥ3 n (7) Mꜥ wr n wr.w Nm3rt m3ꜥ-
ḥrw m ḥd r 3bdw îw dd.ty îpwty.w-ny-sw.t wr.w r-ḥnꜥ≠f ḥr dp.w(t) ꜥ3.t
nn r3-ꜥ≠sn[5] ḥnꜥ n3 îpwty.w n p3 wr ꜥ3 n Mꜥ r dî.t[6] ḥtp≠f m ꜥḥ (8) šps ḥm n
Rs-wd3 r îr.t dd.ty[7] ꜥb.w≠f îmy [nîw.t n?] T3-wr ḥft msy wp.t-r3 îr.t ꜥb.w≠f
snṯr.tw sw m r3.w n pr-dw3.t sp-4[8] smn n.t-ꜥ.w≠f m (9) ḥ3 n sš.w mî dd.t.n
nb nṯr.w sꜥḥꜥ n≠f ꜥḥꜥ m înr 3bw ḥr wd.t n ꜥImn-rn≠f r dî.t ḥtp≠f m ḥm.w
nṯr.w r km nḥḥ d.t

tp-rd n smn p3 ḥnty n Wsîr wr ꜥ3 n Mꜥ (10) Nm3rt m3ꜥ-ḥrw s3 Mḥ.t-n-
wsḥ.t m3ꜥ.t-ḥrw nty m 3bdw

în n p3 t3 mḥ.t(y) în n3 rwdw n p3 wr ꜥ3 n Mꜥ î-îy îrm p3 twt ḥ3s.t(y)
Ḥ3r sdm-ꜥš 3ḥ-ꜥImn-k3-nḫt m3ꜥ-[ḥrw] ḥ3s.ty (11) Ḥ3r 3ḥ-Ptḥ-k3-nḫt m3ꜥ-[ḥrw]
ḥd dbn n 15 dd.t.n ḥm≠f ḥr≠sn ḥd dbn n 20 dmd ḥd dbn n 35

wp-s.t

nty r db3 t3y s3-t3 n 50 nty m ww q3 rsy 3bdw dd.tw n≠f W3ḥ- (12)
ny.t-sw.t ḥd dbn n 6

nty m îmn.t[9] m sdf(?) n p3 ḥn nty m 3bdw 3ḥ s3t3 n 50 îr n{n}[10] ḥd dbn
(n) 4

dmd 3ḥ.w nmḥ.w[11] n t3y s.t 2 m ww q3 rsy 3bdw ḥnꜥ ww q3 (13)
mḥ.t(y) 3bdw 3ḥ st3 n 100 îr n{n} ḥd dbn (n) 10

3ḥwty P3-wr s3 (...)[12] ḥm≠f ꜥI-îr-b3k ḥm≠f B(w)-pw-ꜥImn-ḥ3 ḥm≠f N3-
šn.w-bnr.w[13] ḥm≠f Dnî.t-n-Ḥr dmd (14) s n 5 îr n ḥd dbn (n) 4
qd.t 1

îḥ n 10 îr n ḥd dbn (n) 2(?)

mnî≠sn P3-šr-n-Mw.t (m3ꜥ-)ḥrw s3 Ḥr-s3-3s.t m3ꜥ-(ḥrw) îr n{n} ḥd qd.t
6 2/3

k3m nty m ww q3 mḥ.t(y) 3bdw îr n ḥd dbn (n) 2

k3rî Ḥr-ms m3ꜥ-ḥrw s3 Pn-mnḫ (15) îr n{n} ḥd qd.t 6 2/3

sḥt N-mr-îw m3ꜥ-ḥrw s3 Šd-Ḥr-n-p3-îrr≠f[14] m3ꜥ-ḥrw mw.t≠f T3-qn m3ꜥ.
t-ḥrw îr n ḥd qd.t 6 2/3

sḥt Ns-t3-T3y.t m3ꜥ-ḥrw mw.t≠f T3-dî-Mw.t m3ꜥ.t-ḥrw

ḥm.t T3-dî-3s.t m3ꜥ.t-ḥrw s3.t n Nb.t-ḥp.t m3ꜥ-ḥrw mw.t≠s ꜥIn[...](16)-
îm3ḥ m3ꜥ.t-ḥrw

ḥm.t T3-pt(î)-ꜥImn m3ꜥ.t-ḥrw s3.t n P3-nḥsy m3ꜥ-ḥrw mw.t≠s T-n.t-
Rnnwt.t m3ꜥ.t-ḥrw {m3ꜥ-ḥrw}

bîty.w s n 5 wꜥ nb (ḥd) qd.t 6 2/3

db3 p3 (5) s îr n ḥd dbn (n) 3 2/3 (sic)[15] sw3d r p3 pr-ḥd n Wsîr
mtw gs ḥn n bî.t pr n p3 pr-ḥd (17) n Wsîr m mn.t r p3 ḥtp-nṯr
n Wsîr wr ꜥ3 n Mꜥ Nm3rt m3ꜥ-ḥrw r-šꜥ nḥḥ d.t n b3k n p3y (5) n

bìty.w ì-sw3d̲.tw p3y≠w ḥd̲ r p3 pr-ḥd̲ n Wsìr ìw bn-ìw≠w mwt
ìw bn-ìw≠w 3q[16]

f3ì-sntr (18) s n 5 wꜥ nb ḥd̲ qd.t 6 2/3

  ìr n ḥd̲ dbn (n) 3 2/3 (sic) sw3d̲ r pr-ḥd̲ n Wsìr mtw t3 qd.t 5 sntr
pr n pr-ḥd̲ n Wsìr m mn.t r p3 ḥtp-ntr n Wsìr wr ꜥ3 n Mꜥ Nm3rt
m3ꜥ-ḫrw mw.t≠f Mḥ.t-n-wsḫ.t m3ꜥ.t-ḫrw r-šꜥ nḥḥ d̲.t n (19) b3k n
p3(y) 5 f3ì-sntr ì-(s)w3d̲.tw p3y≠w ḥd̲ r pr-ḥd̲ n Wsìr ìw bn-ìw≠w
mwt ìw bn-ìw≠w 3q

ꜥnt̲ s n wꜥ ìr n ḥd̲ qd.t 6 2/3

  sw3d̲ r pr-ḥd̲ n Wsìr mtw gs hn n sgnn (20) st3 pr n pr-ḥd̲ n Wsìr
m mn.t r p3 ḫ3bs n Wsìr wr ꜥ3 n Mꜥ Nm3rt m3ꜥ-ḫrw mw.t≠f Mḥ.t-n-
wsḫ.t m3ꜥ.t-ḫrw r-šꜥ nḥḥ (d̲.t) n b3k n p3 ꜥnt̲ ì-sw3d̲.tw p3(y)≠f ḥd̲
r pr-ḥd̲ n Wsìr ìw bn-ìw≠f mwt ìw (21) bn-ìw≠f 3q

dd s n wꜥ[17]

  ꜥrt(?)[18] s n 2 wꜥ nb ḥd̲ qd.t 6 2/3

  ps-šꜥ s n 1/4 ìr n ḥd̲ qd.t 1.t (2/3) sw3d̲ r pr-ḥd̲ n Wsìr

  mtw t3y ìt bty pr m mn.t m t ḥnq.t (n) šnꜥ.t m (22) [t3] šnw.ty n
Wsìr ḥnꜥ ꜥrt(?) n Wsìr r p3 ḥtp-ntr n Wsìr wr ꜥ3 n Mꜥ Nm3rt
m3ꜥ-ḫrw mw.t≠f Mḥ.t-n-wsḫ.t m3ꜥ.t-ḫrw r-šꜥ nḥḥ d̲.t n b3k n
p3y [2][19] ꜥrt(?) ps-šꜥ ì-sw3d̲.tw p3y≠w ḥd̲ r pr-ḥd̲ n Wsìr (23)
[r-(?)] ḥnꜥ n3 šmw n t3y 3ḫ ḥr s3t3 n 100 nty šm r t3 šnw.ty n
Wsìr n-ḫr rnp.t ìw bn-ìw≠w mwt ìw bn-ìw≠w 3q

dmd̲ p3 ḥd̲ (n) n3 rmt.t nty sw3d̲ r pr-ḥd̲ n Wsìr (24) ḥd̲ dbn (n) 8 qd.t
7 2/3 2/3 ìr n s 12 1/4 ì-ìr[20] b3k.w pr n pr-ḥd̲ n Wsìr r p3 ḥtp-ntr n
Wsìr wr ꜥ3 n Mꜥ wr (n) n3 wr.w Nm3rt m3ꜥ-ḫrw s3 wr ꜥ3 n Mꜥ Šš3nq
m3ꜥ-ḫrw mw.t≠f Mḥ.t-n-wsḫ.t m3ꜥ.t-ḫrw r-šꜥ (25) nḥḥ d̲.t

dmd̲ p3 ḥtp-ntr n p3 ḫnty n Wsìr wr ꜥ3 n Mꜥ {m3ꜥ-ḫrw} Nm3rt m3ꜥ-ḫrw
s3 Mḥ.t-n-wsḫ.t m3ꜥ.t-ḫrw nty m 3bd̲w

3ḫ s3t3 n 100

s s.t n 25

k3m n wꜥ

ḥd̲ ḫ3wy n wꜥ

hbn.t n šms n wꜥ

w3ḫ-mw (26) [...]

[...].... ìr n ḥd̲ dbn (n) [...][21]

[... "Will you allow] (1) the Great Chief of Chiefs Sheshonq the justified, his son, [to rest] in the place of the blessed spirits beside his father?
Will you allow him to [magnify] his beauty in the city of Tawer opposite
He-whose-waking-is-sound (Osiris)? Will you cause that he be revered
in order to attain[1] old age, while his son (2) remains afterward? Will you
cause that he be favored with the festivals of His Majesty in receiving victory, joined as co-partner?"[2]

Very favorable response by this great god.

Then again he said before this great god: "My good lord, will you kill the (3) superior of the army, the sergeant, the scribe, the agent, any messenger, or anyone sent on business into the country who will seize the property of this statue[3] of the Osiris, Great Chief of the Ma, Namlot, the justified, son of Mehetemweskhet, the justified, which is in Abydos? (4) Any person who will subtract from his divine offerings—whether from his fields, his people, from his cattle, his garden, any of his offerings, or any of his funerary service—will you enact[4] your great and powerful wrath against them, against their wives (5) and their children?"

Favorable response by this great god.

His Majesty then kissed the ground before him. Then His Majesty said: "May you be justified, Sheshonq, the justified, the Great Chief of the Ma, Chief of Chiefs, my great one, together with everyone loyal to you, (6) your army likewise, since Amon-Re King of the Gods has praised you concerning all that you have done for your father. You shall attain old age, enduring on earth, with your heirs (following) in your position forever."

His Majesty then dispatched the statue of the Osiris, Great Chief of (7) the Ma, Chief of Chiefs, Namlot, the justified, northward to Abydos, numerous royal messengers having been assigned accompanying it with many boats beyond counting[5] together with the messengers of the Great Chief of the Ma in order to cause[6] that it rest in the noble palace, (8) the shrine of Him-whose-waking-is-sound, and in order to ensure that its purification be given[7] in the [city of (?)] Tawer at the time of the presentation of the ritual "opening of the mouth." Its purification was made, and it was censed with the spells of the robing room, four times.[8] Its rituals were established (9) in the scribal office in accordance with that which the Lord of the Gods had said. A stela of Elephantine stone was erected for it bearing the decree of Him-whose-name-is-hidden (Amon) in order to cause that it rest in the shrines of the gods unto the completion of forever and ever.

Regulations for the maintenance of the statue of the Osiris, Great Chief of the Ma, (10) Namlot, the justified, son of Mehetemweskhet, the justified, which is in Abydos.

Brought from the north land by the agents of the Great Chief of the Ma who came with the image, the foreigner of Syria, the servant Akhamonkanakht, the justified, and the foreigner (11) of Syria, Akhptahkanakht, the justified: 15 *deben* of silver. What His Majesty gave in addition to them: 20 *deben* of silver.

Total: 35 *deben* of silver.

Its itemization:

Corresponding value of these 50 *arouras* of field that are in the high
    district south of Abydos, known as "Enduring (12) of Kingship":
      6 *deben* of silver.

Those in the (north?-)west,[9] being fed (?) by the well that is in Abydos: 50 *arouras* of field, amounting to[10] 4 *deben* of silver.

Total of private[11] fields of these two places in the high district south of Abydos and the high district (13) north of Abydos: 100 *arouras* of field, amounting to 10 *deben* of silver.

The cultivator Pawer son of (…),[12] his slave Iirbak, his slave Bupua-monkhai, his slave Nashenubeniu,[13] his slave Denitenhor.

Total: (14) 5 men, amounting to 4 *deben,* 1 *kite* of silver.

Ten oxen, amounting to 2 (?) *deben* of silver.

Their herdsman Pasherenmut, the justified, son of Horsiese, the justi-fied, amounting to 6 2/3 *kite* of silver.

The garden that is in the high district north of Abydos, amounting to 2 *deben* of silver.

The gardener Hormose, the justified, son of Penmenekh, (15) amount-ing to 6 2/3 *kite* of silver.

The weaver Nemeriu, the justified, son of Shedhorenpaireref,[14] the justified, his mother being Taqen, the justified, amounting to 6 2/3 *kite* of silver.

The weaver Nestatait, the justified, his mother being Tadimut, the justified;

The slave Tadiese, the justified, daughter of Nebethepet, the justified, her mother being In[..] (16)-imakh, the justified;

The slave Tapetiamon, the justified, daughter of Panehsy, the justified, her mother being Tanetrenenutet, the justified.

Beekeepers, 5 men, each one 6 2/3 *kite* (of silver);
dispersement for the (five) men amounting to 3 2/3 (*sic*)[15] *deben* of silver, remitted to the treasury of Osiris; and 1/2 *hin* of honey should be issued from the treasury (17) of Osiris daily for the divine offerings of the Osiris, Great Chief of the Ma, Namlot, the justified, forever and ever as the production of these (five) beekeepers, whose salaries are remitted to the treasury of Osiris, while they shall not die, while they shall not perish.[16]

Thurifers, (18) 5 men, each one 6 2/3 *kite* of silver;
amounting to 3 2/3 (*sic*) *deben* of silver, remitted to the treasury of Osiris; and the 5 *kite* of incense should be issued from the treasury of Osiris daily for the divine offerings of the Osiris, Great Chief of the Ma, Namlot, the justified, his mother being Mehetemweskhet, the justified, forever and ever as (19) the production of these 5 thurifers, whose salaries are remitted to the treasury of Osiris, while they shall not die, while they shall not perish.

Oilman, one man, amounting to 6 2/3 *kite* of silver;
remitted to the treasury of Osiris; and 1/2 *hin* of fuel (20) oil should be issued from the treasury of Osiris daily for the lamp of

the Osiris, Great Chief of the Ma, Namlot, the justified, his mother
being Mehetemweskhet, the justified, forever and ever as the production of the oilman, whose salary is remitted to the treasury of
Osiris, while he shall not die, while (21) he shall not perish.

What one man[17] gave:

Brewers (?),[18] 2 men, each one 6 2/3 *kite* of silver;

Confectioner, 1/4 man, amounting to 1 (2/3) silver *kite,* remitted
to the treasury of Osiris;

And this barley and emmer should be issued daily as bread and
beer of the storehouse from (22) the double granary of Osiris
and the brewery (?) of Osiris for the divine offerings of the
Osiris, Great Chief of the Ma, Namlot, the justified, his mother
being Mehetemweskhet, the justified, forever and ever as the
production of these [2][19] brewers and confectioner, whose
salaries are remitted to the treasury of Osiris, (23) together
with the harvest of this field on 100 *arouras,* which goes to
the double granary of Osiris yearly, while they shall not die,
while they shall not perish.

Total of the salaries of the persons that are remitted to the treasury of
Osiris: (24) 8 *deben,* 7 2/3 + 2/3 *kite* of silver; amounting to 12
1/4 men. Their production shall be issued specifically[20] from the
treasury of Osiris for the divine offerings of the Osiris, Great Chief
of the Ma, Chief of the Chiefs, Namlot, the justified, son of the
Great Chief of the Ma, Sheshonq, the justified, his mother being
Mehetemweskhet, the justified, for(25)ever and ever.

Total of the divine offerings of the statue of the Osiris, Great Chief of
the Ma, {the justified} Namlot, the justified, son of Mehetemweskhet, the justified, which is in Abydos:

100 *arouras* of field

25 men and women

1 garden

1 silver altar

1 service vessel

[…] libation (26)

[…]… amounting to [… (?)][21] *deben* of silver.

NOTES

1. Cf. line 6; Blackman translated "until the attaining of old age."

2. Literally, "united in a single act/instance."

3. An unambiguous writing of ḫnty "statue" appears in line 6, with the synonym twt "image" in line 10. Kitchen 1986, 285 (§239) n. 248, considered this a
portable image for cultic processions.

4. The infinitive ỉr.t is consistently written ỉrr in the text (lines 4, 7, 8), perhaps
a simple error in transcription from the original hieratic draft.

5. So Blackman 1941, following a suggestion of Gunn. Written rdỉ.t⸗sn.

6. As in line 9, purpose is indicated by r + infinitive; Blackman translated "it was caused to rest/repose."

7. A periphrastic construction with ỉr, rather than a second tense. For the latter, see line 24.

8. Contra Blackman 1941, 88 n. 36, who read hrw 4 "(for) four days." As Blackman concedes, fourfold repetion of formulae is customary. The slight variation in the carving of sp "instance" (lines 2 and 8) is not significant; cf. the varying writings of ẖnty in lines 3 and 6.

9. The following summation "of these two places" lists fields south and north of Abydos, so the western plot must be "northwest."

10. Written redundantly ỉr nn in lines 12–15, as is typical for the Third Intermediate Period; cf. Erman and Grapow 1926–63, 1:111/7.

11. For nmḥ "private, unencumbered," see Baer 1962, 26 n. 10 (ȝḥ.t nmḥ nꜥ "field free and clear"); and discussion in Théodoridès 1965, 122ff. Blackman translated "tenanted land."

12. Left blank on the stela.

13. Blackman read Nȝ-šn.w-mḥ.w.

14. Blackman read Mḥ-Ḥr-n-pȝ-ỉrr⸗f.

15. In lines 16 and 18, 2/3 is carved in error for 1/3.

16. As noted by Blackman 1941, 94, this formula is found only where services are performed by relays of anonymous staff members. Such services are perpetual and not terminated by the death or destruction of any specific individual. Grammatically, the form ỉ-swȝḏ.tw could be a second tense: "It is without their dying, without their perishing, that their salaries shall be remitted to the treasury of Osiris."

17. Presumably Sheshonq.

18. So Blackman 1941, 91 n. 77, for the term in lines 21–22. Alternatively, this may be a writing of šnꜥ "storehouse, storehouse worker" (Erman and Grapow 1926–63, 4:507–8) written differently at the end of line 21.

19. Restored following the pattern in lines 17 and 19. Blackman 1941, 91 n. 81, hesitantly suggested wḏȝ "cellar."

20. Second tense ỉ-ỉr + noun + infinitive, contra Blackman, who translated as a future relative "whose contributions shall pass out from the treasury."

21. Since wp-s.t (line 11, "literally, "dividing it") generally indicates an itemization of a previously mentioned sum, the final total might be expected to again yield 35 *deben*. The reading of many numbers, however, is uncertain, and others seem incorrectly carved; see lines 14, 16, 18, and 21. Moreover, the "individual gift" in lines 21ff. need not be included in the 35 *deben*. Blackman viewed all services and values mentioned after wp-s.t as supplemental to the foundation gift of 35 *deben*.

III

DYNASTY XXII

A. SHESHONQ I

42. BUBASTIS BLOCK

This small limestone fragment with partial cartouches is the single attestation of the dynasty's founder in his reputed (Manethonian) dynastic seat. The text is copied in Naville 1891, 46.

[... Ḥḏ]-ḫpr-[Rꜥ]-stp-n-Rꜥ (2) [...] Ššnq [mrỉ-ʾImn]
[... Hedj]kheper[re]-setepenre (2) [...] Sheshonq, [beloved of Amon].

43. LARGER DAKHLEH STELA
(S. ASHMOLEAN 1894. 107A)

This hieratic stela records an oracular decision by Sutekh (Seth) in regard to a local dispute over named wells and irrigated property, conducted before a Meshwesh commander dispatched by the palace to restore order in the oases. Obtained (with the Smaller Dakhleh Stela of Piye, no. 146 below) in 1894 by Captain H. G. Lyons in the village of Mut in the Dakhleh Oasis, the stela is notable for its preservation of distinctly Libyan names and titles. The limestone stela measures 37 in. (94 cm) in height by 26 in. (66 cm) in width and contains a lunette scene with hieroglyphic labels and 20 lines of hieratic text. A secondary docket in hieratic has been inserted in the lunette, recording the disposition of springs associated with a local well named Tenetsar.

Texts, translation, and commentary appear in Gardiner 1933, 19–30 and pls. V–VII (hieroglyphic transcription); supplementing the original publication in Spiegelberg 1899, 12–21 (with photo); and Breasted 1906–7, 4:359–61 §§725–28. See Kitchen 1986, 290 §247.

LUNETTE SCENE OF ORACLE; HIEROGLYPHIC TEXTS

At Right: Before a garlanded shrine with figures of Hathor, Count Wayhaset raises lamp

[ḥ₃.ty-ꜥ W₃]yḥ₃(2)[s₃]t (n) (3) t₃ (4) Wḥ₃.t

[Count Wa]yha(2)[se]t of the (3) Land of (4) the Oasis.

Behind Count: Petitioner in act of adoration

ḥm-nṯr [n] Swtḫ Nsy-B₃st.t m₃ꜥ-ḫrw (2) s₃ P₃-dî≠w

The prophet [of] Sutekh, Nesubast, the justified, (2) son of Patiou.

Left of Shrine (facing right): Two standing women representing the rival claimants excluded in lines 15–16; second (sister-in-law of Nesubast) labeled

ḥm.t ḥm-nṯr n Swtḫ P₃-tî-B₃st.t (2) s₃ P₃-dî≠w m₃ꜥ-ḫrw

Wife of the prophet of Sutekh, Patibast (2) son of Patiou, the justified.

In Lower Register at Right: Two women (wife and mother-in-law of Nesubast?) beat tambourines

ḥm.t nb(.t) p.t (sic.) šmꜥy(.t) [n Swtḫ? …] (2) m₃ꜥ.t-ḫrw s₃.t [šmꜥy(.t)]
(n) Swtḫ […] m₃ꜥ.t-ḫrw

Wife and housewife, chantress [of Sutekh (?) …], the justified, daughter
of [the chantress] of Sutekh […], the justified.

At Left of Shrine: Hieratic docket of secondary oracle (cf. lines 10, 13–14)

ḏd p₃ nṯr ꜥ₃ [mn] wbn 2 m-ḏr.t Tî-n.t-s₃yr t₃ ḫnm(.t) Pr Ḥr Sḫm.t wp-
tw wꜥ

The Great God said: "[There are not] two springs belonging to Tenetsar, the well of the 'estate of Horus and Sakhmet,' but rather one."

MAIN TEXT

(1) ḥsb.t 5.t ₃bd 4 pr.t sw 16 n ny-sw.t Pr-ꜥ₃[1] ꜥnḫ wḏ₃ snb Š₃š₃q₃ ꜥnḫ
wḏ₃ snb mry ꜣImn hrw pn îw s₃ n ms[2] (n) n₃ Mꜥ.w (2) ꜥ[₃] qꜥḥy₃ ḥm-nṯr
Ḥw.t-Ḥr nb.t[4] Ḥw.t-Sḫm ḫrp ḥm(.w)-nṯr n Ḥr Sḫm.t nb(.t)[4] Pr-ḏ₃ḏ₃[5] ḥm-nṯr
n Swtḫ nb[4] Wḥ₃.t îmy-r₃ bꜥḥ.w (3) îmy-r₃ št₃wy.w[6] ḥ₃.ty-ꜥ W₃ywḥ₃s₃t n p₃
t₃ 2 n Wḥ₃.t îw≠f (m) dmî S₃-wḥ₃.t[7] m-ḫt wḏ sw Pr-ꜥ₃ ꜥnḫ wḏ₃ snb r spd
p₃ t₃ Wḥ₃.t (4) m-ḫt gm[.tw] îw wn≠f n ꜥ n ḫrwy îw≠f b₃g₃s₃

hrw n šmy r sîp n₃ wbny.w n₃ ḫnm(5)y.wt[8] nty (n) S₃-wḥ₃.t ḫnm.wt
ḥbs.w(.t) ḫnm.wt ww (r)-nty sw pḥ.w î (=r) ptrî p₃ wbn ḫnm.t Wbn(6)[-Rꜥ
m]-ḫt ḏd ḥm-nṯr n Swtḫ Nsy-sw-B₃st.t s₃ P₃-dî≠(w) m-b₃ḥ≠f r-ḏd

ptrî wꜥ ḥ₃y fḫ[y] îw≠s d(y) (m) q₃îw p₃y wbn n Wnb-Rꜥ m₃ꜥ sw t₃y
(7) [ḫnm.t] (n) Pr-Rꜥ nty tw≠k q₃îw n≠s îw ḫnm.t nmḥwyw

(t₃y) îw nsy-sw T₃y≠w-Ḥnw.t mw.t≠s Ḥnw.t-nṯr.w t₃y≠î mw.t îw ḥm-
nṯr ḥ₃.ty-ꜥ W₃ywḥ₃s₃t ḏd n≠f ꜥḥꜥ m-b₃ḥ Swtḫ (8) [st₃w(?)] s.t hrw pn[9] sḫꜥ

ḥm n nṯr pn špsy Swtḫ ꜥꜣ pḥ.ty sꜣ n Nw.t pꜣy nṯr ꜥꜣ (m) ḥsb.t 5.t ꜣbd 4 pr.t
sw 25 m ḥbꜣf nfr Wršw ỉw ḥꜣ.ty-ꜥ Wꜣywḥꜣsꜣt ꜥḥꜥ m-bꜣḥ

ḏd (9) [S]wtḫ pꜣy nṯr ꜥꜣ mꜣꜥ.tw Nsy-sw-Bꜣst.t sꜣ Pꜣ-dỉ(ꜣw) tꜣ ḥꜣy nty
mḥ-ỉmnt.t n pꜣy wbn ḫnmy.t Wbn-Rꜥ tꜣy ḫnmy.t (n) Pr-Rꜥ nty (n) Sꜣ-wḥꜣ.t
nsy-sw Tꜣyꜣw-Ḥnw.t tꜣyꜣf mw.t (10) [ỉ]-smn sw nꜣf pꜣ ḥꜣ¹⁰

ḏd pꜣ nṯr ꜥꜣ mn wbn 2 m-[ḏr].t Wbn-Rꜥ tꜣy ḫnmy.t n(.t) Pr-Rꜥ nty (m)
Sꜣ-wḥꜣ.t wp-tw wꜥ wbn wꜥ.tw gm.twꜣf ḥr-n tꜣy ꜥyrꜣ(.t)¹¹ dn-

(11) y.w n nꜣ ḫnmy.wt kꜣm.w n Pr-Rꜥ ỉ-wt rwḏw ꜥnḫꜣf sꜣ Swtḫ-nḫt
ỉ(= r)-ḫ.t tꜣy dny Pr-ꜥꜣ ꜥnḫ wḏꜣ snb Pꜣ-sbꜣ-ḫꜥ-(n)-Nỉw.t ꜥnḫ wḏꜣ snb
pꜣ nṯr ꜥꜣ (m) ḥsb.t 19.t¹²

ḏd Swtḫ (12) pꜣy nṯr ꜥꜣ ỉr wbn nb nty m [ww] n tꜣ ỉꜣd.t¹³ pꜣ nty [...] m
ww n ỉmnt.t Sꜣ-wḥꜣ.t st ỉwꜥ.w fḫy.w (m) nꜣ wbn(.w) n Ḥwy ḥr.tw r-rꜣw ỉw
mw nmḥwy.w nꜣ.w m(13)n mw Pr-ꜥꜣ ꜥnḫ wḏꜣ snb ỉmꜣw nsy-sw pꜣ nmḥw
nty-ỉwꜣf ỉn.tꜣw [r]-bnr pꜣ ḥꜣ¹⁴

ḏd pꜣ nṯr ỉr nꜣ wbny(.w) ỉ-stꜣw Nsy-sw-Bꜣst.t (14) sꜣ Pꜣ-dỉꜣ(w) ỉr-rꜣw
ỉwꜣf ỉn.tꜣw r-bnr [...] ỉwtn ḥnꜥ pꜣ wbn Tꜣyꜣw-Ḥnw.t tꜣyꜣf mw.t smn s.t nꜣ
f ỉw-ỉwꜣw smn¹⁵ n sꜣ (n) sꜣꜣf (15) ỉwꜥ (n) ỉwꜥ.wꜣf ḥm.tꜣf ḥrd.wꜣf ỉw mn
ky šrỉ n[m]ḥw ỉw nsy-sw Tꜣyꜣw-Ḥnw.t ỉw-ỉwꜣf pšỉꜣw ỉm.w wp-tw (16)
Nsy-sw-Bꜣst.t sꜣ Pꜣ-dỉꜣw ỉ.nꜣf Swtḫ pꜣy nṯr ꜥꜣ m-bꜣḥ [mtr.w] qn.w ꜥꜣꜣ

ỉmy-rn.w
ḥm-nṯr Swtḫ nb Wḥꜣ.t ḥꜣ.ty-pꜥt¹⁶
ḥꜣ(17)w.ty Wꜣywḥꜣsꜣt
mꜣtỉwꜣhꜣr¹⁷ Pꜣ-wrdw
mꜣtỉwꜣhꜣr Wꜣywkꜣsꜣhꜣr
mꜣtỉwꜣhꜣr Tỉ-n.t-[...](18)-tỉ
mꜣtỉwꜣhꜣr Kꜣywhꜣm
ḥry qrꜥy Pꜣ-dỉ-Wp-[wꜣw.t(?)]¹⁸
mnḫ¹⁹ ꜥnḫyꜣf sꜣ Nꜣyꜣf-nb.w-nḫt
ỉt-nṯr sš ḫtmw Pꜣ-dỉꜣw sꜣ Kꜣnꜣ
(19) ỉt-nṯr sš ḥw.t-nṯr Tnr-Swtḫ sꜣ Sr-Ḏḥwty
ỉt-nṯr⁴ sš Pꜣ-kꜣmw [sꜣ ...]
[...] sꜣ Pꜣ-dỉꜣw
ỉt-nṯr Tỉ[... sꜣ ...]
ỉt-nṯr Qry-Swtḫ sꜣ ꜥnḫyꜣf
(20) ḥm-[nṯr] n ḥw.t²⁰ ꜣImn Pn-ꜣImn sꜣ Pꜣ-dỉꜣw
wn Pꜣ-ꜥnḫ sꜣ Pn-Gb{g}²¹
wn Pꜣ-wnšw [sꜣ ...]
[... sꜣ ..]mwr[...]

(1) Regnal year 5, month 4 of winter, day 16 of the king and pharaoh,¹
l.p.h., Shesho(n)q, l.p.h., beloved of Amon. On this day there came the
son of the Chief² of the Ma, (2) district chief,³ prophet of Hathor, Lady⁴ of
Diospolis Parva (Hû), overseer⁴ of prophets of Horus and Sakhmet, Lady⁴

of Perdjadja (Abu Tisht),[5] prophet of Sutekh, Lord[4] of the Oasis, overseer of inundated lands, (3) overseer of scrub-lands,[6] Count Wayhaset of the Two Lands of the Oasis (Kharga and Dakhleh), when he was in the town of Mut[7] after Pharaoh, l.p.h., dispatched him to restore order in the land of the Oasis (4) after [it was] discovered that it was in a state of conflict and rebellion.

On the day of going to inspect the springs and wells[8] (5) that are in Mut, both covered wells and irrigation wells: he arrived to inspect the spring-fed well of Weben(6)[-Re] after the prophet of Sutekh, Nesubast son of Patiou, said before him:

"Look, a sheet of flood-water has been released that is here in the vicinity of this spring of Weben-Re. Examine it, this (7) [well] of the region "estate of Re," in whose vicinity you are, whether it is a private well belonging to my mother Tayuhenut, whose mother was Henutneteru";

while the prophet and Count Wayhaset said to him: "Stand in the presence of Sutekh and (8) [claim (?)] it."

On this day[9] there occurred the processional appearance of the Majesty of this noble god Sutekh, great of strength, son of Nut, this great god, in regnal year 5, month 4 of winter, day 25, in his beautiful festival of "Spending the Day," while Count Wahaset was standing in the divine presence.

Then said (9) [S]utekh, this great god: "Nesubast son of Patiou is vindicated. The sheet of flood-water that is northwest of this spring-fed well, Weben-Re, this well of the 'estate of Re' that is in Mut, belongs to Tayuhenut, his mother. (10) Confirm it for him at this time."[10]

Then said the great god: "There are not two springs be[longing] to Weben-Re, this well of the 'estate of Re' that is in Mut, but rather one spring alone was found on that scroll of the (11) cadastral register[11] of the wells and the gardens of the 'estate of Re' that the agent Ankhef son of Sutekh-nakht issued in accordance with this register of Pharaoh, l.p.h., Pseusennes (I), l.p.h., the great god, in regnal year 19."[12]

Then said Sutekh, (12) this great god: "As for every spring that is in the [region] of the tell,[13] (more specifically) the one that [lies (?)] in the region to the west of Mut, they are derivatives (lit., "inheritors") released from the so-called 'Springs of Huy' since they are private waters. (13) There is no water of Pharaoh, l.p.h., among them. They belong to the private individual who will irrigate from them at this time."[14]

Then said the god: "As for the springs regarding which Nesubast (14) son of Patiou has made a claim, he shall irrigate from them [to …] the ground, together with the spring of Tayuhenut, his mother. Confirm them for him, and they shall be confirmed[15] for the son of his son, (15) the heir of his heirs, his wife, and his children, while there is no other son of private status belonging to Tayuhenut who shall have a share among them but only (16) Nesubast son of Patiou." So said Sutekh, this great god, in the presence of numerous [witnesses].

The list thereof:

The prophet of Sutekh, Lord of the Oasis, First among Patricians[16] and (17) leader, Wayhaset.

The matwaher,[17] Pawered.

The matwaher, Wayukasahar.

The matwaher, Tenet[…](18)ti.

The matwaher, Kayuham.

The captain of shield-bearers, Padiwep[wawet(?)].[18]

The cadet,[19] Ankhef son of Nayefnebunakht.

The God's Father and scribe of sealed documents, Patiou son of Kana.

(19) The God's Father and temple scribe, Tel-Sutekh son of Serthoth.

The God's Father[4] and scribe, Pakamu [son of …].

[The …, …] son of Patiou.

The God's Father, Ti[… son of …].

The God's Father, Qeri-Sutekh son of Ankhef.

(20) The prophet of the temple[20] of Amon, Penamon the son of Patiou.

The doorkeeper, Paankh son of Pengeb.[21]

The doorkeeper, Pawenesh [son of …].

[The …, … son of …]mur[…].

NOTES

1. This example is often stated—wrongly—to be the earliest instance of "Pharaoh NN," with the title Pr-ꜥꜣ prefixed to the king's nomen; see Gardiner 1933, 20 and 23. On this basis, the identification with Sheshonq I was disputed by Jacquet-Gordon 1979, 180–82, who preferred Sheshonq III. However, the title Pr-ꜥꜣ is already attested for Siamon of Dynasty XXI in the Karnak Priestly Annals (no. 9.3B).

2. The text preserves an example of the Berber title mas "chief" generally translated in Egyptian texts by wr—or its ideogram, which might be read in either Egyptian or Libyan, first recognized by Erman 1883, 69 n. 1. See further Erman and Grapow 1926–63, 2:142/9; Spiegelberg 1899, 16 n. 1; Bates 1970 [orig. 1914], 83; and Gardiner 1933, 23. A full survey of the examples is found in Yoyotte 1961a, 123–24.

3. For the title and its evolution, see Vernus 1977, 182.

4. Ignored in translation by Gardiner.

5. For the locality, see Gardiner 1947, 2:35*; Vernus 1977, 182.

6. For the term, see Gardiner 1948, 32; Vernus 1977, 179–93 (esp. 182).

7. So identified by Gardiner 1933, 24 n. to line 3.

8. For the terminology regarding wells and springs (Gardiner: "flowing well"), see Gardiner 1933, 20–21.

9. Signs in some disorder; see Gardiner 1933, 25–26, who, however, rearranges passages unnecessarily.

10. Here and in line 13, taken by Gardiner as a writing of hrw "day."

11. See ʿr.t "scroll," Erman and Grapow 1926–63 1:208–9; and dnỉ.t "cadastral register," Erman and Grapow 1926–63 5:466/6.

12. The attribution of this date to the reign of Pseusennes I was first recognized by Daressy 1917a, 10. Previous commentators had ascribed the regnal year to Sheshonq I; cf. Breasted 1906–7 4:359 §725; and Gauthier 1914, 310 n. 1.

13. For the term "tell, mound," see Gardiner 1948, 33.

14. The wells are determined to be private and not crown property and thus are at the disposal of any citizen who might "lead off" the water for irrigation; see Gardiner 1933, 26–27.

15. For the passage and grammar, see Wente 1961, 121.

16. For the title, see Edel 1980, 43 (§7); Clère 1983, 92, §F.

17. Libyan title of unknown meaning.

18. So Spiegelberg; ending unread by Gardiner.

19. Or "novice" in religious associations and perhaps "recruit" in military contexts; see Gardiner 1933, 27; Erichsen 1954, 163.

20. So Spiegelberg and text; Gardiner emends to ḥm-[nṯr] n ʾImn-ʾIp.t "prophet of Amonemope."

21. For late writings of Geb with an extra, final g/k; see Gardiner 1933, 28; Erichsen 1954, 577.

44. DEIR EL-BAHRI CACHE (DB 320): INTERMENT OF DJEDPTAHIUEFANKH

Recording the presentation of linen to the temple of Amon in regnal years 5, 10, and 11 of Sheshonq I, dockets on the mummy wrappings of the priest Djedptahiuefankh provide a *terminus post quem* for the last opening of the celebrated cache of royal mummies at Deir el-Bahri until its discovery in 1881. Formerly thought to be the crag-tomb of Queen Inhapi noted in dockets of the reign of Siamon, Deir el-Bahari tomb 320 is now recognized to be the family tomb of the high priest Pinedjem II, into which the royal mummies were moved only after the death of Djedptahiuefankh. As the linen epigraphs date the manufacture of the cloth and not the burial, the final interment in the cache could date from any time between years 11 and 21. On his funerary papyrus, Djedptahiuefankh is elevated in rank to Second Prophet of Amon and king's-son of the Lord of the Two Lands.

For the texts and translations, see Maspero 1889, 573; Gauthier 1914, 307–9 and 321 §LVI; Breasted 1906–7, 4:394 §§699–700; Thomas 1966, 253, 263 nn. 66–67; and Reeves 1990, 239 (and 183–99 for DB 320). For the funerary papyrus, see A. Edwards 1883, 85–87. See Kitchen 1986, 288–89 §§242 and 244. For the standard format of bandage inscriptions, see Kitchen 1986, 411–16, excursus A.

I. INTERIOR COFFIN LID

ḥm-nṯr 3-nw n ʾImn-Rꜥ ny-sw.t nṯr.w ꜥꜣ qꜥḥ(.t)[1] sꜣ ny-sw.t n Rꜥ-ms-s(w) Ḏd-Ptḥ-ỉw⸗f-ꜥnḫ

Third Prophet of Amon-Re, King of the Gods, district chief,[1] king's-son of Rameses, Djedptahiuefankh.

II. SHOULDER STRAPS OF MUMMY

ỉr.n{n} ḥm-nṯr tpy n ʾImn-Rꜥ (2) ny-sw.t nṯr.w ʾIwpwtỉ mꜣꜥ-ḫrw

Made by the First Prophet of Amon-Re, (2) King of the Gods, Iuput, the justified.

III. MUMMY BANDAGE DEDICATIONS

(a) mnḫ.t šps.t ỉr.n{n}[2] ny-sw.t bỉ.ty nb tꜣ.wy Ḥḏ-ḫpr-Rꜥ-stp-n-Rꜥ sꜣ Rꜥ nb ḫꜥ.w Ššnq mrỉ-ʾImn n ỉt⸗f ʾImn ḥsb.t 5 (2) mnḫ.t šps.t [ỉr.n{n} ḥm-nṯr tpy n ʾImn-Rꜥ ỉmy-rꜣ mšꜥ wr Mꜥ[3] ʾIwpwṯ mꜣꜥ-ḫrw sꜣ ny-sw.t nb tꜣ.wy Ššnq mrỉ-ʾImn n ỉt⸗f ʾImn ḥsb.t 5]

(b) mnḫ.t šps.t ỉr.n{n} ny-sw.t bỉ.ty nb tꜣ.wy Ḥḏ-ḫpr-Rꜥ-stp-n-Rꜥ sꜣ Rꜥ nb ḫꜥ.w Ššnq mrỉ-ʾImn n ỉt⸗f ʾImn ḥsb.t 10 (2) mnḫ.t šps.t ỉr.n{n} ḥm-nṯr tpy n ʾImn-Rꜥ ỉmy-rꜣ mšꜥ wr Mꜥ ʾIwpwṯ mꜣꜥ-ḫrw sꜣ ny-sw.t nb tꜣ.wy Ššnq mrỉ-ʾImn n ỉt⸗f ʾImn ḥsb.t 10

(c) mnḫ.t šps.t ỉr.n{n} ny-sw.t bỉ.ty nb tꜣ.wy Ḥḏ-ḫpr-Rꜥ-stp-n-Rꜥ sꜣ Rꜥ nb ḫꜥ.w Ššnq mrỉ-ʾImn n ỉt⸗f ʾImn ḥsb.t 11 (2) mnḫ.t šps.t ỉr.n{n} ḥm-nṯr tpy n ʾImn-Rꜥ ỉmy-rꜣ mšꜥ wr Mꜥ ʾIwpwṯ mꜣꜥ-ḫrw sꜣ ny-sw.t nb tꜣ.wy Ššnq mrỉ-ʾImn n ỉt⸗f ʾImn ḥsb.t 11

Noble cloth that the King of Upper and Lower Egypt, Lord of the Two Lands, Hedjkheperre-setepenre, Son of Re, Lord of Diadems, Sheshonq (I), beloved of Amon, made[2] for his father Amon in regnal year 5 (variants: year 10/year 11). (2) Noble cloth that the First Prophet of Amon-Re, general and Chief of the Ma,[3] Iuput, the justified, royal son of the Lord of the Two Lands, Sheshonq, beloved of Amon, made for his father Amon in regnal year 5 (variants: year 10/year 11).

NOTES

1. Revised reading following Breasted. Maspero and Edwards copied ꜥḥ/ḥꜥ. For ꜥꜣ qꜥḥ.t, see Erman and Grapow 1926–63, 5:20/10.

2. The wording signifies that the king commissioned and dedicated the fabric.

3. Breasted ignored the ethnic designation Ma to read "commander in chief of the army."

45. HERACLEOPOLIS ALTAR OF PRINCE NAMLOT
(CAIRO JDE 39410)

This dark granite altar block (.57 m high by .56 m wide by .59 m deep), discovered in 1907 in Heracleopolis (Ihnasya el-Medina), records the restoration of daily cattle offerings to the local ram-headed deity Harsaphes by the prince and general Namlot. The text is unique in providing a detailed inventory of the annual levy, specifying the capitation, or individual assessment, upon officials and towns responsible for oxen deliveries in particular months. The introductory section follows the standard narrative format of the *Königsnovelle,* in which the king seeks benefactions for the gods. The king's fragmentary epithet in line 1 regarding "Asiatics" may refer to his victorious Palestinian campaign. While the text presents ruler and prince in a purely classical style, the special regard for the deity of Heracleopolis reflects the long establishment of Libyan military colonies in the region. Sides A and B of the altar have been reworked as a Ptolemaic gaming board and a Coptic offering table, respectively. The text begins on side C in sixteen horizontal lines and concludes on side D in thirteen vertical columns followed a blank space.

Text and translation appear in Tresson 1938, 817–40 and plate; Kamal 1909, 37–38; Maspero 1909, 38–40; Daressy 1913, 133–35, §V; and Kitchen 1986, 290–91 §247, 575 §508. Partial translations are provided by Vernus 1987, 107–8; Redford 1972, 153–56; see the review by Cazelles 1974, 159.

SIDE C: SIXTEEN HORIZONTAL LINES

(1) [...] Skty.w ny-sw.t bỉ.ty nb tꜣ.wy Ḥd-ḫpr-Rꜥ-stp-n-Rꜥ sꜣ Rꜥ nb ḫꜥ.w Ššnq mrỉ-ꜣImn mỉ Rꜥ

(2) [ỉst] ḥm≠f ꜥnḫ wdꜣ s(nb) ḫḥy sp nb n ꜣḫ.w r ỉr.w n ỉt≠f Ḥry-š≠f ny-sw.t tꜣ.wy nb Ḥnn-ny-sw.t wnw m ỉb≠f tỉ sw m

(3) ny-sw.t ỉy ỉn sꜣ ny-sw.t ỉmy-rꜣ mšꜥ Nꜣmꜣrtỉ m-bꜣḥ ḥm≠f ḏd≠f ỉr pr Ḥry-š≠f ny-sw.t tꜣ.wy sw ꜣb (4) r ỉḥ n ỉmny.t gm.n≠ỉ sw wꜣw r ḏꜣmy wn m-bꜣḥ m hꜣw (5) ḏr.tyw nfr pw dỉ pr≠f

ḏd ỉn ḥm≠f ḥs tw kꜣ≠ỉ sꜣ≠ỉ pw pr m ḫnty≠ỉ ỉn

(6) ỉb≠k mỉ ỉb wtt swỉ ḫꜥ.w≠ỉ pw m rnpỉ ỉn ỉt≠ỉ Ḥry-š≠f ny-sw.t tꜣ.wy nb Ḥnn-ny-sw.t smnḫ pr (7) nb m rꜣ≠k m pr≠f r nḥḥ

ỉr.(t)² wḏ m stp-sꜣ ꜥnḫ wdꜣ s(nb) r spd pr Ḥry-š≠f ny-sw.t tꜣ.wy nb Ḥnn-ny-sw.t r dỉ.t (8) mn ỉḥ pn n ỉmny.t ỉm≠f mỉ ỉry.t m hꜣw ḏr.tyw ỉr.(t)² wḏ m ššw (9) r spd≠f ỉw≠tw ḥtrỉ pꜣy ỉḥ n ỉmny.t r nꜣ nỉ.wt dmỉ.w wḥ(ꜣ). w n Ḥnn-ny-sw.t (10) n(n) sp n ỉwhꜣ ỉm≠w n ws.n≠fꜣ mỉ nḥḥ ḏ.t ny-sw.t bỉ.ty nb tꜣ.wy Ḥd-ḫpr-Rꜥ-stp-n-Rꜥ sꜣ Rꜥ nb ḫꜥ.w Ššnq mrỉ-ꜣImn dỉ ꜥnḫ (11) mỉ Rꜥ ḏ.t

tp n ḥtrỉ m-ty 365 n ỉḥ n ḥr rnp.t šꜣꜥ pḥr n ḏ.t

(12) pꜣ ỉmy-rꜣ mšꜥ n Ḫnn-ny-sw.t tp⸗f ỉḥ n 60
tpy ꜣḫ.t r ỉbt 2 ꜣḫ.t

nb(.t) pr ḫry(.t) wr ḫnr.t n Ḥry-š⸗f ny-sw.t tꜣ.wy sꜣ.t n wr ꜥꜣ n Mꜥ ꜣs.t-
    m-Ḥb.t ỉḥ n 3
(13) pꜣ ꜥꜣ n Twhr.w n Wsr-mꜣꜥ.t-Rꜥ ỉḥ n 10
pꜣ ꜥꜣ n Twhr.w n Ḫnn-ny-sw.t ỉḥ n 10
pꜣ ḥm-nṯr n Stḫ nb Sw ỉḥ n 10
ỉbt 3 ꜣḫ.t

(14) pꜣ ꜥꜣ n wšꜣ.w ỉḥ.w n pr Ḥry-š⸗f ny-sw.t tꜣ.wy ỉḥ n 10
pr sḫm(?)-bꜣḫ ỉḥ n 6
pꜣ sš ḥw.t-nṯr n pr Ḥry-š⸗f ny-sw.t tꜣ.wy ỉḥ n 10
pꜣ ỉdnw n ḥw.t-nṯr ỉḥ n 1
nꜣ (15) [...] n pr [pn(?)] ỉḥ n 3
ỉbt 4 ꜣḫ.t

pꜣ ḥm-nṯr n Ḥry-š⸗f ny-sw.t tꜣ.wy ỉḥ n 7
pꜣ ỉdnw nꜣ šsp.wt n pr pn ỉḥ n 1
pꜣ ḥry šsp.wt n pr pn ỉḥ n 1
(16) [...]
[tpy pr.t]

pꜣ [...] šsp.t ỉḥ n 4
pꜣ [... n pꜣ] ỉmy-rꜣ mšꜥ ỉḥ n 8
pꜣ ỉmy-rꜣ šsp n šsp[.w] n pꜣ ỉmy-rꜣ mšꜥ ỉḥ n 8
pꜣ (Side D: 13 vertical columns) (17) [... ỉḥ] n 10
ỉbt 2 pr.t

pꜣ ḥry-pḏ.wt n ꜥḥꜣ.wt n pꜣ ỉmy-rꜣ mšꜥ ỉḥ n 10
pꜣ ꜥꜣ n pr n pr n pꜣ ỉmy-rꜣ mšꜥ ỉḥ n 5
[...] (18) [...]
[ỉbt 3] pr.t

pꜣ sš mšꜥ n pꜣ nḫt n Mr-mšꜥ⸗f ỉḥ n 5
nꜣ ꜥꜣ.w n wḥm.w n Mr-mšꜥ⸗f ỉḥ n 6
pꜣ sš mšꜥ n pꜣ [...]
(19) [...] Ḫnn-ny-sw.t ỉḥ n 2
pꜣ ḥry strps.w n pr n pꜣ ỉmy-rꜣ mšꜥ ỉḥ n 5
pꜣ ḥry šms n pr Ḥry-š⸗f ỉḥ n 1
ỉbt 4 pr.t

(20) [... dmỉ] Pꜣ-sgrỉ-n-Ḥw.t-Tỉ.t dmỉ Tꜣ-ꜥ.t-pꜣ-qn-pꜣ-mšꜥ ỉḥ n 3

dmỉ Pr-Wsỉr ỉḥ n 2
dmỉ Tꜣ-wḥ.t-Sw dmỉ [...]
(21) [...] dmỉ Pꜣ-sgr-n-ꜥr ỉḥ n 1
dmỉ Pꜣ-bḫn-n-pꜣ-Nḥsy ỉḥ n 2
tpy šmw

dmỉ Pꜣ-bḫn-[...] ỉḥ n [...]
(22) [... dmỉ] Pꜣ-bḫn-n-nfr-rnp.t ỉḥ n 1
dmỉ Tꜣ-ỉꜣ.t-p-pꜣ-[dỉ(?)]-Bꜣs.t ỉḥ n 1
dmỉ Pr-ꜥpr(?)-ỉt ỉḥ n 1 dmỉ Pr-Wꜣḏ ỉḥ n 1
dmỉ Tꜣ-šꜣ.t-rs(?) ỉḥ n 1
[...] (23) [...]
dmỉ ꜣIꜣ.t-šꜣ-ḫry-ỉs ỉḥ n 2
dmỉ Pr-nbỉ.t ỉḥ n 1
dmỉ Ḥw.t-Mnṯ(w) ỉḥ n 3
ỉbt 2 šmw
dmỉ Tꜣ-wḥ.t-knỉ.t ỉḥ n 1
[dmỉ ...] (24) [...].w ỉḥ n 1
dmỉ Tꜣ-ỉꜣ.t-tꜣt ỉḥ n 1
dmỉ ꜣIꜣ.t-n-wꜥb ỉḥ n 1
dmỉ Ḥw.t-nbs ỉḥ n 2
dmỉ Ḥw.t-nḏs.t ỉḥ n 1
dmỉ Tꜣ-wḥ.t-ỉm(?) ỉḥ n [...]
(25) [...]
[dmỉ] Nkrw ỉḥ n 1
dmỉ Pꜣ-ỉh-n-Šd-sw-Ḫnsw ỉḥ n 1
dmỉ Pꜣ-ỉh-n-Nb-smn ỉḥ n 1
dmỉ Pꜣ-ỉh-n-Pn-Rꜥ ỉḥ n 1
[...] (26) [...] ꜥ.t n pꜣ ỉmy-rꜣ mšꜥ ỉḥ n 2
n(ꜣ) ỉrw-ḏꜣḏꜣ.w[4] ỉḥ n 1
ỉbt 3 šmw

pꜣ ỉdnw n tꜣ s.t sš n pꜣ ỉmy-rꜣ mšꜥ ỉḥ n 2
pꜣ ỉmy-rꜣ [...] (27) [...]
pꜣ ỉmy-rꜣ ꜥb n ꜥnḫ.w n pr Ḥry-šＺf ỉḥ n 1
n(ꜣ) ḫmty.w ḥnꜥ bỉn.tyw ỉḥ n 1
n(ꜣ) kꜣm.w ḥnꜥ n(ꜣ) yꜥ.w ỉḥ n 1
pꜣ ỉmy-rꜣ ỉw [...]
(28) [... ỉḥ] n 1
n(ꜣ) ḥm.w mrkbt ỉḥ n 1
pꜣ ḥm-nṯr tpy n ꜣImn wꜥb.t n Ḥsb(?)-nḏm.t ỉḥ n 1 n(ꜣ) snỉ.w ỉḥ n 1
    n(ꜣ) ḫr.tyw-nṯr ỉḥ n 1
n(ꜣ) qd.w ỉqd.w ỉḥ n 1

[ỉbt 4 šmw]

(29) [... dmỉ ...]r ỉḥ n 4
pꜣ ḥm-nṯr tpy n Ḥry-š⸗f Rꜥ-ms-s(w) ỉḥ n 1
dỉw ḥry.w rnp.t

(1) [... who defeats (?)] the Asiatics, the King of Upper and Lower Egypt, Lord of the Two Lands, Hedjkheperre-setepenre, Son of Re, Lord of Diadems, Sheshonq (I), beloved of Amon, like Re.

(2) Now, His Majesty, l.p.h., seeks any occasion for benefactions so as to do them for his father Harsaphes, King of the Two Lands, Lord of Heracleopolis, it having been on his mind since he has been (3) king. Then came the prince and general Namlot before His Majesty.

He said: "As for the estate of Harsaphes, King of the Two Lands, it has ceased (4) regarding the daily ox-offering. I found it fallen into ruin from how it was formerly in the time of the (5) ancestors. It would be good to cause it to proceed."

Then said His Majesty: "May my *ka*-spirit praise you, O my son, who came forth from me! (6) Your heart is like the heart of the one who begot it.[1] It is my very body renewed. It is my father Harsaphes, King of the Two Lands, the Lord of Heracleopolis, who renders effective everything that comes forth (7) from your mouth in his estate forever."

A decree was made[2] in the palace, l.p.h., to equip the estate of Harsaphes, King of the Two Lands, the Lord of Heracleopolis, in order to establish (8) this daily ox-offering in it as had been done in the time of the ancestors. A decree was made[2] comprising the costs (9) to equip it. This daily ox-offering was levied upon the cities, towns, and settlements of Heracleopolis (10) without an instance of default among them. It cannot be discontinued[3] accordingly, forever and ever. The King of Upper and Lower Egypt, Lord of the Two Lands, Hedjkheperre-setepenre, Son of Re, Lord of Diadems, Sheshonq, beloved of Amon, given life (11) like Re forever.

Capitation of the levy pertaining to the 365 oxen throughout the year for the cycle of eternity:

(12) The general of Heracleopolis, his capitation: 60 oxen.
For the first month of Inundation to month 2 of Inundation.

The Lady of the house, the chief superior of the harem of Harsaphes, King of the Two Lands, the Lord of Heracleopolis, daughter of the great chief of the Ma, Isetemkheb: 3 oxen.
(13) The chief of the "Hittite troops" of Usimaꜥre: 10 oxen.
The chief of the "Hittite troops" of Heracleopolis: 10 oxen.
The prophet of Seth, Lord of Su: 10 oxen.

For month 3 of Inundation.

(14) [The chief of] ox-fatteners of the estate of Harsaphes, King of the Two Lands: 10 oxen.
The high priestess of Heracleopolis: 6 oxen.
The temple scribe of the estate of Harsaphes, King of the Two Lands: 10 oxen.
The deputy of the temple: 1 ox.
The (15) [...] of [this?] estate: 3 oxen.
For month 4 of Inundation.

The prophet of Harsaphes, King of the Two Lands: 7 oxen.
The deputy of the reception rooms of this estate: 1 ox.
The chief of the reception rooms of this estate: 1 ox.
(16) [...]
[For the first month of winter.]

The [... of] the reception room: 4 oxen.
The [... of the] general: 8 oxen.
The reception room overseer of the reception rooms of the general: 8 oxen.
The (17) [...]: 10 [oxen.]
For month 2 of winter.

The chief of archers of the warships of the general: 10 oxen.
The majordomo of the house of the general: 5 oxen.
[...] (18) [...]
[For month 3] of winter.

The army scribe of the fortress "Beloved of His Army": 5 oxen.
The chief of heralds of "Beloved of His Army": 6 oxen.
The army scribe of the [...]
(19) [...] of Heracleopolis: 2 oxen.
The chief of .... of the house of the general: 5 oxen.
The chief retainer of the estate of Harsaphes: 1 ox.
For month 4 of winter.

(20) [... The town] "The Quieter" of "The Mansion of Tiye"; the town "The Chamber of the Valiant One of the Army": 3 oxen.
The town Busiris: 2 oxen.
The town "The Settlement of Su"; the town [...]
(21) [...]; the town "The Quieter of the Goat": 1 ox.
The town "The Castle of the Nubian": 2 oxen.

For the first month of summer.

The town "The Castle of [. . ."]: [. . .] oxen.
(22) [. . . The town "The] Castle of Neferrenpet": 1 ox.
The town "The mound of Pedubast (?)": 1 ox.
The town "The Equipping (?) House of the Father": 1 ox.
The town "House of the Papyrus Scepter (?)": 1 ox.
The town *Tashatres:* 1 ox.
[. . .] (23) [. . .]
The town "Mound of *Shaheris*": 2 oxen.
The town "House of the Flame": 1 ox.
The town "Mansion of Montu": 3 oxen.
For month 2 of summer.

The town "The Settlement of *Kenit*": 1 ox.
[The town . . .] (24) [. . .]: 1 ox.
The town "The Mound of *Tchat*": 1 ox.
The town "Mound of Purity": 1 ox.
The town "Mansion of the Zizyphus Tree": 2 oxen.
The town "The Lesser Mansion": 1 ox.
The town "The Settlement of the Bark": [. . .] oxen.
(25) [. . .]
[The town] *Nekeru:* 1 ox.
The town "The Camp of Shedsukhonsu": 1 ox.
The town "The Camp of Nebsemen": 1 ox.
The town "The Camp of Penre": 1 ox.
[. . .] (26) [. . . supervisor (?) of the] chamber of the general: 2 oxen.
Those who acted as supervisors (?)[4]: 1 ox.
For month 3 of summer.

The deputy of the archive of the general: 2 oxen.
The overseer of [. . .] (27) [. . .]
The overseer of goatherds of the estate of Harsaphes: 1 ox.
The coppersmiths and the harpists: 1 ox.
The gardeners and the washers: 1 ox.
The overseer of gelders (?) [. . .]
(28) [. . .]: 1 ox.
The chariot craftsmen: 1 ox.
The First Prophet of Amon of the sanctuary of Reckoning (?) Pleasure:
    1 ox.
The chariot warriors: 1 ox.
The stone masons: 1 ox.
The potters and the builders: 1 ox.

[For month 4 of summer]

(29) [The town of ....]r: 4 oxen.
The First Prophet of Harsaphes, Rameses: 1 ox.
For the five epagomenal days.

NOTES
1. For this passage, see Jansen-Winkeln 1992, 147–49.
2. Narrative infinitive.
3. Or n(n) ws n≠f "without discontinuity to it"
4. Tresson: "Les fabricants de tête."

46. APIS EMBALMING BED

Although memorials from the Memphite Serapeum, the burial complex of the sacred Apis bull, are a primary source for the later Third Intermediate Period, no Twenty-First Dynasty Apis burials have yet been discovered, nor any Twenty-Second Dynasty burials before the reign of Osorkon II. That such burials occurred is certain, however, as proved by the discovery at Mitrahina in 1878 of an Apis embalming table, part of a new embalming house commissioned by Sheshonq I. The rectangular calcite table comprises three blocks, with the inscribed stone measuring 1.90 m in length, .50 m in height, and 1.5 m in width. A scene on the south side depicts the name of Apis flanked by the cartouches of Sheshonq I and figures of the High Priest of Ptah on the right and Anubis on the left. The High Priest wears the traditional leopard skin and side-lock of his office and holds a scepter and adze, while Anubis elevates a lustration vase, pouring water over the central names.

For the texts, translation, and discussion, see Brugsch 1878, 38–41; 1883–91, 817 and 948–49; Dimick 1958, 188–89; Kees 1962, 145–46; Vercoutter 1962, 57; Porter and Moss 1981, 841–42. See Kitchen 1986, 291 §248, 489 table 20.

CENTRAL APIS TEXT
Wsîr Ḥp Tm Ḥr n spy[1]
Osiris, Apis, Atum and Horus in a single instance.[1]

FLANKING CARTOUCHES
Ḥḏ-ḫpr-Rꜥ-stp-n-Rꜥ (2) Ššnq mrî-ʾImn
Hedjkheperre-setepenre, (2) Sheshonq, beloved of Amon.

LABEL FOR THE MEMPHITE HIGH PRIEST

wr ḫrp ḥmww (2) s(t)m [n Ptḥ] (3) Šd-s(w)-Nfr-tm (4) mꜣꜥ-ḫrw sꜣ wr (5) ḫrp ḥmww ꜥnḫ≠(6)f-n-Sḫm.t mꜣꜥ-ḫrw (7) ir wp.(t)-rꜣ n it≠f Wsir-Ḥp (8) in iwn-mw.t≠f wꜥb m wr […]

"Chief of Master-craftsmen" (2) and *setem*-priest [of Ptah], Shedsunefer-tem, (4) the justified, son of the "Chief (5) of Master-craftsmen," Ankhef(6)ensakhmet, the justified. (7) Enacting the opening of the mouth ritual for his father Osiris-Apis (8) by the "pillar of his mother"-priest, the pure one in the great house […]

LABEL FOR ANUBIS

ꜣInpw imy wt ḫnty [sḥ nṯr] (2) ir nw Wsir-Ḥp sp 4

Anubis, who is in the mummy bandages, foremost of [the divine embalming booth.] (2) Performing ministrations for Osiris-Apis, four times.

HORIZONTAL BAND

rdi.t m ḥr n wr ḫrp ḥmww s(t)m Šd-s(w)-Nfr-tm mꜣꜥ-ḫrw (2) in ḥm≠f r spd wꜥb.t n it≠f Wsir-Ḥp m kꜣ.t mnḫ.t

Orders were given to the "Chief of Master-craftsmen" and *setem*-priest, Shedsunefertem, the justified, (2) by His Majesty to provide an embalming place for his father Osiris-Apis consisting of excellent construction.

NOTE

1. Following Kees; Brugsch translated "Osiris-Apis-Tum-Hor-en-sopi" as a single divine name, while Vercoutter translated "Atum-Horus of Sep." For identifications of Osiris-Apis as the revived Atum-Horus, see Otto 1938, 27 and 31.

47. GEBEL ES-SILSILAH QUARRY STELA NO. 100

At the quarry of Gebel es-Silsilah, Sheshonq's building campaign is recorded on a formal stela with a cavetto cornice and winged sundisk above a tableau of the King and Prince Iuput introduced by Mut before Amon, Re, and Ptah. The monument is provided with fifty-seven columns of text, including the "signature" and depiction of the kneeling artist: twenty-seven brief columns of labels (lines 1–3 and 8–31), four vertical dedicatory framing bands (lines 4–7), seven horizontal lines extolling the titles and quarry activities of Sheshonq and Iuput (lines 32–38), and nineteen short vertical lines recording the expedition of year 21 (lines 39–56), concluding with the artist's name and titles (lines 56–57). Carved on a sandstone cliff[1] bordering the Nile and facing riverine traffic, the stela measures 2.93 m. high by 2.53 m. wide. The text of year 21 records the latest known date of King Sheshonq I and details the initial construction work on the colonnaded "Great Court" ("Mansion of Hedjkheperre-setepenre in Thebes") before the Second Pylon at Karnak as well as unfulfilled plans for a First Pylon, subsequently built by Nectanebo. Of this major construction by Sheshonq, only portions of the "Bubastite Portal" were decorated before the king's death and the resultant abandonment of the work. Characteristic of the unusual status of the military high priests of this period is the depiction of Prince Iuput in comparable scale to that of the king, his all but equal prominence in the laudatory texts (lines 5, 7, and 36–38), and his request for the royal prerogatives of "valor and victory" (line 38).

A corrected text copy, translation, and publication history are found in Caminos 1952, 46–61, replacing Breasted 1906–7, 4:344–47 §§701–8, and the thoroughly obsolete interpretation in Revillout 1899, 180–81. An English translation of the obsolete analysis of Brugsch has been reissued in Brugsch 1996, 377–79. See further Epigraphic Survey 1954, vii–x; Nims 1955, 115; 1965, 78–79; and Kitchen 1986, 301–2 §260.

A. Labels (Lines 1–31)

Symmetrical Labels to Winged Disk (Lines 1–2)
    Bḥd.t(y) nṯr ꜥꜣ
    Behdetite, the Great God.

Symmetrical "Bandeau" Text of King (Line 3):
    ꜥnḫ ny-sw.t bỉ.ty nb tꜣ.wy Ḥd-ḫpr-Rꜥ-stp-n-Rꜥ sꜣ Rꜥ nb ḫꜥ.w Ššnq mrỉ-ʾImn ꜥnḫ ḏ.t
    Long live the King of Upper and Lower Egypt, Lord of the Two Lands, Hedjkheperre-setepenre, Son of Re, Lord of Diadems, Sheshonq, beloved of Amon, living forever.

Symmetrical Inner Dedication Bands (Lines 4 and 6):
    ꜥnḫ Ḥr Kꜣ-nḫt-mrỉ-Rꜥ sḫꜥ≠f[2] m ny-sw.t r smꜣ tꜣ.wy ny-sw.t bỉ.ty nb tꜣ.wy nb ỉr.(t) ḫt Ḥd-ḫpr-Rꜥ-stp-n-Rꜥ sꜣ Rꜥ n ḫ.t≠f mr≠f Šš(n)q mrỉ-ʾImn dỉ ꜥnḫ mỉ Rꜥ ḏ.t
    Long live the Horus "Strong Bull, beloved of Re, whom he (Re) made manifest[2] as king in order to unite the Two Lands," the King of Upper and Lower Egypt, Lord of the Two Lands, Lord of ritual performance, Hedjkheperre-setepenre, bodily Son of Re, whom he (Re) loves, Shesho(n)q, beloved of Amon, given life like Re forever.

Symmetrical Outer Dedication Bands (Lines 5 and 7):
    ỉr.n{n}[3] ḥm-nṯr tp(y) n ʾImn-Rꜥ ny-sw.t nṯr.w ỉmy-rꜣ mšꜥ wr ḫꜣw.ty ʾIwpwt mꜣꜥ-ḫrw nty ḫꜣ.t n mšꜥ ꜥꜣ[4] n Šmꜥ r-ḏr.w sꜣ ny-sw.t nb tꜣ.wy Ššnq mrỉ-ʾImn

Made by[3] the First Prophet of Amon-Re, King of the Gods, great general and leader Iuput, the justified, who is at the head of all the great armies[4] of Upper Egypt, royal son of the Lord of the Two Lands, Sheshonq, beloved of Amon.

Mut Addresses Sheshonq (Lines 8–15):

ḏd-mdw ỉn Mw.t wr(.t) nb(.t) ʾIšrw ḥnw.t (9) nṯr.w nb.w (10) ny-sw.t bỉ.ty Ḥd-ḫpr-Rᶜ-stp-n-Rᶜ (11) sꜣ Rᶜ Šš(n)q mrỉ-ʾImn (12) dỉ.n≠(ỉ)[5] ᶜnḫ ḏd wꜣs nb s(n)yb nb (13) sꜣ ḥꜣ≠k m ᶜnḫ ḏd wꜣs nb s(n)yb nb ꜣw.t-ỉb nb ḥꜣs.wt nb ḫr tb.ty≠k (14) mỉ r≠k ḥr ḥw.t-ᶜꜣ(.t) (15) dỉ.n≠(ỉ) mꜣꜣ≠k n ỉt≠k ʾImn

Words said by Mut the great, Lady of Asheru, Mistress of (9) all the gods: "O King of Upper and Lower Egypt, Hedjkheperre-setepenre, (11) Son of Re, Shesho(n)q, beloved of Amon, (12) I have granted[5] all life, stability, and dominion, and all health, (13) with protection behind you as all life, stability, and dominion, all health, and all joy, all foreign lands being beneath your sandals. (14) Come, then, into the temple. (15) I have caused that you see your father Amon."

Speech of Amon-Re (Lines 16–18):

ḏd-mdw ỉn ʾImn-Rᶜ nb ns.wt tꜣ.wy ḫnty (17) ʾIp.t-s.wt (18) dỉ.n≠(ỉ)[5] qn(ỉ) nḫt.w ᶜšꜣ wr.t

Words said by Amon-Re, Lord of the Thrones of the Two Lands, Foremost of (17) Karnak: (18) "Thus I have granted[5] valor and very many victories."

Speech of Re-Horachty-Atum (Lines 19–22):

ḏd-mdw ỉn Rᶜ-Ḥr-ꜣḫ.ty Tm (20) nb tꜣ.wy ʾIwn(y) (21) nṯr ᶜꜣ nb p.t (22) dỉ.n≠(ỉ)[5] ḥḥ (n) ḥb-sd ḥfn.t m rnp.wt

Words said by Re-Horachty-Atum, (20) Lord of the Two Lands, the Heliopolitan, (21) the Great God, Lord of heaven (22): "Thus I have granted[5] millions of jubilees and a hundred-thousand of years."

Speech of Ptah-Nun (Lines 23–26):

ḏd-mdw ỉn Ptḥ-Nwn wr (24) n[6] ỉt nṯr.w nb.w nfr ḥr (25) ms psḏ.t ᶜꜣ(.t) (26) dỉ.n≠(ỉ) n≠k tꜣ.w[7] nb ḥtp.w

Words said by Ptah-Nun the great, being[6] the father of all the gods, beautiful of face, who fashioned the Great Ennead: "To you I have given all lands[7] in peace."

Label for Prince Iuput (Lines 27–31):

ḥm-nṯr tp(y) n ʾImn-Rᶜ ny-sw.t nṯr.w ỉmy-rꜣ mšᶜ (28) wr ḥꜣw.ty ʾIwpwt mꜣᶜ-ḫrw (29) sꜣ ny-sw.t nb tꜣ.wy Šš(n)q mrỉ-ʾImn (30) ᶜnḫ wḏꜣ snb qn(ỉ) nḫt.w (31) ỉr.nn[8] snṯr n nb≠f

First Prophet of Amon-Re, King of the Gods, great general (28) and leader Iuput, the justified, (29) royal son of the Lord of the Two Lands, Shesho(n)q, beloved of Amon, (30) (to whom be) life, prosperity, health, valor and victories! (31) Making[8] incense for his lord.

B. MAIN BODY OF TEXT ("MIDDLE PORTION," LINES 32–38)

(32) nb.ty ḫꜥ m sḫm.ty mỉ Ḥr sꜣ ꜣs.t sḥtp nṯr.w m mꜣꜥ.t Ḥr-nbw sḫm pḥ.ty ḫ(wỉ) pḏ.t psḏ.t wr n nḫt.w (m) tꜣ.w nb.w nṯr nfr Rꜥ m (33) ỉrw≠f mstwt n Ḥr-ꜣḫ.ty rdỉ sw ꞽImn ḥr ns.t≠f r smnḫ šꜣꜥ.n≠f r grg Km.t n wḥm ny-sw.t bỉ.ty Ḥd-ḫpr-Rꜥ-stp-n-Rꜥ (34) ỉr.n{n}≠fꜣ wp[9] ḥꜣ.t m mꜣwy n šꜣꜥ kꜣ.t ỉr.n{n}ꜣ sꜣ Rꜥ Šš(n)q mrỉ-ꞽImn ỉ-ỉr mnw n ỉt≠f ꞽImn-Rꜥ nb ns.wt tꜣ.wy ỉr≠f ḥb(.w)-sd (n) Rꜥ (35) rnp.wt n Tm ꜥnḫ.tỉ ḏ.t pꜣy≠ỉ nb nfr dỉ≠k ḏd[10] ỉw m ḥḥ.w nw rnp.wt ꜣḫ[11] (n) pꜣ ỉr n ꞽImn mty≠k[12] ḥr ỉr(.t) n≠ỉ ny.t-sw.t ꜥꜣ(.t) (36) ỉr.n{n}≠fꜣ wp[9] ḥꜣ.t m mꜣwy n šꜣꜥ kꜣ.t ỉr.n{n}ꜣ ḥm-nṯr tp(y) n ꞽImn-Rꜥ ny-sw.t nṯr.w ỉmy-rꜣ mšꜥ wr ḥꜣw.ty ꞽIwpwtỉ mꜣꜥ-ḫrw (37) nty ḥꜣ.t n mšꜥ ꜥꜣ n Šmꜥ r-ḏr.w sꜣ ny-sw.t nb tꜣ.wy Šš(n)q mrỉ-ꞽImn n nb≠f n ꞽImn-Rꜥ ny-sw.t nṯr.w ỉr n≠f ꜥnḫ wḏꜣ snb ꜥḥꜥ q(ꜣ) qn(ỉ) (38) nḫt ỉꜣw ꜥꜣ m wꜣs pꜣy≠ỉ nb nfr dỉ≠k ḏd[10] ỉw m ḥḥ.w nw rnp.wt ꜣḫ[11] (n) pꜣ ỉrr n ꞽImn mty≠k[12] ḥr ỉr(.t) n≠ỉ qn(ỉ) nḫt

(32) The Two Ladies: "He who appears in the double crown like Horus son of Isis, pacifying the gods with Truth"; Horus of Gold: "Powerful of strength, who strikes the Nine Bows, great of victories (in) all lands, the Good God, Re in (33) his essential form, descendant of Horachty; Amon placed him upon his throne in order to perfect what he had initiated and to found Egypt once more"; the King of Upper and Lower Egypt, Hedj-kheperre-setepenre. (34) He opened[9] the quarry anew specifically for the beginning of the construction work that the son of Re, Shesho(n)q, beloved of Amon, who makes monuments for his father Amon-Re, Lord of the Thrones of the Two Lands, did[3] that he might achieve the jubilees of Re (35) and the years of Atum, living forever. "My good lord, may you cause that those who come in millions of years say[10]: 'It is profitable[11] (for) the one who acts for Amon.' May you be agreeable[12] concerning making for me a great kingship." (36) He opened[9] the quarry anew specifically for the beginning of the construction work that the First Prophet of Amon-Re, King of the Gods, great general and leader Iuput, the justified, (37) who is at the head of the great army of the entirety of Upper Egypt, royal son of the Lord of the Two Lands, Shesho(n)q, beloved of Amon, did[3] for his lord and for Amon-Re, King of the Gods, who made for him life, prosperity, and health, a long lifetime, valor, (38) victory, and great old age in dominion. "My good lord, may you cause that those who come in millions of years say[10]: 'It is profitable[11] (for) the one who acts for Amon.' May you be agreeable[12] concerning making for me valor and victory."

C. Expedition of Year 21 ("Bottom Portion," Lines 39–57)

(39) ḥsb.t 21 ȝbd 2 šmw hrw pn ỉw[13] ḥm≠f (m) pȝ ẖnw n (40) Pr-ȝs.t pȝ kȝ ꜥȝ Rꜥ-Ḥr-ȝẖ.ty[14] wḏ.n ḥm≠f r (41) dỉ m ḥr n ỉt-nṯr n ʾImn-Rꜥ ny-sw.t nṯr.w ḥry-sš(tȝ)[15] (42) (n) Pr Rꜥ-Ḥr-ȝẖ.ty ỉmy-rȝ kȝ.t (m) mnw nb tȝ.wy Ḥr-m-sȝ(43)≠f mȝꜥ-ẖrw[16] r ḥwỉ mkỉ[17] kȝ.t nb.t (ỉw≠)s r ḥr Sbk[18] n ẖȝt (44) stp n.t Ḥn(y).t r ỉr mnw ꜥȝ.w wr.t n pr n ỉt≠f (45) šps ʾImn-Rꜥ nb ns.wt tȝ.wy ỉn ḥm≠f dỉ tp-rd r (46) qd bẖn.wt ꜥȝ.wt wr.t nty (m) snt[19] r Sḫd-Nỉw.t[20] (47) m sꜥḥꜥ ꜥȝ.wy≠f n ḥḥ (n) mḥ r ỉr wsẖ(.t) ḥb-sd (48) n pr n ỉt≠f ʾImn-Rꜥ ny-sw.t nṯr.w r pḥr≠s n ḥny.t wȝḏy.t (49) ỉy m ḥtp n nỉw.t rsy.t r b(w) ẖr(y) ḥm≠f (ỉ)n ỉt-nṯr n ʾImn-Rꜥ (50) ny-sw.t nṯr.w ḥry-sš(tȝ)[15] n Pr Rꜥ-Ḥr-ȝẖ.ty ỉmy-rȝ kȝ.t m Ḥw.t-Ḥd-ẖpr-Rꜥ-stp-n-Rꜥ-m-Wȝs(.t)[21] (51) wr mr(w.t) (m)-bȝḥ nb≠f ỉr ẖ.t nb tȝ.wy Ḥr-m-sȝ(52)≠f mȝꜥ-ẖrw ḏd≠f ḏdd.t≠k nb ẖpr≠sn pȝ(y)(53)≠ỉ nb nfr nn sḏr m grḥ nn ꜥꜥ(w)[22] (54) sw(t) m hrw wpw ẖws kȝ.wt[23] nḥḥ nn (55) wrd dỉ ḥsy ḥr ny-sw.t fq.tw≠f m ẖt nw (56) ḥḏ nbw ms≠f spd-ḥr ḥm-nṯr Pȝ-ḥkȝ-nfr ỉr mnw n ʾImn m ỉt≠f (57) wḥm≠f sw

(39) Regnal year 21, second month of summer. On this day, while[13] His Majesty was in the residence of (40) "The estate of Isis," the great *ka*-spirit of Re-Horachty,[14] His Majesty commanded to (41) charge the God's Father of Amon-Re, King of the Gods, the overseer of secrets[15] (42) (of) the estate of Re-Horachty and overseer of works in the monuments of the Lord of the Two Lands, Horemsaef (43), the justified,[16] to safeguard and protect[17] every construction work that is in the sight of Sobek[18] in the (44) choicest quarry of Gebel es-Silsilah (Ḫny/Ḫnw "The Place of Rowing") and to make very great monuments for the estate of his noble father (45) Amon-Re, Lord of the Thrones of the Two Lands. It was His Majesty who gave stipulations to (46) build very great pylon towers that are similar to[19] "Illuminating-Thebes"[20] (47) by erecting its door-leaves of millions of cubits and to make a jubilee court (48) for the house of his father Amon-Re, King of the Gods, and to surround it with statues and a colonnade. (49) Coming in peace from the Southern City (Thebes) to the place where the king was by the God's Father of Amon-Re, (50) King of the Gods, the overseer of secrets[15] of the estate of Re-Horachty and overseer of works in the "Mansion of Hedjkheperre-setepenre in Thebes,"[21] (51) great of love before his Lord of ritual performance, the Lord of the Two Lands, Horemsaef (52), the justified. He said: "(As for) all that which you said, they have happened, my (53) good lord, without sleeping by night nor slumbering[22] (54) by day, but only erecting the eternal constructions[23] without (55) wearying." Praise before the king caused that he be rewarded with items of (56) silver and gold. His clever offspring, the prophet Pahekanefer, who made the monument for Amon as (in the capacity of) his father. (57) May he equal him.

NOTES

1. For a general discussion of the site, see Caminos and James 1963, 1–10.

2. Caminos (1952, 51, textual note to line 4) wrongly disregards the causative force of sḫꜥ and translates "he arises as King" (48). See Kruchten 1986, 77–78, for this term of installation.

3. Written redundantly ỉr.nn as is typical for Dynasty XXII; cf. Erman and Grapow 1926–63, 1:111/7; Caminos 1952, 51–52, textual note to line 5.

4. Following the correct orthography of lines 7 and 37; cluttered with otiose signs in line 5. For the title, see S. British Museum 8 (Sheshonq II Nile Statue, no. 66).

5. Caminos assumes a consistent elipse of n≠k, but cf. line 26, where the dative is expressed. For the translation "Thus," see Hoch 1995, §149 end.

6. N for "m of equivalence," as is common. Caminos tacitly reads the signs ntf twice as ntf ỉt "he is the father," but such labels contain epithets, not declarative sentences.

7. For the tag, see Erman and Grapow 1926–63, 5:220/3.

8. An error for the infinitive ỉr.t; see Caminos 1953, 53, textual note to line 31. See further Jansen-Winkeln 1989, 237–39.

9. Paraphrastic construction with ỉr, literally: "He made an opening."

10. Written ḏdtw.

11. Without emended dative: "Beneficial is the one who acts for Amon" or "It is profitable to act for Amon."

12. So Caminos (1952, 54 textual note to line 35), following Gardiner's hesitant identification with Demotic mt(r)ỉ; cf. Erichsen 1954, 190. Breasted 1906–7, 4:346–47 §§704–5, translated "bear witness." Far less likely is the suggestion by Jansen-Winkeln that the writing is defective for mtn "to reward" (Erman and Grapow 1926–63, 2:170), here construed without an object; see Jansen-Winkeln 1989, 237–39.

13. Following dates and hrw pn, ỉw and adverbial predicate are common, representing either a circumstantial or main clause. Late Egyptian account texts indicate that these should be circumstantial; see Kitchen 1975–90, 1:244 (baking account 1,3) and 245 (2,1 ỉw tw rather than the pronominal compound twtw).

14. Unknown royal Delta (?) residence; see Gauthier 1925–31, 2:41 and 3:148; Caminos 1952, 55, textual note to line 40. On the basis of the borrowed epithet ("the great *ka*-spirit of Re-Horachty") used to describe Piramesses in the later years of Rameses II, Kitchen (1986, 301 n. 314) suggests "a new country residence south of Tanis proper and on the north side of Pi-Ramesse, bounded by the estate of Edjo" (= Isis).

15. For the defective spelling, see Caminos 1952, 55, textual note to line 41; versus Erman and Grapow 1926–63, 3:483/10. Unremarked by Caminos, the suggestion had already been made by Breasted 1906–7, 4:347 §§706 and 708.

16. Incorrectly carved, with mỉ-biliteral for ḫrw.

17. For the abbreviated writing of mkỉ in the common compound ḫwỉ mkỉ, see Caminos 1952, 56, textual note to line 43.

18. Sobek is the chief local god, who thus has divine oversight of the quarry; see Caminos and James 1963, 22, 26, 37, 43, etc. ("Sobek, Lord of Silsilah"). Cami-

nos, however, takes the passage as an odd parenthetical intrusion ("—and it was to be above Suchus—" [1952, 50]), implying that the work should be conducted beyond the jurisdiction of the god. This nuance is not supported by the text.

19. For the reading, see Nims 1965, 79; Erman and Grapow 1926–63, 3:457. Unread and untranslated by Caminos and Breasted. Earlier translations suggested "dressed stone"; see Caminos 1952, 56–57, textual note to line 46.

20. Name of the Second Pylon at Karnak, here wrongly written with ḥm for ḥd-biliteral.

21. Name of the First Court at Thebes; see Nims 1955, 115.

22. Erman and Grapow 1926–63, 1:169/8.

23. Erman and Grapow 1926–63, 3:249/1.

48. THE BUBASTITE PORTAL AT KARNAK: RELIEFS OF SHESHONQ I

The only sections decorated under Sheshonq I in the king's great colonnaded First Court at Karnak, this set of reliefs comprises seven scenes and a dedicatory inscription. The most famous of these is the large-scale victory relief on the outer (southern) facade recording the king's Palestinian campaign (see 1 Kgs 14:25–26; 2 Chr 12:2–4, 9), with its list of approximately 150 captured enemy towns. The transliteration, translation, and suggested identifications for this list have long been a source of interest to both Egyptologists and scholars of biblical history. Other decoration was confined to the inner (northern) face of the architrave and the supporting pilasters flanking the two columns of the gateway and attached to the small temple of Rameses III (on the west) and the Second Pylon (on the east). Particularly notable on the pilaster reliefs, as on Sheshonq's Gebel es-Silsilah Stela (above, no. 47), is the unusual prominence of Iuput, the prince, high priest, and general, depicted on an equal scale with the king in every scene—even in the lowest registers, where "the space was so small that he had to be literally crowded in."[1]

For the texts, see Epigraphic Survey 1954, vii–xiii, and plates 1–12 (line sequences often reordered below for thematic consistency); Porter and Moss 1972, 34–36. Translation (of victory relief only) in Kitchen 1999, 433–40; and Breasted 1906–7, 4:348–57. A brief synopsis appears in Pritchard 1987, 96–97. Wilson 2005 appeared after the present manuscript was closed. Conquered place names are now listed in Aḥituv 1984.[2] Composed in a mixture of Middle and Late Egyptian, the texts of the victory relief include many conventional phrases borrowed from earlier monuments. The regnal year date of the Palestinian campaign is uncertain; for earlier suggestions, see Gauthier 1914, 310. For the artistic depiction, see Fazzini 1988, 6 and 30 and pl. I. An English translation of the obsolete analysis of Brugsch has been reissued in Brugsch 1996, 375–77. See Kitchen 1986, 296–300 §§254–58, 301–2 §260, and excursus E, 432–47 §§398–415.

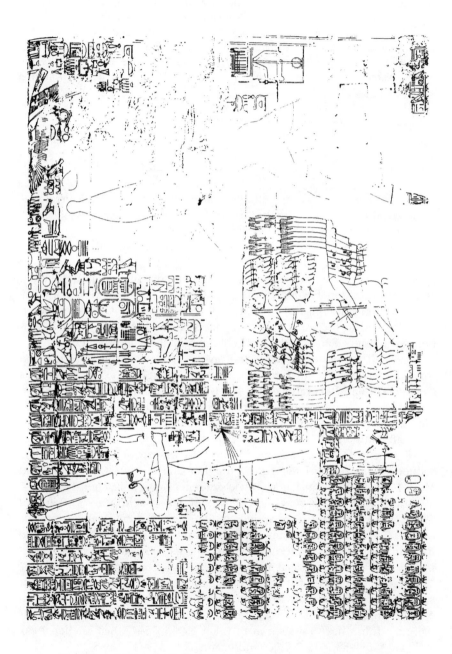

Sheshonq I Victory Relief, Epigraphic Survey 1954, plate 3.

A. Dedication (Architrave, Northern Face: Key Plans K 344)
Text = Epigraphic Survey 1954, pl. 12
　　(1) ꜥnḫ Ḥr kꜣ nḫt mrꜣ Rꜥ sḫꜥ≠f m ny-sw.t r smꜣ tꜣ.wy ny-sw.t bꜣ.ty nb tꜣ.wy nb ḫpš Ḥd-ḫpr-Rꜥ-[stp-n-Rꜥ ...]
　　(2) ꜥnḫ Nb.ty ḫꜥ m sḫm.t(y) mꜣ Ḥr sꜣ ꜣs.t sḥtp nṯr.w m mꜣꜥ.t [sꜣ] Rꜥ n ḫ.t≠f mr[≠f] Ššnq mrꜣ-ʾImn wḫm ms.n≠f ʾIp.[t]-s.[wt] m [mꜣw.t ...] s[t]nw [..]≠f r [ꜣ]r.t n ꜣmy.w-ḫꜣ.t≠f psḏ.t ꜥꜣ.t n Wꜣs.t hry ḥr ꜣr.n≠f swḏ≠sn ny.t-sw.t n [ny-sw.t bꜣ].ty nb tꜣ.wy nb ḫpš Ḥd-ḫpr-Rꜥ-stp-n-Rꜥ ꜣr.n≠f dꜣ ꜥnḫ ḏd wꜣs mꜣ Rꜥ ḏ.t
　　(3) ꜥnḫ Ḥr-nbw sḫm pḥ.ty ḫ(wꜣ) pḏ.t psḏ.t wr nḫt.w m tꜣ.w nb.w [ny-sw.t bꜣ.ty] nb ꜣr.(t) ḫ.t Ḥd-ḫpr-Rꜥ-stp-n-Rꜥ ny-sw.t nḫt rs-tp nḫt [... ḥm]≠f r dꜣ.t tp-rd n ꜣr sw swsḫ ḥw.t-nṯr≠f m ꜣw n ḥḥ.w nṯr≠s nb nṯr.w ḫꜥy ꜣm≠s sr.n≠f nḫt.w n sꜣ≠f mr≠f nb ḫꜥ.w Ššnq mrꜣ-ʾImn ꜣr n≠f ḥb.w-sdꜣ ꜥꜣ wr.t mꜣ Rꜥ ḏ.t

　　(1) Long live the Horus: "Strong Bull, beloved of Re, whom he (Re) made manifest as king in order to unite the Two Lands"; the King of Upper and Lower Egypt, Lord of the Two Lands, Lord of the strong arm, Hedj-kheperre-setepenre [...]
　　(2) Long live the Two Ladies: "He who appears in the double crown like Horus son of Isis, pacifying the gods with Truth"; bodily [Son] of Re, whom [he (Re)] loves, Sheshonq, beloved of Amon, who has refashioned for him Karnak a[new ...] distinguished [...] him to act for those before him, while the Great Ennead is content because of what he has done, so that they transfer kingship to [the King of Upper] and Lower Egypt, Lord of the Two Lands, Lord of the strong arm, Hedjkheperre-setepenre, he having attained the state of being granted life, stability, and dominion like Re forever.
　　(3) Long live the Horus of Gold: "Powerful of strength, who strikes the Nine Bows, great of victories in all lands"; [the King of Upper and Lower Egypt], Lord of ritual performance, Hedjkheperre-setepenre, the victorious king vigilant for victory [...] His [Majesty] to give stipulations for the one who made him (Amon) to widen his temple by an extent of millions, with its god, the Lord of Gods, appearing in it, since he (Amon) foretold victories for his son whom he loves, the Lord of Diadems, Sheshonq, beloved of Amon, so as to make for him very many jubilees[3] like Re forever.

B. Western Pilaster Scenes (Northern Face: Key Plans K 340–43)
Text = Epigraphic Survey 1954, pl. 10 (top to bottom)

(1) Upper Register (= Epigraphic Survey 1954, pl. 10 C; K 340)
Sheshonq I receiving jubilees from Amon-Re and attended by his son the high priest Iuput. Amon-Re offers to Sheshonq's nose the year sign from which depend the glyphs of jubilees, life, stability, and dominion.

Label for the Winged Disk above the Scene (line 5)

Bḥd.t(y) nṯr ꜥꜣ sꜣb šw pr m ꜣḫ.t dỉ≠f ꜥnḫ ḏd wꜣs snb nb mỉ Rꜥ [ḏ.t]

The Behdetite, the great god with dappled plumage who comes forth from the horizon. May he grant all life, stability, dominion, and health like Re, [forever].

Label for Amon (lines 1–4)

ꜣImn-Rꜥ ny-sw.t nṯr.w (2) nb p.t sꜣ ꜥnḫ ḏd wꜣs snb nb ḥꜣ≠f mỉ Rꜥ (3) dỉ.n≠(ỉ) n≠kⁿ⁴ rnp.wt ꜥꜣꜣ m ḥb.w-sdⁿ³ mỉ Rꜥ (4) dỉ.n≠(ỉ) n≠k ꜥnḫ ḏd wꜣs nb r šr.t≠k nṯr nfr

Amon-Re, King of the Gods, (2) Lord of heaven. The protection of all life, stability, dominion, and health is behind him like Re. (3) "Thus I have given to you[4] many years in jubilees[3] like Re. (4) Thus I have given to you all life, stability, and dominion to your nose, O Good God."

Label for the King (lines 6–9)

ny-sw.t bỉ.ty nb ỉr.(t) ḫ.t Ḥd-ḫpr-Rꜥ-stp-n-Rꜥ (7) sꜣ Rꜥ n ḫ.t≠f mr≠f Ššnq mrỉ-ꜣImn (8) tỉ.t Rꜥ ḫnty tꜣ.wy mr(y) nb nṯr.w (9) dỉ ꜥnḫ ḏd wꜣs nb snb nb mỉ Rꜥ ḏ.t sꜣ ꜥnḫ ḏd wꜣs nb ḥꜣ≠f nb mỉ Rꜥ

The King of Upper and Lower Egypt, Lord of ritual performance, Hedj-kheperre-setepenre, (7) bodily Son of Re, whom he (Re) loves, Sheshonq, beloved of Amon, (8) image of Re, Foremost of the Two Lands, beloved of the Lord of the Gods, given all life, stability, and dominion, and all health like Re forever. The protection of all life, stability, and dominion is all around him like Re.

Label for High Priest Iuput (lines 10–11)

ḥm-nṯr tp(y) n ꜣImn-Rꜥ ny-sw.t nṯr.w ỉmy-rꜣ mšꜥ wr ḥꜣw.ty (11) ꜣIw[p]wt [mꜣꜥ-ḥrw] sꜣ ny-sw.t nb tꜣ.wy Ššn[q mrỉ]-ꜣI[mn]

First Prophet of Amon-Re, King of the Gods, great general and leader (ll) Iuput, [the justified,] royal son of the Lord of the Two Lands, Sheshonq, beloved of Amon.

(2) Middle Register (= Epigraphic Survey 1954, pl. 10 B; K 341)

Sheshonq I receiving life from Montu-Re and attended by his son the high priest Iuput. Montu holds three glyphs of life before the king's face as Iuput burns incense.

Label for the Protective Vulture above the Scene (line 6)

Wꜣḏy.t nb.(t) P (ḥnw.t) Dp P nb.(t) p.t ḥnw.t nṯr.w dỉ≠s ꜥnḫ ḏd wꜣs nb mỉ Rꜥ ḏ.t

Edjo, Lady of Pe, (Mistress) of Dep and Pe, Lady of heaven, Mistress of the gods. May she grant all life, stability, and dominion like Re forever.

Label for Montu (lines 2–5)

ḏd-mdw ỉn Mnṯ (3)-Rˁ nb Wȝs.t sȝ ˁnḫ ḏd wȝs (4) dỉ.n⸗(ỉ) n⸗k ˁnḫ ḏd
wȝs nb snb nb (5) dỉ.n⸗(ỉ) n⸗k tȝ.w nb.w m ḥtp

Recitation by Montu (3)-Re, Lord of Thebes. The protection of life,
stability, and dominion (is behind him). (4) "Thus I have given to you all
life, stability, and dominion, and all health. (5) Thus I have given to you
all lands in peace."

Label for the King (lines 7–9)

nb tȝ.wy Ḥḏ-ḫpr-Rˁ-stp-n-Rˁ (8) nb ḫˁ.w Ššnq mrỉ-ˀImn (9) dỉ ˁnḫ ḏd
wȝs nb mỉ Rˁ

Lord of the Two Lands, Hedjkheperre-setepenre, (8) Lord of Diadems,
Sheshonq, beloved of Amon, (9) given all life, stability, and dominion like
Re.

Label for Iuput (lines 1 and 10–11)

ỉr snṯr ˁntỉw dỉ⸗f ˁnḫ s(nb) (10) ḥm-nṯr tp(y) n ˀImn-Rˁ ny-sw.t nṯr.
w ỉmy-rȝ mšˁ wr n Šmˁy ḫȝw.ty (11) ˀIwpwṯ mȝˁ-ḫrw sȝ ny-sw.t nb tȝ.wy
[Šš]n[q] mrỉ-ˀImn

Making incense of myrrh so that he (Montu) might grant life and
health. (10) First Prophet of Amon-Re, King of the Gods, great general of
Upper Egypt and leader (ll) Iuput, the justified, royal son of the Lord of
the Two Lands, Sheshonq, beloved of Amon.

(3) Bottom Register (= Epigraphic Survey 1954, pl. 10 A; K 342): Sheshonq I
suckled by Hathor and attended by his son the high priest Iuput.

Label for the Protective Falcon above the Scene (line 5)

Bḥd.t(y) nṯr ˁȝ sȝb šw pr m ȝḫ.t nb p.t [nb Msn] dỉ⸗f ˁnḫ ḏd wȝs nb
mỉ Rˁ ḏ.t

The Behdetite, the great god with dappled plumage who comes forth
from the horizon, Lord of heaven, [Lord of Mesen.] May he grant all life,
stability, and dominion like Re forever.

Label for Hathor (lines 2–4)

ḏd-mdw ỉ(n) (3) Ḥw.t-Ḥr ḥr(y.t)-ỉb Wȝs.t ỉnk (4) mw.t⸗k sˁnḫ tw m
ḥḏ.t⸗ỉ sȝ ˁnḫ ḏd wȝs ḫȝ⸗s

Recitation by (3) Hathor, resident in Thebes: "I am (4) your mother,
who vivifies you by my milk." The protection of life, stability, and dominion is behind her.

Label for the King (lines 6–9)

nṯr nfr Ḥd-ḫpr-Rꜥ-stp-n-Rꜥ (7) sꜣ Rꜥ Ššnq mrỉ-ʾImn (8) dỉ ꜥnḫ ḏd wꜣs nb (9) mỉ Rꜥ ḏ.t

The Good God Hedjkheperre-setepenre, (8) Son of Re, Sheshonq, beloved of Amon, (9) given all life, stability, and dominion like Re forever.

Label for Iuput (lines 1 and 10–11)

ỉr sšš.ty n Ḥw.t-Ḥr nb.t dỉ≠s qn nḫt (10) ḥm-nṯr tp(y) n ʾImn-Rꜥ ny-sw.t nṯr.w ỉmy-rꜣ mšꜥ wr n Šmꜥy ḫꜣw.ty (11) ʾIwpwt mꜣꜥ-ḫrw sꜣ ny-sw.t nb tꜣ.wy Ššnq mrỉ-ʾImn dỉ ꜥnḫ

Playing two sistra for Hathor the Lady, so that she might grant valor and victory. (10) First Prophet of Amon-Re, King of the Gods, great general of Upper Egypt and leader (11) Iuput, the justified, royal son of the Lord of the Two Lands, Sheshonq, beloved of Amon, given life.

(4) Base Label to All Three Scenes (pl. 10A, lines 12–13 = K 343)

mry dỉ ꜥnḫ ḏd wꜣs s(nb) nb ꜣw.t-ỉb≠f ḫꜥwy ḥr s.t Ḥr sšm ꜥnḫ.w nb.w mỉ Rꜥ ḏ.t (13) sp tpy (n) wḥm ḥb-sdꜣ ỉr n≠f ꜥꜣ wr.t mỉ Rꜥ ḏ.t

(Sheshonq) beloved (of Amon, Montu, and Hathor represented above), given all life, stability, dominion, and health, joyfully appearing upon the throne of Horus, who leads all the living like Re forever. (13) First occasion (of) repeating the jubilee,[3] so as to make for him very many like Re forever.

C. EASTERN PILASTER SCENES (NORTHERN FACE: KEY PLANS K 345–47)
Text = Epigraphic Survey 1954, pl. 11 (top to bottom)

(1) Upper Register (= Epigraphic Survey 1954, pl. 11 C; K 345): Sheshonq I receiving jubilees from Amon-Re and attended by his son the high priest Iuput. Amon-Re offers to Shoshonq's nose the year sign from which depend the glyphs of jubilees, life, stability, and dominion.

Label for the Winged Disk above the Scene (line 4)

[B]ḥd[.t(y)] nṯr ꜥꜣ sꜣb šw nb p.t nb Msn pr m ꜣḫ.t dỉ≠f ꜥnḫ ḏd wꜣs snb nb ꜣw.t-ỉb nb.t mỉ Rꜥ ḏ.t

The Behdetite, the great god with dappled plumage, Lord of heaven, Lord of Mesen, who comes forth from the horizon. May he grant all life, stability, dominion, and health and all joy like Re forever.

Label for Amon (lines 1–3)

ʾImn-Rꜥ nb p.t sꜣ ꜥnḫ ḏd [wꜣs] nb ḫꜣ≠f nb (2) ḏd-mdw dỉ.n≠(ỉ) n≠k rnp.wt ꜥꜣ m ꜣw.t-ỉb (3) r šr.t≠k nṯr nfr

Amon-Re, King of the Gods, Lord of heaven. The protection of all life, stability, and [dominion] is all around him. (2) Recitation: "Thus I have given to you many years in joy (3) to your nose, O Good God."

Label for the King (lines 5–7)

nṯr nfr nb t3.wy Ḥd-ḫpr-Rᶜ-stp-n-Rᶜ (6) s3 Rᶜ nb ḫᶜ.w Ššnq mrỉ-ʾImn (7) dỉ ᶜnḫ ḏd w3s nb mỉ Rᶜ ḏ.t s3 ᶜnḫ ḏd w3s nb ḫ3⸗f nb mỉ Rᶜ ḏ.t

The Good God, Lord of the Two Lands, Hedjkheperre-setepenre, (6) Son of Re, Lord of Diadems, Sheshonq, beloved of Amon, (7) given all life, stability, and dominion like Re forever. The protection of all life, stability, and dominion is all around him like Re forever.

Label for High Priest Iuput (lines 8–9)

ḥm-nṯr tp(y) n ʾImn-Rᶜ ny-sw.t nṯr.w ỉmy-r3 mšᶜ wr ḫ3w.ty (9) ʾIwpwtỉ m3ᶜ-ḫrw s3 ny-sw.t nb t3.wy Ššnq mrỉ-ʾImn

First Prophet of Amon-Re, King of the Gods, great general and leader (9) Iuput, the justified, royal son of the Lord of the Two Lands, Sheshonq, beloved of Amon.

(2) Middle Register (= Epigraphic Survey 1954, pl. 11 B; K 346): Sheshonq I embraced by Khonsu and attended by his son the high priest Iuput (very fragmentary).

Label for the Protective Vulture above the Scene (line 5)

Nḫb.t ḥd.t Nḫn nb.(t) [p.t] dỉ⸗s [ᶜnḫ] ḏd w3s snb nb 3w.t-ỉb nb.t mỉ Rᶜ ḏ.t

Nekhbet, the white one of Nekhen, Lady of [heaven]. May she grant all life, stability, dominion, and health and all joy like Re forever.

Label for Khonsu (lines 1–4)

ḏd-mdw ỉn Ḫnsw (2) m W3s.t Nfr-ḥtp dỉ⸗ỉ mn ḫᶜ[.w] (3) ḥr [tp]⸗k [...] (4) dỉ.n(⸗ỉ) n⸗k ᶜnḫ ḏd w3s nb [...]

Recitation by Khonsu (2) in Thebes, Neferhotep: "I shall cause that the diadems be firm (3) upon your [head ...] (4) Thus I have given to you all life, stability, and dominion [...]."

Label for the King (unnumbered lines a–b)

nb t3.wy Ḥd-[ḫpr]-Rᶜ-[stp-n-Rᶜ] (b) nb ḫᶜ.w [Ššnq mrỉ]-ʾImn [...]

Lord of the Two Lands, Hedjkheperre-[setepenre], (b) Lord of Diadems, [Sheshonq, beloved of] Amon [...]

Label for Iuput (lines 6–7)

ḥm-nṯr tp(y) n ʾImn-Rᶜ ny-sw.t nṯr[.w ...] (7) ʾIwpwṯ m3ᶜ-ḫrw [...]

First Prophet of Amon-Re, King of the Gods, [...] (b) Iuput, the justified, [...]

(3) Bottom Register (= Epigraphic Survey 1954, pl. 11 A; K 347): Sheshonq
I suckled by Mut and attended by his son the high priest Iuput (very fragmentary).

Label for the Protective Falcon above the Scene (line 3)
    Bḥd.t(y) nṯr ꜥꜣ sꜣb šw nb p.t nb Msn dỉ≠f ꜥnḫ [ḏd wꜣs nb ...]
    The Behdetite, the great god with dappled plumage, Lord of heaven,
Lord of Mesen. May he grant [all] life, [stability, and dominion ...]

Label for Mut (lines 1–2)
    Mw.t nb.(t) (2) p.t ḥnw.t nṯr.w
    Mut, Lady (2) of heaven, Mistress of the gods.

Label for the King (lines 4–6)
    nṯr nfr nb tꜣ.wy Ḥd-ḫpr-Rꜥ-stp-n-Rꜥ (7) sꜣ Rꜥ nb ḫꜥ.w Ššnq mrỉ-ʾImn
(8) dỉ ꜥnḫ ḏd wꜣs mỉ Rꜥ
    The Good God, Lord of the Two Lands, Hedjkheperre-setepenre, (5)
Son of Re, Sheshonq, beloved of Amon, (6) given life, stability, and dominion like Re.

Label for Iuput (l. 7)
    [ḥm-nṯr tp(y) n ʾImn-Rꜥ ny-sw.t nṯr.w ỉmy-rꜣ] mšꜥ wr ḥꜣw.ty ʾIw[p]wtỉ
[mꜣꜥ]-ḫrw
    [First Prophet of Amon-Re, King of the Gods,] great general and leader
Iuput, the justified [...]

(4) Lost Base Label to All Three Scenes (= K 348)
    [mry dỉ ꜥnḫ ḏd wꜣs nb ...]
    [(Sheshonq) beloved (of Amon, Khonsu, and Mut), given all life, stabil-
ity, and dominion ...]

D. VICTORY RELIEF (SOUTHERN FACADE: KEY PLANS K 361)
Text = Epigraphic Survey 1954, pls. 2–9; complete scene on pl. 3

    Striding Sheshonq I, followed by the royal *ka*-spirit on a standard,
smites a group of kneeling, submissive enemies before Amon and a goddess personifying Thebes, each deity leading by a tether five registers of
plundered cities symbolized as bound captives. Further captive towns
formed a base line trodden beneath the pharaoh's feet. Amon offers the
King the sword of victory (line 9).

Label for the Protective Falcon above the Scene (line 30)
[Bḥd].t(y) nṯr ꜥꜣ sꜣb šw pr m ꜣḫ.t nb p.t [nb] Msn ḫnty Ḥbnw⁵ ḫnty ꞌI[t]r.
t Mḥw dꞽ≠f ꜥnḫ ḏd wꜣs nb snb nb [nḫ]t nb mꞽ [Rꜥ] ḏ.t
The Behdetite, the great god with dappled plumage who comes forth
from the horizon, Lord of heaven, [Lord] of Mesen, foremost of Minya,⁵
foremost of the Lower Egyptian shrine. May he grant all life, stability,
dominion, all health and all [victor]y like [Re] forever.

Label for Central Scene (lines 1–4)
sqr wr.w ꞌIwn.tyw (2) Sty.w ḫꜣs.wt nb.(t) (3) štꜣ.t⁶ tꜣ.w nb.w Fnḫ.[w]
(4) ḫꜣs.wt⁷ pḥw.w Sṯ.[t]
Smiting the chiefs of the Nubian (2) tribesmen, of all (3) inaccessible⁶
foreign lands, of all the lands of the Phoenicians, (4) and foreign lands⁷ of
the Asiatic back-country.

Label for Amon (line 10)
ḏd-mdw ꞽn ꞌImn-Rꜥ nb ns.wt tꜣ.wy ḫnty ꞌIp.t-s.wt nb p.t ḥqꜣ Wꜣs.t
Recitation by Amon-Re, Lord of the Thrones of the Two Lands, Foremost of Karnak, Lord of heaven, Ruler of Thebes.

Behind Amon
ꜥnḫ ḏd wꜣs nb ḥꜣ≠f nb mꞽ Rꜥ ḏ[.t]
(The protection of) all life, stability, and dominion is all around him
like Re forever.

Speech of Amon (lines 5–9)
[ḏd-md]w ꞽy.w m ḥtp sꜣ(≠ꞽ) mry(≠ꞽ)
nṯr nfr nb ꞽr.(t) ḫ.t
[ny-sw.t bꞽ.ty nb tꜣ.wy]⁸
Ḥḏ-ḫpr-Rꜥ-stp-n-Rꜥ [...] Ḥr kꜣ nḫt sḫm pḥ.ty
ꞽw ḥ(wꞽ).n≠k tꜣ.w ḫꜣs.wt

(6) [ḏd-mdw] ꞽw ptpt.n≠k ꞌIwn.tyw Sty.w
sḫm.n šꜥ[.t≠k] m Mnty.w ḥry.w šꜥ m ꜣt.t nb.(t)
bꜣw≠k nḫt[.w r(?)] tꜣ.w nb.w

(7) [ḏd-mdw] ꞽw wḏ.n≠k m nḫt.w ꞽy.n≠k m qn smꜣ.n≠k [tꜣ.w]
psw.n≠(ꞽ) n≠k ḫꜣs.wt [nb.t] ḥm.w Km.t
wn wꜣ r tkk t(ꜣ)š[.w≠k] rdꞽ.n≠(ꞽ) dmꜣ tp.w≠sn

(8) ḏd-mdw dꞽ≠ꞽ⁹ nḫt.w m [rꜣ]-ꜥ.wy≠k
tꜣ.w nb.w ḫꜣs.t nb.(t) dmḏ [ḥr] tb.ty[≠k]
ḥry.t≠k r ḏr sḫn.w(t) fd.t n.t [p.t]

hmhm.t n ḥm⸗k ḫt pḏ.t psḏ.t
[snḏ]⸗k sd.n⸗s ỉb.w ḫ3s.wt
ỉw⸗k m Ḥr ḥr tp t3.wy
(9) ḏd-mdw ỉw⸗k m wnwn ḥr ḫfty.w⸗k
tỉ.n⸗k sbỉ.w r⸗k
šsp [n]⸗k ḫpš ny-sw.t nḫt
ḥ(wỉ).n ḥḏ⸗k wr.w ḫ3s.wt

[Recitation]: "Welcome, my son, my beloved,
The Good God, Lord of ritual performance,
[King of Upper and Lower Egypt, Lord of the Two Lands],[8]
Hedjkheperre-setepenre [...] Horus, the strong bull, powerful of
strength!
You have struck the lands and the foreign countries."

(6) [Recitation]: "You have trampled the Nubian tribesmen,
and [your] sword has overpowered the Bedouin upon the sands at
every moment,
your wrath victorious [against] all lands."

(7) [Recitation]: "You set out in victory, and you have returned in valor,
having united [the lands,]
since I have burned for you [all] foreign lands who were ignorant of
Egypt and who had fallen into the practice of attacking [your]
boundaries, and I have caused that their heads be cut off."

(8) Recitation: "I gave[9] victory to the [feats] of your arms,
all lands, all foreign countries united [under] [your] sandals,
dread of you extending to the four supports of [heaven],
the war cry of Your Majesty pervading the Nine Bows.
Fear of you—it has broken the hearts of the foreign countries.
You are a Horus over the Two Lands."

(9) Recitation: "You are treading upon your enemies,
having struck down those who rebelled against you.
Receive for yourself the sword, O victorious King,
for your mace has struck the chiefs of the foreign countries."

Speech of Amon (lines 11–24):
ḏd-mdw ỉw ỉb⸗ỉ nḏm wr m3⸗ỉ nḫt.w⸗k
(12) ḏd-mdw s3(⸗ỉ) Ššnq mrỉ-ʾImn mr⸗ỉ
(13) ḏd-mdw pr⸗k[10] (14) ỉm⸗ỉ (15) r ỉr[11] nḏty⸗ỉ
m3⸗ỉ 3ḫ sḫr⸗k

sḫpr.n≠k [ȝ]ḫ.w r pr≠i
smn.n≠k [niw.t]≠i n.t Wȝs.t
s.t wr.t nty ib≠i ḥr≠s

(16) šȝˁ.n≠k ir mnw m ʾIwnw Šmˁ ḥnˁ ʾIwnw Mḥw
niw.t nb.t mit.t iry n nṯr imy spȝ.t≠f
ir.n≠k ḥw.t-nṯr≠i n.t ḥḥ.w n rnp.wt
[sb]ȝ.w ḥr≠s m ḏˁmw n t[wt]≠i (17) im¹²
ḥr≠k ḥr [ȝ]wi ˁḥˁ≠k ḫft(w)
[ˁnḫ].w sḫḏy.w [p]sd.[w]¹³ ḥr [ḥqȝ.t(?)]≠k
sm[n]≠i [s].t≠k (18) r ny-sw.t nb pȝy≠w¹⁴

ḫ(wi).n≠k tȝ nb m ḫpš≠i
qn m sp [n] nḫt
rdi.n≠i [ḥry.t(?)]≠k ḫ[r] Mnty(19).w Sṯ.t ḫȝs.t nb.t
nšny.n ḥḥ≠k m sḏ.t r pḥ.wy≠w
iw≠sn¹⁵ ˁḥȝ r tȝ nb dmḏ
sk.n s ḥm≠k n (= m) [Mn]ṯtw¹⁶ (20) wsr titi ḫfty.w≠f
ḥḏ≠k sqr.n≠f ḥȝk.w≠k ˁȝm.w ḥr ḫȝs.wt wȝ
sḫm.n ȝḫ.t≠k im≠sn

ir.n≠i [n≠]k t(ȝ)š.w(21)≠k r s.t-ib≠k¹⁶
di≠i iw n≠k rsy.w m ks mḥty.w n wr bȝ.w≠k
ir.n≠k ḫȝy.t ˁȝ.t m t[p].w≠sn nn ḏr.w≠sn¹⁶
(22) ḫr.w m-ḫt in.(t)≠sn
wn m ˁšȝ ḫpr m iwt.t
ȝq m-ḫt mi nty nn ms.tw≠w
ḫȝs.wt nb.(t) iw [n]n ṯ(23)nw
sḫtm.n s ḥm≠k m km n ȝ.t

iw mḏd≠i¹⁷ n≠k btš.w r≠k
ȝir≠(i) n≠k ˁȝm.w
mšˁ.w nw Mˁtn¹⁸ smȝ(24).n≠i s iry ḥr tb.ty≠k
ink it≠k nb nṯr.w ʾImn-Rˁ nb ns.wt tȝ.wy
sšm wˁ n why.n sp≠f
rdi≠i sḫȝ.tw qn≠k m n-ḫt¹⁹ m ȝw[.t] ḏ.t

Recitation: "My heart is very happy when I see your victories."
(12) Recitation: "My son, Sheshonq, beloved of Amon, my beloved."
(13) Recitation: "You came forth¹⁰ (14) from me (15) in order to be¹¹
my protector.

I have seen the excellence of your plan,
for you have created benefactions regarding my house,

and you have established my [city] of Thebes,
the Great Place in which my heart is.

(16) In Southern Heliopolis and Northern Heliopolis
and every city likewise you have begun to make monuments for the
god in his district,
    and you have made my temple of Millions of Years, the [gateways]
    in it being electrum, for my [image] (17) therein.[12]
    May you be satisfied concerning the [length] of your lifetime accord-
ingly,
    with the living, illuminated and shining[13] under your [rule],
    since I have [established] your [throne] (18) more than that of any king
who existed in the past.[14]

    With my mighty sword, you have struck every land in a feat of victory,
    and I have placed [terror (?)] of you upon the Bedouins (19) of Asia
and all foreign lands.
    As flame, your fiery blast has raged against their rear,
    fighting[15] against every confederated land.
    Your Majesty has destroyed them just as Montu,[16] (20) the mighty, who
tramples his enemies.
    Your mace—it has smitten your opponents, the Asiatics in the distant
foreign lands,
    your uraeus having overpowered them.

    I have made for you your boundaries (21) exactly in accordance with
your desire,[16]
    causing that there come to you the southerners in bowing and the
northerners because of the greatness of your wrath.
    You have made a great slaughter among their [chiefs], utterly without
limit,[16]
    (22) they being fallen throughout their valleys,
    those who had been a multitude having become a nonentity,
    having perished in the aftermath, like those unborn.
    Every country that has come without (23) number—Your Majesty
has destroyed them in the completion of a moment.

    I have struck[17] for you those who rebelled against you,
    suppressing for you the Asiatics.
    The armies of Mitanni[18]—I have slain (24) those belonging to them
beneath your sandals.
    I am your father, the Lord of the Gods, Amon-Re, Lord of the Thrones
of the Two Lands,

the unique leader, whose action cannot fail.

I have caused that your valor be remembered hereafter[19] for the extent of eternity."

Label for the Goddess Thebes (lines 25–28)

ḏd-mdw ỉn Wȝs.t nḫt (26) nb.(t) ḫpš ḥnw.t n.(t) ḫȝs.wt nb.(t) (27) ḏd-mdw dỉ.n≠(ỉ) n≠k tȝ.w nb.w ḫȝs.wt nb.(t) štȝ.wt[6] ᵓIwn.tyw Sty.w Ḫnty-ḥn-[nfr] (28) ḏd-mdw dỉ.n≠(ỉ) n≠k ḫȝs.wt nb.(t) pḥw.w S̱t.t Ḥȝ.w-nb.wt[20] r [...] (29) ḏd-mdw m wḏ.n ỉt≠f

Recitation by Thebes the Victorious, (26) Lady of the strong arm, Mistress of all foreign lands. (27) Recitation: "Thus I have given to you all lands and all inaccessible[6] foreign countries, the Nubian tribesmen of Lower Nubia." (28) Recitation: "Thus I have given to you all foreign lands, the Asiatic back-country, the Aegean islands,[20] to [...] (29) Recitation: as his father commanded."

Label for Nekhbet Vulture atop Lotus Blossoms, Who Presents Sign of Life to the Horus Name of the King (unnumbered line a)

[mr]y Nḫb.t dỉ≠s ʿnḫ ḏd wȝs mỉ Rʿ

Beloved of Nekhbet. May she grant life, stability, and dominion like Re.

Label for Sheshonq (unnumbered lines b–e and 31–33)

ʿnḫ[21] Ḥr kȝ nḫt mrỉ-Rʿ sḫʿ≠f m ny-sw.t r smȝ tȝ.wy (c) ny-sw.t bỉ.ty nb tȝ.wy nb ỉr.(t) ḫ.t [Ḥḏ-ḫpr-Rʿ-stp-n-Rʿ (d) sȝ Rʿ n ḫ.t≠f mr≠f Ššnq mrỉ-ᵓImn (e) dỉ ʿnḫ ḏd wȝs snb mỉ Rʿ ḏ.t (31) ny-sw.t nṯr [nfr] wr bȝ.w ḫ(wỉ) ḫȝs.wt pḥ sw (32) ỉr m ḫpš≠f r rḫ tȝ.wy[22] (33) sqr.n ḫḏ≠f wr(.w) ḫȝs.wt Ḥr [...][23] nb [ỉr.(t)] ḫt [sȝ ʿnḫ ḏd wȝs nb] ḫȝ≠f nb mỉ Rʿ ḏ.t

Long live[21] the Horus: "Strong Bull, beloved of Re, whom he (Re) made manifest as king in order to unite the Two Lands"; (c) the King of Upper and Lower Egypt, Lord of the Two Lands, Lord of ritual performance, [Hedjkheper]re-setepenre (d) bodily Son of Re, whom he (Re) loves, Sheshonq, beloved of Amon (e) given life, stability, dominion, and health like Re forever. (31) The King, [Good] God, great of wrath, who smites the foreign lands that attack him, (32) who acts with his strong arm so that the Two Lands might know,[22] (33) and whose mace has smitten the chief(s) of foreign lands. Horus, [...][23] the Lord of ritual performance. [The protection of all life, stability, and dominion] is all around him like Re forever.

Label for the Royal *Ka* Positioned behind the King (lines 34–35)

kȝ ny-sw.t ʿnḫ ḫnty (35) ḏbȝ.t ḫnty pr-dwȝ[.t] dỉ ʿnḫ [ḏd wȝs] nb [...] kȝ [Ḥr kȝ nḫt mrỉ-Rʿ sḫʿ≠f m ny-sw.t r smȝ] tȝ.wy

The living royal *ka*-spirit, foremost of (35) the robing room, foremost of the morning room, given all life, [stability, and dominion ...] The *ka*-spirit of [the Horus: "Strong Bull, beloved of Re, whom he (Re) made manifest as king in order to] unite the Two Lands."

Base-Line Label below Central Scene (line 36)
sḫ[w] nn ḫȝs.wt rsy[.t] mḥty.t [sqr.n ḥm⸗f ỉry ḫȝy.t ỉm⸗sn n rḫ tnw ỉn ḥr].w⸗sn m [sqr.w-ʿnḫ r mḥ šnʿ n ỉt⸗f ʾI]mn-Rʿ m ʾIp.t-s.wt m [wḏ]⸗f tp(y) [n n]ḫt.w[24]

Gathering these southern and northern foreign lands [that His Majesty has struck, a great slaughter being made among them, the number not being known.] Their [inhabitant]s [are carried off] as [living captives to fill the magazine of his father,] Amon-Re in Karnak in his first [campaign of] victory.[24]

E. GREAT TOPOGRAPHICAL LIST

Section 1: List of Captured Name Rings Led by Amon
Rows I–V, nos. 1–65, including traditional Nine Bows (Row I, nos. 1–9).[25] For readings, see Kitchen 1986, 433–39 §§399–403; citations of Aḥituv 1984 list in notes below.

Tȝ-šmʿw (2) Tȝ-mḥw (3) ʾIwn.tyw St.t (4) [Tḥnw] (5) S[ḫ.t-(ʾI)ȝm] (6) Mn[ty.w nw St.t] (7) Pḏ.tyw-Šw (8) Šȝ.t (9) Ḥȝ.w-nb.wt[25] (10) mỉt.t ʿ[ȝmw] (11) Gȝ[ḏ.t(?)] (12) M[q]ȝ[ḏ](?) (13) Rwbȝtỉ[26] (row II, 14) Tȝʿnkỉȝ (15) Šȝnmʿỉȝ (16) Bȝtšȝnrỉȝ[27] (17) Rwḫȝbỉȝ[28] (18) Ḥȝpwrwmỉȝ (19) ʾIdrmȝ (20) [...] (21) Šȝwȝdy (22) Mʿḫʿnmʿ[29] (23) Qbʿȝnȝ (24) Bȝtḫwȝrwn (25) Qȝdtm (26) ʾIywrwn (row III, 27) Mʿkdỉw (28) ʾIdyrw (29) Yudhmʿrwk[30] (30) [Ḥb]rt(?) (31) Ḥȝỉȝnm (32) ʿȝrȝnȝ (33) Bȝrwmȝ (34) Ḏȝdptrw (35) Y[w]lḫȝmȝ (36) Bȝtʿȝrwmȝm (37) Kȝqȝrwy (38) Šȝỉwkȝ (39) Bȝttpw[ḫ?]ȝ[31] (row IV, 40) ʾIbȝrwỉȝ (41) [...] (42) [...] (43) [...] (44) [...] (45) Bȝtḏbỉ[...][32] (46) ..[...] (47) [...]ỉ[..] (48) Kk[...] (49) [...] (50) [...] (51) Ssḏ[...] (52) [...] (row V, 53) [P]nwỉȝrw[33] (54) Ḥȝdšȝtȝt[34] (55) Pȝ-ktṭ[35] (56) ʾIdmỉȝȝ[36] (57) Ḏȝ[m]rwmȝ (58) [Mg]drw[37] (59) [T?]rwdỉȝ (60) [...]nȝrw (61) [...]ỉ[.] (62) [...] (63) [...] (64) Ḥȝ[...]ȝpn[38] (65) Pȝʿȝmʿq[39]

Upper Egypt (2) Lower Egypt (3) Tribesmen of Lower Nubia (4) [Libya] (5) [The Western Oases] (6) [Bedouin of Asia] (7) [The Eastern Desert] (8) Upper Nubia (9) the Aegean Islands/Northern Perimeter[25]
(10) Copy of the (defeated) A[siatics]: (11) Gaza[a] (12) Maqqed(ah)(?)[b]

---

a. Aḥituv 1984, 997–98: "Gaza."
b. Aḥituv 1984, 101–2: "Gezer." Aḥituv restores [Q]ȝ[d]ȝ[r].

(13) Rubuti[c,26] (=? Rabbah in Josh 15:60) (row II, 14) Taanach[d] (15) Shu-nem[e] (16) Beth-shan[f,27] (17) Rehob[g,28] (18) Hapharaim[h] (19) Adoraim[i] (20) [...] (21) ...[j] (22) Mahanaim[k,29] (= ? Tulul edh-Dhahab) (23) Gibeon[l] (24) Beth-Horon[m] (25) Kiriathaim[n] (= Kiriath-jearim) (26) Ajalon[o] (row III, 27) Megiddo[p] (28) Adar[q] (29) "King's-Monument"[r,30] (30) [Heb]el(?) (31) Hanem[s] (32) Aruna[t] (= Khirbet ʿAra) (33) Borim[u] (= Khirbet Burim) (34) Giti-padalla[v] (= Jett) (35) Yehem[w] (= Khirbet Yemma/Tell Yaham) (36) Beth-Olam/Beth-Aruma (?)[x] (37) ...[y] (38) Socoh[z] (= Khirbet Shuweiket er-Ras) (39) Beth-Tappu[ah?][aa,31] (row IV, 40) Abel[ab] (41) [...] (42) [...] (43) [...] (44) [...] (45) Beth-saba/soba(?)[ac,32] (46) [...] (47) [...] (48) ..[...] (49) [...] (50) [...] (51) ...[...] (52) [...] (row V, 53) Penuel[ad,33] (= ? Tulul edh-Dhahab) (54) "New (town)"[ae,34] (55) ...[35] (= ? Succoth)[af] (56) Adam(ah)[ag,36]

---

c. Aḥituv 1984, 165–67: "Rubute."

d. Aḥituv 1984, 184–85: "Taanach."

e. Aḥituv 1984, 176–77: "Shunem."

f. Aḥituv 1984, 78–79: "Beth-Shean."

g. Aḥituv 1984, 164–65: "Rehob (3)."

h. Aḥituv 1984, 114–15: "Ḥapharaim."

i. Aḥituv 1984, 52: "Adoraim."

j. Aḥituv 1984, 184: "Šȝ-wȝ-d-y[ ]."

k. Aḥituv 1984, 134: "Mahanaim."

l. Aḥituv 1984, 102: "Gibeon."

m. Aḥituv 1984, 77: "Beth-Horon."

n. Aḥituv 1984, 126: "Kiriathaim."

o. Aḥituv 1984, 55: "Aijalon."

p. Aḥituv 1984, 139–40: "Megiddo." Cf. the fragmentary stela of Sheshonq I excavated at Megiddo, no. 51.

q. Aḥituv 1984, 51: "Adar (3)" ("Threshing-floor").

r. Aḥituv 1984, 197: "Yad Hamelek."

s. Aḥituv 1984, 110: "Ḥān(e)m."

t. Aḥituv 1984, 67: "ʿAruna."

u. Aḥituv 1984, 81: "Borim."

v. Aḥituv 1984, 97: "Gath, Gath-Padalla."

w. Aḥituv 1984, 197–98: "Yaham."

x. Aḥituv 1984, 77: "Beth-ʿOlam."

y. Aḥituv 1984, 124: "Ka/Uqaruya."

z. Aḥituv 1984, 178–79: "Socho."

aa. Aḥituv 1984, 80 "Beth-Tapu[aḥ]."

ab. Aḥituv 1984, 47: "Abel (7)."

ac. Aḥituv 1984, 78: "Beth-Ṣb[..]."

ad. Aḥituv 1984, 154: "Penuel."

ae. Aḥituv 1984, 108: "Ḥadashah."

af. Aḥituv 1984, 179: "Succoth."

ag. Aḥituv 1984, 50: "Adam."

(57) Zemaraim[ah] (= Josh 18:23) (58) [Mig]dol[ai,37] (59) [Ti]rza(?)[aj] (= Tell el-Farʿah) (60) […]… (61) […] (62) […] (63) […] (64) Hapin[ak,38] (65) "The Valley"[al] (= Esdraelon/Jezreel)[39]

Section 2: List of Captured Name Rings Led by Thebes
    Rows VI–X, nos. 66–150. Nos. 105–108 = Berlin 2094; photos in Königliche Museen zu Berlin 1899, 228–29; 1895, 16 and pl. 41; Oriental Institute photo B 296. For readings, see Kitchen 1986, 439–41 §§404–8.

ʿȝíȝdȝmíȝ (67) ʾInȝrwí (68) Pȝ-ḫȝqrwíȝ[40] (69) Ftywšȝíȝ[41] (70) ʾIrȝhrwrw[42] (71) Pȝ-ḥwqrwíȝ (72) ʾIwbȝrȝmʿ[43] (73) Šȝbȝrwṯ (74) n Gbȝrwy[44] (75) Šȝbȝrwṯ (76) Wȝrȝkyt (77) Pȝ-ḫȝqrwíȝ (78) n ʿȝdȝyt[45] (79) Dd[..]íȝ (80) Ḏȝpȝqíȝ (81) Mʿ[..]íȝ (82) Tȝp[w?…] (row VII, 83) Gȝnȝít (84) Pȝ-nȝgbw (85) ʿdȝnsṯ[46] (86) Tȝšdnȝw[47] (87) Pȝ-ḫȝqrwt (88) Šȝnȝíȝ (89) Hȝqȝ (90) Pȝ-nȝgbw (91) Wȝhtrwwȝk[..] (92) Pȝ-nȝgbw (93) ʾIšȝḫȝtít (94) Pȝ-ḫȝgrwy (95) Ḥȝnynyíȝ[48] (96) Pȝ-ḫȝgrwíȝ (97) ʾIrwqȝd (98) ʾIwdȝmt[36] (99) Ḥȝnȝnyy[48] (100) ʾIwdrȝíȝ (101) Pȝ-ḫȝgrw (102) Ṯrwwȝn (103) Ḥȝydbíȝ[49] (104) Šȝrwnrwím (105) [Ḥȝ]y[d]bȝ[íȝ] (106) Dywȝṯy (107) Ḥȝqrwmʿ (108) ʿȝrwdíȝt (109) Rwbȝṯ (110) ʿȝrwdíȝy (111) n Bȝṯṯ (112) Ywrȝḫmʿ[50] (113) […]í[..] (114) […] (115) […] (116) ʾIwdyȝ[r?..] (row IX, 117) ʾIwdr[…] (118) […]bȝyíȝ (119) […]ḥgíȝ (120) [..]ȝrywk (121) Frȝtmʿíȝ[51] (122) ʾIwbȝrȝ (123) Bȝírwrȝdȝ[52] (124) Bȝt-ʿnṯ (125) Šȝrȝḫȝnȝ (126) ʾIrmʿṯnȝ[53] (127) Grwnȝí[54] (128) ʾIwdȝm (129) […]rḫȝṯ (130) Ḥȝ[?..]rȝí (131) Mʿrw[…] (132) ʾIrwr[m?] (133) Ywrdȝ (ROW X, 134) […] (135) […] (136) […] (137) […] (138) […] (139) Ywrḥm (140) ʾIwnyny (141) […] (142) ȝ[…]g[…] (143) […] (144) […] (145) Mʿk[t?] (146) ʾI[…]dy[…] (147) […] (148) […] (149) […]ȝ (150) Ywrwdn[55]

ʿEsem[am] (= Umm el-ʿAzam) (67) …[an] (68) "The Field[40] (69) (of) Photeis"[ao] (= Khirbet Futeis/Tell el ʿUseifir)[41] (70) El-hillel[ap] (cf. Jehallel in 1 Chr 4:16)[42] (71) "The Field (72) (of) Abram"[aq,43] (73) "Shibboleth/Stream (74) of Gabri"[ar,44] (75) "Shibboleth/Stream (76) (of) Urikit"[as] (77) "The

---

ah. Aḥituv 1984, 204: "Zemaraim."
ai. Aḥituv 1984, 141: "Migdal (2)."
aj. Aḥituv 1984, 190: "Tirzah."
ak. Aḥituv 1984, 119: "Ḥap(i)n."
al. Aḥituv 1984, 93: "Emeq, The Valley."
am. Aḥituv 1984, 93: "ʿEsem."
an. Aḥituv 1984, 60: "Anmar/l." Aḥituv copies ʾInmrwí.
ao. Aḥituv 1984, 111: "Ḥagar-Paṭṭish."
ap. Aḥituv 1984, 91–92: "Elhillel." Aḥituv (92 n. 1), denies link with Jehallel.
aq. Aḥituv 1984, 109: "Ḥagar-Abelim."
ar. Aḥituv 1984, 94: "Gabri, The Brook of."
as. Aḥituv 1984, 194: "Urikit, The Brook of Urikit."

Field (78) of Strength"[at],[45] (79) … (80) Sapek[au] (?; cf. 1 Sam 30:28) (81) …[…] (82) Tapp[uah?][av] (row VII, 83) Gath/Ginti[aw] (84) "The Negev/Dry-Country (85) (of) the ʿEznite"[ax] (?; cf. 2 Sam 23:8)[46] (86) …[ay,47] (87) "The Field (88) (of) Ashna"[az] (?, cf. Josh 15:33, 43) (89) Haqaq (?)[ba] (90) "The Negev/Dry-Country (91) (of) …"[bb] (92) "The Negev/Dry-Country (93) (of) the Shuh(ath)ites"[bc] (?; cf. 1 Chr 4:11) (94) "The Field (95) (of) Hanan"[bd,48] (cf. Ben-Hanan in 1 Chr 4:20) (96) "The Field (97) (of) El-gad"[be] (cf. Hazer Gaddah in Josh 15:27) (98) "Land[bf,36] (99) (of) Hanan"[bg,48] (row VIII, 100) Adar[bh] (= ? Hazar-addar) (101) "The Field (102) (of) Tilon"[bi] (cf. 1 Chr 4:20) (103) "The Highlands (?)[49] (104) (of) …"[bj] (105) "The Highlands (?) (106) (of) David (?)"[bk] (107) "Fields (108) (of) Arad- (109) Rabbath/Great Arad"[bl] (= Tell Arad) (110) "Arad (111) of the House (112) (of) Jeroham"[bm] (= ? Tell el-Milh)[50] (113) […] (114) […] (115) […] (116) Ada[r?][bn] (row IX, 117) Adar[bo] (118) [..]… (119) […]… (120) […]… (121) …[bp,51] (122) Abel[bq] (123) "Well of the Almond(?)-Tree"[br,52] (124) Beth-Anat[bs] (cf. ? Josh 15:59)

---

at. Ahituv 1984, 110: "Hagar-N-ʿꜣ-dꜣ-y-tꜣ."
au. Ahituv 1984, 179: "Ṣapiq."
av. Ahituv 1984, 188: "Tapp[uah]."
aw. Ahituv 1984, 95: "Gan."
ax. Ahituv 1984, 149: "Negeb-ʿAṣihut." Ahituv (n. 421) denies link with ʿEznite.
ay. Ahituv 1984, 188: "Taš()dnu."
az. Ahituv 1984, 111: "Hagar-Shani."
ba. Ahituv 1984, 106 "Haqhaq?"
bb. Ahituv 1984, 149: "Negeb-Whtwrk."
bc. Ahituv 1984, 149: "Negeb-Ašuhat."
bd. Ahituv 1984, 110: "Hagar-Hanan."
be. Ahituv 1984, 110: "Hagar-Elgad." Ahituv (n. 250) denies link with Hazer Gaddah.
bf. Ahituv 1984, 54: "Adumim" (2-3).
bg. Ahituv 1984, 114: "Hanan(i)."
bh. Ahituv 1984, 47: "Adar (4-6)."
bi. Ahituv 1984, 110: "Hagar-Tolon."
bj. Ahituv 1984, 110: "Hꜣ-y-d-b Rw-n-rw."
bk. Ahituv 1984, 111: "[Hꜣ]-y-d-bꜣ Dy-wꜣ-t." For discussion, see Kitchen 1997, 29–44; Shanks 1999a, 34–35; 1999b, 10–12.
bl. Ahituv 1984, 66: "Arad the Great."
bm. Ahituv 1984, 65: "Arad of the House of Jeroham."
bn. Ahituv 1984, 47: "Adar (4–6)." Properly restored?
bo. Ahituv 1984, 47: "Adar (4–6)." Dittography from no. 116?
bp. Ahituv 1984, 93–94: "F()l()tam."
bq. Ahituv 1984, 47: "Abel (8)."
br. Ahituv 1984, 74: "Be'er-Luz."
bs. Ahituv 1984, 76: "Beth-Anath (2)."

(125) Sharuhen[bt] (cf. Josh 19:6) (126) El-mat(t)an[bu,53] (127) Goren[bv,54] (128) Adam[bw] (129) [...]... (130) ... (131) ...[...] (132) El-ra[m?][bx] (cf. 1 Chr 2:9, 27) (133) Yurza[by] (= ? Tell Jemmeh) (row X, 134) [...] (135) [...] (136) [...] (137) [...] (138) [...] (139) Jeroham[bz] (cf. Jerahme-el in 1 Chr 2:9) (140) Onam[ca] (cf. 1 Chr 2:26) (141) [...] (142) ..[...] (143) [...] (144) [...] (145) Maacah[cb] (?, cf 1 Chr 2:48) (146) ...[...][cc] (147) [...] (148) [...] (149) [...] (150) Jordan[cd,55]

Section 3: List of Captured Name Rings below Central Scene
    Row XI, nos. 1a–5a. For readings, see Kitchen 1986, 441–42 §408.

Š3rwdd (2a) Rph3 (3a) Rbwn (4a) ʿngrwn[56] (5a) H3m[57]
Sharudad[ce] (2a) Raphia[cf] (3a) Laban[cg] (4a) Ain-Goren[ch,56] (5a) Ham[ci,57]

NOTES
    1. George R. Hughes, "Stages of the Decoration of the Portal," in Epigraphic Survey 1954, ix.
    2. Incorporated as "List XXXIV"; see Aḥituv 1984, 20–21 and pl. III. One must disregard the suggestion that the first four lines of the list are written in a boustrophedon or retrograde fashion (denied in Kitchen 1986, 587 § 536).
    3. Purely prospective wishes, since Sheshonq did not celebrate a jubilee; see Kitchen 1986, 302 n. 322; Wente 1976, 277–78; and Murnane 1981, 371. Kitchen translates pl. 10A, line 13, end: "May there be made for him many more, like Re forever."
    4. If the Middle Egyptian sḏm.n≠f is to be taken seriously in this stereotyped phrase, translate this and subsequent examples: "To you I have given...." But cf. G. Silsilah 100 (text 47 n. 5 above), for instances of this expression without adverbial adjuncts.

    bt. Aḥituv 1984, 171–73: "Sharuhen."
    bu. Aḥituv 1984, 92: "Elmattan."
    bv. Aḥituv 1984, 104: "Goren."
    bw. Aḥituv 1984, 54: "Adumim" (2–3).
    bx. Aḥituv 1984, 92: "Elr[o'i]/Elr[am]."
    by. Aḥituv 1984, 202–3: "Yūrṣa."
    bz. Aḥituv 1984, 202: "Yeroham."
    ca. Aḥituv 1984, 60: " 'Anan."
    cb. Aḥituv 1984, 133: "Maacha[th?]." Aḥituv (n. 339) denies a link with 1 Chr 2:48.
    cc. Aḥituv 1984, 47: "Adar (4–6)", restores 'Idy[r], but the final traces do not fit.
    cd. Aḥituv 1984, 202: "Yurd(a)n."
    ce. Aḥituv 1984, 184: "Šarudad."
    cf. The name has been wrongly omitted from Aḥituv 1984, 161–62: "Rapiḫu."
    cg. Aḥituv 1984, 129: "Laban (2)."
    ch. Aḥituv 1984, 56: "ʿAin-Goren."
    ci. Aḥituv 1984, 105–6: "Ham (2)."

5. See Gauthier 1925–31, 4:25, the metropolis of the XVIth Upper Egyptian (Oryx) nome, modern Minya.

6. Literally, "secret/unknown."

7. The Epigraphic Survey's unpublished "Dictionary Sheets" restore [nb.(t)] "all" after ḫȝs.wt, but the sign is not indicated on pl. 3.

8. Traces of the bee wings above the break assure the restoration of [ny-sw.t bỉ.ty]; [nb tȝ.wy] is restored as the usual companion phrase.

9. Although the initial portion of Amon's speech utilizes only classic Middle Egyptian past narrative sḏm.n≠f forms, the corresponding Late Egyptian sḏm≠f form appears here and in following passages. Less likely in line 8, read dỉ.n≠ỉ (n)ḫt.w, assuming the loss of a second n.

10. Or: prr≠k ỉm≠ỉ "From me you came forth." For the emphatic use of the Late Egyptian sḏm≠f form with verbs of motion, see Wente 1969, 1–14.

11. Written ỉrr for the infinitive ỉr.t.

12. Kitchen 1986, 302, translates: "You have made my Temple of Millions of Years, its doorways (?) [adorned?] with electrum for my [image?] therein."

13. The Epigraphic Survey's "Dictionary Sheets" have "apparently not psḏ"; but traces of s, d, and the determinative are clear.

14. Cf. Erman and Grapow 1926–63, 1:494–95.

15. Although the pronoun is plural, the antecedent is more likely the collective "blast/fire" (hh) rather than "their rear."

16. Marking the emphasized adverbial adjunct of the Middle Egyptian sḏm.n≠f. To maintain line coherence, the sentences have not been cleft, using instead the emphatic terms "just, exactly, utterly."

17. For Middle Egyptian narrative ỉw sḏm.n≠f.

18. Despite frequent remarks on the anachronism of this reference to the defunct *political* entity of Mitanni (e.g., Breasted 1906–7, 4:349 §710), the term may well have survived as a general *geographic* reference (for remote Asia), paralleling common contemporary preference for the anachronyms Ceylon, Burma, Congo, and so forth. There is no justification for dismissing his records as "vague" or "unhistorical," and a narrative of the conquest—albeit fragmentary (Karnak Stela)—does exist; contra J. Wilson in Pritchard 1969, 263–64.

19. For n-m-ḫt; Erman and Grapow 1926–63, 3:346. The Epigraphic Survey's "Dictionary Sheets" read r dỉ.t≠ỉ and translate "until I have caused that your valor be remembered...."

20. For the evolution of the term, see Uphill 1965–66, 410–20.

21. Reading the ꜥnḫ sign offered by Nekhbet before the Horus name.

22. For the idiom, see Epigraphic Survey 1986, 90 n. d and pl. 28 (line 4).

23. Space left uncarved where epithet ṯmȝ-ꜥ "strong armed" is expected (Epigraphic Survey's "Dictionary Sheets").

24. For the restorations, see Epigraphic Survey 1986, 52–53 n. hh and pls. 15 (40) and 17 (25).

25. The traditional listing of peoples subject to the Egyptian king; see Uphill 1965–66, 393–420.

26. For the Semitic element *rabīt "great" (nos. 13, 109), see Hoch 1994, 204 §277.

27. For the element *bēta, "house, clan" (nos. 16, 24, 36, 45, 110–12, 124), see Hoch 1994, 113–15 §144.

28. For the element *raḫābu "broad, open space," see Hoch 1994, 206–7, §280.

29. "Encampment"; see Hoch 1994, 149 §192.

30. For the element *yōd "hand, monument, stela," see Hoch 1994, 57–58 §63. For the element *malku "king," see Hoch 1994, 144–45 §187.

31. Or Bʒttpw[t] = Ain Tuba?; see Kitchen 1986, 436 n. 68; denied by Aḥituv, p. 80. For the element *tappūḫa "apple," see Hoch 1994, 377 § 563 ("House of the Apple").

32. Cf. ? Seboʿim of Neh 11:34; see Kitchen 1986, 437 n. 74.

33. See Kitchen 1986, 438 §402. For the Semitic element *el (u) "god" (nos. 53, 70, 96–97, 126), see Hoch 1994, 27–28 §16.

34. For the element *ḫadītata "new," see Hoch 1994, 238–39 §329 (who connects nos. 53–54).

35. Kitchen (1986, 438 §402) takes the sparrow (Gardiner Sign List G 37) following Pʒ as nḏs with the value of n + z/s, and reads "daringly" Pʒ-n-Skt "The one of Succoth." However, the sparrow is most likely a component (ideogram/determinative) of the common word ktt "little," chosen by the scribe for its phonetic value; see Erman and Grapow 1926–63, 5:147–48.

36. For *adāmat "land" (nos. 98–99 and? 56), see Hoch 1994, 46 §41.

37. For *magdala "tower," see Hoch 1994, 169–70 §224.

38. See Kitchen 1986, 439 n. 81.

39. For the element *amqu/amaq "valley/plain," see Hoch 1994, 69 §74.

40. For the term *ḫaql/*ḫalq "field/territory" (nos. 68–69, 71–72, 77–78, 87–88, 94–95, 96–97, 107), see Hoch 1994, 235–37 §326. The correct translation of the term was first noted by Spiegelberg but wrongly rejected by Burchardt and Noth, followed by Kitchen 1986, 439 §404.

41. Hoch (1994, 278 §398) suggests that the initial f and t are misplaced in a name *Ywšʒftʒ < *ṭapata "to judge."

42. For the element *hillēl "to praise," see Hoch 1994, 216 §298 ("He-praises-El/El-is-praised").

43. See Breasted 1904, 22–36, esp. 36. For the element *abu "father," see Hoch 1994, 18–19 §2. For *râma "to be high/exalted," see 204–5 §278.

44. For *šibbōlet "flowing stream/torrent" (nos. 73 and 75), see Hoch 1994, 276 §396. For the adjunct ngbry, see Hoch 1994, 200 §270, who suggests Šbrt Ngb ry "The-Negeb-Is-Well-Watered-Brook."

45. For *Uzziya < "strength, might," see Hoch 1994, 88 §107.

46. See Kitchen 1986, 440 and n. 91; denied by Aḥituv 1984, 149 n. 421. For *nagbu "The Negev/Dry-country" (nos. 84, 90, 92, and 74), see Hoch 1994, 196 §263.

47. Hoch (1994, 317–18 §457) reads Qʒpnʒ "Byblos" with folk etymology < *kappa "palm, sole." Byblos was beyond the scope of Sheshonq's campaign and is unlikely to be named here. For Sheshonq's diplomatic relations with the city, see Kitchen 1986, 292 §250.

48. For *Hanani/Hananya < "to be gracious" (nos. 95 and 99), see Hoch 1994, 230 §319.

49. For *hidab "highlands (?)" (nos. 103–4, 105–6), see Hoch 1994, 224 §307.

50. For PN *Yuroḫam < verb "to be compassionate" (nos. 112 and 139), see Hoch 1994, 54 §56.

51. Related (?) to the clan Pelet (1 Chr 2:33); see Kitchen 1986, 441 §407 and n. 99.

52. For *biru "well," see Hoch 1994, 91 §112; for *luz "almond (?) tree," see 199 §268.

53. For the element *mattān "gift," see Hoch 1994, 176 §235 ("Gift of El").

54. For the element *goren "threshing floor" (nos. 127 and 4b), see Hoch 1994, 377 §563.

55. Kitchen (1986, 441 §408) admits the obvious similarity to Jordan but suggests a Southwest Palestinian name like Yorda. The identification with Jordan was first suggested by Legrain; see Breasted 1906–7, 4:354.

56. "Well of the Threshing Floor"; for *êna "well," see Hoch 1994, 71–72 §79; for *goren "threshing floor," see 377 §563.

57. Also in the lists of Tuthmosis III; see Gauthier 1925–31, 4:1–2.

49. KARNAK SANCTUARY BLOCK

The text is found on a detached block from the south wall of the North Peristyle Court (VI), northwest of the bark sanctuary of Philip Arrhidaeus. For the location, see PM II (1972), p. 92 (264), and pl. XI (264). The block contains the record of an oracular consultation in the adjacent Karnak sanctuary complex, stipulating Amon's protections and exemptions for Sheshonq's Memphite temple estate (cf. the provisions of the Abydos Stela of Sheshonq I for his father Namlot), with likely reference to the "Bubastite" First Court at Karnak. Conflation with adjoining texts of Taharqa (no. 155 below) led to erroneous suggestions of a Nubian campaign by Sheshonq I.

Text and discussion in Vernus 1975, 1–66, esp. 10–11 and 13–20; with an older copy in Müller 1910, 143–53, with figs. 52–53, block Db, second text only (Blocks I and J = Osorkon II; all others = Taharqa). Chicago Oriental Institute photo 8581. Text adjoins, and previously conflated with,

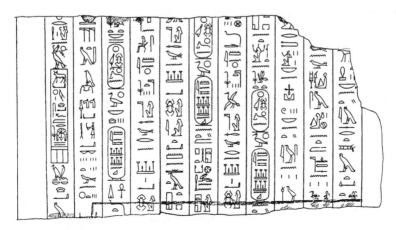

Drawing after Müller 1910, 147–48, as joined in Vernus 1975, 11

later Taharqa inscriptions. Obsolete translation and discussion in Kitchen 1986, 293 §251 and 302 §260 (see 558 §471 and 575 §509); Breasted 1906–7, 4:357–58 §§723–24.

TEXT

(1) [ḥsb.t …] ẖr ḥm n Ḥr k3 nḫt mri-Rꜥ sḫꜥ≠f m ny-sw.t r sm3 t3.wy nb.ty ḫꜥ m [sḫm.ty]

(2) [mi Ḥr s3 3s.t sḥt]p nt̠r.w m m3ꜥ.t Ḥr-nbw sḫm pḥ.ty ḫ(wi) pd̠.t psd̠.t wr (n) nḫt.w [m]

(3) [t3.w nb.w] ny-sw.t bi.ty nb t3.wy Ḥd̠-ḫpr-Rꜥ-stp-n-Rꜥ s3 Rꜥ nb ḫꜥ.w Ššnq mri-ꜣImn di ꜥnḫ d̠.t [hrw]

(4) [pn n sḫꜥ] nt̠r pn šps ꜣImn-Rꜥ ny-sw.t nt̠r.w nt̠r ꜥ3 wr n š3ꜥ ḫpr[1] [d̠d]

(5) [ꜣImn-Rꜥ ny-sw.t nt̠r.w] p3 nt̠r ꜥ3 wr n š3ꜥ ḫpr i(w)≠i di.t mn t3 ḥw.t [n.t]

(6) [ḥḥ n rnp.wt n(.t) ny-sw.t bi.ty] Ḥd̠-ḫpr-Rꜥ-stp-n-Rꜥ s3 Rꜥ Ššnq mri-ꜣImn nty m Ḥw.t-k3-Ptḥ mi(?)[2] wnn ḥw.t≠i n.t]

(7) [ḥḥ n rnp.wt nty m ꜣIp.t-sw].t3 d̠d ꜣImn-Rꜥ ny-sw.t nt̠r.w p3 nt̠r ꜥ3 wr n š3ꜥ ḫpr [iw≠i]

(8) [… t3] ḥw.t n.t ḥḥ n rnp.wt n(.t) ny-sw.t bi.ty Ḥd̠-ḫpr-Rꜥ-stp-n-Rꜥ s3 Rꜥ Ššnq mri-ꜣImn nty [m]

(9) [Ḥw.t-k3-Ptḥ ..].. rmt̠.w nb n wnd̠w.w[4] nb nty-iw≠sn wd̠[5] […]

(10) […]≠f n wr-ḥrp-ḥm.(t) s(t)m[6] nw niw.t(?) nt(y) m ḥtp-nt̠r≠sn 3ḫ[.wt …]

(11) […] s3b ḫtm.w[7] nb nty im≠s r tm di.t t[ḥi …]

TRANSLATION

(1) [Regnal year …] under the Majesty of the Horus: "Strong Bull, beloved of Re, whom he (Re) made manifest as king in order to unite the Two Lands"; the Two Ladies: "He who appears in [the double crown]

(2) [like Horus son of Isis, pacify]ing the gods with Maat"; the Horus of Gold: "Powerful of strength, who strikes the Nine Bows, great of victories [in]

(3) [all lands]"; the King of Upper and Lower Egypt, Lord of the Two Lands, Hedjkheperre-setepenre, Son of Re, Lord of Diadems, Sheshonq, beloved of Amon, given life forever. [This day]

(4) [of the processional appearance of] this noble god, Amon-Re, King of the Gods, the very great god of the beginning of creation.[1] [There said]

(5) [Amon-Re, King of the Gods,] the very great god of the beginning of creation: "I shall cause to endure the Mansion [of]

(6) [Millions of Years of the King of Upper and Lower Egypt,] Hedj-kheperre-setepenre, Son of Re, Sheshonq, beloved of Amon, which is in Memphis just as[2] there exists my Mansion [of]

(7) [Millions of Years that is in Karna]k.[3] There said Amon-Re, King of the Gods, the very great god of the beginning of creation: ["I shall]

(8) [... the] Mansion of Millions of Years of the King of Upper and Lower Egypt, Hedjkheperre-setepenre, Son of Re, Sheshonq, beloved of Amon, which is [in]

(9) [Memphis ...].. all people of any sort[4] who will dispatch[5] [...]

(10) [...] his [...] for the Memphite high priest of Ptah, the *setem*-priest[6] of the city (?), which are as their divine offering (of) field[s ...]

(11) [...] every judge and chancellor[7] who is in it in order not to allow that [...] trans[gress ...]

NOTES

1. For the epithet, see Erman and Grapow 1926–63, 4:406/7; and Kruchten 1986, 28 n. 1.

2. The text has ḥm, probably an error for mỉ; see Vernus 1975, 16 text n.i.

3. For restoration, see Vernus 1975, 16, text n. j. This would be a direct reference to Sheshonq's colonnaded First Court at Karnak, including the Bubastite Portal.

4. See Kruchten 1986, 286.

5. Or "who will order [...]."

6. For these titles of the Memphite high priest, see Maystre 1949, 84–89.

7. Vernus reads ẖn ḥtm.t nb(.t) "among every sealed thing."

50. KARNAK VICTORY STELA
(CAIRO JdE 59635)

The text derives from fragments of a round-topped, yellow sandstone stela once measuring over a meter in height. In the upper vignette, two bas-relief scenes depicted Sheshonq I and the high priest Iuput offering wine to Amon (on the right) and Khonsu (on the left). Below the tableau are eleven broken lines, most lacking the beginning and end. Initial pieces were found in 1894 by Legrain in the antiquities storage of the Opet temple, and additional fragments were discovered in Karnak "Hall K." The text followed the format of a *Königsnovelle*, detailing the royal response to a provocation in the Bitter Lakes region that culminated in the invasion of Palestine. Text without photo in Legrain 1904, 38–39 §21; Grdseloff 1947a, 95–97. Partial translation and discussion in Kitchen 1986, 294 §253 and 302 §260; Grdseloff 1947a; and Breasted 1906–7, 4:358 §724A. Discrepancies in the early copies have required collation by myself in Cairo.

RIGHTHAND SCENE

Label for Winged Disk

Bḥd.t(y) nṯr ꜥꜣ sꜣb šw (2) dỉ ꜥnḫ ḏd wꜣs[1] (3) ḏd-mdw[1] dỉ.n(≥ỉ) n≥k tꜣ.w nb ḫꜣs.wt nb(.t) dmḏ m ḫfꜥ≥k wr[.w[1] ...]

The Behdetite, great god with dappled plumage, (2) who gives life, stability, and dominion.[1] (3) Recitation:[1] "Thus I have placed for you all lands and all foreign countries gathered within your grasp, the chief[s[1] ...]."

Label for Amon

dỉ.n(≠ỉ) n≠k ḥb.w-sd m ꜥnḫ ḏd wꜣs nb (2) ꜣImn-Rꜥ nb ns.wt tꜣ.wy ḫnty ꜣIp.t-s.wt (3) nb p.t ḥqꜣ Wꜣs.t

"Thus I have given to you jubilees comprising all life, stability, and dominion." (2) Amon-Re, Lord of the thrones of the Two Lands, foremost of Karnak, (3) Lord of heaven, Ruler of Thebes.

Label for Sheshonq

nb tꜣ.wy Ḥḏ-ḫpr-Rꜥ-stp-n-Rꜥ (2) nb ḫꜥ.w Ššnq mrỉ-ꜣImn

Lord of the Two Lands, Hedjkheperre-setepenre, Lord of Diadems, Sheshonq, beloved of Amon.

Label for Iuput

ḥm-nṯr tp(y) n ꜣImn-Rꜥ (2) ny-sw.t nṯr.w ỉmy-rꜣ mšꜥ (3) wr ḥꜣw.ty ꜣIwpwt mꜣꜥ-ḫrw (4) sꜣ ny-sw.t n nb tꜣ.wy (5) Ššnq mrỉ-ꜣImn

First Prophet of Amon-Re, (2) King of the Gods, great general and (3) leader Iuput, the justified, (4) royal son of the Lord of the Two Lands, (5) Sheshonq, beloved of Amon.

Label for Scene

dỉ.t ỉrp n ỉt≠f ꜣImn-Rꜥ ỉr.n≠f dỉ ꜥnḫ

Giving wine to his father Amon-Re, he having attained the state of being given life.

Label for Winged Disk

[Bḥd.t(y)] nṯr ꜥꜣ sꜣb šw

[The Behdetite,] great god with dappled plumage.

Label for Khonsu

Ḫ[n]sw m Wꜣs.t[1] Nfr-ḥtp (2) dỉ.[n≠ỉ] n≠k ny.t-sw.t n Rꜥ

Khonsu in Thebes,[1] Neferhotep. (2) "[Thus I have] given to you the kingship of Re."

Label for Sheshonq

nb tꜣ.wy Ḥḏ-ḫpr-Rꜥ-stp-n-Rꜥ (2) nb ḫꜥ.w Ššn[q] mrỉ-ꜣImn

Lord of the Two Lands, Hedjkheperre-setepenre, (2) Lord of Diadems, Sheshon[q], beloved of Amon.

Label for Iuput
    ḥm-nṯr tp(y) n ʾI[mn-Rꜥ ...]
    First Prophet of A[mon-Re, ...]

BODY OF STELA

The text consists of three separate fragments a–c (right to left), with central fragment b the most complete. Fragments a and c each have sections of three lines, and b preserves portions of ten. The precise placement of right fragment a is uncertain. Line numbers are revised; Legrain's initial publication of fragment b ignores lines 1–3a, and Grdseloff reproduces only portions of lines 4–10.

(1c) [...]≠k n [...]
(2b) [...n]ꜣ ḥm.w-nṯr tp.w (2c) n ʾImn-Rꜥ ny-sw.t nṯr.w [...]
(3a) [...] nḫt? mrî Rꜥ s[...](3b) [...]w≠k m-dî≠w nḫt (3c) n tꜣ² ny-sw.t bî.ty nb tꜣ.wy [...]
(4a) [...] tꜣ.w Sṯ.t nb tꜣ.wy Ḥd-[ḫpr]-Rꜥ-[stp-n-Rꜥ nb ḫꜥ.w Ššnq ...] (4b) mry [ʾImn-Rꜥ ny-sw.t] nṯr.w dî ꜥnḫ ḏ.t îsk gm.n [ḥm≠îꜣ³ ...]
(5a) [... s]mꜣ[≠sn³ nꜣ≠î mšꜥ.w ḥnꜥ? nꜣ](5b)y≠î ḫꜣwty.w mḥ în ḥm≠f ḥr≠sn³ [...]
(6b) [... mî?] mr≠sn ḏd în ḥm≠f n šnwy≠f [nty m-ḫt≠f]³
(7b) [...] nꜣy sp.w ḫsy.w îr.n≠sn ḏd în≠sn [ḫr ḥm≠f³...]
(8b) [pr în ḥm≠f ... tî-n.t]-ḥtr.w≠f m-ḫt≠f n rḫ≠sn îst [...]
(9b) [...] îr.n{n} ḥm≠f ḫꜣy.t ꜥꜣ.t îm≠sn î[...]
(10b) [smꜣ].n≠f sn ḥr mr sp.t Km-wr în{n} ît≠f ʾI[mn-Rꜥ]
(11b) [⁴...] ꜥb≠sn n≠î ḫꜣ.w n qny [nḫt.w ...]⁵

(1c) [...] your ... to/for [...]
(2b) [...] the First [Prophets] (2c) of Amon-Re, King of the Gods, [...]
(3a) [...] strong?, beloved of Re, [...] (3b) [...] you [...] with them victory (3b) in the land,² the King of Upper and Lower Egypt, Lord of the Two Lands, [...]
(4a) [...] lands of Asia, Lord of the Two Lands, Hedj[kheper]re-[setepenre, Lord of Diadems, Sheshonq ...] (4b) beloved of [Amon-Re, King] of the Gods, given life forever. Now [My Majesty]³ discovered [that ...]
(5a) [... they] killed [... my soldiers and?] (5b) my leaders. Then His Majesty pondered concerning them³ [...]
6b) [... as?] they desire. Then His Majesty said to his entourage [that was in his following³]:
(7b) ["Behold ...] these wretched deeds that they have done." Then they said [before His Majesty³: "..."]
(8b) [Then His Majesty went forth ...], his chariotry following him, without their knowing. Now [...]

(9b) [...] Among them His Majesty made a great slaughter [...]

(10b) and he [slew] them ashore on the bank of the Bitter Lakes. It was his father A[mon-Re]

(11b) [who[4] ...] they offer to me thousands of (instances of) valor [and victories...][5]

NOTES

1. Passage ignored by Legrain.

2. The word tȝ survives at the end of block 3b, below "n" of block 3c. For the phrase among Sheshonq's royal titles, cf. his Golden Horus name: "great of victories in all lands."

3. Following the restoration of Grdseloff 1947a, 95–96.

4. Kitchen restores "[who decreed the victory for him...]."

5. For the common pairing of qn(ỉ) nḫt.w; see Gebel es-Silsilah Quarry Stela No. 100 (no. 47), lines 18, 30, and 37–38.

51. MEGIDDO STELA FRAGMENT
(ROCKEFELLER MUSEUM, JERUSALEM, NO. I.3554)

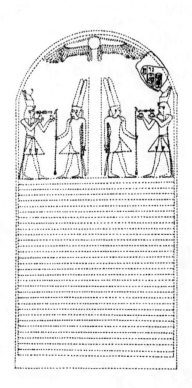

Measuring 50 cm thick and 70 cm high from the base of the cartouches to the top of the curved summit, this irregular, badly weathered limestone block represents a small portion of the upper right scene of a stela perhaps originally 250 cm high. Recovered at Megiddo in 1925 from the excavation dump left by the Gottlieb Schumacher expedition (1903–5), the fragment

Reconstruction after Fisher 1929, 15 and 13

was fortuitously saved from reuse as building masonry. The significance of the piece derives derives strictly from its findspot, corroborating the capture of Megiddo as noted in the Karnak Victory Relief (row III, no. 27).

Primary publication and reconstruction in Fisher 1929, 12–16; with revised archaeological considerations in Lamon and Shipton 1939, 60 (fig. 70) and 61. Original reports of the chance discovery of the fragment by an Egyptian workman are recounted in Larson 1990, 1–3. See also Pritchard 1987, 97; Kitchen 1986, 299 §257.

The fragment contains only the labels of a lost upper vignette recording the speech of a deity and the titles of the king.

SPEECH OF DEITY (AMON?)

[dỉ.n≥ỉ n≥k] ꜥnḫ ḏd [wꜣs] nb

"[Thus I have given to you] all life, stability, [and dominion.]"

TITLES OF SHESHONQ

nṯr nfr Ḥd-ḫpr-Rꜥ-stp[-n-]Rꜥ (2) nb ỉr.(t) [ḫ.t] Ššnq mrỉ-ꜣImn

The Good God, Hedjkheperre-setepenre, (2) Lord of [ritual] performance, Sheshonq, beloved of Amon.

52. BYBLOS STATUE

This broken throne (25 cm by 22 cm) of Egyptian grey granite derives from a seated statue of the king, dedicated in the great temple of Byblos. Probably from the temple esplanade, the statue's precise findspot is uncertain. The piece was formerly in the Loytved collection in Beirut. The texts include Sheshonq's pharaonic titulary and a secondary Phoenician dedication by Abibaal, king of Byblos. Abibaal's claim to have caused the statue

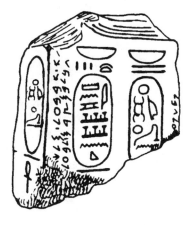

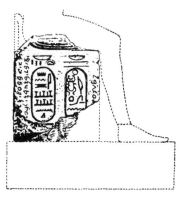

Drawing after Montet 1928, 53.

Reconstruction after Dussaud 1924, 145.

to be brought from Egypt echoes the haughty tone of his predecessor in The Voyage of Wenamon. Unlike the Megiddo stela, Sheshonq's statue dedication confirms an alliance rather than a conquest; see Kitchen 1986, 292–93 §250.93

Citations in Porter and Moss 1927–51, 388. Photo in Clermont-Ganneau 1903, 74–78 and pl. II; squeeze and drawings in Dussaud 1924, 145–47 §5 and pl. XLII; Montet 1928, 53–57, §31.

Further explications of the Phoenician text are found in Albright 1947, 153, 157–58; Hermann 1958, 15–17, 31; Donner and Röllig 1962–64, 1:1 §5; 2:7–8 §5; and Gibson 1971–82, 3:19–21 and 182 fig. 4. The text is restored on the basis of the similar Byblos statue of Osorkon I.

ROYAL TITLES (RIGHT SIDE)

nb t3.wy Ḥd-ḫpr-Rʿ-stp-n-Rʿ (2) nb ḫʿ.w Ššnq mrỉ-ʾImn

Lord of the Two Lands, Hedjkheperre-setepenre, (2) Lord of Diadems, Sheshonq, beloved of Amon.

ROYAL TITLES (BACK)

See Montet 1928, 54 and 53 fig. 17 (partial copy)

[…] Ḥd-ḫpr-Rʿ-stp-n-Rʿ (2) [… Ššnq mrỉ-ʾImn] (3) ʿnḫ [ḏ.t]

[…] Hedjkheperre-setepenre, (2) […, Sheshonq, beloved of Amon,] (3) living [forever.]

PHOENICIAN TEXT (ON SIDE OF THRONE AROUND CARTOUCHES)

[mš(?) z y]bʾ. ʾbbʿl. mlk [gbl. b yḥmlk(?). (2) mlk] gbl. b mṣrm. l bʿl[t. gbl. ʾdtw. tʾrk. bʿlt. gbl. ymt. ʾbbʿl. wšntw.] ʿl gbl

[Statue (?) that] Abibaal, king [of Byblos, son of Yeḥimilk (?), (2) king of] Byblos, had brought from Egypt for Baal[at-Gebal ("Lady of Byblos"), his mistress. May Baalat-Gebal lengthen the days of Abibaal and his (regnal) years] over Byblos!

53. EL-HIBEH TEMPLE RELIEFS
(HEIDELBERG AND *IN SITU*)

Constructed and decorated by Sheshonq I, the Amon temple of el-Hibeh was the northernmost dependency of the high priest of Theban Amon in the Third Intermediate Period. Surveyed by Kamal and Daressy in 1901, the site was excavated by Hermann Ranke in 1913–14; see Porter and Moss 1927–51, 4:124. For the scenes and texts, see Kamal 1901, 84–91; Daressy 1901a, 154–56; Ranke 1926, 58–68 and pls. 19–24; Feucht 1978, 69–77 and pls. 21–22; 1981, 105–17 and pl. 2; and Fazzini 1988, 6. See Kitchen 1986, 291 §248, 302 §260, and 576 §510.

A. Victory Relief

Heidelberg Inv. No. 1970 (formerly Heidelberg and Freiburg). Eleven sandstone fragments (1.40 m. high by 2.17 m. wide) from the north wall of the interior of the temple forecourt depict a triumphal scene of Sheshonq. Contra Kitchen 1986, 302 §260, the fragments of the triumphal relief were not lost but were hidden during World War I and subsequently divided. The Freiburg pieces were transferred to Heidelberg in 1966. The king, wearing the *hemhem*-crown, raises his left arm (with lost mace) and extends his right hand to grasp (now lost) enemies. A figure of Montu once offered jubilees and life to the nose of the king (cf. Bubastite Portal upper pilaster scenes). Behind Sheshonq stood the royal *ka*-spirit. See Ranke 1926, 50 and pl. 20; Feucht 1981, 105–17.

Texts before King

[…] dỉ/nḫt (2) […] Mntw
[…] give/victory (2) […] Montu

Label for King

[ny-sw.t bỉ.]ty [Ḥḏ]¹-ḫpr-Rꜥ-stp-n-Rꜥ (2) s[ꜣ Rꜥ] Ššnq mrỉ-ꜣỉmn (3) dỉ ꜥnḫ ḏd wꜣs m[ỉ] Rꜥ (4) Ḥr tmꜣ-ꜥ nb ỉr.(t) ḫ.t (5) sꜣ ꜥnḫ ḏd wꜣs ḥꜣ⸗f mỉ Rꜥ [ḏ.t]

[The King of Upper and Lower Egy]pt, Hedjkheperre-setepenre, (2) Son of Re, Sheshonq, beloved of Amon, (3) given life, stability, and dominion like Re. (4) Horus with powerful arm, Lord of ritual performance. (5) The protection of life, stability, and dominion is behind him like Re [forever].

Associated Fragments = Label for Scene² (Heidelberg inventory nos. 1345 + 1346). See Feucht 1981, 113

sqr […] (2+) [Mn]t.w St.t nw ḫꜣs.wt [..]
Striking the […] (2+) […] Asian [Bedo]uin of foreign countries […]

B. Second Victory Scene, North Wall

King before god; only feet and partial texts preserved. See Feucht 1981, 114

King

[dỉ.t] t [n] ỉt⸗f ỉr.n⸗f dỉ ꜥnḫ

[Offering] bread [to] his father, he having attained the state of being given life.

God

dỉ.n(⸗ỉ) n⸗k tꜣ.w nb.w m [ḫtp³...] —4 lines lost— [dỉ.n(⸗ỉ)] n⸗k qn(ỉ) [nḫt⁴ r ḫꜣs.wt] nb(.t) St.t ḥr m dm.t⸗k

"To you (I) have given all lands in [peace³...] —4 lines lost— To you [(I) have given] valor [and victory⁴ over] all [foreign countries], with Asia fallen by means of your sword."

C. Victory Relief, First Pillared Hall: Rear Wall, Left
See Daressy 1901a, 155–56; Feucht 1981, 116. Sheshonq offers kneeling enemies to a seated deity. Below are traces of an inscription and a row of captured towns, of which only two of the Nine Bows were preserved.

Text
[...]. rdỉ≠s[... nn?] rḫ ṯnw ḥr[(y).w] sqr.w-ꜥnḫ r ꜥꜣ [...]
[...]. it (?) cause [...], while the number of the affiliates of the prisoners is [not?] known due to the greatness [of ...]

Name Rings
Sḫ.t-(ʾI)ꜣm [...] Pḏ.tyw[-Šw] [...]
The Western Oases [...] The Eastern Desert [...]

D. Pillar Scene, First Pillared Hall: First Pillar on Left
King embraces Amon, who offers the palm branch of life. See Kamal 1901, 87; Daressy 1901a, 155; and Feucht 1981, 114–15.

Winged Disk above Scene
Bḥd.t(y) nṯr ꜥꜣ nb p.t
The Behdetite, great god, Lord of heaven.

Amon
dỉ.n(≠ỉ) n≠k ꜥḥꜥ n Rꜥ m p.[t] ny.t-sw.t≠k ny.t-sw.t (2) [...] mw nb.w [...] (3) [...] nḫt r mḥ.t Tꜣ-St̞.t snḏ n šfy.t≠k (4) šsp≠k ꜥnḫ ḏd wꜣs [nb] rnp.wt [ꜥšꜣ] m[ỉ ...]

"To you I have given the lifetime of Re in heaven. Your kingship is the kingship of (2) [...] all waters [...] (3) victory over the north, with Asia fearful of your dignity. (4) You have received [all] life, stability, and dominion, with [numerous] years like [...]."

King
[ny-sw.t bỉ.]ty nb tꜣ.wy [nb ỉr.(t) ḫ.t] Ḥd-ḫpr-Rꜥ-stp-n-Rꜥ (2) [sꜣ Rꜥ] Ššnq mrỉ-ʾImn (3) ꜥnḫ nb snb nb [ḫꜣ≠f ...]

[The King of Upper and Lower Egy]pt, Lord of the Two Lands, [Lord of ritual performance], Hedjkheperre-setepenre, (2) [Son of Re], Sheshonq, beloved of Amon. (3) All life, all health [is behind him ...]

E. Pillar Scene, First Pillared Hall: First Pillar on Left; Adjacent Face to Preceding
The king offers incense to hawk-headed deity. See Daressy 1901a, 155.

Lost Vulture above Scene
Nḫb.t [...]   Nekhbet.

Deity
[... dỉ.n(ⸯ̉) nⸯk ḥb].w-[sd] qn.t ꜥš3 wr.t (2) nb 3w.t-ỉb nb ḫrⸯ[ỉ]
["To you I have given] many and very numerous [jubilees,] (2) O Lord of all joy deriving from [me."]

King
ntr nfr spd sḫr[.w ...] smnḫ pr n ỉtⸯf [ʾImn-Rꜥ ...] (2) ny-sw.t bỉ.ty nb t3.wy Ḥd-ḫpr-Rꜥ-stp-n-Rꜥ (3) [...] Ššnq mrỉ-ʾImn (4) [...] dỉ ꜥnḫ mỉ Rꜥ d̲.t
The Good God, clever of plan[s ...] who embellished the house of his father, [Amon-Re ..]; (2) the King of Upper and Lower Egypt, Lord of the Two Lands, Hedjkheperre-setepenre, (3) [...] Sheshonq, beloved of Amon, (4) [...] given life like Re forever.

F. Pillar Scene, First Pillared Hall: West Row, Second Pillar from North, South Face
King offers floral collar and two pectorals to Horus. See Ranke 1926, 65 and pls. 19/1 and 21/4; Porter and Moss 1927–51, 4:124.

Horus
[...] m ḥḥ.wⸯf⁵ (2) dỉ.n(ⸯ̉) nⸯk ꜥnḫ d̲d w3s nb ḫꜥ.wy ḥr s.t Ḥr [sšm ꜥnḫ.w]
[...] by/with his millions.⁵ (2) "To you I have given all life, stability, and dominion, appearance upon the throne of Horus, [who leads the living."]

King with Double Crown
[...] Ḥd-ḫpr-[Rꜥ]-stp-n-Rꜥ (2) [...] Ššnq [mrỉ-ʾImn]
[...] Hedjkheper[re]-setepenre, (2) [...] Sheshonq, [beloved of Amon]

G. Pillar Scene, First Pillared Hall: West Row, Second Pillar from North, East Face
King offers incense to Atum. See Ranke 1926, pl. 21/3; Porter and Moss 1927–51, 4:124. For Iuput text, cf. Daressy 1901a, 156.

Atum
[dỉ.n(ⸯ̉) nⸯk ...] ḫrⸯỉ (2) [... Tm nb] p.t⁵ (3) dỉ.n(ⸯ̉) nⸯk ny.t-sw.t n(.t) Rꜥ rnp.wt n.t Tm

["To you I have given ...] deriving from me." (2) [... Atum, Lord of] heaven.⁵ (3) "To you I have given the kingship of Re, the years of Atum."

King
　　[...] n ỉt≠f Tm(?)⁵ [...] nn ḫpr mỉt.t≠f ỉr (2) [...] ...n≠f⁵ n≠sn ḥtp-nṯr (3) [...] Ḥd-ḫpr-Rꜥ-stp-n-Rꜥ (4) [... Ššnq mrỉ-ʾImn] (5) dỉ ꜥnḫ [dd wꜣs mỉ Rꜥ]
　　[...] for his father Atum (?)⁵ [...] there does not exist his equal who made (2) [...] he ...⁵ for them divine offerings. (3) [...] Hedjkheperre-setepenre, (4) [... Sheshonq, beloved of Amon] (5) given life, [stability, and dominion like Re.]

Baseline Text of Prince Iuput
　　ḥm-nṯr tp(y) n ʾImn-Rꜥ ny-sw.t nṯr.w ỉmy-rꜣ mšꜥ wr tp(y) n ḥm≠f sꜣ ny-sw.t n Rꜥmss ḫꜣw.ty ʾIwpwt
　　First Prophet of Amon-Re, King of the Gods, premier great general of His Majesty, king's son of Rameses and leader Iuput.

H. PILLAR SCENE, FIRST PILLARED HALL: FIRST PILLAR ON RIGHT, LEFT PORTION
　　Ram-headed Amon extends sword of victory to king in blue crown. See Kamal 1901, 86–87 (miscopied and mistakenly attributed to Osorkon I); Daressy 1901a, 154.

Amon
　　dỉ.n(≠ỉ) n≠k tꜣ.w nb.w m ḥtp.w ḫꜣs.t nb(.t) ḥr tb.ty≠k (2) dỉ.n(≠ỉ) n≠k S[ṯ.]t ꜥꜣ.w wr.w (3) ʾImn ꜥꜣ hmhm.wt nb Dhm(4).t [...] rn [...] nṯr ꜥꜣ nb n nrw (4) šsp n[≠k ḫpš ...]
　　"To you I have given all lands in peace, every foreign country being beneath your sandals. (2) To you I have given Nubia, the great ones and the chiefs." (3) Amon, great of war-cries, Lord of el-Hibeh, (4) [...] name [...] Great God, Lord of terror. (4) "Receive for [yourself the sword ..."]

King
　　ny-sw.t bỉ.ty Ḥd-ḫpr-Rꜥ-stp-n-Rꜥ (2) sꜣ Rꜥ nb ḫꜥ.w Ššnq [mrỉ-ʾImn]
　　The King of Upper and Lower Egypt, Hedjkheperre-setepenre, (2) Son of Re, Lord of Diadems, Sheshonq, [beloved of Amon.]

I. PILLAR SCENE, FIRST PILLARED HALL: FIRST PILLAR ON RIGHT, RIGHT PORTION
　　King offers *nemset*-jugs to Re. See Kamal 1901, 87.

Nekhbet Vulture above Scene
　　Nḫ[b.t ḥd.t Nḫ]n dỉ≠s ꜥnḫ dd wꜣs
　　Nekh[bet, the White One of Nekhe]n, may she give life, stability, and dominion.

Re
    dỉ.n(≠ỉ) n≠k ḥtp.w d̠ỉ₃.w nb (2) Rꜥ ntr ꜥ₃ nb p.t
    "To you I have given all offerings and foodstuffs." (2) Re, the Great God, Lord of heaven.

King
    ntr nfr ḫꜥ m ḥq₃ ḥr s.t n(.t) ỉt≠f Rꜥ (2) ny-sw.t bỉ.ty Ḥd-ḫpr-Rꜥ-stp-n-Rꜥ (3) s₃ Rꜥ Ššnq mrỉ-ꜣImn (4) [ḫ]ꜥwy m ny-sw.t bỉ.ty ḥr s.t (5) Ḥr n.t [ꜥnḫ.w]
    The Good God, who has appeared as ruler on the throne of his father Re; (2) the King of Upper and Lower Egypt, Hedjkheperre-setepenre, (3) Son of Re, Sheshonq, beloved of Amon, (4) who has appeared as King of Upper and Lower Egypt on the Horus throne (5) of [the living.]

J. Pillar Scene, First Pillared Hall: Second Pillar on Right
    King presents two oil jars to lion-headed goddess. See Daressy 1901a, 155.

Goddess
    dỉ.n(≠ỉ) n≠k ny.t-sw.t n(.t) Rꜥ rnp.wt n.t Tm
    "To you I have given the kingship of Re, the years of Atum."

Legend
    dỉ.t md̠[.t] n mw.t≠f ỉr.n≠s dỉ ꜥnḫ
    Giving oil to his mother, she having granted the state of being given life.

K. Roof Tile, First Pillared Hall
    Flying vultures grasping ostrich plumes between flanking bands of text. See Kamal 1901, 87; Daressy 1901a, 155.

    mrỉ-ꜣImn ꜥ₃ hmhm.(w)t dỉ ꜥnḫ d̠d w₃s snb nb mỉ Rꜥ d̠.t
    Beloved of Amon, great of war-cries, given life, stability, dominion, and health like Re forever.

L. Unplaced Blocks, Vertical Inscriptions
    See Daressy 1901a, 156. For Iuput text, cf. scene G above.

Text of Iuput
    [...] nb≠ỉ n nb(≠ỉ?) (2) mỉ Rꜥ nḥḥ d̠.t (3) ḥm-ntr tp(y) n ꜣImn-Rꜥ ny-sw.t ntr.w ỉmy-r₃ mšꜥ wr tp(y) n ḥm≠f h₃w.ty [ꜣIwpwt̠]

[…] my lord for my (?) lord (2) like Re forever and ever. (3) First Prophet of Amon-Re, King of the Gods, premier great general of His Majesty and leader [Iuput].

Text of Amon-Re

ḏd-mdw dỉ.n(∗ỉ) n∗k pḥ.ty n Mnṯ pš.t n [nb.wy] (2) ḏd-mdw ỉn ʾImn-Rᶜ ny-sw.t nṯr.w nṯr ᶜꜣ nb p.t (3) nṯr [..] ṯs psḏ.t ỉr nty qꜣmw […]

Recitation: "To you I have given the strength of Montu, the division of [the two lords."] (2) Recitation by Amon-Re, King of the Gods, Great God, Lord of heaven, (3) god […] who raised the Ennead, who made that which is created […]

Block from Door Support

Running king with hes-vases: ỉṯ.t [ḥp.t[6]] ẖnp qbḥw ỉr.n∗f dỉ ᶜnḫ

Taking [the oar[6]], presenting cool water, he having attained the state of being given life.

M. PILLAR SCENES FROM SECOND PILLARED HALL

Heidelberg Inventory Nos. 562 + 922. Thickness and adjoining face of one pillar with two scenes of the king before a deity. Description and texts in Feucht 1978, 69–77 and pls. 21–22; Otto 1964, 18, 94, and pl. 18; and Ranke 1926, 52 and pls. 19/2 and 21/1. Texts restored from further blocks recorded in unpublished Ranke manuscript indicated by « ».

King Offers Incense before Goddess (Heidelberg Inv. No. 562)

Goddess

«ꜣs.t (2) wr.t (3) mw.t[7] nṯr (4) dỉ.n∗ỉ n∗k rn∗k mỉ Rᶜ ḏ.t»

«Isis (2) the great, (3) mother[7] of the god. (4) "To you I have given your name like Re forever."»

King

«ny-sw.t bỉ.ty nb tꜣ.wy nb ỉr.(t) ḫ.t Ḥḏ-ḫpr-Rᶜ-»stp-n-Rᶜ (2) «sꜣ Rᶜ n ḫ.t∗f mr∗f Ššn»q mrỉ-ʾImn (3) sꜣ ᶜnḫ […] (4) ỉr(.t) snṯr n mw.t[∗f ꜣs.t ỉr.n∗f dỉ ᶜnḫ]

«The King of Upper and Lower Egypt, Lord of the Two Lands, Lord of ritual performance, Hedjkheperre»-setepenre, (2) «bodily Son of Re, whom he (Re) loves, Sheshon»q, «beloved of Amon». (3) The protection of life […] (4) Making incense for [his] mother [Isis, he having attained the state of being given life.]

King with Blue Crown and Crook Stands before God (Heidelberg Inv. No. 922 + Unidentified Block)

Nekhbet Vulture above Scene

«Nḫb.t ḥḏ.t Nḫn» [dỉ ≠s] ʿnḫ ḏd [mỉ] Rʿ

«Nekhbet, the White One of Nekhen,» [may she give] life and stability [like] Re.

God Shepes

«dỉ.n≠(ỉ) n≠k ḥb.w-sd (2) qn.w wr wr (3) ḏd-mdw ỉn Šps nṯr ʿ3» nb n nrw wr bỉ3.wt

«"I have given to you (2) very, very numerous jubilees." (3) Recitation by Shepes, the Great God,» Lord of terror, great of wonders.

King

«nb t3.wy Ḥḏ-ḫpr-Rʿ-stp-n-Rʿ (2) nb ḫpš Ššnq mrỉ-ʾImn» (3) dỉ ʿnḫ w3s mỉ Rʿ

«Lord of the Two Lands, Hedjkheperre-setepenre, (2) Lord of the strong arm, Sheshonq, beloved of Amon», (3) given life and dominion like Re.

NOTES

1. Feucht (1981, 109) misunderstands the value of the missing crown (Ḥd) in the cartouche and reads Ḫpr-[n]-Rʿ-stp-n-Rʿ.

2. Ranke's suggestion that a corresponding scene on the south wall depicted a victory over Nubia is denied by Feucht (1981, 114) on the grounds that interior reliefs reflect actual history. Former evidence of Nubian tribute (in the Karnak Sanctuary blocks) has been reattributed to Taharqa; see Vernus 1975, 1–66. But see Amon's speech on the facade of the Bubastite Portal (p. 201–2, line 6 above).

3. Cf. the speech of Montu-Re on the Bubastite Portal, western pilaster, middle register (p. 197 above).

4. Feucht (1981, 114), following Ranke, restored qn[.n≠k ḫ3s.wt] nb "that [you] be victorious over all [lands]."

5. Signs unclear on available copy.

6. For restoration, see Erman and Grapow 1935–53, 3:88 (for 1926–63, 3:290/14).

7. Feucht (1978, 71 n. 9) fails to recognize Ranke's transcription of the common title "God's Mother."

54. CARTONNAGE OF HOR
(FITZWILLIAM MUSEUM, CAMBRIDGE E.8.1896)

Horizontal text bands between vertical columns of Book of the Dead Spell 125 give the owner's name, titles, filiation and record his participation in Sheshonq's Palestinian campaign. For the (poorly written) text, see Quibell 1898, 12, 20, and pl. XXXA, 1 (two horizontal bands), with an additional portion of the coffin on pl. XXVIII (judgment scene); and Jansen-Winkeln 1985, 252–54, text B 5. The significance of the text was first noted in Müller 1901, 280–302 (but military participation was wrongly attributed to Hor's father); and Breasted 1906–7, 4:348, b. See Kitchen 1986, 299 n. 304; and 575 §510.

(1A) First Horizontal Band, Right Edge to Center

ḥm-nṯr ꜣImn-Rꜥ ny-sw.t nṯr.w Ḥr mꜣꜥ-ḫrw sꜣ ỉmy-rꜣ nỉw.t ṯꜣty ꜣIꜥꜣ mꜣꜥ-ḫrw

Prophet of Amon-Re, King of the Gods, Hor, the justified, son of the overseer of the city and vizier, Iaa, the justified.

Drawings after Quibell and Spiegelberg 1898, pl. XXXA.

(1B) First Horizontal Band, Left Edge to Center (Retrograde)

[ḥm-nṯr] ꜣImn-Rꜥ ny-sw.t nṯr.w sš (ny-sw.t)[1] mꜣꜥ m[ry≠f šmš] ny-sw.t r nmt.wt≠f ḥr ḫꜣs.wt Rṯnw

[Prophet] of Amon-Re, King of the Gods, genuine (royal)[1] scribe, whom [he] loves, [who followed] the king on his expedition in the foreign lands of Syria-Palestine.

(2) Second Horizontal Band (Retrograde)

ḥm-nṯr ꜣImn-Rꜥ ny-sw.t nṯr.w ꜥqy r p.t mꜣꜣ ỉmy≠s rḫ sštꜣ.w m ḏsr.t ꜣḫ.t[2] Ḥr mꜣꜥ-ḫrw[3] sꜣ [ꜣIꜥꜣ][3]

Prophet of Amon-Re, King of the Gods, one who enters into heaven, who sees the one who is in it, who knows the secrets in the sacred place of the horizon,[2] Hor, the justified,[3] son of [Ia]a.

NOTES

1. Haplography, read ny-sw.t twice.
2. The epithets indicate that Hor has access to the temple shrine and the divine statue within it.
3. Copy unclear, but reading likely. Text unread by Jansen-Winkeln after ꜣḫ.t.

55. CANOPIC CHEST
(BERLIN 11000)

Though provided with negligible text, the chest is here included as the only certain survivor of the lost royal burial. Of Egyptian alabaster and in square naos form, the box is covered by a lid provided with cavetto cornice and torus moldings (base: 48 cm x 48 cm x 53 cm; lid: 58 cm x 54.5 cm x 17.5 cm). The interior is carved into four compartments, approximately 15 cm in diameter. On each lateral side, Isis and Nephthys enfold their wings across the surface. Text appears only on the front, with slight damage from a crowbar once used in prying off the lid. The roof of the lid is decorated with a spread vulture facing the front; the separate head is now lost. Serpents are carved along the side edges.

The chest was donated to the Berlin Museum in 1891 by Julius Issac without acquisition information. Possible burial sites include Thebes, Tanis, Bubastis, Memphis, or Heracleopolis. A Theban origin is suggested by Capart 1941, 254, but questioned by Yoyotte 1988b, 42 and 47 n. 9.

For discussion and text, see Dodson 1994a, 83–85 (cat. 44), 131, 178–79, and pls. XXXVII–XXXVIII; Königliche Museen zu Berlin 1899, 232; 1895, 16 and pl. 42 (with lost vulture head); Oriental Institute photo B 54. Supposed canopic jars of Sheshonq I at Tanis have been reattributed to the new Sheshonq IV, see Dodson 1994a, 83–84 (cat. 50/1–2), 93–94, 178–79, plate XLIII; 1994b, 53–58. See Kitchen 1995, xxv–vi §Y; 1986, 545 §452.

ROYAL NAMES

[nb] ḫʿ[.w] Ḥd-ḫpr-Rʿ-stp-n-Rʿ (2) nb tȝ.wy Ššnq mrỉ-ʾImn (3) [dỉ] ʿnḫ (4) mỉ Rʿ ḏ.t

[The Lord of] Diadem[s], Hedjkheperre-setepenre, (2) Lord of the Two Lands, Sheshonq, beloved of Amon, (3) [given] life (4) like Re forever.

B. OSORKON I

56. THE BUBASTITE PORTAL AT KARNAK: RELIEFS OF OSORKON I

Continuing the decoration of his father's colonnaded court, Osorkon added three scenes on the west face of the eastern pilaster of the "Bubastite Portal." In contrast to the reliefs of Sheshonq I, no space is accorded either the high priest Iuput or his successor Sheshonq (II), son of Osorkon I.

For the texts, see Epigraphic Survey 1954, x and pls. 13–15 (line sequences often reordered below for thematic consistency); Porter and

Moss 1972, 36 (§129). For the artistic depiction, see Fazzini 1988, 10, 31, and pl. VII. For brief discussion, see Kitchen 1986, 305 §264.

(1) Upper Register (= Epigraphic Survey 1954, Pl. 15; Key Plans K 349A)
Osorkon I receiving symbols of dominion and power from Amon-Re.

Label for the Vulture above the Scene (line 4)
Nḫb.t ḥḏ.t Nḫn nb.(t) p.t dỉ≠s[1] ꜥnḫ ḏd wꜣs nb snb nb ꜣw.t-ỉb nb.(t) mỉ Rꜥ ḏ.t
Nekhbet, the White One of Nekhen, Lady of heaven. May she grant all life, stability, and dominion, all health and all joy like Re forever.

Label for Amon (lines 1–3)
ḏd-mdw ỉn ʾImn-Rꜥ ny-sw.t nṯr.w nb p.t sꜣ ꜥnḫ ḏd wꜣs s(nb)[1] nb ḫꜣ≠f nb mỉ Rꜥ (2) ḏd-mdw dỉ.n≠(ỉ) n≠k ḫpš≠ỉ pḥty≠ỉ (3) dỉ.n≠(ỉ) n≠k rnp.wt ꜥꜣ m ꜥnḫ ḏd wꜣs nb
Recitation by Amon-Re, King of the Gods, Lord of heaven. The protection of all life, stability, dominion, and health[1] is all around him like Re. (2) Recitation: "To you I have given my sword and my power." (3) "To you I have given many years in all life, stability, and dominion."

Label for the King (lines 5–8)
nb tꜣ.wy Sḫm-ḫpr-Rꜥ-stp-n-Rꜥ (6) nb ḫpš Wsrkn mrỉ-ʾImn dỉ ꜥnḫ ḏ.t (7) stp ʾImn (8) m-ḫnt ḥḥ.w sꜣ ꜥnḫ ḏd wꜣs nb snb nb ḫꜣ≠f nb mỉ Rꜥ
The Lord of the Two Lands, Sekhemkheperre-setepenre, (6) Lord of the strong arm, Osorkon, beloved of Amon, given life forever, (7) whom Amon chose (8) from among the millions. The protection of all life, stability, and dominion and all health is all around him like Re.

(2) Middle Register (= Epigraphic Survey 1954, Pl. 14; Key Plans K 349B)
Osorkon I given life by Khnum and suckled by Hathor.

Labels for the Vulture above the Scene (lines 8–9)
Wꜣḏy.t nb.t P ḥnw.t Dp P nb.(t) p.t ḥnw.t nṯr[.w] dỉ[≠s] ꜥnḫ ḏd wꜣs snb nb ꜣw.t-ỉb nb mỉ Rꜥ ḏ.t (9) Wꜣḏy.t nb.(t) p.t dỉ≠s ꜥnḫ wꜣs
Edjo, Lady of Pe, Mistress of Dep and Pe, Lady of heaven, Mistress of the god[s]. May [she] grant all life, stability, dominion, and health and all joy like Re forever. (9) Edjo, Lady of heaven. May she grant life and dominion.

Label for Khnum (lines 1–2)
ḏd-mdw ỉn Ḥnm nṯr ꜥꜣ qd nty.w […] (2) ḏd-mdw dỉ.n≠(ỉ) n≠k ꜥnḫ ḏd wꜣs nb ḫr≠ỉ snb nb ḫr≠ỉ

Recitation by Khnum, the great god, who fashioned those who [...] (2) Recitation: "To you I have given all life, stability, and dominion deriving from me and all health deriving from me."

Label for the King before Khnum (lines 6–7)

ntr nfr nb ỉr.(t) ḫt Sḥm-ḫpr-Rʿ-stp-n-Rʿ (7) sꜣ Rʿ n ḫt⸗f Wsrkn mrỉ-ʾImn

The Good God, Lord of ritual performance, Sekhemkheperre-setepenre, (7) bodily Son of Re, Osorkon, beloved of Amon.

Label for Hathor (lines 3–5)

ḏd-mdw ỉn Ḥw.t-Ḥr nb.(t) p.t (4) ḏd-mdw sꜣ n ḫt⸗ỉ (4) mr⸗ỉ Wsrkn mrỉ-ʾImn sḫpr.n⸗ỉ tw r ḥqꜣ ʿꜣ n Km.t r nb n šnw.n ỉtn

Recitation by Hathor, Lady of heaven. (4) Recitation: "O son of my body, (5) whom I love, Osorkon, beloved of Amon. I created you specifically to be the great ruler of Egypt, to be the lord of the circuit of the solar disk."

Label for the King before Hathor (unnumbered lines a–b)

ny-[sw.t] bỉ.ty nb tꜣ.wy Sḥm-ḫpr-Rʿ-stp-n-Rʿ (b) sꜣ Rʿ nb ḫʿ.w Wsrk[n] mrỉ-ʾImn

The King of [Upper] and Lower Egypt, Lord of the Two Lands, Sekhemkheperre-setepenre, (b) Son of Re, Lord of Diadems, Osork[on], beloved of Amon.

Between Two Addorsed Figures of King

sꜣ ʿnḫ ḏd wꜣs nb snb nb hꜣ⸗f nb mỉ Rʿ

The protection of all life, stability, and dominion and all health is all around him like Re.

(3) Bottom Register (= Epigraphic Survey 1954, Pl. 13; Key Plans K 349C)

Osorkon I crowned by Amon-Re and Mut.

Label for the Winged Disk above the Scene (line 7)

[Bḥd.t(y) nṯr ʿꜣ sꜣb šw nb p.t] nb Msn pr m ꜣḫt dỉ⸗f ʿnḫ ḏd wꜣs nb snb ꜣw.t-ỉb nb mỉ Rʿ ḏ.t

[The Behdetite, the great god with dappled plumage, Lord of heaven,] Lord of Mesen, who comes forth from the horizon. May he grant all life, stability, and dominion, all health and all joy like Re forever.

Below Disk (unnumbered lines a–b)

Bḥd.t(y) nb p.t (b) dỉ ʿnḫ

The Behdetite, Lord of heaven, who gives life.

Label for Amon (ll. 1–2)

[ḏd-mdw ỉn] ꜣImn-Rꜥ [...] (2) [smn.n²]≠ỉ ꜣtf n Rꜥ ḥr tp[≠k]

[Recitation by] Amon-Re, [...] (2) "[Thus] I [have affixed²] the *atef*-crown of Re atop [your] head."

Label for the King (lines 8–10)

ny-sw.t bỉ.ty nb tꜣ.wy Sḫm-ḫpr-Rꜥ-stp-n-Rꜥ (9) sꜣ Rꜥ nb ḫꜥ.w Wsrkn mrỉ-ꜣImn (10) dỉ ꜥnḫ mỉ Rꜥ

The King of Upper and Lower Egypt, Lord of the Two Lands, Sekhem-kheperre-setepenre, (9) Son of Re, Lord of Diadems, Osorkon, beloved of Amon, (10) given life like Re.

Label for Mut (lines 3–6)

ḏd-mdw ỉn Mw.t nb.t p.t (4) ḥnw.t nṯr.w ỉnk mw.t≠k qmꜣ nfr(.w)≠k r dỉ≠ỉ t[w] m nb wꜥ n ḥnmm.t ḫꜣs.wt nb.t ḥr tbty≠k mỉ Rꜥ ḏt (5) ḏd-mdw dỉ.n(≠ỉ) n≠k rnp.wt m ḥb.w-sd m ꜥnḫ ḏd wꜣs nb (6) dỉ≠ỉ mn ꜣtf n Rꜥ ḥr tp≠k mỉ wnn≠f ḥr tp n Rꜥ

Recitation by Mut, Lady of heaven, (4) Mistress of the gods: "I am your mother who created your beauty in order that I might place you as unique lord of humanity, with all foreign countries (being) under your sandals like Re forever. (5) Recitation: "Thus I have given to you years in jubilee and in all life, stability, and dominion. (6) Thus I have affixed the *atef*-crown atop your head as it is atop the head of Re."

(4) Base Label to All Three Scenes (= Epigraphic Survey 1954, Pl. 13, Lines 11–12 = K 349D)

[mry dỉ ꜥnḫ] ḏd wꜣs snb nb ꜣw-ỉb≠f [ḫ]ꜥ.wy m ny-sw.t bỉ.ty ḥr s.t Ḥr sšm ꜥnḫ.w nb.w [mỉ] Rꜥ ḏt (12) [wḥm] ḥb.w-[s]dꜣ ỉr n≠f ꜥꜣ wr.w⁴ ꜣw.t-ỉb≠f ḥnꜥ kꜣ≠f mỉ Rꜥ ḏt

[(Osorkon) beloved (of Amon-Re, Khnum, Hathor, and Mut, above), given] all [life,] stability, dominion, and health, joyfully appearing as the King of Upper and Lower Egypt upon the throne of Horus, who leads all the living [like] Re forever. (12) [Repeating] the jubilee³ so as to make for him very many,⁴ while he is joyful with his *ka*-spirit like Re forever.

NOTES

1. Taking the s below wꜣs as an abbreviation for snb. Or read as phonetic complement to wꜣs as elsewhere.

2. Or restore [ḏd-mdw dỉ.n]≠ỉ (Recitation: "Thus I have placed...").

3. Purely prospective wishes, as Osorkon celebrated no jubilees.

4. Or read ỉr≠(w) n≠f ꜥꜣ wr.w "may there be made for him many more"; cf. Kitchen 1986, 302 n. 322, 305 n. 344.

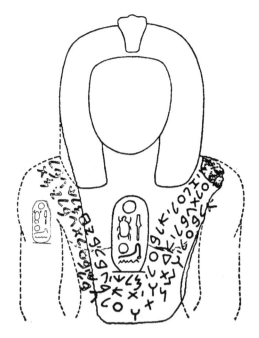

Drawing after Hermann 1958, 18.

57. BYBLOS STATUE
(S. LOUVRE AO. 9502)

Following the diplomatic precedent of his father, Osorkon I dedicated a statue of himself to the great temple of Byblos. Recovered from the temple esplanade, preserved elements of the seated (?) statue of the king include the torso, base, upper arm, and additional small fragments in reddish Mokattam sandstone.[1] The height of the surviving bust measures 60 cm. In 1882,[2] the torso, base, and a (now-lost) fragment of the belt were in the Meuricoffre collection in Naples. In 1910, the torso and base were sold by Canessa to the Peytel collection in Paris, and the bust was acquired by the Louvre in 1925. Further fragments were excavated at the Byblos temple by Montet and Dunand. The texts include pharaonic titulary and a secondary Phoenician dedication by Elibaal, king of Byblos.

For the texts and photos, see Wiedemann 1895, 14 §14; 1912, 14 §X.B; Lair-Dubreuil and Sambon 1910, 3 and pl. 1 (no. 3); Dussaud 1925, 101–17 and pl. XXV; Montet 1928, 49–54 §30 and pls. XXXVI–XXXVIII; and Dunand 1939, 17–18, no. 1048, and fig. 7; with further citations in Porter and Moss 1927–51, 7:388. See also Stierlin and Ziegler 1987, 201; Association française d'action artistique 1987, 166–67 (no. 43); and Kitchen 1986, 308–9 §267.

Further explications of the Phoenician text are found in Albright 1947, 153 and 158 §IV; Hermann 1958, 17–18 and 32 §4; Donner and Röllig 1962–64 1:1 no. 6; 2:8 no. 6; and Gibson 1971–82, 3:21–22 and pl. II, no. 1.

ROYAL TITLES (TORSO)
    Sḫm-ḫpr-Rˁ-stp-n-Rˁ   Sekhemkheperre-setepenre.

ROYAL TITLES (RIGHT ARM)
    See Dunand 1939, 1:18, fig. 7.
    Sḫm-ḫpr-Rˁ-stp-n-Rˁ   Sekhemkheperre-setepenre.

ROYAL TITLES (BASE)
    ny-sw.t bỉ.ty nb tȝ.wy Sḫm-ḫpr-Rˁ-stp-n-Rˁ dỉ ˁnḫ
    The King of Upper and Lower Egypt, Lord of the Two Lands, Sekhem-kheperre-setepenre, given life.

ROYAL TITLES (BACK PILLAR)
    ˁnḫ Ḥr kȝ nḫt mrỉ-Rˁ
    Long live the Horus: "Strong bull, beloved of Re."

Royal Titles (Belt)
    Wsỉ[rkn] mrỉ-ʾImn   Oso[rkon], beloved of Amon.

Royal Titles (Kilt; see Montet 1928, 49–50 no. 26)
    W[sỉrkn] mrỉ-ʾImn   O[sorkon], beloved of Amon.

Royal Titles (Backrest of Throne?; see Montet 1928, 49–50 no. 27)
    sȝ Rˁ   Son of Re.

Royal Titles (Unplaced Fragment; see Montet 1928, 49–51 no. 28)
    [nb ḫˁ].w [Wsrkn mrỉ-ʾI]mn
    [Lord of Diadem]s, [Osorkon, beloved of A]mon.

Phoenician Text (on Torso around Cartouche)
    mš. z pˁl. ʾlbˁl. mlk. gbl. b yḥ[mlk. mlk. gbl.] (2) [l b]ˁlt. gbl. ʾdtw. tʾrk. bˁlt[. gbl.] (3) [ymt. ʾ]lbˁl. wšntw. ˁl [gbl]
    Statue that Elibaal, King of Byblos, son of Yehi[milk, King of Byblos,] made (2) [for B]aalat-Gebal ("Lady of Byblos"), his mistress. May Baalat [-Gebal] lengthen (3) [the days of E]libaal and his (regnal) years over [Byblos]!

58. EL-HIBEH TEMPLE RELIEFS

In the reign of Osorkon I, five relief scenes were added to the east facade of the back wall of the el-Hibeh temple to complete the decoration begun by Sheshonq I. Surveyed by Kamal in 1901, the site was excavated by Hermann Ranke from 1913 to 1914; see Porter and Moss 1927–51, 4:124. For the scenes and texts, see Kamal 1901, 87–89. For the site, see Ranke 1926, 58–68 and pls. 19–24. Cited without discussion in Kitchen 1986, 304 §263. Relief IV preserves traces of a unique variant of Osorkon's royal protocol. First translation.

I. On the left, the king holding a scepter and flower consecrates a pile of offerings to a standing, ibis-headed Thoth wearing a lunar disk and crescent and carrying *was*-scepter and ankh.

Label for Thoth

[Ḏḥwty …] ḫnty Ḥsr.t (2) […] Wsrkn dỉ.n⸗(ỉ) (3) [n⸗k … Mȝ⸗].t (4) […] mỉ Rꜥ rꜥ nb

[Thoth …], Foremost of the Hermopolite necropolis, (2) […] Osorkon. "Thus I have given (3) [to you …] Maat (4) […] like Re, every day."

Label for King

[…]⸗sn ḥw.wt (2) […] nȝ ḥm.w-nṯr (3) […]⸗s[n] smn smȝ (4) […].w m ḥw.t (5) […] n Rꜥ (6) [… Sḫm-ḫpr-Rꜥ]-stp-n-Rꜥ (7) [… Wsrkn mrỉ-ʾImn] (8) [nṯr(?)] nfr

[…] their mansions (2) […] the prophets (3) […] their […], established and united (4) […] in the mansion (5) […] of Re. (6) [… Sekhemkheperre]-setepenre, (7) [… Osorkon, beloved of Amon], (8) the Good [God (?)].

II. On the left, the king wearing an *atef*-crown presents two vases to an enthroned, ram-headed Khnum wearing a disk and uraeus.

Label for Khnum

[…] sȝ⸗f mr⸗f (2) […] ḥtp(?) (3) […] mrỉ-ʾImn (4) […] (5) […] (6) […] nb.w

[…] his son, whom he loves, (2) […] offering (?) (3) […] beloved of Amon, (4) […] (5) […] (6) all […].

Label for King

[… nb tȝ].wy Sḫm-ḫpr-Rꜥ-stp-n-Rꜥ (2) sȝ Rꜥ [nb ḫꜥ.w] Wsrkn mrỉ-ʾImn (3) […] (4) dỉ ꜥnḫ ḏd mỉ Rꜥ rꜥ nb (5) sȝ n ꜥnḫ nb snb nb ȝw.t-[ỉb nb.t ḫȝ⸗f …]

[... Lord of the Two] Lands, Sekhemkheperre-setepenre, (2) Son of Re, [Lord of Diadems,] Osorkon, beloved of Amon, (3) [...], (4) given life and stability like Re every day. (5) The protection of all life, all health, and [all] joy [is behind him ...].

III. On the left, the king in blue crown extends three censers in his right hand and three libation jars in his left before a standing, hawk-headed Khonsu-in-Thebes Neferhotep wearing a disk and carrying a scepter and ankh.

Label for Khonsu
[Ḫn]sw m W3s.t Nfr-ḥtp (2) [dd-mdw(?)] rdỉ.(3) n≠(ỉ) n≠k ḥb[.w]-sd (4) [...] n nṯr.w (5) nb ḥp (6) [...] r Nỉw.t (7) dỉ.n≠(ỉ) n≠k t3 nb sḫ.t [nb.t]
[Kh]onsu in Thebes, Neferhotep. (2) [Recitation (?):] "Thus I have given (3) to you jubilees (4) [...] of the gods, (5) lord of law (6) [...] to Thebes ('The City'). (7) Thus I have given to you every land and [every] field."

Label for King
ny-sw.t [bỉ.ty(?)] ꜥnḫ nṯr nfr ṯ[...] (2) psḏ.t nb (3) [...] (4) [s3 n ...] snb [... ḥ3≠f ...]
The King of Upper [and Lower Egypt (?)]. Long live the Good God, [...] (2) Ennead, Lord (3) [of ...]. (4) [The protection of ...] and health [... is behind him...].

Label for Scene
ỉr.t snṯr mw qbḥw n ỉt≠f rnp.wt(?)3[...]
Making incense and cool water for his father and fresh plants (?)[...].

IV. On the left, the king offers vases to Mut in a double crown, carrying a papyrus scepter.

Label for Mut
[dỉ.n≠(ỉ) n≠k] ḥtp(.w) nb ḏf[3.w nb] ḫr≠ỉ (2) [Mw.t w]r(?) nb(.t) ꞽŠrw ỉr.t nṯr.w nb (3) [...]
["Thus I have given to you all offerings and [all] food[stuffs] deriving from me." (2) [Mut, the gre]at(?), the Lady of Asheru, eye of all the gods (3) [...].

Label for King
[...] nb≠s t3[.wy4 ...]s[...] mỉ w3ḏ5 Rꜥ (2) [Ḥr k3] nḫt [mrỉ]-Rꜥ [...] M3ꜥ.t6 (3) [ny-sw.t bỉ.ty] nb t3.wy Sḫm-ḫpr-Rꜥ-stp-n-Rꜥ (4) [...] s3 Rꜥ nb ḫꜥ.w [Wsrkn] mrỉ-ꞽImn (5) [dỉ ꜥnḫ ...] (6) stp-s3≠f mrỉ ỉt≠f nb t3.wy mr Rꜥ [...]
[...] its lord, the Two [Lands (?)4...]...[...] as Re flourishes5; (2) [Horus:] "Strong [bull, beloved of] Re, [...] Maat;6 (3) [the King of Upper and Lower

Egypt], Lord of the Two Lands, Sekhemkheperre-setepenre, (4) [...] Son of
Re, Lord of Diadems, [Osorkon], beloved of Amon, (5) [given life ...] (6) protected, beloved of his father, Lord of the Two Lands, beloved of Re [...].

V. On the right, the king offers Maat to an enthroned Amon-Re before a
table of offerings.

Label for Amon
     (1–3) [...] (4) [...] ḏr [...] (5) [...] s.t Tm (6) [...nf]r n ỉb n nṯr.w ḥr
ỉr.(t).n⸗f nb
     (1–3) [...] (4) [...] since [...] (5) [...] the throne of Atum (6) [...goo]d
in the hearts of the gods because of all that he has done.

Label for King
     [ny-sw.t bỉ.ty(?)] nb t3.wy [Sḫm-ḫpr]-Rᶜ-stp-n-Rᶜ (2) [s3 Rᶜ] nb ḫᶜ.w
[Wsrkn mrỉ-ʾImn] (3) [dỉ ᶜnḫ ...]
     [The King of Upper and Lower Egypt (?),] Lord of the Two Lands,
[Sekhemkheper]re-setepenre, (2) [Son of Re,] Lord of Diadems, [Osorkon,
beloved of Amon,] (3) [given life ...].

Label for Scene
     [...] ḥnq M3ᶜ.t n nb M3ᶜ.t
     [...] Offering Maat to the Lord of Maat.

NOTES
     1. See Montet 1928, 53. Wrongly stated to be red granite in Donner and Röllig
1962–64, 2:8; following Dunand 1939 1:18.
     2. See Wiedemann 1912, 14; versus Montet 1928, 51, who records 1881.
     3. For possible readings, see Daumas 1988, 400.
     4. Or read Šmᶜ "Upper Egypt."
     5. Or read w3ḏ for wḏ as often: "according to Re's command."
     6. Or copying error by Kamal for determinative of seated Re?

59. BUBASTIS TEMPLE INSCRIPTIONS: BASTET TEMPLE

Bubastis (Tell Basta near the modern city of Zagazig) is the reputed
family seat of Dynasty XXII in the accounts of the historian Manetho, and
the city witnessed significant construction during the early reigns of the
dynasty. While Sheshonq I is attested locally by but a single block (see
above, no. 42), Osorkon I added a monumental granite gateway and
hypostyle hall to the central temple of Bastet and erected a smaller temple
of Atum later described by Herodotus as a shrine of Hermes (Herodotus
2.138). Osorkon II would choose the great temple of Bastet to record his

jubilee in his twenty-second year; see below, no. 78. See Kitchen 1986, 303–4 §262.

This is the first translation. For the texts, see Naville 1891, 47 and pls. XVIII (= XXXIX.M) and XXXIX–XL. Unless otherwise noted, references to the plates below are to Naville 1891. Reconstruction in Van Siclen 1985, 36 fig. 5, to which add Louvre E 10591 (= B 55) in Association française d'action artistique 1987, 168–69 no. 44. For University of Pennsylvania E 224 [= Naville 1891, pl. XL.B], see Myśliwiec 1988, 15, 114, and pl. XXa. For discussion, see Van Siclen 1985, 35; Habachi 1957, 55–56; and Kitchen 1986, 304 §262. For scenes added by Osorkon II below the central winged disk, see below, pp. 339–40.

I. GRANITE GATEWAY TO TEMPLE ENCLOSURE

A. Bottom Left, Register x + 1: King offers incense and water to Bastet and Horhekenu (pl. XXXIX.O, P, Q, R)

Label for King
    ny-sw.t bỉ.ty nb tȝ.wy (2) Sḫm-ḫpr-Rꜥ-stp-n-Rꜥ (3) Wsỉrkn mrỉ-ʾImn (4) dỉ ꜥnḫ ḏd wȝs ȝw.t-ỉb mỉ Rꜥ ḏ.t (5) sȝ [ꜥnḫ hȝ≠f mỉ Rꜥ] (6) ỉr(.t) snṯr n mw.t≠f Bȝst.t
    King of Upper and Lower Egypt, Lord of the Two Lands, (2) Sekhem-kheperre-setepenre, (3) Osorkon, beloved of Amon, (4) given life, stability, dominion, and joy like Re forever. (5) The protection [of life is behind him like Re]. (6) Making incense for his mother Bastet.

Label for Bastet
    ḏd-mdw ỉn Bȝst.t ꜥȝ(.t) nb(.t) Bȝs.t (2) dỉ.n≠(ỉ)
    n≠k ꜥnḫ ḏd wȝs nb (3) dỉ.n≠(ỉ) n≠k ḥb.w-sd n Rꜥ rnp.wt[1] n.t Tm
    Recitation by Bastet the great, Lady of Bubastis: (2) "Thus I have given to you all life, stability, and dominion. (3) Thus I have given to you the jubilees of Re, the years[1] of Atum."

Label for Horhekenu
    ḏd-mdw ỉn Ḥr-(2)ḥknw nb mk (3) dỉ.n≠(ỉ) n≠k ḫȝs.t nb ḫr tb.ty≠k (4) dỉ.n≠(ỉ) n≠k [...] mỉ Rꜥ ny-sw.t tȝ[.wy]
    Recitation by Hor(2)hekenu, Lord of protection: (3) "Thus I have given to you every foreign land under your sandals. (4) Thus I have given to you [...] like Re, King of the Two [Lands."]

B. Left, Register x + 2: King offers unguent to Bastet and Montu (pl. XXXIX. M, N, O)

Label for King

ny-sw.t bỉ.ty nb tꜣ.w nb (2) Sḫm-ḫpr-Rʿ-stp-n-Rʿ (3) Wsỉrkn mrỉ-ʾImn (4) dỉ ʿnḫ ḏd wꜣs snb mỉ Rʿ ḏ.t (5) sꜣ [ʿnḫ] ḥꜣ=f mỉ Rʿ (6) rdỉ.t[2] [mrḥ.t n mw.t=f] Bꜣst.t nb(.t) Bꜣs.t ỉr=s[3] dỉ ʿnḫ mỉ Rʿ ḏ.t

King of Upper and Lower Egypt, Lord of all lands, (2) Sekhemkheperre-setepenre, (3) Osorkon, beloved of Amon, (4) given life, stability, dominion, and health like Re forever. (5) The protection [of life] is behind him like Re. (6) Giving[2] [unguent to his mother] Bastet, Lady of Bubastis, so that she[3] might make the gift of living like Re forever.

Label for Bastet

ḏd-mdw ỉn Bꜣst.t nb(.t) Bꜣs.t (2) dỉ.n=(ỉ) n=k hrw.w(?) n ỉr=k (3) dỉ.n=(ỉ) n=k ḥb.w-sd ʿšꜣ wr(.t) mỉ Rʿ (4) dỉ.n=(ỉ)
n=k ʿnḫ wꜣs nb (5) dỉ.n=(ỉ) n=k tꜣ nb m ḥtp

Recitation by Bastet, Lady of Bubastis: (2) "Thus I have given to you the days (?) of your passing. (3) Thus I have given to you very many jubilees like Re. (4) Thus I have given to you all life and dominion. (5) Thus I have given to you every land in peace."

Label for Montu

ḏd-mdw ỉn Mnṯw (2) ḥr(y)-ỉb (3) [Bꜣ]s.t [...] nb p.t (4) dỉ.n=(ỉ) n=k qn(ỉ) nḫt nb

Recitation by Montu, (2) resident in (3) [Buba]stis, [...] Lord of heaven: (4) "Thus I have given to you all valor and victory."

C. Left, Register x + 3: King offers the Eye of Horus to Bastet and Mahes (pl. XXXIX.J, K, L, M, N)

Label for King

ny-sw.t bỉ.ty nb ỉr.(t) ḫ.t (2) Sḫm-ḫpr-Rʿ-stp[-n-Rʿ] (3) [Wsỉrkn mrỉ-ʾImn] (4) [dỉ ʿnḫ ...] (5) [sꜣ] ʿnḫ wꜣs nb snb nb mỉ Rʿ ḏ.t (6) rdỉ.t[2] wḏꜣ.t n mw.t=f Bꜣst.t nb(.t) Bꜣs.t [ỉr=s] dỉ ʿnḫ

King of Upper and Lower Egypt, Lord of ritual performance, (2) Sekhemkheperre-setepenre, (3) [Osorkon, beloved of Amon,] (4) [given life, ...] (5) [The protection of] all life, dominion, and all health like Re forever. (6) Giving[2] the Eye of Horus to his mother Bastet, Lady of Bubastis, [so that she might attain] the state of being given life.

Label for Bastet

ḏd-mdw ỉn Bꜣst.t (2) nb(.t) Bꜣs.t ỉr.t Rʿ (3)
dỉ.n=(ỉ) n=k nḥḥ m [...] ḥqꜣ ꜣw.t-ỉb

Recitation by Bastet, (2) Lady of Bubastis, the eye of Re: (3) "Thus I have given to you an eternity as [...] ruler of joy."

Label for Mahes
M3ỉ-ḥs (2) dỉ.n≠(ỉ) n≠k ꜥnḫ w3s
Mahes: (2) "Thus I have given to you life and dominion."

D. Left, Register x + 4: King offers the Eye of Horus to Re and goddess
(pl. XXXIX.H, J)

Label for King
[ny-sw].t [bỉ.t]y nb ỉr.(t) ḫ.t (2) Sḫm-ḫpr-Rꜥ-stp-n-Rꜥ (3) W[s]ỉrkn [mrỉ]-
ꜣImn] (4) dỉ ꜥnḫ [...] (5) ḥnq wd3.t n ỉt≠f ỉr≠f dỉ ꜥnḫ mỉ Rꜥ d̠.t
[King of Upper and Lower] Egypt, Lord of ritual performance, (2)
Sekhemkheperre-setepenre, (3) O[s]orkon, [beloved of] Amon, (4) given
life [...] (5) Offering the Eye of Horus to his father so that he might attain
the state of being given life like Re forever.

Label for Re
d̠d-mdw ỉn Rꜥ nt̠r ꜥ3
Recitation by Re, the great god.

Label for Goddess
[...] ỉr.t ỉt≠k
[...] which your father made.

E. Left, Register x + 5: King before lost deities
[Sḫm-ḫpr-Rꜥ]-stp-n-Rꜥ (2) [Ws]ỉrkn [mrỉ-ꜣImn] (3) [dỉ] ꜥnḫ
Sekhemkheperre]-setepenre, (2) [Os]orkon, [beloved of Amon,] (3)
[given] life.

F. Bottom Right, Register x + 1: King offers Eye of Horus to Mut and Hathor
(pl. XL.R, S)

Label for King
[...] dỉ.t wd3.t (n) Mw.t B3s.t [...]
[...] Giving the Eye of Horus (to) Mut of Bubastis [...]

Label for Hathor
[d̠d-mdw ỉn] Ḥw.t-Ḥr nb(.t) Tp-ỉḥ.w
[Recitation by] Hathor, Lady of Aphroditopolis.

G. Right, Register x + 2: King (lost) before Bastet (pl. XL.G)

Label for Bastet
d̠d-mdw ỉn B3st.t ꜥ3(.t) nb(.t) B3s.t (2) ỉr.t Rꜥ nb(.t) p.t ḥnw.t nt̠r.w (3)

dỉ.n꞊(ỉ) n꞊k ꜥnḫ ḏd wꜣs nb […] (4) dỉ.n꞊(ỉ) n꞊k tꜣ nb m ḥtp (5) dỉ.n꞊(ỉ) n꞊k qn(ỉ) nḫt [nb]

Recitation by Bastet the great, Lady of Bubastis, (2) the eye of Re, Lady of heaven, Mistress of the gods: (3) "Thus I have given to you all life, stability, and dominion […]. (4) Thus I have given to you every land in peace. (5) Thus I have given to you [all] valor and victory."

H. Right, Register x + 3: King offers Eye of Horus to Bastet (XL.E)

Label for Winged Disk
Bḥd.ty   The Behdedite.

Label for King
ny-sw.t bỉ.ty nb tꜣ.wy (2) Sḫm-ḫpr-Rꜥ-stp-n-Rꜥ (3) Wsỉrkn mrỉ-ʾImn (4) dỉ ꜥnḫ

King of Upper and Lower Egypt, Lord of the Two Lands, (2) Sekhem-kheperre-setepenre, (3) Osorkon, beloved of Amon, (4) given life.

Label for Bastet
Bꜣst.t ỉr.t Ḥr (2) dỉ.n(꞊ỉ) n꞊k ꜥnḫ ḏd wꜣs (3) dỉ.n꞊(ỉ) n꞊k snb nb

Bastet, the Eye of Horus. (2) "Thus I have given to you life, stability, and dominion. (3) Thus I have given to you all health."

I. Right, Register x + 4: King offers Maat to Amon-Re and Mut (pl. XL.D, E + Louvre 10591 = B 55)

Label for King
ny-sw.t bỉ.ty nb tꜣ.wy (2) Sḫm-ḫpr-Rꜥ-stp-n-Rꜥ (3) Wsỉrkn mrỉ-ʾImn (4) dỉ ꜥnḫ (5) ḥnq Mꜣꜥ.t (n) ỉt꞊f ỉr꞊f dỉ ꜥnḫ mỉ [Rꜥ] ḏ.t

King of Upper and Lower Egypt, Lord of the Two Lands, (2) Sekhem-kheperre-setepenre, (3) Osorkon, beloved of Amon, (4) given life. (5) Offering Maat (to) his father so that he might attain the state of being given life like [Re] forever.

Label for Amon-Re
ḏd-mdw ỉn ʾImn-Rꜥ (2) [ny-sw.t nṯr].w nb p.t ḥr(y)-ỉb Bꜣs.t (3) [dỉ. n꞊(ỉ) n]꞊k [..] m[….] (4) dỉ.n꞊(ỉ) n꞊k qn(ỉ) nḫt

Recitation by Amon-Re, (2) [King of the God]s, Lord of heaven, resident in Bubastis. (3) ["Thus I have given to] you […] in (?) [..] (4) Thus I have given to you valor and victory.

Label for Mut
  ḏdd-mdw în Mw.t nb(.t) [p.t] (2) dî.n≠(î) n≠k sḫ.wt(?) [..]
  Recitation by Mut, Lady [of heaven] (2) "Thus I have given to you fields (?) […]."

J. Right, Register x + 4 (adjoining inner face at right angle): King before Mut (pl. XL.D)

Label for King
  nṯr nfr nb t3.wy nb ḫpš (2) Sḫm-ḫpr-Rᶜ-stp-n-Rᶜ (3) W[s]î[rkn mrî-] ʾI[mn]
  The Good God, Lord of the Two Lands, Lord of the strong arm, (2) Sekhemkheperre-setepenre, (3) O[s]o[rkon, beloved of] A[mon.]

Label for Mut
  ḏd-mdw în Mw.t ḥnw.t nṯr.w (2) dî.n≠(î) n≠k ᶜnḫ w3s nb 3w.t-[îb …]
  Recitation by Mut, Mistress of the gods: (2) "Thus I have given to you all life and dominion and joy […]."

K. Right, Register x + 5: King (lost) offers to Nefertum (pl. XXXIX.C)

Label for Nefertum
  ḏd-mdw în] Nfr-tm s3 Sḫm.t (2) [… nb] p.t
  [Recitation by] Nefertum, son of Sakhmet (2) [… Lord] of heaven.

L. Right, Register x + 5: King (lost) before Bastet and Sopdu (pl. XL.N)

Label for Bastet
  ḏd-mdw în B3st.t ᶜ3(.t) nb(.t) [B3s.t]
  Recitation by Bastet the great, Lady of Bubastis.

Label for Sopdu
  Spd nb (2) î3bt.t (3) dî.n≠(î) n≠k ptr≠k […]
  Sopdu, Lord (2) of the East: (3) "Thus I have granted to you that you see […]"

M. Unplaced Scene: King offers incense and offerings to Bastet (pl. XXXIX. A)

Label for Bastet
  [ḏd-mdw în] B3st.t ḥry(.t)-sšt3 (2) [n Tm nb(.t) p.t ḥn]w.t t3.wy⁴ (3) [dî. n≠(î) n≠k ḥb.w-sd⁵] ᶜš3.t

[Recitation by] Bastet, who is over the secrets (2) [of Atum, Lady of heaven, Mist]ress of the Two Lands.⁴ (3) "Thus I have given to you numerous [jubilees."]⁵

N. Unplaced Scene: King before male deity (pl. XXXIX.D)

Statement of deity
    [dỉ.n≠(ỉ)] n≠k ḫpš n qn(ỉ) nḫt t3.w ḫ3s.t ḥr tb.ty≠k (2) dỉ≠ỉ mn rn≠k ḥr ỉr.n≠k m ḫnw pr≠ỉ n […]
    ["Thus I have given] to you the scimitar of valor and victory and all foreign lands beneath your sandals (2) so that I might establish your name concerning what you have done within my house of […]."

O. Unplaced Scenes: Two Registers

Above: King before Thoth (?) with palm branch (pl. XXXIX.E)

Statement of deity
    [dỉ.n≠(ỉ) n≠k] ꜥnḫ dd w3s nb n d.t
    ["Thus I have given to you] all life, stability and dominion forever."

Below: King before Nefertum

Label for King
    ntr nfr nb t3.wy nb ỉr.(t) ḫ.t (2) Sḫm-ḫpr-Rꜥ-stp-n-Rꜥ (3) [Wsỉrkn mrỉ-]ʾI[mn]
    The Good God, Lord of the Two Lands, Lord of ritual performance, (2) Sekhemkheperre-setepenre, (3) [Osorkon, beloved of] A[mon.]

Label for Nefertum
    dd-mdw ỉn Nfr-tm
    Recitation by Nefertum.

P. Unplaced Scene: Behind the king, Thoth records years on a palm branch (pl. XXXIX.F)

Label for Thoth
    mr≠ỉ
    My beloved.

Label behind King
    ꜥnḫ h3≠f [mỉ] Rꜥ
    [The protection of] life is behind him [like] Re.

THE LIBYAN ANARCHY

Q. Unplaced Scene: Shrine beside royal cartouche (pl. XXXIX.G)
    nb t3.wy Sḫm-[ḫpr]-Rꜥ-[stp-n-Rꜥ]
    Lord of the Two Lands, Sekhem[kheper]re-[setepenre.]

R. Unplaced Scene: King (lost) before Mut (pl. XXXIX.I)

Label for Mut
    ḏd-mdw în Mw.t wr.t nb(.t) ꜣIšrw (2) [dî].n⸗(î) [n⸗]k [t3(?)] nb m [ḥt]p(?)
    Recitation by Mut, the great, Lady of Asheru: (2) "Thus I have [given to] you every [land (?)] in [pea]ce(?)."

S. Three Adjacent Unplaced Scenes

(1) King (lost) before Amon-Re, Re-Horachty, and Ptah (pl. XL.A)

Label for Amon-Re
    ḏd-mdw în ꜣImn-Rꜥ nb ns.wt t3.wy ḫnty (2) ꜣIp.t-s.wt
    Recitation by Amon-Re, Lord of the Thrones of the Two Lands, Foremost of (2) Karnak.

Label for Re-Horachty
    Rꜥ-Ḥr-3ḫ.ty ḥr(y)-îb B3s.t (2) dî.n⸗(î) n⸗k ny.t-sw.t ꜥ3.t n qn(î) nḫt
    Re-Horachty, resident in Bubastis: (2) "Thus I have given to you a great kingship in valor and victory."

Label for Ptah
    ḏd-mdw în Ptḥ ꜥ3 rsy înb(2)⸗f nb ꜥnḫ-t3.wy ḥr(y)-îb B3s.t (3) dî.n⸗(î) n⸗k ḥb.w-sd ꜥš3
    Recitation by Ptah the great, south of his wall (2), Lord of Ankh-Tawy, resident in Bubastis: (3) "Thus I have given to you numerous jubilees."

(2) King offers before Atum and Shu (pl. XL.A, B [= University of Pennsylvania E. 224], C?)

Label for King
    ny-sw.t bî.ty nb t3.wy [Sḫm]-ḫpr-Rꜥ-stp-n-Rꜥ (2) s3 Rꜥ Wsîrkn mrî-ꜣImn (3) dî ꜥnḫ mî Rꜥ ḏ.t (4) [...] n ît⸗f ꜣImn[6] îr n⸗f dî ꜥnḫ
    King of Upper and Lower Egypt, Lord of the Two Lands, [Sekhem]kheperre-setepenre, (2) son of Re, Osorkon, beloved of Amon, (3) given life like Re forever. (4) [...] for his father Amon,[6] who made for him the state of being given life.

Label for Atum
    ḏd-mdw ỉn Tm nb ʾIwnw (2) nṯr ꜥꜣ nb p.t ḥr(y)-ỉb Bꜣs.t (3) [...] (4) dỉ.n≠(ỉ) n≠k ꜥnḫ ḏd wꜣs nb mỉ Rꜥ
    Recitation by Atum, Lord of Heliopolis, (2) great god, Lord of heaven, resident in Bubastis: (3) [...] (4) "Thus I have given to you all life, stability, and dominion like Re."

Label for Shu
    ḏd-mdw ỉn Šw sꜣ Rꜥ nṯr ꜥꜣ (2) ḥr(y)-ỉb Bꜣs.t (3) dỉ.n≠(ỉ) n≠k ny.t-sw.t ꜥꜣ.t m ꜣw.t-ỉb
    Recitation by Shu, son of Re, great god, (2) resident in Bubastis: (3) "Thus I have given to you a great kingship in joy."

(3) Lower Register: Titles of king before Ptah and goddess

Label for King
    Sḫm-ḫpr-Rꜥ-[stp-n-Rꜥ] (2) [Wsỉrkn mrỉ-ʾImn
    Sekhemkheperre-[setepenre], (2) [Osorkon, beloved of] Amon.

Label for Ptah
    ḏd-mdw ỉn (2) Ptḥ
    Recitation by (2) Ptah.

Label for Goddess
    ḏd-mdw ỉn [...] ḥnw.t nṯr.w
    Recitation by [...], Mistress of the gods.

T. Unplaced Scenes

(1) King (lost) before Khonsu (pl. XL.H)

Label for Khonsu
    [... dỉ.n≠(ỉ) n≠k tꜣ nb] m ḥtp ḫꜣs.t nb(.t) ḫr tb.ty≠k [...]
    [... "Thus I have given to you every land] in peace, every foreign land beneath your sandals [...]."

(2) King offers unguent before Edjo and lost deity

Label for King
    nb tꜣ.wy Sḫm-ḫpr-Rꜥ-stp-n-Rꜥ (2) nb ḫꜥ[.w] Wsỉrkn mrỉ-ʾImn (3) [dỉ ꜥnḫ] mỉ Rꜥ ḏ.t (4) sꜣ ꜥnḫ wꜣs [ḫꜣ≠f ...]
    Lord of the Two Lands, Sekhemkheperre-setepenre, (2) Lord of

Diadem[s], Osorkon, beloved of Amon, (3) [given life] like Re forever. (4) The protection of life and dominion [is behind him ...]

Label for Edjo
  dỉ⸗s ꜥnḫ wꜣs
  May she give life and dominion.

Label for Deity
  dỉ.n⸗(ỉ) n⸗k rnp.wt ꜥšꜣ mỉ Rꜥ
  "Thus I have given to you numerous years like Re."

U. Unplaced Scene: King offers incense and water before Nephthys (pl. XL.I, K)

Label for King
  [...] nb ỉr.(t) ḫ.t (2) [...] Sḫm-ḫpr-Rꜥ-stp-n-Rꜥ (3) [...] Wsỉrkn [mrỉ-ʾImn] (4) [dỉ ꜥnḫ] ḏd wꜣs [mỉ Rꜥ ḏ.t] (5) sꜣ ḥꜣ[⸗f ...] (6) ỉr.t snṯr [n ... ỉr⸗f] (7) dỉ ꜥnḫ [...]
  [...] Lord of ritual performance, (2) Sekhemkheperre-setepenre, (3) [...] Osorkon, [beloved of Amon,] (4) [given life,] stability, and dominion [like Re forever.] (5) Protection is behind [him ...] (6) Making incense [for ... so that he might attain] (7) the state of being given life [...].

Label for Nephthys
  [ḏd]-mdw ỉn Nb(.t)-ḥw.t nb(.t) p.t (2) dỉ.n⸗(ỉ) n⸗k qn(ỉ) nḫt
  [Recitation] by Nephthys, Lady of heaven: (2) "Thus I have given to you valor and victory."

V. Unplaced Scenes

(1) King offers to deities (lost) (pl. XL.O)
  [... sꜣ ꜥnḫ ḥꜣ⸗f] mỉ [Rꜥ] (2) [...] ỉr⸗f dỉ ꜥnḫ mỉ Rꜥ
  [... The protection of life is behind him] like [Re.] (2) [...] so that he might attain the state of being given life like Re.

(2) Lower register: King before deity

Label for King
  ny-sw.t bỉ.ty nb tꜣ.wy (2) Sḫm-ḫpr-Rꜥ-stp-n-Rꜥ (3) Wsỉrkn mrỉ-ʾImn (4) dỉ ꜥnḫ ḏd wꜣs snb nb mỉ Rꜥ
  King of Upper and Lower Egypt, Lord of the Two Lands, (2) Sekhemkheperre-setepenre, (3) Osorkon, beloved of Amon, (4) given life, stability, dominion, and all health like Re.

Label for deity

dỉ.n⸗(ỉ) n⸗k ꜥnḫ ḏd [wꜣs ...] (2) dỉ.n⸗(ỉ) n⸗k [...]

"Thus I have given to you life, stability, and [dominion ...] (2) Thus I have given to you [...]."

W. Unplaced Scene: King offers to deities (lost) (pl. XL.P)

Label for Winged Disk

Bḥd.ty [dỉ] ꜥnḫ

The Behdedite [who gives] life.

Label for King

[sꜣ] ꜥnḫ wꜣs ḥꜣ⸗f mỉ Rꜥ

[The protection] of life and dominion is behind him like Re.

X. Unplaced Scene: Montu (pl. XL.Q)

Label for Montu

[ḏd-mdw ỉn Mntw nṯr] (2) ꜥꜣ ḥr(y)-ỉb Bꜣs.t

[Recitation by Montu], (2) great [god] resident in Bubastis.

II. HYPOSTYLE HALL COLUMNS.

Perhaps of Middle Kingdom date, reworked and reinscribed in Ramesside and Libyan periods. See Naville 1891, 10–12, 48–49, and pls. V–VII, IX, XXIII–XXIV, and XLI.A–C; Roeder 1924, 2:228 (10834); Boreux 1932, 1:59–61; Porter and Moss 1927–51, 4:29; Habachi 1957, 61–67, pls. XVIII–XX. Suggested to be the original work of Osorkon I in Van Siclen 1994, 324 n. 23, the columns are variously ascribed to a local temple of Middle Kingdom date in Arnold 1996, 1:39–54, and to post–Dynasty XIX in Haynes 1996, 1:399–408. Four large Hathor capitals (above 7 feet high) in Boston (Museum of Fine Arts 89.555; Oriental Institute photos 37294–95), Louvre, British Museum (1107), Berlin (10834). Fifth example in Sydney recut under Osorkon II, whose cartouches are added to the side of all examples.

Top, Example in Berlin (Roeder 1924, 2:228, Side A = Naville 1891, pl. XLI. B, misidentified as a capital underside on 48 and 66)

(1) [...] Sḥm-ḫpr-Rꜥ-stp-n-Rꜥ (2) [W]s[ỉ]rkn mrỉ-[ʾIm]n (3) dỉ ꜥnḫ mỉ Rꜥ ḏ.t (4) mry [...] nṯr.t nb(.t) p.t ḥnw.t nṯr.w

Sekhemkheperre-setepenre, (2) [O]s[o]rkon, beloved of [Am]on, (3) given life like Re forever, (4) beloved of [...] the goddess, the Lady of heaven, Mistress of the gods.

Bottom, Example in Berlin (Roeder 1924, 2:228, Side B = Naville 1891, 48 and pl. XLI.A)

(1) ny-sw.t bì.ty nb ìr.(t) ḥ.t nb t3.wy Sḥm-ḫpr-Rˁ-stp-n-Rˁ dì ˁnḫ (2) mry-B3st.t ˁ3(.t) nb(.t) B3s.t ìr.t Ḥr ìr mk n ìtⸯs Rˁ

The King of Upper and Lower Egypt, Lord of ritual performance, Lord of the Two Lands, Sekhemkheperre-setepenre, given life, (2) beloved of Bastet the great, Lady of Bubastis, the Eye of Horus who makes protection for her father Re.

Bottom (?), Unplaced Example (Naville 1891, pl. XLI.C)

(1) s3 Rˁ n ḥ.tⸯf mrⸯf nb ḫˁ.w Wsìr[kn] mrì-ʾImn [dì ˁnḫ] (2) [mry] B3st. t ˁ3.t nb(.t) B3s.t wr(.t) wsr(.t) p.t

Bodily son of Re, whom he loves, Lord of Diadems, Osor[kon], beloved of Amon, [given life], (2) [beloved of] Bastet the great, Lady of Bubastis, the great one, the powerful one of heaven.

III. Black "Basalt" Pedestal (Naville 1891, pl. XLI.D)

See Kitchen 1986, 303 §261.

Vertical Cartouches and Flanking Horizontal Titularies

(1) [ny-sw.t bì.ty] nb t3.wy Sḥm-ḫpr-Rˁ-stp-n-Rˁ (2) [s3 Rˁ] nb ḫˁ.w Wsìrkn mrì-ʾImn (3) Ḥr k3 nḫt mrì-Rˁ rdì.n s(w) Tm ḥr ns.tⸯf r grg t3.wy ny-sw.t bì.ty Sḥm-ḫpr-Rˁ-stp-n-Rˁ s3 Rˁ Wsìrkn mrì-ʾImn mrì-B3st.t nb(.t) B3s.t dì [ˁnḫ ...] (4) Ḥr k3 nḫt mrì-Rˁ [...]

[The King of Upper and Lower Egypt], Lord of the Two Lands, Sekhemkheperre-setepenre, (2) [Son of Re,] Lord of Diadems, Osorkon, beloved of Amon; (3) Horus: "Strong bull, beloved of Re, whom Atum placed upon his throne to found the Two Lands"; King of Upper and Lower Egypt, Sekhemkheperre-setepenre, Son of Re, Osorkon, beloved of Amon, beloved of Bastet, Lady of Bubastis, given [life ...] (4) Horus: "Strong bull, beloved of Re, [...]

NOTES

1. Naville 1891 miscopies as ḏbˁ.w "10,000's."

2. Naville miscopies ìr(.t) dì.t "Making the giving"; for rdì.t, see pl. XLI.E.

3. Cf. Osorkon II Jubilee reliefs, Wall B/C, Register 3, southern inner wall (Naville 1892, pl. IX/7–13), where the king offers ìrⸯf dì ˁnḫ mì Rˁ ḏ.t "so that he might attain the state of being given life like Re forever."

4. For the restoration, see Naville 1891, pl. XLI.E.

5. For the restoration, see Naville 1891, pl. XLI.A.

6. The mention of Amon, rather than Atum, makes questionable the placement of block XLI.C.

60. BUBASTIS TEMPLE INSCRIPTIONS: ATUM TEMPLE

The small temple of Atum, fashioned from reworked blocks of Rameses II some "three furlongs" from the main precinct of Bastet, was excavated by Naville in one week during the 1887–1889 field seasons. A red granite pillar (Cairo no. 675) now reduced to twenty-nine small fragments was engraved on four sides with a record of the first Osorkon's expenditures for all the temples of Egypt during his initial four years. Despite the lamentable state of the text, the preserved sums are extraordinary and likely derive in part from the spoils of his father's victorious Palestinian campaign. A graffito from the Khonsu temple at Thebes likely records an instance of the king's early munificence (see below, no. 61).

This is the first complete translation. Discussion and texts in Naville 1891, 48, 60–62, and pls. L–LII, with errata on viii. Unless otherwise noted, references to the plates below are to Naville 1891. A selective translation appears in Breasted 1906–7, 4:362–66 §§729–37. For the identification of the small temple of Atum, see Habachi 1957, 119–20; for its identification, see Van Siclen 1985, 32 no. 5. See Kitchen 1986, 303–4 §262.

A. Relief Block (pl. L.A)

King aboard bark of Atum, with Bastet, Heka (Ḥkȝ), Wepwawet (Wp-wȝ.wt), and leonine oarsman (Ḏr.t "Hand").

Labels for King
    Sḫm-ḫpr-Rᶜ-stp-n-Rᶜ (2) Wsỉrkn mrỉ-ʾImn (3) Sḫm-ḫpr-Rᶜ-stp-n-Rᶜ (4) […]
    Sekhemkheperre-setepenre, (2) Osorkon, beloved of Amon, (3) Sekhemkheperre-setepenre, (4) […]

B. Relief Blocks (pl. L.B, C)

(1) King aboard bark of Atum, with Bastet (Bȝst.t), Heka, Wepwawet (ḏd-mdw ỉn Wp-wȝ.wt "Recitation by Wepwawet"), and leonine oarsman.

Labels for King
    nb [tȝ.wy Sḫm]-ḫpr-Rᶜ-stp-[n]-Rᶜ (2) nb ḫᶜ.w Wsỉrkn mrỉ-ʾImn (3) nb [tȝ.wy …]
    Lord of the [Two Lands], [Sekhem]kheperre-setep[en]re, (2) Lord of Diadems, Osorkon, beloved of Amon, (3) Lord of the [Two Lands …]

(2) Lower Register: King, protected by Sakhmet, offers Eye of Horus to Atum, Shu, and Tefnut.

Label for Sakhmet
   Sḫm.t nb(.t) p.t
   Sakhmet, Lady of heaven.

Label for King
   Sḫm-ḫpr-Rᶜ-stp-n-Rᶜ (2) Wsỉrkn mrỉ-ʾImn
   Sekhemkheperre-setepenre, (2) Osorkon, beloved of Amon.

Label for Atum
   Tm nb m ʾIwnw (2) dỉ.n≠(ỉ) n≠k snb nb
   Atum, Lord in Heliopolis: (2) "Thus I have given to you all health."

Label for Shu
   ḏd-mdw ỉn Šw sȝ Rᶜ (2) dỉ.n≠(ỉ) n≠k qn(ỉ) nḫt
   Recitation by Shu, son of Re: (2) "Thus I have given to you valor and
victory."

Label for Tefnut
   ḏd-mdw ỉn Tfnw.t (2) ḥnw.t psḏ.t
   Recitation by Tefnut, (2) Mistress of the Ennead.

C. Fragmentary Relief Blocks

(1) Below Winged Disk (pl. L.D)
   ḏd-mdw ỉn [...]
   Recitation by [...]

(2) Bastet on Bark of Atum
   [Bȝst.t ... ḥnw.t] nṯr.w (2) [...]s[...]
   [Bastet ... Mistress] of the gods (2) [...]

(3) Goddess Protects King (lost) (pl. L.F)
   [sȝ ᶜnḫ] ḥȝ≠f nb mỉ Rᶜ
   [The protection of life] is all around him like Re.

(4) King before Deity (pl. L.G)

Label for King
   nb tȝ.wy Sḫm-ḫpr-Rᶜ-stp-n-Rᶜ (2) nb ḫᶜ.w Wsỉrkn mrỉ-ʾImn (2) [sȝ ...]
nb [ḥȝ≠f ...]
   Lord of the Two Lands, Sekhemkheperre-setepenre, (2) Lord of Diadems, Osorkon, beloved of Amon. (3) [The protection of] all [... is behind
him ...].

D. Pillar Recording Temple Donations (Cairo 675)

(1) Fragmentary Vignette of King with Deities, Introductory Text Below (pl. LI.B,C). See Kitchen 1986, 303 n. 325.

[ḥsb.t 5(?) ỉbt ... sw][1] 21 h3.t šsp nḥḥ d.t [ẖ]r [... Ḥr nbw nḫt ḫpš d]r pd.t psd.t ỉty ỉṯ t3.w nb.w ny-sw.t bỉ.ty [...] (2) nb t3.wy Sḫm-ḫpr-Rᶜ-stp-n-Rᶜ [...] (3) .... [...]

[Regnal year 5 (?), month ..., day][1] 21, beginning of receiving eternity and unendingness [und]er [... The Golden Horus: "Strong in might, who re]pels the Nine Bows, Sovereign who seizes all lands"; The King of Upper and Lower Egypt, [...], (2) Lord of the Two Lands, Sekhemkheperre-setepenre, [...] (3) ... [...]

(2) Main Body of Text (pl. LI.G1–2)

[...]... d.t⸗w ḥtp m s.t⸗sn ỉb⸗w nb n(n) s.t r⸗sn ḫft rnp.wt h3y dr rk bỉ.tyw ḥr h3.t n(n) mỉ.ty⸗k m t3 pn nṯr nb mn ḥr ns.t⸗f ḥnm⸗f ỉw[n]n⸗f m 3w.t-ỉb [ỉw⸗tw ḥr]² bs⸗k r (2) [ny-sw.t(?) ...]... r⸗k ḥws ḥw.wt⸗sn sᶜš3 ḥnw⸗sn n nbw ḥd ᶜ3.t nb(.t) m3ᶜ.t t ṯ ḥm⸗f ḥr³ tp-rd n⸗s n ỉrw⸗f n Ḫnty-Ḥsr. t šhw mnw.w ỉr.n ny-sw.t bỉ.ty nb t3.wy (3) [Sḫm-ḫpr-Rᶜ-stp-n-Rᶜ n nṯr.w nṯr.w]t [nb nw] nỉw.t nb(.t) Šmᶜw Mḥw m ḫ[sb.t 1].t tpy [pr.t] sw 7 r ḥsb.t 4 ỉbt 4 šmw sw 25 ỉr n rnp.t 3 ỉbd 3 hrw 16 rdỉ ḥm⸗f r pr n ỉt⸗f Rᶜ-Ḥr-3ḫ.ty nbw-nfr qḥqḥ ḥd šps n Tm-Ḫprỉ wr ʾỉwnw nbw-nfr n qm3 šsp 1 ḥsbd m3ᶜ ḥtp-dỉ-ny-sw.t⁴ 10 ỉr (n) nbw-nfr dbn 15,345 ḥd dbn 14,150 ḥsbd m3ᶜ (4) [... dmd dbn ...+] 4,000 qrḥ.t(?) ỉr n dbn 100,000 rdỉ m-b3ḥ Rᶜ-Ḥr-3ḫ.ty Tm wtt t3.wy⸗f šhn⁵ ỉr n nbw-nfr dbn 5,010 ḥd dbn 30,720 ḥsbd m3ᶜ dbn 1,600 ḥm.t km dbn 5,000 ḥd ỉr (n) dbn 100,000 rdỉ m-b3ḥ Ḥw.t-Ḥr nb(.t) ḥtp m Ḥtp⁶ nbw-nfr ḥd šhn rdỉ n-b3ḥ mw.t ḥr sšš.t⸗s nbw-nfr ḥd šhn ḥd n qḥqḥ ḥd rdỉ n-b3ḥ⁷ Ḥry-š⸗f ḫnty ʾỉwnw nbw-nfr ḥd šhn rdỉ n-b3ḥ Dḥwty ḫnty Ḥw.t-sr⁸ nbw-nfr ḥd šhn rdỉ n-b3ḥ B3st.t ḫnty Ḥw.t-sr nbw-nfr šhn rdỉ n-b3ḥ Dḥwty ḥr(y)-ỉb Ḥw.t-Ḥr⁹ nbw-nfr ḥd (5) [šhn ...] nbw-nfr [...] ḥd dbn 9,000 ḥm.t km dbn 30,000 ḥtr⸗f Dsds Knmwt m ỉrp šdḥ Ḥmy Swny¹⁰ m-mỉt.t ỉry r ḥw ḥw.t⸗f mỉ mdw⸗st rdỉ ḥm⸗f r pr Rᶜ ḥnᶜ psd.t⸗f ḥd ḥry-sd.t 3 nbw-nfr m tỉprt(?) 3 ḥd dw 3 ḥtp.t 3 ᶜḥw 17 dd.t 1 šnw(?) 1 ᶜ 2 h3(y) 10 h[n] 1 nms.t 1 wdḥ 1 nbw-nfr ᶜḥw 3 wdḥ 1 3ᶜn 2 šhtp ᶜ3 2 h3(y) 6 [...] šhtp(?) 1 nbw-nfr [..] ḥs[bd m3ᶜ] (6) [...]f [...] dbn 332,000 [...] dr⸗f dbn 594,300 rdỉ ḥm⸗f r pr ʾỉmn-Rᶜ ny-sw.t nṯr.w nbỉ ḥm⸗f šhtp(?) f3ỉ-ḥ.t(?)⸗sn d.t⸗f nbw-nfr ḥd n qm3 ỉr (n) nbw-nfr dbn 183[+x] ḥd dbn 1,900 [+ x] ḥm.t km dbn [...] nbw šḫr[...] ... k3r(?)⸗f šhtp nbw-nfr n [qm3(?) ...] ḥd h3(y) [...]stt(?) 40 [+ x ...]tns [...] 30 [+ x ...] m [...] (7) [...].w ʾỉmn [...] 10 [+ x...] mn Ḥw.t-Ḥr 7 [...]

[...]... their bodies resting in their places. (As for) all their wishes, they are not concerned with them according to the years revealed since the time of previous kings. There is not your like in this land. Every god remains upon his throne, uniting with his shrine in joy, [since][2] you are inducted to be (2) [king (?) ...]... regarding you, building their mansions, multiplying their vessels of gold, silver, and every genuine precious stone. His Majesty occupied himself[3] with regulations for it in his inherent role of Foremost One of the Hermopolite necropolis (Thoth). Summary of the monuments made by the King of Upper and Lower Egypt, Lord of the Two Lands, (3) [Sekhemkheperre-setepenre for all the gods and goddess]es [of] every city of Upper and Lower Egypt from re[gnal year 1], first month of [winter], day 7 to regnal year 4, month 4 of summer, day 25, amounting to three years, three months, and sixteen days.

His Majesty gave to the estate of his father Re-Horachty:
Of beaten fine gold: a noble shrine of Atum-Khepri, chief of Heliopolis
Of hammered fine gold: 1 statue of the prostrate king
Of genuine lapis lazuli: 10 royal sphinxes with offering trays[4]
Amounting to: 15,345 *deben* of fine gold
14,150 *deben* of silver
[...] of genuine lapis lazuli (4)
[Total: X+]4,000 [*deben*]

Vessels amounting to 100,000 *deben,* placed before Re-Horachty-Atum, who begat his two chicks.

Donation[5] amounting to: 5,010 *deben* of fine gold
30,720 *deben* of silver
1,600 *deben* of genuine lapis lazuli
5,000 *deben* of black copper

A shrine amounting to 100,000 *deben,* placed before Hathor Nebet-Hetepet in Hetepet.[6]

Donation of fine gold, and silver, placed before Mut bearing her sistrum.

Donation of fine gold and silver: a shrine of beaten silver, placed before[7] Harsaphes, Foremost of Heliopolis.

Donation of fine gold and silver, placed before Thoth, Foremost of the Mansion of the Prince.[8]

Donation of fine gold and silver, placed before Bastet, Foremost of the Mansion of the Prince.

Donation of fine gold, placed before Thoth, resident in the Mansion of Horus.[9]

[Donation] of fine gold and silver: (5)
    [... *deben* of] fine gold
    9,000 *deben* of silver
    30,000 *deben* of black copper

He levied the Dakhleh and Kharga oases in regard to wine, pomegranate wine, wine of Hemy, and wine of Syene[10] likewise in order to equip his mansion in accordance with their words.

His Majesty gave to the estate of Re and his Ennead:
Of silver: 3 torchieres
Of fine gold, comprising: 3 chariots (?)
Of silver: 3 jars
                3 offering stands
                17 braziers
                1 flat dish
                1 cartouche vessel
                2 bowls
                10 altars
                1 *hin*-jug
                1 spouted vessel
                1 offering stand
Of fine gold: 3 braziers
                1 offering stand
                2 divine apes
                2 large censers
                6 altars
                [...]
                1 fourfold censer
Of fine gold: [...]
Of [genuine] lapis [lazuli] (6)
[...] 332,000 *deben,* its full extent: 594,300 *deben.*

His Majesty gave to the estate of Amon-Re, King of the Gods:
His Majesty fashioned a censing statue bearing their offerings (?), its body being of hammered fine gold and silver, amounting (to) 183 [+x] *deben* of fine gold, 1,900 [+ x] *deben* of silver, and [...] *deben* of black copper.
    Of gold: a [...]..., its shrine and censer of [hammered (?)] fine gold
    Of silver: an altar

[…]… 40[+ x …]… […] 30[+ x …] comprising […] (7) […] Amon […]
10 [+ x …]… Hathor 7 […]

(3) Block A, Fragmentary and Uncertain Traces (pl. LI.A)
[…] nḥḫ(?) 3,000 nbw-nfr […] (2) […] … ḥm≠f m ỉ[…] (3) […] … rdỉ
ḥm≠f ḏd-mdw ỉn ḥm≠f t[…]tw ḥrw sḫ[…] ỉb nb[…] (4) […] … nb ḫȝs.t
Sḫm-ḫpr-Rˁ-stp-n-Rˁ […] (5) […] … sḥtp.w nṯr ỉr n nbw-nfr dbn 140[+x
…] (6) […] … nbw-nfr ḥḏ […] ḥḏ rdỉ ḥm≠f […] (7) […] … ḫsbd mȝˁ wˁȝ
60[+x …]

[…] eternity (?): 3,000 of fine gold […] (2) […]… His Majesty in …[…]
(3) […] that His majesty gave. Recitation by His Majesty: …[…] day …[…]
every heart […] (4) […] Lord of foreign lands Sekhemkheperre-setepenre
[…] (5) […]… divine censers amounting to 140[+x] *deben* of fine gold […]
(6) […] fine gold and silver […] silver that His Majesty gave […] (7) […]…
genuine lapis lazuli, 60[+x …] pails […]

(4) Block D, Fragmentary and Uncertain Traces (pl. LI.D)
[…] rḫ≠k […] pw Ḏḥwty (2) […] rk.w bỉ.tyw ˁȝ.w n mr≠f ḥqȝ […]n […]
You know that Thoth is […] (2) […] times of the great kings whom
he loved, the ruler […]

(5) Block E, Fragmentary and Uncertain Traces (pl. LI.E)
[…]… nbw-nfr mdw 30 [+x …] (2) […] pḫr.t(?) n.t mw […] (3)
[…]…[…]
[…]… fine gold: 30[+x] staves (2) […] remedies (?) of water […] (3)
[…]…[…]

(6) Blocks C2, F, and G3, Fragmentary Vertical Columns (right to left; pl.
LI.C2, F, G3)
[… nb ḥˁ].w Ws[ỉ]rkn mrỉ-[ʾI]mn m-bȝḥ […] nbw-[nfr …] ḫȝ(y) 2 nbw-
nfr qỉs-ˁnḫ ḥḏ 7 rdỉ.n ḥm[≠f ..] (2) […]ṱ.t nbw-nfr ḥḏ n qmȝ […] nbw-nfr
737[+x … rdỉ ḥm≠f r pr bȝ nb] Ḏd ḫ[nˁ] psḏ.t≠f nt[…] 1[+x]…[…] (3) […]≠f
m […]

[…Lord of Diadem]s, Os[o]rkon, beloved of [A]mon before [… fine]
gold […] (2) 2 altars; of fine gold and *qes*-ankh stone: 7 shrines that [His]
Majesty gave […] (2) […] (goddess) of hammered fine gold and silver […]
fine gold 737[+x … His Majesty gave to the estate of the Ram of] Mendes
and his Ennead: one [+x…] (3) […] his […]

(7) Block A, Fragmentary Vertical Columns (right to left; pl. LII.A)
[…] ny-sw.t bỉ.ty nb tȝ.wy Sḫm-ḫpr-Rˁ-stp-n-Rˁ sȝ Rˁ Wsỉrkn mrỉ-ʾImn
[…] (2) […] 100,000 nb [..].t nbw-nfr dmḏ ḫnty […] (3) […] nbw-nfr ḫsbd

mꜣꜥ wꜥꜣ ḥḏ [...] dmḏ [...] (4) [...] 100,000 nbw-nfr wꜥꜣ rdỉ.n ḥm≠f m-bꜣḥ nb [...] (5) [...] nb tỉ-šps [...]pt [...] nbw-nfr ꜥꜣ [...] Rꜥ nb [...]

[...] The King of Upper and Lower Egypt, Lord of the Two Lands, Sekhemkheperre-setepenre, son of Re, Osorkon, beloved of Amon [...] (2) [...] 100,000 ...[...] fine gold, total from out of [...] (3) [...] fine gold and genuine lapis lazuli: pails of silver [...] total [...] (4) [...] 100,000; of fine gold: a pail that His Majesty placed before the lord [...] (5) [...] *tishepes*-trees [...]... [...] fine gold and precious stones [...] Re, lord [...]

(8) Block L, Fragmentary Vertical Columns (right to left; pl. LII. L)
    [...]≠f dbn [...] (2) [...]
    [...] his [...] *deben* [...] (2) [...]

(9) Block M1, Fragmentary Vertical Columns (right to left; pl. LII.M1)
    [...] nbw-nfr [...] (2) [...] rdỉ m-bꜣḥ Ḥr ḫnty rnp.wt(?) nb mꜣꜥ.t(?) nbw-nfr [...] (3) [...] mdw nṯr(?) 1 wꜥꜣ 4 ḥḏ ḫꜣy 3 nbw-nfr sšm n ꜣImn-ꜣIpy ḥr fꜣỉ [...]
    [...] fine gold [...] (2) [...] placed before Horus, foremost of years (?), lord of Maat (?); of fine gold [...] (3) [...] 1 divine staff (?), 4 pails; of silver: 3 altars, of fine gold: an image of Amon of Opet bearing [...]

(10) Block C2, Fragmentary Vertical Columns (left to right; pl. LII.C2)
    [...] w[...].t sꜥdw [...] (2) [... x+] 41 ḥḏ dbn 2,000,000 (3) [...]
    [...] ... fatten (?) [...] (2) [... x+] 41, of silver: two million *deben* (3) [...]

(11) Block E, Fragmentary Vertical Column (left to right; pl. LII.E)
    [...] ... 3,000 [+x...]
    [...]... 3,000 [+x ...]

(12) Block F, Fragmentary Vertical Columns (left to right; pl. LII.F)
    [... rdỉ] ḥm≠f m-b[ꜣḥ ...] (2) [...] ḫꜣy(?) 2 [+x ...]
    [... that] His Majesty [placed] before [...] (2) [...] altars (?) 2 [+x ...]

(13) Block I2, Fragmentary Vertical Columns (left to right; pl. LII. I 2)
    [...]... šbw rꜣ-pr.w n nṯr.w nb.w [...] (2) [...] nbw-nfr ḥḏ dbn 2,300,000 [+x ...] (3) [...].w 990 [+ x...] mꜣꜥ [...] (4) [...] 600,000 [+ x...] (5) [...]
    [...] ... food offering of the temples of all the gods [...] (2) [...] fine gold and silver: 2,300,000 [+ x] *deben* [...] (3) [...] 990 [+ x ...] genuine [...] (4) [...] 600,000 [+ x ...] (5) [...]

(14) Block G, Horizontal Columns (left to right; pl. LII.G)
    [... ny-sw.t] bỉ.ty Sḫm-ḫpr-Rꜥ-stp-n-Rꜥ sꜣ Rꜥ [Wsỉrkn mrỉ-ꜣImn ...]

(2) [...]... nmt.t m ...[...] (3) [...] nbw-nfr ḥd ỉw [...] (4) [...] ḥm n [...] (5) [...] smȝ m sy[...]

[... The King of Upper] and Lower Egypt, Sekhemkheperre-setepenre, son of Re, [Osorkon, beloved of Amon ...] (2) [...] step in ...[...] (3) [...] fine gold, silver while [...] (4) [...] the Majesty of [...] (5) [...] united with [...]

(15) Block K, Horizontal Columns (left to right; pl. LII.K)

[...] (2) [...] rdỉ.n ḥm[ꜥf ...] (3) [... rdỉ.n] ḥmꜥf m-bȝḥ ꜣIw[ꜥs-ꜥȝꜥs¹¹ ...] (4) [...]m[...]

[...] (2) [... His] Majesty gave [...] (3) [...that] His Majesty placed before Ious[âas¹¹...] (4) [...]

(16) Blocks I3 and O2, Horizontal Columns (left to right; pl. LII.I3, O2)

[...] (2) [...]...[...] (3) [...] sḥw [...] (4) [...p]r.t 5 hrw 5 ...[...] (5) [... w]ꜥȝ n ḫprr 1 n [...] (6) [...] nbw-nfr sḥtpy [...] (7) [...] ḫnty nb nbw-nfr [...] (8) [...] wꜥȝ n [...] (9) [... wꜥ]ȝ rdỉ.n [ḥmꜥf m-bȝḥ ...] (10) [...] rdỉ.n [ḥmꜥf m-bȝḥ ...]

[...] (2) [...]...[...] (3) [...] summary [...] (4) [...] of winter day 5, five days ...[...] (5) [...] 1 scarab pail of [...] (6) [...] of fine gold: a fourfold censer [...] (7) [...] foremost of the lord of fine gold [...] (8) [...] pail of [...] (9) [... a pa]il placed by [His Majesty before ...] (10) [...] placed by [His Majesty before ...]

(17) Blocks B, C1, D, and M2, Fragmentary Horizontal Columns, Reverse of Main Preserved Text Face (pl. LII.B, C1, D)

Scene of King before Lost Deities Followed by Goddess and Montu

Label for Goddess
[...] ntr(.t) ꜥȝ(.t) ḥnw.t sḫ.t ntr [...]
[...] the great goddess, Mistress of the divine field [...]

Label for Deity
dỉ≠ỉ n≠k ḥb.w-sd mỉ Rꜥ
"Thus I have given to you jubilees like Re."

Label for King
[...] ỉr n≠f dỉ ꜥnḫ
[...] to make for himself the state of being given life.

Label for Deity
[...] ḏ.t   [...] eternity.

Main Text, Reverse of Donation Text (pl. LII.C1, D, M 2): Record of "afflictions," perhaps motivating the subsequent donation list

ḥsb.t 4(.t) ỉbd 2 pr.t [sw] 10 [+x...] ḫ|r ...] Ḥr [nbw] nḫt [ḫpš dr pḏ.t
psḏ.t (2) ỉty ỉṯ t3.w nb.w ...] ny-sw.t bỉ.ty [...] (3) [...] mw.t[≠f ...] (4) [...]
ḥr(y)-tp [...] (5) [...]t[...]

Regnal year 4, month 2 of winter, day 10[+x] under [...] The [Golden]
Horus: "Strong [in might, who repels the Nine Bows, (2) Sovereign who
seizes all lands," ...] The King of Upper and Lower Egypt, [... (3) his]
mother [...] (4) [...] chief [...] (5) [...]

Main Text, Fragment H (pl. LII.H)

[...] n šn(?)≠sn [...] (2) [...] n ỉ3.t šr sb3 n nỉw.t rsy(?) Mḥw [...] (3) [...]
tpy s3 [...].. tpy [...] n qm3 ỉt≠f ỉ3[d.t(?) ...] (4) [... ỉ]3d.t≠f ỉw ỉ[...] (5) [...]...
n ỉ3.t ms nfr(?) mn.ṯ b3(?)≠k [...] (6) [...]...f [...]

[...] of their circuit (?) [...] (2) [...] of the mound of child of the southern city (?), Lower Egypt [...] (3) [...] first [...] son [...] first [...] of his
father's creation of the aff[l]iction (?) ...] (4) [...] his affliction, while [...] (5)
[...] of the enduring mound of good (?) birth. Your ba-spirit [...] (6) [...]

Main Text, Fragments I1 and O1 (pl. LII.I1, O1)

[...] n ꜥnw sq3≠s ..[...] (2) [...] sḫr hy ḥr≠sn [...] (3) [...]... hn n št3.t[12]
ỉw [...] (4) [...] n Rꜥ ḏs≠f wn šsr ꜥ3(?)[13] pḥ|ty ...] (5) [...]... h3≠k ḥm≠k [...]
(6) [...] ỉ3d.t≠f ỉw [...] (7) [...] sḫtm.ṯ ỉ[...] (8) [... ỉ3]d.t≠f ỉw ỉ3[d.t(?) ...] (9)
[...] 3ḫꜥ n ꜥn.t≠f [...] (10) [...] ny-sw.t wḏ≠f [...] (11) [...] ỉ3d.t [...]

[...] of Tura to exalt it ...[...] (2) [...] Drive away, fall upon them [...]
(3) [...]... chest of the Secret One[12] while [...] (4) [...] of Re himself. An
arrow (of) the Great One[13] of Strength was [...] (5) [...]... Back! Retreat!
[...] (6) [...] his affliction, while [...] (7) [...] destroyed [...] (8) [...] his
affliction while the affliction [...] (9) [...] scratch with his claw [...] (10)
[...] the king. He commanded [...] (11) [...] affliction [...]

Main Text, Fragment N (pl. LII.N)

[...] ... h[...] (2) [...] nb(?) sḫ.t nṯr Ḥry-š≠f(?) ḥr ỉr [...] (3) [...]... nb≠f
m 3w.t n ḏt (4) [...]...[...]

[...]... [...] (2) [...] lord (?) of the divine field, Harsaphes (?) making
[...] (3) [...]... his lord in the extent of eternity [...] (4) [...]...[...]

NOTES
    1. The date with "day 21" should follow "day 25" of the last month of the
fourth year (pl. LI.G1, line 3) and must be in year 5 or later.
    2. Restoration following Breasted 1906–7, 4:363 n. a.
    3. Coptic ⲬⲒϨⲟ; see Crum 1939, 648a.
    4. Cf. Daumas 1988, 1:67, no. 1183.

5. See Erman and Grapow 1926–63, 4:217/17.

6. For the Heliopolitan goddess and a differing analysis of this passage, see Vandier 1964, 75 (document B XXXVI);1965, 144.

7. Correction of copy following Breasted 1906–7, 4:364 n. a, with substitution of phonetic n-b₃ḥ for m-b₃ḥ as elsewhere in this line.

8. Designation of the temple of Re at Heliopolis.

9. Designation of Mesen/Silê.

10. Two towns in the western Delta near Lake Mareotis.

11. For this goddess of Heliopolis, see Vandier 1964, 55–146.

12. Later an epithet of the vulture goddess of el-Kab.

13. If correctly analyzed, an epithet of Seth, the source or victim of the affliction. Or read šsr≠t "your (fem.) arrow of strength." The use of the ending t could be second-person feminine throughout the text, although second-person masculine appears as well.

61. KHONSU TEMPLE GRAFFITO

In the first court of the Khonsu temple at Thebes, seven fragmentary vertical lines dated to Osorkon I are inscribed on column 20, just west of the portico entrance leading to the temple interior. If the broken regnal date should be restored as year 4, the graffito would provide additional confirmation of the Bubastite record of Osorkon's large donations to the temples in his first four years.

For the text and translation, see Epigraphic Survey 1981, fig. 7 (for location), pl. 134, and pp. 20–21. See Kitchen 1984, 85; 1986, 576 §511.

ḥsb.t 2[+x ... ḫr ḥm n ny-sw.t bἰ.ty nb] t₃.wy Sḫm-ḫpr-Rˁ-stp-n-Rˁ s₃ Rˁ nb ḫˁ.w [Ws]ἰ[rkn] mrἰ-ʾImn (2) [...] (3) [...] (4) [...ˁ₃.w(?)] n ˁš sḫkr. t m (5) [... n]ḫt.w rnp.wt ˁš₃ m (6) [ny-sw.t ...] nṯr pn šps Ḫ[n]sw (7) [...] Ḫnsw m W₃s.t Nfr-ḥtp

Regnal year 2 [+ x ... under the Majesty of the King of Upper and Lower Egypt, Lord] of the Two Lands, Sekhemkheperre-setepenre, the son of Re, Lord of Diadems, [Os]o[rkon], beloved of Amon. (2) [...] (3) [...] (4) [... doors (?)] of cedar, ornamented with (5) [precious metals (?) ... in return for victo]ries (?) and many years as (6) [king ...] this august god, Kh[on]su (7) [...] Khonsu in Thebes Neferhotep.

62. DONATION STELA FOR THE GOD'S FATHER HORY
(MMA 10.176.42)

This round-topped limestone stela (70 cm x 59 cm) includes a lunette scene of Osorkon I offering fields to the Heliopolitan deities Re-Horachty and Nebet-Hetepet, with accompanying labels in vertical hieroglyphs and a hieratic decree comprising eight horizontal lines. The hieratic text is notable for its extensive quotation of the royal titulary, with a unique attestation of Osorkon's "Nebty" name and, with texts from Bubastis (above, pp. 248, 251, and 257), the King's Horus and Golden Horus names. Unlike typical donation stelae, the text records a formal, royal proclamation rather than a private benefaction confirmed by local authority. The royal decree represents not a new donation but a transferral of landed revenue from servants of the high priest of Heliopolis to the benefit of the patrician and priest Hory. The detailed description of the boundaries of the transferred plot anticipates the legal formulary of later Demotic (and derived Aramaic) land sales. The stela was acquired by the Metropolitan Museum of Art in New York in 1910 through the Rogers Fund.

As the published text is illegible, a new collation was undertaken based on personal inspection and photography courtesy of Catharine Roehrig, Associate Curator of the Department of Egyptian Art of the Metropolitan Museum. James P. Allen, Curator of Egyptian Art, kindly examined damaged sections of the final line. For a provisional discussion of the text and translation, see El-Alfi 1992, 13–19; Vandier 1968, 137–38; and Meeks 1979a, 633–34, 646, and 666 (no. 22.2.6). See Kitchen 1986, 303–4 §§263–64.

LUNETTE SCENE: KING BEFORE RE-HORACHTY AND (HATHOR) NEBET-HETEPET

Label for King

ntr nfr nb (2) t3.wy nb (3) îr.t ḫt (4) Wsîrkn mrî-ʾImn dî ʿnḫ nb ḏd w3s nb mî Rʿ ḏ.t (5) rdî.t sḫ.t îr=f dî ʿnḫ

The Good God, Lord of (2) the Two Lands, Lord of (3) ritual performance, (4) Osorkon beloved of Amon, given all life and all stability and dominion like Re forever. (5) Giving field(s) so that he might attain the state of being given life.

Label for Re-Horachty

Rʿ-Ḥr-3ḫ.ty (2) ḏd-mdw[1] dî.n=(î) n=k (3) ʿnḫ ḏd w3s nb (4) ḫr=î

Re-Horachty. (2) Recitation:[1] "Thus I have given to you (3) all life, stability, and dominion (4) deriving from me."

Label for Nebet-Hetepet

Nb.t-Ḥtp.t (2) Rʿ.t-Tm.t pr.(t) m Tm

Nebet-Hetepet, (2) the female Re-Atum, come forth from Atum.

MAIN TEXT

[ḥsb].t 6(.t) ʿnḫ Ḥr k3 nḫt mrî-Rʿ rdî.n s(w) Tm ḥr ns.t=f r grg t3.wy nb.ty s3 ḫpr.w wr b3.wt Ḥr-nbw nḫt (2) ḫpš dr pḏ.t psḏ.t ny-sw.t bî.ty nb t3.wy Sḫm-ḫpr-Rʿ-stp-n-Rʿ s3 Rʿ nb ḫʿ.(w) Wsîrkn mrî-ʾImn ḏd m ḥr wr-m₃₃.w² (3) sḥtp ỉb n Rˁ s₃ ny-sw.t ỉmy-r₃ mšˁ ḥ₃w.ty Ḏd-Ptḥ-ỉw≠f-ˁnḫ mw.t≠f T₃-šr.(t)-n-ỉˁḫ₃ ḥnˁ n₃ sš.w sḥnwy.w (4) n pr Rˁ r dỉ.t t₃ 3 st₃.t ₃ḥ.t nt.t (m) drp.w⁴ n p₃ s₃w ₃ḫ.w n wr-m₃₃(.w) n p₃ šˁd⁵ ỉ-ỉr (5) h₃(ỉ) m-ˁq₃ t₃ ḥn.t⁶ n t₃ ḥw.t Rˁ-ms-s(w) n pr Rˁ m sw₃w n t₃ m₃w.(t) n p₃ ḫft-ḥr ỉw rsy ỉtrw ˁ₃ (6) mḥ.ty ỉtrw ˁ₃ ỉmnt.t ỉtrw ˁ₃ ḥnˁ p₃ ˁḏ šˁ nty n rmn n≠f⁷ ỉ₃b.t t₃ bỉ₃.t⁸ ˁ₃.t nt.t m-ˁqy t₃ (7) ḥn.t n t₃ ḥw.t Rˁ-ms-s(w) n pr Rˁ r dỉ.t s n s₃ḥ ỉt-ntr⁹ n ỉt-ntr ḥ₃.ty-pˁ.t¹⁰ n ʾIwnw Ḥry s₃ ʾImn-m(8) -ḥ₃.t ỉr.n ˁnḫ≠s-n-pypy¹¹ mnmn wḏ.(t) tn m sbỉ [n sḏ].t¹² smnḫ¹³ s m ˁ(?)¹⁴ k₃.w

[Regnal] year 6. Long live the Horus: "Strong bull, beloved of Re, whom Atum placed upon his throne to found the Two Lands"; The Two Ladies: "Magnifying forms, great of wonders"; The Golden Horus: "Strong in (2) might, who repels the Nine Bows"; King of Upper and Lower Egypt, Lord of the Two Lands, Sekhemkheperre-setepenre, Son of Re, Lord of Diadems, Osorkon, beloved of Amon. It was commanded to the Greatest of Seers² (high priest of Heliopolis), (3) who pacifies the heart of Re, the Prince, general, and leader Djedptahiuefankh, whose mother is Tashereniah,³ together with the scribes of the administrators (4) of the estate of Re (of Heliopolis) to grant the three *arouras* [approximately 2 acres] of field that provide subvention⁴ for the guardian of the cultivation of the Greatest of Seers and for the woodcutter⁵ and that (5) descend opposite the swampy lake⁶ of the Mansion of Rameses in the estate of Re in the region of the new land of the dromos,

whose south is: the great river,
(6) north: the great river,
west: the great river and the desert margin of sand that is adjacent to it,⁷
east: the great quarry⁸ that is opposite the (7) swampy lake of the Mansion of Rameses in the estate of Re,

in order to give it as God's Father's prebend⁹ to the God's Father and First among Patricians¹⁰ of Heliopolis, Hory, son of Amonem(8)hat, born by Ankhesenpepi.¹¹ The one who upsets this decree is one who perishes [by fi]re;¹² the one who confirms¹³ it has the means¹⁴ of sustenance.

NOTES

1. Each column of the god's statement is headed by ḏd-mdw "recitation," serving as punctuation for the quotation; cf. the speeches of Amon in the Bubastite Portal Reliefs of Sheshonq I.

2. At the end of the line, El-Alfi read n ʾIwnw "of Heliopolis."

3. El-Alfi read the final element as ₃s.t "Isis."

4. For the term drp.w, see Erman and Grapow 1926–63, 5:477; Meeks 1979a, 646 n. 184; and the Donation Stela of Washtihat (OIM 10511), no. 86, line 3. El-Alfi read r-r q₃.w "beside the high land."

5. Erman and Grapow 1926–63, 4:423/1.

6. For the term, see Gardiner 1948, 29.

7. Literally, "as a side to it"; Erman and Grapow 1926–63, 2:418; unread by El-Alfi.

8. Erman and Grapow 1926–63, 1:438/14. El-Alfi translated "well."

9. For the use of s3ḥ as "land endowment/prebend," see Meeks 1979a, 646 n. 185. Meeks (646) assumes that the land is not transferred but serves "simultaneously" to support the dependents of the high priest and Hory. The terminology, however, indicates a change of both category and beneficiary: the land that currently serves as subvention (drp.w) for guardian and woodcutter is to be given instead as prebend (s3ḥ) to Hory.

10. Misread by Meeks, Kitchen, and El-Alfi as ḥ3.ty-ᶜ "mayor." For the title, see Edel 1980, 41–46; Clère 1983, 92 §F; and the Larger Dakhleh Stela, line 16.

11. The reading of this damaged section was confirmed through personal inspection by James P. Allen.

12. Or "one who is a burnt offering"; cf. Erman and Grapow 1926–63, 4:376/14, and the curse of P. BM 10188 (Bremner-Rhind), col. 27/9. Traces of the determinative remain.

13. For the use of smnḫ "confirm/perfect" and mnmn "upset/shift" with wḏ.(t) tn "this decree", see The Chronicle of Prince Osorkon, no. 82, pl. 16, line 53.

14. Or "in the condition of (having) sustenance." Reading of signs suggested by James P. Allen. El-Alfi read rw (if so, possible use of lion hieroglyph for nb "lord"; cf. Erman and Grapow 1926–63, 2:227, 5:92/5–9).

63. STELA OF PASHEDBASTET
(S. UNIVERSITY COLLEGE, LONDON 14496)

Formerly assumed to record the highest regnal date of Osorkon I, this limestone stela contains an unusual *Königsnovelle* for a private individual, recording the donor's pious acts. The stone, purchased by Petrie in Abydos, is now 33 cm high by 36 cm wide. The upper vignette is lost except for the remains of feet advancing from the right. Seven lines of text are preserved, with the right and (blank) bottom edges broken.

For the text and discussion, see Jacquet-Gordon 1967, 63–68 with pl. XI; Stewart 1983, p. 4 (no. 4) and pl. 3; Petrie 1905b, 241–42; and Kitchen 1986, 110–11 §89, 305 §263, 307–8 §266, and table 14.

(1) [ḥsb.t ... 3bd ...] prt sw 26[1] ḥr ḥm n ny-sw.t bỉ.ty nb t3.wy Sḫm-ḫpr-Rᶜ-stp-n-Rᶜ s3 Rᶜ nb ḫᶜ.w Ws[rk]n mrỉ-ʾImn ᶜnḫ [ḏ].t

(2) [hrw pn] wn-ỉn ḥm-nṯr 4-nw n ʾImn-Rᶜ ny-sw.t nṯr.w s3 ny-sw.t n Rᶜ-ms-s(w)[2] wr (n) n3 Mᶜḥ3s3-

(3) [wn][3] ḥ3w.ty P3-šd-B3st.t m3ᶜ-ḫrw ḥr swtwt≠f ḥr ḫ3s.t ᶜḥᶜ.n≠f gm

(4) [≠f?] wḏ n r3-st3w r-gs dhn Ḥ3p-nb≠s[4] mỉ ỉnn m r3-st3w r-gs ᶜn[ḫ]

(5) -]t3.wy[5] wn-ỉn≠f ḏsr≠s pḫr≠s m wḏ.w rdỉ.t n≠s 3ḥ.wt ..[6]

(6) [wn-]ỉ[n≠f] w3ḥ n≠s ỉmny.w(t) m ḥtp.w-nṯr (n) t.w ḥnq.wt ỉrp.w snṯr.w qbḥ

(7) [.w ...] ḥr hrw n nb≠f Wsỉr ḫnty ʾImnty.w nb ꜣbdw m ḏ.t ḏ.t

[Regnal year ..., month ..] of winter, day 26[1] under the Majesty of the King of Upper and Lower Egypt, Lord of the Two Lands, Sekhemkheperre-setepenre, Son of Re, Lord of Diadems, Oso[rko]n, beloved of Amon, living [for]ever. (2) [On this day,] the Fourth Prophet of Amon-Re, King of the Gods, the royal son of Rameses,[2] chief (of) the Mahas(3)[un][3] and leader, Pashedbastet, the justified, was strolling upon the desert edge. Then he found (4) a stela of the necropolis beside the peak of Hapnebes[4] like those that are brought from the necropolis beside Ankh-(5)Tawy.[5] He cleared/sanctified[6] it, surrounded it with boundary stones, and gave fields to it. ... [7] (6) [He] established for it daily offerings as a divine offering of bread, beer, wine, incense, cold water, (7) [and ...] daily for his lord, Osiris, Foremost of the Westerners, Lord of Abydos, throughout eternity.

NOTES

1. Petrie misread the signs of pr.t sw 26 as "year 36." See Jacquet-Gordon 1967, 63–64. With the elimination of this date, Jacquet-Gordon accepts Manetho's figure of only fifteen years for Osorkon I, although Kitchen (1986, 110–11 §89) maintains a reign of thirty-five years on other evidence.

2. See Gauthier 1918a, 257–60; and Meeks 1979a, 632 n. 105.

3. Libyan ethnic (= ? Μασσύλιοι); see Spiegelberg 1917b, 114. The rare name appears in two Dynasty XXII Theban attestations for Fourth Prophets of Amon-Re. Cf. Karnak statue (CGC 42218) of Patimut, whose ancestor Nesy (mother's grandfather) is said to be Fourth Prophet and wr ꜥꜣ n Mhswn ḥꜣw.ty "great chief of Mahasun and leader" (reign of Sheshonq I); see Kitchen 1986, 224 §188. Following Legrain, Jansen-Winkeln (1:112, 114–15 n. 6, 2:491–92, and pls. 26–27) would read the final wn as a Seth determinative in CGC 42218.

4. "She who hides her Lord"; necropolis of Abydos, bounded by a chain of hills; see Jacquet-Gordon 1967, 64–65. Contra Jacquet-Gordon, the name is also used of a portion of the Memphite necropolis, see Ray 1976, 147–48.

5. Clear reference to contemporary pillaging of Memphite cemeteries for stone as building material; see Jacquet-Gordon 1967, 65.

6. For the term in this passage, see Hoffmeier 1985, 205–6.

7. Unclear traces, ignored by previous translators.

64. MUMMY OF NAKHTEFMUT

With the reattribution of the stela of Pashedbastet from year 36, the highest attested regnal date for Osorkon I is provided by a docket of year 33 on the mummy linen of the priest Nakhtefmut (E). The God's Father was interred in a shaft tomb beneath the northern storerooms of the Ramesseum, which served as a cemetery during Dynasty XXII. A stamped leather *menat* pendant attached to straps on the mummy's chest bears the cartouches of Osorkon I, whose name reappears on similar counterpoises throughout this cemetery. While the docket likely dates the linen rather than the burial, the high year date can refer only to Osorkon I, not Pseusennes I or Amonemope a century earlier. A second docket of year 3 may refer to an ephemeral co-regent, Sheshonq II. As is typical of the period, Nakhtefmut records his paternal genealogy within the traditional funerary prayer on the central band of his cartonnage coffin.

For the texts and discussion, see Quibell 1898, 10–11 and pls. XVI–XVIII. The coffin of Nakhtefmut is now in Cambridge (E.64.1896); see Vassilika 1995, cover and 92–93 (misidentified as the Fourth Prophet of Amon). See Kitchen 1986, 110 §89 and 308 §266.

LINEN BANDAGE OF THE THIRD LAYER OF WRAPPING
ḥsb.t 3
Regnal year 3 (of Sheshonq II?)

LARGE LINEN CLOTH OF THE FIFTH LAYER OF WRAPPING
ḥsb.t 33
Regnal year 33 (of Osorkon I)

MENAT COUNTERPOISE
nṯr [nfr] Sḫm-ḫpr-Rꜥ-stp-n-Rꜥ sꜣ Rꜥ Wsrkn mrἰ-ʾImn
The [Good] God, Sekhemkheperre-setepenre, son of Re, Osorkon, beloved of Amon.

CENTRAL TEXT BAND OF COFFIN
ḥtp dἰ ny-sw.t Rꜥ-Ḥr-ꜣḫ.ty Wsἰr-Skr nb šty.t dἰ≠sn ḫꜣ m t ḥnq.t kꜣ.w ꜣpd.w ḫꜣ m mnḫ.t mrḥ.t ḫꜣ m ḥtp.w ḏfꜣ.w n Wsἰr ἰt-nṯr mrἰ wn ꜥꜣ.wy nw p.t[1] (n) ʾIp.t-s.wt Nḫt≠f-Mw.t mꜣꜥ-ḫrw sꜣ mἰ-nn Ns-pr-Nbw.t mꜣꜥ-ḫrw sꜣ mἰ-nn Šd-ʾImn-(m)-ḥꜣ.t mꜣꜥ-ḫrw sꜣ mἰ-nn Ḏd-Ḥns mꜣꜥ-ḫrw sꜣ ḥm-nṯr n ʾImn ἰmy-wnw.t≠f ḥr sꜣ 4-nw Ns-pꜣ-ḥr-n-ḥꜣ.t mꜣꜥ-ḫrw

A offering that the king gives to Re-Horachty and Osiris-Sokar, Lord of the Shrine, that they might give a thousand of bread, beer, oxen, and fowl, a thousand of cloth and oil, a thousand of offerings and foodstuffs to the Osiris, beloved God's Father, opener of the doors of heaven[1] of Karnak, Nakhtefmut, the justified, son of the similarly titled Nespernebut, the justified, son of the similarly titled Shedamonemhat, the justified, son of the similarly titled Djedkhons, the justified, son of the prophet of Amon and astronomer priest for the fourth phyle, Nespaherenhat, the justified.

COUNTERPOISE FROM RAMESSEUM BURIAL, KING BEFORE AMON (QUIBELL 1898, PL. XVIII)
nṯr [nfr] Sḫm-ḫpr-Rꜥ-stp-n-Rꜥ sꜣ Rꜥ Wsrkn mrἰ-ʾImn (2) mrἰ-ʾImn-Rꜥ nb p.t ny-sw.t nṯr.w dἰ ꜥnḫ
The [Good] God, Sekhemkheperre-setepenre, son of Re, Osorkon,

beloved of Amon, (2) beloved of Amon-Re, Lord of heaven, King of the Gods, given life.

NOTE

1. A designation of the sanctuary doors of Karnak temple.

C. SHESHONQ II

65. GRAFFITO OF HIGH PRIEST SHESHONQ (II)

This worn inscription was carved in vertical columns at the back of the first court of Luxor, behind the statues of Rameses II. The text is notable for its mention of a "chantress of the Residence" associated not simply with Amon, but with the First Prophet. The mention of "his son" in line 4 should refer to a son of Sheshonq II, and, if correctly restored, the line suggests a familial relationship between this son and the chantress whose name he perpetuates. The son's name is lost, although a female ascendant, Shepen-wepet, is noted as an associate of the estate of the First Prophet.

This is the first translation. For the text, see Daressy 1913, 133. See Kitchen 1986, 306 §265.

(1) ỉr.n{n} ḥm-nṯr tp(y) n ʾImn-Rꜥ ny-sw.t nṯr.w Ššw(n)q mꜣꜥ-ḫrw

(2) sꜣ ny-sw.t [nb tꜣ.wy] Wsỉrkn mrỉ-ʾImn [...]¹

(3) dỉ.n≠ỉ n ḥs.t n.(t) ḫnw² n ḥm-nṯr tp(y) Ḏd-ꜣs.t-

(4) ỉw≠s-ꜥnḫ sꜣ≠f [s]ꜥnḫ [rn≠s] ṯꜣ(ỉ)-sry.t n Pr-ꜥꜣ ꜥnḫ wḏꜣ snb [...]

(5) [...] Šp-n-wp.t mꜣꜥ.(t)-ḫrw n pꜣ pr ḥm-nṯr tp(y) n ʾImn

(1) Made by the First Prophet of Amon-Re, King of the Gods, Shesho(n)q (II), the justified, (2) royal son of the [Lord of the Two Lands], Osorkon (I), beloved of Amon, [...]¹ (3) which I gave to the chantress of the Residence² of the First Prophet, Djedese(4)iuesankh, while his son [causes her name] to live, the standard bearer of Pharaoh, l.p.h., [...] (5) [... born of the ...] Shepenwepet, the justified, of the estate of the First Prophet of Amon.

NOTES

1. Daressy restored dỉ ꜥnḫ mỉ Rꜥ ḏ.t "given life like Re forever."
2. For the title, see Ritner 1998, 85–90.

66. NILE-GOD STATUE DEDICATED BY HIGH PRIEST SHESHONQ (II)
(S. BRITISH MUSEUM 8)

Measuring 7.25 feet (2.21 m) in height, this sandstone statue of the inundation deity Hapi[1] was likely the latest of three[2] high quality statues erected in Karnak by the high priest and heir apparent Sheshonq II, son of Osorkon I. The historical import of the text lies in its genealogy, which reveals that Sheshonq united in himself the royal bloodlines of Dynasties XXI and XXII through the marriage of Osorkon, son of the founder of Dynasty XXII, to princess Maatkare "B," daughter of Pseusennes II, final ruler of the preceding dynasty. Sheshonq's expectation of succession is indicated by the consistent use of cartouches to enclose his name, although his primary title remains "First Prophet of Amon-Re." In this practice, Sheshonq followed the custom of Dynasty XXI, emulating his maternal grandfather's rise from high priest to Pharaoh. Sheshonq's prayers for long life were unanswered. He predeceased his father and was buried in the ancestral tomb of Pseusennes I at Tanis as Heqakheperre-setepenre Sheshonq, beloved of Amon (see below, no. 68).

The statue depicts Hapi striding with an outstretched table of offerings. Sheshonq is carved in relief in the "negative space" behind the deity's left leg, dressed in a panther skin and holding his hands in adoration. Despite the cartouches, he wears no uraeus. In varying states of preservation, the same text is carved five times on the statue: on the table, above Sheshonq, on the back pillar, and twice around the base. The piece was acquired by the British Museum in 1821 from the H. Salt collection.

For the texts, see Lepsius 1842, pl. XV, a–g, Maspero 1889, 734–36; and Breasted 1906–7, 4:367–68 §§738–40 (wrongly dated to Takelot I by both authors). Discussion includes Gauthier 1914, 299 §II, 300 §V, and 331 §D; Budge 1909, 211; Legrain 1908, 89; and Yorke and Leake 1827, 11 and pl. I, fig. 3. See Kitchen 1986, 8 §5, 60 §49(i), 117 §93 (wrongly styled Sheshonq "C"), 119–20 §94, 195 §157, 284 §238, and 306–7 §265.

LABEL ON EDGES OF OFFERING TABLE, RIGHT OF SPOUT

ỉr.n{n} ḥm-nṯr tp(y) n ꜣImn-Rꜥ ny-sw.t nṯr.w Ššnq mrỉ-ꜣImn n nb≠f (2) ꜣImn-Rꜥ nb ns.wt tꜣ.wy ḫnt(y) ꜣIp.t-s.wt r d[bḥ ꜥnḫ wḏꜣ s(nb) ...]

Made by the First Prophet of Amon-Re, King of the Gods, Sheshonq, beloved of Amon, for his lord (2) Amon-Re, Lord of the Thrones of the Two Lands, Foremost of Karnak, in order to be[seech life, prosperity, health, ...]

LABEL ABOVE SHESHONQ

ỉr.n{n} ḥm-nṯr tp(y) n ꜣImn-Rꜥ ny-sw.t nṯr.w Šš(n)q mrỉ-ꜣImn n nb≠f ꜣImn-Rꜥ ny-sw.t nṯr.w r dbḥ ꜥnḫ wḏꜣ s(nb) ꜥḥꜥ q(ꜣ) ỉꜣw.t ꜥꜣ(.t) nfr(.t) qn nḫt r tꜣ nb ḫꜣs.t nb(.t) sp [wꜥ nꜥš ḫpš nb qn][3]

Made by the First Prophet of Amon-Re, King of the Gods, Sheshonq, beloved of Amon, for his lord Amon-Re, King of the Gods, in order to beseech life, prosperity, health, a long lifetime, advanced and goodly old age, valor, and victory against every land and every foreign land [in a single] feat of [strength, and all valiant might.]³

BACK PILLAR

ir.n{n} ḥm-nṯr tp(y) n ʾImn-Rꜥ ny-sw.t nṯr.w Ššnq mrí-ʾImn n nb≠f ʾImn-Rꜥ nb ns.wt tꜣ.wy ḫnt(y) ʾIp.t-s.wt r dbḥ ꜥnḫ wḏꜣ s(nb) ꜥḥꜥ q(ꜣ) íꜣw. t ꜥꜣ(.t) nfr(.t) qn nḫt r tꜣ nb ḫꜣs.t nb(.t) sp [wꜥ nꜥš] ḫpš nb qn (2) ín.t tꜣ≠f⁴ (n) nb n{w} Šmꜥw Mḥw ḥꜣw.ty Ššnq mrí-ʾImn nty (m) ḥꜣ.t nꜣ mšꜥ.w ꜥꜣ.w n Km.t r-ḏr.w sꜣ ny-sw.t nb tꜣ.wy nb ír.(t) ḫ.t Wsírkn mrí-ʾImn mw.t≠f Mꜣꜥ. t-kꜣ-Rꜥ sꜣ.t ny-sw.t nb tꜣ.wy Ḥr-Pꜣ-sbꜣ-ḫꜥ-n-Níw.t mrí-ʾImn dí ꜥnḫ ḏd wꜣs mí Rꜥ ḏ.t

Made by the First Prophet of Amon-Re, King of the Gods, Sheshonq, beloved of Amon, for his lord Amon-Re, Lord of the Thrones of the Two Lands, Foremost of Karnak, in order to beseech life, prosperity, health, a long lifetime, advanced and goodly old age, valor, and victory against every land and every foreign land [in a single] feat of [strength,] and all valiant might. (2) What his land brings⁴ to the Lord of Upper and Lower Egypt, the leader Sheshonq, beloved of Amon, who is at the head of all the great armies of Egypt, royal son of the Lord of the Two Lands, Lord of ritual performance, Osorkon, beloved of Amon, whose mother is Maatkare, princess of the Lord of the Two Lands, Hor-Pseusennes (II), beloved of Amon, given life, stability, and dominion like Re forever.

STATUE BASE, STATUE'S RIGHT

ꜥnḫ ḥm-nṯr tp(y) (n) ʾImn-Rꜥ ny-sw.t nṯr.w (2) Šš(n)q [mrí-ʾImn] n nb≠f ʾImn-Rꜥ nb ns.wt tꜣ.wy ḫnt(y) ʾIp.t-s.wt r dbḥ ꜥnḫ wḏꜣ s(nb) ꜥḥꜥ q(ꜣ) íꜣw.t ꜥꜣ(.t) nfr(.t) qn nḫt r tꜣ nb ḫꜣs.t nb(.t) sp wꜥ nꜥš ḫpš nb qn (3) [ín.t tꜣ≠f (n)] nb n{w} Šmꜥw Mḥw ḥꜣw.ty Šš(n)q mrí-ʾImn dí ꜥnḫ ḏd wꜣs mí Rꜥ

Long live the First Prophet of Amon-Re, King of the Gods, (2) Sheshonq, [beloved of Amon], for his lord Amon-Re, Lord of the Thrones of the Two Lands, Foremost of Karnak, in order to beseech life, prosperity, health, a long lifetime, advanced and goodly old age, valor, and victory against every land and every foreign land in a single feat of strength, and all valiant might. (3) [What his land brings to] the Lord of Upper and Lower Egypt, the leader Sheshonq, beloved of Amon, given life, stability, and dominion like Re.

STATUE BASE, STATUE'S LEFT

ꜥnḫ ḥm-nṯr tp(y) (n) ʾI[mn]-Rꜥ [ny-sw.t nṯr.w] (2) [Šš(n)q mrí-ʾImn n nb≠f ʾImn-Rꜥ nb ns.wt tꜣ.wy ḫnt(y) ʾIp.t-s.wt r dbḥ ꜥnḫ wḏꜣ s(nb) ꜥḥꜥ q(ꜣ) íꜣw.t ꜥꜣ(.t)] nfr.(t) qn nḫt r tꜣ nb ḫꜣs.t nb(.t) sp wꜥ nꜥš ḫpš nb qn (3) [ín.t tꜣ≠f (n) nb n{w} Šmꜥw Mḥw] ḥꜣw.ty Šš(n)q mrí-ʾImn

Long live the First Prophet of A[mon]-Re, [King of the Gods,] (2)

[Sheshonq, beloved of Amon, for his lord Amon-Re, Lord of the Thrones of the Two Lands, Foremost of Karnak, in order to beseech life, prosperity, health, a long lifetime, advanced] and goodly [old age], valor, and victory against every land and every foreign land in a single feat of strength, and all valiant might. (3) [What his land brings to the Lord of Upper and Lower Egypt,] the leader Sheshonq, beloved of Amon.

TEXT OF HAPI

dd-mdw in Ḥʿpy it nṯr.w nb ḥw sms ḏfꜣw bʿḥw tꜣ.wy m kꜣ.w⸗f dd ʿnḫ dr mꜣr iwḥʿ ḏw.wy m fd⸗f sn r ḥr ʿn r mr⸗f di⸗(i) šn.wty ḥr gsgs ḫrp sn ḥm-nṯr tp(y) n ʾImn-[Rʿ] ny-sw.t [nṯr.w] Ššnq mri-ʾImn

Recitation by Hapi, father of the Gods, lord of foodstuffs, who brings forth sustenance, who inundates the Two Lands with his provisions, who grants life and dispels want, who drenches the two mountain banks with his sweat, who passes forward or backward as he wishes: "I shall cause the two granaries to overflow while the First Prophet of Amon-[Re], King of [the Gods,] Sheshonq, beloved of Amon, administers them."

NOTES

1.The term "Nile God" is disputed in Baines 1985, 83–116 (without mention of the BM statue). The awkward replacement "fecundity figure" is rejected here, since the statue is certainly of Hapi, who, as the inundation, is exclusively related to the Nile.

2. For the reattribution of a fourth statue, see Kitchen 1986, 576 §511.

3. Restored from the base inscriptions. Maspero translates: "la fois où il a manié le sabre, c'est un maître de vaillance."

4. Maspero translates: "qui conduit sa terre"; Breasted: "to take captive his land."

67. DURHAM BES STATUE
(ALNWICK CASTLE N 313)

Formerly in the collection of Alnwick Castle, this broken arragonite statue of the god Bes now measures 21.6 cm in height and is preserved only from the waist down. On the top and sides of the statue base a hiero-glyphic inscription records the donors as the high priest Sheshonq (II), son and later co-regent of Osorkon I, together with the future high priest Harsiese (A), son of Sheshonq (II) and Nes(ta)nebtasheru (B). As Harsiese did not directly succeed his father as high priest but followed Smendes (III) after a decade, Kitchen assumes that the mention of Sheshonq must be a posthumous commemoration of the new pontiff's lineage and claim in the early years of Osorkon II. Harsiese, however, is only a junior prophet on this statue, and the figure should be dated to the pontificate of his father. Like her husband and son, the lady Nesnebtasheru is associated with the cult of Theban Amon as a chantress of the Residence.

Although often repeated, the published texts and translations have been incompatible, requiring collations by both Jansen-Winkeln and myself based on new photographs and personal inspection courtesy of John Ruffle, Keeper of The Oriental Museum, The University of Durham. In the original copies by Birch, only the name of Osorkon I appears in a cartouche, and the pontiff Sheshonq's title is simply "First Prophet of Amon-Re, King of the Gods." In contrast, Legrain, Gauthier and Kitchen wrongly cite the statue as evidence of Sheshonq's royal pretensions, with cartouches and titles identical to—and conflated with—those on the British Museum Nile statue (see above, no. 66). Birch, Legrain, and others are also in error with regard to Harsiese's title, which is only "Prophet of Amon-Re" on this statue, never "First Prophet." While some deficiencies in Birch's printed text are evident from divergent transcription and transliteration, his copy is generally accurate. A further conflation by Legrain (with the Denon Papyri) has led to the false assertion that the statue preserves the mention of a secondary wife of Sheshonq, Nes-ta-wedjat-akhet, mother of a prophet Osorkon. No such wife or son is mentioned on this statue. A stylistic analysis of the figure by Romano inadvertently couples a portion of the Birch transcription with the incongruent analysis of Kitchen (following Legrain).

For the published texts, see Jansen-Winkeln, 1995a, 129–35; contrast Birch 1880, 33–34 (no. 313), with Legrain 1908, 160; the latter followed in Gauthier 1914, 331 §E; Peterson 1970–71, 17–18 §XXVII; and inconsistently in Romano 1989, 2:575–77 (but disregard bibliographic errors on Birch volume and erroneous inclusion of Ballod reference). For the Denon Papyri and Nes-ta-wedjat-akhet, see Gauthier 1914, 331 n. 2; and Maspero 1889, 736–37. See Kitchen 1986, 117 §93, 119 §94, 307 §265, and 314 §272.

TEXT ON UPPER SURFACE, BEGINNING AT BACK LEFT, FROM TAIL

ỉr.n{n} ḥm-nṯr tp(y) n ʾImn-Rꜥ ny-sw.t nṯr.w Šš(nq) (2, left side) mꜣꜥ-ḥrw sꜣ ny-sw.t nb tꜣ.wy[1] Wsrkn mrỉ-ʾImn ḥr[2] sꜣ⸗f ḥm-nṯr n (3, front) [ʾI]mn-[Rꜥ] ny-sw.t nṯr.w Ḥr-sꜣ-ꜣs.t mꜣꜥ-ḥrw mw.t⸗[f] ḥs.(t) m ẖnw (4, right side) ḥry tꜣ.wy[3] Ns-nb(.t)-ʾIšrw[4] mꜣꜥ.t-ḥrw n ẖnw.t⸗f ꜣs.t ḥr(y.t)-ỉb Nṯr.t[5] (5, back right) dỉ[6] ꜥnḫ wḏꜣ s(nb) snỉ(?)

Made by the First Prophet of Amon-Re, King of the Gods, Shesh(onq), (2) the justified, royal son of the Lord of the Two Lands,[1] Osorkon, beloved of Amon, on behalf of[2] his son, the Prophet of (3) [A]mon-[Re], King of the Gods, Harsiese, the justified, [whose] mother is the chantress in the Residence (4) of the Chief of the Two Lands,[3] Nesnebtasheru,[4] the justified, for his mistress Isis, resident in Coptos,[5] (5) who gives life,[6] prosperity, health, and passage (?).

TEXT AROUND BASE, BEGINNING AT CENTER (RIGHT TO LEFT):

[...] ꜥnḫ n [...][7] ḥm-nṯr tp(y) n ʾImn-Rꜥ ny-sw.t [nṯr].w (2, right side)

ỉmy-rꜣ m[š꜄]⁸ wr ḫꜣw.ty Ššn(q) mꜣꜥ-ḫrw sꜣ ny-sw.t nb tꜣ.wy Wsỉrkn mrỉ-
ʾImn (3, back side) [ḫr] sꜣ≠f ḥm-nṯr⁹ n ʾImn-Rꜥ ny-sw.t nṯr.w Ḥr-sꜣ-ꜣs.t
mꜣꜥ-ḫrw mw.t≠f ḥs.(t) (4, left side) m ḫnw ḥry tꜣ.wy¹⁰ Ns-nb(.t)-ʾIšrw mꜣꜥ.
t-ḫrw n ḫnw.t≠f ꜣs.t nb(.t) Gbtyw dỉ≠s ꜥnḫ wḏꜣ¹¹ [snb ....]

   [...] life for [...]⁷ the First Prophet of Amon-Re, King of the Gods,
(2) great general⁸ and leader, Sheshon(q), the justified, royal son of the
Lord of the Two Lands, Osorkon, beloved of Amon, (3) [on behalf of] his
son, the Prophet⁹ of Amon-Re, King of the Gods, Harsiese, the justified,
whose mother is the chantress (4) in the Residence of the Chief of the Two
Lands,¹⁰ Nesnebtasheru, the justified, for his mistress Isis, Lady of Coptos,
that she might give life, prosperity,¹¹ [and health ...]

NOTES
   1. Birch copied nb tꜣ(.wy).
   1. Unread by Birch and copied as a redundant sꜣ sꜣ≠f by Jansen-Winkeln, the
current reading is confirmed by Ruffle.
   2. Perhaps read ḥs.(t) m ḫnw p.t tꜣ "chantress in the Residence of heaven and
earth." Birch copied this title as ḥs.(t) m ḫnm.t and translated "the singer in the
inner place." The title seems a variant of the "chantresses of the Interior/Residence"
associated with the Theban Amon, who have been assumed to be virgins. Here,
however, the chantress is both married and the mother of a son. For these chantresses, see Ritner 1998, 85–90.
   3. Birch placed Ns- in the break.
   4. Nṯr.t (Šmꜥ), the "Divine One (of the South)," a theological name for Coptos.
   5. Birch copied dỉ dỉ-ꜥnḫ ꜥnḫ "who gives vivification and life."
   6. Birch copied ꜥnḫ≠s n. Jansen-Winkeln divided the line, restoring [ỉr.n{n}]
"made by" as the initial section before "First Prophet" and placing ꜥnḫ≠s n [...] at
the text's conclusion.
   7. Unread by Birch but visible on photos.
   8. Birch copied ḥm-nṯr tp(y) "First Prophet."
   10. Birch copied the second example of the mother's title as ḥs.(t) m p.t "singer
in heaven."
   11. Birch copied ꜥnḫ.tỉ.

68. INSCRIPTIONS FROM THE BURIAL OF HEQAKHEPERRE

   In the antechamber of the tomb of Pseusennes I at Tanis, a falcon-
headed silver coffin (inv. no. 211) of one Heqakheperre Sheshonq was
interred intrusively. Preserved as heirlooms accompanying the burial were
a pectoral (inv. no. 219) of Sheshonq "B," inscribed before his accession
as Sheshonq I, as well as a pair of bracelets (inv. nos. 226–27) in the name
of Sheshonq as king. The absence of later-dated heirlooms suggests that
Heqakheperre should be identified as an ephemeral Sheshonq II, son and
co-regent of Osorkon I. The retention of the elder Sheshonq's standard
titulary on his canopic equipment (see above, no. 55) invalidates any

equation of Hedjkheperre (Sheshonq I) with Heqakheperre (Sheshonq II), contra Gardiner 1961, 448.

For the texts, see Montet 1951, 37–38 and pls. XVII–XX (coffin); 43–45 fig. 13 and pls. XXVIII–XXIX (pectoral and bracelets); 1942, 60–62, frontispiece, and pl. XII (coffin); 68–72 and pls. XXI and XXIII (pectoral and bracelets). Color photos appear in Stierlin 1997, 186–87 (coffin) and 192–95 (bracelet and pectoral). See Kitchen 1986, 117–18 §93 and 545 §452.

I. SILVER COFFIN OF HEQAKHEPERRE SHESHONQ II

A. Flanking Horizontal Bands
    (1) Wsỉr ny-sw.t Ššnq mrỉ-ʾImn pw mꜣꜥ
    (2) Ḥqꜣ-ḫpr-Rꜥ-stp-n-Rꜥ (3) Ššnq mrỉ-ʾImn
Justified is the Osiris, King Sheshonq, beloved of Amon.
(2) Heqakheperre-setepenre (4) Sheshonq, beloved of Amon.

B. Central Vertical Band
Wsỉr ny-sw.t Ššnq mrỉ-ʾImn šsp n≠k t m Ḥw.t-kꜣ-Ptḥ qbḥw ḥtp.w m ʾIwnw pr bꜣ≠k ꜥnḫ n ḫpr nb m mr≠f mꜣꜣ≠k ʾItn ḫꜥ n wỉꜣ≠f dỉ≠f rꜥ nb n ḏ.t

Osiris King Sheshonq, beloved of Amon, take for yourself bread in Memphis, cool water and offerings in Heliopolis. May your living *ba*-spirit go forth in any transformation as it wishes. May you see the sun disk risen in his bark, when he presents (himself) daily, forever.

II. PECTORAL INSCRIPTION OF SHESHONQ B IN TWO SECTIONS BELOW THE SOLAR BARK OF AMON-RE
ʾImn-Rꜥ Ḥr-ꜣḫ.ty ḏꜣỉ p.t rꜥ nb (2) r ḫw wr ꜥꜣ n Mꜥ wr (3) n wr.w Šš(n)q mꜣꜥ-ḫrw sꜣ n (4) wr ꜥꜣ n Mꜥ Nmꜣrt
Amon-Re Horachty crosses the sky each day (2) to protect the Great Chief of the Ma, the Chief (3) of Chiefs, Shesho(n)q, the justified, son of (4) the Great Chief of the Ma, Namlot.

III. TWO BRACELETS OF SHESHONQ I, EACH WITH ROYAL TITULARY
    (1) ny-sw.t bỉ.ty nb tꜣ.wy Ḥḏ-ḫpr-Rꜥ-stp-n-Rꜥ (2) sꜣ Rꜥ nb ḫꜥ.w Ššnq mrỉ-ʾImn (3) dỉ ꜥnḫ mỉ Rꜥ ḏ.t
The King of Upper and Lower Egypt, Lord of the Two Lands, Hedj-kheperre-setepenre, (2) Son of Re, Lord of Diadems, Sheshonq, beloved of Amon, (3) given life like Re forever.

D. TAKELOT I

69. APANAGE STELA OF IUWELOT
(CAIRO JdE 31882)

Often mentioned in studies of Egyptian law, economics, or for the once-controversial filiation of Iuwelot with Osorkon I (rather than III), this round-topped red granite stela was discovered intact in the great court of Karnak in 1897 near the temple of Seti II. The stela measures 2.67 m in height, 1.25 m in width, and 0.38 m at its middle thickness. Though undated, the monument belongs to the reign of Takelot I, here as elsewhere conspicuous by his insignificance. In keeping with the contemporary vogue for judicial oracles, this testament of Iuwelot is expressed as an oracular pronouncement by Amon-Re ratifying his high priest's endowment of "ap(p)anage," or land assigned as financial support for a junior member of the royal family. Here the beneficiary is his son Khaemwese and his heirs, to the exclusion of Iuwelot's other children, such as Wasaka-wasa (see below, no. 71). More significant is the express disinheritance of Iuwelot's powerful siblings, including his successor as high priest, Smendes (III), and the ignored Takelot I. Iuwelot's concern may have been well founded, as Khaemwese never attained his father's status at Karnak, and Takelot's son, Osorkon II, made the advancement of his own heirs a dynastic policy (see below, no. 74).

The bulk of Iuwelot's legacy derived from incremental purchases from two extended families, the descendants of Iken and those of the brothers Paikesh and Djedkhonsuiuefankh. In its phraseology, the stela demonstrates the early existence of legal instruments and terminology that would become standardized in Demotic contracts of the Saite and Hellenistic eras. The curses that conclude the stela are not the customary stereotyped "boilerplate" but exceptionally vigorous threats of the loss of property, family, and health for any violator and his assistants.

This is the first integral translation. Formerly Cairo Temporary Registration 28/5/24/2. For the text, see Legrain 1897, 12–16; with a partial translation (excluding conclusion) in Erman 1897, 19–24; Breasted 1906–7, 4:405 §795 (wrongly dated to Osorkon III); Pirenne and van de Walle 1937, 43–65; and Sottas 1913, 161–65 (concluding imprecations).

For commentary on legal matters, see Griffith 1909, 13–14; Moret 1901, 30–31; and Seidl 1951, 29, 39 n. 163, 47 n. 220, and 59 n. 300. A thoroughly obsolete interpretation appears in Revillout 1899, 367–75.

For economic studies, see Baer 1962, 25–45 ("late Dynasty XXIII," following Breasted 1906–7); Janssen 1975, 530–31; and Meeks 1979a, 682.

For dating, see Kees 1964, 93–100; 1953, 195–97; von Beckerath 1966, 46 (no. 16); Drioton and Vandier 1962, 533, 562, and 674; and Jacquet-Gordon 1967, 66–67. See Kitchen 1986, 110–11 §89, 121 §96, 195 §157, 219–20 §184, 306 §265, 310 §269, and 311–12 §270.

<small>BENEATH CENTRAL WINGED DISK, TWO OFFERING SCENES</small>

<small>I. ON RIGHT, IUWELOT DRESSED IN A PANTHER SKIN OFFERS MAAT TO AMON AND MUT</small>

Label for Iuwelot
    ḥm-nṯr tp(y) n ᵓImn-Rᶜ ny-sw.t nṯr.w ỉmy-rȝ (2) mšᶜ wr ḫȝw.ty ᵓIwwr(3)ỉt mȝᶜ-ḫrw sȝ ny-sw.t nb-tȝ.wy (4) Wsỉrkn mrỉ-ᵓImn
    First Prophet of Amon-Re, King of the Gods, great (2) general and leader, Iuw(3)elot, the justified, royal son of the Lord of the Two Lands, (4) Osorkon, beloved of Amon.

Label for Amon-Re
    ḏd-mdw ỉn ᵓImn-Rᶜ nb p.t ḥqȝ Wȝs.t
    Recitation by Amon-Re, Lord of heaven, Ruler of Thebes.

Label for Mut
    ḏd-mdw ỉn Mw.t wr.t nb.(t) ᵓIšrw ỉr.(t) (2) Rᶜ ḥnw.t nṯr.w (3) bȝq.(t)[1] tȝ.wy
    Recitation by Mut the great, Lady of Asheru, Eye (2) of Re, Mistress of the Gods, (3) who makes radiant[1] the Two Lands.

<small>II. ON LEFT, IUWELOT DRESSED IN A PANTHER SKIN OFFERS MAAT TO AMON AND KHONSU</small>

Label for Iuwelot
    ḥm-nṯr tp(y) n ᵓImn-Rᶜ ny-sw.t nṯr.w ỉmy-rȝ (2) mšᶜ wr ḫȝw.t(y) ᵓIw(3)wrỉt mȝᶜ-ḫrw sȝ ny-sw.t nb-tȝ.wy (4) Wsỉrkn mrỉ-ᵓImn
    First Prophet of Amon-Re, King of the Gods, great (2) general and leader, Iu(3)welot, the justified, royal son of the Lord of the Two Lands, (4) Osorkon, beloved of Amon.

Label for Amon-Re
    ḏd-mdw ỉn ᵓImn-Rᶜ nb ns.wt tȝ.wy
    Recitation by Amon-Re, Lord of the Thrones of the Two Lands.

Label for Khonsu
    ḏd-mdw ỉn Ḫnsw (2) m Wȝs.t Nfr-ḥtp (3) Ḥr nb ȝw.t-ỉb
    Recitation by Khonsu (2) in Thebes Neferhotep, (3) the Horus, Lord of joy.

III. Main Text

d̠d ’Imn-R‘ ny-sw.t nt̠r.w pꜣ nt̠r ‘ꜣ wr m šꜣ‘ ḫpr

ỉr tꜣ s.t n sḫ.wt ỉ-grg ḥm-nt̠r tp(y) n ’Imn-R‘ ny-sw.t nt̠r.w ỉmy-rꜣ mš‘ wr ḥꜣw.t(y) ’Iwwrỉt̠ mꜣ‘-ḫrw nty (m) ḫꜣ.t nꜣy mš‘.w ‘ꜣ.w n (2) Šm‘ r-d̠r≠w (n) tꜣ q‘ḥ Sꜣwty² nty m ww n tꜣ qꜣꜣ mḥt ỉmnt.t n.t ỉw ’Iꜣ.t-nfr.tꜣ ḫr.tw r≠s ỉw≠f n ỉḥwn m rk ỉt≠f ny-sw.t Wsỉrkn mrỉ-’Imn (3) n ḥsb.t 10 ꜣbd 4 šmw ‘rqy

tꜣy 556 n stꜣ.t ꜣḥ.(t) nmḥ.w n‘⁴ nty r-qꜣ¡w n≠s nꜣy≠w šd.(w)t nꜣy≠w šn.w nꜣy(4)≠s ỉꜣw.t mnmn.t ỉ-ỉn≠f r-d̠bꜣ ḥd̠ m-dỉ nꜣ nmḥ.w n pꜣ tꜣ n ỉb ḥr(ỉ) ỉw mn sp n ḫr-gs⁵ n-ỉm≠w

ỉw dỉ≠f ỉn.t(w) nꜣ dnỉ.w n nꜣy ꜣḥ.wt (5) (n) pr ’Imn nty m-dỉ nꜣ sš.(w) ḥsb ỉt n pr ’Imn n nꜣ q‘ḥ.w n Šm‘ d̠r(≠w)

ỉw dỉ≠f wỉꜣ¡≠w⁶ (r) nꜣ ꜣḥ.(wt) ỉ-dỉ≠f ḥd̠ r-d̠bꜣ(.t)≠w ỉwd nꜣ ꜣḥ.(wt) (n) pr ’Imn pꜣ ‘ḥ‘y (6) n ꜣḥ.(wt) Pr-‘ꜣ ‘nḫ wd̠ꜣ s(nb) mỉt.t ỉw dỉ≠w grḥ n≠f tꜣy 556 n stꜣ.t ꜣḥ.(t) nmḥ.w n‘ ḥn‘ nꜣy≠w šd.(w)t nꜣy≠w šn.w

ỉw≠w ỉr.w m sš (7) m-dỉ nꜣ sḥn.w n pr ’Imn n nꜣy≠w s.wt sš m pꜣ sḫr n dỉ s.t n≠f ỉ-ỉr nꜣy≠w nb.w

ỉw s nb m rn≠f n nꜣ ỉr dỉ.t n≠f ꜣḥ.t ḥn‘ pꜣ sḫr (8) n dỉ.t n≠w ḥd̠ r-d̠bꜣ. t≠w ỉ-ỉr≠f

ỉmy-rn≠w

tꜣ s.t n w‘b n ’Imn Ns-Ḫnsw mꜣ‘-ḫrw sꜣ Ḥrỉ mꜣ‘-ḫrw sꜣ ‘nḫ≠f-n-Ḫnsw mꜣ‘-ḫrw ꜣḥ.(t) nmḥ.w n‘ stꜣ.t 137 ꜣ(9)ḥ.(t) tnỉ⁷ stꜣ.t 99 dmd ꜣḥ.(t) stꜣ.t 236 šd.t 1 nh.t 8 bnỉ.t 6 ỉr n ḥd̠ dbn 8 qd.t 2/3⁸

tꜣ s.t n

mnḥ⁹ D̠d-Mw.t-ỉw≠f-‘nḫ mꜣ‘-ḫrw sꜣ ’Ikn mꜣ‘-ḫrw ꜣḥ.(t) n(10)mḥ.w n‘ stꜣ.t 66 ꜣḥ.(t) štꜣ tnỉ stꜣ.t 5 dmd ꜣḥ.(t) stꜣ.t 71 šd.t 3 bnỉ.t ‘ꜣ.t 26 bnỉ.t šr.t 50 nh.t 3 ỉr n ḥd̠ dbn 4 qd.t 1 2/3 1/4

mnḥ ’I‘ḥ-ms (11) mꜣ‘-ḫrw sꜣ D̠d-Mw.t-ỉw≠f-‘nḫ mꜣ‘-ḫrw ḥn‘ nꜣ ẖrd.w n Pꜣ-šr-Mw.t mꜣ‘-ḫrw sꜣ D̠d-Ḫnsw-ỉw≠f-‘nḫ mꜣ‘-ḫrw ꜣḥ.(t) štꜣ tnỉ stꜣ.t 64 ꜣḥ.(t) nmḥ.w n‘ stꜣ.t 5 dmd ꜣḥ.(t) (stꜣ.t) 69 (12) ỉr n ḥd̠ dbn 1 qd.t 5

qr‘ Pn-ỉmn sꜣ Pꜣ-ỉkš mꜣ‘-ḫrw ḥn‘ mnḥ Ns-mr-Ḥr mꜣ‘-ḫrw sꜣ D̠d-Ḫnsw-ỉw≠f-‘nḫ mꜣ‘-ḫrw ꜣḥ.(t) štꜣ tnỉ stꜣ.t 30 ỉr n ḥd̠ qd.t 6

‘nḫ.(t) n.(t) nỉw.t Tꜣ-(13)šr.(t)-n-’I‘ḥ mꜣ‘.t-ḫrw tꜣ ḥm.t n.(t) w‘b n ’Imn Šꜣw-’Imn-ỉm≠f mꜣ‘-ḫrw ꜣḥ.(t) štꜣ tnỉ stꜣ.t 10 ỉr n ḥd̠ qd.t 1(?)

mnḥ Kꜣpwf mꜣ‘-ḫrw sꜣ Qꜣ-’Imn mꜣ‘-ḫrw ꜣḥ.(t) nmḥ.w n‘ stꜣ.t 14 (14) ꜣḥ.(t) štꜣ tnỉ stꜣ.t 23 dmd ꜣḥ.(t) stꜣ.t 37 ỉr n ḥd̠ dbn 1 qd.t 1/4

ḥny Tꜣw≠w-ỉw mꜣ‘-ḫrw n pꜣ ỉmy-rꜣ ỉḥ.w n ’Imn ꜣḥ.(t) štꜣ tnỉ stꜣ.t 3 ỉr n ḥd̠ (qd.t) 2/3

(15) mnḥ Ḥrỉ mꜣ‘-ḫrw sꜣ Šꜣmꜣgꜣ mꜣ‘-ḫrw ḥn‘ tꜣy ḥm.t (n.t) Pn-’Imn mꜣ‘-ḫrw sꜣ Šꜣmꜣgꜣ mꜣ‘-ḫrw ꜣḥ.(t) štꜣ tnỉ stꜣ.t 45 ỉr n ḥd̠ qd.t 8

qr‘ ’I‘ḥ-wbn mꜣ‘-ḫrw sꜣ Pꜣ-dỉ-(16)Ḫnsw mꜣ‘-ḫrw ꜣḥ.(t) nmḥ.w n‘ stꜣ. t 8 ꜣḥ.(t) štꜣ tnỉ stꜣ.t 2 dmd ꜣḥ.(t) stꜣ.t 10 ỉr n ḥd̠ qd.t 3 2/3

mnḥ Knmt̠whr mꜣ‘-ḫrw sꜣ ’Ikn mꜣ‘-ḫrw ꜣḥ.(t) stꜣ.t 1 ỉr n ḥd̠ qd.t 1/2

(17) mnḥ Dd-Ḥr-ỉw≠f-ꜥnḫ mꜣꜥ-ḫrw sꜣ Ns-tꜣ-nṯr.t-tn mꜣꜥ.t-ḫrw ꜣḥ.(t) nmḥ.t nꜥ stꜣ.t 3 ꜣḥ.(t) štꜣ tnỉ stꜣ.t 2 dmd ꜣḥ.(t) stꜣ.t 5 ỉr n ḥd qd.t 1 2/3

mnḥ Pꜣ-wn mꜣꜥ-ḫrw sꜣ ꜣIkn mꜣꜥ-ḫrw (18) ꜣḥ.(t) nmḥ.(w) nꜥ stꜣ.t 15 ỉr n ḥd qd.t 6

ꜥnḫ.(t) n.(t) nỉw.t Ns-Ḫnsw mꜣꜥ.t-ḫrw sꜣ.t ꜣIkn mꜣꜥ-ḫrw ḥnꜥ sꜣ≠s Dḥwty-ms mꜣꜥ-ḫrw sꜣ≠s Pꜣ-dỉ-Ḫnsw mꜣꜥ-ḫrw sꜣ≠s Knmtwhr mꜣꜥ-ḫrw ꜣḥ.(t) nmḥ.w nꜥ (19) stꜣ.t 8 ꜣḥ.(t) štꜣ tnỉ stꜣ.t 2 dmd ꜣḥ.(t) stꜣ.t 10 ỉr n ḥd qd.t 3 2/3

mnḥ Dd-Ḫnsw mꜣꜥ-ḫrw sꜣ ꜣIkn mꜣꜥ-ḫrw ꜣḥ.(t) nmḥ.(w) nꜥ stꜣ.t 1 ꜣḥ.(t) štꜣ tnỉ stꜣ.t 1 dmd (20) ꜣḥ.(t) stꜣ.t 2 ỉr n ḥd qd.t 2/3

mnḥ Nsỉ[10] mꜣꜥ-ḫrw (sꜣ?)[11] ꜣIwwksr mꜣꜥ-ḫrw ꜣḥ.(t) nmḥ.w nꜥ stꜣ.t 5 ꜣḥ.(t) štꜣ tnỉ stꜣ.t 2 dmd ꜣḥ.(t) stꜣ.t 7 šd.t 1 ỉr n ḥd qd.t 2 (21) 2/3

mnḥ Dd-Mw.t-ỉw≠f-ꜥnḫ mꜣꜥ-ḫrw sꜣ ꜣIkn mꜣꜥ-ḫrw ꜣḥ.(t) nmḥ.w nꜥ stꜣ. t 5 ỉr n ḥd qd.t 2 1/2

nꜣ ḥm.w ḥm.wt ỉ-ỉn≠f r-dbꜣ ḥd m-dỉ nꜣ nmḥ.w n pꜣ tꜣ n (22) mỉt.t s s.t 32 ỉr n ḥd dbn 15 qd.t 1/3 ḥnꜥ pꜣy 3 ḥm.w n ꜥ mḥt ỉ-dỉ≠f ḥr≠s

dmd ꜣḥ.(t) šbn stꜣ.t 556

s s.t 35

nꜣy≠w šd.wt nꜣy≠w šn.w (23) nꜣy≠w ỉꜣw.t mnmn.t

ỉw≠ỉ smn≠w n ḥm-nṯr n ꜣImn-Rꜥ ny-sw.t nṯr.w ꜥꜣ n qꜥḥ Ḫꜥ-n-Wꜣs.t mꜣꜥ-ḫrw pꜣy≠f šrỉ ỉ-ms n≠f sꜣ.t n sꜣ ny-sw.t (24) Tꜣ-dnỉ.t-n-Bꜣst.t mꜣꜥ.t-ḫrw r-ḫt nḥḥ

ỉw bn-ỉr nꜣ k.(t)-ḫ.t ḥrd.w ỉ-ms.w n≠f m rꜣ-pw nꜣ ḥrd.w n pꜣy≠f ỉt dr.w (25) rḫ ꜥq ḥr-r≠w[12] r pš n-ỉm≠w ḥr sꜣ dwꜣ wp-s.t m-dỉ Ḫꜥ-n-Wꜣs.t mꜣꜥ-ḫrw pꜣy ḥm-nṯr n ꜣImn-Rꜥ ny-sw.t nṯr.w ꜥꜣ n qꜥḥ

dỉ s.t n≠f pꜣy≠f ỉt (26) ỉ-ỉr≠f dỉ s.t ꜥn n sꜣ n sꜣ≠f ỉwꜥ n ỉwꜥ≠f ỉw≠ỉ m-dỉ≠w n nḫt n ḏ.t

ỉw ỉr pꜣ nt-ỉw≠f mnmn wḏ.t tn wḫꜣ pw wꜣww (27) r ḫsf ḏd.wt≠ỉ

ỉw≠ỉ r ḫꜥr ḥr-ꜥ r th(ꜣ) kꜣ≠ỉ nḏ.n≠ỉ sdgꜣ ḫꜣ≠ỉ m-ḫt ḥn.ty db ꜥw sp ỉm≠f n(n) wn≠f nym wḫd≠f bꜣ.w n dd≠ỉ ỉw≠ỉ r rdỉ.t (28) ḫpr≠f m ḥr ỉw ỉwꜥꜥw≠f m-dỉ ky ỉr.ty≠f ḥr dgꜣ≠w ỉw≠f m tp (ḥr) mꜣs.ty[13] r swdꜣ n≠f ỉw ỉt.tw ḥm.t≠f r-ḫft-ḥr≠f (29) ḥꜥ.w≠f nb ꜣbḫ m ḥr ꜥb ỉw≠f m ꜣq n ḏt nn ỉw≠f (m) nty wn mrỉ.w≠f ḥr(y)-rw.ty[14] n≠w pw snnty≠f[15] (30) m ḥm.w nḫty.w≠f[16] ỉw≠f ḥr (dd) mꜣꜥ-ḫrw kꜣ≠k nn sdm≠ỉ n wꜣww r th(ꜣ) wḏ.t tn hn≠ỉ ỉm≠s ỉw(31)≠ỉ r mdd ššr≠ỉ ḥr ỉmy-s.t-ꜥ≠f tp r tꜣ[17] ḥr s.t-ꜥ ꜥ.wy≠ỉ ỉw≠f n ỉr.t Ḥr sḫm≠s ỉm≠f ỉw drp≠ỉ (32) sw m ỉwf n ḥd dd.wt≠ỉ ỉw≠ỉ[18] m swḥw ḥr nḥd≠s r ḥꜥ.w≠f tm snwḫ m b(w)-wr ḥr sḥtp ỉb≠ỉ

There has said Amon-Re, King of the Gods, the very great god since the beginning of creation:

"As for the situation of the fields that the First Prophet of Amon-Re, King of the Gods, great general and leader, Iuwelot, the justified, who is at the head of these great armies of (2) Upper Egypt in their entirety, put into production (in) the district of Siut[2] that is in the territory of the high cultivation northwest of the island "The Good Mound,"[3] as it is called, when he was a youth in the reign of his father King Osorkon, beloved of Amon, (3) in regnal year 10, month 4 of summer, last day,

(that is) these 556 *arouras* of field privately owned with clear title,[4] to which appertain their cisterns, their trees, their (4) flocks, and their herds, which he purchased from the private owners of the country with satisfied heart and without an instance of unfairness[5] among them,

whereas he has caused that there be brought the land-registers of these fields (5) (of) the estate of Amon that are in the possession of the grain-reckoning scribes of the estate of Amon of all the districts of Upper Egypt,

and whereas he has caused that former title be relinquished[6] to the fields that he purchased among the fields of the estate of Amon and the field allotment (6) of Pharaoh, l.p.h., likewise, and whereas they have ceded to him these 556 *arouras* of field privately owned with clear title together with their cisterns and their trees,

they being recorded (7) with the administrators of the estate of Amon of their respective chancelleries as to the particulars of conveying them to him which their owners had done,

with every man named of those who had conveyed fields to him together with the particulars (8) of the payment to them of silver in return for them which he had done,

Their List:

The place of the priest of Amon, Neskhonsu, the justified, son of Hori, the justified, son of Ankhefenkhonsu, the justified: 137 *arouras* of field privately owned with clear title, (9) 99 *arouras* of "tired"[7] field, total: 236 *arouras* of field, 1 cistern, 8 sycamore trees, 6 date palms, amounting to 8 *deben*, 2/3[8] *kite* of silver;

The place of:

the cadet[9] Djedmutiuefankh, the justified, son of Iken, the justified: 66 *arouras* of field (10) privately owned with clear title, 5 *arouras* of "scrub and tired" field, total: 71 *arouras* of field, 3 cisterns, 26 large date palms, 50 small date palms, 3 sycamore trees, amounting to 4 *deben,* 1 and 11/12 *kite* of silver;

the cadet Ahmose, (11) the justified, son of Djedmutiuefankh, the justified, together with the childeren of Pashermut, the justified, son of Djedmutiuefankh, the justified: 64 *arouras* of "scrub and tired" field, 5 *arouras* of field privately owned with clear title, total: 69 (*arouras*) of field, (12) amounting to 1 *deben* and 5 *kite* of silver;

the shield-bearer Penamon son of Paikesh, the justified, together with the cadet Nesmerhor, the justified, son of Djedkhonsuiuefankh, the justi-fied: 30 *arouras* of "scrub and tired" field, amounting to 6 *kite* of silver;

the citizeness Ta(13)sherieniah, the justified, the wife of the priest of Amon Shaamonimef, the justified: 10 *arouras* of "scrub and tired" field, amounting to 1 (?) *kite* of silver;

the cadet Kapef, the justified, son of Qaamon, the justified: 14 *arouras* of field privately owned with clear title, (14) 23 *arouras* of "scrub and tired" field, total: 37 *arouras* of field, amounting to 1 *deben* and 1/4 *kite* of silver;

the oarsman Tjauiu, the justified, of the overseer of cattle of Amon: 3 *arouras* of "scrub and tired" field, amounting to 2/3 (*kite*) of silver;

(15) the cadet Hori, the justified, son of Shamaga, the justified, together with this wife of Penamon, the justified, son of Shamaga, the justified: 45 *arouras* of "scrub and tired" field, amounting to 8 *kite* of silver;

the shield-bearer Iahweben, the justified, son of Padi(16)khonsu, the justified: 8 *arouras* of field privately owned with clear title, 2 *arouras* of "scrub and tired" field, total: 10 *arouras* of field, amounting to 3 2/3 *kite* of silver;

the cadet Kenmetchweher, the justified, son of Iken, the justified: 1 *aroura* of field, amounting to 1/2 *kite* of silver;

(17) the cadet Djedhoriuefankh, the justified, son of (the woman) Nestanetereten, the justified: 3 *arouras* of field privately owned with clear title, 2 *arouras* of "scrub and tired" field, total: 5 *arouras* of field, amounting to 1 2/3 *kite* of silver;

the cadet Pawen, the justified, son of Iken, the justified: (18) 15 *arouras* of field privately owned with clear title, amounting to 6 *kite* of silver;

the citizeness Neskhonsu, the justified, daughter of Iken, the justified, together with her son Djehutymes, the justified, her son Padikhonsu, the justified, and her son Kenmetchweher, the justified: 8 *arouras* of field privately owned with clear title, (19) 2 *arouras* of "scrub and tired" field, total: 10 *arouras* of field, amounting to 3 2/3 *kite* of silver;

the cadet Djedkhonsu, the justified, son of Iken, the justified: 1 *aroura* of field privately owned with clear title, 1 *aroura* of "scrub and tired" field, total: (20) 2 *arouras* of field, amounting to 2/3 *kite* of silver;

the cadet Nesi,[10] the justified, (son of?)[11] Iuwakasar, the justified: 5 *arouras* of field privately owned with clear title, 2 *arouras* of "scrub and tired" field, total: 7 *arouras* of field, 1 cistern, amounting to 2 2/3 *kite* of silver;

(21) the cadet Djedmutiuefankh, the justified, son of Iken, the justified, 5 *arouras* of field privately owned with clear title, amounting to 2 1/2 *kite* of silver;

the male and female slaves whom he purchased from the private owners of the country in (22) like manner: 32 men and women, amounting to 15 *deben* and 1/3 *kite* of silver;

together with these three slaves of the northern region whom he added to it;

total: 556 *arouras* of various categories of fields
        35 men and women
        their cisterns, their trees, (23) their flocks, their herds;

I confirm them for the prophet of Amon-Re, King of the Gods, the district chief, Khaemwese, the justified, his son born to him by the prince's daughter (24) Tadenitenbast, the justified, throughout eternity, while neither the other children who have been born to him nor all of the children of his father (25) will be able to enter upon them[12] to divide them after the morning of inventorying them with Khaemwese, the justified, this prophet of Amon-Re, King of the Gods, and district chief. His father gave them to him; (26) yet again he shall give them to the son of his son, the heir of his heir, while I am with them as guarantor forever.

As for the one who will shift this stela, he is a fool who is sunk to (27) opposing that which I have said. I shall be enraged straightaway regarding the transgression of my plan that I have considered and sheltered behind me throughout the limits of eternity. Blame remains in him. He will not exist. Who will suffer the wrath that I vent? I shall cause (28) that he become a victim, his inheritance in the possession of another while his eyes behold it, as he sits with his head on his knees[13] until the death of him. His wife is seized in his presence, (29) while all his limbs are pervaded with impurity; he is as one who is destroyed in body. He will not come forth as one who has adherents. He is excluded[14] from them, with his support[15] (30) become (only) slaves and his entreaties,[16] as he begs: "May your spirit be justified," (but) I shall not listen to one who is sunk to transgressing this stela to which I have assented. I (31) shall shoot my arrow at his helper, (who is) overthrown[17] beneath the stroke of my arms. He will be given over to the Eye of Horus that it might have power over him, after I have offered (32) him as flesh for the injury of that which I have said, while I[18] am the wind causing that it (the arrow) bite into his collected limbs, searing in intensity, slaking my desire.

NOTES

1. See Erman and Grapow 1926–63, 1:425/14 (attested as Hellenistic).

2. Following Erman and Breasted, commentators have wrongly assumed that Iuwelot's military authority over Upper Egypt extended only to "the region of Siut" (cf. Kitchen 1986, 311 §270). However, r-dr⸗w can only mean "entirely" (literally, "to their, i.e. the armies', limit") and not "to the border of," and the mention of Siut locates the fields, not the combined armies of Upper Egypt. For the expression, see the Nile statue of Sheshonq II, above, p. 266. Thus contra Kees 1964, 95, there is no contradiction between the Apanage Stela and S. BM 1224, which styles Iuwelot "great general of the Two Lands in its entirety."

3. For the pairing of ỉw and ỉꜣ.t, see Erman and Grapow 1926–63, 1:26, 47. Erman understood "northwest (of) N.t-ỉw, called ꜣỉꜣ.t-nfr.t. Breasted interpreted N.t-ỉw as an unusual writing of "Thebes" (followed in Kitchen 1986, 306 §265, 311

§270). The diagonal stroke following the genitive n.t is likely accidental; see Blackman 1941, 90.

4. Literally, "of freemen and smooth"; see Baer 1962, 26 n. 10. In line 17, the property of Djedhoriuefankh derives from fields of a "freewoman" (nmḥ.t), his mother. The terminology has been recognized as underlying later Demotic formulary; see Thompson 1940, 74–75 (nmḥ); and Spiegelberg 1931, 104 n. 6 (nꜥ).

5. See Erman and Grapow 1926–63, 5:193/2.

6. Literally, "be far from," anticipating Demotic formulary, as recognized by Moret 1901, 31 n. 1, with reference to Revillout 1897, 447–48.

7. Low-quality or encumbered land; see Baer 1962, 26 n. 10; and Gardiner 1948, 29 n. 1.

8. Read qd.t 1 1/4 by Borchardt; see Erman 1897, 20 n. 4.

9. Signifying "youth," the term may indicate military ("cadet") or priestly rank ("novice").

10. Given a feminine determinative, presumably in error.

11. Or understand "cadet(s) Nesi, the justified, and Iuwakasar"?

12. An idiom signifying "to have the right of disposal regarding them," as clarified by the following phrase. For the idiom, see Vernus 1978, 122–23; and Menu 1980, 142.

13. The posture of mourning.

14. Literally, "on the outside of them."

15. Literally, "foundation."

16. Or "slaves whom he entreated/trusts." For the term nḥty, see Gilula 1977, 295–96. Sottas translated "esclaves qui prieront pour lui (ainsi)," which is grammatically unacceptable.

17. Literally, "head to earth."

18. For the corrected reading of the signs, see Sethe 1929, 93 n. 4.

70. THE SOLAR HYMN OF IUWELOT
(S. BM 1224)

The lunette of this round-topped limestone stela, measuring 1 ft 11 in. (58.5 cm) in height by 1 ft 4 in. in width, depicts the high priest Iuwelot, son of Osorkon I, and his wife kneeling in adoration of the solar bark, which bears the disk of Re-Horachty. Above the bark, two apes adore the rising sun and an *oudjat*-eye, while a fish and frog appear beneath the stern and prow, respectively. Below the lunette, nine hieroglyphic lines record the high priest's solar hymn, a variant of the popular religious genre grouped collectively as Book of the Dead spell 15.[1]

This is the first complete translation. For a photo and description of the stela, see Fazzini 1988, 27, 35, and pl. XLIII.1; Budge 1909, 215 (no. 777) and pl. XXVIII; with further discussion and additional references in Kees 1953, 195–96; 1964, 95; and Jansen-Winkeln 1985, 1:257 (B.7). Photo courtesy of The British Museum, with the kind assistance of W. Vivian Davies and R. B. Parkinson. See Kitchen 1986, 311 n. 385 (§270) and 576 §512.

Two Baboons, Each with Tag
dwȝ.t   "Adoration."

Label for Iuwelot

[dw]ȝ.t Rᶜ-Ḥr-ȝḫ.ty ḫft wbn≠f in Wsir (2) ḥm-nṯr tp(y) n ʾImn ʾIwwriwt
mȝᶜ-ḫrw (3) sȝ ny-sw.t Wsirkn mri-ʾImn
[Ador]ing Re-Horachty when he rises by the Osiris, (2) First Prophet of
Amon, Iuwelot, the justified, (3) royal son of Osorkon (I), beloved of Amon.

Label for Iuwelot's Wife

sn.t≠f mr.(t)≠f šmᶜy.t n.(t) ʾImn (2) šps.(t) T(ȝ)-dny.t mȝᶜ-(ḫrw)²
His sister ("wife") whom he loves, the chantress of Amon, (2) the
noble lady, Tadenit, the justified.²

Solar Hymn

dwȝ.t Rᶜ-Ḥr-ȝḫ.ty ḫft wbn≠f in Wsir ḥm-nṯr tp(y) n ʾImn-Rᶜ ny-sw.t nṯr.
w ts hp.w nfr.w m tȝ Šmᶜw (2) imy-rȝ mšᶜ wr n tȝ r-ḏr.w≠f ḥȝw.ty ʾIwwriwt
mȝᶜ-ḫrw sȝ ny-sw.t n nb tȝ.wy Wsirkn mri-ʾImn ḏd≠f
i(ȝ)ȝw.w n≠k wbn m iȝbt.t
Rᶜ di≠f s(w) m sḏ.t
bȝ wr sšp.n≠f tȝ.wy
mḥ.n≠f šn m i[r](4)w bik šps
ḥdi.n≠f sts.w
n(n) ḏr.w n dm(ȝ).ty≠f
ḥy sp-2 r nṯr nb
n(n) irw m (5) nṯr.w ᶜȝ.w
ir.ty wr ᶜnḥ.wy n tȝ.wy
šw m qd≠f sḫm nṯr(y) ms s(w) ḏs≠f
s(6)ḥḏ tȝ nb m iwnw≠f
ḥry sp-2 r rḫ s.t≠f
n(n) ir.t mȝȝ sšt(ȝ)≠f

wbkȝ (7) ywᶜ≠k mn.t
dr≠k ḏw.(t) nb.(t) ḥr≠i
di≠k ḏf(d)≠k m gs-dpw.(t)⁴
ḫsr≠k (8) snn.w≠i
ᶜp≠(i) r p.t m-ᶜb ḥȝbs.w
ḥnm≠(i) m iḫiḫ.w
šm≠i r ʾIwnw r-gs S(9)[kr]
[ni]s(?) m wᶜ n šmsy.(w)≠f
bn.tw⁴ ḥḥ≠(i) m ḥḏ.w m-bȝḥ-ᶜ.wy wrd-ib

Adoring Re-Horachty when he rises by the Osiris, First Prophet of

Amon-Re, King of the Gods, he who devises good laws in Upper Egypt, (2) great general of the entire land and leader, Iuwelot, the justified, royal son of the Lord of the Two Lands, Osorkon (I), beloved of Amon, who says: (3)

"Praises be to you, O he who rises in the East,
O Re, when he manifests himself in flame,
great ram-spirit, having illuminated the Two Lands,
having completed the (heavenly) circuit in the form of (4) a noble falcon,
and having spanned the clouds,
with no limit to his two wings,
being more exalted than any god,
without form among (5) the common gods,
the great eyes and ears of the Two Lands,
though devoid of shape,
the divine power who gave birth to himself,
who (6) illumines all lands with his features,
yet whose place is far from being known,
since no eye can behold his mystery.

O illuminator,[3] (7) may you wash away my wrongdoing,
may you drive away all evil from me.
May you place the pupil of your eye as a protective bulwark,
may your might dispel (8) my impurities,
that I might fly up to heaven amidst the stars,
that I might unite with the twilight.
May I go to Heliopolis beside (9) S[okar,]
[summon]ed(?) as one of his followers,
my neck garlanded[4] with onions
in the presence of the Weary-hearted One (Osiris)."

NOTES
    1. See Allen 1974, 12–26.
    2. Budge (1919, 215) read Shepset-tent, while Kitchen (1986, 311) read T(a)denit(enbast). No text is lost.
    3. Or wbk (w)ỉ "illuminate me."
    4. The word, determined with an arm and Gardiner Sign List F 10, perhaps should be linked to Erman and Grapow 1926–63, 1:456/14 and 3:442/4 "to grasp/enclose" or similar. Blackman (1914, 33b) translated "catch hold (?)."

71. PECTORAL OF WASAKAWASA, SON OF HIGH PRIEST IUWELOT

Made of electrum, this pectoral is of typical naos form, with the god Thoth shown standing before twin offering tables. Now in the Petrie

Museum of University College, London, this item of personal jewelry is the only attestation for Wasakawasa, whose prominence is based exclusively, and rather redundantly, upon his father's status as high priest of Amon.

Text publication in Petrie 1905b, 264–65, fig. 108 (wrongly claimed to be high priest); 1917, pl. 51, K. For discussion, see Jacquet-Gordon 1967, 67 n. 3; contra Petrie 1905b, 264, and Kees 1964, 100. See Kitchen 1986, 197 §157 and 311 n. 385.

LABEL FOR THOTH

ḏd-mdw ỉn Ḏḥwty (2) nb Ḥmnw (3) nṯr ꜥꜣ nb p.t (4) dỉ≠(ỉ) ꜥnḫ wḏꜣ s(nb) n sꜣ n ḥm-nṯr tp(y) n ꜣImn Wꜣsꜣkwꜣsꜣ (5) mꜣꜥ-ḫrw sꜣ n ḥm-nṯr tp(y) n ꜣImn ꜣIwwrỉt mꜣꜥ-ḫrw

Recitation by Thoth, (2) Lord of Hermopolis, (3) Great God, Lord of heaven: (4) "I shall give life, prosperity, and health to the son of the First Prophet of Amon, Wasakawasa, (5) the justified, son of the First Prophet of Amon, Iuwelot, the justified."

72. SERAPEUM BLOCK
(S. LOUVRE IM 157?)

Measuring .46 m in height, .48 m in width, and .09 m in depth, this calcite block contains two royal cartouches and the name of a high priest of Memphis associated with the burial of an Apis bull. Formerly assigned to the reign of Takelot II, it is now attributed to Takelot I following reanalysis of the Tanite tomb inscriptions. Such ambiguity reflects the general lack of originality in contemporary titularies, whereby "Hedjkheperre-setepenre Takelot (I), beloved of Amon" must be distinguished from an identical title string for Takelot II only by the latter's addition of "Son of Isis."

For the texts, see Malinine, Posener, and Vercoutter 1968, 18 and plate (no. 19). See Kitchen 1995, xxiii, correcting 1986, 327 §289.

TWO VERTICAL CARTOUCHES

[…] nb tꜣ.wy Ḥḏ-ḫpr-Rꜥ-stp-n-Rꜥ (2) [… nb] ḫꜥ.w Tkrỉwt mry-ꜣImn

[…] Lord of the Two Lands, Hedjkheperre-setepenre, (2) [… Lord] of diadems, Takelot, beloved of Amon.

LOWER HORIZONTAL BAND

ḥs-mr≠f wr ḫrp ḥmww n Ptḥ Mr-n-Ptḥ mꜣꜥ-ḫrw

His beloved favorite, "Chief of Master-craftsmen" of Ptah (high priest of Memphis), Merenptah, the justified.

73. TANITE TOMB INSCRIPTIONS
THE THRONE NAME AND BURIAL OF TAKELOT I

As interpreted by its excavator Montet, Chamber III of the tomb of
Osorkon II in the Amon temple precinct at Tanis represented an intrusive
burial of the successor, Takelot II. New translations of a scene from the east
wall of the chamber prove, however, that the burial is that of Osorkon's
father, Takelot I, whose titulary was previously uncertain. Inscriptions
from objects within the chamber confirm the elder Takelot's throne name,
clearly distinguished from that of his namesake only by the latter's addition
of "son of Isis."

For the texts and their proper interpretation, see Jansen-Winkeln 1987,
253–58, superseding Montet 1947, 81–85 and pl. XXXVIII; 1942, 8–10,
14–15. See further the translation and discussion in Kitchen 1995, xxii–xxiii
§§U–V, replacing 1986, 95–97 §§76–77 and 332–33 §294 (ii).

I. Cartouches Painted on the Reused Middle Kingdom Sarcophagus of Imeny
(Montet 1942, 14–15; 1947, 82 fig. 26)

Ḥd-ḫpr-Rᶜ-stp-n-Rᶜ Tkrȋt mry-ʾImn
Hedjkheperre-setepenre, Takelot, beloved of Amon.

II. Approximately 360 Ushebti Inscriptions, Each Bearing the Royal Name
(Montet 1942, 14–15; 1947, 83 fig. 27 and pl. LVI, E; Association française
d'action artistique 1987, 148–49 no. 32)

Wsȋr ny-sw.t Tkrȋt mry-ʾImn
The Osiris King Takelot, beloved of Amon.

III. Single Ushebti with an Extended Inscription (Montet 1947, 83, fig. 27)

ȋw wšbt.w (r) wšb n nb(2)≠w f3 p3 tw ȋ3bt.t (3) r-ḥr p3 tw ȋmnt.t rdȋ.
t w3(.t) (4) ḥmt.t r ḥr.t (n) Wsȋr ny-sw.t Tkrȋt mry-ʾImn
The ushebtis will respond to their lord (2) to carry the mountain of the
East (3) upon the mountain of the West to give a (4) planned[1] route to the
sky (for) the Osiris King Takelot, beloved of Amon.

IV. Gold Plaque (Montet 1947, pl. LVI, A)

ny-sw.t bȋ.ty Ḥd-ḫpr-Rᶜ-stp-n-Rᶜ s3 Rᶜ Tkrȋt mry-ʾImn
The King of Upper and Lower Egypt, Hedjkheperre-setepenre, Son of
Re, Takelot, beloved of Amon.

V. Dedication Inscription of Osorkon II for His Deceased Father

Osorkon II Adores Osiris and Edjo (Montet 1947, pl. XXXVIII)
[ȋr].n{n} ny-sw.t bȋ.ty nb t3.wy Wsr-m3ᶜ.t-Rᶜ-stp-n-ʾImn s3 Rᶜ nb ḫᶜ.w

Wsỉrkn mrỉ-ʾImn [r smnḫ] Wsỉr ny-sw.t (2) Tkrỉt mry-ʾImn m ḥw.t⸗f tn ntt [m ḫ]nw n ʾItn dỉ ḥtp⸗f m ḥw.t tn m sȝḫ (3) ʾImn-rn⸗f mỉ ỉrr.w n sȝ (n) ȝḫ.wt n ỉṯ⸗f [r] smnḫ ỉr kȝ⸗f stwt r wḏ.n Ḥr-sȝ-ȝs.t (4) n ỉṯ⸗f Wnn-nfr wȝḏ. wy ḥr ỉb⸗ỉ n nb nṯr.w

[Made] by the King of Upper and Lower Egypt, Lord of the Two Lands, Usimaꜥresetepenamon, Son of Re, Lord of Diadems, Osorkon, beloved of Amon, [to benefit] the Osiris King (2) Takelot, beloved of Amon, in this his Mansion that is [in]² the Residence of Aton, to cause that he rest in this Mansion in the vicinity of (3) Him-whose-name-is-hidden³ according to the making by a son of benefactions for his father [in order to] benefit him who made his *ka,* equal to what Horus son of Isis commanded (4) for his father Wennefer. How pleasant it is in my heart for the Lord of the Gods!

Label for Osorkon II

Wsỉr Wsr-mȝꜥ.t-Rꜥ-stp-n-ʾImn (2) ny-sw.t Wsỉrkn mrỉ-ʾImn (3) sȝ ḥr smnḫ (4) qmȝ sw

The Osiris Usimaꜥresetepenamon, (2) King Osorkon, beloved of Amon, (3) a son benefiting (4) the one who created him.

Label for Osiris

ḏd-mdw ỉn Wsỉr⁴ (2) nṯr ꜥȝ n ḏ.t

Recitation by Osiris (2) the great god of eternity.

Label for Edjo as a Uraeus

Wȝḏy.t nb(.t) P

Edjo, the Lady of Pe.

NOTES

1. Montet translates "unknown road."
2. Kitchen translates "which is [an abo]de."
3. Epithet of Amon.
4. Jansen-Winkeln (1987, 255 and 256) transliterates ȝstjrt(!).

E. OSORKON II

74. PHILADELPHIA-CAIRO STATUE
(S. PHILADELPHIA E 16199 + CAIRO JdE 37489¹)

The grey granite statue (123 cm) depicts the kneeling king presenting a stela with a votive inscription. From the main Amon temple at Tanis (north of the central aisle between Pylons II and III), the statue is preserved in three fragments (head, torso, and stela), with substantial damage to the edges.

Of the Cairo fragments, the stela was discovered by Mariette before 1863, and Petrie excavated the kneeling torso in 1884. Philadelphia acquired the unprovenienced head from an antiquities dealer in 1926.[2] Both the statue typology and the text correspond to a formal oracular consultation within the local Amon temple, perhaps shortly after Osorkon's coronation. The text sets forth an official regnal "program," treating religious, dynastic, and military affairs. Of particular interest is the king's intention to establish his own sons in all the prominent offices of the country, including the still-significant lineage chieftainships of the Meshwesh (line 8).[3] Given the royal interest in Libyan matters, the reference to hostile Pyt-Libyans (line 16) is intriguing. Osorkon's fears regarding family fragmentation (line 12) were realized not long after his death, with the schism of the related Dynasty XXIII.

The stela inscription originally comprised twenty-four-plus lines, of which only twenty-one fragmentary lines remain, lacking the beginnings and ends of lines. Cartouches appear on the left shoulder and in the "negative space" between the stela and torso, with the titulary around the base. Left and right designations are from the perspective of the statue, not the viewer.

Texts, translations, photos, and publication history appear in Jacquet-Gordon 1960, 12–23. See also P. Vernus in Association française d'action artistique 1987, 108; Kitchen 1986, 317 §276. Earlier translations are found in Daressy 1896b, 49–51; Griffith in Griffith, Petrie, and Murray 1888, 21 (titulary only); Breasted 1906–7, 4:370–71 §§745–47. Artistic analysis and the first announcement of the join of the head (Philadelphia) to the body with stela (Cairo) appear in Bothmer 1960, 3–11: "the finest statue of an otherwise bleak period in the history of Egyptian sculpture in the round" (11).

CARTOUCHE ON LEFT SHOULDER
    W[sỉrkn] mrỉ-ʾImn sꜣ Bꜣst.t
    Osorkon, beloved of Amon, Son of Bastet

NEGATIVE SPACE ("BRIDGE") CONNECTING STELA TO TORSO

Right Side
    ny-sw.t bỉ.ty nb tꜣ.wy Wsr-mꜣꜥ.t-Rꜥ-stp-n-ʾImn[4] sꜣ Rꜥ nb ḫꜥ.w Wsỉrkn mrỉ-ʾImn sꜣ Bꜣst.t dỉ ꜥnḫ ḏd wꜣs ꜣw.t-ỉb nb mỉ Rꜥ ḏ.t
    The King of Upper and Lower Egypt, Lord of the Two Lands, Usimaꜥ-resetepenamon,[4] Son of Re, Lord of Diadems, Osorkon, beloved of Amon, Son of Bastet, given all life, stability, dominion, and joy like Re forever.

Left Side
    ny-sw.t bỉ.ty nb tꜣ.wy Wsr-mꜣꜥ.t-Rꜥ-stp-n-ʾImn[4] sꜣ Rꜥ nb ḫꜥ.w Wsỉrkn mrỉ-ʾImn sꜣ Bꜣst.t dỉ ꜥnḫ ḏd wꜣs snb nb mỉ Rꜥ ḏ.t

The King of Upper and Lower Egypt, Lord of the Two Lands, Usimaᶜ-resetepenamon,⁴ Son of Re, Lord of Diadems, Osorkon, beloved of Amon, Son of Bastet, given all life, stability, dominion, and health like Re forever.

BASE (TWO FACING BANDS OF INSCRIPTION BEGINNING AT CENTER)

Right Side (right to left)

[ᶜnḫ Ḥr kꜣ nḫt mrỉ-Mꜣᶜ.t ...] mn wsr≠f (?) ... ḫᶜ [m?] Wꜣs.t nb tꜣ[.wy(?) ...] Nb.ty smꜣ pš.ty mỉ sꜣ ꜣs.t sḥtp nṯr.w [m ỉr mꜣᶜ.t⁵ ... ny-sw.t bỉ.ty Wsr-mᶜꜣ.t-Rᶜ-stp-n-ʾImn sꜣ Rᶜ Wsỉrkn mrỉ-ʾImn sꜣ Bꜣst.t dỉ ᶜnḫ]

[Long live the Horus: "Strong Bull Beloved of Maat ...] whose might endures (?) ... appearing [in] Thebes, Lord of the [Two (?)] Land[s ...";] The Two Ladies: "He who unites the two divisions like the son of Isis, who pacifies the gods [by performing justice"⁵;... the King of Upper and Lower Egypt, Usimaᶜresetepenamon, Son of Re, Osorkon, beloved of Amon, Son of Bastet, given life.]

Left Side (left to right)

[ᶜnḫ Ḥr kꜣ nḫt mrỉ-Mꜣᶜ.t ... sḫᶜ sw Rᶜ r ny-sw].t tꜣ.wy Ḥr-nbw sḫm pḥty ḫ(wỉ) ḫft(y)≠f wsr fꜣw⁶ [... ny-sw.t bỉ.ty Wsr-mꜣᶜ.t-Rᶜ-stp-n-ʾImn sꜣ Rᶜ Wsỉrkn mrỉ-ʾImn sꜣ Bꜣst.t dỉ ᶜnḫ]

[Long live the Horus: "Strong Bull Beloved of Maat ... whom Re made manifest to be] King of the Two Lands"; Horus of Gold: "Powerful of strength, who strikes his enemy, mighty in splendor⁶"; [... the King of Upper and Lower Egypt, Usimaᶜresetepenamon, Son of Re, Osorkon, beloved of Amon, Son of Bastet, given life.]

STELA

(1) [...]ḫ[..] nb ḥ.wt⁷ [m]n [..] tp [...ỉw≠k ỉr⁸]

(2) [... nkt(?)] nb nfr nty-ỉw≠w nfr n≠[ỉ] mtw≠w [nfr(?)⁹] n≠ỉ ꜣmy(?) [...]

(3) [...] .. ḥwỉ n-ỉm≠w ỉw≠k šd≠ỉ¹⁰ r sḥd n ʾImn Pꜣ-Rᶜ [Ptḥ]

(4) [Bꜣst.t nb Pr-] Bꜣst.t Wsỉr Ḥr ꜣs.t nṯr nb nṯr.t nb.t n p.t tꜣ ỉw≠k šd≠

(5) [ỉ r nꜣy≠]w sḥd r nꜣy≠w bꜣ.w ỉw≠k pḥr ḥꜣ.t(y)≠ỉ¹¹ r ỉr md.t [nb(.t)]

(6) [nfr.t m]tw¹² ʾImn Pꜣ-Rᶜ Ptḥ Bꜣst.t Wsỉr Ḥr ꜣs.t ḥr n≠ỉ n-ỉm≠w

(7) [ỉw≠k tꜣ]s tꜣy≠ỉ pr.t mwy pr m ḥᶜ.w≠ỉ [r ḫpr(?)]

(8) [ḥqꜣ].w [ᶜ]ꜣ.w n Km.t ỉry.w-pᶜ.t ḥm.w-nṯr tpy.w n ʾImn ny-sw.t nṯr.w wr.w¹³ ᶜꜣ.w n Mᶜ¹⁴ [wr.w]

(9) [ᶜꜣ.w n ḫ]ꜣs.ty≠w ḥm.w-nṯr n Ḥry-š≠f ny-sw.t-tꜣ.wy ỉw wdꜣ≠ỉ hꜣ ḫrw≠ỉ¹⁵ n [...]n[...]

(10) [... ỉ]w≠k pḥr ḥꜣ.t(y)≠w m-sꜣ sꜣ Rᶜ Wsỉrkn mrỉ-ʾImn sꜣ Bꜣst.t ỉw≠k dỉ.ṯ≠w ḥr [šm(?) ḥr]

(11) [t3yₑỉ mỉ].t¹⁶ ỉwₑk smn n3yₑy ḫrd.w ḥr n3y.w [...¹⁷]

(12) [... ỉ]w-dỉₑỉ nₑw nn bq3 ỉb n sn snₑf [ỉr(?) ḥm.t-ny-sw.t]

(13) [s3.t-ny-sw.t] Krmᶜ ỉwₑk dỉ ᶜḥᶜₑs m-b3hₑỉ n n3y(ₑy) ḥb.w-sd [nb.w]

(14) [ỉwₑk dỉ] ᶜnḫ n3yₑs ḫrd.w t3y.w n3yₑs [ḫrd.w s-ḥm.wt]

(15) [ỉwₑk¹⁸ h3b]ₑsn ḫ3.t mšᶜ.w mtwₑw ᶜn nₑỉ smỉ [ḥr(?)]

(16) [... n3]¹⁹ Pywd²⁰ ỉ-ỉr ỉy r sỉ[kn(?) ...]

(17) [...] ᶜ3 wᶜb ỉwₑk sḫtḫtₑw ỉwₑk s[...]

(18) [...]n ḥr n h3n3.w(ₑỉ)²¹ r h3n3.w n [...]

(19) [...] n p3 t3 ỉwₑf 3s ỉwₑk dỉ[.tₑw(?) ḥr šm(?)]

(20) [ḥr (?)] t3yₑy mỉ.t²² nt(y)-ỉw 3[...]

(21) [...] ... n n3yₑy ...[...]

(1) [...] ... every [...] mansion⁷ enduring [...] upon [... You will do⁸]

(2) every good [thing (?)] that will be good for me, so that they will [be good (?)⁹] for me ...[...]

(3) [...] strikes them. You will save me¹⁰ from the censure of Amon, Pre, Ptah],

(4) [Bastet, Lady of Bu]lbastis, Osiris, Horus, Isis, and of every god and every goddess of heaven and earth. You will save

(5) [me from their] censure and from their wrath. You will incline my heart¹¹ to do everything

(6) [good] so that¹² Amon, Pre, Ptah, Bastet, Osiris, Horus, and Isis are content with me by means of them.

(7) [You will] fashion my seed, the semen come forth from my body [to become]

(8) the great [ruler]s of Egypt, the Hereditary Princes, First Prophets of Amon, King of the Gods, great chiefs¹³ of the Ma,¹⁴ [great]

(9) [chiefs] of the foreigners, and prophets of Harsaphes, King of the Two Lands, after I have commanded (it). May my voice¹⁵ descend to [...]

(10) [...] You will incline their hearts toward (lit., "after") the Son of Re, Osorkon, beloved of Amon, Son of Bastet. You will keep them [walking upon]

(11) [my] path.¹⁶ You will establish my children upon their [offices¹⁷]

(12) [... that] I gave to them, without a brother being resentful of his brother. [As for the royal wife]

(13) [and royal daughter] Karoma, you will cause her to stand before me in [all] my jubilee festivals.

(14) [You will cause] that her male and her [female] children live.

(15) [You¹⁸ will send] them at the head of armies so that they return to me report [concerning (?)]

(16) [the]¹⁹ *Pyt*-Libyans,²⁰ who have come to destroy (?) [...]

(17) [...] great of purification. You will repel them; you will [...]

(18) [...] the sight of (my) followers²¹ against the followers of [...]

(19) [...] of the earth as he hurries. You will keep [them walking (?)]
(20) [upon (?)] my path[22] that [...]
(21) [...] ... of/for my [...]

NOTES

1. Equals CGC 1040; see Borchardt 1911–36, 4:34-36 and pl. 161.

2. See Mariette 1887, 15 § XII; Petrie 1885, 15 no. 75; 25 §30; and pls. VI no. 41; XIV fig. 3; and plan no. 75; Griffith in Griffith, Petrie, and Murray 1888, 21; Bothmer 1960, 3 and 4 n. 1; and Jacquet-Gordon 1960, 12.

3. Contra Jacquet-Gordon 1960, 23, there is no reason to conclude that the Meshwesh had become fully Egyptianized and that "there was no real link binding them to their country of origin or to the related tribes which had remained behind there." On the contrary, Osorkon's continued "non-Egyptianized" interest in Meshwesh status designations proves the court to be less assimilated than generally believed.

4. Jacquet-Gordon vocalizes "Usimaʿrēʿmiamūn," wrongly substituting "beloved" (mrỉ/mi) for "chosen" (stp/setep).

5. Jacquet-Gordon prefers "as (being) one who acts justly" due to the lack of an infinitival ending (-t) on ỉr, but cf. line 5.

6. Written ȝwf; cf. Erman and Grapow 1926–63, 1:575/9 for common phrase and metathesis.

7. A reference to the temple setting of the oracular procedure?

8. Following standard translations, the form ỉw≠k + infinitive is translated as an injunctive future, although the oracular form might favor the interrogative: "Will you..." Cf. The Abydos Stela of Sheshonq I, above, no. 41. Here, however, there is no recorded response from the god, suggesting instead a procedure like that of the oracular amuletic decrees. See Edwards 1960.

9. Traces noted with caution by Jacquet-Gordon 1960, 18.

10. The object of the infinitive is correctly written as a suffix pronoun, contra Jacquet-Gordon 1960, 18.

11. Lit. "encircle/enchant the heart." For the idiom, see Ritner 1993b, 66–67.

12. Following a hesitant suggestion of Černý, Jacquet-Gordon restores [nty-ỉw≠w], with nfr.t at the end of line 5. The traces and the translation fit the conjunctive.

13. Ideographically written with figure of chief wearing feather, or read the Berber title ms (mas)?

14. Abbreviated writing with throwstick.

15. So Jacquet-Gordon; Breasted reads ḥm "servant."

16. Literally, "set them in [motion upon my] path"; see Erman and Grapow 1926–63, 2:468/14 for the causitive formation. The statement reflects the common Egyptian idiom of personal behavior as the "path" of life.

17. Restore s.wt or ỉȝw.wt "seats/offices."

18. Jacquet-Gordon first restored ỉw≠ỉ, which is unexpected in this series of oracular statements; see Jacquet-Gordon 1960, 23, Postscript.

19. Or restore [ỉr nȝ] Pywd "As for the Pyt-Libyans"? So Jacquet-Gordon 1960, 23, Postscript.

20. For the Pyt or Pyudu Libyans, see Graefe 1975, 13–17.

21. Equals hnw, "associates/followers," Erman and Grapow 1926–63, 1:494/1–
4; this example cited as "Dyn. 22."
22. Restored following lines 10–11.

75. BYBLOS STATUE

While no statue of Takelot I has been recovered from Byblos, his
successor emulated the diplomatic policy of Sheshonq I and Osorkon I in
presenting a self-representation to the great temple of the Phoenician city.
The throne and lower body of a seated statue of the king were excavated
within the temple proper, east of Hall D, and have a preserved height of
.86 m. Parallel royal titles are carved in three columns on the lateral sides
of the throne (left side with traces only), and a further titulary appears
along the throne's border. No Phoenician inscription is preserved.

For the texts and photo, see Dunand 1939, 115–17 no. 1741; 1937, pl.
XLIII; with a citation in Porter and Moss 1927–51, 388. See Kitchen 1986,
324 §283.

ROYAL TITLES ON LATERAL SIDES
ny-sw.t bỉ.ty Wsr-m3ꜥ.t-Rꜥ-stp-n-ꞌImn (2) s3 Rꜥ Wsrkn mrỉ-ꞌImn s3 B3st.
t (3) mry-3s.t wr.t [mw.t-]nṯr
The King of Upper and Lower Egypt, Usimaꜥresetepenamon, (2) Son
of Re, Osorkon, beloved of Amon, Son of Bastet, (3) beloved of Isis the
great, the God's [Mother].

ROYAL TITLES ON THRONE EDGES (TOP = A, FRONT = B)
ny-sw.t bỉ.ty nb t3.wy Wsr-m3ꜥ.t-Rꜥ-stp-n-ꞌImn s3 Rꜥ Wsỉrkn mrỉ-ꞌImn
(b) nṯr nfr nb t3.wy Wsỉrkn mrỉ-ꞌImn mry 3s.t wr.t [mw.t-] nṯr
The King of Upper and Lower Egypt, Lord of the Two Lands, Usimaꜥresetepenamon, Son of Re, Osorkon, beloved of Amon, (b) the Good God,
Lord of the Two Lands, Osorkon, beloved of Amon, beloved of Isis the
great, the God's [Mother].

76. KARNAK SANCTUARY BLOCKS

The text is found on two *in situ* adjoining blocks from the south wall
of the North Court (VI), northwest of the bark sanctuary of Philip Arrhidaeus. For the location, see Porter and Moss 1927–51, 2:92 (264) and pl.
XI (264). Largely effaced by a superimposed relief of Taharqa, the inscriptions record a fragmentary decree of Osorkon II detailing stipulations for
the temple personnel of Thebes, carved near the sanctuary for the benefit
of its intended audience.[1]

Text and discussion appear in 1975, 1–66, esp. 2, 20–26, and pl. II
(§B); with an older copy in Müller 1910, 151 figs. 57–58, blocks I–J only.

See also Kitchen 1986, 320 §278. Chicago Oriental Institute photos 5209, 6164, and 8742.

(1) [ḥsb.t …] ḫr ḥm n Ḥr kꜣ nḫt] mrỉ-Mꜣꜥ.t sḫꜥ sw R[ꜥ] r ny-sw.t tꜣ.wy Nb.ty smꜣ pš.ty mỉ sꜣ ꜣs.t dmd nꜰf sḫm.ty m ḥtp dhn

(2) […² Ḥr-nbw w]r pḥty ḫ(wỉ) Mnty.w ws[r fꜣw] ny-sw.t bỉ.ty nb tꜣ.wy nb ỉr.(t) ḫ.t Wsr-mꜣꜥ.t-Rꜥ-stp-n-ꜣImn

(3) [sꜣ Rꜥ Wsỉrkn mrỉ-ꜣImn sꜣ Bꜣst.t dỉ ꜥnḫ ḏ.t wḏ.t ꜣwy] m ḥm n stp-sꜣ r pr ꜣImn-Rꜥ nb [p.t? ḫnty] ꜣIp.t-s.wt r [dỉ.]t [m] ḫr n rmṯ[.w(?)]³ … ꜣImn-]Rꜥ pr(?) ny-sw.t

(4) […] sḏm ỉn rmṯ.w n tꜣ.wy [wḏ].t tn ỉr.n ḥmꜰf [r] pr n ỉtꜰf [ꜣI]mn-Rꜥ m ḏd wḏ.n ḥmꜰf r

(5) […] wꜥb m ḥw.t-nṯr n.t ꜣImn[-Rꜥ] ḫ[n]⁴ r.w-pr.w m Wꜣs.t m s[md. t(?)]ꜰs[n] (r)-ꜣw wp ỉ-[ỉ]r

(6) […] hrw n ḥb wꜣḏ pr⁵ m tpy šmw […] ỉw […]

(7) […]m n ḥmꜰf ỉr.n{n} ỉmy-rꜣ Šmꜥ Pꜣ[-…]

(8) […] m ḫw [..]

(1) [Regnal year … under the Majesty of Horus: "Strong Bull] Beloved of Maat, whom Re made manifest to be King of the Two Lands"; The-Two-Ladies: "He who unites the two divisions like the son of Isis, who has joined to himself the double crown in peace, appointed by

(2) […"²; Horus-of-Gold: "Powerful] of strength, who strikes the Bedouin, mighty in splendor"; the King of Upper and Lower Egypt, Lord of the Two Lands, Lord of ritual performance, Usimaꜥre-setepenamon,

(3) [Son of Re, Osorkon, beloved of Amon, Son of Bastet, given life forever. Decree promulgated] in the majesty of the palace regarding the estate of Amon-Re, Lord of [heaven (?), Foremost of] Karnak to instruct the people³ [… Amon-]Re the royal palace

(4) […] Then the people of the Two Lands heard this [decree] that His Majesty made [regarding] the estate of his father Amon-Re in saying: "His Majesty has commanded regarding

(5) [… to be (?)] wab-priest in the temple of Amon-[Re], to provision⁴ the temples in Thebes with their complete personnel. Inventory made

(6) […] day of the festival: "To make the house flourish"⁵ in the first month of summer […] while […]

(7) […] of/for His Majesty that was done by the Overseer of Upper Egypt, Pa[….]

(8) […] in exemption […]

NOTES
1. See Vernus 1975, 25–26, although there is no obvious reference to oracular procedure, in contrast to adjacent inscriptions of Sheshonq I and Taharqa. Note that Sheshonq blocks also record temple exemptions.

2. Vernus (1975, 22 textual note b) restores the unattested epithet: dhn [sw ...
r ḥq3 t3.wy] "whom the god ... has appointed to be ruler of the Two Lands."
   3. Late writing of rmṯ with vulture head? Or read ꜥ[q.w] "those who enter"?
   4. See Vernus 1975, 23 textual note l.
   5. See Vernus 1975, 23–24 textual note o.

77. SUPPOSED "JUBILEE STELA"

Now in a private collection in New York, this round-topped stela
(about 60 cm high) was formerly in the collection of Russian Count Gregor
Stroganoff. Dated to year 22, the stela has been associated with Osorkon's
jubilee reliefs of the same year at Bubastis. The text, however, proves to
be a private dedication, not a royal inscription, and no link to the jubilee or Bubastis can be demonstrated. The lunette scene depicts Osorkon
holding an unguent jar at an offering table before the mummiform Osiris,
who is followed by Horus and Isis (3s.t). In an unusual representation, the
winged sun disk atop the scene extends protective arms to flank the head
and *atef*-crown of Osiris. Behind Osiris the symbols for "dominion and
life" are repeated twice (w3s ꜥnḫ w3s ꜥnḫ). The bottom portion of the stela
has been sawed off, and only two lines of text and the head of the private
donor are preserved. For the text and discussion, see von Beckerath 1996,
19–22; Marucchi 1923, 77–88; Porter and Moss 1927–51, 4:29.

LABEL FOR KING
    Wsr-m3ꜥ.t-Rꜥ-stp-[n]-ʾImn (2) Wsrkn mrỉ-ʾImn
    Usimaꜥresetepenamon, (2) Osorkon, beloved of Amon.

LABEL FOR OSIRIS
    Wsỉr nb Ḏdw   Osiris, Lord of Busiris.

TEXT
    (1) ḥsb.t 22 ḫr ny-sw.t bỉ.ty nb t3.wy Wsr-m3ꜥ.t-Rꜥ-stp-n-ʾImn s3 Rꜥ nb
n¹ ḫꜥ.w Wsrkn mrỉ-ʾImn ꜥnḫ mrỉ-Wsỉr Ḥr 3s.t
    (2) [ḥnq(?)] P3-ỉr(?)-Mw.t² ỉn³ Wsỉr Ḥr 3s.t dỉ n≠f⁴ ꜥnḫ wḏ3 s(nb) ꜥḥꜥw⁵
q3ỉ ỉ3w.t nfr.(t) mr.(t) ḥs.(t) Pr-ꜥ3 n
    (3) [...]

    (1) Regnal year 22 under the King of Upper and Lower Egypt, Lord
of the Two Lands, Usimaꜥresetepenamon, Son of Re, Lord of¹ Diadems,
Osorkon, beloved of Amon, who lives, beloved of Osiris, Horus, and Isis.
    (2) [Donation by (?)] Pairmut (?)² to³ Osiris, Horus, and Isis, who give
to him⁴ life, prosperity, health, a long lifetime,⁵ goodly old age, love, and
praise of Pharaoh for
    (3) [...]

NOTES

1. An atypical writing of this epithet with an indirect genitive.
2. For the suggested reading, see von Beckerath 1996, 20.
3. The writing ỉn is perhaps a conflation of the name determinative with a following dative.
4. The signs are displaced and read n dỉ⸗f. Or understand "for the giving (to) him of life, etc."
5. Von Beckerath (1996, 22) misreads ꜥḥꜥw "lifetime" as sḫm "power."

78. BUBASTIS JUBILEE RELIEFS AND ASSOCIATED MONUMENTS ("FESTIVAL HALL," HYPOSTYLE HALL, NAOS)

Scenes of Osorkon's royal jubilee celebrated in year 22 (ca. 853 B.C.E.) are depicted upon a monumental red granite gateway (formerly known as a "Festival Hall") located between the first and second courts of the great temple of Bubastis. Roughly one-third of the decorated blocks are preserved, with the greatest loss from North Wall E. All stone is reworked from Ramesside and earlier constructions. Particular historical importance has been attached to §§III.H (hall construction) and III.I (jubilee date). Incorporating elements from New Kingdom, and perhaps even Old Kingdom, "Heb-Sed" ceremonies, the Osorkon reliefs provide the most detailed evidence for this pivotal ritual of divine kingship, designed to reinvigorate the waning powers of an elder king. Consisting primarily of (many previously untranslated) brief tags and labels, the jubilee texts nevertheless explain the accompanying ritual actions and, on occasion, record hymns and invocations. In §II.B.2 the king is said to have "overthrown the Libyans," while Horus of Libya appears as a patron of the jubilee in §III.E.5. The traditional nature of Osorkon's festival has been used to support the contention that the Libyan dynasty was thoroughly Egyptianized.

This is the first complete translation. The initial discovery is reported in Naville 1891. For the texts, see Naville 1892; Porter and Moss 1927–51, 4:28–29; with additional discoveries in Habachi 1957, 59–70. Partial translations and discussion appear in Barta 1978, 25–42 and pls. I–IV; and Uphill 1965, 365–83. Individual blocks were removed to the British Museum, Berlin, the Louvre, and the University of Pennsylvania at Philadelphia; see Budge 1909, 212 (BM1105 = Naville 1892, pl. XXIII/5) and 213 (BM 1077 = Naville 1892, pl. XVI/8); Königlichen Museen zu Berlin 1899, 229–30 (10838 = Naville 1892, pl. III/13; 10837 = Naville 1892, pl. XI/6); Boreux 1932, 1:59–61 (E 10592 = B 53); and Association française d'action artistique 1987, 170–71 (no. 45). For the artistic depictions, see Fazzini 1988, 10, 32, and pls. XI–XV.

Reconstruction of the walls and register numbering (from the base) here follow the extensive revisions by Barta.[1] Further revisions have been suggested by Kuraszkiewicz 1996, 79–93. The order of reading any individual wall is from bottom to top; so Uphill 1965, 366, following Naville 1892, 9.[2] The sequence of walls is disputed; here flanking walls are paired in succession (A + D; B/C + E/F).[3] See Kitchen 1986, 320–22 §§279–80. Unless otherwise noted, all references to plates are to Naville 1892.

NOTES TO INTRODUCTION

1. Barta's study is acknowledged without further critical comment in Kitchen 1986, 577 §514.

2. Note, however, that this order is reversed in other ritual reliefs; cf. Nelson 1949, 202–4 (Karnak reliefs of Seti I). See also the cautionary remarks of Barta 1978, 34, and the clear top to bottom order of the deities on Naville 1892, pl. X/3.

3. Naville orders the walls in strict sequence A–F. Uphill's reinterpretation is self-contradictory, first insisting that paired walls should be viewed together (1965, 366–67), then isolating wall D from its companion A (p. 380). A more systematic analysis of complementary sections is found in Barta, pp. 34-42.

§I. NAVILLE'S WALL A: EASTERN OUTER FACE

A. Bottom, Register 1: Edjo with papyrus scepter behind king (pls. III/14, left-15, and XXVIII; Naville 1892, 9; Uphill 1965, 370). Facing right (toward entrance). Lost figure of Bastet (?) before king; cf. §IIA (pl. XVII, right 13–15).

Label for Edjo
    ḏd-mdw ỉn W3ḏy.t [ḥr(y.t)]-ỉb B3s.t (2) dỉ≠(ỉ) n≠k ʿnḫ w3s nb mỉ Rʿ
    Recitation by Edjo, [resi]dent in Bubastis: (2) "I shall give to you all life and dominion like Re."

Behind King (cf. §II A for restoration)
    s3 ḫ3[≠k mỉ Rʿ]
    Protection is behind [you like Re.]

B. Register 2: Thoth (?) offers jubilees and glyph of years (pls. III/14, right, and XXVIII; Naville 1892, 9; Uphill 1965, 370). Facing right.

    dỉ≠(ỉ) n≠k ʿnḫ w3s nb mỉ Rʿ d.t
    "I shall give to you all life and dominion like Re forever."

Behind God
    [s3 ...] snb nb mỉ Rʿ
    [The protection of ... and] all health like Re.

C. Register 3: Offering Clepsydra[1] (pls. III [= Naville 1891, pl. XLII.A], XXVIII, and cf. XVI; Naville 1892, 9–10; Uphill 1965, 370). Facing right. Pl. III/13 = Berlin 10838; see Königliche Museen zu Berlin 1899, 229–30; Porter and Moss 1927–51, 4:28; Oriental Institute photo 1786 (purchased from Dr. Franz Stoedtner); misidentified as British Museum (1077) in Naville 1891, 66 n. to pl. XLII.A.

Nekhbet (pl. III/13)

[…] (2) dỉ.n⸗(ỉ) n⸗k […] m ꜥnḫ [wꜣs(?)] nb

[…] (2) "I have given to you […] in all life and [dominion (?)]."

King before Nekhbet

Wsr-mꜣꜥ.t-Rꜥ-stp-n-ʾImn (2) Wsỉrkn mrỉ-ʾImn sꜣ Bꜣst.t (3) dỉ šb.t[1] (n) mw.t⸗f Nḫb.t ỉr.n⸗s dỉ ꜥnḫ wꜣs mỉ Rꜥ (4) sꜣ ḥꜣ⸗k m ꜥnḫ wꜣs mỉ Rꜥ

Usimaꜥresetepenamon, (2) Osorkon, beloved of Amon, Son of Bastet. (3) Giving a clepsydra[1] (to) his mother Nekhbet, she having granted life and dominion like Re. (4) Protection is behind you, consisting of life and dominion like Re.

Queen

ḥm.t ny-sw.t Krꜥmꜥ (2) ꜥnḫ wꜣs mỉ Rꜥ ḏ.t

Queen Karoama. (2) Life and dominion like Re forever.

Two Priests behind Royal Figures in Shrine (pl. III/12; cf. XVI)

s(t)m (2) r[dỉ].t [š]b.t [n ny-sw.t]

Setem-priest. (2) Giving a clepsydra [to the king.]

Three Smaller Registers outside Shrine, from Top (pl. III/12)

(a) Cloaked figure with baton

ỉry-nṯr[2] (2) dỉ ꜥnḫ wꜣs (3) dỉ ꜥnḫ

He who pertains to the god,[2] (2) given life and dominion, (3) given life.

Two conversing priests at head of (lost) file

r tꜣ (2) ḏd-mdw dỉ (r) tꜣ (3) r tꜣ

"To the ground!" (2) Recitation: Placing on the ground. (3) "To the ground!"

(b) Two conversing priests at head of file

r tꜣ (2) ḏd-mdw dỉ (r) tꜣ (3) r tꜣ (4) [ṯ.t] n.t pr-ꜥnḫ

"To the ground!" (2) Recitation: Placing on the ground. (3) "To the ground!" (4) [Staff] of the Scriptorium.

(c) File of priests
      [ḥry].w³ ḥk3.w ṯ.t n.t pr-ꜥnḫ
      [Chief]³ Magicians. Staff of the Scriptorium.

D. Register 4: Procession to First Pavilion (pls. II/11–13 and XXVIII; Naville 1892, 11; Uphill 1965, 370). Facing right. Led by "Hereditary Prince" (rpꜥ.t) with staff, two "friends" (smr) with fans.

Conversing Priests
      r t3 (2) ḏd-mdw (3) r t3 (4) r t3 (5) ḏd-mdw (6) r t3
      "To the ground!" (2) Recitation. (3) "To the ground!" (4) "To the ground!" (5) Recitation. (6) "To the ground!"

Followed by two viziers (t3.ty), "Hereditary Prince" (rpꜥ.t) with staves, prophet (ḥm-nṯr) bearing haunch or scorpion symbol (?), and three "friends" (smr)

E. Registers 5–6: Procession to First Pavilion (pls. II/10–11 and XXVIII; cf. pl. XIII; Naville 1892, 12; Uphill 1965, 370–71; see Barta 1978, 35; color photo in Wildung 1997, 171). Facing right. Led by "God's Mother of Assiut" (mw.t-nṯr n S3wty), followed by two prophets (ḥm-nṯr), first bearing Horus standard, second with pḏ-ꜥḥꜥ-staff; then portable shrine of Wepwawet, carried by six priests, with attendant priest in panther skin and chief lector priest (ḥry-ḥb.t ḥry-tp) with scroll. In subregister 6 above, nine prophets (ḥm-nṯr) carry standards.

Label for Scene
      šsp tp w3.t ḥr nṯr r wsḫ.t
      Setting out on the road bearing the god to the broad court.

Label for Wepwawet
      [...] ḥr [...].t (2) Wp-w3.wt nb S3w(ty) (3) Wp-w3.wt Mḥw dỉ ꜥnḫ (4) dỉ≠f ꜥnḫ ḏd w3s 3w.t-ỉb mỉ Rꜥ ḏ.t
      [...] on [...]. (2) Wepwawet, Lord of Assiut, (3) Wepwawet of Lower Egypt, given life. (4) May he give life, stability, dominion, and joy like Re forever.

Label for King
      ḫꜥ [...] šsp tp w3.t r (2) ḥtp (ḥr) tnt3.t ḥb-sd (3) ḫꜥ m pr-wr ỉr≠f dỉ ꜥnḫ (4) nb ḫꜥ.w Wsỉrkn mrỉ-ʾImn s3 B3st.t [dỉ] ꜥnḫ w3s [...] (3) dỉ ꜥnḫ w3s ḥ3 nb mỉ Rꜥ
      Appearing [...] Setting out on the road to (2) rest (on) the jubilee baldachino. (3) Appearing in the Sanctuary of Upper Egypt that he might

attain the state of being given life. (4) Lord of Diadems, Osorkon, beloved of Amon, Son of Bastet, [given] life and dominion […] (5), given life and stability all around like Re.

Queen
    [ḥm.t ny-sw.t] Krˤmˤ
    [Queen] Karoama.

F. Register 7: Procession to Broad Court (pls. II/7–9, bottom, and XXVIII; Naville 1892, 14; Uphill 1965, 371). Facing right. Nineteen prophets (ḥm-nṯr) bearing nome standards, followed by two viziers (ṯȝ.ty).

Label for Procession
    nȝ šms[.w] Ḥr
    The Followers of Horus.

G. Registers 8–9. Scene in Broad Court (pls. II/4–9 and XXVIII; Naville 1892, 13–14; Uphill 1965, 371; Barta 1978, 35–36). Courtiers facing left; king facing right. In center of court, platform with adoring plebs (rḫy.t) along base, reached by staircases at cardinal points: ḫnd.t rsy.t "staircase of the south"; ḫnd.t mḥ.t "staircase of the north"; ḫnd.t imn.ty "staircase of the west"; ḫnd.t iȝb.t "staircase of the east." Beneath protective gestures of flanking gods, king with double crown, crook, and flail seated on throne that is depicted four times for each direction.

Amon and Tatenen Flank Osorkon Facing to the South
    [ʾImn] (2) [Wsr-mȝˤ.t]-Rˤ-[stp-n-ʾImn] (3) Tȝ-ṯnn
    [Amon] (2) [Usimaˤre[setepenamon] (3) Tatenen

Atum and Horus (?) Flank Throne
    Tm (2) [Ḥr?] (3) [sp 4] ḥr r mḥty
    Atum (2) [Horus?] (3) Four times, facing the north.

Khepri and Geb Flank Throne
    Ḫpri (2) Gb (3) sp 3 [sic?] ḥr r imnt.t
    Khepri (2) Geb (3) Three [sic?] times, facing the west.

Nephthys and Isis Flank Throne
    Nb.t-ḥw.t (2) ȝs.t (3) sp 4 ḥr r iȝb.t
    Nephthys (2) Isis (3) Four times facing the east.

Three chamberlains (imy-ḫnt)[4] approach dais with standard of Amon, standard of Atum (Tm), and sphinx of royal *ka*-spirit (Ḥr on *serekh*).

Retrograde (?) recitation by following priest, labeled: r sm₃ [p.]t To unite heaven.

ḏd-mdw ḫꜥ Ḥr ḥtp ḥr s.t≠f rsy.t r ḫpr.tỉ (2) {ḏd-mdw}⁵ sm₃ p.t r t₃ sp 4

Recitation: Horus has appeared, seated upon his southern throne until there occurs (2) the unification⁵ of heaven to earth! Four times.

Beside Amon standard + file of queen and three princesses (subregister 9).

ʾImn-Rꜥ nb ns.[wt] t₃.wy […] mr≠f tw w₃ḥ≠f tw (2) ʾImn-Rꜥ nb ns.wt t₃.wy […] Krꜥmꜥ (3) ꜥnḫ.tỉ (4) mỉ Rꜥ (5) s₃.t ny-sw.t (6) s₃.t ny-sw.t (7) s₃.t ny-sw.t

Amon-Re, Lord of the Thrones of the Two Lands […]. He loves you; he has established you. (2) Amon-Re, Lord of the Thrones of the Two Lands […]. Karoama, (3) living (4) like Re. (5) Princess (6) Princess (7) Princess

Five prostrate figures in five rows on right, before dais: three termed chamberlains (ỉmy.w-ḫnt), one "great ones and friends" (wr.w smr.w), and one "great ones of Upper and Lower Egypt" (wr.w Šmꜥ Mḥw).

H. Register 10. Procession to Jubilee Palace (pls. I/4–6 and XXVIII; Naville 1892, 14–15; Uphill 1965, 371–72). Facing right. Procession led by ỉry-nṯr (2) dỉ ꜥnḫ "He who pertains to the god, (2) given life."

Followed by two clapping priests—šsp.t n.t dḥn.t "chorus of clappers"—and four conversing priests: r t₃ (2) r t₃ (3) r t₃ (4) r t₃ "To the ground!" (2) "To the ground!" (3) "To the ground!" (4) "To the ground!"

Thereafter one friend (smr), one majordomo (ỉmy-r₃ pr wr), a bearer of insignia (ẖry-nws)⁶ with oar, two viziers (t₃.ty), a chamberlain (ỉmy-ḫnt) with lotus (?) scepter, the high priest of Heliopolis (wr-m₃.w), and two stolist priests (sm₃ty).

I. Registers 11–12: Procession to Jubilee Palace (pls. I/3–6 and XXVIII; Naville 1892, 14; Uphill 1965, 372; and Barta 1978, 36–37). Facing right. In two subregisters. At base, shrine of Wepwawet led by "God's Mother of Assiut" ([mw.t-nṯr n S₃wtỉy); corresponds to register 5. Two following prophets, six porters, two attendants in panther skins, and chief lector priest (ẖry-ḥb.t ḥry-tp) with scroll. In subregister 12 above, two-plus prophets (ḥm-nṯr) carry standards.

Label for Wepwawet

[… dỉ≠f ꜥnḫ ḏd w₃s ₃w.t-ỉb] mỉ Rꜥ ḏ.t sp-2

[… May he give life, stability, dominion, and joy] like Re forever and ever!

Label for King
wḏȝ ỉn ny-sw.t r ḥtp ḥr tnṯȝ.t ḥb-sd (2) ẖry-ḥb.(t) ḫft ỉy ḥr tnṯȝ.t ḥb-sd
šṯ⁷ (3) [...] (4) [sȝ ꜥnḫ ...] mỉ Rꜥ

Proceeding by the king to rest on the jubilee baldachino, (2) while the
lector priest when coming upon the jubilee baldachino...⁷ (3) [...] (4) [The
protection of life ...] like Re.

J. Register 13. Procession to Jubilee Palace (pls. I/5 and XXVIII; Naville
1892, 15; Uphill 1965, 372). Facing left. Behind mr.t-goddess, ꜥnḫ-glyph
carries Horus standard extending year glyph, ḏd-glyph carries bow, and
[wȝs]-glyph carries Wepwawet standard. Each armed glyph provided with
legend "given life" (dỉ ꜥnḫ).

K. Register 14: Procession to Jubilee Palace (pls. I/5 top and XXVIII; Naville
1892, 15; Uphill 1965, 372; for rearrangement as separate register, see Barta
1978, 31 and pl. I). Seated "Souls of Pe" (bȝ.w P).

L. Register 15: Procession to Jubilee Palace (lost; see Barta 1978, 31 and
pl. I)

M. Registers 16–17: Procession to Jubilee Palace (pls. I/1–2 and 5, XXVIII;
Naville 1892, 15; Uphill 1965, 372). In two subregisters. Courtiers facing
left; king and bearer of insignia facing right. Behind enthroned king are
Nekhbet (Nḫb.t), Edjo (Wȝḏy.t), Horus, and Seth. Before king the ỉmy-
wt-standard and a kneeling bearer of insignia (ẖry-nws) with crook and
canes.

Label for King
nṯr nfr Wsr-mȝꜥ.t-Rꜥ[-stp-n-]ʾỈ[mn] (2) sȝ Rꜥ [Wsỉrkn] mrỉ-ʾImn [sȝ Bȝst.
t] (3) dỉ ꜥnḫ wȝs

The Good God, Usimaꜥre[setepen]a[mon,] (2) Son of Re, [Osorkon,]
beloved of Amon, [Son of Bastet,] (3) given life and dominion.

Before Dais
[...] ꜥnḫw n ỉt≠k (2) [ʾImn-Rꜥ nb] ns.wt tȝ.wy ḥsỉ (3) [...] tw
[...] living for your father (2) [Amon-Re, Lord of the] Thrones of the
Two Lands, praise (3) [...] you.

Three chamberlains (ỉmy-ẖnt) bring standards of Amon, Atum, and the royal
ka-spirit (cf. register 8) before bearer of insignia (ẖry-nws) with scepters.

Facing Right, Figure with Staff and Chief Lector Priest
ḏd-mdw ỉn ẖr(y)-ḥb.(t) ḥry-tp [...] (2) sr ny-sw.t ỉn [...]

298 THE LIBYAN ANARCHY

Recitation by the chief lector priest: [...] (2) Announcing the king by [...]

In upper subregister 17, kneeling priestess who pacifies (shtp), queen, and three princesses.

NOTES TO §I. WALL A

1. Traditional identification denied in Sambin 1988. For the Osorkon jubilee examples, see Sambin 1988, 14–15 and 439 pl. III.

2. Uphill 1965, 370, reads ntr r(3) "the god's mouth." High priest of Bubastis? So Naville 1891, 14 and 29.

3. Uphill 1965, 370, reads hr.w hk3, but cf. pl. IX/13 and Naville 1891, 10.

4. For "chamberlains," see Epigraphic Survey 1980, 44 n. e; Erman and Grapow 1926–63, 1:75/1; Lesko 1982–90, 1:31: "courtier"; and Naville 1891, 14: "those of the first hall."

5. So Barta 1978, 36, treating the second dd-mdw (line 3) as a visual marker of speech. Cf. the speech of Amon (lines 5–9) on the Victory Relief of Sheshonq I at Karnak, no. 48, pp. 201–2.

6. For "bearers of insignia," see Epigraphic Survey 1980, 51 n. d.

7. Uphill 1965, 372, translates "reads" (< šd).

§II. NAVILLE'S WALL D: WESTERN OUTER FACE.

A. Bottom, Register 1: King between Bastet and Seshat (pl. XVII, right 13–15, XXVIII; Naville 1892, 26; Uphill 1965, 380). Facing left (toward entrance).

Label for Lost Figure of Bastet
di≠(i) n≠k nrw m ib.w [...] (2) di≠(i) n≠k šfy.t m [...] (3) dd-mdw in B3st.t [...]
"I shall give to you terror in the hearts [of men]. (2) I shall give to you respect in [the hearts/bodies ...]." (3) Recitation by Bastet [...]

Label for King
ʿnh ntr nfr nb t3.wy nb [ir h.t] (2) Wsr-m3ʿ.t-Rʿ-stp-[n]-ʾImn (3) Wsirk[n] mri-ʾImn s3 B3st.t (4) di ʿnh [..] (5) s3 h3≠k mi Rʿ
Long live the Good God, Lord of the Two Lands, Lord [of ritual performance,] (2) Usimaʿresetepenamon, (3) Osorkon, beloved of Amon, Son of Bastet, (4) given life [...] (5) Protection is behind you like Re.

Label for Seshat
dd-mdw in Sš3.t hr(y.t)-ib B3s.t (2) di≠(i) n≠k ʿnh w3s nb mi Rʿ
Recitation by Seshat, resident in Bubastis: "I shall give to you all life and dominion like Re."

B. Register 2: King Receives Jubilees, Life, and Glyph of Years from Bastet, Thoth, and Horhekenu (?) (pl. XVII, left 10–13, and XXVIII; Naville 1892, 26; Uphill 1965, 380–81). King facing left.

Label for Bastet

dỉ⸗(ỉ) ꜥnḫ wȝs r fnd⸗k (2) dỉ⸗(ỉ) n⸗k rnp.wt n(.t) Rꜥ (3) Bȝst.t ꜥȝ(.t) nb(.t) Bȝs.t (4) dỉ⸗(ỉ) n⸗k [...] (5) dỉ⸗(ỉ) n⸗k ꜥnḫ wȝs [...]

"I shall give life and dominion to your nose. (2) I shall give to you the years of Re." (3) Bastet, the great, Lady of Bubastis. (4) "I shall give to you [...] (5) I shall give to you life and dominion [...]."

Between Bastet and King

[dỉ]⸗s n⸗k ḥb.w-sd n [rnp.t?] 12 n wꜥ nb [...] ỉw⸗k ḫꜥ.t (2) ḥr s.t Ḥr sḫr⸗k Ṯḥnw (m) tn(ỉ?)⸗k pr ỉm⸗ỉ

She [will give] to you jubilees of 12 [years] each [...], you apppearing (2) on the Horus throne, having overthrown the Libyans by your might (?), which came forth from me.

Label for King Receiving Jubilees[1] from Bastet

nṯr nfr (2) Wsr-mȝꜥ.t-Rꜥ-stp-n-ʾImn (3) Wsỉrkn mrỉ-ʾImn sȝ Bȝst.t (4) dỉ ꜥnḫ wȝs mỉ Rꜥ ḏ.t (5) dỉ ꜥnḫ nb mỉ Rꜥ (6) sȝ ḫȝ⸗k m ꜥnḫ wȝs [mỉ Rꜥ]

The Good God, (2) Usimaꜥresetepenamon, (3) Osorkon, beloved of Amon, Son of Bastet, (4) given life and dominion like Re forever, (5) given all life like Re. (6) Protection is behind you, consisting of life and dominion [like Re].

Label for Thoth

sš⸗(ỉ) n⸗k ḥb(.w)-sd (2) n Rꜥ rnp.wt n (3) Tm (4) ḏd-mdw (ỉ)n Ḏḥwty (5) nb Ḥmnw (6) ḥr(y)-ỉb Bȝs.t

"I shall inscribe for you the jubilees (2) of Re, the years of (3) Atum." (4) Recitation by Thoth, (5) Lord of Ashmunein, (6) resident in Bubastis.

Label for Horhekenu (?)

dỉ⸗(ỉ) n⸗k ḥb-sd ꜥšȝ wr[.t ...] (2) [...] nṯr [ꜥȝ] nb p.t ḥr(y)-ỉb Bȝs.t [...]

"I shall give to you very many jubilees [...]." (2) [... Great] God, Lord of heaven, resident in Bubastis.

C. Register 3: Offering Clepsydra (pls. XVI, XXVIII; Naville 1892, 26; Uphill 1965, 381). Facing left. Pl. XVI/8 = British Museum 1077; cf. Budge 1909, 213; Porter and Moss 1927–51, 4:29.

King before Lost Edjo

[Wsr]-mȝꜥ.t-[Rꜥ-stp-n-ʾI]mn (2) Wsỉrkn mrỉ-ʾImn sȝ Bȝst.t (3) dỉ šb.t n

mw.t[≠f W3ḏy.t ...] (4) s3 ḫ3≠k m ꜥnḫ w3s mỉ Rꜥ
[Usi]maꜥ[resetepena]mon, (2) Osorkon, beloved of Amon, Son of Bastet.
(3) Giving a clepsydra to [his] mother [Edjo ...] (4) Protection is behind
you, consisting of life and dominion like Re.

Queen
    ḥm.t ny-sw.t Krꜥmꜥ (2) ꜥnḫ w3s nb mỉ Rꜥ ḏ.t
    Queen Karoama. (2) All life and dominion like Re forever.

Two Priests behind Royal Figures in Shrine
    s(t)m (2) rdỉ.t šb.t n ny-sw.t
    Setem-priest. (2) Giving a clepsydra to the king.

Three Smaller Registers outside Shrine, from Top

    (a) Three princesses labeled collectively "royal children" (ms.w ny-sw.t)
         and each individually as "royal child" (ms ny-sw.t)

    (b) Two drummers (cf. pl. XI, 6 = Back Wall C) and attendant figure
         (cf. pl. XIV, 1 = Wall D, register 11). For musical scenes, see Man-
         niche 1991, 68–70.
         sq.t (2) ḥq3 (3) (ỉ)m(y) šnḏ.t Skr (?)
         Beating (the drum). (2) Controller (of the oversized drum). (3) Loin-
         cloth wearer of Sokar (?).

    (c) Chanters
         dḫn.w (2) šsp.t n.t dḫn.t
         Giving the beat. (2) The chorus of clappers.

D. Register 4: Dignitaries Standing, Kneeling, and Prone (pls. XV/8–9 and
XXVIII; Naville 1892, 26; Uphill 1965, 381; for addition of pl. XXV/vi to this
register, see Barta 1978, 31 and pl. I; cf. Naville 1891, 30). Facing left.

From Right: Seated figures labeled "chiefs" (wr.w), four standing figures,
then protrate figures
    [sn t3 ỉ]n wr.w
    [Kissing the ground by] the chiefs.

At Far Left: remains of two prostrate figures (pl. XXV/vi; remove from pl.
XXX; p. 30 and Uphill, p. 377)
    [sn t3 ỉn] ỉmy.w-ḫnt (2) sꜥḥ.w
    [Kissing the ground by] chamberlains and (2) dignitaries.

Behind Prone Figures (pl. XXV/vi; remove from pl. XXX and cf. pl. XIV/1; Naville 1892, 30 and Uphill 1965, 377)

ḏd-mdw ḥs hy [ḥb(?)²] (2) hy Ptḥ[-Tꜣnn …] (3) ḏd-mdw ỉn ḥ[s(?) …]

Recitation: "Praise, hail to [the festival (?)²], (2) hail to Ptah-[Tenen …] (3) Recitation by the singer (?) […]

E. Register 5: Procession of Singers (pl. XXV/vi; remove from pl. XXX and cf. pl. XIV/1; Naville 1892, 30; Uphill 1965, 377; see Barta 1978, 31, 36, and pl. I). Facing left. Three women labeled "singers" (šmꜥy.wt) with gazelle wands, plant headresses,³ and ankhs.

Text for Women

[…] ỉry.w(?) […] (2) ḫꜥ Ḥr šsp.n≠f šw.ty ny-sw.t Wsr-mꜣꜥ.t-Rꜥ-stp-n-ꜣImn (3) ḏd-mdw ỉhy ḥb-sd ỉhy ḫpr ḥb-sd (n) Ptḥ (4) [-Tꜣnn]

[…] companions (?) […] (2) "Horus has appeared, having taken the double plumes: King Usimaꜥresetepenamon!" (3) Recitation: "Hail to the jubilee, hail to the occurence of the jubilee of Ptah (4) [-Tenen!"]

F. Register 6: Agricultural Ritual (pls. XV/6–7 bottom and XXVIII; Naville 1892, 27; Uphill 1965, 381; for addition of pl. XXV/vi to this register, see Barta 1978, 31 and pl. I)

Facing Left: Woman with plant headdress and lost figures labeled "peasants" (sḫty.w): pḥrr n […] Running about […]

(a) Single line
m-bꜣḥ ny-sw.t […]
Before the king […]

(b) Above figure
ỉmy-tw [ꜣḥ.wt] (2) dỉ ꜥnḫ […]
Between [the fields]. (2) Given life […]

(c) Above figures
[sḫty(?)].w pḥrr≠sn ỉmy-tw ꜣḥ.wt
[Peasant]s (?), as they go about between the fields.

Facing Right: File of five councilors with staves (pl. XXV/vi and remove from pl. XXX; Naville 1892, 30; Uphill 1965, 377)

ḏꜣḏꜣ.t (2) n(.t) ḥnr.t (3) wr(.w) (4) ꜥnḫ.w

Magistrates (2) of the council chamber, (3) chiefs of (4) the living (?).

G. Register 7: Dignitaries Standing, Kneeling, and Prone (pls. XV/6–7 middle and XXVIII; Naville 1892, 26–27; Uphill 1965, 381; for addition of pl. XXV/vi to this register, see Barta 1978, 31 and pl. I). Facing left. At far left (pl. XXV/vi), feet of standing women, then (pl. XV/6) standing figures with plumes, labeled "Nubian tribesmen" (ʾIwn.tyw St.t).

Two Rows of Seated Figures

    rdỉ.t ʾIwn.tyw [St.t m-bȝḥ(?)] (2) rdỉ.t nȝ qnb.tyw šᶜ4 m-bȝḥ

    Placing the [Nubian] tribesmen [in the royal presence (?).] (2) Placing the judges of the sand[4] in the royal presence.

Four Rows of Prostrate Figures

    sn tȝ ỉn (2) ʾIwn.tyw St.t (3) nȝ qnb.tyw (4) šᶜ

    Kissing the ground by (2) the Nubian tribesmen, (3) the judges of the sand.

H. Register 8: Rejoicing in City (pls. XV/4 bottom, 6–7 top, and XXVIII; Naville 1892, 27; Uphill 1965, 381). At left, file of priestesses with *hes*-vases. Males labeled "peasants" (sḫty.w) before female singers (?), two male dancers, female flautist, priest in panther skin.

Beside Flautist

    dỉ≠ỉ ḏd (2) [Ws]ỉrkn [mrỉ]-ʾI[mn sȝ] Bȝst.t (3) mỉ Rᶜ

    I shall cause that (2) Osorkon, [beloved] of A[mon, Son of] Bastet, be established (3) like Re.

Above Dancers

    dỉ ᶜnḫ mỉ Rᶜ

    Given life like Re.

I. Register 9: Rejoicing in City; Bes Ritualist (pls. XV/4 top–5 and XXVIII; Naville 1892, 27–28; Uphill 1965, 381). Texts obscure and suggested to be in foreign languages. See Romano 1989, 2:578–81.

Register 9, Naville 1892, pl. XV/5.

At Left: Two men with loops, followed by seated man, bull, acrobats
dỉ ꜥnḫ (2) wꜥbỉ nms.t≠k m nbw sb.t[≠k] m d̠ꜥmw [sꜣ.t Mntỉ.w dỉ≠s n≠k qbḥlw ỉtỉ mỉ mr nt̠r (?)[5]
Given life. (2) Pure are your ewers of gold and [your] libation jars of electrum. [The daughter of the Bedouin, may she give to you cool] water, O sovereign as the god desires (?).[5]

Behind Acrobats
ỉr hnw sp 4 (2) d̠d-mdw pḫt(?) pḫt dp.t[6] (3) Ḥr kꜣ nḫt mn mꜣꜥ.t
Beating the breast—4 times. (2) Recitation: … taste (?)[6] (3) Horus, the strong bull, firm of truth.

Man in Adoration: Before kneeling men beating breast, two standing figures, and Bes-masked priest
Adoring Man
ỉr n≠k wn-[ḫr(?)]
Make for yourself the reve[lation(?)].

Above Gesturing Men
rdỉ.(t) ns(y).t n pr.t[7] ỉn (ỉbḫ) pr.t wꜣwꜣ sw wꜣwꜣ
Giving pods (?) of seeds[7] by the (garner). As for the seed, roast it in a roasting.

Behind Lion-Masked Figure: Two subregisters of kneeling men beating breast
ỉr hnw (2) rḫy.t
Beating the breast (2) by the plebs.

J. Register 10: Rejoicing in City; Female Chorus (pls. XIV bottom and XXVIII; Naville 1892, 28; Uphill 1965, 381). At right, female clappers and drummer. At left, three pairs of kneeling women chant and gesticulate.

Over Left Pair
qꜣ-qꜣ-tꜣ sn-d̠r-qꜣt[8] (2) dỉ ꜥnḫ wꜣs snb nb mỉ Rꜥ
…[8] (2) Given all life, dominion, and health like Re.

Over Middle, Facing Pair
ỉr.(t) ỉr.t[9] (2) dỉ ꜥnḫ ḥb.w-sd ꜥšꜣ wr.t mỉ Rꜥ d̠.t (3) snb nb ꜣw.t-ỉb nb rꜥ nb
Eye to eye.[9] (2) Given life and very many jubilees like Re forever. (3) All health, all joy, every day.

K. Register 11: Rejoicing in City (pls. XIV/1 and 3 and XXVIII; Naville 1892, 28; Uphill 1965, 381). Facing right.

Text at Right Edge
   ḫ3s.t nb(.t) ẖr ḥ3.t⸗sn (2) ẖr nms.wt n (nbw) s(3)b.wt n d͑mw
   All foreign lands carry their best, (2) bearing jugs in (gold) and (3) libation jars in electrum.

Label for King (?) and Official
   pr.t ḥ3 (2) ỉn ny-sw.t
   Going back (2) by the king.

Label for Three Princesses (ms.w ny-sw.t)
   ms.w ny-sw.t sw3 ỉr s.t
   Princesses who pass by to prepare the throne.

Two Following Attendants
   (ỉ)m(y) šnḏ.t Skr (?) (2) sẖm
   Loincloth wearer of Sokar (?). (2) Controller.

Text at Left Edge
   nṯr.w tp ỉ3.t⸗sn ẖr wmny (2) n ny-sw.t ẖr s.t-wr.t
   The gods upon their standards on the right side (2) of the king on the great throne.

L. Register 12: Rejoicing in City (pls. XIV/1 and 3 and XXVIII; Naville 1892, 28–29; Uphill 1965, 381). Facing left.

From Left, Four Rows of Prostrate Dignitaries
   sn (2) t3 (3) m-b3ḥ (4) ỉn (5) (ỉ)m(y).w-ẖnt (6) s͑ḥ.w ny-sw.t (7) smr.w (8) wr.w
   Kissing (2) the ground (3) in the royal presence (4) by (5) chamberlains, (6) royal dignitaries, (7) friends, (8) and chiefs.

Behind Prone Figures
   ḏd-mdw ḥs ỉhy tnt3(.t) (2) hy s.t wr.t
   Recitation: "Praise, hail to the baldachino, (2) hail to the great throne!"

Prostrate Man Adores Ptah-Tenen
   Twnn (2) ỉr⸗f hnw sp 4
   Tenen. (2) He will beat the breast—4 times.

Two Seated Men
    ḏd-mdw ḥs
    Recitation: "Praise!"[10]

Two Priestesses with *Hes*-Vases
    dỉ ʿnḫ (2) mỉ Rʿ ḏ.t
    Given life (2) like Re forever.

M. Register 13: Rejoicing in City (pls. XIV/1–3, XXVIII; Naville 1892, 29; Uphill 1965, 381–82). Facing left. At left, three women (styled rwtt) with gazelle wands, plant headresses, and ankhs. Cf. pl. XXV/vi.

Text for Women
    ḫʿ Ḥr šsp.n≠f šw.ty (2) ny-sw.t Wsỉrkn mrỉ-ʾImn sȝ Bȝst.t dỉ ʿnḫ nb
    "Horus has appeared, having taken the double plumes: (2) King Osorkon, beloved of Amon, Son of Bastet, given all life!"

Four Similar Women (Styled rwtt), Two with Sistra
    ḏd-mdw ỉḥy ḥb-sd ỉḥy (2) ḫpr ḥb-sd n Ptḥ-Tȝnn
    Recitation: "Hail jubilee, hail (2) occurrence of the jubilee of Ptah-Tenen!"

Three Chiefs with Ostrich Eggs (?)[11]
    rdỉ.t ḥms n(ȝ) wr.w [m-bȝḥ?] (2) wr.w dỉ ḫȝ
    Causing the chiefs to sit [in the royal presence (?).] (2) Chiefs placed behind.

N. Register 14: Rejoicing in City (pls. XIV/1–2, XXVIII; Naville 1892, 29; see Barta 1978, 37). Facing left. Procession of glyphs for life, stability, and dominion, each carrying a divine standard and "given life" (dỉ ʿnḫ). At head of procession, Falcon of Horus, Hesat cow of Isis, and mr.t-goddess with broken legend: "bring back and return" (ỉn ỉy). For restoration, cf. pl. IX/1–6.

O. Registers 15–16: Procession (pl. XIII/iv; remove from pl. XXIX; Naville 1892, 18; Habachi 1957, 61–62; Uphill 1965, 367; for placement, see Barta 1978, 31, 37, and pl. I). In two subregisters. Facing right. Cf. pl. II/10–11. In upper subregister 16, three prophets (ḥm-nṯr), each bearing jackal standards; then portable shrine of Wepwawet, carried by four-plus priests, with two attendant priests at side.

Label for Wepwawet
    Wp-wȝ.wt nb Sȝw(ty) (2) Wp-wȝ.wt Mḥw

Wepwawet, Lord of Assiut, (2) Wepwawet of Lower Egypt.

Label for King (Habachi 1957, 62)
    nṯr nfr Wsr-mꜣꜥ.t-Rꜥ-stp-n-ʾImn (2) [sꜣ] Rꜥ (3) dỉ ꜥnḫ (4) sꜣ ꜥnḫ [...]
    The Good God, Usimaꜥresetepenamon, (2) [Son of] Re, (3) given life.
(4) The protection of life [...].

Queen (Habachi 1957, 62)
    ḥm.t ny-sw.t Krꜥmꜥ (2) ꜥnḫ wꜣs(?)
    Queen Karoama. (2) Life and dominion (?).

P. Register 17 (Habachi 1957, 62; Uphill 1965, 367; for placement, see Barta 1978, 31 and pl. I). Cf. pls. IX/4–5 and XIV/1. Falcon of Horus (bỉk n Ḥr) followed by Hesat cow of Isis (ꜣs.t). Uraeus frieze above scene.

NOTES TO §II. WALL D
    1. The jubilee glyph is miscopied in Naville 1892 as a "clepsydra"; see Sambin 1988, 15.
    2. So Naville 1891, 30; or restore tntꜣ(.t) "baldachino"; cf. pl. XIV/1.
    3. For plant headdresses, see Desroches-Noblecourt 1956, 197–204 (association with gazelle heads on 203); and Epigraphic Survey 1980, 52. The gazelle wands were misinterpreted as "lotus flowers" by Naville and Uphill.
    4. Assumed to be a designation of desert chieftains.
    5. For a parallel to the beginning of the passage, see Epigraphic Survey 1980, 46 and pl. 32.
    6. Incomprehensible. Foreign language or incantation?
    7. A variant of this text appears in Epigraphic Survey 1980, 47 and pl. 34: "He has given to me a pod of seeds, so has done the garner-man. As for the pod of seeds, I have roasted it with a roasting." If comprehensible to the contemporary scribes, this ancient text might have been understood as ending with glossolalia or ululation. Naville suggested that the text was a magical incantation.
    8. Garbled for qꜣ tꜣ qꜣ.t sḏr≠k qꜣ.t. "what should be exalted is exalted. May you spend the evening being exalted." See Epigraphic Survey 1980, 47 and pl. 36.
    9. Garbled or revised from "My eyes are bloodshot from staring." See Epigraphic Survey 1980, 47 and pl. 36.
    10. Or "Recitation (by) the singer"; cf. register 4 above (pl. XXV/vi).
    11. Or egg-shaped ewers? For the association of ostrich eggs with cult and Libyan tribute, see Conwell 1987, 25–34.

§III. NAVILLE'S WALLS B/C: SOUTHERN INNER WALL AND CONTINUATION ON WEST INNER FACE

A. Register 1

On Projecting Post: Souls of Nekhen (pl. XXVI/iv and adjust on pl. XXIX;

Uphill 1965, 373. n. 31; for placement, see Barta 1978, 31, 37, and pl. II)

[…]… pr≠s (2) b3.w Nḫn dỉ≠sn [snb(?)…]

[…] … her house (?) (2) Souls of Nekhen as they give [health (?)…]

On Inner Wall: King Ascends Dais (pl. IX/1–6 and adjust on pl. XXIX; Naville 1892, 23 n. 8; Uphill 1965, 376; for placement, see Barta 1978, 31–32, 37–38, and pl. II). In two subregisters. In bottom subregister, procession of standards carried by glyphs for ʿnḫ, dd, and w3s. Labels 1–3 face left, 4–12 right, and 13–20 left.

Standards

Wp-w3.wt šms bỉ.ty (2) Nḫn ny-sw.t (3) dỉ≠f ʿnḫ nb (4) [..]n.w Stš(?) (5) S33.t (6) b3.w (7) šms.w Ḥr (8) Ḥr-Ḫnty-ỉr.ty (9) ỉ3b.t (10) Wp-w3.wt Šmʿw (11) mr.t (12) Ḥs3.t 3s.t (13) bỉk (14) Ḥs3.t 3s.t (15) Šmʿw (?) (16) ỉmn.t(?) (17) Wp-w3.wt Šmʿw (18) […] ỉwn.t (19) Ḏḥwty (20) Ḥr

Wepwawet, follower of the King of Lower Egypt (2) Nekhen of the King (3) May he give all life. (4) […]… of Seth (?) (5) Seshat (6) Souls (7) Followers of Horus (8) Hor-Khentyirty (9) East (10) Wepwawet of Upper Egypt (11) Music goddess, (12) Hesat cow of Isis (13) Falcon (14) Hesat cow of Isis (15) Upper Egypt (?) (16) West (?) (17) Wepwawet of Upper Egypt (18) […] She of Dendera (?) (19) Thoth (20) Horus

Upper Subregister: King with flanking attendants

[…] tnt3.t (2) [… ḥb-sd ʿ3 wr].t mỉ Rʿ

[…] baldachino. (2) […] very [many jubilees] like Re.

Beside Dais: Souls of Nekhen (b3.w Nḫn) and Pe (b3.w P) and rows of Uraei

Souls of Pe (pl. XXVI/v and XXIX)

[b3.w P] dỉ≠sn snb

[Souls of Pe] as they give health.

B. Register 2

On Projecting Post (pl. XIII/vi and XXIX; see Barta 1978, pl. II)

[…] (2) … nwb […] (3) […] ỉwn.w≠s … nw […] (4) […] nw T3-ntr ỉwn […] (5) […] … n nwb […]

[…] (2) […] … gold […] (3) […] its pillars … of […] (4) […] of God's-Land, pillar […] (5) […] .. of gold […].

On Inner Wall: King before Shrine (pl. IX/11–13 and adjust on pl. XXIX; Naville 1892, 18; Uphill 1965, 374; for placement, see Barta 1978, 31, 38, and pl. II). King faces Bastet (B3st.t) on right

wḏꜣ [ỉn ny-sw.t r ḥtp …] (2) Wsr-mꜣꜥ.t-Rꜥ-stp-n-ʾImn (3) [Ws]ỉ[rkn]
mrỉ-ʾImn sꜣ Bꜣst.t (4) mrỉ-Rꜥ stp n ʾImn (5) dỉ ꜥnḫ

Proceeding [by the king to rest …] (2) Usimaꜥresetepenamon, (3)
[Os]o[rkon,] beloved of Amon, Son of Bastet, (4) beloved of Re, chosen of
Amon, (5) given life.

Within Shrine: King faces Bastet (Bꜣst.t) on right
Wsr-mꜣꜥ.t-Rꜥ-stp-n-ʾImn (2) [Ws]ỉrkn mrỉ-ʾImn sꜣ Bꜣst.t dỉ ꜥnḫ mỉ Rꜥ
ḏ.t ỉr […] (3) dỉ ꜥnḫ

Usimaꜥresetepenamon, (2) [Os]orkon, beloved of Amon, Son of Bastet,
given life like Re forever. Making […] (3) given life.

Wepwawet Standard
Wp-wꜣ.wt nb Sꜣwt(y) (2) Wp-wꜣ.wt Mḥw
Wepwawet Lord of Assiut. (2) Wepwawet of Lower Egypt.

In Upper Subregister: Three prophets (ḥm-nṯr) carry Wepwawet standards

Behind Broken Figure of King
[…] mỉ Rꜥ (2) ꜥnḫ […]
[…] like Re. (2) Life […]

Before King
ꜥḥꜥ ỉn [ny-sw.t …]
Waiting by the [king in …]

Text of Lost Magicians
ḥry.w-ḥkꜣ ḏḏ≠sn […] (2) ỉhy ḥb.w-sd n Ḥr ḏ.t sp-2 ỉhy ḥb.w-sd n […]
(3) Ḥr nṯr[.w] pr-ꜥnḫ pḥr≠sn ny-sw.t sp […] m […]

The chief magicians, as they say: […] (2) "Hail, jubilees of Horus, forever and ever! Hail, jubilees of […] (3) Horus." The gods of the scriptorium
as they go around the king […] times in […].

Procession (pls. XIII/ii and XXIX, continued on Wall C, pl. XIII/iii and
XXXI; for placement, see Barta 1978, 31 and pls. II–III)

Above Standard Bearers
[…] ꜥnḫ ḏd wꜣs mỉ Rꜥ ḏ.t […] dỉ≠s n≠k ḥfn.w m ḥb.w-sd ḥr s.t [Ḥr
…]

[…] life, stability and dominion like Re forever. […] "May she give to
you hundreds of thousands of jubilees upon the [Horus] throne […]."

In Upper Register: Two Boats
   Beside Left
      nṯr ꜥꜣ ḫnty ḥb.w-sd
      Great God, Foremost of jubilees.
   In Band Above
      [...] nb sḫ.t≠k (2) wn.t(ỉ) ḥr(3)≠ỉ ꜥnḫ.t(ỉ) ḏ.t
      [...] lord of your field, (2) you existing before (3) me, living forever.

C. Register 3

On Projecting Post: King Offers Incense (pl. XIII/i and XXIX; see Barta 1978, pl. II). In two subregisters. Facing right.

Beside King
      [...] (2) Wsỉrkn mrỉ-ʾImn sꜣ Bꜣst.t (3) mr-ʾImn r (4) [ny-sw.t] nb (5) dỉ ꜥnḫ
      [...] (2) Osorkon, beloved of Amon, Son of Bastet, (3) whom Amon loves more than (4) any [king], (5) given life.

Upper Subregister: Kneeling Magicians (ḥry.w-[ḥkꜣ.w])
      ỉr hnw ỉn ḥr(y).w-ḥkꜣ.w
      Beating the breast by the chief magicians.

On Inner Wall: King Offers Incense to Cult Poles (pl. IX/7–13 and adjust on pl. XXIX; Naville 1892, 21–22; Uphill 1965, 374–75; for placement, see Barta 1978, 32 and pl. II). In three subregisters. In lowest subregister, procession to left by twenty-six-plus priests in panther skins and carrying geographical standards. In central field, king offers incense to cult poles provided with offerings, followed by Hermopolitan high priest of Thoth (ḫrp-ns.ty) and overseer of treasurers of the palace (mr-ḫtmw/sḏꜣw.ty-ꜥḥ). In upper subregister, three-plus prophets (ḥm-nṯr) in panther skins carry standards.

King before Bastet (Bꜣst.t) and Cult Pillars
      nṯr nfr Wsr-mꜣꜥ.t-Rꜥ-stp-n-ʾImn (2) sꜣ Rꜥ Wsỉrkn mrỉ-ʾImn sꜣ Bꜣst.t (3) sꜣ mr n Tm (4) dỉ ꜥnḫ (5) ỉr snṯr ỉr≠f dỉ ꜥnḫ mỉ Rꜥ ḏ.t
      The Good God, Usimaꜥreseteepenamon, (2) Son of Re, Osorkon, beloved of Amon, Son of Bastet, (3) beloved son of Atum, (4) given life. (5) Making incense so that he might achieve the state of being given life like Re forever.

Before Wepwawet Pole with Twelve Walking Jackals
      Wp-wꜣ.wt Šmꜥ ḫrp tꜣ.wy nṯr.w ḥr(.yw)-ỉb [...]

Wepwawet of Upper Egypt, who administers the Two Lands and the gods who are resident in [...]

Before Jackal Pole with Two Entwined Serpents

[...] sn.w n ỉtr.t ḫnt.t ỉnb.w dỉ≠f ꜥnḫ nb mỉ Rꜥ ḏ.t

[...] poles of the shrine before the walls. May he give all life like Re forever.

Before Forked Pole with Eight Rams

nṯr ꜥꜣ ỉmy ḥb-sd.w [...] nṯr [...] nb dỉ≠f qn(ỉ) [...]pr nb

The great god who is in the jubilees, [...] god [...] all [...]. May he give valor [...] all [...].

Before Bull-Headed Pole

kꜣ ʾIwnw ḫnt(y) Ḥw.t-ꜥꜣ.t ḥr(y)-tp nṯr.w nb dỉ≠f ꜣw.t-ỉb nb mỉ Rꜥ rꜥ nb[1]

The bull of Heliopolis, Foremost of "Great House" (sanctuary of Heliopolis), chief of all the gods. May he give all joy like Re every day.[1]

Before Bull-Headed ỉwn-Pillar

Ḥb(y) ʾIwnw ḫnty pr-wr dỉ≠f ḏd wꜣs nb ḫr≠f mỉ Rꜥ ḏ.t

The Festive One of Heliopolis, Foremost of the Sanctuary of Upper Egypt. May he give all stability and dominion deriving from him like Re forever.

Before ỉwn-Pillar

ỉwn ỉmy ʾIwnw ḫnty ḥb.w-sd dỉ≠f ỉr n[≠f ...]

The pillar that is in Heliopolis, Foremost of the jubilees. May he grant the making for [him of ...].

Before Phoenix-Pillar

bn[w] ỉmy ʾIwnw ḫnty Ḥw.t-bnw dỉ≠f ỉr.t ḥb.w-sd ꜥšꜣ wr.t

The phoenix that is in Heliopolis, Foremost of the Mansion of the Phoenix. May he grant the enactment of very many jubilees.

Before Second Phoenix(?)-Pillar

[...] m ʾIwnw ḫnty Ḥw.t-bnw dỉ≠f ỉr.t ḥb(.w)-sd ꜥšꜣ wr.t

[...] in Heliopolis, Foremost of the Mansion of the Phoenix. May he grant the enactment of very many jubilee(s).

Before Pole

[...] ḥb[.w]-sd dỉ ꜥnḫ msḏr.wy nṯr.wy nḫt ỉwf≠k

[...] jubilee[s], who vivifies the ears of the two gods and fortifies your flesh.

Before Lost Pole
    [...] ḥb.w-sd dỉ⸗s rnp.wt nḥḥ m ꜣw.t-ỉb
    [...] jubilees. May she give infinite years in joy.

D. Register 4

On Projecting Post: King and Queen before Divine Symbols (pl. IVbis, 13; ignored by Barta 1978, 32, but see pl. II). Titles and plumes of queen preserved at bottom of block.
    ḏd [mdw ỉn ...] (2) [... Wsỉrkn?] (3) ḥm.t ny-sw.t [Krꜥmꜥ] (4) ꜥnḫ.tỉ
    Recitation [by ...] (2) [... Osorkon(?).] (3) Queen [Karoama], (4) living.

On Inner Wall B and Back Wall C (pls. VIII/25–27 and XII/8–10; adjust on pls. XXIX and XXI; Naville 1892, 23; Uphill 1965, 375; ignored by Barta 1978, 32, but see pls. II–III). Text fragments below rows of divine shrines; lines 3–10 beside prone emblem of Nefertem.
    mꜥn[ḏ.t? ...] (2) nb [...] (3+) ḏd-mdw ỉn ꜣInpw [...] (4+) nḏm ḫnt(y) Ḥw.t [ḥb-sd ...] (5+) kꜣrỉ [...] (6+) pr.t ꜥnḫ Rꜥ (7+) wtt.n [sw] (8+) psḏ.t rnn. n⸗(ỉ) (9+) sw r ny-sw.t tꜣ.wy r ḥqꜣ (10+) šn.n ỉtn dỉ ꜥnḫ nb (11+ = Wall C, pl. XII/8) Ḫns m (12+) Wꜣs.t Nfr-ḥtp (13+) dỉ.n⸗(ỉ) n⸗k [...] (14+) mỉ Rꜥ (15+, pl. XII/10) dỉ.[n⸗(ỉ) n⸗k ...] (16+)⸗ỉ nb [...] (17+) ntk [...] (18+) mry Mꜣꜥ.t [...]
    Day-bark (?) [...] (2) lord [...] (3+) Recitation by Anubis [...] (4+) sweet, Foremost of the Mansion of [the Jubilee ...] (5+) Shrine [of ...] (6+) "The living seed of Re, (7+) [whom] the Ennead begat, (8+) whom I nursed (9+) to be King of the Two Lands, to be ruler of (10+) what the disk encircles, given all life." (11+) Khonsu (12+) in Thebes, Neferhotep. (13+) "I have given to you [...] (14+) like Re." (15+) ["I have] given [to you ...] (16+) all my [...] (17+) You are [...] (18+) beloved of Maat [...]."

Wall C, Bottom of Register (pl. XXVI/iii; see Barta 1978, pl. III). King in festival robe.
    [...]... mỉ [Rꜥ] (2) [sꜣ ḥꜣ]⸗k nb (m) ꜥnḫ wꜣs
    [...]... like [Re]. (2) [Protection] all [around] you (consisting of) life and dominion.

E. Register 5

(a) On Projecting Post: King Offers Incense, Followed by Queen (pl. IVbis/13 and adjust on pl. XXIX; Naville 1892, 16; Uphill 1965, 372; for placement, see Barta 1978, 32, 39, and pl. II). Lower subregister. Facing right.

Label before Northern Shrines

wdn ḫ.t nb nfr wʿb ỉn ny-sw.t [Wsr]-mꜣʿ.t-Rʿ-stp-n-ʾImn n nṯr.w nb ỉtr.
t [mhy.t]

Offering everything good and pure by King [Usi]maʿresetepenamon to
all the gods of the [northern] row of shrines.

Label for King

Wsr-mꜣʿ.t-Rʿ-stp-n-ʾImn (2) Wsỉrkn mrỉ-ʾImn sꜣ Bꜣst.t (3) dỉ ʿnḫ mỉ
Rʿ ḏ.t (4) ỉr snṯr n nṯr.w (5) nṯr.wt nb.w ḥb.w-sd ỉr≠f dỉ ʿnḫ (6) sꜣ ḫꜣ≠k
m ny.t-sw.t ʿꜣ.t

Usimaʿresetepenamon, (2) Osorkon, beloved of Amon, Son of Bastet,
(3) given life like Re forever. (4) Making incense for all the gods (5) and
goddesses of the jubilees, so that he might attain the state of being given
life. (6) Protection is behind you as great kingship.

Queen with Sistrum and Menat

ḥm.t ny-sw.t sꜣ.t ny-sw.t (2) Krʿmʿ

Queen and Royal daughter (2) Karoama.

On Inner and Back Wall: Double Rows of Shrines (ỉtr.t) (pls. VII/18–20,
VIII/24–27, and XII/8–10, and adjust on pls. XXIX and XXXI; Naville 1892,
20–21; Uphill 1965, 375–76; for placement, see Barta 1978, 32 and pl. II).
Lower subregister. Gods face left. Before (below) each row is depicted a
pile of offerings.

Lower Egyptian Row (32+ Shrines)

[...] (2) Ptḥ (2a) nb Mꜣʿ.t (3) Ḥr ḫnty (3b) Ḥm dỉ≠f ʿnḫ nb ḫ(ꜣc)r≠f
mỉ Rʿ (4) Dp.t² nb.t p.t ḥnw.t tꜣ.wy (4b) ḥr(y).t-ỉb ḥb-sd (4c) dỉ≠s qn (4d)
nḫt nb (5) Mrḥy³ (5b) ḫnty ḥb-sd (5c) dỉ≠f ʿnḫ wꜣs nb (5d) dỉ≠f ꜣw.t-ỉb
nb (6) Sbk (6b) dỉ≠f ʿnḫ wꜣs nb (6c) dỉ≠f snb nb (6d) dỉ≠f ꜣw.t-ỉb nb (7)
Ḥpḥp⁴ nṯr ʿꜣ (7b) ḫnty ḥb-sd (7c) dỉ≠f ḥtp.w nb (7d) dỉ≠f ḏfꜣ.w nb (8) ꜣs.t
wr.t (8b) ḥr(y).t-ỉb ḥb-sd (8c) dỉ≠f (sic) qn nb (8d) dỉ≠f (sic) nḫt nb (9)
ʾIn-ḥr-Šw sꜣ Rʿ nṯr ʿꜣ ḫnty ḥb-sd dỉ≠f nḥḥ (10) N.t ḫnty(.t) (10b) ḥb-sd dỉ≠s
(10c) ʿnḫ wꜣs (11) Ḥr Tḥnw (11b) ḫnty ḥb-sd nṯr ʿꜣ nb p.t (11c) dỉ≠f ʿnḫ
wꜣs (12) Py.t⁵ (12b) nb.t p.t ḥnw.t tꜣ.wy (12c) [...] (13+ = pl. VIII/24–26)
[...] (14+) [...] (15+) [...] (16+) [...] (17+) Rs-wḏꜣ [...] (17+b) dỉ≠f ʿnḫ wꜣs
(18+) Ḥr [...] (19+) [Ḥr ...] (19+b) dỉ≠f q[n nb] (19+c) dỉ≠f nḫt nb (20+) Ḥr
nṯr ʿꜣ (20+b) ḫnty ḥb-sd (20+c) dỉ≠f snb nb (20+d) dỉ≠f ꜣw.t-ỉb nb (21+)
St (21+b) dỉ≠f ʿnḫ wꜣs nb (21+c) dỉ≠f ḥw nb (21+d) dỉ≠f ḏfꜣ.w nb (22+)
Ḏḥwty (22+b) ḫnty ḥb-sd (22+c) dỉ≠f qn nb (22+d) dỉ≠f [nḫ]t nb (23+) [...]
(23+b) ḫnty ḥb-sd (23+c) dỉ≠f ꜣw.t-ỉb (23+d) dỉ≠f ʿnḫ wꜣs nb (24+) Ḥr nṯr
ʿꜣ (24+b) ḫnty ḥb-sd (24+c) dỉ≠f ʿnḫ wꜣs nb (24+d) dỉ≠f snb nb (25+ =
Wall C, pl. XII/8) Sbk Šd.t (25+b) m ḥr-ỉb Št.t (25+c) nṯr ʿꜣ nb p.t (25+d)

dỉ⸗f ꜥnḫ wꜣs nb (26+) Ḥr ꜥꜣ (26+b) nṯr ꜥꜣ nb p.t (26+c) dỉ⸗f ꜥnḫ wꜣs nb (26+d) ḫr⸗f ḏ.t (27+) […] (28+) […] (28+b) ḫnty ḥb-sd (28+c) dỉ⸗f ꜥnḫ wꜣs nb (28+d) dỉ⸗f snb nb (29+) […] (29+b) nṯr ꜥꜣ nb p.t (29+c) [dỉ⸗f …] nb (29+d) […] (30+) Ḥqs nṯr ꜥꜣ (30+b) ḫnty ḥb-sd (30+c) dỉ⸗f qn nb (30+d) dỉ⸗f df ꜣ.w nb (31+) Ḥpḥp nṯr ꜥꜣ (31+b) ḫnty ḥb-sd (31+c) dỉ⸗f snb nb (31+d) dỉ⸗f ꜣw.t-ỉb nb (32+) […]

[…] (2) Ptah, (2b) Lord of Truth. (3) Horus, Foremost of (3b) Letopolis. May he give all life deriving (3c) from him like Re. (4) She of Dep,[2] Lady of heaven, Mistress of the Two Lands, (4b) resident at the jubilee. (4c) May she give all valor (4d) and all victory. (5) Merhy,[3] (5b) Foremost of the jubilee. (5c) May he give all life and dominion. (5d) May he give all joy. (6) Sobek. (6b) May he give all life and dominion. (6c) May he give all health. (6d) May he give all joy. (7) Hephep,[4] the great god, (7b) Foremost of the jubilee. (7c) May he give all offerings. (7d) May he give all foodstuffs. (8) Isis the Great, (8b) resident at the jubilee. (8c) May he [sic] give all valor. (8d) May he [sic] give all victory. (9) Onuris-Shu, (9b) son of Re, the great god, (9c) Foremost of the jubilee. (9d) May he give eternity. (10) Neith, Foremost (10b) of the jubilee. May she give (10d) life and dominion. (11) Horus of Libya, (11b) Foremost of the jubilee, (11c) the great god, Lord of heaven. (11d) May he give life and dominion. (12) She of Pe,[5] (12b) Lady of heaven, Mistress of the Two Lands. (12c) […] (13+) […] (14+) […] (15+) […] (16+) […] (17+) He-whose-Waking-Is-Sound […] (17+b) May he give life and dominion. (18+) Horus […] (19+) [Horus? of …], (19+b) May he give [all] va[lor.] (19+c) May he give all victory. (20+) Horus, the great god, (20+b) Foremost of the jubilee. (20+c) May he give all health. (20+d) May he give all joy. (21+) Set. (21+b) May he give all life and dominion. (21+c) May he give all sustenance. (21+d) May he give all foodstuffs. (22+) Thoth, (22+b) Foremost of the jubilee. (22+c) May he give all valor. (22+d) May he give all [victor]y. (23+) […], (23+b) Foremost of the jubilee. (23+c) May he give joy. (23+d) May he give all life and dominion. (24+) Horus, the great god, (24+b) Foremost of the jubilee. (24+c) May he give all life and dominion. (24+d) May he give all health. (25+) Sobek of Crocodilopolis, (25+b) in the midst of Crocodilopolis, (25+b) the great god, Lord of heaven. (25+d) May he give all life and dominion. (26+) Horus the elder, (26+b) the great god, Lord of heaven. (26+c) May he give all life and dominion (26+c) deriving from him forever. (27+) […] (28+) […], (28+b) Foremost of the jubilee. (28+c) May he give all life and dominion. (28+d) May he give all health. (29+) […], (29+b) the great god, Lord of heaven. (29+c) [May he give] all […] (29+d) […] (30+) Heqes, the great god, (30+b) Foremost of the jubilee. (30+c) May he give all valor. (30+d) May he give all foodstuffs. (31+) Hephep, the great god, (31+b) Foremost of the jubilee. (31+c) May he give health. (31+d) May he give all joy. (32+) […]

(b) On Projecting Post: King Offers Incense, Followed by Queen (pl. IVbis/12–13 and adjust on pl. XXIX; Naville 1892, 16; Uphill 1965, 372; for placement, see Barta 1978, 32 and pl. II). Upper subregister. Facing right.

Label before Southern Shrines
    wdn ḫ.t nb [nfr wᶜb in ny-sw.t Wsr-mȝᶜ.t-Rᶜ-]stp-n-[ʾI]mn n nṯr.w nb itr.t rsy.t (2) ms wḏḥw […] (3) wḏ.n ḥm[≠f …] (4) rdi.t ms mr n […] (5) wȝḏ-wr […]
    Offering everything [good and pure by King Usimaᶜreʾ]setepen[a]mon to all the gods of the southern row of shrines. (2) Fashioning an altar […] (3) [His] Majesty commanded […] (4) causing to fashion (?) what was desired of […] (5) the sea […]

Label for King
    Wsr-mȝᶜ.t-Rᶜ-stp-n-ʾImn (2) Wsirkn mri-ʾImn sȝ Bȝst.t (3) di ᶜnḫ mi Rᶜ (4) ir sntr n nṯr.w nṯr.wt (5) nb.w ḥb.w-sd ir≠f di ᶜnḫ nb
    Usimaᶜresetepenamon, (2) Osorkon, beloved of Amon, Son of Bastet, (3) given life like Re. (4) Making incense for all the gods and goddesses (5) of the jubilees, so that he might attain the state of being given all life.

Queen with (Lost) Sistrum and Menat
    Krᶜmᶜ   Karoama

On Inner and Back Wall: Double Rows of Shrines (itr.t) (pls. VII/17–20, VIII/19 and 23–27, and XII/7–10, and adjust on pls. XXIX and XXXI; Naville 1892, 18–20; Uphill 1965, 375–76; for placement, see Barta 1978, 32 and pl. II). Upper subregister. Gods face left. Before (below) each row is depicted a pile of offerings.

Upper Egyptian Row (31+ Shrines)
    […] (2) [Wr.t]-Ḥkȝ.(w) (2b) […] (3) Ws[ir] Ḫnty (3b) ʾImn.tyw nṯr ᶜȝ (3c) nb […] nb.t (3d) di ᶜnḫ […] (4) Ḥw.t-Ḥr nb(.t) ʾIwn.t (4b-d) […] (5) [Mw.t nb.t] ʾIšr.t (5b) […] (5c) [di≠s] ᶜnḫ wȝs (5d) [di≠s] snb (6) [Mntw-Rᶜ] nb Mȝt (6b) [di≠f] qn nb (7) [Ḥr-m-ȝḫ.t nb] ʾIwnw (7b) [di≠f] nḫt nb (8) [Mntw nb] Wȝs.t (8b) […] (9) Ḫnsw m Wȝs.t Nfr-ḥtp(9b).w≠f nb (10) Ḫnmw nb (10b) Šȝs-ḥtp (10c) di≠[f …]≠f nb (10d) di≠[f …]≠f nb (11) [Mnw nb] ʾIp(w) di≠f ᶜnḫ (11b) […] (12) Sb[k …] nb (12b) nṯr[.w? …] (12c-d) […] (13+ = pl. VIII/19 & 24) […] (14+) ʾInpw […] (14+b) ḫnty [ḥb-sd] (14+c) di[≠f …] (14+d) nb […] (15+) Rᶜ⁶ […] (15+b) […] (15+c) di[≠f …] (15+d) […] (16+) Ḥr […] (16+b) nṯr ᶜȝ (16+c) di≠f […] (16+d) di≠f […] (17+) Ḥr […] (17+b) nṯr ᶜȝ (17+c) di[≠f …] (18+) […] (19+) [… di](19+b)≠f snb nb (20+) ʾImy-wt (21+) Bnbt⁷ nṯr ᶜȝ (21+b) [ḫnty] ḥb-sd (21+c) […] (22+) […] (22+b) […] (22+c) di≠f ᶜnḫ wȝs nb (22+d) di≠f ȝw.t-ib nb.t (23+) Gb it

(23+b) nṯr.w ḫnty (23+c) ḥb-sd dỉꜥf (23+d) nḫt nb (24+) Srq[.t] (24+b) dỉꜥs ꜥnḫ wȝs nb (25+ = Wall C, pl. XII/7–8) Ḥr-mr.ty (25+b) ḫnty ḥb-sd (25+c) dỉꜥf nḥḥ m (25+d) ny-sw.t tȝ.wy ḏ.t sp-2 (26+) Nbty nb tȝ (26+b) Šmꜥ nṯr ꜥȝ (26+c) dỉꜥf qn nb (26+d) dỉꜥf nḫt.w nb (27+) Wȝb.wy(?)[8] ḫnty (27+b) ḥb-sd dỉꜥf (27+c) ꜥnḫ wȝs nb (27+d) mỉ Rꜥ ḏ.t (28+) Ḥȝ (28+b) nb ỉmnt. t (28+c) dỉꜥf ꜥnḫ wȝs nb (28+d) mỉ Rꜥ rꜥ nb (29+) Rsy nṯr ꜥȝ (29+b) ḫnty ḥb-sd (29+c) dỉꜥf ꜥnḫ wȝs (29+d) dỉꜥf snb (30+) Stḫ (30+b) ḫnty ḥb-sd (30+c) dỉꜥf ꜥnḫ wȝs (31+) [...]

[...] (2) [She-who-Is-Great-of]-Magic. (2b) [...] (3) Osiris, Foremost of (3b) the Westerners, the great god, (3c) Lord of all [...], (3d) given life [...]. (4) Hathor, Lady of Dendera (4b-d) [...]. (5) [Mut, Lady of] Asheru, (5b) [...]. (5c) [May she give] life and dominion. (5d) [May she give] health. (6) [Montu-Re,] Lord of Medamud. (6b) [May he give] all valor. (7) [Harmakhis, Lord] of Heliopolis. (7b) [May he give] all victory. (8) [Montu, Lord of] Thebes. (8b) [...] (9) Khonsu in Thebes, (9b) all whose satisfactions are good (var. of Neferhotep). (10) Khnum, Lord (10b) of Shashotep. (10c) May [he give] all his [...]. (10d) May [he give] all his [...]. (11) [Min, Lord] of Akhmim. May he give life (11b) [...] (12) Sob[ek ...], Lord (12b) of the god[s (?) ...]. (12c-d) [...] (13+) [...] (14+) Anubis [...], (14b) Foremost [of the jubilee,] (14+c) May [he] give [...] (14+d) all [...]. (15+) Re[6] [....] (15+b) [...] (15+c) May [he] give [...] (15+d) [...] (16+) Horus [...], (16+b) the great god. (16+c) May he give [...] (17+) Horus [...]. (17+b) the great god. (17+c) May [he] give [...] (18+) [...] (19+) [... May] (19+b) he give all health. (20+) He-who-is-in-His-Bandages. (21+) Benbet,[7] the great god, (21+b) [Foremost] of the jubilee. (21+c) [...] (22+) [...] (22+b) [...] (22+c) May he give all life and dominion. (22+d) May he give all joy. (23+) Geb, father (23+b) of the gods, Foremost (23+c) of the jubilee. May he give (23+d) all victory. (24+) Selqet. (24+b) May she give all life and dominion. (25+) Hor-merty, (25+b) Foremost of the jubilee. (25+c) May he give eternity as (25+d) King of the Two Lands, forever and ever. (26+) The Ombite, Lord of Upper (26+b) Egypt, the great god. (26+c) May he give all valor. (26+d) May he give all victories. (27+) God of the (19th) Oxyrhynchite Nome,[8] Foremost (27+b) of the jubilee. May he give (27+c) all life and dominion (27+d) like Re, forever. (28+) Ha, (28+b) Lord of the West. (28+c) May he give all life and dominion, (28+d) like Re, every day. (29+) The Southwind, the great god, (29+b) Foremost of the jubilee. (29+c) May he give life and dominion. (29+d) May he give health. (30+) Seth, (30+b) Foremost of the jubilee. (30+c) May he give life and dominion. (31+) [...]

F. Register 6

On Projecting Post (pl. IVbis/4 and 12, and adjust on pl. XXIX; Naville

1892, 16–17; Uphill 1965, 373; for placement, see Barta 1978, 32 and pl. II). In multiple subregisters. At left, two subregisters, each with Anubis and serpent shrine.

Shrine of Anubis
    ʾInpw nb (2) sḥd⁹ nb p.t (3) dı͗≠f ꜥnḫ wꜣs (4) nb snb nb
Anubis, the Lord of (2) illumination,⁹ Lord of heaven. (3) May he give all life and dominion (4) and all health.

Behind Shrines
    [… dı͗?] bꜣ.w P Nḫn ı͗tr.t Šmꜥ Mḥw ḥḥ.w m rnp.wt (n) ny-sw.t bı͗.ty Wsr-mꜣꜥ.t-Rꜥ-stp-n-ʾImn ḥb.w-sd ꜥšꜣ wr.t
    [… May] the souls of Pe, Nekhen, and the rows of shrines of Upper and Lower Egypt [give (?)] millions of years (to) the King of Upper and Lower Egypt, Usimaꜥresetepenamon, and very many jubilees.

Twelve Prophets in Panther Skins with "Egg" Libation Vessels, in Four Subregisters (Three Prophets Each), from Top
    [ḥm.w-nṯr] bꜣ.w P (2) [ḥm.w-nṯr bꜣ.w Nḫn] (3) ḥm.w-nṯr ı͗tr.t [Šmꜥ] (3) ḥm.w-nṯr ı͗tr.t [Mḥw]
    [Prophets of] the souls of Pe. (2) [Prophets of the souls of Nekhen.] (3) Prophets of the row of shrines of [Upper Egypt.] (4) Prophets of the row of shrines of [Lower Egypt.]¹⁰

King Offers Maat
    rdı͗.t Mꜣꜥ.t […] (2) nṯr nfr [Wsr-mꜣꜥ.t]-Rꜥ-[stp-n-ʾImn] (3) [Wsı͗rkn mrı͗]-ʾImn sꜣ Bꜣst.t (4) dı͗ ꜥnḫ
    Giving Maat […] (2) The Good God, [Usimaꜥ]re[setepenamon,] (2) [Osorkon, beloved of] Amon, Son of Bastet, (3) given life.

Queen with Ankh
    [ḥm.t] ny-sw.t [sꜣ.t ny-sw.t] (2) Krꜥmꜥ
    Queen [and Princess] (2) Karoama.

On Inner (B) and Back (C) Walls (pls. VII/4, 16–17, 19, VIII/19 and 21–23, XII/7, and XI/6, and adjust on pls. XXIX and XXXI; Naville 1892, 18–19; Uphill 1965, 375; for placement, see Barta 1978, 32, 39, and pls. II and III). In two subregisters. Two parallel rows of offerings and shrines of Ram or Falcon-headed gods, with further offerings below shrines. Upper row of shrines lost.

Label beside Upper Offerings
    ı͗r.t ḥtp-dı͗-ny-sw.t (n) nṯr.w ḫnty ḥw.wt nṯr.w n ḥb-sd

Making an "offering that the king gives" for the gods who are foremost of the mansions of the gods of the jubilee.

Label beside Lower Offerings

[ìr].t ḥtp-dỉ-ny-sw.t (n) nṯr.w ḫnty ḥw.wt nṯr.w [n ḥb-sd]

[Making] an "offering that the king gives" for the gods who are foremost of the mansions of the gods [of the jubilee.]

Lower Row of Fifteen Shrines

nṯr ꜥꜣ ḫnty ḥb-sd (1b) dỉ≠f ꜥnḫ wꜣs nb (2) nṯr ꜥꜣ ḫnty ḥb-sd (2b) dỉ≠f snb nb mỉ Rꜥ (3) nṯr ꜥꜣ ḫnty ḥb-sd (3b) dỉ≠f ꜥnḫ wꜣs nb (4) nṯr ꜥꜣ ḫnty ḥb-sd (4b) dỉ≠f qn nb (5) nṯr ꜥꜣ nb ḥb-sd (5b) dỉ≠f nḫt nb (6) nṯr ꜥꜣ nb ḥb-sd (6b) dỉ≠f ḥtp.w nb (7) nṯr ꜥꜣ nb ḥb-sd (7b) dỉ≠f df3.w nb (8) nṯr ꜥꜣ nb ḥb-sd (8b) dỉ(≠f) ꜥnḫ wꜣs nb (9) nṯr ꜥꜣ nb ḥb-sd (9b) dỉ≠f qn nb (10) nṯr ꜥꜣ nb ḥb-sd (10b) dỉ≠f nḫt nb (11) nṯr ꜥꜣ ḫnty ḥb-sd (11b) dỉ≠f ꜥnḫ wꜣs nb (12) nṯr ꜥꜣ nb ḥb-sd (12b) dỉ≠f ny.t-sw.t ꜥꜣ.t (13) nṯr ꜥꜣ nb ḥb-sd (13b) [dỉ≠f ...] (14) nṯr ꜥꜣ nb ḥb-sd (14b) [dỉ≠f] snb nb (15) nṯr ꜥꜣ nb ḥb-sd (15b) dỉ≠f ḏd wꜣs nb

The great god, Foremost of the jubilee. (1b) May he give all life and dominion. (2) The great god, Foremost of the jubilee. (2b) May he give all health like Re. (3) The great god, Foremost of the jubilee. (3b) May he give all life and dominion. (4) The great god, Foremost of the jubilee. (4b) May he give all valor. (5) The great god, lord of the jubilee. (5b) May he give all victory. (6) The great god, lord of the jubilee. (6b) May he give all offerings. (7) The great god, lord of the jubilee. (7b) May he give all foodstuffs. (8) The great god, lord of the jubilee. (8b) May he give all life and dominion. (9) The great god, lord of the jubilee. (9b) May he give all valor. (10) The great god, lord of the jubilee. (10b) May he give all victory. (11) The great god, Foremost of the jubilee. (11b) May he give all life and dominion. (12) The great god, lord of the jubilee. (12b) May he give a great kingship. (13) The great god, lord of the jubilee. (13b) [May he give ...] (14) The great god, lord of the jubilee. (14b) [May he give] all health. (15) The great god, lord of the jubilee. (15b) May he give all stability and dominion.

Procession of King: Preceded by Shrine of Wepwawet and Two Files of Priests (pl. VIII/22–23; head of procession on Wall C, pl. XII/7; Naville 1892, 23–24; Uphill 1965, 376). In two subregisters.

Lower Subregister, Facing Right: Five-plus priests who carry drums and staff lead procession, two labeled "friends" (smr), one with harp (?) labeled "divine brother" (sn-nṯr).[11] Thereafter, priests in filets and panther skins carrying staves.

ỉm(y)-ḫt Ḥȝ (2) wḥm Ḥr(?)[12] (3) wr ḥts(?)[13] (4) wr mȝ.w (5) smȝty (6) s(t)m (7) ḥdtp (< ḥtp) (8 = Wall B, pl. VIII/23) ḥtp (9) sȝ bỉ.ty (10) sš ny-sw.t rȝ-ʿ-šs n (11) t̠.t pr-ʿnḫ (12) [sȝ] ny-sw.t (13) sȝ bỉ.ty (14) ḥr(y).w-ḥkȝ. w (15) smr.w

Attendant of Ha (priest of seventh nome of Lower Egypt) (2) herald of Horus (?)[12] (3) Great of favor (?)[13] (4) Greatest of Seers (high priest of Heliopolis) (5) stolist (6) *setem* (7) offering-priest (?) (8) offering-priest (?) (9) amulet man of the Lower Egyptian king (10) royal document scribes (11) of the staff of the scriptorium (12) [amulet man] of the Upper Egyptian King (13) amulet man of the Lower Egyptian King (14) chief magicians (15) friends.

Upper Subregister, Facing Right: Four-plus priests within border of shrine precede "God's Mother of Assiut" ([mw.t-nt̠r n] Sȝwty), followed by two prophets bearing standards (cf. pls. II/10–11 and XIII) Then portable shrine of Wepwawet carried by priests, with attendant chief lector priest with scroll.

King in Festival Robe
   [...]... ʿḫ ny-sw.t pn (2) [sȝ] ʿnḫ d̠d wȝs mỉ Rʿ
   [...]... this royal palace. (2) [The protection of] life, stability, and dominion like Re.

King in Shrine Offers Clepsydra (pl. XI/6; Naville 1892, 24; Uphill 1965, 377 §VI; = Berlin 10837; see Königliche Museen zu Berlin 1899, 229–30; Porter and Moss 1927–51, 4:29). Facing left. Two *setem*-priests (s(t)m) in panther skins stand behind the king; one gives a clypsedra to the king (cf. pl. XVI) on a platform.

King
   [Wsr-mȝʿ.t-Rʿ-stp-n-ʾImn] (2) [Wsỉrkn mrỉ-ʾImn sȝ Bȝst.t] (3) dỉ ʿnḫ wȝs
   [Usimaʿresetepenamon,] (2) [Osorkon, beloved of Amon, son of Bastet,] (3) given life and dominion.

Label for Scene
   ny-sw.t nd̠r m-ʿ s(t)m
   The king takes possession from the *setem*-priest.

Purification Ceremony: King in festival robe and Upper Egyptian crown pours water from hands on priest, while five priests with "egg" vessels perform "baptism of Pharaoh" (contra inverse explanation, Naville 1892, 24). Small figure of Bastet (Bȝst.t) before king's face.

King

 nṯr nfr (2) [Wsr-mȝꜥ.t-Rꜥ-stp-n-]ʾI[mn] (3) ḥry(?) Bȝs.t r (4) s.t nb

The Good God, (2) [Usimaꜥresetepen]a[mon], (3) chief(?) of Bubastis more than (4) any place.

Before King

wdn sꜥb [...] ny-sw.t

Making offering and cleansing [...] the king.

Above Purifying Priests

wꜥb sp-2 sp-4

"Be pure! Be pure!"—4 times.

Labels for Priests, from Top

s(t)m ỉr(.t) ꜥb wꜥb m sp-4 (2) ỉmy-ḫt Hȝ ỉr.t ꜥb wꜥb sp-2 sp-4 (3) ỉmy-ḫnt ỉr.t ꜥb wꜥb sp-2 sp-4 (4) wr ḥts(?) ỉr(.t) ꜥb wꜥb sp-2 sp-[4] (5) [...] ỉr(.t) ꜥb wꜥb sp-2 sp-[4]

Setem-priest; making purification: "Be pure! Be pure!"—4 times. (2) Attendant of Ha (priest of seventh nome of Lower Egypt); making purification: "Be pure! Be pure!"—4 times. (3) Chamberlain; making purification: "Be pure! Be pure!"—4 times. (4) Great of favor (?); making purification: "Be pure! Be pure!"—[4] times. (5) [...]; making purification: "Be pure! Be pure!"—[4] times.

G. Register 7

On Projecting Post: King Passes Shrines and Enters "Hall of Eating" (pl. IV/2–4 and adjust on pl. XXIX; Naville 1892, 17; Uphill 1965, 373; for placement, see Barta 1978, 32, 40, and pl. II). In two subregisters.

Shrines with Mummiform Figures Wearing White and Red Crown (cf. register 6)

[Wsỉr ḫnty ʾImn].tyw dỉ≠f ꜥnḫ wȝs (2) Ḥr ḫnt ḥb-sd dỉ≠f qn nb

[Osiris, Foremost of the West]erners. May he give life and dominion. (2) Horus, Foremost of the jubilee. May he give all valor.

Upper Subregister

[... dỉ≠f ḥt]p(?) nb ḫr≠f (2) [...] m ny-sw.t tȝ.wy ḏ.t

[... May he give] all [satisfac]tion (?) deriving from him. (2) [...] as King of the Two Lands forever.

Label for Scene

ḫꜥ m sḥ n wnm r sḫꜥ ḥm n nṯr p[n] šps ʾImn-Rꜥ nb ns.wt tȝ.wy r ḥtp m

(2) m{sic} s.t≠f m Ḥw.t ḥb-sd

Appearing in the Hall of Eating in order to make the processional appearance of the majesty of this noble god Amon-Re, Lord of the Thrones of the Two Lands, in order to rest in (2) his place in the Mansion of the Jubilee.

King, Facing Right, Dresssed in Robe and Crown of Upper Egypt, Faced by Smaller Figure of Bastet (B3st.t)

nṯr nfr nb t3.wy Wsr-m3ꜥ.t-Rꜥ-stp-n-ʾImn (2) s3 Rꜥ mr≠f Wsỉrkn mrỉ-ʾImn s3 B3st.t (3) mr n Rꜥ m sk(t.t) (4) dỉ ꜥnḫ mỉ Rꜥ ḏ.t (5) s3 ꜥnḫ [... h3≠f] mỉ Rꜥ ḏ.t

The Good God, Lord of the Two Lands, Usimaꜥresetepenamon, (2) Son of Re, whom he loves, Osorkon, beloved of Amon, Son of Bastet, (3) beloved of Re in the night bark, (4) given life like Re forever. (5) The protection of life [and ... is behind him] like Re forever.

On Inner Wall B (pl. V/2 & 4–7; adjust on pl. XXIX; Naville 1892, 18; Uphill 1965, 373, wrongly cited in n. 33 as pl. XXVI, no. 5). King and queen before elaborate bark of Amon carried by porters.

King

[... Wsỉrkn mrỉ-ʾImn s3 B3st.t] dỉ ꜥnḫ
[... Osorkon, beloved of Amon, Son of Bastet], given life.

Queen

ḥm.t ny-sw.t s3.t ny-sw.t wr.t Krꜥmꜥ (2) ꜥnḫ.t(ỉ) ḏ.t
Great royal wife and princess, Karoama, (2) living forever.

Texts Flanking Shrine of Amon

(1) ḏd-mdw ỉn ʾImn-Rꜥ ny-sw.t nṯr.w dỉ[.n≠(ỉ) n](2)≠k ḥḥ.w m ḥb[.w]-sd (3) rnp.wt≠k nḥḥ ḏ.t [ḥr] (4) s.t Ḥr n.t ꜥnḫ.[w] (5) 3w.t-ỉb [mỉ] Rꜥ [ḏ.t] (6; behind shrine) [...]... (7) [...] dỉ.n≠(ỉ) n≠k (8) [...]≠f

Recitation by Amon-Re, King of the Gods: "[I have] given [to] (2) you millions of jubilees, (3) your years eternal and forever [upon] (4) the Horus throne of the living, (5) and joy [like] Re [forever]." (6) [...]... (7) [...] "I have given to you (8) [...] his [...]."

Label for Lost Oryx Sacrifice (pl. XIII/v; lower register, and adjust on pl. XXIX; Naville 1892, 18; for placement, see Barta 1978, 32 and pl. II)

[... sm314] (2) m3-ḥḏ.w n ỉt≠f ʾImn-Rꜥ [...] (3) ỉr n≠f {n≠f}15 ḥm≠f ỉr.n≠f dỉ ꜥnḫ (4) nṯr nfr nb ỉr.(t) ḫ.t Wsr-m3ꜥ.t-Rꜥ-stp-n-ʾImn (5) s3 Rꜥ n ẖ.t≠f mr≠f [Wsỉrkn mrỉ]-ʾImn s3 B3st.t (6) rdỉ.n ʾImn ḥq3.t m [...] (7) dỉ ꜥnḫ ḏd w3s mỉ Rꜥ ḏ.t

[... Slaying¹⁴] (2) oryx for his father Amon-Re, [...] (3) which His Majesty did for him,¹⁵ he having attained the state of being given life. (4) The Good God, Lord of ritual performance, Usimaʿresetepenamon, (5) bodily Son of Re, whom he loves, [Osorkon, beloved of] Amon, Son of Bastet, (6) [to whom] Amon gave rulership in [Egypt ...], (7) given life, stability, and dominion like Re forever.

Queen

rpʿ.t wr.t ḥs.wt ḥnw.t n [Šmʿ] Mḥw [ḥm.t ny-sw.t wr.t] (2) mr≠f nb(.t) t3.wy Krʿmʿ (3) ʿnḫ[.tỉ] dd[.tỉ ...]

Princess, great of praises, Mistress of [Upper] and Lower Egypt, [great royal wife] (2) whom he loves, Lady of the Two Lands, Karoama, (3) living and enduring [...]

Back Wall C (pl. XI/4–6; and adjust on pl. XXI; Naville 1892, 24; Uphill, 377–78). In three subregisters. Facing left.

First Subregister: Procession of conversing priests and musicians, from right

šsp.t n.t (2) dḫn.w(t) (3) sq m srw (4) srw (5) r t3 (6) dd-mdw r t3 (7) r t3 (8) dd-mdw r t3 (9) s3 t3

Chorus of (2) clappers. (3) Beating the drum. (4) drum. (5) "To the ground!" (6) Recitation: "To the ground!" (7) "To the ground!" (8) Recitation: "To the ground!" (9) Protecting the earth.

Second Subregister: Seated and prone dignitaries (cf. pl. XV)

[sn] t3 [ỉn ...]

[Kissing] the ground [by ...]

Standing Man (b3ty) behind Prone Figures, Raising Double Loop
dd-mdw h3 tn
Recitation: "Back!"

Top Subregister: Two priests, one with jackal standard (ḥm-ntr pfy "that prophet") and one (ḥm-ntr) with vase, followed by three plumed Nubian tribesmen (ʾIwn.tyw St.t); cf. pl. XV/6.

H. Register 8

On Projecting Post (pl. IV/1–2 [= Naville 1891, pl. XLII.C], and adjust on pl. XXIX; Naville 1892, 17; Uphill 1965, 373). Queen and three princesses.

[ḥm.t ny-sw.t s3.t ny-sw.t Krʿmʿ] (2) ʿnḫ.tỉ s(nb).tỉ (3) s3.t ny-sw.t n ḥ.t≠f mr≠f (4) T3-š3ʿ-ḫpr m3ʿ.t-ḫrw (5) s3.t ny-sw.t n ḥ.t≠f mr≠f (6) Krʿmʿ m3ʿ.t-ḫrw (7) s3.t ny-sw.t n ḥ.t≠f mr≠f (8) [...] ʾI-ỉrmr m3ʿ.t-ḫrw

[Queen and Princess Karoama,] (2) living and healthy. (3) Princess of his body, whom he loves, (4) Tashakheper, the justified. (5) Princess of his body, whom he loves, (6) Karoama, the justified. (7) Princess of his body, whom he loves, (8) [...] Irmer, the justified.

On Inner Wall B (pl. V/5; adjust on pl. XXIX). Facing right. File of priests and two groups of priestesses.

Before First File of Priestesses
    [...] m-ḫt sw‘b sḫn.t
    [...] after purifying the resting-place.

Before Second File of Priestesses
    [...] pr-’Imn ḫft sw‘b sḫn.t
    [...] temple of Amon, while purifying the resting-place.

King before Processional Bark of Amon (pl. VI/10–11 and adjust on pl. XXIX; Naville 1892, 18; Uphill 1965, 374; see also Kitchen 1986, 322 §280; and Breasted 1906–7, 4:371 §748)

Label for King
    Ḥr k3 nḫt mrỉ-M3‘.t (2) ny-sw.t bỉ.ty nb t3.wy Wsr-m3‘.t-R‘-stp-n-’Imn (3) s3 R‘ n ẖ.t≠f Wsỉr[kn] mrỉ-’Imn s3 B3st.t (4) dỉ [‘nḫ] mỉ R‘ ḏ.t
    Horus: "Strong Bull Beloved of Maat," (2) the King of Upper and Lower Egypt, Lord of the Two Lands, Usima‘resetepenamon, (3) bodily Son of Re, Osor[kon], beloved of Amon, Son of Bastet, (4) given [life] like Re forever.

Label before Shrine of Amon
    ḫ‘ ỉn ḥm n nṯr pn šps [šsp[16]] (2) tp w3.t r ḥtp m ḥw.t ḥb (3)-sd ỉr.n ḥm≠f m m3w.t n ỉt[≠f ...] (4) sbt.w≠s nb.w m ḏ‘mw wḫ3.w [...] (5) dỉ ‘nḫ ḏd w3s [...]
    Appearance by the Majesty of this noble god. [Setting out[16]] (2) on the road to rest in the Mansion of the Jubilee ("Festival Hall") (3) that His Majesty made anew for [his fathe]r [...] (4), all its walls of electrum, its columns [of ...,] (5) given life, stability and dominion [...]

Label behind Shrine of Amon
    ḏd-mdw ỉn ’Imn-R‘ nb ns.wt t3.wy [...] (2) n s3≠f mr≠f Wsr-m3‘.t-R‘-[stp-n-’Imn [...] (3)≠k wỉ m mnw≠k [...]ỉ [...] (4) m ỉsw ỉr≠w m ḥḥ.w m ḥb.w-sd (5) s3 R‘ Wsỉrkn mrỉ-’Imn s3 B3st.t [...]
    Recitation by Amon-Re, Lord of the Thrones of the Two Lands [...] (2) to his son, whom he loves, Usima‘re[setepen]amon: "You [...] (3) me in

your monument [...] (4) as the reward for them, being millions of jubilees [...] (5) Son of Re, Osorkon, beloved of Amon, Son of Bastet [...].

Procession of Clappers and Censing (pl. XIII/v; adjust on pl. XXIX; for placement, see Barta 1978, 32 and pl. II). In two subregisters. In lower subregister, three chanters followed by a priest censing. Above, traces of feet, linked by Naville with pl. XIII/iv, relocated by Barta to Wall D, registers 15–16.

Label for Chanters
    dḫn (2) în šsp.t (3) n.t dḫn.(4)wt
    Giving the beat (2) by the chorus (3) of (4) clappers.

Label for Thurifer
    ḥnq sntr în ḫr(y)-ḥȝ.t n ny-sw.t
    Censing by the one who precedes the king.

Wall C. Rites in the Tomb (pl. X/1–5; adjust on pl. XXXI; Naville 1892, 25; Uphill 1965, 378; for placement, see Barta 1978, 32 and pl. III). Pl. X/3 = Louvre E 10592; see Association française d'action artistique 1987, 170–71 (no. 45). In four subregisters. King and procession facing left. In bottom subregister, four priests in filets including *setem*-priest (s(t)m) with staff and "estate inspector" (sḥd-pr) with knives(?). Then "praised one" (ḥs.ty) with crook, chief lector priest (ḥry-ḥb.t ḥry-tp) with scroll, ending with two men carrying knife and bolt of cloth. Second subregister, at right, king in shrine facing three rows of four gods.

Label for King in Robe with Crook and Flail
    nṯr nfr Wsr-mȝꜥ.t-Rꜥ-stp-n-ʾImn (2) sȝ Rꜥ W[s]îrkn mrî-ʾImn sȝ Bȝst.t (3) dî ꜥnḫ mî Rꜥ
    The Good God, Usimaꜥreseteenamon, (2) Son of Re, O[s]orkon, beloved of Amon, Son of Bastet, (3) given life like Re.

Label for Scene
    ḥtp m-ḫnw îs.t îr≠f [dî ꜥnḫ]
    Resting within the tomb that he might attain [the state of being given life.]

Gods, from Top
    Rꜥ (2) Tm (3) Šw (4) Tfn.t (5) Gb (6) Nw.t (7) Wsîr (8) Ḥr (9) Swty (10) ȝs.t (11) Nb.t-Ḥw.t (12) Kȝ-ny-sw.t
    Re (2) Atum (3) Shu (4) Tefnut (5) Geb (6) Nut (7) Osiris (8) Horus (9) Seth (10) Isis (11) Nephthys (12) the royal *ka*-spirit (holding *imiut*-emblem)

King in Robes Holds Cup for Myrrh (?), Facing Smaller Figure of Bastet
(B3st.t)
    [Wsr-m3ʿ.t-Rʿ-stp-n-ʾImn Wsỉrkn mrỉ-ʾImn s3 B3st.t] (2) dỉ ʿnḫ mỉ Rʿ
(3) s3 ḫ3⸗k mỉ Rʿ
    [Usimaʿresetepenamon, Osorkon, beloved of Amon, Son of Bastet,] (2)
given life like Re. (3) Protection is behind you like Re.

Label for Scene
    [...].t n šsp ʿntyw(?) [...]
    [...] for receiving myrrh(?) [...]

Before King: Three subregisters of fileted priests carrying ushebti-like
images on poles

    Bottom Subregister, Names over Images
        Nb.t-Ḥw.t (2) B3.t (3) [...] ỉrr(?) (4) Ḥry šns⸗f (5) Wp-s.t (6) Ḥry.t
        n h3w(?) (7) Sḥtp Nb.wy (8) 3ḫ.t
        Nephthys (2) Bat (3) [...] who acts (?) (4) Chief of his offering
        bread (5) Opener of the Place (6) Chief of time (?) (7) Pacifier of
        the Two Lords (8) The Effective One

    Middle Subregister
        Šsmw (2) Ḥr-3ḫ.ty (3) B3.ty[17] (4) Šns (5) ʿnn-ḥr (6) ʿʿ.wy-Ḥr (7)
        šspw (8) [...]
        Shesmu (2) Horachty (3) Baty[17] (4) Offering bread (5) He whose
        face is turned back (6) Arms of Horus (7) Image (8) [...]

    Upper Register: Nineteen-plus priests in panther skins with unlabeled
    "ushebti-standards"; above, frieze of "life" (ʿnḫ), stability (ḏd), and
    dominion (w3s).

I. Register 9.

On Projecting Post and Wall B (pl. VI/i and ii; adjust from bottom register
on pl. XXIX; Uphill 1965, 373; for placement, see Barta 1978, 32 and pl.
II). Facing right. King escorted by Thoth and other gods.

King, Facing Smaller Figure of Bastet (B3[st.t]), Escorted by Thoth
    [Wsr-m3ʿ.t-Rʿ-stp-n-ʾImn] (2) Wsỉrkn mrỉ-[ʾImn s3 B3st.t] (3) dỉ ʿnḫ w3s
    [Usimaʿresetepenamon], (2) Osorkon, beloved of [Amon, Son of
Bastet,] (3) given life and dominion.

Above Thoth

[...] wꜣḏ bs(?) r ḥtp (2) [ḥr] tnṯꜣ.t (3) šps m bꜣḥ (4) [pꜣ]ỉw≠k(?) nb ꜣImn (5) [...]

[...] fresh [...]. Being inducted (?) to rest (2) [upon the] noble balda-chino (3) in the presence of (4) [yo]ur (?) lord Amon (5) [...]

King between Two Gods

[Wsr-mꜣꜥ.t-Rꜥ-stp-n-ꜣImn] (2) Wsỉrkn mrỉ-[ꜣImn sꜣ Bꜣst.t] (3) dỉ ꜥnḫ wꜣs

[Usimaꜥresetepenamon], (2) Osorkon, beloved of [Amon, Son of Bastet,] (3) given life and dominion.

Scene of "Appearance in the Temple" (pl. VI/8–11 [= Naville 1891, 50–51 and pl.XLII.B], and adjust on pl. XXIX; Naville 1892, 4; Uphill 1965, 373–74; see Barta 1978, 32, 41, and pl. II). Adapted from an older source; closely paralleled by Soleb relief of Amonhotep III. Retrograde main text. For the text, translation, and discussion, see Van Siclen 1973, 295–99; Breasted 1906–7, 4:372–73 §§749–51. A thoroughly obsolete interpretation appears in Revillout 1899, 184–85 (equating Osorkon II with Sargon II). See also Kitchen 1986, 320–22 §§279–80; Vernus 1975, 25–26. Cf. Lepsius 1849–59, 3:pl. 86b. Facing right.

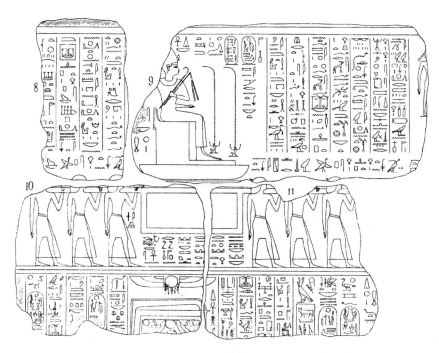

Scene of "Appearance in the Temple," Naville 1892, pl. VI/8–11.

Label for King: Seated on litter before two glyphs for millions of years (text between lines 4 and 5 of framing decree)

nṯr nfr (2) Wsr-m3ꜥ.t-Rꜥ-stp-n-ʾImn mr.n ʾImn (r)[18] ny-sw.t nb (3) Wsỉrkn mrỉ-ʾImn s3 B3st.t (4) s3 Rꜥ stp n (5) Tm (6) dỉ ꜥnḫ nb (7) [s3 ꜥnḫ ḏd w3s] s[nb] nb mỉ Rꜥ

The Good God, (2) Usimaꜥresetepenamon, whom Amon loves more than[18] any king, (3) Osorkon, beloved of Amon, Son of Bastet, (4) Son of Re, chosen of (5) Atum, (6) given all life. (7) [The protection of] all [life, stability, dominion, and] health like Re.

Label for Scene (above ỉmy-ḫnt porters on each side of king)

[…] ỉmy-r3 pr(?) (2) f3.t ny-sw.t ḥr ḥtp ḥr sp3 wḏ3 r ꜥḥ ỉn ny-sw.t (3) f3.t ny-sw.t ḥr sp3 […]

[…] Steward (2) Carrying the king, sitting on the litter, proceeding to the palace by the king. (3) Carrying the king on the litter […]

Below Litter (six vertical columns)

t3.w nb ḫ3s.t nb(.t) (2) Rtnw ḥr(y).t (3) Rtnw [ḫ]r(y).t (4) ḫ3s.t nb(.t) št3 (5) r rd.wy nṯr pn nfr (6) rḫy.t nb ꜥnḫ≠sn

All lands, all foreign countries, (2) upper Syria-Palestine, (3) lower Syria-Palestine, (4) all remote foreign countries (5) are at the feet of this Good God. (6) All living citizens.

Main Text

(1) ḥsb.t 22 3bd 4 3ḫ.t[19] ḫꜥ m ḥw.t-nṯr n(.t) ʾImn nt[y]
(2) m ḥw.t ḥb-sd ḥtp ḥr sp3 šsp ḫw t3.wy ỉn[20] ny-sw.t
(3) ḥw.t ḫnỉ.t n(.t) pr-ʾImn ḥnꜥ ḥw.t ḥm.wt nb(.t) n(.t)
(4) nỉw.ty≠f[21] nty m ḥm.wt ḏr h(3)w ỉt.w≠f
(5) ỉw≠sn m ḥm.wt m pr nb ḥtr(.w) ḥr b3k≠sn
(6) ḥr rnp.t ỉst ḥm≠f ḥr ḥḥy sp ꜥ3 n 3ḫ.w
(7) n ỉt≠f ʾImn-Rꜥ ḫft sr≠f ḥb-sd tpy n s3≠f ḥtp
(8) ḥr ns.t≠f sr≠f n≠f ꜥ3 wr.w m W3s.t nb.t
(9) pḏ.t psḏ.t ḏd-ḫr ny-sw.t m-b3ḥ ỉt≠f ʾImn ỉw ḥw.n≠(ỉ) W3s.t
(10) ḥr q3≠s ḥr wsḫ≠s wꜥb.t dỉ.tỉ n nb≠s nn ḏ3w-t3 r≠
(11) s ỉn rwḏw.w n.w pr ny-sw.t ḫw rmt.w≠s n ḥn.ty ḥr rn wr n nṯr nfr

(1) Regnal year 22, month 4 of Inundation.[19] Appearance in the temple of Amon that (2) is in the Mansion of the Jubilee; sitting upon the litter; initiating the protection of the Two Lands by[20] the king. (3) Exempting the harem of the estate of Amon together with all the women of (4) his two cities[21] who had been servants since the time of his forefathers, (5) being servants in any estate, who were taxed concerning their labor (6) annually.

Now, as His Majesty was seeking a great deed of benefit for (7) his father Amon-Re, since he (Amon-Re) had announced a first jubilee for his son who sits (8) upon his throne, and he (Amon-Re) had announced for him very many in Thebes, the Lady of (9) the Nine Bows, the king thus said in the presence of his father Amon: "I have exempted Thebes (10) in her length and her breadth, while she is clear from legal claim and granted to her lord, with no interference against (11) her by agents of the royal palace, so that her people might be exempted to the ends of time by the great name of the Good God."

King Enters Palace with ḫkr-Ornamentation (pl. IVbis/14–15, and adjust from projecting post on pl. XXIX; Naville 1892, 16; Uphill 1965, 372; for placement, see Barta 1978, 32, 41, and pl. II)

Label for Scene

ḥtp m ʿḥ ỉn ny-sw.t ḫft ỉy.t ḥr ỉr.t ỉrr.wt m [...]

Resting in the palace by the king when coming to perform what is to be done in [...]

NOTES TO §III. WALLS B/C

1. Versus Uphill 1965, 375, who reads "like the lord Re."

2. Epithet of Edjo; Erman and Grapow 1926–63, 5:443/2.

3. Mrḥw, a god in bull form; Erman and Grapow 1926–63, 2:112/5. Uphill 1965, 376, has Merky (sic), and, following Naville, suggests identification with Apis/Hapi.

4. Erman and Grapow 1926–63, 3:71/3.

5. Epithet of Edjo; Erman and Grapow 1926–63, 1:489/11.

6. Or read Ḫ[nsw] "Kh[onsu]," as Naville 1892, 20.

7. Uphill 1965, 376, misreads "Bebtet."

8. See Helck 1974, 118–21.

9. Cf. Ritner 1985, 149–55.

10. Contra Uphill (1965, 373), the twelve prophets are not the "spirits of Pe."

11. Labels are placed before, not after, the designated figure. Uphill (1965, 376) wrongly assigned this label to the preceding "friend" carrying a staff; see Naville 1892, 23. For the sn-nṯr musician associated with funerals, see Altenmüller 1978, 18–20, who translated the title "united with the deified one."

12. Or m wḥm [...] "repeating [...]."

13. Cf. Erman and Grapow 1926–63, 3:202–03; but generally in feminine. Or read wr sḫm or wr ʿḥ≠s? For the paleography, see Naville 1892, 17 n. 4.

14. For the idiom and rite, see Derchain 1962.

15. Dittography. Note the loss of the same dative in line 6.

16. For the idiom, see Erman and Grapow 1926–63, 3:533/13; Naville 1892, pls. II and III.

17. Epithet of Osiris; see Erman and Grapow 1926–63, 1:417/3.

18. For the restoration, cf. the inscriptions of Kheruef, in Epigraphic Survey 1980, pl. 54, l: mr.n≠f r ny-sw.t [nb]. The loss of the preposition r is constant in these jubilee texts in the common recitation dỉ (r) t3 "Placing on the ground."

19. The celebration of a jubilee before year 30 suggests an appropriation by Osorkon of the (7/8?) years of Takelot I; see Naville 1892, 6; Hornung and Staehelin 1974, 55. For the absolute date of the jubilee, see Kitchen 1986, 320 §279 and n. 424 (ca. 853 B.C.E.); contra E. Uphill 1965, 382–83 (844 B.C.E.); 1967, 61–62 (ca. 839/838 B.C.E.).

20. The n of ỉn has been moved to the beginning of the next line.

21. Distinct from Soleb version, probable reference to Bubastis and Thebes.

§IV. NAVILLE'S WALLS E/F.

A. Register 1 (pl. XIX/1–2 and adjust on pl. XXX; Naville 1892, 32; Uphill 1965, 377; for placement, see Barta 1978, 32 and pl. IV). At left edge, king and procession face left. In three subregisters.

Scene 1: King in red crown, holding mace and staff, faces smaller image of Bastet (B3st.t) and is preceded by priestess named "chief of singers" wr.(t) ḥs.(wt).

 nṯr nfr (2) Wsr-m3ꜥ.t-Rꜥ-stp-n-ʾImn (3) Wsỉrkn mrỉ-ʾImn s3 B3st.t

The Good God, (2) Usimaꜥresetepenamon, (3) Osorkon, beloved of Amon, Son of Bastet.

Decree (?) Subdivided into Two Vertical Subcolumns in Old Kingdom Fashion

[...]d(?) Ḥr wḏ≠f nb ỉr≠f (2) wỉ3 nṯr [...] (3) ḫd [...]

[...]... Horus his every command regarding it: (2) the divine bark [...] (3) go downstream [...]

In Lowest Subregister: Procession led by bearer of insignia (ḥry-nws), followed by chamberlain (ỉmy-ḫnt), friend ([s]mr), and setem-priest (sm).

Scene 2: King in red crown, holding ankh, faces smaller image of Bastet. Labels of king and Bastet lost.

Recitation by King (?)

ḏd-mdw ms ṯn [...]

Recitation: "Betake yourselves [...]!"

Facing King, Upper Subregister: Two priests making obsequies

b3 [Ptḥ(?)]-Tnn

The ba-spirit(?) of [Ptah]-Tenen.

Text of Priests

ḏd-mdw mr pn [...] (2) ḏd-mdw w3ḥ m p [...]

Recitation: This love [...] (2) Recitation: "Place in the [...]."

Facing King, Middle Subregister: Two priests making obsequies
[...] (2) t3.w [...] (3) ḥnw.t t3.w [...]
[...] (2) lands [...] (3) Mistress of the lands [...]

Lowest Subregister: Procession led by friend (smr), followed by bearer of insignia (ḫry-nws).

Behind King, Upper Subregister: Four-plus priests labeled "followers of Horus" (šms.w-Ḥr) carry divine standards

Label for Scene
šsp ḫr nṯr tp-w3.t ỉr tp-w3.t[1]
Setting out bearing the god on the road at the beginning of the road.

Lower Subregister: Procession led by bearer of insignia (ḫry-nws), followed by chamberlain (ỉmy-ḫnt) and "friend" (s[mr]) or *setem*-priest (s[(t)ml]).

Scene 3 (pl. XX/5, lower register; ignored by Barta 1978, 32, but cf. pl. IV). Lost except for label for lost figure: "the unique one carrying the sack" wꜥ ḫr(y) ḥn.[2] Cf. pl. XIX/5.

Wall F (pl. XXV/i and adjust on pl. XXXI). Three subregisters of priests facing right. Single figure in lowest subregister labeled lector priest (ḫry-ḥb.t). Upper sub-register: [...] sḥ [...] Hall

B. Register 2

On Projecting Post (pls. XVIII/12–13 and XXX; Naville 1892, 29; Uphill 1965, 376). Large horizontal inscription.
    (1) [...] ḫꜥ mỉ [Rꜥ ...] nb t3.wy Wsr-m3ꜥ.t-Rꜥ-stp-n-ỉmn s3 Rꜥ nb ḫꜥ.w [Wsỉrkn mrỉ-ỉmn s3 B3st.t ...]
    (2) [...] wḏb [...] mw wr t3.wy m ḥt≠f ḥr dbḥ [...]
    (3) [...]≠f m ḥr.w mỉ [Rꜥ ...] ḥr nb mr n wỉ3 sty.w m ḥr≠sn [...]
    (4) [...].w [...]w m ꜥntyw bg(3)w m mw [...]

    (1) [...] appearing like [Re ...] Lord of the Two Lands, Usimaꜥresetepenamon, son of Re, Lord of Diadems, [Osorkon, beloved of Amon, Son of Bastet ...]
    (2) [...] shore [...] great water, the Two Lands behind him pleading for [...]

(3) [...] his [...] in faces like [Re ...], everyone love of the bark, the rays in their faces [...]

(4) [...] with myrrh, shipwrecked in water [...]

On Inner Wall E, Right to Left

Scene 1 (pl. XIX/5 + XX/5; Naville 1892, 30–32; Uphill 1965, 377; for placement, see Barta 1978, 32 and pl. IV). Pl. XX/5 = University of Pennsylvania E 226. In three subregisters. Movement to left.

In Lowest Subregister (pl. XX/5): Three dwarves with forked sticks serving as police (s°š3), first labeled "chief" (ḥ3ty). Followed by two lector priests (ḥry-ḥb.t).

In Middle Subregister: Man presents bow to another, followed by *setem*-priest (s(t)m)
ḏd-mdw ḥr p(3) îy bî.ty
Recitation at the coming of the King of Lower Egypt.

In Upper Subregister: Sitting man faces four-plus advancing figures, including "opener of the mouth" (wn-r3) and "the unique one carrying the sack" (w° ḥr(y) ḥn).[2]

Scene 2 (pl. XXV/v; Naville 1892, 32). Facing left. King in red crown follows porters carrying solar (?) bark, labeled: R° m (?) [wî3≠f(?)] Re in (?) [his bark?].

King
nṯr nfr [Ws]îrkn mrî-ʾImn
The Good God, [Os]orkon, beloved of Amon.

Scene 3 (pl. XXV/ii + XIX/1–2; Naville 1892, 32; for join, see Barta 1978, pl. IV). Facing left. File of nine-plus priests, led by "the unique one carrying the sack" (w° ḥr(y) ḥn).

Label for Scene (pl. XXV/ii)
[...] m °ḥ° î3b.t n s.t≠f
[...] in the position left of his seat.

Wall F (pl. XXV/i). Three prone figures ([...] m [..]), with lost text above: [...] b

C. Register 3

On Projecting Post (pl. XVIII/10–11 and 13, and pl. XXX; Naville 1892, 29; Uphill 1965, 376). Facing left. File of six-plus priests, including "He who pertains to the god" (ỉry-nṯr, cf. pl. III/12, §I. C), king's acquaintance (rḫ ny-sw.t), brothers (sn.w), and prophets (ḥm.w-nṯr).

On Inner Wall E, Right to Left (pls. XIX/5 top + XXV/v top). File of eight-plus priests without preserved texts. Then seated king in red crown preceded by priest with Nekhen standard (pl. XXVII/vi bottom)

    […] n (2) nṯr nfr Wsr-mꜣꜥ.t-Rꜥ-stp-n-ʾImn […] (3) ḫr […] m Nḫn n [ny-sw.t(?)]³ …]

    […] for (?) (2) the Good God, Usimaʿresetepenamon, […] (3) bearing [the standard (?) …] in Nekhen of [the King (?)³ …]

King in Shrine (pls. XX/vi and XXX; Naville 1892, 31–32). At right behind shrine, priests in three subregisters face right. In middle subregister, two prone figures followed by three standing figures labeled in retrograde "common priests" (ꜥšꜣ)⁴ and "opener of the mouth" (wn-rꜣ). In upper subregister, "the unique one carrying the sack" (wꜥ ḫr(y) ḥn, retrograde).

    dỉ wn ꜥšꜣ (2) [rꜣ(?) …] Ḥꜣ.t šd ḏꜥ […]

    Causing the common priests (?) to open (2) [the mouth (?) …] Mendes extract (?) …[…]

King in Robe and Red Crown Enthroned in Shrine Facing Smaller Figure of Bastet (Bꜣst.t)

    Wsr-mꜣꜥ.t-Rꜥ-stp-n-ʾImn (2) Wsỉrkn mrỉ-ʾImn sꜣ Bꜣst.t (3) dỉ ꜥnḫ

    Usimaʿresetepenamon, (2) Osorkon, beloved of Amon, Son of Bastet, (3) given life.

Below Shrine: Subregister with three priests labeled "prophets" (ḥm.w-nṯr)

Wall F (pl. XXIV/10; Naville 1892, 31–32; Uphill, 377). In two subregisters. Standing figure above; below, kneeling bearer of insignia (ḫry-nws) on stepped platform holds knife and staff.

    nṯr nfr t[…] ꜥꜣ […] ḫr(y)-nws

    The Good God […] great […] bearer of insignia.

D. Register 4

On Projecting Post (pl. XXV/iii; Naville 1892, 29; Uphill 1965, 376). Facing left. King in robe and red crown carries crook, followed by two fan-bearers and figure with bow (?).

Label for King

[...] Wsỉrkn mrỉ-ʾImn sꜣ Bꜣst.t (2) dỉ ꜥnḫ wꜣs

[...] Osorkon, beloved of Amon, Son of Bastet, (2) given life and dominion.

On Inner Wall E, Right to Left (pls. XIX/4 + XX/4 + XXVII/vi top + XX/3 and 6; Naville 1892, 32; for placement, see Barta 1978, 33 and pl. IV). In two subregisters. Enthroned king faces left; two figures seated behind face right (including ḥry-nws "bearer of insignia" with staves?). Below (pl. XX/4), file of six-plus priests advance left, including chamberlain (ỉmy-ḫnt), "friend" (smr), crew member (ỉmy-ỉs), and bearer of insignia (ḥry-nws). Head of file with staff (pl. XXVII/vi) and "Nekhen of the King standard" met by prone figure and chanting priestess.

ḏd-mdw hꜣ-snḏ (2) [...] p[...]

Recitation: "Hail and respect!" (2) [...]...[...]

At Far Left (pl. XX/3 and 6): Procession of four-plus priests advance left, labeled "lectors" (ẖr(y)-ḥb.(t)).

Wall F (pl. XXIV/9; Naville 1892, 34; Uphill 1965, 377; for placement, see Barta 1978, 33 and pl. III). In two subregisters. In upper subregister, from right, priest with falcon standard follows "the unique one carrying the sack" (wꜥ ẖr(y) ḥn, retrograde) advancing left. Before them, two prostrating "brothers who lie down and stand" (sn sḏr ꜥḥꜥ). A figure (rn "name/someone") pours from a jug.

Two Kneeling Figures with Adze (?), Partially Retrograde Text

ḥms.t tp r(w)dw ḥr mḥt (2) ḏd-mdw ꜥḥꜥ wn rꜣ

Sitting on the staircase at the north. (2) Recitation: "Stand, open the mouth."

In Lower Subregister, from Right: *Setem*-priest (s(t)m) in panther skin advances left, behind two pairs of facing dancers (?).

pẖr/dbn ḥr mḥt ny-sw.t (2) ḏd-mdw ꜥḥꜥ wn rꜣ (3) ḏd-mdw ꜥḥꜥ wn rꜣ

Turning about on the north of the king. (2) Recitation: "Stand, open the mouth." (3) Recitation: "Stand, open the mouth."

E. Register 5

On Projecting Post (pl. XXVI/vi). Facing left. King in robe and red crown and carrying crook and flail advances left from doorway, followed by striding figure with staff. Single cartouche effaced.

Fragmentary Text at Left (pl. XXV/iv bottom; ignored by Barta 1978, 33, but cf. pl. IV). Retrograde.
[...] h₃ nṯr.w [...]
[...] Hail gods [...]!

Wall F (pl. XXIII/7–8 + XXIV/7 and 9; Naville 1892, 34; Uphill 1965, 377; for placement, see Barta 1978, 33, 38–39, and pl. III). Pl. XXIII/7 = University of Pennsylvania E 225. In three subregisters. At left edge, king in robe and red crown and carrying crook and flail advances right, toward smaller figure of Bastet (B₃st.t):
Wsr-m₃ᶜ.t-Rᶜ-stp-n-ʾImn (2) Wsỉrkn mrỉ-ʾImn s₃ B₃st.t (3) dỉ ᶜnḫ mỉ Rᶜ ḏ.t
Usimaᶜreseteпenamon, (2) Osorkon, beloved of Amon, Son of Bastet, (3) given life like Re forever.

Label for Scene
pr h₃ ỉnb(.w)⁵
Going out around the wall(s).⁵

Before King: File of officials in middle subregister, including bearer of insignia (ḥry-nws), chamberlain (ỉmy[-ḫnt]), and setem-priest (s(t)m). In upper subregister, two opposed processions of standard bearers meet at central label:
šsp ḥr nṯr [...] ỉr r(w)dw⁶
Setting out carrying the god [...] to the staircase.⁶

In bottom subregister (pl. XXIV/7 and 9), file of eight-plus priests, including "amulet man of the Lower Egyptian King" ([s₃] bỉ.ty) and lector priest (ḥr(y)-ḥb.(t)). At right, label: šsp [...] Setting out [..]

F. Register 6

On Projecting Post (pl. XVIII/9 + XXV/iv; Uphill 1965, 376; for placement, see Barta 1978, 33 and pl. IV). In three subregisters. On right, enthroned king in shrine faces smaller figure of Bastet (B₃st.t). Standards before shrine labeled "followers of Horus" (šms.w Ḥr).

Label for King
Wsr-m₃ᶜ.t-Rᶜ-stp-n-ʾImn (2) Wsỉrkn mrỉ-ʾImn s₃ B₃st.t
Usimaᶜreseteпenamon, (2) Osorkon, beloved of Amon, Son of Bastet

Label before Lost File of Officials in Upper Subregister
ỉy ỉr tp r(w)dw

Coming to the top of the staircase.

In middle subregister, figures including bearer of insignia (ḫr(y)-nws), "name/someone" (rn), and fragmentary labels:
  šsp [...] (2) îmy n[..] (3) ḏd-mdw s[...]
  Setting out [...] (2) which is in [...]. (3) Recitation: [...]

At bottom (pl. XXV/iv), file of priests including prophet (ḥm-nṯr):
  ḏd-[mdw] h₃-[s]nḏ
  Recitation: "Hail and respect!"

Wall F (pl. XXIII/5–7; Naville 1892, 34; Uphill 1965, 377; for placement, see Barta 1978, 33, adding top of XXIII/7, and pl. III). Pl. XXIII/5 = British Museum 1105; cf. Budge 1909, 212–13; Porter and Moss 1927–51, 4:29. In three subregisters.

At left edge, stepped shrine with enthroned king in robe and red crown and carrying flail, facing smaller image of Bastet (B₃st.t):
  Wsr-m₃ꜥ.t-Rꜥ-stp-n-ʾImn (2) Wsîrkn mrî-ʾImn s₃ B₃st.t (3) dî ꜥnḫ mî Rꜥ (4) ꜥ₃ ḥr s.t
  Usimaꜥresetepenamon, (2) Osorkon, beloved of Amon, Son of Bastet, (3) given life like Re, (4) great upon the throne.

In bottom subregister, from right, official with staff faces gesturing male and two females with retrograde inscription:
  ms[.w] ny-sw.t (2) ḥr(y).w [...] (3) d(y) ḫr(y)-ḥb.(t)
  Royal children (2) who are in charge of [...]: (3) "Here, lector!"
Two priests with papyrus flank glyph for offering (ḥtp).

In middle subregister, setem-priest (s(t)m) acts as door opener (wn ꜥ₃.wy) and recites offering prayer:
  ḥtp dî ny-sw.t
  An "offering that the king gives."

Three runners approach two officials with maces:
  r t₃ ḥr p(₃) šm pr(?) m ḥtp n nṯr.w
  "To the ground—at the coming and going (?) in peace of the gods."

In upper subregister, file of six men advance to glyph of "six-weave cloth" (sîs)[7] labeled (retrograde):
  šn nṯr B₃st.t în w₃ḥ r t₃
  The divine ring/hair (?) of Bastet, brought and placed upon the ground.

G. Register 7

On Projecting Post, Offering Table of Fish and Fowl (pl. XVIII/7–9; Naville 1892, 33–34; Uphill 1965, 376–77; for placement, see Barta 1978, 33, 40–41, and pl. IV). Facing right. Individual sections of six compartments: standing man holding bird and fish in center, two labels in boxes above, four below. Each offered bird and fish associated with specific divinity. Second category highly obscure: priestly titles, materials, and dates? From top right.

    (1) Stš (b) spr wr(?) (c) Stš (d) šm (e) (ỉ)m(y)-[ḫt] St[š] (f) s[w]
    (2) Ȝs.t (b) wꜥ wr-ḫb(?) (c) Stš (d) rȝ (e) [...] (f) ꜥḥȝ
    (3) Stš (b) špt⁸ (c) [...] (d) sȝ (e) [...] (f) sw
    (4) Stš (b) ḫr(y)-ꜥ (c) Ḥr (d) ꜥq (e) [Nb.t]-Ḥw.t (f) ỉn.t
    (5) Ḏḥwty (b) ḫr(y) ... (c) (ỉ)m(y)-ḫt Stš (d) ỉm (e) Ḥr (f) ḫfm
    (6) Ḏḥwty (b) ḫr(y)-[nw]s(?) (c–f) [...]

    (1) Seth: (b) great petitioner (?). (c) Seth: (d) šm-bird. (e) Follower (?) of Seth: (f) sw-fish.
    (2) Isis: (b) great unique one of the festival (?). (c) Seth: (d) ro-goose (e) [...]: (f) perch.
    (3) Seth: (b) angry one (?).⁸ (c) [...]: (d) sȝ-goose. (e) [...]: (f) sw-fish.
    (4) Seth: (b) assistant. (c) Horus: (d) ꜥq-goose. (e) Nephthys: (f) tilapia fish.
    (5) Thoth: (b) bearer ... (c) Follower (?) of Seth: (d) ỉm-bird. (e) Horus: (f) ḫfm-fish.
    (6) Thoth: (b) bearer of [insign]ia (?). (c–f) [...].

Wall F, Continuation of Table (pl. XXII/4–6; Naville 1892, 33–34; Uphill 1965, 376–77; for placement, see Barta 1978, 33 and pl. III). Facing right. Remains of eleven-plus offering scenes.
    (1) [...]
    (2) [Nb.t]-Ḥw.t (b) ḥb n Rꜥ (c) [Nb.t]-Ḥw.t (d) P (e) Ḥr (f) [...]
    (3) Ḏḥwty (b) hrw n ṯḥn (c) Stš (d) ṯrp (e) Ḏḥwty (f) [...]
    (4) Ḥr (b) ỉȝ(.t) (c) [Nb.t]-Ḥw.t (d) stḥ (e) [Nb.t]-Ḥw.t (f) [...]
    (5) Ḏḥwty (b) bỉ.t Mḥw (c) Ḏḥwty (d) sȝ(?) (e) Ḏḥwty (f) [...]
    (6) Stš (b) mꜥ[(?)...] (c) Ḥr (d) rd (e) [Nb.t]-Ḥw.t (f) [...]
    (7) [...] (b) ỉty [P](?) (c) Ḏḥwty (d) sȝ(?) (e–f) [...]
    (8–11) [...]

    (1) [...].
    (2) Nephthys: (b) festival of Re. (c) Nephthys: (d) Pe-goose. (e) Horus: (f) [...].
    (3) Thoth: (b) day of faience. (c) Seth: (d) ṯrp-duck. (e) Thoth: (f) [...].

(4) Horus: (b) i̯ꜣ.t-plant. (c) Nephthys: (d) stḥ-goose. (e) Nephthys:
(f) […].
(5) Thoth: (b) Northern honey. (c) Thoth: (d) sꜣ-goose (?). (e) Thoth:
(f) […].
(6) Seth: (b) …[…] (c) Horus: (d) rd-goose. (e) Nephthys: (f) […].
(7) […] (b) sovereign of Pe (?). (c) Thoth: (d) sꜣ-goose (?). (e-f) […].
(8–11) […].

H. Register 8

On Projecting Post. Continuation of Table (pl. XVIII/7–8; Naville 1892,
33–34; Uphill 1965, 376–77; for placement, see Barta 1978, 33 and pl. IV).
Facing right. Like scenes of register 7, but man carries bird on head, not in
raised hand. Remains of five-plus scenes.
   (1) […] (b) […] (c) Nb.t-Ḥw.t (d) stḥ (e) Nb.t-Ḥw.t (f) ḥm.t
   (2) […] (b) […] (c) ꜣs.t (d) ḥtm (e) ꜣs.t (f) šp.t
   (3) […] (b) […] (c) […] (d) […] (e) Ḏḥwty (f) s(w)
   (4) […] (b) […] (c) […] (d) […] (e) ꜣs.t (f) ꜥḥꜣ
   (5) […] (b) […] (c) […] (d) […] (e) Ḏḥwty (f) s(w)

   (1) […] (b) […] (c) Nephthys: (d) stḥ-goose. (e) Nephthys: (f) ḥm.t-fish.
   (2) […] (b) […] (c) Isis: (d) ḥtm-bird. (e) Isis: (f) puffer-fish.
   (3) […] (b) […] (c) […] (d) […] (e) Thoth: (f) sw-fish.
   (4) […] (b) […] (c) […] (d) […] (e) Isis: (f) perch.
   (5) […] (b) […] (c) […] (d) […] (e) Thoth: (f) sw-fish.

On Inner Wall E (pl. XXVII/iv; for placement, see Barta 1978, 33, 41, pl. IV).
In two subregisters. In lower subregister, a file of priests advances to the
right, including lector-priest (ẖr(y)-ḥb.(t)), two palace administrators (ẖrp-
ꜥḥ), a "friend" (smr), and the bearer of insignia (ẖr(y)-nws) with knives (?).

In upper subregister, four men pull rope of bird trap (?):
   ꜥḏ ꜥḏ ꜥḏ
   "Secure!" "Secure!" "Secure!"

Label for Scene (retrograde)
   […] s r ẖnn.t
   […] it regarding birds.

Wall F. Continuation of Table of Fish and Fowl Offerings (pl. XXII/2–3
[XXII/2 = Naville 1891, pl. XIX]; Naville 1892, 33–34; Uphill 1965, 376–77;
for placement, see Barta 1978, 33, 41, and pl. III). Facing right. At right edge
in three subregisters (pl. XXII/3), three figures face file of offering bearers.

Above: Lector priest (ḫr(y)-ḥb.(t)) recites list
    srnp.t r3
    "Renewing fowl"

Middle: Figure offers bird
    dỉ šsp […]
    "Causing to receive […]"

Bottom: Figure with baton or list
    dỉ ꜥd̲ Ḥr š[…]
    "Causing Horus to be secure …[…]."

Remains of Eight-Plus Offering Scenes
    (1) Ḥr (b) bỉ.ty (c) Ḥr (d) rd (e) Ḥr (f) s[w]
    (2) Stš (b) sn(w) (c) Stš (d) r3 (e) S[tš] (f) […]
    (3) Stš (b) sn(w) (c) Stš (d-f) […]
    —loss of about five scenes—
    (4+) Stš (b) … (c) Stš (d) nm (e) Stš (f) ꜥḥ3
    (5+) Wsỉr (b) ỉty P(?) (c) Stš (d) n(ỉ)w (e) Wsỉr (f) ꜥḥ3
    (6+) Ḫnty-ỉr.ty (b) wn (c) Ḫnty-ỉr.ty (d) ḥn.t (e) Ḫnty-ỉr.ty (f) ḥm.t
    (7+) 3s.t (b) sḫm(?) Mw.t (c) 3s.t (d) ḥtm (e) 3s.t (f) šp.t
    (8+) Stš (b) md̲(.t) (c) Stš (d) r3 (e) Stš (f) ꜥḥ3

    (1) Horus: (b) honey. (c) Horus: (d) rd-goose. (e) Horus: (f) sw-fish.
    (2) Seth: (b) offering bread. (c) Seth: (d) ro-goose. (e) Seth: (f) […].
    (3) Seth: (b) offering bread. (c) Seth: (d-f) […].
    —loss of about five scenes—
    (4+) Seth: (b) … (c) Seth: (d) nm-heron. (e) Seth: (f) perch.
    (5+) Osiris: (b) sovereign of Pe (?). (c) Seth: (d) ostrich. (e) Osiris: (f)
perch.
    (6+) Khenty-irty: (b) opener. (c) Khenty-irty: (d) pelican. (e) Khenty-
irty: (f) ḥm.t-fish.
    (7+) Isis: (b) authority (?) of Mut. (c) Isis: (d) ḥtm-bird. (e) Isis: (f)
puffer-fish.
    (8+) Seth: (b) salve. (c) Seth: (d) ro-goose. (e) Seth: (f) perch.

I. Register 9

Wall F (pl. XXI/1–3 [pl. XXI/2 = Naville 1891, pl. XIX]; Naville 1892, 34–35;
for placement, see Barta 1978, 33, 42, and pl. III). In three subregisters.
Facing right. Two scenes of stepped shrine with enthroned king in robe
and red crown and carrying flail, facing smaller image of Bastet (B3st.t).

Scene at Right, Label for King
  Wsr-mꜣꜥ.t-Rꜥ-stp-n-ʾImn (2) [Wsỉrkn] mrỉ-ʾImn sꜣ Bꜣst.t (3) dỉ ꜥnḫ
  Usimaꜥresetepenamon, (2) [Osorkon], beloved of Amon, Son of Bastet,
(3) given life.

In middle subregister, two fan-bearers mount stairs of shrine beneath label:
  pr dỉ šw.ty ḥr s.t
  House of putting the fans on the throne.

Two figures follow, each labeled "name/someone" (rn), with speech above
(retrograde):
  ḏd-mdw tp ḥr tp ḫr n ḥm
  Recitation: "Head down, head down, to the Majesty!"

At bottom, a file of four-plus priests advances to the right, including *setem*-
priest (s(t)m) and bearer of insignia (ḫr(y)-nws).

Scene at Left, Label for King
  Wsr-mꜣꜥ.t-Rꜥ-stp-n-ʾImn (2) [Wsỉrkn] mrỉ-ʾImn sꜣ Bꜣst.t (3) dỉ ꜥnḫ
  Usimaꜥresetepenamon, (2) [Osorkon], beloved of Amon, Son of Bastet,
(3) given life.

In upper subregister, a file of four porters with standards previously labeled
"followers of Horus."

In middle subregister, two adoring figures face away from king, each labeled
"name/someone" (rn). At foot of stairs, *setem*-priest (s(t)m) recites:
  mỉ ḫr nṯr […]
  "Come, bearing the god […]!"

Label for Scene
  swꜣ r tp r(w)dw
  Passing to the top of the stairs.

At bottom, a file of four-plus priests advances to the right, including *setem*-
priest ([s](t)m) and two lectors (ḫr(y)-ḥb.(t)).

NOTES TO §IV. WALLS E/F
  1. For the idiom, cf. pl. II/11 (§I.E).
  2. See Naville 1892, 31; Erman and Grapow 1926–63, 3:367/15. Written retrograde. Uphill (1965, 377) wrongly read qnỉ "sash."
  3. Very uncertain, but cf. §III, Walls B/C, register 1, inner wall (pl. IX, 1).
Naville's copy ends with a questionable pelt determinative.

4. Versus Naville 1892, 32, who translated "herald" < ꜥš "to cry."

5. Versus Naville 1892, 34 (followed by Uphill 1965, 377), who translated "House of the North." See Barta 1978, 39.

6. Uphill (1965, 377) translated "Receiving the god in the house of the staircase."

7. See Erman and Grapow 1926–63, 4:40/8–9.

8. See the priestly title in Erman and Grapow 1926–63, 4:454/15–16.

§V. UNPLACED FRAGMENTS IGNORED BY BARTA AND OTHERS

A. Pl. XXVII/i. King with cup kneels before addorsed figures of seated deities (Amon?) with ankh and *was*-scepter.

B. Pl. XXVII/ii. Larger and smaller male figures advance to right.

C. Pl. XXVII/iii (cf. Wall A, registers 11–12)

Lector Priest Faces Right
[…]f[.]t […] (2) [ḫr(y)-ḥb.(t)] ḫr(y)-t[p] ḏd-mdw […]
[…]…[…] (2) Chief [lector priest]. Recitation: […]

Above Priest
[…] ỉy m ḥtp […]
[…] "Welcome" […]

Label for Scene behind Priest
[wḏ3(?)] ỉn ny-sw.t r ḥtp ḥr [tnt3.t ḥb-sd(?)]
[Proceeding (?)] by the king to rest on the [jubilee baldachino (?)]

D. Pl. XXVII/v (cf. Wall A, registers 5–6). Three-plus porters of Wepwawet shrine advance to right.

Above Porters
[šsp tp w3.t ḥr ntr] r wsḫ.t
[Setting out on the road bearing the god] to the broad court.

§VI. ADDITIONS TO THE GRANITE GATEWAY OF OSORKON I
Scenes added below central winged disk. See Naville 1891, pl. XL.L, M.

A. Below Right Wing of Disk: King (Lost) before Deity

Label for King
ntr nfr nb t3.wy (2) Wsr-m3ꜥ.t-Rꜥ-stp-n-ʾImn (3) Wsỉrkn mrỉ-ʾImn s3 B3st.t (3) [dỉ ꜥnḫ] nb [mỉ] Rꜥ

The Good God, Lord of the Two Lands, Usimaʿresetepenamon, (2) Osorkon, beloved of Amon, Son of Bastet, (3) [given] all [life like] Re.

Label for Deity
　　dỉ.n≠(ỉ) n≠k qn nḫt [...] (2) dỉ.n≠(ỉ) n≠k ny.t-sw.t [ʿȝ.t] n (< m) [qn(ỉ) nḫt]
　　"I have given to you valor and victory [...] (2) "I have given to you a [great] kingship in [valor and victory."][1]

B. Below Left Wing of Disk: King (Lost) before Deity

Label for King
　　nṯr nfr nb tȝ.wy (2) Wsr-mȝʿ.t-Rʿ-[stp-n-]ʾImn (3) Wsỉr[kn] mrỉ-ʾImn sȝ Bȝst.t (4) dỉ ʿnḫ nb [mỉ] Rʿ
　　The Good God, Lord of the Two Lands, (2) Usimaʿre[setepen]amon, (3) Osor[kon], beloved of Amon, Son of Bastet, (4) given all life [like] Re.

Label for Deity
　　dỉ.n≠(ỉ) n≠k pḥty [...] (2) dỉ.n≠(ỉ) n≠k [...]
　　"I have given to you strength [...] (2) "I have given to you [...]."

NOTE TO §VI. GRANITE GATEWAY OF OSORKON I
　　1. For the restoration, cf. Naville 1891, pl. XL.A.

§VII. HYPOSTYLE HALL COLUMNS.
　　Perhaps of Middle Kingdom date, reworked and reinscribed in Rames-side and Libyan periods. See Naville 1891, 10–12, 48–49, and pls. V–VII, IX, XXIII–XXIV; Roeder 1924, 2:228 (10834); Boreux 1932, 1:59–61; Porter and Moss 1927–51, 4:29; Habachi 1957, 61–70, pls. XVII–XX. Suggested to be the original work of Osorkon I in Van Siclen 1994, 324 n. 23, the columns are variously ascribed to a local temple of Middle Kingdom date in Arnold 1996 and to post-Dynasty XIX in Haynes 1996. Five large Hathor capitals (above 7 ft high) in Boston (MFA 89.555; Oriental Institute photos 37294–95), Louvre, British Museum (1107), Berlin (10834), and Nicholas Museum of the University of Sydney (see Habachi 1957, 65–66). Various papyrus-bud capitals and four palm leaf capitals (including British Museum 1065). Each engraved on sides with double cartouches:
　　Wsr-mȝʿ.t-Rʿ-stp-n-ʾImn (2) Wsỉrkn mrỉ-ʾImn
　　Usimaʿresetepenamon, (2) Osorkon, beloved of Amon.

§VIII. TEMPLE NAOS (CAIRO 70006 = JdE 35130).
　　Speckled red granite, 66 cm high. Found 60 m east of temple. Made in two pieces; only upper portion with cavetto cornice and torus molding sur-

vives. On both sides Osorkon II in kilt stands bent over in the act of opening (?) the shrine. Just below torus molding is flanking parallel dedication text, beginning at center and continuing to rear. For texts, see Roeder 1914, 24–25 and pl. 65a; Daressy 1901b, 132, §CLXXXIII; and Habachi 1957, 60.

Cartouche before the King
    Wsr-mЗᶜ.t-Rᶜ-stp-n-ʾImn
    Usimaᶜresetepenamon

Dedication Text, Left Exemplar
    [ᶜnḫ Ḥr kЗ nḫt] mrî-MЗᶜ.t sḫᶜ [sw] Rᶜ r ny-sw.t tЗ.wy Nb.ty smЗ (2) pš.ty mî sЗ Зs.t sḫtp nṯr.w m îr mЗᶜ.t ny-sw.t bî.ty Wsr-mЗᶜ.t-Rᶜ-stp-n-ʾImn sЗ Rᶜ Wsîrkn mrî-ʾImn sЗ BЗst.t îr.n≠f m mnw≠f n mw.t≠f BЗst.t nb(.t) (3) [p.t ḥnw.t tЗ.wy îr.t n≠s s.t m ...]
    [Long live the Horus: "Strong Bull,] beloved of Maat, [whom] Re caused to appear in glory to be King of the Two Lands," The-Two-Ladies: "He who unites (2) the two divisions like the son of Isis, who pacifies the gods by performing justice," the King of Upper and Lower Egypt, Usimaᶜresete-penamon, Son of Re, Osorkon, beloved of Amon, Son of Bastet. As his monument he made for his mother Bastet, Lady (3) [of heaven, Mistress of the Two Lands, the making for her of a shrine in ...]

Dedication Text, Right Exemplar
    [ᶜnḫ Ḥr kЗ nḫt mrî-MЗᶜ.t ...] (2) [...] ny-sw.t bî.ty Wsr-mЗᶜ.t-Rᶜ-stp-n-ʾImn sЗ Rᶜ mry[≠f] Wsîrkn [mrî-ʾImn] sЗ [BЗst.t] îr.n≠f m mnw≠f n mw.t≠f BЗst.t nb(.t) p.t ḥnw.t tЗ.wy (3) îr.t n≠s s.t m [...]
    [Long live the Horus: "Strong Bull,] beloved of Maat, ...] (2) [...,"] the King of Upper and Lower Egypt, Usimaᶜresetepenamon, Son of Re, whom [he] loves, Osorkon, [beloved of Amon], Son of [Bastet]. As his monument he made for his mother Bastet, Lady of heaven, Mistress of the Two Lands, (3) the making for her of a shrine in [...]

79. MAHES TEMPLE ("PORTICO OF OSORKON")

Inscriptions from a small temple at Bubastis erected by Osorkon II some 60 m north of the Great Temple of Bastet. This is the first complete translation; see Habachi 1957, Plan. For the site and texts, see Habachi 1957, 45–55 and pls. XI.B, XII, XIII.A; Naville 1891, 49–50 and pl. XLI.E–H; and Kitchen 1986, 319 §277.

A. CORNER BLOCK, LONGER SIDE
(Naville 1891, 50 and pl. XLI.E; Habachi 1957, 52–53). King offers *wedjat*-eye to Bastet.

Label for Disk with Pendant Uraei and Ankhs above Scene
Bḥd.t(y) (2) dỉ ꜥnḫ
The Behdetite, (2) who gives life.

Label for Bastet
dỉ.n≠(ỉ) n≠k t꜍ nb m w꜍ḥ tp (2) dỉ.n≠(ỉ) n≠k pḥ.ty nb mỉ Rꜥ (3) ḏd-mdw ỉn B꜍st.t ḥry(.t)-sšt꜍ (4) n Tm nb(.t) p.t ḥnw.t t꜍.wy
"I have given to you all lands in subjugation ('bowing the head'). (2) I have given to you all strength like Re." (3) Recitation by Bastet, who is over the secrets (4) of Atum, Lady of heaven, Mistress of the Two Lands.

Label for King
ny-sw.t bỉ.ty nb t꜍.wy nb ḫꜥ.w (2) Wsr-m꜍ꜥ.t-Rꜥ-stp-n-ʾImn (3) Wsỉrkn mrỉ-ʾImn s꜍ B꜍st.t (4) dỉ ꜥnḫ w꜍s nb mỉ Rꜥ ḏ.t (5) s꜍ ḥ꜍[≠f ...]
The King of Upper and Lower Egypt, Lord of the Two Lands, Lord of Diadems, (2) Usimaꜥresetepenamon, (3) Osorkon, beloved of Amon, Son of Bastet, (4) given all life and dominion like Re forever. (5) Protection is behind [him ...].

Label for Scene
rdỉ.t wd[꜍.t n mw.t≠f B꜍st.t nb(.t) B꜍s.t ỉr≠s dỉ ꜥnḫ][1]
Giving the *wedjat*-eye [to his mother Bastet, Lady of Bubastis, that she might make the state of being given life.][1]

B. Corner Block, Shorter Side
(Naville 1891, 50 and pl. XLI.H; Habachi 1957, 52–53, and pl. XIII. A). Hor-hekenu offers sign of life to nose of king.

Label for God
ḏd-mdw ỉn Ḥr-ḥknw
Recitation by Hor-hekenu.

Label for King
ny-sw.t bỉ.ty nb ỉr.(t) ḫ.t (2) Wsr²-m꜍ꜥ.t-Rꜥ-stp-n-ʾImn (3) Wsỉrkn mrỉ-ʾImn s꜍ B꜍st.t (4) dỉ ꜥnḫ w꜍s mỉ Rꜥ ḏ.t (5) s꜍ [ḥ꜍≠f ...]
The King of Upper and Lower Egypt, Lord of ritual performance, (2) Usimaꜥresetepenamon,[2] (3) Osorkon, beloved of Amon, Son of Bastet, (4) given life and dominion like Re forever. (5) Protection is [behind him ...].

C. Column Drums.
(Habachi 1957, 48–54 and figs. 14.A–D) Framed rectangular inscriptions beneath heaven sign. Four vertical lines of text; Horus name, beloved of Mahes, faces nomen and prenomen of Osorkon II.

Column 1 (fig. 14.A): Inscription on Upper Portion of Drum

Ḥr kꜣ [nḫt] mrỉ-Mꜣꜥ.t (2) mry Mꜣỉ-ḥs [nb Bꜣs].t dỉ ꜥnḫ (3) ny-sw.t bỉ.ty nb tꜣ.wy Wsr-mꜣꜥ.t-Rꜥ-stp-n-ꜣImn (4) sꜣ Rꜥ nb ḫꜥ.w Wsỉrkn [mrỉ] ꜣImn [sꜣ B]ꜣst.t

The Horus: "[Strong] Bull, beloved of Maat," (2) beloved of Mahes, [Lord of Bubas]tis, given life; (3) the King of Upper and Lower Egypt, Lord of the Two Lands, Usimaꜥresetepenamon, (4) Son of Re, Lord of Diadems, Osorkon, [beloved of] Amon, [Son of Ba]stet.

Column 4 (fig. 14.B)

Ḥr kꜣ nḫt mrỉ-Mꜣꜥ.t (2) mry Mꜣỉ-ḥs ꜥꜣ nb Bꜣs.t dỉ ꜥnḫ (3) ny-sw.t bỉ.ty nb tꜣ.wy Wsr-[mꜣꜥ.t]-Rꜥ-stp-n-ꜣI[mn] (4) [sꜣ Rꜥ nb ḫꜥ.w Wsỉrkn mrỉ-ꜣImn sꜣ Bꜣst.t]

The Horus: "Strong Bull, beloved of Maat," (2) beloved of Mahes, the great, Lord of Bubastis, given life; (3) the King of Upper and Lower Egypt, Lord of the Two Lands, Usi[maꜥ]resetepena[mon], (4) [Son of Re, Lord of Diadems, Osorkon, beloved of Amon, Son of Bastet.]

Column 8 (fig. 14.C = Naville 1891, 49 and pl. XLI.G[3]): Inscription on Middle Portion of Drum

Ḥr kꜣ nḫt mrỉ-Mꜣꜥ.t (2) mry Mꜣỉ-ḥs sꜣ Bꜣst.t dỉ ꜥnḫ (3) ny-sw.t bỉ.ty [Wsr-mꜣꜥ.t]-Rꜥ-[stp-n-]ꜣI[mn] (4) [sꜣ Rꜥ nb ḫꜥ.w Wsỉrkn mrỉ-ꜣImn sꜣ Bꜣst.t]

The Horus: "Strong Bull, beloved of Maat," (2) beloved of Mahes, son of Bastet, given life; (3) the King of Upper and Lower Egypt, [Usimaꜥ]re[se-tepen]a[mon], (4) [Son of Re, Lord of Diadems, Osorkon, beloved of Amon, Son of Bastet.]

Column 10 (fig. 14.D): Inscription on Upper Portion of Drum

[Ḥr kꜣ nḫt mrỉ-Mꜣꜥ.t (2) mry Mꜣỉ-ḥs … dỉ ꜥnḫ] (3) ny-sw.t bỉ.ty nb tꜣ.wy [Wsr-mꜥꜣ.t]-Rꜥ-[stp-n-]ꜣI[mn] (4) sꜣ Rꜥ nb ḫꜥ.w [Wsỉrkn mrỉ-ꜣImn sꜣ Bꜣst.t]

[The Horus: "Strong Bull, beloved of Maat," (2) beloved of Mahes, …, given life;] (3) the King of Upper and Lower Egypt, Lord of the Two Lands, [Usimaꜥ]re[setepenamon], (4) Son of Re, Lord of Diadems, [Osorkon, beloved of Amon, Son of Bastet.]

D. ISOLATED BLOCK
(Naville 1891, 49 and pl. XLI.F)
    [...] kꜣ(.w) nw ḥr≠ỉ [...] (2) [...] gm(?).n kꜣ[...]
    [...] bulls of my sight [...] (2) [...] the *ka*-spirit (?) found (?) [...]

E. DORSAL PILLAR OF USURPED RED LIMESTONE COLOSSAL STATUE
(Habachi 1957, 56–57 and pl. XV.A; Naville 1891, 58 and pl. XLIX.D; Porter and Moss 1927–51, 4:28)

[... Nb.ty sm3 pš.ty mỉ s3 3s.t] sḥtp nṯr.w m ỉr m3ꜥ.t [ny-sw.t] bỉ.ty [Wsr-
m3ꜥ.t-Rꜥ-stp-n-ꜣImn s3 Rꜥ Wsỉrkn mrỉ-ꜣImn s3 B3st.t ...]

[... The-Two-Ladies: "He who unites the two divisions like the son
of Isis,] who pacifies the gods by performing justice"; the King of [Upper]
and Lower Egypt, [Usimaꜥresetepenamon, Son of Re, Osorkon, beloved of
Amon, Son of Bastet, ...]

NOTES
    1. For restoration, cf. Osorkon I example, Naville 1891, pl. XXXIX.K and M.
    2. Initial element carved as reed-leaf, from original Ramesside cartouche.
    3. Contra Habachi 1957, 47, who suggested an identification with column 4
despite differences in text and orientation.

80. DONATION STELA OF DJEDPTAHIUEFANKH
(CAIRO JDE 45327)

Few land donation stelae are as explicit in detail as this record of an
oracular transaction enacted by Prince Namlot "C," high priest of Heracleopolis and future Theban pontiff, on behalf of a local priest of Ptah in
the reign of Osorkon II. While most donation stelae record only the details
of the gift itself, this stela reveals the mode of transmission and proves
donation texts to be but a subset of oracular records. Found at Tell Minia
el-Shorafa, about 15 km south of Helwan in the vicinity of Heracleopolis,
the round-topped stela measures 0.86 m in height and 0.53 m in width.
As is often the case with such monuments, the surface was only summarily smoothed below the inscription, indicating its use as a field marker. In
the lunette, an enshrined figure of Ptah is followed by a standing Sakhmet
and the water-lily emblem of Nefertem. In adoration before the Memphite
triad stand Osorkon II, his son Namlot, and the priestly donor. Osorkon's
depiction is a simple matter of protocol, as the oracular ceremony was
performed by the high priest Namlot, not the absent king. In return for
the gift of 42 1/2 *arouras* to the temple estate, the donor retains economic
benefits (to defray the continued cost of his funerary cult undertaken by
the temple), while the intermediary is rewarded with divine blessings of
life and health. The boundary specifications of the gift include mention of
"fields of the Sherden," perhaps old feudal holdings allotted to mercenaries
drawn from this group of former "Sea Peoples."
    Formerly Cairo 27/1/21/2. For the text, translation, and discussion, see
Iversen 1941, 3–18; Daressy 1915, 140–43; Menu 1998, 141–43; and Meeks
1979a, 609, 616, 627, 628, 633–35, 638, 645–46, and 667 (no. 22.5.16). See
Kitchen 1986, 106 §86, 196 §157, and 322 §281.

LABEL FOR PTAH

    [Ptḥ pꜣ nṯr ꜥꜣ] nb ꜥnḫ-tꜣ.wy

    [Ptah, the great god,] Lord of Ankh-Tawy.

LABEL FOR SAKHMET

    Sḫm.t ꜥꜣ.t mrỉ-Ptḥ nb.(t) p.t ḥnw.t nṯr.w nb.w

    Sakhmet the great, beloved of Ptah, Lady of heaven, Mistress of all the gods.

LABEL FOR THE EMBLEM OF NEFERTEM

    [Nfr-tm ...] s[... nṯr].w(?) nb

    [Nefertem, ...] who [...] all the [god]s (?).

LABEL FOR THE KING

    [... Wsr-mꜣꜥ.t-Rꜥ]-stp-n-ʾImn (2) [...] Wsỉrkn [mrỉ-ʾImn sꜣ Bꜣst.t] (3) dỉ⸗ỉ n⸗k Mꜣꜥ.t rꜥ nb rḫ.kwỉ ḥtp⸗k ḥr⸗s

    [...] Usimaꜥreseteptenamon, (2) [...] Osorkon, beloved of Amon, Son of Bastet. (3) "I have given to you Maat every day, since I know that you are satisfied because of it."

LABEL FOR THE INTERMEDIARY NAMLOT "C"

    [ḥm-nṯr tp(y) n] Ḥr(y)-šfy.t (2) [...] ny-sw.t tꜣ.wy ỉmy-r mšꜥ (3) [ḫꜣw. ty N]mꜣrṯ

    [First Prophet of] Harsaphes, (2) [...] King of the Two Lands, the general and (3) [leader, N]amlot.

LABEL FOR THE DONOR

    ḥm-nṯr ỉt-nṯr sš ḥsb ỉḥ n pr Ptḥ Ḏd-Ptḥ-ỉw⸗f-ꜥnḫ mꜣꜥ-ḫrw

    Prophet and God's Father, cattle counting scribe of the estate of Ptah, Djedptahiuefankh, the justified.

MAIN TEXT

    (1) ḥsb.t 16.(t) ḫr ḥm n ny-sw.t bỉ.ty nb tꜣ.wy Wsr-mꜣꜥ.t-Rꜥ-stp-n-ʾImn sꜣ Rꜥ nb ḫꜥ.w Wsỉrkn mrỉ-ʾImn sꜣ Bꜣst.t mrỉ-Ptḥ dỉ ꜥnḫ mỉ Rꜥ ḏt m ḥb Ptḥ p(ꜣy)⸗f nb nfr m ḥb⸗f nfr (n) msy.t

    (2) hrw pn n ḥnq ꜣḥ.t stꜣ.t [42 1/2] m swꜣ.w n dmỉ [(Pr)-Sḫm-ḫpr-(Rꜥ) ...] dmḏ 7 n [...] (3) [...] dmḏ 15 dmḏ drw⸗f 42 rmny ỉw rsy⸗f pꜣ (ỉ)hꜣy n Ḏd-ʾI[mn]-ỉw⸗f-ꜥnḫ sꜣ ʾI-ỉr-sw-[ỉt⸗f] m[ḫ.t⸗f ꜣḥ].wt Tꜣy-[...] (4) ỉꜣb.t⸗f ꜣḥ.wt Šꜣrdnꜣ.w m-ḏr.t ḥm-nṯr Ḥr mꜣꜥ-ḫrw ỉmnt.t⸗f ꜣḥ.t pr Ptḥ nty nb⸗f ỉt-nṯr {n ỉt-nṯr}¹ ḥry sštꜣ n pr Ptḥ sš ḥw.t-nṯr sš ḥsb ỉḥ n pr Ptḥ (5) Ḏd-Ptḥ-ỉw⸗f-ꜥnḫ sꜣ ḥm-nṯr Ns-Mn ỉ-ỉr ḥm-nṯr tp(y) n Ḥr(y)-šfy.t ny-sw.t tꜣ.wy wr ꜥꜣ n (Pr)-Sḫm-ḫpr-(Rꜥ) ỉmy-r mšꜥ ḫꜣw.ty Nmꜣrtỉ sꜣ n nb tꜣ.wy Wsỉrkn mrỉ-ʾImn sꜣ Bꜣst.t mw.t⸗f (6) Ḏd-Mw.t-ỉw⸗s-ꜥnḫ mꜣꜥ.t-ḫrw ỉw⸗f wḥm⸗f m-bꜣḥ Ptḥ pꜣy

nṯr ꜥꜣ m ḏd pꜣy≠ỉ nb nfr ỉw≠k šsp pꜣy ḥmkw (< ḥnq) n ꜣḥ.t ỉ-dỉ n≠k (7) ỉt-nṯr {n ỉt-nṯr}[1] ḥry sštꜣ n (pr) Ptḥ sš ḥw.t-nṯr sš ḥsb ỉḥ n pr Ptḥ ḥm-nṯr Ḏd-Ptḥ-ỉw≠f-ꜥnḫ m šsp nfr n-ḏr.t≠ỉ ỉw≠k dỉ n≠ỉ pꜣ(y)≠f ḏbꜣ n ꜥnḫ wḏꜣ snb ꜥḥꜥ q(y) ỉꜣw.t ꜥꜣ.(t) [nfr.t] (8) mtw≠f ḫꜣm.tw≠f r šꜣꜥ nḥḥ ḏ.t ꜥḥꜥ.n pꜣy nṯr ꜥꜣ hnn wr sp-2 wḥm ḏd≠f pꜣy≠ỉ nb nfr ỉw≠k ḫdb rmṯ.w nb wnḏw nb (9) n pꜣ tꜣ ḏr≠f[3] nty-ỉw≠w th(ỉ)≠f m-dỉ≠f r šꜣꜥ nḥḥ ḏ.t ỉw≠k šꜥd rn.w n pꜣ tꜣ ḏr≠f ỉw Sḫm.t m-sꜣ ḥm.t≠w Nfr-tm m-sꜣ ẖrd≠w ꜥḥꜥ.n pꜣy nṯr ꜥꜣ hnn wr sp-2

Regnal year 16 under the Majesty of the King of Upper and Lower Egypt, the Lord of the Two Lands, Usimaꜥresetepenamon, Son of Re, Lord of Diadems, Osorkon (II), beloved of Amon, Son of Bastet, beloved of Ptah, given life like Re forever, in the festival of Ptah, his good lord, in his beautiful festival of the evening meal.

(2) On this day of offering [42 1/2] *arouras* of field in the region of the town [(Per)sekhemkheper(re) ...] totaling 7 of [...] (3) totaling 15, with a final total of 42 and 1/2 *arouras,*

whose south is: the stable of Djedamoniuefankh, son of Irsuitef,

[whose] north is: the fields of Tay[...],

(4) whose east is: the fields of the Sherden, under the control of the prophet Hor, the justified,

whose west is: the field of the estate of Ptah, whose possessor is the God's Father,[1] Overseer of Secrets of the estate of Ptah, temple scribe, cattle counting scribe of the estate of Ptah, (5) Djedptahiue-fankh, the justified, son of the prophet Nesmin, the justified,

which was made by[2] the prophet of Harsaphes, King of the Two Lands, the Great Chief of (Per)sekhemkheper(re), the general and leader, Namlot ("C"), son of the Lord of the Two Lands, Osorkon, beloved of Amon, Son of Bastet, whose mother is (6) Djedmutiuesankh, the justified, while he repeats it before Ptah, this great god, saying:

"My good lord, will you accept this donation of field that (7) the God's Father,[1] Overseer of Secrets of the (estate) of Ptah, temple scribe, cattle counting scribe of the estate of Ptah, and prophet Djedptahiuefankh has given to you with a good acceptance from my hand? Will you give to me its recompense of life, prosperity, health, long lifetime, and [goodly] advanced old age, (8) and he (the donor) may retain control of it forever and ever?"

Then this great god assented fervently. Again he said:

"My good lord, will you kill any person of any sort (9) in the entire land[3] who will transgress it with respect to him forever and ever? Will you eradicate their names from the entire land, while Sakhmet pursues their wives and Nefertem pursues their children?"

Then this great god assented fervently.

NOTES

1. Redundantly written ỉt-nṯr n ỉt-nṯr in lines 4 and 7; the title is written correctly in the lunette label for Djedptahiuefankh.

2. The term introduces the intermediary who "makes" the transaction before the oracle.

3. For the phraseology, see the parallel in the Oracular Decree Preserving the Property of Maatkare (B), no. 40, lines 5+x and 7+x.

81. THE DIRGE OF GENERAL PASHERENESE

At the west entrance to the tomb of Osorkon II at Tanis appears an unusual scene of private grief within a royal context. On the left thickness, the general Pasherenese is depicted barefoot and with hands placed atop his head in an attitude of mourning. Before him, six incised lines record his dirge in a terse script that has elicited varying translations. The burial site of Tanis is designated as "Thebes, the divine district," and the tomb itself is a "mansion of millions of years." A final note records that it was Kapes, mother of Osorkon II, who sponsored the general's addition to the tomb.

For the text and translations, see Montet 1947, 71–73 and pls. XXII–XXIII; Loret 1942, 97–106; and P. Vernus in Association française d'action artistique 1987, 109. See Kitchen 1986, 94 §74 and 311 §270.

ỉmy-rꜣ mšꜥ wr (n) nꜣ ỉs.wt n Šmꜥ Mḥw Pꜣ-šr-n-ꜣs.t sꜣ Ḥr nḥwꜣ(ỉ) (2) nꜣk nn snỉ-ḫwtꜣ[1] n(n) wrd m ḥḥy ḥrꜣk ỉbꜣ(ỉ) ꜣtp m (3) hm(h)m (n)-ḏr sḫꜣꜣ(ỉ) nfr.wꜣk dỉꜣỉ swr.tw m ḥm (n) nbꜣ(ỉ) r fqꜣ.w m ḥ.tꜣ (4) swdꜣꜣ(ỉ) nbꜣ(ỉ) r nỉw.tꜣf Wꜣs.t spꜣ.t nṯr.(t)ꜣ[3] mrr ỉbꜣf ꜥr bꜣꜣf (5) r s.t wnnꜣf[4] ḥw.t nt ḥḥ n rnp.wt pꜣ ny-sw.t nṯr(y) ḥtp ḥr s.tꜣf bꜣꜣf (6) ẖnm ḥr(y).t nb tꜣ.wy Wsỉrkn mrỉ-ʾImn ỉr nꜣf Kꜣpws

Great general of the troops of Upper and Lower Egypt, Pasherenese son of Hori: "I have grieved for you without ceasing,[1] without wearying in yearning for the sight of you, my heart burdened with cries when I have recalled your goodness. I have caused that one be exalted more by being a slave of my lord than by the rewards of property.[2] I have conveyed my lord to his city, Thebes-the-divine-district,[3] which his heart loved, so that his *ba*-spirit might mount up to the place of his existence,[4] the mansion of millions of years. The divine king is on his throne, and his *ba*-spirit is joined with the firmament: the Lord of the Two Lands, Osorkon, beloved of Amon. Kapes has acted for him.

NOTES

1. For the unusual expression, see Erman and Grapow 1926–63, 3:250/1. Perhaps literally, "without the passing of forbearance(?)," with metathesis ḥwt from wḥd, Erman and Grapow 1926–63, 1:355/15–16 (note identical determinatives).

2. Montet translates: "J'ai fait en sorte de t'agrandir par toute sorte de service

plus que par des offrandes en nature," which requires the cumbersome analysis: dỉ≄ỉ swr≄(ỉ) tw ("I have caused that I exalt you"). Vernus translates ḥm "body/ slave" as "personality": "Je veux faire qu'on trouve plus à s'enrichir dans la person-naité de mon maître que dans des advantages matériels."

3. A designation of Tanis, the Thebes of the North; see Loret 1942, 101–2.

4. Or read s.t wn(n) n≄f "the place that belongs to him."

F. TAKELOT II

82. THE CHRONICLE OF PRINCE OSORKON ("B")

By virtue of its length and unconventional phraseology, the chronicle of the high priest and heir-apparent Osorkon (B), eldest son of Takelot II, is one of the most significant sources for the history of Libyan period Egypt. The extensive texts illustrate the beginnings of internal dissension and political fragmentation, document contemporary religious reliance on oracles and curses, and provide detailed economic data on goods and ser-vices. Occupying most of the interior surface of the Bubastite Portal, the annals are divided into three distinct sections.

The earliest record, from year 11 of Takelot, covers the southeast wall of the gateway and comprises thirty-six lines of primary text beside and beneath a large dual relief scene of Osorkon offering Maat to Amon, who embraces King Takelot. The main inscription details Osorkon's triumphant return, retaliations, and benefactions after the first of what would become many expulsions from Thebes. For most of his tenure, the sometime high priest would be confined to the royal court and el-Hibeh, the northernmost dependency of the estate of Theban Amon.

Osorkon's unprecedented remarks that he acted so that he might attain his father's throne (line 53) are more elaborately developed in the initial section of the next record, dating to the following year. Begun on the inte-rior west wall and continued onto the adjacent southwest wall, the second inscription of forty-one lines was provided with a large dual relief scene of Osorkon offering bread to Amon of Karnak, now without the intervention of Takelot II. An initial encomium of Osorkon justifies the pontiff's fre-quent absence from Thebes and includes a remarkable mock titulary, with epithets incorporating the key elements of Horus, the Two Ladies, Golden Horus, King of Upper and Lower Egypt, and Son of Re.

Subsequent sections from years 15 to 24 of Takelot II and 22 to 28 of Sheshonq III detail the failure of Osorkon's ambitions. A Theban revolt by an unnamed usurper at the very end of year 15 entailed nine years of exile, culminating in a grand military expedition in year 24 and oracular consultations during which Osorkon reminded court representatives of his expectations and frustrations (lines 7–8) and denounced the complicity of Thebes and Amon himself (line 17). As evidenced by the donation stela for his sister Karoama (no. 84), the peace lasted into the next and final year of Takelot's reign. With the death of his father, Osorkon's troubles multiplied. Passed over for the kingship in favor of his younger brother Sheshonq (III), who may have assumed the throne during one of the high priest's infrequent travels to the south, Osorkon was driven from Thebes as well by his collateral cousin and counter-pontiff, Harsiese (B), his probable opponent in all earlier conflicts. Osorkon would not return to authority at Thebes until twenty-two years later, although his control remained intermittent, with Harsiese attested in years 25–26, replaced again by Osorkon in year 28. A detailed list of Osorkon's benefactions during the disputed years comprises the bulk of the second, propagandistic, inscription, concluding with a curse on his (deceased?) opponent's memory.

The chronicle's ultimate section, an addendum of year 29, marks Osorkon's last appearance in Thebes for a decade during which a new counter-pontiff, Takelot (E), controlled the rebellious city. At approximately eighty years of age, Osorkon made a final military return to Thebes in year 39, as recorded in the Karnak Priestly Annals (no. 9.7, pp. 52–54) and the Theban Nile Level Records (no. 7.22, p. 38).

For the texts, see Epigraphic Survey 1954, x–xi, fig. 1 (for location), and pls. 1B and 16–22 (vignette line sequences reordered below for thematic consistency). For supplemental text copies, translation, and commentary, see Caminos 1958; Jansen-Winkeln 1985, 290–94; Porter and Moss 1972, 35–36 (§125 = Key Plans K 354–56, year 11; §127 = K 350–52, yrs. 12–15; §126 = K 353, yrs. 22–29); all replacing Breasted 1906–7, 4:377–86 §§756–70. See Kitchen 1986, 106–7 §86; 181–82 §148; 196 §157; 199–200 §162; 330–33 §§292–94; 338–39 §299; 578 §516; and 1995, xxiii–xxv §§W–X and xxxi §BB.

(1) INSCRIPTION OF YEAR 11 OF TAKELOT II (EPIGRAPHIC SURVEY 1954, PLS. 16–19)

Upper Register, Addorsed Scenes: Amon embraces Takelot II while Osorkon offers Maat (Epigraphic Survey 1954, pl. 17)

Righthand Label for the King (lines 2–3)
    nṯr nfr Tkrt mrỉ-ʾImn sꜣ ꜣs.t dỉ ꜥnḫ (3) mry ʾImn-Rꜥ pꜣw.ty tꜣ.wy
    The Good God, Takelot (II), beloved of Amon, Son of Isis, given life, (3) beloved of Amon-Re, the Primordial One of the Two Lands.

Central Label for the King (line 8)
    ny-sw.t bỉ.ty nb tꜣ.wy nb ỉr.(t) ḫ.t Ḥḏ-ḫpr-Rꜥ-stp-n-Rꜥ sꜣ Rꜥ nb ḫꜥ.w

T̲krỉwt mrỉ-ʾImn sꜣ ꜣs.t mry ʾImn-Rꜥ nb ns.wt tꜣ.wy nb p.t ḫnt(y) ʾIp.t-s.wt dỉ ꜥnḫ mỉ Rꜥ d̲.t

(8) The King of Upper and Lower Egypt, Lord of the Two Lands, Lord of ritual performance, Hedjkheperre-setepenre, Son of Re, Lord of Diadems, Takelot, beloved of Amon, Son of Isis, beloved of Amon-Re, Lord of the Thrones of the Two Lands, Lord of heaven, Foremost of Karnak, given life like Re forever.

Righthand Label for Prince Osorkon (lines 4–7 and 1)

ḥs-mr≠f[1] ḥm-nt̲r tp(y) n ʾImn-Rꜥ ny-sw.t nt̲r.w ỉmy-rꜣ mšꜥ (5) wr ḥꜣw.ty n tꜣ d̲r≠f sꜣ ny-sw.t (6) ỉry-pꜥ.t ḥꜣ.ty-ꜥ[2] Wsỉrkn sꜣ (7) ny-sw.t bỉ.ty nb tꜣ.wy T̲krỉwt mrỉ-ʾImn sꜣ ꜣs.t dỉ ꜥnḫ d̲.t (1) [rdỉ.t Mꜣ]ꜥ.t ḥs wỉ nt̲r.w [ḥr≠s]

The one praised and beloved[1] of him (Takelot), the First Prophet of Amon-Re, King of the Gods, great (5) general and leader of the entire land, the Prince, (6) hereditary noble and count,[2] Osorkon, son of (7) the King of Upper and Lower Egypt, Lord of the Two Lands, Takelot, beloved of Amon, Son of Isis, given life forever. (1) [Offering Maʾat so that the Gods might praise me [because of it].

Lefthand Label for the King (lines 10–11)

nt̲r nfr T̲krỉwt mrỉ-ʾImn sꜣ ꜣs.t dỉ ꜥnḫ (11) mry ʾImn-Rꜥ nb ns.wt tꜣ.wy
The Good God, Takelot, beloved of Amon, Son of Isis, given life, (11) beloved of Amon-Re, Lord of the Thrones of the Two Lands.

Lefthand Label for Prince Osorkon (lines 12–17 and 9)

ḥm-nt̲r tp(y) n ʾImn ỉmy-rꜣ mšꜥ wr ḥꜣw.ty (13) Wsỉrkn mꜣꜥ-ḫrw ms n ḥm.t ny-sw.t wr.(t) (14) Krmꜥmꜥ mrỉ-Mw.t ꜥnḫ.tỉ sꜣ.t n (15) ḥm-nt̲r tp(y) n ʾImn-Rꜥ ny-sw.t nt̲r.w ỉmy-rꜣ mšꜥ (16) n Ḥnn-ny-sw.t ḥꜣ.wty Nmꜣrt̲ (17) sꜣ ny-sw.t (n) nb tꜣ.wy Wsỉrkn mrỉ-ʾImn sꜣ Bꜣst.t dỉ ꜥnḫ (9) rdỉ.t Mꜣꜥ.t n nb Mꜣꜥ.t shtp≠f m ꜥrq(?) ꜥry.t(?)≠f[3]

The First Prophet of Amon, great general and leader, (13) Osorkon, the justified, born of the great royal wife (14) Karomama, beloved of Mut, who yet lives, the daughter of (15) the First Prophet of Amon-Re, King of the Gods, and general (16) of Heracleopolis, the leader Namlot, (17) royal son of the Lord of the Two Lands, Osorkon, beloved of Amon, Son of Bastet, given life. (9) Offering Maat to the Lord of Maat, so that he might be satisfied by the fulfilment of his stipulations(?).[3]

Main Text of Year 11 of Takelot II (Epigraphic Survey 1954, pls. 16–19, lines 18–53; Kitchen 1986, 330–31 §292)

(18) ḥsb.t 11.(t) tp(y) pr.t sw 1 ḫr ḥm n ny-sw.t bỉ.ty Ḥd̲-ḫpr-Rꜥ-stp-n-Rꜥ [sꜣ Rꜥ T̲krỉwt mrỉ-ʾImn sꜣ ꜣs.t] mry-[ʾImn-Rꜥ] nb ns.wt tꜣ.wy Mw.t wr.(t) nb.(t) [p.t(?)] Ḫnsw m Wꜣs.t Nfr-ḥtp dỉ ꜥnḫ mỉ Rꜥ d̲.t

s[k] ỉmy-r3 Šmꜥw ḥr(y)-tp t3.wy ỉr.nn ᾽Imn m ỉbⱶf ḏs[ⱶf ḥm-nṯr tp(y) n] ᾽Imn m W3s.t ỉmy-r3 mšꜥ wr n t3 ḏrⱶf ḥ3w.ty Wsỉrk[n] ms [n] ỉry.(t)-pꜥ.t wr.(t) ḥs.wt ḥm.t ny-sw.t wr.(t) nb.(t) t3.wy [Kr]mꜥmꜥ [mrỉ-Mw.t] ꜥnḫ.tỉ m ḫnwⱶf m qn(ỉ) nḫt ḥr(y)-tp t3š.wⱶf T3-dhn.t-n.t-᾽Imn (19) -ꜥ3-hmhm.t k3.tw rⱶs [sk] sw m [ỉry-]pꜥ.t [ḫ3.ty-ꜥ2 ... wr] wr.w s3 [s]msw n Wr.ty-Ḥk3.w smỉ nⱶf T[3-Šmꜥw] spr nⱶf T3-Mḥw ỉw snḏ.tⱶf pḥr.t4 ỉm[ⱶsn b3]kⱶsn r ꜥr(r)y.tⱶf n ꜥ3w n pḥ.ty ⱶf w[d(ỉ) n]ⱶf nb ns.wt t3.wy

ỉst ỉr s3 ny-sw.t ỉry-[pꜥ.t] ḫ3.ty-ꜥ2 Wsỉrkn n(n) rⱶf ỉbⱶf ꜥq.w m nn nn wn ỉmⱶf n ḏḏⱶf ꜥ3ⱶỉ ỉm (20) [š]r(?)5 sy m ỉbⱶf ḏḏ k3ⱶf nb m rp(?)[...]6 ḫfty wp.tyⱶfy ỉ3.t ḥm-nṯr tp(y) n ᾽Imn nb nḥḥ [ỉr ḏ].t ỉw rn-wrⱶf tp sp.tyⱶf mỉ ḥḏ.t [n.(t) mw].tⱶf ỉmy-tw r3-ỉbⱶf7 m prⱶf m ḫ.t rḫ.w(y) sw n ꜥḥ3 ḥr ỉš.tⱶf r k3 ḥr (21) [b3wy] ḥr ỉdr.wⱶf pḥr sw m [... mỉ sm]n ḥ3 nw.wⱶs ỉwⱶf 3w-[ỉbⱶ f ...]s[...] spr r dmỉ m mrw.(t) [s]ḥ3 rmt.wⱶf nbⱶf šps wr nḏs wꜥ ᾽Ip.t-s.wt m ỉbⱶf r nṯr m k.t nỉw.t8 ḥr(y).t mw(22)[ⱶf(?) ỉr.nⱶf ḫnty(?) t]p [ỉ]tr(w) ḥr [ḥ]b[y.t] n.t tp-tr.[w]ⱶf n(n) sp wꜥ th(ỉ).nⱶf nw mỉ ỉꜥḥ m [nmt].tⱶf

ḥr m-ḫt dwn s(y) W3s.t n nbnb t3 [nṯr.w] ỉmy.wⱶs sḏm ỉn nṯr ꜥ3 nỉs nⱶf ỉw nⱶf b3 mnḫ Ḥnn-ny-sw.t m rnⱶf m dd [ỉbⱶf] (23) drⱶf ỉsf.t prⱶf r-ḥ3 m [tp n] mšꜥⱶf mỉ [Ḥr] pr m 3ḫ-bỉ.t sk sw r dmỉ Ḥmnw ḥr ỉr.t ḥss nbⱶf nb Ḥmnw nb md.w-[nṯr] ḥr shrr nb.w n.w T3-Šmꜥw sn ꜥḥ.wⱶsn sm3w(y) mꜥḥꜥ.(w)tⱶsn swꜥb (24) ḫ[m.w]ⱶsn r dw.w nb.w sꜥḥꜥ ỉnb.(w)ⱶs[n] m m3w. t [g]rg ḫb3.w m nỉw.t nb.(t) n.w T3-Šmꜥw [d]r rq.wⱶf n.w ḫnw t3 pn wn w3 (r) ḫnn m rkⱶf ỉr.nⱶf ḫnty [...] m ꜥq[y9 ...] (25) [...] m3ꜥ nwy m [ḥ]tp rdỉ r t3 r [W3s].t nḫt ꜥqⱶf m-ḫnwⱶs [m] ḫ rp.t10 nṯr.w ỉmy.wⱶs m ršw ššpⱶf [mn]d.tyⱶs n.w ḏꜥmw snqⱶf m ỉrt.tⱶs ꜥ[qⱶsn nⱶf] m ꜥnḫ w3s ddⱶs nⱶf (26) [qn(ỉ)ⱶs n]ḫt.wⱶs

ḫpr sw wnnⱶf ỉm ḥr ỉr.t ḥss.wt nb nṯr.w ᾽Imn-Rꜥ nb ns.wt t3.wy ḥr ms(ỉ) [wdn].w ḫ.t n nḫt.wⱶf n ᾽Imn p3 nṯr ꜥ3 ḏd sw mỉ nⱶk ꜥ.wyⱶf ḥr ḥḥ m ḫ.t ḥtp.w m b(w) nb nfr r dỉ.t m3ꜥꜥ (27) ḥtp.w-nṯr r ꜥ3 wr.(t) m ḫ.t nb.(t) nfr.(t) wꜥb.(t) nḏm.t bnr.t ꜥpr.(t) m ḏbꜥ.w ḫ3.w n(n) dr-ꜥⱶⱶsn m ỉmny.[t] n.t rꜥ nb m h3w ḥr wn m b3ḥ

ỉ[y.t] p[w] ỉr.n ỉmy-r3 Šmꜥw Wsỉrkn r ḥm n nṯr pn šps m ḫbⱶf nfr m Nḥb-k3.(w) (28) [tpy] pr.t sw 1 sḥꜥ n nṯr pn šps nb nṯr.w nb.w ᾽Imn-Rꜥ ny-sw.t nṯr.w p3 nṯr ḏr-ꜥ(.wy) ỉs ḥm-nṯr tp(y) n ᾽Imn Wsỉ[r]kn m ỉrwⱶf m ỉwn-mw.tⱶf ḥr [... š]m m ḥrⱶf nⱶf m bỉ3.t nfr.t ỉ[yⱶsn r] ḥw.t-nṯr n-mrw. t sr nⱶf nḫt.w (29) [m tp n] mšꜥ ⱶf ỉwⱶf ḥnnⱶf wr sp-2 ḫft ḏd.tⱶf mỉ ỉt ỉ3m nⱶf s3ⱶf

ỉy.(t) pw ỉn ḥm.w-nṯr ỉt.w-nṯr wꜥb.w ḥr(y).w-ḥb.t n.w ᾽Imn wnw. t ḥw.t-nṯr [mỉ q]dⱶs ḥr ꜥnḫ.w r ỉmy-r3 Šmꜥw nỉw.t tn r 3wⱶs m ꜥ.wⱶs nb wⱶs nb m t3y.w (30) [ḥm.wt] dmd m sp wꜥ t ḏdⱶsn m r3 wꜥ (ḥr) [ỉr].t sbḥ. w r ỉmy-r3 Šmꜥw r-nt[t] mn[tk nḏ]ty qn(ỉ) n nṯr.w nb.w dhn tw ᾽Imn [m] s3 smsw11 n wttⱶk stp.nⱶf tw m q3b ḥfn.w r ỉr.t mrr ỉbⱶf ḏr (31) [ỉs]t wnnⱶn ḥr nḫ.tⱶk sḏmⱶn s.t-ỉbⱶk rⱶf mk ỉn.nⱶf [t]lw [nⱶn] r dr m3ỉrⱶn ḥr ws ỉg[p] m-ꜥqⱶn ḏr nty t3 pn w3 (r) mḥw hp.wⱶf sbỉ ḥr ꜥ (32) [sbỉ].w r nbⱶsn m wn

m sr.w≠f šsp [g]s.t nb m r.w-pr.w≠f r ḥd sḫr.[w]≠f w3ḥ nb hdn r ʿr.t r s3q n.t-
ʿ ḫw.wt-nṯr w3 r ḫ3[q].t n(n) 3 m rḫ [ny-sw].t ỉw (33) [≠k r smn(?) r.w]-pr.w
m ḫ3.t ỉry m ʿ[3].t(?) n.(t) p3w.t tp.(t) nỉw.t ḫpr≠s¹² mstyw Wsỉr [...] hb tw
m t3 wn ḏd.tw ỉr.t Rʿ r≠s w3 r tḫn df≠s¹³ ỉw r≠f t3 pn mỉ m [m] ḥm[≠k ...]
ʿḥʿ≠k (34) [...]r[...]r [...]≠k sbỉ.w [...] msdm.t≠s pw trw n.w ỉr.t¹⁴ r≠s¹² ḫpr
sw qn r ỉr.t¹⁴ sw ḫʿ.w≠k b3q [...] ʿḥʿw Ḥ[r(?) ...] mỉ wn≠s

(35) ʿḥʿ.n ḏ[d] ỉ[n] [ỉmy-r3] Šmʿw sbỉ ỉn n≠ỉ th.t≠f nb ʿ n.w tp.w-ʿ [...]
ỉr.t Rʿ ʿḥʿ.n ỉn.tw≠sn n≠f ḥr-[ʿ] m sq(r).w-ʿnḫ mỉ ḥtr.w n.w ḏ[nḫ].w ʿḥʿ].
n sḫ[r]≠f n≠f s.t rdỉ.t m(36)s≠[sn] mỉ ʿrw grḥ ḫ.t-[ḫ3wy] rkḥ ʿḥ.w ỉm [ʿḥʿ.n
ỉn≠w ʿḥ.w (?) r s]m3≠sn⁹ mỉ ʿḥ.w n.w pr.t Spd.t rkḥ.tw s nb m sḏ.t m s.t
bt3w≠f [ỉ-ỉr≠f r(?) nỉw].t⁹ W3s.t ʿḥʿ.n rdỉ.[n≠f ỉn.t](37)w [n≠f] ms.w bw3.
w [n.w ḫ]nw t3 p[n nty] m rḫ ḫ.t [r] dỉ.t [ḥms≠sn ḥr] s.t ỉt.w≠sn m ỉb mr
n mrw.(t) smnḫ [t3] r tp≠f ʿ ʿḥʿ.n ḏd.n≠f n≠sn m3 m [... t]ḥ.tw(y)≠f(y) sw
n [...] (38) [...≠s]n b(w)-wʿb [...] pw [ḏ.]t(?)⁹ s3w ḫpr mỉt.t t ḏd.tw nḫḫ
[pw W3s.t] nb≠s pw ḏt Rʿ pw ʾIwnw Šmʿw 3ḫ.t≠f twy ỉmy t3 pn mk 3 [...
wʿ]b(?)⁹ ỉm≠s rn≠s (39) [...] šw sỉ3.n≠ỉ ỉst ḥs wỉ nṯr.w≠s ḥr≠[s] dỉ≠s[n ...]t
n≠s

ỉr.t[w] wḏ.t ḥr rn≠ỉ m ḥm-nṯr tp(y) n [ʾI]mn-[Rʿ ny-sw].t nṯr.w Wsỉrkn r
ḥn pr ʾImn-Rʿ ny-sw.t nṯr.w [pr Mw.t wr.(t) nb.(t) ʾIšr]w pr [Ḫn]sw m [W3s.
t] Nfr-[ḥtp] (40) pr Mn[ṯ(w)] nb W3s.t ỉp.t M3ʿ.t ḥw.wt r.w-pr.w sḏf3≠f r dỉ.[t]
wnn≠sn r ʿḥʿ≠sn r dỉ.[t ḫ3]w ḥr ỉry.t (m) ḥw ḥtp.wt ḥr≠sn m 3w ḏ.t nḫḫ
r ts [r]mt.[w≠s]n mnmn.w(t)≠sn ʿḥw.wt≠s[n] (41) mn r sḫr.w≠sn ỉw smd.
t≠s[n] nb ḫw(ỉ) m[k(ỉ)] n(n) rdỉ.t ḏ3.tw r≠sn ỉ[n s] nb ỉn ḫ3.ty-ʿ nb sr nb
rwḏw nb n pr ny-sw.t ʿnḫ wḏ3 s(nb) r k3.t nb.(t) ỉrr.t m t3 pn r dr≠f wp.t
b3k≠[sn] (42) m nn n r.w-pr.w

ḥnʿ ỉr.t wḏ.[t 2]-nw.t r ḥn≠[s]n [...]msrw [...]nb r di.[t ḥtp.w-nṯr ... t3ỉ].
w(?)⁵ m-ḫnw p3 pr n ḥm-nṯr tp(y) n ʾImn r [pr ʾImn(?)]⁵ m ỉr.t n-šš w m
[r.w-pr.w(?)]≠sn⁵ r p3 ḥtp-nṯr m snṯr (43) bỉ[.t] w3 r ʿḥʿ ỉw n3 f[3ỉ.w] snṯr
bỉty.w fḫ

rḫ rn [ỉ]ry≠w

dỉ.w r t3 rmny.t nty r-ḫt p3 ḥry [s3w] sš ḥd dbn 21 qd.t 1.(t)

dỉ.(w) r n3 [... nty r]-ḫt n3 smsw h3y.t ḫ3.t n3 šw(44)ty.w [p3] ḥm-nṯr n
Mw.t nty r-ḫt p3 [sš] šʿ.t n t3 [ḥm.t-nṯr n] Mw.t ḥd dbn 30

n3 rmt.w P3-nb.(t)-tp-ỉḥ.w ḥd dbn 18 qd.t 1/2

p3 [...] m p3 ỉmy-r3 pr.wy-ḥd nty pr n ḥt[r⁹ ḥd] dbn 5 dmd dbn 23 qd.t
1/2

dỉ.w r [t]3 (45) [rmny.t n.t pr(?)]⁵ ʾImn mỉt.t ḥd dbn 20 [+ x] qd.t 2.(t)

ḥr dm[d] nty pr m p3 pr n p3 [ḥm]-nṯr tp(y) [n] ʾI[mn r] pr ʾImn m ḫ[t]r¹⁵
r [t]n{r}w¹⁶ rnp.t [ḥd dbn ...] qd.t 3.(t) 1/2

ḥnʿ w3ḥ p3[y≠]s[n] ḥt[p.w-n]ṯr nm 2 wn t3ỉ≠w m(46)-ḫnw [s]t3 mtr dỉ.t
r s.t≠sn

ḫ[nʿ] ỉr.t wḏ.t [r] ḥn twy st3.(t) d[g]lm r-w3ḥ.n≠ỉ m m3w.(t) r [ʾIm]n-Rʿ
ny-sw.t nṯr[.w]

[rḫ] rn îry

nȝ w‘b[.w] îmy[.w] ȝbd≠sn m pr ʾImn m (47) ḫr[.t rnp.t dg]m ḥn 440 [+ 45]

pȝ pr n nbw [n] ʾI[m]n [d]gm ḥn 365 m ḫr.t rnp.t

tȝ wm.t šs dgm 365

dmd smȝ sqnn n d[g]m ḥn 1215 îr n dgm (48) [ḫ]ḏ(?)⁵ [...] 43 [+ x] ît⁹ [...]

ḫ[n‘ îr.t] w[ḏ.t] r smn [x+] 70 rmṯ r s.t≠w mtr.(w) [nty] ṯȝ(î) n tȝ rmny.t n.(t) pr ʾImn (r)-ḫt pȝ îmy-rȝ pr

ḥn‘ îr.t wḏ.t r ḥn [t]wy ḥtp.(t)-nṯr n ȝpd.w r-wȝḥ.n≠î (49) m mȝw.(t) [m ḥm-nṯr tp(y) n ʾI]mn(?)⁵ [... r‘] nb n Mw.t wr.t nb.[t ʾIšr]w Mntw-R‘ nb Wȝs.t ʾImn-m-ʾIp.t ṯȝ(y) nṯr.w

rḫ rn îry

ḥtp-nṯr [n] Mw.t wr.t nb.t ʾIšrw n rdî≠î [r]ȝ [...]

ḥtp-nṯr n Mntw-[R‘] n r‘ nb rȝ [1] (50) ḥtp-nṯr [n ʾImn-m-ʾIp].t r‘ [nb r]ȝ 1 m dmd ḫr.t rnp.t rȝ 730

îw grg.n≠î ḥ(ȝ)mw≠sn m dd≠î ḥd dbn 16 1/2 rmṯ.w s 30 tȝy≠sn wnm. t sms r pȝ pr n pȝ ḥm-nṯr tp(y) n ʾImn (m) ḫr.t (51) [rnp.t ... x +] 425 [ḥn‘] tm rdî.t th.tw [...≠s]n ḥr mw ḥr tȝ m pȝ [pr n] sbî ḏ.t   ḥn‘ îr.t wḏ.t r tm dî.(t) nȝ w‘b.w îmy(≠w) ȝbd≠sn n [pr] ʾIm[n ...] m wsḫ.t n.(t) sš ḥm.t nb.(t) ḫpr≠f m [...] (52) [... r mk(î)] ḥw(î) nȝ îry.w-‘ȝ [n pr] ʾImn [n]ȝ [n]f. w wîȝ pr ʾImn mît.t r [t]m [dî.t] dî≠[s]n snw n wd(î) n nȝy≠s[n] ‘ḥ‘.w ḥr tp îtrw ḥr mr.t nb.(t) n nîw.[t] nb.(t) [ḏ.t]⁵

îw [îr].n≠î n ʾImn n îb mr [ḥr tp] (53) ‘nḫ wḏ s(nb) n ît≠î sȝ R‘ Ṯkrîwt mrî-ʾImn sȝ ȝs.t ‘nḫ ḏ.t [r] dî.[t] ḫ‘(î) kȝ≠f r wnn≠î¹⁷ ḥr ns.t≠f rḫ.kwî nṯr n nṯr.w n [Wȝs.]t(?) n îr≠(î) m ḥm≠f

îr smnḫ.tw(y).f(y) wḏ.t t[n r tm t]ḥ(î) wḏ.t.n≠î n ḥḏ.n≠f sḫr.w≠î wnn[≠f r] mwt≠f ḥr ḥs.t n.t ʾImn pȝy≠sn nb îr pȝ [nty-]îw≠f mnmn wḏ.t tn îr.n≠î ḫr≠f n š‘.t n ʾImn-R‘ sḫm.n nbî.t îm≠f n.w Mw.t m nšn≠s n(n) sȝ≠f r wḏb sȝ≠f îw rn≠î mn wȝḥ m ȝw ḏ.t

(18) Regnal year 11, first month of winter, day 1, under the Majesty of the King of Upper and Lower Egypt, Hedjkheperre-setepenre, [Son of Re, Takelot, beloved of Amon, Son of Isis,] beloved of [Amon-Re,] Lord of the Thrones of the Two Lands, of Mut the great, the Lady [of heaven(?)], and of Khonsu in Thebes Neferhotep, given life like Re forever.

Now, the Overseer of Upper Egypt and chief of the Two Lands, whom Amon appointed in accordance with his own desire, [the First Prophet of] Amon in Thebes, the great general of the entire land and leader, Osorko[n], born [of] the hereditary noble, great of favor, the great royal wife, Lady of the Two Lands, [Karo]mama, [beloved of Mut,] who yet lives, was in his residence in valor and victory over his boundaries, (at) "The Peak of Amon, (19) Great of War-Shout," so it shall be called. Now, he was a hereditary noble [and count,[2] ... greatest] of the great, the eldest son of the two uraei "Great of Magic," one to whom [Upper] Egypt reported, one to whom Lower Egypt petitioned, since fear of him encircled[4] [them,] with their imposts at his gate because of the greatness of his strength, which the Lord of the Thrones of the Two Lands imparted [to] him.

Now, regarding the Prince, hereditary noble and count[2] Osorkon, his heart was by no means in agreement with this (situation). There was no fault in him. He did not say: "May I be greater thereby." (20) It was ignominious (?)[5] in his heart, for his soul said: "The lord is ...[...][6] the enemy who will divide the office of First Prophet of Amon, Lord of eternity, [who made] infinity." His great name was upon his lips like his [mother's] milk within his stomach,[7] when he came forth from the womb. How much more knowledgeable was he in fighting for his property than even a bull upon (21) [the field of combat] for its herds. He was one who circled about in [... like a go]ose about its nestlings. He was joyful [...]...[...] arriving at the town through the desire that its people, both great and small, might remember its noble lord, since the Unique One of Karnak was in his heart more than a god in another city[8] that was loyal to (22) [him. He would sail southward (?) o]n the river bearing festal offerings of his (Amon's) calendrical festivals. Not once did he miss a period of time, even as the moon in its [cour]se.

Now after Thebes rose up against the protector of the land and the [gods] who were in it, the great god heard the appeal (made) to him. The beneficient ram of Heracleopolis came to him (Osorkon) in his (Amon's) name, as the granting of his (Amon's) wish (23) that he (Osorkon) might repulse wrongdoing. He came forth at [the head] of his army like [Horus] come forth from Chemmis. Now, he was at the town of Hermopolis doing what is praised of its lord (Thoth), the Lord of Hermopolis, Lord of the [Divine] Words, and making content the lords of Upper Egypt. Their braziers were set up, their tombs renewed, their sh[rines] purified (24) against all evils, their walls erected anew, what had been destroyed in every city of Upper Egypt was refounded, and the enemies of the interior of this land, who had fallen into disturbance in his reign, were repulsed. He sailed southward [...] opposite[9] [...] (25) [...] navigating the stream in peace, and putting to land at [Thebe]s the Victorious. He entered within it [as] the child of the Maiden,[10] while the gods who were within it rejoiced as he received her breasts of electrum, suckling her milk so that it enter[ed into him] as life and dominion, while she gave to him (26) [her valor and] her victories.

It happened that he was there doing what is praised of the Lord of the gods, Amon-Re, Lord of the Thrones of the Two Lands, and presenting [offerings] and the booty of his victories to Amon, the great god. He was the one who said (the ritual recitation): "Take to yourself," his hands bearing millions of things and offerings consisting of everything good in order to give a present of (27) divine offerings in very great abundance, consisting of everything good, pure, pleasant, and sweet, supplied by the tens of thousands and thousands without end as the daily offering of each day in excess of what had existed previously.

Then came the Overseer of Upper Egypt Osorkon to the Majesty of this noble god in his goodly festival of Nehebkau ("Yoking the *ka*-spirits") (28) [on the first] month of winter, day 1. There occurred the processional appearance of this noble god, Lord of all the gods, Amon-Re, King of the Gods, the god of the primeval time. Now, the First Prophet of Amon Osorkon was in his capacity as "Pillar-of-his-Mother" priest, bearing [...], while the god was] going forward to him as a goodly oracle. [They] returned to the temple in order to predict for him victories (29) [at the head of] his army. He (Amon) assented very greatly in accordance with what he (Osorkon) said, like a father whose son is dear to him.

Then came the prophets, God's Fathers, common priests, lector priests of Amon, and the temple staff [in] its entirety bearing bouquets for the Overseer of Upper Egypt, (together with) this whole city, in all its districts and all its quarters, the men (30) [and women] united in one occasion. Now they said with one accord, crying out to the Overseer of Upper Egypt, thus: "You are the valiant protector of all the gods, for Amon has appointed you [as] the eldest son[11] of the one who begot you. From the midst of hundreds of thousands he has chosen you in order to enact fully that which his heart desires. (31) [No]w we beseech you, since we hear of your affection regarding him. Behold, he has brought you [to us] in order to dispel our misery by putting an end to the cloudburst confronting us; since this land has fallen into a state of drowning, its laws having perished at the hands of (32) [those who rebel]led against their lord, even those who had been his officials, while every palette-bearing scribe in his temples would harm his ordinances, which the Lord of the Calamus (Thoth) had set down on the scroll, and would destroy the customary rituals of the temples that had fallen into a state of plunder. Yet it was not in the knowledge of the king. (33) [You shall establish (?)] the temples as before, in the gr[eatness (?)] of the first primeval time of Thebes, when it came into being.[12] O true image of Osiris, [...] who sent you into the land that is called the "Eye of Re," which has fallen into a state of injury to its pupil.[13] What, then, would this land be like without [you]? [...] when you stand (34) [...] you [...] rebels [...] The ocherous blood of him[14] who acted against it (the Eye of Re)[12] is its eye-paint. It happened that evil befell the one[14] who did it, although you are innocent [...] lifetime of H[orus (?) ... Let Thebes be punished (?)[5]] according to its fault."

(35) Then the [Overseer] of Upper Egypt said: "Go and bring to me every transgressor against him (Amon) and the records of the ancestors

[…] the Eye of Re." Then they were brought to him directly as prisoners like yoked (birds) with pinioned wings. [Then] he struck them down for him (Amon), causing (36) that they be carried like goats on the night of the [Evening] Sacrifice when braziers are kindled. [Then they brought braziers (?)] to sacrifice them[9] like the braziers of the (festival) Going Forth of Sothis, with the result that every one was burned with fire in the place of his crime [that had been committed against (?) the] city[9] of Thebes. Then [he] caused that there be [brought to him] (37) the children of the magnates of the interior of this land who were knowledgeable [in order to] cause [that they occupy the] positions of their fathers with a willing heart through the desire of improving the [land] beyond its former condition. Then he said to them: "See, now, [the fate of (?)] him who will transgress him (Amon) for […] (38) […] them purity. […] is eternal.[9] Beware lest the same thing happen. Now, it is said that [Thebes is] everlasting, and eternal is its lord. He is Re of Upper Egyptian Heliopolis, this effective Eye of his that is in this land. Behold, […] purity (?)[9] is in it, its name (39) […] the light that I have perceived. Now, its gods praise me concerning [it], while they cause […] for it.

Let there be made a decree in my name as First Prophet of Amon-[Re, King] of the Gods, Osorkon, in order to provision the estate of Amon-Re, King of the Gods, [the estate of Mut the great, Lady of Ash]eru, the estate of [Khon]su in [Thebes], Nefer[hotep], (40) the estate of Mon[tu], Lord of Thebes, the hidden shrine of Maat, and the primary and secondary temples of its supply, in order to cause that they be in their proper standing and to provide an increase over what had been done (regarding) sustenance and offerings for them throughout the length of eternity and infinity, in order to organize their personnel, their herds, and their fields, (41) established according to their ordinances. All their staffs are exempted and protected, without allowing that they be interfered with by any man, by any count, any official, any agent of the royal palace, l.p.h., regarding any work that is done in this entire land, except for [their] work (42) in these temples.

Together with making a [seco]nd decree in order to provision them […] every […] in order to give [the divine offerings that are to be taken (?)][5] from within the estate of the First Prophet of Amon to [the estate of Amon (?)][5] as that which should be done in a profitable manner in their [temples (?)][5] with regard to the divine offering consisting of incense (43) and honey, but which is fallen into a state of abeyance, since the thurifers and bee-keepers have been disbanded.

The list thereof:

What is given to the domain that is under the authority of the chief of records: 21 *deben* and 1 *kite* of silver.

What is given to the […, who are] under the authority of the elders of the portal who are before the merchants, (44) and [the] prophet of

Mut, who is under the authority of the letter [scribe] of the [prophetess of] Mut: 30 *deben* of silver.

The people of Aphroditopolis (Atfih): 18 *deben* and 1/2 *kite* of silver;

The [...] from the Overseer of the Double Treasury, which is issued from the (annual) levy[9]: 5 *deben* [of silver;]

Total: 23 *deben* and 1/2 *kite* (of silver).

What is given to the (45) [domain of the estate (?)][5] of Amon likewise: 20 [+x] *deben* and 2 *kite* of silver;

In addition to the total that is issued from the estate of the First Prophet [of] Amon [to] the estate of Amon from the levy[15] per[16] year: [... *deben*] and 3 and 1/2 *kite* [of silver];

Together with adding their [divine] offerings (of) 2 *nem*-vases, which had been taken from (46) the corresponding illumination (allowance) given to their offices;

To[gether with] making a (third) decree [in order to] provision this castor oil illumination that I have added anew with respect to [Amon]-Re, King of the Gods.

The list thereof:

The priests who are on monthy service in the estate of Amon throughout (47) the course of [the year:] 4[85] *hin* of castor;

The House of Gold [of] Amon: 365 *hin* of castor in the course of the year;

The Gateway of Alabaster: 365 (*hin*) of castor;

Sum-total: 1215 *hin* of castor oil, amounting to (48) 43 [+x *hin*] of castor [for light]ing(?),[5] (equalling the value of?) [...] of barley.[9]

Together [with making a] (fourth) decree in order to establish [x+] 70 people at their proper offices, who are to be taken from the domain of the estate of Amon that is under the authority of the steward.

Together with making a (fifth) decree in order to provision this divine offering of birds that I have added (49) anew [as the First Prophet of] Amon (?)[5] [...] daily for Mut the great, Lady [of Asher]u, Montu-Re, Lord of Thebes, Amonemope, the most virile of the gods.

The list thereof:

The divine offering [of] Mut the great, Lady of Asheru, deriving from my (personal) gift: [...] geese.

The divine offering of Montu-[Re] for each day: [1] goose;

(50) and the divine offering [of Amon(em)ope] daily: 1 goose;

totaling 730 geese per year.

I have founded their aviaries by my gift of 16 1/2 *deben* of silver and a staff of 30 men, their nestling-feed owing from the estate of the First Prophet of Amon (in) the course (51) [of the year, amounting to] 425 [+x ...], together with preventing one from transgressing [...] them on water or on land in the [estate of] Him who Traverses Eternity (Amon).

Together with making a (sixth) decree in order to prevent the priests
who are on monthly service in the estate of Amon [...] in the hall of a
scribe of any craft so that he might become [...] (52) [... in order to pro-
tect] and exempt the door-keepers [of the estate] of Amon, and [the] sailors
of the sacred barge of the estate of Amon likewise in order to prevent
them from paying departure tax for their ships on the river at any harbor
of any city [forever (?)].[5]

I have [acted] for Amon with a willing heart [on behalf of] (53) the
life, prosperity, and health of my father, the Son of Re, Takelot, beloved of
Amon, Son of Isis, living forever, [in order] to cause that his *ka*-spirit rejoice
and in order that I might be[17] upon his throne, since I know the god of the
gods of [Thebes (?)], and I do not act in ignorance of him.

As for the one who shall confirm this decree [so as not] to transgress
that which I have commanded, while not harming my ordinances, [he]
shall be even [until] his death in the favor of Amon, their lord. (But,) as for
the one who shall upset this decree that I have made, may he fall to the
slaughter of Amon-Re, the flame of Mut having overpowered him in her
raging. His son shall not succeed him. My name is established and enduring throughout the length of eternity."

(2) INSCRIPTION OF YEARS 12 AND 15–24 OF TAKELOT II

Upper Register, Addorsed Scenes: Amon receives bread offering from high
priest Osorkon (Epigraphic Survey 1954, pl. 20)

Righthand Label for Amon (lines 1–3)
    ḏd-mdw ỉn ʾImn-Rꜥ-Ḥr-ꜣḫ.ty nṯr ꜥꜣ (2) ḫr(y) nṯr.w (3) ḏd-mdw dỉ.n≠(ỉ)
n≠k nḫt.w nb ḫr≠ỉ
    Recitation by Amon-Re-Horachty, the great god, (2) chief of the gods.
(3) Recitation: "Thus I have given to you all victories deriving from me."

Righthand Label for Prince Osorkon (lines 4–8)
    ḥm-nṯr tp(y) n ʾImn-Rꜥ ny-sw.t nṯr.w ỉmy-rꜣ mšꜥ (5) wr ḫꜣw.ty Wsỉrkn
mꜣꜥ-ḫrw (6) sꜣ ny-sw.t n nb tꜣ.wy Ṯkr[ỉw]t mrỉ-ʾImn sꜣ ꜣs.t ꜥnḫ ḏ.t (7) ms
n≠f ỉry.(t)-pꜥ.t wr.(t) ḥs.w(t) ḥnw.t n (8) Šmꜥw Mḥw ḥm.t ny-sw.t wr.(t)
Kr[mꜥ]mꜥ mrỉ-Mw.t mꜣꜥ.(t)-ḫrw
    The First Prophet of Amon-Re, King of the Gods, great (5) general
and leader, Osorkon, the justified, (6) royal son of the Lord of the Two
Lands, Takelot, beloved of Amon, Son of Isis, living forever, (7) to whom
the hereditary noble, great of favor, mistress of (8) Upper and Lower
Egypt, the great royal wife, Karo[ma]ma, beloved of Mut, the justified,
gave birth.

Central Label for Osorkon (line 9)

wnn k3 ny-sw.t nb t3.wy [Ḥd-ḫpr]-Rᶜ-stp-n-Rᶜ s3 Rᶜ [Ṯkr]ỉw[t] mrỉ-ʾImn s3 3s.t wnn ʾIp.t-s.wt n s3≠f ḥr(y)-[tp t3.wy Wsỉrkn] m3ᶜ-ḫrw

So long as there exists the royal *ka*-spirit of the Lord of the Two Lands, [Hedjkheper]re-setepenre, Son of Re, [Takelot], beloved of Amon, Son of Isis, so shall Karnak exist for his son, the chief [of the Two Lands, Osorkon], the justified.

Lefthand Label for Amon (lines 1–3)

dd-mdw ỉn ʾImn-Rᶜ nb ns.wt t3.wy nb p.t (2) ḫnty ʾIp.t-s.wt (3) dd-mdw dỉ.n≠(ỉ) n≠k qn(ỉ) nb ḫr≠ỉ

Recitation by Amon-Re, Lord of the Thrones of the Two Lands, Lord of heaven, (2) Foremost of Karnak. (3) Recitation: "Thus I have given to you all valor deriving from me."

Lefthand Label for Prince Osorkon (lines 4–8)

ḥm-ntr tp(y) n ʾImn-Rᶜ ny-sw.t ntr.w ỉmy-r3 mšᶜ (5) wr ḫ3w.ty Wsỉrkn m3ᶜ-ḫrw (6) s3 ny-sw.t n nb t3.wy Ṯkrỉwt mrỉ-ʾImn s3 3s.t ᶜnḫ d.t (7) s3 sms(w) wp-ḥ.t (8) n ḥm.t ny-sw.t wr.(t) Kr(m)ᶜ[mᶜ] mrỉ-Mw.t m3ᶜ.(t)-ḫrw

The First Prophet of Amon-Re, King of the Gods, great (5) general and leader, Osorkon, the justified, (6) royal son of the Lord of the Two Lands, Takelot, beloved of Amon, Son of Isis, living forever, (7) eldest son and firstborn (8) of the great royal wife, Karo(m)a[ma], beloved of Mut, the justified.

Main Text of Year 12 of Takelot II (Epigraphic Survey 1954, pl. 21, lines 1–6; Kitchen 1986, 331 §292)

ḥsb.t 12.(t) tp(y) 3ḫ.t sw 9 ḫr ḥm n Ḥr K3 nḫt ḫᶜ [m] W3s.t [ny-sw].t bỉ.ty nb t3.wy nb ỉr.(t) ḫ.t Ḥd-ḫpr-Rᶜ-stp-n-Rᶜ s3 Rᶜ n ḫ.t≠f Ṯkrỉwt mrỉ-ʾImn s3 3s.t mry ʾImn-Rᶜ nb ns.wt t3.[wy] k3 mw.t≠f ny-sw.t ntr.w nb p.t ḫnty ʾIp.t-s.wt Mw.t wr.t nb.(t) ʾIš[rw] Ḫnsw m W3s.t Nfr-ḥtp dỉ ᶜnḫ mỉ Rᶜ d.t

ỉst r≠f wn s3≠f smsw ḫr(y)-tp t3.wy [ḥm-ntr tp(y) n ʾImn-Rᶜ] ny-sw.t ntr. w ỉmy-r3 mšᶜ wr ḫ3w.ty Wsỉrkn m3ᶜ-ḫrw [...] r mrr≠f mỉ Šw r-gs Rᶜ (2) ḫr shtp ỉb n W3dy.t nb.(t)≠f m ḥr.t hrw n mr(w).t smnḫ t3š[.w≠f] ndm st(ỉ) m šny.t mỉ nḫb wr ỉry fnd n ntr nb

[tỉ sw(?)][18] m ḥwn ỉqr bnr mrw.t mỉ Ḥr pr m 3ḫ-bỉ.t ᶜq n tk[k] t3š.w≠f n s3 k3 nḫt mỉ dr.ty m ỉry.w-p.t

shm pḥ.ty [r-g]s(?)[19] Nb.ty ỉwᶜ mnḫ n shm.ty

mw(y) n Ḥr-nbw m3.t(w) m ḫᶜ.w≠f ḥr [w]ry.t mỉ sb3 ḫr sšd (3) Ḥr dw3. t m ḫ3b(3)s snn≠f m wr swḥ.t sbq.t tỉ.t n.t ny-sw.t bỉ.ty

hr.w m g(3)wy n m3≠f ḫft s3 Rᶜ ḫᶜ.w ᶜnḫ n s3 3s.t m9 [wn(?)] m3ᶜ.t 3 m3ᶜ-ḫrw m gs(y).w≠f mỉ s3 Wsỉr wp ḥ.t ỉm≠f n wr.t ḥs.wt [qm]ꜣ.n wr.[t] ḥts nfr.w≠f m ḥr(y)-ỉb ꜥḥ.(t) wr.t šdd.n≠s m ỉrt.t≠s [m]-ḫnw Pr-nw

rnn.n ny-sw.t ḥr šnb.t≠f m Pr-wr Pr-nsr sḏr≠f ỉmy-tw Wr.ty-Ḥkꜣ.w≠sn m ḥr.t hrw (4) Rr.t nṯr.w ḥnk.t rs-tp≠sn ḥr≠f šꜥ wꜣḥ r[d.wy]≠f ḥr sꜣt(w) m-ḫnw≠s (r) rdw n s.t wr.t

ḥꜣ.ty-ꜥ m wḏꜥ md.w(t) ꜥq.(t) m ꜥnḫ.wy≠f n.t-ꜥ m stp-[sꜣ] ḫpr r [sꜣ]ỉ(r.t)≠f ḥr≠s [sḫr.w≠f] nb ḫpr≠s[n] m ḫ.wt bỉ.tyw

ỉw pꜣ.n≠f wp.t rꜣ≠f r ḏd ꜣỉmn ỉw≠f m nḫn [bḥ]s qn(ỉ) ḥr mn.ty n mw.t≠f ḥr st(ỉ) ḥn≠f m ḫ.t r ỉr.t mrr≠f rḫ.n≠f (5) my n pr ỉm≠f bs.n≠f

ỉst ꜥq(ꜣ)w m⁹ [...] r sḫr nb n ỉb≠f ḫ.t≠f mḫ n tꜣy≠f mrw.t šfy.t≠f ḫt ḫꜥ.w≠f ỉw [...] wr≠f r nṯr.w

ḥꜣ n≠f ꜣḫw≠[f] nb ỉr≠f ḥr mw≠f ꜣm n≠f [...] sbꜣ.n nb≠f ḫpr≠f n Ḥr tmꜥ-ꜥ n.{t} tꜣ.wy tm.w ḫnḫn n≠f ḥnmm.t mw.t ỉꜣm.t-ỉb ḥr rdỉ.t t n ḥqr ḏbꜣ ḥꜣw ỉy ḥr bg(ꜣw) (6) n mꜣỉr nḏ.ty šntꜣy.t qn(ỉ) n rs-tp ḥr ḫ.wt r.w-pr.w rwd-ỉb n šms Wꜣs.t

ỉy.n≠f m nw n 3 m rnp.t ꜥḫꜣy.w≠f wdn ḥr ḥby.(t)≠s dỉ≠f s(y) m ḥb.t tnw [...] m ḫꜥꜥw n pꜣ mꜣ≠f ḥr sḥb ḥtp.w≠s sdfꜣ ḥꜣ.wt≠s m ḫ.t nb.(t) nfr.t wꜥb.t bnr.t nḏm.t rdỉ.t ḥꜣwy ḥr ỉmny.t≠s [n].t rꜥ nb n ỉb n g(ꜣ).t qmꜣ sy

Regnal year 12, first month of Inundation, day 9, under the Majesty of the Horus "Strong Bull, appearing in Thebes"; the King of [Upper] and Lower Egypt, Lord of the Two Lands, Lord of ritual performance, Hedj-kheperre-setepenre, bodily Son of Re, Takelot (II), beloved of Amon, Son of Isis, beloved of Amon-Re, Lord of the Thrones of the Two Lands, bull of his mother, King of the Gods, Lord of heaven, Foremost of Karnak, of Mut the great, Lady of Asheru, and of Khonsu in Thebes Neferhotep, given life like Re forever.

Now then, his eldest son, the chief of the Two Lands, [the First Prophet of Amon-Re,] King of the Gods, the great general and leader, Osorkon, the justified, was [beside his father in the palace (?)] in accordance with his (Takelot's) desire, like Shu beside Re, (2) pacifying the heart of Edjo, his lady, in the course of every day through the desire of confirming [his] boundaries—a sweet-scented one among the courtiers, like the great lotus that accompanies the nose of every god.

[Now he][18] was an excellent youth, sweetly beloved like Horus come forth from Chemmis, who charges among those who would violate his boundaries as the son of the (royal) Strong Bull, just as a kite among aerial flocks;

one powerful of strength [be]side (?)[19] the Two Ladies, the beneficent heir of the double crown;

the seed of the Golden Horus, whose body upon the chariot is viewed as a flashing star, (3) a Horus of the morning among the starry firmament;

whose semblance is that of a chief, the legitimate egg and image of the King of Upper and Lower Egypt;

at the sight of whom faces are dazzled as before the Son of Re, the living body of the son of Isis in[9] [very (?)] truth, one who is great in justification among his neighbors like the son of Osiris;

the firstborn of (the queen) "She who is great of favor," one whose beauty "She who is great of charm" [crea]ted in the midst of the great palace, one whom she suckled with her milk within the Lower Egyptian shrine at Dep;

one whom the king cradled upon his breast in the Upper Egyptian shrines at el-Kab and Pe so that he might sleep between their two uraei "Great of Magic" in the course of every day, while Reret and the gods of the bedroom watched over him until his feet were placed on the ground within it at the steps of the great throne;

foremost in judging matters that reached his ears, while rituals in the palace transpire according to his understanding concerning them, with all [his plans] being realized throughout generations of kings.

He had already opened his mouth to say: "Amon," when he was but a child, a [cal]f embraced upon the lap of his mother yet reeking, but he was provided with a body to enact what he (Amon) wishes, since he (Amon) knows (5) the progeny of the one who came forth from him (Amon), whom he (Amon) had inducted.

Now, [he is] one who is precise in[9] [...] regarding every plan of his (Amon's) heart, his body being filled with his (Amon's) love, his (Amon's) dignity pervading his limbs, since [he knows (?)] that he (Amon) is greater than the (other) gods;

one for whom all [his] efficacy was prepared so that he might be loyal to him (Amon); one for whom there was grasped [...]; one whom his lord instructed so that he might become the strong-armed Horus of the entire Two Lands; one to whom humanity submissively approaches; a kindhearted mother giving bread to the hungry, clothing the naked, coming at the cry (6) of the wretched; a protector of the widow, valorous in watching over the property of the temples, steadfast in serving Thebes.

On three occasions during the year he returned with his ships burdened with its (Thebes') festival offerings, so that he might set it in festivity every [...] in joy at the sight of him making festal its offering stones, provisioning its altars with everything good, pure, pleasant, and sweet, and granting an increase in its daily offerings of each day through thought for the shrine of the one who created it.

Main Text of Years 15–24 of Takelot II (Epigraphic Survey 1954, pl. 21, lines
7–20 and pl. 22, line 1; Kitchen 1986, 331–32 §293, 546–50 §§454–61)

ỉr m-ḫt ḥsb.t 15.(t) ȝbd 4 šmw sw 25 ḥr ḥm n ỉt≠f šps nṯr ḥqȝ Wȝs.t n
ꜥm p.t ỉꜥḥ[20] nšn n p.t(?)[21] ḫpr m tȝ pn mỉ […]ȝ[…] ms.w bšt.w wd(ỉ)≠sn
ḫȝꜥy.t m Šmꜥw Mḥw [… n] wrḏ.n≠f n ꜥḫȝ r ỉmytw≠sn mỉ Ḥr m-ḫt ỉt≠f rnp.
wt snỉ n(n) ḫsf-ꜥ wꜥ ḥr ỉt.t 2-nw≠f

ỉy ỉn nṯr ꜥȝ ḥr(y)-ỉb ʾIp.t-s.wt r (8) sḫȝ sȝ≠f r nbnb pr ỉm≠f ḥtp≠f n ỉb≠f
n sšm.[w]≠f mnḫ r ḥb.w≠f nb nfr.w ꜥḥꜥ.n ḏd ỉn ỉmy-rȝ Šmꜥw pn n sr.w≠f
smr.w [šny.t(?)] n.t ỉt≠f nty r-gs≠f mt(n) r≠f wn≠tn m stp.w-rȝ n{.t} wtt [wy
… m] rk≠f pw gr≠sn ḥr mḥy≠f m rk≠ỉ n(n) ꜥḫȝ≠tn ḥr mn(ỉ)≠f pw tȝw m
ḥ.t rd.wy ḥr šm.t ḥw.wt-nṯr m sn(ỉ)-mn.t (9) ḫpr.t[22] m tp(y).t n≠sn mỉ wr≠s
r spȝ.wt grg≠s mỉ-m […]≠tn ḫpr ḥqȝ≠s wꜥ m ȝbd ḏ.t≠ỉ p(ȝ)q ỉnt≠ỉ th(ỉ)≠f
ḥr [sȝỉ(r).t]{(?)[23] ḥr≠s rꜥ nb n gm≠ỉ sḫr.w n rḫ snb≠s m rw.ty [dbḥ(?) ḥr≠s n
pȝ][5] nṯr ḥr wdn n≠f ḥr≠s m kȝ.w n dd≠f[24] r šḥtp≠f [m mr].t Rꜥ pw Ḥr-ȝḫ.ty
(3)ḫ.t≠f twy ỉmy tȝ pn ḫpr wpš≠f s(y) r sšp tȝ [k]k …n…ꜥḫ …f […]

(10) sk gr.t ꜥrq.n≠f ḏd md.(t) tn ḥr sḏm.w≠f ỉb≠sn nḏm [ḥr≠s] r [ḫ].t
[nb.(t) … ḏd≠sn …] tỉ.t [… sḫr.w(?)]≠k nb ḫpr≠sn ỉr gr.t ḥtp n≠n nṯr mȝꜥ≠f
tȝ ḥr≠k ntn ḥȝ.t(y)[-ꜥ(?) …] ȝḫ ḥm(w) nfr ḥȝt.(t) m-ꜥ ỉmy-ỉr.ty qn(ỉ) mnḫ
kȝ.t qn(ỉ) m ỉr.t≠s tr nb ḥtp-nṯr sỉn m ꜥ ḥr≠k ỉn.tw ỉb≠k r≠sn ḥȝ.t ḥtp nn
ỉr.n≠f[24] (11) dỉ.ḥr≠k n≠f mỉ dỉ≠f n≠k ȝḫ pȝ dỉ n pȝ dỉ ỉw≠[n] r ȝw≠ỉb ḥr≠k
n(n) ḫft(y).w≠k tm wn ȝḫ n≠n gr.t […] šf.t≠f ỉr.n≠f s(y) n nty r ḫpr

ꜥḥꜥ.n ḏd n≠sn ỉn ỉmy-rȝ Šmꜥw pn ỉm[ỉ snhy.tw(?)] mšꜥ≠n m b(w) wꜥ
ḥws≠n n≠f wḏy.t ꜥḥꜥ.n ỉr(w) mỉ ḏ[d]≠f ȝtp.ḥr≠sn r ꜥḥꜥy.w≠f m ḥ.wt≠f nb
ỉptn ḫft gs.wyw≠f nb m ms.w ny-sw.t ꜥȝ.w sr.w (12) nty m-ḫt≠f m tȝy.w
ḥm.wt šny.t n.t wtt≠f mšꜥ≠f šms.w≠f n(n) wn ḏr-ꜥ≠sn ỉw gr.t ꜥḥꜥy.w ꜥšȝ.t
n wꜥ nb ỉm wdn≠sn ḥr wdn.w ḥr nḫ(ỉ) n≠f qn(ỉ) ꜥḥꜥy.w m […]≠sn n(n)
rḫ tnw≠sn pr.w-ḥr-mw(?) mỉ ꜥšȝ.t≠sn s nb ḥr snṯr≠f n(n) ḏr.w n ḥry.wt-
mw n.w ỉy.(w) ḏs≠sn k.t-ḫt ꜥšȝ.t n.(t) mšꜥ [ḥr ỉ]trw(?) […] (13) ḥr ȝw n
mȝꜥ-ḫrw≠f m ỉb≠sn mỉ sȝ Wsỉr ꜥḥꜥ.n dỉ≠f s(w) r mr.(t) ỉs.wt m hy mnmn
n≠f tȝ.wy m-ḫt≠f ḥr nhm r ḥr(y).t wb[ḫ] p.t n mȝꜥw nfr n.{t} mḥy.t mỉt.t (n)
ỉr.n≠s n≠f r tnw sp mȝ.tw ḥt3[.w …] rꜥ mw mỉ sbȝ.w r ḥ.t n ḥ.t n Nw.t mỉ Ḥr
ḫnty m rkḥ ḥr(ỉ)w ỉ[w]ꜥ≠f m mȝꜥ-ḫrw ỉdb.w nhm ꜥd.w m ršw r (w)d(ỉ)≠f
r tȝ n Wȝs.t (m) ḥȝ.t ꜥḥꜥy.[w≠f] Wsr-ḥȝ.t (n) ʾImn […] (14) nš.t n.(t) mšꜥ≠f
mỉ qbḥ nhp≠f r nw n ȝḫ.t ỉy≠sn ḥr≠f m ỉb mr r dbḥ n≠f nḫt

ꜥḥꜥ.n gm≠sn Wȝs.t ḥr qmȝ hnw ʾIp.t-s.wt (ḥr) dḫn [n≠f] m[ỉ] dḫn n mr.t
ḥr sp spr n≠s ḥp[25] [ỉry] nb sšm m wr≠f m p.t-nṯr ỉwn-mw.t≠f m ʾIwnw
Šmꜥw ꜥḥꜥ.n ỉr.n≠f ꜥȝb.t [ꜥȝ.t n n]b≠f nṯr≠f šps wr r nṯr.w ʾImn-Rꜥ nb ns.wt
tȝ.wy psḏ.t ỉmy.(t) ʾIp.t-s.wt nb.w p.t [tȝ] s[d] m rȝ m ꜥ[ȝb.t m] (15) wndw
gḥs.w n(ỉ)ȝw.w mȝ-ḥḏ.w rȝ.w šd.w m dbꜥ.w ḥȝ.w ȝpd.w š[ȝ5 …] ḥr≠f ḥr
ḥn(ỉ) ỉnw r ws[ḫ.wt] n.t pr≠[f] bn[26] rȝ-ꜥ m b(w) nb nfr t ḥ[nq.t n(n) tn]w≠sn
mr.w bꜥḥ m ỉrp [ỉrt].t nḏb.w(t) n dq(r).w rnp(ỉ).w bỉ.t šdḥ mỉt.t ỉry ḏdm.
t [n.t ꜥn]ty.w sn[ṯr].w ꜥḥꜥ.[n] rdỉ.n≠f mȝꜥ nn m ḥtp-ỉb qnn […] (16) nṯr ꜥȝ
ỉmy Wȝs.t

sḫꜥ n nṯr pn šps r sḫr ꜥꜣb.t≥f tn psḏ.t≥f m ꜣw.(t)-ỉb ḥr šsp≥s m(?) [...
d]d(?) ḥr nṯr ꜥꜣ ỉn ḥm-nṯr tp(y) n ʾImn Wsỉrkn [(m) ḥꜣ.t] mšꜥ≥f ḥr dd m sw3š
[ʾImn] nṯr [ꜥꜣ] ỉn ỉw wn ḥr(y)-tp≥k n[b(?) ... k]y m ḥr[y ...] gr≥k r ỉw≥f nỉw.
wt m swḥ(ꜣ) spꜣ.wt [m ḫnnw nšn m]⁵ wꜥ nb ỉm [s] nb ỉm≥sn ḥr (dd) ỉnk
ỉt≥ỉ tꜣ p[n ...] (17) ỉn ỉw ỉr.n≥k r Wꜣs.t mỉ ỉr.t≥k r≥sn nmꜥ≥s twt≥k ỉm ḫpr
spꜣ.t≥f [m snỉ-mn.t(?)]⁵ ... pꜣly≥sn nb r-ꜣw m wn mꜣꜥ.t ỉw [...] ḥry(?) ḥr(?)
[... ṯ]s≥k n≥[s]n mkꜣ tỉ n ꜥš [...] n rꜣ-ꜥ n šn[.t] ỉtn≥k mꜣ≥sn d(ꜣ)ỉr≥s ḥr≥k n
sf≥k ḥr [...]w nṯr.w nb.w r dỉ.t≥s m ꜥ.wy≥k r šw[≥s] m [...] (18) mkꜣ tw n
nb md.w nṯr šꜣꜥ mꜣwy r[n] tꜣ.wy ỉr.n≥f rn [... nỉw].t⁵ nb.(t) r≥s r dỉ.(t) tꜣ r
dr≥f ḥr (dd) ỉmỉ⁵ tꜣ [... ỉry].w(?) dỉ≥f ỉmny.t n ꜣbd [... Wꜣs].t(?) [...].ṯ(w)≥s
m hrw wꜥ wꜣḥ kꜣ≥k šps wr [...]≥k ỉtn≥k nty m ḥr(y).t nfr n tꜣ pn ḥtp≥k m
s[f(?)]²⁷ ḥr≥k [...] (19) dr.ḥr≥k sf≥n ḥr≥s m[...]≥k sḏm≥sn [... ỉn ỉ]w psd
n≥k ỉr.t Rꜥ ḥr≥ỉ ꜥnḫ≥ỉ [...] ỉr≥k ỉn ỉw psd [n≥ỉ ỉr.t Rꜥ ḥr≥k(?)]⁵ ...] ꜥnḫ
m(w)t tp rꜣ≥k n ḥsf.ṯ(w) ꜥ≥k m p.t m tꜣ [...] ḏꜣm.w m ṯnw šꜥ ḥr mnfy.t [...]
(20) [...] r≥sn m [...pꜣy]≥ỉ ḥpš r snḫt Wꜣs.t gm [...] kꜣ nb ḥnꜥ [...] n nb nṯr.
w⁹ mḥ≥ỉ dr msw.(t)≥ỉ r mỉn r⁹ [...] nb pꜣ nb nṯr.w [...]ḥꜣ nb m nḏ.ty ntk
[...] (pl. 22, line 1) [...] pw nkn.n≥f ḥḥ.w n dd kꜣ≥k nṯr.w nb.w n.w p.t tꜣ
stꜣ r≥f ỉy n ḫrw≥f m [ḥr(y).t-ỉb n] ꜥꜣꜣ.t ỉn pꜣ nṯr ꜥꜣ ỉw≥f hnn≥f wr [...].
n≥f n≥sn dhn≥f nb≥sn mỉn r [... ḥp]lr n ỉry [...] ꜥḥꜥ.n rdỉ.n≥f sw m [...]

Now afterwards, in regnal year 15, fourth month of summer, day 25,
under the Majesty of his noble father, the god who rules Thebes, the sky
did not swallow the moon (in an eclipse),²⁰ although a great (?) convul-
sion²¹ occurred in this land like [...] the children of rebellion, as they
inflicted civil strife in Upper and Lower Egypt [...] He did [not] weary
of fighting among them even as Horus following his father, while years
passed when there was no restraining one from seizing his fellow.

The great god resident in Karnak came in order to (8) remind his
son (Takelot II) to protect the one who came forth from him (Osorkon),
since he (Amon) was pleased in his heart with his (Osorkon's) excellent
guidance regarding all his (Amon's) goodly festivals. Then this Overseer
of Upper Egypt said to his officials, friends, and the [entourage (?)] of his
father who were beside him: "Behold, now, you are the counselors of him
who begot [me ...] It is the case that [... in] his time, yet they have ceased
being loyal to him in my time. You shall not fight because it would mean
his death. 'While breath is in the body, the legs yet walk'—the temples are
in ongoing distress, (9) it having occurred²² in the chief of them (Thebes)
in proportion to its being greater than the (other) nomes. How will it be
refounded? Your [...] have come to pass, with its ruler alone during the
month, while my body is thin and I am afflicted, since he has transgressed
the [wisdom (?)]²³ concerning it every day. I have discovered no plans for
knowing how to heal it outside of [begging (?) on its behalf to the]⁵ god
and offering to him on its behalf with sustenance that he has given²⁴ in

order to pacify him—that is Re-Horachty—[with what is desired:] this Effective Eye (Thebes) of his that is in this land. May it happen that he rekindle it in order to enlighten the darkened land with his brazier (?) [...]." (10) Now, then, he finished delivering this speech to his listeners, while their hearts were glad [on account of it] more than [any]thing. [... They said "...] O image [....] all your [plans,] may they come to pass. If, then, god is gracious to us, let him set straight the land under you. You are the Prince [...] the effective one, the good rudder, the prow rope in the hand of the valiant captain, one excellent of work, one valiant in doing it at any time, for the divine offerings have been speedily brought by hand before you. May your thoughts be brought to bear upon them. These are the best offerings that he has made.[24] (11) Thus you should give to him according as he has given to you. Giving to the giver is profitable. [We] shall be joyful on account of you, without your enemies—who are nonexistent. Would that we had, moreover, [...] his dignity. It is for those yet to be that he has done it."

Then there was said to them by this Overseer of Upper Egypt: "Let our army [be marshalled] in one place so that we might put together for him an expedition." Then it was done in accordance with what he had said. Thus they loaded his ships with all these things of his before all his partisans, comprising the royal children, the grandees, and officials (12) who were accompanying him, both male and female, and the entourage of his progenitor, his army and his followers, with no limit to them. As for the ships, moreover, in each one of them was a multitude, burdened with offerings and praying that he have valor, with the ships in [...] their [...], whose number was unknown, and (as for) the sailors, as many as there were, everyone was bearing his incense. There was no end to the flotilla of those who came of their own volition, with other multitudes of troops [on the] river (?) [...] (13) because of the extent of his justification in their hearts, like (that of) the son of Osiris. Then he went on board, while the crews were in exultation, so that the Two Lands quaked behind him, shouting up to heaven. The sky brightened even with the goodly breeze of the north wind, the duplicate of what it had provided for him at each occasion when sails were seen [...] on[9] the water like the stars on the belly of the body of Nut, as when Horus sails southward in the Feast of Burning, prepared for his inher[itance] in triumph, with the river banks shouting and the desert edges in joy until he put to land at Thebes in front of [his] ships and the sacred Userhat barge of Amon [...] (14) with the fluttering of his army like (that of) a bird pond when it swarms at the season of Inundation, as they came before him with willing heart to beg victory for him.

Then they found Thebes creating jubilation, with Karnak clapping a beat [for him] like the clap of the songstress on the occasion when the runner approaches her,[25] and with every functionary who was important in "God's Heaven" (Thebes?) and the "Pillar-of-his-Mother" priest in Upper

Egyptian Heliopolis. Then he made a [great] oblation [for] his lord, his noble god, greater than the (other) gods, Amon-Re, Lord of the Thrones of the Two Lands, and for the Ennead that is in Karnak, the Lords of heaven [and earth], being surrounded with an o[blation consisting of] (15) short-horned cattle, gazelles, ibexes, oryxes, fattened geese in tens of thousands and thousands, and birds of the mar[sh[5] ...] Thus he conveyed the tribute to the broad halls of [his] temple estate, with no[26] end to every benefaction: bread and beer [without] their number, basins overflowing with wine [and mil]k, the grounds with fruits and vegetables, honey, pomegranate wine, and likewise heaps [of] myrrh and incense. Then he offered these with a contented heart, valiant [...] (16) the great god who is in Thebes.

There occurred the processional appearance of this noble god in order to accept this oblation of his, while his Ennead was in joy at receiving it in (?) [...] The First Prophet of Amon, Osorkon, spoke (?) before the great god [in front of] his army, saying while extolling [Amon] the [great] god: "Is there anyone who is your chief [...] another as superior [...], that you should be silent with respect to his coming, although the cities were in uproar, the nomes [in turmoil, with disturbance in][5] each one of them, and every man within them saying: 'I am the one who will seize this land.' [...] (17) Have you acted against Thebes as you have acted against them? When it was unjust, then you were agreeable to it, so that his nome came to be [in distress (?)][5] ...] their lord altogether in very truth. The [...] superior (?) over (?) [...] whom you have elevated for them. Pay heed to the call [...] to the extent of that which your disk encircles, since they have seen its (Thebes') subjugation beneath you, while you have not been lenient concerning [...] all the gods, in order to put it (Thebes) in your hands so that [it] might be free [from harm (?)] (18) Pay heed to the Lord of the Divine Words (Thoth), who first thought of the name of the Two Lands after he had made the name [of Thebes (?) ...] every [cit]y[5] with respect to it in order to cause the entire land to say: 'Let[5] the land [...] companions (?). May he give daily offerings per month [... Theb]es (?) [...], it being [...] in one day.' As your very noble *ka*-spirit endures, [...] your [...], your disk that is in the sky, it goes well for this land when you are satisfied with h[umility (?)][27] before you [...] (19) Thus you should dispel our leniency concerning it (Thebes) [...] your [...], since they have heard [... Does] the Eye of Re shine for you because of me? As I live, [...] which you have made. Does [the Eye of Re] shine [for me because of you?[5] ...], since life and death are upon your mouth, nor can you be repelled in heaven or on earth [...] troops numerous as the sands as well as infantry [...] (20) [...] regarding them in [...] my strong arm will strengthen Thebes, [...] find [...] every bull together with [...] of the Lord of the gods,[9] since I have been anxious since my birth until today regarding[9] [...] every [...] the Lord of the gods [...] every [...] as a protector. You are [...] (pl. 22, line 1) He is [...], since he has injured millions because of what your *ka*-spirit and all the gods of heaven and earth said."

The great god drew toward him and came toward his voice in [the midst of] the multitude, and he assented greatly [...] He has [...] for them, since he has appointed their lord today in order to [... become] as a companion [...] Then he placed him as [...].

Main Text Subsequent to Revolt of Harsiese at Accession of Sheshonq III (Epigraphic Survey 1954, pl. 22, lines 2–21; Kitchen 1986, 332 §294)

[...] n sb(ỉ).w ḥr≠f n ḏd wꜥ ỉr [... m] rꜣ-ꜥ m wry.w n.w ḫnw tꜣ pn ḫpr wnn≠f ỉm m wꜥw tm ḫp(r) wꜥ n mrỉ [ḥnꜥ≠f(?)...] hrw ḫp(r) sḏm.t nfr.t ỉy.t m Wꜣs.t r snḏm ỉb≠f wr ḏd ꜣw ỉb≠k n(n) ḫf.tyw≠k s[r] n≠k nṯr ꜥꜣ ḫpr sḫꜣ ḏd≠k n≠f [...] (3) [...] mk ỉr≠f ḏd.t≠k n pḥ nw dỉ.ḥr≠k pr.w m šms≠f m mḥ ỉb≠k n mšꜥ m kꜣ(ỉ) sḫr.w n ꜥḥꜣ mdw≠k pw rn wr [n ꞽmn(?) ...] qꜣb ꜥꜣb. wt n bꜣ ỉr st snḏ≠f ꜥq.[t] m ḥ.t nb.(t) ḥr tm mḥ n≠f sr.n≠f ỉw n≠[f p].t m tꜣw nb mrr≠f r (w)ḏ(ỉ)≠f r tꜣ m Wꜣs.t

[...] (4) nb ꜥꜣ ꞽmn ḥtp m nḫt.w≠f psḏ.t≠f ḥꜥꜥ.w ꜥq≠f m-ḫnw≠s smꜣ≠f ḥꜥ.w≠[f m] mw ḥr(y)-ỉb n ꜣḫ.t wnn≠f ỉm≠s m wỉn [... ꜥḥꜥ.n ỉr.n≠f ḥtp. w-nṯr m ḥꜣw ḥr wn] m-bꜣḥ m ḥ.t nb.(t) nfr.t wꜥb.t ḏd.n p.t qmꜣ.n tꜣ sḫpr. n ỉr.{t} wnn.t sḫm.t.n≠f ỉr.(t) n≠f ḫnty m ḥḥ.w n.w ḫ.wt mỉ nt.t r ḥb≠f nfr n.{w} ꞽp.t rs(y).t [...] n≠f n nb r ḏr [...]w[...] n nb tꜣ.wy(?) [...] (5) wꜣb.wt ỉwḥ m qmỉ ḥ(wỉ).t Ḥꜥpy ḥr sꜣtw nb m snf n ỉwꜣ.w wnḏw.w ꜥ.wt ḫꜣs.t n(n) rḫ tnw≠sn qbḥ.(w) m tnw [šꜥ(?)²⁸ ...] ḥr≠f ḥm.w-nṯr ꜥꜣ.w ỉt.w-nṯr ꜥꜣ.w [...] ỉ[mn wnw.t] ḥw.t-nṯr mỉ-[q]d≠sn n mꜣ[w.t(?)]²⁹ ... dỉ≠f(?)] pḥ ỉwty.w nty.w ỉm≠sn m dd≠f n≠sn

ꜥḥꜥ.n ḏd.n≠f n≠sn ỉr.t m bỉꜣ.t n wr.t m [...] p(3) nṯr ꜥꜣ n [...] (6) r rdỉ. t rḫ sy ỉw.w m ḥḥ.w n.w rnp.wt n pꜣy pr (n) sbb nḥḥ ḥnꜥ ḏ.t r dỉ.t snḏ≠[f] m-ḫnw ḥ.t≠sn n wr n bꜣ.w≠f ḥr s ỉ[n ꞽmn(?) mꜥ]n spr n≠f ḥr≠s n(n) wḥm ꜣbd [...] dỉ ts nb n.w ḥtp.w-nṯr n ꞽmn ḥnꜥ psḏ.t≠f

ḥnꜥ ḏd ỉrw sḥw(y) (n) sp nb n ꜣḫ.w ỉr.n≠ỉ n≠sn m mꜣwy šꜣꜥ n ḥsb.t 11 ḥr ḥm n ỉt≠ỉ šps ny-sw.t bỉ.ty sꜣ Rꜥ [Ṯkrỉwt] mrỉ-ꞽmn (7) r ḥsb.t 28 ḥr ḥm n ny-sw.t bỉ.ty Wsr-mꜣꜥ.t-Rꜥ-stp-n-Rꜥ sꜣ Rꜥ Ššnq mrỉ-ꞽmn sꜣ Bꜣst.t dỉ ꜥnḫ ḏ.t rḫ ỉr[y]

[...] ỉ[p].t n ḫsbd mꜣꜥ 2

twt n Ḥr(y)-š≠f [1(?)]

[... n Ṯkrỉwt mrỉ-ꞽmn(?)]³⁰ ꜥnḫ ḏ.t

ꜥnty.w šw ḥqꜣ.t 2

snṯr wꜣḏ [ḥb]n.(t) ꜥꜣ.(t) 50

bỉ.t (ḥbn.t) ꜥꜣ.(t) 50

b(ꜣ)q (ḥbn.t) ꜥꜣ.(t) 50

dỉ≠f r gꜣ(ỉ).t n.(t) ꞽmn ns.(ty) tꜣ.wy m Ḥw.(t)-bnbn

[nbw]-nfr dbn 6 qd.(t) 6.(t)

ḫ[s]bd [mꜣꜥ] dbn 25

nšm.t mꜣʿ.t (dbn) 1
ḥsb.t 24 ꜣbd 4 […]
(8) ỉn.w=f m-bꜣḥ ʾImn
nbw-nfr m Ḫnt(y)-ḥn-nfr dbn 3
wḏꜣ n nbw-nfr ḥr ḫsbd mꜣʿ 10 [+ x]
[… ṯ]bnk 1 dmd 2 nty n=sn
wꜣḥ [n mꜣw.(t)]
[…] nty ḥr=f nbw-nfr qd.(t) 5.(t) 1/6
ḫsbd mꜣʿ rp.t Mꜣʿ.t 1.(t) mss(?)[31] sꜣwy ḥr=f m nbw-nfr ỉr (n) dbn 1 qd.(t) 8.(t) 1/3
š[…] dbn 4 qd.t 3.(t)
mḫnm.t mꜣʿ ỉn(r) 1 ỉr (n) dbn 65 [+ x …]
dỉ=f r ṯs p(ꜣ) sḥtp […]
(9) dd=f m-bꜣḥ Mnṯ(w) nb Wꜣs.t dbn 20
dỉ=f m-[bꜣḥ] Mw.t wr.t nb.t ʾIšr(w) ḥmt
[…] ḥ[nq].t hn 100 ỉr (n) sšrw ḥqꜣ.t 2.t rʿ nb
[… nbw]-nfr [m Ḫn]ty-ḥn-nfr ẖr ḥḏwy[.t] 2.t m wʿ nb mḥ 3 ỉr (n) dbn 150
ỉr.n=f n=sn st[ꜣ].t sšny[32] m wꜣḥ n mꜣw.(t) (n) ẖr.t rnp.t hn 365 ỉr (n) nḏm.t n ḏtm.t ẖꜣr 23 [+ x …]
(10) wp-s.t
nty pr m tꜣ qꜣḥ.t Ḥw.t r [dỉ(?)] n=w ṯꜣ.tw=w (r) rw[.ty …]
[…] tꜣ štꜣ.(t) rsy.(t) m-ẖnw nꜣ šʿd.w-s[m] n pꜣ ḥm-nṯr tp(y) n ʾImn r […]
[… pꜣ sš ḥsb] ỉt n tꜣ štꜣ.(t) rsy.(t) ḥḏ dbn 4 qd.t 2.(t) pꜣ sš
ḥsb ỉt n tꜣ qꜣḥ.t Ḥw.t ḥḏ dbn 1 [+ 3(?)] qd.t 2.(t) dmd ḥḏ dbn 4 (sic) qd.t 4.(t) m ẖr.t rnp.t
wꜣḥ [n] (11) mꜣw.(t) r ḫꜣw.t Rʿ tp-ḥw.t n pr ʾImn sqn dgm hn 5
m ꜣbd nb ḫpr […]
[…] dbn 3 qd.t 3.(t)
ʿn[t]yw šw tp tꜣ Nḥsy ẖꜣr 3 ḥqꜣ.t 2.(t)
ḥmt dbn 1,000 rnp.[t nb …]
[dỉ(?)]=f m rnp.t ṯn m-bꜣḥ ʾImn-Rʿ ny-sw.t nṯr.w pꜣ nṯr ʿꜣ n ḏr-ʿ ḥḏ ḥtp sšn n 1 ỉr (n) dbn 200
sḥw sšrw n wꜣḥ m mꜣw.(t) ỉr.[n] (12) ḥm-nṯr tp(y) n ʾImn-[Rʿ] ny-sw.t [nṯr.w ḥꜣ]w.ty W[s]ỉrkn šꜣʿ-n ḥsb.t 22 r ḥsb.t 28 […]
[… ẖꜣr x +] 6 ḥqꜣ.t 3.(t) m ẖr.t rnp.t
ʿd šʿ 3 rʿ nb m-bꜣḥ nṯr pn ỉr (n) sšrw […]
[…]
[…] rꜣ […]
wnm.t sms sšrw ẖꜣr 35 ḥqꜣ.t 1.(t)
dmd ḥtp.[w]-nṯr [n] nṯr [p]n sšrw ẖꜣr 828 ḥqꜣ.t 2.(t)
wꜣḥ n mꜣw.(t) r pꜣ ḫn(ỉ) n ʾImn (n) ḥsb.t 23.(t)

šḥm.t 110 (13) ỉr (n) [sš]r ḫȝr [x +] 411 ḥqȝ.t 3.(t)
[ḥsb].t 24.(t)
wȝḥ [n] mȝw.(t) r pȝ ḥtp ʿȝ wʿb n [ʾI]mn […]
[…] ḫr.t hrw sšrw ḫȝr 1
(n) ʾImn-Rʿ ỉmy pr≠f ḥr s.t wr.t ḫr.t hrw sšrw ḥqȝ.t […]
[…] sšrw ḥqȝ.t 3.(t)
    dmd ḥtp.[w]-nṯr […]
[… n] ʾImn m wȝḥ n mȝw.(t) ḫr.t hrw sšrw [ḫȝr x ḥqȝ.t x 1/]20 1/40
(n) Mw.t wr.t nb.t ʾIšr(w) m ḫr.t hrw sšrw ḥqȝ.t 3.(t)
(n) Mw.[t] nb.t p.t ḥr(y.t) s.t wr.t ḫr.t hrw sšrw ḥqȝ.t 1.(t)
    n[t]y (14) m ḥnq.t r pȝy≠s ʿš n ḥmt rʿ nb sšrw ḥqȝ.t 2.(t) 1/2
    dmd nty mȝʿ m-bȝḥ [nṯr.t tn sšrw ḥqȝ.t 3.(t) 1/2
[…]
[(n) Ḫnsw] m Wȝs.t Nfr-ḥtp ḫr.t hrw sšrw ḥqȝ.t 1.(t) 1/2
(n) Ḫ[nsw] nb Mȝʿ.t ḥr(y) s.t wr.t ḫr.t hrw [sšrw …]
(n) Ḫns]w p(ȝ) ỉr sḫr.w […]
[…] wr rʿ nb sšrw […]
    dmd […]
[…] ḫr.t hrw sšrw ḥqȝ.t 3.(t) 1/4
wȝḥ n mȝw.(t) m-bȝḥ Mnṯ(w) nb [Wȝ]s.t sšrw ḥqȝ.t 2.(t) 1/2 1/4 1/10
[+ x]³³
    nty n ḥnq.t m-bȝḥ nṯr p[n] m ḫr.t hrw sšrw ḥqȝ.t 1.(t) 1/2
    dmd ḫr.t hrw sšrw ḫȝr 1 1/20 1/[x …]
(15) ḥtp.w-nṯr n Mȝʿ.t sȝ.t Rʿ ẖnm ʾImn ḫr.t hrw sšrw [ḥqȝ].t 1.(t) 1/20
1/40
(n) ʾImn-(m)-ʾIp.t ḫr.t hrw [sšrw …]
[…] ḥtp.w-nṯr m [wȝ]ḥ n [mȝ]w.(t) [n Wsỉ]r nb ȝbdw ḫr.t hrw [sšrw …]
[…] ḫr.t hrw sšrw ḥqȝ.t 1.(t)
(n) ʾImn-(m)-ʾIp.t(?) […]
[…] p(ȝ) ỉw m ʾIn-Mw.t ḫr.t hrw sšrw ḥqȝ.t 1.(t)
(n) Nmty nb Ḏwf(y) ḫr.t hrw sšrw ḥqȝ.t 1.(t)
(n) Nḥm.(t)-ʿwȝy ḥn[w …] ḫr.t hrw sšrw ḥqȝ.t 1.(t)
dmd ḥtp.w-nṯr (16) n ʾImn-Rʿ nb ns.wt tȝ.wy ḥnʿ psd.t≠f ḫr.t hrw
    wȝḥ n mȝw.(t) sšrw ḫȝr 22 1/8 1/10 ỉr (n) ḫȝr 1 [+ x …]
    wȝḥ n mȝw.(t) (n) Mnṯ(w) nb [Wȝs.t sš]rw ḫȝr 60 rȝ šd […]
    [… sw]n.t m wȝḥ n mȝw.(t) n […]
[…] ʾI[p].t-s.wt sšrw ḫȝr 30 […]
[… n]ty wȝḥ r pȝ ḥn(ỉ) n ʾImn n rnp.t tn s[ḥm].t 112 ỉr (n) sšrw ḫȝr
2,749
dmd m [wȝ]ḥ n ḥsb.t 24.(t) sšrw ḫȝr 8,039 ḥqȝ.t 2.(t)

(17) ḥtp.w-nṯr n ʾImn-Rʿ ny-sw.t nṯr.w pȝ nṯr ʿȝ n dr-ʿ
wȝḥ n mȝw.(t) n ḥsb.t 25.(t) ḫr.t hrw rȝ […]

[.. t3 g3(i).t ꜥ3.t] šps.(t) ỉr (n) sšrw ẖr 10 [+x] ḥq3.[t] 2.(t)

    bỉ.t hn 665 n [...]

[...] m rnp.t ṯn sšr[w ...]

ḥtp.w-nṯr [...]

[dmd m w3ḫ n m3]lw.(t) n ꞌImn-Rꜥ nb ns.wt t3.wy ḥnꜥ psḏ.t≠f š3ꜥ-n ḥsb.

t 22 r ḥsb.t 28 sšrw ẖr 11,616 ḥq3.t 1.(t) 1/20 1/80

    ḥtp.(w)-nṯr n Mw.t wr.t nb.(t) ꞌIšr(w) ẖr.t hrw k3 1 ỉr (n) k3 365 (18)

m ẖr.t rnp.t

    wp-s.t

p3 ḥm-nṯr tp(y) n ꞌImn (m)-ẖnw t3 mḏ.t n pr ꞌImn k[39 ...]

[... ḥml-nṯr tp(y) n ꞌImn [k]3 [...] dmd k3 [3]65 m-b3ḥ Mw.t wr.[t] nb.t

[ꞌIšr(w) m ẖr.t rnp.t(?) ...]

    [...] m-ẖnw p3 [...]

    [...] p3 [ḥm-nṯr tp(y) n] ꞌImn m snṯr bỉ.t ḥḏ dbn 62 [+x ...]

t3 st3.t (n) nḥḥ n ꞌImn nty ḥsb.ṯ n [n]3 sr.w

        ḥḏ dbn 40 qd.(t) 2.(t) 1/2

        (n) n3 Š3sw (19) n Pr-nb-tp-ỉḥ.w ḥḏ dbn 6 qd.(t) 1/2

n3 ḫ3w.w n [t]3 st3.t sšn32 n3 [...]

    [... ꞌImn-Rꜥ ny-sw.t nṯr.w p3 nṯr ꜥ3] n ḏr-ꜥ nty pr m-ḏr.t n3 wḫꜥ.w (n)

n3 ḥn.wt(?)34 [...]

    [...] hn 365 ỉr (n) ḥḏ [dbn ...]

    [...] Mnṯ(w)-Rꜥ nb W3s.t qꜥḥ Ḫnty-Mnw m-ḏr.t p3 sš [š]ꜥ.t n t3 ḥm.t-nṯr

n Mw.t ḥḏ dbn 36 qd.t 5.(t)

n3 [...].t [... p3 ỉmy-r3] št3.w35 bỉ.t hn 365 (20) ỉr (n) ḥḏ dbn 3 qd.(t)

6.(t) 1/2 dmd ḥḏ dbn 40 qd.(t) 1.(t) 1/2 dmd ẖr.t

        rnp.t ḥḏ dbn 195 [qd.t ...]

    [...] n pr.wy-ḥḏ n ḥm-[nṯr] tp(y) n [ꞌI]mn

    dỉ≠f(?) m(?)9 [...]

    [...] bỉ.t hn 1,000 dỉ r pr.wy-ḥḏ n pr ꞌImn

    w3ḥ [n] m3w.(t) n t3 g3(ỉ).t ꜥ3.t šp[s n ꞌImn ...]3[... r ṯn]w rnp.t m-ḏr.t

p3 ḥ3.ty-ꜥ n Pr-Sḫm-ḫpr-Rꜥ

        ỉw3 tp(y) 2

ꜥḥꜥ.n ỉr.t(w) wḏ.t ḥr≠sn m [ḏd ỉr p3 ntly [ỉ]w≠f smnḫ ỉr.n≠(ỉ) nb n

ꜥq.w≠sn36 (21) tm.n≠f37 th(ỉ) m wḏ.t.n≠ỉ38 ḥr ꞌImn ḥnꜥ psḏ.t≠f wnn≠f wnn

r3-pr pn ỉwty [sk] n ḏ.t mk dỉ≠ỉ 3ḫ.w≠f s m [3w.t-ỉb(?)] ỉr≠ỉ n≠f m ỉb mr.t

ỉr≠ỉ n psḏ.t[≠f] mỉ[t.t] ỉry rḫ.k(w)ỉ mr[.t nṯr.w ...] n ḫpr [...] ḫpr [... ỉr p3

nty-ỉw≠f ỉr r (?) r.w]-pr.w≠sn pgs.tw39 m-ḫt sḫ3≠f m pry.w nṯr.w ỉw [rn≠ỉ]

w3ḥ ḥr ỉr.n≠ỉ n p3y pr ḏ.t

(2) [...] of those who rebelled against him. Not one said: "Make [...]
also" among the great ones of the interior of this land. It happened that
he was there alone, in order that not one friend be [with him (?) ...] the
day. It happened that good news came from Thebes in order to comfort

his heart greatly, saying: "Be joyful, for you have no enemies. What the great god foretold for you has happened. Recall that you said to him [...] (3) Behold, he has done that which you said, although the moment has not arrived. Thus you shall provide an increase in his service. Do not put your trust in the army; do not devise plans for fighting. The great name [of Amon (?)] is your staff. [...] Double oblations for the soul who made them. Fear of him has penetrated every body, precluding disregard of him, since he has predicted that the sky would come to [him] with every sort of wind that he desired in order that he put to land at Thebes."

[...] (4) the great Lord Amon being pleased with his victories, his Ennead rejoicing as he entered within it (Thebes) and provided [his] limbs [with] water in the midst of (the season of) Inundation. He was in it (Thebes) casting aside [his former opponents (?) ... Then he made divine offerings in excess of what had existed] previously, consisting of every-thing good and pure that heaven has given, that the earth has produced and that the one who made existence has created, which he (Osorkon) had neglected to do for him beforehand, consisting of millions of things in accordance with what is proper for his goodly Southern Opet festival. He [...] for the Lord of the universe [...] for the Lord of the Two Lands (?) [...] (5) the hillocks being moistened with aromatic gum, the surge of an inundation on every piece of ground consisting of the blood of oxen, short-horned cattle and desert flocks whose number is unknown, and of waterfowl numerous as the [sands (?)[28] ...] before him (Amon), and the great prophets and the great God's Fathers [... priests and lector priests (?) of] A[mon and the staff] of the temple in its [entirety] a[new (?)[29] ... he caused (?)] those who lacked to attain the status of those who were pos-sessors among them by his gift to them.

Then he said to them: "Perform, now, a wondrous deed because of the greatness of [...] the great god. [...] did not [...] (6) in order to let those who are to come for millions of years to this estate of Him who Traverses Eternity and Infinity know it, and in order to place fear [of him] within their bodies because of the greatness of his wrath concerning it (Thebes). It is [Amon (?) who pun]ishes (?) the one who petitions him concerning it. A month will not recur [...] allowing any pilfering of the divine offerings of Amon and his Ennead."

Together with the statement: "Make a compilation of every instance of benefactions that I have done for them anew beginning in regnal year 11 under the Majesty of my noble father, the King of Upper and Lower Egypt, Son of Re, [Takelot], beloved of Amon (7) to regnal year 28 under the Maj-esty of the King of Upper and Lower Egypt, Usima're-setepenre, Son of Re, Sheshonq (III), beloved of Amon, Son of Bastet, given life forever.

The list thereof:

[...] two chalices of genuine lapis lazuli;

[1?] statue of Harsaphes;

[... of Takelot, beloved of Amon(?)],[30] living forever;

2 *heqat* of dry myrrh;

50 large *heben* of fresh incense;

50 large (*heben*) of honey;

50 large (*heben*) of olive oil;

What he gave to the shrine of Amon, the Enthroned One of the Two Lands in the Mansion of the Benben:

6 *deben* and 6 *kite* of fine gold;

25 *deben* of [genuine] lapis lazuli;

1 (*deben*) of genuine feldspar.

Regnal year 24, month 4 of [...] (of Takelot II):

(8) His tribute before Amon:

3 *deben* of fine gold from Lower Nubia;

10 [+ x] amuletic pectorals of fine gold and genuine lapis lazuli;

[...] and 1 vase; totaling 2 that are for them.

[New] endowment:

[...] that is upon it, 5 1/6 *kite* of fine gold;

1 statue of Maat of genuine lapis lazuli, with a sash (?)[31] upon it consisting of fine gold, amounting to 1 *deben* and 8 1/3 *kite*;

4 *deben* 3 *kite* of [...]

1 block of genuine red jasper, amounting to 65 [+x] *deben*.

What he gave to organize the giving of offerings: [...].

(9) What he gave before Montu, Lord of Thebes: 20 *deben*.

What he gave [before] Mut the great, the Lady of Asheru: [...] of copper.
[...]

100 *hin* of beer, amounting to 2 *heqat* of grain every day.
[...]

[... of] fine gold from Lower Nubia, with 2 lamps, each one being 3 cubits, amounting to 150 *deben*;

As a new endowment he made for them a lotus-shaped lamp[32] and in the course of the year 365 *hin* (of fuel-oil), amounting to 23 [+x] sacks of carob seed in heaps;

(10) Their specification:

What is issued from the district of Hû in order to [be given (?)] to them, when they are taken outside [...]

[...] the Southern Region from within the grass-cutters of the First Prophet of Amon to [...]

[... the] grain [reckoning scribe] of the Southern Region: 4 *deben* and 2 *kite* of silver;

and the grain reckoning scribe of the district of Hû: 4 (?) *deben* and 2 *kite* of silver; totaling 4 (*sic, for 8?*) *deben* and 4 *kite* of silver in the course of the year.

New (11) endowment for the altar of Re (on) the roof of the temple of Amon: 5 *hin* of castor oil in every month that there might occur [...]

> [...] 3 *deben* and 3 *kite*;
>
> 3 sacks and 2 *heqat* of first-class dry myrrh of the land of Nubia;
>
> 1,000 *deben* of copper [every] year [...]

What he [gave (?)] this year before Amon-Re, King of the Gods, the great god of the primeval time:

> 1 silver lotus-style offering table, amounting to 200 *deben*.

Compilation of items comprising new endowments, which were made by (12) the First Prophet of Amon-[Re], King of the [Gods,] and leader, Osorkon, beginning in regnal year 22 (of Sheshonq III) to regnal year 28 [...]:

> [...] 6 [+ x sacks] and 3 *heqat* of [...] in the course of the year;
>
> 3 cakes of fat every day before this god, amounting to [...] of grain;
>
> [...]
>
> [...] geese [...]
>
> nestling-feed: 35 sacks and 1 *heqat* of grain.
>
> Total of the divine offerings [for] this god: 828 sacks and 2 *heqat* of grain.

New endowment for the harim of Amon (in) regnal year 23:

> 110 women, (13) amounting to 411 [+x] sacks and 3 *heqat* of grain.

[Regnal] year 24:

New endowment for the great pure offering table of Amon [...]

[....] daily: 1 sack of grain.

(For) Amon-Re, who is in his temple in the sanctuary, daily: [...] *heqat* of grain.

> [...] three *heqat* of grain.
>
> Total of the divine offerings [for ...]

[... for] Amon as a new endowment daily: [x sacks] and [x +] 1/20 1/40 [*heqat*] of grain.

(For) Mut the great, the Lady of Asheru, daily: 3 *heqat* of grain.

(For) Mut, Lady of heaven, who is in the sanctuary, daily: 1 *heqat* of grain;

> what is (14) for the beer destined for her copper jug, every day: 2 1/2 *heqat* of grain;
>
> Total of what is offered before [this goddess: 3 1/2 *heqat* of grain.]

[...]

[(For) Khonsu] in Thebes Neferhotep daily: 1 1/2 *heqat* of grain.

(For) Kh[onsu], Lord of Maat, in the sanctuary, daily: [... of grain.]

[(For) Khons]u, the maker of plans [...]

[(For) ...] the great, every day [...] of grain.

> Total of [...]

[...] daily: 3 1/4 *heqat* of grain.

New endowment before Montu, Lord of [The]bes: 2 1/2 1/4 1/10 [+x][33]
heqat of grain;

what is for beer before this god daily: 1 1/2 *heqat* of grain; totaling
daily 1 1/20 1/[x] sacks of grain.

(15) Divine offerings for Maat, daughter of Re united with Amon, daily:
1 1/20 1/40 [*heqat*] of grain.

(For) Amon(em)ope daily: [... of grain.]

[...]

Divine offerings as a new endowment [for Osiri]s, Lord of Abydos, daily
[... of grain.]

[...] daily: 1 *heqat* of grain.

(For) Amon(em)ope(?) [...]

[...] the island of In-mut daily: 1 *heqat* of grain.

(For) Nemty, Lord of Djufy, daily: 1 *heqat* of grain.

(For) Nehemaway ("She-who-rescues-the-robbed") of the Residence
[...], daily: 1 *heqat* of grain.

Total of the divine offerings (16) for Amon-Re, Lord of the Thrones of
the Two Lands, and his Ennead daily.

New endowment: 22 1/8 1/10 sacks of grain, amounting to 1 [+
x] sacks [...]

New endowment (for) Montu, Lord of [Thebes]: 60 sacks of grain;

[...] fattened geese.

[...] of the sixth-day festival as a new endowment for [...]

[...] Karnak: 30 sacks of grain [...]

[...] which is endowed for the harim of Amon in this year: 112 women,
amounting to 2,749 sacks of grain.

Total of the endowment for regnal year 24 (of Sheshonq III): 8,039
sacks and 2 *heqat*.

(17) Divine offerings for Amon-Re, King of the Gods, the great god of
the primeval time.

New endowment in regnal year 25 (of Sheshonq III), daily: [...] geese.

[...]

[... the great] and noble [shrine], amounting to 10 [+x] sacks and 2 *heqat*
of grain;

665 *hin* of honey for [...]

[...] in this year: [...] of grain.

[...]

Divine offerings [for ...]

[...]

[Total of] new [endowments] for Amon-Re, Lord of the Thrones of the
Two Lands, and his Ennead, beginning in regnal year 22 (of Takelot

II) to regnal year 28 (of Sheshonq III): 11,616 sacks and 1 1/20 1/80
beqat of grain.
Divine offerings for Mut the great, the Lady of Asheru, daily: 1 bull,
amounting to 365 bulls (18) in the course of the year.
Their specification:
The First Prophet of Amon, from within the stable of the estate of
Amon: [...] b[ulls];[9]
[...]
[...] the First Prophet of Amon: [...] bulls; totalling [3]65 bulls before
Mut the great, the Lady of [Asheru in the course of the year.]
[...] from within the [...]
[...] the [First Prophet of] Amon, consisting of incense and honey: 62
[+x] *deben* of silver [...]
The sesame(?)-oil lamp of Amon that is reckoned to [the] officials:
> 40 *deben* and 2 1/2 *kite* of silver;
> and to the Shasu Bedouin (19) of Aphroditopolis (Atfih): 6 *deben*
> and 1/2 *kite* of silver.
The incense pellets for the lotus-shaped lamp,[32] the [...]
[...]
[...Amon-Re, King of the Gods, the great god] of the primeval
time, which is issued through the agency of the fishermen of the
marshes (?)[34] [...]
[...] 365 *hin,* amounting to [... *deben*] of silver.
[...]
[...] Montu-Re, Lord of Thebes, of the district of Akhmim, through the
agency of the letter scribe of the Prophetess of Mut: 36 *deben* and 5
kite of silver.
The [...]
[The overseer of] scrub-lands:[35] 365 *hin* of honey, (20) amounting to
3 *deben* and 6 1/2 *kite* of silver; totaling 40 *deben* and 1 1/2 *kite* of
silver; totaling in the course of the year: 195 *deben* and [... *kite*] of
silver [...].
[...] of the Double Treasury of the First Prophet of Amon.
What he gave (?) as (?)[9] [...]
[...] 1,000 *hin* of honey, given to the Double Treasury of the estate
of Amon.
New endowment for the great and noble shrine [of Amon ... each]
year through the agency of the mayor of Persekhemkheperre: 2 first-
class oxen.
Then a decree was made concerning them [saying: "As for the one
who] will confirm all that I have done for their provisions,[36] (21) not having[37] transgressed against what I have decreed[38] for Amon and his Ennead,
he shall exist as long as there exists this temple, which is indestructible

forever. Behold, I have presented his benefactions with the result that men [are in joy (?)]. It is with a willing heart that I have acted for him and for his Ennead likewise, since I know that which [the gods] desire [...] to happen [...] happen [... As for the one who will act against (?)] their temples, may one spit[39] when he is remembered in the houses of the gods. My [name] is enduring because of what I have done in this house, forever."

(3) FINAL ADDENDUM IN YEAR 29 OF SHESHONQ III (EPIGRAPHIC SURVEY 1954, PL. 22, LINE 22; KITCHEN 1986, 338–39 §299)

(22) ḥsb.t 29.(t) ḥtp.w-ntr n ʾImn-Rꜥ nb ns.wt tꜣ.wy m Ḥw.t-bnw(?) wꜣḥ n mꜣw.(t) ỉkw (ḥqꜣ.t) 1.(t) ḫdw[40] (ḥqꜣ.t) 1.(t) ỉr (n) bd.t ḥqꜣ.t 2.(t) m ḫr.t hrw n.t rꜥ nb

Regnal year 29. Divine offerings for Amon-Re, Lord of the Thrones of the Two Lands in The Mansion of the Phoenix (?). New endowment: 1 (*heqat*) of sesame and 1 (*heqat*) of *khedju*-bread,[40] amounting to 2 *heqat* of emmer in the course of every day.

NOTES

1. For the compound "his praised and beloved one," see Erman and Grapow 1926–63, 3:156/22.

2. In the traditional title string of ỉry-pꜥ.t ḥꜣ.ty-ꜥ "hereditary noble and count" (lines 6 and 19), the word should be distinguished from the similarly written ḥꜣw.ty "leader" (conflated by Caminos), found in the combination "great general and leader" (lines 5 and 12).

3. Caminos read the final enigmatic signs mr.ty(?)⸗f "(with) what he will like (?)." For the logogram ꜥrq, see Erman and Grapow 1926–63, 1:212 ("completion"). The same glyph with a stroke may be read ꜥr.t or ꜥ "document," with reference to these terms in lines 32 and 35, or perhaps wḏ.t "decree," with reference to line 39.

4. For notions of "encircling," see Ritner 1993b, 57–67.

5. Restoration suggested with hesitation by Caminos.

6. Or read nb m rm[y ḥr] ḫfty wp.ty⸗fy ỉꜣ.t "The lord is be[wailing] the enemy who will divide the office"?

7. Versus Caminos, who emends to ỉmy.t-rꜣ "utterance."

8. As a resident of distant el-Hibeh, Osorkon is at pains to stress his special devotion to Amon of Thebes rather than to his local deity, Harsaphes of Heracleopolis (depicted as Amon's messenger in line 22). Harsaphes is surely the "god in the other loyal city."

9. Copied traces unread by Caminos.

10. The "Maiden" is the personification of Thebes; cf. the depiction of Thebes the Victorious on the Bubastite Portal victory relief of Sheshonq I, line 25, above, p. 205.

11. Legal, as well as biological, term indicating "trustee."

12. Caminos read tꜣ "land."

13. Caminos, overlooking the resumptive pronoun (r⸗s) and common phrase wꜣ r "fallen into a state" (cf. lines 24, 31, 32), read r swꜣ r-tḫn ḏf⸗s "in order to banish the injurer of its pupil."

14. Ignoring feminine ending as otiose, or read "she who acted" with indictment of Thebes as sponsor of evil.

15. For the annual levy (ḫtr), see Redford 1972, 145–54.

16. Carving error of r for ṯ, or phonetic spelling with nr for l; see Caminos 1958, 60–61 §84t.

17. Or, with Caminos, "until I am on his throne." See Gardiner 1999, 126, §163.11.

18. Restoration suggested by Jansen-Winkeln 1985, 291–93.

19. Traces fit m or gs; unread by Caminos; Jansen-Winkeln 1985 suggested mỉ(?).

20. For previous discussions of this passage, see Caminos 1958, 88–89; and the remarks of Kitchen 1986, 181–82, 331 n. 488 and (rebutting recent attempts to revive the notion of an eclipse) 546–50 §§454–61. Contra Caminos (1958, 89), this phrase constitutes the main clause, with the following passage "concessive." An ill-omened eclipse did not occur, yet a calamity occurred nonetheless.

21. Carved simply as "n" + bookroll; see Caminos 1958, 90, who posits the emended readings ⁽ȝ "great" or n p.t "of the sky." Or, without emendation, read nšn n mdȝ.t ḫpr "a disturbance (worthy) of record occurred."

22. Caminos (1958, 93) suggested that the carver omitted a long section of text with the (lost) feminine antecedent of the Old Perfective ḫpr.ṯ being "Thebes." The direct antecedent should, however, be mn.t "sickness" in the compound sn(ỉ)-mn.t "distress/calamity," and no text need be lost.

23. Cf. [sȝ]lỉ(r.t)≠f ḫr≠s (also followed by sḫr.w) on pl. 21, line 4.

24. Osorkon returns to the service of Amon that which the creator has himself produced. The statements in lines 9–11 express the theological basis for offering scenes in which god and king provide reciprocal offerings; see Ritner 1993a, 193.

25. The simile may refer to the jubilee ritual during which the king performs a public race. For the ritual and its musical accompaniment, see the Bubastis Jubilee Reliefs of Osorkon II, above, no. 78. Caminos translates sp as "threshing floor (?)."

26. Unique example of the Late Egyptian negative in these inscriptions.

27. If correctly restored, the passage would indicate that as Amon requires Thebes to be submissive, so Osorkon must not be. For sf(n), "leniency, undue mildness, meekness," see Caminos 1958, 107–8 n. r.

28. Cf. pl. 21, line 19 for the restoration.

29. The traces suggest n + reversed mȝ-sickle and bookroll, as in pl. 22, line 16.

30. Only the end of the cartouche is preserved. As the benefactions under Sheshonq III begin on pl. 22, line 12, the royal reference should be to Takelot II.

31. See Meeks 1980–82, 1:172, no. 77.1873. Caminos read m sȝwy "with gold alloy"; disputed by Harris 1961, 39 n. 8.

32. Although Caminos (1958, 131 n. cc) knew of no surviving examples of such lamps, the burial chamber of Tutankhamon provided two famous examples; see Edwards 1976, unnumbered pages 81 and 83.

33. Caminos read 2 1/4 1/6 1/x.

34. See Erman and Grapow 1926–63, 3:105/1. Caminos suggested ḫnttyw (Erman and Grapow 1926–63, 3:122/2) "and the slaughterers."

35. For the restoration, see Vernus 1977, 183 §10. The same title appears in The Larger Dakhleh Stela (S. Ashmolean 1894. 107a), no. 43, pp. 174 and 176.

36. Unread by Caminos; see Erman and Grapow 1926–63, 1:232, bottom (abbreviated writing).

37. Caminos discounted the "herring-bone" carving, here read as "n."

38. Although the preceding list details Osorkon's gifts to Amon and his Ennead, Caminos read wḏ.t n≠ỉ "what has been commanded to me."

39. Cf. the curse against social enemies in Papyrus Bremner Rhind, col. 27/3: "He will be spat upon each time that he is remembered"; discussed in Ritner 1993b, 87.

40. A special type of dough and the bread baked from it; see Meeks 1980–82, 1:172, no. 77.3004.

83. KARNAK GRAFFITO OF HORI
(LOUVRE E. 3336 = C 258)

Dated four months and ten days after the beginning of The Chronicle of Prince Osorkon, the inscription of Hori was carved on a window architrave of the central hall of Thutmose III's Akh-menu chapel, which served as the Karnak sanctuary during the Libyan era. Like the Karnak Priestly Annals inscribed in the same structure, the text of Hori concerns the priest's right of entry into the sanctuary. Unlike the Annals, however, Hori's graffito records not an induction but a petition for the restoration of privileges before the newly triumphant Osorkon. The circumstances perhaps reflect the competing factions among the Theban clergy, noted elsewhere in Osorkon's chronicle and in the Karnak Oracular Text against Harsiese (no. 85). Hori's claims by right of descent are significant, illustrating the beginnings of the "priestly caste system" of the Late Period.

For the text and translations, see Daressy 1913, 130–31; Kruchten 1989, 246, 257–63, and pls. 14 and 32 (labeled Louvre E 336); Kees 1953, 254–55; Daumas 1980, 283–84; Schott, 1950, 985, no. 144; and Breasted 1906–7, 4:374–75 §§752–54 (Graffito of Harsiese [sic]). See Kitchen 1986, 331 §292.

(1) ḥsb.t 11.(t) ḫr ḥm (n) ny-sw.t nb t3.wy Tkrỉwt mrỉ-ỉmn s3 3s.t dỉ ꜥnḫ ḏ.t tp(y) šmw sw 11 hrw n spr r W3s.t nḫt ỉr.t Rꜥ ḥnw.t r3.w-pr.w 3ḫ.t pw n.t ỉmn-rn≠f

(2) nỉw.t≠f n s3b-sš.(w) ỉn ḥm-nṯr tp(y) n ỉmn-Rꜥ ny-sw.t nṯr.w ỉmy-r3 mšꜥ wr ḫ3w.ty Wsỉrkn m3ꜥ-ḫrw s3 ny-sw.t n nb t3.wy Tkrỉwt mrỉ-ỉmn s3 3s.t ꜥnḫ ḏ.t m ḫb≠f nfr (n) tp(y) šmw ỉy

(3) ỉn wꜥb ꜥq n pr ỉmn ỉmy-3bd≠f n 3ḫ-mnw ḥr s3 3-nw Ḥrỉ s3 mỉ-nn [ꜥnḫ≠f]-n-Ḫnsw m3ꜥ-ḫrw m-b3ḥ p(3) ỉmy-r3 Šmꜥw r ḏd ỉnk wꜥb ꜥq n ỉp.t-s.wt ỉnk s3 n

(4) ḥm.w-nṯr ꜥ3.w n ỉmn ḥr mw.t≠ỉ s3 n wꜥb mty n sbḥ.t Šmꜥw nty ḏr-ḫnt ỉw ỉt.(w) n.w ỉt.w≠(ỉ) n ỉt-nṯr m33 sšt3 n P3w.ty-t3.wy šsp

(5) t3y≠î h d3≠î m-îr îsq n(y)-wî W3s.t ms≠î m-ḫnw≠s bn înk h(3) îwn3 dd.în≠[f] îr.tw¹ m

(6) wd.n≠k nb îy în ḥm-nṯr n ᵓImn-Rᶜ ny-sw.t nṯr.w rwdw ᶜ3 sš šᶜ.(t) n nb t3.wy Nb-nṯr.w(?) s3 Ḥrî ᶜḥᶜ.n≠f wᶜb≠f n š wᶜb swᶜb≠f

(7) n bd Šrp.t² šsp w3.t r 3ḫ-mnw t3 3ḫ.t n.t p.t pr.(t) îm r ᶜḥ3³ ᶜḥ.t n.t b3 ḥry šfy.t⁴ hy.t n.t

(8) b3⁵ d3î p.t snî n≠f ᶜ3.wy 3ḫ.t n.(t) P3w.ty-t3.wy m33 sšt3 Ḥr stî pr≠f ḫr rš(w.t) îb≠f nhm pḫ.n≠f Nw.t ḥry.{kw}t⁶ dg(3)≠f îmy≠f

(1) Regnal year 11 under the Majesty of the King, Lord of the Two Lands, Takelot (II), beloved of Amon, Son of Isis, given life. The first month of summer, day 11: the day of arriving at Thebes the Victorious, the Eye of Re, the Mistress of temples—it is the horizon of Him whose name is hidden,

(2) his city of recreation—by the First Prophet of Amon-Re, King of the Gods, great general and leader, Osorkon, the justified, royal son of the Lord of the Two Lands, Takelot (II), beloved of Amon, Son of Isis, living forever, in his beautiful festival of the first month of summer. There

(3) came the *wab*-priest with right of entrance belonging to the estate of Amon, the priest on monthly service in the Akh-menu shrine for the third phyle, Hori, son of the similarly titled [Ankhef]enkhonsu, the justified, into the presence of the Overseer of Upper Egypt in order to say: "I am a *wab*-priest with right of entrance belonging to Karnak. I am the son of

(4) great prophets of Amon on my mother's side, the son of a conscientious *wab*-priest of "the Gateway of Upper Egypt" (Thebes) in previous times, while the father of my fathers was a God's Father who beheld the mysteries of the Primeval One of the Two Lands. Accept

(5) my certificate, so that I might cross over (into the temple sanctuary). Do not delay! I am of Thebes; I was born within it. I am not an interloper." Then (he) said: "Let it be done¹ in accordance with

(6) all that you have commanded." Then came the prophet of Amon-Re, King of the Gods, the great agent and letter scribe of the Lord of the Two Lands, Nebnetcheru (?), son of Hori. Then he purified him (*wab*-priest Hori) in the pure lake, and he made him pure

(7) with natron of the Wadi Natrûn.² One took the road to the Akh-menu sanctuary, the horizon of heaven. One went forth from it to the "Place of Battle,"³ the palace of the *ba*-spirit whose dignity is exalted,⁴ the hall of (8) the Ram-spirit⁵ who traverses heaven. The doors of the horizon of the Primeval One of the Two Lands were opened for him. One saw the mystery of the luminous Horus. He went forth in joy, with his heart exulting, since he had reached the distant⁶ heaven and seen the one who is in it.

NOTES

1. The passage is here taken as the response of Osorkon, following the emendation of Daressy and Kees. Kruchten analyzed the passage as a final question by Hori: *in irr.tw m wd.n≠k nb* "Is it in accordance with all that you (Osorkon) have commanded that one has acted?"

2. A late spelling deriving from a hieratic error for the older Štp.t "Wadi Natrûn"; see Erman and Grapow 1926–63, 4:528/34; Ritner 1986, 193–94.

3. A section of the Akh-menu chapel, perhaps the open "New Year's court" or the inner cella. The name probably evokes the primordial site of the defeat of chaos; see Daumas 1980, 283–84.

4. The epithet puns on the name of the deity Harsaphes of Heracleopolis; see Erman and Grapow 1926–63, 4:457/1.

5. The term constitutes a pun on *ba*-ram and *ba*-spirit.

6. Ignored in all commentaries, the otiose "k" seems a visual marker of the Old Perfective, anticipating Demotic practice.

84. DONATION STELA FOR PRINCESS KAROAMA
(CAIRO JDE 36159)

Deriving from the small Karnak temple of "Osiris the Giver of Life (Wsîr p3 dd ʿnḫ), Lord of Eternity (nb ḏ.t)," this round-topped stela was recovered from illegal diggers by G. Legrain in 1902 and is notable for its unique representation. In the lunette, Amon and his son Khonsu stand behind a small altar, adored by the chantress Karoama, whose upper body projects from beneath the raised lid of a large paneled (funerary?) chest. Her left arm is raised in worship, while the right holds a papyrus roll, presumably a copy of the decree on her behalf. While Maspero has interpreted the scene as recording a posthumous endowment (*wakf*) for the funerary cult of the princess, Meeks (1979a, 612) and Fazzini (1988, 16) believed that the stela commemorates the establishment of her dowry. The explicit role of her brother, the high priest Osorkon, as intermediary in the donation is to be compared with the prominence accorded lineage chiefs on many donation stelae from the Delta. This benefaction for Karoama securely attests to the presence of Osorkon in Thebes in year 25 of his father, just prior to the latter's death and the ensuing usurpation of the pontifical office by Harsiese (B). Osorkon would not return to Thebes as high priest for over twenty years.

For the text (formerly Cairo 9/6/24/1), see Legrain 1903, 183 and the "note additionnelle" by G. Maspero on 185–86; Breasted 1906–7, 4:375–76 §755; with discussion and photo in Fazzini 1988, 4, 16, 34, and pl. XXXIII.2; Menu 1998, 143; and Spiegelberg 1913, 23*–24* (n. 2). For additional discussions of the text, see Meeks 1979a, 611, 612, 641, 646, and 667 no. 22.7.25; Caminos 1958, 110–11; and 1949, 255–59. See Kitchen 1986, 329 §290 n. 474, and 332 §294 (1). See further Kitchen 1995, xxiii §W.

Label for Amon

ʾImn-Rᶜ nb ns.wt tȝ.wy ḫnt(y) ʾIp.t-s.wt

Amon-Re, Lord of the Thrones of the Two Lands, Foremost of Karnak.

Label for Khonsu

Ḥnsw nfr-ḥtp

Khonsu Neferhotep

Label for Karoama

ḥs.(t) n.(t) ẖnw (n) ʾImn[1] sȝ.t ny-sw.t Krᶜmᶜ

The chantress of the Residence of Amon, the princess Karoama.

Main Text

(1) ḥsb.t 25.(t) ny-sw.t bỉ.ty Tkrrtỉ ᶜnḫ ḏ.t ḥm-nṯr tp(y) (n)

(2) ʾImn Wsrkn hȝr(w) pn smn

(3) tȝ 35 n stȝ.t ȝḥ.t n wḏb nmḥ[2] n

(4) ḥs.(t) n.(t) ẖn n ʾImn[1] sȝ.t ny-sw.t Krᶜmᶜ

Regnal year 25 (of) the King of Upper and Lower Egypt, Takelot (II), living forever, and the First Prophet of (2) Amon, Osorkon. On this day there was established (3) the 35 *arouras* of riverine and private[2] fields for (4) the chantress of the Residence of Amon,[1] the princess Karoama.

NOTES

1. For such chantresses, see the Funerary Stela of Tafabart (no. 5), p. 32, and Ritner 1998, 85–90.

2. For the term, see the Apanage Stela of Iuwelot, n. 4.

85. KARNAK ORACULAR TEXT AGAINST HARSIESE

Evidence of the competing factions surrounding rival high priests Osorkon (B) and Harsiese (B) may survive on a worn sandstone block, found inverted and reused in the foundations of the south wall of the axial passage of the Third Pylon at Karnak. Missing its introduction and date, the text records an oracular procedure conducted before Amon on behalf of Theban *wab*-priests, members of the lesser clergy, regarding fiscal abuses by higher clergy and bureaucrats. Once erected in the center of Karnak, near the customary site of oracular consultations, the copy of the divine decree served as a "public posting" for the concerned parties. Style and orthography indicate a date in Dynasty XXII, with specific terminology echoed in the Chronicle of Prince Osorkon. The priests' complaint that administrators have "transformed haves into have-nots" (line x+5) finds its inverse counterpart in Osorkon's claims to have caused "the have-nots to attain the status of the haves among them" after the revolt of Harsiese in the reign of Sheshonq III (pl. 22, line 5). Harsiese himself seems to appear in the Karnak oracle, not in the capacity of high priest, but as the southern administrator with the archaic title "Magnate of the Ten of Upper Egypt," who is summoned to witness and enforce the decision of Amon in favor of the petitioners (x+7). Vernus has suggested that the document reveals Osorkon's partisans to have been among the lower clergy, in contrast to Harsiese's support among the local elite. The text was left *in situ* and reburied following its discovery in 1968, and no measurements are available.

For the text, translation, and discussion, see Vernus 1980, 215–33 and pl. LIII; and Serge Sauneron and Jacques Vérité 1969, 271–74. See Kitchen 1986, 578 §517.

[…] (x+1) […] n [p]r(?) ḥr […] n […] (x+2) […].n(?) ḫpr ḥn ꜥ≠n pr.w≠n ḥr […] ḥr psd≠n … ḥr m[… n]ḥr.w(?) … (x+3) […]≠n ỉw≠n m ḥm.w 3ḫ n [nb≠sn dd ỉry]≠ỉ ỉry≠ỉ m 3.t mtn n3 ỉry.w (x+4) md3.t ḥr šsr gs≠n skm(w) ỉn≠sn shy nn shw(?)≠n[1] ḫft ḥsb n [ḥr.t] rnp.t [g3]w(?)≠n ḥr s.t-ḥr≠sn ỉy(x+5)≠sn m ḥ3q m spy r 3w≠f šsp≠sn nsp.w shpr≠sn nty.w m ỉwty.(w) [ꜥ]wn-r3 ḥr≠n (x+6) ỉw sšm≠n m ḥ3w n≠ỉ ỉw≠k ḥr ḥrw≠n ḥsf≠k 3d.w m 3.t≠sn ḥnn wr sp-2 ỉn p3 nṯr ꜥ3 (x+7) ꜥḥꜥ.n rdỉ.n≠f nỉs.tw r wr md Šmꜥw[2] ḥsf n nỉw.t Ḥr-s3-3s.t sr.w rwd.w n.w Šmꜥw wd(ỉ) shr.w m-[ḫ]t (x+8) r.w-pr.w r ỉr wšb3 ḥr s3mw.w n k3≠f dw3.w Rꜥ r ḥ.t Nw.t wdy.t Skt.t sqd.t Mꜥnd. t (x+9) ỉs.t≠sn[4] f3(ỉ) ḥr≠sn dw3 nṯr n k3≠f ḥn.t≠sn ms[nḥ] m dd ỉw≠n rwỉ t3 [s]r[w.t(?)] ỉ-t3y n (x+10) p3 ỉmy-r3 št3.w[5] ḥn≠ n3 k.(t)-ḥ.t nwt nty šmỉ [r] p3 pr-ḥd n p3 ḥm-nṯr tp(y) n ꜣImn nn rdỉ≠n ỉw [nty nb r] sm(x+11)ỉ m-b3ḥ m-3w d.t ḥnn ḥr≠s wr sp-2 pr nb m r3≠sn wd.t n.t nṯr pn šps ꜣImn-Rꜥ ny-sw.t nṯr.w wr [(n) š3ꜥ (n) ḫpr] (x+12) ỉr.w [r ḥ]n n3 wꜥb.w n pr ꜣImn pr Mw.t pr Ḫnsw ḥr mw ḥr t3 tm d3(ỉ) [t3] r≠sn m 3w d.t ỉw ỉr [p3] (x+13) [nty ỉw≠f] smnḫ wd[.t] tn r rdỉ.(t) wnn≠s ỉw≠f ḥr ḥs.t n.(t) nb nṯr.w ỉw k3≠f s[mn]6 s3≠f r [s.t≠f]7 (x+14) [ỉr p3 nty ỉw≠f r th(ỉ)≠s] m-dỉ≠[sn] (r) 3w db ꜥ≠f ḥr nṯr m nỉw.t≠[f] wr ḥs[.tw≠f(?) …] (x+15) […] ỉw […]

[…] (x+1) "[…] going on […]…[…]

(x+2) […] our (?) […] It happened that our activity was restricted, our revenues for […] on our backs … […] fled (?)

(x+3) […] us, we being servants useful to [their lord, saying: 'I shall act]; I shall act,' at an instant. Behold, the (x+4) bookkeepers are killing our half (share), which they have caused to end in ruin. We shall not collect[1] what conforms to the account for the [course] of the year, and we are deprived under their supervision. They have come (x+5) as plunderers for the entire remainder. They have taken up the sword, and they have transformed 'haves' into 'have-nots,' being greedy concerning us. (x+6) Our condition is one of 'Would that I had.' May you come at our plea so that you might repel the wrathful ones in their decisive moment."

Very strong agreement by the great god.

(x+7) Then he (Amon?) caused that there be summoned the "Magnate of the Ten of Upper Egypt"[2] who maintains order in the city, Harsiese, and the officials and agents of Upper Egypt who issue directives throughout (x+8) the temples, in order to act as advocates[3] for those (priests) who bless his *ka*-spirit and who adore Re at the belly of Nut during the procession of the Night Barge and the sailing of the Day Barge, (x+9) while their crews[4] lifted their faces to thank god for his *ka*-spirit, their faces turned about in saying: "We shall withold the [cloth (?)] that is taken for (x+10) the overseer of scrub-lands[5] and the other woven material that goes [to] the treasury of the First Prophet of Amon. We shall not allow [anyone] to come [to] (x+11) complain in the divine presence for the length of eternity."

Very strong agreement concerning it, (namely,) everything that came forth from their mouth.

Decree of this great and noble god, Amon-Re, King of the Gods, the great one [since the beginning of creation,] (x+12) which was made [to or]ganize the *wab*-priests of the estate of Amon, the estate of Mut, and the estate of Khonsu, whether on water or on land, to prevent interfering with them for the length of eternity, while as for [the] (x+13) [one who will] confirm the decree, in order to cause that it be in effect, he shall be in the favor of the Lord of the Gods. His *ka*-spirit shall en[dure],[6] and his son shall be in [his position.][7] (x+14) [As for the one who will transgress it] with regard to [them] all, his blame shall be before the god in [his] city, greatly, while [he is] repulsed (?) [...] (x+15) [...] while [...]

NOTES
    1. Vernus emended to n{n} sḥwy≠n "we have not collected"; see 1980, 220–21. Or read nn sksk≠n "we shall not destroy."
    2. Vernus 1980, 222–23, read wr šmꜤ 10 (= md̲). Harsiese bears the same title in the Karnak Priestly Annals, text no. 9.2 (p. 49).
    3. Literally, "to make answer for," meaning "to protect."
    4. Vernus read (mỉ) qd≠sn. The nautical term "gang, crew," regularly associated with the solar barge, is here used for the collective *wab*-priests.
    5. See Vernus 1977, 183 §11.
    6. The determinative indicates the customary smn; Vernus suggested ḥr wꜣḥ(?).
    7. Vernus restored ns.t≠f.

Chicago OIM 10511.

G. SHESHONQ III

86. DONATION STELA OF WASHTIHAT (A)
(CHICAGO OIM 10511)

The stela, purchased by J. H. Breasted from the Cairo Antiquities dealer Maurice Nahman on 22 November 1919, measures 41.1 cm in height, 26.2 cm at its greatest (bottom) width, and approximately 6.2 cm in thickness. The lunette scene depicts a winged disk above standing figures of Osiris, Horus, and Isis, with the donor represented only by his name, carved in three short hieratic lines at the right edge. A text of seven inscribed hieratic lines details the donation and provides the earliest use within a donation stela of the standard "donkey curse" directed against potential transgressors. The stela is suggested by Meeks to derive from the Western Delta. Traces of red pigment adhere in the carved hieratic signs and line divisions.

This is the first integral publication of the stela. The author thanks the Director of the Oriental Institute for permission to publish the stela and John Larson, museum archivist, for the reproduced photograph. For discussions of the text, see Meeks 1979a, 627, 646, and 668 no. 22.8.3; and Yoyotte 1961a, 144 n. 7. See Kitchen 1986, 335 §296.

LABEL FOR OSIRIS
　　Wsỉr ḫnty ꜣImnt.t
　　Osiris, Foremost of the West

LABEL FOR HORUS
　　Ḥr sꜣ ꜣs.t
　　Horus son of Isis

LABEL FOR ISIS
　　ꜣs.t wr(.t) nṯr(.t) ꜥꜣ(.t)
　　Isis the great, the great goddess

DONOR REPRESENTED BY NAME ONLY BEFORE OSIRIS:
　　Wꜣš(2)ꜣtỉhꜣ(3)t[1]
　　Washtihat

MAIN TEXT
　　[ḥs]b.t 3 ḫr ḥm n ny-sw.t bỉ.ty nb tꜣ.wy Wsr-mꜣꜥ.t-Rꜥ-stp-n-Rꜥ (2) sꜣ [Rꜥ] Ššꜣ(n)q sꜣ Bꜣst.t mrỉ-ꜣImn ỉw Wꜣššꜣtỉ[h](3)ꜣtỉw dỉ.t [t]ꜣw stꜣ.t 10 n ꜣḥ.t n drp. w (n) wꜥb (4) n ỉt-nṯr wꜥb ḫꜣmww Ḥr sꜣ(?) Pꜣpꜣyw(?)[2] (5) n tꜣw sḫ.t nty

ḏd n⸗s wndw.t³ îr p³ (6) nty-îw⸗f th³⸗w nk s(w) ꜥ³.w nk ꜥ³.w (7) ḥm.t⸗f nk ḥm.t⸗f ẖrd.w⸗f ...⁴

[Regnal] year 3 under the Majesty of the King of Upper and Lower Egypt, Lord of the Two Lands, Usimaꜥre-setepenre, (2) Son of [Re], Sheshonq (III), Son of Bastet, beloved of Amon, while Washtih(3)at gives that 10 *arouras* of field as priestly subvention (4) for the God's Father, priest and carpenter Hori, son (?) of Papaiou (?)² (5) from that field which is called "the depression."³ As for the one (6) who will transgress them, may donkeys rape him, may donkeys rape (7) his wife, may his wife rape his children... ⁴

NOTES

1. For the form of the name, cf. Cairo JdE 30972, line 2, in Maspero 1893, 84, translated below, no. 105.

2. Or take the initial P³ as the possessive prefix "he of/son of" Paiou; cf. the Donation Stela of the Libu Chief Titaru (Brooklyn Museum 67.119) and the Donation Stela of Bakenatum (MMA 55.144.6), below, nos. 104 and 149.

3. For the term, see Gardiner 1948, 31.

4. The final traces are damaged and unclear. With minor variations, this "donkey curse" is attested from Ramesside times and is adopted in donation decrees from the reigns of Sheshonq III to that of Tefnakht. See Sottas, 1913, 149–50, 166, and 168; Janssen 1968, 171–72; and Marciniak 1974, 70–71 and pls. XI–XIA (for Ramesside antecedents).

87. DONATION STELA OF BAKENNEFY (A)
(CAIRO JdE 45610)

This limestone round-topped stela, measuring 0.40 m in height by 0.33 m in width, was recovered from reused building material in Heliopolis. The text preserves a donation made by Bakennefy (A), the presumptive heir of Sheshonq III. Bakennefy must have predeceased his father, who was succeeded by a junior son, Pamiu. In the lunette, a winged disk twice labeled hovers over an image of heaven with ten stars above a scene of Bakennefy offering to Osiris, Horus, and Isis.

For the texts, translation, and discussion, see Daressy 1916, 61–62; and Menu 1998, 143–44. For additional discussion of the text, see Meeks 1979a, 610, 627, 628, 645, and 668 (22.8.14). See Kitchen 1986, 344 §305, 477 table 10, and 490 table 21B.

LABEL FOR WINGED DISK
  Bḥd.(ty) nṯr ꜥ³
  The Behdedite, the great god.

LABEL FOR OSIRIS
ḏd-mdw ỉn Wsỉr
Recitation by Osiris.

LABEL FOR HORUS
ḏd-mdw [ỉn Ḥr]
Recitation [by Horus.]

LABEL FOR ISIS
ḏd-mdw ỉn 3s.t ᵓIw⸗s-ˤ3⸗s
Recitation by Isis-Iousâas.[1]

LABEL FOR PRINCE BAKENNEFY
ỉry-pˤ.t wr tp ḥm⸗f B3k-n-[nfy]
The first great Hereditary Prince of His Majesty, Baken[nefy.]

MAIN TEXT
ḥsb.t 14.(t) ḥr ḥm n ny-sw.t bỉ.ty nb t3.wy Wsr-m3ˤ.t-Rˤ-stp-n-Rˤ s3 Rˤ
nb ḫˤ.w Ššnq s3 [B3st.t] dỉ ˤnḫ mỉ Rˤ ḏ.t (2) ỉry-pˤ.t wr ḥr(y)-tp t3.wy s3
ny-sw.t s3 smsw n nb t3.wy ḫ3w.t(y) B3k-n-nfy (3) [s3 T3]-dỉ-B3st.t mw.t⸗s
T3-dỉ-B3st.t ḥnq n² 3ḥ.t st3.t 10 m shn (4) n wˤb p3 wb33 P3-šr-3s.t-dỉ s3⸗f
Ns-Wn-nfr n dmỉ P3-sbty-n-Šš[nq]

Regnal year 14 under the Majesty of the King of Upper and Lower
Egypt, Lord of the Two Lands, Usimaˤre-setepenre, Son of Re, Lord of
diadems, Sheshonq (III), Son of [Bastet], given life like Re forever. (2)
The great Hereditary Prince, Chief of the Two Lands, royal son and eldest
son of the Lord of the Two Lands and leader, Bakennefy (A), (3) [son of
Ta]dibastet whose mother is Tadibastet, donates 10 *arouras* of field into
the authority (4) of the *wab*-priest and butler, Padiesedi, whose son is
Neswennefer, in the town of "The Wall of Shesho[nq]."

NOTES
    1. For this goddess at Heliopolis, see Vandier 1964, 69–70.
    2. The Late Egyptian text employs the direct object marker later standard in
Demotic and Coptic.
    3. Read p3 ỉ3b.t "of the east" by Menu.

88. DONATION STELA OF THE MENDESIAN CHIEF HORNAKHT
(BROOKLYN MUSEUM 67.118)

Deriving from the important Delta site of Mendes, this limestone
stela records a donation of land for the support of a cultic flautist during
the reign of Sheshonq III. Reflecting relative tribal autonomy, the king is

replaced as intermediary by the local lineage chief of the Ma (Meshwesh), as is typical for the reigns of Sheshonq III and V. The round-topped stela measures 52.3 cm. in height, 32.3 cm in width, and approximately 6.5 cm in depth. In the lunette, a winged disk with pendant uraeai fills the space above the hieroglyph for heaven. In the main field, the chief Hornakht, distinguished by the Meshwesh plume worn horizontally in the hair, offers the sign for "fields" to the gods Harpocrates, Osiris, Banebdjed ("The Ram of Mendes"), and the latter's consort, Hatmehyt. Behind the chieftain, the beneficiary is depicted dressed like the chief in kilt and transparent over-kilt, but in conformity to his duties he is shaven bald and plays a double pipe. Accompanying each figure is a brief identifying legend in cursive hieroglyphs. Below the tableau, seven engraved hieratic lines record the text of the donation. This donation by Hornakht is paralleled in year 21 of Iuput II by a donation of Hornakht's son and successor Smendes to a certain Gemnefhorbak, probable son of the earlier beneficiary and also a temple affiliate of Harpocrates; see no. 121.

For the texts, photographs, and discussion, see Kitchen 1969–70, 59–67 and figs. 1–3; Yoyotte 1961a, 125 (no. 9); Fazzini 1988, 16, 34, and pl. XXXIII.1; and Meeks 1979a, 614, 627, 628, 633, 644, 651, and 668 no. 22.8.22. See Kitchen 1986, 345 §306, 491 table 22A, and 543 §449.

LABEL FOR THE WINGED DISK
> Bḥd.t(y) dỉ ꜥnḫ[1]
> The Behdedite, who gives life.[1]

LABEL FOR OSIRIS
> ḏd-mdw ỉn Wšỉr (2) dỉ ꜥnḫ
> Recitation by Osiris, (2) who gives life.

LABEL FOR BANEBDJED
> ḏd-mdw ỉn Bꜣ-nb-Ḏd.t
> Recitation by the Ram, Lord of Mendes (Banebdjed).

LABEL FOR HATMEHYT
> ḏd-mdw ỉn Ḥꜣ.t-mḥy.t
> Recitation by Hatmehyt.

LABEL FOR HORNAKHT
> wr ꜥꜣ ḥꜣ.wty (2) Ḥr-nḫt mꜣꜥ-ḫrw
> The Great Chief and leader, (2) Hornakht, the justified.

LABEL FOR FLAUTIST
> wḏn(wy) Ḥr-p(ꜣ)-ḫrd (2) ꜥnḫ-Ḥr-p(ꜣ)-ḫrd

The flautist of Harpocrates, (2) Ankhhorpakhered.

MAIN TEXT

(1) ḥsb.t 22.t (n.t) Pr-ꜥꜣ Šꜣšꜣnq ḥnk n Ḥr-pꜣ-ẖrd ḥr(y)-ỉb Ḏd.t m-ḏr.t n wr ꜥꜣ (n) Mꜥ ḥꜣ.wty Ḥr-(2)nḫt sꜣ n wr (ꜥꜣ n) Mꜥ Ns-Ḫb.t ꜣḥ.t stꜣ.t 10 dỉw n wḏnwy n Ḥr-p(ꜣ)-ẖrd ꜥnḫ-Ḥr-(pꜣ)-ẖrd (3) sꜣ n ḥry wḏnwy n Bꜣ-nb-Ḏd.t Gm-n≠f-Ḥr-bꜣkỉ ỉw≠w mn m-dỉ≠f r nḥḥ (4) ḏ.t pꜣ nty-ỉw≠f tꜣ≠w m-dỉ≠f (nk sw ꜥꜣ) nk ꜥꜣ ḥm.t≠f nk ḥm.t≠f ẖrd≠f[2] ỉw Bꜣ-nb-n-Ḏd.t nṯr (5) ꜥꜣ nb ꜥnḫ Ḥꜣ.t-mḥy.t Ḥr-pꜣ-ẖrd š≤d≠f m ḥsq tp≠f ỉw-bn-ỉw≠w dỉ šsp n≠f (6) šrỉ≠f ꜥꜣ ỉw pꜣ nty-ỉw≠f wḫꜣ tꜣy≠f nfr.t ỉw≠f mn m pꜣ tꜣ (7) mỉ-qd s nṯr.w mtw≠w dỉ pꜣy≠f šrỉ r tꜣy≠f s.t

Regnal year 22 (of) Pharaoh Sheshonq (III). A donation for Harpocrates, resident in Mendes, through the agency of the Great Chief of the Ma (Meshwesh) and leader, Hor(2)nakht, son of the (Great) Chief of the Ma, Neskhebit, (comprising) 10 *arouras* of field that are given to the flautist of Harpocrates, Ankhhor(pa)khered, (3) son of the chief flautist of the Ram, Lord of Mendes (Banebdjed), Gemnefhorbak, they remaining in his possession forever (4) and ever. The one who shall take them from him, (may a donkey rape him), may a donkey rape his wife, may his wife rape his child;[2] while the Ram, Lord of Mendes, the great god, (5) Lord of life, and Hatmehyt and Harpocrates shall slaughter him by cutting off his head; and they shall not allow his eldest son (6) to succeed him. The one who shall seek his welfare, (however), he shall abide in the land (7) like a man of the gods, and they shall place his son in his office.

NOTES

1. The tag dỉ ꜥnḫ is written twice, beside each ureaus. The ꜥnḫ-sign on the left is miscarved as a reed-leaf (ỉ).

2. The standard "donkey curse" has been truncated and the final word summarily carved (perhaps read sꜣ≠f "his son"). For this curse, see the discussion on the Donation Stela of Washtihat (Chicago OIM 10511), no. 86, n. 4.

89. FIRST SERAPEUM STELA OF PADIESE
(LOUVRE S. IM 3749)

The round-topped limestone stela, which measures .73 m in height by .45 m in width by .108 m in depth, contains the official commemoration of the burial of an Apis bull in year 28 of Sheshonq III. Beneath a winged disk, the lunette shows Apis as a standing, bull-headed man holding ankh and scepters and being adored by Padiese and his two sons. Given primary position as high priest of Ptah, Padiese is, however, indicated exclusively by his Libyan lineage rank, and he wears the distinctive, horizontal Meshwesh feather in his hair. The important sacerdotal title is instead transferred to his eldest son, Peftchauawybast, so that Padiese assumes quasi-royal

status between deity and high priest. Such incongruities prove the continued strength of Libyan ethnic bonds beneath a veneer of Egyptianization
and reflect Padiese's claim to the office by direct lineal descent from the
royal family. See also Padiese's later Serapeum stelae under Pamiu, below,
nos. 94–95.

For the texts, see Malinine, Posener, and Vercoutter 1968, 19–20 and pl.
VII (no. 21); Breasted 1906–7, 4:386–88 §§771–74. See Kitchen 1986, 193–94
§155 and 340–41 §301.

BELOW WINGED DISK

sw mḥ m ỉr wn≠f[1]

He is filled with what would make his existence.[1]

HORIZONTAL BAND BELOW DISK

ḥsb.t 28 (n.t) ny-sw.t bỉ.ty Wsr-mꜣꜥ.t-Rꜥ-stp-n-ʾImn sꜣ (Rꜥ) nb ḫꜥ.w
Šš(n)q mrỉ-ʾImn sꜣ-Bꜣst.t nṯr ḥqꜣ ʾIwnw

Regnal year 28 of the King of Upper and Lower Egypt, Usimaꜥre-setepenamon, Son of (Re), Lord of diadems, Sheshonq, beloved of Amon, Son
of Bastet, the god, ruler of Heliopolis.

LABEL FOR FIGURES

ḏd-mdw ỉn (2) Ḥp tm ꜥb.w≠f tp≠f (3) dỉ≠f s(nb) ꜥnḫ wḏꜣ n wr ꜥꜣ n
Mꜥ (4) Pꜣ-dỉ-ꜣs.t mꜣꜥ-ḫrw sꜣ n wr ꜥꜣ (5) n Mꜥ Ṯk(6)rỉwt mꜣꜥ-ḫrw mw.t≠f
Ṯs-Bꜣst.t-pr.(w) mꜣꜥ.(t)-ḫrw sꜣ n ỉry-pꜥ.t wr tp n ḥm≠f[2] (7) Ššnq mꜣꜥ-ḫrw
sꜣ ny-sw.t n nb tꜣ.wy (8) Wsrkn mrỉ-ʾImn dỉ ꜥnḫ

ḥs-mr≠f[3] wr (9) ḫrp ḥmww n Ptḥ Pꜣy≠f-tꜣw-(m)-ꜥ.wy-Bꜣst.t mꜣꜥ-ḫrw sꜣ
n wr ꜥꜣ n Mꜥ Pꜣ-dỉ-ꜣs.t mꜣꜥ-ḫrw (10) ỉr.n{n} Tꜣ-ỉry.(t)

ḥs-mr≠f s(t)m (11) n Ptḥ Ṯkrỉwt mꜣꜥ-ḫrw sꜣ n wr ꜥꜣ n Mꜥ Pꜣ-dỉ-ꜣs.t
mꜣꜥ-ḫrw ỉr.n{n} Ḥr≠s

Recitation by (2) Apis, whose two horns of his head are sharp. (3)
May he give health, life, and prosperity to the Great Chief of the Ma, (4)
Padiese, the justified, son of the Great Chief (5) of the Ma, Tak(6)elot ("B"),
the justified, and whose mother is Tchesbastetperu, the justified, son of the
first great Hereditary Prince of His Majesty,[2] (7) Sheshonq ("D"), the justified, royal son of the Lord of the Two Lands, (8) Osorkon (II), beloved of
Amon, given life.

His beloved favorite,[3] "Chief (9) of Master-craftsmen" of Ptah (high
priest of Memphis), Peftchauawybast, the justified, son of the Great Chief
of the Ma, Padiese, the justified, (10) born of Tairy.

His beloved favorite, the *setem*-priest (11) of Ptah, Takelot ("D"), the
justified, son of the Great Chief of the Ma, Padiese, the justified, born of
Heres.

MAIN TEXT

(1) ḥsb.t 28 (n.t) ny-sw.t bἰ.ty nb tȝ.wy Wsr-mȝˁ.t-Rˁ-stp-n-ʔImn sȝ Rˁ nb ḫˁ.w Ššnq mrἰ-ʔImn sȝ-Bȝst.t nṯr ḥqȝ ʔIwnw dἰ ˁnḫ mἰ Rˁ ḏ.t (2) ḥs-mr≠f wr ˁȝ n Mˁ Pȝ-dἰ-ȝs.t mȝˁ-ḫrw sȝ n wr ˁȝ n Mˁ Ṯkrἰwt mȝˁ-ḫrw mw.t≠f Ṯs-Bȝst.t-pr.(w) (3) mȝˁ.(t)-ḫrw sȝ n ἰry-pˁ.t wr tp n ḥm≠f Ššnq mȝˁ-ḫrw sȝ ny-sw.t n nb tȝ.wy Wsr-mȝˁ.t-Rˁ-stp-n-ʔImn⁴ dἰ ˁnḫ mἰ Rˁ ḥs-mr≠f wr ḫrp (4) ḥmww n Ptḥ Pȝy≠f-tȝw-(m)-ˁ.wy-Bȝst.t mȝˁ-ḫrw sȝ n wr ˁȝ n Mˁ Pȝ-dἰ-ȝs.t mȝˁ-ḫrw mw.t≠f Tȝ-ἰry.(t) (5) mȝˁ.(t)-ḫrw sȝ.t n wr ˁȝ n Mˁ Ṯkrἰwt mȝˁ-ḫrw⁵ ḥs-mr≠f s(t)m n Ptḥ Ṯkrἰwt mȝˁ(6)-ḫrw sȝ (n) wr ˁȝ n Mˁ Pȝ-dἰ-ȝs.t mȝˁ-ḫrw ἰr.n{n} Hr≠s mȝˁ.t-ḫrw [...]

Regnal year 28 of the King of Upper and Lower Egypt, Lord of the Two Lands, Usimaˁre-setepenamon, Son of Re, Lord of diadems, Sheshonq, beloved of Amon, Son of Bastet, the god, ruler of Heliopolis, given life like Re forever. (2) His beloved favorite, the Great Chief of the Ma, Padiese, the justified, son of the Great Chief of the Ma, Takelot ("B"), the justified, and whose mother is Tchesbastetperu, (3) the justified, son of the first great Hereditary Prince of His Majesty, Sheshonq ("D"), the justified, royal son of the Lord of the Two Lands, Usimaˁre-setepenamon,⁴ given life like Re. His beloved favorite, "Chief of Master-(4)craftsmen" of Ptah, Peftchauawy-bast, the justified, son of the Great Chief of the Ma, Padiese, the justified, and whose mother is Tairy, (5) the justified, daughter of the Great Chief of the Ma, Takelot ("B"), the justified.⁵ His beloved favorite, the *setem*-priest of Ptah, Takelot ("D"), the justified, (6) son of the Great Chief of the Ma, Padiese, the justified, born of Heres, the justified [...].

NOTES

1. Paralleled in Serapeum Stela catalogue no. 23, the phrase is unregistered in Erman and Grapow 1926–63, and the translation is provisional. If correctly analyzed, Padiese declares the fulfillment of his obligations for the embalming of Apis.

2. Miscarved as ḥm n "the Majesty of"; cf. line 3 of the main text.

3. In all cases, the beloved favorite of Apis.

4. The prenomen of Osorkon II.

5. Padiese's parents were full or half siblings; see Černý 1954, 23–24.

90. GATEWAY OF SHESHONQ III AT TANIS

One of the greater builders at the capital at Tanis, Sheshonq III sponsored the construction of a grand pylon gateway of granite to serve as the entrance into the enclosed temple precinct of Amon. Blocks of Rameses II from nearby Per-Rameses were reused and reworked, although the decoration and inscriptions remained incomplete. Only brief sections of text survive, but these are sufficient to establish the royal attribution.

For the texts, translation, and discussion, see Goyon in Montet 1960, 13–22 and pls. 9–13. See Kitchen 1986, 343 §304.

I. West Face, North Tower
Register II: Above an unlabeled scene of the king before Amon and Mut
Label for Hathor Who Follows Amon
> ḏd-mdw ỉn Ḥw.t-Ḥr nb.(t) nh.t […]
> Recitation by Hathor, Lady of the sycamore […]

West Face, South Tower
Register II: Above an unlabeled scene of the king before Amon and Khonsu
Label for Min-Amon
> ḏd-mdw [ỉn Mnw-ʾImn …] (2) […] n s.t(3)≠f …[…] (4) [dỉ.n≠(ỉ) n≠k(?)
> …] nb […] nb (5) […] nb […] nb
> Recitation by [Min-Amon …] (2) […] to his place (3) …[…] (4) ["Thus
I have given to you (?)] all […] all […] (5) all […] and all […]."

II. Interior Face of South Tower, West End
Register I
Label for the King before Amon
> sꜣ Rꜥ nb [tꜣ.wy(?) …]
> Son of Re, Lord of [the Two Lands (?) …]

Register II
Label for Disk with Pendant Uraei
> Bḥd.t(y)   The Behdedite

Label for the King before Ptah
> [ny-sw.t] bỉ.ty Wsr-mꜣꜥ.t-Rꜥ-stp-n-Rꜥ (2) sꜣ Rꜥ Šš(n)q mrỉ-ʾImn sꜣ Bꜣst.t
> nṯr ḥqꜣ ʾIwnw (3) […] n Ptḥ-Tꜣnn
> The King of [Upper] and Lower Egypt, Usimaꜥre-setepenamon, (2)
Son of Re, Sheshonq, beloved of Amon, Son of Bastet, the god, ruler of
Heliopolis. (3) […] for Ptah-Tanen.

Register III
Label for the King, Who Receives Life from a Lost God
> […] Wsr-mꜣꜥ.t-Rꜥ-stp-n-Rꜥ (2) […] Šš(n)q mrỉ-ʾImn sꜣ Bꜣst.t nṯr ḥqꜣ
> ʾIwnw
> […] Usimaꜥre-setepenamon, (2) […] Sheshonq, beloved of Amon, Son
of Bastet, the god, ruler of Heliopolis.

III. Interior Face of South Tower, East End
Register I: The king, protected by Bastet, offers Maat to Amon, Mut, and
Khonsu
> dỉ.(t) mꜣꜥ.t n ỉt≠f
> Giving Maat to his father.

Register II: Beside barks of Amon, Mut, and Khonsu
Label for Nekhbet Vulture
Nḫb.t ḥḏ.t Nḫn (2) dỉ ꜥnḫ wꜣs mỉ Rꜥ ḏ.t
Nekhbet, the White One of Nekhen, (2) who gives life and dominion like Re forever.

IV. INTERIOR FACE OF NORTH TOWER, EAST END

Label for Thoth
ḏd-mdw ỉn Ḏḥwty nb Ḥmnw (2) mꜣꜥ psḏ.t
Recitation by Thoth, Lord of Hermopolis, (2) who presents the Ennead.

Label for Nephthys
ḏd-mdw ỉn Nb.t-ḥw.t (2) dỉ.n≠(ỉ) n≠k ꜥḥꜥw (n) Rꜥ [...] n Rꜥ mr≠(ỉ)
Recitation by Nephthys: (2) "Thus I have given to you the lifetime of Re, the [...] of Re, my beloved.

V. ISOLATED BLOCK
dỉ.n≠(ỉ) n≠k ḥb ꜥšꜣ wr mỉ Rꜥ
"Thus I have given to you very many festivals like Re."

H. DOCUMENTS OF THE NEWLY RECOGNIZED SHESHONQ IV
(CA. 786–773 B.C.E.)

Objects formerly thought to exhibit unusual variants of the standard titulary of Sheshonq I (Hedjkheperre-setepenre, Sheshonq) have now been reattributed to a much later Sheshonq (Hedjkheperre-setepenre, Sheshonq, beloved of Amon, Son of Bastet, the god, ruler of Heliopolis), who will have ruled for the final twelve to thirteen years once attributed to Sheshonq III. This new Sheshonq "IV" is not to be confused with the controversial king traditionally given that number, who is renumbered as Sheshonq "VI" (so that Kitchen's Sheshonq VI becomes Sheshonq "VII"). For these reattributions, see Kitchen 1995, xxv–xxvi §Y.

91. CANOPIC JARS FROM TANITE TOMB (V) OF SHESHONQ III

A secondary burial in the tomb of Sheshonq III at Tanis included a sarcophagus and two fragmentary canopic jars. For the texts, see Dodson 1994, 83–84 (cat. 50/1–2), 93–94, 178–79, pl. XLIII; 1993, 53–58; revising 1988, 229–31. See Kitchen 1995, xxv-vi §Y; 1986, 545 §452.

JAR I
ḏd-mdw ỉn Ḥpw [...]

Recitation by Hapi [...]

JAR 2

ḏd-mdw ỉn [...] (2) Wsỉr Ḥd-ḫpr-Rʿ-stp-n-Rʿ ny-sw.t Ššnq mrỉ-ʾImn sꜣ Bꜣst.t nṯr ḥqꜣ ʾIwnw

Recitation by [...] (2) The Osiris, Hedjkheperre-setepenre, King She-shonq, beloved of Amon, Son of Bastet, the god, ruler of Heliopolis

92. DONATION STELA OF GREAT CHIEF NIUMATEPED (A)
(S. HERMITAGE 5630)

Now in St. Petersburg, this round-topped stela measures 46 cm in height and was purchased at Giza in 1911 for the Turaev collection. The stela probably derives from the West Delta residence of the Great Chief of the Libu, Niumateped (A). In the cursorily carved lunette, the Great Chief, distinguished by his erect Libu plume, stands before an altar and the deities Shu and Tefnut. The space behind the Great Chief is occupied by a large quiver. The lunette has no labels, and the text is in hieratic, with an addition inserted above line 4. The format of the donation text parallels those of Sheshonq V ("Regnal year X, while NN donates...").

For the text, see Turaev 1912, 2 and pl. I; Yoyotte 1961a, 142–43 §29, Document A; and Meeks 1979a, 616, 641, 652, and 666 (no. 22.1.10). See Kitchen 1986, 291 §249; 1995, xxv–xxvi §Y.

(1) ḥsb.t 10.t ḥr ḥm n ny-sw.t bỉ.ty nb tꜣ.wy (2) Ḥd-ḫpr-Rʿ-stp-n-Rʿ sꜣ Rʿ Ššnq nṯr ḥqꜣ (3) ʾIwnw ỉw wr ʿꜣ n Rbw Nꜣywmꜣtỉ ỉwpd(4)ỉ ḥnq ꜣḥ.t stꜣ.t 10.(t) n Šw Tfnw.t (4bis) m pꜣ tꜣ n Pr-ʿꜣ ʿnḫ wḏꜣ snb (5) mn≠w mn pꜣ šw šꜣʿ (6) nḥḥ ḏt ỉw (= r) nꜣy.w wʿb.w ʾI-ỉr≠f-ʿꜣ-n-qm ʾImn-(m)-ʾIp.t

(1) Regnal year 10 under the Majesty of the King of Upper and Lower Egypt, Lord of the Two Lands, (2) Hedjkheperre-setepenre, Son of Re, Sheshonq, the god, ruler of (3) Heliopolis, while the Great Chief of the Libu, Niumateped (4) donates 10 *arouras* of field to Shu and Tefnut (4 bis) from the land of Pharaoh, l.p.h. (5) May they remain just as the sunlight remains for(6)ever and ever with respect to these priests, Iirefaaenqem and Amon(em)ope.

I. PAMIU

The brief rule of Pamiu "The Cat" was confined to the north, and his claim to be "the god, ruler of Thebes," can indicate only his control of Tanis, the "northern Thebes." His name (commonly, if improperly, styled Pimay) displays the dynastic allegiance to the goddess Bastet of Bubastis. Contemporary monuments include construction and tomb debris from Tanis, five Serapeum stelae, and a bronze statuette. A donation stela from Bubastis may be dated in his name, but former attributions of scarabs and a Brooklyn papyrus from the Thebaid (16.205) are now discounted. A Serapeum Stela (Louvre no. 26) names his successor Sheshonq V as his son. A magical healing stela may date from the period before his accession (p. 69).

For the texts and an excellent overview of the reign of Pamiu, see Yoyotte 1988a, 155–78 and pls. 2–6. See Kitchen 1986, 348–49 §308; 1995, xxvi §Y (revising 1986 103 §83 and 348 n. 588).

93. BLOCKS 24–25 FROM THE SACRED LAKE AT TANIS

Among the blocks reused in the sacred lake of Tanis and recovered by P. Montet, nos. 24–25 retain vestiges of the cartouche of Pamiu, providing meager proof of his construction at the dynastic capital. Both blocks are of limestone, and no. 24 (broken and now lost) measured 26 cm in height by 31/36 cm in width, while no. 25 (Inv. Mag. 221) measures 65.5 cm in length by 16.4 in height by 65.5 cm in depth. The relative simplicity of the nomen on these blocks anticipates the archaizing style of Dynasties XXIV–XXVI. Contrast the more typical, and prolix, nomen on his British Museum statuette. For the texts, see Yoyotte, 1988a, 161–64 and pl. 3.

BLOCK 24

[Pȝ]-mỉ(w) [mrỉ(?)]-Ḥr [...]
[Pa]miu, [beloved of (?)] Horus [...]

BLOCK 25

[dwȝ(?)] nṯr [sp(?)] 4 P(ȝ)-mỉ[(w) ...]
[Adoring (?)] god 4 [times (?)]. Pamiu

94. SECOND SERAPEUM VOTIVE STELA OF PADIESE
(LOUVRE STELA IM 3697, CAT. NO. 22)

From the Serapeum catacombs derive a series of votive stelae recording the burial in year 2 of Pamiu of a sacred bull installed twenty-six years earlier in the reign of Sheshonq III. Two were erected by the Memphite pontiff Padiese (text nos. 94–95) and three by lesser clergy (text nos. 96–97). One of the latter group, discovered by Mohammed Ibrahim Aly in 1986, remains unpublished. Most of the stelae have not been fully translated. For the texts, see Malinine, Posener, and Vercoutter 1968, 21–23 and pls. VIII–IX (nos. 22–25); and Yoyotte 1988a, 160; 1961, 124. See Kitchen 1986, 102 §82, 193–94 §155, and 348 §308.

The Second Stela of Padiese is a round-topped limestone stela that measures .87 m in height by .455 m in width by .09 m in depth. Beneath a winged disk, the lunette shows Apis as a standing, bull-headed man followed by the goddess of the West and adored by three figures. The first of these is Padiese, high priest of Memphis, who wears the sacerdotal leopard skin but displays his Libyan ethnicity with unshaved head, prone Meshwesh feather, and titles reflecting his rank in the tribal lineage rather than the Egyptian priesthood. While technically high priest of one of the most prominent and powerful institutions in the country, Padiese seems to have preferred his Libyan associations, deferring Egyptian priestly honors to his sons Peftchauawybast and Harsiese (H). The latter son follows in the proper guise of the *setem*-priest, with sidelock, leopard skin, and scepter. A third figure is largely broken away. Both Padiese and Harsiese maintained their Libyan connections even in their tombs, where each is styled "Great Chief of the Ma" (Badawi 1944, 181; 1956, 157–58). Labels and the main text are in carved hieroglyphs, with later additions in black ink. Translated in Breasted 1906–7, 4:390–91 §§778–81.

LABEL BESIDE APIS
    ḥtp dî ny-sw.t Wsîr (2) Ḥp Ḫnt(y) îmnt.t nṯr ꜥꜣ
    An offering that the king gives (to) Osiris(2)-Apis, Foremost of the West, the great god.

LABEL FOR GODDESS
    ḏd-mdw în ᵓIr≠s-îmnt.t
    Recitation by She-(who)-makes-the-West.

LABEL FOR PADIESE
    wr ꜥꜣ nꜣ Mꜥ.w (2) Pꜣ-dî-ꜣs.t mꜣꜥ-ḫrw (3) sꜣ wr ꜥꜣ n nꜣ Mꜥ(4)šwꜣš Ṯk(5)rîwt mꜣꜥ-ḫrw
    Great Chief of the Ma, (2) Padiese, the justified, (3) son of the Great Chief of the Me(4)shwesh, Tak(5)elot, the justified.

LABEL FOR HARSIESE
    s(t)m n Ptḥ Ḥr-sꜣ(2)-ꜣst [mꜣꜥ-ḫrw]
    The *setem*-priest of Ptah, Harsi(2)ese, [the justified].

INK ADDITION BETWEEN APIS AND PADIESE
    Ḥp-î-îr-ꜥꜣ-wꜣ (2) sꜣ ꜥn-n-Mw.t (3) ḏ.t nḥḥ
    Hapiiraawa, (2) son of Anenmut, (3) forever and ever.

MAIN TEXT
    [ḥsb].t 2.(t) ꜣbd 2 n pr.t sw 1 ḫr ḥm n ny-sw.t bî.ty nb tꜣ.wy Wsr-mꜣꜥ.

t-Rᶜ-stp-n-(ʾI)mn dỉ ᶜnḫ sȝ Rᶜ nb ḫᶜ.w (2) [Pȝ]-my(w) [mrỉ-ʾImn] dỉ ᶜnḫ ḏd
wȝs mỉ Rᶜ ḏ.t mry Ḥp Ḫnt(y) ỉmnt.t nṯr ᶜȝ hrw pw(ȝ)[y s]tȝ nṯr m ḥtp r ỉmnt.
t nfr.t qrs.t(w)≠f m ẖr.t-nṯr rdỉ.t ḥtp≠f m ḥw.t(4)≠f n[.t] nḥḥ m s.t≠f n.t ḏ.t sk
ms.tw≠f (m) ḥsb.t 28.(t) r h(ȝ)w ḥm (5) [n] ny-sw.t bỉ.ty Wsr-mȝᶜ.t-Rᶜ-stp-
n-Rᶜ sȝ Rᶜ Ššnq mrỉ-ʾImn nṯr ḥqȝ ʾIwnw mȝᶜ-ḫrw ỉw≠sn ḥr ḥḥ nfr.w≠f (6)
m bw nb n.w Tȝ-mḥy gm.n.tw≠f r Ḥw.t-šd-ȝbd¹ m-ḫt (7) ȝbd 3 phr≠sn (mỉ)
rm.w ỉdḥ ỉȝ.(t) nb.(t) n.w Tȝ-mḥy bs.(8)tw≠f r Ḥw.t-kȝ-Ptḥ ḫr ỉt≠f Ptḥ rsy
ỉnb≠f ỉn wr ḫrp ḥmww stm m pr Ptḥ (9) wr ᶜȝ n nȝ Mᶜšwȝš Pȝ-dỉ-ȝs.t sȝ wr
ḫrp ḥmww s(t)m [wr ᶜȝ] (10) n nȝ Mᶜšwȝš Ṯkrỉwt ỉr{.t}.n sȝ.t ny-sw.t n ẖ.t≠f
mr.t≠f Ṯs-Bȝst.t-pr.w (m) ḥsb.t 28 ȝbd 2 n ȝḫ.t ᶜḥᶜ nfr n nṯr pn rnp.t 26

[Regnal] year 2, month 2 of winter, day 1, under the Majesty of the
King of Upper and Lower Egypt, Lord of the Two Lands, Usimaᶜre-setepenamon, given life, Son of Re, Lord of diadems, (2) [Pa]miu, [beloved of
Amon], given life, stability, and dominion like Re forever, beloved of Apis,
Foremost of the West, the great god. On this day (3) occurred the hauling
of the god in peace to the beautiful West so that he might be buried in the
necropolis. It was caused that he rest in his Mansion (4) of eternity, in his
place of infinity. Now, he was born (in) regnal year 28 in the reign of the
Majesty (5) of the King of Upper and Lower Egypt, Usimaᶜre-setepenre,
Son of Re, Sheshonq (III), beloved of Amon, the god, ruler of Heliopolis,
the justified. They sought for his beauty (6) in every place of Lower Egypt.
It was at Hushedabed¹ that he was discovered after (7) three months, as
they went (like) fish of the Delta marshes about every mound of Lower
Egypt. He was installed (8) at Memphis before his father Ptah, South of
His Wall, specifically by the "Chief of Master-craftsmen" (high priest of
Memphis) and *setem*-priest in the estate of Ptah, (9) the Great Chief of the
Meshwesh, Padiese, the son of the "Chief of Master-craftsmen" and *setem*-
priest, [the Great Chief] (10) of the Meshwesh, Takelot (B), and who was
born by the king's bodily daughter, whom he loves, Tchesbastetperu, (in)
regnal year 28, month 2 of Inundation. The goodly lifespan of this god
was 26 years.

NOTE
    1. A site in the Memphite region near Tura; see Gauthier 1925–31, 4:135.

95. THIRD SERAPEUM VOTIVE STELA OF PADIESE
(LOUVRE STELA IM 3736, CAT. NO. 23)

This round-topped limestone stela measures .87 m in height by .46 m
in width by .095 m in depth. Similar in format to text number 94, the stela
again represents Apis and the goddess of the West adored by Padiese,
sporting leopard skin and Libyan feather, and by Harsiese dressed as a

setem-priest. While text 94 stresses the role of Padiese, text 95 favors Harsiese. For bibliography, see the introduction to text 94.

LABEL FOR APIS
        Wsîr-Ḥp (2) Ḫnt(y) îmnt.t nṯr (ʿ3)
        Osiris-Apis, (2) Foremost of the West, the (great) god.

LABELS FOR PADIESE AND HARSIESE
        dî≠f qn(î) nḫt (n) wr n n3 (2) Mʿšw3š (3) P3-dî-3s.t (4) s(t)m n wr
ḫrp ḥmww (5) n Ptḥ (6) Ḥr-s3-3s.t m3ʿ-(ḫrw) (7) îr{.t}.n wr.(t) ḫnr.t (8) m
Mn-nf(9)r St[3]-îr.t¹
        May he give valor and victory to the Chief of the (2) Meshwesh, (3)
Padiese, (4) and to the *setem*-priest of the "Chief of Master-craftsmen" (5)
of Ptah, (6) Harsiese, the justified, (7) who was born by the Chief of the
harim (8) in Memphis, (9) Setairet.¹

STATEMENT OF PADIESE REGARDING APIS
        îw sḥ mḥ m îr wn≠f²
        The (embalming) booth is filled with what would make his existence.²

MAIN TEXT
        [ḥsb.t 2.(t) 3bd 1+] 1 n pr.t sw 1 ḫr ḥm n ny-sw.t bî.ty nb t3.wy Wsr-m3ʿ.
t-Rʿ-stp-n-(ʾI)mn dî ʿnḫ [s3 Rʿ nb ḫʿ.w] (2) [P3]-my(w) [mrî-ʾImn] dî ʿnḫ ḏd
w3s mî Rʿ ḏ.t mry Ḥp Ḫnt(y) îmnt.t nṯr ʿ3 [ḥrw] (3) [pw]y st3 nṯr m ḥtp r
îmnt.t nfr.t qr[s.t(w)≠f m ḥr.t-nṯr] (4) [b]s.tw≠f r Ḥw.t-k3-Ptḥ ḥr ît≠f Ptḥ rsy
înb≠f (m) ḥsb.t 10 [+ 18 3bd 2 n 3ḫ.t] (5) ḥr ḥm n ny-sw.t Wsr-m3ʿ.t-Rʿ-stp-
n-Rʿ s3 Rʿ Ššnq mrî-ʾImn nṯr ḥq3 ʾIwnw [m3ʿ-ḫrw sk ms.tw≠f m] (6) ḥsb.t 28
wnn≠f m î3d(r).w≠f îw≠sn ḫ[ḫ nfr.w≠f m] (7) [bw nb nw T3-m]ḥy ʿḥʿ nfr
n nṯr pn rnp.t 26 în îry-pʿ.t ḥ3.ty-ʿ [...] (8) [...] ḥwn ḥts ḫnt(y) pr.w M3nw
m33 ʿḥm (m) ʿb ḫrp šndy.t nb.t ḫrp [...]³ (9) [wr ḫrp ḥmww st]m Ḥr-s3-3s.t
s3 wr ḫrp ḥmww s(t)m wr ʿ3 n n3 [Mʿ](10)šw3š P3-dî-3s.t îr{.t}.n wr.(t) ḫnr.t
m Mn-nfr [St3](11)-îr.t¹ s3≠f mr≠f Tkrîwt mw.t≠f T3-dî-t3-nb-n-[p].t (12) s3≠f
mr≠f ʿnḫ-P3-dî-3s.t mw.t≠f K3p≠w-s-ḥ3-3s.t
        [Regnal year 2, month] 2 of winter, day 1, under the Majesty of the
King of Upper and Lower Egypt, Lord of the Two Lands, Usimaʿre-setepenamon, given life, [Son of Re, Lord of diadems,] (2) [Pa]miu, [beloved of
Amon], given life, stability, and dominion like Re forever, beloved of Apis,
Foremost of the West, the great god. (3) On [this day] occurred the hauling of the god in peace to the beautiful West so that he might be bur[ied
in the necropolis.] (4) He was installed at Memphis before his father Ptah,
south of his wall, specifically in regnal year 28, [month 2 of Inundation]
(5) under the Majesty of King Usimaʿre-setepenre, Son of Re, Sheshonq
(III), beloved of Amon, the god, ruler of Heliopolis, [the justified. Now,

he was born in] (6) regnal year 28 and was among his herds while they sought [his beauty in] (7) [every place of Lower] Egypt. The goodly lifespan of this god was 26 years. (Made) by the hereditary noble and count, [...] (8) [...] the youth, the favored one, the foremost of the Houses of Manu, he who sees the cult image in the shrine, director of all kilts, director of [...],³ (9) ["Chief of Master-craftsmen" and *setem*]-priest, Harsiese, son of the "Chief of Master-craftsmen" and *setem*-priest, the Great Chief of the [Me](10)shwesh, Padiese, and who was born by the Chief of the harim in Memphis, Setairet,¹ and (by) his son, whom he loves, Takelot, whose mother is Taditanebenpe, (12) and his son, whom he loves, Ankhpadiese, whose mother is Kapushaese.

NOTES

    1. Probably an abbreviation for the common name St₃-îr.t-bîn.t.

    2. Paralleled in Cat. No. 21, the phrase is unregistered in Erman and Grapow 1926–63, and the translation is provisional. If correctly analyzed, Padiese declares the fulfillment of his obligations for the embalming of Apis.

    3. The titles ḥts and ḥrp šndy.t nb.t are archaic revivals, while ḫnt(y) pr.w M₃nw is associated with the high priest of Memphis in Dynasty XIX. The title m₃₃ ꜥḥm (m) ꜥb is not recorded in Erman and Grapow 1926–63 and might be read îr gmḥsw ꜥb "who makes the falcon of the shrine."

96. SERAPEUM VOTIVE STELA OF GOD'S FATHER SENEBEF (LOUVRE STELA IM 4205, CAT. NO. 24)

The rectangular limestone stela measures .43 m in height by .375 m in width by .10 m in depth, and has no lunette or figures. A single line of dedication precedes the main text and additional dedications. For bibliography, see the introduction to text 94.

A.

    [...] s₃ Šd-s(w)-Nfr-tm m₃ꜥ-ḫrw

    [...] son of Shedsunefertem, the justified.

B.

    ḥsb.t 1 [+1 ₃bd 2 pr.t sw 1] ḥr ḥm n ny-sw.t bî.ty Wsr-m₃ꜥ.t-Rꜥ-stp-[n]-ʾIm[n] s₃ Rꜥ nb îr.(t) (2) ḫ.t P₃-my(w) mrî-ʾImn dî ꜥnḫ ḏd w₃s mî Rꜥ ḏ.t mry Ḥp Ḫnt(y) îmnt.t (3) hrw pwy st₃ nṯr pn r îmnt.t nfr.t qrs(4).t(w)꞊f m ḫr.t-nṯr m ḥtp m ḥtp ḫr nṯr nfr ḫr Wsîr ḫr ʾInpw ḫr (5) smy.t îmnt.t sk sḫn. tw꞊f r Ḥw.t-k₃-Ptḥ ḫr ît꞊f (6) Ptḥ rsy înb꞊f (m) ḥsb.t 28 ₃bd 2 n ₃ḫ.t m rkw ḥm n ny-sw.t bî.ty (7) Ššnq mrî-ʾImn nṯr ḥq₃ ʾIwnw m₃ꜥ-ḫrw îr.t.n ît-nṯr ḥr(y)-sš[t₃ ...] pr Ptḥ îmy-s.t-ꜥ (n) s₃ (8) 3-nw ḥm-nṯr Ḥp Ḫnt(y) îmnt.t ḥm-nṯr ʾInpw tp(y) ḏw꞊f ḥm-nṯr Ḏḥwty ḫnt(y) Ḥry-Tḥnw¹ ḥm-nṯr (9) Snb꞊f m₃ꜥ-ḫrw m pr Wsîr n mr [...]n m ḫn.ty rnp.wt

Regnal year 2, [month 2 of winter, day 1,] under the Majesty of the
King of Upper and Lower Egypt, Usima're-setepenamon, Son of Re, Lord
of ritual (2) performance, Pamiu, beloved of Amon, given life, stability, and
dominion like Re forever, beloved of Apis, Foremost of the West. (3) On
this day occurred the hauling of this god to the beautiful West so that he
might be buried (4) in the necropolis in peace, in peace, before the Good
God, before Osiris, before Anubis, and before (5) the western desert. Now,
he was inducted at Hikuptah (Memphis) before his father (6) Ptah, south
of his wall, in regnal year 28, month 2 of Inundation, in the time of the
Majesty of the King of Upper and Lower Egypt, Sheshonq (III), beloved
of Amon, the god, ruler of Heliopolis, the justified. Made by the God's
Father and Chief of Secrets [...] of the estate of Ptah, the acolyte for the
third (8) phyle, prophet of Apis, Foremost of the West, prophet of Anubis
who is upon his mountain, prophet of Thoth, Foremost of the Hermopolitan shrine,[1] and prophet, (9) Senebef, the justified, in the estate of Osiris
through love [...] through the expanse of years.

C.

s3≠f mr≠f (2) w'b dr.t[2] (3) m pr Ptḥ (4) Ḥr-(m)-Ḥby.t m3'-ḫrw (5)
sn≠f shd s(t)m (6) m Ḥw.t Skr (7) [...]-šd-sw m3'-ḫrw (8–11) [...] (12)
[...]p[...]n[...]

His son, whom he loves, (2) who is pure of hands[2] (3) in the estate
of Ptah, (4) Har(em)kheby, the justified; (5) His brother, the inspector of
setem-priests (6) in the Mansion of Sokar, (7) [...]shedsu, the justified;
(8–11) [...] (12) [...]...[...]

NOTES

1. "Bearing Libyans" an ancient cult site of Thoth at Hermopolis (Erman and
Grapow 1926–63, 4:394/11).

2. A priestly title.

97. SERAPEUM VOTIVE STELA OF GOD'S FATHER PADJA
(LOUVRE STELA IM 3441, CAT. NO. 25)

The round-topped limestone stela measures .42 m in height by .335 m
in width by .07 m in depth, with painted scenes and texts. In the lunette,
below a sky glyph and winged disk, King Pamiu is shown offering a cake
to a standing, bull-headed Apis, who is followed by Hathor wearing the
sign for "West" upon her head. Behind Pamiu stands the votary Padja.
The text displays a predilection for cryptic spellings; see Vandier 1965, 97
§E.LXXIII. For bibliography, see the introduction to text 94.

LABEL FOR APIS

Ḥp Ḫnt(y) ỉmnt.t nṯr (ꜥꜣ)

Apis, Foremost of the West, the (great) god.

LABEL FOR HATHOR

Ḥw.t-Ḥr nb.(t) ỉmnt.t [...]

Hathor, Lady of the West, [...].

LABEL FOR KING PAMIU

nb tꜣ.wy Wsr-mꜣꜥ.t-Rꜥ-stp-n-(ꜣI)mn (2) nb ḫꜥ.(w) Pꜣ-my(w) mrỉ-ꜣImn

Lord of the Two Lands, Usimaꜥre-setepenre. (2) Lord of diadems, Pamiu, beloved of Amon.

LABEL FOR PADJA

ỉt-nṯr (n) Ptḥ Pꜣ-ḏꜣ

God's Father of Ptah, Padja.

MAIN TEXT

(1) ḥsb.t 2.(t) ꜣbd 2 pr.t sw 1 ḫr ḥm n ny-sw.t bỉ.ty nb tꜣ.wy Wsr-mꜣꜥ. t-Rꜥ-stp-n-(ꜣI)mn dỉ ꜥnḫ sꜣ Rꜥ nb ḫꜥ.(w) (2) Pꜣ-my(w) mrỉ-ꜣImn dỉ ꜥnḫ ḏd wꜣs mỉ Rꜥ ḏt ỉ Wsỉr-Ḥp Ḫnt(y) ỉmnt.t nṯr (ꜥꜣ) dỉ≠f mn rn (n) (3) ỉt-nṯr (n) Ptḥ ḫnm (n) Ḫnsw pꜣ ḫrd ḥm-nṯr n Nb.t-ḥtp.t n Ḫꜣỉ-nfr shḏ s(t)m (m) Ḥw.t Skr nb nmt.t (4) m Rꜣ-stꜣw Pꜣ-ḏꜣ sꜣ ỉt-nṯr (n) Ptḥ ḫnm (n) Ḫnsw pꜣ ḫrd ḥm-nṯr n Nb.t-ḥtp.t Pꜣ-myw sꜣ n (5) ỉt-nṯr n Ptḥ ḥm-nṯr nn n nṯr.w Skr-m-sꜣ≠f ỉw rn≠w mn m pr≠k

Regnal year 2, month 2 of winter, day 1, under the Majesty of the King of Upper and Lower Egypt, Usimaꜥre-setepenamon, given life, Son of Re, Lord of diadems, (2) Pamiu, beloved of Amon, given life, stability, and dominion like Re forever. "O Osiris-Apis, Foremost of the West, (great) god, may he cause that there remain the name of (3) the God's Father of Ptah, the nurse of Khonsu the child, the prophet of (Hathor) Nebethetepet of Khanefer (Memphis), the inspector of *setem*-priests, (in) the Mansion of Sokar, who has freedom of movement (4) in the Memphite necropolis, Padja, son of the God's Father of Ptah, the nurse of Khonsu the child, the prophet of (Hathor) Nebethetepet, Pamiu, son of (5) the God's Father of Ptah and prophet of these gods, Sokaremsaef, with their names remaining in your house!"

ADDED GRAFITTO

wꜣḥ Mw.t-[...] (2) Pꜣ-dỉ-Nw.t (3) sꜣ≠f [...]

May there endure Mut-[...] (2) Padinut, (3) and his son [...]

98. BRITISH MUSEUM BRONZE STATUE 32747

Evidence of the high quality of bronze work during the Libyan Period, the statuette represents King Pamiu kneeling and offering round vessels for water or wine. Perhaps part of a dyad or portable shrine, the figure measures 25.5 cm in height. Cartouches of the king appear on the belt clasp and on both shoulders. From the common prenomen, the piece was formerly attributed to Rameses II or Pedubast I. For the texts and attribution, see Yoyotte 1988a, 164–66 and pls. 4–5.

BELT CLASP
    Wsr-mȝꜥ.t-Rꜥ-stp-n-Rꜥ   Usimaꜥre-setepenre

LEFT SHOULDER
    Wsr-mȝꜥ.t-Rꜥ-stp-n-Rꜥ   Usimaꜥre-setepenre

RIGHT SHOULDER
    Pȝ-mỉw mrỉ-ꜣImn sȝ Bȝst.t nṯr ḥqȝ Wȝs.t
    Pamiu, beloved of Amon, Son of Bastet, the god, ruler of Thebes.

99. S. LOUVRE E 1139 (= C 275)

Purchased in Cairo in 1907 by G. Bénédite, the round-topped stela is assumed to derive from Memphis due to internal references to local rituals of Sokar. Beneath a disk with pendant uraei, the lunette shows the worshiper and a woman adoring Isis, behind whom stands a large *was*-scepter. Labels and text are in hieroglyphs. The votive stela contains the highest year date for King Pamiu.

The stela is previously untranslated. For the text, see Yoyotte 1988a, 160–61 and pl. 2; Bénédite 1908, 316–17; and Gauthier 1914, 372.

LABEL FOR SOLAR DISK
    Bḥd.t(y) nṯr ꜥȝ
    The Behdedite, the great god.

LABEL FOR MALE WORSHIPER
    dwȝ n nb≠f …
    Adoration of his lady …

LABEL FOR FEMALE WORSHIPER
    dwȝ n nb≠s …
    Adoration of her lady …

MAIN TEXT

(1) ḥsb.t 6.(t) ḫr ḥm n ny-sw.t bỉ.ty nb t3.wy Wsr-m3ꜥ.t-Rꜥ-stp-n-Rꜥ (2) s3 Rꜥ nb ḫꜥ.w P3-mỉw{.t} dỉ ꜥnḫ n dỉ≠f (n) 3s.t t3 (3) nṯr.t dỉ≠s pr b3 P3-tqb (4) rḫ.n≠f ỉw r ḥtp.t n Ḥw.t Rꜥ n ḥb Skr n(n) ḥm(5).t m b(w) mr≠s n≠s{.t}¹ b3 r ḥry n Rꜥ (6) n h(rw) n pḫr ỉnb² (m) m3ꜥ-ḫrw

Regnal year 6 under the Majesty of the King of Upper and Lower Egypt, Lord of the Two Lands, Usimaꜥre-setepenre, (2) Son of Re, Lord of diadems, Pamiu, given life. (The day) of his giving to Isis the (3) goddess so that she might cause that the *ba*-spirit of Patcheqeb go forth, (4) having learned how to come to the offerings of the Mansion of Re on the Festival of Sokar, without retreating (5) from the place that she (Isis) desires for them (the offerings),¹ the *ba*-spirit destined upward to Re (6) on the day of encircling the wall² (in) justification.

NOTES

1. Or "for herself."

2. The ritual circuit during the Sokar festival; for further references, see Ritner 1993b, 59.

100. DONATION STELA
(CAIRO TEMPORARY REGISTRATION 2/2/21/13)

Questionably associated with King Pamiu, the limestone stela from Tell-Basta measures 65 cm in height by 23 cm in width. Poorly carved and worn, the lunette depicts the standard winged disk below a curved sign for heaven. On the left, the lion-headed Bastet with papyrus scepter and disk is followed by hawk-headed Horus son of Isis. On the right, a standing king presents to the deities the hieroglyph for field, here modified to indicate the name of the territory of the Bubastite (eighteenth) nome of Lower Egypt (sḫ.t-nṯr). All texts are in (fairly corrupt) hieroglyphs. The royal nomen is unclear, although the final signs of the published copy suggest Pamiu ([P]3-my). If correctly analyzed, the text records the gift of fields for temple gardeners Iamon and Djedptahiuefankh, offered by a chief gardener and sanctioned by the king.

The stela is previously untranslated. For the text, see Daressy 1915, 145–47; Meeks 1979a, 614, 629, 641, 650, and 669 (22.9.00); and Yoyotte 1988a, 168.

LABEL FOR BASTET

ḏd-mdw ỉn B3st.t nb.(t) p.t (2) dỉ≠ỉ n≠k nḫt

Recitation by Bastet, Lady of heaven: (2) "I have given to you victory."

LABEL FOR HORUS

ḏd-mdw ỉn Ḥr sꜣ ꜣs.t (2) dỉ≠ỉ n≠k qny
Recitation by Horus, son of Isis: (2) "I have given to you valor."

LABEL FOR KING

nb (tꜣ.wy)[1] Wsr-mꜣꜥ.t-Rꜥ-stp-n-Rꜥ (2) nb (ḫꜥ.w)[1] Pꜣ-my(w)(?) mrỉ-ʾImn
Lord (of the Two Lands),[1] Usimaʿre-setepenre. (2) Lord (of diadems),[1]
Pamiu (?), beloved of Amon.

MAIN TEXT

(1) ḥnk ꜣḥ.t stꜣ.t 10.(t) (ỉn) ny-sw.t bỉ.ty Wsr-mꜣꜥ.t-Rꜥ-stp-n-Rꜥ (2) Pꜣ-
my(w)(?) mrỉ-ʾImn (ỉ)t tꜣ.wy ḫꜥ.w(?) (m) mꜣꜥ.t ḥꜣ.t m-m nty ḥnk (n) nꜣ (3)
kꜣrt(y)[2] ḥm-nṯr ʾImn-Rꜥ ny-sw.t nṯr.w ʾI-ʾImn (4) ḥnk nꜣ kꜣrt(y)[2] (n) Bꜣst.t
ꜥꜣ.(t) nb.(t) Bꜣst.t Ḏd-Pt(5)ḥ-ỉw≠f-ꜥnḫ dỉ.n{n} ḫ(ry) kꜣrty[3] ꜥnḫy-n(6)-nm(?)
Bꜣst.t ꜥꜣ.(t) nb.(t) Bꜣst.t mn ḥkꜣ

(1) Offering 10 *arouras* of field (by) the King of Upper and Lower
Egypt, Usimaʿre-setepenre, (2) Pamiu (?), beloved of Amon, who has seized
the Two Lands, having appeared (?) (in) Maat.
    First among those (fields) that are offered (to) the (3) gardeners[2] of the
prophet of Amon-Re, King of the Gods: (to) Iamon;
    (4) Offered (to) the gardeners[2] of Bastet the great, Lady of Bubastis:
(to) Djedpta(5)hiuefankh;
    Given by the chief gardener (?),[3] Ankhyennim (?), of Bastet the great,
Lady of Bubastis, enduring of magic.

NOTES

    1. Left blank.
    2. So Meeks 1979a, 629, 650. Yoyotte (1988a, 168 n. 77) read ṯnfy "dancer."
    3. The text as copied by Daressy is corrupt: ḥkꜣtty.

101. CANOPIC JAR FROM TANIS TOMB II

The disturbed burial in the undecorated Tomb II at Tanis has been
assigned to Pamiu on the basis of a reused limestone canopic jar, 31 cm
in height and 13.5 cm in diameter, inscribed in faded ink with the king's
prenomen. Supporting this identification is the find of a figure of a cat (3.8
cm high) in goldleaf (Cairo JdE 86932b), probable debris from an inscription of the king's name on the destroyed sarcophagus.
    For the text and discussion, see Yoyotte 1988a, 166–68 and pl. 6; and
Dodson 1988, 224–25 and 233.

    ḏd-mdw ỉn ꜣs.t[1] [...] Wsr-mꜣꜥ.t-Rꜥ-[stp-n-Rꜥ ...]
    Recitation by Isis:[1] "[...] O Usimaʿre-[setepenre, ...]"

NOTE

1. Copied by Montet as “Osiris.” For the reading, see Dodson 1988, 224–25.

J. SHESHONQ V

102. BUBASTIS DONATION STELA OF SHESHONQ V (CAIRO JdE 45779)

Now lacking most of the lunette and the lower right corner, the royal donation stela of Sheshonq V yet retains the traces of a rare reversal of the standard decorative scheme of such monuments. Although only the feet are preserved, it is evident that the goddess Bastet stood on the right behind a large beer jug, with the king and the administrator of the gift on the left. The absence of any local intermediary is significant and indicates the direct authority of the king within his home territory. The true beneficiary of the gift was the Bubastite clergy rather than the goddess herself, as the 42 *arouras* (roughly 28 acres) were entailed to finance the cost of only one jug of beer (about 1/2 liter) daily.

The text contains the complete, archaizing titulary employed by Sheshonq V prior to his jubilee. The simplicity of its style, adapted from Old and Middle Kingdom models, marks the beginnings of an official chancellery archaism that will be characteristic of Dynasties XXIV–XXVI. The stela as preserved measures 0.38 m. in height and 0.28 m. in width.

For the text, translation, and discussion, see Daressy 1915, 144–45; Menu 1998, 144–45; and Meeks 1979a, 614, 628–29, 643, 645, 646, 649, 652, and 670 (no. 22.10.00c). See Kitchen 1986, 86–87 §67, 350–51 §§309 and 311.

(1) [Ḥr W]s[r]-pḥ.ty Nb.ty Wsr-pḥ.ty Ḥr-nbw Wsr-pḥ.ty ny-sw.t bỉ.ty ꜥꜣ-ḫpr-Rꜥ sꜣ Rꜥ Šꜣšꜣnq (2) [ỉr=n=f m] mnw n mw.t=f Bꜣst.t nb.t Bꜣs.t ꜣḥ.t sṯꜣ.t 42 ḫnty (3) […] Bꜣst.t tꜣ ḥꜣwrꜥ(?)[1] ẖr ḥnq.t hn 1 m ỉmny.w(t)(4)[=s] n.t rꜥ nb[2] r sḥtp ḥm.t=s ỉm=f r-ḫt rmṯ ḥw.t-nṯr Bꜣst.t Dỉ-Bꜣst.t-p(ꜣ)-snb sꜣ Ns-Bꜣst.t ỉr.n nb.(t)-pr ḥr(y.t)-ḥs(6)[y.wt] Bꜣs.t Tꜣ-dnỉ.t-n-Bꜣst.t

ỉr sry nb rmṯ nb (7) [sm]n=f ḥtp-nṯr (n) hn n ḥnq.t (n) ḥm.t Bꜣs.t wn ms.w=f smn.(8)[w ḥr ns.]wt=sn ms.w n ms.(w)=w smn.w ḥr ns.wt(9)[=sn ỉr sry] nb rmṯ nb th(ỉ)=f ḥtp-nṯr (10) [(n) hn n ḥnq.t (n) ḥm.t Bꜣst].t [nb.(t)] Bꜣs.t dr tḫ=f dỉ.t ḥq(r)=f (11) [… ꜥ(?)]=f ḫsf r=f[3] ḫr Bꜣst.t nb.(t) (12) [Bꜣs.t …] nḥḥ ḥnꜥ ḏ.t rnp.t ꜣbd hrw

(1) The Horus: “Great of Strength,” the Two Ladies: “Great of Strength,” the Horus of Gold: “Great of Strength,” the King of Upper and

Lower Egypt, Aakheperre-setepenre, Son of Re, Sheshonq (V). (2) [He made as] a monument for his mother Bastet, Lady of Bubastis, 42 *arouras* of field at the front of (3) [...] of Bastet, with the revenue[1] supporting 1 *ḥin*-jug of beer in [her] daily offerings (4) of each day[2] in order to satisfy Her Majesty with it, under the supervision of the man of the temple (5) of Bastet, Dibastpaseneb, son of Nesbast, born by the housewife and chief of the singers (6) of Bubastis, Tadenitenbast.

As for any official or any man (7) who confirms the divine endowment of 1 *ḥin*-jug of beer for the Majesty of Bubastis, their children shall be confirmed (8) in their places, with the children of their children confirmed in [their] places. (9) [As for] any official or any man who transgresses the divine endowment (10) [of 1 *ḥin*-jug of beer for the Majesty of Bastet, Lady] of Bubastis, his inebriation shall be dispelled and he shall be made to hunger (11) [...], while he is opposed[3] before Bastet, Lady (12) [of Bubastis ...] forever and ever: year, month, and day!

NOTES

1. Translated by Daressy as "revenue." If correctly copied, the term is perhaps related to ḥwrˁ "to rob"; cf. ˁwȝỉ (Erman and Grapow 1926–63, 1:171), meaning both "to harvest" and "to rob."

2. For the idiom, see The Chronicle of Prince Osorkon, pl. 21, line 6 (p. 361 above).

3. For the restoration, see Erman and Grapow 1926–63, 3:335–36.

103. ERASED DONATION STELA
(CAIRO JdE 85647)

Dating to the reign of Sheshonq V, this round-topped limestone stela derives from Kôm Firîn in the West Delta and measures 49 x 31.5 x 13 cm. The lunette is decorated with addorsed scenes of a Libyan chief offering bread to the deity Heka on the right, while a harpist plays before the goddess Sakhmet on the left. The lunette texts are inscribed in hieroglyphs, with the body of the donation stela in cursive hieratic. The hieroglyphic name of the chief has been hacked out, leaving only traces of his priestly title, and the standing feather that once distinguished his chiefly rank is excised as well. This *damnatio memoriae* is continued within the body of the text itself, where the initial five lines recording all specifics of the donation have been thoroughly erased. The selective damage visited upon the stela is clear evidence of political and personal animosity, indicative of the social turmoil in the waning years of Dynasty XXII. Ironically, the second half recording curses against potential violators has been left intact. The primary interest of the remaining text resides in these elaborate curses, fittingly uttered in a dedication to Heka, the god of magic.

Publication with transcription and photo in Bakir 1943, 75–81 and pls. I–II. See also Meeks 1979a, 638–39, 669 no. 22.10.00a; and Kitchen 1969–70, 60 nn. 6–7 and 65–67. See Kitchen 1986, 351 n. 609.

LABEL FOR WINGED DISK AT TOP OF LUNETTE
Bḥd.t(y) nṯr ꜥꜣ nb p.t
The Behdetite, the great god, Lord of heaven.

CARTOUCHE BELOW DISK, FLANKED BY PENDANT URAEI WITH ANKHS
ꜥꜣ-ḫpr-Rꜥ   Akheperre

LABEL FOR CHIEF
ḥm-nṯr Ḥkꜣ [...]
Prophet of Heka [...]

LABEL FOR HEKA
ḏd-mdw în Ḥkꜣ (2) ḥr(y)-îb ꜥḥ sꜣ tꜣ(ꜣ)y pr m (4) ḥtp qmꜣ Sbk (5) msw Sḫm.t ꜥꜣ.(t) dî[1] ꜥnḫ ḏ.t
Recitation by Heka, (2) resident in the palace, male son (3) come forth in (4) peace, whom Sobek created, (5) born of Sakhmet the great, who gives[1] life forever.

LABEL FOR SAKHMET
ḏd-mdw în Sḫm.t ꜥꜣ.(t) (2) nb.(t) tꜣ.wy[2] nb.(t) ꜣImn.t (3) dî[3] ꜥnḫ ḏd wꜣs nb
Recitation by Sakhmet the great, (2) Lady of the Two Lands,[2] Lady of the West, (3) who gives[3] all life, stability, and dominion.

CENTRAL BAND BETWEEN HEKA AND SAKHMET
ḏd-mdw dî.n≠(î) n≠k dî-ꜥnḫ[4] ḏd wꜣs nb ꜣw.t-îb nb snb nb Šš[nq ...]
Recitation: "Thus I have given to you all vivification,[4] stability, and dominion, all joy and all health, Shesh[onq ...]."

HIERATIC TEXT
(1–5) [... îr pꜣ nty-îw≠f thꜣ nꜣ ꜣḥ](6).wt nk≠f ꜥꜣ nk ꜥꜣ [ḥm.t]≠f nk ḥm.t≠f [ḥ]rd≠[f ḫp]r≠f m šꜥd (n) ny-sw.t ḥsq≠w (7) tp≠f ḥḥ îs≠f îr≠w ꜥḥꜥ≠f (m) tm wnw qrs.tw≠f m wnmy.t b[n] î[mn] sꜣ[≠f] ḥr s.t≠f îw≠f ḫbd (8) n pr ꜣImn pr Rꜥ Ptḥ pr n pꜣ ḥkꜣ ḥr îr pꜣ nty-îw≠f smn [nꜣ] ꜣḥ.wt m[tw≠f] tm ḫb p(9)ꜣy≠w nwḥ.w ḫpr≠f m ḥs n nṯr n nîw.t≠f îw sꜣ≠f mn ḥr ns.t≠f mî mn p.t mî mn tꜣ (10) nn ḫpr ḥ.t nb ḏw r≠f n ḏ.t ḏ.t ...[5] bw.t nṯr nb nṯr.t nb.t mnmn wḏ n [ꜣḥ.t[6] ...]

1–5 [... As for the one who will transgress regarding the field](6)s, may he rape a donkey,[7] may a donkey rape his [wife], may his wife rape [his] child. May he be as one slaughtered for the king. May his head (7) be cut off. May his tomb be searched for (in vain). May his lifetime be made (as) nonexistent, he being buried in the devouring flame. [His] son will not re[main] upon his position, he being hated (8) in the house of Amon, the house(s) of Re and Ptah, and the house of the ruler. But, as for the one who will confirm [the] fields and who will not subtract from (9) their measuring cords, may he be a praised one of his local god. His son will be established on his seat even as heaven is established and even as the earth is established. (10) Nothing evil will happen to him through the body of eternity, (for?)⁵ the abomination of every god and every goddess is to shift a [field] stela⁶ [...].

NOTES
    1. Bakir translates "given life forever."
    2. Omitted from Bakir's transcription (1943, 78).
    3. Elevated on stela, statement of Behdetite? Bakir translates "given life, stability and dominion."
    4. Evidence of fused compound term with dỉ; cf. Coptic **ⲦⲀⲚϨⲞ**. Bakir translates "donation."
    5. Traces unclear and unread by Bakir. Perhaps read ntt "because, for"; see Erman and Grapow 1926–63, 2:354/13.
    6. The wording indicates that the donation stela was erected as a boundary stone.
    7. As noted by Bakir, this inverts the usual phrase "May a donkey rape him."

104. DONATION STELA OF THE LIBU CHIEF TITARU
(BROOKLYN MUSEUM 67.119)

Formerly in the Michaelides collection, the round-topped limestone stela likely derives from Kôm Firin in the West Delta and measures 39.3 cm in height by 18.5 cm in width by 12.5 cm in depth. A winged disk occupies the top of the lunette, while the main field depicts the Libu chief offering the sign for "fields" to two deities on a raised platform: Sakhmet, wearing a disk and holding a "Nefertem" scepter; and the child Heka, shown with disk, flail, and finger to his mouth. Behind the Libu intermediary, distinguished by the plume worn vertically in his hair, is the smaller figure of the beneficiary, who raises his hands in adoration. A cursive hieroglyphic text labels the deity Heka (Ḥkȝ), and a carved hieratic text of eight lines completes the stela. Although intended for the support of the cult of Sakhmet, the donation is made directly to the individual beneficiary. The stela dates to the reign of Sheshonq V.

For the texts, photographs, and discussion, see Kitchen 1969–70, 59–60, 64–67, and fig. 4; Yoyotte 1961a, 144 §32 Document D, and pl. I.2; and Meeks 1979a, 614–16 n. 32, 627, 628, 630, and 670 no. 22.10.15. See Kitchen 1986, 351 §311 and 490 table 21A.

MAIN TEXT

(1) ḥsb.t 15.(t) ḥr ḥm n ny-sw.t bỉ.ty nb t3.wy ꜥ3-ḫpr-Rꜥ-stp-n-Rꜥ (2) s3 Rꜥ nb ḫꜥ.w Š3š3nq mry-ʾImn nṯr ḥq3 W3s.t (3) ỉw wr ꜥ3 n Rbyu Tỉt3rw p3-(n) Dỉdỉ[1] (4) ḥnq 3ḥ.t st3.t 10 n ḥry tnfy n Sḫm.t wr.(t) nb.(t) t3.wy (5) ꜥ.t(?)[2] dmỉ Rwb3gr(?)[3] ỉr n3 (6) nty-ỉw⸗w ḫ3y sḫ.wt mtw⸗w smn p3y wḏ (7) [ỉw⸗w ḥr ḥs.t] Sḫm.t ỉw Sḫm.t r smn n3y⸗w ḥrd.w (8) m sḫ.wt nty-ỉw⸗w n-ỉm⸗w(?) …[…]

Regnal year 15 under the Majesty of the King of Upper and Lower Egypt, the Lord of the Two Lands, Aakheperre-setepenre, (2) Son of Re, Lord of diadems, Sheshonq (V), beloved of Amon, the god, ruler of Thebes, (3) while the Great Chief of the Libu, Titaru, son of Didi,[1] (4) donates 10 *arouras* of field to the chief dancer of Sakhmet the great, Lady of the Two Lands, (5) of the town chamber (?),[2] Rebegar (?).[3] As for those (6) who will measure the fields and confirm this stela, (7) [they will be in the favor of] Sakhmet, and Sakhmet will confirm their children (8) in the fields in which they will be (?) …[…]

NOTES

1. Kitchen, following Yoyotte, interprets the initial p3 as the possessive prefix p3-(n) "he of, son of" Didi. Further possible examples occur in the Donation Stela of Washtihat (Chicago OIM 10511), no. 86 above, and the Donation Stela of Bakenatum (MMA 55.144.6), no. 149 below.
2. Untranslated by Kitchen, who also suggested the reading wsḫ.t "hall."
3. Or read Rws3gr "Resegar."

105. DONATION STELA OF WASHTIHAT (B)
(CAIRO JdE 30972)

From the region of Kom Abu-Billo in the western Delta, this limestone stela, formerly round-topped, now preserves a height of 0.53 m and a width of 0.31 m. Between large framing *was*-scepters, a central figure of Hathor, facing right, is adored by Ker, a Great Chief of the Libu, on the right and the donor Washtihat on the left. The inscriptions of the lunette are in hieroglyphs, while the nine lines of the body of the text are in hieratic. The text is notable for the Libyan names of the principal parties, the military status of the donor, and the clear indications that the transaction occurred during the donor's lifetime. As Washtihat was no farmer, the lands in question may have accrued to him as feudal payment for military service, although the shield-bearers in the Apanage Stela of Iuwelot (text no. 69) received their land as paternal inheritance. Reflecting the relatively unacculturated status of the Libu, the Great Chief's Libyan titles take precedence over his Egyptian ones.

Formerly Cairo Temporary Registration 8/3/25/11. For the text and translation, see Koenig 1982, 111–13; Maspero 1893, 84–86 (hieroglyphic transcription); Müller 1906, 54–55 and pl. 88 (hieratic copy); Yoyotte 1961a, 144 §33; Breasted 1906–7, 4:392–93 §§782–84; Sottas 1913, 151–52 (concluding imprecations); and Meeks 1979a, 615–16 n. 32, 627 n. 82, 641 n. 151, 647–48 nn. 193 and 196, 651 n. 210, and 670 (no. 22.10.19). See Kitchen 1986, 351 §311 and 579 §519.

LABEL FOR THE GREAT CHIEF

dỉ⸗s ꜥnḫ wḏꜣ snb n wr ꜥꜣ n Rbꜣ

May she give life, prosperity, and health to the Great Chief of the Libu (Ker).

LABEL FOR THE DONOR

dỉ⸗s ꜥnḫ wḏꜣ snb n qrꜥ¹ ꜥꜣ n Pr-ꜥꜣ

May she give life, prosperity, and health to the great shield-bearer¹ of Pharaoh.

MAIN TEXT

ḥsb.t 19.t ḫr ḥm n ny-sw.t bỉ.ty ꜥꜣ-ḫpr-Rꜥ dỉ ꜥnḫ ỉw qrꜥ ꜥꜣ (2) n Pr-ꜥꜣ Wꜣštỉhꜣt sꜣ n Wꜣsꜣtỉrwkꜣnꜣỉw²(3) mw.t⸗f Tỉ-n.t-sꜣhꜣrwỉw ḥnk ꜣḫ.wt stꜣ.t 5 r pr Ḥw.t-Ḥr (4) nb.t Mfk.t r-ḫt ḥry wn.w Pꜣ-sꜣ-ꜥqy sꜣ n (5) Pꜣ-qnw mw.t⸗f Spd.t-hr.tỉ r dbḥ n⸗f ꜥnḫ wḏꜣ snb ꜥḥꜥ qꜣ (6) ỉꜣw.t ꜥꜣ.t nfr.t ḥr ḥs.w(t) n nb⸗f wr ꜥꜣ Rb wr ꜥꜣ n Mꜥ ḥꜣw.ty (7) ḥm-nṯr Kr m pr Ḥw.t-Ḥr nb.t Mfk.t mn wꜣḥ r ḏ.t ỉr rmṯ [nb] (8) sš nb nty hꜣb m wp.t n ww dmỉ Pꜣ-Sbk ntwtw³ r thꜣ (9) wḏ.t tn ḫpr⸗w ḫr šꜥd n Ḥw.t-Ḥr mn rn swꜣḥ s(.t) ḏ.t

Regnal year 19 under the Majesty of the King of Upper and Lower Egypt Aakheperre, given life, when the great shield-bearer (2) of Pharaoh, Washtihat son of Wastirkani, (3) whose mother is Tenetsahari, donates 5 *arouras* of field to the estate of Hathor, (4) Lady of Turquoise, under the authority of the overseer of door-keepers, Pasiaqy son of (5) Paqenu, whose mother is Sopdherti, in order to beseech for himself life, prosperity, health, a long (6) lifetime, and an advanced and goodly old age bearing the praises of his lord, the Great Chief of the Libu, the Great Chief of the Ma, leader (7) and prophet, Ker, in the estate of Hathor, Lady of Turquoise, established and enduring forever. As for [any] man (8) or any scribe who is sent on business to the district of the town of Pasobek and who shall transgress against (9) this stela, let them be subject to the slaughter of Hathor. May the name of him who maintains it remain forever.

NOTES

1. For the term, see Hoch 1994, 299–300.

2. Breasted reads Nwꜣhtỉrwkꜣnꜣỉw. In both lines 2 and 4 filiation is expressed by sꜣ n. For the correct reading, see Koenig 1982, 111.

3. Error for conjunctive or nty-ỉw≠w?

106. DONATION STELA OF GREAT CHIEF RUDAMON
(S. IFAO NO. SQ. 14456)

Paralleling the "Erased Donation Stela" (Cairo JdE 85647), this cursorily carved round-topped stela (41 x 30 x 7 cm) likely derives from the western Delta on the basis of the recipient deities Sakhmet and Heka, whose contemporary local cult sites were concentrated in the vicinity of Kôm el-Hisn and Kôm Firîn. Beneath the customary winged disk, the tribal chieftain, wearing both the erect feather of the Libu and the horizontal feather of the Meshwesh, approaches from the right. Usurping the traditional role of pharaoh, he offers the hieroglyph for "field" to the standing deities. Behind the chief, a smaller male personage bears a large jar on his shoulder, perhaps indicative of his occupation as a brewer. Crowned by a disk and ureaus, Sakhmet carries a papyrus scepter and ankh. Behind her, the infant Heka places his finger to his mouth and carries a flail. The texts in the lunette are carved in very cursive hieroglyphs, while the six horizontal lines of the donation text are in hieratic. Style, locale, and regnal year suggest a date under Sheshonq V.

Publication with transcription and photos in Berlandini 1978, 147–63 and pls. XLIV–L. The text is not included in the survey of such stelae by Meeks 1979a. See Kitchen 1986, 580 §521, 599 table *21A.

LABEL FOR SAKHMET
    Sḫm.t Nb.(t) Tꜣ.wy
    Sakhmet, Lady of the Two Lands

LABEL FOR HEKA
    Ḥkꜣ   Heka

LABEL FOR THE LIBU CHIEF
    R(w)d-ʾImn   Rudamon

LABEL FOR THE RECIPIENT
    Tỉ[y]rꜣpnwꜣ   Tilpenwe

MAIN TEXT
    (1) ḥsb.t 30.(t) tpy pr.t sw 1 ỉw wr ꜥꜣ Rby.w wr ḥꜣw.ty R(w)d-ʾImn ỉw...
    (2) pr ỉw ỉt-nṯr(?) Wꜣsꜣšꜣtꜣ sꜣ Dyỉỉwpnwꜣ [mw.t≠f ...]ḥ...

(3) ḥmk[1] [st̠3.t] 5 3[ḥ.t] n ḥm-ntr Ḥk3 p3 šr nty ḥr-[îb][2] ʿḥ s3
(4) [t3y][2] pr [m ḥtp qm3][2] Sbk ms(?) Sḫm.t Tî[y]r3pn[w3] ...
(5) [îr] p3 nty-îw≠f [t]ḥ[3] m [... î]w≠f šm n šʿt [ny-]sw.t
(6) nk≠f ḫrd≠f îw s3≠f [sbî] p3 nty-îw≠f [s]mn wd̠ îw≠f ʿnḫ

(1) Regnal year 30, first month of winter, day 1 (of Sheshonq V), when the Great Chief of the Libu, Chief and Leader Rudamon ..[...]
(2) had come forth, and when the God's Father (?) Weseshte, son of Ti(l)penwe, [whose mother is [...]h[...]
(3) donates[1] 5 [arouras] of f[ield] for the Prophet of Heka the Child, who is [resident in][2] the palace, male
(4) [son] come forth [in peace],[2] whom Sobek [created],[2] born of Sakhmet, Tilpen[we] ...
(5) [As for] the one who will tr[ansgress] in [..., he] will go to the slaughter of the [ki]ng.
(6) May he rape his child. His son [will perish.] The one who will confirm the stela, he will live.

NOTES
    1. For the spelling of ḥnq as ḥm-k3, see Donation Stela Strassburg 1588 (no. 14).
    2. For the restoration, see Cairo JdE 85647, lunette label for Heka.

K. OSORKON IV

107. ARTIFACTS OF OSORKON IV

Attestations of Osorkon IV are scarce, reflecting the relative impotence of this "shadow-pharaoh," the last representative of the "Bubastite" Dynasty XXII reigning from Tanis. Although ruling for some sixteen years, Osorkon was overshadowed in the north by his contemporaries Tefnakht and Bakenrenef of Dynasty XXIV. Contemporary monuments include only a single glazed ring of unknown provenience and a relief block, both now in Leiden, and an electrum aegis from Bubastis, formerly in the Hilton Price collection and now in the Louvre. The ring comprises double cartouches surmounted by solar disk and plumes, providing the prenomen and nomen of the king. The block, similar in style to the Tanite work of Sheshonq V, probably derives from Tanis or Bubastis and preserves the text of a formal investiture scene. The aegis (3.125 in by 3.25 in) depicts the head of Sakhmet flanked by two falcons above a large floral collar and names on the reverse both Osorkon and a Queen Tadibast, his mother or, less likely, his wife. In the abbreviated name "So," Osorkon is probably mentioned in 2 Kgs 17:4 as the Egyptian ruler to whom Hoshea of Israel sent envoys in a vain appeal for assistance against Assyria. In Assyrian records, Osorkon appears as "Shilkanni," king of Egypt, who presented a diplomatic gift of twelve large horses to Sargon II. The last mention of Osorkon is on the Piye Victory Stela of year 21, where the Tanite ruler is shown bowing in submission to the Nubian conqueror.

For the texts, references, and discussion, see Schneider 1985, 261–67 and pl. I; Gauthier 1914, 399–400 §§2.I–IV; and Price 1897, 298 no. 2520. A drawing of the Leiden ring appears in Leemans 1842–1905, 60 and pl. XCVII, no. 330; and Petrie 1905b, 264 fig. 107. The Louvre aegis is illustrated (front only) in Vernier 1907, 115 and pl. XIX.1; and Perrot and Chipiez 1883, 382–83 fig. 314. See Kitchen 1986, 88 §69, 116–17 §92, and 372–76 §§332–36; and the dissenting views in Redford 1986, 317; von Beckerath 1994, 7–8; 1997, 61, 93–94, and 98–99.

I. LEIDEN GLAZED RING (AO 10A)

ny-sw.t bỉ.ty ꜥꜣ-ḫpr-Rꜥ-stp-n-ꜣImn (2) ny-sw.t bỉ.ty Wsrknỉ[1] mrỉ-ꜣImn

King of Upper and Lower Egypt, Aakheperre-setepenamon. (2) King of Upper and Lower Egypt, Osorkon,[1] beloved of Amon.

II. LEIDEN RELIEF BLOCK (F 1971/9.1)

Label for Geb

Gb ỉry-pꜥ.t nṯr.w nṯr (2) [ꜥꜣ ...] (3) [dỉ ꜣ ỉ] n ꜣ k ns.t Gb ỉꜣw.t ꜣItm

Geb, the Hereditary Prince of the gods, the [great] god, (2) [...] (3) "[I have given] to you the throne of Geb, the office of Atum."

Label for King

[nb tꜣ.]wy ꜥꜣ-ḫpr-Rꜥ-stp-n-ꜣImn (2) [sꜣ Rꜥ] Wsrkỉn mrỉ-ꜣImn

[Lord of the Two] Lands, Aakheperre-setepenamon, (2) [Son of Re,] Osorkon, beloved of Amon.

III. LOUVRE AEGIS

sꜣ Rꜥ Wsrk(n)[2] (ꜥnḫ)[2] ḏ.t (2) mw.t nṯr ḥm.t ny-sw.t Tꜣ-dỉ-Bꜣst.t[3] ꜥnḫ.tỉ

Son of Re, Osorko(n)[2] (living)[2] forever. (2) The God's Mother and royal wife Tadibast,[3] who yet lives.

NOTES

1. The order of the signs is actually Swrknỉ, even closer to the Assyrian Shilkanni.

2. Omitted in error by the engraver.

3. The title "royal wife" and personal name are enclosed in a cartouche.

IV

DYNASTY XXIII

A. PEDUBAST I

108. RESTORATION INSCRIPTION OF PASHEDBAST (B)

One of the clearest documents of the peaceful condominium of Dynasties XXII and XIII is found in the dedication of a vestibule door at Pylon X at Karnak. Erected by Pashedbast (B), a younger son of Sheshonq III of Dynasty XXII, the doorway is nonetheless dated in the contemporary reign of Pedubast I of Dynasty XXIII.

For the text, translation, and discussion, see Legrain 1914, 13–14 and 39–40. See Kitchen 1986, 131 §103 and 339 §299.

ny-sw.t bỉ.ty nb tꜣ.wy Wsr-mꜣꜥ.t-Rꜥ-stp-n-ʾImn sꜣ Rꜥ nb ḫꜥ.w Pꜣ-dỉ-Bꜣst.t mrỉ-ʾImn dỉ ꜥnḫ ḏd wꜣs nb ꜣw.t-ỉb nb [ḏ.t] (2) [ỉmy-rꜣ mšꜥ] wr ḥꜣw. ty Pꜣ-šd-Bꜣst.t sꜣ ny-sw.t nb tꜣ.wy [Š]š[nq] mrỉ-ʾImn [mrỉ] ʾImn-Rꜥ nb ns.wt tꜣ.wy [ny-sw.t nṯr].w (3) [ḫnty ʾIp.t-]s.(w)t ỉr.n≠f sbḫ.t ꜥꜣ.t m ỉnr rwḏ.t m-ḫt gm.n≠f sw wꜣw [r wꜣs]

The King of Upper and Lower Egypt, Usimaꜥre-setepenamon, Son of Re, Lord of Diadems, Pedubast (I), given all life stability, dominion, and all joy [forever.] (2) [The] great [general] and leader, Pashedbast (B), king's son of the Lord of the Two Lands, [Sh]esh[onq] (III), beloved of Amon, [beloved of] Amon-Re, Lord of the Thrones of the Two Lands, [King of the Gods], (3) [Foremost in] Karnak. After he found it fallen [into ruin], he made a great portal consisting of hard stone.

109. DONATION STELA OF HARKHEBY
(FLORENCE 7207)

Formerly misattributed to Takelot I, this donation stela from Bubastis is unusual in depicting the beneficiary alone in the lunette, offering a lamp to the deities Bastet and Horus. The likely donor, King Pedubast I, is represented instead by his cartouches that flank the central figure of Bastet. The round-topped stela measures 0.67 m in height, 0.32 m in width, and 0.11 m in depth.

For the texts, translation, and discussion, see Caminos 1969, 42–46; and Menu 1998, 145. For additional discussion of the text, see Meeks 1979a, 609, 614, 627–30, 646, 650, and 671 (23.1.23). See Kitchen 1986, 116 §92 n. 151, 120–21 §95, and 341 §301.

LABEL FOR BASTET

dd-mdw în B3st.t ḥnw.t nṯr.w
Recitation by Bastet, Mistress of the gods.

LABEL FOR HORUS

dd-mdw în Ḥr s3 (2) B3st.t
Recitation by Horus, son of (2) Bastet.

LABEL FOR BENEFICIARY

ḥry k3nty[1] (2) n B3st.t Ḥr-Ḫby
Chief gardener[1] (2) of Bastet, Harkheby.

MAIN TEXT

Wsr-m3.t-R'-stp-n-'Imn (2) P3-dî-B3st.t mrî-'Imn (3) ḥsb.t 23.(t) (4) hrw pn dî ḥnk 3ḥ.w(t) st3.(t) 3 n² (ḥry) k3nty.w n B3st.t Ḥr-Ḫby (5) îr p(3) nty îw≠f th(î) p(3)y wd ḥr s.t≠f îw≠f n š'.t n.(t) ny-sw.t (6) nḫt îw≠f ḥr n nm.t n.(t) Sḫm.t p(3) nty îw≠f th(î) p(3)y wd

Usima're-setepenamon, (2) Pedubast, beloved of Amon. (3) Regnal year 23: (4) On this day there was given a donation of 3 *arouras* to² the (chief) of gardeners, Harkheby. (5) As for the one who will disturb this stela from its place, he is destined for the slaughter of the mighty king. (6) He will fall to the slaughter block of Sakhmet, the one who will disturb this stela.

NOTES

1. For the term, see Meeks 1979a, 629 n. 92, and cf. Erman and Grapow 1926–63, 5:107/8–9.

2. Caminos understood "belonging to" Harkheby, making him the donor rather than the recipient. For discussion, see Meeks 1979a, 629–30.

B. OSORKON III

110. A THEBAN FLOOD RECORDED IN LUXOR TEMPLE

Discovered by Grébaut in 1889, this weathered hieratic graffito of fifty-one lines is incised on two faces at right angles on the southernmost pilaster base separating the forecourt of Amonhotep III from the following hypostyle hall at Luxor temple (Nelson Key Plans 83).[1] The text begins (twenty-one lines) on the western face of the pilaster at the front of the hypostyle, with the continuation (thirty lines) from its left edge onto the northern face of the pilaster at the rear of the forecourt. Composed by the priest and scribe Nakhtefmut (line 9), the text comprises a hymn and reproof to the god Amon, who has inexplicably submerged his sacred city, disrupting human activity and diverting temple ritual (lines 4–8). Nakhefmut is careful to remind the deity that there have been no lapses in temple construction or ritual texts (lines 28–30), cited elsewhere as motives for divine displeasure.[2]

The Luxor inscription corresponds to text 5 of the records of Theban Nile flood levels carved on the western face of the Karnak quay. It is the second highest level recorded, indicating a flood depth of more than two feet (62 cm) above the Luxor temple pavement.[3] For the quay records, see above, text 7.

Presented here is the first complete translation, aided by collation of the original by John C. and Deborah Darnell and the author in 1996. Recently cleaned, the text is now damaged by salts from rising ground water. Text and partial translation in Daressy 1896a, 181–86[4]; with further commentary in Legrain 1896a, 120; Daressy, 1898, 80 §CLIX; Breasted 1906–7, 4:369–70 §§742–44 (lines 1–6 only); Meyer 1907–8, 116; Porter and Moss 1972, 317 (98 a–b); and Chicago Oriental Institute Photos 9091–92. For the reattribution of the text to Osorkon III rather than II, see Gauthier 1914, 382–83 §I; and Daressy 1926, 7–8 n. 3. See Kitchen 1986, 92 n. 38 and 342–43 n. 557.

A. Hypostyle Section = Porter and Moss 1972, 317 (98 b)

(1) ḥsb.t 3.t 3bd 3 pr.t[5] sw 12 ḫr ḥm[6] n ny-sw.t bỉ.ty nb t3.wy Wsr-m3ʿ.t-Rʿ-stp-n-ʾImn ʿnḫ wḏ3 snb s3 Rʿ

(2) Wsrkn mrỉ-ʾImn s3 3s.t[7] dỉ ʿnḫ ḏ.t ỉw bs[8] nwn m tp(?)[9] [...] t3 pn r ḏr.w≠f

(3) ỉqḥ.n≠f[10] tn.wy[11] mỉ sp tpy [...]t[...] t3 pn n sḫm≠f mỉ w3ḏ-wr nn ʿ-(n)-mw[12]

(4) rmṯ r ḫsf 3.t≠f ḥr nb m ḥmwy.w[13] ḥr nỉw.t≠f[14] nšn [...]≠f ḥy [...].. mỉ p.t

(5) r.w-pr.w nb n W3s.t mỉ ḥm.w hrw pn sḫꜥ n ꜣImn n ꜣIp.t p3 w[ỉ3¹⁵] n sšm≠f šp[sy]¹⁶

(6) ꜥq≠f r pr wr n wỉ3≠f r-pr pn nỉw.tyw≠f mỉ nb[y.w] m w3w sbḫ≠

(7) sn pw m p.t ḥr Rꜥ r s3ḫ nṯr pn ꜥ3 m p3 ỉw nfr ḥtp≠f m ꜣIp.t-s.wt

(8) ḏsr nn rḫ≠tw mn ꜣIp.t mỉ p.t¹⁷ r sw3š nṯr ꜥ3 m wr b3.w≠f s3-mr≠f ỉsk wḏ≠f

(9) ỉr.n{n}¹⁸ ḥm-nṯr n ꜣImn-Rꜥ ny-sw.t nṯr.w sš ny-sw.t m pr-ꜥnḫ¹⁶ Nḫt-t3y≠f-Mw.t¹⁹ [s3 ḥm-nṯr …]-nw²⁰ (n) ꜣImn B3k-n-Ḫns

(10) ḏd≠f ỉ nṯr šps ms sw ḏs≠f ỉty n sp3.t(?)≠f ꜥḫ m ḫꜥ[.w(?)]≠f¹⁶ dmḏ ḥr ỉtn≠f mỉ […]

(11) ḫr ḏ.t≠f r sḫ3p sšt3≠f smsw ḫpr m h3.t t3.wy ḥr ḫnty≠f q3mw ḫ.t nb.t

(12) sḥb r.w-pr.w≠f wbny r nḥḥ ḥtpy ḏ.t msb n ḥn [nḥ]ḥ¹⁶

(13) wḥm ms.wt ḥr sšp.t krḥ m ḫprw≠f mnḫ n ỉꜥḫ ỉy n Ḥꜥpy

(14) r bꜥḥ t3.wy sꜥnḫ r3 nb m rwd≠f t3w pw ḥns m sts≠f srq.n≠f ỉḥty

(15) nb pr nsr.w m sty.w≠f ḥr smnḫ ỉr.n≠f nb sḫm ḏsr ỉr(?) n

(16) ḏr.t(?)≠f²¹ ḫpr nṯr.w nṯr.wt ỉm≠f wtt≠f rmt.t ꜥw.t ỉpty.w ḫnn.w ḏd-

(17) mw.t(?)²² nb.t ỉr.t(w) nn r 3w m ḥmw n ỉb≠f ḥr grg t3.wy ỉr pr(?) r(?) šn.t≠f r ḫpr m-ꜥ

(18) nỉw.t≠k W3s.t ỉr.t Rꜥ ḥnw.t t3.w twt pw r ḥry.t ḥry sḫn r≠s m sp tpy

(19) msḫn.t nfr.t n.t B3.wy-dmḏ h3≠f r≠s m ḫ.t Nw.t h3yn3²³ pw n

(20) b3≠f K3-mw.t≠f swr nḫt.w≠f m ḫnty≠s b3wtyw²⁴ s.w

(21) nṯr.w nṯr.wt dmḏ≠sn r≠s ḥr nfr.w[≠s]¹⁶ sthn ḥr nb n m33≠s m ḥp bh²⁵

B. FORECOURT SECTION = PORTER AND MOSS 1972, 317 (98 A)

(22) ḫnm≠s m ꜥntyw nb wrỉ[…] w3ḏ [..]≠sn

(23) s.t-ỉb n nṯr.w r [p.t(?)] pw-trỉ mkw s.t nn n(t)k

(24) [rw]ḏ≠s¹⁶ m ḫnt t3 pn r 3w≠f wbn.tw rꜥ nb ḥr m33 p3 [ỉtn(?)]

(25) ỉḥty(?)≠s m t3w n¹⁶ r3 ḥr≠s ỉt.t r Šmꜥ≠s [… b]ꜥḥ¹⁶

(26) r ḥ.wt-nṯr≠k wr s.t≠k ḏsr m p3wty t3.wy ỉmn.n≠k tw m¹⁶

(27) ḫnw≠s swr mnw≠f […].w […] ny.w-sw.t bỉ.tyw ḥr ỉr

(28) 3ḫ n k3≠k skm.tw ds.t ỉnr.w r s3w.t≠s ḥr

(29) sq3≠s ỉmy.t ḥw.t-nṯr≠k r3≠sn wr s ḫr≠k ḥr ḏd≠k r≠s m r3≠k

(30) ḏs≠k ỉnk ꜣImn ḥtp≠f m ḫnty ỉp.t≠f ḥr r3.w ntry ỉr.n nb mk3.tw

(31) ḫft sḏm.tw²⁶ mỉ ỉmy.w sp3.wt wn≠sn ḥr nỉs≠k rꜥ nb ḥr dr

(32) ḏw nb m nỉw.t≠w qꜥ ỉmw²⁷ wḥm.n≠f ỉy ỉmw²⁷

(33) sšm pn wꜥ3w pw wr nn sḫ3.tw [mỉ.ty]≠f gs ỉpt ꜥ3mw

(34) (ỉ)n w3ḏ-wr ptr sỉ3.tw m-ꜥ ḥnmm.t bss

(35) Ḥꜥpy m wḏ.n≠k ỉn-ỉw≠f smḥ pr≠k m mḏw.t≠f wbn.tw ḫꜥ.tw

(36) m W3s.t rḫ≠sn mỉ m wḥm(?) m qỉ≠f pr≠f h3≠f ḥr sḫr.w

(37) w3ḫ≠f wḏb.w r […] dbn

(38) .n≠f ỉp.t≠k (m) ỉtrw¹⁶ [...]s ẖnn.w m ẖnty≠s [...]

(39) ẖpr ds≠f sẖr.w ḏw pw r [...] ... [...] nỉw.tyw

(40) wr ỉr.n{n} ỉmw m ẖnty nỉw.t≠k [...] wbn [...]

(41) [...] m rkw ny-sw.t Mn-ẖpr-Rꜥ [...]

(42) [...]≠f rḫ≠f nn wnw m-ꜥ≠f wnn ỉty ẖr [...] pr(?)≠k k3

(43) [...] nỉw.t≠k m h3yn3 [...]≠k [...] m ẖnty [...]

(44) [...]

(45) ẖprw n-ỉm≠s wh3 [...]

(46) m rkw s3≠k ny-sw.t bỉ.ty Wsrkn ḥnꜥ sn≠f¹⁶ [ꜣIwpwṯ(?)...]

(47) ỉmw²⁷ ỉt ỉm≠s swr≠k šf(y.t)≠k m ỉb.w(?) nb ẖ3(.wt)≠sn ntt

(48) 3[q] m wḏ≠k nn nḫ[.t²⁸ r] sẖ ḥr≠k²⁹ r≠s wp³⁰ nn mk [...]

(49) [...]

(50) ỉw(?)≠k ỉr≠k ḏd [...]w [...] p3 [ẖrly(?)] [...]

(51) ỉmw²⁷ r tpḥ.t≠f ỉp.t [...]≠s

(1) Regnal year 3, third month (of) winter,⁵ day 12 under the Majesty⁶ of the King of Upper and Lower Egypt, Lord of the Two Lands, Usimaꜥ-resetepenamon, l.p.h., Son of Re,

(2) Osorkon, beloved of Amon, Son of Isis,⁷ given life forever. The flood water of the Abyss welled up⁸ in the first (?)⁹ [...] this entire land.

(3) As at the beginning of time (lit., "the first occasion"), it attained¹⁰ the bordering mountains,¹¹ [...] this land being in its power like the sea. There was no canal¹²

(4) made by (lit., "of") man to repel its intensity, everyone being as fleas¹³ in hisJ city, its raging high [...] as heaven,

(5) every temple of Thebes like swamps. On this day occurred the processional appearance of Amon of Luxor (in) the ba[rk¹⁵] of his au[gust]¹⁶ portable image.

(6) He entered into the shrine (lit., "great house") of his bark of this temple, with his citizens like swimmers in the waves. It was

(7) their petition in heaven before Re to approach this great god in the beautiful island so that he might rest in Karnak

(8) the holy, since it was unknown whether Luxor was (yet) firm like heaven,¹⁷ in order to praise the great god through the greatness of his manifestation. The son-who-loves, then, (here is) his command,

(9) made by¹⁸ the prophet of Amon-Re, King of the Gods, royal scribe in the scriptorium,¹⁶ Nakhtefmut,¹⁹ [son of the ...²⁰ prophet] of Amon, Bakenkhons.

(10) He said: "O noble god who gave birth to himself, sovereign of his nome (?), exalted in his appearance[s]¹⁶, united with his disk like [...]

(11) with his body in order to conceal his secret image! O eldest one, who came to be before the Two Lands at his beginning, who created everything,

(12) who puts his temples in festival, rising forever, setting forever, conducting to the limits [of eter]nity,[16]

(13) who is reborn in the glow of night in his excellent form as the moon, who comes as the Inundation

(14) to flood the Two Lands so as to vivify every mouth with his strength! He is the wind that flies through his firmament, having caused

(15) all throats to breathe, from whose rays the heat goes forth perfecting all that he has made. Sacred power, who acted by means of

(16) his hand,[21] from whom all gods and goddesses came into being! He engendered all mankind, animals, birds, fish, and matter (?),[22]

(17) with all this done by the skill of his heart in founding the Two Lands, having caused that things go forth (?) to his storehouse (?) in order to be in the possession of

(18) your city Thebes, the Eye of Re, mistress of the lands. It is equal to distant heaven, in which one alighted in the beginning of time,

(19) the goodly birth-brick of "Him-Whose-Two-Spirits-Are-United," to which he descends from the body of Nut. It is the dwelling place[23] of

(20) his *ba*-spirit, Kamutef, who augments his victories within it—the primordial one (?)[24] (for) men,

(21) gods and goddesses, to which they gather because of [its] beauty,[16] at the seeing of which every face is brightened, through the running of the one who has fled,[25]

(22) its fragrance all of myrrh, great […] flourish [with] their [flowers (?)],

(23) the favorite place of the gods, more than [heaven (?)]. Who will protect it, if not you,

(24) [that it might gr]ow[16] from the beginning of this land to its full extent, shining each day, seeing the [disk (?)],

(25) its throat (?) with breath for[16] the mouth, its face turned (?) to its Upper Egypt […] flood[16]

(26) into your great temple, your sacred place as the primeval one of the Two Lands, you having hidden yourself[16]

(27) within it, O you whose monuments are magnified […], with kings of Upper and Lower Egypt performing

(28) benefactions for your *ka*-spirit. Completed is the cutting of stones to be its walls,

(29) elevating them within your temple. As for their incantations, they are great before you because of what you said regarding them with your own mouth:

(30) "I am Amon, resting within his chapel because of the divine incantations that the lord made." Be attentive

(31) and listen, please,[26] to those who are in the nomes. They have been summoning you daily about driving out

(32) all evil from their city since the "sea"[27] poured forth, and again it has come forth (as) a sea.[27]

(33) This situation is a great curse! Nothing [like] it can be recalled, with half of Luxor swallowed

(34) by the sea! How is (it) to be perceived by humanity? It is

(35) in accordance with what you have commanded that the Inundation wells up. Will it submerge your temple in its depths while you rise and shine

(36) in Thebes? How will they know when his proper form will return, when he comes and goes according to plan,

(37) depositing sandbanks at [...?]

(38) He has encircled your chapel (with) the river[16] [...] its [...], fish before it [...]

(39) [...] who came into being by himself. It is an evil plan to [...] compel (?) [...] citizens

(40) [...] great [...] which the sea made before your city [...] shine [...]

(41) [...] in the time of King Menkheperre (Tuthmosis III) [...]

(42) his [...] he knew he had nothing. The sovereign was doing [...] your house. Then

(43) [...] your city as the dwelling place [...] you [...] before [...]

(44) [...]

(45) which came into being within it, fail [...]

(46) in the time of your son, the King of Upper and Lower Egypt Osorkon and his brother[16] [Iuput (?) ...]

(47) sea[27] take possession of it (Thebes?), that you might magnify your dignity in all hearts. Their corpses that

(48) have perished as you commanded, there is no prayer[28] [to] dissuade[29] you regarding them. Nor[30] is there protection [...]

(49) [...]

(50) you come (?) that you might do [that which ...] said [...] the [...] heaven [... that there return (?)]

(51) the sea[27] to its cavern-source, and Luxor [...] its [...].

NOTES

1. Wrongly stated to be the "northwest" corner of the hypostyle in Daressy 1896a, 181; followed by Breasted 1906–7, 4:369 n. a. From the central axis of the hypostyle hall, the pilaster stands in the northeast corner; see Porter and Moss 1972, pl. XXXI (98 a–b); and Nelson 1941, pl. XXII (83).

2. Cf. "The Dream of Nectonebo" in Wilcken 1927, 369–74; and Maspero 1967, 285–89.

3. Daressy 1898, 80 § CLIX, correcting 1896a, 186. For earlier texts of the "flood genre," see Baines 1974, 39-54; Breasted 1906–7, 4:308–9, §§627–30 (Gebelein inscription of Smendes), and cf. the stela of Ahmose describing unprecedented

rain, discussed in Foster and Ritner 1996, 1–14, and note the reference to events under Tuthmosis III in line 41, below.

4. Daressy had first discussed the text in a lecture before the Institut Égyptien, 6 December 1895; see Legrain 1896a, 120.

5. Daressy read tpy pr.t "first month of winter/Tybi"), although this date was noted as uncertain already in Legrain 1896b, 120. E. Meyer, aided by a collation by L. Borchardt, emended the date to 3bd 3 pr.t "third month of winter/Phamenoth" (1907–8, 116). The revised dating is followed by Gauthier 1914, 382–83. For discussion, see Gauthier 1914, 383 n. 1.

6. The divine determinative, miscopied by Daressy as a seated deity, is represented by a falcon on a standard throughout the text.

7. For the clear distinction between Osorkon-beloved-of-Amon (III) "Son of Isis" and Osorkon-beloved-of-Amon (II) "Son of Bastet," see Kitchen 1986, 88–94.

8. Erman and Grapow 1926–63, 1:474/5–6.

9. Uncertain traces; tp(?) "first/upon"?

10. Erman and Grapow 1926–63, 1:138/13.

11. Erman and Grapow 1926–63, 5:372/5–6.

12. First recognized by Daressy 1896a, 184 n. 11; see Erman and Grapow 1926–63, 1:159/7; Clère 1983, 95–96; and the full writing in Erichsen 1954, 51.

13. Erman and Grapow 1926–63, 3:281/12. Daressy 1896a, 184, translated "pelicans."

14. Probably "Amon's"; cf. lines 6, 18, and 43.

15. Reading suggested by Breasted 1906–7, 4:369, corroborated by still-visible traces of a bark.

16. Reading courtesy of John C. and Deborah Darnell.

17. If correctly analyzed, the passage suggests a transferral of the cult image from the flooded Luxor to the Karnak temple.

18. For the writing with double n, characteristic of the period, see Erman and Grapow 1926–63, 1:111/7, marked "D. 22"; and Caminos 1952, 51–52, textual note 5.

19. Nḥt determined by a man with stick, not w and strong arm.

20. Second-, Third-, or Fourth-ranked Prophet of Amon.

21. Text copy marked uncertain by Daressy 1896a, 182. If correctly transcribed, a reference to the creator's generative act of masturbation.

22. Text copy marked uncertain by Daressy 1896a, 182. Erman and Grapow 1926–63, 5:634, literally "heaps" of minerals, vegetation, etc.

23. Erman and Grapow 1926–63, 2:484.

24. On the basis of the determinative, taken as a phonetic rendering of p3w.ty (Erman and Grapow 1926–63, 1:496–97), with a common b/p switch. Or (?) metathesis for bw3.t "covert, sporting place" (Erman and Grapow 1926–63, 1:455/1). Daressy 1896a, 185, translated "center(?)."

25. A reference to the heavenly course of the returning sun god? Daressy (1896a, 185) translated: "on ne peut s'en aller l'abandonnant."

26. The phrase was miscopied by Daressy, who translated (1896a, 185): "Un appel t'est fait pour combattre (le mal)." For the emended text, see Caminos 1958, 107 §q; Osing 1983, 356 §u; and Erman and Grapow 1935–53, 2:240, to 1926–63, 2:162/11: mk3.tw ḥft sḏm.tw.

27. Variant spellings of ym "sea/floodwaters" unregistered in Erman and Grapow 1926–63, 1:78/11, and unrecognized by Daressy 1896a, 186 n. 1. This metaphorical use of "sea" corresponds to the mention of w3d̲-wr in lines 3 and 34.

28. Erman and Grapow 1926–63, 2:289.

29. Literally, "to make dumb the face"; see Erman and Grapow 1926–63, 3:474/5–10.

30. "But there is not..."; taken as disjunctive, Erman and Grapow 1926–63, 1:301/21. Or (?) translate "dissuade you regarding them (in) judgment."

111. AKORIS STELA OF OSORKON III

Now lacking its rounded lunette, this limestone stela discovered in 1982 measures 51.0 cm in height, 49.5 cm. in width, and 11.0 cm in depth. The eleven preserved lines of text record a gift of oil by Osorkon III to the local temple of Amon-Re at Akoris (Tehneh) in Middle Egypt and the oracular confirmation of the gift by Amon-Re, Mut, Khonsu, and the local avatar of Amon. The stela is notable primarily for its extensive quotation of Osorkon's titulary, which here includes the designation "high priest of Amon." Despite this addition, Osorkon III probably cannot be identified with the earlier high priest Osorkon (B), son of Takelot II; see Kitchen 1995, xxxi §BB. For royal use of this title, cf. the Titles of the Tanite Priest-King Pseusennes I, no. 29 above.

For the text, photo, and translation, see Den Tomimura in Paleological Association of Japan, Egyptian Committee 1995, 301–6 and pl. 116 (top); and Madoka Suzuki in Paleological Association of Japan 1983, 13–16. See Kitchen 1986, 580 §520.

TEXT

(1) [ḥ]sb.t 3 [+ x 3b]d 3 [... sw] 3 [+x] ḫr ḥm [n ...]

(2) ḫ3s.wt s3 3s.t Ḥr sḫm ḫpš îtî t3.wy [ʿ3] pḥ.ty îty nb(?)

(3) t3.wy m3î ḥs ʿ3 hmhm ḫry.t≠f m ḫ3s.wt mî ʾImn-Rʿ ny-sw.t nt̲r.w wr

(4) ny(.t)-sw.t mî Tm (wr) ḥb(.w)-sd mî Tnn ḥm-nt̲r tp(y) n ʾImn-Rʿ ny-sw.t nt̲r.w ny-sw.t bî.ty nb t3.wy Wsr-m3ʿ.t-Rʿ-stp-n-ʾImn{-Rʿ}[1] nt̲r ḥq3 W3s.t

(5) s3 Rʿ nb ḫʿ.w Wsrk(n) mrî-ʾImn s3 3s.t dî ʿnḫ mî Rʿ d̲.t h3[2] pn smn. ty p3 12 n g3dy[3] n

(6) nḫ(ḫ)[4] r Pr ʾImn-Rʿ-m3î-ḫnty[5] tp t3 mr (ḥr)-ʿ.wy[6] n3 îmy.w-r3[7] mr în ny-sw.t bî.ty nb t3.wy

(7) Wsr-m3ʿ.t-Rʿ-stp-n-ʾImn{-Rʿ}[1] nt̲r ḥq3 W3s.t[8] s3 Rʿ nb ḫʿ.w Wsrk(n) mrî-ʾImn s3 3s.t d̲d ʾImn-Rʿ ny-sw.t nt̲r.w p3 nt̲r ʿ3 wr š3ʿ ḫpr Mw.t wr(.t)

(8) nb(.t) ʾIšrw Ḥnsw m W3s.t Nfr-ḥtp Ḥr nb 3w.t-îb ʾImn-Rʿ-m3î-ḫnty[5] îr p3 nty-îw≠f

(9) mnmn t3 wd̲(.t) ỉw≠f n š'dy n ỉmn-R' ỉw≠f n hh n ḥm n S̲ḫm.t

(10) nn 'q ḫ3.t≠f [r ḥr.t-ntr(?) ... ỉw≠w dỉ.t≠f tp(?)] ḫt

(11) ỉr p3 ỉry smn t3 wd̲(.t) ỉw≠f n ḥsw.t n p3 nb ['ḥ]'(?) q3 m-'≠f mỉ R' d̲.t

TRANSLATION

(1) [Reg]nal year 3 [+x, mon]th 3 [of ...], day 3 [+x] under the Majesty [of ... who ...]

(2) the foreign lands, the Son of Isis, Horus, powerful of arm, who seized the Two Lands, [great of] strength, Sovereign, Lord

(3) of the Two Lands, the wild lion, great of war-shout, terror of whom is in the foreign lands like Amon-Re, King of the Gods, great of

(4) kingship like Atum, (great) of jubilee(s) like (Ptah-)Tenen, First Prophet of Amon-Re, King of the Gods, King of Upper and Lower Egypt, Lord of the Two Lands, Usima'resetepenamon{re},[1] the God, Ruler of Thebes,

(5) Son of Re, Lord of Diadems, Osorko(n), beloved of Amon, Son of Isis, given life like Re forever. On this day[2] there were established the 12 vessels[3] of

(6) oil[4] for the estate of Amon-Re-the-Lion-at-the-South[5] upon the riverbank under the supervision of[6] the harbor masters[7] by the King of Upper and Lower Egypt, Lord of the Two Lands,

(7) Usima'resetepenamon{re},[1] the God, Ruler of Thebes,[8] Son of Re, Lord of Diadems, Osorko(n), beloved of Amon, Son of Isis. There said Amon-Re, King of the Gods, the very great god since the beginning of creation, and Mut, the great,

(8) the Lady of Asheru, and Khonsu-in-Thebes, Neferhotep, the Horus lord of joy, and Amon-Re-the-Lion-at-the-South[5]: "As for the one who will

(9) displace the stela, he shall be subject to the slaughter of Amon-Re; he shall be subject to the fiery blast of the Majesty of Sakhmet.

(10) His corpse shall not enter [the necropolis (?) ... He shall be placed upon (?)] the stake.

(11) As for the one who will confirm the stela, he shall be in the favor of the lord, a long life (?) being his like Re forever.

NOTES

1. In both lines 4 and 7, an intrusive R' appears before ỉmn and after stp-n-, surely deriving from the common prenomen Usima'resetepenre.

2. Phonetic spelling, cf. Coptic ϨΟΟⲨ.

3. So Tomimura, but cf. g3tỉ "oil" Erman and Grapow 1926–63, 5:208/12.

4. Traditionally understood as sesame oil, but see Krauss 1999, 293–98.

5. The local form of Amon at Tehneh; see Yoyotte 1950, 193; and Paleological Association of Japan, Egyptian Committee 1995, 301 n. 2.

6. For the writing, see Černý and Groll 1975, 115. Tomimura understands "by the hands of."

7. Tomimura treats n₃ as a genitive and translates "harbor-master" in the singular.

8. Unlike in line 4, "the God, Ruler of Thebes" is inserted within the cartouche.

C. PEFTCHAUAWYBAST (LOCAL HERACLEOPOLIS DYNASTY)

112. HARSAPHES AND ROYAL STATUES
(BOSTON MFA 06.2408 AND MFA 1977.16)

Symptomatic of the political fragmentation of the later Libyan era are the petty city states of Heracleopolis and Hermopolis, both prominent in the Piye Victory Stela. Each obtained a degree of independence perhaps as early as the reign of Takelot III. While the Hermopolite kingdom of Namlot is otherwise unattested, the rule of Peftchauawybast in Heracleopolis is confirmed by statuary, two coffin inscriptions, and two donation decrees of his tenth year.

I. Harsaphes Statue Boston (MFA 06.2408)

Made of solid gold, the 6 cm statuette of the local ram deity Harsaphes was excavated at Ahnas el-Medineh, the site of ancient Heracleopolis. Below the base is a votive dedication improperly divided by the engraver into three columns. The order given below follows Petrie's rearrangement. Peftchauawybast's insistence upon "true rulership" seems special pleading for a kinglet caught between competing claims of suzerainty. Reflecting contemporary archaizing practice, his prenomen Neferkare recalls that of Pepi II of the Old Kingdom. Imitations of Pepi II's Horus name and prenomen have also been recovered from the sacred lake at Tanis and may be further attestations of Peftchauawybast.

For the text, translation, and discussion, see Petrie 1905a, frontispiece and 18–19; Gauthier 1914, 400; Graefe 1990, 86 n. 8; and Russman 1981, 149–55. For the Tanaite blocks, see Montet 1966, 73–75.

ny-sw.t bỉ.ty Nfr-k₃-Rꜥ s₃ Rꜥ P₃(y)⸗f-t₃w-(m)-ꜥ.wy-B₃s.t¹ mry Ḥry-š⸗f ny-sw.t t₃.wy dỉ ḥq₃ m₃ꜥ.t dỉ ꜥnḫ ḏ.t Sm₃-t₃.wy² dỉ ꜥnḫ wḏ₃ (n) Nfr.wy-B₃s.t

The King of Upper and Lower Egypt, Neferkare, Son of Re, Peftchau-awybast, beloved of Harsaphes, King of the Two Lands, who grants true rulership, given life forever. The Uniter of the Two Lands² gives life and prosperity to Neferwybast.

II. ROYAL STATUE OF PEFTCHAUAWYBAST (BOSTON MFA 1977.16)

This kneeling, royal bronze figure (22 cm in height) wears a "Kushite-like Egyptian royal cap" and on the basis of style is assigned to Neferkare Peftchauawybast. In proportions and regalia it parallels the contemporary faience plaque of Iuput II, with conscious adaptation to official Kushite conventions. For the text, translation, and discussion, see Russman 1981, 149–55.

BELT INSCRIPTION
Nfr-k3-Rᶜ   Neferkare

NOTES
 1. For the correct handcopy of the text, see Russman 1981, 154.
 2. An epithet of Harsaphes.

113. DONATION STELAE OF YEAR 10
(CAIRO JDE 45948 AND TEMPORARY REGISTRATION 11/9/21/14)

Two donation stelae discovered in Ahnas el-Medineh, ancient Heracleopolis, record land donations made by King Peftchauawybast for the support of one or two daughters enrolled as "chantresses of the Residence of Amon." If princess Ilot of Cairo JdE 45948 should be equated with a proposed "[chantress of A]mon (I)lot" in Cairo 11/9/21/14, then the duplicate stelae would prove that such monuments served as actual field markers, a conclusion otherwise supported by the design of their bases. As in the donation stela for Karoama, these decrees record a dowry for a princess depicted alone, with neither king nor intermediary.

For the texts, translation, and discussion, see Daressy 1917b, 43–45; 1921, 138–39; Menu 1998, 145–46; and Graefe 1990, 85–90. For additional discussions of the text, see Meeks 1979a, 609, 612, 616, 627, 630, 646, 652, and 672 (23IX.10a–b). See Kitchen 1986, 181 §147, 234 §198, and 357–58 §319.

I. CAIRO JDE 45948

The round-topped limestone stela measures 0.55 m in height by 0.31 m in width. Below the glyph for heaven, Amon and Mut are adored by the royal daughter and chantress Ilot, the beneficiary of the donation. The lower base (0.21 m) is undecorated and thicker than the rest, being designed as a tenon to support the stela in the ground.

Label for Amon-Re
 dd-mdw ꜣImn-Rᶜ nb (2) ns.wt t3.wy
 Recitation by Amon-Re, Lord (2) of the Thrones of the Two Lands.

Label for Mut
    Mw.t nb.(t) p.t
    Mut, Lady of heaven.

Label for Beneficiary Ilot
    ḥs.(t) (n.t) ẖnw (n) ꜣImn¹ (2) ꜣIrwt (3) ms n (4) ḥm.t ny-sw.t sꜣ.t ny-
    sw.t² Tꜣ-šr.(t)-n.(t)-ꜣs.t ꜥnḫ.tỉ mỉ Rꜥ ḏ.t nḥḥ
    The chantress of the Residence of Amon,¹ (2) Ilot, (3) born of (4) the
    Queen and Princess,² Tasherenese, living like Re forever and ever.

Main Text
    ḥsb.t 10.t ny-sw.t bỉ.ty nb tꜣ.wy Nfr-kꜣ-Rꜥ sꜣ Rꜥ P(ꜣy)≠f-tꜣw-(m)-ꜥ.(wy)-
    Bꜣs.t dỉ ꜥnḫ (2) hrw pn dỉ.t 50 stꜣ.t m swꜣw wḏbꜣ (3) n Pꜣ-ỉhy-n-ẖꜣ.t ỉw≠w
    mn r nḥḥ ḏ.t (4) ỉr pꜣ nty ỉw≠f th(ỉ) wḏ.(t) tn ỉw≠f (r) šꜥ(5)d ꜣImn-Rꜥ ỉw≠f
    n ḥḥ Sẖm.t
    Regnal year 10 (of) the King of Upper and Lower Egypt, Lord of the
    Two Lands, Neferkare, Son of Re, Peftchauawybast, given life. (2) On this
    day there was given 50 *arouras* in the riverbank³ region (3) of the town
    "The-Camp-at-the-Front," they being established forever and ever. (4) As
    for the one who will transgress this stela, he is destined to the slaughter of
    Amon-Re; he is subject to the fiery blast of Sakhmet.

III. CAIRO 11/9/21/14
    The round-topped limestone stela measures 0.49 m in height by 0.28
    m in width. In the lunette, Amon and Mut are adored by the standing vota-
    ress, who holds a sistrum and broad necklace with menat counterpoise.
    A vertical royal cartouche separates the deities and beneficiary. The lower
    base (0.175 m) is undecorated and thicker to serve as a tenon.

Label for Amon-Re
    ꜣImn-Rꜥ nb [ns.wt tꜣ.wy]
    Amon-Re, Lord [of the Thrones of the Two Lands.]

Label for Mut
    [Mw.t] nb.(t) p.t
    [Mut,] Lady of heaven.

Royal Cartouche
    ny-sw.t bỉ.ty [Pꜣ(y)≠f-tꜣw-(m)-ꜥ.(wy)-Bꜣs.t] mry ꜣImn-Rꜥ
    The King of Upper and Lower Egypt, [Peftchauawybast], beloved of
    Amon-Re.

Label for Beneficiary

[ḥs.(t) (n.t) ẖn]w⁴ (2) (n) ʾImn [...]mnrỉt⁵ mw.t(3)[≠s ḥm.t ny-sw.t] Tꜣ-šr.(t)-[n.(t)]-ꜣs.[t ꜥnẖ.tỉ mỉ Rꜥ] ḏ.t

[The chantress of the Residence] (2) of Amon, [...]men-lot,⁵ whose mother (3) is [the Queen] Tasherenese, [living like Re] forever.

Main Text

(1) ḥsb.t 10.t nṯr nfr nb tꜣ.wy nb ỉr ẖ.t Pꜣ(y)≠f-tꜣw-(m)-ꜥ.(wy)-Bꜣs.t dỉ ꜥnẖ m[ỉ Rỉ ḏ.t nḥḥ] (2) hrw pn dỉ.t 50 stꜣ.t ꜣḥ.t (n) ḥs.(t) n.(t) ẖn[w (n) ʾImn ..mnr](3)ỉwṯ⁵ tꜣy≠f šr.t (m) d[d] Pꜣ(y)≠f-tꜣw-(m)-ꜥ.(wy)-Bꜣs.t n dmỉ [n Pꜣ-ỉh](4)y-n-ẖꜣ.t ỉw≠w mn r nḥḥ ḏ.t

Regnal year 10 (of) the Good God, Lord of the Two Lands, Lord of ritual performance, Peftchauawybast, given life like [Re forever and ever.] (2) On this day there was given 50 *arouras* of field for the chantress of the Residence [of Amon, ...men-l](3)ot,⁵ his daughter, as a gift of King Peftchauawybast to the town [of "The-Camp-](4)at-the-Front," they being established forever and ever.

NOTES

1. For such chantresses, see the Funerary Stela of Tafabart, p. 32, and Ritner 1998, 85–90.

2. Following Graefe 1990, 87 n. 13, the sign ny-sw.t serves double duty in the phrase "queen and princess." Daressy understood "wife of the royal prince" (ḥm.t sꜣ ny-sw.t with honorific transposition of ny-sw.t), while Menu understood "daughter of the royal wife" (sꜣ.t ḥm.t ny-sw.t with honorific transposition of ḥm.t ny-sw.t). If Ilot is the daughter of King Peftchauawybast in Cairo 11/9/21/14, she cannot be the daughter of a junior prince (as Daressy) nor the granddaughter of Peftchauawybast's queen (as Menu).

3. Meeks understood "occidental region" (1979a, 630 n. 93).

4. For the restoration, see Graefe 1990, 88. Daressy restored [nb.t] pr "housewife." Meeks and Menu would restore the chantress title in line 2.

5. The identity of the princess and beneficiary is disputed, with Meeks and Menu equating Ilot of JdE 45948 with the "[...]men-lot" of this text by restoring the end of line 2 of her label as [ḥs.(t) (n.t) ẖnw (n)ʾI]mn Rỉt "chantress of the Residence of A]mon, (I)lot." If correct, the restoration of lines 2–3 in the main text should be "chantress of the Residence [of Amon, (I)l]ot, his daughter."

D. RUDAMON

Son of Osorkon III and brother of Takelot III, Rudamon (Amonrud in older works) is attested by only a few citations, and the length of his reign is unknown. His titulary survives on a rock-crystal vase in the Louvre and on minor additions to the peripheral Karnak temple of Osiris Heqa-Djet. Rudamon's genealogy may be reconstructed on the basis of two funerary records of his descendants: a votive inscription of his daughter Nesiterpauti and a coffin fragment naming a great-grandson, Padiamonnebnesuttawy.

114. LOUVRE ROCK CRYSTAL VASE

For the text and bibliography, see Daressy 1897a, 20–21 §CXLII; Gauthier 1914, 392; Pierre 1874–78, 180. See Kitchen 1986, 127 §101 and 360 §322.

ntr nfr Wsr-mȝꜥ.t-Rꜥ-stp-n-ꜣImn (2) nb tȝ.wy Rwd-ꜣImn mrꜣ-ꜣImn

The Good God, Usimaꜥre-setepenamon, (2) The Lord of the Two Lands, Rudamon, beloved of Amon.

115. ADDITIONS TO THE TEMPLE OF OSIRIS HEQA-DJET

Located at the eastern edge of the Karnak enclosure, the small temple of Osiris Heqa-Djet ("Ruler of Eternity") was constructed by Osorkon III, Takelot III, and the divine Adoratrix, Shepenwepet I. One door lintel is carved with an elaborate, stylized presentation of a king's titulary that does not correspond to those of the founders and is thus attributed to Rudamon, who is elsewhere attested at the site by two painted cartouches, inserted somewhat intrusively in earlier carved scenes.

Until the appearance of the long-awaited publication of the temple announced by Kadish and Redford forthcoming, the texts and discussion are available only in Legrain 1900b, 130 (= Oriental Institute photo 9675), 132 (= photos 9641–42), and 134 (= photos 9651–52). Rudamon's titulary at this site is confused with that of Takelot III in von Beckerath 1975, 222.

A. Door Lintel (Legrain Chamber B, Wall A" [1900b, 130])

A central cartouche and "Two Ladies name" is flanked on each side by a depiction of a *serekh,* or palace facade, surmounted by a Horus falcon and enclosing the "Horus name." Each *serekh* is itself flanked by representations of the tutelary goddesses Edjo and Nekhbet on baskets above their respective heraldic plants, signifying "Edjo, Lady of Lower Egypt" (Wȝḏ.t nb.t Mḥw) and "Nekhbet, Lady of Upper Egypt" (Nḫb.t nb.t Šmꜥw). Each goddess offers signs of eternity and dominion to Horus and thus to the king. Readings have been corrected by reference to Oriental Institute photo 9675.

Central Name

[…] Nb.ty ḥkn m mȝꜥ.t (2) ntr nfr Wsr-mȝꜥ.t-Rꜥ nb tȝ.wy (3) mry P(y).t Dp(y).t nb.t Pr-nw[1] ḥnw.t tȝ.wy (4) Nḫb.t ḥḏ.t Nḫn nb.(t) ꜣtr.(t)[2] Šmꜥw

[…] The Two Ladies: "Rejoicing in Maat"; (2) the Good God, Usimaꜥre, Lord of the Two Lands, (3) beloved of She of Pe and Dep, Lady of the Sanctuary of Lower Egypt,[1] Mistress of the Two Lands, (4) and Nekhbet, the White One of Nekhen, Lady of the Sanctuary[2] of Upper Egypt.

Horus Name
    nb mꜣꜥ-ḫrw[3]
    Lord of justification.[3]

Label for Each Edjo and Nekhbet Near Base of Heraldic Plant
    dỉ(2)≠s (3) ꜥnḫ (4) wꜣs[4]
    May (2) she give (3) life and (4) dominion.[4]

B. Painted Cartouches Inserted between Figures of Hathor, Isis, and Neith (Legrain Chamber C, Wall B [1900b, 132])
    Wsr-mꜣꜥ.t-Rꜥ (2) [Rwd]-ʾImn mrỉ-ʾImn
    Usimaꜥre (2) [Rud]amon, beloved of Amon.

C. Painted Cartouche Inserted in Blank Column between Texts of Hapi and Osiris (Legrain Chamber C, Wall D, [1900b, 134])
    [Rwd]-ʾImn mrỉ-ʾImn
    [Rud]amon, beloved of Amon.

NOTES
    1. Miscopied on the left by Legrain as p.t "heaven," followed by a nonexistent blank space. Legrain's copy omits the entire righthand text.
    2. Miscopied by Legrain on the left as ʾIwnw "Heliopolis" and on the right as ꜥḥ "palace."
    3. Kitchen read nb Mꜣꜥ.t "Lord of Maat" (1986, 127 §101, 360 §322).
    4. Legrain copies only dỉ ꜥnḫ for all four versions, omitting all joining text on the outer side of the heraldic plant. The far righthand text of Edjo is broken and reads dỉ(2)[≠s] (3) ꜥnḫ (4) [wꜣs].

116. BURIAL OF PRINCESS NESITERPAUTI
(MEDINET HABU TOMB 21)

During early Dynasty XXV, a daughter of Rudamon was interred in a chamber (1.40 by 3.05 m and 1.70 m high) excavated below the existing flooring of the disused Room 43 at the rear of the great temple of Medinet Habu. A rectangular flooring slab probably found above the tomb bears a painted scene of the princess adoring two depictions of Osiris, and a hieroglyphic label provides the filiation of both the princess and her father. Within the tomb were the remains of a wooden coffin and mummy, gilded faience beads, and four boxes of faience ushebtis (most 9 cm high), all discovered during a re-excavation by the Oriental Institute in 1927. The first excavator, Daressy, wrongly attributed the position of the stone and the contents of the tomb to Ptolemaic modifications. Later publications still cite the block as "reused."

A minor spelling variation of the divine name "Osiris," ubiquitous in late documents and already known in Dynasty XVIII, is first securely dated for the Third Intermediate Period by its appearance on this flooring block. Anthony Leahy has suggested that this inscription marks a chronological *terminus a quo,* indicating a Dynasty XXV or later date for all such Libyan period spellings. With so few dated and so many undated examples, however, the chronological value of this assessment is suspect.

For the discovery and texts, see Daressy 1897a, 20–21 §CXLII; 1897b, 170; Gauthier 1914, 392–94; and Hölscher 1954, 17 (fig. 21) and 32 (Tomb of "Nester"), with unpublished excavation photos P. 12560/Chicago Oriental Institute 647 and P. 12561/Chicago Oriental Institute 648; Porter and Moss 1964, 773 no. 21 and pl. XVI; and Leahy 1979, 141–53. See Kitchen 1986, 127 §101, 356 §318, and 360 §322.

FLOORING BLOCK (CAIRO JdE 33902)

Wsỉr dỉ ꜥnḫ dỉ(2)≠f ḥtp.w nb (n) ḥs.(t)[1] (n.t) ḫn (3) n ꜣImn Ns.t-r(4)-Pꜣw.ty[2] mꜣꜥ.(t)-ḫrw sꜣ.t ny-sw.t nb (5) tꜣ.wy Rwd-ꜣImn mꜣꜥ-ḫrw sꜣ ny-sw.t (6) nb tꜣ.wy Wsrkn mꜣꜥ-ḫrw nb ỉmꜣḫ mw.t≠s ḥm.t ny-sw.t Tꜣ-dỉ-[ꜣImn][3] mꜣꜥ.(t)-ḫrw

Osiris, the giver of life, may he give (2) all offerings to the chantress[1] of the Residence (3) of Amon, Nesiter(4)pauti,[2] the justified, royal daughter of the Lord of (5) the Two Lands, Rudamon, the justified, royal son of (6) the Lord of the Two Lands, Osorkon (III), the justified, the possessor of reverence, while her mother is the royal wife, Tadi[amon],[3] the justified.

365 USHEBTIS

ḥs.(t) (n.t) ḫn n ꜣImn Ns.t-r-Pꜣw.ty[2]

Chantress of the Residence of Amon, Nesiterpauti.[2]

NOTES

1. The three signs ending in "s" are surely miscopied as ꜥnḫ wḏꜣ snb by Daressy 1897a, 20. For the office, see Ritner 1998, 85–90.

2. Read Ns-ṯr by Ranke 1935–77, 1:179, no. 24, followed by Hölscher. Leahy read Ns-ṯr.wy(?).

3. So restored by Daressy.

117. BERLIN COFFIN PLANK 2100

Acquired by Lepsius in western Thebes, this fragment of a wooden coffin (1.18 m in length) names a second daughter of Rudamon and preserves a genealogy that demonstrates the close dynastic link between terminal Dynasty XXIII and the new "kingdom" of Heracleopolis noted in the Victory Stela of Piye. The coffin's owner is a descendant of the local Heracleopolitan kinglet, Peftchauawybast, and his wife Irwedjabastnefu (?), daughter of King Rudamon. Remains of the coffin's decoration include seven side registers with three human-headed and four ram-headed deities.

For the text, see Lepsius 1849–59, 3:258 and pl. 284a; Königliche Museen zu Berlin 1899, 238; Daressy 1897a, 20–21 §CXLII; Breasted 1906–7, 4:430 n. c; and Gauthier 1914, 392–93. See Kitchen 1986, 127 §101, 356 §318, and 360 §322.

[... P3-dỉ-ʾImn]-nb-ns.wt-t3.wy m3ꜥ-ḫrw ỉr[.n] B[...]ḥꜥ-Dw3(?)[1] s3.t ny-sw.t nb t3.wy P(3y)≠f-t3w-ꜥ(.wy)-B3st.t m3ꜥ-ḫrw mw.t≠s nb.(t) pr šps.t s3.t ny-sw.t nb t3.wy Rwd-ʾImn m3ꜥ-ḫrw ʾIr-B3st.t-wḏ3-nfw[2] m3ꜥ.(t)-ḫrw

[... Padiamon]nebnesuttawy, the justified, born by B[...]hadua (?),[1] the royal daughter of the Lord of the Two Lands, Peftchauawybast, the justified, while her mother is the housewife and noble woman, the royal daughter of the Lord of the Two Lands, Rudamon, the justified, Irbastwedjanefu,[2] the justified.

NOTES

1. So read by Gauthier.
2. So Daressy and Gauthier, or read ʾIr-B3st.t-wḏ3-n-t3w? See the cross listing in Kitchen 1986, 506.

GENEALOGY OF RUDAMON

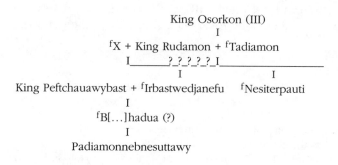

King Osorkon (III)
I
ᶠX + King Rudamon + ᶠTadiamon
I_____?_?_?_?_?_I_____
          I   I
King Peftchauawybast + ᶠIrbastwedjanefu   ᶠNesiterpauti
          I
      ᶠB[...]hadua (?)
          I
   Padiamonnebnesuttawy

E. IUPUT II

118. TELL EL-YAHUDIYEH BARK STAND

The cube of pink granite (50 cm in height) was excavated at Tell el-Yahudiyeh by Naville in 1887 and removed to the Bulak (later Cairo) Museum. On the front side facing images of the kneeling king offer oil (left) and the Eye of Horus (right) to the royal titulary arranged in two columns. At both right and left corners, two figures of the king (labeled by one cartouche apiece) raise their arms to support the representation of heaven.[1]

For the text, see Naville 1890, 10–11 and pl. 1; 1888, 53; Daressy 1908, 203; 1913, 142; and Gauthier 1914, 382 §II. See Kitchen 1986, 124–25 §98 ("statue base"), 341–42 §302, and reattribution to Iuput II on 542 §§446–47.

CENTRAL INSCRIPTION

ny-sw.t bỉ.ty nb tꜣ.wy Wsr-mꜣꜥ.t-Rꜥ-stp-n-ꜣImn (2) sꜣ Rꜥ nb ḫꜥ.w ꜣIwpwt mrỉ-ꜣImn sꜣ Bꜣst.t

The King of Upper and Lower Egypt, Lord of the Two Lands, Usimaꜥre-setepenamon, (2) Son of Re, Lord of Diadems, Iuput, beloved of Amon, Son of Bastet.

LEFT CORNER

Wsr-mꜣ ꜥ.t-Rꜥ-stp-n-ꜣImn (2) ꜣIwpwt mrỉ-ꜣImn sꜣ Bꜣst.t

Usimaꜥre-setepenamon, (2) Iuput, beloved of Amon, Son of Bastet.

RIGHT CORNER

[Wsr-mꜣ ꜥ.t-Rꜥ-stp-n-ꜣImn] (2) ꜣIwpwt mrỉ-ꜣImn sꜣ Bꜣst.t

[Usimaꜥre-setepenamon,] (2) Iuput, beloved of Amon, Son of Bastet.

NOTE

1. For the iconography, see Kurth 1975.

119. THE HOOD PLAQUE
(BROOKLYN 59.17)

This large green glazed faience plaque, 29 cm in height, depicts the ruler of Leontopolis (Tell Moqdam) standing and wearing the blue crown in an artistic style closer to Nubian (Dynasty XXV) representations than to earlier Libyan models. Above and flanking the king appear two cartouches.

For the text and photographs, see Riefstahl 1968, 61 and 106 (no. 59); Edwards and James 1984, 133–34 (fig. 182b); Fazzini 1972, 64–66 and fig. 36; and Sotheby's 1924, 7 (no. 22), and pl. II. See Kitchen 1986, 124–25 §98, 341–42 §302, and reattribution to Iuput II on 542 §§446–47.

[Wsr-]mꜣ ꜥ.t-Rꜥ-[st]p-[n]-Rꜥ (2) ꜣIwpwt mrỉ-ꜣImn sꜣ Bꜣst.t

[Usi]maꜥre-[sete]p[en]re, (2) Iuput, beloved of Amon, Son of Bastet.

120. LEONTOPOLIS BRONZE DOOR HINGE
(CAIRO JdE 38261)

Said to derive from Leontopolis (Tell Moqdam), this bronze hinge was once attached to a monumental gateway. The piece measures 52 cm in length, 11 cm in thickness, and 20 cm in height for the rectangular portion which was attached to the doorleaf, rising to 37 cm for the conical pivot, whose point is now broken. On the panel, a rectangular frame encloses the royal titulary and two small vertical columns below the queen's name. The findspot of the piece has been used by Kitchen to support his argument that Leontopolis was the capital of the XXIIIrd Dynasty. The likely burial of Iuput II in a usurped Ramesside sarcophagus has been discovered in 2007 in Buto (Tell Faraïn) during excavations by the German Archaeological Institute.

For the text, see Daressy 1908, 202–3 (wrongly called JdE 38262); 1931, 628–29; Yoyotte 1953, 190 n.1; and Gauthier 1914, 382 §III. See Kitchen 1986, 124–25 §98, 341–42 §302, and reattribution to Iuput II on 542 §§446–47 ("bronze fragment"). See further Kitchen 1995, xxx §AA.

MAIN TEXT

ny-sw.t bỉ.ty nb t3.wy Wsr-m3ʿ.t-Rʿ-stp-n-ʾImn s3 Rʿ nb ḫʿ(.w) ʾIwpwt mrỉ-ʾImn s3 B3st.t nb ỉr.(t) ḫ.t ḥm.t ny-sw.t wr(.t) Tn.t-k3.t-[w3(?)]¹ dỉ ʿnḫ

The King of Upper and Lower Egypt, Lord of the Two Lands, Usimaʿre-setepenamon, Son of Re, Lord of Diadems, Iuput, beloved of Amon, Son of Bastet, Lord of ritual performance, (and) the Great Royal Wife Tentkat[wa(?)],¹ given life.

VERTICAL ADDITION

dỉ(?)⸗s n⸗ỉ nfr.t Twtw (2) ḥry ỉdnw n W3d.t nb(.t) ʾIm.t² n ỉr s.t nfr(.t)

May she give (?) good things to me, Tutu, (2) chief deputy of Edjo, Lady of Nebêshah,² for making a good place.

NOTES

1. Restoration suggested by Daressy 1908, 202.
2. Tell el-Farʿûn; see Gardiner 1947, 2:171*.

121. DONATION STELA OF SMENDES SON OF HORNAKHT
(GENEVA INV. NO. 23473)

From Mendes (Tell el-Rubʿa), this stela provides the highest known regnal date (year 21) for Iuput II. Measuring 53 cm in height, 32 cm in width, and between 6 and 8 cm in thickness, the stela is dominated by a lunette scene beneath a winged solar disk representing the local chief of the Ma (largely broken away) and the beneficiary offering before Isis suckling Horus and the Ram of Mendes. Below the lunette, eight hieratic lines record the donation of land.

For the text, photograph, and translation, see Chappaz 1982, 71–81; Yoyotte 1958b, 21 fig. 3. For discussion, see Yoyotte 1961a, 125 (document 10) and 132; de Meulenaere and MacKay 1976, 205 no. 107; Meeks 1979a, 614, 631, 633, and 671 no. 23.2.21; and Leahy 1990, 185. See Kitchen 1986, 124–25 §98, 341–42 §302, and reattribution to Iuput II on 542–43 §§446 and 448. See further Kitchen 1995, xxx §AA.

LABEL FOR ISIS
    dd-mdw [ỉn] ꜣs.t wr.t[1]
    Recitation [by] Isis the Great.[1]

LABEL FOR THE RAM OF MENDES
    dd-mdw ỉn Bꜣ-nb-(Dd.t)
    Recitation by the Ram, Lord [of Mendes] (Banebdjed).

LABEL FOR THE DONOR
    [N]s-[b]ꜣ-nb-[Dd.t][2]   Smendes[2]

LABEL FOR THE BENEFICIARY
    Gm-n≠f-[Ḥr]-bꜣk   Gemnefhorbak

MAIN TEXT
    (1) [ḥs]b[.t] 21.t (n) Pr-ꜥꜣ ꜣIwwꜣpwwꜣtỉ ḥnq n
    (2) Ḥr-pꜣ-ẖrd ḥr(y)-ỉb Dd.t m-dr.t wr ꜥꜣ n Mꜥ
    (3) hꜣw.ty Ns-bꜣ-nb-Dd.t sꜣ wr ꜥꜣ (n) Mꜥ hꜣw.ty Ḥr-nḫt
    (4) ỉ-ḥnq≠f n ḥry ỉmy-wnw.t n Ḥr-pꜣ-ẖrd Gm-n≠f-Ḥr-bꜣk
    (5) ꜣḥ.t stꜣ.t 5 m-ẖnw pꜣ šꜣw n tꜣ ꜥ.t Nḥs[y] m-ẖnw
    (6) tꜣ mꜣw.t(?)[3] n wꜥbꜣ[4] ỉr p[ꜣ] n[ty]-ỉw≠f tꜣ(ỉ) pꜣ ḥnk (n) nn n nb(≠f)
    (7) hꜣ(?) ỉꜣd.t [Sḫm.t r-ḥr≠f (?) ...] bn nd.tw≠f[5] n
    (8) [...] ḫ.t bn ṯ(ꜣ)ỉ≠f mw

    (1) Regnal year 21 (of) Pharaoh Iuput (II); a donation to
    (2) Harpocrates, resident in Mendes, through the agency of the Great Chief of the Ma (Meshwesh)
    (3) and leader, Smendes, son of the Great Chief (of) the Ma and leader, Hornakht,
    (4) which he offered to the chief astronomer priest of Harpocrates, Gemnefhorbak,
    (5) (consisting of) 5 *arouras* of field within the meadow land of "The Place[5] of the Nubian" within

(6) the island-land (?)[3] with clear title.[4] As for the one who will take the offering (of) this from (its) lord,

(7) may the plague [of Sakhmet (?)] fall (?) [upon him ...] He will not be saved[6] from

(8) [...] property. He will not obtain water.

NOTES

1. Chappaz reads mw.t-nṯr "the divine mother."

2. Unread by Chappaz, who identifies the figure as king Iuput.

3. Chappaz no longer accepts his published reading s₃tw "land" (personal communication). "Islands" are attested in the names of Delta sites in Demotic documents.

4. Literally, "being pure" (and thus unencumbered). The text anticipates the phraseology of northern Demotic contracts, which substitute wꜥb for Theban nꜥ ("smooth"); cf. the Apanage Stela of Iuwelot, Main Text, l. 3, above, pp. 273, 275, and 278 n. 4. Chappaz translates "land of pure water."

5. The term indicates an enclosed space; cf. ꜥ.t n.t ḫt "orchard, arbor."

6. Chappaz, following Goyon (personal communication), understands bn nd̠.n.tw⸗f [ỉ₃.t]⸗f n [ḫrd.w⸗f] "He will not transmit his office to his children."

F. SHESHONQ "VII" (FORMERLY VI)

122. BRONZE PENDANT, UNIVERSITY COLLEGE, LONDON

The supposed Sheshonq VII (renumbered from "VI" following the discovery of a new Sheshonq "IV") is uniquely attested on a bronze double cartouche pendant from the Petrie collection. The cartouches, crowned by solar disks, are well carved but poorly spelled. As noted by Kitchen, the initial elements W₃s-nṯr may be graphic errors for Wsr-m₃ꜥ, so that the the pendant may represent merely a variant of the titulary of Sheshonq III (Usimaꜥre-setepenamon). This item exemplifies the ambiguity that surrounds much of the era's documentation, with historical reconstruction dependent upon a single, and often disputed, piece of evidence.

For the text and photograph, see Petrie 1905b, 271 fig. 111; 1917, pl. 51, D. See Kitchen 1995, 87 §67; for the reattribution of numbers, see 1995, xxvi §Y.

W₃s-nṯr-Rꜥ-stp-(n)-Rꜥ (2) Šš(nq mrỉ)-ꜣImn nṯr ḥq₃ W₃s.t

Wasneterre-setepenre, (2) Shesho(nq, beloved of) Amon, the god, ruler of Thebes.

V

DYNASTY XXIV

A. THE GREAT CHIEF OSORKON (C) OF SAIS

Great Chief Osorkon (C) bears military and religious titles analogous to those of Tefnakht of Sais and is probably his immediate predecessor. From these titles, it is clear that the territory of Sais had expanded to include neighboring Buto and Kom el-Hisn, so that Osorkon already controlled the core of Tefnakht's future "princedom of the West."

For the texts, translation, and discussion, see Yoyotte 1960, 13–22; and Andreu 1997, 182–83. See Kitchen 1986, 141 §113, 147 §118, 350 §311, 355 §316, and 362 §324.

123. VICTORY TALISMAN
(LOUVRE E. 10943)

A green faience disk with details in black, this amulet of Great Chief Osorkon measures 9.6 cm in height and diameter and 0.8/0.7 cm in thickness. The talisman takes the form of the *shen*-knot symbolizing eternity, within which the youthful sun-god sits upon a lotus flanked by two protective winged uraei offering the *shen*-knot. Around the perimeter, two facing hieroglyphic inscriptions begin above the god's head, providing the deity's speech on the viewer's left, and the titles of Osorkon on the right.

LEFTHAND SPEECH OF SUN-GOD

ḏd-mdw ỉn Rꜥ-Ḥr-ꜣḫ.ty nb p.t ḥr(y)-ỉb ꜣIwnw dỉ(≠ỉ) n≠k pḥ.ty mỉ Mnṯ(w) šfy.t≠k m-ẖnw n tꜣ.wy

Recitation by Re-Horachty, Lord of heaven, resident in Heliopolis: "I have given to you strength like Montu and your dignity within the Two Lands."

435

RIGHTHAND LABEL OF OSORKON

wr ꜥꜣ (n) Mꜥ ḥꜣw.ty ḥm-nṯr N.t ḥm-nṯr n Wꜣḏy.t nb.(t) ꜣImꜣw Wsỉrk(n)
Great Chief of the Ma (Meshwesh) and leader, prophet of Neith,
prophet of Edjo, and of the Lady of Kom el-Hisn, Osorko(n).

124. USHEBTIS
(UNIVERSITY COLLEGE, LONDON NOS. 475–76)

NO. 475

ḏd-mdw ỉn Wsỉr wr ꜥꜣ (2) Mꜥ Wsỉrkn mꜣꜥ-ḫrw
Recitation by the Osiris, Great Chief (2) of the Ma, Osorkon, the justified.

NO. 476

ḏd-mdw ỉn Wsỉr wr [ꜥꜣ] (2) Mꜥ Ws(ỉr)kn
Recitation by the Osiris, [Great] Chief (2) of the Ma, Osorkon.

B. TEFNAKHT

125. FAROUK DONATION STELA OF TEFNAKHT
(S. ABEMAYOR)

Acquired for the collection of King Farouk in 1942 from the antiquities dealer Abemayor, the round-topped stela derives from Tell Faraïn
(Buto). Dimensions and material are unpublished. A winged disk surmounts the figure of Tefnakht offering the sign for field to Neith and
Edjo, while the beneficiary appears behind Tefnakht in the guise of a
scribe. Hieroglyphic labels accompany the figures, and four lines of hieratic text record the donation. Dating to the final years of Sheshonq V,
the stela provides the earliest record of the Great Chief Tefnakht, who
would challenge Piye for the domination of Egypt after the death of the
nominal Tanite monarch.

For the text, see Yoyotte 1961a, 153–54 §§48–49; 1960, 15, 20; and
Meeks 1979a, 616, 627, 628, and 670 (no. 22.10.36). See Kitchen 1986, 355
§316, and 362 §324.

LABEL FOR NEITH

N.t   Neith

LABEL FOR EDJO

Wꜣḏ.t P T(p) dỉ ꜥnḫ wꜣs nb
Edjo of Pe and Dep, who gives all life and dominion.

LABEL FOR GREAT CHIEF TEFNAKHT
   wr ꜥꜣ Mꜥ ḥꜣw.ty wr ꜥꜣ n Rby Tꜣy≠f-nḫt
   Great Chief of the Ma (Meshwesh) and leader, Great Chief of the Libu,
Tefnakht.

LABEL FOR THE BENEFICIARY
   Nḫt-ꜣImn   Nakhtamon

MAIN TEXT
   (1) ḥsb.t 36 ꜣbd 2 šmw sw 14 ỉw wr ꜥꜣ Mꜥ ḥꜣw.ty (2) Tꜣy≠f-nḫt ḥmk[1]
ꜣḥ.t stꜣ.t 10 n pr Wꜣḏy.t nb.(t) (3) P Dp n ḥry ꜥqr[2] Nḫt-ꜣImn ỉw≠w mn(3).
t r nḥḥ ḏ.t sꜣ≠f Kꜣnꜣỉw
   Regnal year 36, month 2 of summer, day 14, while the Great Chief of
the Ma and leader, (2) Tefnakht donates[1] 10 *arouras* of field to the estate
of Edjo, Lady of (3) Pe and Dep for the chief *aker*,[2] Nakhtamon, they being
established (3) forever and ever. His son, Kana.

NOTES
   1. For the spelling of ḥnq as ḥm-kꜣ, see Donation Stela Strassburg 1588, p. 79
above.
   2. For the uncertain (Libyan or Semitic?) title, see Vittmann 1975, 50–51; 1978,
131 n.1 and 160 n. 1; adding the misread example in Habachi 1977, 108 and n. 1
(as noted by Meeks 1980–82, 2:81).

126. DONATION STELA OF TEFNAKHT, GREAT CHIEF OF THE WEST

   Discovered in the home of a local guard at Ibtu near Tell Faraïn
(Buto), the stela dates to the waning days of the nominal rule of Sheshonq
V, whose cartouches were left empty. The true state of political power
in the Delta is indicated by Tefnakht's grandiose title "Great Chief of
the entire land," adopted prior to his conflict with Piye over middle and
southern Egypt. The dimensions and material of the round-topped stela
are unpublished. Framed below a curved glyph for heaven supported on
was-scepters, a winged disk arches over the figure of Tefnakht offering
the sign for field to the enthroned Harendotes, Horus-who-protects-
his-father, patron of Buto, who wears the double crown and holds a
was-scepter and ankh. Tefnakht wears the upright feather of the Libu
chiefs, and behind him the beneficiary appears as a seated harpist. All
texts are in hieroglyphs. Although divisions were made for ten lines of
primary text, only four were completed, and the sculptor ceased carving
in the middle of Tefnakht's name.
   For the text, see Sauneron 1957, 51 and 53–54 figs. 1–2; Yoyotte 1961a,
152–53 §47 and pl. I.1; 1959, 97–98; and Meeks 1979a, 616, 627, 628, 634,

438 THE LIBYAN ANARCHY

638, 651, and 670–71 (no. 22.10.38). See Kitchen 1986, 104–5 §84, 355 §315, and 362 §324.

LABEL FOR HARENDOTES

Ḥr-nd̲-ît≥f nb P (2) dî.n≥î n≥k ꜥnḫ wꜣs nb mî Rꜥ (3) dî.n≥î n≥k snb nb{.t} (4) sꜣ ḫꜣ≥f m ꜥnḫ wꜣs nb{.t}

Horus-who-protects-his-father, Lord of Pe. (2) "Thus I have given to you all life and dominion like Re. (3) I have given to you all health." (4) Protection is behind him consisting of all life and dominion.

LABEL FOR GREAT CHIEF TEFNAKHT

wr ꜥꜣ n{.w} tꜣ d̲r≥f (2) Tꜣ(y)≥f-nḫt (3) ḥnk sḫ.t îr≥f dî ꜥnḫ

Great Chief of the entire land, (2) Tefnakht. (3) Offering field(s) so that he might attain the state of being given life.

LABEL FOR HARPIST BENEFICIARY

îmy-rꜣ ḥs n Ḥr nb P Ḥr(î) (2) sꜣ mî-nn T̲ꜣ(î)-p(ꜣ)-n-P-n-îm≥w

Overseer of singers of Horus, Lord of Pe, Hori, (2) son of the similarly titled Tchaipenpenimu.

MAIN TEXT

1) ḥsb.t[1] 38.(t) ḫr ḥm n ny-sw.t bî.ty nb tꜣ.wy (…)[2] (2) sꜣ Rꜥ (…)[2] hrw pn ḥnk ꜣḫ.t stꜣ.t 10 î-îr (3) wr ꜥꜣ ḫꜣw.ty wr ꜥꜣ n Rby ḥm-nt̲r N.t Wꜣd̲y.t nb.(t) ʾImꜣ[w] m[kꜣ n] (4) P-ꜣ-(î)ḥw.ty[4] mkꜣ n Khtn[5] ḥqꜣ spꜣ.wt îmnt.t Tꜣ(5)(y≥f-nḫt …)[2]

Regnal year[1] 38 under the Majesty of the King of Upper and Lower Egypt, Lord of the Two Lands (…),[2] (2) Son of Re (…).[2] On this day: a donation of 10 *arouras* of field that was made by (3) the Great Chief and leader, the Great Chief of the Libu, prophet of Neith and Edjo, Lady of Kom el-Hisn, *mek*[3] [of] (4) Pahout,[4] *mek*[3] of Keheten,[5] ruler of the nomes of the West, Te(5)(fnakht …).[2]

NOTES

1. The writing of "regnal year" here includes the crossed "x" determinative, characteristic of the revised transliteration ḥsb.t, as recognized by Yoyotte 1961a, 152 n. 3.
2. Text left unfinished by the carver.
3. Libyan title of uncertain meaning, see Yoyotte 1959, 97–100.
4. "The cultivator," a geographic name?
5. Libyan term, designating a geographic area?

127. ATHENS DONATION STELA OF KING TEFNAKHT
(UNNUMBERED)

Acquired by the Museum of Athens in 1881 as a gift from the Demetrio collection in Alexandria, the round-topped limestone stela measures 73 cm high by 40 cm wide. The lunette is surmounted by the customary winged disk, below which are two addorsed scenes of King Tefnakht offering fields to Neith of Sais on the left and to Atum on the right. Between the king and the deities appears a smaller figure of the beneficiary, provided with implements of his office as porter of the temple of Neith. On the left he bears a forked stick for snaring snakes, while on the right he holds both a forked stick and a broom. The figures are accompanied by hieroglyphic labels, and a hieratic text of eleven lines details the donation. Although generally accepted as a monument of Tefnakht I, former Great Chief of the West and opponent of Piye, the stela may date to the reign of his grandson, Tefnakht II, son of Bocchoris, as first suggested by Priese, adopted by Baer, noted by Meeks, but ignored by Kitchen in all editions of *The Third Intermediate Period in Egypt (1100–650 B.C.)*.[1]

For the text, see el-Sayed 1975, 37–53, pl. VII; Spiegelberg 1903, 190–98; Sottas 1913, 152–54; Mallet 1896, 3–6; Petrie 1905b, 314 fig. 133; Priese 1972, 19 n. 19; Baer 1973, 23–24; and Meeks 1979a, 616, 627–28, 641, 643, 646, and 672 (no. 24.1.8). See Kitchen 1986, 372 §332 and 582–83 §526.

LABEL FOR WINGED DISK AT TOP OF LUNETTE
Bḥd.t(y) nṯr ꜥꜣ nb p.t
The Behdetite, the great god, Lord of heaven.

RIGHTHAND SCENE

Label for Atum
Tm ḫn(ty) Ḥꜥp(y)[2] (2) dỉ ꜥnḫ ḏd wꜣs nb ḏ.t
Atum, Foremost of Hapi,[2] (2) who gives all life, stability, and dominion forever.

Label for King Tefnakht
nb ỉr.(t) ḫ.t Špss-Rꜥ Tꜣ(y)⸗f-nḫt dỉ ꜥnḫ wꜣs ḏ.t (2) dỉ.t sḫ.t ỉr⸗s[3] (*sic*) dỉ ꜥnḫ
The Lord of ritual performance, Shepsesre, Tefnakht, given life and dominion forever. (2) Giving field(s) so that he[3] (Atum) might make the gift of life.

Label for Beneficiary
ꜣỉ-ỉr⸗[f-]ꜥꜣ-(n)-[N].t   Ire[f]aaen[n]eith

LEFTHAND SCENE

Label for Neith
   [...] (2) dỉ≠s ꜥnḫ wꜣs nb
   [...] (2) May she give all life and dominion.

Label for King Tefnakht
   [nb ỉr.(t) ḫ.t] Šp[ss]-Rꜥ Tꜣ(y)≠f-nḫt ꜥnḫ ḏ.t (2) dỉ.t sḫ.t ỉr≠s dỉ ꜥnḫ ḏ.t
   [The Lord of ritual performance], Shep[ses]re, Tefnakht, living forever.
(2) Giving field(s) so that she (Neith) might make the gift of eternal life.

Label for Beneficiary
   ꜣ I-ỉr≠f-ꜥꜣ-(n)-N.t   Irefaaenneith

MAIN TEXT
   (1) ḥsb.t 8.(t) ẖr ḥm n ny-sw.t bỉ.ty nb tꜣ.wy Ḥr Sỉꜣ-ẖ.t⁴ ny-sw.t bỉ.ty
Nb.ty Mꜣꜥ-ḫrw Ḥr-nbw [...]⁵ Špss-Rꜥ sꜣ Rꜥ n ẖ.t≠(2)f mr≠f ms n N.t mw.t
nṯr Tꜣy≠f-nḫt hꜣ(w) nfr ỉr.(t) wḏ.t ny-sw.t r dmy (3) Ḥw.t-n.t-Rꜥ-mss⁶ ḫnty
Ḥꜥpy² r ḥmk ꜣḫ.t stꜣ.t (4) 10.t m-ẖnw pꜣw ỉdbw ꜣḫ.t n.(t) wꜣḫ.t Ḥꜥpy⁷ nty-
ỉw≠w ḏd n≠f Tꜣ-mꜣ(5)y n pr N.t nb.(t) Sꜣw.t r-ẖt n ꜥꜣ⁸ (n) N.t ꜣI-ỉr≠f-ꜥꜣ-n-N.t
sꜣ (6) ḥry ꜥꜣ.w n pr N.t nb Sꜣw.t [ꜣI]ry ỉr pꜣ nty-ỉw≠f dỉ.t mn≠w mn sꜣ(7)≠f
r s.t≠f n wꜥ sꜣ n wꜥ⁹ nn sk.t rn≠f r nḥḥ ḏ.t ỉr pꜣ nty-ỉw≠f mn(8)mn≠w bꜣ.w
(n) N.t ḫpr r≠f r nḥḥ ḏ.t nn smn sꜣ≠f r s.t≠f nk s(w) pꜣ (9) ꜥꜣ (nk) pꜣ ꜥꜣ
ḥm.t≠f ẖrd.w≠f šmỉ≠f r hh n rꜣ n Sḫm.t ỉw (≠r) ꜥrq nb n ḏr nṯr.w (10) dmd
pꜣ nty-ỉw≠f ḥb n¹⁰ pꜣy ḥmk (n) N.t ḥb≠w nꜣy≠f ỉt.w qrỉ(s)≠w¹¹ s.t n tꜣ (11)
tꜣ(w.t) bn šsp n≠f ms.w≠f sꜣ.tw r N.t m-ỉr pḫ tꜣ ꜣd.t
   Regnal year 8 under the Majesty of the King of Upper and Lower
Egypt, Lord of the Two Lands, the Horus: "Perceptive of Body"⁴; the King
of Upper and Lower Egypt, the Two Ladies: "The Justified"; the Horus of
Gold: ["..."],⁵ Shepsesre, bodily Son of Re (2), whom he loves, born of
Neith, the God's Mother, Tefnakht. The good day of making a royal decree
regarding the town of The Mansion of Rameses,⁶ which is at the south of
Hapi,² in order to donate 10 *arouras* of field (4) from within that riverbank
field that the Inundation has added,⁷ which is called: "The new (5) land
of the estate of Neith, Lady of Sais," under the authority of the porter⁸ of
Neith, Irefaaenneith, son of (6) the chief porter of the estate of Neith, Lady
of Sais, [I]ry. As for the one who will confirm them, may his son be established (7) in his place, from one son to another⁹ without the destruction of
his name forever and ever. As for the one who will (8) disturb them, the
wrath of Neith comes to be against him forever and ever. His son will not
be confirmed in his office. May the donkey rape him; (9) may the donkey
(rape) his wife and his children. May he go to the fiery blast of the mouth
of Sakhmet and to the oath of the Lord of the universe and (that of) the

gods (10) altogether. The one who will subtract from[10] this donation for Neith, may his moments (of life) be diminished; may he be buried[11] in the (11) flame. His children will not succeed to him. Beware of Neith; do not approach the Angry One!

NOTES

1. Baer's article is cited only in the 1995 preface (xxxiii): "now much-outdated study."

2. Name of the Delta agricultural territory attached to the cult of Neith in the nomes of Sais and Prosopis; see el-Sayed 1975, 39; and Yoyotte 1961a, 155–56 §52.

3. The carver has been influenced by the lefthand label, applied to Neith.

4. El-Sayid read Sἰз-ἰb "Perceptive of Heart" in 1970, 116–18; followed by Kitchen 1986, 372 n. 740. The correct reading is noted by Yoyotte in the hieroglyphic Michaïlides Donation Stela of King Tefnakht (see following text).

5. The Golden Horus name has been omitted.

6. The site of the modern Delta village of Rameses, near Kom Gaef, to be distinguished from the "Mansion of Rameses in the estate of Re" cited in the Donation Stela for the God's Father Hory, p. 260.

7. Literally, "field of the addition of the Inundation," designating "new/island" land created by silt deposited during the annual flood.

8. Erman and Grapow 1926–63, 1:165/2–3, derived from ἰry-ʿз and written similarly to the later spellings of the synonym wnw, Erman and Grapow 1926–63, 1:312/13. See de Meulenaere 1956, 300.

9. For the expression, cf. lines 14–15 of the main text of the Serapeum Stela of Pasenhor, pp. 18–20.

10. Wrongly labeled "sic" by el-Sayed. For the use of ḫb n, see the Abydos Stela of Sheshonq I for His Father Namlot, line 4, pp. 166 and 169.

11. The defectively written word was read by el-Sayed as qrἰ "to draw near," but the determinative suggests qr(s) "to be buried," elsewhere associated with fire in curses; cf. line 7 of the Erased Donation Stela (Cairo JdE 85647), no. 103, pp. 406–7.

128. MICHAÏLIDES DONATION STELA OF KING TEFNAKHT

Formerly in the Michaïlides collection, the undated round-topped stela probably derives from the vicinity of El-Awasgah on the eastern edge of the Delta, approximately 9 km to the northeast of Bubastis and 10 km from Saft el-Henneh. The document attests to the eastern expansion of Saite rule under Shepsesre Tefnakht, since this principality was formerly held by the Great Chief Patchenfy of Saft el-Henneh, as recorded in the Piye Stela of year 21. Dimensions and material are not published. The lunette is framed by *was*-scepters supporting a curved glyph for heaven, beneath which Tefnakht stands in archaizing posture with lowered arms facing Harendotes ("Horus-who-protects-his-father") and lion-headed Edjo, patrons of Buto. Hieroglyphic labels accompany the figures, and eight hieroglyphic lines complete the donation. Like the Athens Stela, this document might date to Tefnakht II, rather than to Tefnakht I, as generally assumed.

For the text, translation (of lines 1–4 only) and discussion, see Yoyotte 1971, 35–45 and figs. 1–2; Priese 1970, 19 n. 19; Baer 1973, 23–24; and Meeks 1979a, 628 and 672 (no. 24.1.0). See Kitchen 1986, 372 §332 and 368 §328 n. 716.

SEREKH FOR TEFNAKHT

Ḥr Sȝ-ḫ.t[1]   Horus: "Perceptive of Body"[1]

LABEL FOR HARENDOTES

Nḏ-ît≠f   He-who-protects-his-father

LABEL FOR EDJO

Wȝḏ.t   Edjo

MAIN TEXT

(1) h(rw) pn n ḥnk ȝḥ.t î[n ny-sw.t] bî.ty Špss-Rꜥ s[ȝ Rꜥ] (2) T(ȝy)≠f-nḫt sȝ N.t n pȝy tš n dmî Tȝ-šn(3)w.t-(n)-ʾInb-ḥḏ[2] stȝ.t 10 r-ḫt îry-ꜥȝ (n) pr Ḥr-(n)-P (4) Pȝ-Ḫȝr(w) sȝ n îry-ꜥȝ (n) pr Ḥr-înḏ-ît≠f(?)[3] (5) îr pȝ nty-[îw≠f dî.t] mn≠f mn sȝ(4)[≠f ḥr s.t ît≠f mî] mȝꜥ Ḥr ḥr s.t ît≠f (7) pȝ nty-îw≠f mnmn≠f sḫm (8) [nbî.t[4] n.t Wȝḏ.t(?) îm≠f ...]

(1) This day of donating fields b[y the King of Upper] and Lower Egypt, Shepsesre, Son [of Re], (2) Tefnakht, Son of Neith, in this district of the town of "The Granary (3) of Memphis"[2]: 10 *arouras* under the authority of the porter of Horus of Pe, (4) Pakharu, son of the porter of the estate of Harendotes.[3] (5) As for the one who [will con]firm it, may [his] son remain (6) [on the seat of his father just as] Horus is justified on the seat of his father. (7) The one who will disturb it, may (8) [the flame[4] of Edjo] overpower [him ...]

NOTES

1. El-Sayed read Sȝ-îb "Perceptive of Heart" in 1970, 116–18.

2. Homophonous writing as "The Tree of Memphis"; for discussion, see Yoyotte 1971, 37–40.

3. Or haplography for "porter of the estate of (Horus of Pe), Harendotes," as suggested by Yoyotte 1971, 37–40 n. 17.

4. For the restoration, see The Chronicle of Prince Osorkon, no. 82, pl. 19, line 53 (pp. 353 and 358 above).

C. BAKENRENEF

Although King Bakenrenef, the Bocchoris of Manetho, is well attested in later literature as an influential lawgiver (Diodorus 1.79 and 94–95) and the recipient of a dire oracle delivered by a prophetic lamb ("The Prophecy of the Lamb"), contemporary monuments of the monarch are few. Manetho lists him as the sole ruler of Dynasty XXIV, indicating that he had succeeded in controlling Memphis, unlike his immediate predecessor and presumed father, Tefnakht. Records of Bakenrenef include four scarabs, a decorated vase excavated from an Etruscan tomb at Tarquinia in Italy in 1895, a painted inscription from the Memphite Serapeum, and several votive stelae discovered at the same site and now in the Louvre. The Serapeum finds derive from the burial of an Apis bull in year 6 of Bakenrenef, his highest attested date. A small limestone cartouche fragment (about 12 cm in height) discovered by Montet at Tanis (San el-Hagar) attests to the king's acquisition of this former capital after the disappearance of Osorkon IV (contra Kitchen 1986, 377; 1995, xxxviii). After the first month of Inundation, day 5, of his sixth year (cf. Serapeum Stela No. 102 [text 137 below]), Bakenrenef was defeated by the Nubian Shabako and reportedly burned alive, although his descendants would continue as local rulers in Sais and reunite the country as Dynasty XXVI.

For the texts, references, and discussion, see Gauthier 1914, 410–12 §§2.I–VIII; Smith 1958, 242 fig. 76 and 285 n. 21 (vase); Petrie 1905b, 316 fig. 134 (Serapeum inscription); Malinine, Posener, and Vercoutter 1968, 75–98 and pls. XXVI–XXXIV (nos. 91–122); Yoyotte 1971, 35–45 (esp. 44–45 and fig. 3); and Breasted 1906–7, 4:447 §884. For additional references to Bakenrenef, see Kákosy 1993, 3–5; and for the "Prophecy of the Lamb," see Zauzich 1983, 165–74 and pl. 2. See Kitchen 1986, 141–43 §114 and 376–77 §§337–38.

129. SCARABS

LOUVRE

ntr nfr nb t3.wy W3ḥ-k3-Rꜥ mrỉ-ʾImn
The Good God, Lord of the Two Lands, Wahkare, beloved of Amon.

LOFTIE COLLECTION

ny-sw.t W3ḥ-k3-Rꜥ   King Wahkare.

DAVIS COLLECTION

ny-sw.t bỉ.ty W3ḥ-k3-Rꜥ ỉty nb
King of Upper and Lower Egypt, Wahkare, sovereign and lord.

G. FRASER COLLECTION
ny-sw.t bỉ.ty W3ḥ-k3-Rᶜ
King of Upper and Lower Egypt, Wahkare.

130. DECORATED VASE FROM TARQUINIA

The king is twice depicted in the upper register within a papyrus grove, led by Thoth and Horus and flanked by Neith and Horus (?). A vertical band with the king's titulary divides the scenes. A lower register depicts bound prisoners and monkeys in a palm grove. A similar but smaller faience vase has been reported in Sicily.

W3ḥ-k3-Rᶜ s3 Rᶜ B3k-n-rn≠f dỉ ᶜnḫ ḏ.t
Wahkare, Son of Re, Bakenrenef, given life forever.

131. SERAPEUM INSCRIPTION

ḥsb.t 6.(t) (n) ny-sw.t bỉ.ty W3ḥ-k3-Rᶜ s3 Rᶜ B3k-n-rn≠f ᶜnḫ ḏ.t
Regnal year 6 of the King of Upper and Lower Egypt, Wahkare, Son of Re, Bakenrenef, living forever.

132. SERAPEUM VOTIVE STELA OF DJEDDJEHUTYIUEFANKH
(LOUVRE STELA IM 1258, CAT. NO. 91)

Consisting of only the damaged lower four lines of text, this limestone stela measures .095 m in height by .13 m in width and .03 m in depth and is inscribed in faded black ink. The text records the date of the opening of the crypt for the deceased Apis and an appeal to the deity.

[...] (x+1) ʾIw≠f-n-t̠3w-ᶜ.(wy)-3s.t mw.t≠f [...](x+2)s ḥsb.t 6.(t) (n) ny-sw.t bỉ.ty W3ḥ-k3-Rᶜ s3 Rᶜ (x+3) B3k-(n)-rn≠f ᶜnḫ ḏ.t my ỉr≠k (n) Ḏd-Ḏḥwty(x+4)[-ỉw]≠f-ᶜnḫ s3 Ḏd-3s.t-ỉw≠f-ᶜnḫ
[...] (x+1) Iuefentchauauiese, whose mother is [...](x+2)s (in) regnal year 6 of the King of Upper and Lower Egypt, Wahkare, Son of Re, (x+3) Bakenrenef, living forever. May you act (for) Djeddjehuty(x+4)[iu]efankh, son of Djedeseiuefankh.

133. SERAPEUM VOTIVE STELA OF ANKHWENNEFER
(LOUVRE STELA IM 2704, CAT. NO. 92)

The round-topped limestone stela measures .18 m in height by .115 m in width and .045 m in depth. In the lunette, the recumbent mummified

Apis, with disk and uraeus, is adored by the standing donor. Five lines of hieroglyphs are traced in black ink.

LABEL FOR APIS

[...] sšm≠f   [...] his image.

LABEL FOR DONOR

ꜥnḫ-Wn-nfr   Ankhwennefer.

MAIN TEXT

(1) ḥsb.t 6.(t) ḏd-mdw în Ḥp-Wsîr sꜣ (2) Gb nṯr ꜥꜣ nb.{t} ʾImnt.t m ḥtp (3) dî≠f ꜥnḫ [snb(?)] nb.{t} n by (4) ꜥnḫ-Wn-nfr ît≠f (5) [...]-Ptḥ mꜣꜥ mî Rꜥ ḏ.t

(1) Regnal year 6. Recitation by Apis-Osiris son of (2) Geb, the great god, Lord of the West in peace. (3) May he give all life [and health (?)] to the stonemason, (4) Ankhwennefer, whose father is (5) [...]ptah, justified like Re forever.

134. SERAPEUM VOTIVE STELA OF PAINMU
(LOUVRE STELA IM 3424, CAT. NO. 93)

The round-topped limestone stela measures .183 m in height by .114 m in width and .042 m in depth. The lunette scene has largely disappeared, although traces remain of Apis beside a table of offerings adored by a standing worshiper with raised hands. Engraved hieroglyphs label Apis and provide three lines of the traditional funerary prayer and a date.

LABEL FOR APIS

Wsîr-Ḥ(2)p   Osiris-Apis.

MAIN TEXT

(1) ḥtp dî ny-sw.t (n) Wsîr-Ḥp (2) Ḫnty ʾImnt.t dî ꜥnḫ (n) ît-nṯr rḫ ny-sw.t Pꜣ-în-mw (3) sꜣ ît-nṯr rḫ ny-sw.t Tꜣ(y)-nfr ḥsb.t (4) 6.(t)

(1) An offering that the king gives (to) Osiris-Apis, (2) Foremost of the West, who gives life (to) the God's Father and king's acquaintance, Painmu (3) son of the God's Father and king's acquaintance, Tchainefer. Regnal year (4) 6.

135. SERAPEUM VOTIVE STELA OF PENTADJER
(LOUVRE STELA IM 2680, CAT. NO. 97)

The round-topped limestone stela, commissioned by the beneficiary's son, measures .226 m in height by .177 m in width by .036 m in depth.

In the lunette, the recumbent Apis crowned with disk and uraeus appears atop a platform beside a table of offerings. Before him kneels the donor. Fragmentary ink labels accompany the figures, and six engraved lines of text contain the traditional funerary offering prayer for humans, here adapted for the deceased Apis and his worshipers. An extra line (6bis) has been painted behind and below the final allotted text space.

LABEL FOR SCENE
&#x12; Wsỉr-[Ḥp …]   O Osiris-[Apis …]

LABEL BEHIND APIS
[…] Ḥr […]   […] Horus […]

LABEL ON PLATFORM
Ḥr(ỉ) s3 Ḥr(ỉ) […]   Hori son of Hori […]

MAIN TEXT

(1) ḥtp dỉ ny-sw.t (n) Ptḥ-Skr dỉ≠f pr.t-ḫrw (m) t ḥnq.t k3.w 3pd.w mnḫ.(t) (2) sntr ỉrp ỉrt.t ḫ.t nb.(t) nfr.(t) wꜥb.(t) (3) n k3 (n) Wsỉr-Ḥp Ḫnty ꜣImnt.t ḥmww b3k (4) n pr d̠.t Pn-t3-d̠r s3≠f (5) sꜥnḫ rn≠f (Dd)-ꜣImn-ỉw≠f-ꜥnḫ ỉr.n nb.(t) pr D̠d-Ḥꜥp(y)(6)-ỉ(w)s≠ꜥnḫ ḥsb.t 6.(t) s3≠f ꜣImn-ḥr (6bis) […] s3 […] Wn-nfr s3 wꜥb (n) P[t]ḥ […]

(1) An offering that the king gives (to) Ptah-Sokar, so that he might give an invocation offering consisting of bread, beer, beef, fowl, cloth, (2) incense, wine, milk, and everything good and pure (3) to the *ka*-spirit of Osiris-Apis, Foremost of the West, and to the craftsman and servant (4) of the estate, Pentadjer, whose son (5) causes his name to live: (Djed)amoniuefankh, born of the housewife Djedhapi(6)iuesankh. Regnal year 6. His son Amonher (6bis) […] son of […] Wennefer, son of the *wab*-priest of Ptah […].

136. SERAPEUM VOTIVE STELA OF PA-AA
(LOUVRE STELA IM 3592, CAT. NO. 101)

The limestone stela takes the form of the hieroglyphic sign for "offering," with the royal cartouche and date carved in the upper projection. It measures .28 m in height by .225 m in width by .065 m in depth. In the upper register, mummiform Apis rests upon a sledge upon a base. Eight hieroglyphic lines fill the upper register, and five are arranged in prepared horizontal lines. Design and text contain archaizing features.

UPPER REGISTER

(1) B3k-n-rn≠f (2) ḥsb.t 6.(t) (3) ḥtp dỉ ny-sw.t (4) (n) Wsỉr-Ḥ(5)p (6) Ḫnty ꜣImnt.t (7) dỉ ꜥnḫ (n) ḥr(y)-ꜥ3 (8) P3-ꜥ3

(1) Bakenrenef, (2) regnal year 6. (3) An offering that the king gives (4) (to) Osiris-(5)Apis, (6) Foremost of the West, (7) who gives life to the chief porter, (8) Pa-aa.

LOWER REGISTER

(1) ḥtp dỉ ny-sw.t ḥtp (dỉ n) ꜣInpw dỉ≠f pr.t-ḫrw (m) t ḥnq.t k3.w 3pd. w šs mnḫ.(t) ỉrp ỉḫ.t nb.(t) (2) nfr.(t) wꜥb.(t) n k3 n ỉm3ḫ(w) rḫ ny-sw.t ḥr(y)-ꜥ3 pr (3) B3st.t nb.(t) ꜥnḫ-t3.wy P3-ꜥ3 s3 n ꜥ3 (n) (4) B3st.t nb.(t) ꜥnḫ-t3.wy P3-dpw-dỉ≠s.t(?)[1] mw.t≠f Pn-(5)ꜥqr ẖnm m ꜥnḫ mỉ ꜥnḫ rḫ nb pr B3st.t nb.(t) ꜥnḫ-t3.wy (6) [...][2] ḥm.t

(1) An offering that the king gives, and an offering (that is given) to Anubis, so that he might give an invocation offering (consisting of) bread, beer, beef, fowl, alabaster, cloth, wine, and everything (2) good and pure to the *ka*-spirit of the revered one and king's acquaintance, the chief porter of the estate of (3) Bastet, Lady of Ankh-Tawy, Pa-aa, son of the porter of (4) Bastet, Lady of Ankh-Tawy, Padepudies (?),[1] whose mother is Pen(5)aqer, united with life, like the life of every one who is knowledge-able in the estate of Bastet, Lady of Ankh-Tawy. (6) [... his][2] wife.

NOTES

1. As read by Ranke 1935–77, 1:126 no. 20.
2. Left blank.

137. SERAPEUM VOTIVE STELA OF PASHERENESE
(LOUVRE STELA SN 22, CAT. NO. 102)

This poorly executed round-topped limestone stela measures .169 m in height by .141 m in width by .031 m in depth. Engraved on both sides, the stela shows on the recto a standing figure of the bull-headed Apis, adored by three smaller figures. On a small upper register three men carry standards of Wepwawet, Horus, and Thoth. The verso contains a solar disk and six lines of text, continued in paint after the middle of line 2.

RECTO

Labels for Men Following the Donor

Ḥr-Ḏḥwty s3 Ḥr-Ḥp (2) ꜥ3 Ptḥ-[...]

Hordjehuty son of Horhapi. (2) The porter, Ptah-[...]

Label for Apis and Donor
(1) ḏd-mdw ỉn Ḥp dỉ≠f ꜥnḫ wꜣs n (2) Pꜣ-šr-n-ꜣs.t sꜣ Pꜣ-šr-n-Ptḥ
Recitation by Apis, as he gives life and dominion to (2) Pasherenese, son of Pasherenptah.

Verso

Label in Upper Register
Pꜣ-šr-n-ꜣs.t   Pasherenese

Painted Text on Edges
(left edge) ḥtp dỉ ny-sw.t (n) Wsỉr-(right edge)-Ḥp [Ḫnty] ꜣImnt.t
An offering that the king gives (to) Osiris(right edge)-Apis, Foremost of the West.

Main Text
(1) ḥtp dỉ ny-sw.t (n) Ptḥ-Skr dỉ≠f pr.t-ḫrw (m) t ḥnq.t (2) kꜣ.w ꜣpd.w nb.{t} ḥr wḏḥw≠sn n rꜥ nb n kꜣ (n) Wsỉr-(3)Ḥp Ḫnty ꜣImnt.t dỉ≠f ꜥnḫ wꜣs nb.{t} ꜣw.(t)-ỉb nb.(t) (4) ḏd snb nb ḏ.t n Pꜣ-šr-n-ꜣs.t sꜣ n Pꜣ(5)-šr-n-Ptḥ ỉw pꜣy nṯr ꜥꜣ ỉr.t š[m?] r Km(y).tꜣ ḥsb.t 6.(t) tpy ꜣḫ.t sw 5.{t}

(1) An offering that the king gives (to) Ptah-Sokar, so that he might give an invocation offering consisting of all bread, beer, (2) beef, fowl, on their offering tables every day to the *ka*-spirit of Osiris-(3)Apis, Foremost of the West, so that he might give all life and dominion, all joy, (4) all stability and health forever to Pasherenese, son of Pa(5)sherenptah, since this great god went to the Serapeum[3] in regnal year 6, first month of Inundation, day 5.

Notes
3. Abbreviation for Kmy.t; see Vercoutter 1962, 31.

138. TANIS CARTOUCHE FRAGMENT

[... Bꜣk-n]-rn≠f   [... Baken]renef.

VI

DYNASTY XXV

THE ROYAL GENEALOGY OF DYNASTY XXV

139. ASPALTA ELECTION STELA
(CAIRO JdE 48866)

Although two generations later than the primary focus of this volume, the Aspalta Election Stela (ca. 593 B.C.E.) illuminates one mechanism for selecting Nubian royalty and provides a retrospective, if damaged, matrilineal genealogy for Dynasty XXV. The stela serves as a Nubian counterpart to the patriarchial, Libyan stela of Pasenhor and conforms to the account of Nubian monarchy recorded by Diodorus (3.5.1).

For the texts, translation, and discussion, see Grimal 1981a, vii–xv, 21–35, and pls. V–VII; Eide et al. 1994, 232–52; Schäfer 1905, 81–100; Roeder 1961, 3380–91; Budge 1912, lxxxix–xcvii and 89–104; Priese 1972, 99–124; John Wilson in Pritchard 1969, 447–48; and Porter and Moss 1927–51, 7:217–18. For the Cushite Dynasty, see Dunham and Macadam 1949, 139–49. See Kitchen 1986, 165 §132 n. 344.

LABEL FOR AMON

ḏd-mdw ỉn ᵓImn (n) Np(ꜣ).t sꜣ⸗(ỉ) mry⸗(ỉ) (2) [ᵓIsprtꜣ] dỉ⸗ỉ n⸗k ḫꜥ.(w) (3) n Rꜥ ny.t-sw.t⸗f ḥr ns.t⸗f (4) smn.n⸗ỉ Nb.ty m tp⸗k (5) mỉ smn p.t ḥr sḫn.wt 4 (6) ꜥnḫ.tỉ wꜣs.tỉ mꜣꜥ.tỉ rnp.(tỉ) mỉ Rꜥ (7) ḏt tꜣ.w nb ḫꜣs.wt nb.(t) dmḏ ḥr (8) ṯbw.ty⸗k

Recitation by Amon of Napata: "My beloved son, (2) [Aspalta], I have given to you the appearance in glory (3) of Re and his kingship upon his throne. (4) I have established the Two Ladies at your brow (5) just as heaven is established upon the 4 supports, (6) while you live, have dominion, are justified and rejuvenated like Re (7) forever, with all lands and every foreign country gathered beneath (8) your sandals."

LABEL FOR MUT

ḏd-mdw ỉn Mw.t nb.(t) p.t dỉ≠(ỉ) (n)≠k (2) ꜥnḫ wꜣs nb snb nb ꜣw.t-ỉb nb ḏ.t

Recitation by Mut, Lady of heaven. "I shall give to you (2) all life and dominion, all health and all joy forever."

LABEL FOR THE QUEEN

ḏd-mdw ỉn sn.(t) ny-sw.t mw.t ny-sw.t ḥnw.t n.(t) Kš [Nnsrsꜣ] ỉy.n≠(ỉ) ḫr≠k ʾImn-Rꜥ nb ns.(w)t tꜣ.wy nṯr ꜥꜣ (2) ḫnt(y) ʾIp.t≠f rḫ rn≠f dỉ qn(ỉ) (n) nty ḥr mw≠f smn≠k sꜣ≠k mry≠k (3) [ʾIsprtꜣ] ꜥnḫ ḏ.t m ỉꜣ.t tw tp.t n.t Rꜥ wr≠f ỉm≠s (4) r nṯr.w nb sꜥšꜣ≠k rnp.wt≠f n ꜥnḫ ḥr-tp (tꜣ) mỉ ʾItn n p.t (5) dỉ≠k n≠f ꜥnḫ wꜣs nb ḫrỉ≠k snb nb ḫrỉ≠k ꜣw.t-ỉb nb ḫrỉ≠k ḫꜥ.(w) ḥr s.t Ḥr ḏ.t

Recitation by the king's sister and king's mother, the Mistress of Kush, [Ñasalsa]. "I have come before you, O Amon-Re, Lord of the Thrones of the Two Lands, great god, (2) Foremost of his harem, who knows his name and who gives valor to the one who is loyal to him. May you establish your beloved son (3) [Aspalta], living forever, in this chief office of Re, so that he might be greater in it (4) than all the gods. May you multiply his years of life on earth like (those of) the sun disk in heaven. May you give to him all life and dominion issuing from you, all health issuing from you, all joy issuing from you and appearance upon the throne of Horus forever."

MAIN TEXT

(1) ḥsb.t 1.(t) ꜣbd 2 pr.t sw 15 ḫr ḥm (n) Ḥr nfr ḫꜥ.(w) Nbty nfr ḫꜥ.(w) Ḥr-nbw wsr ỉb ny-sw.t bỉ.ty nb tꜣ.wy [Mry-kꜣ-Rꜥ] sꜣ Rꜥ nb ḫꜥ.w [ʾIsprtꜣ] mry ʾImn-Rꜥ nb ns.(w)t tꜣ.wy ḫr(y)-ỉb Ḏw-wꜥb

ỉsk ỉr≠f (2) mšꜥ n.{w} ḥm≠f r-ꜣw≠f m-ḫnw dmỉ Ḏw-wꜥb rn≠f nṯr ỉm≠f Ddwn ḫnty Tꜣ-Stỉ nṯr pw n Kš m-ḫt mn bỉk ḥr srḫ(3)≠f

ỉsk wn ṯs.w nt(y) mḥ-ỉb m-q(ꜣ)b mšꜥ.w n.w ḥm≠f s 6 ỉw wn ṯs.w nt(y) mḥ-ỉb ỉmy.(w)-rꜣ ḫtm.t s 6 ỉsk ỉr≠f wn (4) ỉmy.w-rꜣ mḏꜣ.t nt(y) mḥ-ỉb s 6 ỉsk wn sry.w ỉmy-rꜣ ḫtmw n.{t} pr ny-sw.t s 7

ꜥḥꜥ.n ḏd≠sn n mšꜥ r-ꜣw≠f mỉ≠n sḫꜥ≠n (5) nb≠n mỉ ỉꜣd.t nn mnỉw≠sn wn.ỉn mšꜥ pn mḥ.t wr sp-2 ḥr ḏd ỉw nb≠n d(y) ḥnꜥ≠n n{n} rḫ≠n sw ḫꜣ (6) rḫ≠n sw ꜥq≠n ḫr≠f bꜣk≠n n≠f mỉ bꜣk tꜣ.wy n Ḥr sꜣ ꜣs.t m-ḫt ḥtp≠f ḥr ns.t ỉt≠f Wsỉr dỉ≠n ỉꜣw n Wꜣḏ.tyt(7)≠f

ꜥḥꜥ.n ḏd.ỉn wꜥ n snw≠f ỉm≠sn nn rḫ sw b(w)-nb wp(w) Rꜥ pw ḏs≠f wnn≠f ḥr ḥsr≠f ḏw nb {ỉ}r≠f n b(w) nb nty ỉw≠f ỉm

ꜥḥꜥ.n ḏd.ỉn (8) wꜥ n snw≠f n-ỉm≠sn ỉw Rꜥ ḥtp≠f m ꜥnḫ.t ỉw stnw≠f sw m ḥr(y)-ỉb≠n

ꜥḥꜥ.n ḏd wꜥ n snw≠f n-ỉm≠sn mꜣꜥ.t pw wp.(t) pw n.t Rꜥ dr ḫpr (9) p.t dr ḫpr stnw ny-sw.t rdỉ.n≠f sw n sꜣ≠f mrỉ≠f ḥr nty twt pw n Rꜥ ny-sw.t ỉmy ꜥnḫ.w ỉn rdỉ sw Rꜥ m tꜣ pn m mr(w.t) grg tꜣ pn ꜥḥꜥ.n ḏd.ỉn (10) wꜥ n snw≠f n-ỉm≠sn ỉw Rꜥ n ꜥq≠f m{-n} p.t ỉw ns.t≠f šw m ḥqꜣ ỉw ỉꜣw.t≠f t(y) mnḫ m ꜥ.wy≠f rdỉ.n≠f sw n sꜣ≠f mrỉ≠f ḥr nty Rꜥ rḫ ḥr ḏd ỉr≠f hꜣp.w nfr.w ḥr ns.t≠f

(11) wn.ỉn mšꜥ pn r-ꜣw≠f ḥr mḥ.t ḥr ḏd nb≠n d(y) ḫnꜥ≠n n{n} rḫ≠n sw wn.ỉn mšꜥ.w n.w ḥm≠f ḏd r-ꜣw≠sn m rꜣ wꜥ ỉgr wn nṯr pn ʾImn-Rꜥ nb ns.(wt) tꜣ.wy ḥr(y)-ỉb Ḏw-wꜥb nṯr pw n Kš m(12)ỉ≠n šm≠n ḫr≠f nn ỉr≠n md.t m ḥm≠f nn nfr md.t ỉry m ḥm≠f mꜥr sp m-ꜥ nṯr nṯr pw n ny.w-sw.t n.(w) Kš ḏr rk Rꜥ ntf sšm n wnn (13) ny.(t)-sw.t n.(t) Kš m ꜥ.wy≠f rdỉ.n≠f n sꜣ≠f mr≠f dỉ≠n ỉ(ꜣ)wy n ḥr≠f sn≠n tꜣ ḥr ḫ.t≠{s}n ḏd≠n m-ḫft-ḥr≠f ỉy≠n ḥr≠k ʾImn dỉ≠k n≠n nb≠n r sꜥnḫ≠n r qd rꜣ.w-pr.w n nṯr.(w) nṯr.(w)t nb.w n.w Šmꜥw Mḥw r wꜣḥ (14) ḥtp.w-nṯr≠sn n(n) ỉr≠n md.(w)t m ḥm≠k ntk pw sšm n n(n) mꜥr md.t ỉry m ḥm≠k

ꜥḥꜥ.n ḏd.ỉn mšꜥ pn r-ꜣw≠f ḥrw nfr pw m sšrw mꜣꜥ ḥḥ n sp

šm pw ỉr.n nꜣ ts{s}.w n.w ḥm≠f (15) ḥnꜥ nꜣ smr.w n.w pr ny-sw.t r ḥw.t-nṯr n.t ʾImn gm≠sn ḥm.w-nṯr wꜥb.w ꜥꜣ.w ꜥḥꜥ.(w) pḥr ḥw.t-nṯr ḏd≠sn n≠sn ỉw m nṯr pn ʾImn-Rꜥ ḥr(y)-ỉb Ḏw-wꜥb r rdỉ.t dỉ≠f n≠n nb≠n r sꜥnḫ≠n r qd rꜣ.w-pr.w (16) n.w nṯr.w nṯr.(w)t nb.(w) n.(w) Šmꜥw Mḥw r wꜣḥ ḥtp. w-nṯr≠sn nn ỉr≠n md.wt m ḥm nṯr pn ntf sšm n

ꜥ(q) pw ỉr.n nꜣ ḥm.w-nṯr wꜥb.w ꜥꜣ.w r ḥw.t-nṯr ỉr rꜣ≠s nb n ỉr ꜥbw≠f sntr≠f

ꜥ(q) pw ỉr.n nꜣ ts(17).w n.w ḥm≠f ḥnꜥ nꜣ sry.w n.(w) pr ny-sw.t r ḥw.t-nṯr rdỉ.n≠sn ḥr ḫ.t≠sn m-bꜣḥ nṯr pn ḏd≠sn ỉy≠n ḥr≠k ʾImn-Rꜥ nb ns.(wt) tꜣ.wy ḥr(y)-ỉb Ḏw-wꜥb dỉ≠k n≠n ny-sw.t r sꜥnḫ≠n r qd rꜣ.(w)-pr.(w) n.(w) nṯr.w n.w Šmꜥw Mḥw r wꜣḥ ḥtp.(w)-nṯr ỉꜣw.t t(y) (18) mnḫ m ꜥ.wy≠k dỉ≠k s.(t) n sꜣ≠k mrỉ≠k

ꜥḥꜥ.n wꜣḥ≠sn sn.w ny-sw.t m-bꜣḥ nṯr pn n{n} ỉt.n≠f wꜥ ỉm≠sn wꜣḥ m 2-nw n sp sn ny-sw.t sꜣ ʾImn ms.n Mw.t nb.(t) p.t sꜣ Rꜥ [ʾIsprtꜣ] ꜥnḫ ḏ.t

ꜥḥꜥ.n ḏd.ỉn nṯr (19) pn ʾImn-Rꜥ nb ns.(wt) tꜣ.wy ntf pw ny-sw.t nb≠tn ntf pw sꜥnḫ tn ntf pw qd rꜣ-pr nb n Šmꜥw Mḥw ntf wꜣḥ ḥtp.w-nṯr≠sn ỉt≠f pw sꜣ≠ỉ sꜣ Rꜥ [Snkꜣỉmnskn]¹ mꜣꜥ ḥrw mw.t≠f sn.(t) ny-sw.t mw.t ny-sw.t ḥnw.t n.(t) Kš (20) sꜣ.t Rꜥ [Nnsrsꜣ] ꜥnḫ ḏ.t mw.t≠s sn.(t) ny-sw.t dwꜣ.t-nṯr n.(t) ʾImn-Rꜥ ny-sw.t nṯr.w n Wꜣs.t [ʾImn-ỉr-dỉ-s] mꜣꜥ.(t) ḥrw mw.t≠s sn.(t) ny-sw.t [...] mꜣꜥ.(t) ḥrw mw.t≠s sn.(t) ny-sw.t [...] mꜣꜥ.(t) ḥrw mw.t≠s sn.(t) ny-sw.t [...] mꜣꜥ.(t) ḥrw mw.t≠s sn.(t) ny-sw.t [...] (21) mꜣꜥ.(t) ḥrw mw.t≠s sn.(t) ny-sw.t ḥnw.t n.(t) Kš [Kꜣtỉmꜣr(?)] mꜣꜥ.(t) ḥrw ntf nb≠tn

wnn nꜣy ts.w n.w ḥm≠f ḥnꜥ sry.w n.(w) pr ny-sw.t ḥr rdỉ.t≠sn ḥr ḫ.t≠sn m-bꜣḥ nṯr pn ḥr sn tꜣ wr sp-2 ḥr rdỉ.t ỉꜣ(w) n nṯr pn ḥr (22) qn(ỉ) ỉr≠f n sꜣ≠f mrỉ≠f ny-sw.t bỉ.ty [ʾIsprtꜣ] ꜥnḫ ḏ.t

ꜥq pw ỉr.n ḥm≠f ḫ(=r) ḫꜥ(ỉ.t) m-bꜣḥ ỉt≠f ʾImn-Rꜥ nb ns.(wt) tꜣ.wy gm.n≠f sdn nb n.w ny.w-sw.t n.(w) Kš ḥnꜥ wꜣs.w≠sn wꜣḥ m-bꜣḥ nṯr pn wnn ḥm≠f ḏd m-bꜣḥ nṯr (23) pn mỉ n≠ỉ ʾImn-Rꜥ nb ns.(wt) tꜣ.wy ḥr(y)-ỉb Ḏw-wꜥb dỉ≠k n≠ỉ ỉꜣw.t t(y) mnḫ nn sw m ỉb≠ỉ n ꜥꜣ n mr(w.t)≠k dỉ-k n≠ỉ sdn r mr ỉb≠k ḥnꜥ wꜣs

ꜥḥꜥ.n ḏd.ỉn nṯr pn ỉw n≠k sdn n sn≠k ny-sw.t bỉ.ty [ʾInrỉmn] m3ꜥ ḫrw
(24) {m3ꜥ ḫrw} mn≠f m tp≠k mỉ mn sḫm.ty ḥr tp≠k ỉw w3s.(t)≠f m ḏr.t≠k
sḫr≠s ḫfty.w≠k nb

ꜥḥꜥ.n ḥꜥ.ỉn ḥm≠f m [sdn sn≠f ny-sw.t bỉ.ty ʾInrỉmn] m3ꜥ ḫrw rdỉ.n≠f
w3s.(t)≠f m ḏr.t≠f wn.ỉn ḥm≠f rdỉ.t sw ḥr ḫ.t m-b3ḥ nṯr (25) pn ḥr sn t3 wr
sp-2 ḏd≠f mỉ n≠ỉ ʾImn-Rꜥ nb ns.(wt) t3.wy ḥr(y)-ỉb Ḏw-wꜥb nṯr wr bnr
mr(w).t sḏm sprw n≠f m t3 3.t ḏ[d ...] n≠[ỉ(?)] dỉ≠k ꜥnḫ ḏd w3s nb snb nb
3w.t-ỉb nb.t mỉ Rꜥ ḏ.t ỉ3w.(t) ꜥ3.(t) nfr.(t) (26) dỉ≠k s3(ỉ) [q]nw(?) m h3 Rꜥ
n{n} rdỉ.n≠k sḏr [...] ỉm≠f dỉ≠k [...] sw [...] ỉr [...].w≠sn m ḫf(3w)y dỉ≠k
mr(w).t≠ỉ m-ḫnw Kš šf(y.t) (27) pw T3 Mḥw [...] nty ỉw (= r) ỉb≠f dỉ≠k
mrw.t≠(ỉ) m ỉw(?)≠s[n ...] ỉw≠w ḫt [...]

ḏd.ỉn nṯr pn [...]≠k r-3w≠sn nn ḏd≠k h3 n≠ỉ r≠s r nḥḥ ḏ.t

(28) pr.(t) pw ỉr.n ḥm≠f [m] ḥw.t-nṯr r-ḫnw mš ꜥ≠f mỉ wbn [Rꜥ] wn.ỉn
mš ꜥ≠f r-3w≠f ḥr nhm wr sp-2 [...] ỉb≠sn nḏm r ꜥ3 wr.(t) ḥr rdỉ.t ỉ3w n ḥm≠f
ḏd≠sn (29) ỉy m ḥtp n[≠n ... m-ḫn]w≠n mỉ rnp.wt Ḥr m-ḫnw mš ꜥ≠k ḫꜥ.tỉ
ḥr s.t Ḥr mỉ Rꜥ ḏ.t

rnp.t tn n.t ḫꜥ ḥm≠f ỉm≠s ꜥḥꜥ.n w3ḥ.n≠f ḥb.w (30) [...]≠sn [...] 3bd [...]
pr[.t ...] ḥm≠f [...] ỉt [...] ḥr.tw r≠f(?) ḥnq.t [ꜥš]² 40 šw 100 dmḏ ḥnq.t 140

(1) Regnal year 1, month two of winter, day 15, under the Majesty
of the Horus: "Beautiful of Epiphanies"; the Two Ladies: "Beautiful of
Epiphanies"; the Horus of Gold: "Powerful of Heart"; the King of Upper
and Lower Egypt, Lord of the Two Lands, [Merikare], the Son of Re, Lord of
Diadems, [Aspalta], beloved of Amon-Re, Lord of the Thrones of the Two
Lands, resident in Gebel Barkal.

Now then, (2) the entire army of His Majesty was in the city whose
name is Gebel Barkal and in which the god is Dedwen, the foremost of
Nubia—for he is the god of Cush—after the falcon was established in his
(funerary) memorial. (3)

Now, the trusted commanders in the midst of the armies of His Majesty
were six men. The trusted commanders and overseers of fortresses were
six men. Now then, (4) the trusted chief secretaries were six men. Now,
the officials and chief treasurers of the palace were seven men.

Then they said to the entire army: "Come, let us (5), being like a herd
without its herdsman, cause our lord to appear in glory!" This army then
considered it very seriously, saying: "Our lord is here with us, but we do
not know him. If only (6) we might know him, so that we might enter
bearing him and render service to him just as the Two Lands render service
to Horus, the son of Isis, after he sat upon the throne of his father Osiris,
and so that we might give praise to his double (7) uraei!"

Then one said to his fellow among them: "There is none who knows
him unless it be Re himself. He averts every evil from him wherever he
might be."

Then one said (8) to his fellow among them: "Re sets in the land of life; he has already elevated him in our midst."

Then one said to his fellow among them: "That is true. It has been the decision of Re since (9) heaven came into being and since the royal crown came into being. He gave it to his beloved son because the king is the image of Re among the living. Is it through a desire to reestablish this land that Re will grant it to this land?"

Then one said (10) to his fellow among them: "Has not Re entered into heaven? His throne is empty of a ruler. His excellent office here is in his hands. He gave it to his beloved son because Re knows that he shall enact good laws upon his throne."

(11) This entire army then considered it, saying: "Our lord is here with us, but we do not know him." The armies of His Majesty then said altogether with one voice: "Yet there is this god Amon-Re, Lord of the Thrones of the Two Lands, resident in Gebel Barkal. He is the god of Cush. (12) Come, let us go before him! We shall not do anything in ignorance of him. No matter will be good that is done in ignorance of him, but a deed is successful through the agency of the god. He has been the god of the kings of Cush since the time of Re. He is the one who will guide us. (13) In his hands is the kingship of Cush, which he has given to his beloved son. Let us give praise to his face and kiss the ground on our bellies, saying before him: 'We have come before you, O Amon, so that you might give to us our lord in order to vivify us, to build the temples of all the gods and goddesses of Upper and Lower Egypt, and to establish (14) their divine offerings. We shall not do anything in ignorance of you. It is you who will guide us. No matter is successful that is done in ignorance of you.'"

Then this entire army said: "It is a good speech in very truth, a million times over!"

The commanders of His Majesty then went (15) with the courtiers of the palace to the temple of Amon, and they found the prophets and major priests waiting round about the temple, and they said to them: "Now let this god, Amon-Re, resident in Gebel Barkal, come in order to cause that he give to us our lord to vivify us, to build the temples (16) of all the gods and goddesses of Upper and Lower Egypt, and to establish their divine offerings. We shall not do anything in ignorance of this god. He is the one who will guide us."

The prophets and major priests then entered into the temple to perform all its rituals of making his purification and his censing.

The commanders (17) of His Majesty and the officials of the palace then entered into the temple, and they placed themselves upon their bellies in the presence of this god, saying: "We have come before you, O Amon-Re, Lord of the Thrones of the Two Lands, resident in Gebel Barkal, so that you might give us a king in order to vivify us, to build the temples of the gods of Upper and Lower Egypt, and to establish the divine offerings. The excellent office here (18) is in your hands; may you give it to your son whom you love."

Then they placed the royal brethren in the presence of this god, but he did not take one of them. There was placed a second time the royal brother, the son of Amon, born of Mut, the Lady of heaven, the Son of Re, [Aspalta], living forever.

Then this god, (19) Amon-Re, Lord of the Thrones of the Two Lands, resident in Gebel Barkal, said: "He is the king, your lord. It is he who will vivify you. It is he who will build all the temples of Upper and Lower Egypt. It is he who will endow their divine offerings. His father is my son, the Son of Re, [Senkamanisken],[1] the justified, while his mother is the king's sister and king's mother, the Mistress of Cush, (20) the Daughter of Re, [Ñasalsa], living forever, whose mother is the king's sister, the Divine Votaress of Amon-Re, King of the Gods, in Thebes, [Amonardis II], the justified, whose mother was the king's sister [...], the justified, whose mother was the king's sister [...], the justified, whose mother was the king's sister [...], the justified, whose mother was the king's sister [...] (21), the justified, whose mother was the king's sister and Mistress of Cush, [Katimala (?)], the justified. He is your lord."

These commanders of His Majesty and the officials of the palace placed themselves upon their bellies in the presence of this god, kissing the ground very fervently and giving praise to this god because of (22) the valor that he had made for his beloved son, the King of Upper and Lower Egypt, [Aspalta], living forever.

His Majesty then entered in order to appear in glory in the presence of his father Amon-Re, Lord of the Thrones of the Two Lands, and he found every crown of the kings of Cush together with their scepters placed before this god. In the presence of this god His Majesty said: (23) "Come to me, O Amon-Re, Lord of the Thrones of the Two Lands, resident in Gebel Barkal! May you give to me the excellent office here, although it was not my intent, through the greatness of your love. May you give me the crown in accordance with your desire, together with the scepter."

Then this god said: "Yours is the crown of your brother, the King of Upper and Lower Egypt, [Anlamani], the justified. (24) May it remain upon your head just as the double crown remains on your head. His scepter is in your hand. May it overthrow all your enemies."

Then His Majesty appeared in glory in [the crown of his brother, the King of Upper and Lower Egypt, Anlamani], the justified, after he had placed his scepter in his hand. And His Majesty placed himself on his belly in the presence of (25) this god, kissing the ground very fervently, saying: "Come to me, O Amon-Re, Lord of the Thrones of the Two Lands, resident in Gebel Barkal, great god, sweetly beloved, who hears the one who petitions him at once, who said [...] to [me (?).] May you grant all life, stability, and dominion, all health and joy like Re forever, and a great and good, lengthy old age. (26) May you give the wisdom [and va]lor (?) from the reign of Re, without allowing [...] to slumber in it. May you give [...] it [...] their enemies (?) as snakes. May you place love of me within Cush. It is the dignity (27) of Lower Egypt [...] which is according to his wish. May you place love of me in their islands (?) [...], while they pervade [...]."

Then this god said: "[I shall grant (?)] your [wishes (?)] in their entirety. There is nothing concerning which you will say: 'If only I had!' forever and ever."

(28) His Majesty then went out [from] the temple into the midst of his army like the rising [of Re]. And his entire army shouted very greatly [...], with their hearts extremely happy, giving praise to His Majesty, saying: "Come in peace, [our] lord [...] in our midst, like the years of Horus in the midst of your army, while you appear in glory upon the throne of Horus forever!"

This year in which His Majesty appeared in glory: then he established festivals (30) [...] their [...] month [...] of winter, [day ...] His Majesty [...] called (?) ["...] of the Father": 40 [jugs][2] and 100 jars of beer, for a total of 140 vessels of beer.

NOTES

1. For the identification of Aspalta's father, see Dunham and Macadam 1949, 142 and 149. Wilson restores "Inle-Amon" (Anlamani), the predecessor and elder brother of Aspalta whose name belongs in line 23.

2. For the restoration, see "The Dream Stela of Tanwetamani," line 9.

GENEALOGY OF DYNASTY XXV AS GIVEN BY THE ASPALTA ELECTION STELA

Royal Sister and Mistress of Cush [Katimala (?)]
I
Royal Sister [...] (reigns of Lords C and D at El Kurru)
I
Royal Sister [...] (reigns of brothers Alara and Kashta)
I
Royal Sister [...] (reigns of brothers Piye and Shabako)
I
Taharqa + Royal Sister [Tekahatamani or other]
I
Divine Votaress Amonardis II (reigns of Tanwetamani and Atlanersa)
I
? + Senkamaniskeñ + Ñasalsa
I   I
Anlamani   Aspalta

A. KATIMALA

140. SEMNA INSCRIPTION OF QUEEN KATIMALA
(KHARTOUM NATIONAL MUSEUM)

West of the central doorway on the facade of the New Kingdom temple of Semna, the original decoration was cut away and replaced by a scene of a slim Nubian queen and her attendant offering to the goddess Isis. The first queen since Hatshepsut to style herself "King of Upper and Lower Egypt," the obscure ruler Katimala typically has been assigned to the later Meroitic period of Nubian history. In both its artistic style and Late Egyptian language, however, the inscription certainly predates the archaizing Classicism begun under Piye, as recognized in unpublished lectures by Klaus Baer. After initial disagreement, the pre-Meroitic redating is now accepted in recent editions of the inscription. Katimala, whose name corresponds to the Meroitic *Kdi-mel(ye)*, or "beautiful woman," is most likely an ancestor of the Napatan Dynasty XXV. Her prominence is in accord with the matriarchal character of Nubian society evident in Napatan records and in the Meroitic institution of *Kandake* ("Candace"), or queen regnant.

The text records the conclusion of turbulent events instigated by an enemy Makaresh following a tranquil period under her predecessors, who, with Katimala, are probably to be identified with the unknown "Lords" A through D buried in the earliest royal tombs at El Kurru. The royal genealogy of Aspalta notes six generations of female antecedents, ending with a "king's sister and Mistress of Cush" who could well be Katimala, approximately 850 B.C.E. In its righteous tenor, the text's insistence upon devotion to Amon is typical for Libyan-era Egypt and anticipates the zealous narratives of Piye. The difficulties of the inexpertly carved text have precluded full analysis. The following first translation is indebted to the study by Klaus Baer.

For the texts, translation, and discussion, see Caminos 1998, 20–27 and pls. 4, 6–7, and 14–17; 1994, 73–80; 1964b, 85 ("more likely Meroitic"); Dunham and Janssen 1960, 9–11 and pls. 11, 13–14; Grapow 1940, 24–41; de Wit and Mertens 1962, 140; and Eide et al. 1994, 42–47. An unpublished copy of the inscription was made by Breasted in 1907 (notebook 9, 60–61; and supplemental notebook, 48–51), in association with Oriental Institute photos 3348–50 (dated Dynasty XXV?). Cf. Kitchen 1986, 150 §120 n. 283.

LABEL FOR ISIS

ḏd ỉn ȝs.t mw.t nṯr ỉr.(t) (2) Rˁ ḥnw.t nṯr.w nb.w šsp.(3)n⸗(ỉ) ḥtp.t[1] n ḥm.t ny-sw.t wr.t sȝ.t ny-sw.t (4) Kȝ[tỉmȝl …]

Said by Isis, the God's Mother, the eye (2) of Re, the Mistress of all the gods: "I have accepted (3) the floral offering[1] of the king's great wife and king's daughter, Ka[timala ...]"

LABEL FOR KATIMALA

ḥm.t ny-sw.t wr.t s3.t ny-sw.t K3ty(2)m3r2 m3ꜥ.t-ḫrw ỉmy šsp≠s ḥtp.(t)≠ (ỉ) (3) ny-sw.t bỉ.ty ḥm.t ny-sw.t wr.t s3.t ny-sw.t (4) s3 wḏ3.t nb.(t) n.(t) ꜥnḫ ḥ3≠s

The king's great wife and king's daughter, Kati(2)mala,[2] the justified: "May she accept (my) floral offering." (3) The King of Upper and Lower Egypt, the king's great wife and king's daughter. (4) Protection and all security of life are behind her.

MAIN TEXT

(1) ḥsb.t 14.(t) (3bd) 2 pr.t sw 9 ḏd ỉn ḥm≠f n(=m) ḥm.t ny-sw.t wr.t s3.t ny-sw.t K3tym3r2 m3ꜥ.t-ḫrw tw≠n (r) tnw3 ỉw bn tw≠n b3ky m-ḫnw n3 b3k.w n.(w) 'Imn ỉw wn (2) ḫf(ty.w) ỉw mnỉ≠w dỉ.t ḫpr t3 md.t n t3 rnp.t ỉ-ḫpr n≠n ỉw mn≠(ỉ) dỉ.t ḫpr≠s{w} ỉr-r≠w ỉw bn mn≠w dỉ.t ḫpr≠(s) n≠n ỉw wn wr ỉw ꜥw(3)≠f nbw ḥd mtw≠f ỉry 'Imn s[ḫw]r(?) (3) qm3y ỉm≠ỉ ḫf[(ty) wꜥr].w(?) ỉry(.t) b3k n 'Imn p3 ỉr≠ỉ ỉw b(w)-pw≠ỉ sḫ3wy t3 md.t ỉ-ḫpr r≠ỉ m t3 rnp.t m-ḏr h3n≠ỉ n 'Imn ỉ3d ꜥw3[y nbw ḫld p3 (4) dỉw n3y≠ỉ ỉt.w ỉ-šsp≠(ỉ) n≠w sỉn n≠ỉ m-ḫt wỉ(3)wỉ(3)≠f ỉw≠ỉ ỉr≠f m ḏw.w nbw ỉ-ỉr≠ỉ 3m m t3 rnp.t ỉy(3) nḫt ḥk3y [(n) p3] nṯr

ḥr ḏd(5)≠ỉ (n) mꜥb3 n wry.(w) ntỉy ...]ỉ[...] bỉn p3 pr-ꜥ3 qq m ḫpš≠f ỉstw nfr snd ỉrm ḫ3ꜥ pḥ.wy r-ḥ3.ty ḫrwy mỉ-qd p3 wn n3y≠[ỉ] ỉt.w ỉ-(6)šsp≠ (ỉ) n≠w ỉr.(t)≠f ḥr ỉ-ỉr≠(ỉ) [...] t3 rnp.t ḥr t3 md.t ỉ-ḫpr ỉr≠ỉ ḥr ỉry n3y≠(ỉ) ỉt.w ỉ-wn ssnḏ n3(y)≠w ḫrwy.(w) nb wn≠w ḥms ỉw≠w nfr ỉ[rm n3]y≠w ḥm.(w)t (7) nfr ỉr.(t) bỉn m-dỉ p3 [ntỉy bw-ỉr≠f 3m ỉm≠f bỉn ỉr.(t) bỉn m-dỉ rḫy.(t) ỉw≠f 3m ỉw≠f r dỉ.(t) p3 nty ꜥnḫ pt(r)ỉ≠n pꜥ[.t ... n3]y≠w bỉn (8) ỉw≠w ꜥnḫ bỉn ỉr.(t) nfr (n) ꜥḏ3ỉw p3-ḏd4 nṯr ỉr ỉ(= r) ỉr.(t) ꜥnḫ ỉry nfr ỉstw nfr ỉr.(t) n 'Imn k3y t3 ỉw bn t3y≠f s.t ỉwn3 ḥr ỉry p3 nty ỉr.(t) (n) 'Imn k.t s.t ḥr p[tr]ỉ [...] š3ꜥ (9) p3 h3(w) ỉw ns-sw5 hy.w(t) (n.t) [n]3y≠ỉ ỉt.w ỉstw bỉn ḫrp t3y ḥrp.(t) n.(t) 'Imn m mn.t nfr šꜥ.t n t3 ḥrp.(t) n.(t) 'Imn mỉ-qd p3 [ỉ-ỉr] M3k3(10)r3š3 ỉw ỉ-ỉr n3 rmt.w nb n nỉw.t sḫwr M3k3r3š3 m mn.t ỉw dmỉ n≠f mỉ-qd ꜥdn ỉw b(w)-pwy [... p3]y≠f bỉn (11) pḥw r ḥ3.ty≠f6 mỉ-qd p3 [n]tỉy pḥ r ḥ3.ty (n) p3 mš3 p3 ỉr nfr n t3 ḏr≠f bỉn ỉr.(t) n≠f p3 nty bwt(?) ...[...] (12) n≠n(?) w[...] ny.[t]≠sw.t(?) wry.[t ...] ꜥ3 qnqn [...] rḫ≠ỉ ỉw≠ỉ ỉr.(t) ...[...] (13) tn r≠ỉ mỉ rn≠ỉ ỉ-ỉr≠w ...[...] ỉr(y)≠[w]

(1) Regnal year 14, (month) 2 of winter, day 9. Said by His Majesty, namely, the king's great wife and king's daughter, Katimala,[2] the justified: "Where shall we turn[3] when we do not serve among the servants of Amon, since there are (2) enemies who have continually caused to happen in this

year the matter that has happened to us, while I have continually caused it to happen against them, although they will not continue to cause (it) to happen to us, even though there is a chief who has stolen gold and silver and makes Amon [accur]sed (?), (2) the one who has created me?

The enemy has [fled]. It was acting as servant for Amon that I did, while I have not recalled the matter that happened against me in this year from the time that I relied upon Amon, who attacks the robber [of gold and silv]er. The (4) one whom my fathers, whom I succeeded, had appointed, hastened to me after he was unsuccessful, and I accomplished it in the Mountains of Gold. Now, in this year I understood that the magic of [the] god is indeed powerful.

Now, I said (5) to the 30 chiefs who […]: 'Wretched is the pharaoh who is stripped of his power. Is it good to fear and to turn tail before the enemy like that which my fathers, whom (6) I succeeded, used to do? Now, I [spent (?)] the year only engaged in the matter that happened against me. Now as for my fathers, who used to terrify all their enemies, they used to dwell happily [with] their wives. (7) It is good to do evil to the one whom he (Amon) does not know. It is bad to do evil to the subjects while he knows. He will appoint the one who lives. We have seen the patricians (?) […] their evil, (8) while they were alive. It is bad to do good falsely. Thus said[4] the god, who acts to make life: 'Do good!' Is it good to make for Amon another land that is not his place? Now as for the one who makes for Amon another place, now look, […] until (9) today, while he is found in[5] the annals of my fathers. Is it bad to offer this offering cattle to Amon daily? Or good to slaughter the offering cattle of Amon like that [which] Maka(10)resh [did], when daily all the people of the city cursed Makaresh, destruction having befallen him likewise, when […] did not […] his evil, (11) which entered into his heart[6] like that which entered into the heart of the army? He who does good for the entire land, it is bad to do to him that which is abominated (?) […] (12) to us (?) […] a great kingship (?) […] great […] fighting […] I know I shall do …[…] (13) this […] against me like my name. They did …[…] pertaining to them."

NOTES
1. Erman and Grapow 1926–63, 3:196/1–3. Caminos, who translated only these labels, read shtp, requiring the substitution of "n" and "s," the reversal of "p" and "t," and an unusual combination of optative and imperative.
2. The carving does not carefully distinguish "t" from "r," and the queen's name seems written "Karimala" in the label and "Katimala" in the main text. However, Caminos's preference for "Karimala" is excluded by the Meroitic equivalent of the name.
3. Erman and Grapow 1926–63, 5:373/14.
4. Coptic ⲡⲉϫⲉ.

5. Literally, "he belongs to the annals. . . . "
6. Meaning "to think of, conceive." The idiom recurs in the Demotic romance of Setna I, col. 5/26.

B. KASHTA

141. ELEPHANTINE STELA
(CAIRO JDE 41013)

This lunette fragment from a granite round-topped stela was excavated by Maspero in the great temple of Elephantine, to the northeast of the gateway of Alexander. Now measuring approximately 20 cm in height by 6 cm in thickness, the stela had an original width of approximately 35 cm. At the summit of the lunette, a winged disk and pendant uraeus surmount the texts and lost representations of the local divine triad of Khnum, Satet, and Anukis, while, on the viewer's right, an *oudjat*-eye protects the titles and image of the king. The damaged royal stela of uncertain purpose preserves the only sculpted representation of the Nubian Kashta and establishes the presence of Nubian authority in Upper Egypt prior to the famous campaign of Piye. Kashta's Egyptian reign is otherwise attested in the "Karnak Priestly Annals" (text 31) and by a bronze aegis, now in a private collection, whose counterpoise is engraved with a scene representing the king (K3št) being suckled by the goddess Mut, the consort of Theban Amon. Contra Kitchen, these Theban attestations are probably associated with the accession of Kashta's daughter Amonardis (I) as "heiress-apparent" to the God's Wife Shepenwepet I, daughter of Osorkon III.

For the text, translation, and discussion, see Leclant 1963, 74–81; Priese 1970, 16–17; and Eide et al. 1994, 42–47. See Kitchen 1986, 151 §122 (who ignores Priese's identification of the Karnak Priestly Annals text 31) and 581 §522.

LABEL FOR KHNUM
 Ḫnm-Rˁ (2) nb qbḥw
 Khnum-Re, (2) Lord of the cataract region.

LABEL FOR SATET
  St.t nb.(t) 3b[w]
  Satet, Lady of Elephantine.

(1) ny-sw.t bỉ.ty N(y)-mȝꜥ.t-Rꜥ (2) sȝ Rꜥ nb tȝ.wy Kȝšt (3) mry (Ḫnm St.t ꜥnq.t)[1] ꜥnḫ ḏ.t

The King of Upper and Lower Egypt, Nimaꜥre, (2) Son of Re, Lord of the Two Lands, Kashta, (3) beloved (of Khnum, Satis, and Anukis),[1] living forever.

NOTE

1. No divine names were carved. The lost representations of the deities served as both illustration and text.

142. WADI GASUS INSCRIPTION

Some 15 km from the Red Sea, an expedition of quarriers or prospectors left a terse inscription in two vertical columns on a rock face of the remote Wadi Gasus (26°33'N 34°02'E). The subject of much chronological speculation, the inscription is included here as a cautionary presentation to show the equivocal nature of its evidence. Each column of the text contains a date followed by the cartouche of a Divine Votaress of Amon, celebate princesses who secured the allegiance of Thebes to the crown by providing "a politically harmless titular head for the domain of Amun" (Baer 1973, 20). Corresponding regnal dates identify the votaresses with Shepenwepet I (daughter of Osorkon III) and Amonardis I (daughter of Kashta). The regnal dates had long been assigned to the votaresses themselves, until reinterpretation of the text by Christophe, Bierbrier, and Kitchen linked the dates to the (unmentioned) rulers Piye and either Takelot III or Iuput II.

As countered by Baer and Wente, however, the use of regnal years by God's Wives of this period is hardly surprising, since these figures adopted many features of royalty, including cartouches, a "female Horus" prenomen, and even jubilee festivals—which necessarily presuppose a regnal year count. The "usurpation" of royal regnal dates in quarry inscriptions by semi-independent local rulers during an era of political competition finds a direct counterpart in the Hatnub graffiti of the First Intermediate Period. If, as Christophe notes (1952–53, 143 n. 1), regnal dates of unspecified sovereigns are not unusual at the beginning of texts, it is nonetheless unparalleled for a regnal date followed by a cartouche to be understood as anything other than the date of the royal individual named in the cartouche. Current consensus may favor the Christophe hypothesis, but the argumentation is dubious and chronological deductions based upon it are unprovable speculation. Far more reasonable is the conclusion that Amonardis I was adopted as junior votaress in the eighth year of Shepenwepet I, at the instigation of Kashta in his first year at Thebes (see the Elephantine

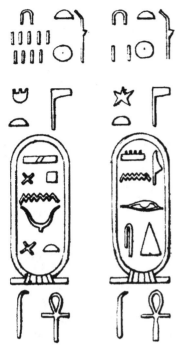

Corrected from Schweinfurth
1885, plate II.

Stela of Kashta, p. 459). The inscription of the twelfth year of Amonardis should thus fall within the reign of her father Kashta (ca. 13–19 years) and not that of her brother Piye.

For the text and discussion, see Schweinfurth 1885; Christophe 1952–53, 141–52; Baer 1973, 20; and Wente 1976, 276. See Kitchen 1986, 175–778 §§143–45, 359–60 §321, 543–44 §450, and 581 §522.

(1) ḥsb.t 12.(t)[1] dwȝ.t-nṯr ᵓImn-ỉr-dỉ-s(y) ꜥnḫ.tỉ

Regnal year 12[1] (of?) the Divine Votaress Amonardis (I), the living.

(2) ḥsb.t 19.(t) ḥm.t-nṯr Šp-n-wp.(t) ꜥnḫ.tỉ

Regnal year 19 (of?) the God's Wife Shepenwepet (I), the living.

NOTE
1. Originally read 13; for the revised reading, see Christophe 1952–53, 143.

C. PIYE

143. GEBEL BARKAL STELA NO. 26 OF YEAR 3

This sandstone stela was discovered broken and toppled from its base in the colonnaded court B 501 constructed by Piye at Napata (Gebel Barkal). The main body of the text is lost, and the surviving upper section measures 123 cm in width by 130 cm in height. The lunette of the round-topped stela is surmounted by a winged disk above a depiction of Piye offering a necklace and pectoral to a seated, ram-headed Amon, who is followed by standing figures of Mut and Khonsu. Amon extends his hands to the king, offering two crowns: the "Blue Crown" associated with ritual and battle; and the Lower Egyptian crown representing territory claimed, if not yet controlled, by the Nubian ruler. The original figure of the king has been erased and replaced, and the cartouches have been attacked by chisel throughout the text. Such erasures are common on Dynasty XXV monuments in Nubia and derive from the punitive invasion of the Saite ruler Psametik II in 593 B.C.E.

Dated to regnal year 3 in the fragmentary penultimate line, the stela is the earliest record of Piye's reign. What is preserved of the main body of the text displays the initial form of the king's titulary, which imitates that of the legendary conqueror Thutmose III, whose ancient local stela ("the Gebel Barkal Stela") was re-erected beside Piye's in court B 501. Piye's later titularies would imitate those of Rameses II and, in his "archaizing" phase, the Old Kingdom ruler Snefru. In sharp contrast to the famous Victory Stela of year 21, composed in anachronistic Middle Egyptian, Stela 26 is written in contemporary Late Egyptian. The lengthy speeches of Amon and Piye in the lunette well reflect the current political conditions, with multiple Libyan chiefs and kings whom Piye claims to dominate. The single word in the final line suggests that the primary text once had the literary form of a *Königsnovelle,* in which the king is informed of a situation requiring royal attention. The "Victory Stela" begins in similar fashion, and, like its more famous counterpart, Stela 26 may have related a campaign of Piye against his northern opponents. Gilula has noted the similarity of Amon's speech to the text of Jer 1:4–5, but the Egyptian god's speech follows standard New Kingdom phraseology, and the text does not use Middle Egyptian emphatic forms.

For the text, translation, and discussion, see Reisner 1931, 89–100 and pls. V–VI; Gilula 1967, 114; Priese 1970, 24–28; Eide et al. 1994, 55–62; and Grimal 1986, 217–19 and minor references on 742. See Kitchen 1986, 369 §329 and 582 §523.

SPEECH OF AMON

(1) dd-mdw (ỉ)n ʾImn-Rᶜ nb ns.wt t3.wy dhn wᶜb ḥr (2) s3ẕf mrẕf [Py mrỉ-ʾImn¹] ddẕ ỉ rẕk m (3) ẖ.t n.(t) mw.tẕk ỉwẕk r ḥq3 n Km.(t) (4) rḫẕ ỉ tw m mwy wnnẕk (5) m swḥ.t ỉwẕk r (6) nb ỉr.(t).nẕ ỉ šsp nẕk wr.ty sḫᶜ² (7) Rᶜ m sp tp(y) nfr ỉt ḥr s(8)mnḫ s3ẕf ỉnk wd nẕk nm pšẕf r-ḥnᶜẕk (9) ỉnk nb p.t dỉẕ ỉ n Rᶜ dỉẕf (10) n ms.wẕf m nṯr.w r-mn rmṯ.w ỉnk dd nẕk n.t-ᶜ nm pšẕf s(y) (11) r-ḥnᶜẕk n(n) wd ky ny-sw.t (12) ỉnk dỉ ny-sw.t n mrẕ ỉ

(1) Recitation by Amon-Re, Lord of the Thrones of the Two Lands, of the Pure Peak (Gebel Barkal), to (2) his son, whom he loves, [Piye, beloved of Amon¹]: "I said concerning you (while you were) in (3) the body of your mother, that you would be the ruler of Egypt. (4) I recognized you in the semen when you were (5) in the egg, that you would be (6) lord of what I have made. Receive for yourself the double diadem, (7) which Re made manifest² on the goodly first occasion. A father benefits (8) his son. I am the one who has decreed (the kingship) for you. Who will share with you? (9) I am the lord of heaven. What I have given to Re, he

has given (10) to his children among the gods as well as (among) men. I
am the one who gives to you the duty. Who will share it (11) with you?
There is no one who can decree another king. (12) I am the one who
appoints a king as I please."

SPEECH OF MUT
      (14) ḏd-mdw (ỉ)n Mw.t nb.(t) p.t šsp n≠k ḫꜥ.w m-ꜥ ꜣImn rḫ≠ỉ ỉb≠f
r(?)≠k ḏd≠f r≠k ꜥnḫ n≠k m ny-sw.t (14bis) [ꜥn]ḫ≠k ḏ.t
      (14) Recitation by Mut, the Lady of heaven: "Receive to yourself the
crowns from the hand of Amon. I know his thoughts concerning you.
He has said concerning you that you possess life as king, (14bis) living
forever."

SPEECH OF KHONSU
      (15) ḏd-mdw (ỉ)n Ḫnsw mds(?) šsp n≠k ỉꜥr.ty m-ꜥ ỉt≠k ꜣImn
      (15) Recitation by Khonsu the forceful (?): "Receive for yourself the
two uraei from the hand of your father Amon."

LABEL FOR PIYE
      (a) Py (b) sꜣ n ꜥnḫ ḥꜣ≠k mỉ Rꜥ ḏ.t
      (a) Piye. (b) The protection of life is behind you like Re forever.

SPEECH OF PIYE
      (16) [sꜣ Rꜥ Py mrỉ-ꜣImn] (17) ḏd≠f dỉ n≠ỉ ꜣImn n Np.(t) (18) ỉr ḥqꜣ n
ḫꜣs.t nb.(t) pꜣ nty tw≠ỉ ḏd n≠f ntk wr ỉw≠f ỉr wr pꜣ nty tw≠ỉ (19) ḏd n≠(f)
bn ntk wr ỉ(w)nꜣ b(w)-ỉr≠f ỉr wrꜣ dỉ n≠ỉ ꜣImn m Wꜣs.t ỉr ḥqꜣ n Km.t pꜣ
nty tw≠ỉ (20) ḏd [n≠f ỉr ḫꜥ ỉr≠f ḫꜥ pꜣ] nty tw≠ỉ ḏd n≠f m-ỉr ḫꜥ b(w)-ỉr≠f
ḫꜥ pꜣ nty (21) tw≠ỉ dỉ ḥr≠ỉ r≠f nb mn qỉ n ḫf pꜣy≠f dmỉ ỉw (22) bn sw m
ḏr.t≠ỉ ỉ(w)nꜣ⁴ nṯr.w ỉr.w ny-sw.t rmt.w ỉr.w ny-sw.t (23) ỉn ꜣImn ỉr (w)ỉ
pꜣ nty b(w)-p(w) nꜣ ḥꜣ.tyw ỉr≠f⁵ ỉn≠w n≠ỉ wr.(t)-ḥkꜣ.(w) (24) ỉr≠s wn(?)
[...] ꜥḥꜥ(w) nfr
      (16) [The Son of Re, Piye, beloved of Amon] (17), says: "Amon of
Napata appointed me (18) to be ruler of every foreign land. The one to
whom I say: 'You are chief,' he becomes chief. The one to whom I (19)
say: 'You are not chief,' he does not become chief.³ Amon in Thebes
appointed me to be ruler in Egypt. The one [to whom] I (20) say: '[Appear
(as king),' he appears. The] one to whom I say: 'Do not appear,' he does
not appear. Each one (21) to whom I turn my attention, there is no way
to plunder his town, unless (22) it be by my hand.⁴ Gods make a king,
men make a king, (23) (but) it is Amon who made me, the one whom the
leaders did not make.⁵ I was brought the (crown) Great of Magic, (24) and
it has caused there to be [...] a good lifetime.

MAIN TEXT

(25) ꜥnḫ Ḥr kꜣ nḫt ḫꜥ m Np.(t) Nb.ty Wꜣḫ ny.t-sw.t mꜣ Rꜥ m p.t Ḥr-nbw ḏsr ḫꜥ.(w) sḫm pḥ.ty ꜥnḫ ḥr nb n mꜣꜣ≠f mꜣ ꜣḫ.ty ny-sw.t bꜣ.ty nb tꜣ.wy [Mn-ḫpr-Rꜥ] sꜣ Rꜥ nb ḫꜥ.(w) (26) [Py mrꜣ-ʾImn] nṯr nfr ny-sw.t ny.w-sw.t ḥqꜣ ḥqꜣ.w ꜣty ꜣt tꜣ.w nb sḫm pḥ.ty ꜣtf≠f ny.w-sw.t m tp≠f ḫsf m sḫm≠f ꜥn ꜣrw mꜣ Rꜥ m p.t ḫꜥ.w mꜣ ꜣḫ.ty dꜣ≠f sw (27) [...] wꜣs bꜣꜣw.t m qmꜣ.t(w)≠f šꜣꜥ nꜣ(?) [... qm]ꜣ Ḏḥwty [...]≠sn r ny.t-sw.t wꜥ wꜥ.ty swsḫ Kš dꜣ ḥry.t≠f m nb ḫꜣs.wt n(n) wn ꜥbꜥ wr (28) sḫ≠sn rꜣ≠sn [...] ꜣr.ty sḫd dꜥr≠sn štꜣ.(w) ḥr mꜣꜣ ḥr dḫ[n.w] (29) rḫ ʾImn [... dꜣ ꜥnḫ] mꜣ [Rꜥ] ḏ.t [ḥsb.t] 3.(t) ꜣbd [...] (30) ꜣw.[tw r ḏd n ḥm≠f ...]⁶

(25) Long live the Horus: "Strong bull appearing in Napata"; the Two Ladies: "Enduring of kingship like Re in heaven"; the Golden Horus: "Of holy appearance, of powerful strength, at whose sight everyone lives as (at the sight of) the Horizon-dweller," the King of Upper and Lower Egypt, Lord of the Two Lands, [Menkheperre], Son of Re, Lord of Diadem(s), (26) [Piye, beloved of Amon], the Good God, king of kings, ruler of rulers, sovereign who seizes all lands, of powerful strength, whose royal *atef*-crown is upon his head, who repels by means of his strength, whose form is beautiful like (that of) Re in heaven, with appearances like (those of) the Horizon-dweller when he manifests himself, (27) [...] of dominion, with wonders when he was created, beginning with the [...] which Thoth created [...] them concerning kingship, the singly unique one, who widened (the boundaries of) Kush, whose terror placed (him) as lord of foreign lands, without boasting of greatness, (28) when they were deaf to their speech [...] whose eyes illuminate their secret thoughts, looking at the hid[den things] (29) that Amon knows, [... given life] like [Re] forever. [Regnal year] 3, month [....]: (30) [one] came [to say to His Majesty ...]⁶

NOTES

1. Traces of the erased cartouche were read by Reisner 1931, 94.

2. The text puns on the terms for crowns/diadems (ḫꜥ.w) and for "make manifest/cause to appear" (sḫꜥ) as king.

3. All writings of "chief" show a figure wearing a feather, indicating that Libyan chiefs are meant; see Priese 1970, 26–27.

4. Literally, "when (22) it is not by my hand."

5. Reisner and Priese emend unnecessarily to: pꜣ nty (n) nꜣ ḥꜣ.tyw b(w)-p(w)≠f ꜣr n≠ꜣ ꜣnw "the one (among) the leaders who has not made tribute for me."

6. For the reading and interpretation of lines 28–30, see Priese 1970, 25.

144. GEBEL BARKAL STELA 29 + 30 OF YEARS 3–4 (CAIRO 47085 + BERLIN 1068)

Grey granite fragments dispersed over the area of the temple complex of Gebel Barkal are all that remain of a major stela of Piye recounting the events of years 3 and 4. One fragment brought to Berlin in 1845 by Lepsius is now lost, a casualty of the Second World War. Additional fragments were recovered by the Reisner expeditions from 1915 to 1920. The content preserved in the meager fragments parallels that of the later "Victory Stela" of year 21. Piye and his armies are mentioned making offerings and celebrating the Opet festival of Amon at Thebes. Thereafter, in year 4, the Nubians sail northward and encounter "the armies of the Northland." Like Stela 26 of year 3, this Stela 29 + 30 suggests that Piye's territorial ambitions were repeatedly challenged by northern forces, perhaps in alliance with the incipient realm of the Saite Great Chief of the West.

For the texts, translation, and discussion, see Priese 1970, 28–30; Erman 1891, 126; Schäfer 1905, 78–79, Loukianoff 1926, 88–89; and Reisner 1931, 82 (nos. 29 and 30). See Kitchen 1986, 369 §329 and 582 §523.

CAIRO FRAGMENT 47085
    (x+1) [...] dỉ ʾImn q(ȝ) [...]
    (x+2) [...] ns Py ỉw tm [...]
    (x+3) [... ḫ]b tp(y) ȝḫ.t sw 14 ḥn(ꜥ) ḥm-nṯr tp(y) (n) ʾImn [...]

    (x+1) [...] Amon caused to be high [...]
    (x+2) [...] belonging to Piye, while not [...]
    (x+3) [... the festi]val of the first month of Inundation, day 14, together with the First Prophet of Amon [...]

BERLIN FRAGMENT 1068
    (x+1) [... mšꜥ].w n [Py ...]
    (x+2) [...] wȝ.t(?) n nbw r ḥr≠f ỉw≠sn [...]
    (x+3) [...] r ʾIp.t n ȝbd 2 ȝḫ.t ḥsb.t 4.(t) ḫr [ḥm] n [...]
    (x+4) [...] wdn.w ꜥȝ.w m-bȝḥ≠f ḥd≠s[n ...]
    (x+5) [... m]šꜥ.w n p(ȝ) Tȝ-Mḥw [...]

    (x+1) [... arm]ies of [Piye ...]
    (x+2) [...] path (?) of gold toward him, while they [...]
    (x+3) [... procession of Amon (?)] to the Opet-shrine in month 2 of Inundation. Regnal year 4 under the [Majesty] of [...]
    (x+4) [...] numerous offerings before him. They sailed north [...]
    (x+5) [... ar]mies of the Northland [...]

145. VICTORY STELA
(CAIRO JDE 48862+47086–47089)

Piye's pretensions to imperial control over the petty kingdoms of Libyan Egypt, as expressed in his programmatic stela of year 3, were

Lunette of Piye Victory Stela, Budge 1912, li.

severely challenged in his twentieth year of rule. The southern expansion of the independent Saite state ruled by Tefnakht, Great Chief of the
West and a lineage chieftain of the Libu, had extended beyond the critical
city of Memphis and gained the fealty of princes in the East Delta and
in Upper Egypt as far as Hermopolis, with only the beleaguered city of
Heracleopolis yet unconquered. Informed that half of Egypt had fallen to
Tefnakht's control, with the remaining Thebaid implicitly threatened, Piye
dispatched a force northward to join his Egyptian commanders. Despite
initial victories, Piye's forces failed to seize Hermopolis or to lift the siege
of Heracleopolis. The king himself felt compelled to lead a new invasion
that successfully advanced as far northward as the Delta town of Athribis,
where he received the personal submission of most northern rulers. After
a failed counterassault at Mosdai, Tefnakht sued for peace by diplomatic
messenger while remaining in Sais, secure in his western possessions.
Neither Piye nor his Nubian successors were able to eradicate the Saite
dynasty or the other petty kingdoms within their nominal control, and
the descendants of Tefnakht would form both the ill-fated Dynasty XXIV
and the illustrious Dynasty XXVI, which reunified Egypt and suppressed
Libyan, Nubian, and Assyrian incursions.

The Piye Victory Stela is justly famous as a unique work of royal historical propaganda. The legitimacy of Piye's rule is indicated not merely
by expressions of divine approval, royal victory, and obsequious flattery
but by conscious attempts to present the Nubian ruler as truly Egyptian,
while his Libyan opponents are debased and unclean outsiders who sport
feathers, eat fish, and are uncircumcised. Like the Mahdi of the nineteenth
century, Piye led an Egyptian campaign that was both military invasion
and religious pilgrimage designed to "cleanse" a debased aristocracy. Piye's
zeal in the cause of Amon is explicit, with a detailed "holiness code" for
his soldiers and a military itinerary dependent upon the celebration of religious festivals. Composed in classical Middle Egyptian, the language of the
stela also serves the theme of cultural revival, and the exceptional lapses
into the common vernacular are intentionally placed in the speeches of
vanquished Libyans. As implied in the concluding line, this literary revival
was certainly the work of Nubian-allied Thebans who would have been

familiar with local Ramesside monuments that stigmatized the ancestral Libyans as uncircumcised, feather-wearing barbarians.

Discovered in 1862 within the temple of Gebel Barkal at the Nubian capital of Napata, the grey granite round-topped stela measures 1.80 m. high, 1.84 m. wide, and 0.43 m. in thickness. Additional fragments discovered in situ by Reisner from 1915–1920 are now joined to the stela, which was attacked in antiquity during the invasion of Psametik II. In the lunette, Piye stands below a solar disk with double pendant uraei and before an enthroned Amon followed by his standing consort, Mut. Splayed on either side of the central group, two registers of vanquished Libyan rulers make obeisance to the victorious king. While three of these registers depict the conclusion of the narration, with eight prostrate rulers grouped by rank "kissing the ground" in submission (cf. lines 77, 99, 114–17, and 148–49), the upper righthand register illustrates the surrender of Namlot, ruler of Hermopolis (line 58), through the intervention of the royal wives (lines 33–44). Although Namlot does not grovel like his confederates, his status is consciously inverted as the queen occupies the male position at the head of the register (cf. the gender-based insult in lines 149–50). Following afterward, Namlot adopts the standard position and gesture of a queen with raised sistrum, and, like a mere servant, he leads a horse on a tether. The main text comprises 159 lines, distributed over the front (lines 1–34), lefthand (35–76), back (77–117), and righthand (118–59) surfaces.

For the text, translations and discussion, see Grimal 1981b; Schäfer 1905, 1–56; Lichtheim 1973–80, 3:66–84; Eide et al. 1994, 62–119; Budge 1912, xi–lxxv and 1–70; and Breasted 1906–7, 4:406–44 §§796–883. Further discussion is found in Logan and Westenholz 1971–72, 111–19; Kahn 1999, 5–6; Priese 1972, 99–124; 1970, 30–32; Gardiner 1935, 219–23; Spalinger 1979a, 273–301; 1981, 37–58. For geographic terms in the stela, one should consult Gomaà 1974. For the discovery, see M. Mariette 1863, 413–22; Rougé 1863, 94–127; and Loukianoff 1926, 86–89. See Kitchen 1986, 362–68 §§324–28 and 582 §523.

LABEL FOR ENTHRONED AMON-RE

[dd-mdw i]n ꜣImn-Rꜥ nb ns.wt tꜣ.wy ḫnty ꜣIp.t-[s.wt] (2) [ḫr(y)-ib] Ḏw-wꜥb (3) di.n⸗(i) n⸗k tꜣ Nḥsy(?)[1] [...] ḫft(?) mi it⸗k Rꜥ [ḏ.t(?)]

[Recitation] by Amon-Re, Lord of the Thrones of the Two Lands, Foremost of Karnak, (2) [resident in] "the Pure Mountain" (Gebel Barkal): (3) "To you I have given the land of the Nubians (?)[1] [...] accordingly (?), like your father Re [forever (?).]

LABEL FOR MUT

[M]w.t nb.(t) ꜣIšr(w)
[M]ut, Lady of Asheru.

LABEL FOR PIYE
> ny-sw.t bỉ.ty sȝ Rᶜ Py
> The King of Upper and Lower Egypt, the Son of Re, Piye.

LABEL FOR QUEEN REPRESENTING INTERCESSORS BEFORE PIYE
> ḥm.wt ny-sw.t (2) ḥtp r≠k Ḥr [nb ᶜḥ …].w n šr(ỉ) ny-sw.t Wnw
> Royal wives. (2) "Peace be with you, O Horus, [Lord of the palace² …].
> The king has not belittled Hermopolis."

LABEL FOR NAMLOT WITH SISTRUM AND HORSE
> ny-sw.t Nmȝrṯ   King Namlot.

LABELS FOR THREE BOWING KINGS WITH CAP-CROWNS AND URAEUS
> ny-sw.t Wsrkn (2) ny-sw.t ᵓIwpt (3) ny-sw.t P(ȝy)≠f-ṯȝw-ᶜ.wy-Bȝst.t
> King Osorkon (IV). (2) King Iuput (II). (3) King Peftchauawybast.

LABELS FOR TWO BOWING GREAT CHIEFS WEARING MESHWESH FEATHERS
> wr ᶜȝ n Mᶜ (2) ᵓIwkȝnšȝy (3) wr ᶜȝ n Mᶜ (4) Ḏd-ᵓImn-ỉw≠f-ᶜnḫ
> The Great Chief of the Ma, (2) Akanosh. (3) The Great Chief of the Ma,
> (4) Djedamoniuefankh.

LABEL FOR BOWING PRINCE WITH SIDELOCK
> [ỉry-pᶜ.t Pȝ-dỉ-ȝs].tỉ
> [The Hereditary Prince Padies]e.

LABEL FOR TWO COUNTS WEARING MESHWESH FEATHERS
> ḥȝty-ᶜ Pȝ-ṯnfy (2) ḥȝty-ᶜ Pȝ-mȝ(ỉ)
> Count Patchenefy. (2) Count Pamai.

MAIN TEXT
> (1) ḥsb.t 21.t ȝbd (tpy) ȝḫ.t ḥr ḥm n ny-sw.t bỉ.ty Py mrỉ-ᵓImn ᶜnḫ ḏ.t
> wḏ ḏd ḥm≠ỉ
>> sḏm m ỉr.n≠ỉ m hȝw r tpy.w-ᶜ
>> ỉnk ny-sw.t tỉ.t nṯr
>> šsp ᶜnḫ n Tm
>> pr m ḥ.t mtn m ḥqȝ
>> snḏ n≠f wr.w r≠f
>> rḫ.n [ỉt≠f] (2) sỉȝ.n mw.t≠f
>> ỉw≠f r ḥqȝ m swḥ.t
>> nṯr nfr mrỉ nṯr.w
>> sȝ Rᶜ ỉr m ᶜ.wy≠f(y)
>> Py mrỉ-ᵓImn

> ỉw.n.tw r ḏd n ḥm≠f ỉw wn wr n ỉmnt.t ḥȝty-ᶜ wr m Ntr Tȝ(y)≠f-nḫtỉ

m (Wꜥ-m-ḫ.w)³ m H̱ꜣsw m Ḥꜥp(y) m [...] (3) m ꜥnw m Pr-nbw m ꞋInb-ḥd
ìt.n≠f ìmnt.t m mì qd≠f m pḥww r ꞋIt-tꜣ.wy ḫnty n mšꜥ ꜥšꜣ tꜣ.wy dmd m-
ḫt≠f ḥꜣty.w-ꜥ ḥqꜣ.w ḥw.wt m tsm.w m ìry rd.wy≠f(y)

n ḫtm.n sbt.t [ꜥꜣ.wy≠s m] (4) spꜣ.wt n.w Šmꜥw Mrì-Tm Pr-Sḥm-ḫpr-Rꜥ
Ḥw.t-ntr-Sbk Pr-mḏ Tkꜣnš dmì nb n ìmnt.t sn≠sn ꜥꜣ.wy n snḏ≠f ꜥn≠f sw
r spꜣ.wt ìꜣbt.t wn≠sn n≠f mì nn Ḥw.t-bnw Tꜣy≠w-ḏꜣy.t Ḥw.t-ny-sw.t Pr-
nb.(t)-tp-ìḥ.t

mk [sw ḥr] (5) gwꜣ r (Ḥw.t)-nn-ny-sw.t ìr.n≠f sw m sd-m-rꜣ⁴ n(n)
rdì.(t) pr pr.w n(n) rdì.(t) ꜥq ꜥq.w ḥr ꜥḥꜣ mì rꜥ nb ḫꜣy.n≠f sw m pḥr≠s nb
ḫꜣ.ty-ꜥ nb rḫ sꜣ.(t)≠f dì≠f s nb ḥms ḥr pš≠f m ḥꜣty.w-ꜥ ḥqꜣ.w ḥw.wt

ꜥḥꜥ.n sḏm [ḥm≠f nn] (6) m wr-ìb sbì ìb≠f ꜣw

wn nn n wr.w ḥꜣty.w-ꜥ ìmy.(w)-rꜣ mšꜥ nty m nìw.t≠sn h(ꜣ)b n ḥm≠f
mì rꜥ nb m ḏd

ìn ìw gr.n≠k r sḫm Tꜣ-Šmꜥw spꜣ.wt n.w ḫnw Tꜣ(y)≠f-nḫt m ìt n ḥr≠f
n gm≠f ḫsf ꜥ≠f Nmꜣrt [ḥqꜣ n Ḫmnw] (7) ḥꜣ.ty-ꜥ n Ḥw.t-wr.(t) ìw sḫnn.n≠f
sbt.t n Nfrws(y) wḥn.n≠f nìw.t≠f ds≠f m snḏ n ìt n≠f sw r gwꜣ r k.t nìw.
t mk sw šm r wn m ìry rd.wy≠f(y) wìꜣn.n≠f mw n ḥm≠f ꜥḥꜥ≠f ḥn(ꜥ)≠f mì
wꜥ m [šms.w≠f m] (8) spꜣ.t n.t Wꜣsb dì≠f n≠f fq(ꜣ).w r ḏd ìb≠f m ḫ.t nb.(t)
gm.(t).n≠f

ꜥḥꜥ.n h(ꜣ)b.n ḥm≠f n ḥꜣty.w-ꜥ ìmy.w-rꜣ mšꜥ nty ḥr Km.t ts Pꜣ-wꜣrmꜣ
ḥnꜥ ts Rwꜥmrskny⁵ ḥnꜥ ts nb n.w ḥm≠f nty ḥr Km.t

sbì m sk ts ꜥḥꜣ pḥr gwꜣ r≠s (9) ḥꜣq rmt.w≠s mnmn.(t)≠s ꜥḥꜥy.(w)≠s
ḥr-tp ìtr(w) m rdì.t pr ꜥḥwty.w r sḫ.t m rdì.t skꜣ skꜣ.w gwꜣ r ḫnt(y) n Wnw
ꜥḥꜣ r≠s mì rꜥ nb

ꜥḥꜥ.n≠sn (ḥr) ìr.t mìt.t

ꜥḥꜥ.n ḥm≠f sbì mšꜥ r Km.t ḥr ḥn≠sn wr sp-2

ìm[y] h(ꜣì) m (10) grḥ m sḫr n ḥbꜥ ꜥḥꜣ≠tn ḫft mꜣꜣ sr n≠f ꜥḥꜣ m wꜣ ìr
ḏd≠f sìn n mšꜥ t-n.t-ḥtr.w n k.t nìw.t ìḫ ḥms≠tn r ìw mšꜥ≠f ꜥḥꜣ≠tn ḫft ḏd≠f
ìr wn gr nḫ.w≠f m k.t nìw.t ìmy (11) sìn.tw n≠sn ḥꜣty.w-ꜥ nn ìn.n≠f r
nḫw≠f Tḥnw mšꜥ n mḥ-ìb ìmy sr.tw n≠sn ꜥḥꜣ m tp-ꜥ ḏd

n rḫ≠n ꜥš n≠f m snh mšꜥ nḥb qnw tp n ìḥ(w)≠k

ì-(12)ìr sk m ꜥḥꜣ rḫ n≠k ꞋImn pꜣ ntr wḏ n

ìr spr≠tn r ḥnw n Wꜣs.t ḫft-ḥr-n ꞋIp.t-s.wt ꜥq≠tn m mw wꜥb tn m ìtr(w)
wnḫ tn m tpy⁶ šrm pḏ.t sfḫ ꜥḥꜣw⁷ m ꜥbꜥ (13) wr m nb pḥty n wn pḥty n
tr m ḥm≠f ìr≠f sꜣw≠ꜥ m nḫt-ꜥ ìw ꜥšꜣ dì≠s(n) sꜣ n ꜥnd.w ìw wꜥ ìt≠f s 1000
ntš tn m mw n.w ḥꜣw.w(t)≠f sn≠tn tꜣ ḫft-ḥr≠f ḏd(14)≠tn n≠f ìmy n≠n wꜣ.t
ꜥḥꜣ≠n m šw.t ḥpš≠k ḏꜣmw wḏ.n≠k ḫpr hd≠f nhdh(d) n≠f ꜥšꜣ

ꜥḥꜥ.n rdì.n≠sn⁸ (s.t) ḥr ḥ.t≠sn m-bꜣḥ ḥm≠f

ìn rn≠k ìr≠f n≠n ḫpš

sḫ≠k mnì mšꜥ≠k

t≠k m ḥ.t≠n ḥr wꜣ.t nb.(t)

ḥ(n)q.t≠k (15) ꜥḥm (ì)ꜣb≠n

ìn qn(ì)≠k dì n≠n ḫpš nr.tw n sḫꜣ rn≠k

n km.n mšꜥ ts≠f m ḥm.ty
nm mît.t≠k îm
ntk ny-sw.t nḫt îr m ꜥ.wy≠f(y)
îmy-rꜣ n.{w} kꜣ.t ꜥḥꜣ

nꜥ pw îr.n≠sn m (16) ḫd spr≠sn r Wꜣs.t îr.n≠sn mî dd.t nb n ḥm≠f nꜥ
pw îr.n≠sn m ḫd ḥr îtr(w) gm≠sn ꜥḥꜥw.w qn(î).w îw m ḫnty ḥr mšꜥ ḫnw.
w ts.wt qn(î) nb n.{t} Tꜣ-Mḥw spd m ḫꜥy.w n.w rꜣ-ꜥ-ḫt (17) r ꜥḥꜣ r mšꜥ (n)
ḥm≠f

ꜥḥꜥ.n îr(w) ḫꜣy.t ꜥꜣ.t îm≠sn n rḫ(w) tnw ḥꜣq mšꜥ≠sn ḥnꜥ ꜥḥꜥw≠sn în
m sqr.w-ꜥnḫ r b(w) ḥr ḥm≠f šm pw îr.n≠sn r ḫnty n (Ḥw.t)-nn-ny-sw.t ḥr
sr ꜥḥꜣ

r dî.t rḫ ḥꜣ.tyw-ꜥ ḥnꜥ ny.w-sw.t n.w Tꜣ-Mḥw îs

ny-sw.t Nmꜣrt ḥn(ꜥ) (18) ny-sw.t ꜣIwwpt wr n Mꜥ Ššnq n Pr-Wsîr-nb-
Ddw ḥnꜥ wr ꜥꜣ n Mꜥ Dd-ꜣImn-îw≠f-ꜥnḫ n Pr-Bꜣ-nb-Dd.t ḥnꜥ sꜣ≠f sms(w)
nty m îmy-rꜣ mšꜥ n Pr-Dḥwty-wp-rḥwy mšꜥ n îry-pꜥ.t Bꜣk-n-nfy ḥnꜥ sꜣ≠f
sms(w) wr n Mꜥ (19) Ns-nꜣ-ꜥꜣy.(w) m Ḥsbw wr nb tꜣî mḥ.t nty m Tꜣ-Mḥw
ḥnꜥ ny-sw.t Wsrkn nty m Pr-Bꜣst.t ḥnꜥ ww n Rꜥ-nfr ḥꜣty-ꜥ nb ḥqꜣ.w-ḥw.wt
ḥr îmnt.t ḥr îꜣbt.t îw.w ḥr(y).w-îb dmd ḥr mw wꜥ m îry rd.wy n wr ꜥꜣ n
ꜣImn.t ḥqꜣ ḥw.wt (n) Tꜣ-Mḥw ḥm-nṯr (n) N.t nb.(t) Sꜣ(w).t (20) s(t)m n Ptḥ
Tꜣ(y)≠f-nḫtî

pr.(t) pw îr.n≠sn r≠sn ꜥḥꜥ.n≠sn (ḥr) îr.(t) ḫꜣy.t ꜥꜣ.t îm≠sn wr r ḫ.t
nb.(t) ḥꜣq(w) ꜥḥꜥw.w≠sn ḥr îtr(w) dꜣ(î.t) pw îr.n spy mn(î) ḥr îmnt.t m
h(ꜣ)w Pr-pgꜣ

ḫd r≠f tꜣ dwꜣ sp-2 dꜣ(î).n mšꜥ n ḥm≠f (21) r≠sn ꜣbḫ mšꜥ n mšꜥ

ꜥḥꜥ.n smꜣ≠sn rmṯ îm≠sn ꜥšꜣ s{m}sm.w n rḫ(w) tnw nhdh(d) ḫpr m spy
wꜥr≠sn r Tꜣ-Mḥw m šḫ.t q(ꜣ).t qsn.(t) r ḫ.t nb.(t)

rḫ ḫꜣy.(t) îr.t n-îm≠sn

rmṯ s (…)⁹ (22)

(w)ꜥr ny-sw.t Nmꜣrt m ḫnty r rsy ḫft dd.tw n≠f Ḥmnw m ḫnty n ḫrwy.
w m-ꜥ mšꜥ.w n.w ḥm≠f ḥꜣq(w) rmṯ.w≠f mnmn.(t)≠f

ꜥḥꜥ.n ꜥq.n≠f r ḫnty n Wnw mšꜥ.w n.w ḥm≠f ḥr-tp îtr(w) ḥr mry.(t)
(23) n.t Wnw

ꜥḥꜥ.n sdm≠sn sw šn.n≠sn Wnw ḥr îfd≠s n(n)¹⁰ rdî pr pr.w n(n) rdî ꜥq
ꜥq.w h(ꜣ)b.n≠sn r smî n ḥm n ny-sw.t bî.ty Py mrî-ꜣImn dî ꜥnḫ m hd nb
îr.n≠sn m nḫt nb n ḥm≠f

ꜥḥꜥ.n ḥm≠f ḫ≠r ḥr≠s mî ꜣby

în-îw rdî(24).n≠sn sp spy m mšꜥ.w n.w Tꜣ-Mḥw r dî.t pr pr îm≠sn
r sdd wdy.(t)≠f tm rdî.t mt≠sn r sk pḥw≠sn ꜥnḫ≠î mr (w)î Rꜥ ḥs wî ît≠î
ꜣImn îw≠î r ḫd ds≠î whn≠î (25) îr.n≠f dî≠î ḫt≠f ꜥḥꜣ r-ḫt nḥḥ îr ḥr-sꜣ îr(w)
îr.w n.w wp-rnp.t wdn≠î n ît≠(î) ꜣImn m ḥb≠f nfr îr≠f ḫꜥꜥ≠f nfr n.{w} wp-
rnp.t wd≠f (w)î m ḥtp r mꜣꜣ ꜣImn m ḥb nfr n.{w} ḥb ꜣIp.t sḫꜥ≠î sw m sšm≠f

(26) r ʾIp.t rsy.t m ḥb=f nfr n.{w} ḥb ʾIp.t grḥ m ḥb mn m Wꜣs.t ỉr n=f Rʿ m sp tp(y) sẖʿ=ỉ sw r pr=f ḥtp ḥr ns.t=f h(rw) sʿq nṯr ꜣbd 3 ꜣḫ.t sw 2 dỉ=ỉ dp Tꜣ-Mḥw dp.(t) ḏbʿ.w=ỉ

ʿḥʿ.n mšʿ wn dy ḥr (27) Km.t sḏm pꜣ ẖʿr ỉr.n ḥm=f r=sn ʿḥʿ.n=sn ʿḥꜣ r Wꜣsb Pr-mḏd ỉṯ(ỉ)=sn sw mỉ gp n mw h(ꜣ)b=sn ẖr ḥm=f n ḥtp ỉb=f ḥr=s

ʿḥʿ.n=sn ʿḥꜣ r tꜣ thn wr nẖt.w gm=sn sw mḥ.tỉ (28) m mšʿ.w m qn(ỉ) nb n.w Tꜣ-Mḥw

ʿḥʿ.n ỉr.t(w) ỉwn n ms r=s sẖnn(w) sꜣ.w(t)=s ỉr(w) ẖꜣy.(t) ʿꜣ.t ỉm=sn n(n) rẖ(w) tnw ḥnʿ sꜣ n wr n Mʿ Tꜣ(y)=f-nẖt

ʿḥʿ.n h(ꜣ)b=sn n ḥm=f ḥr=s n ḥtp ỉb=f r=s

(29) ʿḥʿ.n=sn (ḥr) ʿḥꜣ r Ḥw.t-bnw wn ẖnw=s ʿq mšʿ.w n.w ḥm=f r=s

ʿḥʿ.n h(ꜣ)b=sn n ḥm=f n ḥtp ỉb=f r=s

ꜣbd (tpy) ꜣḫ.t sw 9 ỉy.(t) pw ỉr.n ḥm=f m ḫd(ỉ) r Wꜣs.t ḥts.n=f ḥb ʾImn m ḥb ʾIp.t nʿ pw ỉr.n ḥm=f m (30) ḫd(ỉ) r dmỉ.(t) n.t Wnw pr.(t) ḥm=f m sny.t n.t wỉꜣ nḥb m s{m}sm.w ṯs m wry.wt šf(y).t ḥm=f r pḥw St.tyw ỉb nb ẖr sdꜣw=f

ʿḥʿ.n ḥm=f (ḥr) pr m ḫꜣʿ r ms(31)dd mšʿ=f ẖʿr r=s(n) mỉ ꜣby ỉn-ỉw mn=sn[11] ʿḥꜣ=tn nn wḏf wp.(t)=ỉ ỉn rnp.t ḥts pḥwy dd snḏ=ỉ m Tꜣ-Mḥw ỉr.(t) n=sn sḫ.t q(ꜣ).t qsn.(t) m ḥ(wỉ)

ỉr.t=f n=f ỉmꜣw r ỉmnt.t-rs Ḫmnw gwꜣ r=s (32) mỉ rʿ nb ỉr.t ṯrry r ḥbs sbty ṯs(ỉ.t) bꜣk r sḫy sty.w ḥr štỉ.t ẖꜣʿ.w ḥr ẖꜣʿ ʿn.w ḥr smꜣ rmṯ.(w) ỉm=sn mỉ rʿ nb

ḫpr.n hrw.w ỉw Wnw sḥwꜣ=s n fnḏ gꜣ(w) m ẖn(33)m=s

ʿḥʿ.n Wnw (ḥr) rdỉ.t sw ḥr ẖ.t=s (ḥr) snmḥ ḫft-ḥr-n bỉ.ty[12] ỉpwty.w (ḥr) pr.(t) h(ꜣỉ.t) ẖr ḫ.t nb.(t) nfr.(t) mꜣꜣ nbw ʿꜣ.t nb.(t) šps.(t) ḥbs.w m pds ḫʿ wn ḥr-tp=f ỉʿrʿ.t dd šf(y).t=f n(n) ꜣb n hrw.w ʿšꜣ ḥr smmḥ (<snmḥ) n wrr.(t)=f

ʿḥʿ.n rdỉ.t(w) ỉw(t) (34) ḥm.t=f ḥm.t ny-sw.t sꜣ.t ny-sw.t Ns-Ṯ(ꜣ)-n.t-Mḥw[13] r snmmḥ (<snmḥ) n ḥm.wt ny-sw.t ỉp.t ny-sw.t sꜣ.wt ny-sw.t sn.wt ny-sw.t rdỉ.n=s (sy) ḥr ẖ.t=s m pr ḥm.wt ḫft-ḥr-n ḥm.wt ny-sw.t

mỉ (t)n n=ỉ ḥm.wt ny-sw.t sꜣ.wt ny-sw.t sn.wt ny-sw.t sḥtp=tn Ḥr nb ʿḥ wr bꜣw=f ʿꜣ mꜣʿ-ẖrw=f ỉmy (35) [...]=f [...]=ỉ mk sw [...] (36) [...] sw mk [...]n[...]ỉw s[...] (37) n=f pẖr=[f] r=f n dwꜣ sw [...]m[...]

(38) [... s(?)]ḏfꜣỉ[...] (39) [...]n[...] n ʿnḫ m [...] (40) [...]mỉ[....] (41) [...] mḥ=sn(?) m ꜣḫ.t [...] dwꜣ [n?]=f (42) [...] ḥm.wt ny-sw.t sn.wt ny-sw.t [... rdỉ.n=s]n s.(t) (ḥr) ẖ.t=sn (43) [m-bꜣḥ ḥm=f ...]m ḥm.[w]t ny-sw.t [...] ḥqꜣ n Ḥw.t-wr.(t) (44) [...] n nỉw.t=f(?) ḥqꜣ (45) [...] m (46) [...] m ḥqꜣ (47) [...] m nỉw.t(?) (48) [...] (49) [...] n wš(?) [...](50)w r b(w) ẖr(y) ḥm=[f m]dw(?) n=f ḥm[=f]

n[m...] (51) mw.t=k nm sšm tw sp-2 nm ỉr sšm tw sp-2 nm sšm tw [...](52).n=k wꜣ.t n.(t) ʿnḫ ỉn-ỉw ỉs ḥ(w)y p.t m šsr wnn=ỉ [...] (53) rsy.w m ksw mḥty.w (ḏd) ỉmy n m-m šw.t=k ỉs wn=s bỉn ny-sw.t(?) [Wnw ỉy(?)][14] (54) ẖr ḥtp.w=f ḥmw pw ỉb sʿg(ꜣ)=f nb=f n nt.t m bꜣw nṯr mꜣꜣ.

n≠f ḫ.t m qbb.w m(?) ỉb [...] (55) n(n) ỉȝw mȝȝ m-ꜥ ỉt≠f spȝ.wt≠k mḥ.tỉ m nḫn.w

ꜥḥꜥ.n≠f rdỉ.n≠f sw ḫr ḫ.(t)≠f m-bȝḥ ḥm≠f

[ḥtp r≠k] (56) Ḥr nb ꜥḫ ỉn bȝw≠k ỉr s.(t) r≠ỉ ỉnk wꜥ m ḥm.w ny-sw.t ḥtr m bȝk.w r pr-ḥḏ (n) ỉ[mny].t [ỉ](57)p bȝk≠sn ỉr.n≠(ỉ) n≠k m ḫȝw r≠sn

ꜥḥꜥ.(n) mȝꜥ.n≠f ḥḏ nbw ḫsbd mfk(ȝ.t) ḥm.t ꜥȝ.t nb.(t) ꜥšȝ

(58) ꜥḥꜥ.n mḥ(w) pr-ḥḏ m ỉnw pn ỉn.n≠f ssm m wnm.t sšš.t m ỉȝb.t sšš.t n.t nbw ḫsbd

ꜥḥꜥ.n sḫꜥ (59) (ḥm)≠f m ꜥḥ≠f wḏȝ r pr Ḏḥwty nb Ḥmnw smȝ.n≠f ỉwȝ.w wnḏw.w ȝpd.w n ỉt≠f Ḏḥwty nb Ḥmnw Ḥmnyw m pr Ḥm(60)nyw

wn.ỉn mšꜥ.w n.w Wnw ḥr nhm ḫnw dd≠sn

nfr w(y) Ḥr ḥtp m (61) nỉw.t≠f sȝ Rꜥ Py

ỉr≠k n≠n ḥbs(d) mỉ ḥw(ỉ)≠k Wnw

wḏȝ pw ỉr.n ḥm≠f r (62) pr n ny-sw.t Nmȝrṯ šm.n≠f (r) ꜥ.t nb.(t) n.t pr ny-sw.t pr-ḥḏ≠f wḏȝ.w≠f rdỉ.n≠f stȝ.n.tw (63) n≠f ḥm.wt ny-sw.t sȝ.wt ny-sw.t wn.ỉn≠sn (ḥr) swȝš ḥm≠f m ḫ.wt ḥm.wt n dȝ.n ḥm≠f ḥr≠f r(63)≠sn wḏȝ pw ỉr.n ḥm≠f r ỉḥ(w) n.{w} s{m}sm.w wḏȝ.w n.{t} nfr.w mȝȝ.n≠f [...] (64) sḥqr≠sn dd≠f

ꜥnḫ≠ỉ mr (w)ỉ Rꜥ ḫwn fnd≠ỉ m ꜥnḫ qsn.w(y) nn ḥr ỉb≠ỉ sḫ(66)qr s{m}sm.w≠ỉ r btȝ nb ỉr.n≠k m kf(ȝ) ỉb≠k mtr.(t) n≠ỉ tw snd n≠k gs(67)wy. w≠k ỉn-ỉw ḫm.n≠k šw.t nṯr ḥr≠ỉ n wh(ỉ) n≠f sp≠ỉ ḫȝ ỉr s.(t) n≠ỉ (68) k[y] n rḫ≠ỉ n ts≠ỉ sw ḥr≠s ỉnk ms m ḫ.t sḫpr m swḥ.t nṯr.(t) mt(69)wt nṯr ỉm≠ỉ wȝḥ kȝ≠f n ỉr≠ỉ m ḥm≠f ntf wḏ n≠ỉ ỉr.t

ꜥḥꜥ.n sỉp(w) ḫ.t≠f r pr-ḥḏ (70) šnw.wt≠f r ḥtp-nṯr n.{t} ʾImn m ʾIp.t-s.wt

ỉy.(t) pw ỉr.n ḥqȝ n (Ḥw.t)-nn-ny-sw.t P(ȝy)≠f-ṯȝw-ꜥ.wy-Bȝst.t ḥr ỉnw (71) r Pr-ꜥȝ nbw ḥḏ ꜥȝ.t nb.(t) m s{m}sm.w m stp n ỉḥ(w) rdỉ.n≠f sw ḫr ḫ.t≠f m-bȝḥ ḥm≠f dd≠f

ỉnd-ḥr≠k Ḥr (72) ny-sw.t nḫt kȝ hd kȝ.w

šd wỉ dwȝ.t mḏ.kwỉ m kk(w)

dd n≠ỉ ḥḏ(73)d ḥr≠f

n gm.n≠ỉ mrỉ n hrw qsn.(t)[15]

ꜥḥꜥ.t(y)f(y) m hrw n ꜥḥȝ

wp(w) ntk pȝ ny-sw.t nḫt

kfȝ.(74)n≠k kk(w) ḥr≠ỉ

ỉw≠ỉ r bȝkỉ ḥnꜥ hr.wt≠ỉ

(Ḥw.t)-nn-ny-sw.t ḥtr (75) r ꜥry.t≠k

twt ỉs Ḥr-ȝḫ.ty ḥr(y)-tp ỉḫm.w-sk

wnn≠f wnn≠k m ny-sw.t

n(n) sk≠f (76) n(n) sk≠k

ny-sw.t bỉ.ty Py ꜥnḫ ḏ.t

ḥd pw ỉr.n ḥm≠f r wp.t mr r-gs R3(77)-ḥn.t gm.n≠f Pr-Sḥm-ḫpr-Rˁ
s3.w(t)≠f ṯs.(w) ḫtm≠f ḥtm.(w) mḥ.(w) m qn(ỉ) nb n.{t} T3-mḥw
　ˁḥˁ.n ḥm≠f h(3)b n≠sn m ḏd
　　ˁnḫ.w m mt sp-2 šw3(78)[.w] ḥwr.w ˁnḫ.w m mt
　　ỉr sn(ỉ) 3.t n(n) wn n≠ỉ mk tn m ỉp ḫr.w
　　ḫr(y) db̠ˁ pw n ny-sw.t
　　m šnˁ sb3.w n.w ˁnḫ≠tn r sm3 m nm.t n.(t) hrw pn
　　m mr mt r msdd ˁnḫ (79) [… ˁ]nḫ ḫft-ḥr n t3 ḏr≠f

　ˁḥˁ.n h(3)b.n≠sn n ḥm≠f r ḏd
　　mk šw.t nṯr ḥr-tp≠k
　　s3 Nw.t dỉ≠f n≠k ˁ.wy≠f
　　k3 ỉb≠k ḫpr ḥr-ˁ
　　mỉ pr m r3 n nṯr
　　mk sw ms.tw≠k n nṯr ḥr m33≠n m r3-ˁ.wy≠k
　　mk nỉw.t≠k ḫtm.w≠f (80) […]≠k ỉm
　　ˁq ˁq.(w) ỉm pr pr.w
　　ỉr ḥm≠f (m) mrr≠f

　ˁḥˁ.n≠sn pr ḥn(ˁ) s3 n wr n Mˁ T3(y)≠f-nḫt ˁq pw ỉr.n mšˁ.w n.w
ḥm≠f r≠s n sm3.n≠f wˁ m rmṯ nb gm.n≠f (81) [ỉm …].w ḥn(ˁ) ḥtm.w r ḫtm
ỉš.(t)≠f sỉp(w) pr.w-ḥḏ≠f r pr-ḥḏ šnw.wt≠f r ḥtp.w-nṯr n ỉt≠f ʾImn-Rˁ nb
ns.wt t3.wy nˁ pw ỉr.n ḥm≠f m ḥḏ gm.n≠f Mr-Tm pr Skr nb sḫd ḫtm.n≠s
ỉw(t.t) pḫ≠s dỉ.n≠s ˁḥ3 m ỉb≠s šsp(82) sn […]m sn snḏ šf.t ḫtm.n≠s r3≠sn
　ˁḥˁ.n h(3)b n≠sn ḥm≠f m ḏd
　　mtn w3.t sn.t m ḥr≠tn stp≠tn r mrr≠tn
　　wn ˁnḫ≠tn ḫtm mt≠tn
　　n(n) sn(ỉ) ḥm≠ỉ ḥr nỉw.t ḫtm.tw

　ˁḥˁ.n wn.n≠sn ḥr-ˁ ˁq.n ḥm≠f r ḥnw n nỉw.t tn m3ˁ.n≠f (83) ˁ(3)b.[t
ˁ3.t n ʾIm]nḥy ḫnt(y) Shḏ sỉp(w) pr-ḥḏ≠f šnw.wt≠f r ḥtp.w-nṯr n ʾImn m
ʾIp.t-s.wt ḥd pw ỉr.n ḥm≠f r ʾIt-t3.wy gm.n≠f sbt.t ḫtm.(t) ỉnb.w mḥ.(w) m
mšˁ.w qn(ỉ.w) n.w T3-Mḥw ˁḥˁ.n sn≠sn ḫtm.w rdỉ.n≠sn (st) ḥr ẖ.t(84)≠sn
m-b3[ḥ ḥm≠f ḏd.n≠sn] n ḥm≠f
　　wḏ n≠k ỉt≠k ỉwˁ.(t)≠f
　　ntk t3.wy ntk ỉm≠sn
　　ntk nb nt.t ḥr-s3 t3

　wḏ3 pw ỉr.n ḥm≠f r dỉ.t m3ˁ ˁ3b.t ˁ3.t n nṯr.w ỉmy.w nỉw.t tn m ỉw3.w
wnḏw 3pd.w ẖ.t nb.(t) nfr.(t) wˁb.(t) ˁḥˁ.n sỉp(w) pr-ḥḏ≠f r pr-ḥḏ šnw.wt≠f
r ḥtp.w-nṯr (85) n ỉt≠f ʾImn[-R]ˁ nb ns.wt t3.wy ḥd pw ỉr.n ḥm≠f r ʾInb]-ḥḏ
　ˁḥˁ.n h(3)b.n≠f n≠sn m ḏd ỉm(y) ḫtm ỉm(y) ˁḥ3 ḥnw Šw m sp tp(y)
ˁq ˁq≠f pr pr≠f n(n) ḫsf.tw šm.w wdn≠ỉ ˁ3b.t n Ptḥ n nṯr.w ỉmy.w ʾInb-ḥḏ

drp≠ỉ Skr m št3(y).t m3≠ỉ Rsy-ỉnb≠f ḥd≠ỉ m ḥtp (86) [...].w ᵓInb-ḥd ꜥd snb
n rm.tw nḫn.w m3 m r≠f tn sp3.wt tp-rsy n sm3.tw wꜥ nb ỉm wp sbỉ.w wꜥ3
ḥr nṯr ỉr.t(w) nm.t m ḫ3k.w-ỉb

ꜥḥꜥ.n ḥtm≠sn ḥtm≠sn dỉ≠sn pr mšꜥ.w r nhy m mšꜥ.w n.w ḥm≠f m
ḥmw.w ỉmy.w-r3 qd sqd.wt (87) ỉy [... r] mry.t n.t ᵓInb-ḥd ỉs wr pf n
S3(w).(t) spr r ᵓInb-ḥd m wḥ3 ḥr ḥn n mšꜥ≠f ḫn.w≠f tp nb n mšꜥ≠f tp rmṯ.
w 8,000 ḥr ḥn n≠sn wr sp-2

mk Mn-nfr mḥ.(w) m mšꜥ m tp nb n.w T3-Mḥw ỉt bd.(t) pr.(t) nb.(t)
šnw.wt ngsgs ḫꜥy.w nb n.w (88) [r3-ꜥ-ḫt ... s]bt.t qd(w) ṯsm.(t) wr.(t) m ỉr.t
n ḥm.t rḫ.t(ỉ) ỉtr(w) m pḫr ỉ3bt.t n(n) gm.tw ꜥḥ3 ỉm md.w d(y) mḥ.(w) m
ỉw3.w pr-ḥd ꜥpr.(w) m ḥ.t nb.(t) ḥd nbw ḥm.t ḥbs snṯr bỉ.t sft šm≠ỉ dỉ≠ỉ
ḫ.t n wr.w Mḥw wn≠ỉ n≠sn sp3.wt≠sn¹⁶ ḫpr≠ỉ m (89) [...] hrw.w r ỉy≠ỉ

ḥms pw ỉr.n≠f ḥr ssm.t n nḥty.n≠f wrry.(t)≠f ḥd pw ỉr.n≠f m snd n
ḥm≠f ḥd t3 r≠f dw3 sp-2 spr ḥm≠f r ᵓInb-ḥd mn.n≠f ḥr mḥ.t≠s gm.n≠f mw
ꜥr r s3w.w(t) ꜥḥꜥ.w mn r (90) [...] Mn-nfr ꜥḥꜥ.n ḥm≠f m33 s(w) m nḫt.w sbt.
t ḥy m qd n m3w.(t) ṯsm.w(t) ꜥpr.(t) m nḫt n gm.tw w3.t n.t ꜥḥ3 r≠s

wn.ỉn s nb ḥr dd r3≠f m mšꜥ.w n.w ḥm≠f m tp-rd nb n ꜥḥ3 s nb ḥr dd
ỉmy gw3≠n (91) [r Mn-nfr] mk mšꜥ≠s ꜥš3 k.t-ḫ.t ḥr dd ỉr st3 r≠s sḥy≠n s3tw
r s3w.(t)≠s snḥ≠n b3k sꜥḥꜥ≠n ḫt-t3w ỉr≠n ḥt3t m drw.w r≠s pš≠tn sw m nn
r gs≠s nb m ṯrtr ḥnꜥ (92) [...] ḥr mḥ.t≠s r ṯs.(t) s3tw ḥr s3w.(t)≠s gm≠n w3.t
n.t rd.wy≠n

ꜥḥꜥ.n ḥm≠f ḫꜥr r≠s mỉ 3by dd≠f

ꜥnḫ≠ỉ mr (w)ỉ Rꜥ ḥs wỉ ỉt≠ỉ ᵓImn qm.n≠ỉ (= gm.n≠ỉ) ḫpr nn ḫr≠s
m wd.(t) n.t ᵓImn nn pw dd rmṯ(93)[.w nb n.w T3-Mḥw] ḥnꜥ sp3.wt rsy.w
wn≠sn n≠f m w3w n rdỉ.n≠sn ᵓImn m ỉb≠sn n rḫ≠sn wd.n≠f ỉr.n≠f sw r
rdỉ.t b3w≠f rdỉ.t m33.tw šf(y).t≠f ỉw≠ỉ r ỉṯ≠s mỉ gp n mw ỉw wd n≠ỉ (94)
[ỉt≠ỉ ᵓImn]

ꜥḥꜥ.n rdỉ.n≠f wd ꜥḥꜥy.w≠f mšꜥ≠f r ꜥḥ3 r mry.t n.t Mn-nfr ỉn.n≠sn n≠f
d3(y) nb mḫn.(t) nb.(t) shry.(t) nb.(t) ꜥḥꜥ.w mỉ ꜥš3≠sn wn mn r mry.t n.t
Mn-nfr ḫ3t.t mn m pr.w≠s (95) [...]w nds rm≠f m mšꜥ nb n ḥm≠f nꜥ(ỉ.t)
ḥm≠f r sk ds≠f ꜥḥꜥ.w mỉ ꜥš3≠sn wd ḥm≠f n mšꜥ≠f

n ḥr≠tn r≠s snb s3w.(wt) ꜥq pr.w ḥr(y)-tp ỉtr(w) ỉr ꜥq wꜥ ỉm≠tn ḥr
s3w.(t) n(n) ꜥḥꜥ.tw m h3w≠f (96) [...] n(n) ḥsf tn ṯs.wt ḥs(y) pw gr ḥtm≠n
Šmꜥ(w) mn≠n Mḥw ḥms≠n m Mḫ3y.(t)-t3.wy

ꜥḥꜥ.n ỉt.t(w) Mn-nfr mỉ gp n mw sm3(w) rmṯ ỉm≠s ꜥš3 ḥnꜥ ỉn m sqr-
ꜥnḫ r b(w) ḥr(y) ḥm≠f ỉr m-(97)[ḫt t3 ḫld 2-nw n hrw ḫpr rdỉ.n ḥm≠f šm
rmṯ.(w) r≠s ḥr ḥw(ỉ) r-pr.w n nṯr n≠f dsr-ꜥ ḥr ḥm.w nṯr.w drp qbḥ.w (n)
d3d3.t Ḥw.t-k3-Ptḥ swꜥb Mn-nfr m ḥsmn snṯr dỉ.t wꜥb.w r s.t-rd.wy≠sn wd3
ḥm≠f r pr (98) [Ptḥ] ỉr.t ꜥbw≠f m pr dw3.t ỉr.t n≠f n.t-ꜥ nb ỉr.wt n ny-sw.t
ꜥq≠f r ḥw.t-nṯr ỉr.t ꜥ3b.t ꜥ3.t n ỉt≠f Ptḥ Rsy-ỉnb≠f m ỉw3.w wnd.w 3pd.w ḫ.t
nb.(t) nfr.(t) wd3 pw ỉr.n ḥm≠f r pr≠f ꜥḥꜥ.n sdm sp3.t nb.(t) nt.t m ww n
Mn-nfr Ḥry-p(3)-dmy Pny(99)-n3-ỉwꜥꜥ P(3)-bḫn-n-Byw T3-wḥy-By.t sn≠sn
ḥtm.w≠w wꜥr≠sn m wꜥr n rḫ.tw b(w) šm≠sn ỉm

ỉy pw ỉr.n ny-sw.t ’Iwpṯ ḥnꜥ wr n Mꜥ ’Iwk3nšw ḥnꜥ ỉry-pꜥ.t P(3)-dỉ-
3s.tỉ (100) ḥnꜥ ḥ3.tyw-ꜥ nb n.w T3-Mḥw ḥr ỉnw≠sn r m33 nfr.w ḥm≠f

ꜥḥꜥ.n sỉp(w) pr-ḥḏ.w ḥnꜥ šnw.wt n.w Mn-nfr ỉr.(w) r ḥtp-nṯr n ’Imn n
Ptḥ n psḏ.t ỉmy.w Ḥw.t-k3-Ptḥ

ḥḏ ỉr≠f t3 dw3 sp-2 wḏ3 ḥm≠f r ỉ3bt.t ỉr.(t) ꜥbw n Tm m Ḥr-ꜥḥ3 (101)
psḏ.t m Pr-psḏ.t ỉmḫ.t nṯr.w ỉm≠s m ỉw3.w wnḏ.w 3pd.w dỉ≠sn ꜥnḫ wḏ3
snb n ny-sw.t bỉ.ty Py ꜥnḫ ḏ.t

wḏ3 ḥm≠f r ’Iwnw ḥr ḏw pf n Ḥr-ꜥḥ3 ḥr mtn n.{t} Sp(3)¹⁷ r Ḥr-ꜥḥ3 wḏ3
ḥm≠f r ỉm3w nty ḥr ỉmnt.t ’Ity ỉr(w) ꜥbw≠f swꜥb≠f m-ỉb (102) Š-qbḥ ỉꜥ(ỉ)
ḥr≠f m ỉtr(w) n.{t} Nnw ỉꜥ(ỉ) Rꜥ ḥr≠f ỉm wḏ3 r šꜥy q(3) m ’Iwnw ỉr.t ꜥ3b.t
ꜥ3.t ḥr šꜥ q(3) m ’Iwnw ḫft-ḥr-n Rꜥ m wbn≠f m ỉḫ.(w) ḥḏ.w ỉrt.(t) ꜥntyw snṯr
ḫ3w (103) nb nḏm st(ỉ) ỉy m wḏ3 r pr Rꜥ ꜥq r ḥw.t-nṯr m ỉy(3)w sp-2 ḥr(y)-
ḥb ḥr(y)-tp (ḥr) dw3 nṯr ḫsf sḥdy.w r ny-sw.t ỉr.t pr dw3.t ts sdb swꜥb≠f m
snṯr qbḥw ms n≠f ꜥnḫ.w n.w Ḥw.t-bnbn ỉn n≠f ꜥnḫ.w ts (104) ḫnd r sšd wr
r m33 Rꜥ m Ḥw.t-bnbn ny-sw.t ḏs≠f ꜥḥꜥ.(w) m wꜥ.(w) sd s.wy(t) sn(ỉ) ꜥ3.wy
m33 ỉt≠f Rꜥ m Ḥw.t-bnbn ḥrp mꜥ(n)d.(t) n Rꜥ skt.n n Tm ỉn ꜥ3.wy w3ḥ sỉn
db ꜥ (105) m ḫtm n ny-sw.t ḏs≠f ḥn n wꜥb.w ỉnk sỉp.n≠ỉ ḫtm n ꜥq.n ky r≠s
m ny-sw.t nb ꜥḥꜥ.t(y)≠f(y) rdỉ.n≠sn (s.t) ḥr ḥ.t≠sn m-b3ḥ ḥm≠f m ḏd r mn
w3ḥ n(n) sk Ḥr mry ’Iwnw ỉy m ꜥq r pr Tm šms ꜥnty(106)w (n) twt n ỉt≠f
Tm-Ḫprỉ wr ’Iwnw ỉy.n ny-sw.t Wsrkn r m33 nfr.w ḥm≠f

ḥḏ r≠f t3 dw3 sp-2 wḏ3 ḥm≠f r mry.t tp ꜥḥꜥy.w≠f ḏ3(ỉ.t) r mry.t n.t Km-
wr ỉr.t ỉm3w n ḥm≠f ḥr rsy K3hny ḥr ỉ3bt.t (107) n.t Km-wr ỉy pw ỉr.n nn n
ny.w-sw.t ḥ3.tyw-ꜥ n.w T3-Mḥw wr.w nb t3(ỉ) mḥ.t t3ty nb wr nb rḫ ny-sw.t
nb m ỉmnt.t m ỉ3bt.t m ỉw.w ḥr(y).w-ỉb r m33 nfr.w ḥm≠f wn.ỉn ỉry-pꜥ.t
P3-dỉ-3s.t rdỉ sw ḥr ḥ.t≠f m-(108)b3ḥ-ꜥ ḥm≠f ḏd≠f

mỉ r Km-wr m3≠k Ḫnty-ḫty ḫw tk¹⁸ Ḥwy.t sm3ꜥ≠k ꜥ3b.t n Ḥr m pr≠f
m ỉw3.w wnḏ.w 3pd.w ꜥq≠k r pr≠ỉ sn(ỉ) n≠k pr-ḥḏ≠ỉ dwn≠(ỉ) tw m ḫ.t
ỉt≠ỉ dỉ≠ỉ n≠k nbw r ḏr.w ỉb≠k m(109)fk.(t) twt n ḥr≠k ssm.wt qnw m tp
n ỉḥ(w) ḥ3.wty n šmm.t

wḏ3 pw ỉr.n ḥm≠f r pr Ḥr Ḫnty-ḫt(y) r dỉ.t m3ꜥ ỉw3.w wnḏ.w 3pd.w n
ỉt≠f Ḥr Ḫnty-ḫty nb Km-wr wḏ3 ḥm≠f r pr n ỉry-pꜥ.t P3-dỉ-3s.t ꜥ(3)b≠f n≠f m
ḥḏ nbw (110) ḫsbd mfk.(t) ꜥḥꜥ(w) wr m ḫ.t nb.(t) ḥbs.w šs ny-sw.t m tnw
nb 3ty.wt sḥn.wt m p(3)g.(t) ꜥnt(yw) mrḥ.(t) m ḫbḫb ḥtr.w m t3y.w ḥm.wt
m ḥ3.wty nb n ỉḥ(w)≠f swꜥb.n≠f sw m ꜥnḫ nṯr ḫft-ḥr-(n) nn n ny.w-sw.t
wr.w ꜥ3.w n.w T3-(111)Mḥw

wꜥ nb ỉm ḥ3p≠f s{m}sm.w(t)≠f ỉmn n≠f š3w≠f k3 mt≠f n mt n ỉt≠f
k3.n≠ỉ nn r wf3≠tn b3k ỉm m rḫ≠tn nb m-ꜥ≠ỉ k3 ḏd≠tn ỉmn.n≠ỉ r ḥm≠f m
ḥ.t nb.(t) (112) n pr ỉt≠ỉ nbw ỉḥ.w m ꜥ3.t m ỉp.wt nb.(t) mnfy.w(t) m ỉry-
dr.ty nbw m ỉry-ḫḫ bb.w stwr.(w) m ꜥ3.t s3.(w) n.w ꜥ.t nb.(t) m3ḥ.w n.(w)
tp š3qy.w n.(w) msḏr ḥkr.w nb n.(w) ny-sw.t ḥn.(w) nb n.w wꜥb ny-sw.t
m nbw ꜥ3.t nb.(t) nn r-3w ꜥ(3)b.n≠ỉ (113) m-b3ḥ šs-ny-sw.t ḥbs.w m ḥ3.w
m tp nb n n3y.t≠ỉ ỉw≠ỉ rḫ.kw(ỉ) ḥtp≠k ḥr≠s wḏ3 r šmm.t stp≠k mrr≠k m
s{m}sm.w(t) nb.(t) 3bb≠k

ꜥḥꜥ.n ḥmꜣf (ḥr) ỉr.t mỉt.t ḏd.ỉn nn n ny.w-sw.t ḥꜣ.tyw-ꜥ ḥr ḥmꜣf wḏ
n r nỉw.wtꜣn wnꜣn (114) pr-ḥḏꜣn stpꜣn r mrr ỉbꜣk ỉnꜣn nꜣk tp.w n.w
šmm.(t)ꜣn ḥꜣ.wty(w) n.w s{m}sm.w(t)ꜣn ꜥḥꜥ.n ḥmꜣf (ḥr) ỉr.t mỉt.t
rḫ rn ỉry

ny-sw.t Wsrkn m Pr-Bꜣst.t ww n Rꜥ-nfr
ny-sw.t ꜣIwwpṯ m Ṯ-n.t-rm.w Tꜣ-ꜥn
ḥꜣ.ty-ꜥ Ḏd-ꜣImn-ỉ(w)ꜣf-ꜥnḫ (115) m Pr-Bꜣ-nb-Ḏd.t Tꜣ-šnw.t-Rꜥ
sꜣꜣf smsm (<smsw) ỉmy-rꜣ mšꜥ m Pr-Ḏhwty-wp-rḥwy ꜥnḫ-Ḥr
ḥꜣ.ty-ꜥ ꜣIwkꜣnš m Ṯb-nṯr m m Pr-ḥby.(t) m Smꜣ-Bḥd.t
ḥꜣ.ty-ꜥ wr n Mꜥ Pꜣ-ṯnf(y) m Pr-Spd m Šnw.t-n-ꜣInb-ḥḏ
(116) ḥꜣ.ty-ꜥ wr n Mꜥ Pꜣ-mꜣ(y) m Pr-Wsỉr-nb-Ḏdw
ḥꜣ.ty-ꜥ wr n Mꜥ Ns-nꜣ-ỉs.ty[19] m Ḥsbw
ḥꜣ.ty-ꜥ wr n Mꜥ Nḫt-Ḥr-nꜣ-šn.w m Pr-grr
wr n Mꜥ Pn-Tꜣ-wr.t
wr n Mꜥ Pn-T(ꜣ)-bḫn.t
ḥm-nṯr Ḥr nb Ḫm (117) Pꜣ-dỉ-Ḥr-smꜣ-tꜣ.wy
ḥꜣ.ty-ꜥ Ḥr-Bs m Pr-Sḫm.t-nb.(t)-Sꜣ.t Pr-Sḫm.t-nb.(t)-Rꜣ-ḥsꜣwy
ḥꜣ.ty-ꜥ Ḏd-Ḥyw m Ḫnt(y)-nfr
ḥꜣ.ty-ꜥ Pꜣ-Bꜣs m Ḥr-ꜥḥꜥ m Pr-Ḥꜥp(y)

ḫr ỉnwꜣsn nb nfr (118) [... nb]w ḫ[ḏ ...] ꜣ[tỉy.[w]t sḥn.tỉ [m p(ꜣ)]g.(t)
ꜥntyw m (119) ḫb[ḫb ...] m šꜣw nfr ḥtr.w (120) [m ṯꜣy.w ḥm.wt m ḥꜣw.ty
nb n ỉḫ(w)ꜣf[20] ...]

[ỉr ḥr-sꜣ] nn ỉw.n.tw r ḏd (121) n ḥm[ꜣf ...] mšꜥ(?) [...] sw ỉnb(122).
wꜣ[f n snḏ(?)]ꜣk [...] dỉꜣf ḥ.t m pr-ḥḏꜣ[f ꜥḥꜥy.wꜣf ḥr-tp] ỉtr(w) sḏr.nꜣf Msd
(123) m mšꜥ.w s[...]bꜣf [...]

ꜥḥꜥ.n rdỉ.n ḥmꜣf šm mšꜥꜣf (124) ḥr mꜣꜣ ḫpr.(t) ỉm m mnfy.(t) n.(t)
ỉry-pꜥ.t Pꜣ-dỉ-ꜣs.t ỉw.n.(t)w r smỉ (125) n ḥmꜣf m ḏd sꜣmꜣnꜣn[21] rmt nb
gmꜣn ỉm wn.ỉn ḥmꜣf rdỉ sw n fq(ꜣ) (126) n ỉry-pꜥ.t Pꜣ-dỉ-ꜣs.t ꜥḥꜥ.n sḏm
sw wr n Mꜥ Tꜣ(y)ꜣf-nḫtỉ rdỉ (127) ỉw ỉpwty r b(w) ḫr(y) ḥmꜣf m swnswn
m ḏd

ḥtp rꜣk n mꜣꜣ.nꜣỉ ḥrꜣk m (128) hrw.w n.w šp.(t) n ꜥḥꜥ.(n)ꜣỉ ḫft hhꜣk
nrꜣỉ n šfy.tꜣk ỉs ntk Nbty ḫnt(y) Tꜣ-Šmꜥw Mnṯ(w) (129) kꜣ nḫt ꜥ ỉr nỉw.t
nb.(t) dỉꜣk ḥrꜣk rꜣs n gm.nꜣk bꜣk ỉm r pḥ.nꜣỉ ỉw.n w n.w wꜣḏ-(130)wr ỉwꜣ
ỉ snḏ.kwỉ n bꜣwꜣk ḥr md.t p(ꜣy)ꜣf[17] nbỉ ỉr ḫft(y) rꜣỉ ỉn-ỉw n qbḥ (131)
ỉb n ḥmꜣk m nn ỉr.nꜣk rꜣỉ ỉnk ỉs ḥr(y) dbꜥ mꜣꜥ n sḥꜣk wỉ r dꜣr btꜣꜣ(ỉ)
ḫꜣy m (132) ỉwsw rḫ m qd.t q(ꜣ)bꜣk s.t nꜣỉ m ḥmt wꜣḥ pr.t ꜥbꜣk sw n tr
(ỉ)m(y) wḥ(133)ꜣ mnw r wꜣb.wyꜣf(y) wꜣḥ kꜣꜣk ḥr(y.t)ꜣk m ḥ.tꜣỉ snḏ.tꜣk
m-ꜥb qs.(w)ꜣỉ n ḥms.nꜣỉ m (134) ꜥ.(t)-ḥnq.t n ms.tw nꜣỉ bnỉ.t wnmꜣỉ ỉs t
n ḥqr s(w)ỉꜣỉ[22] mw m (135) ỉb.(t) dr hrw pf sḏmꜣk rnꜣỉ dḥr.(t) m qs.wꜣỉ
tpꜣỉ wšr.(w) ḥbs(136).wꜣỉ ḥtꜣ.(w) r sḥtp.tw nꜣỉ N.t ꜣw ḥp.(t) ỉn.nꜣk rꜣỉ
ḥrꜣk rꜣỉ gr ỉn rnp.t s(137)pḥꜣ kꜣꜣỉ swꜥb bꜣk m ṯsꜣf ỉmy šsp.ṯ(w) ḥ.tꜣỉ r
pr-ḥḏ m (138) nbw ḥnꜥ ꜥꜣ.t nb.(t) ḥꜣ.tyw ỉs n.w s{m}sm.w(t) ḏbꜣ.w m ḥ.t

nb.(t)²³ ỉmy ỉw n≠ỉ ỉ(139)pwty m sỉn dr≠f snḏ.t m ỉb≠ỉ k3 pr≠ỉ r ḥw.t-nṯr
m-ḫr≠f (r) sw‘b≠ỉ m ‘nḫ (140) nṯr

rdỉ.n ḥm≠f šm ḫr(y)-ḥb.(t) ḥr(y)-tp P3-dỉ-’Imn-(nb)-ns.wt-t3.wy ỉmy-r3
mš‘ P3-wrm3⁵ fq(141).n≠f sw m ḥḏ nbw ḥbs.w ‘3.t nb.(t) šps.(t) pr.n≠f r
ḥw.t-nṯr dw3.n≠f nṯr s(142)w‘b.n≠f sw m ‘nḫ nṯr m ḏd

n(n) th(ỉ)≠ỉ wḏ ny-sw.t n(n) wỉn≠ỉ (143) ḏd.t ḥm≠f n(n) ỉr≠ỉ ỉw r
ḫ3.ty-‘ m ḥm≠k ỉr≠ỉ m ḏd(144).t.n ny-sw.t n(n) th(ỉ)≠ỉ wḏ.n≠f
‘ḥ‘.n ḥm≠f ḥr ḫr≠s

ỉy.n.tw r ḏd (145) n ḥm≠f Ḥw.t-nṯr-Sbk sn≠s{n} ḫtm≠s Mtnw rdỉ ḥr
ḥ.t≠s n(n) wn (146) sp3.t ḫtm.tw r ḥm≠f m sp3.wt n.w Šm‘w Mḥw ỉmnt.t
ỉ3bt.t ỉw.w ḫr(y).w-ỉb ḥr ḥ.t≠sn n snḏ.t≠f ḥr (147) rdỉ.t m3‘ ḥ.t≠sn r b(w)
ḫr(y) ḥm≠f mỉ nḏ.wt n.t ‘ḥ

ḥḏ r≠f t3 dw3 (148) sp-2 ỉy.n nn n ḥq3 2 n.w Šm‘w ḥq3 2 n.w Mḥw m
ỉ‘r‘.wt r sn t3 n b3w (149) ḥm≠f ỉs gr nn n ny.w-sw.t ḫ3.tyw-‘ n.w T3-Mḥw
ỉy r m33 nfrw ḥm≠f rd.wy(150)≠sn m rd.wy ḥm.wt²⁴ n ‘q.n≠sn r pr ny-sw.t
ḏr-nt.t wnn≠sn m ‘m‘(151).w ḥn‘ wnm rm.w bw.t pw n.t pr ny-sw.t ỉs ny-
sw.t Nm3rt ‘q(152)≠f r pr ny-sw.t ḏr-nt.t wnn≠f m w‘b n wnm≠f rm.w ‘ḥ‘.
n ḥmt (153) r rd.wy≠sn w‘ m ‘q (r) pr ny-sw.t

‘ḥ‘.n 3tp(w) ‘ḥ‘.w m ḥḏ nbw ḥmty (154) ḥbs.w ḫ.t nb.(t) n.w T3-Mḥw
m3‘.w nb n Ḥ3r ḫ3w nb n t3 nṯr ḫnt(y) (155) pw ỉr.n ḥm≠f ỉb≠f 3w gs.wy≠
f(y) nb ḥr nhm ỉmnt.t ỉ3bt.t šsp≠sn sr ḥr (156) nhm m h(3)w ḥm≠f
ḫnw nhm ḏd≠sn

p3 ḥq3 tr sp-2 (157) Py p3 ḥq3 tr
ỉw≠k ỉy.tw ḫ3q.n≠k T3-Mḥw
ỉr≠k k3.(158)w m ḥm.wt
nḏm ỉb n mw.t ms tỉ t3y st(y).t ỉm≠k
ỉmy.w ỉn.t ỉr n≠s ỉ(3)wy ỉdy.t (159) ms k3
ỉw≠k r nḥḥ nḫt≠k mn
p3 ḥq3 mrỉ-W3s.t

(1) Regnal year 21, first month of Inundation, under the Majesty of the
King of Upper and Lower Egypt, Piye, beloved of Amon, living forever.
The decree that My Majesty has spoken:
"Hear what I have done in exceeding the ancestors.
I am the king, the representation of god,
the living image of Atum,
who issued from the womb marked as ruler,
who is feared by those greater than he,
[whose father] knew (2) and whose mother perceived
even in the egg that he would be ruler,
the Good God, beloved of the gods,

> the Son of Re, who acts with his two arms,
> Piye, beloved of Amon."

One came to say to His Majesty: "The Chief of the West, the count and chief in Behbeit el-Hagar, Tefnakht, is in the (Harpoon)³ nome, in the nome of Xois, in Hapi, in [...], (3) in the marshy region of Kom el-Hisn, in Per-noub and in the nome of Memphis. He has seized the West even in its entirety, from the northern coastal marshes to Lisht, sailing southward with a sizable army, while the Two Lands are united behind him, and the counts and rulers of estates are as dogs at his heels.

No stronghold has closed [its doors in] (4) the nomes of Upper Egypt: Meidum, the Fort of Osorkon I, Crocodilopolis (Medinet el-Faiyum), Oxyrhynchus (el-Bahnasa), and Takinash. Every city of the West has opened doors just through fear of him. When he turned about to the nomes of the East, then they opened to him likewise: the Mansion of the Phoenix, el-Hibeh, the Mansion of the King, and Aphroditopolis (Atfih).

Behold, [he is] (5) beleaguering Heracleopolis (Ihnasya el-Medina), and he has made himself an enclosing uroborous,⁴ not allowing goers to go nor allowing entrants to enter, while fighting every day. In its full circuit he has measured it, with every count knowing his (assigned) wall, while he stations every man among the counts and rulers of estates to besiege his section."

Then [His Majesty] heard [this] (6) defiantly, laughing and amused.

But these chiefs, counts and generals who were in their cities were sending word to His Majesty daily, saying:

"Have you been silent so as to ignore Upper Egypt and the nomes of the Residence, while Tefnakht seizes what is before him, having found no resistance? Namlot, [ruler of Hermopolis], (7) count of Hutweret, has thrown down the wall of Nefrusy. He has demolished his own city through fear of the one who would seize it for himself in order to beleaguer another city. Behold, he has gone to be a subordinate at his (Tefnakht's) heels, having shrugged off allegiance to His Majesty. He stands with him just like one of [his followers] (8) in the nome of Oxyrhynchus, while he (Tefnakht) gives to him rewards as his desire dictates from among everything that he has found."

Then His Majesty sent word to the counts and generals who were in Egypt, the commander Pawerem, and the commander Lamersekny,⁵ and every commander of His Majesty who was in Egypt:

"Proceed in battle formation, engage in combat, encircle and beleaguer it! (9) Capture its people, its herds, its ships upon the river! Do not allow the cultivators to go forth to the fields! Do not allow the plowmen to plow! Beleaguer the frontier of the Hare nome; fight against it every day!"

Then they did likewise.

Then His Majesty sent an army to Egypt, charging them forcefully:

"Do not attack at (10) night in the manner of a game. You should fight when there is sight. Announce battle to him from afar! If he should say: 'Wait for the troops and cavalry of another city,' then may you sit until his army comes. Fight when he says. If, further, his supporters are in another city, let (11) one wait for them. The counts, these whom he has brought to support him, and the trusted Libyan troops, let one announce battle to them in advance, saying:

'O you whom we do not know how to address in mustering the troops! Yoke the best steeds of your stable! (12) Line up in battle formation! Be informed that Amon is the god who sent us!'

When you arrive within Thebes before Karnak, you should enter into the water. Purify yourselves in the river! Clothe yourselves in the best linen![6] Lay down the bow, withdraw the arrow![7] Do not boast of (13) greatness as a possessor of strength! The mighty has no strength in ignorance of him (Amon), for he makes the broken-armed strong-armed. (Thus) do multitudes turn tail to the few; one seizes a thousand men. Sprinkle yourselves with the water of his altars. You should kiss the ground before him and you should say (14) to him: 'Give us passage, that we might fight in the shadow of your strong arm! The corps of recruits whom you have sent, let its onslaught occur while multitudes tremble before it.'"

Then they placed[8] (themselves) on their bellies before His Majesty, (saying):

> "It is your name that will serve as our strong arm,
> your counsel that brings your army to port,
> with your bread in our bellies on every passage,
> and your beer (15) quenching our thirst.
> It is your valor that provides our strong arm,
> so that one is terrified at the mention of your name.
> No army profits whose commander is a coward.
> Who is your equal there?
> You are a mighty king, who acts with his two arms,
> the master of the art of war."

They then went sailing (16) northward and they arrived at Thebes; they did exactly as His Majesty had said. They then went sailing northward on the river, finding that numerous ships had come southward with soldiers, sailors, and troops of every valiant warrior of Lower Egypt equipped with weapons of warfare (17) to fight against the army of His Majesty.

Then a great slaughter was made among them, in incalculable numbers. Their army and their ships were captured and brought away as captives to the place where His Majesty was. They then advanced to the frontier of Heracleopolis, announcing battle.

List of the counts and kings of Lower Egypt:

King Namlot and (18) King Iuput; Chief of the Ma, Sheshonq, of Busiris;

Great Chief of the Ma, Djedamoniuefankh, of Mendes and his eldest son, who was the general of Hermopolis Parva; the army of Hereditary Prince Bakennefy and his eldest son, the Chief of the Ma, (19) Nesnaiu, in Hesebu; every plume-wearing chief who was in Lower Egypt; and King Osorkon (IV), who was in Bubastis and the district of Ranefer; with every count and ruler of estates in the West, in the East and the islands in between being united in a single alliance as subordinates at the heels of the Great Chief of the West, the ruler of estates of Lower Egypt, the prophet of Neith, Lady of Sais, (20) the *setem*-priest of Ptah, Tefnakht.

They then went forth against them. Then they made a great slaughter among them, greater than anything, and their ships on the river were captured. The remnant then crossed over, landing on the West in the vicinity of Perpega.

As the land lightened and the morning dawned, the army of His Majesty crossed over (21) against them, so that army joined battle with army.

Then they slew numerous men among them together with horses in incalculable numbers, with trembling occurring in the remnant so that they fled to Lower Egypt from a beating more severe and painful than anything.

List of the slaughter which was made among them.

Men: (...)[9] persons. (22) (Horses: ...)

King Namlot fled upstream to the South when he was told: "Hermopolis is faced with enemies from the troops of His Majesty, with its people and its herds captured."

Then he entered into Hermopolis while the troops of His Majesty were on the river and the bank (23) of the Hare nome.

Then they heard it and surrounded the Hare nome on its four sides, without[10] letting those who would go out go out nor letting those who would enter enter. They sent word explicitly to report to the Majesty of the King of Upper and Lower Egypt, Piye, beloved of Amon, given life, detailing every attack that they had made, detailing every victory of His Majesty.

Then His Majesty raged because of it like a panther: "Have they allowed (24) a remnant to remain among the troops of Lower Egypt so as to let go an escapee among them to relate his campaign, not killing them to exterminate the last of them? As I live, as Re loves me, as my father Amon favors me, I shall go northward myself, that I might overturn (25) what he has done, that I might cause that he retreat from fighting for the course of eternity! After the rites of the New Year are performed, when I offer to my father Amon in his beautiful festival, when he makes his beautiful appearance of the New Year, let him send me in peace to behold Amon in the beautiful festival of the Opet feast, that I might convey his image in procession (26) to Luxor temple in his beautiful festival of "The Night

Feast of Opet" and the festival of "Abiding in Thebes" that Re devised for him in the primordial time, that I might convey him in procession to his house in order to rest on his throne on the day of ushering in the god in the third month of Inundation season, day 2, and that I might make Lower Egypt taste the taste of my fingers."

Then the troops who were there in (27) Egypt heard the raging that His Majesty had made against them.

Then they fought against Oxyrhynchus of the Oxyrhynchite nome, taking it like a burst of water and sending word before His Majesty, but his heart was not appeased because of it.

Then they fought against "The Peak, Great of Victories," finding it filled (28) with troops comprising every valiant warrior of Lower Egypt.

Then a battering ram was employed against it, so that its walls were demolished and a great slaughter made among them in incalculable numbers, including the son of the Chief of the Ma, Tefnakht.

Then they sent word to His Majesty because of it, but his heart was not appeased regarding it.

(29) Then they fought against Hutbenu, so that its interior was opened and the troops of His Majesty entered into it.

Then they sent word to His Majesty, but his heart was not appeased regarding it.

First month of Inundation season, day 9. His Majesty then came sailing northward to Thebes. At the feast of Opet, he celebrated the festival of Amon. His Majesty then went (30) sailing northward to the quay of the Hare nome. His Majesty came out of the cabin of the barge, the horses were yoked, the chariots were mounted, so that the grandeur of His Majesty extended to the hinterlands of the Asiatics, and every heart was quaking before him.

Then His Majesty burst forth to revile (31) his army, raging at it like a panther: "Do they endure[11] while your combat is such that my business is delayed? It is the year for finalizing a conclusion, for placing fear of me in Lower Egypt, and for inflicting upon them a severe and painful defeat by striking."

He made for himself a camp at the southwest of Hermopolis, keeping a stranglehold on it (32) daily. A talus was made to clothe the wall, and a platform was erected to elevate the archers when shooting and the slingers when slinging stones, slaying the people among them daily. Days passed, and Hermopolis became foul to the nose, deprived of (33) its ability to breathe.

Then Hermopolis threw itself upon its belly, pleading before the King of Lower Egypt,[12] while messengers came and went bearing everything beautiful to behold: gold, every sort of precious gemstone, clothing by the chest, and the diadem that had been on his brow, the uraeus that had inspired respect of him, without ceasing for numerous days, imploring his crown.

Then One (King Namlot) sent (34) his wife, the royal wife and royal daughter, Nestanetmehu,[13] to implore the royal wives, the royal concubines, the royal daughters, and the royal sisters, and she threw herself upon her belly in the women's house before the royal women:

"Come to me, royal wives, royal daughters, and royal sisters! May you appease Horus, Lord of the palace, whose wrath is great, whose vindication is grand! Cause (35) that he [...] me. Behold, he [...] (36) [...] him. Behold, [...]... [Speak (?)] (37) to him, so that [he] might then turn about to the one who praises him. [...]"

(38) [...] provision [...] (39) [...] of life in [...] (40) [...] (41) [...] they filled (?) with what was efficacious [...] praise him (42) [...] the royal wives, the royal sisters [... They threw] themselves upon their bellies (43) [before His Majesty ...] the royal wives [... Namlot,] ruler of Hutweret.(44) [...] for his city (?), the ruler (45) [...] (46) [...] as ruler (47) [...] in the city (?) (48) [...] (49) [...] through lack of [...] (50) [...] to the place where [His] Majesty was. [His] Majesty spoke (?) to him [...]:

"Who [...] (51) your mother? Who has guided you? Who has guided you? Who, then, has guided you? Who has guided you [so that you have abandoned] (52) the path of life? Has heaven then rained with arrows? I was [content] (53) when Southerners bowed down and Northerners (said): 'Place us within your shade!' Was it bad that the King (?) [of Hermopolis came (?)][14] (54) bearing his offerings? The heart is a rudder, which capsizes its owner by what issues from the wrath of god, when he has seen flame in the cool waters in (?) the heart. [...] (55) There is no adult who is seen with his father, for your nomes are filled (only) with children."

Then he threw himself on his belly in the presence of His Majesty: "[Peace be with you,] (56) Horus, Lord of the palace! It is your wrath that has done this against me. I am one of the king's servants who pays taxes to the treasury as daily offerings. (57) Make a reckoning of their taxes. I have provided for you far more than they."

Then he presented silver, gold, lapis lazuli, turquoise, copper, and every sort of gemstone in great quantity.

(58) Then the treasury was filled with this tribute, and he brought a horse with his right hand and a sistrum in his left—a sistrum of gold and lapis lazuli.

Then His Majesty appeared in splendor (59) from his palace, proceeding to the temple of Thoth, Lord of Hermopolis, and he sacrificed long-horned cattle, short-horned cattle, and fowl for his father Thoth, Lord of Hermopolis, and the Ogdoad in the temple of the (60) Ogdoad.

The troops of the Hare nome proceeded to shout and sing, saying:

"How beautiful is Horus, appeased (61) in his city,

The Son of Re, Piye!
May you celebrate for us a jubilee,
As you protect the Hare nome!"

His Majesty then proceeded to (62) the house of King Namlot, and he went into every chamber of the palace, his treasury and his storehouses. He caused that there be presented (63) to him the royal wives and the royal daughters. They proceeded to hail His Majesty with feminine wiles, but His Majesty did not pay attention (64) to them. His Majesty then proceeded to the stable of the horses and the quarters of the foals. When he saw [that] (65) they were starved, he said: "As I live, as Re loves me, as my nose is rejuvenated with life, how much more painful it is in my heart (66) that my horses have been starved than any other crime that you have committed at your discretion. Your neighbor's fear of you is testimony for me. (67) Are you unaware that the shadow of god is over me and that my deeds have not failed because of him? If only another had done it to me, (68) whom I did not know, whom I had not rebuked because of it! I am one fashioned in the womb and created in the egg of god, with the seed (69) of god within me! As his *ka*-spirit endures, I have not acted in ignorance of him! He is the one who commanded me to act!"

Then his property was assigned to the treasury (70) and his granary to the endowment of Amon in Karnak.

The ruler of Heracleopolis, Peftchauawybast, then came bearing tribute (71) to Pharaoh: gold, silver, every sort of gemstone, and the pick of the horses of the stable. He threw himself upon his belly in the presence of His Majesty, saying:

"Hail to you, Horus, (72) mighty king, bull who attacks bulls!
The netherworld has seized me, and I am deep in darkness!
O you who give me the enlightenment (73) of your face,
I cannot find a friend on a day of distress,[15]
who will stand up on a day of fighting,
except for you, O mighty king!
From me you have stripped away (74) the darkness.
I shall be a servant together with my property, while Heracleopolis
     is levied with taxes (75) for your domain.
You are indeed Horakhty, chief of the imperishable stars!
As he exists, so do you exist as king.
He will not perish, (76) nor will you perish,
O King of Upper and Lower Egypt, Piye, living forever!"

His Majesty then sailed northward to the opening of the canal beside (77) Illahun, and he found Per-Sekhemkheperre with its ramparts heightened, its fortress closed, and filled with every valiant warrior of Lower Egypt.

Then His Majesty sent word to them saying:

"O living dead! O living dead!
O miserable (78) wretches! O living dead!
If the moment passes without opening to me,
behold, you belong to the tally of the fallen!
Such is the one subjected to royal punishment.
Do not bar the gates of your life so as to confront the slaughter
    block of this day!
Do not desire death so as to hate life!
(79) [Choose (?)] life in the presence of the entire land!"
Then they sent word to His Majesty, saying:
"Behold, the shadow of god is upon you.
The son of Nut, may he give to you his arms,
then your wish will come to pass directly
like what issues from the mouth of the god.
Behold, you are born of god,
because we see (it) by the actions of your arms.
Behold, as for your city and its fortifications,
(80) [do what pleases] you with them.
May entrants enter and goers go;
may His Majesty do what he will."
Then they came out with a son of the Chief of the Ma, Tefnakht. The troops of His Majesty then entered into it, without his slaying anyone among all the people whom he found (81) [there. ...] men and treasurers to seal his possessions, while his treasuries were assigned to the treasury, and his granaries to the endowment of his father Amon-Re, Lord of the Thrones of the Two Lands. His Majesty then went sailing northward, and he found that in Meidum, the House of Sokar, Lord of Illumination, had been closed, not having been attacked, and had intent to fight. [...] seized (82) them; fear [overpowered?] them; awe sealed their mouths.
Then His Majesty sent word to them, saying:
"Behold, two ways are before you; choose as you wish.
Open, you will live; close, you will die.
My Majesty will not pass by a closed city!"
Then they opened to him directly, and His Majesty entered within this city, and he presented (83) a [great] offering [to] Imenhy, Foremost of Illumination. Its treasury and granaries were assigned to the endowment of Amon in Karnak. His Majesty then sailed north to Lisht, and he found the stronghold closed and the walls filled with valiant troops of Lower Egypt.
Then they opened the fortifications and they threw themselves on their bellies (84) in the presence of [His Majesty, and they said to] His Majesty:
"Your father has entrusted to you his legacy.
Yours are the Two Lands, and yours those in them.

You are the Lord of what is upon earth."

His Majesty then proceeded to have a great offering presented to the gods who are in this city, consisting of long-horned cattle, short-horned cattle, fowl and everything good and pure. Then its treasury was assigned to the treasury and its granaries to the endowment of (85) his father Amon-[Re, Lord of the Thrones of the Two Lands. His Majesty then sailed northward to] Memphis.

Then he sent word to them, saying: "Do not close; do not fight, O residence of Shu from the primordial time! The entrant—let him enter; the goer—let him go! No traveler will be hindered. I shall offer an oblation to Ptah and the gods who are in the Memphite nome; I shall make offering to Sokar in his sanctuary; I shall behold (Ptah) South-of-His-Wall; and I shall sail northward in peace, (86) [while the people] of Memphis are safe and sound and children are not mourned. Look, then, to the nomes of the South. None among them has been slain except for the rebels who blasphemed god, so that a slaughter was made among the traitors."

Then they closed their fortification, and they sent out troops against some of the troops of His Majesty, who were but craftsmen, architects, and sailors (87) who had come [... to] the harbor of Memphis. Now that Chief of Sais arrived in Memphis at night, ordering his soldiers, his sailors, all the elite of his army, a total of 8,000 men, ordering them firmly:

"Behold, Memphis is filled with troops comprising all the elite of Lower Egypt, with barley, emmer, every sort of grain, with the granaries overflowing, and with every sort of weapon (88) [of war. It is protected (?) by a] stronghold; a great battlement has been built as a work of skillful craftsmanship; the river encircles its east, and fighting will not be found there. The stables here are filled with oxen, the treasuries supplied with everything: silver, gold, copper, clothing, incense, honey, and oil. I shall go that I might give things to the Chiefs of Lower Egypt, that I might open for them their nomes,[16] and that I might become (89) [...] days until I return."

He then mounted upon his horse, as he did not trust his chariot. He then went northward in fear of His Majesty. As the land lightened and the morning dawned, His Majesty arrived at Memphis. When he moored on its north, he found the water risen to the ramparts, with ships moored at (90) [the houses of] Memphis.

Then His Majesty saw that it was strong, the enclosure walls high with new construction, and the battlements supplied in strength. No way of attacking it was found. Every man proceeded to state his opinion among the troops of His Majesty, entailing every tactic of fighting, with every man saying, "Let us lay siege (91) [to Memphis.] Behold, its army is numerous," while others were saying, "Make a ramp against it so that we elevate the ground to its ramparts. Let us put together a (siege) platform, erecting masts and using sails as walls for it. Let us divide it by this means on every side of it, with talus and (92) [...] on its north, to elevate the ground to its rampart so that we might find a path for our feet."

Then His Majesty raged against it like a panther, saying:

"As I live, as Re loves me, as my father Amon favors me, I have discovered that this has happened for it by the command of Amon. This is what [all] men (93) [of Lower Egypt] and the nomes of the South say: 'Let them open to him from afar! They do not place Amon in their hearts, nor do they know what he has commanded. He has done it expressly to give evidence of his wrath and to cause that his grandeur be seen.' I shall seize it like a cloudburst; [my father Amon] has commanded me."

(94) Then he sent his ships and his troops to assault the harbor of Memphis, and they brought away for him every boat, every ferry, every pleasure boat, as many ships as were moored at the harbor of Memphis with prow rope fastened among its houses. (95) [There was not] a common soldier who wept among the entire army of His Majesty. His Majesty himself went to arrange the battle formation of the ships, as many as they were. His Majesty commanded his army:

"Forward against it! Mount the ramparts! Enter the houses atop the river! If one among you enters over the rampart, no one will stand in his way, (96) [...] no troops will repel you. It would be vile, then, that we should seal Upper Egypt, moor at Lower Egypt, and yet sit in siege at "The Balance of the Two Lands."

Then Memphis was taken like a cloudburst, with numerous people slain within it, in addition to those brought as prisoners to the place where His Majesty was. Now (97) [after the land] lightened and a second day occurred, His Majesty sent men into it, protecting the temples of the god for him, consecrating the shrines of the gods, offering cool water to the divine tribunal of Hikuptah, purifying Memphis with natron and incense, and putting priests in their assigned places. His Majesty proceeded to the estate of (98) [Ptah], his purification was performed in the robing room, and there was performed for him every ritual that is performed for a king. He entered into the temple. A great offering was made to his father Ptah, South-of-His-Wall, consisting of long-horned cattle, short-horned cattle, fowl, and everything good. His Majesty then returned to his house.

Then every nome that was in the region of Memphis heard (it): Heripademi, Peni(99)naiua, The Fort of Biu, and The Oasis of Bit, opening their fortifications and fleeing in flight, and no one knew where they went.

King Iuput then came together with the Chief of the Ma, Akanosh, and the Hereditary Prince, Padiese, (100) and all the counts of Lower Egypt, bearing their tribute in order to behold the beauty of His Majesty.

Then the treasuries and granaries of Memphis were assigned, made over to the endowments of Amon, of Ptah, and of the Ennead that is in Hikuptah.

As the land lightened and the morning dawned, His Majesty proceeded to the East. An offering to Atum was made in Babylon (Old Cairo) (101), to the Ennead in the estate of the Ennead, and to the cavern and the gods within it, consisting of long-horned cattle, short-horned cattle, and fowl, so that they might give life, prosperity, and health to the King of Upper and Lower Egypt, Piye, living forever.

His Majesty proceeded to Heliopolis over that mountain of Babylon on the road of the god Sepa[17] to Babylon. His Majesty proceeded to the camp that is on the west of Ity, his purification was performed, he was purified in the midst of (102) the Lake of Cool Water, and his face was washed in the river of Nun where Re washed his face.

Proceeding to the High Sand in Heliopolis. Making a great offering on the High Sand in Heliopolis in the sight of Re at his rising, consisting of white oxen, milk, myrrh, incense, and (103) every sort of sweet-smelling perfume pellets. Coming in procession to the estate of Re. Entering into the temple in great acclamation, with lector priests adoring god and ritually repelling enemies from the king. Performing the rites of the robing room. Tying on the *sedeb*-garment. Purifying him with incense and cool water. Presenting to him bouquets of the Mansion of the *Benben*-mound. Bringing to him amulets of life. Mounting (104) the stairway to the great window to behold Re in the Mansion of the *Benben*-mound, while the king himself stood alone. Breaking the seals of the doorbolts. Opening the doors. Seeing his father Re in the Mansion of the *Benben*-mound. Consecrating the morning-bark for Re and the evening-bark for Atum. Bringing the doors back into position. Applying the clay. Sealing (105) with the king's own seal. Giving orders to the priests: "I myself have inspected the seal. No other can enter into it, among all the kings who may arise." Before His Majesty they placed themselves on their bellies, saying: "(It is) to be established and enduring without fail, O Horus, beloved of Heliopolis!" Coming and entering the estate of Atum. Presenting myrrh (106) to the image of his father Atum-Khepri, the great one of Heliopolis. King Osorkon (IV) came expressly to behold the beauty of His Majesty.

As the land lightened and the morning dawned, His Majesty proceeded to the harbor at the head of his ships and crossed over to the harbor of the nome of Athribis, and the camp of His Majesty was made on the south of Kaheny, on the east (107) of the nome of Athribis. Then there came these kings and counts of Lower Egypt, all the plume-wearing chiefs, all viziers, all chiefs, all royal confidants, from the West, from the East and from the islands in between, to behold the beauty of His Majesty. Then the Hereditary Prince Padiese threw himself upon his belly in (108) the presence of His Majesty, saying:

"Come to Athribis, that you might behold the god Khentykhety, that the goddess Khuyt might protect you,[18] that you might present an offering to Horus in his temple, consisting of long-horned cattle, short-horned cattle, and fowl. May you enter into my house, for my treasury is open to you. I shall gratify you with my ancestral property, and I shall give you gold to the limits of your desire, turquoise (109) heaped up before you, and many horses from the best of the stable, the foremost of the stall."

His Majesty then proceeded to the estate of Horus Khentykhety to have long-horned cattle, short-horned cattle, and fowl presented to his father Horus Khentykhety, Lord of Athribis. His Majesty proceeded to the house of Hereditary Prince Padiese, who presented him with silver, gold, (110) lapis lazuli, turquoise, a great heap of everything, clothing of royal linen of every thread count, couches spread with fine linen, myrrh, unguent in jars, and horses both male and female, being all the foremost of his stable. He purified himself by a divine oath even in the sight of these kings and great chiefs of Lower (111) Egypt:

"Anyone here who conceals his horses or who hides for himself his worth, he shall die the death of his father! I have said this just so that you might testify for me, your humble servant, in all that you know that I possess. You should say whether I have hidden from His Majesty anything (112) of my father's house: gold ingots, gemstones, every sort of vase, armlets, gold bracelets, necklaces, collars inlaid with gemstones, amulets of every limb, garland crowns for the head, rings for the ears, every royal adornment, all the vessels of the king's purification in gold and every sort of gemstone. All of these I have presented (113) in the royal presence, and clothing of royal linen by the thousands, being all the best of my weaving workshop. I know that you will be satisfied with it. Proceed to the stall, choose what you wish among all the horses that you desire."

Then His Majesty did likewise. These kings and counts said before His Majesty: "Send us to our towns that we might open (114) our treasuries, that we might choose in accordance with what your heart desires, and that we might bring to you the best of our stalls, the foremost of our horses." Then His Majesty did likewise.

The list of them:

> King Osorkon (IV) in Bubastis and the district of Ranefer,
> King Iuput (II) in Leontopolis (Tell Moqdam) and Taan,
> Count Djedamoniuefankh (115) in Mendes and the Granary of Re,
> His eldest son, the general in Hermopolis Parva, Ankhhor,
> Count Akanosh in Sebennytos, in Iseopolis (Behbeit el-Hagar),
>   and Diospolis Inferior,
> Count and Chief of the Ma, Patchenefy in Saft el-Henneh and in
>   the Granary of Memphis,
> (116) Count and Chief of the Ma, Pamai in Busiris,

Count and Chief of the Ma, Nesnaiu[19] in Hesebu,
Count and Chief of the Ma, Nakhthornashenu in Pergerer,
Chief of the Ma, Pentaweret,
Chief of the Ma, Pentabekhnet,
Prophet of Horus, Lord of Letopolis (Ausim), (117) Padihorsomtus,
Count Horbes in the estate of Sakhmet, Lady of Eset, and the estate
    of Sakhmet, Lady of Rahesu,
Count Djedkhiu in Khentnefer,
Count Pabasa in Babylon (Old Cairo) and in Atar el-Nabi,
bearing all their good tribute (118) [...] of gold, silver, [...] couches spread
[with fine] linen, myrrh in (119) jars, [...] of good value, horses (120) [both
male and female, being all the foremost of his stable[20] ...]

[Now after]wards, one came to say (121) to [His] Majesty [...] army (?)
[...] him [his] walls (122) [through fear (?)] of you, while he has set fire to
his treasury [and to his ships on] the river. He has reinforced Mosdai (123)
with soldiers even while he [...].

Then His Majesty sent his army (124) to see what had happened there
among the troops of the Hereditary Prince Padiese. They returned to report
(125) to His Majesty, saying: "We slew[21] every man whom we found there."
Then His Majesty gave it as a gift (126) to the Hereditary Prince Padiese.

Then the Chief of the Ma Tefnakht heard it and sent (127) a messenger
in fawning supplication to the place where His Majesty was, saying:

"Peace be with you! I cannot look upon your face in (128) days of
shame. I cannot stand before your fiery blast, for I am terrified of your
grandeur. Indeed, you are the Ombite (Seth), Lord of Upper Egypt, Montu,
(129) the strong-armed bull! To whatever city you might turn your attention, you cannot not find me, your humble servant, until I have reached
the islands of the sea, (130) for I am fearful of your wrath, saying: 'His[17]
flame is hostile to me.' Is not the heart of Your Majesty cooled (131) by
these things that you have done to me? I am indeed one justly reproached,
but you did not smite me commensurably with my crime. Weigh with (132)
the balance, ascertain with the weights! May you multiply them for me in
triplicate, (but) leave the seed that you may harvest it in season. Do not
tear out (133) the grove to its roots! As your ka-spirit endures, terror of
you is in my body, fear of you is within my bones! I cannot sit in (134)
the beer hall, nor has the harp been played for me. For I have eaten bread
in hunger, I have drunk[22] water in (135) thirst, since that day when you
heard my name! Bitterness is in my bones, my head is balding, my clothing
(136) rags, until Neith is appeased toward me! Long is the course that you
have brought upon me, and your face is against me yet. It is a year (137)
for purging my soul. Cleanse the servant of his fault! Let my property be
received into the treasury: (138) gold and every sort of gemstone, even
the foremost of the horses, repayments in every kind.[23] Send to me (139)

a messenger in haste, that he might dispel fear from my heart! Then I shall go to the temple in his sight to cleanse myself by a divine (140) oath.

When His Majesty sent the chief lector priest Padiamon(neb)nesuttawy and the general Pawerem,[5] he (Tefnakht) presented (141) him with silver, gold, clothing, and every sort of precious gemstone. When he went into the temple, he praised god and (142) cleansed himself by a divine oath, saying:

"I shall not transgress the royal command. I shall not thrust aside (143) that which His Majesty says. I shall not do wrong to a count without your knowledge. I shall act in accordance with what (144) the king has said. I shall not transgress what he has commanded."

Then His Majesty was satisfied concerning it.

One came to say (145) to His Majesty: "Crocodilopolis has opened its fortress and Aphroditopolis is placed upon its belly. There is no (146) nome sealed against His Majesty among the nomes of the South and North, while the West, the East and the islands in between are upon their bellies through fear of him, (147) having their property sent to the place where His Majesty is, like servants of the palace."

As the land lightened and the morning (148) dawned, these two rulers of Upper Egypt and two rulers of Lower Egypt, those entitled to royal uraei, came to kiss the ground because of the wrathful power (149) of His Majesty. Now, however, these kings and counts of Lower Egypt who came to behold the beauty of His Majesty, their legs (150) were like the legs of women.[24] They could not enter into the palace since they were uncircumcised (151) and eaters of fish—such is an abomination of the palace. However, King Namlot entered (152) into the palace since he was pure and did not eat fish. Three stood (153) in their positions while one entered the palace.

Then the ships were loaded with silver, gold, copper, (154) clothing and everything of Lower Egypt, every product of Syria, every incense pellet of god's land. (155) His Majesty then sailed southward with his heart gladdened and all those on both sides of him shouting. The West and East took up the announcement, (156) shouting round about His Majesty.

The chant of jubilation which they said:
"O mighty ruler, O mighty ruler! (157) Piye, O mighty ruler!
You return having conquered Lower Egypt;
making bulls (158) into women!
Happy is the heart of the mother who bore you,
and of the male whose seed is within you!
Those in the Nile valley praise her,
the cow (159) who gave birth to a bull!

You are eternal, your victory enduring,
O ruler beloved of Thebes!"

NOTES

1. The damaged bird glyph perhaps represents the traditional Middle Egyptian term for Piye's Nubian kingdom. A clear nḥ-bird appears in line 11.

2. The restoration by Breasted follows Nestanetmehu's speech in line 34 and Namlot's speech in lines 55–56. The position of the speech on the lunette suggests that the speaker is the depicted queen, not Namlot.

3. Incompletely carved. For the geographic identification of this series of nomes, see Yoyotte 1961a, 154. For the name of the Harpoon nome, see Helck 1974, 153; for the "Bull of the Desert" (Xoite) nome, see 163–67.

4. Literally, "tail-in-mouth," designating a snake biting its tail, a symbolic enclosure both protective and hostile. For the religious context of this passage, see Ritner 1984b, 219–20.

5. The names of Piye's commanders, Lamersekny and Pawerem, are often considered Libyan, but the latter is a late spelling of the purely Egyptian name and title Pȝ-wr-mȝȝ.w; see Erichsen 1954, 94; correcting Dixon 1964, 127; and Caminos, 1972, 208.

6. See Erman and Grapow 1926–63, 5:292/15–16. Grimal read tp-š (291/17).

7. A conscious paraphrase of a passage from the classical Middle Kingdom literary "Tale of Sinuhe" (B 274); see Gardiner 1935, 220 n. 3. For other adaptations of classical passages, see Logan and Westenholz 1971–72, 111.

8. In lines 14 and 105 the scribe has used contemporary phonetic spelling (rtỉ < rdỉ) and not transposed passive forms, contra Kahn 1999, 5–6.

9. The engraver has left spaces blank for the insertion of battlefield tallies, but these were never added.

10. A direct parallel of line 5, the passage demonstrates the lack of clear separation between negative forms, contra Spalinger 1979b, 66–80, who also admits exceptions to his interpretation.

11. Lichtheim assumed an error for mn≠tn "Are you continuing to fight..." Grimal assumed an error for a book-roll determinative: "Is this the manner of your fighting."

12. The Hermopolitans acknowledge Piye's legitimacy as ruler of Lower Egypt (bỉ.ty) and thus make supplication to his crown.

13. "She of the One of Lower Egypt"; reading following Rougé, Kitchen, and sense. The reading "Nestent" ("She of the One of") adopted by Breasted, Lichtheim, and Grimal is senseless and does not account for the final signs.

14. Restoration following the suggestion of Lichtheim (1973–80, 3:82 n. 50).

15. A conscious paraphrase of a passage from the classical Middle Kingdom literary text "The Instructions of Amonemhat I"; see Gardiner 1934, 482.

16. Tefnakht vows to restore northern towns to their local rulers in return for defensive assistance against Piye.

17. On the deity's mythological journey from Heliopolis, see the conclusion of Horus Cippus Text C, above, p. 72; and Ritner 1990b, 167–68.

18. In contrast to Piye's exalted addresses in classic Middle Egyptian, the speech of his Libyan foes reflects common, contemporary grammar. In line 108, Padiese's speech includes a writing of the Demotic dependent pronoun tk, and in

line 130, Tefnakht uses the possessive adjective p(ꜣy)≠f, not the Middle Egyptian demonstrative pf, as taken by Lichtheim 1973–80, 3:79.

19. Ns-nꜣ-ỉs.ty is carved in error for Ns-nꜣ-ꜥꜣy.(w); cf. line 19.
20. Restored following line 110.
21. The contemporary spelling of smꜣ > sꜣm.
22. The contemporary spelling of swr > s(w)ỉ; Coptic **CⲰ**. In these passages, Tefnakht uses the Late Egyptian past- and present-tense constructions.
23. Or, following an early suggestion of Griffith, "horses, adorned with everything."
24. Trembling in fear.

146. SMALLER DAKHLEH STELA
(S. ASHMOLEAN MUSEUM 1894. 107B)

Like the larger limestone monument of Dynasty XXII, this sandstone stela was discovered in 1894 by Captain H. G. Lyons in the village of Mut in the Dakhleh Oasis. With maximum dimensions measuring 81.5 cm in height by 39.5 cm in width by 12 cm in depth, the stela has suffered the loss of a large fragment from the upper left corner, damaging both the lunette scene and the ends of the first eight lines. The document records a private donation of loaves by an oasis official for his deceased (?) father, confirmed by a tribal intermediary during the reign of the Nubian king Piye. The unambiguous hieratic writing of Piye (Py) in this text was instrumental in the reanalysis of the royal name, formerly read as Piankhy. In the lunette scene, framed by the heaven sign resting on *was*-scepters, a chief with upright Libu plume offers flowers and a libation vessel to the falcon-headed Sutekh (the Lower Egyptian pronunciation of Seth), lord of the oasis, and a now-lost goddess. Between the Libyan chief and the deities are a pile of offerings with vessel and offering stand. Contrary to usual practice, hieratic—not hieroglyphic—labels accompany the surviving figures, and a preliminary hieratic statement of authorship is separated by a horizontal dividing line from the sixteen hieratic lines that complete the text of the donation. Although dressed in Libu fashion, the local dynast is chieftain of the "Shamin," a tribe or subclan attested uniquely here.

Texts, translation, and commentary appear in Janssen 1968, 165–72 and pls. XXV–XXVA; Spiegelberg 1903, 194–96 (with photo); Sottas 1913, 150; and and Meeks 1979a, 634, 651–52, and 672 no. 23.XV.24. See Kitchen 1986, 371 §331.

LABEL FOR SUTEKH (SETH) AND LIBYAN CHIEF

ḏd-mdw ỉn Swtḫ[1] ꜥꜣ pḥty (2) sꜣ n Nw.t (3) dỉ≠f qn(ỉ) nḫt n (4) wr ꜥꜣ Šꜣ(m)ỉwn[2] Ns(5)-Ḏḥwty

Recitation by Sutekh,[1] great of strength, (2) son of Nut. (3) May he give valor and victory to (4) the Great Chief of the Sha(m)in,[2] Nes(5)djheuty.

MAIN TEXT

(1) ỉrỉ.n{n}³ Ḥr-n-t3-bỉ3 s3 P3y-(dd)-ʾImn(?)⁴ [sš ḫtm ...]

(2) ḥsb.t 24.(t) 3bd 3 3ḥ.t sw 10 (n.t) Pr-ˁ3 Py s3 3s.t mrỉ-[ʾImn ...]

(3) wr ˁ3 n3 Š3mỉwn Ns-sw-Ḏḥwty h3[(w) pn ...]

(4) p3 t3y⁵ bd.t ˁq.w 5 n ỉmn.(t) m-ḫnw [... r-ḫt(?)]

(5) ỉt-ntr n ʾImn ḥm-ntr 2-nw n Sḫm.t sš sḫn pr ʾImn [...]

(6) s3 ˁnḫ-Ḥr s3 Ḫ3ˁ≠w-s(w) ỉ-ỉr ỉt-ntr n [ʾImn-Rˁ ny-sw.t]

(7) ntr.w sš ḫtm m wḥ3.t Ḥr-(n)-t3-bỉ(3) s3 P3y-d[d-ʾImn(?) ...]

(8) m grg p3 bnr⁶ n P3y-dd-ʾImn(?) p3y≠f ỉt n ỉr[...]

(9) ≠f ỉ dr.t n3 ḥry.w ˁ dd≠f m h3(w) pn st smn n≠f r

(10) nḥḥ d.t ỉr p3 sš ḫtm m wḥ3.t ḥnˁ p3 sḫn

(11) ḥnˁ p3 sr nty-ỉw≠f smn t3 wd.t ỉw≠f ḥr ḥs.(t)

(12) n.(t) ʾImn-Rˁ ỉw s3≠f šsp n≠f ỉr p3 nty-ỉw≠f

(13) st3.t≠f⁷ ỉw≠f (n) šˁd n ʾImn-Rˁ ỉw≠f (n) h3h3 Sḫm.t st⁸

(14) ḫrwy n Wsỉr nb 3bdw ḥnˁ s3 n s3≠f nḥḥ d.t

(15) nk sw ˁ3.w nk ˁ3.w ḥm.t≠f nk ḥm.t≠f ḥrd≠f

(16) p3 mtr sš Dd-3s.t-ỉw≠f-ˁnḫ s3 n Pn-...p...(?) p3

(17) sš⁹ n p3 sš ḫtm m wḥ3.t ỉrỉ.n{n}³ Ḥr-n-t3-bỉ3 sš ḫtm

(1) Made by¹ Horentabia, son of Pai(ded)amon (?),⁴ [scribe of the seal ...]

(2) Regnal year 24, month 3 of Inundation, day 10 (of) Pharaoh Piye, Son of Isis, beloved of [Amon ... and of] (3) the Great Chief of the Shamin, Nesdjheuty. On [this] day [there was established] (4) the 5 containers⁵ of emmer loaves as a daily offering within [... under the authority of] (5) the God's Father of Amon, Second Prophet of Sakhmet and administrative scribe of the estate of Amon, [...] (6) son of Ankhhor son of Khausu, which was made by the God's Father of [Amon-Re, King] (7) of the Gods, the scribe of the seal in the Oasis, Hor(en)tabia, son of Paide[damon (?) ...] (8) in the outer settlement⁶ for Paidedamon (?), his father, for his ...[...] (9) at the disposition of the chiefs of the place. He said on this day: "They are confirmed to him for(10)ever and ever. As for the scribe of the seal in the Oasis and the administrator (11) and the official who will confirm the decree, he shall be in the favor (12) of Amon-Re, and his son shall succeed him. As for the one who will (13) not comply,⁷ he shall be subject to the slaughter of Amon-Re; he shall be subject to the fiery blast of Sakhmet. He is⁸ (14) an enemy of Osiris, Lord of Abydos, together with the son of his son forever and ever. (15) May donkeys rape him, may donkeys rape his wife, may his wife rape his child."

(16) The witness scribe, Djedeseiuefankh, son of Pen..p... (?), the (17) scribe⁹ of the scribe of the seal in the Oasis.

Made by³ Horentabia, scribe of the seal.

NOTES

1. For Sutekh as the Lower Egyptian pronunciation of "Seth," see Gunn and Gardiner 1918, 44; and Velde 1967, 3.

2. The tribal name was read Š3s3(?) "Shasu" Bedouin by Spiegelberg and followed by Giveon 1971, 198–99. To judge from the photograph, the missing "m" may be present to the right of Š3, following the pattern of inversions in the lunette writings.

3. The writing is a variant of the typically redundant Libyan Period spelling îr.n{n}.

4. Reading suggested with hesitation by Janssen 1968. The full writing appears in line 8.

5. See Erman and Grapow 1926–63, 5:349/5. For earlier discussions of the uncertain term, see Janssen 1968, 168 n. k.

6. Perhaps a reference to the outer (Kharga) and inner (Dakhleh) Oases, as noted by Janssen (1968, 169–70).

7. Literally, "reverse himself." The phraseology anticipates Demotic usage; see Sethe 1920, 198, §78b, 397, §25.

8. Error for sw.

9. Janssen (1968, 171 n. jj) read sš šˁ.t "letter/dispatch scribe," but cf. the writing of "scribe" in line 16 (p3 mtr sš).

147. FUNERARY STELA OF QUEEN TABIRY
(KHARTOUM 1901)

The granite stela of Tabiry, chief queen of Piye and daughter of his uncle and predecessor Alara, preserves the only historical inscription found at the royal necropolis of El Kurru north of Gebel Barkal. Recovered from the queen's tumulus (El Kurru tomb 53), the unusual ovoid stela resembles the base of a large scarab and measures approximately 18.5 cm at its greatest height and 12.5 cm at its greatest width. The upper field of the stela depicts Tabiry in Nubian dress standing before an altar and adoring the enthroned Osiris, who is followed by Isis.

The primary interest of the stela consists of the filiation and titles of Tabiry, one of five wives associated with Piye. Tabiry's epithet "the great one of the foreigners" (ḫ3s.tyw with female determinative) led Reisner to postulate Libyan ethnicity for the queen and dynasty. A Libyan origin of Dynasty XXV now seems unlikely, but the queen's title is unusual. Piye's Gebel Barkal Stela 26 does equate the term "ruler of foreign land(s)" (ḥq3 n ḫ3s.t) with Libyan chiefs, so that some link (biological or political) between the queen and northern Libyans is possible. If correctly understood, the concluding lines of the text record a unique declaration by the queen, who takes responsibility for the misdeeds of her life. Such an admission is uncharacteristic of Egyptian funerary texts and may reflect the "hyper-religiosity" of Piye's court, otherwise evident in the king's great "Victory Stela."

For the text and discussion, see Dunham 1950, 87, 90 fig. 29f, and pl. 30A; Eide et al. 1994, 119–20; Reisner 1921, 27–28; Macadam 1949, 121–23; and Dunham and Macadam 1949, 147 no. 72. See Kitchen 1986, 149 §120 n. 282.

LABEL FOR OSIRIS
     Wsỉr   Osiris

LABEL FOR ISIS
     Ꜣs.t dỉ ꜥnḫ
     Isis, who gives life.

LABEL FOR TABIRY
     ḥm.t ny-sw.t TꜢb(2)ỉry[1]
     Queen Tab(2)iry.[1]

MAIN TEXT
     (1) ḥtp dỉ ny-sw.t n Wsỉr Ḫnty ʾImnt.t nṯr ꜥꜢ (2) nb Ꜣbdw dỉ∸f t ḥnq.t snṯr ꜥntyw (3) n ḥm.t ny-sw.t ꜥꜢ.t sꜢ.t ʾIrrꜢ sꜢ.t n (4) KꜢsq.t ḥm.t ny-sw.t ꜥꜢ.t tp.t n ḥm∸f Py dỉ ꜥnḫ (5) TꜢ-bỉry tꜢ ꜥꜢ.t ḫꜢs.tyw W(6)dꜢ∸s …[2] rn m-sꜢ mr s(y) Py (7) Wsỉr ḥm.t ny-sw.t TꜢ-bỉry mry (8) ỉnk mrỉ ỉt∸(ỉ) nꜢ ỉry∸ỉ (m) mn.t[3] (9) n hrw.(w) ỉpn nꜢ ỉry∸ỉ
     (1) An offering that the king gives to Osiris, Foremost of the West, the great god, (2) Lord of Abydos, so that he might give bread, beer, incense, and myrrh (3) to the great royal wife, daughter of Alara and daughter of (4) Kasaqa, the chief great royal wife of his Majesty Piye, given life, (5) Tabiry, the great one of (female) foreigners, with We(6)djas ….[2] being (her) name after Piye fell in love with her. (7) The Osiris and royal wife Tabiry, the beloved. (8) "I am beloved of (my) father. Those things that I have done wrong[3] (9) in these days (of my life) are what I have done."

NOTES
     1. The name may correspond to the Demotic TꜢ-ble.t, "The blind one." Macadam sought to link the queen's name (bỉry) with Demotic writings of the tribal name "Blemmye" (Blḫ-mwt).
     2. A semicursive group unrecognized by the textual editor.
     3. For the unusual final remark, cf. the idiom ỉr mn.t "to do wrong" (Erman and Grapow 1926–63, 2:67/13).

D. SHABAKO

148. VICTORY SCARAB OF SHABAKO
(ROM 910.28.1)

The underside of this large glazed steatite scarab (9 cm x 6.8 cm) is provided with nine lines of text commemorating the Nubian king's victories over rebels in Egypt, the deserts, and foreign lands. Like earlier examples from the reign of Amonhotep III, such scarabs were the equivalent of official medals, presented by the king to select officials and courtiers. First noted in Syria, the scarab was acquired in Jerusalem in May 1910 by the Royal Ontario Museum, Toronto, with the registration number 1718.

For the text, translation, and discussion, see Maspero 1906, 142; Müller 1914, 49–52; Alt 1915, 43–45; and Eide et al. 1994, 123–25. Suggestions of forgery raised by Maspero and Alt were disproved by Yoyotte 1956, 457–76; 1958c, 206–10. See Kitchen 1986, 379 §340.

(1) [ʿnḫ Ḥr] sbq¹ t3.wy Ḥr-nbw sbq t3.wy (2) ny-sw.t bỉ.ty Nfr-k3-Rʿ s3 Rʿ Š3b3k3 dỉ ʿnḫ (3) mry ʾImn r ny-sw.t nb{.t} ḫpr{.t} ḏr (4) w3ḥ²
t3 sm3.n≠f³ sb(ỉ).w r≠f m Šmʿw Mḥw (5) m ḫ3s.t nb(.t) ḫry.w šʿy.w bdš(6).w r≠f ḫr n š≠f ỉy(7)≠sn ḏs≠sn m sq(ỉ).w-ʿnḫ n(8)ḏr.n wʿ snw≠f ỉm≠sn ḫr ỉr(.t) n≠f⁴ (9) 3ḫ.t n.t ỉt≠f n ʿ3 n mr≠f sw

(1) [Long live the Horus:] "He who blesses² the Two Lands," the Golden Horus, "He who blesses the Two Lands," (2) the King of Upper and Lower Egypt, Neferkare, Son of Re, Shabako, given life, (3) whom Amon loves more than any king who has existed since the establishment of (4) the earth.²

He has slain³ those who rebelled against him in Upper Egypt and Lower Egypt (5) and in every foreign land, while the sand-dwelling Bedouin who (6) revolted against him are fallen to his slaughter. (7) They themselves come as prisoners because (8) each has seized his fellow among them, enacting for him (Shabako)⁴ (9) the benefaction of his father through the greatness of his love for him.

NOTES
1. Reading sb3q "to illuminate, bless" (Erman and Grapow 1926–63, 4:86–87). See Grimal 1986, 320 n. 1033.
2. For wḥʿ t3, see Erman and Grapow 1926–63, 1:349/11; see Yoyotte 1958c, 206–10.
3. Emphatic form stressing "in Upper Egypt and Lower Egypt," etc.
4. Or, as Müller and Kitchen: "for he (the king) had performed (ỉr.n≠f) benefactions for his father...."

149. DONATION STELA OF BAKENATUM
(MMA 55.144.6)

The defeat of Bocchoris by Shabako and the Nubian ruler's temporary control of the Saite region is well-illustrated by this donation stela acknowledging his authority in Buto and dated four years after his capture of Memphis. Political circumstances may be responsible for the suppression of any titles associated with the donor Bakenatum, and the absence of any later stelae dated to Shabako suggests that his control of the west Delta was brief, succeeded by the rule of the Saite king Tefnakht II. The round-topped stela is .35 m. in height and depicts Shabako wearing the double crown and offering the hieroglyph for fields to the carved name of Ptah and the following standing figures of Horus and Edjo, patrons of Buto. The lunette texts are in hieroglyphs, while the main text comprises six lines of hieratic.

For the text, translation, and discussion, see Brugsch 1896, 83–84; Hornung 1999, 135 fig. 48 (photo); Sottas 1913, 154; Gomaà 1974, 59 n. 52; and Meeks 1979a, 616, 618, 634, 644, and 673 (no. 25.4.6). See Kitchen 1986, 379 §340.

LABEL FOR (UNDEPICTED) PTAH
Ptḥ dỉ ꜥnḫ
Ptah who gives life.

LABEL FOR HORUS
Ḥr n P dỉ ꜥnḫ
Horus of Pe who gives life.

LABEL FOR EDJO
Wꜣḏy.t   Edjo.

LABEL FOR KING
Šꜣbꜣkꜣ (2) dỉ ꜥnḫ
Shabako, given life.

MAIN TEXT
(1) ḥsb.t 6.(t) ḫr ḥm n ny-sw.t bỉ.ty Nfr-kꜣ-Rꜥ sꜣ Rꜥ Šꜣbꜣkꜣ ꜥnḫ wḏꜣ [snb]¹ (2) hrw pn ḥnq ꜣḥ.t stꜣ.t 20 ỉ-ỉr Bꜣk-n-Tm (3) p(ꜣ)-nꜣ Ḥtp-Bꜣst.t n Pꜣ-rwrwsꜣ p(ꜣ)-nꜣ Pꜣy≠f-tꜣw-ꜥ.wy(4)-Ḥr ỉw≠w mn r nḥḥ ḏ.t pꜣ nty-ỉw≠f (r) (5) th(ỉ) pꜣy ꜣḥ.t ỉw≠f r šꜥ.(t) n.(t) ny-sw.t ỉw≠f sḫ[r] n [tꜣ] (6) nm.t n Sḫm.t

(1) Regnal year 6 under the Majesty of the King of Upper and Lower Egypt, Neferkare, Son of Re, Shabako, l.p.[h.].¹ (2) On this day: a donation of 20 *arouras* of field that was made by Bakenatum, (3) son of² Hetep-

bastet, for Parurusa, son of[2] Peftchauaui(4)hor, they being established forever and ever. The one who will transgress this field, he is destined to the slaughter of the king, being struck down upon [the] (6) slaughter block of Sakhmet.

NOTES

1. Brugsch read W₃ḏy.t [mrỉ] "beloved of Edjo."

2. For the possessive prefix used to indicate filiation, see The Donation Stela of Washtihat (OIM 10511) and The Donation Stela of the Libu Chief Titaru (Brooklyn Museum 67.119), pp. 384–85 and 408 above.

150. KARNAK RESTORATION INSCRIPTION

On the Fourth Pylon at Karnak (west face of the north tower), Shabako recorded his restoration of this great gateway of Tuthmosis IV, explicitly funded by plunder from his reconquest of the north. Shabako's text was itself restored under Alexander or the subsequent Ptolemies.

For the text, photo, and translation, see Leclant 1951, 104–13; Breasted 1906–7, 4:454 §889; and Barguet 1962, 90 and 310. See Kitchen 1986, 379–80 §340.

[Ḥr sbq t₃.wy ... Š₃b₃k₃ ... ỉr.n≠f n mnw≠f n ỉt≠f] ʾImn-Rˁ nb ns.wt t₃.wy ẖnty ʾIp.t-s.wt sm₃wy sb₃ ˁ₃ šps ʾImn-Rˁ sẖm šfy.t ỉr.t n≠f mk.t ˁ₃.t m nbw-nfr ỉn.n ḥm n ny-sw.t bỉ.ty Nfr-k₃-Rˁ s₃ Rˁ Š₃b₃k₃ mry-ʾImn ˁnẖ ḏ.t m nẖt.wt wḏ.t.n ỉt≠f ʾImn hy.t ˁ₃.t mk.tw m nbw nfr wẖ₃.wy b₃k m ḏˁmw spr. wy ẖr(y).w m ḥḏ wˁb ỉr≠f dỉ ˁnẖ mỉ Rˁ ḏ.t

[The Horus: "He who blesses the Two Lands," ... Shabako, ... He made as a monument for his father] Amon-Re, Lord of the Thrones of the Two Lands, Foremost of Karnak, the restoration of the great and noble gateway "Amon is Powerful of Respect," making for it a great protective overlay in fine gold that the Majesty of the King of Upper and Lower Egypt, Neferkare, Son of Re, Shabako, beloved of Amon, living forever, had brought away in victories that his father Amon-Re had ordained, and a great portico overlaid in fine gold with two columns[1] worked in electrum and two supporting bases in pure silver, so that he might attain the state of being given life like Re forever.

NOTE

1. The portico before the Fourth Pylon had two columns plated with electrum and silver; see Leclant 1951, 112.

151. NINEVEH CLAY STAMP SEALS
(BRITISH MUSEUM 51–9–2,43 AND 81–2–4,352)

Two fragmentary clay sealings, excavated by Austen Layard at Nineveh (Kuyunjik), bear dual impressions of Assyrian and Egyptian seals once attached to documents of a presumably diplomatic nature. The lost documents have been surmised to have been copies of a treaty concluded between Shabako and either Sennacherib or Sargon II of Assyria. If Sargon II, the documents could be linked to events of 712 B.C.E. and the extradition of the fugitive Iamani of Ashdod from Egypt to Assyria, effected during the following reign of Shebitku. The Egyptian seal is certainly royal and bears the image of Shabako in the canonical posture of a king smiting his enemies. Wearing the Red Crown of Lower Egypt, Shabako raises a mace above the lost figure of an enemy. A missing divine figure, or perhaps the scarab image of the seal itself,[1] rewards the king's gesture. One Egyptian seal measures 1 inch square and the other 1.25 inch by .75 inch.

For the texts, translation, and discussion, see Hall 1913, 290 §§2775 and 2776 (nos. 84884 and 84527); Gauthier 1916, 17 §XVII; Budge 1974, 249–50 (BM 51–9–2,43 and 81–2–4,352); Newberry 1905, 187 and pl. XXXVIII, no. 7; Bezold 1889–99, 4:1784; Layard 1853, 156–59. See Kitchen 1986, 144 §115, 380 §341, and 583–84 §527 (with chronological revisions in Frame, 1999, 40 and 52–54).

LABEL FOR THE DEITY
dỉ.n≠(ỉ) n≠k [ḫ3s.wt nb.w(t)][2]
"I have given to you [all foreign countries.]"[2]

LABEL FOR THE KING

nṯr nfr Š3b3k3 (2) nb ỉr.(t) (3) ḥ.t (4) s3 ꜥnḫ ḥ3≠f
The Good God, Shabako, (2) the Lord of ritual (3) performance. (4) The protection of life is around him.

BM 51-9-2, 43 after Hall 1913, 290.

NOTES
1. There is little room for a deity; cf. Hodjash and Berlev 1994, 131.
2. Restoration following Budge 1893, 249.

152. KAWA TEMPLE B INSCRIPTION

Aside from the royal tomb at El Kurru, what scant evidence exists for Nubian construction under Shabako is limited to nine column drums reused in Temple B at Kawa. Reassembled and plastered as column 4 of this temple in the reign of the Meroitic ruler Harsiotef, the drums originally formed portions of two columns at the site. Each original column (A and B) bore two sets of an identical inscription, staggered at different heights.

For the texts, translations, and discussion, see Macadam 1955, 46–48. See Kitchen 1986, 382 §344.

COMPOSITE TEXT BASED ON COLUMN A, SUPPLEMENTED BY B

[ny-sw.t bỉ.ty] Nfr-k3-[Rᶜ] s3 Rᶜ Š3b3k3 ỉr.n≠f m mnw≠f n mw.t≠f ᶜnq. t ỉr≠f dỉ ᶜnḫ [d.t]

[The King of Upper and Lower Egypt], Neferka[re], Son of Re, Shabako. For his mother Anunkis he made (it) as his monument, so that he might attain the state of being given life [forever].

E. SHEBITKU

153. MEMPHIS STATUE
(CAIRO CG 655)

The rare monuments of Shebitku include two works recovered from Memphis: a seated statue of the king, now fragmentary and headless; and an unpublished block from an otherwise lost structure. The black granite statue, 1.32 m. in height, was found near the south gate of the great temple of Ptah. On the rear of the throne, the king's *serekh* is flanked by Thoth and Horus above a scene of enemies bound to the hieroglyph for "unification."

For the texts and discussion, see Gauthier 1916, 29–30 §III; Borchardt 1911–36, 3:2 and pl. 121; and Porter and Moss 1981, 837 (statue) and 839 (block). See Kitchen 1986, 386 §347.

BELT

Š3b3t3k3 mrỉ-Ptḥ

Shebitku, beloved of Ptah.

FRONT, LEFT OF THRONE

Ḥr dd ḫᶜ.w ny-sw.t bỉ.ty Š3b3t3k3 mry Ptḥ ᶜnḫ d.t

The Horus: "Enduring of Epiphanies"; the King of Upper and Lower Egypt, Shebitku, beloved of Ptah, living forever.

LEFT SIDE OF THRONE

Ḥr dd ḫᶜ.w (2) ny-sw.t bỉ.ty Š3b3t3k3 (3) w3s ᶜnḫ nb (4) [...] t3.w [nb] (5) ḫ3s.t nb.t r (6) ntr nfr pn

The Horus: "Enduring of Epiphanies"; (2) the King of Upper and

Lower Egypt, Shebitku, (3) (to whom be) all dominion and life. (4) [... all] lands (5) and every foreign country to (6) this Good God.

REAR OF THRONE

Label for Thoth
    nb Ḥmnw
    The Lord of Hermopolis.

Label for Horus
    Bḥd.t[y]   The Behdedite.

Royal Titles
    Ḥr ḏd ḫꜥ.w (2) Šꜣbꜣtꜣkꜣ
    The Horus: "Enduring of Epiphanies"; (2) Shebitku.

Bound Prisoners
    rḫy.t ḫꜣ[.w](2)-nb.wt[1]
    The plebeians and inhabitants of the isles.[1]

NOTE
    1. For the shifting identification of this geographic term, see Uphill 1965–66, 393–420.

154. KARNAK CHAPEL
(BERLIN 1480)

Shebitku's chapel for Amon by the sacred lake at Karnak is now destroyed except for a doorway in Berlin and an isolated block in New Haven (Yale 14.1949). In most instances, the royal name in the cartouche has been roughly erased, leaving only the words "Re" and "beloved of Amon." On the exterior lintel of the Berlin door are addorsed scenes of seated Amon offering life and dominion to the king's *serekh,* while two registers of fecundity figures bring offerings toward the portal. Restating rather than merely illustrating the text, the attendant representations exemplify the symbiotic relationship between pictographic text and vignette that is uniquely Egyptian. The royal *serekh* establishes Shebitku as the patron of the monument, in return for which Amon grants life and dominion and to which he sends his divine emissaries of fertility.

    For the texts and discussion, see Lepsius 1849–59, 5:pls. 3–4; Sethe 1900, 40–42; Gauthier 1916, 29 §II; Leclant 1965, 59–61 §16 and pls. 36–37; Porter and Moss 1972, 223 §T. See Kitchen 1986, 383 §345 (mislabeled "Osiris-chapel") and 386 §347.

EXTERIOR, LINTEL

Label for Amon

ʾImn(2)-Rᶜ nb ns.(w)t t3.wy nṯr ᶜ3 nb p.t

Amon(2)-Re, Lord of the Thrones of the Two Lands, the great god, Lord of heaven.

The Royal *Serekh*

Ḥr ḏd ḫᶜ.(w)

The Horus: "Enduring of Epiphanies"

Label for Righthand Field Goddess

ḏd-mdw în.n≠(î) n≠k (2) {ḏd-mdw} ḥw nb (3) îmy T3-Mḥw

Recitation: "Thus I have brought to you (2) all food (3) that is in Lower Egypt."

Label for Lefthand Field Goddess

ḏd-mdw în.n≠(î) n≠k (2) {ḏd-mdw} ḫ.t nb.t nfr.t ḫr≠î (3) Npr(î)

Recitation: "Thus I have brought to you (2) everything good issuing from me (3) and Nepri (the grain deity)."

EXTERIOR, RIGHT SIDE

ḏd-mdw nṯr nfr Ḏd-k3.w-Rᶜ îr.n≠(î) mḥ.t pr≠î m ḥtp.w ḏf3.w (n)-mr(w.t) nfr nw sb3.w n.w îr.(t) n≠(î) ḫ.t-nṯr dî.n≠(î) n≠k ᶜnḫ ḏ.t

(2) ḏd-mdw ʾImn-Rᶜ ḫnt(y) ʾIp.t-s.wt sᶜš3.n≠(î) n≠k ny-sw.t bî.ty Š3b3t3k3 mrî-ʾImn ᶜnḫ ḏ.t tnw n.w ᶜ.wt m t (n) šnᶜ ḥr wr n ḥtp.w-nṯr

Recitation: "O Good God, Djedkaure, I have filled my house with offerings and foodstuffs through the desire that these doorways of enacting ritual for me might be good. I have given to you life forever."

(2) Recitation: "O Amon-Re, Foremost of Karnak, the King of Upper and Lower Egypt, Shebitku, beloved of Amon, living forever, has multiplied for you the number of chambers with bread of the storehouse in consideration of the quantity of divine offerings."

EXTERIOR, LEFT SIDE

ḏd-mdw ny-sw.t bî.ty Ḏd-k3.w-Rᶜ s3≠î îrr ḥss.t≠î rḫ mrr.t≠(î) dî.n≠(î) n≠k ᶜnḫ ḏd w3s nb snb nb Š3b3t3k3 dî ᶜnḫ

(2) ḏd-mdw ʾImn-Rᶜ nb ns.(w)t t3.wy [îr n]≠k s3≠k Š3b3t3k3 mrî-ʾImn dî ᶜnḫ mnw pn nfr wᶜb n-mr(w.t) îr≠f (n)≠k ḥtp.w-nṯr îmn(y).t n.t rᶜ nb mî ᶜš3≠s

Recitation: "O King of Upper and Lower Egypt, Djedkaure, my son, who does what I praise and who knows what I desire, I have given to you all life, stability, and dominion, and all health, O Shebitku, given life."

(2) Recitation: "O Amon-Re, Lord of the Thrones of the Two Lands, your son Shebitku, beloved of Amon, given life, [has made for] you this beautiful, pure monument through the desire that he might make for you divine offerings and the daily offering of each day, as numerous as it may be."

INTERIOR, RIGHT SIDE

ꜥnḫ Ḥr ḏd ḫꜥ.w ny-sw.t bỉ.ty Ḏd-kꜣ.w-Rꜥ mry ꜣImn (2) ꜥnḫ sꜣ Rꜥ mꜣꜥ ḫꜥ ḥr ns.t≠f Šꜣbꜣtꜣkꜣ mrỉ-ꜣImn dỉ ꜥnḫ ḏ.t (3) Nb.ty sḫꜥ mꜣꜥ.t mry tꜣ.wy ny-sw.t bỉ.ty Ḏd-kꜣ.w-Rꜥ mry ꜣImn-Rꜥ nb ns.(w)t tꜣ.wy dỉ ꜥnḫ nb ḏ.t (4) Ḥr-nbw ḥr(w) ḥr nḫt sꜣ Rꜥ Šꜣbꜣtꜣkꜣ mrỉ-ꜣImn-Rꜥ nb ns.(w)t tꜣ.wy dỉ ꜥnḫ nb ḏ.t

Long live the Horus: "Enduring of Epiphanies"; the King of Upper and Lower Egypt, Djedkaure, beloved of Amon. (2) Long live the true Son of Re, appearing in glory upon his throne, Shebitku, beloved of Amon, given life forever. (3) The Two Ladies: "He who causes Maat to appear, Beloved of the Two Lands"; the King of Upper and Lower Egypt, Djedkaure, beloved of Amon-Re, Lord of the Thrones of the Two Lands, given all life forever. (4) The Horus of Gold: "He who is pleased by victory"; the Son of Re, Shebitku, beloved of Amon-Re, Lord of the Thrones of the Two Lands, given all life forever.

INTERIOR, LEFT SIDE

ꜥnḫ Ḥr ḏd ḫꜥ.w ny-sw.t bỉ.ty Ḏd-kꜣ.w-Rꜥ mry ꜣImn (2) ꜥnḫ sꜣ Rꜥ mꜣꜥ ḫꜥ ḥr ns.t≠f Šꜣbꜣtꜣkꜣ mrỉ-ꜣImn dỉ ꜥnḫ ḏ.t (3) Nb.ty ꜥꜣ šf.t m tꜣ.w nb ny-sw.t bỉ.ty Ḏd-kꜣ.w-Rꜥ mry ꜣImn-Rꜥ nb ns.(w)t tꜣ.wy dỉ ꜥnḫ nb ḏ.t (4) Ḥr-nbw ꜥꜣ ḫpš ḫ[wỉ] pḏ.t [ps]ḏ.t sꜣ Rꜥ Šꜣbꜣtꜣkꜣ mrỉ-ꜣImn-Rꜥ nb ns.(w)t tꜣ.wy dỉ ꜥnḫ nb ḏ.t

Long live the Horus: "Enduring of Epiphanies"; the King of Upper and Lower Egypt, Djedkaure, beloved of Amon. (2) Long live the true Son of Re, appearing in glory upon his throne, Shebitku, beloved of Amon, given life forever. (3) The Two Ladies: "He whose Respect is Great in All Lands"; the King of Upper and Lower Egypt, Djedkaure, beloved of Amon-Re, Lord of the Thrones of the Two Lands, given all life forever. (4) The Horus of Gold: "He whose Strength is Great, who Smites the Nine Bows"; the Son of Re, Shebitku, beloved of Amon-Re, Lord of the Thrones of the Two Lands, given all life forever.

EAST WALL (DESTROYED)

The King offers a bouquet to Amon and Khonsu.

Label for Nekhbet as a Protective Vulture

Nḫb.t [P.t Dp.t nb.t p.t ḥnw.t Pr-wr]

Nekhbet, [she of Pe and Dep, Lady of heaven, Mistress of the Upper Egyptian shrine at el-Kab.]

Label for Amon

ḏd-mdw în ʾImn-Rᶜ ny-sw.t nṯr.w nb p.t ḥr(y)-tp psḏ.t ᶜȝ.t (2) sȝ≠(î) n ḫ.t≠(î) mry≠(î) Šȝbȝtȝkȝ mrî-ʾImn dî ᶜnḫ ḏ.t (3) dî.n≠(î) n≠k ᶜnḫ ḏd wȝs r fnd≠k pw (4) [...] mrr [...] ᶜnḫ≠f ḏ.t (5) dî.n≠(î) [n≠k] ḥb.w ᶜšȝ

Recitation by Amon-Re, King of the Gods, Lord of heaven, Chief of the Great Ennead: (2) "O my bodily son, my beloved, Shebitku, beloved of Amon, given life forever. (3) Thus I have given to you all life, stability, and dominion to this nose of yours. (4) [...] love [...] that he might live forever. (5) Thus I have given [to you] many jubilees."

Label for Khonsu

ḏd-mdw în Ḥnsw m Wȝs.t Nfr-ḥtp (2) sȝ≠(î) n ḫ.t≠(î) mry≠(î) ny-sw.t bî.ty Šȝbȝtȝkȝ mrî-ʾImn dî.n≠(î) n≠k (3) ny.t-sw.t tȝ.wy m îsw mnw [p]n nfr îr.n≠k n≠(î) (4) dî.n≠(î) n≠k ᶜḥᶜ(w) n Rᶜ m p.t

Recitation by Khonsu in Thebes, Neferhotep: (2) "O my bodily son, my beloved, King of Upper and Lower Egypt, Shebitku, beloved of Amon, thus I have given to you (3) kingship of the Two Lands in exchange for this beautiful monument that you have made for me. (4) Thus I have given to you the lifetime of Re in heaven."

Label for the King

ny-sw.t bî.ty Ḏd-kȝ.w-Rᶜ (2) sȝ Rᶜ Šȝbȝtȝkȝ mrî-ʾImn (3) dî ᶜnḫ ḏ.t (4) nb ȝw.t-îb ḥqȝ Wȝs.t (5) ît(î) tȝ.wy m mȝᶜ ḫrw

The King of Upper and Lower Egypt, Djedkaure, the Son of Re, Shebitku, beloved of Amon, given life forever, the possessor of joy, the ruler of Thebes, (5) who has seized the Two Lands in justification.

WEST WALL (BERLIN 1480)

The King offers bread to Amon and Mut.

Label for Edjo as a Protective Vulture

Wȝḏy.t P.t Dp.t nb.t p.t ḥnw.t Pr-nw

Edjo, she of Pe and Dep, Lady of heaven, Mistress of the Lower Egyptian shrine at Dep.

Label for Amon

ḏd-mdw în ʾImn-Rᶜ nb ns.(w)t tȝ.wy sȝ≠(î) n ḫ.t≠(î) mry≠(î) ny-sw.t bî.ty Šȝbȝtȝkȝ mrî-ʾImn (2) bnr.wy mrw.t≠k ḫr≠î îb≠(î) ḫᶜ[ᶜ ...] îr n≠(î) nfr.[w] (3) ḥʿ.(w) ḥr ns.t Tm mỉ Rʿ ḏ.t (4) dỉ.n≥(ỉ) n≥k t3.w nb m [ksw(?)] ḥ3s.t nb ḥr ṯbw.ty≥k

Recitation by Amon-Re, Lord of the Thrones of the Two Lands: "O my bodily son, my beloved, King of Upper and Lower Egypt, Shebitku, beloved of Amon, (2) how sweet is the love of you issuing from me, while my heart rejoices [over] the one who has done good things for me, (3) appearing in glory on the throne of Atum like Re forever! (4) Thus I have given to you all lands in [bowing (?)], with all foreign countries beneath your sandals."

Label for Mut

ḏd-mdw ỉn Mw.t wr.(t) ʾỈšr(w) (2) s3≥(ỉ) n ḥ.t≥(ỉ) mry≥(ỉ) Š3b3t3k3 mrỉ-ʾỈmn (3) mḥn≥k mỉ Nb-r-ḏr (4) dỉ≥ỉ nr≥k [m] ḥ3s.wt rsy.t mḥ.tyw ḥr [snḏ(?)≥k]

Recitation by Mut, the great one of Asheru. (2) "O my bodily son, my beloved, Shebitku, beloved of Amon, (3) your coiled uraeus is like that of the Lord of the Universe. (4) I have placed terror of you [in] the southern foreign countries, while the northern ones possess [fear (?) of you]."

Label for the King

ny-sw.t bỉ.ty Ḏd-k3.w-Rʿ (2) s3 Rʿ Š3b3t3k3 mrỉ-ʾỈmn (3) dỉ ʿnḫ ḏ.t (4) nb 3w.t-ỉb ḥq3 W3s.t (5) ỉt(ỉ) t3.wy m m3ʿ ḫrw (6) sq(r) t ḥḏ n ỉt≥f ʾỈmn-Rʿ ỉr≥f dỉ ʿnḫ

The King of Upper and Lower Egypt, Djedkaure, the Son of Re, Shebitku, beloved of Amon, given life forever, the possessor of joy, the ruler of Thebes, (5) who has seized the Two Lands in justification. (6) Consecrating white bread for his father Amon-Re, so that he might attain the state of being given life.

F. TAHARQA

155. KARNAK SANCTUARY BLOCKS

The fragmentary reliefs and texts are carved on *in situ* and dismantled blocks from the south wall of the North Peristyle Court (VI), northwest of the bark sanctuary of Philip Arrhidaeus. For the location, see Porter and Moss 1972, 92 (264) and pl. XI (264). Three representations depict Taharqa in the act of offering; the figure on §B is surcharged over an exemption decree of Osorkon II (see above, pp. 288–90). Conflation of §J2 with the adjoining §J1 led to erroneous suggestions of a Nubian campaign by Sheshonq I (above, text 49). The three texts comprise a grand hymn, paralleled in the papyrus and tablet of Neskhons (Cairo 58032 and 46891) and in the papyrus of Pinedjem (Cairo 58033), followed by two prayers promising offerings to the god Amon. The texts are composed in Late Egyptian. In the initial hymn, Taharqa requests protection from Amon against unspecified troubles, spells, and afflictions of the Evil Eye. The phraseology recalls that of contemporary "Oracular Amuletic Decrees" and later "Self-Dedications" designed for commoners, in which the suppliant declares himself a servant of the god in exchange for divine protection (see lines 14 and 17–18). Taharqa's deference to Amon is explicit, for the god alone is both king-maker, selecting an unknown candidate from among his territories (line 4), and uncommanded commander (19) whose every wish is incumbent upon the monarch (20).

Texts, translation, and discussion are found in Vernus 1975, 1–66, esp. 1–12 and 26–59; and Eide et al. 1994, 181–90; with an older copy in Müller 1910, 143–53. Obsolete translation and discussion (as Sheshonq I text) appear in Kitchen 1986, 293 §251 and 302 §260 (see 558 §471 and 575 §509); and Breasted 1906–7, 4:357–58 §§723–24. Chicago Oriental Institute photos 5206, 5209, 6164, 8580–81, and 8741–42.

I. Taharqa Consecrates Offerings to Amon-Re
The king stands before sections of three slaughtered bulls and registers of vegetables, wine, bread, and fowl (Vernus 1975, 2–5 and pl. III; Müller 1910, 144 fig. 49 Ac and pl. 43).

Label for Scene
 rdỉ.t ꜥꜣb.t n ỉt≠f ᵓImn-Rꜥ nb ns.wt tꜣ.wy [ỉr]≠f [dỉ ꜥnḫ]
 Giving an oblation to his father Amon-Re, Lord of the Thrones of the Two Lands, [so that] he [might attain the state of being given life].

Behind King
 [sꜣ ꜥnḫ ḏd wꜣs nb ḥꜣ≠f(?)] nb
 [The protection of all life, stability, and dominion is] all [around him (?)].

Label for Cattle
 [n]g(ꜣ)
 [Lo]ng-horned oxen.

Amon Hymn from the Eastern Edge of the South Wall (§§C and J2)
 (1) [... nṯr pn šps nb nṯr.w nb.w ᵓImn-Rꜥ nb ns.wt tꜣ.wy ḫnlty ᵓIp.t-s.wt bꜣ šps wbn m ḥr(y).t [št³ ms].w ꜥšꜣ ḫpr.w n rḫ.tw bs≠f ỉr p.t twꜣ s(y) n bꜣ≠f ḥnp tꜣ.wy [m] rn≠f sḫm šps mry.ty šfy.ty wsr [m ḫ]ꜥꜥ[.w≠f nb fꜣw] sḫm ḫpr ḫpr ḫpr.w nb m ḫpr≠f ỉtn wr ḥꜣy
 (2) [psḏ.t dỉ≠f sw ꜥnḫ ḥr nb ḏꜣy ḥr(y)].t n wrd.[n]≠f dwꜣ.ty sp-2 n.t-ꜥ≠f

mn nḫḫ wr îty ꜥnḫ m mꜣꜥ.t wr wr.w ꜥꜣ n ꜥꜣ.w wr sw r nṯr.w îw wsr≠f în
[pḥ.wy ḏ].t wr (n) šꜣꜥ (n) ḫpr ît tꜣ.wy m nḫt.w≠f nḫḫ sb

(3)[b ḏ.t ît ît.w] mw.t mw.wt stn(î) sw r psḏ.t bîꜣy.ty sr îy.t b(w)-ḫpr.
t kꜣ.t[≠f pw(?)]¹ nḫḫ ḏ.t ny-sw.t bî.ty ꜣImn-Rꜥ nb ns.wt tꜣ.wy nb p.t tꜣ mw
dw.w ḫ[r]≠f n sꜣ≠k mr≠k ny-sw.t bî.ty [Ḥw-Nfr-tm-Rꜥ]² sꜣ Rꜥ [Thrq]² [mrî]
ꜣImn-Rꜥ nb ns.wt tꜣ.wy [...] î[wꜥ] n Šmꜥw Mḥw dî ꜥnḫ nb ḏd wꜣs nb snb
nb ꜣw.(t)-îb nb.(t) mî Rꜥ ḏ.t

(4) [...] md.t mî ꜥꜣ≠s dî≠k n≠î Šmꜥw Mḥw stp≠k wî (m)-ḫnw[≠sn
dî]≠k ḏd≠w tꜣ.wy≠î îs î-îr ꜣImn îr Pr-ꜥꜣ n p(ꜣ) nt(y) mr≠f sw dî≠k gm≠î
s(y) ḏd p(ꜣ) dî≠k ꜥq≠f p[(ꜣy) ...] rmṯ.w î-wn b(w)-rḫ≠w s(y) ḥr≠î î

(5) [ꜣImn ...] î p(ꜣ) nt(y) b(w)-îr≠f ḫꜣꜥ tꜣ îr≠f îw≠s n gs î ꜣImn m-[îr
...]≠k n-îm≠w îw≠k sḏm≠w n≠î mtw≠k [...]

(6) [... bî]n.t m-îr dî ꜥq≠î r md.t îw msd≠k s(y) p[... wꜣ].t(?)≠î m-îr
dî îr≠î p(ꜣ) nt(y) ms[d≠k s(y) ...]

(7) [...] m-dî≠kꜣ ḥr îrm≠(î)⁴ înk (r)-ntt înk p(ꜣy)≠k šr îw ntk î-[wtt(?)
ḫp]r nb⁵ mn nkt îw [...]

(8) [...] ḫnw n ꜣImn nꜣy sr≠k n≠î nn îw b(w)-îr.t≠k⁶ dî ḫꜥ≠î m [ny-
sw.t ...]

(9) [...] n⁷ Ḥꜥp(y) ꜥꜣ n p(ꜣ)y≠î hꜣw îꜣw n≠î tꜣ p.t îw≠s n ꜥdⁿ îw≠s ꜥšꜣ
[n ḥw(?)⁹...]

(10) [... tꜣ.w(?) îw b]n înk sw îw-nꜣ my s.t ḥr≠î dr≠w îw [...]

(11) [...] r≠î¹⁰ î-nw r≠f ...[...] r [ꜣI]mn¹¹ ntf p(ꜣ) îr nfr [...]

(12) [... n]ḥm wî r šnw nḥm wî r md.t îr.t¹² bîn.t nb my ḏd≠w r[≠î
...]

(13) [...] t hnq.t kꜣ.w ꜣpd.w îw ḫꜣty≠î nḏm my fꜣî≠î n≠k nkt nb n p(ꜣ)
nt(y) p(ꜣy)[≠î(?)] îry(?)¹⁰ [...]

(14) [...] mr îr p(ꜣ) nt(y) b(w)-p(w) Pr-ꜥꜣ nb îr≠f îw≠î m-dî≠k n bꜣk
îw≠k šnꜥ n≠(î) nꜣ [...]

(15) [...] mn p(ꜣ) nt(y)-îw≠f ꜥmḏ≠w î ꜣImn p(ꜣ) îr≠î n pꜣ tꜣ Nḥs(y)
î-dî[≠k(?)]

(16) [n≠î ... ꜣ]ḫw(?) my îr≠î sw n p(ꜣy)≠k înw n p(ꜣ) tꜣ Ḫꜣr î-ꜥmḏ≠w
r-r≠k î ꜣIm[n]

(17) [... nꜣ]ly≠î ḥm.wt my ꜥnḫ nꜣ(y)≠î ḥrd.w ꜥmḏ n≠î pꜣ mwt r≠w nḥm
wî r rꜣ¹³ [...]

(18) [...] n rꜣ≠w¹³ mtw≠k pnꜥ≠w r ḏꜣḏꜣ≠w ḫꜥ.w≠w ḥr(y) îr dî ꜥnḫ
p(ꜣy)≠f bꜣk în [...]

(19) [...] îw nb sp-2 î ꜣImn mn p(ꜣ) nt(y)-îw≠f wꜣḥ n≠k sḥn ntk p(ꜣ)
nt(y) wꜣḥ

(20) [sḥn ...] îw¹⁴ p(ꜣ) nt(y)-îw≠k ḏd n≠î m-šm n-îm≠k sp-2 îw≠î šm
m [t]ꜣ [ꜣt]¹⁵

(21) [...] î ꜣImn mn îr.t bîn.t¹⁶ n tꜣ md.t î-îr≠k î¹⁷ p(ꜣ) nt(y) [...]

(1) [… this noble God, Lord of all the Gods, Amon-Re, Lord of the Thrones of the Two Lands, fore]most of Karnak, noble *ba*-spirit who shines in the sky, [secret of imag]es, numerous of manifestations, whose arcane form is unknown, who made heaven, who elevated it for his *ba*-spirit, who has delimited the Two Lands [by] his name, noble power, beloved, revered, mighty [in his appear]ances, [lord of magnificence], powerful of manifestation, from whose manifestation all manifestations are manifest, the great solar disk who radiates

(2) [light, who shows himself so that everyone might live, who crosses the sky] without wearying each morning, whose custom is fixed, the great elder, the sovereign who lives on Maat, greatest of the great, grandest of the grand, greater than the gods, whose might is come having attained the [limits] of eternity, the great one since the beginning of creation, who takes possession of the Two Lands by his victories, infinite one, who

(3) traverses [eternity, father of fathers,] mother of mothers, who distinguished himself from the Ennead, oracular one, who predicts that which is coming before it has occurred, [whose] work [is][1] eternity and infinity, the King of Upper and Lower Egypt, Amon-Re, Lord of the Thrones of the Two Lands, Lord of heaven, earth, water, and mountains. He declares, namely, your son whom you love, the King of Upper and Lower Egypt, [Khunefertemre],[2] Son of Re, [Taharqa,[2] beloved of] Amon-Re, Lord of the Thrones of the Two Lands, […] the heir of Upper and Lower Egypt, given all life, all stability and dominion, all health and all joy like Re forever:

(4) "[…] a matter in accordance with its importance. You have given to me Upper and Lower Egypt. You have chosen me from within [them.] You [have caused] that they, my Two Lands, say: 'Amon makes Pharaoh precisely the one whom he desires.' You have caused me to discover that he whom you have caused to accede is […] people who had not known about me. O

(5) [Amon, …], O he who does not abandon what he has done when it is but half (finished), O Amon, do [not …] yourself with them. You will hear them for me and you will […]

(6) […] evil. Do not let me enter into a matter that you hate. […] my [path (?)]. Do not let me do that which you hate. […]

(7) […] with you.[3] Now as for me, myself,[4] I am your son, while you are the one who [begat (?)] all[5] [that has come into being]. There is nothing that […]

(8) are […] the Residence of Amon. You foretold that for me when you had not yet[6] caused that I appear as [king …]

(9) […] in[7] a great Inundation in my reign. Grant to me heaven in plenitude[8] and in an abundance [of rain (?)[9] …]

(10) [… lands (?) that] are not mine. Place them beneath me in their entirety, while […]

(11) [...] at me[10] [...] Look at him ...[...] at Amon.[11] He is the one who has done good [...]

(12) [...] Protect me against troubles. Protect me against any matter of the Evil Eye.[12] Let them say regarding [me ...]

(13) [...] bread, beer, oxen, and fowl, while my heart is happy. Let me offer up to you everything consisting of what my (?) fellow (?)[10] [...]

(14) [...] desire to do that which no pharaoh has done, since I am with you as a servant. You will repel for me the [...]

(15) [...] There is no one who will divert them. O Amon, what I have done in the land of Nubia, which [you (?)] gave

(16) [to me (?) ... is (?)] benefactions (?). Let me make it as your tribute of the land of Syria, which has been diverted from you. O Amon,

(17) [... protect (?)] my wives. Let my children live; divert for my sake death from them. Save me from the spell[13] of [...]

(18) [...] of their spells,[13] and you should reverse them on their own heads. Superior, who causes his servant to live [...]

(19) [...] all [...]! O Amon, there is no one who shall give orders to you. You are the one who gives

(20) [orders ...] whereas[14] the (order) that you shall say to me: 'Get going!,' I shall go at that [instant].[15]

(21) [...] O Amon, there can be no Evil Eye[16] in the matter that you have done regarding[17] the one who [...]

II. Fragmentary Prayer from the West Section of the South Wall (§§H, Fa, I, and K)

(1) [...]≥ỉ [...] (2) [...]tỉ[...] (3) [...] ms [...]..n.w ... (4) [...]≥ỉ ỉn[w ...] (5) [...] ‹3 [...] wr ỉt(?) [...] (6) [...] ḥn t3≥ỉ šmm.t my ‹ḥ‹≥ỉ ḥn≥w ỉw≥ỉ [...] (7) [...] dỉ≥k n≥ỉ my ḏrỉ≥f q(3)s sw my nfr≥f my [...] ỉn≥ỉ n≥k p3 [...] ỉ ʾImn p3w.ty n [...] (8) [... n] Nḥsy my ỉn≥ỉ sw n≥k n p(3) t3 Nḥsy [...] ʾIkš ỉ ʾImn my ỉr[≥ỉ(?) ...] ỉr n≥k b3k hb n3y[≥ỉ ...] (9) [...].w nkt nb nt(y) ỉy n≥k n p(3y)≥k t3 Nḥsy p(3)y≥k k[... n3y≥k] k3.w dšr.w n3y≥k ḥrp.w n3y≥k m3.w-ḥd n3y≥k ḥn n 3by.w[18] [...] (10) [...] n[3y]≥k qwq.w p(3)y≥k stỉ p(3)y≥k š‹ w‹b n3y≥[k ...] n3 b‹.w qy.w n m3m3 [...] (11) [... n]3 mnw n p(3)y≥k ḥtp-nṯr [...] (x + 1) [... ỉ ʾImn] ỉ3w n≥ỉ ḥpš n n3 rmṯ.w ỉ3w [n≥ỉ ...] (x + 2) [... dn]ỉ.t ỉ ʾImn ỉ3w n≥ỉ ‹q.w ỉ ʾImn [...] (x + 3) [... ỉ] ʾI[m]n my ỉw p(3) Ḥ‹py [...]

(1) [...] I [..] (2) [...] (3) [...] birth/child [...] (4) I [...] bring/tribute [...] (5) great [...] great one, father (?) [...] (6) [...] in my magazine/stable. Let me stand within them while I [...] (7) [...] that you gave to me. Let it be firm; bind it. Let it be good; let [...] that I bring to you the [...] O Amon, primeval one of [...] (8) [... of] Nubia. Let me bring it to you from the land of Nubia [...] Cush. O Amon, let [me (?)] do [...] act for you as a servant, sending my [...] (9) [...] everything that comes to you from your

land of Nubia: your [..., your] red cattle, your consecrated cattle, your gazelles, your panther skins,[18] [...] (10) [...] your dôm-palm fruits, your Nubian ochre, your pure sand, your [...], the long branches of the dôm-palm, [...] (11) [...] the fixed offerings of your divine endowment [...] (x + 1) [... O, Amon,] grant to me the domination of mankind. Grant [to me ...] (x + 2) [...] vase. O Amon, grant to me bread. O Amon, [...] (x + 3) [... O] Amon, let the Inundation come [...]

III. FRAGMENTARY PRAYER FROM THE WEST SECTION OF THE SOUTH WALL (§§D, G, AND A)

Beneath the vulture Nekhbet offering the sign for life, the standing king wears an *atef*-crown (see Müller 1910, 144 fig. 49; miscopied in Vernus 1975, 6 fig. 5) and presents a figure of Maat.

Label for Nekhbet

Nḫb.t ḥd.t Nḫn dỉ⸗s ꜥnḫ

Nekhbet, the white one of Nekhen. May she give life.

Label for the King

[...] r ỉr.t⸗f nb sp-2 ỉw n3y⸗ỉ [...] (2) ny-sw.t bỉ.ty [Ḥw-Nfr-tm-Rꜥ] (3) s3 Rꜥ [Thrq] dỉ ꜥnḫ w3s d.t

[...] regarding all that he has done, two times, while my [...]. (2) The King of Upper and Lower Egypt, [Khunefertemre], (3) Son of Re, [Taharqa], given life and dominion forever.

Prayer behind King

ỉmy dỉ⸗ỉ ỉn.w s.t n⸗k ỉw ḥ3.ty⸗ỉ ndm (n) n3 ỉr⸗k n⸗ỉ nb my ỉw⸗[ỉ r ḥry] ḫr⸗k my šm⸗ỉ [r-ḫ]ry ḥr⸗k [...] r ỉr.t n⸗ỉ ḫpr [...] p(3) nt(y) n3-nfr [...]

Let me cause them to be brought to you, since my heart is happy (for) all that you have done for me. Let [me] come [up] before you; let me go up before you [...] in order to make for me the occurrence of [...] that which is good [...]

NOTES

1. Restoration suggested by Vernus 1975, 36 §y, who preferred the less grammatical k3.t[⸗f nb].

2. Erased by order of Psametik II, the cartouches were restored in paint and plaster in the Ptolemaic period. Traces were still evident to Rosellini in 1832; see Vernus 1975, 5.

3. Translated "with me" by Vernus 1975, 31.

4. For discussion of the passage, see Vernus 1975, 39–40 §as.

5. Miscopied as k in Vernus 1975, 29; see 3 fig. 2 and 41 §at.

6. For the writing and discussion, see Vernus 1975, 41–42 §aw.

7. Supplied from Müller 1910, 146 fig. 51.

8. Literally, "fat"; for the pairing of terms for "fat" (ḥpn; ḏdꜣ) and "numerous" (ꜥšꜣ); see the Hatnub graffiti, 17/6, 20/19, 24/3, and 26/7, noted in Anthes 1928, 47 §19.

9. For the restoration, and the association of Nubian rains and high inundations, see Vernus 1975, 43 §aaa.

10. Supplied from Müller 1910, 147 fig. 52.

11. So Vernus, contra Müller, who read smn.

12. Vernus 1975, 44 §aae, dismissed the writing of ỉr.t as an error for md.t bỉn.t, but cf. line 21: ỉr.t bỉn.t n tꜣ md.t.

13. Vernus does not recognize the reference to magic; for the reversal of hostile magic (pnꜥ ḥkꜣ.w), see Ritner 1993b, 21 n. 85, 168 n. 780, and 213 n. 987.

14. Taken as a phonetic writing of ỉr "as for" by Vernus 1975, 47 §aau.

15. Restoration suggested by Vernus 1975, 48 §aau.

16. Or "evil doing"; cf. line 12.

17. Taken as a writing of r "regarding" by Vernus 1975, 48 §aav.

18. Section copied by Champollion, now lost.

156. MEDINET HABU STELA
(CAIRO JdE 36410)

Discovered in the *sebakh* works at Medinet Habu in 1902, the round-topped stela of Taharqa is of limestone and measures .60 m high by .36 m wide. Within a lunette framed by *was*-scepters supporting a curved sign for heaven, a winged disk hovers over a scene of the king offering vessels of milk to an enthroned Amon and the standing goddess Mut. Below the scene are six lines of text recording royal sponsorship of the renovation of the ruined enclosure wall of the small temple of the Ennead. The text is composed in classical Middle Egyptian, with archaizing plurals. Recorded as inventory no. 36140 by Carter, the stela is listed (correctly?) as JdE 36410 by Leclant.

For the text, see Carter 1903, 178–80, with an appended translation by G. Maspero on 180; Hölscher 1939, 34 and 53; and Leclant 1965, 154 §43F and 346–47. A duplicate copy in London, signaled in Gauthier 1918b, 190, was purchased by A. Gardiner and donated in 1941 to the Ashmolean Museum at Oxford (no. 1132). See Kitchen 1986, 388 §349 and n. 836.

LABEL FOR THE KING

sꜣ Rꜥ Thrq (2) dỉ ꜥnḫ [mỉ Rꜥ] ḏ.t (3) ḥnq ỉrt.t n ỉt⸗f ꜣImn-Rꜥ[1]

The Son of Re, Taharqa, (2) given life [like Re] forever. (3) Offering milk to his father Amon-Re.[1]

LABEL FOR MUT

Mw.t nb.(t) p.t ḥnw.t tꜣ.wy

Mut, Lady of heaven, Mistress of the Two Lands.

MAIN TEXT

(1) ḥsb.t 3.(t) ḫr ḥm n ny-sw.t bỉ.ty Ḥw-Nfr-tm-Rꜥ sꜣ Rꜥ Thrq dỉ ꜥnḫ mỉ Rꜥ ḏ.t (2) ỉr.n≠f m mnw≠f n ỉt.w≠f nṯr.w nṯr.w(t)² nb.wꜣ ꜣ3.t-Tꜣw-mw(3). tꜣ smꜣ(wy) sbty ỉr.t.n ỉt.w≠f tpy.w-ꜥ n nṯr.w nṯr.w(t)² (4) nb.wꜣ ꜣ3.t-Tꜣw-mw.tꜣ pḫr ḫꜣ ḥw.t-nṯr≠sn m sbt(y) n (5) db.t m kꜣ.t mnḫ.(t) n.(t) ḏ.t ỉst gm.n ḥm≠f wꜣw r ḏꜥmꜣ pr h(6)ꜣ m b(w) ḏsr ḥr gs≠s mḫt.t sḏsr.n≠f s.t ḏsr. t n nb≠s ỉr≠f dỉ ꜥnḫ ḏ.tꜣ

(1) Regnal year 3 under the Majesty of the King of Upper and Lower Egypt, Khunefertemre, Son of Re, Taharqa, given life like Re forever. (2) It was as a monument for his ancestors, the gods and goddesses,² lords³ of the mound of Djême,⁴ that he made (3) the renovation of the enclosure wall that his ancestral fathers had made for the gods and goddesses,² (4) lords³ of the mound of Djême,⁴ surrounding their temple with an enclosure wall of (5) brick, in construction perfect for eternity. Now as His Majesty had found (it) fallen into ruin,⁵ so that one might exit and (6) enter the sanctuary on its northern side, he reconsecrated the holy place for its lord so that he might attain the state of being given life forever.⁶

NOTES

1. Although glossed by Carter as a carving error, the orientation of the name Amon-Re is reversed to serve as a label for the seated deity.

2. Contra Maspero, the writing of six nṯr-signs in lines 2 and 3 represents two sets of plurals, not a defective spelling for nine nṯr-signs. The writing would still represent the Ennead, a group composed of male and female deities.

3. Or "all the gods and goddesses of the mound of Djême."

4. For the theological significance of the "mound" of Djême, burial site of the primordial Ogdoad, see Fazzini 1988, 11 and 22–23.

5. For the New Kingdom reinterpretation of older wꜣs as ḏꜥm, see Foster and Ritner 1996, 6 n. 28.

6. The Ashmolean stela differs from the Cairo text only at the conclusion, expanding ỉr≠f dỉ ꜥnḫ ḏ.t to ỉr≠f dỉ ꜥnḫ ḏd wꜣs mỉ Rꜥ ḏ.t "so that he might attain the state of being given life, stability, and dominion like Re forever."

157. A MEMPHITE DONATION
(CAIRO JdE 36861)

This record of royal donations to a small Amon shrine near Memphis is one of the rare attestations of Taharqa north of the Thebaid. Broken into six pieces, the calcite donation stela measures 1.35 by 0.54 m and depicts in its lunette identical addorsed scenes of Taharqa offering the sign for "field" to Amon and Mut beneath an overarching winged disk. The text is a mixture of Late and Middle Egyptian, with numerous errors in carving.

For the text, translation, and discussion, see Meeks 1979b, 221–59 and pl. XXXVIII. See Kitchen 1986, 389 §350 and 585 §529.

LABEL FOR THE WINGED DISK

Bḥd.t(y) nṯr ꜥꜣ dỉ ꜥnḫ
The Behdedite, the great god who gives life.

LABEL FOR AMON

ʾImn-Rꜥ ḫnt(y) ḥw.wt-nṯr.w
Amon-Re, foremost of the temples.

LABEL FOR MUT

Mw.t ḫnt(y) ḥw.wt-nṯr.w
Mut, foremost of the temples.

JOINT SPEECH BY DEITIES

ḏd-mdw dỉ.n≠(ỉ) n≠k ꜥnḫ wꜣs nb snb nb nṯr nfr T[hrq]
Recitation: "Thus I have given to you all life and dominion and all health, O Good God [Taharqa]."

LABEL FOR THE KING

nṯr nfr T[hrq] (2) dỉ ꜥnḫ (3) sꜣ ꜥnḫ ḥꜣ≠f nb (4) ḥnk sḫ.t n ỉt≠f
The Good God [Taharqa], (2) given life. (3) The protection of life is all around him. (4) Offering fields to his father.

MAIN TEXT

(1) [ꜥnḫ] Ḥr [q(ꜣ) ḫꜥ.w Nb.ty q(ꜣ) ḫꜥ.w Ḥr-nbw ḫw tꜣ.wy ny-sw].t bỉ.ty [Ḥw-Nfr-tm]-Rꜥ [sꜣ Rꜥ] T[hrq] ꜥnḫ ḏt ỉr.n≠f m mnw≠f (2) (n) ỉt≠f ʾImn-Rꜥ ḫnt(y) ḥw.wt-nṯr.w

ỉs(t) gỉm.n ḥm≠f rꜣ-pr pn wꜣ.tw r wꜣs(ꜣ){m} nn wn ḫ.t nb.t ỉm ḫsf dỉ ḥm≠f m ḥr n ỉmy-rꜣ kꜣ.t nb.t (4) n.t ẖnw≠f ḥnꜥ ḥmw.w nb n.{t} ḥm≠f [sqỉd. tw≠f mỉ ỉmy≠f ḥr-ḥꜣ.t (5) ꜥḥꜥ qd pr pn (n) ỉt≠f ʾImn-Rꜥ [ḫnt(y) ḥw].wt-nṯr. w m ỉn(r) ḥḏ nfr ꜥnw (6) [n]f[r] sw r ỉmy≠f ḥr-ḥꜣ.t ỉ[…]r(7)≠f [...] m ḥw.t≠f ỉn [...]m[..]m[...] ḥnꜥ ssm nb n ḫ.t(8)-nṯr.w≠f mḥ.t m wꜥ nb n mꜣꜥ.t [...] grg. wt nb.t mn r s.wt≠sn m ḥḏ (9) ḥm.t qrḥ.w(t) nb.t mn r s.wt≠s[n] nn ḏr.w≠sn qd≠f ꜥmt(?)≠f¹ wḏꜣ.w(10)≠f mḥ.t m pr.t nb.t nḏm.t

dỉ≠f n≠f ḥḏ dbn 30 [n bꜣk(?)] nꜣ wḫꜥ.(w) n.(w) Mn-nfr m-ḏr tꜣ ḫsf.(t) (11) n.(t) Mn-nfr

ỉmy-rn≠w

p3 14² ꜣbd.w ḥḏ dbn 24

ms(w.t)³ Wsỉr [ḥḏ dbn 4]

mn dbn 2

dmḏ ḥḏ dbn 30 ỉr.w ỉḥ 38

dỉ≠f n≠f pꜣ mr m (=n) mšꜥ nty m-bꜣḥ≠f ḥr (12) mnḫ.t snṯr bỉ.t nḥḥ ḥnꜥ pꜣ ỉ[…] n pꜣ ḥtp-nṯr n Ptḥ pꜣ nṯr ꜥꜣ nty pr n pr ꜣ'Imn-Rꜥ (13) ḫnt(y) ḥw.wt-nṯr.w

dỉ≠f n≠f ỉwf psỉ dỉ≠f n≠f ꜥq.w 6 n ḥr.(t) hrw n nꜣ twt.w n ḥm(14)≠f{f} n pꜣ ꜥmt(?)[1] rsy n pr Ptḥ dỉ≠f n≠f qb.w (ỉ)ꜥb[.w …] n pr Ptḥ

dỉ≠f n≠f nḥḥ hn 44 nꜣ Kmt dỉ≠f n≠f (15) [nḥ]ḥ hn 23 n ḥr.t ꜣbd ḥr tꜣ mr.t Mn-n[fr m-ꜥ(?)] nꜣ ḥry.w šwty.w dỉ≠f n≠f snṯr hn (16) 2

dỉ≠f n≠f ꜣḥ.wt stꜣ.t n 467 rmn

ỉmy-rn≠w

 [nty m sw]w n pr ꜣ'Imn-Rꜥ ḫnt(y) ḥw.wt-nṯr.w stꜣ.t n 120 (17) ḥnꜥ
  mr šn.w

 nty m sww (n) tꜣ […].t stꜣ.t n 66 rmn

 nty m sww n pꜣ bḫ(n) (18) sꜥrq(?)[4] stꜣ.t 50

 nty m sww (n) Tꜣ-ḥw.t-pꜣ-[…]

 nty m sww (n) Tꜣ-ḥw.t-Mꜣỉ (19) stꜣ.t 110

 nty n sww (n) ꜣ'Iḫnw stꜣ.t 32

 dmd stꜣ.t 4[6]7 rmn

dỉ≠f n≠f ỉḥ.w 20 kꜣ 1 (20) ỉw pꜣ ꜣḫy nn pꜣ mr mšꜥ […] dỉ≠f n≠f srỉw 30

n-dr.t (21) ḥm-nṯr Ptḥ ḥm-nṯr ꜣ'Imn-Rꜥ ḫnt(y) ḥw.wt-nṯr.[w …] sꜣ ḥm-nṯr […] Nḫt

ỉw pꜣ nty-ỉw(22)≠f smn tꜣy wd.(t) ỉr.n ḥm-nṯr ỉw[≠f] ỉr nꜣ [ḥs].w n Ptḥ-Skr ỉw pꜣ nty(23)-ỉw≠f thꜣ tꜣy wd.(t) ỉr[.n ḥm≠f n] ỉt≠f ꜣ'I[mn-Rꜥ ḫnt(y) ḥw.wt-nṯr.w ỉ]w≠f [r] (24) šꜥd n Ptḥ-Skr ꜣ'Imn-Rꜥ ḫnt(y) ḥw.wt-nṯr.[w] ḥr šꜥd ny-sw.t […] nḥḥ ḏ.t r ḏr.t n [ḥm]-nṯr [Ptḥ(?)]

(1) [Long live] the Horus: ["Exalted of Epiphanies"; the Two Ladies: "Exalted of Epiphanies"; the Horus of Gold: "Protector of the Two Lands"; the King of] Upper and Lower Egypt, [Khunefertem]re, the Son of Re, [Taharqa], living forever. As his monument for (2) his father Amon-Re, foremost of the temples, he made (the following):

Now, His Majesty found this shrine fallen into ruin, (3) with nothing in it protected. His Majesty gave orders to the overseer of all works (4) of his residence together with all the craftsmen of His Majesty that it should be built as it had been previously. (5) Then this house of his father Amon-Re, [foremost of] the temples, was built in good white Tura calcite. (6) It was better than it had been previously. […] (7) him […] in his temple by […] together with every procedure of (8) his divine rituals completed individually and properly […], all the utensils established in their places in both silver and (9) copper, and all the vessels established in their places, in unlimited quantities. He constructed its …,[1] its magazines being filled with all sorts of sweet fruits.

He gave to him 30 *deben* of silver [as the produce (?) of] the fishermen of Memphis under the authority of the civil defense (11) of Memphis.

Their list:

the 14[2] months: 24 *deben* of silver,
the Birth (?)[3] of Osiris: [4 *deben* of silver,]
remaining: 2 *deben* ,
Total: 30 *deben* of silver, equivalent to 38 oxen.

He gave to him "The Canal of the Army," which is before him, yielding (12) clothing, incense, honey, and oil, together with the [...] of the divine endowment of Ptah, the great god, which is issued to the estate of Amon-Re, foremost of the temples.

He gave to him a *deben* of cooked meat. He gave to him 6 loaves in the course of every day for the statues of His Majesty (14) in the southern ...[1] of the estate of Ptah. He gave to him beer jugs and cups [...] of the estate of Ptah.

He gave to him 44 *hin* of oil of the Egyptians. He gave to him (15) 23 *hin* of oil in the course of the month at the harbor of Memphis [from] the chief merchants. He gave to him (16) 2 *hin* of incense.

He gave to him 467 1/2 *arouras* of field.

Their list:

[what is in the] territory of the estate of Amon-Re, foremost of the temples: 120 *arouras,* (17) together with the "Canal of the Trees,"
what is in the territory of "The [...]": 66 1/2 *arouras* of field,
what is in the territory of "The Completed (?)[4] (18) Villa": 50 *arouras,*
what is in the territory of "The Temple of the [..." ...],
what is in the territory of "The Temple of the Lion": 110 *arouras,*
what is in the territory of Akhni: 32 *arouras,*
Total: 467 1/2 *arouras.*

He gave to him 20 oxen and 1 bull, (20) while the pasture for these is "The Canal of the Army" [...] He gave to him 30 geese.

Under the authority of (21) the prophet of Ptah and prophet of Amon-Re, foremost of the temples, [...], son of the prophet of [...], Nakht,

while as for the one who will (22) confirm this decree that His Majesty has made, [he] will do [what is praised by] Ptah-Sokar, whereas the one who will violate this decree that [His Majesty] has made [for] his father Amon-[Re, foremost of the temples,] he will [be subject to] (24) the slaughter of Ptah-Sokar and Amon-Re, foremost of the temples, at the slaughter of the King [...] forever and ever, under the authority of the prophet of [Ptah (?)].

NOTES
1. An unknown institution of the estate of Ptah.
2. Perhaps an error for 12.
3. Meeks suggested: "fashioning an Osiris."
4. Meeks suggested a derivation from sg3 "hillock, fortification"

158. NAPATA INSCRIPTIONS

At the Cushite capital of Napata beside the sacred peak of Gebel Barkal, Taharqa erected a granite statue of himself and a bark stand within the central Amon temple, and he restored the adjacent shrine of Mut, whose New Kingdom construction he deemed inferior. The prominence accorded Theban Amon in Taharqa's reliefs reflects the history of the cult, transplanted to Nubia during the New Kingdom and thus only secondarily "resident" at Gebel Barkal, the "Karnak of Amon of Napata" (ʾIp.t-s.wt ʾImn Np3.t). More significantly, the scenes underscore the theological link between Napata and Thebes and the resultant divine justification for the imperial claims of Dynasty XXV. Secondary reliefs are purposefully chosen, depicting Egyptian deities with mythological links to Nubia (Tefnut, Onuris) as well as transported cults (Amon of Kawa) and native Nubian divinities (Dedwen). In the Mut temple celebrating divine queenship, complementary scenes of Taharqa's mother Abar and Chief Queen Tekahatamani appear on facing walls. A representative selection of Taharqa's Napatan texts follows.

For the texts, translation, and discussion, see Lepsius 1849–59, 5:pls. 5–13; Dunham 1970, 12, 17, 20, and pls. VII–VIII and XXIX; Breasted 1906–7, 4:457–58 §§897–900; and Schäfer 1897, 98–99; Breasted photos 2999–3002 and 3018–33. See Kitchen 1986, 390 §350.

GREAT AMON TEMPLE (B 500)

I. Statue of Taharqa (Merowe Museum 11)

Back Pillar
Ḥr q(3) ẖꜥ.w Nb.ty q(3) ẖꜥ.w Ḥr-nbw ẖw t3.wy Ḥw-Nfr-tm-Rꜥ s3 Rꜥ n ẖ.t⸗f mry⸗f Thrq mry ʾImn (n) Np(3).t ẖr(y)-îb Ḏw-wꜥb dî ꜥnẖ ḏ.t
The Horus: "Exalted of Epiphanies"; the Two Ladies: "Exalted of Epiphanies"; the Horus of Gold: "Protector of the Two Lands"; Khunefertemre, the bodily Son of Re, whom he loves, Taharqa, beloved of Amon of Napata, resident in Gebel Barkal, given life forever.

Base
nṯr nfr Thrq (2) mry ʾImn-Rꜥ
The Good God, Taharqa, (2) beloved of Amon-Re.

II. Symmetrical Bandeau Text of Granite Bark Stand (still *in situ* but with fragments in Boston)

ꜥnḫ Ḥr q(ꜣ) ḫꜥ.w Nb.ty q(ꜣ) ḫꜥ.w Ḥr-nbw ḫw tꜣ.wy ny-sw.t bỉ.ty nb tꜣ.wy Ḥw-Nfr-tm-Rꜥ sꜣ Rꜥ Thrq ꜥnḫ ḏ.t ỉr.n≠f m mnw≠f n ỉt≠f ꞌImn-Rꜥ nb ns.wt tꜣ.wy nṯr ꜥꜣ ḥr(y)-ỉb Tꜣ-Stỉ mꜣꜣt p r ḥtp ḥr≠f m ꜥḥ≠f n sp ḫpr mỉt.t ḥr nṯr.w nb.w ꜥnḫ wꜣs nb ḥr≠f m ỉsw ḫꜥ.(w) ḥr s.t Ḥr ḏ.t

Long live the Horus: "Exalted of Epiphanies"; the Two Ladies: "Exalted of Epiphanies"; the Horus of Gold: "Protector of the Two Lands"; the King of Upper and Lower Egypt, Lord of the Two Lands, Khunefertemre, the Son of Re, Taharqa, living forever. As his monument for his father, Amon-Re, Lord of the Thrones of the Two Lands, the great god, resident in Nubia, he made this granite pedestal on which to rest in his palace. Never had the like been done under any of the god(-king)s, with all life and dominion issuing from him as reward, in addition to appearing in glory on the throne of Horus forever.

Symmetrical Side Text

nṯr nfr Thrq twꜣ.n≠f ỉt≠f nṯr ꜥꜣ nb Tꜣ-Stỉ rdỉ.{n}n≠f sw ḥr s.t≠f n.t Np(ꜣ.t) ỉn qꜣ ḫꜥ.(w) ỉr≠f ꜥnḫ ḏ.t

The Good God, Taharqa has elevated his father, the great god, Lord of Nubia, since he had placed him upon his throne of Napata. It is "Exalted of Epiphanies" who will attain the state of being given life.

Symmetrical Side Text

Ḥr-nbw Thrq rdỉ.n≠f ꞌImn m ḥr(y) p≠f nṯr špss srwd≠f ns.t≠f ꜣw.(t)-ỉb ḥr≠f ny.t-sw.t ꜥꜣ.(t) (m) ỉsw m ꜥnḫ ḏ.t

The Horus of Gold, Taharqa, has placed Amon as one who is on his pedestal, while the noble god makes firm his throne, with joy issuing from him and a great kingship as reward in eternal life.

Symmetrical Side Text, Spoken by Hapi of the South and North

ḏd-mdw (ỉn) nṯr.wy Thrq dỉ.n≠(ỉ) n≠k ḏfꜣw nb pr (ỉ)m≠ỉ smꜣ≠ỉ n≠k tꜣ.wy m ḥtp mỉ Rꜥ ḏ.t

Recitation (by) the two gods: "O Taharqa, thus I have given to you all foodstuffs that come forth from me, as I unite the Two Lands in peace for you like Re forever."

Side Text

ḏd-mdw ỉn nb ns.wt tꜣ.wy ḥr(y)-ỉb Ḏw-wꜥb dỉ≠f ꜥnḫ wꜣs nb n ny-sw.t bỉ.ty Ḥw-Nfr-tm-Rꜥ sꜣ Rꜥ Thrq ꜥnḫ ḏ.t

Recitation by the Lord of the Thrones of the Two Lands, resident in Gebel Barkal, as he gives all life and dominion to the King of Upper and Lower Egypt, Khunefertemre, the Son of Re, Taharqa, living forever.

Side Text
ḏd-mdw ỉn ʾImn-Rᶜ ḥr(y)-ỉb Ḏw-wᶜb dỉ≠f ᶜnḫ wȝs nb n ny-sw.t bỉ.ty
Ḥw-Nfr-tm-Rᶜ sȝ Rᶜ Thrq ᶜnḫ ḏ.t

Recitation by Amon-Re, resident in Gebel Barkal, as he gives all life
and dominion to the King of Upper and Lower Egypt, Khunefertemre, the
Son of Re, Taharqa, living forever.

Mut Temple B 300: Third Hall

I. Lintel and Side of Bes Columns
ᶜnḫ nṯr nfr qmȝ.n Rᶜ wtt.n Ḥmnw ny-sw.t bỉ.ty nb tȝ.wy Ḥw-Nfr-tm-Rᶜ
sȝ [Rᶜ ...] (2) ny-sw.t bỉ.ty nb tȝ.wy Ḥw-Nfr-tm-Rᶜ sȝ Rᶜ nb ḫᶜ.w Thrq mrỉ-
Ḥw.t-Ḥr ḥnw.t tȝ.wy dỉ ᶜnḫ nb ḏ.t

Long live the Good God, whom Re created, whom the Ogdoad begat,
the King of Upper and Lower Egypt, Lord of the Two Lands, Khunefertemre, the Son [of Re, ...] (2) The King of Upper and Lower Egypt, Lord of
the Two Lands, Khunefertemre, the Son of Re, Lord of diadems, Taharqa,
beloved of Hathor, Mistress of the Two Lands, given all life forever.

Back of Bes Column, with Royal Titles before Edjo
Wḏȝy.t dỉ≠s ᶜnḫ wȝs nb snb nb ȝw.t-ỉb nb ḏ.t (2) ny-sw.t bỉ.ty nb tȝ.wy
Ḥw-Nfr-tm-Rᶜ sȝ Rᶜ Thrq mrỉ-Ns.wt(y)-tȝ.wy dỉ ᶜnḫ ḏ.t

Edjo, as she gives all life and dominion, all health and all joy forever.
(2) The King of Upper and Lower Egypt, Lord of the Two Lands, Khunefertemre, the Son of Re, Taharqa, beloved of Him of the Thrones of the
Two Lands, given life forever.

II. Upper Bandeau Text, Facing Right
ᶜnḫ Ḥr q(ȝ) ḫᶜ.w Nb.ty q(ȝ) ḫᶜ.w Ḥr-nbw ḫw tȝ.wy ny-sw.t bỉ.ty nb
tȝ.wy nb ỉr.(t) ḫt Ḥw-Nfr-tm-Rᶜ sȝ Rᶜ nb ḫᶜ.w Thrq ᶜnḫ ḏ.t ỉr.n≠f m mnw≠f
n mw.t≠f Mw.t nb.(t) p.t ḥnw.t Tȝ-Stỉ qd≠f pr≠s sᶜȝ≠f ḥw.t-nṯr≠s m-mȝw.(t)
m ỉnr ḥḏ nfr (n) r(w)d.(t) dỉ≠s n≠f ᶜnḫ nb ḫr≠s ḏd nb ḫr≠s wȝs nb ḫr[≠s
...]

Long live the Horus: "Exalted of Epiphanies"; the Two Ladies:
"Exalted of Epiphanies"; the Horus of Gold: "Protector of the Two Lands";
the King of Upper and Lower Egypt, Lord of the Two Lands, Lord of ritual
performance, Khunefertemre, the Son of Re, Lord of diadems, Taharqa,
living forever. As his monument for his mother Mut, Lady of heaven,
Mistress of Nubia, he made: his building her house and his enlarging her
temple anew in good white sandstone, so that she might give to him all
life issuing from her, all stability issuing from her, and all dominion issuing from [her ...]

III. Upper Bandeau Text, Facing Left

ꜥnḫ Ḥr q(3) ḫꜥ.w Nb.ty q(3) ḫꜥ.w Ḥr-nbw ḫw t3.wy ny-sw.t bỉ.ty nb
t3.wy nb ỉr.(t) ḫ.t Ḥw-Nfr-tm-Rꜥ s3 Rꜥ nb ḫꜥ.w Thrq ꜥnḫ ḏ.t ỉr.n≠f m mnw≠f
n mw.t≠f Mw.t (n) Np(3).t qd≠f n≠s ḥw.t-nṯr n m3w.(t) m ỉnr ꜥn ḥḏ nfr (n)
r(w)d.(t) ỉs(t) gm.n ḥm≠f ḥw.t-nṯr tn qd m ỉnr m-ꜥ tpy.w-ꜥ m k3.t nḏs.(t)
wn ỉn ḥm≠f (ḥr) rdỉ.(t) qd.tw ḥw.t-nṯr tn m k3.t mnḫ.t n ḏ.t dỉ ꜥnḫ w3s
[mỉ] Rꜥ [ḏ.t]

Long live the Horus: "Exalted of Epiphanies"; the Two Ladies: "Exalted
of Epiphanies"; the Horus of Gold: "Protector of the Two Lands"; the King
of Upper and Lower Egypt, Lord of the Two Lands, Lord of ritual performance, Khunefertemre, the Son of Re, Lord of diadems, Taharqa, living
forever. As his monument for his mother Mut of Napata he made: his building for her the temple anew in beautiful, good white sandstone. Whereas
His Majesty found this temple built in stone by the ancestors as an inferior
construction, His Majesty then caused that this temple be (re)built as an
excellent, eternal construction, while he is granted life and dominion [like]
Re [forever.]

IV. Southeast Wall: Taharqa offers incense to Onuris and Tefnut.

Label for Onuris

ʾIn-ḥr (2) ḏd-mdw dỉ.n≠(ỉ) n≠k ꜥnḫ w3s nb (3) ḏd-mdw dỉ.n≠(ỉ) n≠k
3w.(t)-ỉb nb.(t)

Onuris. (2) Recitation: "Thus I have given to you all life and dominion." (3) Recitation: "Thus I have given to you all joy."

Label for Tefnut

Tfnw.t s3.t Rꜥ (2) ḏd-mdw dỉ≠(ỉ) ꜥnḫ w3s

Tefnut, the daughter of Re. (2) Recitation: "I shall give life and dominion."

Label for the King

nṯr nfr nb t3.wy nb ỉr.(t) ḫ.t (2) ny-sw.t bỉ.ty Ḥw-Nfr-tm-Rꜥ (3) s3 Rꜥ
Thrq (4) dỉ ꜥnḫ ḏd [w3s] (5) ỉr.(t) snṯr

The Good God, Lord of the Two Lands, Lord of ritual performance, (2)
the King of Upper and Lower Egypt, Khunefertemre, the Son of Re, Taharqa, (4) given life, stability, [and dominion.] (5) Making incense.

V. Fragmentary Southwest Wall

Label for Amon

ʾImn-Rꜥ nb ns.(w)t t3.wy ḫnt(y) ʾIp.t-s.(2)wt (3) ḏd-mdw dỉ.n≠(ỉ) n≠k
snb nb

Amon-Re, Lord of the Thrones of the Two Lands, Foremost of (2) Karnak. (3) Recitation: "Thus I have given to you all health."

VI. East Wall: Taharqa and his primary wife Tekahatamani offer to Amon and Mut within the Gebel Barkal shrine distinguished by a projecting uraeus.

Label for Amon

ḏd-mdw ỉn ʾImn-Rꜥ nb ns.(w)t tꜣ.wy ḥr(y)-ỉb Ḏw-wꜥb (2) dỉ ꜥnḫ ḏd wꜣs nb

Recitation by Amon-Re, Lord of the Thrones of the Two Lands, resident in Gebel Barkal, (2) who gives all life, stability, and dominion.

Label for Mut

ḏd-mdw ỉn Mw.t nb.(t) Tꜣ-Stỉ (2) ʾImn-Rꜥ nb ns.(w)t tꜣ.wy ḥr(y)-ỉb Ḏw-wꜥb (3) sꜣ≠k mrỉ≠k sꜣ Rꜥ Thrq ꜥnḫ ḏ.t dỉ≠k (n)≠f ꜥnḫ ḏd wꜣs nb ḫr≠ỉ snb nb ḫr≠ỉ mỉ Rꜥ ḏ.t

Recitation by Mut, the Lady of Nubia: (2) "O Amon-Re, Lord of the Thrones of the Two Lands, resident in Gebel Barkal, (3) as for your son whom you love, the Son of Re, Taharqa, living forever, may you give to him all life, stability, and dominion issuing from me and all health issuing from me like Re forever.

Label for the King

ny-sw.t bỉ.ty Ḫw-Nfr-tm-Rꜥ (2) sꜣ Rꜥ Thrq (3) dỉ ꜥnḫ wꜣs

The King of Upper and Lower Egypt, Khunefertemre, (2) the Son of Re, Taharqa, (3) given life and dominion.

Label for the Queen

ḏd-mdw ỉn ỉry.t-pꜥ.t wr.(t) ḥsw.(t)(2) ḥnw.t ḥm.t nb.(t) sn.t ny-sw.t ḥm.t ny-sw.t mrỉ≠f (3) Dỉkht-ʾImn ỉr.t sš(4)š.(t) n ḫr≠k (5) nfr ʾImn-Rꜥ nb ns.(w)t tꜣ.wy ḥr(y)-ỉb Ḏw-wꜥb sꜣ≠k mrỉ≠k sꜣ Rꜥ Thrq dỉ≠k sw m ny-sw.t n nḥḥ Ḥr wꜣḫ(?) n ꜥnḫ ḏ.t

Recitation by the Hereditary Princess, whose praises are great, (2) the mistress of all wives, the king's sister and king's wife, whom he loves, (3) Tekahatamani, who plays the (4) sistrum before your beautiful face: (5) "O Amon-Re, Lord of the Thrones of the Two Lands, resident in Gebel Barkal, as for your son whom you love, the Son of Re, Taharqa, may you place him as king forever, a Horus whose life endures (?) forever.

VII. West Wall: Taharqa, followed by his mother Abar, offers Maat to Amon and Mut.

Label for Amon

ʾImn-Rˁ nb ns.(w)t tꜣ.wy ḫnt(y) ʾIp.t-s.(2)wt (3) ḏd-mdw dỉ.n≠(ỉ) n≠k ˁnḫ wꜣs nb

Amon-Re, Lord of the Thrones of the Two Lands, Foremost of (2) Karnak. (3) Recitation: "Thus I have given to you all life and dominion."

Label for Mut

Mw.t nb.(t) p.t (2) ḏd-mdw dỉ.n≠(ỉ) n≠k ꜣw.(t)-ỉb nb.(t) 3) ḏd-mdw dỉ.n≠(ỉ) n≠k ˁnḫ wꜣs nb ḫr≠ỉ snb nb ḫr≠ỉ ḫˁ.tỉ m ny-sw.t bỉ.ty [...]

Mut, the Lady of heaven. (2) Recitation: "Thus I have given to you all joy." (3) Recitation: "Thus I have given to you all life and dominion issuing from me, all health issuing from me, while you have appeared in glory as King of Upper and Lower Egypt [...]."

Label for the King

nṯr nfr nb tꜣ.wy nb ỉr.(t) ḫ.t (2) ny-sw.t bỉ.ty Ḥw-Nfr-tm-Rˁ (3) sꜣ Rˁ Thrq (4) dỉ ˁnḫ mỉ Rˁ

The Good God, Lord of the Two Lands, Lord of ritual performance, (2) the King of Upper and Lower Egypt, Khunefertemre, the Son of Re, Taharqa, (4) given life like Re.

Label for the Queen Mother

ỉry.t-pˁ.t wr.(t) ḥs(2)w.(t) ḥnw.t tꜣ.wy (3) wr.t nb.(t) tꜣ.w nb ḫꜣs.wt nb.(t) (4) mw.t ny-sw.t sn.t ny-sw.t [ʾI]br ỉỉ.n≠(ỉ) ḫr≠k [... ʾIb]r ˁnḫ ḏ.t

The Hereditary Princess, whose praises are great, (2) the mistress of the Two Lands, (3) the great one, the Lady of all lands and all foreign countries, (4) the king's mother and king's sister, [A]bar. "Thus I have come before you [... Ab]ar, living forever.

VIII. Back (North) Wall, Doorway to Central Sanctuary

Symmetrical Label for Winged Disk

Bḥd.t(y) nṯr ˁꜣ

The Behdedite, the great god.

Right of Doorway

Hr q(3) ḫˁ.w Nb.ty q(3) ḫˁ.w ny-sw.t bỉ.ty nb tꜣ.wy Ḥw-Nfr-tm-Rˁ [mrỉ] ʾImn-Rˁ nb [ns.wt tꜣ.wy ... dỉ ˁnḫ ...] mỉ Rˁ (2) Hr-nbw ḫw tꜣ.wy sꜣ Rˁ n ḫ.t≠f mrỉ≠f nb ḫˁ.w Thrq [mrỉ] Mw.t nb.(t) p.t [ḥnw.t(?)] nṯr[.w ...] ḏ.t

The Horus: "Exalted of Epiphanies"; the Two Ladies: "Exalted of Epiphanies"; the King of Upper and Lower Egypt, Lord of the Two Lands, Khunefertemre, [beloved of] Amon-Re, Lord of [the Thrones of the Two Lands ... , given life ...] like Re. (2) The Horus of Gold: "Protector of the

Two Lands"; the bodily Son of Re, whom he loves, the Lord of diadems, Taharqa, [beloved of] Mut, Lady of heaven, [Mistress (?)] of the god[s ...] forever.

Left of Doorway

Ḥr q(3) ḫꜥ.w Nb.ty q(3) ḫꜥ.w ny-sw.t bỉ.ty nb tꜣ.wy Ḥw-Nfr-tm-Rꜥ [mrỉ] ꜣImn-Rꜥ nb ns.[wt tꜣ.wy ... dỉ ꜥnḫ ... mỉ Rꜥ] (2) Ḥr-nbw ḫw tꜣ.wy sꜣ Rꜥ n ḫ.t≠f mrỉ≠f nb ḫꜥ.w Thrq [mrỉ] Mw.t nb.(t) p.t [...]

The Horus: "Exalted of Epiphanies"; the Two Ladies: "Exalted of Epiphanies"; the King of Upper and Lower Egypt, Lord of the Two Lands, Khunefertemre, [beloved of] Amon-Re, Lord of the throne[s of the Two Lands ... , given life ... like Re.] (2) The Horus of Gold: "Protector of the Two Lands"; the bodily Son of Re, whom he loves, the Lord of diadems, Taharqa, [beloved of] Mut, Lady of heaven [...]

Scene Right of Doorway

Label for Mut

Mw.t (n) Np(ꜣ).t (2) ḏd-mdw ỉr pt(r)≠k mrr.(t) nṯr.wt nfr.(w)t ꜥnḫ≠s ḏt

Mut of Napata. (2) Recitation: "If you see the one whom the beautiful goddesses love, she lives forever."

Label for King

ny-sw.t bỉ.ty nb tꜣ.wy Ḥw-Nfr-tm-Rꜥ (2) sꜣ Rꜥ nb ḫꜥ.w Thrq (3) mꜣꜣ nṯr sp 4

The King of Upper and Lower Egypt, Lord of the Two Lands, Khunefertemre, (2) the Son of Re, Lord of diadems, Taharqa. (3) Beholding the deity. 4 times.

Scene Left of Doorway

Label for Hathor

Ḥw.t-Ḥr ḥnw.t tꜣ.wy (2) ḏd-mdw dỉ.n≠(ỉ) n≠k ꜥnḫ wꜣs nb snb nb ḫt nb.(t) ḏt

Hathor, Mistress of the Two Lands. (2) Recitation: "Thus I have given to you all life and dominion, all health and everything forever."

Label for King

ny-sw.t bỉ.ty nb tꜣ.wy Ḥw-Nfr-tm-Rꜥ (2) sꜣ Rꜥ nb ḫꜥ.w Thrq (3) dwꜣ nṯr sp 4

The King of Upper and Lower Egypt, Lord of the Two Lands, Khunefertemre, (2) the Son of Re, Lord of diadems, Taharqa. (3) Adoring the deity. 4 times.

Western Side-Chapel

I. Bandeau Text
ꜥnḫ Ḥr q(ꜣ) ḫꜥ.w Nb.ty q(ꜣ) ḫꜥ.w Ḥr-nbw ḫw tꜣ.wy ny-sw.t bi̓.ty nb tꜣ.wy nb i̓r.(t) ḫ.t Ḥw-Nfr-tm-Rꜥ sꜣ Rꜥ n ḫ.t⸗f mri̓⸗f Thrq ꜥnḫ ḏ.t i̓r.n⸗f m mnw⸗f n mw.t⸗[f] Mw.t i̓r.t Rꜥ nb.t p.t ḥnw.t nṯr.w ḥr(y.t)-i̓b Np(ꜣ).t qd pr⸗s m i̓nr ḥḏ nfr (n) rwḏ.(t)

Long live the Horus: "Exalted of Epiphanies"; the Two Ladies: "Exalted of Epiphanies"; the Horus of Gold: "Protector of the Two Lands"; the King of Upper and Lower Egypt, Lord of the Two Lands, Lord of ritual performance, Khunefertemre, the bodily Son of Re, whom he loves, Taharqa, living forever. As his monument for [his] mother Mut, the Eye of Re, Lady of heaven, Mistress of the gods, resident in Napata, he made: the building of her house in good white sandstone.

II. East Wall: The king, followed by Mut, offers milk to Amon of Kawa, bread to Dedwen, and Maat to Re-Horachty.

Label for Amon
ꜣImn-Rꜥ (n) Gm-ꜣItn (2) ḏd-mdw di̓.n⸗(i̓) n⸗k ꜥnḫ wꜣs nb

Amon-Re of Gematon. (2) Recitation: "Thus I have given to you all life and dominion."

Label for Mut
ḏd-mdw i̓n Mw.t wr.(t) (2) nb.(t) ꜣIšr (3) ḏd-mdw di̓.n⸗(i̓) n⸗k rnp.wt Ḥr m bi̓ty ny.t-sw.t⸗f r Dp [...]

Recitation by Mut, the great, (2) Lady of Asheru. (3) Recitation: "Thus I have given to you the years of Horus as King of Lower Egypt and his kingship at Dep.

Label for the King
nṯr nfr nb tꜣ.wy nb i̓r.(t) ḫ.t (2) ny-sw.t bi̓.ty Ḥw-Nfr-tm-Rꜥ (3) sꜣ Rꜥ Thrq (4) di̓ ꜥnḫ (5) mi̓ Rꜥ (6) ḥnk i̓rt.t [...]

The Good God, Lord of the Two Lands, Lord of ritual performance, (2) the King of Upper and Lower Egypt, Khunefertemre, (3) the Son of Re, Tahar-qa, (4) given life (5) like Re. (6) Offering milk [...].

Label for Dedwen
ḏd-mdw (i̓n) Ddwn ḫnt(y) Tꜣ-Sti̓ (2) di̓ ꜥnḫ wꜣs (3) mi̓ Rꜥ

Recitation (by) Dedwen, foremost of Nubia, (2) who gives life and dominion (3) like Re.

Label for the King

nb t3.wy Ḥw-Nfr-tm-Rᶜ (2) nb ḫᶜ.w Thrq (3) dỉ ᶜnḫ nb (4) mỉ Rᶜ ḏ.t (5) nṯr nfr qn(ỉ) mỉ Mnṯ(w) nb pḥ.ty ny-sw.t bỉ.ty s3 Rᶜ Thrq [...] (6) sq(r) [t ḥḏ ...]

The Lord of the Two Lands, Khunefertemre, (2) the Lord of diadems, Taharqa, (3) given all life (4) like Re forever. (5) The Good God, valiant like Montu, Lord of strength, the King of Upper and Lower Egypt, the Son of Re, Taharqa, [...] (6) Consecrating [white bread ...]

Label for Re-Horachty

Rᶜ-Ḥr-3ḫ.ty ḥry nṯr.w (2) ḏd-mdw dỉ.n≠(ỉ) n≠k ᶜnḫ w3s nb (3) ḏd-mdw dỉ.n≠(ỉ) n≠k ᶜnḫ w3s nb snb nb [...]

Re-Horachty, chief of the gods. (2) Recitation: "Thus I have given to you all life and dominion." (3) Recitation: "Thus I have given to you all life and dominion and all health [...]."

Label for the King

nṯr nfr nb t3.wy nb ỉr.(t) ḫ.t (2) s3 Rᶜ Thrq (3) dỉ ᶜnḫ ḏd w3s (4) mỉ Rᶜ ḏ.t (5) nṯr nfr nb t3.wy nb ỉr.(t) ḫ.t nb ḫ3s.wt [...]

The Good God, Lord of the Two Lands, Lord of ritual performance, (2) the Son of Re, Taharqa, (3) given life, stability, and dominion (4) like Re forever. (5) The Good God, Lord of the Two Lands, Lord of ritual performance, Lord of foreign countries [...]

EASTERN SIDE-CHAPEL

West Wall: Thoth recites before twelve seated deities.

ḏd-mdw ỉn nb Ḥmnw nb mdw-nṯr n psḏ.t [...] Ḥw-Nfr-tm-Rᶜ (2) s3 Rᶜ nb ḫᶜ.w Thrq ᶜnḫ ḏ.t dỉ≠n n≠f [...] (3) nḫt r Mḥt.t ỉr sš.w nb Ḥmnw [...] (4) tw m ḏd.t≠k nb (5) ntk Ḥmnw mn r nḥḥ sp-2 r ḏ.t sp-2

Recitation by the Lord of Hermopolis, Lord of Hieroglyphs, to the Ennead [...] Khunefertemre, (2) the Son of Re, Lord of diadems, Taharqa, living forever. Let us give to him [...] (3) victory against the North. May the scribes of the Lord of Hermopolis act [...] (4) you in accordance with all that you have said. Yours is Hermopolis, enduring (5) forever and ever!

159. KAWA RELIEF OF THE TRADITIONAL "LIBYAN SMITING SCENE"

Both halves of the divided rear wall of the first court of Temple T at Kawa bear colossal reliefs of the king as a rampant sphinx trampling defeated Libyan chiefs. Deities representing the west survey the scene approvingly, beside tallied files of captured herds and the forlorn wife and children of the Libyan ruler. The reliefs of this western wall are direct

Kawa Temple T Scene, Macadam 1955, plate IXb.

copies of traditional scenes found with little variation in the Old Kingdom valley temples of Sahure and Neuserre at Abusir and of Unas, Pepi I, and Pepi II at Saqqara. The imagery was maintained into the late Middle Kingdom as well, and related scenes have recently been identified at Thebes at the Deir el-Bahari temple of Montuhotep II. The surprising uniformity of these representations and text—with identical names for defeated Libyans over a span of two millennia—has served as a cautionary example against the uncritical acceptance of Egyptian historical reliefs. Far from being common, however, the stereotypical use of such a detailed, "historical" scene is unique and may reflect a cultic need to express mastery over Egypt's elusive, pastoral western neighbors. In the absence of contemporary encounters, an older record was reused in specific temple contexts.

The recurrence of the scene at Kawa is easily explained, since artists from the Memphite area were sent by the king to design the temple, as noted in Kawa Stela IV, lines 20–22. For Taharqa, the ancient scene would have had contemporary propagandistic value, bolstering his dynasty's claim to be the legitimate heir to Egyptian tradition, in contrast to its Libyan adversaries. In surely related actions, Taharqa supplied the same temple with "male and female servants from among the children of the rulers of the Libyans" (Kawa Stela III, line 22) and maidservants who had been "wives of chieftains of Lower Egypt" (Kawa Stela VI, line 20).

For the scenes, texts, and discussion, see Macadam 1955, 61, 63–65, and pls. IX and XLVIII–XLIX; and Ritner 2008, 305–14. For earlier examples of the standard Libyan scene, see the discussion and bibliography in Stockfisch 1996, 315–25. The Montuhotep example (OIM 8856) was first noted by Ritner 1996. Cf. Kitchen 1986, 389 and n. 844.

LABEL FOR THE RIGHTHAND (NORTH) SCENE

[ptpt ḫ]3s.wt nb.w(t)
[Trampling] all foreign lands.

LABEL BESIDE ANIMAL FILES

dbḥ ḥtp.w n (2) p.t Thrq (3) [...].t ꜣw.t-îb⸗f ḏ.t

Requirements of the altars of (2) heaven of Taharqa. (3) [...] so that his heart be elated forever.

LABEL FOR THE LIBYAN WIFE AND CHILDREN

Ḥw-ît⸗[s] (2) Wsꜣ (3) [Wnî]

Khuites. (2) Wesa. (3) [Weni.]

LABEL FOR DOOR FRAME

[...] nn ît n [...] ît(?) Ḥr nḫt(?) [...] (2) [...] ꜥnḫ wꜣs nb snb nb ꜣw.t-îb nb n sꜣ Rꜥ Th[rq ...]

[...] without seizing [...] which Horus the mighty (?) seized (?) [...] (2) [...] all life and dominion, all health and all joy to the Son of Re, Taharqa [...]

LABEL FOR LEFTHAND (SOUTH) SCENE

ptpt ḫꜣs.wt nb.w(t)

Trampling all foreign lands.

LABEL BESIDE ANIMAL FILES

ḥ(ꜣ)q.n⸗f ꜥw.t⸗sn (2) mnmn.(t)⸗sn nb.(t) (3) [... ḫꜣq].n⸗f ḫꜣs.wt bšd.w dî⸗f îr⸗sn šm.(t) ts[m.wᶦ ...]

He captured all their flocks (2) and herds. (3) [...] He has [captured (?)] the foreign lands that had revolted, causing them to walk at heel like dogs[1] [...].

LABEL FOR THE LIBYAN WIFE AND CHILDREN

Ḥw-ît⸗s (2) Wsꜣ (3) Wnî

Khuites. (2) Wesa. (3) Weni.

LABEL FOR DOOR FRAME

[... ꜥrq(?)].n⸗f ît.t [...] n [...] (2) [...] ꜥnḫ wꜣs nb [s]n[b nb] ꜣw.t-îb nb n sꜣ Rꜥ Thr[q ...]

[...] He has completed (?) seizing [...] (2) [...] all life and dominion, all health and all joy to the Son of Re, Taharqa [...]

NOTE

1. Literally, to "do the dog-walk." The passage is a paraphrase of the classical Instructions of Amonemhat; see Macadam 1955, 64–65, and cf. the Victory Stela of Piye, line 3. The passage is found also on the door frame to the Kawa hypostyle hall: "He has slaughtered the Temehu-Libyans, he has restrained the Asiatics, he has [captured (?)] the foreign countries that had revolted, causing them to do the

dog-walk, while the [sand-dweller]s, whose place is unknown, come fearful of the king's slaughter" (Macadam 1955, pl. XI).

160. KAWA STELA III
(NY CARLSBERG GLYPTOTEK ÆIN 1707)

Measuring 1.31 m by 0.71 m by 0.29 m., the grey granite round-topped stela was discovered *in situ* in the first court of Temple T at Kawa in Nubia, the ancient Gem(pa)aton. Although broken, the text is virtually complete and preserves the record of gifts presented by Taharqa to the temple of Gematon from his second to eighth years. In addition to the expected gifts of gold, silver, and copper utensils and other basic materials such as incense, wax, linen, and timber, Taharqa's scribes noted the politically significant assignment to the temple staff of "children of the rulers of the Libyans" (line 22). Clearly intended to demonstrate Taharqa's imperial control over the feudal polities of the north, the statement is nonetheless a tacit acknowledgment of the Nubian dynasty's failure to suppress local divisions within a reintegrated kingdom and is indicative of a philosophy of government not far removed from that proclaimed by Piye in his third year (Gebel Barkal Stela 26).

Imitating archaic practice, each section is introduced by an oversized palm branch signifying "regnal year," with the date indicated not by following numbers but by notches in the midsection of the branch itself. In the classically inspired lunette, flanking inscriptions of the royal titulary receive the signs of life and eternity from small figures of Amon and Nekhbet on the right and Anukis and Edjo on the left. Above the scene are the outspread wings of the Behdedite below the glyph for heaven. Despite the conscious attempts at formal classicism in design, the language of the stela lapses frequently into Late Egyptian spellings and grammar.

For the text, translation, and discussion, see Macadam 1949, 4–14 and pls. 5–6; and the revisions noted in the review by Clère 1951, 174–80. See Kitchen 1986, 167 §134, 169 §136, and 388 §349.

SYMMETRICAL LABEL FOR THE OVERARCHING WINGS
    Bḥd.t(y)   The Behdedite.

LABEL FOR AMON OFFERING LIFE TO THE ROYAL *SEREKH*
    ʾImn-Rˤ (n) Gm-ʾItn
    Amon-Re of Gematon.

LABEL FOR NEKHBET OFFERING ETERNITY TO THE ROYAL PRENOMEN
    Nḫb.t (2) dỉ⸗s (3) ˤnḫ wȝs
    Nekhbet, (2) as she gives (3) life and dominion.

ROYAL TITULARY

ꜥnḫ Ḥr q(3) ḫꜥ.w (2) ny-sw.t bἰ.ty Ḥw-Nfr-tm-Rꜥ (3) mry psḏ.t (4) nb
t3.wy Thrq (5) dἰ ꜥnḫ nb ḏd w3s (6) mἰ Rꜥ ḏ.t

Long live the Horus: "Exalted of Epiphanies"; (2) the King of Upper
and Lower Egypt, Khunefertemre, (3) beloved of the Ennead, (4) the Lord
of the Two Lands, Taharqa, (5) given all life, stability, and dominion (6)
like Re forever.

LABEL FOR ANUKIS OFFERING LIFE TO THE ROYAL *SEREKH*

ꜥnq.t nb.(t) St.t
Anukis, Lady of Sehel.

LABEL FOR EDJO OFFERING ETERNITY TO THE ROYAL PRENOMEN

W3ḏy.t (2) dἰ⸗s (3) ꜥnḫ w3s
Edjo, (2) as she gives (3) life and dominion.

ROYAL TITULARY

ꜥnḫ Ḥr q(3) ḫꜥ.w (2) ny-sw.t bἰ.ty Ḥw-Nfr-tm-Rꜥ (3) mry psḏ.t (4) nb
t3.wy Thrq (5) dἰ ꜥnḫ nb ḏd w3s (6) mἰ Rꜥ ḏ.t

Long live the Horus: "Exalted of Epiphanies"; (2) the King of Upper
and Lower Egypt, Khunefertemre, (3) beloved of the Ennead, (4) the Lord
of the Two Lands, Taharqa, (5) given all life, stability, and dominion (6)
like Re forever.

MAIN TEXT

(1) ḥsb.t [2.t] (n.t) Ḥr q(3) ḫꜥ.w Nb.ty q(3) ḫꜥ.w Ḥr-nbw ḫw t3.wy ny-
sw.t bἰ.ty Ḥw-Nfr-tm-Rꜥ s3 Rꜥ Thrq ꜥnḫ ḏ.t ἰr.n⸗f m mnw⸗f n ἰt[⸗f ꜢImn]-Rꜥ
nb Gm-ꜢItn

  ḥḏ ḫ3y.t 1 ἰr n dbn (2) 220
  nbw sḥtpy 1 ἰr n dbn 10
  nbw nms.t 1 ἰr n dbn 10 qd.t 5
  nbw wn.(t)-ḫ(r) 1 ἰr n dbn (1) qd.t 2
  ḥmt š3m 7
  p(3)g.(t) ḫyrd 50 šnd.t 38 (3) r(w)dy 12 mnḫ.t 20 ἰr n 120
  ḫsbd rp(y).t M3ꜥ.t 1
  pr.t ꜥwnw 1200
  nh.t snṯr
  sr (4) 1
  bnw 1

ἰr⸗f dἰ ꜥnḫ nb ḏd nb snb nb 3w.t-ἰb nb.(t) ἰr.t ḥḥ m ḥb-sd ꜥš3 wr.(t)
ḫꜥ.w m ny-sw.t bἰ.ty ḥr s.t Ḥr mἰ Rꜥ ḏ.t

(5) ḥsb.t 3.(t) (n.t) ny-sw.t bỉ.ty Thrq ꜥnḫ ḏ.t ỉr.n≠f m mnw≠f n ỉt≠f
ʾImn-Rꜥ nb Gm-ʾItn
    ḥḏ ḫꜣ(w)y.t 1
    nhp ḫꜣy(w).t 1
    nms.t (m) ḥr (n) šf.t 50
    ḥmt šw 20
    ḫꜣwy.(t) ꜥꜣ.(t) 20
    ḥmt dn(ỉ)(6).t 30
    ḥmt pšny 14
    ḥmt ꜥꜣgny 3
    ḥmt dnỉ.t n ḫ(y) ꜥꜣ 1
    ḥmt wḫꜣ.t ꜥꜣ.t 1
    mnḫ dbn 50
    mr[ḫ]w dbn 20
    snṯr ꜥq.w 7
    rdnw 5
    ỉmy.w-wnw.t 4
    mrḫw 2

(7) ḥsb.t 4.(t) (n.t) ny-sw.t bỉ.ty Thrq ꜥnḫ ḏ.t ỉr.n≠f m mnw≠f n ỉt≠f
ʾImn-Rꜥ nb Gm-ʾItn
    nbw dbn 100
    ḥḏ nms.t 5 m ḥr šf[.t] ỉr n dbn 8
    ḥḏ nms.t 1 ỉr n dbn 15
    nbw ḥs 1 ḥr≠s m ḥr n šf.t (8) ỉr n dbn 7
    nbw nms.t 1 ḥr≠s m ḥr n šf.t ỉr n dbn 3 qd.t 5.(t)
    ḥmt ḫr(y)-stꜣ 1
    ḥmt ḫꜣwy.(t) 3
    ḥmt sšn n ḫꜣwy.(t)[1] 3
    ḥmt ꜥgny 3 ỉr n dbn 9
    ḥdwy.(t) 3
ỉr≠f dỉ ꜥnḫ ḏd wꜣs nb snb nb ꜣw.t-ỉb nb.(t) ḏ.t

(9) ḥsb.t 5.(t) (n.t) ny-sw.t bỉ.ty Thrq ꜥnḫ ḏ.t ỉr.n≠f m mnw≠f n ỉt≠f
ʾImn-Rꜥ nb Gm-ʾItn
    nbw bb.t 1 ỉr n nbw dbn 21 qd.t 6.(t)
    ḫsbd dbn 15 qd.t (1)
    ỉnꜣq mꜣꜥ dbn 56
    mfk(ꜣ).(t) dbn 61
    ḫyrd 10 šnd.(t) 5 rwḏ 5 hꜣrtỉ 20 ỉr n 40

(10) ḥsb.t 6.(t) (n.t) ny-sw.t bỉ.ty Thrq ꜥnḫ ḏ.t ỉr.n≠f m mnw≠f n ỉt≠f
ʾImn-Rꜥ nb Gm-ʾItn

nbw ḥbs 1 ỉw tw(t) n ny-sw.t sš ḫr≠f ỉr n dbn 5 qd.(t) (1)
ḥḏ nbw ḏbꜥ.(t) 1
ỉr≠f dỉ ꜥnḫ ḏd wꜣs nb snb nb ꜣw.t-ỉb nb.(t) mỉ Rꜥ ḏ.t

(11) ḥsb.t 7.(t) (n.t) ny-sw.t bỉ.ty Thrq ꜥnḫ ḏ.t ỉr.n≠f m mnw≠f n ỉt≠f
ꜣImn-Rꜥ nb Gm-ꜣItn
nbw sḥtpy n ḫꜣ.ty 1
nbw bỉk 1 ỉw twt [n] ny-[sw.t] m-bꜣḥ≠f ỉw≠w ḥr rnp.t
nbw sšp n ḥr (n) šf.t 1 ḥnꜥ rp(ỉ).(t) nr ỉw≠w ḥr wꜥ.t (12) rnp.t
nbw šp(s) n Ḫnsw ỉw≠wᴮ ḥr wꜥ.t rnp.t
nbw twt n ꜣImn-Rꜥ nb Gm-ꜣItn ỉw šwꜣ[b] 2 ḥr ḏrw.w≠f twt n ny-
sw.t m-bꜣḥ≠f
(13) nbw msy.(t) 1
nbw ḥr n šf.t ḥr ỉꜣ.t 1
nbw ḥr n šf.t ḥr bỉnr.t 3
nbw špš n ꜣImn-Rꜥ [nb] Gm-ꜣItn ḥr bỉnr.t 1
nbw rp(y).t ꜣs.t 1 ỉr n (14) nbw dbn 11 qd.t 3.(t) 1/2
ỉsh(ꜣ) 2
ỉr.n sꜣ Rꜥ Thrq ꜥnḫ ḏ.t n ỉt≠f ꜣImn-Rꜥ nb [G]m-ꜣItn ỉr≠f dỉ ꜥnḫ nb ḏd nb
wꜣs nb snb nb ꜣw.t-ỉb nb.(t) mỉ Rꜥ ḏ.t

(15) ḥsb.t 8.(t) (n.t) ny-sw.t bỉ.ty Thrq ꜥnḫ ḏ.t ỉr.n≠f m mnw≠f (n)
ꜣImn-Rꜥ nb Gm-ꜣItn
ḥmt twt n ny-sw.t ỉw≠f smꜣ ḫꜣs.wt ḥbs.w≠f 6
ḥḏ (16) nbw ỉbry.w 8
pꜣ grg n pꜣ rꜣ-pr n mꜣ(w.t) r-qd ḥm≠f
nbw hd[n] 1
nbw ḥs.t 1
nbw nms.t 1
nbw ꜥbš 2
nbw (17) šnb.t 1
nbw sp.t snṯr 1
nbw šfd 1
ḥḏ ḫꜣy.t ḫ(y.t) 1
twt n ny-sw.t ḥr≠s m nbw 1
nbw twt n Ḥꜥp(y) nty ḥr≠s 1
ỉr n nbw ỉpd 10 (18) ỉr n nbw dbn 51 qd.t 4.(t)
ḥḏ ḥtp 1
ḥḏ ḫꜣwy.(t) 15
ḥḏ ḫꜣwy.(t) ḫ(y.t) 1
ḥḏ sḥtp 1
ḥḏ ḥs.t 1
ḥḏ sp.t snṯr 1

ḥḏ šf(19)d 1
ḥḏ šnb.(t) 1
ḥḏ msy.t 1
ḥḏ ʿbš 1
ḥḏ qb.t 1
ḥḏ ḥm.t 2
ḥḏ wšm 4
ḥḏ sšn 1
ḥḏ pšny (20) 1
ḥḏ wdḥ 1
ḥḏ hn n wp-rȝ 1 nt.t îm≠f
    ḥḏ dš(r).ty 4
    ḥḏ bs 2
    ḥḏ ʿrf 2
    ḥḏ rrm 4
    îms 4
    (21) îr n dbḥ.(t) 17
ḥḏ ḥḏ.t 1 îr n dbn 1891 qd.t (1.t)
nbw p(ȝ)g n tȝ(î) 35
ḫt nb šnd.(t) ʿš šwȝb

smn.n≠f ḥtp.(22)w-nṯr sḏfȝ ḫȝwy.w(t)≠f swȝḏ šnʿ≠f m ḥm.w ḥm.wt m ms.w ḥqȝ.w n.w Tḥn.w (23) grg ḥw.t-nṯr tn îr.(t).n≠f n≠f (n)-mȝw.(t) mḥ.n≠f sw m ḫny.wt ʿȝ šḫm.w≠sn m ʿ.wy≠sn r sšš n (24) ḫr≠f nfr îr≠f n≠f îswy m nn m rdî.(t) n≠f ʿnḫ nb ḫr≠f ḏd nb ḫr≠f wȝs nb ḫr≠f snb nb ḫr≠f (25) ȝw.t-îb nb.(t) ḫr≠f îr≠f ḥḥ m ḥb.(w)-sd ʿȝ wr.(t) ḫʿ ḥr s.t Ḥr n.t ʿnḫ. w ȝw-îb≠f ḥnʿ kȝ≠f mî Rʿ ḏ.t nḥḥ

(1) Regnal year [2] (of) the Horus: "Exalted of Epiphanies"; the Two Ladies: "Exalted of Epiphanies"; the Horus of Gold: "Protector of the Two Lands"; the King of Upper and Lower Egypt, Khunefertemre, the Son of Re, Taharqa, living forever. As his monument for [his] father [Amon]-Re, Lord of Gematon, he made:

    1 silver altar, amounting to (2) 220 *deben,*
    1 gold censer, amounting to 10 *deben,*
    1 gold ewer, amounting to 10 *deben* and 5 *kite,*
    1 gold mirror, amounting to a *deben* and 2 *kite,*
    7 large bronze vessels,
    50 veils, 38 kilts, (3) 12 garments, and 20 clothes of fine linen
        amounting to 120,
    1 lapis lazuli figure of Maat,
    1200 cypress seeds,
    an incense tree of sycamore,

1 (4) drum,

1 harp,

so that he might attain the state of being given all life, all stability, all health, all joy, and the celebration of millions of jubilee festivals, most numerously, appearing in glory as King of Upper and Lower Egypt upon the throne of Horus like Re forever.

(5) Regnal year 3 (of) the King of Upper and Lower Egypt, Taharqa, living forever. As his monument for his father Amon-Re, Lord of Gematon, he made:

1 silver vase,

1 cover of the vase,

50 ewers with a ram's face,

20 bronze jars,

20 large vases,

30 bronze (6) bowls,

14 bronze vessels,

3 bronze ring-stands,

1 bronze bowl of great height,

1 great bronze cauldron,

50 *deben* of wax,

20 *deben* of bitumen,

7 loaves of incense,

5 of laudanum,

4 astrologer priests,

2 astronomical instruments.

(7) Regnal year 4 (of) the King of Upper and Lower Egypt, Taharqa, living forever. As his monument for his father Amon-Re, Lord of Gematon, he made:

100 *deben* of gold,

5 silver ewers with ram's faces, amounting to 8 *deben*,

1 silver ewer, amounting to 15 *deben*,

1 gold offering vase, whose face is a ram's face, (8) amounting to
7 *deben*,

1 gold ewer, whose face is a ram's face, amounting to 3 *deben* and
5 *kite*,

1 bronze brazier-stand,

3 bronze vases,

3 bronze *nymphea lotuses* for vases,[1]

3 bronze ring-stands, amounting to 9 *deben*,

3 lamps,

so that he might attain the state of being given all life, stability, and dominion, all health and all joy forever.

(9) Regnal year 5 (of) the King of Upper and Lower Egypt, Taharqa, living forever. As his monument for his father Amon-Re, Lord of Gematon, he made:

> 1 gold collar, amounting to 21 *deben* and 6 *kite* of gold,
> 15 *deben* and a *kite* of lapis lazuli,
> 56 *deben* of real tin,
> 61 *deben* of turquoise,
> 10 veils, 5 kilts, 5 garments, and 20 cloths, amounting to 40.

(10) Regnal year 6 (of) the King of Upper and Lower Egypt, Taharqa, living forever. As his monument for his father Amon-Re, Lord of Gematon, he made:

> 1 gold covering with an image of the king drawn upon it, amount-
>   ing to 5 *deben* and a *kite*,
> 1 silver and gold signet-ring,

so that he might attain the state of being given all life, stability, and dominion, all health and all joy like Re forever.

(11) Regnal year 7 (of) the King of Upper and Lower Egypt, Taharqa, living forever. As his monument for his father Amon-Re, Lord of Gematon, he made:

> 1 gold censer in the form of the forepart of a lion,
> 1 gold falcon with an image of the king before it, both being on
>   a year-sign,
> 1 gold criosphinx together with a figure of a vulture, both being
>   on a (12) year-sign,
> a gold statuette of Khonsu, being[2] on a year-sign,
> a gold image of Amon-Re, Lord of Gematon, with two persea trees
>   at its edges and an image of the king before it,
> (13) 1 gold dish,
> 1 gold ram's head on a standard,
> 3 gold ram's heads on date palms,
> 1 gold statuette of Amon-Re, [Lord] of Gematon, on a date palm,
> 1 gold figure of Isis, amounting to (14) 11 *deben* and 3 1/2 *kite*
>   of gold,
> 2 linen strips,

which the Son of Re, Taharqa, living forever, made for his father Amon-Re, Lord of [Ge]maton, so that he might attain the state of being given all life, all stability, all dominion, all health, and all joy like Re forever.

(15) Regnal year 8 (of) the King of Upper and Lower Egypt, Taharqa,

living forever. As his monument for Amon-Re, Lord of Gematon, he made:

> 1 bronze image of the king slaying the foreign lands, and its 6 garments,
> 8 silver (16) and gold unguent jars,
> the equipment of the new temple that His Majesty built:
>> 1 gold broom,
>> 1 gold offering vase,
>> 1 gold ewer,
>> 2 gold vessels,
>> 1 gold (17) trumpet,
>> 1 gold incense measure,
>> 1 gold incense burner,
>> 1 tall silver altar,
>>> with 1 gold image of the king on it,
>>> and 1 gold image of Hapi that is on it,
>> amounting to 10 gold articles, (18) amounting to 51 *deben* and 4 *kite* of gold,
> 1 silver offering stand,
> 15 silver vases,
> 1 tall silver vase,
> 1 silver censer,
> 1 silver offering vase,
> 1 silver incense measure,
> 1 silver incense burner, (19)
> 1 silver trumpet,
> 1 silver dish,
> 1 silver vessel,
> 1 silver beer jar,
> 2 silver pots,
> 4 silver situlae,
> 1 silver *nymphea lotus* cup,
> 1 silver (20) vessel,
> 1 silver pitcher,
> 1 silver chest for the Opening the Mouth Ritual, and its contents:
>> 4 silver "red pots,"
>> 2 silver torches,
>> 2 silver bags,
>> 4 silver myrrh containers,
>> 4 scepters,
>> (21) amounting to 17 implements,
> 1 silver shrine, amounting to 1891 *deben* and a *kite*,
> 35 thin sheets of gold for engraving (?),
> and every sort of timber: acacia, cedar, and persea.

He established the endowment (22) of the god precisely with its altars provisioned, its magazines supplied with male and female servants from among the children of the rulers of the Libyans, (23) and this temple, which he had made for him, founded anew. He filled it with numerous chantresses, with their sistra in their hands, in order to play before (24) his beautiful face just so that he might repay him for this by giving to him all life issuing from him, all stability issuing from him, all dominion issuing from him, all health issuing from him, (25) all joy issuing from him, and that he might celebrate millions of jubilee festivals, most numerously, appearing in glory upon the Horus throne of the living, being joyful with his *ka*-spirit, like Re forever and ever.

NOTES
   1. So Macadam; or read wdn n ḫȝwy.(t) "offering holders of/for vessels"?
   2. The scribe has carelessly recopied the plural of line 11.

161. KAWA STELA IV
(MEROWE MUSEUM NO. 52)

Discovered *in situ* in the first court of Temple T at Kawa in Nubia, the grey granite round-topped stela measures 2.08 m by 0.81 m by 0.35 m. The text recounts Taharqa's reconstruction of the ruined Kawa temple, the ancient Gempaaton, which he had visited as a youth over six years previously when summoned to Egypt from Nubia to join his elder brother, the former king Shebitku. Dated in the sixth year of Taharqa, the stela was erected following the completion—rather than the instigation—of the work, as noted in lines 22–26. Royal gifts during and after the course of reconstruction are recorded in Kawa Stela III, and the rebuilt temple would not be dedicated formally until year 10, as documented by Kawa Stela VII. A mistranslation of lines 12–13 of the stela reinforced belief in a supposed co-regency between Shebitku and Taharqa, since the latter was thought to have been summoned northward in his own first regnal year. Correctly translated, however, Taharqa's action in his first year was to recall his former visit, not to undertake it.

In the lunette, a winged disk hovers below the curved sign for heaven supported by two *was*-scepters and over a dual scene of Taharqa offering to Amon and Anukis. The texts are largely symmetrical, differing only to indicate the offering of wine on the right and bread on the left. On the right, Taharqa wears the distinctive Cushite headband while Anukis has the double crown. On the left the situation is somewhat reversed, with Taharqa wearing the double crown and Anukis bearing her own unique headdress.

For the text, translations, and discussions, see Macadam 1949, 14–21 and pls. 7–8; and the revisions noted in the review by Clère 1951, 176–77; Leclant and Yoyotte 1952, 15–27; Rainey 1976, 38–41; and Eide et al. 1994, 135–45. See Kitchen 1986, 149 §120, 157–58 §127, 160 §129, 164–72 §§132–37, 388 §349; 1995, xli §KK.

LABEL FOR WINGED DISK

Bḥd.t(y) nṯr ꜥꜣ nb p.t
The Behdedite, great god, lord of heaven.

LABEL FOR AMON

ꜣImn-Rꜥ Gm-ꜣItn (2) nṯr ꜥꜣ nb p.t (3) ḏd-mdw dỉ.n≠(ỉ) n≠k ꜥnḫ wꜣs nb
Amon-Re of Gematon, (2) great god, lord of heaven. (3) Recitation: "Thus I have given to you all life and dominion."

LABEL FOR ANUKIS

ꜥnq.t (2) ḏd-mdw dỉ.n≠(ỉ) n≠k ꜥnḫ wꜣs nb snb nb ꜣw.t-ỉb nb mỉ Rꜥ ḏ.t
Anukis. (2) Recitation: "Thus I have given to you all life and dominion, all health and all joy like Re forever."

LABEL FOR THE KING

nṯr nfr nb tꜣ.wy nb ỉr.(t) ḫ.t (2) Thrq (3) dỉ ꜥnḫ (4) sꜣ ꜥnḫ nb ḥꜣ≠f mỉ Rꜥ ḏ.t
The Good God, Lord of the Two Lands, Lord of ritual performance, (2) Taharqa, (3) given life. (4) The protection of all life is around him like Re forever.

LABEL FOR THE RIGHTHAND SCENE

rdỉ.t ỉrp n ỉt≠f ꜣImn ỉr≠f dỉ-ꜥnḫ
Giving wine to his father Amon, so that he might attain the state of being given life.

LABEL FOR LEFTHAND SCENE

sq(r) t ḥḏ n ỉt≠f ꜣImn ỉr≠f dỉ-ꜥnḫ
Consecrating white bread for his father Amon so that he might attain the state of being given life.

MAIN TEXT

(1) ḥsb.t 6.t ḫr ḥm n Ḥr q(ꜣ) ḫꜥ.w Nb.ty q(ꜣ) ḫꜥ.w Ḥr-nbw ḫw tꜣ.wy ny-sw.t bỉ.ty Ḫw-Nfr-tm-Rꜥ sꜣ Thrq ꜥnḫ ḏ.t mrỉ-Mꜣꜥ.t rdỉ (2) n≠f ꜣImn Mꜣꜥ.t ꜥnḫ ḏ.t

ỉst ḥm≠f m nb rnpỉ pr-ꜥ qn(ỉ) wꜥw ny-sw.t sḫm n(n) mỉt.t≠f ḥq(ꜣ) mỉ Tm mr.w(t)≠f (3) ḥr pḥr tꜣ.w mỉ Rꜥ ḫꜥꜥ≠f m p.t sꜣ Rꜥ mỉ ꜣIn-ḥr.(t) ny.t-sw.t≠f m ḫḫ mỉ Tꜣ-twnn wn (4) nm.t wsḫ tb.wy h(ꜣ)b sšr≠f sḫm≠f wr.w

ptpt dw.w m-s₃ ḫrw(5).w≠f ꜥḥ₃ ḥr ḫpš≠f sm₃ ḥfn.w wnn ḥr nb ggwy n m₃≠f
ḥꜥꜥ n≠f bw-nb.w m ḫꜥ≠f (6) ꜥḥ₃ m ỉb≠f rꜥ nb n whs.n≠f ḥm.t≠f pw sḫnw ḥr
b₃k.w r₃-ꜥ-ḫt rn≠f pḫr m t₃.w ḥr (7) ḫ₃s.t nb.(t) m qn(ỉ) n ḫpš≠f qn(ỉ)

ỉs ḥm≠f m T₃-Stỉ m ḥwn nfr sn ny-sw.t bnr mr(w.t) ỉw.(t) pw ỉr.n≠f m
(8) ḫd r W₃s.t m-q(₃)b ḥwn.w nfr.w ḥ(₃)b.n ḥm≠f ny-sw.t Š₃b₃t₃k₃ m₃ꜥ-ḫrw
m-s₃≠w r T₃-Stỉ wnn≠f (9) ỉm ḫnꜥ≠f mr.n≠f sw r sn.w≠f sw₃≠f¹ r sp₃.t tn
n.t ꜣImn Gm-p₃-ꜣItn sn≠f² t₃ r rw.ty ḥw.t-nṯr ḫnꜥ (10) mšꜥ n ḥm≠f ḫd r-ḫnꜥ≠f
gm.n≠f ḥw.t-nṯr tn qd.tw m db.(w)t pḫ.n q₃₃.t (11) ỉr(y)≠w tp-ḥw.t≠s (ỉ)ꜥꜥ
m ₃ḫ.t r tr n rnp.t snd.(t) n ḫpr ḫ(wỉ).t₃ wnn ỉb n ḥm≠f w₃ r (12) dw ḥr≠s
r ḫꜥ ḥm≠f m ny-sw.t ḫꜥ ny-sw.t ḫꜥ bỉ.ty smn Nb.ty tp≠f ḫpr rn≠f m Ḥr q(₃)
ḫꜥ.w sḫ₃.n≠f ḥw.t-nṯr (13) tn m₃.n≠f m ḥwn m rnp.t tp.(t) n.t ḫꜥ≠f

dd ỉn ḥm≠f n smr.w≠f mk ỉb≠ỉ r qd ḥw.t-nṯr (14) n.(t) ỉt≠ỉ ꜣImn-Rꜥ
Gm-p₃-ꜣItn ḥr-nt.t wnn≠s qd.tw m db.(w)t (ỉ)ꜥꜥ.tw m ₃ḫ.t nn r≠f (15) nfr
ḥr ỉb≠w⁴ wn nṯr pn m s.t tn n(n) rḫ ỉr.t.n ḫ(w)y.t ntf pw swd₃ r₃-pr pn r
ḫpr.(t) ḫꜥ≠ỉ m ny-sw.t (16) rḫ.n≠f nt.t ỉr.n≠(ỉ) n≠f mnw s₃≠f ỉm m₃≠k n≠ỉ
w.t≠ỉ (17) ỉn sn≠sn smsw⁵ s₃ Rꜥ ꜣIrrỉ m₃ꜥ-ḫrw m dd nṯr pn rḫ nt.t ḥr mw≠f
ḫyḫy ỉw n ꜥš n≠f (18) m₃≠k n≠ỉ r ḫ.t n.(t) gs.wy.w(t)≠ỉ smn≠k ms.w≠sn
tp t₃ ỉr≠k n≠sn mỉ ỉr.n≠k n≠ỉ dỉ≠k spr≠sn r b(w)(19)-nfr sdm.n≠f n dd.t≠f
r≠n sꜥḥꜥ.n≠f wỉ m ny-sw.t mỉ dd.n≠f n≠f nfr.wy ỉs ỉr.t n ỉr qb (20) ỉs ỉb
n ỉrr n ỉr n≠f

dd.n≠sn ḫft ḥm≠f wn m₃ꜥ.t pw dd.t≠k nb s₃≠f ỉm(y)≠k smnḫ mnw.w≠f
rdỉ.n ḥm≠f (21) šm mšꜥ≠f⁶ r Gm-(p₃)-ꜣItn ḫnꜥ ỉs.w(t) ꜥ₃ ḥmww.w nfr.w
n(n) rḫ tnw≠sn ỉmy-r₃ k₃.t ỉm ḫ(22)nꜥ≠sn r ḫrp k₃.t m r₃-pr pn ỉs ḥm≠f
m-ḥnw ꜣInb-ḥd

ꜥḥꜥ.n qd ḥw.t-nṯr tn m ỉnr ḥd nfr n rwd.t mn(23)ḫ.tw rwd.tw ỉr.tw m
k₃.t nḥḥ ḥr≠s r ỉmnt.t pr m nbw wḫ₃y.w m nbw ꜥrw(24).w ỉr(y)≠w m ḥd
qd bḫn.w≠s sꜥḥꜥ sb₃.w≠s ḫt.tw ḥr rn wr n ḥm≠f wd mn.w≠s ꜥ₃ (25) m t₃
šd š.w≠s ḫnꜥ ḥw.t-ḥsmn≠s⁷ mḥ.tw m dbḥ.w≠s n.w ḥd nbw (26) ḥmt nn rḫ
tnw ỉr(y)≠w rdỉ ḥtp nṯr pn m-ḥnw≠s ₃ḫ mnḫ d.t (27) ỉswy m nn m ꜥnḫ
w₃s ḫꜥ ḥr s.t Ḥr d.t

(1) Regnal year 6 under the Majesty of the Horus: "Exalted of Epiphanies"; the Two Ladies: "Exalted of Epiphanies"; the Horus of Gold:
"Protector of the Two Lands"; the King of Upper and Lower Egypt, Khunefertemre, the Son of Re, Taharqa, living forever, beloved of Maat, to whom
Amon gives Maat, living forever.

Now, His Majesty is a master of rejuvenation, a champion, one
uniquely valiant, a powerful king who has no equal, a ruler like Atum,
love of whom (3) pervades the lands like Re when he appears in the sky,
a Son of Re like Onuris, whose kingship is infinite like Tatenen, with open
(4) stride, wide(-spread) sandals, who sends forth his arrow that he might
overpower chiefs, who tramples the mountains in pursuit of his enemies,
(5) who fights with his strong arm, slaying hundreds of thousands, at the

sight of whom every face is dazzled, for whom everyone rejoices when he appears (6) with fighting in his heart daily. He does not weary, since providing for the works of war is his skill, his name pervading the lands and (7) every foreign country by means of the valor of his valiant strong arm.

Now, His Majesty was in Nubia as a goodly youth, a king's brother, sweetly beloved. He came (8) northward to Thebes in the midst of the goodly youths for whom His Majesty, King Shebitku, the justified, had sent word to Nubia, so that he might be (9) there with him, since he loved him more than all his brothers. As soon as he passed[1] into this district of Amon of Gempaaton, he kissed[2] the ground at the gates of the temple together with (10) the army of His Majesty that had come north with him. He found this temple built with bricks, but with a (11) mound deriving from them having reached its roof, which had been covered over with earth at the time of a dreadful year through the occurrence of rainfall.[3] The heart of His Majesty was fallen into (12) a state of sadness concerning it until His Majesty appeared as king, crowned as King of Upper and Lower Egypt, when the double crown had been established upon his head, and his name became the Horus "Exalted of Epiphanies." It was in the first year of his reign that he recalled this temple (13) that he had seen as a youth.

His Majesty then said to his courtiers: "Behold, my desire is to rebuild the temple (14) of my father Amon-Re of Gempaaton, because it was built with bricks but is covered over with earth, which is (15) unacceptable.[4] This god has been in this situation because what the rain had done was unknown. It is he who has safeguarded this temple until it happened that I appeared as king, (16) since he knows that I have made for him a monument, for his son am I, whom he has begotten, since the mothers of my mother were dedicated to him (17) by their elder[5] brother, the Son of Re, Alara, the justified, with the words: 'This god knows who is loyal to him. Hasten, O he who comes to the one who calls to him! (18) May you look after the wombs of my female relatives for me; may you establish their children on earth; may you act for them as you have acted for me; may you cause that they attain (19) prosperity.' As he hearkened to what he said regarding us, so he elevated me as king just as he had said to him. How good it is, then, (for me now) to act for the one who has acted! For refreshed (20) is the heart of him who acts for the one who has acted for him."

Before His Majesty they said: "All that you have said is the very truth, for you are his son, who embellishes his monuments." His Majesty sent (21) his army[6] expressly to Gem(pa)aton together with numerous work crews and good craftsmen in incalculable numbers, an architect being there (22) with them to direct the work in this temple—for His Majesty was in Memphis.

Then this temple was built in good white sandstone, excellent, (23) firm, and made as an eternal construction, with its face toward the west, the house in gold, the columns in gold, the inlays (?) (24) on them in silver, while its pylon towers were built, its portals were erected, being engraved with the great name of His Majesty, its numerous groves were planted (25) in the ground, its lakes were dug, in addition to its house of natron[7] filled with its implements of silver, gold, (26) and bronze in incalculable numbers, and this god was caused to rest within it, glorious and effective forever, (27) with the reward for this being life and dominion and appearance in glory upon the throne of Horus forever.

NOTES

1. Rainey has misread the text as sn.n(!)≠f r sp3.t n.t 'Imn.

2. The scribe has carved a horizontal "s" in place of the expected bookroll determinative.

3. Macadam provided a loose translation: "having been covered over with earth at a time of year when one feared the occurrence of rainfall," attributing the dirt covering to human agency as a form of weak protection. However, rain is named as the cause of the mudslide in line 15.

4. Literally, "not good in hearts."

5. Macadam read the term as wr "Chief," at this date an unlikely combination with the formal Pharaonic titles adopted by the Cushites.

6. The unusual spelling appears also in Demotic; see Erichsen 1954, 181.

7. The term designates the purification chapel of the temple.

162. THE EXTRAORDINARY HIGH NILE IN TAHARQA'S YEAR 6 (THE KAWA V, COPTOS, MATAANA, AND TANIS STELAE)

Preserved in four exemplars, Taharqa's formal record of the great flood in his sixth year corresponds to the highest flood level carved on the western face of the Karnak quay (texts 34–35), marking the highest inundation known from antiquity. Although 0.055 m higher than the disastrous flood a century earlier in the third year of Osorkon III (text 5), this inundation is proclaimed a beneficial "wonder" on behalf of the Nubian king. In a propagandistic exercise of ancient "spin-doctoring," the overwhelming flood is interpreted as one of four miracles, entailing as well the riddance of rats and snakes, the predation of locusts, and the destructive south wind, so that the king acquires an extraordinary harvest in time to be witnessed by his proud mother on her first visit to the king in Egypt.

The most complete version is found on the grey granite Stela Kawa V (Ny Carlsberg Glyptotek ÆIN 1712), discovered *in situ* in the first court of Temple T at Kawa in Nubia and measuring 2.02 m by 1.22 m by 0.31 m. In the lunette, below the sign for heaven supported by two *was*-scepters, a solar disk spreads its wings above addorsed scenes of Taharqa offering wine jars to Amon in human form on the right and bread to ram-headed

Amon on the left. In both scenes Taharqa's mother Abar stands behind her son and raises a sistrum.

The first recognized copy of the text, discovered in successive excavations at Tanis by Mariette, Petrie, and Montet, is fragmentary and contains only the conclusion. Two further, abbreviated copies in the Cairo Museum describe the flood but include neither the king's response nor mention of his mother's visit from Nubia. The grey granite Coptos version (Cairo JdE 48440) measures 1.08m by 0.57 m by 0.35 m and depicts Taharqa offering fields to Min, Horus, and "Isis the great, Lady of heaven." The smaller pink granite Mataana version (Cairo JdE 38269) measures 0.88 m by 0.53 m by 0.35 m and shows addorsed scenes of Taharqa offering fields to the god "Hemen, Lord of Hefat, who gives all life, dominion, all health, all joy, all lands, and all foreign countries." The "Behdedite, great god, Lord of heaven, who gives life and dominion," appears atop the lunette on both Cairo stelae. The great flood was celebrated also by an issue of commemorative scarabs proclaiming Taharqa "beloved of Hapi, Lord of food."

For the collated texts, translations, and discussion, see Macadam 1949, 22–32 and pls. 9–10; with the revisions noted in the review by Clère 1951, 175; Eide et al. 1994, 145–58; Rainey 1976, 38–41; Griffith 1938, 423–30; Kuentz 1938, 430–32; Vikientieff 1930 (Coptos and Mataana); Leclant and Yoyotte 1952, 15–27; 1949, 28–37, 90 pls. II–III (Tanis and Louvre scarab N. 632); Petrie 1888, 12, 29–30, and pl. 9; and Breasted 1906–7, 4:455–57 §§892–96 (Tanis Stela). Line numbers follow Kawa Stela V; additions from parallel texts are placed in <>. See Kitchen 1986, 157–58 §127, 164–72 §§132–37, 387–89 §§348–49, and 585 §529.

LABEL FOR WINGED DISK
Bḥd.t(y) nṯr ꜥꜣ nb p.t
The Behdedite, the great god, lord of heaven.

RIGHHAND SCENE

Label for Amon of Thebes
ꜣImn-Rꜥ nb ns.wt tꜣ.wy (2) nb p.t (3) ḏd-mdw dî.n≠î n≠k ꜥnḫ wꜣs nb ḏd.t nb ꜣw.t-îb nb mî Rꜥ ḏ.t
Amon-Re, Lord of the Thrones of the Two Lands, (2) Lord of heaven. (3) Recitation: "Thus I have given to you all life and dominion, all stability and all joy like Re forever."

Label for the King
nṯr nfr nb tꜣ.wy (2) Ḥw-Nfr-tm-Rꜥ (3) sꜣ Rꜥ n ḥ.t≠f (4) Thrq (5) dî ꜥnḫ nb mî Rꜥ (6) ḏ.t (7) rdî.t îrp n ît≠f ꜣImn îr≠f dî ꜥnḫ
The Good God, Lord of the Two Lands, (2) Khunefertemre, (3) bodily

Son of Re, (4) Taharqa, (5) given all life like Re (6) forever. (7) Giving wine to his father Amon so that he might attain the state of being given life.

Label for the Queen Mother

mw.t ny-sw.t (2) ˀIbꜣr (3) ỉr.t sšš.t n ỉt⸗s ỉr⸗s dỉ ꜥnḫ

The Queen Mother, (2) Abar. (3) Playing the sistrum for her father so that she might attain the state of being given life.

LEFTHAND SCENE

Label for the Ram-Headed Amon

ˀImn-Rꜥ (2) (n) Gm-ˀItn (3) ḏd-mdw dỉ.n⸗ỉ n⸗k ꜥnḫ wꜣs nb snb nb ꜣw.t-ỉb nb mỉ Rꜥ ḏ.t

Amon-Re (2) of Gematon (Kawa). (3) Recitation: "Thus I have given to you all life and dominion, all health and all joy like Re forever."

Label for the King

nṯr nfr nb tꜣ.wy (2) Ḥw-Nfr-tm-Rꜥ (3) sꜣ Rꜥ n ḫ.t⸗f (4) Thrq (5) dỉ ꜥnḫ nb mỉ Rꜥ (6) ḏ.t (7) sq(r) t ḥḏ n ỉt⸗f ˀImn ỉr⸗f dỉ ꜥnḫ

The Good God, Lord of the Two Lands, (2) Khunefertemre, (3) bodily Son of Re, (4) Taharqa, (5) given all life like Re (6) forever. (7) Consecrating white bread for his father Amon so that he might attain the state of being given life.

Label for the Queen Mother

mw.t ny-sw.t (2) ˀIbꜣr (3) ỉr.t sšš.t n ỉt⸗s ỉr⸗s dỉ ꜥnḫ

The Queen Mother, (2) Abar. (3) Playing the sistrum for her father so that she might attain the state of being given life.

MAIN TEXT

(1) ḥsb.t 6.t ḫr ḥm n Ḥr q(ꜣ) ḫꜥ.w Nb.ty q(ꜣ) ḫꜥ.w Ḥr-nbw ḫw tꜣ.wy ny-sw.t bỉ.ty [Ḥw-Nfr-tm-Rꜥ] <nṯr nfr sꜣ ˀImn-Rꜥ tỉ.t ꜣḫ.t n.t Tm pr.t wꜥb.t pr.t ḫnty⸗f qmꜣ.n Rsy-ỉnb⸗f nfr.w⸗f ms.n Mw.t nb.t p.t wꜥ nṯry pr m ỉwf. w nṯr bỉ.ty nn ḫpr mỉ.ty⸗f dmḏ.n psḏ.t r rnn[⸗f] r snq[⸗f r] ḫnm[⸗f] ỉt tꜣ.w wꜥf pḏ.t psḏ.t ny-sw.t bỉ.ty Ḥr tmꜣ ꜥ nb tꜣ.wy nb ỉr.(t) ḫ.t> sꜣ Rꜥ [Thrq] ꜥnḫ ḏ.t mrỉ-Mꜣꜥ.t rdỉ n⸗f ˀImn Mꜣꜥ.t¹ ꜥnḫ ḏ.t

<ỉ>sk <r⸗f> ḥm⸗f mr nṯr pw (2) wrš⸗f m hrw sḏr⸗f m grḥ ḥr ḥḥ ꜣḫ.wt n nṯr.w ḥr qd rꜣ.w-pr.w⸗sn wꜣ r mrḫ ḥr ms sšm.w⸗sn mỉ sp tp(y) ḥr qd šnꜥ.w⸗sn ḥr sḏfꜣ (3) ḫꜥ.wt⸗sn ḥr smꜣꜥ n⸗sn ḥtp.w-nṯr m ḫ.t nb.(t) ḥr ỉr.t wdḥw.(w)⸗sn m ḏꜥmw ḥḏ ḥm.t

ỉs<k> gr ḥtp ỉb n ḥm⸗f m ỉr.t n⸗sn ꜣḫ.wt rꜥ nb wnn tꜣ pn ḥr bꜥḥw (4) m rk⸗f mỉ wnn⸗f m m h(ꜣ)w Nb-r-ḏr s nb sḏr r šsp n<n> ḏd ḥw n⸗ỉ r-s(y)² Mꜣꜥ.t bs.tw m-ḫt ỉdb.w ỉsf.t ḏdm m sꜣṯw wnn (5) bỉꜣ.wt ḫpr m rk ḥm⸗f m

ḥsb.t 6.(t) n.t ḫꜥ⸗f n pꜣ.tw mꜣꜣ mỉt.t ỉry ḏr rk ỉmy.w-ḥꜣ.t n-ꜥꜣ-n mr sw ỉt⸗f
ꜣImn-Rꜥ wnn ḥm⸗f ḥr (6) dbḥ Ḥꜥp(y) m-ꜥ ỉt⸗f ꜣImn-Rꜥ nb ns.wt tꜣ.wy ḥr
tm rdỉ ḫpr šwꜣ m rk⸗f

ỉs gr ḫ.t nb.(t) prr ḥr sp.ty ḥm⸗f dd ỉt⸗f ꜣImn ḫpr⸗sn ḥr-ꜥ.w(y) ḫpr.
n tr n ḥw(ỉ).t (7) Ḥꜥp(y) wnn⸗f ḥr ḥw(ỉ).t m b(w)-wr rꜥ nb ỉr.n⸗f hrw.w
ꜥšꜣ ḥr ḥw(ỉ).t m mḥ 1 rꜥ nb ꜥq.n⸗f dw.w Tꜣ-Šmꜥw ḥr-tp.n⸗f ỉꜣ.wt Tꜣ-Mḥw
wnn tꜣ m Nnw m nn(ỉ) nn tn(ỉ) (8) mꜣw.t r ỉtrw ḥwỉ.n⸗f m mḥ 21 šsp 1
ḏbꜥ 2 1/2 r dmỉ.t n.(t) Wꜣs.t rdỉ.n ḥm⸗f ỉn.tw n⸗f gnw.wt n.t tp(y).w-ꜥ ḥr
mꜣꜥ Ḥꜥp(y) ḫpr m hꜣ(w)⸗sn n<n> gm.tw mỉt.t ỉry ỉm

(9) ỉs gr ḥw(ỉ) p.t m Tꜣ-Stỉ sthn.n⸗s dw.w r-dr⸗sn wnn s nb n.w Tꜣ-Stỉ
bꜥḥ m ḫ.t nb.(t) wnn Km.t m ḫb nfr dwꜣ⸗sn nṯr n ḥm⸗fꜣ wnn ỉb n ḥm⸗f
nfr r ḫ.t nb.(t) m ỉr n⸗f ỉt⸗f (10) ꜣImn ḥr rdỉ.(t) mꜣꜥ ḥtp.w-nṯr n nṯr.w nb.w
ỉb⸗f ꜣw m ỉr n⸗f ỉt⸗fꜣ

sw ḥm⸗f ḏd⸗f ỉr n⸗ỉ ỉt⸗ỉ ꜣImn-Rꜥ nb ns.wt tꜣ.wy bỉꜣ.t tnꜣ 4.t nfr.t m-
ḥnw rnp.t wꜥ.t m ḥsb.t 6.(t) n.t ḫꜥ⸗ỉ m ny-sw.t [n pꜣ.tw mꜣꜣ] (11) mỉt.t ḏr
ỉmy.w-ḥꜣ.t ỉw.n Ḥꜥp(y) m ỉt ỉḥ.w bꜥḥ.n⸗f tꜣ pn r-ꜣw⸗f nn gm mỉt.t⸗f ḥr
sš.w m rk ḏr.tyw nn ḏd sdm⸗ỉꜣ m-ꜥ ỉt⸗ỉ rdỉ.n⸗f (12) n⸗ỉ sḥ.t nfr.t r-ꜣw⸗s
smꜣ.n⸗f ḥdqq.w ỉmy.w-tꜣ wn m q(ꜣ)b⸗s ḫsf.n⸗f wnm n sꜣnḥm.w r⸗s nn
rdỉ.n⸗f ꜥwꜣ s.t rsyw (13) ꜥwꜣ.n⸗ỉ šmw r šnw.wt nn rḫ tnw ỉry m ỉt Šmꜥw
ỉt Mḥw pr.t nb rwd ḥr sꜣ tꜣ

ỉỉ.n⸗ỉ ỉs m Tꜣ-Stỉ m-q(ꜣ)b sn.w ny-sw.t ts.n ḥm⸗f (14) ỉm wnn⸗ỉ ḥnꜥ⸗f
mr.n⸗f (w)ỉ r sn.w⸗f nb r ms.w⸗f nb tn(ỉ).kw(ỉ) r⸗sn ḥr ḥm⸗f phr.n⸗ỉ
ỉb.w pꜥ.t mr(w).t⸗ỉ ḥr ḥr nb (15) ššp.n⸗ỉ ḫꜥ m ꜣInb-ḥd m-ḫt ḥr(ỉ) bỉk r p.t
wḏ n⸗ỉ ỉt⸗ỉ ꜣImn dỉ.(t) tꜣ.w nb ḫꜣs.t nb.(t) ḥr tb.wy⸗ỉ rsy r Rtḥ-Qb.tꜣ mḥt.
t r Qb(16)ḥ.(w)-Ḥrꜣ ỉꜣbt.t r wbn Rꜥ ỉmnt.t r ḥtp.t⸗f ỉm⸗[s]

s[k mw.t⸗ỉ] m Tꜣ-Stỉ m sn.(t) ny-sw.t bnr mr(w).t mw.t ny-sw.t ꜣIbꜣr
ꜥnḫ.tỉ ỉs gr.t ḥr(ỉ).n(17)⸗ỉ ḥr⸗s m ḥwn n rnp.t 20 m ỉw.n⸗ỉ ḥnꜥ ḥm⸗f r
Tꜣ-Mḥw

ꜥḥꜥ.n ỉw.n⸗s m ḥd r mꜣꜣ⸗ỉ m-ḫt ḥn(18)ty rnp.wt gm.n⸗s wỉ ḫꜥ.kw(ỉ)
ḥr s.t Ḥr ššp.n⸗ỉ ḫꜥ.w n Rꜥ ḫnm.n Wꜣḏ.ty m tp⸗ỉꜣ nṯr.w nb.w m sꜣ ḫꜥ.w⸗ỉ
wnn⸗s ḫꜥꜥ.tw r ꜥꜣ (19) wr.(t) m-ḫt mꜣꜣ nfr.w ḥm⸗f mỉ mꜣꜣ ꜣs.t sꜣ⸗s Ḥr
ḫꜥ.(w) ḥr s.t ỉt⸗f Wsỉr m-ḫt wnn⸗f m ḥwn m-ḫnw sš n ꜣḫ-bỉ.ty (20) wnn
Šmꜥw Mḥw ḫꜣs.t nb.t dhn⸗sn tꜣ n mw.t ny-sw.t tn ỉw⸗sn m ḫb r ꜥꜣ wr.(t)
wr.w⸗sn m-ꜥb šr(ỉ).w⸗sn nhm⸗sn n mw.t ny-sw.t tn (21) m ḏd

ỉw ꜣs.t ššp.n⸗s Ḥr mỉ mw.t ny-sw.t ḫnm.n⸗s sꜣ⸗s ny-sw.t bỉ.ty Thrq
ꜥnḫ ḏ.t nṯr.w mrỉ wnn⸗k ꜥnḫ.tỉ r nḥḥ m wḏ.n ỉt⸗k ꜣImn nṯr (22) mnḫ mr mr
sw rḫ nty ḥr mw⸗f rdỉ ḫnm tw mw.t⸗k m ḥtp mꜣꜥ⸗s nfr.w ỉr.n⸗f n⸗k ny-sw.t
nḫt ꜥnḫ tw snb tw mỉ ꜥnḫ Ḥr n mw.t⸗f ꜣs.t wnn⸗k ḫꜥ.tỉ ḥr s.t Ḥr ḏ.t nḥḥ

(1) Regnal year 6 under the Majesty of the Horus: "Exalted of Epiphanies"; the Two Ladies: "Exalted of Epiphanies"; the Horus of Gold:
"Protector of the Two Lands"; the King of Upper and Lower Egypt, [Khune-
fertemre,] <the Good God, son of Amon-Re, the effective image of Atum,

the pure seed that came forth from him, whose beauty (Ptah) South-of-His-Wall created, whom Mut, Lady of heaven, bore, the divinely unique one who came forth from the god's flesh, a king of Lower Egypt whose like does not exist, to nurse, to suckle, and to rear whom the Ennead assembled, who has seized the lands, who has curbed the Nine Bows, the King of Upper and Lower Egypt, the Horus who is mighty of arm, the Lord of the Two Lands, the Lord of ritual performance,> the Son of Re, [Taharqa], living forever, beloved of Maat, to whom Amon gives Maat,[1] living forever.

Now, <then,> His Majesty is one who loves god, (2) spending the day and passing the night seeking benefactions for the gods, rebuilding their temples that had fallen into decay, refashioning their images as in primordial times, building their storehouses, provisioning their (3) altars, assigning to them divine endowments consisting of everything, and making their offering stands of electrum, silver, and copper.

Now, further, the heart of His Majesty is satisfied precisely by performing benefactions for them daily. This land is overflowing (4) in his time, just as it was in the era of the Lord of the Universe, with every man sleeping until dawn without a care at all,[2] for Maat has been introduced throughout the banks and wrongdoing pinned to the ground. (5) In His Majesty's time, in the sixth regnal year of his epiphany, wonders have occurred whose like has not been seen since the time of the ancestors, so greatly does his father Amon love him. His Majesty had been (6) requesting an inundation from his father Amon-Re, Lord of the Thrones of the Two Lands, to prevent the occurrence of famine in his time.

Indeed, everything that issues from upon the lips of His Majesty, straightaway his father Amon causes that they happen. When the season occurred for the rising (7) of the inundation, it was rising abundantly every day. It spent many days rising even at the rate of one cubit per day. As it entered into the mountains of Upper Egypt, so it overtopped the mounds of Lower Egypt. The land was within the primordial ocean, the inert waters, and one could not distinguish (8) islands from the river. When it rose by 21 cubits, 1 palm, and 2 1/2 fingers at the harbor of Thebes, His Majesty caused that there be brought to him the ancestral annals to see if such an inundation had occurred in their era, but without anything similar being found there.

(9) Moreover, the sky rained in Nubia, and it made all the mountains glisten. As everyone of Nubia was overflowing with everything, so Egypt was in happy festival, thanking god for His Majesty.[3] The heart of His Majesty was happier than anything at what his father (10) Amon had done for him, causing divine endowments to be presented to all the gods, his heart elated at what his father Amon had done for him.[4]

His Majesty said: "My father Amon-Re, Lord of the Thrones of the Two

Lands, has made for me these[5] 4 beautiful wonders within a single year in the sixth regnal year of my epiphany as king. Nothing (11) similar [has been seen] since the forefathers. When the inundation came like a cattle thief, it flooded this entire land. Nothing similar can be found in the writings from the time of the ancients, and there is none who says: 'I heard[6] (it) from my father.' He has given (12) to me a thoroughly good cultivation: as he has slain the rats and the snakes in its midst, so he has repelled from it the voracity of locusts. He has prevented the south wind from reaping it, (13) so that I have reaped the harvest for the granaries, in incalculable numbers, of Upper Egyptian barley, Lower Egyptian barley, and every seed that grows on the surface of the earth.

Now, I came from Nubia in the midst of the royal brethren whom His Majesty had called up (14) from there, so that I might be with him, since he loved me more than any of his brothers and more than any of his children, with the result that I was more distinguished than they by His Majesty. I had captivated the hearts of the patricians, even as love of me was with everyone. (15) It was after the falcon had departed to heaven that I received the crown in Memphis, when my father Amon commanded me to place all lands and all foreign countries beneath my sandals, southward to Retehu-Qabet,[7] northward to the Cool (16) Waters of Horus,[8] eastward to the rising of the sun, and westward to the place in which it sets.

[Now, my mother] was in Nubia as the king's sister, sweetly beloved, the Queen Mother, Abar, the living. Moreover, I had departed (17) from her as a youth of 20 years, when I came with His Majesty to Lower Egypt.

Then she came sailing northward to see me after an interval (18) of years, and she found me crowned upon the throne of Horus, having received the diadems of Re, the two uraei joined at my head,[9] and all the gods serving as the protection of my limbs. She was exceedingly joyful (19) after beholding the beauty of His Majesty, just as when Isis beheld her son Horus crowned upon the throne of his father Osiris, after he had been but a youth within the swamp of Chemmis. (20) Upper and Lower Egypt and every foreign country were bowing to the ground for this Queen Mother, being exceedingly festive—their elders in company with their juniors—as they acclaimed this Queen Mother, (21) saying:

"Isis has received Horus even as the Queen Mother has been united with her son. O King of Upper and Lower Egypt, Taharqa, living forever, beloved of the gods <and goddesses>, you are ever-living specifically by command of your father Amon, the (22) excellent god, who loves the one who loves him, who recognizes the one who is loyal to him, and who has caused that your mother be united with you in peace that she might behold the good things that he has made for you. O mighty king, live and be healthy just as Horus lives for his mother Isis! Forever and ever you appear in glory upon the throne of Horus!

NOTES

1. The Coptos stela has a lacuna probably to be restored [mrỉ-Mnw nb Gb.tyw] "beloved of Min, Lord of Coptos," and the Mataana stela has mrỉ-Ḥmn nb Ḥf(3).t "beloved of Hemen, Lord of Hefat."

2. Literally, "without saying: 'If only I had' at all." For the final phrase, the Coptos stela substitutes r ḫ.t nb.(t) "regarding anything."

3. The Coptos and Mataana stelae substitute ny-sw.t "king."

4. The Coptos stela concludes by adding ỉr≠f dỉ ꜥnḫ ḏd wȝs nb ḫꜥ.w ḥr s.t Ḥr mỉ Rꜥ ḏ.t "that he might attain the state of being given all life, stability, and dominion, and appearances upon the throne of Horus like Re forever." The Mataana stela concludes with ỉr n≠f ꜣImn [...] m sȝ≠f [... ꜥnḫ] nb ḫr≠f [ḏd] nb ḫr≠f wȝs nb [ḫr≠f ...] ḫꜥ m ny-sw.t bỉ.ty [ḫr s.t Ḥr mỉ Rꜥ] ḏ.t "which Amon has made for him [....] as his son [... granting] all [life] issuing from him, all [stability] from him, and all dominion [from him ...] and appearance as King of Upper and Lower Egypt [upon the throne of Horus like Re] forever."

5. Contra Leclant and Yoyotte (1952, 16) and Kitchen (1986, 168), the translation "these 4 wonders" is certain, as the number is attributive (4.t), and the great inundation cannot be automatically excluded as a wonder since it is explicitly mentioned *first* within this section as "a cattle thief, having flooded this entire land." The wonders thus include: (1) the unprecedented flood; (2) the removal of rats, snakes and locusts; (3) the diversion of the south wind; and (4) the remarkable harvest.

6. Beginning of the fragmentary Tanis Stela.

7. An African tribe and later the designation of a portion of the world ocean. For discussion, see Zibelius 1972, 159.

8. The northern limits of the inhabitable world.

9. Double uraei form the distinctive headband of Kushite rulers, perhaps indicating sovereignty over Egypt and Nubia.

163. KAWA STELA VI
(MEROWE MUSEUM NO. 53)

Recording Taharqa's gifts to the Gem(pa)aton temple in years 8–10, Kawa Stela VI is the pendant to Stela III of years 2–8. From the first court of Kawa's Temple T, the broken grey granite round-topped stela measures 1.82 m by 0.85 m by 0.30 m. In the damaged lunette appear the remains of a dual scene of Taharqa offering to Amon. As in Stela III, the text is subdivided by oversized palm branches signifying "regnal year," with notches in mid-branch corresponding to the year number. Following the enumeration of yearly gifts, the text restates much of Kawa Stela IV, with its mention of the king's discovery and repair of the temple and the dynastic link to the cult of Amon through the female descendants of Taharqa's ancestor Alara. The stela's non-Egyptian emphasis upon maternal ancestors reflects the distinctly matrilineal Cushite society. The deportation of foreign princes recalls the earlier policy of Thutmose III, and the subservice of Libyan queens echoes the depiction of the Old Kingdom "Libyan Smiting Scene" revived for this temple. The language is primarily Middle Egyptian with occasional Late Egyptian lapses.

For the text, translations, and discussions, see Macadam 1949, 32–40 and pls. 11–12; the revisions noted in the review by Clère 1951, 177–79; Leclant and Yoyotte 1952, 27–29; and Eide et al. 1994, 164–76. See Kitchen 1986, 149 §120 and 389 §349.

RIGHTHAND SCENE

Label for Amon of Gebel Barkal
[ʾImn-Rꜥ nb D̲w]-wꜥb (2) [d̲d-mdw] dỉ.n≠(ỉ) n≠k ꜥnḫ wꜣs nb snb nb mỉ Rꜥ d̲.t
[Amon-Re of Gebel]-Barkal. (2) [Recitation.] "Thus I have given to you all life and dominion and all health like Re forever."

Label for the King
[…] (2) [sꜣ ꜥnḫ nb ḥꜣ≠f] mỉ [Rꜥ] d̲.t (3) sq(r) t ḥd̲ n ỉt≠f ʾImn ỉr≠f dỉ-ꜥnḫ
[…] (2) [The protection of all life is around him] like [Re] forever. (3) Consecrating white bread for his father Amon so that he might attain the state of being given life.

LEFTHAND SCENE

Label for Amon of Gematon
[ʾImn-Rꜥ nb Gm-ʾItn] (2) [d̲d-mdw] dỉ.n≠(ỉ) n≠k ꜥnḫ wꜣs nb d̲d nb ꜣw.t-ỉb nb.(t) d̲.t
[Amon-Re of Gematon]. (2) [Recitation.] "Thus I have given to you all life and dominion, all stability and all joy like Re forever."

Label for the King
[… n ỉt≠f ʾImn ỉr≠f] dỉ ꜥnḫ
[… for his father Amon so that he might attain] the state of being given life.

MAIN TEXT
(1) ḥsb.t 8.(t) (n.t) ny-sw.t bỉ.ty Ḫw-Nfr-tm-Rꜥ sꜣ Rꜥ Thrq ꜥnḫ d̲.t ỉr.n≠f m mnw≠f n ỉt≠f ʾImn-Rꜥ nb Gm-ʾItn
    ḥmt ḥtp 1
    ḥmt kꜣ-ḫr-kꜣ ḥr ꜣꜥꜥny 2 [10(?)+]1
    […].w [x+]10
    […] (2) 54
    ḥmt ḫꜣ-rnp.t 50

ḥmt dnỉ.t 15

ḥmt sft 50

ḥmt ʿš 5

ḥmt ʿš ḫy 1

ḥmt qb.t ʿꜣ.t 4

ḥmt ỉrsꜣ 10

ḥmt sšš.t 1

ḥmt [...](ꜣ)ꜣ 1

ḥmt šfd 3

ḥmt tꜣ(ỉ).t¹ 3

ḥmt ḥs.t 7

ḥmt dꜣdꜣ.t 1

ḥmt g(ꜣ)š 5

wḫꜣ n ḫr(y)-stꜣ 1

ḥmt mn(4).t 1

ḥmt ḫdww 5

ḥmt ḫꜣwy.(t) 3

ḥmt nḥm.t 1

ḥmt ʿgny 1

ḥmt ʿ 1

ḥmt wšꜣm 1

ḥmt ʿgny n ḫꜣwy ḫy 1

(5) ḥmt ḥmt n pḥd 1

ḥmt ỉkn 1

    ỉr n ḥmt 281 ỉr n dbn 7815

ḫrd 8

dꜣ(y).t 57

ttfᴮ 2

ḫt-tꜣw n bn(r.t) (6) 16

ỉfd 4

nw.t n.(t) nwḥ 4

ḫt n nbs 56

ʿntyw šw ḫꜣr(?) 15

ḥd (ỉ)ʿn 1

ḥmt s.t-mn(w) 2

    ỉr {n}n dbn (7) 1545

qny dbn 550

ỉr.n ny-sw.t bỉ.ty Thrq ʿnḫ ḏ.t n ỉt⸗f ʾImn-Rʿ nb Gm-ʾItn ỉr⸗f dỉ ʿnḫ nb ḏd wꜣs nb snb nb ꜣw.t-ỉb nb.(t) mỉ Rʿ ḏ.t nḥḥ

(8) ḥsb.t 9.(t) (n.t) ny-sw.t bỉ.ty Thrq ʿnḫ ḏ.t ỉr.n⸗f m mnw⸗f n ỉt⸗f ʾImn-Rʿ nb Gm-ʾItn

    nbw dbn 651

nbw snb 1 ỉr n dbn 9

ḥḏ dbn 3200

ḥḏ ḏr.t n (9) snb 1

ḥḏ šw ỉw sp.t≠w n nbw 2

ḥḏ tf ꜥrꜥr n nbw 1

ḥḏ tk3 2

ḥḏ bꜥ-ꜥ3 n ỉmy-wnw.t 1

(10) ḥw 1 n ḥḏ nbw

ḥmt šw 2

ḥmt qb.t 1

ḥmt ḫ3y.t 10

mḫ≠s-pns≠s3 1

pr.t ꜥwnw 1000

ḥmt dbn 1(11)3456

ḥḏ n smn⁴ 2 ỉr n ḥḏ dbn 200 dbn 4 qd.t 4 1/2

ḥmt ḫ3wy.(t) 10

sšny (1)

hn 147

ỉr≠f dỉ ꜥnḫ ḏd w3s mỉ Rꜥ ḏ.t

(12) ḥsb.t 10.(t) (n.t) ny-sw.t bỉ.ty Thrq ꜥnḫ ḏ.t ỉr.n≠f m mn(w)≠f n ỉt≠f ʾImn-Rꜥ nb Gm-ʾItn

nbw dbn 15

wšb.w(t) dbn 500

qny dbn 106

ḥsbd n sš dbn 2000

(13) mnḫ 500 dbn

ṯḥy dbn 100

tḥn krṯ 10

ỉns mnḫ.t 100

ỉdmỉ mnḫ.t 200

g3r3bw ỉw≠w ỉnḥ 35

r3dny (14) ꜥq.w 5

nbw p(3)g (n) t3(ỉ) 60

nbw (ḥr) ḫ3s.t≠f dbn 300

ḫt nb ꜥš3 nn rḫ ṯnw ỉr(y)≠w m ꜥš mr šnd.t

sṯḥn nỉw.t≠f r-3w≠s (15) m šnwy.w nb rdỉ.n≠f k3ry.w r≠s m stp.w n.w Ḏsḏs mỉt.t ỉr(y)≠w m rmṯ.w n.w T3-Mḥw qd ḥw.t-nṯr≠f w3.t r mr(16)ḥw m ỉn(r) nfr n rwḏ.(t) m-ḫt gm.n sw ḥm≠f qd.ṯw m tb.(t) pḥ.n q3y.t tp-ḥw.t≠s qd.n≠f sw m ỉnr m k3.t mnḫ.t n p3.(17)tw m33 mỉt.t ḏr nṯr.w r hrw pn ỉr.n≠f sw m ỉnr nfr rwḏ mnḫ sꜥḥꜥ wḥ(3).w ḫt m nbw nfr ꜥrw≠sn m ḥḏ qd bḫn. w≠s m (18) ỉr.t r nfr sꜥḥꜥ sb3.w≠s m ꜥš m3ꜥ qr m ḥmt St.t ḫt.tw ḥr rn wr n ḥm≠f m-ꜥ sš.w nb ỉqr m ḏbꜥ.w≠sn ḫt.tw m-ꜥ ḥmww.w (19) nfr.w sn≠sn

ỉr.t.n tp(y).w-ꜥ sw3ḏ šnꜥꜥs sḏf3 ḫ3wy.wꜥs mḥ.nꜥf s.t m wdḥw.w n.w ḥd
nbw ḥmt Sṯ.t ꜥ3.t nb.(t) m3ꜥ.t n(n) rḫ ṯnw⸗sn mḥ.nꜥf (s.t) m (20) mr.(t)
ꜥš3.t rdỉ.nꜥf ḥm.w r⸗s m ḥm.wt wr.w n.w T3-Mḥw ḫ3m ỉrp m ỉ3rr.wt n.w
nỉw.t tn ꜥš3 s.t r Ḏsḏs rdỉ.nꜥf k3ry.w r⸗sn m k3ry.w nfr.w n.w (21) Mnty.w
Sṯ.t mḥ.nꜥf ḥw.t-nṯr tn m wꜥb.w r⸗s m s rḫ r3⸗sn m ms.w wr.w n.w t3 nb
mḥ.nꜥf prꜥf m ḫnw.w r sšš n ḥrꜥf nfr

ỉr.n (22) ḥmꜥf nw n-ꜥ3.(t)-n mrꜥf ỉtꜥf ʾImn-Rꜥ nb Gm-ʾItn ḥr rḫ.nꜥf
mnḫꜥf ḥr ỉbꜥf ḥḥ ỉw n ꜥš nꜥf ḥr bỉ3.t ỉr.(t).nꜥf nꜥf mw.tꜥf m ẖ.t n ms.(t)⸗s
ḥn.tw nꜥf mw.t n.(t) mw.tꜥf ỉn sn⸗s smsw s3 Rꜥ ʾIrr (23) [m3ꜥ-ḫrw] m ḏd
ỉ nṯr mnḫ ḫ(3)ḫ ỉw n ꜥš nꜥf m3⸗k nꜥỉ r sn.tꜥỉ ḥm.t ms.(t)⸗ỉ ḥnꜥ⸗ỉ m ẖ.t
wꜥ.t ỉr.nꜥk⁵ n⸗s mỉ ỉr.nꜥk n ỉr nꜥk n bỉ3.t nn s(y) ḥr ỉb.w n(n) nḥd r⸗s
ỉn k3wy.w shm⸗k n⸗ỉ w3w3 ḏw r⸗ỉ sꜥḥꜥ(24).nꜥk wỉ m ny-sw.t ỉr⸗k n
sn.(t)⸗ỉ mỉt.t nw stn.n⸗k ms.w⸗s m t3 pn dỉ⸗f sprꜥf r bw-nfr ḫꜥ.(w) m
ny-sw.t mỉ ỉr.n⸗k n⸗ỉ sḏm.nꜥf n ḏd.t⸗f nb.t n(n) ḏ3.t m3ꜥ r⁶ mdw.w⸗f nb
rdỉ⸗f nꜥf s3⸗f snw⸗f s3 Rꜥ Thrq ꜥnḫ ḏ.t ny-sw.t (25) [...] r sḫ3 rnꜥf r smnḫ
mnw.w⸗f r srwḏ twt.w⸗f r ḫt rnꜥf ḥr r3-pr r nỉs rn n mw.wt⸗f tpy.w(t)-ꜥ r
smn n⸗sn pr.t-ḫrw r dỉ.(t) n⸗sn ḥm.w-k3 ꜥš3 špss m ẖ.t nb.(t) ỉrꜥf dỉ ꜥnḫ
nb mỉ Rꜥ ḏ.t

(1) Regnal year 8 (of) the King of Upper and Lower Egypt, Khunefertemre, the Son of Re, Taharqa, living forever. As his monument for his
father Amon-Re, Lord of Gematon, he made:

    1 bronze altar,
    11(+?) bronze Choiak vessels bearing two apes (each),
    10 [+x ...],
    (2) 54 (+?) [...],
    50 bronze "thousand-year" vessels,
    15 bronze bowls,
    50 bronze knives,
    5 bronze beer jugs,
    1 tall bronze beer jug,
    4 large bronze beer jars,
    10 bronze Cypriot-style (?) vessels,
    1 bronze sistrum,
    1 bronze [...], (3)
    3 bronze incense burners,
    3 bronze tweezers,[1]
    7 bronze offering vases,
    1 bronze drinking mug,
    5 bronze beer pots,
    1 column for a brazier-stand,
    1 bronze (4) smelting brazier,
    5 bronze lamps,

3 bronze vases,
1 bronze lily-bud vase,
1 bronze ring-stand,
1 bronze bowl,
1 bronze situla,
1 bronze ring-stand for a tall altar,
(5) 1 bronze implement for chopping,
1 bronze hoe,
    amounting to 281 bronze objects amounting to 7815 *deben*,
8 veils,
57 robes,
2 "overflowing" cloths,[2]
16 masts of date-palm wood, (6)
4 four-weave cloths,
4 skeins of thread,
56 logs of zizyphus-wood,
15 sacks (?) of dried myrrh,
1 silver writing tablet,
2 bronze furnaces
    amounting to (7) 1545 *deben*,
550 *deben* of yellow ochre,

which the King of Upper and Lower Egypt, Taharqa, living forever, made for his father Amon-Re, Lord of Gematon, so that he might attain the state of being given all life, all stability and dominion, all health, and all joy like Re forever and ever.

(8) Regnal year 9 (of) the King of Upper and Lower Egypt, Taharqa, living forever. As his monument for his father Amon-Re, Lord of Gematon, he made:

651 *deben* of gold,
1 golden fan, amounting to 9 *deben*,
3200 *deben* of silver,
1 silver handle for (9) a fan,
2 silver jars, whose rims are of gold,
1 silver saw (?), worked in gold,
2 silver lamps,
1 silver astronomer's star-sighting staff,
(10) 1 fan of silver and gold,
2 bronze jars,
1 bronze beer jar,
10 bronze altars,
1 clepsydra (?),[3]
1000 cypress seeds,

(11) 13456 *deben* of silver,
silver for 2 geese,[4] amounting to 200 *deben* of silver, being 4 *deben*
     and 4 1/2 *kite* (of gold).
10 bronze vessels,
a *nymphea lotus* vessel,
147 jugs,
so that he might attain the state of being given life, stability, and dominion
like Re forever.

(12) Regnal year 10 (of) the King of Upper and Lower Egypt, Taharqa,
living forever. As his monument for his father Amon-Re, Lord of Gematon,
he made:
15 *deben* of gold,
500 *deben* of beads,
106 *deben* of yellow ochre,
2000 *deben* of lapis lazuli for painting,
(13) 500 *deben* of wax,
100 *deben* of …,
10 faience containers,
100 cloths of scarlet linen,
200 cloths of red linen,
35 plaited cloths that are embroidered at the edges,
5 (14) loaves of laudanum,
60 thin sheets of gold for engraving (?),
300 *deben* of gold of the gold regions,
and all abundant timber, in incalculable numbers, in cedar, juniper,
     and acacia.
His entire city was caused to glisten (15) with all kinds of trees. To it
he appointed gardeners from among the very best of Bahriya Oasis and
the same from among the people of Lower Egypt. His temple, which had
fallen into ruin, was rebuilt (16) in good white sandstone after His Majesty found it built in brick, but with a mound having reached its roof. In
stone he rebuilt it, as an excellent work whose (17) like has not been seen
since (the time of) the gods until today. In excellent good white sandstone
he made it. The columns were erected, overlaid in beautiful gold, their
inlays (?) in silver. Its pylons were built in (18) good execution. Its doors
were erected in true cedar, the bolts in Asiatic bronze, engraved with the
great name of His Majesty through the agency of all manner of skillful-
fingered scribes and engraved through the agency of good craftsmen (19)
who surpassed what the ancients had done. Its storehouse was supplied,
and its altars were provisioned. As he filled it with offering tables of silver, gold, and Asiatic bronze and every sort of gemstone in incalculable
numbers, so he filled it with (20) numerous servants. To it he appointed

maidservants from among the wives of the Chiefs of Lower Egypt. Wine is pressed from the vines of this city; they are more abundant than (those of) the Bahriya Oasis. To them he appointed gardeners from among the good gardeners (21) of the tribesmen of Asia. As he filled this temple with priests for it, comprised of men who know their spells from among the children of the Chiefs of every land, so he filled his house with chantresses to play before his beautiful face.

It was through of (22) the greatness of his love of his father Amon-Re, Lord of Gematon, that His Majesty did this, because he recognized that he was excellent in his opinion, (namely) the one who hastens, who comes to the one who calls to him, and because of the wonder that he (Amon) made for him (Taharqa) when his mother was in the womb, before she had been born, when the mother of his mother was dedicated to him by her elder brother, the Son of Re, Alara, (23) [the justified,] with the words: "O excellent god! Hasten, O he who comes to the one who calls to him! May you look after my sister-wife for me, she who was born together with me in a single womb. You have acted[5] for her just as you have acted for the one who acted for you, as a wonder unimagined, unbelieved by plotters, when you repelled for me evil plots against me, and you elevated (24) me as king. May you act for my sister similarly, having distinguished her children in this land"—with the result that he caused that he attained prosperity, appearing in glory as king—"just as you have done for me." As he hearkened to all that he said without disregarding[6] any of his words, so he appointed for him his (grand)son, his double, the Son of Re, Taharqa, living forever, a king (25) [...] in order to commemorate his name, to embellish his monuments, to keep his statues in repair, to engrave his name upon the temple, and to pronounce the names of his ancestral mothers, to establish invocation offerings for them, to provide them with numerous funerary priests, they being rich in all things, so that he might attain the state of being given all life like Re forever.

NOTES
1. See Clère 1957, 157–58.
2. Blankets?
3. Literally, "fill it, empty it," see Clère 1951, 178–79.
4. Funds for the sacred geese of Amon.
5. Macadam ignores the past tense: "Do thou act for her...."
6. Literally, "without turning the temple against."

164. KAWA STELA VII
(NY CARLSBERG ÆIN 1713)

Blackened by fire so that much of the surface has flaked away, the grey granite stela measures 1.925 m by 0.839 m by 0.263 m and, like all the other Kawa stelae of Taharqa, was found *in situ* within the first court of Temple T. The monument is dated to regnal year 10 and records the formal dedication of the restored Gempaaton temple. In the lunette, below the customary images of heaven and the winged disk, are symmetrical scenes of Taharqa offering bread to Amon of Karnak on the right and Amon of Kawa on the left.

For the text, translation, and discussions, see Macadam 1949, 41–44 and pls. 13–14; the revisions noted in the review by Clère 1951, 179; and and Eide et al. 1994, 176–81. See Kitchen 1986, 389 §349.

SYMMETRICAL LABEL FOR WINGED DISK
Bḥd.t(y) nṯr ꜥꜣ
The Behdedite, the great god.

RIGHTHAND SCENE

Label for Amon of Karnak
ʾImn-Rꜥ nb ns.wt tꜣ.wy (2) dỉ ꜥnḫ ḏd wꜣs ꜣw.t-ỉb mỉ Rꜥ
Amon-Re, Lord of the Thrones of the Two Lands, (2) who gives life, stability, dominion, and joy like Re.

Label for the King
nṯr nfr nb tꜣ.wy Thrq dỉ ꜥnḫ (2) sꜣ ꜥnḫ hꜣ≥f mỉ Rꜥ (3) dỉ.(t) šꜥ.t n ỉt≥f
The Good God, Lord of the Two Lands, Taharqa, given life. (2) The protection of life is around him like Re. (3) Giving a loaf to his father.

LEFTHAND SCENE

Label for Amon of Kawa
ʾImn-Rꜥ Gm-ʾItn (2) dỉ ꜥnḫ ḏd wꜣs ꜣw.t-ỉb mỉ Rꜥ
Amon-Re of Gematon, (2) who gives life, stability, dominion, and joy like Re.

Label for the King
nṯr nfr nb ỉr.(t) ḫ.t Th[rq dỉ ꜥnḫ] (2) [sꜣ ꜥnḫ hꜣ]≥f [mỉ Rꜥ] (3) sq(r) t ḥḏ n ỉt≥f
The Good God, Lord of ritual performance, Taha[rqa, given life.] (2)

[The protection of life is around] him [like Re.] (3) Consecrating white bread for his father.

MAIN TEXT

(1) ḥsb.t 10.t tp(y) ȝḫ.t sw 1 ḫr ḥm n Ḥr q(ȝ) ḫꜥ.w Nb.ty q(ȝ) ḫꜥ.w Ḥr-nbw ḫw tȝ.wy ny-sw.t bỉ.ty Ḫw-Nfr-tm-Rꜥ sȝ Rꜥ Th[rq dỉ ꜥnḫ mỉ Rꜥ ḏ.t]

(2) sꜥḫꜥ wpš rdỉ.(t)[1] pr n nb≠f ny-sw.t bỉ.ty Thrq ꜥnḫ ḏ.t ỉr.n≠f m mnw≠f ḥw.t-nṯr n.t ỉt≠f ʾImn wr ḥr-ỉb ȝḫ.t[2] ḥws.tw m (3) ỉn(r) m mnw n ḏ.t qd ỉnb.w sꜥḫꜥ wḫ.w mn rwḏ r nḥḥ ỉw gr wḏ.n ḥm≠f r dỉ.(t) ḫn[ty] (4) ꜥš mȝꜥ n Ḫnty-š r sꜥḫꜥ snw.w≠f m ḥw.t-nṯr tn ỉr.t.n ḥm≠f n ỉt≠f ʾImn rdỉ.t r bḫn[.w n.(w) ḥw.t-nṯr] ỉr.t.n ḥm≠f (5) n ỉt≠f šd[1] mw qbḥ (n) ḫȝy.w sḥtp ỉb n ʾImn wr ỉr.(t)[1] n≠f šnꜥ.t n ḥtp.w(t)-nṯr ỉr.t.n ḥm≠f m [...] ꜥq.w≠f

(6) ỉsk r≠f ỉr ḥm≠f ny-sw.t pw qn(ỉ) nfr sḫr.w mꜥr sp.w stp.n sw ỉt≠f ʾImn m [...][3] m rḫ.(7)n≠f ỉb≠f r qd ḥw.t-nṯr r smnḫ rȝ.w-pr.w sk ḥm≠f r d[mỉ n ʾInb-ḥḏ(?) ḥr ỉr.t ḥss.t ỉt≠f] ʾI[m]n [ꜥḫꜥ.n ḏd.n≠f n smr].w≠f ỉr (8) nf rḫ.n ḥm≠ỉ m ḥw.t-nṯr n.t ỉt≠ỉ ʾImn-Rꜥ Gm-ʾI[tn ...] ỉw ỉr.n ḥm≠ỉ (9) pr ỉt≠ỉ ʾImn wr qd m [ỉnr ḥḏ nfr n rwḏ.t mnḫ.tw rwḏ.tw[4] ...]

[...] ḥr ḥm≠f r mn (10) r wȝḫ mrỉ-Ptḥ ỉw[≠f r ...]≠sn r ỉr.t mỉ (11) šȝꜥ. n ḥm≠[f ...] nbw [...] rdỉ.t[1] ḥtp nṯr ỉm (12) [...] ḏ.t qd m ḏbȝ.t (13) [... n]t.t r-gs wn m ḏbȝ.t n (14) [...] n sȝ nḏ ỉt≠f ỉr.n≠f n ỉr n≠f (15) [... ỉswy m nn m ꜥnḫ wȝs]5 nb.w ḫꜥ m ny-sw.t bỉ.ty ḥr s.t Ḥr ḏ.t

(1) Regnal year 10, first month of Inundation, day 1, under the Majesty of the Horus: "Exalted of Epiphanies"; the Two Ladies: "Exalted of Epiphanies"; the Horus of Gold: "Protector of the Two Lands"; the King of Upper and Lower Egypt, Khunefertemre, the Son of Re, Tah[arqa, given life like Re forever.]

(2) Erecting, sprinkling, and presenting[1] the house to its lord. The King of Upper and Lower Egypt, Khunefertemre, the Son of Re, Taharqa, living forever, made as his monument the temple of his father Amon the great, resident in the Horizon,[2] being formed from (3) stone as an eternal monument, with the walls built, the columns erected, enduring and firm for eternity. Further, His Majesty commanded that (4) genuine cedar of Lebanon be ferried downstream in order to erect his flagpoles at this temple that His Majesty had made for his father Amon, being placed at the pylon towers [of the temple] that His Majesty had made (5) for his father. There were dug[1] the cool waters that satisfy the heart of Amon the great. A storehouse was made[1] for him for the endowment offerings that His Majesty had made for his father, consisting of [...] his loaves.

(6) Now, then, as for His Majesty, he is a valiant king whose plans are good, whose deeds are successful. It was from among [the royal brethren (?)][3] that his father Amon selected him when (7) he recognized his desire to build the temple and to embellish the shrines.

Now, His Majesty was at the [town of Memphis (?), doing what his father] Amon [praised. Then he said to] his courtiers: "As for (8) that which My Majesty knows about the temple of my father Amon-Re of Gem[aton …] My Majesty has made (9) the house of my father Amon the great, built in [good white sandstone, excellent and firm[4] …"]

[…] under His Majesty to remain (10) and to endure. The beloved one of Ptah will […] them to do as (11) [His] Majesty had begun […] gold […] The god was caused to rest[1] within it (12) […] forever, built in brick (13) […] which is beside what was in brick for (14) […] of a son who protects his father. It is for the one who acted for him that he has acted. (15) [… the reward for this being] all [life and dominion,][5] and appearance in glory upon the throne of Horus forever.

NOTES

1. Narrative infinitive construction.

2. Contra Macadam, who assumes this to be a sportive writing of Gematon. The designation of an older Aton shrine as a "horizon" is unexceptional.

3. Perhaps restore "the children of his father." The surviving determinative is of a seated person.

4. Restored following Kawa Stela IV, lines 22–23.

5. Restored following Kawa Stela IV, line 27.

165. SERAPEUM VOTIVE STELA OF SENEBEF
(LOUVRE STELA IM 2640, CAT. NO. 125)

The brief votive stela is one of at least seven monuments associated with the burial of the second Apis bull to serve under Taharqa, which died at twenty years of age during the first Assyrian invasion. Due to turbulent conditions, its replacement would not be installed for two years.

The lunette is framed by *was*-scepters supporting heaven, within which the *setem*-priest Senebef, clothed in a panther skin, addresses an anthropomorphic, bull-headed Apis, standing within a shrine. The hieroglyphic stela is of limestone and measures 0.529 m by 0.273 m by 0.074 m.

For the text, translation, and discussion, see Malinine, Posener, and Vercoutter 1968, 99–100 and pl. XXXV; Vercoutter 1960, 71; Depuydt 1994, 23–25; and Breasted 1906–7, 4:465–66 §§917–18. See Kitchen 1986, 162 §131, 392 §353, and 489 table 20.

LABEL FOR APIS
Wsỉr-Ḥp   Osiris-Apis.

LABEL FOR SENEBEF
s(t)m ḥm-nṯr Ptḥ Snb≠f
The *setem*-priest and Prophet of Ptah, Senebef.

MAIN TEXT

(1) ḥsb.t 24.(t) ꜣbd 4 pr.t sw 23 ḫr ḥm (n) ny-sw.t bỉ.ty Thrq ꜥnḫ ḏ.t (2) stꜣ nṯr m ḥtp r ʾImnt.t nfr.t ỉn ỉry-pꜥ.t ḥꜣ.ty-ꜥ s(t)m ḥrp šnḏw.t nb (3) ḥm-nṯr Ptḥ ỉt-nṯr Snb≠f sꜣ n ỉt-nṯr s(t)m sḥḏ s(t)m¹ ꜥnḫ-Wn-nfr (4) ms n Nꜣ-ꜥꜣ-tꜣy≠s-nḫt sn≠f ỉt-nṯr s(t)m sḥḏ s(t)m¹ (5) Pth-ḥtp

(1) Regnal year 24, month 4 of winter, day 23, under the Majesty of the King of Upper and Lower Egypt, Taharqa, living forever: (2) the hauling of the god in peace to the beautiful west by the Hereditary Prince and Count, the *setem*-priest and director of all kilts, (3) the Prophet of Ptah and God's Father, Senebef, son of the God's Father, *setem*-priest and inspector of *setem*-priests (?),[1] Ankhwennefer, (4) born of Naatesnakht, together with his brother, the God's Father, *setem*-priest and inspector of *setem*-priests (?),[1] (5) Ptahhotep.

NOTE

1. Breasted translated "divine father of Sekhetre," a supposed Memphite shrine perhaps linked to the temple of Sahure at Abusir. For the translation adopted here, see Malinine, Posener, and Vercoutter 1968, 25 n. 1.

166. MUT TEMPLE INSCRIPTIONS OF MONTUEMHAT

Throughout the later years of Nubian rule in Egypt, primary authority in southern Upper Egypt was held by Montuemhat, Fourth Prophet of Amon, Mayor of Thebes, Governor of Upper Egypt, and local king in all but name from Elephantine to Hermopolis. Montuemhat's lengthy autobiography, detailing his benefactions to the gods on a truly royal scale, is found on the walls of a crypt in the temple of Mut at Karnak. The cause for such extensive restorations and renovations would seem to be the disastrous Assyrian invasion of 667/666 B.C.E., entailing purification (B.3) after destruction (B.4), sieges (B.13), rebellions (B.14), general neglect (B.19, A.5), and ruin (A.6, A.9, A.34). In conformity with late Egyptian theology, this period "when the whole land was in upheaval" is termed a "divine lesson" that required Montuemhat to return Upper Egypt to the "path of its god" (B.11).

As recognized by Breasted and Leclant, the traditional textual arrangement is incorrect. The scene accompanying the longer inscriptions has been separated as "Text C," and the biographical "Text B" should precede the inventory of "Text A." Below a series of registers of cult images depicting forms of Mut of Asheru, her "august libation vase," Horus, Sakhmet, Re-Horachty, Amon, and four baboons that herald sunrise, Taharqa and the family of Montuemhat adore the resident goddess, who stands behind a laden altar.

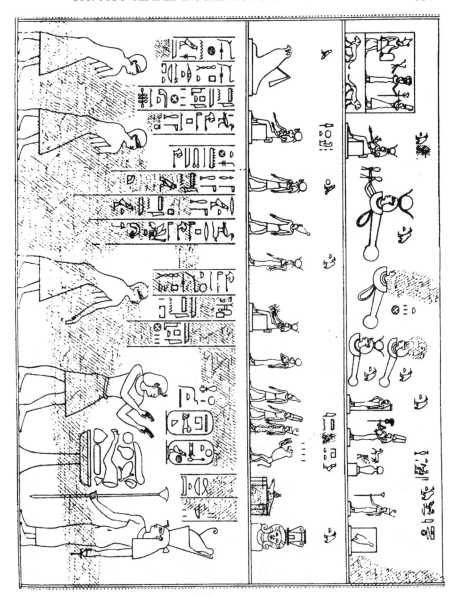

Mut Temple, Montuemhat Text C, after Mariette 1875, plate 43.

For the texts, discussion, and translation, see Leclant 1961, 193–238 (document 44; with full bibliography); Mariette 1982b [orig. 1875], 64–66 and pls. 42–44; and Breasted 1906–7, 4:458–65 §§901–16. Signs noted by early copyists but no longer visible to Leclant are not bracketed. See Kitchen 1986, 397–400 §358–59.

I. TEXT C (EAST WALL)

Label for Mut

[Mw.t] wr.[t] nb.t p.(t) (2) [ỉr.t Rˁ] ḥnw.t nṯr.w nb.(w)

[Mut], the great, lady of heaven, (2) [the Eye of Re], Mistress of all the gods.

Label for Taharqa

[ny-sw.t bỉ.ty] Ḫw-Nfr-tm-Rˁ (2) [sȝ Rˁ] Thrq [dỉ ˁnḫ] mỉ Rˁ ḏ.t

[The King of Upper and Lower Egypt], Khunefertemre, (2) [Son of Re], Taharqa, (3) [given life] like Re forever.

Label for Nesptah A, Father of Montuemhat

[ḥm-nṯr ʾImn] m ʾIp.t-s.wt (2) sš [ḥw.t-nṯr] m pr ʾImn (3) ḥȝ.ty-ˁ n Nỉw.t Ns-Ptḥ

[The prophet of Amon] in Karnak, (2) [temple] scribe in the estate of Amon, (3) and Mayor of Thebes, Nesptah.

Label for Montuemhat

sȝ≠f ỉry-pˁ.t ḥȝ.ty-ˁ ḫtmw bỉ.ty smr [wˁ.t(y) n m](2)rw.t ḥm-nṯr [4]-nw ʾImn m [ʾIp.t-s.wt …] (3) nṯr ˁȝ ḥm-nṯr ʾImn m [ʾI]p.t-(4)rsy.t Mnṯ(w)-m-ḥȝ.t

His son, the Hereditary Prince and Count, royal seal bearer, beloved [unique] friend, (2) [Fourth] Prophet of Amon in [Karnak …], (3) the great god, and Prophet of Amon in Luxor, (4) Montuemhat.

Label for Nesptah B, Son of Montuemhat

sȝ ḥȝ.ty-ˁ pn ḥm-nṯr [4]-nw (2) ʾImn m ʾIp.t-s.wt mt(y) n sȝ (3) Ns-Ptḥ ỉr.n nb.t pr (4) Ns-Ḫnsw mȝˁ-[ḫrw]

The son of this Count, the [Fourth] Prophet (2) of Amon in Karnak and phylarch, (3) Nesptah, born of the housewife, (4) Neskhonsu, the justified.

II. TEXT B (NORTH LATERAL WALL)

[ỉry-pˁ.t ḥȝ.ty-ˁ ḫtmw bỉ.ty smr wˁ.t(y) ỉmy-rȝ ḥm.w-nṯr] nṯr.w nb ḥm-nṯr 4-nw ʾImn ḥȝ.ty-ˁ n Nỉw.t ỉmy-rȝ Šmˁw [mỉ qd≠s] Mnṯ(w)-m-ḥȝ.t s(nb) sȝ ḥm-nṯr ʾImn ḥȝ.ty-ˁ n Nỉw.t Ns-Ptḥ mȝˁ-ḫrw [ḏd≠f] ỉw ms.n(2)[≠ỉ wȝ ˁȝ šps n Mw.t(?) …] m mḥ 80 m ȝw≠s m ˁš mȝˁ n tp ḫtyw pr wr m ḏˁmw mḥ m ˁȝ.t nb.(t) mȝˁ.t […] wr n hrw […] ˁpr (3) […] ỉw≠(ỉ) swˁb ḥw.wt-nṯr nb.w(t) ḫt spȝ.wt Šmˁw r-ḏr≠s mỉ nt.t r swˁb rȝ.w-pr.w […] m-ḫt ḫpr (4) […] m Šmˁw[1] ỉw šrḫr (< ḫrḫr) pw k[.t-ḫ.wt(?) …]ṯ(?) ỉw nn r-ȝw rdỉ.n≠(ỉ) m ḥr.w≠tn nn ḫnw ỉm n ˁbˁ (5) [… nn] ỉ(w)-ms nn grg n s.t-rȝ≠ỉ ḥnw.t≠ỉ sšȝ.tw (< šsȝ.tw) m ỉr.t.n≠ỉ nb.(t) hrw-r Wȝs.t [ȝḫ.t] ỉmn rn≠f ỉr.t Rˁ ḥnw.t [rȝ.w-pr.w][2]

(6) [...]≠s sḥtp.n≠(ỉ) nb≠s nṯrỉ m ḥ.t-ỉb≠f ỉw3.w r wr wnḏw r nfr dỉ≠ỉ
ḥ.[t n] nb≠ỉ n b(w)-nfr (7) [... ỉw rdỉ.n≠ỉ ḫpr nb≠ỉ] ḥr ḥr šbw≠ỉ ḥtp-nṯr≠ỉ
mỉ m3ꜥ≠f tp-tr nb r sw≠sn [ỉ]w sꜥš3.n≠(ỉ) ꜥḥꜥw [...] (8) [...] bk3 šnw.wt≠f
m tp.w ỉḥ.(t)≠f ḥḏ.w r tr≠sn sḫnt.w r sw≠sn sḥb≠sn (9) [...] m dmḏy.t≠f
r sḥb pr m ḏf3w≠f ḥm.w-nṯr wꜥb.w ḥr [dw3] nṯr wnw.t ḥw.t-nṯr (10) [...]r
m-ḫt sp3.wt wr.w nḏs.w [ḥtp] ḥr ỉr.t.n Ḥꜥp(y) n nỉw.t≠ỉ t3 m nḏ3.t nỉw.wt
sp3.wt m qn

(11) [...] sb3 nṯr ỉs pw ỉw dỉ.[n≠ỉ Šm]ꜥw ḥr w3.t nṯr≠s t3 r-ḏr≠f m r3-ꜥ-
pnꜥ n wr n (12) [... 3]ḫw≠ỉ n ꜥ3 n mnḫ≠ỉ ḥr [ỉb nb≠ỉ(?)] ỉy m rsy shr≠ỉ m
tp.w-[rd(?)]≠ỉ ỉy m (13) [...] ꜥq.w m pr grḥ m hrw3 (14) [... ỉr.n(?)]≠ỉ b(w)
mnḫ n nỉw.t≠ỉ dr.[n≠ỉ] bṯn.w m sp3.wt Šmꜥw [...] nw (15) [...]

[...] šms nṯr≠f nn 3b sn ḥw.t m33 ỉm≠s ḥḏ nb ḥtm ḥr ḏbꜥ.(t≠ỉ) (16) [...]
ỉry.w≠ỉ m ḥw.t-nṯr [...] 3b r nmt.t nb≠ỉ s3≠ỉ r-ḥnꜥ(17)[≠ỉ ... tw]lr wꜥb k3≠f
šḥd ḥm.[w]-nṯr m W3s.t mt(y) n s3 Ns-Ptḥ snb ms.w(18)[≠ỉ ...] wn.w ḥm-nṯr
rḫ s.t-rdwy≠[ỉ] wrš≠ỉ ḥr ḥḥ sḏr≠[ỉ ḥr] ḏꜥr ḥr ḥḥ (19) [... ḥr sḫ]3 sn.w ḥr nỉs
[šm(?)].w ḥr ṯs n.t-ꜥ w3 r stp[t] (20) [...] rḫ.kwỉ mrrw [nṯr.w rm]t ỉr.n≠ỉ nw
m qnw n ḫpš≠ỉ (21) [...] hrw-r s3≠ỉ ḥry ns.t≠ỉ ỉwꜥ≠ỉ ỉqr nḏr sb3.t≠ỉ ỉmy-r3
(22) [...] ww≠f ḥr b3k n≠f gs.w≠f s nb (23) [...] b3w

ỉsw nw ḥr nb nṯr.w ʾImn wr ḥq3 (24) [... ḫ]r Mw.t nb.t p.t ỉr.t Rꜥ Ḥnsw
nṯr wr pr m nnw ḥr Mnṯ(w) nb W3s.t psḏ.t ꜥ3.t (25) [... ḫ]r ḥnw.t≠n ḥr
šms.w ḥm.t≠s ḥr psḏ.t ỉmy.w ḥw.t Mw.t ꜥnḫ nfr nn šnw m 3w.(t)-ỉb (26)
[... qr]s.t nfr.t ỉ3w.t w3ḥ ỉwꜥ≠n mnḫ [m]n ḥr ns.t≠n s3ḫ(27)[≠sn ... n]fr.
t ḥꜥ.w≠n tm r ỉry.w≠sn rn≠n mn [...]≠n(?) ḥs.wt≠n (28) [...]≠n ḏḏ≠f d(y)
m pr≠t s[ḫ]3≠n s[mn(?) ...]r[...] ỉy.w ḏr-nt.t mr (29) [...] m ỉmn.w sn [...]
ḥnw.t≠n m ỉr.t n≠s (30) [... ḥm-nṯr 1+] 3-nw ʾImn m ʾIp.t-s.wt [ḥ3.ty-ꜥ n
Nỉw.t] ỉmy-r3 Šmꜥw mỉ [qd]≠s (31) [Mnṯ(w)-m-ḥ3.t s(nb) ...] d(y) m ḥw.t
Mw.t (32) [... ḥm-nṯr] 4-nw ʾImn ḥ3.ty-ꜥ n Nỉw.t ỉmy-r3 Šmꜥw mỉ [qd]≠s
Mnṯ(w)-[m-ḥ3.t s(nb)] (33) [... šms(?)].w n.w ḥnw.t≠n Mw.t nb.t p.t ỉr.t Rꜥ
ỉmy.(t) ḥ3.[t ...]

(34) [...] qꜥḥ n≠(ỉ) ꜥ.wy≠tn m ḥtp-dỉ-ny-sw.t m-ḫt wdn [...]

[The Hereditary Prince and Count, royal seal bearer, unique friend,
overseer of the prophets] of all the gods, Fourth Prophet of Amon, Mayor
of Thebes, overseer of Upper Egypt [in its entirety], Montuemhat, the
healthy, son of the prophet of Amon and Mayor of Thebes, Nesptah (A),
the justified, [who says:] "[I] fashioned (2) [the great and noble bark of
Mut (?) ...], being 80 cubits in its length, in genuine pinewood of the
Lebanese hillsides, with the naos in electrum inlaid with every sort of
genuine gemstone. [...] many days [...] equipped (3) [...], while I purified all the temples throughout the nomes of Upper Egypt to its full extent
in accordance with the ritual scroll "Purifying Temples" [...] after there
happened (4) [...] in Upper Egypt,[1] when it was the case that [others (?)]
were destroyed. [...] As for all of these things that I have brought to your

attention, there is no boastful statement among them, (5) [... no] half-truth, nor falsehood in my declaration, for my mistress is aware of all that I have done outside of Thebes, [the horizon] of Amon, the Eye of Re, the Mistress of [temples.][2]

(6) [As for Thebes, I ...] its [...]. With his favorites I contented its divine lord: long-horned cattle in quantity, short-horned cattle in quality, while I placed the property [of] my lord in a good state. (7) [... I caused that my lord be] pleased with my food offerings and my divine offerings in accordance with his direction at every seasonal feast on their appointed days. I multiplied the quantity of [...] (8) [...] so that his granaries were swollen with the best of his fields, brought downstream in their season or upstream in their days, while they made festive (9) [the ...] in his festival cycle in order to make the temple festive with his foodstuffs, while the prophets and *wab*-priests [adored] god, and the temple staff (10) [...] throughout the nomes, as both the powerful and humble [were satisfied] because of what the Inundation had done for my city, with the land overflowing, cities and nomes in abundance.

(11) [...] It was indeed a divine lesson. [I] placed Upper Egypt on the path of its god, when the whole land was in upheaval, because of the greatness of (12) [...] my effectiveness, the magnitude of my excellence in [the heart of my lord (?)] who came from the south and whom I pleased by my [regulations (?)] that came from (13) [Nubia (?) ... allow/prevent (?)] those who enter going out by night or day.[3] (14) [...] I [acted as] an excellent refuge for my city, and I expelled the rebels from the nomes of Upper Egypt [...] these (15) [...]

[I was one who was (?) ...] serving his god without ceasing, opening the temple and beholding him who is in it, with every shrine sealed with my seal (16) [...] my companions in the temple [...] staying at the footsteps of my lord, my son with (17) [me ...], whose *ka*-spirit is cleansed and pure, the inspector of prophets in Thebes, the phylarch Nesptah, the healthy, while [my younger (?)] children (18) [...] who were prophets knew [my] position, for I spent the day searching and spent the night investigating and searching (19) [...] recalling those who passed by and summoning those who [left (?)], confirming the duties that had fallen into neglect. (20) [...] I know what [god and men] love; with the force of my strong arm I did these. (21) [...] apart from my son, who occupies my position, my excellent heir who adheres to my instruction, the overseer of (22) [...] his territories working for him, every man of his neighbors (23) [...] the wrathful manifestation.

The rewards for these deriving from the lord of the gods, Amon the great, the ruler (24) [of ...], deriving from Mut, the lady of heaven, the Eye of Re, and Khonsu the great god who came forth from the Abyss, and deriving from Montu, the lord of Thebes, and the great Ennead (25) [...]

deriving from our mistress, deriving from the entourage of Her Majesty, deriving from the Ennead who are in the temple of Mut, are a good life without care, joy, (26) [...], a good burial, a prolonged old age, and our excellent heirs secure in our positions so that they attain (27) [...] a good [burial (?)], with our bodies complete in their components, our names secure [...] our praises (28) [...] our [...] that he be enduring here in your temple, our memory [established (?) ...] for those who will come, since love (29) [...] among those that are hidden, open (?) [...] our mistress with what is done for her (30) [... the] Fourth Prophet of Amon in Karnak, [Mayor of Thebes,] overseer of Upper Egypt in its [entirety], (31) [Montuemhat, the healthy, ...] here in the temple of Mut (32) [...] the Fourth [Prophet] of Amon, Mayor of Thebes, overseer of Upper Egypt in its [entirety], Montu[emhat, the healthy,] (33) [... entourage (?)] of our mistress Mut, lady of heaven, Eye of Re, who is at the front of [...]

(34) [...] Bend your arms for me in the funerary invocation after offering [...]

TEXT A (SOUTH LATERAL WALL)

[... d]bḥ.w(t)-ḥtp nb.(t) mî Rᶜ [...] (2) [...] nfr nḫḫ [...] (3) [...] (4) [...] îb 2 wn r nṯr wᶜ.ty îw sḫpr.n≠(î) (s.t) m îb 4 mî nt.t r (5) [... m-ḫt ḥn].ty rnp.wt w3 r stpt

îw sḫᶜ.n≠(î) Mnw-ʾImn r ḫtyw≠f m pr W3s.t m ḥb≠f nfr (6) [ḫtyw ... w3 r mr]ḥw îw sm3ᶜ.n≠(î) ᶜ3b.t (n) n3 nṯr.w 8 n 3bd 2 šmw sw 28 mr (< mî) nt.t r (7) [...] m d̠ᶜmw ᶜ3.t nb.(t) šps.(t)

îw ms.n≠(î) sšm-ḫw n Ḫnsw p(3) ḫrd mk.t m nbw tî.t≠f nb.(t) m (8) [înr m3ᶜ⁴ ...] ḫᶜ.w⁵ îw îr.n≠(î) bḥd(w) n nṯr pn mn.(t)y m ḥd wᶜb ḥpw (9) [... mî w]nn.t (m) n.t-ᶜ.w≠f nb [r d]r≠sn m-ḫt ḥn.ty rnp.wt w3 r mrḥw

îw (10) [...n≠(î) ... î]pl.wt št3.w≠s î[...] d̠.t r ᶜḥᶜw≠s mî nt.t r sîp.t wr.(t) îw qd.n≠(î) ḥw.t-nṯr≠s m înr (11) [... ᶜ3.w≠s m] ᶜš m3ᶜ qd.t nbd m ḥm.t St.t ḥpw îr(y).t m d̠ᶜmw q(3)r.wt s.w (12) [...] nbw mḥ m ᶜ3.t nb.(t) îw sᶜḥᶜ.n≠(î) n≠s [ḥly.w[t] m wḥ3 24 m înr ḥd nfr n rwd̠.(t) ḥb (13) [...] îw ḫws.n≠(î) š≠s wᶜb nfr m înr ḥd nfr n rwd̠.(t) îw sᶜḥᶜ.n≠(î) n≠s šnᶜ≠s r b3k ḥtp-nṯr≠s îm îw s≠š3.n≠(î) wd̠ḥw.(14)[w≠s ...]

îw sm3(wy).n≠(î) p3 sšm-ḫw (n) Ḫnsw-m-W3s.t Nfr-ḥtp Ḫnsw (w)ts-ḫᶜ.(w) nṯr.wy m ḥd [mḥ] m ᶜ3.t nb.(t) m3ᶜ.t îw sᶜš3.n≠(î) wd̠ḥw.w≠sn m ḥd nbw ḥm.t (15) [ḥsmn ...] Ḫnsw wn nḫ(w) Ḫnsw p3 îr sḫr.w m tî.t≠sn m d̠ᶜmw mî wnn ḥr-ḫ3.t

îw ḫws.n≠(î) š wᶜb n Mnṯ(w) nb W3s.t m înr ḥd nfr n rwd̠.(t) mî (16) [wnn ḥr-ḫ3.t ...] r shd̠ pr≠f ᶜ3 šps îm îw sᶜš3≠(î) wd̠ḥw.w≠f m ḥd nbw ḥm.t ḥsmn

îw ms.n≠(î) Ḥnw.t wᶜ.t grg W3s.t W3s.t nḫ.t nb.(t) ḫpš m tî.t(17)[≠s ...] wr

îw ms.n≠(î) sšm-ḫw n B3st.t ḥr(y.t)-îb W3s.t ḥr nbî.w m d̠ᶜmw ᶜ3.t

nb.(t) mꜣꜥ.(t) ỉw ms.n≠(ỉ) sšm-ḫw n Ptḥ wbn n mꜣꜣ≠f m nbw (18) [...]
wdḥw.w≠sn nfr r wnn ḫr-ḥꜣ.t

ỉw ms.n≠(ỉ) [sšm-ḫw] (n) Ḥw.t-Ḥr nb.(t) ᵓIn(r).ty [...] ḥd m tỉ.t≠sn
dsr.t mỉ nt.t r sỉp.t wr.(t) ỉw (19) [...n≠(ỉ) ... ꜥꜣ].t nb.(t) mꜣꜥ wꜥ ỉm nb ḥr
nbỉ 2

ỉw ms.n≠(ỉ) sšm-ḫw n ᵓImn nb ns.(w)t tꜣ.wy ḫr(y)-ỉb Wꜣs.t sšm-ḫw n
Ḥnsw ḥsb ꜥḥꜥw sšm-ḫw n ᵓImn nb ns.(w)t tꜣ.wy (20) [... wꜥ] ỉm nb ḥr nbỉ
2 ỉw ms.n≠(ỉ) pꜣ ỉb-ỉb n Dsr-kꜣ-Rꜥ mꜣꜥ-ḫrw m ḏꜥmw ꜥꜣ.t nb.(t) ḥr nbỉ 2
mỉ wnn≠f ḥꜣ.t (21) [ỉw ms.n≠(ỉ) sšm-ḫw n ...] Ḥnsw ḫr(y)-ỉb ᵓIꜣ.t-Tꜣmw.t
m tỉ.t≠sn m ḏꜥmw ḥr [n]bỉ 2 ỉw ms.n≠(ỉ) tꜣ ꜥꜣ.t (n.t) Pꜣ-ḫnty⁶ m tỉ.t≠s dsr.
t smꜣw(y).n≠(ỉ) ḥw.t-ntr≠s mr (< mỉ) wnn≠s ḥꜣ.t

(22) [ỉw smꜣw(y).n≠(ỉ) sbty(?) n ḥw.t-ntr n.t Ḥn]sw m ỉnr ḥd nfr (n)
rwḏ.(t) r ḥsf wꜣw ỉtr(w) ḥr≠f m ỉw≠f ỉw mḏḥ.n≠(ỉ) ḫn(23)[q.t ...] n nb≠f
ỉm ḥb≠f nfr n ꜣbd 4 ꜣḫ.t sw 25 ỉw smꜣw(y).n≠(ỉ) sbty n ḥw.t-ntr n.t ᵓImn m
ᵓIp.t-s.wt smꜥr(24)[.n≠(ỉ) ... ỉw sꜥḥꜥ(?)].n≠(ỉ) tsm.wt ỉm wꜣḥ r tꜣ qd.n≠(ỉ)
s.t m ḏbꜣ[.t] mỉ gm.n≠(ỉ) nfr r ỉr.t tp-ꜥ

(25) [... ỉw ms.]n≠ỉ pꜣ kꜣ n Mꜣd(w) m tỉ.t≠f dsr.t qd.[n]≠ỉ ḥw.t≠f nfr
s(y) r ỉm(y)≠s (26) [ḥꜣ.t ... ỉw smꜣwy].n≠ỉ ḥw.t-ntr n.t Mntw nb [Mꜣd(w)
m] ꜥš mꜣꜥ [... ỉw shld.n≠(ỉ) sbꜣ.w≠s r nfr ỉw (27) [...n≠(ỉ) ...] n Mnw ḫr(y)
ḥtyw≠f [m] spꜣ.t Ntr.wy m ḏꜥmw nfr r wnn≠f ḥr-ḥꜣ.t ỉw (28) [...n≠(ỉ) ...
n] Ḥr nb ḫꜣs.(w)t ḫr(y)-ỉb IJmḫm⁷ ỉw ms.n≠ỉ sšm-ḫw n Ḥr-Mn(w) (29)
[...] nb

ỉw ms.n≠ỉ Ḏḥwty ḫnty n.{t} p.t m tỉ.[t]≠f dsr.t mk.t [m nbw(?)] (30) [...
ỉw] ms.n≠ỉ sšm-ḫw n Ḏḥwty ḫnty Ḥw.t-ỉbt.t [...] m ḏꜥmw (31) [...]

[ỉw ms.n]≠ỉ tỉ.t nb.(t) n.(t) Wsỉr ms.n≠(ỉ) sn [ḫr]-tp≠sn m nỉw.t≠ỉ
r-ꜣw[≠sn] m ỉr(y).w≠sn (32) [... ỉw qd.n≠ỉ] ḥw.t-[ntr]≠sn shḏ≠(ỉ) wdḥw.
w≠sn nfr r wnn ḥr-ḥꜣ.t ỉw qd.n≠(ỉ) š wꜥb n ḥw.t-ntr n.(t) ꜣs.t n [ꜣ]b[d]w
(33) [...] ỉw ms.n≠(ỉ) wỉꜣ n Wsỉr m spꜣ.t tn m mḥ 26 n ꜥš mꜣꜥ mỉ n.t-ꜥ≠s
mt(r).t m-ḫt gm.n≠(ỉ) (sw) m šnd[.t ...] ỉw šꜣ[ꜥ.n≠ỉ(?)] (34) [... m] ḏbꜣ.
t m-ḫt gm.n≠(ỉ) wꜣ r fḫ sꜣ≠ỉ r-ḫ[nꜥ≠ỉ ...] dr rdỉ.n [≠ỉ ...] ntr mt(y) n sꜣ
[Ns-Ptḥ snb]

[...] all cultic necessities like Re [...] (2) [...] of goodly youth [...] (3) [...]
(4) [...] two dancers being present per individual god, I increased them
to four dancers like that which is in accordance with [...] (5) [... after] a
span of years of having fallen into neglect.

I caused Min-Amon to appear in procession to his terrace in the estate
of Thebes in his beautiful festival (6) [of the terrace ... fallen into] decay. I
renewed the offerings of the Ogdoad in month 2 of summer, day 28, like
that which is in accordance with (7) [...] in electrum and every sort of
precious gemstone.

I fashioned the holy bark of Khonsu the child, overlaid with gold, with
each of its images in (8) [genuine semiprecious stone⁴ ...] sacred crowns.⁵

I made a portable throne for this god, with legs in pure silver, the inlaid figures (9) [... like] what was in all his cultic regulations in their entirety after a span of years of having fallen into decay.

I (10) [...] her secret chambers [...] eternally with respect to her wealth, like that which is in accordance with the great inventory scroll. I built her temple in stone (11) [... its doors of] genuine Aleppo pinewood, banded with Asiatic copper, the attached inlaid figures in electrum, the doorbolts and bars (12) [...] gold inlaid with every sort of gemstone. I erected for her a portico with 24 columns in good white sandstone, made festive (?) (13) [...] I constructed her beautiful, pure lake in good white sandstone. I erected for her her labor establishment in order to produce her divine offerings within it. I multiplied [her] offering tables (14) [...].

I renewed the holy bark of Khonsu-in-Thebes-Neferhotep and of Khonsu exalted of appearances, the two gods being in silver [inlaid] with every sort of genuine gemstone. I multiplied their offering tables in silver, gold, copper, (15) [and bronze. ...] Khonsu the Protective Entity and Khonsu the Authority in their images of electrum as they had been previously.

I constructed the pure lake of Montu, lord of Thebes, in good white sandstone as (16) [it had been previously ...] in order to illuminate his great and noble house by means of it. I multiplied his offering tables in silver, gold, copper, and bronze.

I fashioned the Unique Mistress, the founder of Thebes, Thebes the Victorious, Lady of the strong arm, in [her] image (17) [...] great.

I fashioned the holy bark of Bastet, resident in Thebes, on carrying poles of electrum and every sort of genuine gemstone. I fashioned the holy bark of Ptah who shines that he be seen in gold (18) [... I made] their offering tables better than they had been previously.

I fashioned [the holy bark] of Hathor, lady of Gebelein, [...] brilliant in their sacred images like that which is in accordance with the great inventory scroll. I (19) [...] every sort of genuine gemstone, each one of them on two carrying poles.

I fashioned the holy bark of Amon, Lord of the Thrones of the Two Lands, resident in Thebes, the holy bark of Khonsu who reckons lifetimes, and the holy bark of Amon, Lord of the Thrones of the Two Lands, (20) [...] each one of them on two carrying poles.

I fashioned the beloved oracular statue of Amonhotep I, the justified, in electrum and every sort of gemstone on two carrying poles as it had been previously. (21) [I fashioned the holy bark of ... and] Khonsu, resident in the mound of Djeme, in their images of electrum on two carrying poles. I fashioned the Great One of the Southern Section[6] in her sacred image, and I renewed her temple as it had been previously.

(22) [I restored the enclosure wall (?) of the temple of] Khonsu in good

white sandstone in order to repel the waves of the river from it when it rises. I hewed the tabernacle (23) [...] for his lord therein on his beautiful festival of month 4 of Inundation, day 25. I restored the enclosure wall of the temple of Amon in Karnak, and [I] improved (24) [...] I [erected (?)] the ramparts there that were lying on the ground, and I rebuilt them of brick as I had found them, better than what the ancestors had done.

(25) [...] I [fashioned] the bull of Medamud in his sacred image, and I built his temple better than it had been (26) [previously ...] I [restored] the temple of Montu, lord of [Medamud, in] genuine pinewood [...] I made its gateways beautifully resplendent. I [...] for Min who is upon his terrace in the Coptite nome in electrum, better than it had been previously. (27) [I ... for] Horus the lord of foreign lands, resident in Khemkhem.[7] I fashioned the holy bark of Hor-Min (29) [...] all [...].

I fashioned Thoth, foremost of heaven, in his sacred image, overlaid [with gold (?)] (30) [...] I fashioned the holy bark of Thoth, foremost of the Mansion of the Net[8] [...] in electrum (31) [...]

I [fashioned] every image of Osiris. On their behalf I fashioned them in my city in [their] entirety with what pertains to them. (32) [... I built] their temples and I made their offering tables more beautifully resplendent than they had been previously. I built the pure lake of the temple of Isis in Abydos (33) [...] I fashioned the bark of Osiris in this nome, comprising 26 cubits of genuine pinewood in accordance with its precise cultic regulations after I had found it in acacia-wood [... I] began (?) (34) [... in] brick after I had found it fallen into ruin, while my son has been with [me ...] since [I] have given [offerings to (?)] the god, the phylarch [Nesptah, the healthy.]

NOTES

1. This passage has been considered a reference to the Assyrian sack of Thebes in 667/666 B.C.E. and restored "after there had been [an invasion of unclean foreigners in] Upper Egypt" (Breasted) or "after there had been [a profanation] in Upper Egypt" (Rougé and Wreszinski).

2. Restored after the Karnak Graffito of Hori (Louvre E. 3336), no. 83, line 1.

3. A possible reference to a siege; cf. the Victory Stela of Piye (no. 145 above), lines 5, 23, and 80.

4. Restored from S. Berlin 17271, Main Inscription, line 7.

5. The text depicts three distinct crowns: the double-plumed crown and *Atef* (of Amon?) and the lunar crescent of Khonsu.

6. The name Pꜣ-ḫnty designates a quarter of Thebes; see Leclant 1961, 226.

7. Unknown locality.

8. The temple of Thoth at Hermopolis Magna.

167. NEW YEAR'S TALISMAN OF MONTUEMHAT
(PRIVATE COLLECTION)

Executed in blue-green glassy faience, this ex-voto on behalf of Montuemhat, Fourth Prophet of Amon, mayor and effective ruler of Thebes, parallels examples otherwise restricted to the benefit of royalty. An elaborate composite symbol of "life, stability, and dominion," the damaged figure originally measured 24 cm by 11.3 cm by 1.8 cm and is inscribed on the shaft of the *was*-scepter with good wishes of health, joy, and prosperity for the New Year. The talisman for "the Overseer of Upper Egypt in its entirety" is indicative of the extraordinary prominence of the man recorded by the Assyrians on the Rassam cylinder to be "king of Thebes." The lower fragment of a comparable piece for Montuemhat is now in the Brooklyn Museum (16.580.165).

For the text, translation, and discussion, see Berlandini 1994; for parallel wishes in temple contexts, see Germond 1986.

wp ʾImn-[R]ꜥ rnp.t nfr.(t) rnp.t ꜥ[nḫ]¹ rnp.t ꜣw.(t)-íb rnp.t ḥḥ rnp.t ḥfn. w n ḥm-nṯr 4-nw (n) ʾImn ímy-rꜣ ḥm.w-nṯr (n) nṯr.w nb.(w) ḥꜣ.ty-ꜥ wr m Wꜣs.t ímy-rꜣ Šmꜥw mí-qd≠s Mnṯ-m-ḥꜣ.t s(nb)

May Amon-[R]e open a good year, a year of l[ife],¹ a year of joy, a year of millions, a year of hundreds of thousands, for the Fourth Prophet of Amon, the overseer of prophets of all the gods, the Great Mayor in Thebes, the Overseer of Upper Egypt in its entirety, Montuemhat, (to whom be) health!

NOTE

1. Unread by Berlandini, the traces show a vertical sign with circular top, corresponding to the shape of the talisman itself. For the requested "year of life," see Germond 1986, 20–21.

G. TANWETAMANI

168. NAPATA STATUES
(TOLEDO MUSEUM 49.105 AND MEROWE MUSEUM 17)

Recovered from a cache of statues north of the First Pylon of the main temple of Gebel Barkal, these now-headless figures preserve the titulary of the last Nubian ruler of Egypt. Damaged during the invasion of Psametik II, the statues were interred beneath a later Meroitic pavement.

For the texts and discussion, see Dunham 1970, 17, 20–21, and pls. IX–XI; and Porter and Moss 1927–51, 7:221 (the Toledo example is wrongly located in Boston). See Kitchen 1986, 399 §359.

BELT

ntr nfr T3nw3tỉmn dỉ ꜥnḫ
The Good God, Tanwetamani, given life.

BACK PILLAR

Ḥr w3ḥ mr.wt ny-sw.t bỉ.ty B3-k3-Rꜥ s3 Rꜥ T3nw3tỉmn mry ꜣImn Np(3. t) ḥr(y)-ỉb t3 wꜥb dỉ ꜥnḫ mỉ Rꜥ ḏ.t
The Horus: "Enduring of Love"; the King of Upper and Lower Egypt, Bakare, the Son of Re, Tanwetamani, beloved of Amon of Napata, resident in Gebel Barkal,[1] given life like Re forever.[2]

BASE OF TOLEDO STATUE

ny-sw.t bỉ.ty nb t3.wy B3-k3-Rꜥ (2) s3 Rꜥ mrỉ≠f T3nw3tỉmn (3) dỉ ꜥnḫ ḏ.t (4) mry ꜣImn Np(3.t) ḥr(y)-ỉb t3 wꜥb
The King of Upper and Lower Egypt, Bakare, the Son of Re, whom he loves, Tanwetamani, (3) given life forever, (4) beloved of Amon of Napata, resident in Gebel Barkal.[1]

NOTES

1. "The Pure Land" rather than the expected "Pure Mountain."
2. The Merowe statue lacks the phrase "like Re," and the final word is damaged on the Toledo statue.

169. DREAM STELA
(CAIRO JDE 48863)

Discovered in 1862 together with the Victory Stela of Piye and the Aspalta Election Stela at the temple of Gebel Barkal, the granite Dream Stela of Tanwetamani measures 1.32 m by 0.72 m and details the accession of the king, predicted by a prophetic dream, and his subsequent victories and religious procession through Egypt in imitation of his ancestor Piye. Tanwetamani's conscious imitation of his more illustrious predecessor is particularly evident when, rebuffed at a Delta fortress, he contemplates employing an earthen talus (line 27) such as that once used successfully by Piye (Victory Stela, line 32). But whereas Piye seized the treasuries of submissive dynasts, the weakened Tanwetamani rewards them with "bread, beer, and everything good" (line 39). In the lunette a winged disk surmounts addorsed scenes of the king and a queen offering to Amon, who is shown ram-headed on the right and fully anthropomorphic on

the left. Tanwetamanai is accompanied by two royal women: Qalhata, the
probable Queen Mother qualified as "Mistress of Nubia," and Piyearty (formerly read Piankharty), who is further "king's wife and Mistress of Egypt."
Tanwetamani's Egyptian adventure, contemporary with the beginning
of the reign of Psametik I, lasted less than a year. The destructive, third
Assyrian invasion and the shrewd policies of Psametik brought an end to
a century of Nubian authority in Egypt.

For the text, translation, and discussion, see Grimal 1981a, vii–xv, 3–20,
and pls. I–IV; Eide et al. 1994, 193–209; Schäfer 1905, 57–77; Roeder 1961,
369–79; Budge 1912, lxxv–ix and 71–88; Priese 1972, 99–124; Breasted
1906–7, 4:467–73 §§919–34; and Porter and Moss 1927–51, 7:217–18. See
Kitchen 1986, 173 §139, 393–94 §354, and 587 §533.

LABEL FOR RAM-HEADED AMON OF GEBEL BARKAL

ʾImn-Rꜥ nb ns.(w)t tꜣ.wy ḥr(y)-ỉb (Ḏw)-wꜥb (2) ḏd-mdw dỉ.n≠(ỉ) n≠k
ꜥnḫ wꜣs nb (3) ḏd-mdw dỉ.n≠(ỉ) n≠k ḫꜥ(w) m ny-sw.t bỉ.ty ḥr s.t Ḥr n.t
ꜥnḫ.w mỉ Rꜥ ḏ.t

Amon-Re, Lord of the Thrones of the Two Lands, resident in (Gebel)
Barkal. (2) Recitation: "Thus I have given to you all health and dominion."
(3) Recitation: "Thus I have given to you appearance in glory as King of
Upper and Lower Egypt upon the throne of Horus of the living like Re
forever."

LABEL FOR THE KING

ny-sw.t bỉ.ty nb tꜣ.wy Bꜣ-kꜣ-Rꜥ (2) sꜣ Rꜥ nb ḫꜥ.w Tꜣnwꜣtỉmn (3) mrỉ-
ʾImn (4) dỉ ꜥnḫ mỉ Rꜥ (5) rdỉ.(t) wḏꜣ n ỉt≠f

The King of Upper and Lower Egypt, Lord of the Two Lands, Bakare,
(2) the Son of Re, Lord of Diadems, Tanwetamani, (3) beloved of Amon,
(4) given life like Re. (5) Giving an amuletic necklace to his father.

LABEL FOR THE QUEEN

sn.t ny-sw.t ḥnw.t n.(t) Tꜣ-Stỉ (2) Qrhtꜣt (3) ỉr.(t) sš.(t)

The king's sister, Mistress of Nubia, (2) Qalhata. (3) Playing the sistrum.

LABEL FOR HUMAN-HEADED AMON OF KARNAK

ʾImn-Rꜥ nb ns.(w)t tꜣ.wy ḥr(y)-ỉb ʾIp.t-s.wt (2) ḏd-mdw dỉ.n≠(ỉ) n≠k
ꜥnḫ wꜣs nb (3) ḏd-mdw dỉ.n≠(ỉ) n≠k tꜣ.w nb ḫꜣs.wt nb.(t) pḏ.t psḏ.t dmḏ
ḥr tbw.ty≠k ḏ.t

Amon-Re, Lord of the Thrones of the Two Lands, resident in Karnak.
(2) Recitation: "Thus I have given to you all health and dominion." (3)
Recitation: "Thus I have given to you all lands, all foreign countries, and
the Nine Bows gathered beneath your sandals forever."

LABEL FOR THE KING

ny-sw.t bἰ.ty nb t3.wy B3-k3-Rᶜ (2) s3 Rᶜ nb ḫᶜ.w T3nw3tἰmn (3) mrἰ-
ʾImn (4) dἰ ᶜnḫ ḏ.t (5) rdἰ.(t) M3ᶜ.t n ἰt≠f ʾImn ἰr≠f dἰ ᶜnḫ

The King of Upper and Lower Egypt, Lord of the Two Lands, Bakare,
(2) the Son of Re, Lord of Diadems, Tanwetamani, (3) beloved of Amon,
(4) given life forever. (5) Offering Maat to his father Amon so that he might
attain the state of being given life.

LABEL FOR THE QUEEN

sn.t ny-sw.t ḥm.t ny-sw.t ḥnw.t n.(t) Km.t (2) Pyἰrty (3) ἰr.(t) sš.(t)

The king's sister and king's wife, Mistress of Egypt, (2) Piyearty. (3)
Playing the sistrum.

MAIN TEXT

Recto (1) nṯr nfr ḥr(w) m pr≠f Tm pw n rḫy.t nb ᶜb.wy ḥq3 ᶜnḫ.w ἰty
ἰt t3 nb nḫt ḫpš m ḥr(w) ᶜḫ3 ḥs(ἰ) ḥr m ḥr(w) [ḫw]-n(y)-(r)-ḫr nb qn(ἰ)
mἰ Mnṯ(w) ᶜ3 pḥ.ty mἰ M3-ḥs m3ᶜ ἰb mἰ ḫnty Ḥsr.t ḏ3 W3ḏ-wr m-s3 pḥ s(w)
ἰn pḥ.(wy) n p[ḥ sw ἰt.](3)n≠f t3 pn nn ᶜḫ3 nn wn ᶜḥᶜ m ḥs(ἰ)≠f ny-sw.t
bἰ.ty B3-k3-Rᶜ s3 Rᶜ T3nw3tἰmn mrἰ-ʾImn (n) Np(3).t

ḥsb.t 1.(t) n.t sḫᶜ≠f m ny-sw.t [bἰ.ty(?)] (4) m3.n ḥm≠f rswy.(t) m grḥ
ḫf(3w) 2 wᶜ ḥr wnmy≠f ky ḥr ἰ3by≠f nḥs pw ἰr.n ḥm≠f n{n} gm.n≠f s.t ḏd.n
[ḥm≠f ḫpr] (5) nn r≠ἰ ḥr m

ᶜḥᶜ.n wḥm≠s(n) n≠f m ḏd ἰw n≠k T3-Šmᶜw ἰt n≠k T3-Mḥw ἰw Nb.ty
ḫᶜ.(w) m tp≠k rdἰ n≠k t3 m 3w≠f ws[ḫ]≠f [nn] (6) ky psš≠f ḥnᶜ≠k

wn ḥm≠f ḫᶜ.(w) ḥr s.t Ḥr m rnp.t tn pr.(t) pw ἰr.n ḥm≠f m b(w) wnn≠f
ἰm mἰ pr Ḥr m Ḫby.t pr.n≠f m [...] ἰ(7)w n≠f ḫḫ ḫfn pḥr m-s3≠f ḏd.n ḥm≠f
ἰs m3ᶜ pw rwsy.(t) 3ḫ pw n dἰ s(y) m ἰb≠f sḏw n ḥm s(y)

ἰw pw ἰr.n ḥm≠f r Np(3).t nn wn ᶜḥᶜ [m] (8) ḥs(ἰ)≠f spr pw ἰr.n ḥm≠f
r ḥw.t-nṯr n.t ʾImn (n) Np(3).t ḥr(y)-ἰb Ḏw-wᶜb wnn ḥm≠f ἰb≠f nfr m-ḫt
m3≠f ἰt≠f ʾImn-Rᶜ nb ns.(w)t t3.wy ḥr(y)-ἰb Ḏw-wᶜb ἰn.tw n≠f ᶜnḫy n nṯr
p[n] (9) ᶜḥᶜ.n ḥm≠f sḫᶜ ʾImn (n) Np(3).t ἰr≠f n≠f ᶜ3b.t ᶜ3.(t) w3ḫ≠f n≠f ḥb(y.
t) wᶜ.(t) ἰḥ 36 ḥnq.t ᶜš 40 šw 100

ḫd pw ἰr.n ḥm≠f r T3-Mḥw r m33 ἰt≠f (10) ʾImn-rn≠f-r-nṯr.w spr pw
ἰr.n ḥm≠f r 3bw ᶜḥᶜ.n ḥm≠f ḏ3(ἰ) r 3bw spr pw ἰr.n≠f r ḥw.t-nṯr n.t Ḥnm-
Rᶜ nb Qbḥ.t (11) rdἰ.n≠f sḫᶜ nṯr pn ἰr.t(w) n≠f ᶜ3b.t ᶜ3.(t) rdἰ.n≠f t ḥnq.t n
nṯr.w qr.ty sḥtp.n≠f Nwn m tpḥ.t≠f

ḫd pw ἰr.n ḥm≠f r Nἰw.t W3s.t n.t ʾImn wn ḥm≠f (12) ḫd pw r ḫnt(y)
n W3s.t ᶜq pw ἰr.n ḥm≠f r ḥw.t-nṯr n.t ʾImn-Rᶜ nb ns.(w)t t3.wy ἰw ἰr≠f ḥm
(n) snṯ wr ḥnᶜ wnw.t ḥw.t-nṯr n.t ʾImn-Rᶜ (13) nb ns.(w)t t3.wy ἰn≠sn n≠f
ᶜnḫy n ʾImn-rn≠f wn ḥm≠f ἰb≠f ḫᶜᶜ m-ḫt m3≠f ḥw.t-nṯr tn wnn≠f sḫᶜ ʾImn-
Rᶜ nb ns.(w)t t3.wy ἰr.t(w) ḥb ᶜ3 m t3 ḏr≠f

ḫd (14) pw ἰr.n ḥm≠f r T3-Mḥw wn ἰmnt.t ἰ3bt.t ḥr nhm ḫnw nhm
ḏd≠sn ἰy.tw m ḥtp k3≠k m ḥtp r sᶜnḫ t3.wy (15) r sᶜḥᶜ r3.w-pr.w nty w3w.

w r wȝs r smn ꜥḥm.w≠sn m sšm.(w)≠sn r rdî.(t) ḥtp.w-nṯr n nṯr.w nṯr.(w)t
pr.t-ḫrw n ȝḫ(16).w r dî.(t) wꜥb r s.t≠f r îr.(t) ḫ.t nb.t n.w (î)ḫ.wt-nṯr wnn
m îb≠sn r ꜥḥȝ ḫpr≠sn m ḥꜥꜥ

spr (pw) îr.n ḥm≠f r Mn-nfr pr.(t) pw (17) îr.n nȝ ms.w bdš.(t) r ꜥḥȝ
ḥnꜥ ḥm≠f wn ḥm≠f îr.t ḥȝy.t ꜥȝ.(t) îm≠sn nn rḫ tnw≠sn wn ḥm≠f ît Mn-nfr
ꜥq≠f r ḥw.t-nṯr n.t (18) Ptḥ Rsy-înb≠f îr≠f ꜥȝb.t n (ît)≠f Ptḥ-Skr sḥtp≠f Sḫm.
t r mrr≠s wn ḥm≠f îb≠f ȝw r îr.(t) mnw n ît≠f ꜣImn (n) Np(ȝ).t îr≠f wḏ.t
ḥr≠s (19) r Tȝ-Stî r qd n≠f h(ȝ)y.(t) n mȝw.(t) nn gm.tw≠s qd m rk tp(y).w-ꜥ
rdî.n ḥm≠f qd.tw≠s m înr ḫt.tw m nbw (Verso, 20) ṯms≠s m ꜥš kȝp(21).tw
m ꜥnty(w) šw n Pwn.t ꜥȝ.wy îry.t m ḏꜥmw qr(22).ty m tḥty qd.n≠f k.t h(ȝ)y.
t n pr r-ḥȝ r îr.(t) îrt.t(23)≠f n mnmn.(t)≠f ꜥšȝ m db̠ꜥ.w ḫȝ.w št.w mḏ.w nn
rḫ dnw bḥs.w (24) rnpî.(w) nb n.w mw.wt≠sn

îr ḥr-sȝ nn ḫd pw îr.n ḥm≠f r ꜥḥȝ ḥnꜥ wr.w n.w Tȝ-Mḥw (25) ꜥḥꜥ.n≠sn
ꜥq r înb.t≠sn mî [...]rn[...] r bb.t≠sn wn.în ḥm≠f îr.(t) hr(w) ꜥšȝ ḫr≠sn nn
pr wꜥ n-(26)îm≠sn r ꜥḥȝ ḥnꜥ ḥm≠f

ḫnty pw îr.n ḥm≠f r ꜣInb-ḥḏ wnn≠f sndm m ꜥḥ≠f wȝw(ȝ) sḫ ḥnꜥ (27)
îb≠f r rdî.t pḫr mšꜥ≠f r ṯrr(y).t ḥr≠sn ḏd.în îr≠f [...]nn îy.tw r smî n≠f m
ḏd îw nn ꜥȝ.w îy r b(w) (28) ḫr(y) ḥm≠f [îty] nb≠n

ḏd.în ḥm≠f în-îw îy≠sn r ꜥḥȝ în-îw îy≠sn r bȝk [n ḥm]≠î ꜥnḫ≠sn m
tȝ ȝ.t

ḏd.în(29)≠sn ḫft ḥm≠f îy≠sn r bȝk îty nb≠n

ḏd.în ḥm≠f îw nb ḥnꜥ≠î nṯr pn špss ꜣImn-Rꜥ nb ns.(w)t tȝ.wy ḫr(y)-îb
Ḏw-wꜥb nṯr ꜥȝ mnḫ (n) rḫ rn≠f rs-tp (30) ḥr mrr≠f ḏd qn(î) n nty ḥr mw≠f
nn thȝ≠f nty ḥr sḫr.w≠f nn tnmm n sšm.n≠k (sic for f) sw mk ḏd.(t)≠f n≠î
n grḥ (31) mȝȝ≠î m hr(w) ḏd.în ḥm≠f [îw≠w(?)] îr≠w tnw n tȝ ȝ.t

ḏd.n≠sn ḫft ḥm≠f îw≠w d(y) ꜥḥꜥ.(w) r ꜥry.t

pr.(t) pw îr.n ḥm≠f (32) m ꜥḥ≠f [... ḫld(?) mî psd Rꜥ m ȝḫ.t gm.n≠f s.t
rdî.t ḥr ḫ.t≠sn sn tȝ n-ḫft-ḥr≠f ḏd.în ḥm≠f îs mȝꜥ pw pȝ ḏȝîs.n≠f (33) md.t
[...] ḥr≠î ꜥḥꜥ.n r[ȝ≠î(?)] ḫpr wḏ.tn nṯr pw ḫpr≠s ꜥnḫ n≠î mr wî Rꜥ ḥs wî
ꜣImn m pr≠f m mȝȝ≠î nṯr pn špss ꜣImn (34) (n) Npy.t ḥr(y)-îb Ḏw-wꜥb m
wnn≠f ꜥḥꜥ r≠î ḏd≠f n≠î [w]nn≠(î) m sšm≠k r wȝ.t nb.t nn ḏd.(t)≠k ḫȝ n≠î
r≠s¹ sr≠î n≠k dw3w [{n}]n [î]w.t≠f (35) îw≠î mî ḥm ḥr šȝw≠k ḥmww rḫ ḥr
šȝw ḥm≠f nn ḥr[wy.]w(?) dw3w n≠î îw nḫt.w≠k

ꜥḥꜥ.n wšb≠sn n≠f m ḏd mk nṯr pn s(36)r≠f n≠k (n) ḫȝ.t sꜥrq≠f n≠k îw.t
{n-}m nfr mk nn ꜥnw nṯr ḥr pr m rȝ≠f îty nb≠n

ꜥḥꜥ pw îr.t în îry-pꜥ.t ḥȝ.ty-ꜥ n Pr-Spd Pȝ-qrr r md.t ḏd≠f (37) sȝm(<
smȝ)≠k mr≠k sꜥnḫ mr≠k nn db̠ꜥw.tw r nb ḥr mȝꜥ.ty ꜥḥꜥ.n wšb≠sn n≠f m sp
wꜥ ḏd≠sn îmy n≠n ꜥnḫ nb ꜥnḫ nn ꜥnḫ m ḫ(38)m≠k bȝk≠n n≠k mî îwty.w
wꜥ mî ḏd≠k r≠s m sp tp(y) hr(w) swn≠k m ny-sw.t

wn.în îb n ḥm≠f ḥꜥy m-ḫt sdm≠f md.t tn rdî.(39)n≠f n≠sn t ḥnq.t ḫ.t
nb.t nfr.(t)

îr m-ḫt hr(w).w swȝ ḥr nn rdî.n≠sn ḥr ḥ.t≠s[n ...] ḏd.n≠sn îw≠n d(y)
îr≠n ḥr-m îty nb≠n ḏd.în (40) ḥm≠f m ḏd m ḏd.în≠sn ḫft ḥm≠f šm≠n r

nỉw.(w)t≠n sḥn≠n mrỉ.w≠n f3y≠n b3k≠n r ẖnw wn.ỉn ḥm≠f (dỉ.t) šm≠sn
(41) r nỉw.wt≠sn wn.ỉn≠sn m ꜥnḫy.w wnn rs.tyw ḥr ḫd mḥ.tyw ḥr ḫnty r
b(w) ẖr(y) ḥm≠f ḥr ḫ.t nb.t nfr.(t) n.w T3-Šmꜥw df3w nb (42) n.w T3-Mḥw
r sḥtp ỉb n ḥm≠f

wnn ny-sw.t bỉ.ty B3-k3-Rꜥ s3 Rꜥ T3nw3tỉmn ꜥnḫ wd3 snb ḫꜥ.(w) ḥr s.t
Ḥr ḏ.t

Recto (1) The Good God on the day when he came forth—he is Atum
to the subjects, the lord of horns, ruler of the living, the sovereign who
has seized every land, whose arm is victorious on the day of fighting, who
advances forward on the day of (2) combat, lord of valor like Montu, great
of strength like Mahes, true of heart like the one who is foremost of the
Hermopolite necropolis (Thoth), who has crossed the sea in pursuit of the
one one who attacked him, and who has brought an end to the one who
[attacked him.] (3) He has [seized] this land even without fighting, with no
one who can stand in his advance, the King of Upper and Lower Egypt,
Bakare, the Son of Re, Tanwetamani, beloved of Amon of Napata.

Regnal year 1 of his appearance in glory as King of Upper [and Lower
Egypt (?)]. (4) His Majesty saw a dream in the night: two serpents, one on
his right and the other on his left. His Majesty then awoke, and he could
not find them. [His Majesty] said: (5) "Why has this [happened] to me?"

Then they reported to him, saying: "Yours is Upper Egypt; take for
yourself Lower Egypt. The Two Ladies appear in glory on your brow, and
the land is given to you in its length and its [width. There is no] (6) other
who will share it with you."

His Majesty was appearing in glory on the throne of Horus in this year.
His Majesty then went forth from the place where he was just as Horus
went forth from Khemmis. He went forth from [...] even as (7) millions
and hundreds of thousands came to him, going round about after him. His
Majesty said: "Behold, the dream is true. It is beneficial for the one who
puts it in his heart but detrimental for the one who ignores it."

His Majesty then came to Napata, with none standing [in] (8) his
advance. His Majesty then arrived at the temple of Amon of Napata, resident in Gebel Barkal. His Majesty's heart was glad when he beheld his
father Amon-Re, Lord of the Thrones of the Two Lands, resident in Gebel
Barkal, and the floral bouquet of this god was brought to him. (9) Then
His Majesty caused Amon of Napata to appear in procession as he made
for him a great oblation, and he established for him one festival offering
of 36 oxen, 40 jugs, and 100 jars of beer.

His Majesty then sailed downstream toward Lower Egypt to behold
his father, (10) the One whose name is hidden (Amon) from the gods.
His Majesty then arrived at Elephantine. Then His Majesty crossed over to
Elephantine. His Majesty then arrived at the temple of Khnum-Re, Lord of

the Cataract, (11) and he caused that this god appear in procession and that a great oblation be made for him. As he gave bread and beer to the gods of the two caverns, so he satisfied Nun in his cave.

His Majesty then sailed downstream to the city of Thebes of Amon. It was the case that His Majesty (12) sailed downstream to the south of Thebes. His Majesty then entered the temple of Amon-Re, Lord of the Thrones of the Two Lands, while there came to him the Servant of the Great Foundation and the hourly priesthood of the temple of Amon-Re, (13) Lord of the Thrones of the Two Lands, bringing to him the bouquet of Him-whose-name-is-hidden (Amon). His Majesty's heart was in joy when he beheld this temple. He caused Amon-Re, Lord of the Thrones of the Two Lands, to appear in procession, so that a great festival was celebrated in the entire land.

(14) His Majesty then sailed downstream toward Lower Egypt, while the west and east were shouting songs of joy, saying: "You are come in peace, your *ka*-spirit in peace, in order to vivify the Two Lands, (15) to erect the temples that are fallen into ruin, to establish their cult images in their proper state, to give divine endowments to the gods and goddesses and invocation offerings to the blessed (16) dead, to put the priest in his place, and to perform all rites of the divine rituals." Those who had been inclined to fighting became joyful.

His Majesty then arrived at Memphis. (17) The children of revolt then went forth to fight with His Majesty. His Majesty made a great slaughter among them, in incalculable numbers. His Majesty captured Memphis, (18) entering into the temple of Ptah, South of His Wall, and making an oblation for his father Ptah-Sokar, and satisfying Sakhmet in accordance with her desire. His Majesty's heart was elated to make a monument for his father Amon of Napata, and he issued a decree concerning it (19) to Nubia in order to build for him a new portico, not found to have been built in the time of the ancestors. His Majesty caused that it be built specifically of stone, overlaid in gold, (Verso, 20) with its shrine of cedar, censed (21) with dry myrrh of Punt, the doorleaves pertaining to it of electrum, with the (22) hinges of lead. For him he built another portico for a rear exit (23) in order to furnish his milk for his numerous herds, in the tens of thousands, thousands, hundreds, and tens, with incalculable numbers of calves, (24) all the young of their mothers.

Now afterward, His Majesty sailed downstream to fight with the Chiefs of Lower Egypt. (25) Then they entered into their fortification as [vermin slink] into their holes. And His Majesty spent many days by them without one of them going out (26) to fight with His Majesty.

His Majesty then sailed upstream to Memphis. He was seated in his palace, devising (27) with his heart a plan to cause his army to surround them by an earthen talus. And then [...] said that someone had come to report to him, saying: "These Chiefs have come to the place (28) where His Majesty is, [O sovereign, our lord."

And His Majesty said: "Have they come to fight, or have they come to render service [to] my [Majesty] so that they might live at this instant?"

And they said (29) before His Majesty: "They have come to serve, O sovereign, our lord."

And His Majesty said: "The lord is with me, this noble god, Amon-Re, Lord of the Thrones of the Two Lands, resident in Gebel Barkal, the great god, who is beneficial to the one who knows his name, who watches (30) over the one whom he loves, and who gives valor to the one who is loyal to him. He will not mislead the one who bears his counsels, nor can there be a misstep for the one whom he has led. Behold, what he has said to me by night (31) I have seen by day." And His Majesty said: "Where, then, [are they] at this moment?"

Before His Majesty they said: "They are here, waiting at the gate."

His Majesty then went forth (32) from his palace [...] resplendent, even as Re shines in the horizon, and he found them placing themselves upon their bellies and kissing the ground before him. And His Majesty said: "Behold, what he has spoken is true, (33) the matter [...] concerning me. Then the speech [for me (?)] came to fruition; it was the decree of the god that it happen. As Re lives for me and loves me, as Amon praises me in his estate, behold I have seen this noble god Amon (34) of Napata, resident in Gebel Barkal, when he was standing by me saying to me: 'I shall be your guide at every road. There is nothing concerning which[1] you will say: "If only I had!" I shall prophesy for you the morrow before it has come. (35) I shall be like a servant on behalf of your fate, a craftsman knowledgeable concerning the fate of His Majesty. There are no en[emie]s (?) who may appeal to me, so that your victory arrives.'"

Then they answered him saying: "Behold, this god, (36) as he has prophesied for you at the beginning, so he has wrapped up for you what is concluded happily. Behold, the god will not go back on what has come forth from his mouth, O sovereign, our lord."

The Hereditary Prince and Count of Per-Soped, Pakrur, then stood to speak, saying: (37) "Slay whom you wish. Let live whom you wish. The lord cannot be blamed concerning justice." Then they answered him all at once, saying: "Give us life, O lord of life! There is no one who can live in ignorance (38) of you. Let us labor for you like those who have nothing, just as you said regarding it on the first occasion, on the day when you were recognized as king."

The heart of His Majesty rejoiced when he heard this speech, and he gave (39) to them bread, beer, and everything good.

Now when days had passed after these events, they placed themselves upon their bellies [before His Majesty] and said: "Why are we here, then,

O sovereign our lord?" And (40) His Majesty said: "Why?" And they said before His Majesty: "Let us go to our cities that we might administer our subjects and that we might levy our taxes for the Residence." And His Majesty let them go (41) to their cities. And they were as living men. The southerners went downstream, and the northerners went upstream to the place where His Majesty was, bearing every good thing of Upper Egypt and all the produce of Lower Egypt in order to satisfy the heart of the king.

The King of Upper and Lower Egypt, Bakare, the Son of Re, Tanwetamani, will be alive, prosperous, healthy, and appearing in glory upon the throne of Horus forever.

NOTE

1. The passage is read following the Election Stela of Aspalta, no. 139, line 27.

170. DONATION (?) STELA OF ANKHNESITES
(CAIRO JdE 37888)

Although Tanwetamani's true control of Egypt lasted only a year, Theban loyalists continued to date by his reign. This round-topped stela, 0.40 m in height by 0.32 m in width, preserves the latest mention of his rule in Egypt and records a land donation or sale enacted by a chantress of the Residence of Amon for the benefit of a functionary of the Divine Votaress. The stela was purchased in Luxor. The text begins below a standard depiction of the winged disk, labeled "the Behdedite" (Bḥd.ty).

For the text, translation, and discussion, see Legrain 1906, 226–27; Pirenne and van de Walle 1937, 65–68; and Menu 1998, 146–47. For additional discussion of the text, see Meeks 1979a, 611, 612, and 673 (25.7.8). See Kitchen 1986, 399 §359.

ḥsb.t 8.(t) ꜣbd 3 pr.(t) ny-sw.t bỉ.ty [nb] tꜣ.wy Tꜣnwꜣt[ỉmn] dỉ ꜥnḫ ḏ.t (2) hrw pn smn tꜣ 10 stꜣ.t ꜣḫ.t qꜣy.t (3) nmḥ ḥr pr ꜣImn tꜣ qꜥḥ.(t) Ḥw.t-Tnỉ [...] (4) [r-ḫt]¹ pꜣ ỉdn(w) sš ỉmy-ḫnt dwꜣ.t-nṯr ꜣImn Tkn-nfw² (5) sꜣ Gm-ꜣImn ỉ-ỉr ḥs.(t) (n.t) ḥn(w) (n) ꜣImn (6) ꜥnḫ-nꜣs-ỉtꜣs sꜣ.t n tkn³ P(ꜣ)-dỉ-ꜣs.t ỉ-šsp (7) nꜣf nbw dbn [...] ṯms.t⁴ 10.t [...] rsy⁵ ỉꜣw ḥn [s]ld(ꜣ)ỉ wỉꜣ n (8) ꜣImn ꜣIr.t-Ḥr-rꜣw sꜣ P(ꜣ)-dỉ-ꜣIp.t mḥ.(t) pꜣ mw (9) nty šmỉ [r] pḥ n p(ꜣ) dmỉ ỉꜣb.t pꜣ mw p(ꜣ)-n (10) ḥw.t ỉmn.t pꜣ mw nty ḥr pḥ n p(ꜣ) dmỉ ỉr p(ꜣ) nty (11) [ỉwꜣf smnꜣw] ỉwꜣf [ḥ]r [nꜣ] ḥs.w n ꜣImn [...]

Regnal year 8, third month of winter, of the King of Upper and Lower Egypt, [Lord of] the Two Lands, Tanwet[amani], given life forever. (2) On this day there was established 10 *arouras* of high field, (3) privately held, on the estate of Amon in the district of the Mansion of the Elder [...] (4) [under the authority of]¹ the deputy scribe and chamberlain of the Divine Votaress of Amon, Tekennefu,² (5) son of Gemamon, made by the chantress of the Residence of Amon, (6) Ankhnesites, daughter of the petitioner (?)[3] Padiese. What was received (7) from him: [...] *deben* of gold and 10 red cloths.[4] [Its boundaries:]

> south:[5] The islands (?) of the rower who conveys the bark of (8) Amon, Irethorerou, son of Padiipet.
>
> north: The water (9) that goes to reach the town.
>
> east: The water belonging to (10) the temple.
>
> west: The water that reaches the town.

As for the one who (11) [will confirm them], he possesses [the] favor of Amon.

1. Or restore [(m)-ḏr.t] "to the hand/possession of"; see Meeks 1979a, 644.

2. Or Tkn-n≠f-t3w.

3. Literally, "one who approaches." Legrain translated "pedestrian," while Menu suggested "neighbor" or a nautical title.

4. Erman and Grapow 1926–63, 5:369/15. Following Pirenne and van de Walle, Menu read "scribe (of the 10?)."

5. Previous editors have restored [Ḥn]sw s3, following the handcopy of Legrain, which eliminates the southern boundary.

=VII=

DYNASTY XXVI

A. PSAMETIK I

171. ADOPTION STELA OF NITOCRIS
(CAIRO JDE 36327)

Following the defeat and flight of Tanwetamani, Psametik I, the king
of Sais and client ruler for the Assyrian Assurbanipal, carefully consolidated
his control over the fractious Delta polities, subordinating local rulers to
regional "Harbor-masters," loyal only to the king and charged with the oversight and taxation of all riverine traffic. By year 8, Psametik's ascendancy
was unchallenged throughout Egypt, as proved by the pivotal "Adoption
Stela," which marks the return of the Thebaid to central, royal authority
and the effective end of the "Libyan Anarchy." The political role of the
traditional female office known as Divine Votaress or God's Wife had been
elevated by the reign of Osorkon III at the expense of the now-demoted
male office of First Prophet of Amon. Staffed by celibate princesses who
succeeded one other by adoption and whose affairs were managed largely
by stewards, the office of Votaress could not produce a schismatic dynasty
as had the high priesthood. As the forced adoption of Kashta's daughter
Amonardis I by Shepenwepet I of Dynasty XXIII signaled the beginning of
Nubian control of Thebes, so the forced adoption of Psametik's daughter
Nitocris by Shepenwepet II, daughter of Piye, and Amonardis II, daughter
of Taharqa, signaled its termination.

Psametik's incorporation of Thebes was typically careful and deliber-
ate. The rival Nubian claimant to the office of Divine Votaress was not
removed but politically marginalized. As the Election Stela of Aspalta
shows, the irrelevant princess subsequently abandoned her Theban position and returned to the Napatan court, where she bore a daughter. The

575

mayor and once de facto ruler Montuemhat was left in office until his death, although he and his family were required to provide daily and monthly stipends as tribute to the local representative of the new Saite superiority. Discovered by Legrain in the forecourt of Karnak in 1897, the broken red granite stela now has a maximum measurement of 188.4 cm by 145.5 cm by 85 cm, after the loss of its crowning lunette and an indeterminate number of lines.

For the text, translation, and discussion, see Der Manuelian 1994, 297–321; Caminos 1964a, 71–101; and Breasted 1906–7, 4:477–88 §§935–58. See Kitchen 1986, 172–73 §139, 403–4 §364, and 480 table 13.

(1) […] r [s]šš.(t) [n ḥr]≠f m [… m3]3(?) nfr≠f [r]ḫ≠f sw m wdn b3w ỉr≠ỉ n≠f (n)-mr(w.t) ỉr.t n ỉt≠ỉ (2) ỉnk s3≠f tp(y) m‘r ỉt nṯr.w ỉr.t ḫ.t-nṯr.w ỉr≠f n≠f sw r sḫtp ỉb≠f rdỉ.n≠ỉ n≠f s3.t≠ỉ r ḥm.t nṯr sḫwd≠ỉ s.t r ḫpr.w ḫr ḫ3.t≠s smwn r≠f ḥtp≠f ḥr sns.w≠s ḫw(ỉ)≠f t3 n (3) rdỉ n≠f s.t

ỉst gr sḏm.n≠ỉ r-ḏḏ s3.t ny-sw.t ỉm Ḥr q(3) ḫ‘.w nṯr nfr [Thrq] m3‘ ḫrw rdỉ.t.n≠f n sn.t≠f r s3.t≠s wr.t ntt ỉm m dw3.t-nṯr nn r(= ỉw)≠ỉ (r) ỉr.t m tm ỉr.t dr ỉw‘ ḥr ns.t≠f (ḫr)-ntt ỉnk ny-sw.t mrỉ (4) m3‘.t bwt≠ỉ ḏsr.t pw ỉ(w)ms s3 nḏty ỉt≠f ỉt ỉw‘ Gb dmḏ psš.wy m ḥwn k3 rdỉ≠ỉ n≠s s.(t) r s3.t≠s wr.t mr(< mỉ)-nn ỉr.t(w)≠s n sn.t ỉt≠s

ḫr≠sn (5) dhn≠sn t3 dw3≠sn nṯr n ny-sw.t bỉ.ty W3ḫ-ỉb-R‘ ‘nḫ ḏ.t ḏḏ≠sn r mn w3ḥ r ḥn.ty nḥḥ wḏ.t≠k nb.(t) r mn w3ḥ nfr.wy nn ỉr n≠k nṯr 3ḫ.wy ỉr n≠k ỉt≠k rdỉ.n≠f sw m ỉb n mr.n≠f sw3ḫ≠f (6) ỉr sw ḫr-tp t3 (ḫr)-ntt (ỉ)st mr≠f sḫ3 k3≠k ḫ‘‘≠f n dm.tw rn≠k Ḥr ‘3 ỉb ny-sw.t bỉ.ty Psmtk ‘nḫ ḏ.t

ỉr.n≠f n mnw≠f n ỉt≠f ’Imn nb p.t ḥq3 psḏ.t rdỉ.t n≠f s3.t≠f wr.t mrỉ.t≠f N.t-ỉqr.t (7) rn≠s nfr Šp-n-wp.t r ḥm.t nṯr r sšš n ḫr≠f nfr

ḥsb.t 9.(t) tp(y) 3ḫ.t sw 28 pr.(t) m ỉp.t ny-sw.t ỉn s3.t≠f wr.t wnḫ.tỉ m p(3)g.(t) shkr.tw m mfk(3.t) m m3w.(t) šms.w≠s ḫr≠s ‘3 m tnw (8) šn‘.w ḥr sdsr w3.wt≠s šsp w3.t nfr.(t) r tp-š r rdỉ.t ḥr m ḫnty.t r W3s.t ‘ḫ‘.w ḫr≠s m tnw ‘3 ỉsw.t m nḫt.w-‘ 3tp r-3w-r ḫ3w.w ỉry≠w m ḫ.t nb.(t) nfr.t n.t pr ny-sw.t (9) ṯs ỉry≠w m{-m} smr w‘.ty ḫ3.ty-‘ N‘r.t ḫnt.t ỉmy-r3 mš‘ wr ‘3 n mry.t Sm3-t3.wy-t3y≠f-nḫt ỉpw.tyw ḫnty.t r rsy r snfr ‘3b.t tp-‘≠s f3ỉ ḫty ḫt t3w nq‘ r ḫmm.ty≠f (10) t3w bw3 šsp ḫ‘.w≠sn ḫ3.ty-‘ nb ḫr-tp ‘3b.t≠f ‘pr m ḥ.t nb.(t) nfr.t m t ḥnq.t k3.w 3pd.w ỉ(3)q.wt bnr.w sm.w ḥ.t nb.(t) nfr.(t) ỉn gr w‘ dỉ≠f n snw≠f r spr.(t)≠s r W3s.t¹

(11) ḥsb.t 9.(t) 3bd 2 3ḫ.t sw 14 (w)dỉ r t3 r dmỉ n Nỉw.t nṯr.w W3s.t (ḫr) šsp ḫ3.t≠s gm.n≠s W3s.t m ḏ3m.w n.w t3ỉ.w m wp.wt n.t ḥm.wt ‘ḫ‘ ḥr nhm m ḥs(ỉ)≠s sd-m-r3 (12) m k3.w 3pd.w ‘3b.wt wr.w(t) ‘3 m tnw

ḫr≠sn ḏd≠sn ỉy s3.t ny-sw.t N.t-ỉqr.t r pr ’Imn šsp≠f s(y) ḥtp≠f ḫr≠s ỉw s3.t bỉ.ty Šp-n-wp.t r ’Ip.t-s.wt ḥs s(y) nṯr.w ỉmy.(w)≠s ỉw mn w3ḥ mnw nb (13) ny-sw.t bỉ.ty Psmtk ‘nḫ ḏ.t r nḥḥ

ỉw ššp.n ’Imn nb p.t ny-sw.t nṯr.w ỉr.(t) n≠f s3.t≠f Ḥr ‘3 ỉb ‘nḫ ḏ.t r nḥḥ ỉw ḥs.n ’Imn ḥq3 psḏ.t ỉr.(t) n≠f s3≠f Nb.ty nb ‘ ‘nḫ ḏ.t r nḥḥ ỉw mr.n (14)

ʾImn wr nṯr.w îr.(t) n≠f s3≠f Ḥr-nbw qn(î) ʿnḫ ḏ.t r nḥḥ îsw nn ḫr ʾImn
k3 p.ty≠f ḫr Mnt(w) nb ns.(w)t t3.wy m ʿnḫ ḥḥ ḏd ḥḥ w3s ḥḥ snb 3w.(t)-îb
nb ḫr≠sn n s3≠sn mr≠sn ny-sw.t bî.ty nb t3.wy W3ḥ-îb-Rʿ (15) s3 Rʿ Psmtk
ʿnḫ ḏ.t r nḥḥ dî.(t) n≠f ḥn(ʿ) k3≠f dî n≠f Ḥr s.t≠f dî.n≠f Gb îwʿ≠f wnn≠f
ḫnt(y) k3.w ʿnḫ.w nb îst sw m ny-sw.t bî.ty ḫr s.t Ḥr n wḥm k3 r≠f

îr m-ḫt spr≠s r ḥm.t nṯr Šp-n-wp.t (16) m3.n≠s s(y) ḥtp≠s ḥr≠s mr.n≠s
s(y) r ḫ.t nb.(t) îr≠s n≠s îmy.(t)-pr îr.t n≠s ît≠s mw.t≠s ḥn(ʿ) s3.t≠s wr.t
ʾImn-îr-dî-s s3.t ny-sw.t T[hrq] m3ʿ ḫrw îr ḫr≠sn m sš m ḏd rdî.n≠n n≠t
ḫ.t≠n nb.(t) m sḫ.t m nîw.t wnn≠t mn.t ḫr ns.t≠n r mn (17) w3ḥ r ḫn.ty nḥḥ
mtr.w ḥr≠sn m ḥm.w-nṯr wʿb.w smr.w nb n.w ḥw.t-nṯr

rḫ.t n.(t) ḫ.t nb.(t) rdî.t n≠s m dî.w m nîw.wt sp3.wt n.w(t) Šmʿw Mḥw
rdî.t n≠s ḥm≠f m T3-Šmʿw sp3.t 7²

 m ww n Ḥnn-nysw.t sp3.t (18) îw-n3 rn≠s ntt m sww≠s 3ḫ.t st3.
  t 300
 m ww n Pr-mḏd t3 s.t n.(t) P(3y)≠w-T3.wy ntt m sww≠s 3ḫ.t st3.
  t 300
 m ww n Dwn-ʿn.wy t3 s.t n Kwkw ntt m sww≠s (19) 3ḫ.t st3.t 200
 m ww n Wn.t n3 s.wt n.(t) Nsy-Mnw ntt m sww≠s st3.t 500
 m ww n W3ḏy.t Q3y ntt m sww≠s st3.t 300
 m ww n Ḥw.t-sḫm t3 s.t n Ḥr-s3-3s.t ntt m sww≠s (20) st3.t 200
 nn tm dmd sm3 3ḫ.t st3.t 1800 ḥnʿ ḫ.t nb.(t) pr.(t) îm m sḫ.t m nîw.
  t ḥnʿ n3(y)≠w šw.wt ḥnʿ n3(y)≠w mr.w

t ḥnq.t rdî n≠s r ḥw.t-nṯr n.t ʾImn
rdî.t n≠s ḥm-nṯr 4-nw ʾImn h3.ty-ʿ n Nîw.t (21) îmy-rʿ Šmʿw Mnt(w)-
m-ḫ3.t s(nb) t dbn 200 îrt.t hn 5 šʿ.(t) 1 sm ḥtp.t 1 ḥr.t hrw n.t rʿ nb ḥr.t
3bd k3 3 r3 5
rdî.t n≠s s3≠f wr shḏ ḥm.w-nṯr m W3s.t Ns-Ptḥ t dbn 100 îrt.t hn 2 sm
ḥtp.t 1 ḥr.t hrw n.t rʿ nb ḥr.t 3bd (22) šʿ.(t) 15 ḥnq.t hbn.t 10 3ḫ.t n t3 qʿḥ.
t Ṯbw st3.t 100
rdî.t n≠s ḥm.t ḥm-nṯr 4-nw ʾImn Mnt(w)-m-ḫ3.t Wḏ3-rn≠s m3ʿ.t ḫrw t
dbn 100 ḥr.t hrw n.t rʿ nb
rdî.t n≠s ḥm-nṯr tp(y) ʾImn Ḥr-Ḫby.t ḥr.t hrw t dbn 100 îrt.t hn 2 ḥr.t
3bd šʿ.(t) 10 (23) ḥnq.t hbn.t 5 sm ḥtp.t 10
rdî.t n≠s ḥm-nṯr 3-nw ʾImn P3-dî-ʾImn-nb-ns.(w).t-t3.wy ḥr.t hrw t dbn
100 îrt.t hn 2 ḥr.t 3bd ḥnq.t hbn.t 5 šʿ.(t) 10 sm ḥtp.t 10
 dmd sm3 ḥr.t hrw t dbn 600 îrt.t hn 11 šʿ.(t) 2 1/6 sm ḥtp.t 2 2/3 (24)
ḥr.t 3bd k3 3 r3 5 ḥnq.t hn 20 3ḫ.t st3.t 100

 rdî.t n≠s ḥm≠f m Ḥq3-ʿḏ m ḥw.t-nṯr n.t Rʿ-Tm m ḥtp.w-nṯr w3ḥ.n ḥm≠f
bd.t tp(y) ḫ3(r) 3 m-ḫt m3ʿ m-b3ḥ ḥr.t hrw ḥtp nṯr îm

rdỉ.t n≠s m ḥw.wt S3w t dbn 200 (25) Pr-W3ḏ.t t dbn 200 Pr-Ḥw.t-Ḥr-(nb.t)-mfk.(t) t dbn 100 Pr-ỉnby t dbn 50 Pr-Nb.(t)-ʾIm3w t dbn 50 Pr-M3nw t dbn 50 T3-ʿ.t-n.(t)-T̠3r.t t dbn 50 D̠ʿn.t t dbn 100 Pr-Ḥw.t-Ḥr t dbn 100 (26) Pr-B3st.t nb.(t) B3s.t t dbn 100 Ḥw.t-(t3) ḥr(y.t)-ỉb t dbn 200 Ms(y)t t dbn 50 Bỉ3≠s-t3 t dbn 50 Pr-Ḥr(y)-šf-nb-Ḥnn-ny-sw.t t dbn 100 Pr-Spdw t dbn 100 dmḏ sm3 t dbn 1500

rdỉ.t n≠s m T3-Mḥw sp3.t 4

(27) m ww n S3w n3y pr.w n n3 Š3ỉs.w rsy.w ntt m sww(≠s) 3ḥ.t st̠3.t 360

m ww n Bỉ3≠s-t3 t3 ʿ.t n.(t) Nfr-ḥr ntt m sww≠s 3ḥ.t st̠3.t 500

m ww n Gbw (28) T-n.t-t3-wʿ.t-nh.t ntt m sww≠s st̠3.t 240

m ww ḥr(y)-ỉb ʾIwnw P3-sbty-n-Ḥry-s3-Ḏdty ḏd.tw n≠f P3-sbty-n-P3-šr-n-Mw.t-ỉr.t.n(29)-mr.t-wbḫ.t ntt m sww≠f st̠3.t 300

dmḏ sp3.t 4 3ḥ.t st̠3.t 1400 ḥnʿ ḫ.t nb.(t) pr.(t) ỉm m sḫ.t m nỉw.t ḥnʿ n3y≠w šw.w ḥnʿ n3y≠w (30) mr.w

dmḏ sm3 t dbn 2100 sp3.t 11 3ḥ.t st̠3.t 3300 ḏd sp-2 sw3ḏ sp-2 nn sk nn mrḥw nḥḥ sp-2 ḏ.t sp-2

(31) m ww n T3-wr ʾInp ḥnʿ rmt.w≠f nb 3ḥ.wt≠f nb ḫ.t≠f nb.(t) m sḫ.t m nỉ.wt

[Psametik has dedicated his daughter Nitocris as Divine Votaress to Amon] (1) in order to play the sistrum [before] his face in [...] to see his goodness, since he knows him to be weighty of wrath. I acted for him through the desire to act for my father. (2) I am his firstborn son, whom the father of the gods made successful in performing the divine rituals. He begat him for himself in order to satisfy his heart. I have given to him my daughter specifically to be the God's Wife. I have endowed her better than those who existed before her. Surely, then, he will be pleased by her worship and protect the land of (3) the one who gave her to him.

Now, however, I have heard that a king's daughter is already there, of the Horus "Exalted of Epiphanies," the Good God [Taharqa], the justified, whom he had given to his sister to be her eldest daughter and who is there as Divine Votaress. I shall not do the very thing that should not be done and expel an heir from his position, because I am a king who loves (4) Maat, while my special abomination is falsehood, being a son and protector of his father, who has seized the inheritance of Geb and united the two portions (of Egypt) as a youth. Thus I shall give her (Nitocris) to her (Amonardis II) to be her eldest daughter likewise, as she (Amonardis II) was made over to the sister of her father.

Thereupon they (5) bowed to the ground, thanking god for the King of

Upper and Lower Egypt, Wahibre, living forever, and saying: "(It is) to be established and enduring to the limits of eternity! All that you have commanded will be established and enduring! How good is this which god has done for you! How profitable is what your father has done for you! He has placed it in the heart of the one whom he loves so that he in turn might cause (6) the one who begat him to be enduring on earth, because, truly, he desires that your *ka*-spirit be remembered and he rejoices when your name is pronounced: the Horus: 'Great of Heart'; the King of Upper and Lower Egypt, Psametik, living forever."

As his monument for his father Amon, Lord of heaven and ruler of the Ennead, he made: the giving to him of his beloved eldest daughter Nitocris, (7) whose good name is Shepenwepet, to be God's Wife and to play the sistrum before his beautiful face.

Regnal year 9, first month of Inundation, day 28. Departure from the king's private quarters by his eldest daughter, clad in fine linen and adorned with new turquoise, while her retainers, numerous in number, bore her (8) and police cleared her way. Setting out on a good road to the quay in order to head southward to the Theban nome. The ships bearing her were in great number, had crews consisting of strong-armed men, and were loaded up to their bulwarks with every good thing of the royal palace. (9) The commander over them was the unique friend, the mayor of the Heracleopolitan nome, great general and harbor-master, Sematawy-tefnakht, while messengers sailed upstream to the south to arrange for provisions ahead of her. Raising the sail of the mast, with pricking of his (Sematawytefnakht's) nostrils (10) as the winds arose. Taking up their tackle. Every mayor was responsible for his (Sematawytefnakht's) provisions, having been furnished with every good thing, comprising bread, beer, oxen, fowl, leeks, dates, vegetables, and every good thing. One would then yield to the next until she arrived at Thebes.[1]

(11) Regnal year 9, month 2 of Inundation, day 14. Putting to land at the quay of Thebes, while the gods of Thebes welcomed her. She found Thebes with troops of men and crowds of women standing and shouting at her advance, while she was surrounded (12) with oxen, fowl, and abundant provisions, many in number.

Thereupon they said: "May the Upper Egyptian king's daughter Nitocris come to the house of Amon, so that he may receive her and be satisfied with her. May the Lower Egyptian king's daughter Shepenwepet come to Karnak, so that the gods who are in it may praise her, since every monument (13) of the King of Upper and Lower Egypt, Psametik, living forever, is established and enduring forever."

Amon, Lord of heaven, King of the Gods, accepted what his son, the Horus: "Great of Heart," living forever and ever, had done for him. Amon, ruler of the Ennead, praised what his son, the Two Ladies: "Lord of Rank," living forever and ever, had done for him. (14) Amon, the greatest of the gods, loved what his son, the Horus of Gold: "Valiant One," living forever and ever, had done for him. The reward for this issuing from Amon, the bull of his two heavens, and from Montu, Lord of the Thrones of the Two Lands, is life in the millions, stability in the millions, dominion in the millions, and all health and joy issuing from them to their son, whom they love, the King of Upper and Lower Egypt, Lord of the Two Lands, Wahibre, (15) the Son of Re, Psametik, living forever and ever. What was given to him and his ka-spirit: Horus gave to him his throne; Geb gave to him his inheritance. He is at the very forefront of all ka-spirits of the living. Now, he is the King of Upper and Lower Egypt upon the throne of Horus, whom no ka-spirit can duplicate.

Now after she reached the God's Wife Shepenwepet, (16) the latter saw her and was satisfied with her and loved her more than anything. She made over to her the deed of property transfer that her father and mother had made for her, together with her eldest daughter, Amonardis, the king's daughter of [Taharqa], the justified. Their bidding was done in writing, stating: "We have given to you all our property whether in the country or in town. You will be established in our positions, to be established (17) and enduring to the limits of eternity." The witnesses of their bidding were the prophets, wab-priests and all the officials of the temple.

List of everything given to her as a gift from the cities and nomes of Upper and Lower Egypt:

What His Majesty gives to her from seven[2] nomes of Upper Egypt:

from the district of Heracleopolis: an estate (18) called Iuna that is in its territory, 300 arouras of field.

from the district of Oxyrhynchus: the place of Paiutawy that is in its territory, 300 arouras of field.

from the district of the Falcon nome: the place of Kuku that is in its territory, (19) 200 arouras of field.

from the district of the Hare nome: the places of Nesmin that are in its territory, 500 arouras.

from the district of the Aphroditopolite nome: Qay that is in its territory, 300 arouras.

from the district of the Sistrum nome: the place of Harsiese that is in its territory, (20) 200 arouras.

The sum total of all this: 1,800 arouras of field, together with everything that derives from them whether in the country or in town, together with their dry lands and their canals.

Bread and beer given for her to the temple of Amon:

What the Fourth Prophet of Amon, the mayor of Thebes (21) and Overseer of Upper Egypt, Montuemhat, (to whom be) health, gives to her:

200 *deben* of bread, 5 *hin* of milk, 1 cake, and 1 bundle of vegetables in the course of every day, with a monthly requirement of 3 oxen and 5 geese.

What his eldest son, the inspector of prophets in Thebes, Nesptah, gives to her: 100 *deben* of bread, 2 *hin* of milk, and 1 bundle of vegetables in the course of every day, with a monthly requirement of (22) 15 cakes, 10 *heben* of beer, and (the yield of) 100 *arouras* of field in the tract of Antaeopolis (Qaw el-Kebir).

What the wife of the Fourth Prophet of Amon, Montuemhat, Wedjarenes, the justified, gives to her: 100 *deben* of bread in the course of every day.

What the First Prophet of Amon, Harkheby, gives to her as a daily requirement: 100 *deben* of bread and 2 *hin* of milk, with a monthly requirement of 10 cakes, (23) 5 *heben* of beer, and 10 bundles of vegetables.

What the Third Prophet of Amon, Padiamonnebnesuttawy, gives to her as a daily requirement: 100 *deben* of bread and 2 *hin* of milk, with a monthly requirement of 5 *heben* of beer, 10 cakes, and 10 bundles of vegetables.

Sum total: a daily requirement of 600 *deben* of bread, 11 *hin* of milk, 2 1/6 cakes, and 2 2/3 bundles of vegetables, (24) with a monthly requirement of 3 oxen, 5 geese, 20 *hin* of beer, and (the yield of) 100 *arouras* of field.

What His Majesty gives to her from the temple of Re-Atum in the Heliopolitan nome from among the divine offerings that His Majesty has establshed: 3 sacks of first-class emmer after being offered in the divine presence daily, when the god is satisfied with it.

What is given to her from the temples of Sais: 200 *deben* of bread; (25) the estate of Edjo (Buto): 200 *deben* of bread; the estate of Hathor, (Lady) of Turquiose (Kom Abu Billo): 100 *deben* of bread; the estate of the Two Walls: 50 *deben* of bread; the estate of the Lady of Imau (Kom el-Hisn): 50 *deben* of bread; the estate of Manu: 50 *deben* of bread; the chamber of Tchel: 50 *deben* of bread; Tanis: 100 *deben* of bread; the estate of Hathor: 100 *deben* of bread; (26) the estate of Bastet, Lady of Bubastis: 100 *deben* of bread; Athribis: 200 *deben* of bread; Supper-Town: 50 *deben* of bread; Wonder-Bread-Town[3]: 50 *deben* of bread; the estate of Harsaphes, Lord of Heracleopolis: 100 *deben* of bread; the estate of Sopdu (Saft el-Hinna): 100 *deben* of bread.

Sum total: 1500 *deben* of bread.

What is given to her from four nomes of Lower Egypt:
> (27) from the district of Sais: these estates of the southern Bedouin that are in its territory: 360 *arouras* of field.

from the district of Wonder-Bread-Town[3]: the chamber of Neferher
that is in its territory: 500 *arouras* of field.

from the district of Geb: (28) the place belonging to the One of
the Sycamore that is in its territory: 240 *arouras*.

from the middle district of Heliopolis: the wall of Hory, son of
Djedty, called the wall of Pasherinmut, born of (29) Meretweb-
khet, that is in its territory: 300 *arouras*.

Total of the four nomes: 1400 *arouras* of field together with everything
that derives from them whether in the country or in town, together with
their dry lands and their (30) canals.

Sum total: 2100 *deben* of bread and 3300 *arouras* of field from eleven
nomes. Enduring! Flourishing! Without perishing or decay forever and
ever!

Addendum: (31) from the district of Abydos: Inup together with all
its people, all its fields, and all its property whether in the country or in
town.

NOTES

1. Translators have typically interpreted these sentences to mean that supplies
were received from each mayor, who was in charge of his own provisions. However, the term taken as "supplies" certainly means "tackle" in association with ships
and is distinct from the consistent term for the "provisions" expressly arranged by
royal messengers.

2. The text lists only six nomes, and the seventh is added as an addendum
in line 31.

3. Literally: "(the town of) Bread is its Wonder," an unidentified locality.

172. DONATION STELA OF PADIKHONSU
(STELA LOUVRE E. 10572)

Still incompletely published, the Louvre stela of Padikhonsu from the
eighth year of Psametik I preserves the penultimate mention of a Meshwesh chieftain and reflects the careful suppression of these local dynasts
by the Saite monarch during his reunification of Egypt. In Psametik's
thirty-first year, well after the reunification, a final attestation of a "Chief of
the Meshwesh" (ḥry Mꜥ) in the Demotic Rylands Papyrus IX reveals these
once-powerful warlords as reduced to the status of a mere constable of
the police. In the lunette, King Psametik I wears the double crown and
offers the hieroglyph for fields to Hor-Merti, the local god of Horbeit. The
dimensions, lunette, and line numbers remain unpublished.

For the text, translations, and discussion, see Revillout 1892, 237–38;
1895, 413; Yoyotte 1958a, 416–18; and Gomaà 1974, 58 and 99–100; Ritner

1990a, 101–8; Meeks 1979, 636, 647–48, and 674 (no. 26.1.8). See Kitchen 1986, 402 §361 and 460 §429.

LABEL FOR DEITY
Ḥr-Mr.ty   Hor-Merti.

LABEL FOR KING PSAMETIK (I)
 nṯr nfr nb t3.wy Psmṯk
The Good God, Lord of the Two Lands, Psametik.

LABEL FOR SCENE
rdỉ.t sḥ.t (n) ỉt∓f ỉr∓f dỉ ꜥnḫ
Giving field(s) to his father, so that he might attain the state of being given life.

MAIN TEXT
ḥsb.t 8.(t) (n) nṯr nfr nb t3.wy Psmṯk mrỉ-Ḥr nb Šdnw ỉw ỉry-pꜥ.t ḥ3.ty-ꜥ wr ꜥ3 ḥ3.wty P(3)-dỉ-Ḫnsw rdỉ.t ỉḥ.t st3.t 10 n sꜥnḫ[1] (n) ꜥ3[2] (n) t3 ḥtp.(t) n ꜥ3-t3y∓f-nḫt ḥnꜥ sn.w∓f nt.t (n) sḥ.t dmỉ Bt-Ḥr rsy T3-ỉr-t3(?)[3] mḥ.t T3-rb.t-ʾỈmn[4] ỉmn.t ḥry ḥs ꜥ3-kỉ ḥnꜥ P(3)-bs p(3) ḫny[5] ỉ3b.t N(3)-rs.w3 p(3) nty th(ỉ) p(3) sꜥnḫ n3 ꜥ3.w[2] Wsỉr ỉw Ḥr-Mr.ty (r) ḫb p.t∓f (r) ḫb ꜥḥꜥw∓f (r) šꜥt ḥm.t∓f ḫrd.w∓f

Regnal year 8 of the Good God, Lord of the Two Lands, Psametik, beloved of Horus, Lord of Horbeit, while the Hereditary Prince, Count, Great Chief, and leader, Padikhonsu, gives 10 *arouras* of field as an endowment[1] for the porter,[2] being the offering for Aatefnakht and his brothers, which are among the fields of the town of Beithor, (whose borders are)

south: Tairta (?)[3]
north: The Camp[4] of Amon
west: (the lands of) the chief singer Aaki and of Pabasa the rower[5]
east: The enclosures.[3]

The one who will transgress the endowment of the porters[2] of Osiris, Hor-Merti will diminish his heaven, will diminish his lifetime, will slaughter his wife and his children.

NOTES
1. The earliest example of the Demotic term for endowment. For the passage, see Meeks 1979, 648 n. 194; Erichsen 1954, 410–11; and Griffith 1909, 99 n. 3, for an example in the reign of Amasis (year 15).

2. For the writing of "porter" in these stelae, see the Athens Donation Stela of King Tefnakht, no. 127 above.

3. For the geographical terms, see Yoyotte 1958a, 416–18. The specification of boundaries anticipates Demotic convention and is found also in the Donation Stela for the God's Father Hori (MMA 10.176.42, reign of Osorkon I).

4. For the term rb.t "military camp" (Coptic ⲈⲢⲂⲈ), see Yoyotte 1958a, Ritner 1984a, 174 §5; and Erichsen 1954, 244; contra Vleeming, 1987, 156–62 (read rs.t).

5. For the revised reading of Revillout's suggested names "Aaneba" and "Pebespheb," see Yoyotte 1958a, 416; and Gomaà 1974, 99.

173. BLOCK STATUE OF HARBES
(NY CARLSBERG GLYPTOTEK E. 78)

The black granite votive statue of Harbes is provided with a carved "appeal to the living," requesting favors from the priesthood of the temple in which it was erected in return for an earlier land donation. Complementing the information gleaned from the numerous donation stelae, the statue's inscription proves that funerary services were an expected benefit from endowments made during a donor's lifetime. As noted by its editor, the inscription "is one of the very few examples—if not the only—where a private landed donation is mentioned in other texts than the ordinary donation inscriptions." Cartouches of Psametik I are carved on the shoulders, and a funerary prayer appears on the back pillar, duplicated by an obliterated and unpublished inscription at the base. For the text, translation, and discussion, see Iversen 1941, 18–21.

LEFTHAND SHOULDER
W3ḥ-ỉb-Rˁ   Wahibre.

RIGHTHAND SHOULDER
Psmtk   Psametik.

VERTICAL BACK PILLAR
Wsỉr nb Ḏdw nṯr ˁ3 ḫnty ᵓImnt.t nb 3btw pr.t-ḫrw n k3 n Wsỉr Ḥ3rbs ỉr.n Šb-n-3s.t m3ˁ-ḫrw

Osiris, Lord of Busiris, the great god, Foremost of the West, Lord of Abydos, (grant) an invocation offering to the *ka*-spirit of the Osiris Harbes, whom Shebenese, the justified, bore.

MAIN TEXT
(1) ỉmy-r3 ḫtm.w Ḥ3rbsỉ s3 P(3y)≠f-ṯ3w-ˁ.wy-Šw ỉr.n Šb-(n)-3s.t (2) dd≠f ỉ ḥm.w nṯr.w ỉt.w-nṯr wˁb.w ˁq r ḥw.t-nṯr n.t Wsỉr (3) nb Ḏdw r sḥtp Wsỉr m mrr≠f r rdỉ.t 3w.(4)w(t) n nṯr.w msy n 3ḫ.w m rdỉ.t (5) ws dnỉ.w≠ỉ m prr m-b3ḥ m 3ḫ (6) st3.t 60 pf dỉ≠ỉ n≠tn qˁḥ n≠(ỉ) dr.ty≠tn ḫft (7) ỉr.t ḥ.t dm≠tn rn≠ỉ r-gs nṯr ˁ3 nfr n≠tn ỉr.t n≠ỉ ḫ.t

Overseer of the treasurers, Harbes, son of Peftchauauishu, whom Shebenese bore, (2) who says: "O prophets, divine fathers, and priests who enter into the temple of Osiris, (3) Lord of Busiris, in order to satisfy Osiris with what he desires and to give offerings (4) to the gods and meals to the blessed dead, do not (5) allow my share to be cut out from what issues into the divine presence from (6) those 60 *arouras* of field that I gave to you. Bend your hands to me (7) when performing ritual! May you pronounce my name beside the great god. It is good for you to perform ritual for me."

174. THE LIBYAN CAMPAIGN OF PSAMETIK I
(S CAIRO UNNUMBERED)

One of several Saite stelae discovered along the Dashur road at South Saqqara, Stela VII preserves the fragmentary report of a campaign against Libyan incursions by Psametik I shortly after his effective reunification of Egypt. Such an action against western Libyan groups may have been feasible only after the removal of more threatening Assyrian and Nubian invaders, but the political symbolism of this campaign is no less important. Although a descendant of the Libyan chieftain Tefnakht, Psametik followed the later practice of his family in avoiding any reference to such ethnic origins. The conscious suppression of Libyan features seems a response to the "propaganda wars" of the Third Intermediate Period, in which dynasts of Libyan and Nubian ancestry vied for the role of legitimate "Egyptian" ruler. With this stela, the Saite family's Egyptian transformation is complete, and the new ruler is proclaimed a proper pharaoh "who smites the Libyans." The lunette features a central cartouche of the king beneath a winged disk and flanked by images of Edjo and Nekhbet offering dominion and eternity to the royal *serekh*. The stela, lacking its base and the end of all lines, now measures 196 cm by 101 cm by 49 cm and poses many textual uncertainties.

For the text, translations, and discussion, see Der Manuelian 1994, 323–32; and Goedicke 1962, 26–49. See Kitchen 1986, 405 §365.

SYMMETRICAL LABEL FOR THE WINGED DISK
    Bḥd.t(y)   The Behdedite.

CENTRAL CARTOUCHE
    W3ḥ-ỉb-Rꜥ ḥw(ỉ) Tḥnw
    Wahibre, who smites the Tehenu-Libyans.

LABEL FOR EDJO
    W3ḏy.t P.t Dp.t (2) dỉ≠s (3) ꜥnḫ w3s

Edjo, She of Pe and Dep, (2) as she gives (3) life and dominion.

ROYAL *SEREKH*

Ḥr ꜥꜣ ỉb

The Horus: "Great of Heart."

LABEL FOR NEKHBET

Nḫb.t P.t Dp.t (2) dỉ≠s (3) ꜥnḫ wꜣs

Nekhbet, She of Pe and Dep, (2) as she gives (3) life and dominion.

ROYAL *SEREKH*

Ḥr ꜥꜣ ỉb

The Horus: "Great of Heart."

MAIN TEXT

(1) ḥsb.t 11.t ḫr ḥm n ny-sw.t bỉ.ty Wꜣḥ-ỉb-Rꜥ sꜣ Rꜥ Psmṯk ꜥnḫ ḏ.t r nḥḥ [ỉ]w.(t) pw ỉr.n ḥm≠f [m ḥw.t(?) ...] (2) ny-sw.t bỉ.ty Sḥtp-ỉb-Rꜥ mꜣꜥ ḫrw wn ḥm≠f ššp ꜣ.t nfr.t ỉm ḫft mꜣꜣ≠f wr(?) ꜥꜣ(?) rmṯ.w(?)¹ [ḫꜣs.t n.t Tḥnl(3). w nb.t wr.t m ṯꜣy.w ḥm.wt m spꜣ.t nb.(t) n.t ỉmnt.t Mw Ṯmḥ[w ...] (4) m ḥsb.t 10.t

sṯ dm.tw rn n ḥꜣ.tyw-ꜥ n.w nỉw.t nb.t r mḥ(w).t² wr.w [...] ḫr≠s(?)¹ [... ḏd.n ḥm≠f n smr.w nty.w(?)] (5) m-ḫt≠f ỉn ỉw ḥw(ỉ).n Tḥnw [ḥr] ḫꜣs.t≠sn ỉw mḥ(w)t≠sn² mḥ.tꜣ m tnw [ꜥšꜣ(?) ...]

[... ḏd.n] (6) nn n smr[.w] ḫft ḥm≠f ỉr Ptḥ Rsy-ỉnb≠f m wḏ.(t) n nb nb ỉty nb≠n nṯsn [...] (7) nt(y) n Wꜣsb mḥ.t r wꜣḏ-wr ḥꜣk.w-ỉb pw n.w pr ny-sw.t wn≠sn ḥr pšn tꜣ(?) r tr.w [... ỉmy.w-rꜣ mn](8)f(y).t ỉmy.w-rꜣ nw.w ṯs nb n mšꜥ nb n ḥnw ṯs nb s(?)[...]

[... ḏd.n] (9) ḥm≠f n≠sn ỉmy ỉn.tw Mꜥ s nb n ꜥḥꜥ.w n.w [...] mnf(y).t [...] (10) mšꜥ [...] r-dr≠f snḥ r ꜥꜣry.t ỉr.(t) nty.w ỉw (= r) wḏ nb n ḥm≠[ỉ(?) ...]

(11) ḥsb.t 11.(t) ꜣbd tp(y) pr.t sw 7 rdỉ.n ḥm≠f ỉḥ.tw [...] m dꜣ[mw(?) ...] (12) nw nb r ḫꜣs.t sḫ.t ꜥ[rq.t] r šd.wt [...] s nb r [...] tr[...] (13) snṯ sḏr sq(ꜣ) m ỉnb n(n) ḫt n(n) ꜥḥꜣ r [...] (14) ỉw rdỉ≠f šm ṯrr≠s [...] ỉr.n ḥm≠f nn n rdỉ.t [...]

(1) Regnal year 11 under the Majesty of the King of Upper and Lower Egypt, Wahibre, the Son of Re, Psametik, living forever and ever. His Majesty came [from the funerary estate (?) ...] (2) of the King of Upper and Lower Egypt, Sehetepibre (Amonemhat I), the justified. His Majesty had been spending a pleasant time there when he saw a great chief and all the important people (?)¹ [of the desert land of] (3) the Tehenu-Libyans, consisting of both men and women, from every district of the west, both Ma and Temehu Libyans [...] (4) in regnal year 10.

Now, the names of the mayors of every town were pronounced with respect to the tribes[2] and chiefs [...] because of it[1] [... Then His Majesty said to the companions who were (?)] (5) in his following: "Have the Libyans cast their lot with their desert land? Their tribes[2] are filled[3] with [great (?)] numbers of [...]."

[...] (6) These companions [said] before His Majesty: "Ptah, south of his Wall, has made a command to every lord, O sovereign, our lord. It is they who [...] (7) who are in the Oxyrhynchite nome northward to the Mediterranean. They are rebels against the palace. They were dividing the land (?) at the times [..." Then were summoned the overseers of] (8) infantry, overseers of hunters, and every commander of every army of the residence, every commander [...]

[...] (9) His Majesty said to them: "Let the Ma be brought, every man of the combatants, [...] infantry [...] (10) the [...] army in its entirety, who have been mustered at the gate in order to do those things that are in accordance with every command of [my (?)] Majesty [...]"

(11) Regnal year 11, first month of winter, day 7: His Majesty caused that [...] be surrounded with troops (?) [...] (12) every hunter to the desert land of the Siwa Oasis to the wells [...] every man to [...] (13) foundation secured and heightened with a wall without wood and without fighting against [...] (14) after he had caused its talus to go [...]. His Majesty did this for the purpose of causing [...]

NOTES
1. Read by Goedicke but unverified by Der Manuelian.
2. Literally, "families." Der Manuelian rearranged the signs unnecessarily to produce thm "to mobilize."
3. Or "Their tribes of the north are in [great (?)] numbers [...]."

175. FIRST SERAPEUM STELA
(LOUVRE SIM 3733, CAT. NO.192)

Recovered by Mariette from the Saqqara Serapeum in 1852, the round-topped stela records the burial and lifespan of the third, and final, Apis bull serving under Taharqa, born and installed in year 26 after the death of its predecessor in year 24. The Apis survived the second Assyrian invasion and the final expulsion of the Cushites under Tanwetamani and died in the twentieth year of Psametik I. As the bull lived twenty-one years, the stela indicates a length of reign for Taharqa as twenty-six years and some months, with Taharqa's partial twenty-seventh year assigned to Psametik. The stela measures 0.497 m by 0.318 m by 0.095 m and depicts in the damaged lunette Psametik pouring a libation to the Apis bull beneath heaven and a winged disk with pendant uraei.

Formerly Louvre 190. For the text, translation, and discussion, see Mali-nine, Posener, and Vercoutter 1968, 146 and pl. 152; Breasted 1906–7, 4:492 §§959–62; Schmidt 1958, 121–30; Vercoutter 1960, 72–76; and Parker 1960, 267–69 and pl. XXXVIII. See Kitchen 1986, 161–63 §§130–31, 172 §138, 393 §354, and 489 table 20.

SYMMETRICAL LABEL FOR THE WINGED DISK
Bḥd.t(y)   The Behdedite.

LABEL FOR APIS
Ḥp ꜥnḫ Wsỉr Ḫnt(y) ỉmnt.t (2) dỉ.n⸗(ỉ) n⸗k ꜥnḫ wꜣs nb
The living Apis, Osiris, Foremost of the West. (2) "Thus I have given to you all life and dominion."

MAIN TEXT
(1) [ḥsb].t 20.(t) ꜣbd 4 šmw sw 20 ḫr ḥm n ny-sw.t bỉ.ty Wꜣḥ-ỉb-Rꜥ sꜣ Rꜥ n ẖ.t⸗f (2) Psmṯk pr.n ḥm n Ḥp ꜥnḫ r Rꜣ-sṯꜣw (3) nṯr pn m ḥtp r ỉmnt.t nfr.t m ḥsb.t 21.(t) ꜣbd 2 ꜣḫ.t (4) sw 25 ỉsṯ ms.tw⸗f m ḥsb.t 26 (n.t) ny-sw.t (5) Thrq sḫn.tw⸗f r Ḥw.t-kꜣ-Ptḥ m (6) ꜣbd 4 pr.t sw 9 ỉr n rnp.t 21[1]

(1) [Regnal year] 20, month 4 of summer, day 20, under the Majesty of the King of Upper and Lower Egypt, Wahibre, bodily Son of Re, (2) Psame-tik: The Majesty of the living Apis went forth to Saqqara, (3) with this god resting in the beautiful west in regnal year 21, month 2 of Inundation, (4) day 25. Now he had been born in regnal year 26 of King (5) Taharqa, and he was installed in Memphis in (6) month 4 of winter, day 9, amounting to 21 years (of life).[1]

NOTE
1. A scratched addendum of disputed authenticity adds: "20 years, 1 [month], 4 days."

176. THE STATUE OF IBI, CHIEF STEWARD OF NITOCRIS (CAIRO JdE 36158)

The Cairo statue of Ibi serves as a fitting conclusion to the documen-tation of the turbulent Third Intermediate Period. Inscribed in the newly fashionable, spare archaizing style with few determinatives, the text itself represents a break with the Ramesside scribal conventions favored by previous Libyan dynasties. After a brief and traditional prayer on behalf of the chief steward (lines 1–4), the autobiographical text provides an insider's view of the consolidation of Saite power in Thebes. A description of the induction of Princess Nitocris in year 9 (lines 4–10) is followed by King Psametik's confident assessment of his authority in year 26, when at the "invitation" of northern adherents now resident in Upper Egypt he appoints his associate Ibi (lines 11–14) to supplant any Theban claimants to the fief of the once-powerful Montuemhat, who had been allowed to die in office. Political as well as personal motivations are implicit in the complaints of prior mismanagement and Ibi's guiltless devotion to sovereign and mistress. The deliberately paced installation of Saite loyalists was characteristic of Psametik's internal political strategy, and by year 26 no serious opposition remained to a unified Egyptian state. Only four years later papyrus records make the last official mention of a Meshwesh chieftain, now reduced in status to a mere police chief subservient to the royal harbor-master. Both politically and culturally, Egypt had entered a new and vibrant era.

Purchased in Luxor in 1903, the calcite stelephoros statue now measures 0.70 m in height, with the loss of upper torso and head. In the stela's lunette, a solar disk with pendant uraei grants life and is symmetrically labeled "The Behdedite, the great god" (Bḥd.ty nṯr ꜥꜣ). The text is badly worn, especially in the final lines, and the handcopies vary drastically.

For the texts, translation, and discussion, see Graefe 1994, 85–99 and pls. 10–14; Daressy 1904, 94–96; Sander-Hansen 1940, Textanhang 3; Breasted 1906–7, 4:488–91 §§958A–M; Abdel-Hamid 1982, 367–75; and Ritner 1990a, 101–8. See Kitchen 1986, 405 §365 and 587 §534 (as "Aba").

MAIN TEXT

(1) [...] ỉmy-rꜣ pr wr ḥm.t nṯr ꜣIbꜣ sꜣ mrỉ nṯr ꜥnḫ-Ḥr (2) [... mr] tn ḥs tn ꜣImn (3) mr tn Mnt(w) nb Wꜣs.t mỉ [nỉs⸗tn rn(?)]¹ n ... n] nb [tꜣ.wy(?)] ỉm[y-rꜣ pr] (4) wr n ḥnw.t⸗ỉ sꜣ.t⸗f ḥm.t nṯr [N.t-ỉqr.t ... ꜣIbỉ ...]

[ḥsb.t 9.(t) ... sšm(?) sꜣ.t ny-sw.t N.t-ỉqr.t] (5) mrỉ.(t)⸗f ḥs.(t) ꜥꜣ.t (n.t) ḫnw (n) ꜣImn ḥs.t ỉt⸗s mr.(t) mw.t⸗s [ḥm.t ny-sw.t wr.t] Mḫ(y).t-m-wsḫ.t r ḥm.t nṯr dwꜣt.t nṯr ꜣImn [nb ỉp.t]-s.[w]t (6) ỉn ḥry.(w)-ḫb.(t) ḫr(y)-tp sš.(w) mdꜣt-nṯr ḥm.w-nṯr ỉt.w nṯr wꜥb.(w) smr.w ꜥꜣ.w n.w ḥm⸗f m ỉry rd.wy n ḥnw.t⸗sn tꜣ ḏr⸗f m ḫb ꜥꜣ ỉꜥb.w (7) mḥ m pꜥ.wt ḫb hy ḫnf ḫr⸗s ḥtp n ꜣḫ.w wr.t m sꜣ.t⸗f mr.(t)⸗f ḥm.t nṯr N.t-ỉqr.t ꜥnḫ.tỉ wnw.t ḥw.t-nṯr m šms⸗s (8) s nb r ỉry.(t)⸗sn ỉr.t n⸗s n.t-ꜥ nb mỉ ḫpr ḫꜥ.w n nb⸗s nfr ꜣImn mnḫ.[t] dỉ⸗s stw.t mỉ Šw rdỉ.t (9) mꜣꜥ ꜥꜣb.t wr.(t) sšm.n wnw.t ḥw.t-nṯr ḥtp.(t) ḥs.(t) mr.(t) ḥr-tp ꜥnḫ wḏꜣ snb n ỉt⸗s Wꜣḥ-ỉb-Rꜥ ḏꜣ(ỉ).n ḥm.t⸗s (10) r ꜥḥ sndm.(tỉ) m-ḫnw dntꜣ.t⸗s n nbs ỉr.t n mꜣw.t m ḥḏ nbw mḥ m ꜥꜣ.t nb.(t) mꜣꜥ.(t) ỉr.t n⸗s m dỉw

(11) ḥsb.t 26.(t) ꜣbd 3 ꜣḫ.t sw 3 rḫ.n ḥm⸗f qỉ mnf(y).w(t) n.(t) tꜣ⸗n h(ꜣ)b.n ḥm⸗f n wr.w⸗f wn.(w) m-ḫt⸗f (12) nt(y).w m Tꜣ-Šmꜥw ḥm.w-nṯr wꜥb.w n ꜣImn ḥnr.t n.(t) ꜣImn ỉy⸗sn m ḏd sḏm.n ḥm⸗f pr dwꜣ.t nṯr ꜣImn (13) wꜣ r wꜣs n(n) rꜣ ḥry ỉm⸗f (n) ḥnw.t ḏꜣỉs.w⸗f s nb ḥr ỉt.(t) r dd ỉb⸗sn (ỉ)my dhn(14).tw rḫ ny-sw.t ꜣIbꜣ r ỉmy-rꜣ pr wr n ḥm.t nṯr šwy n⸗f ḥ.t⸗s nb.(t) wn.t šm ỉr.(t) tbꜣ (<ḏbꜣ) n kꜣ.w(t)

n(15){n} rdỉ.n≠(ỉ) ỉn.tw n sš.w rwḏ.w nb h(ȝ)b m wp.wt n.(t) pr dwȝ.t
nṯr mỉ ˁšȝ≠sn sḥwy.n≠(ỉ) ḫ.t nb.(t) (16) wn.t š(m) s.w šmsw.t≠f nb.(t) wn
m-ˁ kȝ.w r-gs≠sn mtrỉ.(w) mỉ ḥr hȝ.t mḥ pr.w-ḥḏ≠s m ḥḏ nbw ḥm.t [m]
ḥtm.t nb.(t) n.t (17) pr-ḥḏ bkȝ šnw.wt≠s m ỉt Mḥw bd.t pr.t nb.(t) sˁšȝ.n≠(ỉ)
mḏ.[wt]≠s m ỉwȝ.w tp(y≠w) dỉ≠(ỉ) sr.w≠s ḥtr (18) r tn(w) [...] smn.n≠(ỉ)
ḫ.t nb.(t) m šȝ(y).t m [...] mỉ qỉ≠sn n t[ȝ hȝ.t(?)] ḥrw-r pš.t≠s m ḥw.t-nṯr n.t
ʾImn (19) p(ȝy)≠s ḥrw m ḫr.t-ḥrw m [...] ḥrw≠s [...] ḥw.t≠s n [...] r≠w ḫ.t
ḥr nb≠s ḏbȝ.w≠s nb ḥtp ỉm [ỉr.n≠(ỉ)] (20) wp.wt≠s nb ḥr-ḥȝ ỉr.t.n ny-sw.t
nb tȝ qd.n≠(ỉ) wˁb.t≠s r-gs pr ny-sw.t ḥnr.(t) ʾImn m kȝ.t nḥḥ ḫ.t nb.(t) [...]
m [...] (21) [...] nbw m-ḫnw≠f qd.n≠(ỉ) pr≠s m pr wˁb n ỉt≠s ʾImn ỉr.t n≠s
ỉt≠s Rˁ m sp tp(y) q(ȝw) mḥ 100 wsḫ.t mḥ 100 [...] (22) ḥws m wsḫ.t≠s nb
ˁȝ.wy m ˁš ỉnb.w ỉr m ỉnr sȝt(w)≠f m ỉnr ḫȝ.t nb.(t) gm.(t) m-ḫnw≠f ḫȝw.
w(t)≠f (23) n(n) ḫr.(t) ḥrw-(r?)≠sn h(y).t≠f m ḥḏ mḥ m ˁȝ.t nb.(t) mȝˁ.(t)
sˁḫˁ.n≠(ỉ) ḥw.t-nṯr r-gs≠f n nb≠s Wsỉr Wn-nfr m kȝ.t mnḫ.t nb≠s ỉm≠f [...]
(24) [...] mỉ Rˁ m ȝḫ.t≠f ms.n≠(ỉ) sšmw.w n ḥm≠f m ḥḏ mḥ m ˁȝ.t nb.(t)
mȝˁ.(t) ḥn(ˁ) rp(y).wt n.w ḏ.t≠s m ḥḏ [...] (25) [...] ḥrw pn r-gs nb≠s ˁb r
wn sḫnty(?) s.t [...] wr n≠s(?) wsḫ.t r pḥr 4 s(ȝỉ)≠s ỉm≠f ḫft wḏ ỉt≠s ʾImn r
ỉp.t≠f [ḫ]n(ˁ) ḥnr.(t)≠f wn ḥn(ˁ)≠s m ḥb≠f ỉr≠(ỉ) n≠f wḏb n pȝ.wt ỉr.n≠(ỉ)
mỉt.t≠f r-gs sbȝ ḥry n pr ʾImn s(ȝỉ)≠s ỉm ḥnˁ ỉt≠s m ḥb≠f n tpy šmw sw 1
(26) [...] dwȝ.t-nṯr n nb≠s grg pr≠f m [...] sȝt(w) m [...] nb [...]≠f mȝˁ
ˁȝ.w≠f m ˁš sȝt(w) m pȝq.t ḥftn.t(?) mḥ.t(?) n≠f(?) ms.n≠(ỉ) ḥr-tp ˁnḫ wdȝ
snb n ˁ.wy dwȝ.t-nṯr N.t-ỉqr.t [...].n≠(ỉ) ḥw.t-ḥsmn≠f n mȝ(w.t) ḥws m ỉnr.
w ḫnm.w(t) šn nb r ḫn[p] mw ỉm≠f (27) [...] ḥm.t ny-sw.t wr.t Mḥ.t-n-wsḫ.
t mỉ nn m ḫ.t nb.(t) ỉw qrs ˁȝ.t n wḏḥ.w≠sn m dbḥ.w nb n.w rȝ-pr m ḥḏ
nbw ḥm.t ˁȝ.t nb.(t) wȝḥ.n≠(ỉ) ḥtp.w-nṯr≠sn m t ḥnq.t kȝ ȝpd.w šs mrḥ.t
ỉrp ỉrt.t spr.w rnpỉ.w m [pr] ʾImn [... rˁ(?)] nb (28) [...] N.t-ỉqr.t [...] wȝs(?)
kȝ.w≠sn n(n) ỉw ỉm≠sn n(n) ḫn ỉm n ˁbˁ ḏd-mdw≠ỉ nfr ḏbȝ.tw≠f m nfr ḥr
mdd wȝ.t n.(t) nb≠ỉ ỉr.n≠ỉ ḥr mw n sḫn n ḥnw.t≠(ỉ) ỉwty [...] nt.t nṯr nfr

(1) [...] chief steward of the God's Wife, Ibi, son of the beloved of
god, Ankhhor, (2) [... who says:] "May Amon [love] you and praise you, (3)
and may Montu, Lord of Thebes, love you even as [you hail the name (?)]¹
of the ... of] the Lord [of the Two Lands (?)], the chief [steward] (4) of my
mistress his daughter, the God's Wife [Nitocris, ... Ibi ...]

[Regnal year 9 ... There was conducted the royal daughter Nitocris]
(5) whom he loves, the chief chantress of the Residence of Amon, who
is praised by her father and beloved by her mother, [the great royal wife]
Mehetemweskhet (C), to become the God's Wife and Divine Votaress of
Amon, Lord of Karnak, (6) by the chief lector priests, scribes of the divine
books, Prophets, Fathers of the God, wab-priests, and the great friends of
His Majesty as subordinates at the heels of their mistress, while the entire
land was in great festival, with the bowls (7) filled with festival cakes,
rejoicing and prostration because of her, and satisfaction on account of the

great benefactions through his daughter, whom he loves, the God's Wife Nitocris, who yet lives, and while the temple staff was in her retinue (8) with all men at their duties. There was performed for her every ritual just as occurred in the coronation of her good lord Amon, while she splendidly gave forth rays like Shu. There were presented (9) great offerings. On behalf of the life, prosperity, and health of her father Wahibre the temple staff conducted a floral bouquet of praise and love. Her Majesty crossed over (10) to the palace seated within her palanquin of zizyphus wood, which was newly made with silver and gold and inlaid with every sort of genuine gemstone and which had been made for her as a gift.

(11) Regnal year 26, month 3 of Inundation, day 3. Whereas His Majesty knew the character of the troops of our land, so His Majesty sent word to his officials who had been in his following (12) and who were in Upper Egypt, and the Prophets, the *wab*-priests and the musical troupe of Amon, and they came, saying: 'His Majesty has heard that the estate of the Divine Votaress of Amon (13) has fallen into ruin. There is no supervising voice in it for the Mistress and its disputants, with the result that all men seize things as their hearts dictate. Let one appoint (14) the king's acquaintance Ibi to be chief steward of the God's Wife and to collect for him all her property that has gone missing and make payment for constructions.'

I did not allow the seizure of any scribes or agents who had been sent on business of the estate of the Divine Votaress, however many they were, and I collected everything (16) that had gone missing, including men of her whole retinue who were in the possession of others beside them, with the result that all was precise as formerly, while her treasuries were filled with silver, gold, copper, and every sealed thing of (17) the treasury, and her granaries were swollen with Lower Egyptian barley, emmer, and every sort of grain. I multiplied her cattle pens with long-horned cattle and first-grade cattle, while I caused her officials to be taxed (18) each [...]. I established everything by assessment in [...] as they had been [formerly], apart from her allotment in the temple of Amon (19) on her day, daily, in [...] her day [...] her mansion of [...] regarding them, the property concerning her lord, with all her payments satisfied by means of them. [I conducted] (20) all her business over and above what had been done by any king of the land. I built her refectory beside the royal palace and harem of Amon as an eternal construction, with everything [...] in [...] (21) [...] and gold within it. I built her house in the pure house of her father Amon, being what Re made for her in the primordial occasion: 10 cubits in height and 100 cubits in width [...], (22) constructed in its full width, with door leaves in cedar, walls made in stone, its pavement in stone, with every quarry represented within it, its altars (23) having no necessities far from them, its ceiling in silver inlaid with every sort of genuine gemstone. I erected a temple beside it for her lord Osiris Onnophris in excellent construction, with her lord in it [...] (24) [... shining (?)] like Re in his horizon. I fashioned images of His Majesty in silver inlaid with every sort of genuine gemstone, together with female images of her body in silver [...] (25) [...] today beside her lord, purified from fault, with position advanced (?) [...] great for her (?) in width in order to go about four times, so that she was satisfied with it in accordance with the command of her father Amon regarding his private apartment and his musical troupe who were with her in his festival as I made for him reversion offerings of loaves. I did likewise beside the upper gateway of the estate of Amon so that she was thereby satisfied together with her father in his festival of the first month of summer, day 1.

(26) [...] Divine Votaress for her lord, founding his house with [...] pavement in [...] all [...] its genuine [...], its doors in cedar, pavement in stone chips, a granary (?) and measure (?) for him (?), which I fashioned on behalf of the life, prosperity, and health belonging to the Divine Votaress Nitocris. [I constructed] his Mansion of Natron anew, built with stone and with wells and every sort of tree in order to drink water in it. (27) [...] great royal wife Mehetemweskhet likewise in everything. There were buried multitudes of their vessels comprising all the requirements of the temple in silver, gold, copper, and every sort of gemstone. I established their divine offerings consisting of bread, beer, oxen, fowl, alabaster, oil, wine, milk, ribs, and vegetables in the [estate] of Amon [...] every [day (?)]. (28) [...] Nitocris [...] dominion (?) their *ka*-spirits. There is no wrongdoing among them, no boastful statement, while my recitation was so good that it was repaid with goodness for adhering to the path of my lord. I acted loyally to the command of my mistress, who did not [...] of the Good God.

BACK PILLAR WITH "SAITE FORMULA"

[nṯr nỉw.ty n ...] smr wꜥ.(ty) ỉmy-rꜣ pr wr rḫ ny-sw.t mꜣꜥ ꜣỉbꜣ sꜣ mrỉ nṯr ꜥnḫ-Ḥr mꜣꜥ-ḫrw ỉmy tw ḫꜣ⸗f ḫft kꜣ⸗f m-bꜣḥ⸗f ꜣỈwny pw[2]

[O local god of ...] the unique friend, chief steward, and genuine king's acquaintance, Ibi, son of the beloved of god, Ankhhor, the justified, place yourself behind him even as his *ka*-spirit is before him. He is a Heliopolitan.[2]

NOTE

1. Restored from Montuemhat's statue Berlin 17271, Main Text, line 3.
2. For differing interpretations of this formula, see Junge 1984, 5:357–58.

BIBLIOGRAPHY

Abdallah, Aly O. 1984. An Unusual Private Stela of the Twenty-First Dynasty from Coptos. *JEA* 70:65–72.

Abdel-Hamid, Sayed. 1982. Une nouvelle statue thébaine d'Aba. *CdK* 7:367–75.

Aḥituv, S. 1984. *Canaanite Toponyms in Ancient Egyptian Documents.* Jerusalem: Hebrew University.

Albright, W. F. 1947. The Phoenician Inscriptions of the Tenth Century B.C. from Byblus. *JAOS* 67:153–60.

Allen, Thomas George. 1974. *The Book of the Dead or Going Forth by Day.* SAOC 37. Chicago: University of Chicago Press.

Alt, Albrecht. 1915. Bemerkungen zu dem "historischen" Skarabäus des Königs Schabako. *OLZ* 15:43–45.

Altenmüller, H. 1978. Zur Bedeutung der Harfnerlieder des Alten Reiches. *SAK* 6:1–24.

Andreu, Guillemette. 1997. Talisman d'Osorkon. Pages 182–83 in *L'Égypte ancienne au Louvre.* Edited by Guillemette Andreu, Marie-Hélène Rutschowscaya, and Christiane Ziegler. Paris: Hachette.

Anthes, Rudolf. 1928. *Die Felsinschriften von Hatnub.* UGAÄ 9. Leipzig: Hinrichs.

Arnold, Dieter. 1996. Hypostyle Halls of the Old and Middle Kingdoms? Pages 39–54 in vol. 1 of *Studies in Honor of William Kelly Simpson.* Edited by Peter Der Manuelian. Boston: Museum of Fine Arts.

Assmann, Jan. 1975. *Ägyptische Hymnen und Gebete.* Zurich: Artemis.

———. 1977. *Das Grab der Mutirdis.* Vol. 6 of *Grabung im Asasif 1963–1970.* Mainz am Rhein: von Zabern.

Association française d'action artistique. 1987. *Tanis: L'or des pharaons.* Paris: Galeries Nationales du Grand Palais.

Badawi, Ahmad. 1944. Zwei Denkmäler des grossen Gaugrafen von Memphis Amenophis Ḥwjj. *ASAE* 44:181–206.

———. 1956. Das Grab des Kronprinzen Scheschonk, Sohnes Osorkons II. und Hohenpriesters von Memphis. *ASAE* 54:153–77.

Baer, Klaus. 1962. The Low Price of Land in Ancient Egypt. *JARCE* 1:25–45.

———. 1973. The Libyan and Nubian Kings of Egypt: Notes on the Chronology of Dynasties XXII to XXVI. *JNES* 32:4–25.

Baines, John. 1974. The Inundation Stela of Sebekḥotpe VIII. *AcOr* 36:39–54.

————. 1985. *Fecundity Figures*. Warminster: Aris & Phillips.

Bakir, Abd el-Mohsen. 1943. A Donation Stela of the Twenty-Second Dynasty. *ASAE* 43:75–81.

Barguet, P. 1962. *Le temple d'Amon-Rê à Karnak*. Cairo: IFAO.

Barta, Winfried. 1978. Die Sedfest-Darstellung Osorkons II. im Tempel von Bubastis. *SAK* 6:25–42.

Bates, Oric. 1970 [orig. 1914]. *The Eastern Libyans*. London: Cass.

Beckerath, Jürgen von. 1966. The Nile Level Records at Karnak and Their Importance for the History of the Libyan Period (Dynasties XXII and XXIII). *JARCE* 5:43–55.

————. 1968. Die "Stele der Verbannten" im Museum des Louvre. *RdÉ* 20:7–36.

————. 1975. Amenrudj. *LÄe* 1:222.

————. 1984. *Handbuch der ägyptischen Köningsnamen*. MÄS 20. Munich: Deutscher Kunstverlag.

————. 1994. Osorkon IV = Herakles. *GM* 139:7–8.

————. 1996. Die angebliche Jubiläums-Stele Osorkons II. *GM* 154:19–22.

————. 1997. *Chronologie des pharaonischen Ägypten*. MÄS 46. Mainz am Rhein: von Zabern

Bénédite, Georges. 1908. Quelques objets égyptiens acquis par le Musée du Louvre en 1907. *Gazette des Beaux Arts* 3rd series 40:316–17.

Berlandini, Jocelyne. 1978. Une stèle de donation du dynaste libyen Roudamon. *BIFAO* 78:147–63.

————. 1980. Une stèle d'Horus sur les crocodiles du supérieur des prêtres de Sekhmet, Padiimennebnesouttaouy. *Karnak* 6:235–45.

————. 1994. Un Ânkh/Djed/Ouas pour le Nouvel An de Montouemhat. *BSÉG* 18:5–22.

Bernand, E. 1981. *Recueil des inscriptions grecques du Fayoum*. 3 vols. Leiden: Brill; Cairo: IFAO.

Bezold, Carl. 1889–99. *Catalogue of the Cuneiform Tablets in the Kuyunjik Collection of the British Museum*. 5 vols. London: British Museum.

Bickel, Susanne, Marc Gabolde, and Pierre Tallet. 1998. Des annales héliopolitaines de la Troisième Période intermédiaire. *BIFAO* 98:31–56.

Bierbrier, M. L. 1973. Hrere, Wife of the High Priest Paiankh. *JNES* 32:311.

————. 1975. *The Late New Kingdom in Egypt (c. 1300–664 B.C.)*. Warminster: Aris & Phillips.

Birch, S. 1880. *Catalogue of the Collection of Egyptian Antiquities at Alnwick Castle*. London: Clay, Sons & Taylor.

Blackman, Aylward M. 1914. *The Rock Tombs of Meir*. Vol. 1. London: Egypt Exploration Fund.

————. 1941. The Stela of Shoshenk, Great Chief of the Meshwesh. *JEA* 27:83–95.

Bohleke, Briant. 1997. An Oracular Amuletic Decree of Khonsu in the Cleveland Museum of Art. *JEA* 83:155–67.

Borchardt, Ludwig. 1911–36. *Statuen und Statuetten von Königen und Privatleuten im Museum von Kairo, Nr. 1–1294*. 5 vols. Berlin: Reichsdruckerei.

————. 1932. Ein Stammbaum memphitischer Priester. *SPAW* 24:618–22.

————. 1935. *Die Mittel zur zeitlichen Festlegung von Punkten der ägyptischen Geschichte und ihre Anwendung*. Cairo: privately printed.

Boreux, Charles. 1932. *Guide-Catalogue Sommaire*. 2 vols. Paris: Musées nationaux.

Bothmer, Bernard V. 1960. The Philadelphia-Cairo Statue of Osorkon II (Membra Dispersa III. *JEA* 46:3–11.

Botti, G. 1900. Manuscrits libyens découverts par M. Schiaparelli dans le musée de Turin. *Bulletin de l'Institut Égyptien, Séance du 29 Décembre, 1899*. 10:161–69.

Breasted, James Henry. 1904. The Earliest Occurrence of the Name of Abram. *AJSL* 21:22–36.

———, ed. and trans. 1906–7. *Ancient Records of Egypt: Historical Documents from the Earliest Times to the Persian Conquest*. 5 vols. Chicago: University of Chicago Press.

Brugsch, Emil. 1896. Mittheilungen von Emil Brugsch-Bey. *ZÄS* 34:83–84.

Brugsch, Heinrich Karl. 1878. Ein wichtiges Denkmal aus den Zeiten Königs Šešonq I. *ZÄS* 16:38–41.

———. 1883–91. *Thesaurus Inscriptionum Aegyptiacarum*. 6 vols. Leipzg: Hinrichs.

———. 1996. *Egypt under the Pharaohs*. London: Bracken. Reprint of *A History of Egypt under the Pharaohs*. London: Murray, 1902.

Bruyère, B. 1952. *Notes à propos de quelques objets trouvés en 1939 et 1940*. Vol. 3 of *Rapport sur les fouilles de Deir el Médineh, 1935–1940*. FIFAO 20/3. Cairo: IFAO.

Budge, E. A. Wallis. 1909. *A Guide to the Egyptian Galleries (Sculpture)*. London: British Museum.

———. 1912. *Annals of Nubian Kings*. London: Paul, Trench, Trübner.

———. 1974 [orig. 1894]. *The Mummy*. 2nd ed. New York: Causeway Books.

Caminos, Ricardo A. 1952. Gebel Es-Silsilah No. 100. *JEA* 38:46–61.

———. 1958. *The Chronicle of Prince Osorkon*. AnOr 37. Rome: Pontifical Biblical Institute.

———. 1964a. The Nitocris Adoption Stela. *JEA* 50:71–101.

———. 1964b. Surveying Semna Gharbi. *Kush* 12:82–86.

———. 1969. An Ancient Egyptian Donation Stela in the Archaeological Museum of Florence (Inv. No. 7207). *Centaurus* 14:42–46.

———. 1972. Another Hieratic Manuscript from the Library of Pwerem son of Ḳiḳi (Pap. B.M. 10288). *JEA* 58:205–24.

———. 1994. Notes on Queen Katimala's Inscribed Panel in the Temple of Semna. Pages 73–80 in *Nubie, Soudan, Éthiopie*. Vol. 2 of *Hommages à Jean Leclant*. Edited by Catherine Berger, Gisèle Clerc, and Nicolas Grimal. BdÉ 106/2. Cairo: IFAO.

———. 1998. *The Temple of Semna*. Vol. 1 of *Semna-Kumma*. London: Egypt Exploration Society.

Caminos, Ricardo A., and T. G. H. James. 1963. *The Shrines*. Vol. 1 of *Gebel Es-Silsilah*. ASE 31. London: Egypt Exploration Society.

Capart, Jean. 1941. A propos des fouilles de Tanis. *CdÉ* 16/32:254.

Carter, Howard. 1903. Report of Work Done in Upper Egypt (1902–1903), IV. Stela of Taharka. *ASAE* 4:171–80.

Cazelles, H. 1974. Review of Redford 1972. *RdÉ* 26:159.

Černý, Jaroslav. 1939. *Late Ramesside Letters*. BiAeg 9. Brussels: Fondation Égyptologique Reine Élisabeth.

———. 1942. Le caractère des oushebtis d'après les idées du Nouvel Empire. *BIFAO* 41:126–33.

———. 1946. Studies in the Chronology of the Twenty-First Dynasty. *JEA* 32:24–30.

———. 1954. Consanguineous Marriages in Pharaonic Egypt. *JEA* 40:23–29.

———. 1962. Egyptian Oracles. Pages 35–48 in Parker 1962.

———. 1973. A Community of Workmen at Thebes in the Ramesside Period. BdÉ 50. Cairo: IFAO.

Černý, Jaroslav, and Sarah Israelit Groll. 1975. *A Late Egyptian Grammar*. Rome: Biblical Institute Press.

Chappaz, Jean-Luc. 1982. Une stèle de donation de l'An 21 de Ioupout II au Musée d'art et d'histoire. *Genava* 30:71–81.

Chassinat, Émile. 1935. *Le Temple de Dendara*. Vol. 3. PIFAO 857/3. Cairo: IFAO.

Christophe, Louis-A. 1952–53. La double datation du Ouadi Gassous. *BIE* 35:141–52.

Clère, Jacques J. 1951. Review of Macadam 1949. *BiOr* 8:174–80.

———. 1957. Le nom égyptien des "pincettes." *RdÉ* 11:157–58.

———. 1983. Autobiographie d'un général gouverneur de la Haute Égypte à l'époque saite. *BIFAO* 83:85–100.

Clermont-Ganneau, Charles. 1903. Inscription égypto-phénicienne de Byblos. *Recueil d'Archéologie Orientale* 6:74–78.

Conwell, David. 1987. On Ostrich Eggs and Libyans. *Expedition* 29/3:25–34.

Crum, Walter E. 1939. *A Coptic Dictionary*. Oxford: Clarendon.

Daressy, Georges. 1888. Les carrières de Gebelein et le roi Smendès. *RT* 10:133–38.

———. 1892. Notes et remarques. *RT* 14:20–38.

———. 1896a. Une inondation à Thèbes sous le règne d'Osorkon II. *RT* 18:181–86.

———. 1896b. Inscriptions inédites de la XXIIe dynastie. *RT* 18:43–53.

———. 1897a. Notes et remarques. *RdÉ* 19:20–21.

———. 1897b. *Notice explicative des ruines de Médinet Habou*. Cairo: Imprimerie Nationale.

———. 1898. Notes et remarques. *RT* 20:72–86.

———. 1901. Le temple de Hibeh. *ASAE* 2:154–56.

———. 1903. *Textes et Dessins Magiques: Catalogue général des antiquités égyptiennes du Musée du Caire*. Cairo: IFAO.

———. 1904. Une statue d'Aba. *ASAE* 5:94–96.

———. 1908. Le roi Auput et son domaine. *RT* 30:202–8.

———. 1909. *Cercueils des cachettes royales*. Cairo: IFAO.

———. 1910. Le décret d'Amon en faveur du grand prêtre Pinozem. *RT* 32:175–86.

———. 1913. Notes sur les XXIIe, XXIIIe et XXIVe dynasties. *RT* 35:129–50.

———. 1915. Trois stèles de la période Bubastite. *ASAE* 15:140–47.

———. 1916. Le fils aîné de Chéchanq III. *ASAE* 16:61–62.

———. 1917a. Les rois Psousennes. *RT* 38:9–12.

———. 1917b. Stèle du Roi Pefnifdubast. *ASAE* 17:43–45.

———. 1921. Fragments Héracléopolitains. *ASAE* 21:138–44.

———. 1926. Le voyage d'inspection de M. Grébaut en 1889. *ASAE* 26:1–22.

————. 1931. Léontopolis métropole du XIXe nome de la Basse-Égypte. *BIFAO* 30:625–49.

Daumas, François. 1980. L'interpretation des temples égyptiens anciens à la lumière des temples gréco-romains. *CdK* 6:261–84.

————. 1988. *Valeurs phonétiques des signes hiéroglyphiques d'époque gréco-romaine*. 2 vols. Montpellier: Université de Montpellier.

Depuydt, Leo. 1994. Apis Burials in the Twenty-Fifth Dynasty. *GM* 138:23–25.

Der Manuelian, Peter. 1994. *Living in the Past: Studies in Archaism of the Egyptian Twenty-Sixth Dynasty*. London: Kegan Paul.

Derchain, Philippe. 1962. *Le sacrifice de l'oryx*. Rites égyptiens 1. Brussels: Fondation Égyptologique Reine Élisabeth.

Desroches-Noblecourt, Ch. 1956. Interprétation et datation d'une scène gravée sur deux fragments de récipient en albâtre provenant des fouilles du palais d'Ugarit. Pages 179–220 in *Ugaritica III*. Edited by Claude F. A. Schaeffer. Paris: Geuthner.

Dimick, John. 1958. The Embalming House of the Apis Bulls. *Archaeology* 11:183–89.

Dixon, David M. 1964. The Origin of the Kingdom of Kush. *JEA* 50:121–32.

Dodson, Aidan. 1988. Some Notes Concerning the Royal Tombs at Tanis. *CdÉ* 63:221–33.

————. 1993. A New King Shoshenq Confirmed? *GM* 137:53–58.

————. 1994. *The Canopic Equipment of the Kings of Egypt*. London: Kegan Paul.

Donner, Herbert, and Wolfgang Röllig. 1962–64. *Kanaanäische und Aramäische Inschriften*. 3 vols. Wiesbaden: Harrassowitz.

Drioton, Etienne, 1949. Un orant de style populaire. Pages 255–59 in vol. 1 of *Studi in Memoria di Ippolito Rosellini*. Pisa: Lischi.

Drioton, Etienne, and Jacques Vandier. 1962. *L'Égypte*. 4th ed. Paris: Presses Universitaires de France.

Dunand, Maurice. 1937. *Fouilles de Byblos: Atlas*. Vol. 1. Paris: Geuthner.

————. 1939. *Fouilles de Byblos: Texte*. Vol. 1. Paris: Geuthner.

Dunham, Dows. 1950. *El Kurru*. Vol. 1 of *The Royal Cemeteries of Kush*. Cambridge: Harvard University Press.

————. 1970. *The Barkal Temples*. Boston: Museum of Fine Arts.

Dunham, Dows, and J. M. A. Janssen. 1960. *Semna and Kumma*. Boston: Museum of Fine Arts.

Dunham, Dows, and M. F. Laming Macadam. 1949. Names and Relationships of the Royal Family of Napata. *JEA* 35:139–49.

Dussaud, René. 1924. Les inscriptions phéniciennes du tombeu d'Aḥiram, roi de Byblos. *Syria* 5:135–57.

————. 1925. Dédicace d'une statue d'Osorkon I par Elibaʿal, roi de Byblos. *Syria* 6:101–17.

Edel, Elmar. 1980. Der älteste Beleg für den Titel ḥꜣ.tj-pʿt und sein Weiterleben bis in die römische Zeit hinein. *Serapis* 6:41–46.

Edwards, A. 1883. Relics from the Tomb of the Priest-Kings at Dayr-el-Baharee. *RT* 4:79–87.

Edwards, Iorwerth E. S. Appendix. 1955. *JEA* 41:96–98.

———. 1960. *Oracular Amuletic Decrees of the Late New Kingdom: Hieratic Papyri in the British Museum*. 2 vols. London: British Museum.

———. 1976. *Tutankhamun: His Tomb and Its Treasures*. New York: Metropolitan Museum of Art.

Edwards, Iorwerth E. S., and T. G. H. James. 1984. Egypt. In *The Cambridge Ancient History: Plates to Volume III: The Middle East, the Greek World and the Balkans to the Sixth Century B.C.* Edited by John Boardman. New ed. Cambridge: Cambridge University Press.

Egberts, A. 1991. The Chronology of The Report of Wenamun. *JEA* 77:57–67.

———. 1998. Hard Times: The Chronology of "The Report of Wenamun" Revisted. *ZÄS* 125:93–108.

Eide, Tormund, et al. 1994. *From the Eighth to the Mid-Fifth Century BC*. Vol. 1 of *Fontes historiae Nubiorum: Textual Sources for the History of the Middle Nile Region between the Eighth Century BC and the Sixth Century AD*. Bergen: University of Bergen.

El-Alfi, Mostafa. 1992. A Donation Stela from the Time of Osorkon I. *Discussions in Egyptology* 24:13–19.

el-Sayed, Ramadan. 1970. Tefnakht ou Horus SI3-(IB). *VT* 20:116–18.

———. 1975. *Documents relatifs à Saïs et ses divinités*. BdÉ 69. Cairo: IFAO.

Epigraphic Survey. 1954. *The Bubastite Portal*. Vol. 3 of *Reliefs and Inscriptions at Karnak*. OIP 74. Chicago: University of Chicago Press.

———. 1979. *Scenes of King Herihor in the Court*. The Temple of Khonsu 1. OIP 100. Chicago: Oriental Institute of the University of Chicago.

———. 1980. *The Tomb of Kheruef: Theban Tomb 192*. OIP 102. Chicago: Oriental Institute of the University of Chicago.

———. 1981. *Scenes and Inscriptions in the Court and the First Hypostyle Hall*. The Temple of Khonsu 2. OIP 103. Chicago: Oriental Institute of the University of Chicago.

———. 1986. *The Battle Reliefs of King Sety I*. RIK 4; OIP 107. Chicago: Oriental Institute of the University of Chicago.

———. 1998. *The Facade, Portals, Upper Register Scenes, Columns, Marginalia, and Statuary in the Colonnade Hall*. OIP 116. Chicago: Oriental Institute of the University of Chicago.

Erichsen, Wolja. 1954. *Demotisches Glossar*. Copenhagen: Munksgaard.

Erman, Adolf. 1883. Editorial Note. *ZÄS* 21:69 n. 1.

———. 1891. Bruchstück einer Äthiopenstele. *ZÄS* 29:126.

———. 1897. Zu den Legrain'schen Inschriften. *ZÄS* 35:19–24.

Erman, Adolf, and Hermann Grapow, eds. 1926–63. *Wörterbuch der aegyptischen Sprache*. 7 vols. Leipzig: Hinrichs.

———. 1935–53. *Wörterbuch der ägyptischen Sprache: Die Belegstellen*. 5 vols. Berlin: Akademie.

Fazzini, Richard. 1972. Some Egyptian Reliefs in Brooklyn. *Miscellanea Wilbouriana* 1:33–70.

———. 1988. *Egypt Dynasty XXII–XXV*. Leiden: Brill.

Feucht, Erika. 1978. Zwei Reliefs Scheschonqs I. aus El Hibeh. *SAK* 6:69–77.

———. 1981. Relief Scheschonqs I. beim Erschlagen der Feinde aus El Hibef. *SAK* 9:105–17.

Fischer-Elfert. H. W. 1996. Two Oracle Petitions Addressed to Horus-Khau with Some Notes on the Oracular Amuletic Decrees (P. Berlin P. 8525 and p. 8526). *JEA* 82:129–44.

Fisher, Clarence S. 1929. *The Excavation of Armageddon.* OIC 4. Chicago: University of Chicago Press.

Foster, Karen P., and Robert K. Ritner. 1996. Texts, Storms, and the Thera Eruption. *JNES* 55:1–14.

Frame, Grant. 1999. The Inscription of Sargon II at Tang-i Var. *Or* 68:31–57.

Gardiner, Alan H. 1932. *Late Egyptian Stories.* Brussels: Fondation Égyptologique Reine Élisabeth.

——. 1933. The Dakhleh Stela. *JEA* 19:20–30.

——. 1934. The Earliest Manuscripts of the Instruction of Amenemmes I. Pages 479–96 in part 2 of vol. 1 of *Mélanges Maspero.* MIFAO 66/2. Cairo: IFAO.

——. 1935. Piankhy's Instructions to His Army. *JEA* 21:219–23.

——. 1947. *Ancient Egyptian Onomastica.* 3 vols. Oxford: Oxford University Press.

——. 1948. *The Wilbour Papyrus II: Commentary.* Oxford: The Brooklyn Museum.

——. 1961. *Egypt of the Pharaohs.* Oxford: Clarendon.

——. 1962. The Gods of Thebes as Guarantors of Personal Property. *JEA* 48:57–69.

——. 1999. *Egyptian Grammar.* 3rd edition. Oxford: Ashmolean Museum.

Gauthier, Henri. 1914. *De la XIXe à la XXIVe dynastie.* Vol. 3 of *Le livre des rois d'Égypte, recueil de titres et protocoles royaux.* MIFAO 19. Cairo: IFAO.

——. 1916. *De la XXVe dynastie à la fin des Ptolémées.* Vol. 4 of *Le Livre des rois d'Egypte, recueil de titres et protocoles royaux.* MIFAO 20. Cairo: IFAO.

——. 1918a. Les "Fils Royaux de Ramsès." *ASAE* 18:245–64.

——. 1918b. Les stèles de l'an III de Taharqa de Médinet-Habou. *ASAE* 18:190.

——. 1925–31. *Dictionnaire des noms géographiques contenus dans les textes hiéroglyphiques.* 7 vols. Cairo: IFAO for Société royale de géographie d'Egypte.

Germond, Philippe. 1986. *Les invocations à la Bonne Année au temple d'Edfou.* AH 11. Geneva: Belles-Lettres.

Gibson, John C. L. 1971–82. *Textbook of Syrian Semitic Inscriptions.* 3 vols. Oxford: Clarendon.

Gilula, Mordechai. 1967. An Egyptian Parallel to Jeremiah I 4–5. *VT* 17:114.

——. 1977. Egyptian NḤT = Coptic NAḤTE "To Believe." *JNES* 36:295–96.

Giveon, Raphael. 1971. *Les bédouins Shosou dans les documents égyptiens.* DMOA 18. Leiden: Brill.

Goedicke, H. 1962. Psammetik I. und die Libyer. *MDAIK* 18:26–49.

Golénischeff, Woldemar. 1927. *Papyrus Hiératiques.* Cairo: IFAO.

Gomaà, Farouk. 1974. *Die libyschen Fürstentümer des Deltas vom Tod Osorkons II. bis zur Wiedervereinigung Ägyptens durch Psametik I.* Wiesbaden: Reichert.

Graefe, Erhart. 1975. Der libysche Stammesname *p(j)d(j)/pjt* im spätzeitlichen Onomastikon. *Enchoria* 5:13–17.

——. 1981. *Untersuchungen zur Verwaltung und Geschichte der Institution der Gottesgemahlin des Amun vom Beginn des Neuen Reiches bis zur Spätzeit.* Wiesbaden: Harrassowitz.

600   THE LIBYAN ANARCHY

————. 1990. Eine Seite aus den Notizbüchern von Robert Hay. Pages 85–90 in *Festschrift Jürgen von Beckerath: Zum 70. Geburtstag am 19. Februar 1990.* Edited by Bettina Schmitz and Arne Eggebrecht. HÄB 30. Hildesheim: Gerstenberg.

————. 1994. Der autobiographische Text des Ibi, Obervermögensverwalter der Gottesgemahlin Nitokris, auf Kairo JE 36158. *MDAIK* 50:85–99.

Grapow, Hermann. 1940. Die Inschrift der Königin Katimala am Tempel von Semne. *ZÄS* 76:24–41.

Grdseloff, Bernhard. 1947a. Édôm, d'après les sources égyptiennes. *RHJE* 1:69–99.

————. 1947b. En marge des récentes recherches sur Tanis. I. — Une mention de Tanis sous Ramsès II? II. — Le roi Neferkherès. III. — "Takhpnès" (I. Rois, XI, 19; 20). *ASAE* 47:203–16.

Griffith, Francis Ll. 1909. *Catalogue of the Demotic Papyri in the John Rylands Library Manchester.* Manchester: Manchester University Press.

————. 1937. *Catalogue of the Demotic Graffiti of the Dodecaschoenus.* Oxford: Oxford University Press, 1937.

————. 1938. A Stela of Tirhaqa from Kawa, Dongola Province, Sudan. Pages 423–30 in vol. 1 of *Mélanges Maspero.* MIFAO 66/1. Cairo: IFAO.

Griffith, Francis Ll., W. M. Flinders Petrie, and Alexander S. Murray. 1888. *Tanis, Part 2: Nebesheh (Am) and Defenneh (Tahpanhes).* EEF Memoir 4. London: Trübner.

Grimal, Nicolas-Christophe. 1981a. *Quatre Stèles Napatéennes au Musée du Caire: JE 48863–48868.* MIFAO 106. Cairo: IFAO.

————. 1981b. *La stèle triomphale de Pi('ankh)y au Musée du Caire.* Cairo: IFAO.

————. 1986. *Les termes de la propagande royale égyptienne de la XIXe dynastie à la conquête d'Alexandre.* Paris: Imprimerie Nationale.

Groll, S. 1974. Review of E. F. Wente, *Late Ramesside Letters. RdÉ* 26:168–72.

Gunn, Battiscombe. 1941. Notes on Egyptian Lexicography. *JEA* 27:144–48.

————. 1946. The Split Determined Infinitive. *JEA* 32:92–96.

————. 1955. The Decree of Amonrasonthēr for Neskhons. *JEA* 41:83–105.

Gunn, Battiscombe, and Alan H. Gardiner. 1918. The Expulsion of the Hyksos. *JEA* 5:36–56.

Habachi, Labib. 1957. *Tell Basta.* SASAE 22. Cairo: IFAO.

————. 1972. *The Second Stela of Kamose.* Glückstadt: Augustin.

————. 1977. *Tavole d'offerta are e bacili da libagione n. 22001–22067.* Catalogo del Museo Egizio di Torino 2. Turin: Edizioni d'arte Fratelli Pozzo.

Haigh, Daniel Henry. 1877. Origin of the XXII. Dynasty. *ZÄS* 15:38–40, 64–71.

Hall, H. R. 1913. *Catalogue of Egyptian Scarabs, Etc. in the British Museum.* London: British Museum.

Harris, J. R. 1961. *Lexicographical Studies in Ancient Egyptian Minerals.* Berlin: Akademie.

Haynes, Joyce L. 1996. Redating the Bat Capital in the Museum of Fine Arts, Boston. Pages 399–408 in vol. 1 of *Studies in Honor of William Kelly Simpson.* Edited by Peter Der Manuelian. Boston: Museum of Fine Arts.

Helck, Wolfgang. 1974. *Die altägyptische Gaue.* Wiesbaden: Reichert.

————. 1986. Wenamun. *LÄe* 6:1215–17.

Hermann, Wolfram. 1958. Der historische Ertrag der altbyblischen Königsinschriften. *MIO* 6:14–32.

Hoch, James E. 1994. *Semitic Words in Egyptian Texts of the New Kingdom and Third Intermediate Period.* Princeton: Princeton University Press.
———. 1995. Middle Egyptian Grammar. Missassauga: Benben.
Hodjash, Svetlana, and Oleg Berlev. 1994. A Document for the History of Nome XIV, Lower Egypt, in the Libyan Period. Pages 129–35 in vol. 4 of *Hommages à Jean Leclant.* Edited by Catherine Berger, Gisèle Clerc, and Nicolas Grimal. BdÉ 106/4. Cairo: IFAO.
Hoffmeier, James K. 1985. *Sacred in the Vocabulary of Ancient Egypt.* OBO 59. Fribourg: Universitätsverlag; Göttingen: Vandenhoeck & Ruprecht.
Hölscher, Uvo. 1939. *The Temples of the Eighteenth Dynasty.* Vol. 2 of *The Excavation of Medinet Habu.* OIP 41. Chicago: University of Chicago Press.
———. 1954. *Post-Ramesside Remains.* Vol. 5 of *The Excavation of Medinet Habu.* OIP 66. Chicago: University of Chicago Press.
Hornung, Erik. 1999. *History of Ancient Egypt.* Ithaca, N.Y.: Cornell University Press.
Hornung, Erik, and Elisabeth Staehelin. 1974. *Studien zum Sedfest.* AH 1. Geneva: Belles-Lettres.
Iversen, Erik. 1941. *Two Inscriptions Concerning Private Donations to Temples.* Det Kgl. Danske Videnskabernes Selskab, Historisk-filologiske Meddelelser 27/5. Copenhagen: Munksgaard.
———. 1996. Remarks on "An Unusual Private Stela of the Twenty-First Dynasty from Coptos." *JEA* 82:213–14.
Jacquet-Gordon, Helen K. 1960. The Inscriptions on the Philadelphia-Cairo Statue of Osorkon II. *JEA* 46:12–23.
———. 1965–66. Two Stelae of Horus-on-the-Crocodiles. *ABM* 7:53–64.
———. 1967. The Illusory Year 36 of Osorkon I. *JEA* 53:63–68.
———. 1979. Deux graffiti de l'époque libyenne sur le toit du temple de Khonsou à Karnak. Pages 167–83 in vol. 1 of *Hommages à la mémoire de Serge Sauneron: 1927–1976.* BdÉ 81. Cairo: IFAO.
———. 2004. *The Graffiti on the Khonsu Temple Roof at Karnak: A Manifestation of Popular Piety.* OIP 122. Chicago: Oriental Institute of the University of Chicago.
Jansen-Winkeln, Karl. 1985. *Ägyptische Biographien der 22. und 23. Dynastie.* 2 vols. ÄAT 8. Wiesbaden: Harrassowitz.
———. 1987. Thronname und Begräbnis Takeloths I. *VA* 3:253–58.
———. 1989. Zwei Bemerkungen zu Gebel es-Silsila Nr. 100. *JEA* 75:237–39.
———. 1990. Zu den biographischen Texten der 3. Zwischenzeit. *GM* 117/118: 165–80.
———. 1991a. Der Ausdruck wꜥ zꜣ wꜥ. *GM* 123:53–56.
———. 1991b. Review of Kruchten 1989. *BiOr* 48/5–6:765–71.
———. 1992. Das "Zeugende Herz." *LingAeg* 2:147–49.
———. 1995a. Historische Probleme der 3. Zwischenzeit. *JEA* 81:129–49.
———. 1995b. Die Plünderung der Königsgräber des Neuen Reiches. *ZÄS* 122:62–78.
———. 1997. Die thebanischen Gründer der 21. Dynastie. *GM* 157:49–74.
Janssen, Jac. J. 1968. The Smaller Dâkhla Stela. *JEA* 54:165–72.
———. 1975. *Commodity Prices from the Ramesside Period.* Leiden: Brill.

Junge, Friedrich. 1984. Saitische Formel. *LÄe* 5:357–58.

———. 1996. *Einführung in die Grammatik des Neuägyptisch.* Wiesbaden: Harrassowitz.

Kadish, Gerald E. and Donald B. Redford. Forthcoming. *The Twenty-Third Dynasty Chapel of Osiris Ruler of Eternity at Karnak.* Toronto: Society for the Study of Egyptian Antiquities.

Kahn, Dan-El. 1999. A Note on the *sdm.n.f* forms in the Pi(ankh)y Stela. *GM* 172:5–6.

Kákosy, László. 1993. King Bocchoris and the Uraeus Serpent. *Acta Classica Universitatis Scientiarum Debreceniensis* 28:3–5.

Kamal, Ahmed Bey. 1901. Description générale des ruines de Hibé, de son temple et de sa nécropole. *ASAE* 2:84–91.

———. 1909. Un Monument nouveau de Sheshonq Ier. *RT* 31:37–38.

Kees, Hermann. 1953. *Das Priestertum im ägyptischen Staat vom Neuen Reich bis zur Spätzeit.* PÄe 1. Leiden: Brill.

———. 1962. Der Hohepriester von Memphis Schedsunefertem. *ZÄS* 87:140–49.

———. 1964. *Die Hohenpriester des Amun von Karnak bis zum Ende der Äthiopenzeit.* Leiden: Brill.

Kemp, Barry. 1983. *Ancient Egypt: A Social History.* Cambridge: Cambridge University Press.

Kitchen, Kenneth A. 1969–70. Two Donation Stelae in The Brooklyn Museum. *JARCE* 8:59–68.

———. 1975–90. *Ramesside Inscriptions, Historical and Biographical.* 8 vols. Oxford: Blackwell.

———. 1984. Review of Epigraphic Survey 1981. *BiOr* 41:84–85.

———. 1986. *The Third Intermediate Period in Egypt (1100–650 B.C.).* 2nd ed. Warminster: Aris & Phillips.

———. 1993. Review of Kruchten 1989. *JEA* 79:308–9.

———. 1995. *The Third Intermediate Period in Egypt (1100–650 B.C.).* 2nd ed. with new preface. Warminster: Aris & Phillips.

———. 1997. A Possible Mention of David in the Late Tenth Century BCE, and Deity *Dod as Dead as the Dodo? *JSOT* 76:29–44.

———. 1999. *Poetry of Ancient Egypt.* Jonsered: Åströms.

Koenig, Yvan. Notes sur la stèle de donation Caire JE 30972. *ASAE* 68:111–13.

Königliche Museen zu Berlin. 1895. *Aegyptische und Vorderasiatische Alterthümer aus den Königlichen Museen zu Berlin.* Berlin: Mertens.

———. 1899. *Ausführliches Verzeichnis der aegyptischen Altertümer und Gipsabgüsse.* Berlin: Spemann.

Krauss, Rolf. 1999. Nh(h)-Öl = Olivenöl. *MDAIK* 55:293–98.

Kruchten, Jean-Marie. 1986. *Le grand texte oraculaire de Djéhoutymose.* Monographies Reine Élisabeth 5. Brussels: Fondation Égyptologique Reine Élisabeth.

———. 1989. *Les annales des prêtres de karnak (XXI-XXIImes Dynasties) et autres textes contemporains relatifs à l'initiation des prêtres d'Amon.* OLA 32. Leuven: Departement Oriëntalistiek.

Kuentz, C. 1938. Note au précédent article. Pages 430–32 in vol. 1 of *Mélanges Maspero.* MIFAO 66/1. Cairo: Imprimerie de l'Institut Français d'Archéologie Orientale.

Kuraszkiewicz, Kamil O. 1996. Bemerkungen zur Rekonstruction des Jubiläums-portals Osorkons II. *GM* 151:79–93.

Kurth, Dieter. 1975. *Den Himmel Stützen*. Rites égyptiens 2. Brussels: Fondation Égyptologique Reine Élisabeth.

Lamon, Robert S., and Geoffrey M. Shipton. 1939. *Megiddo I*. OIP 42. Chicago: University of Chicago Press.

Larson, John A. 1990. Egypt in Israel: The Discovery of the "Shishak Stela Fragment" at Megiddo. *Oriental Institute News and Notes* 124 (May-June): 1–3.

Lauffray, Jean, Serge Sauneron, and Claude Traunecker. 1975. La tribune du quai de Karnak et sa favissa. *Karnak* 5:43–76.

Layard, Austen H. 1853. *Discoveries in the Ruins of Nineveh and Babylon*. London: Murray.

Leahy, Anthony. 1979. The Name of Osiris Written 𓊪. *SAK* 7:141–53.

———. 1983. The Proper Name Pišanḫuru. *GM* 62:37–48.

———. 1990. The Twenty-Third Dynasty. Pages 185–90 in *Libya and Egypt c1300–750 BC*. Edited by Anthony Leahy. London: SOAS Centre of Near and Middle Eastern Studies and the Society for Libyan Studies.

———. 1992. "May the King Live": The Libyan Rulers in the Onomastic Record. Pages 146–63 in *Studies in Pharaonic Religion and Society in Honour of J. Gwyn Griffiths*. Edited by A. Lloyd. London: Egypt Exploration Society.

Leclant, Jean. 1951. Les Inscriptions "ethiopiennes" sur la porte du IVe pylone du grand temple d'Amon a Karnak. *RdÉ* 8:104–13.

———. 1961. *Montouemhat, quatrième prophète d'Amon, prince de la ville*. BdÉ 35. Cairo: IFAO.

———. 1963. Kashta, Pharaon, en Égypte. *ZÄS* 90:74–81.

———. 1965. *Recherches sur les monuments thébains de la XXVe dynastie dite éthiopienne*. Cairo: IFAO.

Leclant, Jean, and Jean Yoyotte. 1949. Nouveaux Documents Relatifs à l'An VI de Taharqa. *Kêmi* 10:28–42.

———. 1952. Notes d'Histoire et de Civilisation Éthiopiennes. *BIFAO* 51:1–39.

Leemans, Conradus. 1842–1905. *Leyden Rijksmuseum van Oudheden, Monuments égytpiens du Musée d'antiquités des Pays-bas à Leide*. Leiden: Brill.

Lefebvre, Gustave. 1926. Herihor, Vizier. *ASAE* 26:63–68.

Legrain, Georges. 1896a. Les crues du Nil depuis Sheshonq Ier jusqu'à Psametik. *ZÄS* 34:119–21.

———. 1896b. Textes gravés sur le quai de Karnak. *ZÄS* 34:111–18.

———. 1897. Deux stèles trouvées à Karnak en février 1897. *ZÄS* 35:12–19.

———. 1900a. Fragments des annales des prêtres d'Amon. *RT* 22:51–63.

———. 1900b. Le temple et les chapelles d'Osiris à Karnak: Le temple d'Osiris-Hiq-Djeto. *RT* 22:125–36.

———. 1903. Notice sur le temple d'Osiris Neb-Djeto. *ASAE* 4:181–86.

———. 1904. Rapport sur les travaux exécutés à Karnak du 31 Octobre 1902 au 15 Mai 1903. *ASAE* 5:1–43.

———. 1906. Deux stèles inédites. *ASAE* 7:226–27.

———. 1908. Le dossier de la famille Nibnoutirou. *RT* 30:73–90, 160–74.

———. 1909a. Recherches généalogiques. *RT* 31:1–10.

————. 1909b. *Statues et statuettes des rois et de particuliers*. Vol. 2. Catalogue général des antiquités égyptiennes du Musée du Caire 49. Cairo: IFAO.

————. 1914. Au Pylône d'Harmhabi à Karnak (Xe Pylône). *ASAE* 14:13–44.

Lepsius, Carl Richard. 1842. *Auswahl der wichtigsten Urkunden des ägyptischen Alterthums*. Leipzig: Wigand.

————. 1849–59. *Denkmäler aus Aegypten und Aethiopien*. 12 vols. Berlin: Nicolai.

Lesko, L. 1982–90. *A Dictionary of Late Egyptian*. 5 vols. Berkeley, Calif.: Scribe.

Lichtheim, Miriam. 1973–80. *Ancient Egyptian Literature: A Book of Readings*. 3 vols. Berkeley and Los Angeles: University of California Press.

Logan, Thomas J., and Joan Goodnick Westenholz. 1971–72. *Sḏm.f* and *Sḏm.n.f* Forms in the Pey (Piankhy) Inscription. *JARCE* 9:111–19.

Loret, Victor. 1942. La stèle votive du tombeau d'Osorkon II. *Kêmi* 9:97–106.

Loukianoff, Gregoire. 1926. Nouveaux fragments de la stèle de Piankhi. *Ancient Egypt* 11:86–89.

Macadam, Miles F. Laming. 1949. *The Inscriptions: Texts, Plates*. Vol. 1 of *The Temples of Kawa*. London: Griffith Institute.

————. 1955. *History and Archaeology of the Site: Text, Plates*. Vol. 2 of *The Temples of Kawa*. London: Griffith Institute.

Malinine, Michel, Georges Posener, and Jean Vercoutter. 1968. *Catalogue des Stèles du Sérapéum de Memphis*. Paris: Imprimerie Nationale.

Mallet, Dominique. 1896. Quelques monuments égyptiens du Musée d'Athènes. *RT* 18:1–15.

Manniche, Lise. 1991. *Music and Musicians in Ancient Egypt*. London: British Museum Press.

Marciniak, Marek. 1974. *Les inscriptions hiératiques du temple de Thoutmosis III*. Deir el-Bahari 1. Warsaw: PWN Editions Scientifiques de Pologne.

Mariette, Auguste. 1887. Fragments et documents relatifs aux fouilles de Sân. *RT* 9:1–20.

————. 1982a [orig. 1880]. *Catalogue général des monuments d'Abydos découverts pendant les fouilles de cette ville*. Wiesbaden: Harrassowitz.

————. 1982b [orig. 1875]. *Karnak étude topographique et archéologique: Avec un appendice comprenant les principaux textes hiéroglyphiques découverts ou recueillis pendant les fouilles exécutées à Karnak*. Wiesbaden: Harrassowitz.

Mariette, M. 1863. Lettre de M. Aug. Mariette à M. le Vicomte De Rougé sur une stèle trouvée à Gebel-Barkal. *Revue Archéologique* NS 7:413–22.

Marucchi, O. 1923. Di una stela egizia dedicata in occasione del giubileo del faraone Osorkon II. *Atti della Pontifica Accademia Romana di Archeologia, Rendiconti* 1:77–88.

Maspero, Gaston. 1889. *Les momies royales de Déir el-Baharî*. MIFAO 1/4. Paris: Leroux.

————. 1893. Sur deux stèles récemment découverts. *RT* 15:84–86.

————. 1906. Sur un scarabée de Sabacon. *ASAE* 7:142.

————. 1909. Note additionelle. *RT* 31:38–40.

————. 1967. *Popular Stories of Ancient Egypt*. Translation of 1882 edition. New York: University Books.

Maystre, Charles. 1949. Sur les grands prêtres de Ptah. *JNES* 8:84–89.

Meeks, Dimitri. 1980–82. *Année lexicographique*. 3 vols. Paris: Impr. de la Margeride.

———. 1979a. Les donations aux temples dans l'Égypte du 1er Millénaire avant J.-C. Pages 605–87 in *State and Temple Economy in the Ancient Near East: Proceedings of the International Conference Organized by the Katholieke Universiteit Leuven from the 10th to the 14th of April 1978 II*. Edited by Edward Lipiński. OLA 6. Leuven: Departement Oriëntalistiek.

———. 1979b. Une fondation memphite de Taharqa. Pages 219–59 in vol. 1 of *Hommages à la mémoire de Serge Sauneron: 1927–1976*. BdÉ 81. Cairo: IFAO.

Menu, Bernadette. 1980. Note sur les inscriptions de S3-Mwt surnommé Kyky. *RdÉ* 32:141–44.

———. 1998. Fondations et concessions royales de terres en Égypte ancienne. Pages 121–54 in Recherches sur l'histoire juridique, économique et sociale de l'ancienne Égypte. BdÉ 122. Cairo: IFAO.

Meulenaere, Herman de. 1956. Trois personnages Saïtes. *CdE* 31:249–56.

Meulenaere, Herman de, and Pierre MacKay. 1976. *Mendes II*. Warminster: Aris & Phillips.

Meyer, E. 1907–8. Neue Nachträge zur ägyptischen Chronologie. *ZÄS* 44:115–25.

Montet, Pierre. 1928. *Byblos et L'Égypte*. Paris: Geuthner.

———. 1941. *Le drame d'Avaris: Essai sur la pénétration des Sémites en Égypte*. Paris: Geuthner.

———. 1942. La nécropole des rois Tanites, Tombeau I, Tombeau II, Tombeau III. *Kêmi* 9:1–96.

———. 1947. *Les constructions et le tombeau d'Osorkon II à Tanis*. Fouilles de Tanis: Le nécropole royale de Tanis 1. Paris: Jourde et Allard.

———. 1951. *Les constructions et le tombeau de Psousennès à Tanis*. Fouilles de Tanis: Le nécropole royale de Tanis 2. Paris: CNRS.

———. 1960. *Les constructions et le tombeau de Chéchanq III a Tanis*. Fouilles de Tanis: Le nécropole royale de Tanis 3. Paris: CNRS.

Moret, Alexandre. 1901. Un procès de famille sous la XIXe dynastie. *ZÄS* 39:11–39.

———. 1966. *Le Lac Sacré de Tanis*. Paris: Klincksieck.

Müller, W. Max. 1901. Eine neue Inschrift zu den asiatischen Zügen des Pharao Schischaq. *OLZ* 4:280–302.

———. 1906. *Results of a Journey in 1904*. Vol. 1 of *Egyptological Researches*. Washington, D.C.: Carnegie Institution.

———. 1908. Königsnamen der 22. ägyptischen Dynastie. *OLZ* 11:361–63.

———. 1910. Inscriptions of Shoshenq I, Karnak. Pages 143–53 in *Results of a Journey in 1906*. Vol. 2 of *Egyptological Researches*. Washington, D.C.: Carnegie Institution.

———. 1914. Ein historischer Text des Aethiopenkönigs Schabako. *OLZ* 17:49–52.

———. 1921. Aegyptisch-libysches. *OLZ* 24:193–97.

Munier, Henri. 1922. Un achat de terrains au temps du roi Si-Amon. Pages 361–66 in *Recueil d'études égyptologiques dédiées à la mémoire de Jean-François Champollion*. Paris: Librairie Ancienne Honoré Champion.

Munro, Peter. *Die spätägyptischen Totenstelen*. Ägyptologische Forschungen 25. Glückstadt: Augustin, 1973.

Murnane, William J. The Sed-Festival: A Problem in Historical Method. *MDAIK* 37:369–76.

Myśliwiec, K. 1988. Royal Portraiture of the Dynasties XXI–XXX. Mainz am Rhein: von Zabern.

Naville, Edouard. 1888. Les fouilles du Delta pendant l'hiver de 1887. *RT* 10:50–60.

———. 1890. *The Mound of the Jew and the City of Onias.* London: Kegan Paul.

———. 1891. *Bubastis (1887–1889).* London: Kegan Paul.

———. 1892. *Festival-Hall of Osorkon II in the Great Temple of Bubastis (1887–1889).* London: Paul, Trench, Trübner.

Nelson, Harold H. 1941. *Key Plans Showing Locations of Theban Temple Decorations.* OIP 56. Chicago: University of Chicago Press.

———. 1949. Certain Reliefs at Karnak and Medinet Habu and the Ritual of Amenophis I. *JNES* 8:201–32, 310–45.

Newberry, Percy E. 1905. Ancient Egyptian Scarabs. London: n.p.

Nims, Charles F. 1955. Places about Thebes. *JNES* 14:110–23.

———. 1965. *Thebes of the Pharaohs.* New York: Stein & Day.

Oppert, Jules. 1873. Les Inscriptions en langue susienne. Pages 179–228 in vol. 2 of *Mémoires du Congrès international des Orientalistes.* Paris: Maisonneuve.

Osing, Jürgen. 1983. Die Worte von Heliopolis. Pages 347–61 in *Fontes atque pontes: Eine Festgabe für Hellmut Brunner.* Edited by Manfred Görg. ÄAT 5. Wiesbaden: Harrassowitz.

Otto, Eberhard. 1938. *Beiträge zur Geschichte der Stierkulte in Aegypten.* Leipzig: Hinrichs.

———. 1964. *Aus der Sammlung des Ägyptologischen Instituts der Universität Heidelberg.* Berlin: Springer-Verlag.

Paleological Association of Japan. 1983. *Preliminary Report: Second Season of the Excavations at the Site of Akoris, Egypt.* Kyoto: Paleological Association of Japan.

Paleological Association of Japan, Egyptian Committee. 1995. *Akoris: Report of the Excavations at Akoris in Middle Egypt 1981–1992.* Kyoto: Koyo Shjobo.

Parker, Richard A. 1960. The Length of the Reign of Taharqa. *Kush* 8:267–69.

———. 1962. *A Saite Oracle Papyrus from Thebes.* Providence, RI: Brown University.

Payraudeau, Frédéric. 2003. Le fragment no 6 des Annales des prêtres d'Amon à Karnak et une nouvelle branche de la famille de Néseramon. *RdÉ* 53:250–55.

Peet, T. Eric. 1928. The Chronological Problems of the Twentieth Dynasty. *JEA* 14:52–73.

Perrot, Georges, and Charles Chipiez. 1883. *A History of Art in Ancient Egypt.* Translated by Walter Armstrong. London: Chapman & Hall.

Peterson, Bengt Julius. 1970–71. Ausgewählte ägyptische Personennamen nebst prosopographischen Notizen aus Stockholmer Sammlungen. *OrSuec* 19–20:3–22.

Petrie, W. M. Flinders. 1885. *Tanis, Part 1: 1883–84.* EEF Memoir 2. London: Trübner.

———. 1888. *Tanis.* Vol. 2: London: Egypt Exploration Fund.

———. 1905a. *Ehnasya, 1904.* EEF Memoir 26. London: Egypt Exploration Fund.

———. 1905b. *A History of Egypt from the XIXth to the XXXth Dynasties.* A History of Egypt 3. London: Methuen.

———. 1917. *Scarabs and Cylinders with Names*. London: British School of Archaeology in Egypt.

Pierret, Paul. 1874–78. *Recueil d'inscriptions inédites du Musée égyptien du Louvre*. 2 vols. Paris: Franck.

Pirenne, J., and B. van de Walle. 1937. Documents juridiques égyptiens. *Archives d'histoire du droit oriental* 1:3–86.

Porter, Bertha, and Rosalind L. B. Moss. 1927–51. *Topographical Bibliography of Ancient Egyptian Hieroglyphic Texts, Reliefs, and Paintings*. 7 vols. Oxford: Clarendon.

———. 1964. *Royal Tombs and Smaller Cemeteries*. Vol. 1.2 of *Topographical Bibliography of Ancient Egyptian Hieroglyphic Texts, Reliefs, and Paintings*. 2nd ed. Oxford: Clarendon.

———. 1972. *Theban Temples*. Vol. 2 of *Topographical Bibliography of Ancient Egyptian Hieroglyphic Texts, Reliefs, and Paintings*. 2nd ed. Oxford: Clarendon.

———. 1981. *Saqqara to Dahshur*. Vol. 3.2 of *Topographical Bibliography of Ancient Egyptian Hieroglyphic Texts, Reliefs, and Paintings*. 2nd ed. Oxford: Clarendon.

Posener, Georges. 1982. Un Papyrus d'El-Ḥîbeh. *RdÉ* 68:134–38.

Price, F. G. Hilton. 1897. *A Catalogue of the Egyptian Antiquities in the Possession of F. G. Hilton Price*. London: Bernard Quaritch.

Priese, Karl-Heinz. 1970. Der Beginn der kuschitischen Herrschaft in Ägypten. *ZÄS* 98:16–32.

———. 1972. Zur Sprache der ägyptischen Inschriften der Könige von Kusch. *ZÄS* 98:99–124.

Pritchard, James B. 1969. *Ancient Near Eastern Texts Relating to the Old Testament*. 3rd ed. Princeton: Princeton University Press.

———. 1987. *The Harper Atlas of the Bible*. New York: Harper & Row.

Quibell, James Edward. 1898. *The Ramesseum*. Translations and comments by Wilhelm Spiegelberg. Egyptian Research Account 2. London: Quaritch.

Rainey, Anson. 1976. Taharqa and Syntax. *Tel Aviv* 3:38–41.

Ranke, Hermann. 1926. *Koptische Friedhöfe bei Karara und der Amontempel Scheschonks I. bei el Hibe*. Berlin: de Gruyter.

———, ed. 1935–77. *Die ägyptischen Personennamen*. 3 vols. Glückstadt: Augustin.

Ray, J. D. 1976. *The Archive of Ḥor*. Texts from Excavations 2. London: Egypt Exploration Society.

Redford, Donald B. 1972. Studies in Relations between Palestine and Egypt during the First Millennium B.C.: I. The Taxation System of Solomon. Pages 141–56 in *Studies on the Ancient Palestinian World Presented to Professor F. V. Winnett*. Edited by J. W. Wevers and D. B. Redford. Toronto: University of Toronto Press.

———. 1981. Interim Report on the Excavations at East Karnak, 1977–78. *JARCE* 18:11–41.

———. 1983. Interim Report on the Excavations at East Karnak (1981–1982 Seasons). *JSSEA* 13:203–24.

———. 1986. *Pharaonic King-Lists, Annals, and Day-Books*. Mississauga: Benben.

Reeves, Carl Nicholas. 1990. *Valley of the Kings: The Decline of a Royal Necropolis*. London: Kegan Paul.

Reeves, Carl Nicholas, and Richard H. Wilkinson. 1996. *The Complete Valley of the Kings: Tombs and Treasures of Egypt's Greatest Pharaohs*. London: Thames & Hudson.

Reisner, George A. 1921. The Royal Family of Ethiopia. *Museum of Fine Arts Bulletin, Boston* 19:27–28.

———. 1931. Inscribed Monuments from Gebel Barkal. *ZÄS* 66:76–100.

Renouf, P. Le Page. 1891. Who Were the Libyans? *PSBA* 13:599–603.

Revillout, Eugène. 1892. Un papyrus bilingue du temps de Philopator. *PSBA* 14:60–97, 120–32, 229–55.

———. 1895. *Mélanges sur la métrologie, l'économie politique et l'histoire de l'ancienne Égypte*. Paris: Maisonneuve.

———. 1897. *La Propriété sés demembrements la possession et leurs transmissions en droit égyptien comparé aux autres droits de l'antiquité*. Paris: Leroux.

———. 1899. Précis du droit égyptien comparé aux autres droits de l'antiquité. 2 vols. Paris: Giard & Bière.

Riefstahl, Elizabeth. 1968. *Ancient Egyptian Glass and Glazes*. Brooklyn: Brooklyn Museum.

Ritner, Robert K. 1984a. A Property Transfer from the Erbstreit Archives. Pages 171–87 in *Grammata demotika: Festschrift für Erich Lüddeckens zum 15. Juni 1983*. Edited by Heinz-J. Thissen und Karl-Th. Zauzich. Würzburg: Zauzich.

———. 1984b. A Uterine Amulet in the Oriental Institute Collection. *JNES* 43:209–21.

———. 1985. Anubis and the Lunar Disc. *JEA* 71:149–55.

———. 1986. The Site of the Wild Bull-Hunt of Amenophis III. *JEA* 72:193–94.

———. 1989. Horus on the Crocodiles: A Juncture of Religion and Magic. Pages 103–16 in *Religion and Philosophy in Ancient Egypt*. Edited by James P. Allen et al. YES 3. New Haven: Yale University Press.

———. 1990a. The End of the Libyan "Anarchy" in Egypt: P. Rylands IX, cols. 11–12. *Enchoria* 17:101–8.

———. 1990b. Horus Cippus "Text C" and the "Business of Sepa." *VA* 6/3:167–68.

———. 1993a. Egyptian Magic: Questions of Legitimacy, Religious Orthodoxy, and Social Deviance. Pages 189–200 in *Studies in Pharaonic Religion and Society: In Honour of J. Gwyn Griffiths*. Edited by Alan B. Lloyd. London: Egypt Exploration Society.

———. 1993b. *The Mechanics of Ancient Egyptian Magical Practice*. SAOC 54. Chicago: University of Chicago Press.

———. 1994. Denderite Temple Hierarchy and the Family of Theban High Priest Nebwenenef: Block Statue OIM 10729. Pages 205–26 in *For His Ka: Essays Offered in Memory of Klaus Baer*. Edited by David P. Silverman. SAOC 55. Chicago: University of Chicago Press.

———. 1996. A Rediscovered Middle Kingdom Exemplar of the "Libyan Smiting Scene." American Research Center in Egypt Annual Meeting, St. Louis, 13 April.

———. 1998. Fictive Adoptions or Celibate Priestesses? *GM* 164:85–90.

————. 2008. Libyan vs. Nubian as the Ideal Egyptian. Pp. 305–14 in *Egypt and Beyond: Essays Presented to Leonard H. Lesko*. Edited by Stephen E. Thompson and Peter De Manuelian. Providence, R.I.: Brown University.

Roeder, Günther. 1914. *Naos*. CGC. Leipzig: Breitkopf & Härtel.

————. 1961. *Zauberei und Jenseitsglauben im alten Ägypten*. Zurich: Artemis.

————, ed. 1924. *Aegyptische Inschriften aus den Königlichen Museen zu Berlin*. 2 vols. Leipzig: Hinrichs.

Romano, James. 1989. The Bes-Image in Pharaonic Egypt. 2 vols. Ph.D. diss. 1989. New York University.

Roth, Ann Macy. 1983. Some New Texts of Herihor and Ramesses IV in the Great Hypostyle Hall at Karnak. *JNES* 42:43–53.

Rougé, Vicomte E. de. 1863. Inscription historique du Roi Pianchi-Mériamoun. *Revue Archéologique* NS 8:94–127.

Russman, Edna R. 1981. An Egyptian Royal Statuette of the Eighth Century B. C. Pages 149–55 in *Studies in Ancient Egypt, the Aegean, and the Sudan: Essays in Honor of Dows Dunham on the Occasion of His 90th Birthday, June 1, 1980*. Edited by William Kelly Simpson and Whitney M. Davis. Boston: Department of Egyptian and Ancient Near Eastern Art, Museum of Fine Arts.

Ryholt, Kim. 1993. A Pair of Oracle Petitions Addressed to Horus-of-the-Camp. *JEA* 79:189–98.

Sambin, Chantal. 1988. *L'Offrande de la soi-disant "clepsydre": Le symbol šb.t/wnšb/wtt*. StudAeg 11. Budapest: Université Loránd Eötvös de Budapest, Chaire de l'egyptologie.

Sander-Hansen, Constantin E. 1940. *Das Gottesweib des Amun*. Copenhagen: Munksgaard, 1940.

Sauneron, Serge. 1957. Cinq années de recherches épigraphiques en Égypte. *BSFE* 24:45–54.

Sauneron, Serge, and Jacques Vérité 1969. Fouilles dans la zone axiale du IIIe pylône à Karnak. *Kêmi* 19:249–76.

Schäfer, Heinrich. 1897. Ein Tempelgeräth. *ZÄS* 35:98–99.

————. 1905. *Urkunden der älteren Äthiopenkönige*. Urkunden des aegyptischen altertums 3/1–2. 2 vols. Leipzig: Hinrichs.

Schipper, Bern U. 2005. *Die Erzählung des Wenamun*. OBO 209. Fribourg: Academic Press.

Schmidt, G. 1958. Das Jahr des Regierungsantritts König Taharqas. *Kush* 6:121–30.

Schneider, Hans. D. 1985. A Royal Epigone of the 22nd Dynasty. Pages 261–67 in vol. 2 of *Mélanges Gamal Eddin Mokhtar*. Edited by Paule Posener-Kriéger. BdÉ 97/2. Cairo: IFAO.

Schott, Siegfried. 1950. *Altägyptische Festdaten*. Wiesbaden: Steiner.

Schweinfurth, Georg. 1885. *Alte Baureste und hieroglyphische Inschriften im Uadi Gasus mit Bemerkungen von Pr. A. Erman*. Berlin: Königliche Akademie der Wissenschaften.

Seele, Keith C. 1947. Oriental Institute Museum Notes: Horus on the Crocodiles. *JNES* 6:43–52.

Seidl, Erwin. 1951. *Einführung in die ägyptische Rechtsgeschichte bis zum Ende des Neuen Reiches*. ÄF 10. Glückstadt: Augustin.

Sethe, Kurt. 1900. *Thebes.* Vol. 3 of *Denkmäler aus Aegypten und Aethiopien. Text.* Leipzig: Hinrichs.

———. 1920. *Demotische Urkunden zum ägyptischen Bürgschaftsrechte vorzüglich der Ptolemäerzeit.* Leipzig: Teubner.

———. 1929. *Amun und die Acht Urgötter von Hermopolis.* Berlin: Akademie der Wissenschaften.

Shanks, Hershel. 1999a. Has David Been Found in Egypt? *BAR* 25/1:34–35.

———. 1999b. David in Egypt. *BAR* 25/3:10–12.

Simpson, William K., ed. 1973. *The Literature of Ancient Egypt.* New Haven: Yale University Press.

Smith, William Stevenson. 1958. *The Art and Architecture of Ancient Egypt.* Harmondsworth, U.K.: Penguin.

Sotheby's. 1924. *Sotheby's Catalogue: Sale of Hood Collection.* London: Sotheby's.

Sottas, Henri. 1913. *La préservation de la propriété funéraire dans l'ancienne Égypte.* Paris: Librairie Ancienne Honoré Champion.

Spalinger, Anthony. 1979a. The Military Background of the Campaign of Piye (Piankhy). *SAK* 7:273–301.

———. 1979b. The Negatives ⸗ and /\ in the Piye (Piankhy) Stela. *RdÉ* 31:66–80.

———. 1981. Notes on the Military in Egypt during the XXVth Dynasty. *JSSEA* 11:37–58.

Spiegelberg, Wilhelm. 1899. Eine Stele aus der Oase Dachel. *RT* 21:12–21.

———. 1903. Die Tefnachthosstele des Museums von Athen. *RT* 25:190–98.

———. 1913. *Die demotischen Papyri Hauswaldt.* Leipzig: Hinrichs.

———. 1917a. Briefe der 21. Dynastie aus El-Hibe. *ZÄS* 53: 1–30.

———. 1917b. Varia. *ZÄS* 53:91–115.

———. 1920. Neue Schenkungsstelen über Landstiftungen an Tempel. *ZÄS* 56:55–60.

———. 1931. *Die demotischen Papyri Loeb.* Munich: Beck.

Stern, Ludwig. 1883. Die XXII. manethonische Dynastie. *ZÄS* 21:15–26.

Stewart, H. M. 1983. *The Late Period.* Part 3 of *Egyptian Reliefs and Paintings from the Petrie Collection.* Warminster: Aris & Phillips.

Stierlin, Henri. 1997. *The Gold of the Pharaohs.* Paris: Terrail.

Stierlin, Henri, and Christiane Ziegler. 1987. *Tanis: Vergessene Schätze der Pharaonen.* Munich: Hirmer.

Stockfisch, Dagmar. 1996. Bemerkungen zur sog. "libyschen Familie." Pages 315–25 in *Wege öffnen: Festschrift für Rolf Gundlach zum 65. Geburtstag.* Edited by Mechthild Schade-Busch. Wiesbaden: Harrassowitz.

Taylor, John H. 1998. Nodjmet, Payankh and Herihor: The End of the New Kingdom Reconsidered. Pages 1143–55 in *Proceedings of the Seventh International Congress of Egyptologists.* Edited by Christopher J. Eyre. Leuven: Peeters.

Théodoridès, Aristide. 1965. Le Papyrus des Adoptions. *RIDA* 12:79–142.

Thomas, Elizabeth. 1966. *The Royal Necropoleis of Thebes.* Princeton: Morgan.

Thompson, H. 1940. Two Demotic Self-Dedications. *JEA* 26:68–78.

Tresson, Paul. 1938. L'Inscription de Chechanq Ier, au Musée du Caire: Un frappant exemple d'impôt progressif en matière religieuse. Pages 817–40 in vol. 1 of *Mélanges Maspero.* MIFAO 66/1. Cairo: IFAO.

Turaev, Boris. 1912. Nieskol'ko egipetskikh nadpiseï iz moeï kollektsii. *Zapiski Klassitcheskavo Otdeleniya Rousskavo Archeologicheskavo Obschestva* 8:2.

Uphill, Eric. 1965. The Egyptian Sed-Festival Rites. *JNES* 24:365–83.

———. 1965–66. The Nine Bows. *JEOL* 19:393–420.

———. 1967. The Date of Osorkon II's Sed-Festival. *JNES* 26:61–62.

Van Siclen, Charles C., III. 1973. The Accession Date of Amenhotep III and the Jubilee. Appendix A: A Note on the Reign of Osorkon II. *JNES* 32:295–99.

———. 1985. The City of Basta: An Interim Report. *NARCE* 128:28–39.

———. 1994. Nectanebo II's Great Naos for Bastet. Pages 321–32 in *Essays in Egyptology in Honor of Hans Goedicke*. Edited by B. Bryan and D. Lorton. San Antonio: Van Siclen Books.

Vandier, J. 1964. Iousâas et (Hathor)-Nébet-Hétépet. *RdÉ* 16:55–146.

———. 1965. Iousâas et (Hathor)-Nébet-Hétépet. *RdÉ* 17:89–176.

———. 1966. Iousâas et (Hathor)-Nébet-Hétépet. *RdÉ* 18:67–142.

Vassilika, E. 1995. *Egyptian Art*. Fitzwilliam Museum Handbooks. Cambridge: Fitzwilliam Museum.

Velde, Herman te. 1967. *Seth, God of Confusion: A Study of His Role in Egyptian Mythology and Religion*. PÄe 6. Leiden: Brill.

Vercoutter, Jean. 1960. The Napatan Kings and Apis Worship. *Kush* 8:62–76.

———. 1962. *Textes biographiques du Sérapéum de Memphis*. Paris: Librairie Ancienne Honoré Champion.

Vernier, Émile. 1907. *La bijouterie et la joaillerie égyptiennes*. MIFAO 2. Cairo: IFAO.

Vernus, Pascal. 1975. Inscriptions de la troisième période intermédiaire (I). *BIFAO* 75:1–66.

———. 1977. Le mot št3w, "branchages, bosquets, bois." *RdÉ* 29:179–93.

———. 1978. Littérature et autobiographie: Les inscriptions de S3-Mwt surnommé Kyky. *RdÉ* 30:115–46.

———. 1980. Inscriptions de la Troisième Période Intermédiaire (IV): Le texte oraculaire réemployé dans le passage axial du IIIe pylône dans le temple de Karnak. *Karnak* 6:215–33.

Vikientieff, V. 1930. *La Haute Crue du Nil et l'averse de l'an 6 du roi Taharqa*. Cairo: IFAO.

Vittmann, Günther. 1975. Ein neuer Wesir der Spätzeit. *GM* 15:50–51.

———. 1978. *Priester und Beamte im Theben der Spätzeit: Genealog. u. prosopographische Untersuchungen zum thebanischen Priester- u. Beamtentum d. 25. u. 26. Dynastie*. BzÄe 1. Vienna: Afro-Pub.

Vleeming, Sven P. 1987. Two Greek-Demotic Notes. *Enchoria* 15:155–62.

Wente, Edward F. 1961. IWIW·F SDM in Late Egyptian. *JNES* 20:120–23.

———. 1967a. *Late Ramesside Letters*. SAOC 33. Chicago: University of Chicago Press.

———. 1967b. On the Chronology of the Twenty-First Dynasty." *JNES* 26:155–56.

———. 1969. A Late Egyptian Emphatic Tense. *JNES* 28:1–14

———. 1976. Review of Kenneth A. Kitchen, *The Third Intermediate Period in Egypt (1100–650 B.C.)* [1973]. *JNES* 35:275–78.

———. 1990. *Letters from Ancient Egypt*. SBLWAW 1. Atlanta: Scholars Press.

Wiedemann, Alfred. 1895. Varia. *RT* 17:1–17.

————. 1912. Varia. Sphinx 16:11–22.

Wilcken, Ulrich. 1927. *Urkunden der Ptolemäerzeit*. Vol. 1. Berlin: de Gruyter.

Wildung, Dietrich. 1997. *Egypt from Prehistory to the Romans*. Koln: Taschen.

Wilson, Robert R. 1977. *Genealogy and History in the Biblical World*. New Haven: Yale University Press.

Winand, Jean. 1987. *Le voyage d'Ounamon: Index verborum, concordance, relevés grammaticaux*. AegLeo 1. Liege: Centre informatique de philosophie et lettres.

Wit, C. de, and P. Mertens. 1962. The Epigraphic Mission to Kumma and Semna (1961): Report and Results. *Kush* 10:118–49.

Yorke, Ch., and Martin Leake. 1827. *Les principaux monuments égyptiens du Musée Britannique*. London: n.p.

Yoyotte, Jean. 1950. Amon M₃ʾI ḤR ḪNTY à Kawa et à Tehne. *RdÉ* 7:193.

————. 1953. La ville de "Taremou" (Tell el-Muqdâm). *BIFAO* 52:190–92.

————. 1956. Plaidoyer pour l'authenticité du scarabée historique de Shabako. *Bib* 37:457–76.

————. 1958a. Notes de Toponymie Égyptienne. *MDAIK* 16:413–30.

————. 1958b. Promenade à travers les sites anciens du Delta. *BSFE* 25:13–24.

————. 1958c. Sur le scarabée historique de Shabako: Note additionelle. *Bib* 39:206–10.

————. 1959. Un étrange titre d'époque libyenne. *BIFAO* 58:97–100.

————. 1960. Le talisman de la victoire d'Osorkon, Prince de Saïs et autres lieux. *BSFE* 31:13–22.

————. 1961a. Les principautés du Delta au temps de l'anarchie libyenne (Études d'histoire politique). Pages 121–81 in *Orient ancien*. Vol. 1 of *Mélanges Maspero*. MIFAO 66/1 (fascicle 4). Cairo: IFAO.

————. 1961b. Les vierges consacrées d'Amon thébain. *CRAIBL* 1961:43–52.

————. 1971. Notes et documents pour servir à l'histoire de Tanis. *Kêmi* 21:35–45.

————. 1976–77. "Osorkon fils de Mehytouskhé", un pharaon oublié? *BSFE* 77–78:39–54.

————. 1988a. Des lions et de chats: Contribution à la prosopographie de l'époque libyenne. *RdÉ* 39:155–78.

————. 1988b. À propos de Psousennès II. *BSFFT* 1:41–53.

————. 1989. Pharaon Iny. Un roi mystérieux du VIIIe siècle av. J.-C. *CRIPEL* 11:125–30.

Zauzich, K.-Th. 1968. *Die ägyptische Schreibertradition*. Wiesbaden: Harrassowitz.

————. 1983. Das Lamm des Bokchoris. Pages 165–74 in *Papyrus Erzherzog Rainer (P. Rainer Cent.): Festschrift zum 100-jährigen Bestehen der Papyrussammlung der Österreichischen Nationalbibliothek*. Vienna: Brüder Hollinek.

Zibelius, Karola. 1972. *Afrikanische Orts- und Völkernamen in hieroglyphischen und hieratischen Texten*. Wiesbaden: Reichert.

————. 1978. *Ägyptische Siedlungen nach Texten des Alten Reiches*. Wiesbaden: Reichert.

LIBYAN NAMES, NAME ELEMENTS, AND TERMS

GENERAL INDEX

CONTEMPORARY EGYPTIAN PERSONAL NAMES (SELECTED)

Letters and numbers in ( ) follow Kitchen 1986, with additions marked by *. HPA =
High Priest of Amon; GWA = God's Wife of Amon; CR = Chantress of the Residence.
See also Index of Libyan Names, Name Elements, and Terms.

ROYAL NAMES OF OTHER PERIODS AND REGIONS

LANGUAGES

BIBLICAL CITATIONS

CLASSICAL CITATIONS